Fighting the People's War

Fighting the People's War is an unprecedented, panoramic history of the 'citizen armies' of the United Kingdom, Australia, Canada, India, New Zealand and South Africa, the core of the British and Commonwealth Armies in the Second World War. Drawing on new sources to reveal the true wartime experience of the ordinary rank and file, Jonathan Fennell fundamentally challenges our understanding of the war and of the relationship between conflict and socio-political change. He uncovers how fractures on the home front had profound implications for the performance of the British and Commonwealth Armies and he traces how soldiers' political beliefs, many of which emerged as a consequence of their combat experience, proved instrumental to the socio-political changes of the post-war era. *Fighting the People's War* transforms our understanding of how the great battles were won and lost as well as how the post-war societies were forged.

Jonathan Fennell is a Senior Lecturer at the Defence Studies Department at King's College London. He is a Director of the Sir Michael Howard Centre for the History of War and a Director and Co-Founder of the Second World War Research Group. His first book, *Combat and Morale in the North African Campaign* was shortlisted for the Royal Historical Society's Whitfield Prize, was joint runner-up for the Society for Army Historical Research's Templer Medal and was selected as one of *BBC History Magazine*'s 'Books of the Year' 2011.

Armies of the Second World War

This is a major new series of histories of the armies of the key combatants in the Second World War. The books are written by leading military historians and consider key aspects of military activity for each of the major powers, including planning, intelligence, strategy and operations. As with the parallel *Armies of the Great War* series, military and strategic history is considered within the broader context of foreign policy aims and allied strategic relations, national mobilisation and the war's domestic social, political and economic effects.

A full list of titles in the series can be found at:
www.cambridge.org/armiesofworldwarii

Fighting the People's War

The British and Commonwealth Armies and the Second World War

Jonathan Fennell

CAMBRIDGE
UNIVERSITY PRESS

CAMBRIDGE
UNIVERSITY PRESS

University Printing House, Cambridge CB2 8BS, United Kingdom

One Liberty Plaza, 20th Floor, New York, NY 10006, USA

477 Williamstown Road, Port Melbourne, VIC 3207, Australia

314–321, 3rd Floor, Plot 3, Splendor Forum, Jasola District Centre, New Delhi – 110025, India

79 Anson Road, #06–04/06, Singapore 079906

Cambridge University Press is part of the University of Cambridge.

It furthers the University's mission by disseminating knowledge in the pursuit of education, learning, and research at the highest international levels of excellence.

www.cambridge.org
Information on this title: www.cambridge.org/9781107030954
DOI: 10.1017/9781139380881

First published 2019

Printed in the United Kingdom by TJ International Ltd. Padstow Cornwall

A catalogue record for this publication is available from the British Library.

ISBN 978-1-107-03095-4 Hardback

For Anna

CONTENTS

ILLUSTRATIONS

FIGURES

MAPS

TABLES

ACKNOWLEDGEMENTS

When Michael Watson asked me to follow up *Combat and Morale in the North African Campaign* with a book on the British Army, as part of Cambridge's new series on the Armies of the Second World War, I was, of course, delighted. Having spent a few years in the City after completing my doctorate, I was, at the time, still feeling my way back into academia and the opportunity to write a second book for Cambridge University Press seemed too good to be true. I was less sure, however, that, with a number of excellent books recently published on the topic, there was much new to offer in the area. I suggested to Michael that the best way to approach the project might be to look at the British and Commonwealth Armies in their entirety, rather than focusing solely on Britain; no one had yet written a comprehensive history on the subject and much might come out of a comparative analysis. Michael agreed and I got down to work.

Six years later I realise now what a big project this was to take on. Thankfully, my initial concerns about the viability of the topic proved unfounded and as I travelled the world, and explored the vast archives of the Commonwealth, I discovered new sources that have allowed the development of what I hope readers will find to be a far-reaching new history of the British and Commonwealth Armies in the Second World War. I received much help in undertaking this globe-trotting adventure. Jerremie Clyde, from the University of Calgary, helped me get to Canada, courtesy of a seed grant to explore his very interesting project on a 'gamic mode of history'. A grant from the Australian Army History Unit (Reference: HMSP-A/OUT/2012) took me to Australia, and my home institution, King's College London, provided the additional funding to visit the archives in New Zealand. A British Academy Small Research Grant (Reference: SG121399) provided the means for a research trip to South Africa.

On these travels, and in my research in the United Kingdom, I received incredible levels of help, support and hospitality from many people, not all of whom I can mention here.

In Canada, Yves Tremblay, Valerie Casbourn, and the team at the Directorate of History and Heritage, were unceasingly supportive and good-humoured in tracking down file request after file request. Indeed, they have continued to help me find sources for this study over the years since my visit to Ottawa. Bill Rawling and John MacFarlane kindly met me at Library and Archives Canada, and, along with the excellent archivists there, pointed me towards many an interesting source, while Terry Copp very generously shared files from his own extensive collections. Claire Cookson-Hills offered expert research assistance and the team at the Elections Canada Library Service were unhesitatingly co-operative. Doug Delaney, in particular, has been wonderful over the course of researching and writing this book. He very kindly sent me an early version of the bibliography for his new study, *The Imperial Army Project*, and then shared a pre-publication draft of the book. Doug also provided insightful feedback on the Canadian sections of the final manuscript of this study.

In Australia, Andrew Richardson, from the Australian Army History Unit, copied a number of important files in the National Archives for me. Like many young scholars, I received advice from the late Jeffrey Grey. Karl James sent me some hard-to-access literature on the Australian war effort and provided me with helpful advice on other sources, while Peter Dean very kindly shared an early draft of his new book, *MacArthur's Coalition*, and provided helpful feedback on the Australian sections of this manuscript. Susan Garner and the team at the Australian Electoral Commission were enormously helpful in tracking down the raw voting statistics for Australian service personnel during the war. The Archivists at the Australian War Memorial, and at the National Archives of Australia in Canberra, Melbourne and Sydney, were, as I've come to expect from my visits to the Commonwealth, extremely professional and supportive.

In New Zealand, Ian McGibbon and John McLeod very kindly met up with me and pointed out many avenues of investigation regarding the 2NZEF. Donal Raethal and the archivists at Archives New Zealand and the Turnbull Library were unstintingly supportive, especially in relation to getting access to a number of closed files in the Freyberg papers. Peter Cooke provided superb research assistance, while Mary Slater, Carolyn Carr and the librarians at the Defence Library, HQ New Zealand Defence Forces, have quite simply been incredible in brain-storming avenues of investigation and in tracking down sources. Most of all, I'd like to thank John Crawford who has corresponded with me on a number of matters related to the 2NZEF and who very kindly read and provided feedback on the New Zealand sections of this manuscript.

I am fortunate to have a superb network of friends and family in South Africa, one of the numerous blessings of marrying a 'Saffa' and playing rugby for many years. Additionally, my research visit to Pretoria was much enriched by the support of archivists at the UNISA United Party Archives and at the Defence Personnel Archives. I must, however, make special mention of Steve de Agrela and Mariette Boraine, at the South African National Defence Force Documentation Centre. Steve's enthusiastic support and encyclopaedic knowledge of the file series at the Documentation Centre was truly remarkable. Jeremy Seekings has provided sage advice on carrying out the social-class profile of the UDF in this book. Above all, I owe a debt of gratitude to Ian van der Waag, who has provided expert feedback on the South African portions of this manuscript and who has offered much support and advice over the duration of this project.

With regards to the research carried out in the United Kingdom, I must first thank my colleagues at the Defence Studies Department, King's College London. It is hard to imagine a more supportive or good-natured department of scholars in the Academy. I've sat for many an enjoyable hour in Niall Barr's office discussing every aspect of the British and Commonwealth experience during the war. Niall very kindly read an early draft of the manuscript and pointed out many profitable avenues of exploration, as indeed did Alan Allport and Jean Smith, in relation to some of the early chapters. Alan Jeffreys generously and helpfully read the Indian Army sections of the book, while Andrew Stewart and James Kitchen read later drafts of the whole manuscript, making major contributions to the final output with their detailed and thoughtful feedback. Ian Gooderson and Dan Lear shared files from their own research on the war in the Mediterranean, and Gajendra

Singh was most kind in sharing a detailed reading list for the Indian experience in the Second World War. I owe a debt of gratitude to Gary Sheffield, who, cognisant of the theme of the book, contacted me while on a research visit to Canberra and offered to copy a number of files relevant to the project, and Clare Mence, who helped me track down key editions of the *Maple Leaf*. Joe Maiolo very generously explained the intricacies of trying to work out comparative military spending during the interwar years, while innumerable librarians and archivists at the National Archives, Liddell Hart Centre for Military Archives, Imperial War Museum and the British Library have provided support over the years. I must make special mention of Aaron Cripps, Sue Barrett, Tim Pierce, Yvonne Potter and the teams at the Hobson Library, the Joint Services Command and Staff College, and the Trenchard Hall Library, at RAF Cranwell. With their help, I've been able to access a whole host of valuable primary and secondary sources from around the world in the comfort of my own academic institution. If it takes a village to raise a child, it takes an international community of scholars, librarians and archivists to finish a history book!

While acknowledging all this help and support, I must also make it clear that all errors and oversights in this study are my responsibility, and my responsibility alone.

No part of this book would have been written without the truly remarkable love and encouragement of my family. Only the spouse of an academic can fully understand the frustration of trying to share a conversation with a historian in the full 'fog' of book writing, a part of this great adventure that lasted three years! This book is dedicated to my wife Anna, who makes all things fun and possible, and who has brought our two wonderful daughters into the world. The births of our darling Isla and Isabelle, which have book-ended the writing of this work, have brought home to me how much the soldiers sacrificed in the many years they spent away from their families during the war. Finally, I would like to thank my mother and father. They have offered unbelievable love and support throughout the process of researching and writing this book and proofread uncountable drafts. I could not ask for better or more wonderful parents.

As I've engaged with the reports and summaries that encapsulate the concerns expressed in the approximately 17 million letters that form the backbone of this study, the story of the Second World War has become necessarily more human. The war's vastness, technological terrors and geopolitical implications have been contextualised by the much more profound recognition that the war was an experience endured by people, like you and me. It was immediate, quite literally a matter of life and death. I've tried to understand the experience of these soldiers, men like my grandfather and great-uncles who served in the forces and did their duty for Britain. What was it like to carry enormous responsibility, for those around you, and for the future of your country? What was it like to have to kill, to be truly afraid, to be tired beyond endurance? I've closed my eyes and tried to imagine the desperate sudden desire to live on realising death is imminent. I've tried to imagine the depth of grief and longing, and the unfathomable sadness that these men were subject to; in equal measure, I've attempted to reflect on the camaraderie of the front line and the thrill and exhilaration that many felt in combat and in the experience of victory.

And, yet, while I cannot relive these men's experiences, I can attempt to recount and contextualise them here. Rather than simply just telling their story, I trust that this book illustrates their very real agency, the extent to which they shaped their universe, both on the battlefield and in the world that emerged post-1945 and that it demonstrates that ordinary people really did matter. I hope that it will do them justice and that where it explores the trials and tribulations of service, it is respectful and thoughtful in the way it does so.

More than anything, I hope that this book can help readers to understand the meaning of the Second World War. I hope that you enjoy it.

ABBREVIATIONS

AAES	Australian Army Education Service
ABCA	Army Bureau of Current Affairs
ABDA	American British Dutch Australian Command
ACR	Appreciation and Censorship Report
ACS	Army Council Secretariat
AFCC	Australian Field Censorship Company
AGCR	Army Group Censorship Report
ADMS	Assistant Director of Medical Services
AEC	Army Education Corps
AEComm	Australian Electoral Commission
AES	Army Education Scheme
AFHQ	Allied Forces Headquarters
AFV	Armoured Fighting Vehicle
AG	Adjutant-General
AI	Army Intelligence
AIF	Australian Imperial Force
AJHR	Appendix to the Journals of the House of Representatives
AMF	Australian Military Forces
ANZ	Archives New Zealand
ATS	Auxiliary Territorial Service
AWM	Australian War Memorial
AWOL	Absent Without Leave
BEF	British Expeditionary Force

BL	British Library
BLM	Bernard Law Montgomery
Bn	Battalion
BNAF	British North African Force
Brig.	Brigadier
CAB	Records of the Cabinet Office
CAO	Canadian Army Overseas
CATD	Central Army Transit Depot
CGS	Chief of the General Staff
CIGS	Chief of the Imperial General Staff
C-in-C	Commander-in-Chief
CMCR	Canadian Mail Censorship Report
CMHQ	Canadian Military Headquarters
CMF	Central Mediterranean Force
CMF	Citizen Military Force
CO	Commanding Officer
Col.	Colonel
DAG	Deputy Adjutant-General
DCIGS	Deputy Chief of the Imperial General Staff
DCS	Deputy Chief of Staff
DDMS	Deputy Director Medical Services
DEFE	Records of the Ministry of Defence
DFMS	Durban Forces Mail Summary
DGAMS	Director-General of the Army Medical Service
DGAW&E	Director-General of Army Welfare and Education
DHH	Directorate of History and Heritage
DIV. DOCS.	Divisional Documents
DMS	Director Medical Services
DRC	Defence Requirements Committee
DSO	Distinguished Service Order
EAFHQ	East African Forces Headquarters
ECAC	Executive Committee of the Army Council
FCSWR	Field Censor Section Weekly Report
FCR	Field Censorship Report
FO	Records of the Foreign Office
FSR	Field Service Regulations
GDP	Gross Domestic Product
Gen.	General
Gds	Guards

GHQ	General Headquarters
GOC	General Officer Commanding
GOC-in-C	General Officer Commanding-in-Chief
Gp	Group
GSO	General Staff Officer
HNP	*Herenigde* (Re-united) National Party
HQ	Headquarters
IC	Intelligence Corps
ICO	Indian Commissioned Officer
INA	Indian National Army
IOR	India Office Records
IWM	Imperial War Museum
LAC	Library and Archives Canada
LHCMA	Liddell Hart Centre for Military Archives
Lieut.	Lieutenant
Maj.	Major
MC	Military Cross
MCS	Military Censorship Summary
ME	Middle East
MEF	Middle Eastern Forces
MEMCWS	Middle East Military Censorship Weekly Summary
MEFCWS	Middle East Field Censorship Weekly Summary
MI 12	Military Intelligence Section 12
NA	National Archives
NAA	National Archives of Australia
NAAFI	Navy, Army and Air Force Institutes
NCO	Non-Commissioned Officer
n.d.	Not Dated
NGF	New Guinea Force
NRMA	National Resources Mobilisation Act
NYD(N)	Not Yet Diagnosed (Nervous)
NZ	New Zealand
NZEF	New Zealand Expeditionary Force
OB	*Ossewa Brandwag*
OCTU	Officer Corps Training Unit
OR	Other Rank
POW	Prisoner of War
RAC	Royal Armoured Corps
RAF	Royal Air Force

RCAMC	Royal Canadian Army Medical Corps
RO	Routine Order
SA	South Africa
SANDF, DOC	South African National Defence Force, Documentation Centre
SEAC	South-East Asia Command
SIW	Self-Inflicted Wound
SOPAC	South Pacific Area Command
S. of S.	Secretary of State
SWPA	South-West Pacific Area
TA	Territorial Army
TEWTS	Tactical Exercises Without Troops
UAP	United Australia Party
UDF	Union Defence Force
UP	United South African National Party (usually shortened to the United Party)
US	United States
UWH	Union War Histories
VC	Victoria Cross
VD	Venereal Disease
VCIGS	Vice Chief of the Imperial General Staff
WDF	Western Desert Force
WO	Records of the War Office
WOSBs	War Office Selection Boards
WR	War Records

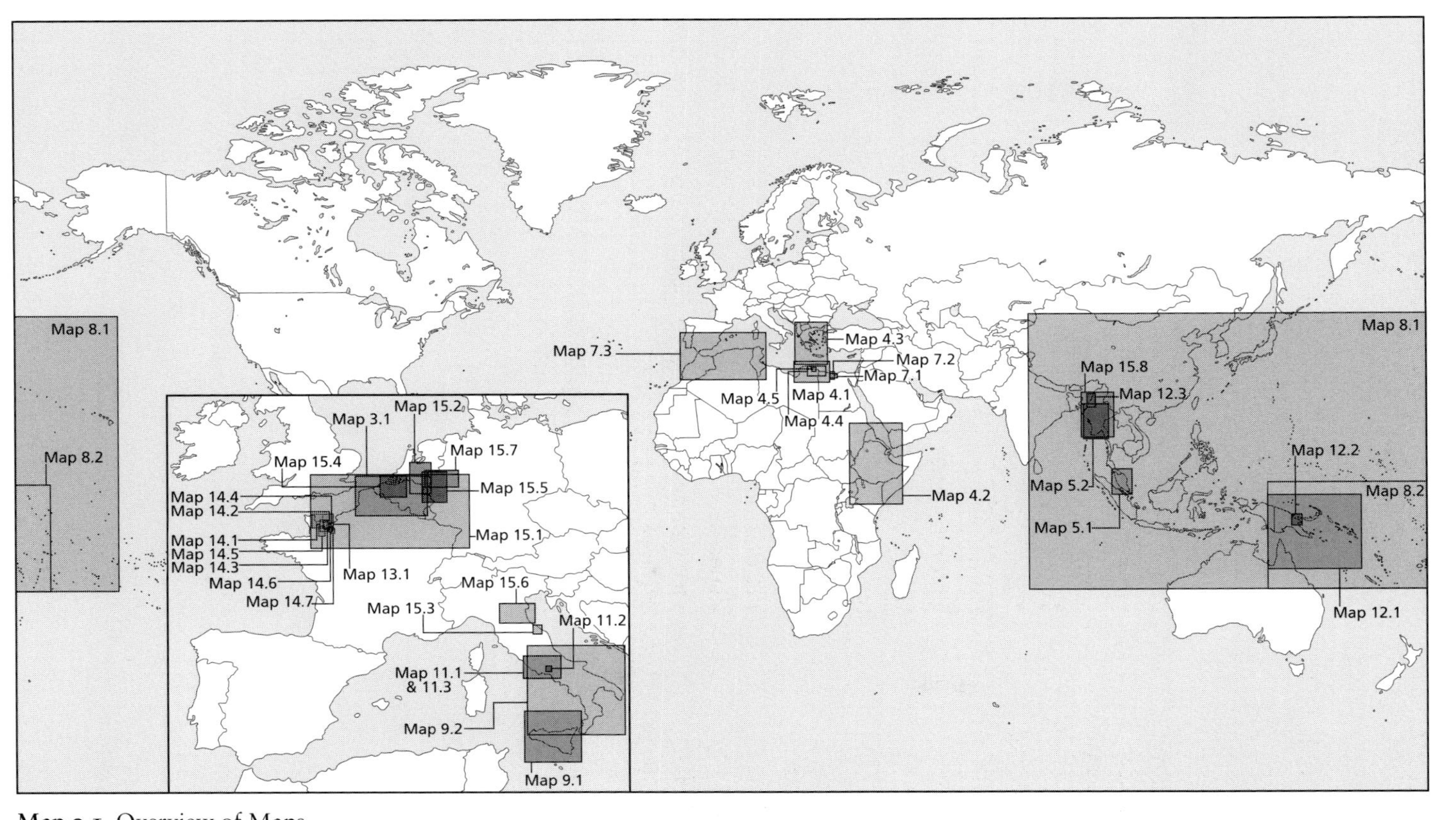

Map 0.1 Overview of Maps

INTRODUCTION

> If an ill-informed or indifferent electorate is a menace to our national safety, so, too, is an Army which neither knows nor cares why it is in arms.
>
> Army Bureau of Current Affairs (ABCA), 21 July 1941.[1]

In citizen armies, it matters enormously that soldiers should, as Oliver Cromwell put it, know what they fight for and love what they know;[2] the fundamentals of victory or defeat 'often have to be sought far from the battlefield, in political, social, and economic factors'.[3] This study explores the British and Commonwealth Armies in the Second World War, a fighting force, at its core, made up of contingents from Britain, Australia, Canada, India, New Zealand and South Africa.[4] The book investigates both the material culture and history of great armies in a world war and also the political, social, and economic factors that influenced their behaviour and experience in the period running up to, during and immediately after the largest conflagration of the twentieth century.[5]

Not only can the behaviour of armies best be understood in their political and social context, but societies too can be more fully comprehended by assessing the conduct of citizens in military service to the state. War might 'not appear a likely context in which to investigate wider societal issues',[6] but, conflict 'can bring into the open so much that is normally latent' and 'concentrate and magnify phenomena for the benefit of the student'.[7] War 'speeds up all processes, wipes out minor distinctions', and can bring 'reality to the surface'.[8] The manner and extent to which states make demands on societies and extract resources, both material and psychological, 'can be instructive: the state's new burst of energy and activity provides a flare of light enabling us to see its features more clearly'.[9]

The clarity that paradoxically can emerge from a study of the chaos of war can contribute to a deeper knowledge of the characteristics of any society. Thus, this book seeks to analyse the terms of citizen soldiers' war participation and locate the history of the Army firmly within the broader domain of twentieth-century British and Commonwealth history.[10] 'Just as we search for the origins of war in the preceding years of peace, we should also consider how the origins of the domestic order may be found in the preceding war'.[11]

When we look at the Second World War in this light, the story of the British Commonwealth, and its armies, reflects a dynamic and contested reality. In many ways, the conflict tore communities apart and created deep divides. While the 'culture of wartime' emphasised 'the interdependency between the individual and the nation', divisions of class, age, gender, ethnicity and race persisted, and, in some situations, were heightened as a consequence of the conflict.[12] In the United Kingdom, competing narratives about the meaning of the war led to the rejection of the pre-war status quo and the 'political revolution' encapsulated in Labour's unexpected landslide victory in the 1945 general election. Similar dynamics were at play in other parts of the Commonwealth. On the defeat of Germany in May 1945, the South African Intelligence Corps conceded that 'the celebrations unfortunately were not national or unanimous in character, indeed from all over South Africa there are reports of intense local dissention occasioned'.[13] Leo Amery, the Secretary of State for India, noted in late 1943 that:

> The fact cannot be ignored that, of all the united nations none has felt less moral incentive to co-operate in the prosecution of war than India. The Indian war effort ... is pretty frankly a mercenary undertaking so far as the vast majority of Indians are concerned ... we have to reckon all the time with strong forces which if not positively pro-Japanese, are certainly anti-British, or at best are indifferent.[14]

Fractures on the home front had profound implications for those fighting on the front line; they need as a consequence to be integrated into the history of battles and campaigns: 'To maintain morale and enthusiasm for the war effort, it was important for the state to propagate a sense of solidarity.' The English, Welsh, Scots and Irish of the British Army; the Australians of British, Irish and other ethnic origins of the Australian Army; the English and French speakers of the Canadian Army; the Punjabis, Madrassis, Bengalis and many others, of the Indian Army; the Pākehā (men of European descent) and Maori of the 2nd New Zealand Expeditionary Force (2NZEF); and the English- and Afrikaans-speakers and Africans of the South African Army, or Union Defence Force (UDF), believed that victory had to be about more than just defeating Germany, Italy and Japan and 'restoring society to its prewar and pre-Depression conditions'. It had to be 'about building an improved modern nation in the postwar world', about building, as some put it, a 'new Jerusalem'.[15]

Such issues lie at the heart of this book. Quite simply, socio-political factors were central to the performance of the British and Commonwealth Armies in the Second World War. The men who fought 'tended to worry far more about the affairs of their families' than about the war more generally.[16] Many soldiers drafted into the Army 'had centuries of disillusionment behind them'.[17] 'Many' more had been told by their parents of the 'unemployment from which the latter suffered after the last war'.[18] The soldiers' own letters attest to the fact that for the majority 'the call from their homes' was 'stronger than comradeship'.[19]

The domestic implications of fractures on the front line were no less dramatic than the military implications of fissures on the home front. There can be little doubt that the state changed profoundly in all the Commonwealth countries as a result of the war.[20] In its most obvious form, Britain lost an empire and developed a fully functioning welfare state.[21] If the political-military crisis of 1940 'had not undone Conservative predominance, England could easily have developed different constitutional forms and a different kind of democracy'.[22] The great military defeats of 1940 to 1942 had consequences that extended far beyond the martial domain; the geopolitical, economic and social implications of military disaster were immense. Moreover, the soldiers' political beliefs, many of which emerged as a consequence of their experience on the front line, were instrumental to the socio-political changes that materialised post-war. Labour's victory in the British election of 1945 was dependent in no small measure on the votes and political influence of soldiers and their families. The story, arguably, was little different for the Australian election of 1943. In New Zealand, the continuation of the great adventure in social citizenship that had been set in motion by Labour's victory in the 1935 general election hinged considerably on the voting preferences of the cohort of citizens who fought in the Second World War. The war nearly destroyed the unity of Canada and South Africa; in the latter case, the conditions for institutionalised apartheid were substantially shaped by the soldiers' experience on the front line. On the Asian subcontinent, the very character of partition and the birth of an independent India and Pakistan in 1947 were influenced by veterans of the war.[23]

The book, therefore, in many ways, challenges familiar understandings of the Second World War and of war and political and social change in the twentieth century more generally. In scholarly, and particularly in public discourse, the conflict is still commonly portrayed as the 'people's war'; a time when citizens and subjects from across Britain and the Empire joined together united 'to save the world' against Nazism.[24] This was the message of contemporary propaganda, which readily evoked notions of 'equality of sacrifice' and national and Imperial unity against a common foe.[25] There is also a consensus that it was experiences on the home front rather than the battlefront that 'laid the basis' for important reforms, most notably the advance of the modern welfare state in the years following the end of hostilities.[26] The book confronts these perceptions and attempts a more nuanced and, where required, a more critical account. As a consequence, it is hoped that a deeper and more contextualised understanding of the place of the Second World War in twentieth-century British and Commonwealth history will emerge.[27]

Writing a New History of the Second World War

Remarkably, there is to date no single-volume history of the British and Commonwealth Armies in the Second World War. Those few studies that have addressed these armies together, from the start to the finish of the war, have done so almost uniquely through the lens of manpower and mobilisation.[28] In contrast, this study sets out to integrate assessments of mobilisation, battle, campaigns and strategy, with considerations of the enormous geopolitical and socio-economic preludes to and consequences of the war. The book, it is argued, fills a significant gap in our understanding of the Second World War.

It has the potential to both disrupt prevailing orthodoxies and build bridges between existing accounts that have become siloed in national- and campaign-focused narratives.

The bedrock of this new study is of course the considerable literature on and around the topic. This body of work can be broken down into three broad categories: studies of national armies;[29] campaign and battle histories that address the British and Commonwealth Armies in multinational perspective;[30] and campaign and battle histories that focus on individual national contributions.[31] As important as these works are to our understanding of the British and Commonwealth Armies in the Second World War, the book aims to go beyond a synthesis of the existing secondary literature.

To do this, the book makes use of a vast array of freshly discovered and underused primary sources to pursue a number of key interlocking strands. In the first instance, it fully embraces a cross-national methodology; the histories of the many components of the British world system make little 'sense on their own'.[32] The basis of 'British power' lay in combining the strength of its overseas components with that of the Imperial centre.[33] The British and Commonwealth Armies were organised and trained to take the field with standard establishments, equipment and procedures; there was a harmonised 'language' of war, as set out in shared doctrine, and a common staff system. They were purposely designed to fight as a multinational team and they must be studied accordingly in that light.[34]

The book, therefore, addresses all the campaigns fought by these great armies: the war in the West and in the East. Too many of the most creative and well-researched analyses of the British and Commonwealth experience in the Second World War focus either on the conflict against Germany or the fight against Japan; David French's seminal *Raising Churchill's Army: The British Army and the War against Germany 1919–1945* is the most obvious example.[35] As Figure 0.1 shows, once Japan entered the conflict in December 1941, significant numbers of British and Commonwealth divisions fought in the Far East and the South-West Pacific Area (SWPA).[36] In the summer of 1940, the Empire had been able to assign the equivalent of just over twenty-three divisions to the Western theatres of war. It would take, due to commitments in the East, four long years before it could do so again, by which time the equivalent of an additional sixteen divisions were

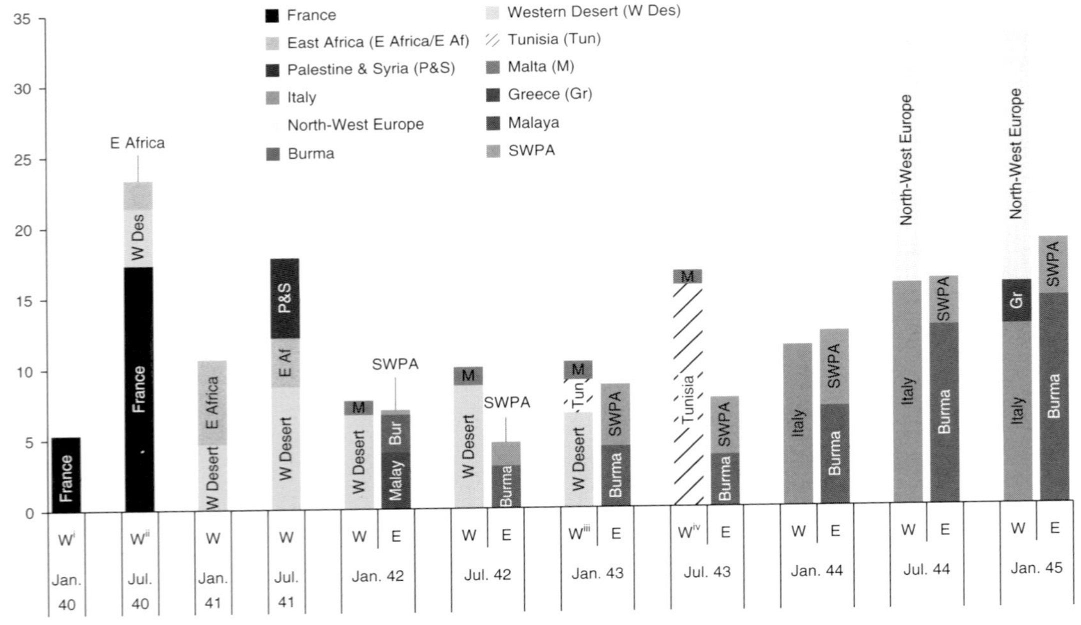

Figure 0.1 British Commonwealth divisions in fighting contact with the Axis, Western and Eastern theatres, 1940–5

[i] 'W' denotes Western theatre; 'E' denotes Eastern theatre.

[ii] Figure for France is for June 1940; by 4 June, 12⅓ divisions had fought in and been evacuated from France and ⅓ division had been captured at Calais. South of the Somme, during June, 4⅔ divisions co-operated with the French, making a total of 17⅓ divisions.

[iii] Strategic reserves in the Middle East (Cyprus, Syria, Iraq and Persia) are not included for January 1943.

[iv] As the Axis threat had 'not been removed on 1 July', Malta is included in the July 1943 figures.

allocated to the fighting in Burma and the SWPA. The Second World War 'ought to be recognized as a global struggle, and particularly as an imperial one, in which apparently disparate British battles and strategic concerns formed part of one interconnected whole'.[37] Acknowledging this aspect of the conflict provides an opportunity to integrate analyses of the wars in the West and the East and to explore the complexities of waging a multi-front multinational global war.

The second key strand to the book is its integrative approach, not only in terms of the literature on the British and Commonwealth Armies in the war, but also in terms of the literature on the political, social and economic histories of Britain and the Commonwealth. In order to chart the military implications of fissures on the home front and the domestic implications of fractures on the front line, the book engages with wider accounts of war and social change and with the political and social histories of the Commonwealth. There is regrettably a 'long-standing division' between social historians of the Second World War and the practitioners of military history. In numerous accounts of social change during the war, 'servicemen are treated as some kind of invisible "Other" whose absence and needs shaped the lives and anxieties of those at home, but otherwise scarcely appear'.[38] This study seeks to build on recent work in this field and address this significant disconnect in the literature.[39]

Finally, the book explores the British and Commonwealth experience in a perhaps more 'democratic' manner than that encountered in existing accounts. While the challenges faced by those in charge of the state and the military institution during the war are necessarily considered, the book takes seriously the agency of ordinary citizen soldiers embroiled in the conflict. Strategy can, and perhaps should, be understood as an iterative multi-level decision-making continuum where decisions on means and ends at each level of war and society can affect decisions on means and ends at all other levels. If we understand strategy in this manner, our comprehension of military and political dynamics is radically dependent on taking account of the often highly contextualised, contingent and interlinked decisions and behaviours not only of those at the top of any organisational or socio-political structure but also of those further down the 'chain of command'.[40] Social and political change is no less dependent on the contribution of ordinary citizens; the 'essence' of the democratic state is, after all, 'accountability to the general public'.[41]

Uncovering the Role of the Citizen Soldier

Studying the British and Commonwealth Armies in this manner poses substantial challenges. Thankfully, the increasing willingness of archives across the Commonwealth to allow digital photography of documents makes an integrated approach, based on extensive travel and primary research, possible – perhaps for the first time. Meaningfully incorporating the story of citizen soldiers into narratives about the outcomes of battles, campaigns and social and political change, however, is a far more intractable problem.

Whereas there is an abundance of sources available regarding the decisions and activities of those at the top of the strategic chain (much of which has been mined in the existing literature), considerably less survives from the bottom. The behaviours expected of soldiers by their political and military leaders exert 'overwhelming dominance over the archival record'. Therefore, 'the influence of an authority-generated model' for understanding warfare, and history for that matter, 'persists even in the most innovative works'.[42] In this sense, it is not surprising that the role of Winston Churchill, and other war leaders, and the decisions of senior commanders in the field, dominate the history of the Second World War.[43] In a similar vein, it is records relating to the size of armies, the movements of men and machines and the productive capacities of combatant nations that mostly survive in archives. The accessibility of such records facilitates the portrayal of war as a complex game of chess, where the interplay between numbers, tactics and ruses decides the outcome of events.

The great military philosopher, Carl von Clausewitz, was not the first to criticise such a mechanistic and potentially deterministic understanding of history.[44] Military practitioners and theorists have long emphasised the relevance of the ordinary man in battle, of 'unquantifiable' and 'intangible' factors.[45] Scholars have addressed the challenge of integrating the 'unquantifiable' and 'intangible' into the history of war in a number of ways. Some works on, for instance, the German and American Armies in the Second World War, use attitudinal surveys to illuminate the experience of the citizen soldier at particular places and periods of time. Such studies, however, are few and far between and their findings are often highly contextualised; their relevance to understanding the attitudes and behaviour of combatants more generally in the Second World War is limited.[46] Most other studies use personal recollections and memoirs to provide impressions of the mood of troops and dynamics within units, but these sources suffer from serious methodological shortcomings, not least the fallibility of individuals' memories, especially where interviews take place decades after the event; additionally, prevailing cultural and social interpretations of the meaning of events can often distort the recollections of historical actors. Contemporaneously recorded diaries or letters are more reliable as historical sources, but it is often difficult to amass a representative sample of such sources for an army. Moreover, as sources they tend by their very nature to be unrepresentative. Men 'who were predisposed to keep detailed accounts of their military service were generally better educated and more articulate than their comrades, which means that they were both more likely to be officers and also, perhaps, more likely to hold idiosyncratic views about the Army'.[47]

This book circumvents these problems by leveraging the processes that the British and Commonwealth Armies themselves used for assessing the personal concerns of troops, their broad social and political perspectives, and their willingness to fight. It interrogates sources such as censorship summaries (of soldiers' mail) (see Appendix 1), morale reports (see Appendix 2) and official statistics on rates of sickness, battle exhaustion, desertion, absence without leave (AWOL) and self-inflicted wounds (SIW) (see Appendix 3).[48] Many of these sources are newly discovered or have been underused in existing accounts.[49] For example, 925 censorship summaries, based on 17 million letters sent between the battle and home fronts during the war, are used in this book. These remarkable sources cover the British Army from 13 June 1941 to 15 October 1945, the Australian Army from 13 June 1941 to 30 June 1945, the Canadian Army from 1 July 1943 to 15 October 1945, the Indian Army from 19 August 1942 to 30 September 1945, the New Zealand Army from 13 June 1941 to 30 September 1945, and the UDF, from 24 October 1940 to 30 June 1945. Operations covered include campaigns in the Middle East (most importantly in East and North Africa and Tunisia), in the Mediterranean (most importantly in Sicily and Italy), in North-West Europe (most importantly in Normandy, the Low Countries and Germany), and in the SWPA (most importantly in New Guinea).

The censorship summaries, which allow the soldiers' story in the Second World War to be told on a level broadly comparable with that of the great statesmen and military commanders, were compiled by

Illustration 0.1 A Soldier of 2/24th Australian Infantry Battalion writes a letter home from an advanced machine-gun post in New Guinea, November 1943. Soldiers' letters were used by the military authorities to produce the censorship reports that form a key part of this book.

assessing the contents of soldiers' letters – and just about every soldier in the Army wrote letters (see Illustration 0.1). The primary purpose of censorship was, of course, security. Soldiers were forbidden to record operational details, such as unit names, troop numbers, movements and casualties in their correspondence, lest such information fall into enemy hands.[50] The censorship reports were primarily designed to assess the effectiveness of the Army's efforts in this regard. They also, however, provided assessments of the soldiers' attitudes and levels of morale.[51] Each day, the censors compiled a report for General Headquarters (GHQ) 'giving broad details of the mail examined during the previous day and forwarding any important submissions' or 'evidence of any abnormal conditions in any particular unit(s)'. The censors would also write directly to the commanding officers of units in order that any irregularities or problems discovered could be 'put right'. A weekly or bi-weekly composite censorship summary, or report, typically addressing a national contingent in an army, was then compiled and sent to relevant HQs. This report was also sent on to Military Intelligence Section 12 (MI 12) in London, which was responsible to the War Office for the administration of army censorship,[52] and to the Army HQs in Wellington, Melbourne, Ottawa, Pretoria and Delhi, where they were distributed to the appropriate directorates and branches for action.[53]

Censorship was undoubtedly unpopular with many troops. The South African censors reckoned, for example, that at least 50 per cent of the men resented that their officers shared in their confidences.[54] The process could delay mail, often by up to three days, and the issue of censorship officers breaching confidence by discussing the contents of the men's mail was periodically raised by troops.[55] As a result, soldiers were often 'sensitive about including affectionate phrases, etc.'[56] Nevertheless, the War Office was convinced that censorship provided a 'fair sample' of the mood of the men.

> It is quite clear, from – inter alia – the express statements of letter writers, that while some men feel constraint in writing where their letters are unit-censored, they write quite freely in green envelopes which are seen only by the Base Censor. Indeed, most writers seem to forget the censor, whether the base censor or their officer – when they write.[57]

It is important to note, that within the terms of the censorship regulations, correspondents retained 'their right' to 'express freely their own opinions'.[58] Indian soldiers, for example, were 'allowed, and indeed, encouraged, to state [their] misgivings about the contemporary political situation, wartime problems that affected [their] famil[ies] and particular official policies'.[59] C. P. Stacey, the Canadian Official Historian, noted in 1941 that censorship reports were 'relatively exhaustive' and were of 'definite interest as source material'. 'It is doubtful', he continued, whether the historian 'will have at his disposal any material which comes closer to affording a genuine cross-section of the thinking of the man in the ranks'. Such sources, he maintained, would act as 'a useful supplement', or 'at times, perhaps, a corrective – to War Diaries and other records of a more official type'.[60]

Stacey believed that the censors made 'every effort to present a justly balanced picture'.[61] The censors themselves, who were 'usually men of some age, with previous military service, and a knowledge of the world and of the ... soldier in particular', certainly felt that the summaries gave 'a valuable picture of the outlook of soldiers' and was an 'adequate guide to the outlook of our armed forces'.[62] The censors in North Africa were adamant that they covered issues widely and deeply, only expressing views that represented a considerable body of opinion among troops, not isolated instances of over-exuberance or ill-temper.[63]

In many ways, therefore, it is hard to overestimate the significance of these sources. From a quantitative perspective, they are based on a highly representative sample of soldiers' mail (17 million letters). Moreover, as the summaries dealt with much more than military matters, and engaged routinely with 'industrial and political issues',[64] these documents provide a window into the attitudes of a substantial section of British and Commonwealth society during the first half of the 1940s. They arguably rank alongside sources such as Gallup Polls, Mass Observation studies and Home Intelligence reports in terms of their significance to historians of the twentieth century.[65]

Other primary sources are used in this study to add to or refine the picture that emerges from censorship summaries and which fill in the gaps where these sources do not survive or where they provide an incomplete picture. Forty-four morale reports are used (see Appendix 2), as are statistics relating to weekly and monthly levels of sickness, battle exhaustion, SIW, desertion and AWOL. These sources, especially the ones of a more quantitative nature, are particularly useful in assessing morale; the real proof of morale and motivation, after all, is the behaviour of soldiers. Indeed, contemporaneous historical sources show that quantitative metrics of this kind provide a very accurate indicator of the levels of morale in an army (see Appendix 3). Thus, where these metrics are available, they are used to develop a nuanced, and perhaps superior, appreciation of fluctuations in troop morale than those described in the censorship summaries.

A wide range of other data is also interrogated. Considerable use is made, for example, of information on the occupations of troops to build the first statistically robust social-class profile of the British and Commonwealth Armies in the Second World War. As those armies that were called on to defend democracy were also periodically required to partake in it, detailed returns showing the voting behaviours of service personnel in the British and Commonwealth Armies during the war are examined too. Elections were held in Australia in 1940 and 1943 (see Illustration 0.2), in South Africa and New Zealand in 1943 and in Canada and the United Kingdom in 1945. A referendum on state

Illustration 0.2 Men of 17th Australian Infantry Brigade, Wau Area, New Guinea, casting their votes in the federal election, 16 August 1943. Detailed statistics of the soldiers' vote survive for many of the national polls that took place during the war. These sources indicate the extent to which citizen soldiers influenced social and political change both during and immediately after the Second World War.

powers was held in Australia in 1944. Due to the exigencies of a world war, troops were often overseas during these periods and considerable efforts were made to ensure that citizen soldiers were given the opportunity to vote. Remarkably, considering the challenges of holding elections during a world war, detailed statistics of the soldiers' vote survive for all bar one of these national polls (the British general election of 1945). In the Australian and South African elections, and the Australian referendum, the soldiers' vote was counted separately, and, accordingly, it is possible to ascertain exactly how this body of electors voted as compared to citizens in general. In the cases of New Zealand and Canada, not only was the soldiers' vote recorded separately, but it was broken down by theatre of operations. The availability of these sources on soldiers' voting choices, offers the chance to gain a deeper insight into the attitudes of citizen soldiers as opposed to those of civilians at key moments in the war. Perhaps more importantly, it also allows this study to gauge the extent to which citizen soldiers influenced social and political change both during and immediately after the Second World War.

Taken together, these sources provide an authoritative insight into many of the key factors that affected citizen soldiers in pursuing victory and building for peace. But, it must be recognised that scholars' judgements can be 'considerably affected' by the 'documents they principally rely on'.[66] The perspectives that emerge from the censorship summaries, morale reports, occupational and medical records and voting behaviours of the troops are, therefore, explored alongside more traditional primary sources, such as the personal papers and correspondence of commanders in the field, planning documents and after-action reports. All of these sources are then interrogated in the context of the wider literature. Where the primary sources support the dominant narrative in the literature, the dominant narrative prevails. Where they challenge it, a new and exciting history of the Second World War emerges.

How the Story Unfolds

In the main, the book is structured chronologically, apart from two thematic chapters, 'The Great Imperial Morale Crisis' and 'Soldiers and Social Change'. The analytical narrative employed highlights structures, patterns, contingencies and the agency of those involved in the momentous events of the Second World War. Chapter 1 assesses the military and political context in which the British Commonwealth, and its armies, entered the Second World War. Much, indeed, depends on an evaluation of the preparedness of the Empire, in terms of its politics and public morale and its military tools, during the interwar period. The balance drawn between 'structure', what seems likely given underlying trends, and '"contingency", those unpredicted and unpredictable historical accidents that can still have profound consequences', drives much of our understanding of the past.[67] An assessment of the interwar

British Army, its materiel, manpower, doctrine, training and organisation, is, therefore, central to our understanding of the 'structural' influences on patterns of victory and defeat in the early years of the war. It was, after all, the British Army that bore the overwhelming burden of the fighting during the first year of the conflict. The great campaigns that followed, in the Middle East, the Far East, the Mediterranean and North-West Europe were largely fought by new citizen armies comprised of volunteers and conscripts from across the Empire.

Chapter 2 assesses the mobilisation process that took place across the Commonwealth at the start of the war. As Sir Ronald Adam, the Adjutant-General of the British Army between 1941 and 1946, wrote, 'men and women remain the most important assets of an Army'.[68] We know, however, remarkably little about those who fought for Britain and the Commonwealth during the Second World War.[69] The chapter explores the highly contested political context of mobilisation, the extent to which citizens mobilised voluntarily for war and the social backgrounds and occupations of those who fought. The more we understand about the men who fought in the British and Commonwealth Armies, the better we can comprehend their behaviour as soldiers.[70] The chapter shows that 'deeply political questions of will and consensus lay at the heart of the mobilization process'.[71] Recruitment and the scale of commitment to the war were, in many ways, dependent on levels of collective and internal political and social cohesion. An investigation of mobilisation across the Commonwealth illuminates the extent to which the process 'acted to either legitimize or contest the authority' of governments and facilitate social and political change.[72]

Part II explores what the historian John Darwin has termed 'the great crisis of empire', the period 1940 to 1942. Darwin has argued persuasively, that the British Empire did not fade slowly into the shadows, reach its apogee in the interwar years and finally succumb to a wave of decolonisation in the 1960s, but that the 'real turning point came with the strategic catastrophe' of the first half of the war.[73] In these years, the British world system 'all but broke up and never fully recovered'. Up until the catastrophic defeats in France, the Middle East, Burma and Malaya, 'it had seemed axiomatic that in one form or another, with more local freedom or less, the bond of empire would hold and the system endure'.[74] The causes of the great military defeats of 1940 to 1942 matter greatly, therefore, as they had consequences that extended far beyond the martial domain. Chapters 3–5 provide an analytical narrative of the campaigns in the West in 1940, the struggle in North Africa and the Middle East and the disasters in Malaya and Burma. Chapter 6 then explores the major themes to emerge in Part II, with an emphasis on the ideological disconnect that developed between the citizen soldier and the state, leading to what is coined 'The Great Imperial Morale Crisis'.

Part III, 'Transformation', engages with the process of rebuilding the British and Commonwealth Armies after the defeats of 1940 to 1942. It explores, in Chapters 7 and 8, how complex and often contradictory imperatives at the political, military strategic, operational and tactical levels combined to drive adaptation and innovation in both the West and the East. With the British and Commonwealth Armies in a state of shock after their performance in Europe, Africa and the Far East, and with Commonwealth governments proving slow to address fundamental political and socio-economic problems across the Empire, the High Command and commanders in the field had to discover ways to win, in spite of what appeared to be insuperable structural problems. The reforms that followed included changes to personnel selection, man-management, welfare and education and a dramatic reorientation of fighting techniques. By controlling operations tightly, instead of relying to a very large extent on initiative, as had been done in the early years of the war, commanders in the field, and General Sir Bernard Law Montgomery in particular, found that they could get more out of the forces available to Britain and the Empire.

Part IV, 'The Limits of Attrition', addresses the hard fighting that developed in the Mediterranean, Burma and New Guinea in 1943 and 1944. As the British and Commonwealth Armies in the West grappled to build on the transformation of late 1942 and adapt methods to the challenges of warfare in the inhospitable terrain of Sicily and Italy (Chapter 9), and as the war dragged on into a fourth year, the countries of the Commonwealth attempted to remobilise their societies for the struggle ahead. This process of remobilisation, explored in Chapter 10, hinged on governments' willingness to manage the war effort in a manner consistent with the aims and political aspirations of citizen soldiers.[75] The unwillingness of Churchill and the Conservative-led Coalition Government in the United Kingdom to countenance implementation of the Beveridge Report, and the inability of Peter Fraser in New Zealand and General Jan Smuts in South Africa to guarantee equality of sacrifice, exacerbated the psychological disengagement of soldiers from the war effort. For the British, this led to morale problems in Italy; the South Africans failed to raise replacements for the loss of 2nd South African Division at Tobruk; and the New Zealanders, in an 'incident of wilful disobedience unprecedented in New Zealand's [and perhaps Imperial] military history', mutinied.[76] Problems on the home front, therefore, significantly undermined morale and combat performance on the battlefront. It was only by largely replacing those formations that had failed at Cassino (see Chapter 11) that a great victory was achieved in Operation 'Diadem' leading to the liberation of Rome.

In the East, 1943 was the 'seminal year' in recalibrating Australian and Indian jungle warfare methods.[77] Chapter 12 outlines the dramatic process of reforming these Armies and how this turnaround resulted in significantly improved performance on the battlefield; Japanese forces were defeated in New Guinea, in the largest military operations ever conducted by Australian forces;[78] and the Indian Army's campaign at Imphal and Kohima resulted in the 'greatest land defeat of the Japanese armed forces in their history'.[79] In both the SWPA and Burma, the form of warfare adopted by the Australian and Indian Armies reflected a hybrid between basic pre-war principles and the approaches that had emerged in 1942 to address 'the great crisis of Empire'. As a consequence, both armies proved exceptionally capable of killing Japanese in battles of attrition but less accomplished in the kinds of rapid exploitation operations that were required for the annihilation of Japanese formations in the field.

Part V plots the final transformation of the British and Commonwealth Armies in the Second World War. D-Day, the invasion of German-occupied Europe, was, as Chapter 13 demonstrates, a considerable success. However, in light of the controversy surrounding the failure to capture Caen on the first day, the chapter explores whether Montgomery and the War Office prepared their men fully for the challenges set them in 'Overlord'. In the case of the Normandy campaign that followed, which is explored in Chapter 14, the British, Canadian and American forces 'destroyed effectively two German armies'.[80] Normandy and North-West Europe was 'one of the last great land battles'.[81] German losses on the Eastern Front during the summer of 1944 came to 1,000 men per division per month. In Normandy, they suffered 2,300 casualties per division per month, losing close to half a million men or about forty-three divisions.[82] For the Anglo-Canadian Armies in Normandy, however, the experience proved largely frustrating. Continued doctrinal weaknesses and high casualties contributed to morale problems, which impacted substantially on the British failure to break out of the bridgehead around Caen and the Canadian's inability to close the vital Falaise Gap in August 1944.[83]

By now, the war had clearly moved into its final phase. The issue was no longer whether the British and Commonwealth Armies would be on the winning side but how to shape victory to support Imperial interests. A quick end to the war, brought about by the successes of the British and Commonwealth Armies, was the only way to sustain the standing and reputation of the Empire;[84] every day that passed saw the exchequer in greater debt to the Americans. Thus, in the wake of Normandy and the continued slow advance in Italy, generals in the field and at the War Office finally developed an approach to restore mobility to the battlefield. As Chapter 15 shows, new doctrine at the tactical and operational levels re-emphasised the importance of initiative and a devolved system of command and control in the British and Commonwealth Armies. Meanwhile, measures to maintain morale were refined and greatly improved. Whereas, in the early years of the war, the cumulative effect of problems on the home front had frequently led to crises in morale, leading in turn to ineffective battlefield performance, by 1945, the British and Commonwealth Armies had effectively insulated themselves from these dynamics. Dramatic campaigns of fire and manoeuvre ensued as 21st Army Group and Eighth Army finally learnt how to conclusively destroy the German Army in battle.

Meanwhile in Burma, Fourteenth Army, in what became the largest land campaign fought by Japan outside China and the longest campaign fought by the British and Commonwealth Armies in the war, outmanoeuvred and outfought a much larger Japanese force than was ever encountered by the Americans in the Pacific.[85] By 1945, the Indian Army was a significantly different force from that which had begun the war. It was flexible, confident, highly motivated, innovative, increasingly culturally representative and highly trained. In more than one respect, it illustrated the extent of the transformation that had taken place in the British and Commonwealth Armies in the Second World War. In spite of ever-present tensions on the home front, an at times hopelessly ineffective citizen army was turned into a competent professional one.

The book concludes, in Part VI, with an exploration of the implications of the soldiers' radicalisation during the war. Chapter 16 investigates the dramatic impact the conflict had on soldiers' political convictions and the role they played in the social and political changes that emerged during and following the Second World War. The chapter shows that for the ordinary soldier, the defeat of Germany, in spite of Churchill's constant urgings, was not an end in itself. For the ordinary citizen soldier, the war was, at heart, about building a better post-war world at home. By exploring the voting behaviours of soldiers in key elections during and after the conflict, and by investigating the role of Indian soldiers in Partition, the chapter shows that the world that emerged post-1945 was to a far greater extent than is commonly understood the product of the beliefs and aspirations of the citizen soldier that had defended the Empire. The chapter demonstrates that as a consequence of the experience of comradeship, interdependence and cohesion on the front line, concepts of fairness and egalitarianism became deeply embedded in those who fought. A spirit of social cohesion emerged from the exigencies of combat cohesion with profound and, in many cases, long-lasting results.

Key Themes

Engaging with a topic of this scale has, of course, required some selectivity in treatment. The battles and campaigns that emerged as most significant from the sources have been given more prominence than those that were of more tangential relevance. The invasion of Madagascar and the Dieppe Raid, for example, receive only passing mention. That is not to say that these operations were fundamentally unimportant, only that a view has been taken that others, such as those that took place in North Africa and Burma around the same time played a greater role in the evolution of Allied operations.

A perhaps contentious choice resulted in the book not dwelling to any extent on the contribution of British and Commonwealth Special Forces. As many historians have argued, their performance was 'mixed at best' and it is arguable that these men would have been better employed as regular line infantry during the conflict. Thus, although the exploits of Orde Wingate's Chindits, to offer just one example, certainly deserve recognition, their contribution was considered less relevant to the overall narrative of the British and Commonwealth Armies developed here.[86]

Very difficult decisions had to be made about detailing the contributions of many others to the war effort. The roles in particular of Colonial soldiers, of soldiers from the Irish Free State and of women in the British and Commonwealth Armies, might ideally have warranted further explicit elaboration. By 1945, there were 473,250 men from the Colonies serving in the military forces of the Empire, with by far the largest contingent coming from East and West Africa.[87] About 43,000 Irishmen from south of the border volunteered to join the British armed forces, in spite of the fact that Éire remained officially neutral in the conflict.[88] Additionally, women served in significant numbers. By June 1943, the British Auxiliary Territorial Service (ATS) numbered no less than 214,420.[89] The majority of these men and women undertook vital roles in support and administration behind the lines. Others made contributions at the 'sharp end'; East and West African soldiers, for example (as we shall see), played a role in the successful prosecution of the East African campaign in 1940/1 and in Burma in 1944 and 1945. Men from south of the Irish border were scattered throughout all categories of unit in the British Army, while many women served in often highly dangerous anti-aircraft units.[90] Their contribution to victory is unquestionable, but a detailed examination of their experience in the Second World War has unfortunately fallen outside the realms of what was possible in this study.[91] The core of the Imperial Armies was always the land forces of Britain, India and the Dominions.[92] About 95 per cent of the over 10 million men who fought as part of the British and Commonwealth Armies originated from these parts of the Empire.[93] This is primarily, although certainly not exclusively, a story about them.

The British and Commonwealth Armies made numerous contributions to the peoples, institutions and states of the British Commonwealth, three of which are given considerable attention in this study: they played a key role in the military defeat of the Axis, albeit to different extents in different theatres at different times; their varying levels of performance at critical moments during the long global conflict were a factor in the declining extent and influence of the Empire; and they functioned as an instrument or conduit of socio-political change in all the countries from which they were recruited. By engaging with these three strands, this study aims to bridge the gap between traditional military histories of the British, Australian, Canadian, Indian, New Zealand and South African Armies in the Second World War and the mainstream political, social and economic histories of those countries. It is hoped that by challenging established narratives on the military history of the Second World War, the end of Empire, and war and social change, this study will make a valuable contribution to our understanding of the Second World War and its place in twentieth-century British and Commonwealth history.

Part I The Military and Political Context

1 INTERWAR

Materiel and Manpower

The story must begin in the interwar years. Much, indeed, depends on an evaluation of the preparedness of Britain, the Commonwealth and its armies during this period. The balance drawn between 'structure', what seems likely given underlying trends, and 'contingency', 'those unpredicted and unpredictable historical accidents that can still have profound consequences', drives much of our understanding of the past.[1] It can also inform the manner in which preparations are made for the future. It is important, in short, to understand those areas where the British and Commonwealth Armies were in decline in the interwar years and recognise where, quite frankly, they were not.[2]

The extent of British and Commonwealth military power during these critical years was a reflection first and foremost of Britain's economic, geopolitical and demographic strengths. Britain provided the vast majority of the funding for the interwar British and Commonwealth Armies and just about all of their equipment. For example, in the financial year 1937/8, Britain spent £265.2 million on defence, while India spent £34.5 million, Canada £7.2 million, Australia £6 million, South Africa £1.7 million and New Zealand £1.6 million.[3] The UK provided '90% of imperial munitions to the end of 1940, a proportion that remained above 60% even after the USA entered the war'.[4]

In terms of military power, Britain remained close to peerless during most of this period.[5] 'No other great power could match its combination of military (mainly naval) and economic strength or its latent ability to coerce its enemies'.[6] Despite the rise of American power, 'it was still widely thought that Britain held the "central place" in the world economy'. She was the world's greatest trader and investor, with the most diverse portfolio and the largest business network. In geopolitical terms, she commanded an intermediate position between Continental Eurasia and the Outer World.

> To be wholly in the Outer World (like the United States) without purchase in Eurasia, was to risk commercial exclusion from the wealthiest and most populated parts of the globe. Without an influence in Continental politics, an Outer power might find the Old World unified against it, driving it into defensive isolation, or threatening it with encirclement and attrition. A purely Continental power, by contrast, was forced into constant territorial rivalry. Its frontiers were always at risk. The fixed costs of its defence were always high. Access to the Outer World was always in doubt. The scope for political and economic freedom was narrow, impeding its economic and social development. But the intermediate power – Britain – had the best of both worlds. It was less exposed to territorial friction. It was hard to isolate and even harder to encircle. It could draw on the products of the Outer World and deny them to the Continent. And, with a modicum of luck or skill, it could ensure that no Continental combination could be formed against it – or, if formed, last long.[7]

Britain was the world's first fully industrialised and urban society. She had the largest global empire the world had ever seen, controlling just under a quarter of the world's land mass, and a similar proportion of the world's population, and she had alliances with other powerful states. In 1939, the combined gross domestic product (GDP) of the British and French empires exceeded that of Germany and Italy by 60 per cent.[8] The *Economist* wrote, in September 1939, that Britain, along with her allies, had similar white populations to Germany and Italy, large colonial populations, double the coal and motor-car production and more than three times the merchant shipping and iron-ore production of Germany.[9]

Contrary to the popular perception that Britain disarmed after the First World War,[10] defence expenditure in the United Kingdom 'stabilised after 1923, even rising in some years and, measured as a percentage of GDP, was not much lower between 1923/4 and 1927/8 than between 1906/7 and 1913/14'. A retrenchment took place during the Depression, but even then, defence spending as a proportion of GDP only fell from 2.9 per cent in 1927/8 to 2.7 per cent in 1930/1. It remained stable at 2.8 per cent between 1931/2 and 1934/5 and then started to grow steadily as Britain gradually rearmed from 1935 onwards.[11]

As national currencies 'were not convertible or stable in value in the 1930s', it is not possible to present a truly accurate picture of British defence expenditure in comparison to its main competitors during this period. Nevertheless, it is feasible to trace defence spending in each national currency, thus giving a sense of 'the rate and scale of change in competitive arms expenditure'.[12] As demonstrated in Table 1.1,[13] from the onset of the international crisis instigated by Hitler's rise to power in 1933, Britain increased its defence expenditure by a factor of twenty-four. By comparison, Germany increased its spending by a multiple of seventy-five; but Germany started from a lower base. The French War Ministry, for example, estimated that Britain (not including the Empire) spent 15.4 billion francs on defence in 1928 compared to the Germans who spent 4.3, barely 28 per cent of the British total.[14] By 1938, French intelligence noted that the only state to exceed British rearmament expenditure was Nazi Germany and, if one added military spending in the Dominions, 'The British empire already ha[d] the largest defence budget in the world.'[15]

Within this context, the British Army ranked second in spending priorities for almost all of the interwar years, its key role in defending the Empire surpassed by the Royal Navy's responsibility for home defence (see Table 1.2).[16] With the end of the First World War, spending on the Army, like in the other two services, had decreased. On 15 August 1919, the War Cabinet decided that it should be assumed that the British Empire would 'not be engaged in any great war during the next ten years' (the Ten Year Rule); thus, whereas expenditure on the Army towards the end of the First World War (1918/19) had been £974 million, in 1921/2 it was £95.1 million and by 1922/3 it was £45.4 million. Spending stabilised around this mark for much of the 1920s and by 1927/8 was still £44.15 million (in a period when prices

Table 1.1 Defence expenditure of the Great Powers, 1931–40 (in millions in each national currency)

Year	Britain (pounds sterling)	France (francs)	Germany (reichsmark)	Italy (lire)	Soviet Union (ruble)	United States (dollars)	Japan (yen)
1931	107.5	13,852	610	5,034	1,790	733	434
1932	103.3	13,814	720	5,049	4,034	703	733
1933	107.6	13,431	750	4,575	4,299	648	873
1934	113.9	11,601	4,093	5,317	5,393	540	955
1935	137.0	12,800	5,492	12,108	8,174	711	1,032
1936	185.9	15,101	10,271	13,078	14,858	914	1,105
1937	256.3	21,580	10,963	12,282	17,481	937	3,953
1938	397.4	29,153	17,247	13,446	23,200	1,030	6,097
1939	719.0	93,687	38,000	24,689	39,200	1,075	6,417
1940	2,600.0		55,900	63,235	56,752	1,498	7,266

were stable or falling). It was only in 1928/9 that there was a reduction in Army expenditure to £40.5 million, when Winston Churchill, who was Chancellor, succeeded in persuading the Committee of Imperial Defence (CID) to implement the Ten Year Rule on a rolling basis.[17]

This new arrangement was to be reviewed each year and was not, Churchill intended, to hamper the development of ideas but to hold back mass production until the situation required it, a challenge and consideration well understood by the Army itself. The Army was, therefore, 'free to experiment' with new weapons and make use of the large stocks of equipment left over from the First World War.[18] Nevertheless, the financial crisis arising from the Great Depression led to further reductions and Army expenditure reached its interwar nadir of £35.9 million in 1932/3. By then, however, with the international political situation deteriorating, the Cabinet cancelled the assumption that there would be no major war for ten years.[19] In 1934, the Defence Requirements Committee (DRC) of the CID identified Germany as Britain's 'ultimate' potential enemy and recommended a programme for dealing with what were described as 'the worst deficiencies' in the armed forces. A Continental expeditionary force consisting of five mechanised divisions supported by fourteen infantry divisions drawn from the Territorial Army (TA) was recommended. Neville Chamberlain, the Chancellor of the Exchequer, accepted that it was essential to have an expeditionary force to keep Germany out of the Low Countries, but he did not believe that Germany would be ready for war in the five-year period being considered by the DRC, and recommended that the Army's programme be spread over a longer period.[20] Subsequent DRC reports again stressed the need to build up the Army, but recognition that 'industry could not fulfil the whole programme without a semi-war organisation to overcome bottlenecks, principally shortages of skilled labour and machine tools', encouraged the Treasury and the Government to prioritise the Royal Air Force (RAF) as a deterrent to German aggression.[21]

In spite of these challenges, the Army's budget bounced back to £44.6 million in 1935/6.[22] The Cabinet approved formal rearmament in February 1936 and thereafter matters began to develop at pace. Army expenditure for 1936/7 was £54.8 million, in 1937/8 it was £77.8 million. With the German occupation of Austria in March 1938, the Government gave full priority to rearmament and that year (1938/9) spending came to £121.4 million. Once it was clear that appeasement and the Munich agreement had failed, the foot was fully taken off the brakes and, on 22 February 1939, the Cabinet approved plans to raise a regular expeditionary force of four infantry and two armoured divisions with an immediate reserve of four TA divisions. After four years of prevarication, the original DRC recommendation had finally been put into action and, on 29 March, the Cabinet signed off on the doubling of the TA from thirteen to twenty-six divisions. It then, on 19 April, approved a plan to increase industrial capacity and reserves of equipment for a thirty-two-division force to be in the field twelve months after the outbreak of war. In 1939/40 expenditure on the Army rose to £242.4 million and by now 'the problem was no longer the availability of finance' (Army expenditure had risen sixfold in the space of five years), but rather how fast this new army could be trained and 'the speed with which industrial capacity could be brought on stream to allow all the money it had been allocated to be spent'.[23]

Defence expenditure elsewhere in the Commonwealth broadly mirrored the trend set in Britain but was not comparable in terms of scale to that of the United Kingdom.[24] In the financial year 1937/8, for example, 'when crucial decisions were being taken in London as to the relative importance of imperial defence and support on land for European allies', Britain spent about 5.6 per cent of its national income on defence, compared to about 1 per cent in Canada, 1 per cent in Australia, 0.8 per cent in New Zealand and 0.4 per cent in South Africa.[25] As a proportion of its central government revenue, India spent about twice as much on defence as Britain (57 per cent, as opposed to 27 per cent), but this expenditure was insufficient to 'modernize the Indian army to European standards'. The British Government, as a result, decided in December 1933, to make an annual contribution of £1.5 million to Indian defence. It increased this figure to £2 million in 1938, with an additional contribution of £5 million towards creating a fully modernised Imperial Reserve Division. It eventually agreed, in 1939, to pay £34 million for a wider modernisation of the Indian Army and, with nearly a third of the British Army stationed in India at any one time (on internal security duties), it can certainly be argued that Indian defence relied significantly 'on British military resources'.[26]

Britain was, therefore, by 1938/9 in a better position with regards to military expenditure than critics sometimes suggest. The decision to ramp up spending and expand the Army had been left late (see Tables 1.1 and 1.2), but the logic of British strategy appeared

Table 1.2 Expenditure by the defence departments and Army share of total defence expenditure, 1924/5 to 1939/40

Financial year	RAF	Army	Navy	Total	Army as % of total
1924/5	14,310	44,765	55,625	114,700	39%
1925/6	15,470	44,250	59,657	119,377	37%
1926/7	15,530	43,600	57,600	116,730	37%
1927/8	15,150	44,150	58,140	117,440	38%
1928/9	16,050	40,500	56,920	113,470	36%
1929/30	16,750	40,500	55,750	113,000	36%
1930/1	17,800	40,150	52,574	110,524	36%
1931/2	17,700	38,520	51,060	107,280	36%
1932/3	17,100	35,880	50,010	102,990	35%
1933/4	16,780	37,592	53,500	107,872	35%
1934/5	17,630	39,660	56,580	113,870	35%
1935/6	27,496	44,647	64,806	136,949	33%
1936/7	50,134	54,848	81,092	186,074	29%
1937/8	82,290	77,877	101,950	262,117	30%
1938/9	133,800	121,361	127,295	382,456	32%
1939/40	294,834	242,438	181,771	719,043	34%

sound; France would hold the line on the Continent, providing time for Britain to build up its strength, mobilise its economy, and train its new army. In the interim, the Royal Navy and RAF would play a dominant role in a Continental conflagration by devastating Germany through blockade and aerial bombardment.[27] The Army was, nevertheless, weaker in terms of materiel than it would ideally have wished, as it took time to build up production from a low base.[28] By September 1939, the Germans had already built 3,890 armoured vehicles; by comparison the British had 146.[29] The regular divisions sent to France in September 1939 were short of vital specialist weapons, ammunition, spare parts and communications equipment.[30] But, Britain and France were catching up fast. In the first half of 1940, the combined Anglo-French production of tanks was 1,412, compared to German production of 558. Between January and May 1940, Anglo-French aircraft production was twice the German production rate.[31] As the Cabinet Secretary remarked as early as December 1938, 'there was nothing much wrong with the scale of Britain's preparations, but "I wish we had started rearming a year earlier"'.[32] In sum, a 'consensus' has emerged that Anglo-French forces, on a material calculation alone, were sufficiently well equipped to avoid defeat and disaster.[33]

In terms of manpower, the British Army was weak, however, certainly in terms of numbers. Whereas the German Army had expanded fivefold between 1932 and 1938, aided considerably by the introduction of conscription in March 1935,[34] numbers in the regular British Army remained static at around 200,000.[35] The TA, a force of part-time volunteer soldiers, the embodiment of Britain's amateur military tradition and long-time distrust of large standing armies, numbered around 130,000.[36] In June 1938, the Regular Army still stood at 197,000, with the TA providing an additional 186,421. Little had changed by June 1939, the British Army, regular and territorial, numbering in the region of 400,000 men. However, by the end of August 1939, with the introduction of conscription in April/May (the first time Britain imposed compulsory military service in peacetime), the call-up of the reserves and the doubling of the TA, the Army had over 700,000 men under arms, in training or carrying out full-time administrative duties.[37] After the declaration of war, the Army could also rely on the manpower of the Raj and the Dominions. Thus, by September 1939, the British and Commonwealth Armies combined numbered over 1.1 million men,[38] compared to a German Army more than three times that size (3.7 million).[39] Britain was, however, allied with France who had by 1939 armed forces numbering about 5 million.[40]

The speed of expansion of the Army had clearly left it vulnerable, the new forces and weapons at its disposal could not be turned into an effective fighting force overnight. But these deficiencies were offset to a significant degree by other factors, one of which was the quality of its commanders. By the start of the Second World War, the leadership of the British Army, in spite of the many criticisms it has since received,[41] was, by any standards, modern, highly professional and had, irrespective of the vacillation of its political masters, been thinking seriously about a Continental war for over a decade. The men who went on to command field-force divisions of the British Army against Germany and Italy in the Second World War were typically young and up-and-coming thrusters. Many were younger than their German counterparts. The vast majority, 92 per cent, had served in the Great War. Only a tiny proportion, 4 per cent, were old enough to have served in the Boer War. Most divisional commanders in the Second World War, therefore, had relatively recent 'personal knowledge of front-line service' and possessed what Napoleon referred to as one of the greatest attributes that any general required, luck (because they had survived the war).[42] They were also broadly competent; 92 per cent of divisional commanders who had served in the First World War had been awarded medals for gallantry or leadership of a high order.[43]

Furthermore, by the interwar years, the British Army had overcome the worst of its innate conservatism and was a relatively meritocratic organisation. Promotion was no longer a function of seniority and the majority of divisional commanders in the Second World War were members of not particularly fashionable line infantry regiments.[44] The abolition of purchase in 1871 and the introduction of competitive entrance examinations at the military academies at Sandhurst and Woolwich 'had caused a slow but inexorable decline in the dominance of the landed squirearchy within the officer corps'. Whereas, in 1860, over half of all incoming Sandhurst cadets had listed their fathers' occupation as 'gentlemen', by 1930, only one in ten did so; this was at a time when almost one-quarter of German Army officers could be described as 'noblemen'.[45]

Senior officers were also highly professional, 98 per cent coming from the regular British Army as opposed to 2 per cent being territorials. As many as 79 per cent had received some form of military higher education before 1939, in most cases a PSC (Passed Staff College), as compared to 49 per cent for divisional commanders in the First World War. Of those who would command corps or armies in the field in North Africa, Italy and North-West Europe, 94 per cent were Staff College graduates. 'Officers who lacked "push", "ambition" and "ruthlessness" did not enter the staff colleges; nor did they succeed there';[46] Sir Edmund Ironside, when commandant at Camberley in 1925, wrote that 'a modern commander must be a highly educated, very fit and very intelligent man'.[47] What applied to senior officers also applied to those at the very top of the military hierarchy; when the Secretary of State for War, Leslie Hore-Belisha, appointed Lord Gort, the future commander of the British Expeditionary Force (BEF), as his military secretary in September 1937, it was welcomed by *The Times* as an indication of his determination to ensure that senior officers were young enough to withstand the physical and mental strains of mechanised warfare, and, perhaps more importantly, 'progressive enough' to find solutions to the problems it was creating.[48]

Doctrine

Not only was the level of preparation of the Army, from a materiel and manpower perspective, more multifaceted than is often recognised, but recent scholarship has also shown that the Army's intellectual (doctrinal) preparation for war was far more advanced, modern and reflective than suggested in the literature.[49] During the interwar years the Army never 'entirely lost sight of the need to fight a European enemy with modern equipment'. Hitler's rise to power and Germany's withdrawal from the League of Nations and the Geneva Disarmament Conference in 1933, persuaded the hierarchy of the Army that 'its main mission was to prepare for a continental land war'. The General Staff 'remained wedded to this priority, and it guided training' for most of the 1930s.[50] In the interwar years, the General Staff issued no fewer than four editions of its main doctrinal manual, the *Field Service Regulations* (*FSR*), the 'tactical bible of all the British Commonwealth armies'. This compared with the two editions of German and French doctrine produced during the same period and was, as one historian has put it, 'itself proof that the British army was trying hard to understand the lessons of the First World War'.[51]

In fact, there is much to indicate that the British Army had identified the key intellectual and doctrinal aspects to the coming war well before 1939. One of the main developments was the rejection by the Army of the attrition-based siege warfare that had characterised engagements on the Western Front. Instead, it sought to ensure speed, mobility and surprise in its battlefield behaviour by embracing modern technology, through the use of tanks, trucks and air power. By 1937, just 6,544 horses and mules remained in service in the Army, compared to 28,244 in 1913. The Royal Artillery was in the process of converting to motorised gun tractors and large numbers of soldiers were being transported by road as more and more infantry platoons were issued with lorries. 'By the time of the invasion of Poland, the British Army in Europe was rather more motorized than the German Army.'[52]

Furthermore, the Army was wedded to the necessity of all arms co-operating in battle to ensure decisive results.[53] Speaking after an exercise in 1927, George Milne, the Chief of the Imperial General Staff (CIGS), noted that 'it is the co-operation of all necessary arms that wins battles' and that this understanding should be the 'basis' for training in the future. 'I want that to be your principle in training', he said, 'combination and co-operation of arms.'[54] All four iterations of *FSR* emphasised the same necessity, for all arms to co-operate intimately in battle; infantry were hopelessly vulnerable without artillery and anti-tank support; the artillery could not conquer territory on its own; and tanks needed infantry and artillery to overcome hostile anti-tank weapons, to open passages through defiles and to consolidate ground gained. A course on inter-service co-operation was taught in the second year at Staff College during the interwar years[55] and the Kirke Report (1932), on the lessons of the First World War, endorsed the doctrine that mobility could be achieved on the battlefield only by combined arms action designed to generate superior firepower.[56]

The emphasis on co-operation extended also to the Army's relationship with the RAF. *FSR* had little to say about the air and land battle,[57] but that did not mean that the necessity for co-operation with an air component was lost on the War Office. During the interwar period there was an ongoing dispute between the General Staff and the Air Staff over who should control the air/land interface. It was in part the Army's obsession with the importance of close air support, as opposed to other more 'strategic' air-power roles, that 'moved the government to establish a separate air service' in the first place.[58] 'Bitter controversy' over the creation of the RAF, its role in Imperial policing and the priority it accorded to independent bombing, meant that most interactions between the Army and RAF during the interwar years were characterised by friction or even open hostility. Nevertheless, each service continued to 'assert that the closest co-operation between air and land forces was essential'. For example, considerable experience was gained from joint exercises during the interwar years where 'many of the rudimentary problems associated with co-ordinating air–ground operations were identified' and solutions learned.[59] The RAF Staff College included lectures on Army Co-Operation in a European War in its syllabus; an Army Co-Operation School ran annual courses for air and army officers; manuals on air/land co-operation were released during the interwar years; and between 1931 and 1934 Wing Commander J. C. Slessor gave a series of lectures at the Staff College at Camberley analysing air operations in the Great War (the lectures were later, in 1936, published as a book titled *Air Power and Armies*).[60]

The problem was not that each service eschewed the need for co-operation, but that they saw co-operation very differently. The General Staff wanted the air force to focus primarily on direct support of land operations (close air support), while the Air Staff thought it could best co-operate with the Army by attacking the enemy's means of production (strategic bombing) or through long-range interdiction of enemy HQs or communication networks.[61] This meant that the RAF placed close air support at the bottom of its priority list, which, in turn, as the war approached, left the General Staff nervous that an 'air striking force would be unavailable to assist ... in its land campaign because it would be off conducting its own bombing operations'. They pointed specifically to recent developments in Spain and China, where the value of aircraft operating in close support of an army had been, in their view, conclusively proven. These differences were not ironed out by the time the war started in September 1939, but, even though the Army entered the war in a less-than-perfect situation with regards to air support, it is clear that it did recognise that air support, as the General Staff expounded in a 1939 report on 'RAF Services for the Field Force', was 'as essential to the operations of the field force as any other form of support'.[62]

Recent research has also shown that command and control in the British Army was far more flexible and decentralised than has generally been acknowledged in the literature.[63] The perception that the interwar British Army fostered an autocratic top-down command and control system that inhibited the initiative and freedom of subordinate commanders has long been part of the historiography. These arguments, however, emerge more from an assessment of practice – how the British Army fought post-1942 – than they do from an explicit exploration of the doctrine used pre-1939.[64] A closer analysis of doctrine in this period, shows that British commanders were, to a far greater extent than commonly understood, encouraged to exercise initiative in battle and trust in their own professional powers of deduction. For example, the 1936 *FSR Volume III: Operations – Higher Formations* stated:

> In dealing with his subordinates, a commander will allot them definite tasks, clearly explaining his intentions, and will then allow them liberty of action in arranging the methods by which they will carry out these tasks. Undue centralisation and interference with subordinates is harmful, since they are apt either to chafe at excessive control or to become afraid of taking responsibility.[65]

The lessons from the First World War could not have been clearer. The Kirke Committee reported in 1932 that for a timely, reactive system for the conduct of battle, 'the idea is that a commander should be able to carry on with his own resources on simple verbal orders or instructions containing the superior's object and general plan, until a change in the general situation again requires the intervention of higher authority on broad lines'.[66]

What was true for senior commanders applied equally to junior officers. *FSR Volume II – Operations General* (1935) stated:

1. An order must contain only what the recipient requires to know, in order to carry out his task. Any attempt to prescribe to a subordinate commander at a distance anything that he, with a fuller knowledge of local conditions, should be able to decide on the spot will be avoided.
2. In framing orders for operations, the general principle is that the object to be attained, with such information as affects its attainment, will be briefly but clearly stated: the actual method of attaining the object will be given in sufficient detail to ensure co-ordination of effort, but so as not to interfere with the initiative of subordinate commanders, who should be left freedom of action in all matters which they can or should arrange for themselves.[67]

The same publication, in an attempt to help commanders manage the chaos of battle, prioritised verbal orders for transmission of the commander's plan, and stressed the importance of cutting out unnecessary detail and repetition, making orders faster to write and easier to digest. Dedicated liaison personnel were also recommended, and, as the war approached, greater efforts were made to make use of wireless communications.[68]

This approach was stressed in training pamphlets. 'Military Training Pamphlet No. 23 (Operations) Part I: General Principles, Fighting Troops and their Characteristics', produced in September 1939, stated that:

> It is essential that a com[man]d[er] shall make his intentions clear to his subordinates ... By this means alone can subordinates be placed in a position where they are able to appreciate how best they can act intelligently and employ the means at

> their disposal to further the interests of the higher com[man] d[er]'s Plan.[69]

It is clear, therefore, that commanders were expected to balance available means with the expressed intentions of their superior officers. In other words, they were required to use their initiative and intelligence and act strategically. British doctrine, at this time, rather than encouraging a system of restrictive control, overwhelmingly embraced directive control: what modern militaries refer to as 'mission command' – a form of command and control not too dissimilar to the arrangements (*Auftragstaktik*) developed by the *Wehrmacht* in the interwar years.[70]

Training and Organisation

The ambition during the interwar years was clearly, therefore, as General Sir Philip Chetwode put it in 1921, 'to evolve a much harder hitting, quicker moving and, above all, a quicker deploying division' than the British Army had ever had before.[71] This ambitious goal was undermined, however, by serious problems with training in the interwar Army. Throughout the 1930s, training programmes had been focused on a European war against a first-class enemy. Nevertheless, the extent and character of these training programmes were not always up to a very high standard. Whereas the British Army had only undergone two-corps-level exercises in the interwar years, the *Reichswehr* held corps manoeuvres on an annual cycle since 1926.[72] The combined forces manoeuvres held in Germany in September 1937 involved 159,000 troops, 25,000 horses, 20,000 vehicles, 800 tanks, 180 batteries of anti-aircraft guns, and 800 aeroplanes. Twenty-eight soldiers were killed in the course of the exercise.[73] By the time the *Wehrmacht* confronted the BEF in 1940 it had also fought in Poland and absorbed the lessons of that campaign.[74]

By contrast, none of the officers who commanded major formations in the British Army in 1939–40 'had any experience of doing so in peacetime manoeuvres' and had, needless to say, not benefited from the experience of the Polish campaign. Senior officers had to make do with other forms of training, such as signals exercises, tactical exercises without troops (TEWTS), war games, and staff tours, which were easier to organise 'but often lacked realism'.

This meant that officers, notwithstanding their involvement in the First World War, had little recent experience in practicing combined arms manoeuvres; brigade and divisional manoeuvres designed to train commanders and units of different arms to co-operate were crammed into a five-week period every year.[75] The situation was no better for territorial units:

> In theory, Territorial units and formations were supposed to undergo tactical training at one of the four weekend camps each unit attended and at their annual camp, which lasted for a fortnight. In reality, combined arms training rarely took place even at the annual camp. So rudimentary was the state of individual training that many Territorials confined their work at camp to unit and sub-unit training. The only training most senior Territorial officers received in combined arms operations took the form of TEWTs, with the result that they rarely had the 'actual chance of seeing the co-operation of all arms'. The result ... was that by 1939 the Territorial knew even less of combined arms practices than the regulars.[76]

The blame for this training deficit does not fall entirely on the Army; funds, equipment and space were not made available during the interwar years to allow for large-scale training on the German model.[77] Nevertheless, such difficulties do not absolve officers at all levels of the British Army from their collective responsibility to assign a greater priority to training. An army that practiced directive control simply had to train, for success in battle rested ultimately on the shoulders of junior and middle-ranking officers tasked with translating a commander's intent into meaningful, intelligent and successful actions in the chaos of battle. With the bridge between understanding and meaningful practice – intensive training – notably absent during the interwar years, there were few opportunities to truly test theory and ensure that the Army was prepared for the hard, practical realities of twentieth-century combat.

The requirement for focused training was compounded by the manner in which the interwar Army was organised. An army that was expected to fight in conditions as varied as the plains of North-West Europe, the jungles of South-East Asia, the deserts of North Africa and the mountains of the North-West Frontier had to be highly flexible.

In light of this challenge, British battalions and divisions were equipped only with those weapons that they needed irrespective of the environment in which they found themselves. Supporting weapons – such as tanks and heavy-, medium- and anti-aircraft artillery – were provided in ancillary units, controlled at corps or army level and deployed where necessary.[78]

This kind of flexibility made sense in the context of an imperial army spread out across the world, but it did leave British commanders 'dangerously dependent on fire-support weapons that they themselves did not control' directly. For example, whereas a German division commander possessed 138 heavy machine guns under his direct control, a British division commander had none. Instead, he had to co-operate with separate machine-gun battalions, which were organised as corps troops. The same situation pertained to light anti-aircraft guns, leaving front-line units vulnerable to enemy close air support unless co-operation was good or the RAF had established air superiority. The problem was no less severe at brigade level; whereas a German brigade commander had direct control over eight artillery pieces, allowing him to lay on a quick fire-plan, using assets under his own immediate control, British brigade commanders, when in need of artillery support, had to go through the time-consuming business of requesting it from the division. The upshot was that a British battalion or brigade commander might enjoy the advantage of considerably heavier artillery support than his German counterpart, due to the fact that British divisions had a greater number of guns, but, 'whether he actually received it, and how quickly it could be delivered, depended upon how well his communications with his supporting gunners were working. If they were not, the construction of a suitable fire-plan could take a great deal of time and significantly retard the tempo of operations.'[79]

Similar problems with co-ordination were evident with regards to the Army's use of armour and air power. By placing tank brigades, made up of slow moving, but heavily armoured, infantry support tanks, in independent formations outside the divisional organisation and by making armoured divisions, made up of more fast-moving 'cruiser' or cavalry tanks, extremely tank 'heavy', with few infantry and artillery units, the General Staff made achieving co-operation more difficult. Matters were no different with regards to the air/land battle. As Major-General Hugh

Massy, the Deputy Chief of the Imperial General Staff (DCIGS), wrote in September 1939:

> The Germans enjoyed unified control of their land and air forces operating together under Army command, whereas the British employed separate commanders for ground and air. For the British method to work efficiently ... perfect co-operation and agreement must be assured and, in the fog of war, such efficiency is always in doubt.[80]

This really was at the heart of the issue; 'the need to generate superior fire-power by co-ordinating the assets of several ... layers of command' was simply more difficult than co-ordinating the actions of units directly under the control of a single commander. Both the German and British armies recognised the need for combined arms warfare and the importance of devolving command and control to key decision makers at the front. But, the organisation of the British Army, as logical as it was in the prevailing circumstances, combined with a deficient training regime, 'threated to reduce the tempo of ... operations', and undermine the power of subordinate commanders to act rapidly on their own initiative.[81]

Politics and Public Morale

In some ways, therefore, Britain, and its Army, the backbone of the British and Commonwealth Armies during the interwar years, was relatively well prepared for the commencement of hostilities in September 1939. In others, it was not. Success and failure on the battlefield were to depend on more than materiel, manpower, doctrine, training and organisation alone, however. It was to rely also on morale,[82] and in a citizen army made up of volunteers and conscripts, the morale of the people mattered a great deal. Here, however, the British world system was undermined by internal political and social weaknesses, many of which had their origins in the memory of the First World War and the impact of the Great Depression.

The experience of the First World War affected in many ways the manner in which war generally was imagined during the interwar years. The 'unprecedented shock' of the vast numbers of war dead 'meant the end of nineteenth-century optimism'. It was 'impossible to wake from four years of warfare as from an ordinary nightmare'.

To deal with the mourning and suffering and the social dislocation, it was vital, in most cases, to 'sustain the meaning of the war' and since the soldiers had fallen in the name of the state, the state had to keep true to their memories. On 19 July 1919, the same day as the great victory parade in London, the Cenotaph was unveiled at Whitehall. Military cemeteries were built on the battlefields of Europe, and beyond, and memorials were set up in soldiers' home towns and villages, bringing the war deep into communities that had escaped the physical destruction of the front. These memorials conveyed 'the fear of oblivion – of forgetting' by occupying highly visible settings in public squares or near important buildings; in New Zealand they were commonly put at the entrance to rugby grounds. The monuments 'evoked the obligation of the postwar nation to remember and live up to the sacrifice made by its combatants'.[83]

For some, the ultimate 'obligation', or meaning of the war and its sacrifices, was the end to all war.[84] Most, however, appeared to crave a 'middle way between isolationism and militarism'.[85] For yet others, veterans, widows, and orphans, the creators and embodiments of 'living memory', the meaning of the war revolved around demands for recognition and gratitude for their sacrifices for the state.[86] In this context, the failure to provide what can broadly be referred to as 'homes fit for heroes' in the interwar years proved particularly damaging for the relationship between the state and its citizens. As the Canadian Stephen Leacock wrote in *The Unsolved Riddle of Social Justice*, 'conscription has its other side. The obligation to die must carry with it the right to live.'[87]

In Britain, the failure to live up to the promises of the 'Great War' struck hard, especially as the 'dark clouds' of unemployment 'hung persistently over the country' for much of the interwar period. Between 1921 and 1939, the official unemployment total never fell below 1 million, and the unofficial total was significantly higher;[88] the average unemployment rate was 14.2 per cent of the working population.[89] Unemployment remained over 2 million a year between 1930 and 1939[90] and the proportion of those unemployed for a year or more increased fivefold between 1929 and 1936.[91] The north of England, Scotland and Wales, key recruiting grounds for the British Army, suffered most.[92] In 1939, 15 per cent of all insured workers in Tyne and Wear were out of work. In Wales, it was 20 per cent; in Northern Ireland, it was 25 per cent.[93] New products and a decline in demand from overseas impacted upon heavy industries and textiles. Nearly half of the rise in unemployment between 1929 and 1932 was in iron and steel, coal, shipbuilding, cotton and mechanical engineering.[94]

By contrast, the traditionally more prosperous Midlands and south-east (especially Birmingham and London) avoided the worst of the Depression due to their diverse portfolio of industries and a rising population.[95] For the 19 million or so workers that were employed during these decades, decreases in wages were compensated for by lower prices; thus living standards rose for many.[96] However, 'it was the unfairness' and unevenness of the Depression that made the period 'so difficult to bear'.[97] These vicissitudes had important psycho-social as well as economic consequences. Where there was a lack of opportunity to work, 'which for considerable numbers of the unemployed persisted hopelessly for many months', there 'was bound, despite the palliatives that were created', to be a weakening of 'morale'.[98] The problem of unemployment was not ameliorated until preparations for war began following the Munich crisis in 1938.[99]

In spite of these challenges, British politics between the wars was remarkably stable. With the exception of two minority Labour governments, which held power for a total of only three years, the Conservatives were continually in office, whether in their own right or as the dominant partner in a coalition, from the armistice in 1918 through to the outbreak of the Second World War.[100] By 1939, with the introduction of universal suffrage, Britain had become a fully fledged democracy, something that could not be said prior to 1914.[101] However, the question remained, to what extent was Britain to be a 'social' democracy?[102] The party of Stanley Baldwin and Chamberlain 'offered a combination of sound financial methods and cautious social progress', but 'showed little of the urgency associated with pre-1914 Liberalism'. For the most part, the Conservative Party 'was resolutely opposed to major extensions of state power, and had little sympathy with the advocates of far-reaching change'.[103] Pressure for a comprehensive social welfare scheme, full employment and corporatist planning had begun in the early 1930s, but these demands had 'foundered' due to practical, but also philosophical considerations; 'that they would require central government to play a new and constitutionally illegitimate role in the direction of national life'.[104] Many, thus, still saw Britain as 'governed by patronage and networks of almost caste-like exclusivity',[105] and there was a widespread feeling that something had gone wrong in the interwar years.[106] Instead of homes fit for heroes, successive governments were perceived as having turned their attention 'to maintaining a land safe for investments' and most of the old economic and political structures, which had seemed so threatened by the First World War, were restored and re-entrenched.[107]

The situation was just as complex, varied and challenging across the Commonwealth. In the decades leading to the outbreak of war, the circumstances that conditioned life in South Africa 'changed dramatically, sometimes traumatically'.[108] South African firms had few investments on the New York stock exchange and, initially at least, South Africa was relatively isolated from the worst effects of the slump. However, as the international prices of South African maize and wool dropped and international and domestic demand for South African goods contracted, many companies cut wages, and bankruptcies and unemployment soared. To add to South Africa's economic woes, the country experienced a period of severe drought in 1931 and 1932[109] and 'most white households', not to mention the millions of black and coloured South Africans, 'suffered hardship, or at least some sort of economic reverse'.[110] According to the report of the Carnegie commission of enquiry into white poverty in South Africa in 1932, almost 200,000 to 300,000, out of a total white population of about 2 million, could be classified as being 'very poor'.[111]

Partly as a response to this economic challenge, the National Party (NP), led by the Prime Minister, General J. B. M. Hertzog, and the South African Party (SAP), led by the leader of the opposition, General Jan Smuts, formed a coalition government in March 1933. In the general election that followed, in May, the Coalition swept the boards, taking 136 of 150 seats in the House of Assembly. In December 1934, the two parties merged to form the United South African National Party (usually shortened to the United Party, or UP), in a party-political reorganisation known as 'Fusion'.[112]

The Fusion Government appeared to solve the key problems facing South Africa. The country experienced steady industrial growth from about 1933 onwards. Between 1932 and 1937, the annual gross national product rose from £217 million to £370 million. There was relatively little increase in the cost of living, so many people experienced real and substantial improvements in living standards. Between 1932 and 1939, well over 100,000 whites found employment.[113] Furthermore, by agreeing upon South Africa's status as a fully self-governing dominion with the King as head of state, Fusion appeared 'to have buried the long-standing quarrel between "republicans" and "loyalists", and paved the way for a (white) South African identity common to both Afrikaners and English'.[114]

The path to an end of 'racialism' (referring to English–Afrikaner antipathy rather than the black–white struggle) and the new found economic prosperity seemed to be confirmed by the result of the 1938 election when the United Party trounced what was left of the old Nationalist party led by D. F. Malan.[115] That is not to say that the spark of Afrikaner nationalism had been extinguished in the interwar years. Although the UP had an overwhelming majority in Parliament, Malan's party steadily increased its support amongst those Afrikaners who felt that fusion threatened their identity.[116] Many saw the solution to the continuing poor-white problem, an issue that impacted especially on the Afrikaner portion of the white community, 'in unified economic, political and cultural action';[117] even in 1939, almost 40 per cent of urbanised male Afrikaners found themselves occupied as manual labourers, mine workers, railway workers and bricklayers.[118] Moreover, 'the social traumas' of poverty in the 1920s and 1930s for white men in a colonial society left 'destructive memories' which 'often pass[ed] down through the generations'.[119]

In Canada, the interwar years were for many a terrible hardship and disappointment.[120] For G. M. Smith, a distinguished soldier and winner of the Military Cross (MC) during the Great War, 'the idealism of youth, and its enthusiasm in fighting for what they considered a good cause, the optimistic spirit which filled the people during the war and reached its climax when the Armistice was signed' had all been 'shattered'. Woodrow Wilson's fourteen points had become 'the fourteen disappointments' and self-determination had become 'selfish determination'.[121] The Depression hit Canada hard. With the United States, Canada experienced the Western world's most severe decline in industrial production and gross national product.[122] Unemployment rose to record levels. In 1929, it had stood at 116,000. By 1932, it had risen to 741,000 and peaked at 826,000 in 1933. It declined to 411,000 in 1937 only to increase again to 529,000 by 1939.[123] Thus, at no stage during the 1930s did unemployment return to anywhere near its pre-Depression level. By 1933, unemployment accounted for fully

20 per cent of the total civilian labour force. In some areas, the figures rose as high as 35 and even 50 per cent.[124] In these circumstances, the unemployed, the destitute, and the sick had to rely on the charity of others, private groups, or government relief; by 1932, more than 1.5 million Canadians, or 15 per cent of the total population, depended on relief; over one-third of Montreal's francophones were on relief by 1933.[125] To make matters worse, the Prairie West also suffered from a climatic disaster, ten years of exceptional and persistent drought, extreme summer and winter temperatures, unusual weather patterns, and grasshopper infestations.[126]

Some feared that these conditions would spark widespread violence or even revolution[127] and, indeed, Canadian politics in the interwar years was highly contentious on multiple levels. The First World War had caused a 'split along racial lines' in Canada. English Canada had supported the introduction of conscription in 1917, French Canada had not.[128] National disunity had been a high price to pay for the 45,000 conscripts that eventually made their way to the battlefields of Europe in 1918. 'It was', as one historian has put it, 'an unhappy nation that saw the war of exhaustion in Europe come to an end in November, 1918.'[129]

The pain and racial bitterness of the war years lingered on into the peace[130] and it was, in many ways, a man who focused on 'national unity' above all else, the leader of the Liberal Party from 1919 to 1948, William Lyon Mackenzie King, that dominated Canadian politics in the interwar years.[131] Mackenzie King was in power between 1921 and 1930 and between 1935 and 1948. He had sided with the anti-conscription lobby in 1917[132] and was also a progressive and a reformer, who opposed conservative forces in Canada and was 'appalled at labour conditions' and 'believed that workers deserved good treatment, fair wages and representation'.[133] In this way, he was able to call on support from Quebec and the left throughout the interwar years, a factor that was crucial as he led minority governments between 1921 and 1930.[134]

Both before and after the depression, Mackenzie King advocated 'social justice' in Canada.[135] Nevertheless, a number of small parties with clear and more radical socialist agendas developed in the provinces during the interwar years,[136] not least due to the fact that the Conservatives and Liberals appeared 'committed to riding out the Depression without disrupting existing financial and state institutions in any fundamental manner'.[137] These movements, often tied to farm organisations, 'protested the adoption of economic policies designed to benefit eastern manufacturers, bankers, and other elite groups at the expense of ordinary producers'. In 1921, the newly formed Progressive Party won the second largest share of seats in the Federal Parliament and in the 1930s, the heirs to the Progressives, the Social Credit Party and the Co-Operative Commonwealth Federation (CCF) made big strides forward with the electorate.[138] If stability of administration was a characteristic of Canadian politics during the interwar years – 'It's King or Chaos' rang the Liberal campaign slogan in 1935 – it masked a groundswell of more radical opinion that wanted the political economy of the country to be significantly reordered.[139]

In Australia, as in the other Commonwealth countries, the war brought an end to a decade of soaring unemployment and social distress.[140] Between 1930 and 1934, more than 20 per cent of wage and salary earners were out of work. To these were added school leavers who failed to find a job; others, mostly women, withdrew from the workforce; and a further group of employees worked reduced hours. By the middle of 1932 as many as 1 million people in a total workforce of a little over 2 million lacked full-time employment.[141] The situation was worse than in Britain; the level of distress was closer to that of Canada, another country that relied heavily on the export of commodities. Immediately after the crash, more than half the country's exports were needed just to meet payments due on foreign loans.[142]

The gulf between the employed and unemployed was a striking feature of the Depression in Australia. Inequalities of wealth and income widened. The 1933 census revealed that unemployed men had on average been out of work for two years. Popular representations of the Depression depicted 'men and women tossed about by inexorable forces, stripped of dignity by constant humiliation and reduced by hunger to passive stupor'. The birth rate dropped to a new low and immigration and population growth slowed considerably. The ruling United Australia Party appeared to be bereft of ideas and was, according to some, dominated by sectional interests; one of its own members described it as 'a sort of government of the feeble for the greedy'.[143] By the end of the decade, both in absolute and proportional terms, unemployment was still higher than it had been in 1929.[144]

In the period between the world wars, politics at the federal level in Australia was dominated by the non-Labor parties, who were in power for all but twenty-six months.[145] In 1916, the Australian Labor Party (ALP), which had been in government from the start of the war, split over its leader's (W. M. Hughes) support for the introduction of conscription. Hughes was expelled from the ALP; but he retained the premiership at the head of a coalition made up of defectors from the Labor Party and their former political opponents, the Liberals. The new party, the Nationalist Party, remained in power until 1923 when it lost its majority but managed to hold on to power by changing its leader and by forming a new coalition with the Country Party (which represented farmers and city businessmen). This coalition remained in office until the end of the decade.[146]

The Labor Party returned to power under James Scullin in the week that the Depression hit Australia. It 'failed both to protect jobs and to protect the jobless'[147] and split again in 1931, five of its members defecting to join the conservatives in a new political grouping that included the Nationalists, called the United Australia Party (UAP). The UAP won the election of December 1931 and remained in power for the rest of the decade. This 'conservative ascendancy' aimed to 'put Australia back on "sound" business lines' after what had been deemed 'Labor's dangerous flirtation with unorthodox and un-British policies' during the Depression.[148]

In New Zealand, the prosperity expected to continue after the First World War did not materialise.[149] During the 1920s, New Zealand sent on average at least 75 per cent of its exports to, and bought 50 per cent of its imports from, Britain. Thus, fluctuations in overseas demand hit New Zealand hard. With the arrival of the Depression, export income nearly halved. The Conservative Government (a coalition between the United Party and the Reform Party) slashed expenditure, provoking anger at its 'seeming indifference to the needs of ordinary people'. The principle of 'no pay without work' – there was no payment of a 'dole' – led to 'massive' public works schemes. The Government 'laid off staff and re-employed them at relief rates'. Arbitration in industrial disputes and union membership ceased to be compulsory, 'giving more power to employers'.[150] In the worst of the crisis, some cohorts of the male population (the Maori) had a rate of unemployment of 40 per cent. More generally, unemployment fluctuated between 12 to 15 per cent for the Depression years. This level of unemployment 'overwhelmed charities and charitable aid boards', etching the image of 'the soup kitchen in popular memory'.[151] Although the experience of the Depression was varied, on the whole it aligned along class and occupational boundaries;[152] this 'left a gulf between the unemployed and the employed, between workers – especially casual labour – and the privileged' and the gap between rich and poor widened.[153]

New Zealand politics during the interwar years, much as was the case elsewhere in the Commonwealth, was dominated by conservative parties. In the 1920s, Labour gained some traction in the cities but mostly failed to garner mainstream support 'until it abandoned its platform of socialisation, especially the nationalisation of land'.[154] The turning point came with the Depression and in November 1935 Labour, led by Michael J. Savage, won a landslide victory. The Labour Party's election manifesto promised to use the 'wonderful resources of the Dominion' to restore 'a decent living standard' to those who had 'been deprived of essentials for the past five years'. It pledged to restructure the economy and to secure a comfortable standard of living for all.[155]

The new Labour Government believed that by increasing the purchasing power of the ordinary New Zealander, through state intervention in the economy and benefits, it would boost the economy, and 'it did'.[156] Recovery from the Depression was 'unusually fast' and by 1938 real GDP per capita had risen by a third.[157] Unemployment remained stubbornly high;[158] nevertheless, Labour managed to change the narrative. It succeeded in closing the gap between rich and poor and through intervention in the economy, reforms to pensions, healthcare and unemployment benefits, culminating in the Social Security Act of 1938, a true social citizenship was born.[159]

In language that would be echoed in the more radical aspects of United States (US) President Franklin D. Roosevelt's four freedoms,[160] Walter Nash, Minister of Finance, argued that:

> There is and can be no freedom in any real sense of the term so long as a large proportion of the population is perpetually faced with the fear of economic and social insecurity. What freedom did the unemployed have, under the last government, to bring up a healthy and happy family? How free were the invalids who had to depend for their livelihood on the charity of others? How much liberty did the old people enjoy – trying to eke out

> a miserable existence on 17s 6d a week? Did the widows and the orphans and the sick appreciate the wonderful heritage of freedom and liberty bequeathed to them? 'Freedom' ... to the Labour Party ... involves above all else the right to enjoy the necessities of life and the amenities of a decent, civilised existence.[161]

By 1939, New Zealand was firmly on the path towards building a progressive society where ordinary people were protected from the inherent uncertainty of the market and freed from anxieties and hardships caused by circumstances over which they had little control.[162]

The same could not be said for India. On the economic front, 'stagnation and mass poverty' remained the 'dominant' feature in most peoples' lives on the subcontinent. Much like Australia and Canada, the fall in worldwide commodity prices due to the Great Depression hit hard. Prices dropped a remarkable 41 per cent between 1929 and 1934; prices of agricultural produce went down 44 per cent between 1929 and 1931 alone. Thus, the Depression 'spelled total disaster' for many of the 'small producers at the bottom of the hierarchy'. To make matters worse, population growth meant that there was less and less new land available for cultivation. The recovery was slow, and in terms of agricultural prices it came only after 1939, when wartime inflation displaced the deflation of the 1930s.[163] With India's weak economic base and largely peasant-based agrarian society, average annual per capita income was extremely low (60 rupees, or £4 10s), nutrition standards were inadequate and much of the population lived at subsistence level. The standard of education was similarly low and there was a widespread lack of trade skills.[164]

The 'plight of large sections of the peasantry', including the better-off strata, led to disenchantment and, in no small part, to the 'massive rural rally around Gandhian Civil Disobedience' in the 1930s.[165] Indeed, the interwar years were dominated by political strife and the growth in calls for Indian independence from Britain.[166] 'Political India' had widely expected that, in exchange for the sacrifices made during the First World War, there would be an increase in India's political status afterwards, at the least to make it a self-governing dominion. Such expectations were rapidly disappointed, leading to over two decades of nationalist, revolutionary and other political activity. Congress finally achieved some real power through the Government of India Act of 1935, which placed the provinces under elected ministers who controlled all provincial departments. But British-appointed governors in the provinces still retained 'special powers', while in Delhi the defence and foreign affairs portfolios were placed outside the control of the legislature and remained in British hands. Congress swept the provincial elections in 1937, perhaps an illustration of challenges to come. Nevertheless, to many, British power seemed secure and Lord Linlithgow, Viceroy of India between 1936 and 1943, was confident that interwar reforms and concessions had been 'best calculated, on a long view, to hold India to the Empire'.[167]

Structure and Contingency

In 1914, the British Army was in a position within two weeks of mobilisation to send five well-equipped and organised divisions to France; in 1939 it would take thirty days to transfer only three divisions to the Continent.[168] In spite of the fact that Britain was less ready for war in 1939 than it had been in 1914, it would be unfair to argue that Britain was totally unprepared for another world war. It is too easy to paint a picture of incompetence across the Channel, in contrast to Britain's enemy, who, with Teutonic efficiency prepared for the next great conflagration. As Adam Tooze has argued, 'we must clearly set aside any idea that the armaments effort of the Third Reich was carefully tailored towards the construction of a motorized "blitzkrieg" juggernaut'.[169]

The British state, a 'warfare state', was one of 'plenty, of armed forces generously supplied with new equipment by new factories ... The context of British action was not, as so often suggested, one of weakness, isolation and austerity, but rather of abundance of key resources.'[170] As propaganda later in the war stressed, Britain was supported by a massive reserve of manpower; 'one out of every five persons in the world is an Indian'.[171] Britain went to war in 1939 allied with France 'in pursuit of great interest, by choice'. She went to war 'believing in victory'.[172]

Furthermore, in spite of the fact that the British Army suffered 744,702 dead and 1,693,262 wounded between 1914 and 1918, and in spite of subsequent claims that 'the best of a generation had disappeared on the Western Front',[173] the British Army that prepared to fight the Second World War was, in the main, led by a cadre of generals that were professional, committed and, by standards of the time, well educated. Britain planned to fight 'the next war, not the last'.[174] The War Office had made considerable efforts to understand the lessons of the First World War and by 1939 had successfully predicted the character of the forthcoming conflict, with its requirement for all-arms co-operation and integration. It had also developed a doctrine that encouraged its commanders to take responsibility in battle and trust their subordinates in a manner more commonly associated with the German Army of the Second World War.[175]

Notwithstanding these many positive factors, the Cabinet's decision to leave an expansion of the Army to the very last moment did inevitably lead to short-term deficiencies, especially in the quality of training – that essential bridge between theory and practice.[176] These military deficiencies were exacerbated by the impacts of the two socio-economic catastrophes of the first years of the twentieth century, the First World War and the Great Depression. War, as Stuart Macintyre has argued, 'is sometimes regarded as a regenerative force', rather like a 'bushfire that consumes energy, burns away the outmoded accretion of habit and allows new, more vigorous growth to occur. The Great War brought no such national revitalization':

> It killed, maimed and incapacitated. It left an incubus of debt that continued to mount as the payments to veterans and war widows continued; even in the depths of the Depression of the early 1930s there were more . . . [citizens] on war benefits than in receipt of social welfare. Its public memorials were a constant reminder of loss but provided little solace to those who mourned, for the ethos of national sacrifice discouraged excessive personal grief as selfish. So, far from strengthening a common purpose, it weakened the attachment to duty: to live for the moment was a common response to the protracted ordeal. The war increased rather than lessened dependence, hardened prejudices, widened divisions.[177]

To make matters worse, the history of employment between the two world wars was the story of 'an almost continuous struggle against adversity'. These vicissitudes had 'important economic and psychological consequences'. 'The lack of opportunity for working, which for considerable numbers of the unemployed persisted hopelessly for many months, was bound, despite the palliatives that were created, to weaken their morale.'[178] For these reasons, in so far as there were structural influences on the events to come, they were 'human' and psychological to a greater extent than 'material'.[179] While it is natural to search for explanations regarding the performance of the British and Commonwealth Armies in the Second World War in the preceding years of peace, too much has been made by historians of the unpreparedness of the Army for a second great global conflagration. A far more nuanced approach, freed where possible from hindsight is required. Defeat and disaster were by no means preordained in 1939; much would depend on the manner in which the state, its leaders and its publics would mobilise and react and adapt to the crisis of the outbreak of war.

2 MOBILISATION

The argument that the Second World War was a 'good' war has led to a 'mythologised version' of the conflict in the public consciousness. The war is remembered as Britain's 'Finest Hour', when people, 'both the "ordinary people" and the privileged put aside their everyday involvements and individual concerns, joined hands, and came to the nation's defence. Public memories of the war continue to recall this as a historical moment when the nation was truly united.'[1] To many, the conflict was 'one of the rare times in the past hundred years when the country lived up to what the British citizens thought it was'.[2] This perception was no less powerful across the Dominions, if not India. It has been argued that the Second World War was for the Australians a genuine 'people's war, a war to abolish the injustice and insecurity' of the interwar years. The Labor Party fought the war in a manner that fostered 'unity' by seeking the consent of the people called on to fight. This approach made 'the sacrifice seem worthwhile'.[3]

However, even in those parts of the Commonwealth where the trials and tribulations of the interwar years were better managed, there was a distinct disconnect between the rhetoric of nations united in a 'people's war' and the reality as it unfolded on the ground. In the United Kingdom, given the cultural memory of the First World War and the highly fractured nature of Britain's class-based society, where structured inequality was produced and reproduced in economic, social, cultural and political relations,[4] this, perhaps, should not be all that much of a surprise. The same applies, in many ways, to the ethnically fragmented dominions of Australia, Canada and South Africa and the quasi-dominion of India, where large proportions of the population, in some cases the majority, were extremely anti-British in sentiment. Thus, when Britain's pledge to support Poland against German aggression was made a reality on 3 September 1939, Britain and the Commonwealth, on the outbreak of a second world war, were forced to face some harsh truths about the cohesion of the Empire.

The Political Context

For Britain, the war began with the country far from being politically united. The mobilisation process to generate a great army to challenge Germany confronted ruling elites, and the state, with a number of profound challenges, not least regarding the limits of their legitimacy. At the start of 1939, the Conservative Party had enjoyed 'a political supremacy which seemed unchallengeable'.[5] However, having staked its reputation on concerted efforts to preserve peace through appeasing Hitler, Neville Chamberlain's Government was dealt a 'severe blow' on the outbreak of war. Chamberlain managed to hold on to power during what became known as the 'Phoney War' (due to the lack of major land operations) by including former opponents, such as Winston Churchill, in his War Cabinet, but Labour refused invitations to join a wartime coalition.[6]

Chamberlain's position became increasingly untenable when major hostilities on land finally commenced. News from the battlefields was not encouraging leading to a two-day debate in the House of Commons, on 7 and 8 May 1940. This moment of high drama ended in a motion of no confidence that the Prime Minister won, although it left him severely weakened. With his own party abandoning him, Chamberlain turned to Labour in the hope of establishing a coalition government, but Labour's hostility to the man who, as either Chancellor or as Prime Minister, had tormented them throughout the 1930s was too deep seated. They refused. Chamberlain was forced to resign and was replaced by Churchill on 10 May, the same day that the battle of France commenced on the Continent.[7] Churchill understood 'that a war to the end could not be fought without the labour movement' and offered the Labour Party yet another opportunity to form a wartime coalition.[8] This time they agreed, accepting two seats in a new five-man War Cabinet and sixteen ministerial positions compared to the

Conservative's fifty-two. 'National unity', at least at the political level, 'had at last been achieved'.[9]

In India, the political context was far more complicated. The commencement of international hostilities sparked a major political problem for the subcontinent.[10] Technically, since India had not yet attained the status of a fully fledged federal dominion, it entered the war by the Viceroy's proclamation. But, a truly national effort required the Indian ministers in the provincial governments to remain at their posts and serve as directed by the Viceroy in Delhi. The Indian National Congress (INC) insisted that Indian support, however, could only be given if the London government renounced imperialism and promised independence. So, when the Viceroy, Lord Linlithgow, offered no more than a post-war review of the 1935 constitution, the Congress ministries in Bombay, Madras, the United Provinces, the Central Provinces, Bihar, Orissa and the North-West Frontier Province followed the Congress High Command's instructions and resigned as a body.[11]

Congress would not support the war effort on the basis of vague or insufficient British promises regarding self-government only to be delivered once the war was won. Linlithgow, therefore, made another more concrete attempt in August 1940 to draw representatives of the INC into the Government. The 'August Offer' promised dominion status at the end of the war, Congress seats in the Viceroy's 'Cabinet', and an advisory council to bring a larger Indian voice into the war effort. The INC again refused. Dominion status, said Jawaharlal Nehru, was 'as dead as a doornail'. India had to be free to leave the Empire-Commonwealth.[12] When such assurances were not forthcoming, two great revolutionary movements emerged on the subcontinent. The first was the 'Quit India' campaign, 'the most widespread internal uprising the Raj ever experienced', a 'chaotic violent movement' that 'arguably was the decisive moment in India's independence struggle'. The second was the formation of the Indian National Army (INA), raised from Indian prisoners of war (POWs) captured by the Japanese with the avowed aim of returning India to self-rule.[13] The Muslim League did decide to support the war effort; thus, the Punjab and Bengal Muslim-dominated governments gave their backing to Britain's war. But, even this not insignificant pledge of support was to create divisions, as, over time, the League sought to leverage its participation in the war in return for the partition of the subcontinent and the creation of an independent and sovereign Pakistan.[14]

The question of unity was as profound, if not quite as extreme, in the Dominions. On the day that Britain declared war on Germany, Mackenzie King, the Canadian Prime Minister, sent a message to Chamberlain enquiring how the Dominion might assist in Britain's hour of need. On 6 September, the British Government outlined its requirements, requesting Canada, for the second time in twenty-five years, to send an expeditionary force to Europe.[15] On 10 September, a week after Britain declared war, the Canadian Parliament unanimously supported Britain's appeal, but there was no widespread enthusiasm at the political level to engage in another great war. 'There were no fiery speeches, no bands, no pretty girls throwing flowers before the troops. No one said that the Allies would be in Berlin in a week, and very few expected anything but a long dirty war.'[16]

In many ways, Canada entered the war a divided country. Since the conscription crisis of 1917–18, French Canadian antipathy to involvement in a 'British' war had been 'the most dangerous theme in Canadian politics'.[17]

> 'Listen', *Québecois* would say to English Canadians, 'do you think Canada would be at war if England were not?' Who could answer affirmatively to this question? It was not enough to say that the Nazis were a menace to everyone, when the United States stayed out of the war ... [Later, it would not be] enough to say that the war was a fight for democracy, when the Soviet Union was an ally of Britain. To Quebec the war was an English war, and if the English Canadians wanted to die for England that was their business. But they had no right to impose their perverse desires on ... French Canadians.[18]

In 1939, around 3.5 million Canadians, out of a population of 11.5 million, referred to themselves as French;[19] Mackenzie King was not prepared to risk national unity by alienating this key constituency.[20] He, thus, 'refused to be drawn into an unfettered war effort', making it clear to his Liberal War Cabinet that 'Canada's war would be one of limited commitment'. The phrase 'limited liability' became intimately associated with the Liberal position. Canada would stand with Britain, but it would safeguard its own needs and security first. Thus, when Canada's military chiefs asked for a $500 million budget, 'the cabinet rejected the demand as too expensive'. The federal Conservatives' calls for 'greater military involvement and sacrifice' fell on stony ground.

The opening months of the conflict saw Canada adopt 'an unheroic, penny-pinching approach to a war that was already looking grim'.[21]

Politics at the provincial level only heightened the sense of discord. Maurice Duplessis, the Premiere in Quebec and leader of the *Union Nationale*, sought to leverage the war in his own favour, stressing that the conflict would be used to transfer power to Ottawa and that conscription would be introduced eventually regardless of the will of French Canada. In late September, Duplessis called a snap election, to be held that October. Here lay the recipe for a fundamental split; as one Liberal minister put it, 'if Duplessis wins, the war is over, so far as Quebec is concerned'. The federal Liberal Party poured money and its big names into the contest. The Quebec ministers in Mackenzie King's Government announced publicly that they would resign if Duplessis won, leaving Quebec powerless in Ottawa, with no one 'to hold off conscription'. The ploy worked; the provincial Liberals enjoyed a landslide victory.[22]

Mitchell Hepburn, the Liberal Premiere in Ontario, was next to revolt. Hepburn, whose relationship with Mackenzie King had progressively deteriorated during the late 1930s, found himself drawing closer to Duplessis in opposition to Ottawa's handling of the war. On 18 January 1940, he moved a resolution in the Ontario legislature regretting that the Federal Government 'had made so little effort to prosecute Canada's duty in the war in the vigorous manner the people of Canada desire to see'. The resolution was passed with 'an overwhelming majority', thus censuring the federal leader.[23]

This 'extraordinary' resolution 'rattled' Mackenzie King. But he managed to use the situation to his advantage. With the federal Liberals having been in power since 1935, an election was due in Canada that year. He used the vote of no confidence in Ontario as the justification to go to the polls. At the opening of Parliament on 25 January, he announced to a stunned House that he could not continue to lead with the threat of disunity unanswered. Parliament would be dissolved that day.[24]

In the election that followed, the Liberals focused on two messages, 'win the war' and 'preserve Canadian unity', while the Conservatives criticised the Government over its 'lacklustre record' and 'stressed the need for a unified national government'.[25] The result of the election was a landslide of 'unprecedented proportions for the Liberals'. Only 40 Conservatives were elected as against 184 Liberals, the largest majority to that date.[26] It was clear that 'few' at home were 'willing to accept the Conservatives' claims that a greater exertion was needed by the Dominion at this point in the war'. Mackenzie King had now no need to form a government of national unity. The Liberals would run the war effort as they saw fit; a policy of 'limited liability' would characterise Canada's war effort. The alternative was to risk the unity of Canada, and that was something Mackenzie King was unwilling to countenance.[27]

Parochial perspectives were no less present in the Antipodes. Australia entered the war with Robert Menzies as Prime Minister in an unstable minority United Australia Party (UAP) government with Country Party support (though not in formal coalition).[28] There was no question, though, of Australia refusing to follow Britain to war. 'Let me be clear on this', said Menzies in a broadcast at the end of April 1939, 'I cannot have a defence of Australia that depends upon British sea-power as its first element ... and at the same time refuse Britain Australian co-operation at a time of common danger. The British countries of the world must stand or fall together.'[29]

Beneath the rhetoric of unity lay a great unease, however. On 3 September 1939, 'Menzies announced on national radio that it was his "melancholy duty" to inform the Australian people that they were at war with Germany.' The war was 'unwelcome' and 'greeted with little of the imperialist enthusiasm so evident among Australians in 1914'. 'Families still mourned lost sons, brothers and husbands. As Australia emerged from the economic hardship of the Depression and sought to build a firmer manufacturing base, war presaged further years of uncertainty.'[30] Indeed, before the war, the Labor opposition, led by John Curtin, had captured the position of many: 'the positive and calmly-considered view of the Australian Labor party', wrote Curtin, was that 'our first duty is to Australia':

> We believe that the best and the most complete contribution we can make, in the present position of the democracies of the world, is to concentrate ourselves on the maintenance of the integrity and the inviolability of this country and the safety of our own people.[31]

Attempts to form a unity government proved even more complicated than in the United Kingdom and Canada. Menzies was keen on a national government and on 12 July he went so far as to offer

Curtin, 'five or possibly six seats in the Cabinet' and even to stand down from the prime ministership 'if his personal occupancy of that office stood in the way'.[32] The majority of the Labor Party, however, was 'clearly against a national government' as it was felt that the party's social objectives were 'incompatible with membership of a coalition' with the UAP.[33] The call for a national government by the UAP was not, as one of the official historians put it, 'a simple uncomplicated search for unity'. 'It sometimes appeared as a genuine, even if perhaps rather glib approach to a unified war effort. At other times the case was presented in a way to discredit the Opposition.'[34]

With Australia's three-year federal electoral cycle, a national poll was due that year. Despite 'considerable opinion' that national unity would be 'impaired' by 'political campaigning', no consensus could be formed among the political parties on how to postpone the poll, which went ahead on 21 September.[35] By this stage, it was 'quite clear' that a 'national government was already outside the scope of practical politics' and that 'it could not be brought into existence by any vote at the general election'. The election, therefore, revolved around the decision to choose a party to govern.[36] The outcome was inconclusive; it resulted in a hung Parliament, with the UAP and Country Party just about hanging on to power.[37]

The scene was now set for Menzies' downfall. As the war dragged on into 1941, with Japanese aggression ever more in evidence, and the list of military disasters in the Mediterranean notching up, the Country Party demanded Menzies' resignation. Menzies in desperation once more called on Labor to form a national government. They refused. On 28 August 1941, he resigned, to be replaced shortly thereafter by the first Labor Federal Government for ten years.[38] Neither the UAP or Labor had welcomed the war,[39] nor had they found a way to work effectively together in the national interest. The war, as elsewhere, had caused as much disunity as unity on the political front in Australia.

Meanwhile in South Africa, the outbreak of war began to tear down the veneer of stability created by the interwar Fusion Government. From a socio-political perspective, the war, quite simply, had nothing but negative consequences for the Union.[40] In a similar vein to India and Canada, South Africa contained a significant proportion of people fundamentally opposed to participation in the conflict. In the circumstances, General J. B. M. Hertzog, the Prime Minister, was adamant that South Africa could and should stay neutral in Britain's war. To decide otherwise, he propounded, would split the Afrikaner people, wreck the racial good feeling that had developed and smooth the path of radical Afrikaner republicanism. But, when Hertzog put his views to the Fusion Cabinet, it voted against him by seven to six.[41] The matter was taken to the House of Assembly where the Deputy Prime Minister, Smuts, proposed a motion in support of the war. He won by a relatively small majority (eighty for and sixty-seven against). Hertzog approached the Governor General, Sir Patrick Duncan, with a request for a special general election. It was declined. Instead, Duncan summoned Smuts to form a government from pro-war members of the United Party (UP) along with support from the Labour and Dominion Parties. On Wednesday 6 September 1939, just three days after Britain, South Africa declared war on Germany.[42]

The Union was going to war as an increasingly divided country.[43] A number of prominent Afrikaner political figures, civil servants and military officers resigned. Popular discord was manifested when a crowd of 70,000 Afrikaners attended an anti-war rally near Pretoria on 8 September, organised by the *Herenigde* (Re-united) National Party (HNP), the nucleus of which consisted of Nationalists who refused to follow Hertzog when the bulk of the original National Party fused with the South African Party to form the UP in 1934.[44] The controversy over the decision to take the country to war led to widespread disillusionment among Afrikaners and a protracted campaign of civil disobedience and even terrorism by dissident Afrikaner organisations such as the *Ossewa Brandwag* (OB), the New Order and the Greyshirts. Anti-war sentiment among some Afrikaners extended even so far as vocal support for the Nazis and for a German victory. The OB, which a government commission later estimated to number around 350,000, was implicated in numerous acts of sabotage and plots to overthrow the Smuts Government.[45] So great was the anti-war clamour in South Africa by 1943, that it was clear to Smuts that he had little option but to hold an election and seek a mandate from the people to continue with the war policy.[46] Smuts won, thanks in no small measure to the soldiers' vote (see Chapter 16). The result, however, 'denoted a massive growth of support' for the HNP; the conflict, by no means, could be described as a 'people's war' in South Africa.[47]

Much as was the case in the Union, the world crisis came at a time of profound hope and potential in the development of New Zealand. On 3 September 1939, Peter Fraser, acting on behalf of the bed-ridden Labour Prime Minister, Michael Savage, issued a statement noting that New Zealand along with Great Britain was now at war with Germany. Two days later, Parliament voted unanimously to confirm the declaration of war and then proceeded with gusto to sing 'God Save the King'. That evening, Savage spoke to the nation from his sick-bed, proclaiming that New Zealand ranged itself beside Britain; 'where she goes, we go, where she stands, we stand'.[48]

The new 'social contract' championed by the Labour Party after its election victory in 1935 came under sustained pressure on the outbreak of the Second World War. Both Fraser (who became the new Labour Prime Minister after Savage's death in March 1940) and Nash 'saw the successful conduct of war as the primary goal of the government'.[49] In Fraser's first address to the Labour Party Conference as Prime Minister, in April 1941, he advocated patience and sacrifice for the duration of the conflict, and pledged the reward of social reconstruction to follow. The ambition of Labour to remove extremes of wealth and poverty should be left 'in abeyance', he declared, for 'if the Nazis win we lose everything, and instead of remaining free men we become nothing more nor less than the slaves of a foreign ruling class'.[50] The planned implementation of universal superannuation, as laid out in the 1938 Social Security Act, was 'whittled down in size'.[51] To prevent inflation, Nash carried out a strict policy of stabilisation of prices and wages, gaining the support of trade unions to check workers' demands for wage rises.[52]

Labour had promised to avoid conflict about equality during the war; powers to conscript wealth were to equal those to conscript men. However, in reality, big business boomed while the standard of living of the ordinary worker broadly stagnated; 'businessmen and manufacturers had guaranteed markets, sure sales, a disciplined labour force with set wages and conditions, and price margins which provided uninterrupted profitability, capital growth, and resources for further investment'.[53] By comparison, for the working class, opportunities 'to be upwardly mobile were poor . . . and even sagged under the . . . Labour government'.[54]

It seemed that Labour, in its desire to create a national war effort, was placing a disproportionate burden on the very constituency that had delivered it power. The parliamentary Labour Party was critical of this approach. Fraser, by comparison, wished to maintain a 'degree of flexibility' in his dealings with industry and the political right in New Zealand.[55] In the circumstances, the opposition National Party, in spite of the misgivings of the parliamentary Labour Party, hoped that party political differences could be put aside and a two-party coalition government formed.

With the fall of France in June 1940, public opinion demanded national unity and on 16 July, Fraser announced the formation of a two-party War Cabinet made up of three Labour (Fraser, Nash and Frederick Jones, the Minister of Defence) and two National representatives (Adam Hamilton, the leader of the National Party, and the former Prime Minster, Gordon Coates). In a constitutionally anomalous arrangement that reflected the split in the Labour Party over how to manage the war effort, New Zealand would have two cabinets; one, a War Cabinet, including the National representatives, would take major war related decisions, and another, a regular Labour Cabinet, would run domestic affairs.[56]

This arrangement pleased few. The Labour Party, in spite of Fraser's efforts, remained opposed to a national government.[57] The National Party was so unimpressed that it removed its leader, Hamilton, and replaced him with Sidney Holland, who declined to take a seat in the War Cabinet that November (Hamilton and Coates remained in their posts regardless).[58] With the fall of Singapore in February 1942, the stakes became even higher. The war was now a direct threat to New Zealand and with increasing strikes and industrial unrest, Fraser turned again to the National Party. He realised, in this time of national crisis, that he could not contain the demands of unions who fully expected the Labour Government to support them against management, and viewed the refusal of the party to do so as a betrayal. Strikes on the home front highlighted the 'glaring contrast' between those 'who, to a greater or lesser extent, were inflicting loss on the community in pursuit of sectional advantage', and the servicemen 'who had volunteered or been conscripted into risking their lives for the common interest'. The 'problem of maintaining industrial discipline' became 'worse than embarrassing for the Government'.[59]

That June, a new War Administration was set up, including seven Labour and six National ministers. The new arrangement, however, was 'as a constitutional device even more anomalous than its predecessor'. In order to ensure that all the Labour ministers kept their portfolios and that each National minister was responsible for some aspect of the direction of the war, considerable overlap of responsibilities was accepted. For example, Labour's Jones remained Minister of Defence while the former Prime Minister and opposition Member of Parliament Coates became Minister of Armed Forces and War Co-ordination. As if to highlight the *ad hoc* nature of the agreement, the existing domestic Cabinet remained in place.[60]

A coherent and straightforward vision for the management of the New Zealand war effort did not materialise that summer. Perhaps unsurprisingly, the new War Administration lasted only until October, when a dispute at the Huntly mines highlighted the fundamental frictions and competing interests inherent in the deal. The stand-off threatened to escalate into a national strike involving 1,200 miners. With Fraser in the United States, the new War Cabinet authorised legal proceedings against the miners (through the Strike and Lockout Emergency Regulations). Holland, deputy chairman of the War Cabinet and Leader of the Opposition, stated that:

> This is a time for the strongest action ... There can be no thought of any arrangement that interferes with the processes of the law by which those who break it are punished ... The question of who is to rule this country must be settled once and for all.[61]

This, surely, was exactly what the National Party had been co-opted into the War Administration to do. However, on returning to New Zealand, Fraser supported a very different course of action to that agreed in his absence. On 21 September, he recommended to a joint meeting of the War Administration and domestic Cabinet that the mines should be taken under state control, the prosecution of the miners be cancelled and that the owners of the mine should be paid a return on their capital for the rest of the war. This was completely unacceptable to Holland, who advocated that the ring-leaders be imprisoned and the rest given forty-eight hours to get back to work or be drafted into the Army. The National Party decided to withdraw from the War Administration and in early October the six National members duly resigned.[62]

Fraser had neither guaranteed a truly egalitarian distribution of wartime sacrifices nor demonstrated the will to control labour when it predictably revolted. He admitted in Parliament that 'the basis of unity in the country' had 'been destroyed – irretrievably destroyed', there could 'be no trust between the two parties now'. 'The best solution', according to Holland, was to hold an election 'as soon as' the war situation permitted.[63]

Mobilisation

The struggle for unity so evident among political elites across the Commonwealth was matched also, in many ways, by citizens' attitudes to mobilisation. The weight of available evidence points to a far less fervent and less deferent population than that which mythically went 'willingly' to war in 1914. Whereas the threat of war had 'inspired unity' in 1914, it did no such thing in 1939. No view of the experience of the British and Commonwealth Armies in the Second World War can be complete without reference to this reality.[64]

In contrast with the delayed introduction and exercise of compulsory powers to regulate the flow and distribution of manpower in the First World War, conscription was introduced in all parts of the United Kingdom, except Northern Ireland, from the outset of the Second World War.[65] Volunteering alone, according to the Official History, was not going to be 'practicable' as it could not guarantee 'the necessary number of recruits would be forthcoming at the time at which they were wanted'. Accordingly, the National Service (Armed Forces) Act was passed on the same day on which war was declared, all men between the ages of 18 and 41 being liable to service.[66]

The Army began the war with a force 'on paper' of around 900,000 men; 232,000 were regulars, 185,000 were in the regular reserves, 34,000 were in the militia (Britain's first ever cohort of peacetime conscripts), 428,000 were in the TA and 21,000 were in the TA Reserve. Only 485,000 of the 'part-time' soldiers had been 'mobilised and embodied' by the outbreak of hostilities. Thus, at the start of September 1939, Britain's Army stood at just over 700,000 men under arms, in training or carrying out full-time administrative duties. Over the course of the conflict, the Army absorbed around 3 million more men, three-quarters of whom were conscripts.[67] The low rate of volunteering can be explained largely by the fact that conscription was introduced immediately in the Second World War (it was introduced in 1916 in the First World War). Nevertheless, those that wished to volunteer before their call-up could do so. Table 2.1 indicates that while there was some willingness to volunteer for the Army in the first few months of the conflict,

Table 2.1 British Army intakes, September 1939–December 1945 (excluding ATS)

Year	Volunteers	Call-up	Total	% Volunteers
1939 (3 Sept.–31 Dec.)	163,400	112,800	276,200	59%
1940	273,300	858,600	1,131,900	24%
1941	82,000	365,700	447,700	18%
1942	68,600	363,000	431,600	16%
1943	53,300	184,000	237,300	22%
1944	37,200	214,700	251,900	15%
1945	33,900	166,800	200,700	17%
Total	711,700	2,265,600	2,977,300	24%

the volunteering impetus was short lived and diminished notably as the war continued.[68] Over the course of the whole war, 711,000 men volunteered for the Army (24 per cent of all men recruited during the period). The equivalent figure for the First World War was 54 per cent; more men volunteered for the Army in the first two months of the First World War than did in the whole of the Second.[69]

Overall, just over 5.5 million men served in the British armed forces during the Second World War; this represented roughly 45 per cent of all men aged 15 to 49 in 1939.[70] A total of 6,146,574 men served in the British armed forces during the First World War, representing roughly 58 per cent of all Scotsmen, Welshmen, and Englishmen and 15 per cent of all Irishmen aged 15 to 49 in 1911.[71] It is evident, therefore, that in the Second World War, the home front and industry received a greater proportion of the country's manpower than in the First. In March 1941, Churchill imposed a ceiling of 2 million on the strength of the Army to ensure that it did not absorb manpower that would be better employed in industry. However, 'with increasing deliveries of American munitions from mid-1941', the ceiling was breached and the number of men in the Army continued to rise, reaching 2,920,000 by June 1945.[72] The balance of manpower allocation between the forces and industry during the Second World War can partly be explained by the more technological, and less manpower-intensive, approach employed by the British armed forces during the Second World War,[73] but the different relationship that existed between citizens and the state also played a role.

The conciliatory approach employed by Ernest Bevin, the Minister for Labour, during the war reflected the understanding that something had changed during the interwar period. Bevin believed that treating labour with a 'heavy hand' would 'antagonise' and in the long run 'impede the war effort'.[74] The process of negotiation that took place between Government, workers and employers as a result, while lauded by many commentators for its efficiency and success,[75] granted individuals and employers a significant degree of freedom and flexibility in the way that they chose to engage with the war effort. For example, the National Service (Armed Forces) Act, made statutory provision for considering claims for exemption from service for reasons of conscience, and for postponement of service on the ground of the serious personal hardship that immediate call-up would entail. Over the course of the war, 59,192 applications as conscientious objectors and 317,762 for postponement of call-up on grounds of severe personal hardship were made by men and heard by the appeals mechanism. This was 4.5 per cent of all registrations under the Military Training and National Service Acts.[76] In addition, the principal firms engaged in contracts and subcontracts for the Government, and in other work which was deemed of importance to the life of the community, could apply for deferment of the call-up of individual workers who were not otherwise exempt by virtue of the schedule of reserved occupations. By the end of 1941, about 6 per cent of all those called up had applications for a deferment made on their behalf. In all, 301,000 deferments were granted, 4 per cent of those who had been called up.[77]

From the beginning of 1942, the system of maintaining certain reserved occupations (e.g. all skilled craftsmen involved in the manufacture of weapons were exempt from military service) was gradually replaced by a process where reservations were granted only on an individual basis. During this later period, 4,722,800 deferment applications were made. These applications fell into three classes: newly registered under the National Service Acts, renewal applications of those who had already received a period of deferment, and those who in consequence of the raising of the age of reservation for their occupations were now liable to be called up.[78] There can be little doubt that industry needed young men of military age to maintain output. Nevertheless, if one accepts that almost all of these applications were made with the consent of the employee and that the employee had the option to volunteer should he not wish for a deferment, it is apparent that a significant proportion of the public, supported by industry and the professions, were less than enthusiastic about serving in the armed forces. Taking into account the percentage of registrations that avoided service for reasons of conscience and hardship (4.5 per cent) and the 1939 to 1941 figures for the percentage of registrations that applied for a deferment (*c*.6 per cent), it is likely that at a minimum 10 per cent of those called up during the war made an effort to avoid military service. If the deferment figures for 1942 to 1945 are included, this figure could be significantly higher. As the Official History on Manpower during the Second World War admitted, with all these 'loopholes' it was certainly 'not surprising' that the call-up scheme produced a 'disappointingly low number of men for the Armed Forces'.[79]

Mobilisation for the war effort in India also cannot be understood outside of the socio-political context. In the highly charged political climate of the subcontinent, conscription was quite simply out of the question. The Indian Army would have to be expanded by volunteerism alone. On a superficial level, the Raj was extremely successful in this endeavour; the Indian Army of the Second World War was to become the largest volunteer army in history.[80] In October 1939, the regular Indian Army had totalled 205,038 men.[81] In the first months of the war, there was little demand for recruitment as London did not expect to need the Indian Army in a European conflagration; by the end of 1939, the Army had only grown by some 15,000 and by June 1940, according to one report, a meagre 23,000 had been recruited, mostly from the 'martial classes' – groups, such as Sikhs and Gurkhas, who, on the basis of their presumed fighting abilities and traditions as well as their proven loyalty to British interests, were considered ideal for military service.[82]

After the fall of France, the situation changed dramatically. Recognising the increasingly global dimensions of the war, the British Government called for a substantial expansion of the Indian Army. In six months it almost doubled in size and did so again in 1941 when the focused tapping of new classes and areas began. It grew by about 73 per cent in 1942. Thereafter, growth slowed dramatically.[83] Nevertheless, by the end of the war, there were more than 1.65 million Indian men in the Indian Army, with hundreds of thousands more recruits serving in auxiliary roles, a grand total of 2.285 million men.[84] This compared favourably to the 1,270,000 Indians who volunteered in the First World War, 827,000 of whom could be described as combatants.[85]

The army of 2.25 million that was created on the subcontinent was no small achievement. However, it came from a population of 390 million, and, thus, represented only a small proportion of potential Indian manpower. At the time, it was estimated that 12,957,811 of India's vast population were between 18 and 30 years old and 'had the required intelligence, aptitude and mechanical sense essential for service in the modern armed forces'. Taking this figure at face value, this means that 18 per cent of available manpower was tapped by the Indian Army during the war.[86] However, the British assessment of available manpower was the product of deeply ingrained racial prejudices and it is likely that a far greater number of Indians could have made excellent soldiers; the 'peasants' of Russia, for example, proved more than capable of mastering the intricacies of modern warfare and there is no reason why Indians could not have done the same. As it transpired, the Army recruited only about 3 per cent of the adult male population of the region in this period.[87]

The largest number of recruits came from the Indian Army's traditional recruiting ground of the Punjab.[88] However, by the summer of 1942, the supply of 'martial class' recruits for further expansion was running out[89] and only a minority of the new men came through the customary routes. Young Jat Sikh farmers, for example, were noticeably under-represented; with food prices rocketing, there were too many incentives for them to stay on the land.[90] Compared to its pre-war expenditure, in real terms the Indian state was spending three times as much money by the end of the war. This had to be paid for and Indians proved largely unwilling to pay high taxes and showed little desire to lend to the state. With taxes and loans failing to raise enough money to meet wartime expenditure, the state resorted to printing money. The amount of currency in circulation multiplied about six and a half times during the war and inflation was the inevitable result.[91] Certain segments of society, especially debtors and farmers, benefited dramatically from this wartime policy.

> Inflation lightened the burden of debts, money rents and land revenue. The same amount of produce in the early 1940s fetched two or three times what it would have earned five years earlier. Old demands, which remained fixed in money

> terms, could therefore be met by selling a half or a third of the produce previously required to meet them. The problem of rural indebtedness, hitherto a focus of government attention and legislation, was by August 1943 (according to the Reserve Bank of India) 'relegated to the background almost to the point of being forgotten' ... Suddenly, a large section of the peasantry received more prosperity than its political leaders might have dared to promise.[92]

Many of the recruits, from 'non-martial' areas such as Madras, Bengal and Bihar, were not in a position to take advantage of these economic opportunities. Only a minority of such men owned land, the majority being tenants, labourers and artisans. Recruits from Madras went up from 3 per cent of the pre-war Army to 17 per cent of wartime recruits. The quarter of a million Madrassis who joined were mostly agricultural labourers, while the Bengali recruits tended to come from towns.[93] Inflation only exacerbated the already difficult position of these wage earners, who made up about a third of the total rural population and the industrial working class. The real wages of factory workers declined by as much as 30 per cent in the period 1939 to 1943. At the same time, the price of grain rose faster than incomes and in Bengal rises in the price of rice lead to hunger and then famine Those who died, an estimated 4 million, were mostly agricultural labourers.[94]

Thus, while 'in a strictly legal sense' the Army was manned by volunteers, in comparison to Britain most recruits were desperate for jobs and 'were forced to join up through necessity'. Many, in fact, were hungry, underweight and undernourished.[95] Morale reports noted that 'a large proportion of the expanded Army ha[d] enlisted, not because of military tradition, but in order to provide for its families',[96] and, indeed, it is noticeable that the Indian upper classes showed little interest in volunteering for the Army.[97]

It is in this context that the much-vaunted expansion of the Indian Army must be understood. The Army 'continually struggled' to meet its recruitment targets.[98] Except for the Gurkhas, almost all the old 'martial classes' quickly began to show signs of indifference. Sikh, Punjabi, Musalman, Pathan and Dogra regiments all struggled to keep their units up to strength. Increased efforts to recruit among these classes produced few returns.[99] Ordinary, 'non-martial' Indians were, therefore, required, but they proved to be mostly 'economic conscripts', and, in general, had little interest in or enthusiasm for Britain's war, even after the Japanese advance into Burma and Eastern India threatened the immediate security of the subcontinent.[100]

In spite of these changes, the martial composition of the front-line Army changed little, and 'despite being very heavily publicized by the army and government as evidence of the army's increased inclusiveness', the new recruits from non-martial areas were mostly kept out of the front line.[101] At the end of the war, only 5 per cent of the infantry in the Indian Army were raised from non-martial classes. The armoured corps was 'almost entirely composed of the martial classes', while only those artillery and air defence regiments recruited from the martial classes were deployed in the front line. The conclusion one must come to, consequently, is that beyond those communities with traditional ties to Britain, the majority were unwilling to commit to the war effort. In the main, it was the poor, the destitute and the needy that made up the bulk of the Indian Army and these men were mostly kept out of the front line as the authorities did not trust their willingness to fight for the Empire. As one historian has put it, 'few lining up to join the army seemed to be driven purely by patriotism. Recruiting officers realized that volunteers were keener on knowing the scope for personal gain.'[102]

The issue of mobilisation was no less complex in the Dominions. In Canada, the introduction of conscription in the last year of the First World War had nearly torn the country apart; only one French Canadian regiment had been sent overseas to fight at the front and it was generally agreed that French-speaking Canadians had 'shirked their obligation as much as possible'.[103] The war, instead of promoting unity and a spirit of collective sacrifice, split Canada in two.[104]

In an attempt to avoid a repeat of the conscription crisis of the First World War, both the leader of the opposition, Dr Robert Manion, and the Prime Minister, Mackenzie King, came out openly, in March 1939, against conscription in any future war. 'So long as this government may be in power', said Mackenzie King, 'no such measure will be enacted.'[105] Mackenzie King had opposed conscription in the First World War, a fact central to his, and the Liberal Party's, continued success in elections in Quebec. In the interests of national unity, therefore, Canada's participation in the Second World War would have to be, just as was the case in India, on a voluntary basis.[106]

Volunteers were encouraged to enlist for the duration of the war on general service (GS) in the newly created Canadian Active Service Force (CASF), which also incorporated activated reserve units alongside those of the smaller regular force, which numbered just more than 4,000; the reserves came to about 51,000 men.[107] About half of the 58,337 men who joined the Canadian Army in September 1939 were from these regular and reserve forces, while civilian recruitment was enhanced by the lack of key munitions industries in Canada and the continuing high unemployment rate.[108]

However, after this initial wave of enthusiasm, recruitment was 'steady but not spectacular', with 2,000 to 6,000 men joining each month.[109] By February 1940, censorship showed that the men of 1st Canadian Division who had already been sent to the UK were extremely disgruntled. 'Boredom, homesickness and a feeling of not being really needed appear to be the main reasons why nearly all these Canadian soldiers grumble', wrote the censors. 'The majority of the writers warn their friends and relations not to join the Army.'[110]

Following the disaster at Dunkirk, recruitment jumped significantly to over 30,000 in June and July 1940. It was clear, nevertheless, that there was little widespread enthusiasm for war among both English-speaking and French-speaking Canadians. The Conservative Party's poor showing in the 1940 federal elections seemed to be due to the fact that they were 'too imperialistic, too aggressive, too likely to press for conscription'. Too many Canadians 'remembered the casualties, the suffering, the internal strife of the Great War'. Few, it would appear, envisaged Mackenzie King as a great war leader, mobilising men and machines.[111]

Canada had spoken; nevertheless, there was a clear need for more manpower if the country was to make a meaningful contribution to the war. With the disasters in France unfolding, the Government passed the National Resources Mobilisation Act (NRMA) in June 1940. This added a second class of soldier to the Canadian Army, conscripts who were reserved for home defence duty only. Initially, only unmarried or widowed men between the ages of 21 and 24, without children, were called up for thirty-days training. Later, compulsory training for NRMA soldiers was extended to four months, which, from 20 March 1941, was conducted with GS recruits. A month later, authority was obtained for conscripts to replace GS soldiers on coast and home defence duties, thereby releasing volunteers for service overseas.

There can be little doubt that conscription and the continued tensions between French- and English-speaking Canadians impacted upon the scale of wartime mobilisation and war enthusiasm.[112] Over the course of the war, 550,694 men volunteered directly into the Canadian Army. This represented 18 per cent of males aged between 15 and 49 in 1941. However, in addition, a further 58,434 men volunteered to transfer from NRMA to GS during the war, taking the figure up to 20 per cent of the male age cohort. Thus, 609,128 of the 708,535 men who served in the Army during the war could be described as volunteers. The Canadian Army was, therefore, on the surface, almost entirely a volunteer force (86 per cent).[113]

It has been argued, however, that a large proportion of 'volunteers' for GS only did so 'at some point after receiving their first notice to report for medical examination under the compulsory mobilization regulations'. Out of almost 200,000 volunteers surveyed in November 1943, 37 per cent reported that they had volunteered only once the call-up had begun. Overall, if one adds those who volunteered to transfer from NRMA to GS during the war, it is likely that 'over 40 percent of all men who served as volunteers in the Canadian army during the war' were 'induced to do so either directly or indirectly through the workings of the NRMA'.[114]

To make matters more complicated, recruitment was not even across the whole of Canada. French Canadians were noticeably less keen to volunteer than their British Canadian compatriots. While one has to recognise that some French-speaking Canadians would have enlisted in provinces other than Quebec (10.1 per cent of those born in Quebec enlisted in other Canadian provinces), only 11 per cent of those aged 15 to 49 in the predominantly French-speaking province volunteered to join the Army during the Second World War from their home province; this compared with 24 per cent from the British provinces of Ontario and British Columbia and 27 and 28 per cent from the Maritime provinces of New Brunswick and Nova Scotia.[115] Quebec also had the lowest rate of volunteer enlistment for the Royal Canadian Navy and Royal Canadian Air Force, while it had the highest rate of conscription (over twice that of Ontario) of any province in Canada; 32 per cent of enlistments in the Army in Quebec were conscripts, as compared to an average of 10 per cent for the rest of the country.[116]

Overall, an adjutant-general's study of October 1944 indicated that in the Canadian Army Overseas, 'some 74 percent of soldiers were English-Canadian or British, 12 percent were French Canadian, and 12.5 percent were of other continental European extraction'.[117] This was in a country where, in 1939, it was estimated that 30 per cent of the population was French Canadian.[118] Native Canadians were even less likely to join up than French Canadians; 'decades of mistreatment at the hands of the Canadian government' made natives 'unreceptive' to 'mobilization initiatives'. By the end of the war, 'only 3,090 Natives had served in the military (including NRMA units) out of a ... population estimated at 126,000 in 1944'.[119]

It is evident that a significant proportion of potential manpower in Canada was not coming forward with enthusiasm to serve. As J. T. Thorson, the Minister of National War Services, put it in 1942, the number of men available for the Army was 'far less than that indicated by statistical estimates'. In mid-1942, he informed the Cabinet War Committee that it was proving 'necessary to send out as many as nine notices to obtain one [NRMA] man'.[120] As Stacey has put it, 'the majority' of men called up applied for deferment.[121] Postponements of compulsory military training for all reasons totalled 246,133 in January 1943.[122] In May 1945, the figure was 267,468, with a further 13,458 applications still waiting a decision. Of the 267,468 postponements granted, only 32,195 were in essential industries, 10,843 were conscientious objectors, with the rest made up of men involved in farming, fishing, lumbering, mining, education and the merchant marine, among other things.[123] The total number of postponements requested during the war came to 746,478, of which 664,525 were approved; 'some of these were for extensions rather than new requests'.[124] By comparison, during the war, only 157,841 conscripts enrolled for training as part of the NRMA; it is clear, in this context, that a significant proportion of available manpower in Canada had little interest in mobilising for the Second World War.[125]

The South African response to mobilisation was remarkably similar to that of Canada. Mindful of the scale of opposition and the growing tensions within South Africa, and 'the apparent risk of civil war',[126] Smuts decided against a fully national war effort and embarked on creating an entirely volunteer army. The state's participation in the war would be reliant on its ability to mobilise popular support.[127]

Table 2.2 Military Pay HQ: attestations to the Union Defence Force, Cape Corps, Indian and Malay Corps and the Native Military Corps, September 1939–March 1945

Year	UDF	% Total	CC	IMC	NMC	Total non-Eur	% Total
1939	3,039	2%	2	0	0	2	0%
1940	62,950	45%	4,365	1,023	5,211	10,599	14%
1941	27,380	20%	10,286	5,336	21,035	36,657	47%
1942	27,061	19%	5,429	1,888	14,808	22,125	29%
1943	10,895	8%	983	52	5,912	6,947	9%
1944	7,311*	5%	7	0	477	680	1%
1945	1,419	1%	0	0	0	476	1%
Total	140,055	100%	21,072	8,299	47,443	77,486	100%

* Figures for July–Sept. 1944 were not available.

In September 1939, South Africa's regular and reserve forces were very low in numbers; the Permanent Force was 5,382 strong and the Active Citizen Force (roughly the equivalent of the TA in Britain) was 13,490.[128] Over the course of the war, 132,194 white men volunteered for the Army, with 186,218 volunteering for the armed forces in total. Out of a possible total of 570,000 white males of military age, 23 per cent volunteered to join the Army and 33 per cent volunteered for the armed services more generally.[129] This compares to the 146,897 white South Africans that fought during the First World War.[130] Participation by black, coloured and Indian South Africans was more limited with 122,254 men volunteering for the Cape Corps, Indian and Malay Corps and the Native Military Corps out of a population about four times bigger than that of white South Africa.[131] Again, this figure compares to black, coloured and Indian service in the First World War, when 107,769 were deployed as auxiliaries in non-combat roles.[132]

Monthly figures for recruitment in South Africa do not appear to have survived. However, in 1944, the War Records Department liaised with the Military Pay HQ to produce quarterly figures for attestations in the South African Defence Forces (see Table 2.2).[133] These figures do not match exactly the records for total enlistments during the war, but they do provide a substantially reliable picture of fluctuations in the rate of recruitment.

Other sources confirm the patterns laid out in Table 2.2 and it does appear that recruitment started off at a steady pace in South Africa. By the end of July 1940, over 42,000 white men had volunteered.

Considering the size of South Africa's white population,[134] this was a significant effort, especially when compared to initial recruitment levels in other Commonwealth countries. Recruitment, just as was the case in Canada, however, varied significantly in line with ethnic background and attitudes towards the legitimacy of the war. Afrikaners, for example, given their predominantly antagonistic attitude towards Britain,[135] and the stance of Malan's National Party, were far less likely to volunteer than their English-speaking compatriots.

There is much uncertainty in the literature over the number of Afrikaans-speakers who served during the war. The Government wished to present the force as a united front and play down differences between Afrikaans- and English-speakers within units. Thus, in official enlistment returns and statistics, there was no differentiation made on the basis of language. E. G. Malherbe, the Director of Military Intelligence during the war, estimated that 'at least 50 per cent of the force' was Afrikaans-speaking, a figure supported by the historian, Albert Grundlingh. S. Patterson believed that Afrikaans speakers made up 'well over half' while Leo Marquand went as far as to contend that 70 per cent had been Afrikaans-speaking.[136]

In an attempt to ascertain a true picture of the level of Afrikaner enlistment during the war, a sample of 1,112 service records from the South African Defence Personnel Archive in Pretoria was compiled.[137] Sixty-seven per cent of the sample had English names as compared to 33 per cent who had Afrikaans names, suggesting that 67 per cent of the Army was English-speaking. However, as an Afrikaans or English surname is not always a reliable indication of background, another assessment was carried out using surnames and religious affiliation. Afrikaner culture is closely associated with the Dutch Reformed and Nederduits Hervornde (NHK) Churches.[138] Thus, it was considered highly likely that those servicemen who described themselves as members of the Dutch Reformed Church or NHK were both culturally and linguistically Afrikaner. Indeed census statistics for the time show that the percentage of Afrikaans-speakers and the percentage of the population that attended Afrikaner churches were almost identical.[139] Those who described themselves as Anglican, Roman Catholic, Jewish, or members of the Free Churches (Methodist, Presbyterian, Wesleyan, Baptist and Congregationalist) were considered English-speaking.[140] Those few cases that were described as Apostolic and Full Gospel were allocated equally between Afrikaans- and English-speaking. The results matched the previous analysis almost exactly – 66 per cent English-speaking as compared to 34 per cent Afrikaans-speaking. It was noticeable that those with Afrikaans names almost always identified themselves as members of the Dutch Reformed Church, while, for example, those with Irish surnames were usually Catholic. In a population where 59 per cent of white men spoke Afrikaans and 41 per cent spoke English, these findings indicate quite clearly that the Union Defence Force (UDF) was disproportionally made up of English-speaking South Africans.[141]

These figures are supported by two studies carried out for the Adjutant-General on religious denominations in the South African Army in 1940 and 1941. These reports, which break the UDF down by religious affiliation, suggest, by use of a similar methodology, that around 73 per cent of the Army was English-speaking, as opposed to 27 per cent who spoke Afrikaans.[142] They also suggest that, broadly speaking, Afrikaners were less likely to serve on the front line. Records relating to the religious denominations of infantry units, as compared to artillery, anti-aircraft, supporting arms (such as the South African Medical Corps and South African Corps of Signals) and base units show that 24 per cent of infantry, 23 per cent of supporting arms, 36 per cent of artillery, 42 per cent of anti-aircraft and 43 per cent of base units were Afrikaans-speaking. Overall, 57 per cent of Afrikaans-speakers were in infantry units as opposed to 71 per cent of English-speakers).[143]

Motivation for enlistment among black and coloured South Africans was perhaps even more complex than it was for white troops. The African National Congress (ANC), churches and chiefs supported the war effort despite misgivings; declarations of loyalty 'were invariably', however, 'accompanied by calls for a more just political system' in South Africa. Support for the war, it was hoped, might bring about political and economic concessions.[144] After an initial reluctance to utilise black troops for the conflict, the Government eventually decided in June 1940 to establish the Non-European Army Services (NEAS). This consisted of the Cape Corps (CC), the Indian and Malay Corps and the Native Military Corps (NMC). These units, in line with traditional government policy, were largely unarmed and restricted to non-combatant roles. This state of affairs did not appeal to average black and coloured South Africans and it is clear that 'structural constraints' in South African society inhibited those whom the Government hoped would enlist. Indeed, for some, 'the real and immediate war was not in Europe or in North Africa, but much closer to home'. Young men who attended recruiting events were heard to ask questions such as 'what had the Government done for them?' and 'what have we to fight for?'[145]

Inequalities in black and white service conditions both illustrated and exacerbated these tensions. Basic pay per diem for recruits in the NMC was 2s 3d for those without, and 2s 6d for those with, dependants. Recruits in the CC and the IMC received 2s 3d per diem while remuneration for whites was 5s a day. In spite of inequalities in pay, 'it appears unequivocally clear that the foremost reason' for black and coloured enlistment was 'the economic factor'. Eighty per cent of black recruitment came from rural areas and of these the majority came from the Transvaal, where farming faced extremely adverse conditions during the war years.[146]

There were, of course, other reasons for black and coloured South Africans to join up. According to the censorship summaries, many of the black men who did attest were proud to join the Army, as they were keen on adventure and saw it as a positive way to demonstrate their manhood. Such comments clearly indicated a certain amount of racial stereotyping; nevertheless, the reports also pointed to a 'large number' of black soldiers who were also motivated by the concept of 'duty'. One private wrote to his wife that 'it is to protect you and other … people that I have to keep the enemy away from this country. After all, South Africa is the land of our birth and we have to protect it.'[147] The overwhelming evidence, however, suggests that the vast majority of black and coloured South Africans had little interest in the war and were put off enlisting by the appalling treatment they received at the hands of the South African state.

Right from the start, therefore, the character of mobilisation in South Africa was driven by socio-political tensions in the Union. To make matters more complicated, a clause in the Union Defence Act of 1913 stipulated that volunteers were not obliged to serve outside of the geographical boundaries of South Africa. This added an extra layer of volunteerism, as men had to take an additional oath to play a full role in the war effort and serve 'anywhere in Africa'. There are no official records of what proportion of men chose to take the 'Africa oath' and serve with the newly created Mobile Field Force (MFF). However, an analysis of the records from the Defence Personnel Archive in Pretoria shows that the vast majority of volunteers, 81 per cent, were awarded the Africa Service Medal, for service outside of South Africa, and, therefore, must have taken the 'Africa oath'.[148]

From the beginning of 1941, the rush of recruits that had accompanied the outbreak of war began to taper off and 'by the middle of the year the UDF was scraping the barrel for fighting soldiers'. So great was the need, that proposals were made to lower the medical requirements for active service and for an increase in pay to entice working men into the Army. Following the fall of Tobruk in June 1942, with the loss of 33,000 Allied prisoners, 10,722 of them South African, another (second) mobilisation was attempted to fill the void in the manpower of the UDF. This recruiting drive, the 'Avenge Tobruk' campaign, focused more on urban areas than previous efforts.[149] Recruitment jumped 46 per cent from the April/June to the July/September quarters of 1942. However, it fell again, by 56 per cent, in the fourth quarter of the year and never really recovered thereafter.[150] By the middle of the war, it was evident that South Africa's willingness to supply the Imperial war effort with manpower had largely petered out.

Australia, due to provisions in the 1903 Australian Defence Act precluding a large Regular Army, started the war, much like the other Dominions, with a tiny regular force, of fewer than 4,000 men, and a limited militia comprising some 70,000 part-time volunteers.[151] The Defence Act, like its equivalent in South Africa, stipulated that the militia could only serve within Australia. As a result, the country had 'to raise an expeditionary force from scratch for overseas service'.[152] Unlike the First World War, when two plebiscites to introduce conscription were defeated by popular votes, not least due to opposition from Irish Catholics,[153] conscription was introduced without consultation at the outbreak of hostilities in 1939. Much like in Canada, the Army divided its new recruits between those who had volunteered and those who were conscripted for service, with conscripts, the Citizen Military Force, limited to service within Australia and volunteers serving overseas, as part of the Second Australian Imperial Force (AIF).[154]

Mobilisation did not get off to a flying start with only a brief surge in enlistments in the first three months after the outbreak of hostilities. By February 1940, voluntary recruitment had dropped to a meagre 217 men per month. In fact, in the first six months of the war, only 21,998 men enlisted, compared with 62,786 during the corresponding period of the First World War. As news from the battlefields became worse and worse, enlistments rose and half of the total figures for the first two years of war were made in a period of three months, June, July and August 1940, after Germany had broken through on the Western Front and France had surrendered.[155] Enlistments during the second half of 1940 were 'sluggish' while recruitment throughout 1941 'proved slower than expected'.[156] In the first two years of war, voluntary enlistments did not reach the totals attained in 1914–16. Up to the end of August 1941, total enlistments in the AIF from a population of 7 million had amounted to 188,587 (~2.7 per cent). In the first two years of the First World War, 307,966 had volunteered from a population of 5 million (~6.2 per cent). Even if the total strength of the Royal Australian Air Force (RAAF) (about 60,000) and the new enlistments in the Navy (about 10,000) are added to the total of volunteers, recruitment was still below the First World War figure.[157]

In an attempt to increase voluntary enlistments, the maximum age limit for the AIF was raised to 40 in 1940, and the minimum lowered to 19 in 1941, and 18 in 1943.[158] By February 1943, to increase the number of Australian soldiers who could be used overseas, 'Australia' was redefined for conscript soldiers so as to include New Guinea, the Philippines and the Netherlands East Indies, a region of active operations that became known as the South-West Pacific Area (SWPA). Racial barriers to enlistment were also relaxed. By September 1945, approximately 3,000 Aborigines and Torres Strait Islanders had served in the military forces.[159] In spite of these efforts, in the second half of the war, between November 1942 and August 1945, fewer than 21,000 new men joined AIF units.[160]

Overall, approximately 686,473 men enlisted in the Australian Army over the course of the Second World War;[161] of these 261,617 enlisted directly into the AIF.[162] This would suggest that about 38 per cent of the Australian Army in the Second World War was made up of volunteers. These men represented about 15 per cent of the male population between the ages of 15 and 49, and 25 per cent of the male population between the ages of 20 and 40 (the recruiting ages for the AIF).[163] However, a further 2,725 men from the pre-war Regular Army and 207,041 men from the Citizen Military Force changed their status to AIF during the conflict by volunteering for overseas service within their units. This means that about 69 per cent of the Australian Army volunteered at some time during the war, representing about 26 per cent of the male population between the ages of 15 and 49, and

45 per cent of the male population between the ages of 20 and 40 (the recruiting ages for the AIF).[164]

To a degree, the poor rate of direct voluntary enlistments into the AIF was matched by what happened in New Zealand. It is not surprising considering the political context, that the process of mobilisation in New Zealand was characterised by divisions, dissent and, ultimately, outright revolt (see Chapter 10 of this volume). Recruitment for the New Zealand Forces commenced on 12 September 1939. By nightfall, enrolments totalled 5,419. Thereafter, the overall response was disappointing. On 11 April 1940, in an attempt to raise the number of voluntary enlistments, the age limit for other ranks was raised from 35 to 40 years.[165] However, it was clear that not enough men were enlisting to keep the Second New Zealand Expeditionary Force (2NZEF) in the field, and, in spite of the fact that 57,000 men had volunteered,[166] conscription, as it had been in November 1916,[167] was introduced on 22 July 1940.[168] The National Service Emergency Regulations demanded that all men aged between 18 and 45 register for military service. During five years of conscription, 306,000 men were called up for service;[169] only 52 per cent of all those called up (including volunteers) during the war ended up serving in military units (194,000 out of 375,000 volunteers and conscripts, 138,000 of whom served in the Army). The remainder were either conscientious objectors, discarded on medical grounds, reserved due to appeals by employers in essential industry or allocated elsewhere for various other reasons.[170] Selection for service was decided by lot, single men being chosen first. Mobilisation proceeded at the rate of about one ballot a month, until, by December 1941, all single men aged 21 to 40 had been called up for overseas service and all single men aged 18 to 45 (excluding those already called for overseas service) were called up for territorial service (in New Zealand).[171]

With the entry of Japan into the war in December 1941, a second phase of mobilisation began. With the inclusion of married men, recruitment rocketed from an average of 2,900 to 7,500 a month. Over 25,000 men and women joined in the month following the Japanese move into South-East Asia. By the end of 1942, all single and married men between the ages of 18 and 45 had been called up. Thereafter, the Army relied on the small accretion of young men coming of military age, around 1,000 a month. It is clear that by the beginning of 1943, the New Zealand Army faced an acute manpower shortage and indeed only a further 35,000 men were called up before the end of the war.[172]

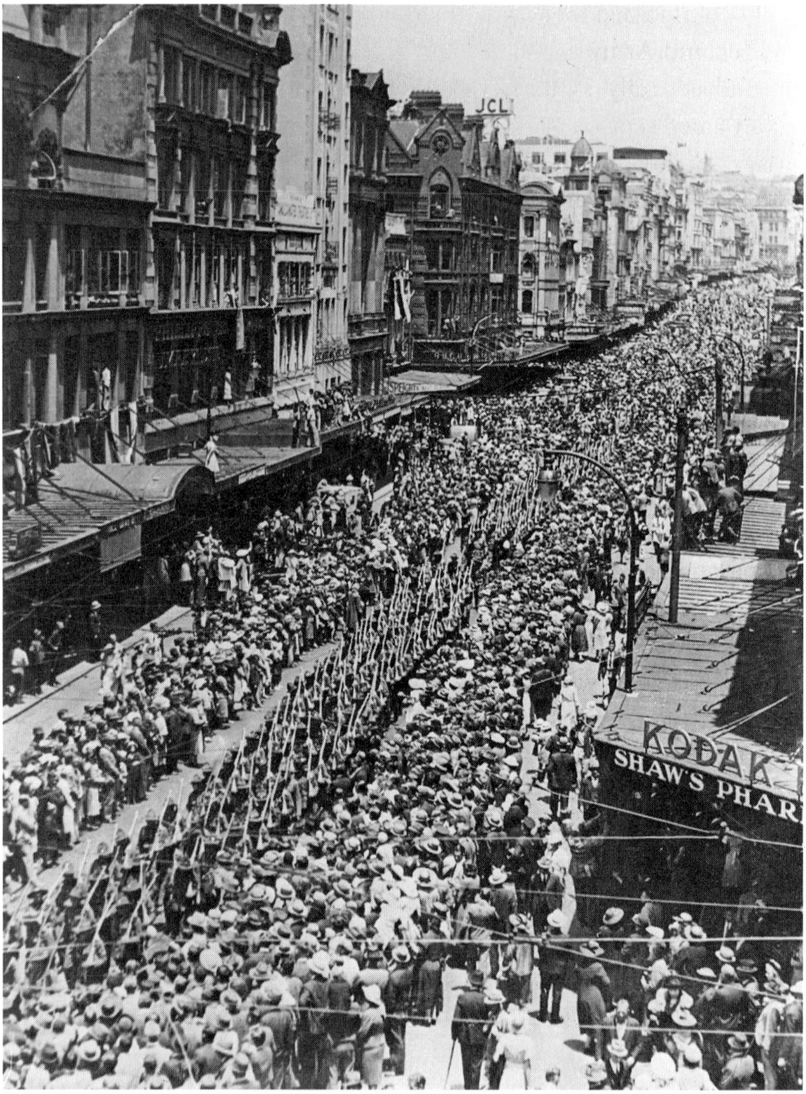

Illustration 2.1 Farewell parade for the 1st Echelon troops of the 2NZEF, Auckland, New Zealand, January 1940. Images like this mask the true level of enthusiasm for the war effort; in total, 47 per cent of all those called up in New Zealand appealed to Armed Forces Appeal Boards to avoid military service.

On the surface, and according to the literature, it appears that there was more enthusiasm to volunteer in New Zealand than perhaps in other Commonwealth countries (see Illustration 2.1).[173] If it is assumed that most of the 57,000 men who volunteered before

22 July 1940 joined the Army, then somewhere up to 41 per cent of the New Zealand Army in the Second World War was made up of volunteers. Indeed, fully 15 per cent of males aged between 15 and 49, and about 19 per cent of those aged between 18 and 45, volunteered for military service.[174] By July 1940, the number of volunteers in New Zealand was just over half of the Australian figure, in spite of the fact that Australia had four times New Zealand's population.[175] Overall, 194,000 men served in the New Zealand armed forces during the war, 51 per cent of the male population aged 15 to 49 and 25 per cent of the total male population.[176] By comparison, 117,000 New Zealanders served in the First World War, about 20 per cent of New Zealand's white male population.[177]

There is a considerable body of evidence, however, that suggests that large sections of New Zealand's population were fundamentally opposed to military service. By June 1942, 60,051 men, or 43 per cent of the total number of men called for territorial service, had lodged appeals against their call-up. In addition, 26,336 men, or 33 per cent of those chosen for overseas service, appealed. Appeals arising out of the conscription of married men with children, June 1942 to February 1943, amounted to 69,365, or a remarkable 71 per cent of the total number chosen. Thereafter, until the end of the war, 10,714, or 31 per cent of those called up, appealed against their service.[178] Such statistics point 'to a significant lack of acceptance of conscription' in New Zealand.[179] In total, 47 per cent of all those called up for military service appealed to Armed Forces Appeal Boards, 1.7 per cent of the total on grounds of conscientious objection. By comparison, only 2.9 per cent of those directed to essential work in industry appealed against their employment to Manpower Appeal Committees (14,450 out of 494,618 decisions and directions).[180]

Equality of Sacrifice?

It does appear that right across the Commonwealth levels of enthusiasm for war reflected levels of public morale, the political context and perceptions of state legitimacy. As the official historian for the New Zealand home front during the war noted in relation to the apparent poor rate of volunteerism:

> They [the men] were bitter that war had arrived for them, who had had no part in making it. Without enthusiasm, they

> accepted that it was necessary to fight the Nazis. They felt that conscription would come sooner or later and they might as well wait for it. With the bleak days of the Depression only a little behind, men who had known relief camps and pannikin bosses had no zest for more mud or for Army sergeants; men who had secured good positions at £5 or £6 a week had no mind to give them up for 7s a day any sooner than they must; men still on relief had little urge to fight for the country that had given them so little. Unemployment was waning, but jobs were still eagerly sought.[181]

One of the Australian official historians painted a similarly bleak picture. The Depression, it was argued, led to the development of a real 'class consciousness'. 'Old ideas of personal security, of class relationships, of investment, development, resources and potentialities, of obligations between creditor and debtor, and of the "just reward" were upset. It left a heritage of distrust, bitterness and resentment.' The ideal of 'mateship', spawned in the trenches of the First World War, was 'dimmed' for the small farmers and wage earners that had suffered most acutely during the Depression. They now put 'personal security' at the forefront of their considerations and this made them 'insensitive to appeals or promises or exhortations'.[182] Manifestations of 'apathy' among the population could be traced back to the Depression; 'many young men, unable to find work' did not feel themselves 'part of the nation'.[183]

These dynamics mattered as the British and Commonwealth Armies were made up disproportionately of those cohorts of society most impacted by the struggles of the Depression, the working- and lower-middle classes.[184] To date, however, only this author has gauged the social-class composition of a national contingent of the British and Commonwealth Armies in the Second World War, that of the 2NZEF. The study showed that the 2NZEF had a disproportionately small percentage (14.8 per cent) of the professional classes as compared to the population at large in New Zealand (25.1 per cent). Skilled workers were also under-represented (23.7 per cent, as opposed to 28.2 per cent). Unskilled workers, by comparison, were represented to a disproportionately high extent (25.5 per cent in the 2NZEF as compared to 12.1 per cent in the general population). It is evident then that the 2NZEF was of lower occupation status than the population at large (see Table 2.3).[185]

Table 2.3 The 2NZEF by social class

Class	Army	1966 Census
I Higher professional	5.3%	5.8%
II Lower professional	9.5%	19.3%
III Clerical & highly skilled	13.3%	13.3%
IV Skilled	23.7%	28.2%
V Semi-skilled	22.7%	21.3%
VI Unskilled	25.5%	12.1%

It is possible to build on the work carried out on the 2NZEF to produce the first comprehensive and statistically robust social-class surveys of the British, Canadian and South African Armies in the Second World War (sufficient data was not found to do the same for the Australian and Indian Armies).[186] The usual method for ascertaining social class categorises groups based on their position in a graded hierarchy of occupations.[187] As Erik Olssen and Maureen Hickey put it, in industrial societies:

> Ideas about careers and occupations fused in complex ways to constitute occupation as a dimension of identity. Occupation also became the key determinant of the work one did, the pay or income one got, the quality of house one lived in and where it was situated, the level of risk of accident or illness, and one's life chances generally.[188]

The five basic social classes used in Britain from 1921 to 1971 were:

I Professional: e.g. doctors, dentists, engineers, writers
II Intermediate: e.g. pharmacists, chemists, teachers, editorial staff
III Skilled: e.g. shop assistants, clerks, lorry drivers
IV Semi-Skilled: e.g. caretakers, railway porters, land workers (misc.)
V Unskilled: e.g. labourers, factory workers (undefined), cleaners.

In October 1944, in preparation for demobilisation, the War Office in the UK presented the Ministry of Labour with a comprehensive breakdown for 2.5 million other ranks in the Army by main occupational classification. This list did not categorise the men by social class. However, by cross-referencing the list with the social-class categories in the 1931 and 1951 censuses, it is possible to build a substantially

Table 2.4 A social-class breakdown of 2.5 million Other Ranks in the British Army, 1944

	Army	General population	
Class	1944*	1931 Census*	1951 Census*
I Professional	0.9%	2.4%	3.3%
II Intermediate	4.4%	13.2%	14.5%
III Skilled	68.4%	48.7%	52.9%
IV Partly skilled	11.3%	18.2%	16.1%
V Unskilled	15.1%	17.5%	13.1%

* Male only.

accurate picture of the social-class make-up of the bulk of the British Army during the Second World War (see Table 2.4).[189]

The sources to carry out a social-class survey of the Canadian Army are available, just as they are in New Zealand and the UK. There were several extensive surveys conducted by the Canadian Adjutant-General's Branch in late 1944 and the autumn of 1945, from which an occupational profile of the Canadian Army can be derived. These surveys, explicitly designed to prepare for the period of demobilisation, questioned soldiers about their pre-war occupations and levels of education as well as their hopes and desires for the post-war world. Special Report No. 180, the most extensive of these surveys, was based on a sample of some 12,000 army personnel (2.4 per cent of the Army).[190] In order to assess the extent to which the Canadian Army was representative of Canadian society more generally, Bernard R. Blishen's occupational-class scale, devised from the findings of the 1951 census, was used to associate each of the occupations listed in Special Report No. 180 with an occupational class (see Table 2.5).[191]

Unfortunately, there are no occupationally based class analyses of South Africa in the 1940s or adjacent decades that are suitable for this study.[192] The sample of service records from the South African Defence Personnel Archive in Pretoria does, however, present an opportunity to compile a social-class profile of the UDF, as it includes details of occupation for those men who served during the war. In order to make an estimation of how representative the troops of the UDF were of South African society more generally, the UDF sample and the *c.*900 discrete occupational categories set out in the 1946 South African census were grouped into classes using, with one key alteration (farmers), the

Table 2.5 The Canadian Army by social class, 1945

		Canada 1951 Census		
Class	Army	English*	French**	Total
I Higher professionals	0.8%	1.3%	0.6%	0.9%
II White collar	9.7%	11.8%	9.5%	10.7%
III White collar + higher blue collar	7.0%	8.3%	4.1%	6.3%
IV Higher blue collar + lower white collar	3.8%	8.5%	5.4%	7.0%
V Skilled trades	38.7%	36.2%	30.6%	34.2%
VI Semi-skilled	19.9%	17.0%	24.5%	19.6%
VII Unskilled	19.9%	16.9%	25.3%	21.3%

* English-speaking.
** French-speaking.

Table 2.6 The Union Defence Force by social class

	Army			South Africa 1946 Census		
Class	English	Afrikaans	Total	English	Afrikaans	Total
I Professional	4.0%	1.2%	3.1%	8.2%	1.4%	4.4%
II Intermediate	10.2%	3.6%	8.0%	18.2%	9.5%	13.5%
III Skilled	74.1%	75.6%	74.6%	66.5%	67.8%	67.2%
IV Partly skilled	8.7%	11.3%	9.6%	5.1%	13.8%	10.0%
V Unskilled	3.1%	8.3%	4.8%	1.8%	7.4%	4.9%

occupational classifications in the 1951 UK census.[193] From this analysis, it was possible to build a social-class breakdown of the UDF in the Second World War (see Table 2.6).[194]

The data presented in Tables 2.3, 2.4, 2.5 and 2.6 show that, certainly in terms of social class, the mix of volunteers and conscripts that made up the British, New Zealand, Canadian and South African contingents of the Commonwealth Armies in the Second World War was not representative of the societies they defended. In the British case, even if it is assumed that all officers (about 6 per cent of those serving in the British Army at any one time)[195] came from social classes I (Professional) and II (Intermediate), which was certainly not the case by 1944, the Army as a whole was not representative in these categories.

An almost identical pattern pertained for the New Zealand and South African Armies and even the Canadian Army (when it is taken into account that the vast majority of the Canadian Army, perhaps 74 per cent, was English-speaking – i.e. 40 per cent of the Army was semi-skilled and unskilled, while only 34 per cent of the English-speaking population was in these categories).[196] This dynamic is hardly surprising considering, for example, that in the UK special deferment schemes were in place for those in finance, the law and many of the medical professions. Moreover, many of the most capable men available for call-up preferred to join either the Royal Navy or the RAF, thus further reducing the number of those from the professional and intermediate classes available to the Army.[197] In 1941, 327,520 out of 2.2 million annual registrants expressed an interest in joining the Navy, and 824,417 the RAF; yet that year those two services only absorbed 92,600 and 174,400 conscripts respectively. Both the Navy and the Air Force 'were spoiled for choice; they could cherry-pick the best and brightest of the bunch'.[198] As a result, Britain's wartime Army was typically made up of shopkeepers, bricklayers, bank clerks, confectioners, bespoke tailors, painters and travelling salesmen.[199] Indeed, this class (III) was clearly over-represented in the British Army; almost 70 per cent of its manpower was made up of skilled workers as compared to about 50 per cent of the overall population.[200]

The picture was not drastically different in South Africa. Only 11 per cent of recruits came from social classes I and II compared to 18 per cent among the white population more generally. This discrepancy was particularly prevalent among English-speakers: only 14 per cent came from social classes I and II compared to 26 per cent in wider society. Skilled workers made up the majority of the UDF: 75 per cent compared to 67 per cent in society. Not all of these skilled workers can be described as particularly affluent, however. Many occupations that would have been considered relatively high status in the 1951 UK census did not carry the same prestige in South Africa, where there was a large base of cheap African labour available. Indeed, no fewer than 77 of the 336 Afrikaner records (23 per cent) were farmers – by far the most represented occupation among Afrikaner recruits.[201] During the war, northern parts of the country were stricken by a devastating drought, which resulted in large-scale crop failures. Localised drought and infestations of 'streak disease' and 'army-worms' also impacted negatively on agriculture throughout these years. Many farmers would have been poor and far from affluent.[202] Prominent military personnel and historians, including Malherbe, Roos and Grundlingh, have all argued that the majority of white volunteers came from the ranks of the poor:

> Small-scale farmers, for instance, enlisted to avoid creditors. Destitute whites who approached welfare and aid societies were often told to enlist rather than beg for assistance. And when the Vaal river flooded the alluvial diamond diggings at Barkly West, many diggers were quick to exchange the uncertainty of prospecting for the greater financial security of armed service.[203]

The censors support this contention, noting that 'a large proportion of letters … particularly those written in Afrikaans, were semi-literate, as far as style, spelling, vocabulary and expression of thought is concerned'.[204] In comparison to Afrikaner enlistment, only thirty-one English-speakers (5 per cent) listed their occupations as farmers, and it does appear that English-speaking recruits were generally more urban and affluent than their Afrikaner compatriots. The most represented occupation among English-speakers was clerk, making up 123 of the 667 records (18 per cent) assessed in this study.

In New Zealand and Canada, it was not skilled but semi-skilled and unskilled classes that were particularly represented in the Army. In both countries, in the context of the remote nature of the war, the extremely fractured political arena, and the high volume of appeals against military service, professional and skilled classes were both more willing and more able than unskilled workers to avoid military service. The 2NZEF and Canadian Army were, to a greater extent than their British and South African equivalents, 'working-class' armies. What evidence there is on the Australian and Indian Armies points to a similar situation. The majority of recruits into the Indian Army, according to Indivar Kamtekar, came from the poor and destitute classes.[205] An Australian Army census taken between 1942 and 1943, showed that employers and the self-employed made up smaller proportions of the Army than they did the population more generally (5.3 per cent compared to 7.4 per cent and 8.1 per cent compared to 13.4 per cent respectively). Employees (i.e. the middle and working classes), made up 86.6 per cent of the Army as compared to 79.2 per cent of the Australian population.[206] As one historian has put it:

> Although combat soldiers and men observing them often noted the great occupational diversity within their ranks, and every infantry battalion probably had its share of intellectual privates and NCOs, [non-commissioned officers] it does seem reasonable to assume that the labouring end of the occupational spectrum was better represented in the front-line than further back, and in the Other Ranks than among the officers.[207]

This observation is supported by information available on Australian Army recruits. They were generally not highly educated; men assessed as requiring attention because they were 'educationally backward' were probably more common than those who had completed a full secondary course, and illiterates were two to three times more prevalent than the university educated. The 1942–3 census found that approximately half the men in the Army had left school at the age of 14. Only 7 per cent had completed a full secondary course; 22 per cent of Australians educated in the 1930s and 1940s tended to finish secondary school. Only 1.4 per cent had a degree or diploma, while about 6 per cent of those educated in the 1930s and 1940s reported having finished university.[208]

Thus, manpower policy, and the degree to which the individual states could compel citizens to serve, played out in the demographic make-up of the British and Commonwealth Armies. In Britain, where special deferment schemes were in place for those in the higher echelons of society, and where many partly skilled and unskilled workers were drafted into the wartime economy, the fighting was left to those in the lower-middle and upper-working classes. In those other countries, where mobilisation was reliant to a greater degree on volunteerism, a larger, if still disproportionately low, fraction of the Army was made up of professional and intermediate classes. It was those most connected to the British world and least able to avoid conscription (by deferment or due to their economic position) that joined up.

These patterns of recruitment matter greatly for 'the incidence of unemployment' in the interwar years 'varied according' to 'social class'. In Britain, at the time of the 1931 census, 'professionals and semi-professionals; employers and managers; clerical workers; foremen and supervisors' accounted for '25.07 per cent of the total workforce but only 8.34 per cent of the unemployed workforce'. By contrast, skilled, semi-skilled and unskilled workers accounted for 74.33 per cent of the total workforce and 91.66 per cent of the unemployed. The incidence of unemployment among the first group of workers varied from 1.31 per cent among employers and managers to 5.06 per cent among clerical workers. By contrast, the incidence of unemployment varied from 11.9 per cent among skilled and semi-skilled workers to 20.51 per cent for unskilled workers.[209] Thus, although it must be recognised that there were a multitude of attitudes towards the Government's interwar record on unemployment, the vast majority of the wartime British Army, the 94.7 per cent that came from social classes III, IV and V, came from those parts of society more affected by the Depression.[210] In New Zealand, Canada, South Africa, Australia and India, unskilled and skilled workers, such as farm and general labourers, also found themselves disproportionately present in the Army. Much as in the UK, these were the men who had suffered most from the vicissitudes of the Depression in the interwar years, with consequent effects on morale, self-worth and motivation.[211]

The Social Contract

It is important, of course, not to overstate the effects of social class on the lack of willingness to serve in a second great war. While it is undoubtedly true that social classes III, IV and V were over-represented in the British and Commonwealth Armies and that this must have had an impact on their commitment and how the Army responded to crises, it cannot be assumed that these classes were homogenous in their approach to the war. Men, in their thousands, did volunteer. Mark Johnston, for example, has highlighted three positive motivations for Australians to join up: a desire for adventure, a sense of the Australian military heritage and, perhaps most importantly of all, duty.[212] Many sources noted the 'seriousness and unusual maturity' of fighting men and it is noticeable that duty, activated by the wartime crisis, played a role in voluntary enlistments across the Commonwealth.[213] Although soldiers rarely talked openly of patriotic duty, 'hardened soldiers' often preferring to 'offer trivial and fabricated reasons, or none at all' for fighting rather than 'confess to patriotic motivation', many did believe that it was vitally important to fight for and defend their country.[214]

It is noticeable, for example, that the vast majority of voluntary enlistments during the war occurred during months where there was either extremely positive or very negative news from the front. Enlistments were, it would appear, strongly related to the events of the war, and the need to defend home and the Empire.[215] Much mobilisation propaganda revolved around this understanding; recruitment material was directed towards big ideas and 'big words', such as the morals and ethics of the war effort.[216] Based on an analysis of the only censorship reports to survive from the first years of the war, the summaries of South African soldiers' mail from East Africa, 1940–41, it does appear that 'big words' and big ideas played a more dominant role in soldiers' willingness to volunteer than is often imagined. There was not a single reference to joining up for economic reasons in this period. One man wrote in May 1941:

> When I joined up it was for the sole benefit of South Africa, and not for pomp and glory, or to get away from civil life, or to see the world at the Government's expense, my whole ideal was to give up all I could to protect and defend South Africa.[217]

In spite of the fact that it was not uncommon for Afrikaners to be ostracised by their families for enlisting,[218] an examination of the censorship summaries again suggests that, especially at the start of the war, those Afrikaners who did join up were highly idealistic, even more so that their more reticent English-speaking compatriots. One man wrote, 'I am helping to fight for the honour of my wife and children and my homeland for I don't want to be a slave under the rule of pigs and men who deny God',[219] while another commented that 'my struggle and my life is for your sake and my duty ... It is a question of life or death and what would become of our land, South Africa.'[220] Another wrote to his wife that he was fighting 'for your freedom – freedom is all'.[221] Some saw their service 'as a martyrdom', while a recurring theme in the men's letters touched on the fact that they saw themselves as the 'true Afrikaners' for they were doing their 'duty' in defending their beloved 'Afrikaner Nation':[222]

> I can tell you another thing and that is we are not fighting for the English alone but also for ourselves. If we have to wait and fight on our own borders when the enemy comes there then we might as well give up. So long as we can fight things out here it is much better for you all. It makes no difference whether we die here or there, but here the fight will not be so unequal as it would be

> there. One must always think of the women and children; how many will perish in airraids [*sic*]. These are things that the Ossewa Bandwag do not consider and they count us as English. I say, the true Afrikaners that I have met are all *here*.[223]

The censors went so far as to suggest that 'one of the most effective forms of propaganda' for the war effort would be 'the granting of Union leave to some of these [Afrikaners]; certainly no better [recruitment] "agents" could be found than those Afrikaners who have taken part in the fighting up north'.[224]

In many ways, therefore, as the South African historian Neil Roos has put it, the act of enlisting 'both embodied and reflected' soldiers' duty as citizens and reflected 'a dialogue about citizenship and patriotism'. The 'big words' set out 'the duties expected' of men, while behind these 'big words' lay 'little stories', motivations relating to the wellbeing of families, loved ones and the community to which soldiers felt emotionally attached.[225]

> From this perspective, the act of volunteering was a political moment that marked the meeting of Big Words and little stories. Some ... might have identified pecuniary need as their main reason for joining, others patriotism, and others yet, peer pressure. However, what was common for all ... was this: the act of volunteering [and enlisting] added layers of duty, obligation and privilege to the social contract that they, like their fathers before them, were busy negotiating with the state.[226]

In this context, the manner in which soldiers, their families and their communities were to be treated by the state during the war would matter greatly. The issues of social justice and fairness would resonate for soldiers throughout the war years and impact greatly on combat performance in the struggles to come.

Rhetoric and Reality

The countries that constituted the main contingents of the British and Commonwealth Armies in the Second World War contained no less than a combined population of 470 million.[227] Nevertheless, the question of mobilisation was to become one of the recurring issues of the war; 'in the end, manpower became the chief limiting factor on Britain's war effort'.[228] The manpower problems that were to become so prevalent from 1942 onwards were not, however, solely an issue of demographics, but more a question of consent. As John Horne has argued in relation to the First World War, the war 'cast doubt on the supposed moral unity of the nation by resuscitating sectional divisions'. Such tensions 'strained the legitimacy of the state and nation and intensified the pressure on governments and military commands' to arbitrate between different perceptions of what was right or wrong and fair or unfair in the context of 'total war'.[229]

Indeed, 'it is easy to forget how deeply segregated the British nation was by class' in the 1940s. The manner in which the Depression shaped the 'terms' of the interaction between the state and its citizens in this period should not be overlooked either.[230] Even in those parts of the Commonwealth where the trials of the interwar years were better managed, there was a distinct disconnect between rhetoric and reality; the war was a contested and deeply divisive experience, a far cry in many ways from a 'People's War'. Additionally, it is important to note that skilled, semi-skilled and unskilled men, the classes that made up the vast majority of the British and Commonwealth Armies, were significantly over-represented in official measures of unemployment during the interwar years.[231] The British and Commonwealth Armies were made up to a significant extent of those men most seriously affected by the Depression.

Britain and the Commonwealth were also far more ethnically and politically divided than is remembered. In the more homogenous societies of the United Kingdom and New Zealand, where a shared sense of British identity was deeply ingrained, governments were able, more or less, to compel their citizens to fight through the introduction of conscription. By comparison, Canada and Australia, with their significant French-speaking and Irish Catholic minorities, restricted conscription to home defence for most of the conflict. South Africa, with its Afrikaner majority among its white population and black majority among all South Africans, and India, where loyalty to Empire 'was at best conditional' and 'at worst non-existent', relied on wholly volunteer armies.[232] In a most basic sense, these conflicting and varied attachments to Empire and the war were borne out in national mobilisation figures (see Table 2.7).[233] Nevertheless, it must be remembered that many cared deeply about the meaning of the war. The act of enlisting reflected soldiers' duty as citizens; it was a 'political moment' that added

Table 2.7 Mobilisation: the British and Commonwealth Armies in the Second World War

	% to Male population aged 15–49			% Army made up of volunteers
Country	Volunteer Army	Army as a whole	Armed Forces	WW2
UK	6%[iii]	28%	45%	24%
NZ	15%	36%	51%	41%
Aus.	26%	38%	52%	69%
Can.	20%	23%	33%	86%
SA[i]	23%	23%	33%	100%
India[ii]	3%	3%	3%	100%

i Figures for South Africa are for white servicemen only out of a total of 570,000 white males of military age.
ii Figures for India are out of the entire male population of India.
iii From 3 Sept. 1939.

layers of duty and obligation to the social contract between citizens and the state.[234] Britain and the Empire was unquestionably made up of a massive number of 'citizens' and 'subjects' it could use in a great war, but it needed to find a way to tap into this resource effectively. In this endeavour, the political and social context and the search for meaning in the war would matter greatly.

Part II The Great Crisis of Empire

3 DEFEAT IN THE WEST

The 'Phoney War'

On the outbreak of war on 3 September 1939, the pre-planned process of sending an expeditionary force to France began to be put into effect. Within five weeks, the Commander-in-Chief (C-in-C) of the BEF, General Lord Gort, had four regular divisions under his command on the Continent: 1st and 2nd Divisions of I Corps, under Lieutenant-General Sir John Dill, and 3rd and 4th Divisions of II Corps, under Lieutenant-General Sir Alan Brooke.[1]

Gort, who until his appointment was the Chief of the Imperial General Staff (CIGS), sat very much at the crossroads of change in the British Army. A Grenadier Guardsman and the son of a viscount, Gort attended the Royal Military College, Sandhurst, in 1905–6. Having performed effectively in staff appointments during the early years of the First World War, he went on to command at battalion and brigade level, earning a reputation for superb leadership and gallantry. He was wounded four times, mentioned in dispatches on eight occasions and awarded the MC, the Distinguished Service Order (DSO) (with two bars) and the Victoria Cross (VC). Following the war, Gort played a key role in the increasing professionalisation of the Army. He attended the Staff College at Camberley on its reopening in 1919 and was invited back as an instructor only two years later. In 1926, he became chief instructor at the senior officers' school at Sheerness; in 1932, he was appointed Director of Military Training in India; and in 1936, he returned once more to the Staff College, this time as Commandant. By 1937, at the age of 50, he was no less than a full general and CIGS.[2]

The BEF, under Gort's command, took over a sector on the Belgium frontier. To its left was General Henri Giraud's Seventh French Army and on its right was General Georges Blanchard's First French Army. Gort and the BEF came under the direct control of General Alphonse Georges, commander of the Armies of the North-East, who was in turn under General Maurice Gamelin, the Supreme Commander of the French Army.[3]

In the months that followed, during the 'Phoney War', the Army looked to rapidly improve its readiness for conflict. Reinforcements poured across the Channel. In December, 5th Division, largely composed of regulars, joined II Corps. In January and February 1940, came the first three territorial divisions; 48th South Midland Division joined I Corps, 50th Northumbrian Division joined II Corps and 51st Highland Division became part of a new III Corps under Lieutenant-General Sir Ronald Adam. This new Corps swelled in numbers with the inclusion of two more territorial divisions, 42nd East Lancashire and 44th Home Counties, in April. That same month, three more 'reserve' territorial divisions, 12th Eastern, 23rd Northumbrian and 46th North Midland and West Riding, with little equipment and almost no training, were sent to France for labour duties and, ideally, to complete their preparations for combat. Thus, by April 1940, the BEF had increased in size to 394,165 men, incorporating five regular and five trained territorial divisions, which made up a fighting establishment of 237,319 men.[4]

In many ways, events unfolded as pre-war plans had anticipated. The BEF made up, as had always been intended, only a small proportion of the Allied Army massing on the Continent. This Army numbered around 3,740,000 and comprised no fewer than 144 divisions: 104 French, 22 Belgian, 8 Dutch and 10 British (not including the untrained 'reserve' divisions). The *Wehrmacht*, by comparison, was made up of 2,760,000 men and just short of 142 divisions, an Allied advantage in terms of manpower of 1.4:1.[5]

The Allied superiority in numbers of men was matched largely, in spite of delays in rearmament, by advantages in materiel. The French alone had 3,254 tanks; the Germans had 2,574. All the French tanks, except for 450 *automitrailleuses de combat* and *de reconnaissance*, were armed with 37mm or 47mm guns while almost 1,500 of the German total had only machine guns or 20mm cannon. The Germans had more numerous anti-tank weapons at their disposal, 12,800 compared to the 7,200 possessed by the French. However, the majority of French tanks were 'generously plated' with 40mm armour. This 'seriously limited the effectiveness of the German anti-tank guns, which with a calibre of 37mm could only penetrate French armour at extremely short ranges'. The German numerical superiority in these weapons was, therefore, 'largely illusory' as most French anti-tank guns could penetrate 'German tanks at most ranges'. The Allies also had the advantage of a greater number of artillery pieces, 14,000 compared to the 7,400 of the Germans.[6]

Where the Allies were less strong was in the air.[7] The Germans employed close to 4,000 aircraft in France in 1940, or ten planes per mile of front;[8] by comparison, in Operation 'Barbarossa' against the Soviet Union in 1941, they would use 3,000, or two planes per mile of front. In France in 1940, the RAF had 182 first-line combat aircraft, 96 bombers and 86 fighters. French air forces numbered some 4,862 aircraft of all types, more than half of which were fighters. However, France's modern front-line aircraft numbered only 523 fighters, 37 bombers, and 118 reconnaissance aircraft (678 aircraft in all).[9]

With the exception of first-line air power, therefore, force-to-force ratios appeared considerably in the Allies' favour, especially considering that they had the advantage also of the defence. Now these forces had to be used effectively to resist the expected German onslaught and prevent a 'knock-out blow', as had been done in 1914. Intelligence estimates throughout the second half of the 1930s had built a coherent picture of the character of the expected German attack. The *Wehrmacht*, it was recognised, placed great emphasis on the speed and manoeuvre of *panzer* divisions supported by a reconstituted *Luftwaffe*.[10] These assessments were reinforced by the findings of the British military mission to Poland in 1939, led by Major-General Sir Carton de Wiart. This series of reports was supplemented by others supplied by escaped Polish officers and pointed again to the conclusion that armoured forces and air power 'played a preponderating part' in German offensive operations. These documents were read closely by the staff at HQ BEF and a series of pamphlets explaining the latest information about German operational techniques were issued to officers in the Field Force.[11] The BEF and the War Office 'had managed to identify all the elements of what was to become Germany's blitzkrieg method – the triad of armoured spearhead, speed of advance, and air support' before the beginning of the German attack in the West.[12]

Where the attack would fall, however, was less certain. It was widely believed that rather than attempt a frontal attack on the Maginot Line, the German onslaught would come with its principal weight through Belgium, as in 1914. Throughout the winter of 1939/40 the French and British High Commands agonised over plans to meet this expected assault. The French, in particular, were determined to avoid a repeat of 1914–18, when war had raged over their industrial northern provinces; they wanted to fight as far as possible on territory outside of their borders. It was decided, as a consequence, that on proof of a German attack, the Allied Armies would advance into Belgium and Holland and make use of the multiple river systems of North-West Europe as strong defensive lines. The final plan for the British Army, Plan D, was to advance to the River Dyle, a narrow stream a short way east of Brussels. Here it would adopt a defensive position between the French First Army, making a similar advance on their right, and the Belgian Army on their left.[13]

The plan was full of risks. The Belgians were publicly neutral; it was, consequently, impossible for Allied commanders openly to discuss proposals with their probable allies. Reconnoitring the land that they would fight on was out of the question too as discovery might provoke the expected German attack.[14] Moreover, an advance into Belgium followed by an encounter battle with the *Wehrmacht* was an extremely complex operation for an army that was largely inexperienced in corps-level manoeuvres and was still desperately trying to make up the training deficit.

This reality was not lost on the commanders of the BEF, who knew that their troops were imperfectly trained; General Sir Edmund Ironside, the new CIGS, had told Gort that his first duty on reaching France was 'to train his army'. In this regard, Gort was only partially successful; although mandatory training procedures for units and formations were introduced in September and October 1939, 'each level of command had sufficient autonomy to vary how best to implement' them. Thus, some formations trained well and others did not. The 3rd Division, for example, held four divisional exercises during this period, each lasting for several days; by comparison, 2nd Division conducted only two short movement exercises. Many formations were also instructed to spend up to 50 per cent of their time preparing fortifications along the Franco-Belgian frontier (defences that Plan D did not envisage utilising). 'The upshot was that on the eve of the German onslaught Gort believed that his regular divisions were still not as well trained as their 1914-vintage counterparts and his Territorials were fit only for static operations.'[15]

The Norwegian Campaign

What was needed most of all, therefore, was time, a commodity that became increasingly scarce as developments elsewhere in Europe began to impact on preparations for the expected onslaught in the West. The Allies' strategy for a long war revolved around the plan to blockade German access to food and raw materials. With this aim in mind, German supplies of Swedish iron ore needed to be cut off; these were known to be exported to Germany via Luleå at the northern end of the Baltic or by rail via Narvik in northern Norway. Narvik was especially important, as during the winter months when Luleå was icebound, it was the sole route for Swedish iron ore to Germany. Furthermore, by making use of Norwegian territorial waters, German ships were able to move with impunity from near the Artic to the Skagerrak, allowing them to circumvent a close blockade of Europe.[16]

Churchill, who on the outbreak of war had been appointed the First Lord of the Admiralty, proposed to mine Norwegian waters to block the route via the coast to the Baltic approaches. The matter was soon subsumed by calls to help Finland in its struggle against the Soviet Union in the Winter War. In late November 1939, the Soviet Union, keen to seize important territory on its north-western borders and emboldened by its non-aggression pact with Germany, had invaded Finland. The British, strongly encouraged by France, decided that supplies and troops should be sent to support the Finns, via Norway. There would, it was hoped, be additional benefits should this approach be pursued. As forces moved to support the Finns, they would, by necessity, 'occupy points vital for the German war economy', most importantly the ports by which iron ore was shipped to Germany.[17]

Before the operation could begin, however, Finland capitulated. The Allies decided to persist regardless, but were pre-empted by the German armed forces, when, on 9 April 1940, the *Wehrmacht* seized Narvik, Trondheim, Bergen and Oslo. The Allies now were faced with the task of landing forces from the sea against an enemy already established on shore, a challenge made harder by the fact that with so many troops deployed in France, there were only a few formations available for another expeditionary force.[18]

Operations began on 14 April, involving landings at two locations over 400 miles apart, one in the area of Trondheim, the other at Narvik. The first of these failed with the forces engaged only lasting two weeks before they had to be evacuated on 3 May.[19] The outcome of this operation was due, according to one report, to no less than:

> A lack of appreciation of the difficulties likely to be encountered; plans concocted from hour to hour without any first-hand knowledge of the situation; choice of troops totally unfitted for such a campaign; loss of essential equipment en route from England; excessive kit (three kit bags per man) which made the Force virtually immobile; the absence of snow-shoes or skis, making movement off the roads impossible; uncertain and inadequate means of communication between Army and Navy; maps out-of-date, difficult to read and received in bulk too late to be distributed; lack of suitable landing-craft; and most important of all, absence of that air parity, if not superiority, which is essential during the early stages of a combined operation.[20]

All of these factors 'made for chaos, and chaos indeed resulted, ending only with an addition to the long list of successful rear-guard actions and evacuations that both disfigure and adorn the early pages of the histories of so many of Britain's wars'.[21]

The actions at Narvik went slightly closer to plan; the town was captured. But with the beginning of the Battle of France on 10 May, an evacuation from Norway became increasingly necessary. By 8 June, all troops had been removed; the experience in Norway served notice, if any was needed, of the challenges that awaited the BEF in the fields of France and Flanders.[22]

The Battle of France

All started well on the Western Front when the German assault eventually materialised. On news of the attack, the BEF advanced into Belgium and by 11 May had reached its positions on the River Dyle. Two days later, British light reconnaissance units came into contact with the enemy for the first time. It soon became clear that the main thrust of the

German offensive was not on the Allied left, as it had been in 1914, but against the French First Army and, above all, its Ninth and Second Armies in the centre of the line. Here, German Army Group A, under General Gerd von Rundstedt, with no fewer than forty-four divisions, and seven of the ten German *panzer* divisions available for *Fall Gelb* (the German attack in the West), advanced south-west through the Ardennes, towards the French frontier in the area of Sedan.[23] In the south, Army Group C, under General Wilhelm von Leeb, with seventeen divisions, none of them armoured, launched a feint against the Maginot Line. In the north, facing the British, French, Belgian and Dutch divisions in the Low Countries was General Fedor von Bock's Army Group B, comprising twenty-eight divisions, including the remaining three *panzer* divisions.[24]

On 15 May, the full force of Army Group B's assault, which was designed to fix the Allied forces in the north, so as not to impede the flanks of the planned breakthrough in the centre, was unleashed on the BEF. 'Ground was lost, and retaken by counter-attack' but by nightfall 'the front was intact'.[25] By now, however, after only five days of the campaign, 'the position on the flanks of the BEF, rather than the actions of the enemy to its front, was chiefly determining events'. In the north, on 14 May, Holland had capitulated, and the French Seventh Army, on the extreme left of the Allied line fell back. To the south of the BEF, at the centre of the Allied line, on the River Meuse, the Germans opened a catastrophic breach in the front of Second and Ninth Armies. The French First Army was also penetrated and the BEF fell back to protect its flanks. Over the next ten days, the *panzer* divisions of Army Group A drove westwards through the shattered French divisions. The threat to the southern and south-western flanks of the BEF now became 'more menacing even than the enemy to the east' – what was supposed to be the front line. The BEF had been positioned in considerable depth; nevertheless, the extent of the German penetration meant that engineers, military police and the three untrained 'reserve' divisions now had to be pressed into service to protect the flanks. By 19 May, there were no French troops between von Rundstedt's spearhead and the sea to the rear of the BEF. The British Army was to all intents and purposes trapped between two German Army Groups; cut off from its base in north-west France, it was in serious danger of complete annihilation.[26]

The *ad hoc* units protecting the BEF's southern flank, much like the French Armies that had disintegrated on the British right, proved no match for Army Group A. By 20 May, little was left of 12th Eastern and 23rd Northumbrian Divisions. The main body of the BEF, which by now had retreated to the Escaut Line (see Map 3.1), generally held on tenaciously. On the afternoon of 21 May, a limited counter-attack by 5th and 50th Northumbrian Divisions (the British reserve) supported by the only tanks attached to the BEF's main body, those of 1st Army Tank Brigade, was launched near Arras on the southern flank. Although the assault sent 'a wave of alarm' through Army Group A, it proved weak at the point of contact with the enemy. Two of 5th and 50th Divisions' four brigades were sent to Arras to strengthen the garrison there. Of the two brigades selected for the counter-attack, one was held in reserve, which meant that only one brigade advanced, and since it held one battalion in reserve the Arras counter-attack was made by little more than two battalions.[27]

The assault was supported by seventy-two tanks, but only sixteen of these vehicles boasted an anti-tank gun. The majority of the BEF's 250 tanks, of which 175 had 2-pounder guns, were in 1st Armoured Division, which had only started to arrive in France in mid-May.[28] The division had been separated from the main body of the BEF by Army Group A's rapid advance, and, as a result, fought under the command of the French Seventh Army. Thus, the main body of the BEF, in spite of the fact that 'on paper' it was the most 'tank-intensive' army in France, only had twenty-five of the powerful medium Matilda II tanks (with 2-pounder anti-tank guns) under its command. Many of these vital weapons broke down during the constant movements of the British retreat and, thus, by the time of the Arras counter-attack, which was the 'only true manoeuvre the BEF was able to make during the campaign', 5th and 50th Northumbrian Divisions were supported by only a handful of medium tanks.[29]

As the BEF's counter-offensive petered out, General Maxim Weygand took over from Gamelin as Supreme Commander of the Allied Forces. He ordered the BEF to fall back to the old frontier positions it had spent the 'Phoney War' preparing. There it was to make ready for a major counter-attack to be launched in conjunction with a northwards thrust by the French from south of the German penetration. By 23 May, the withdrawal was complete. But by now Gort was increasingly short of men, for the BEF was facing threats not only from the east (Army Group B) but also to the south-west and west (Army Group A). Only four divisions defended the line on the frontier to the east. Two divisions and 'whatever *ad hoc* forces [Gort] had been able

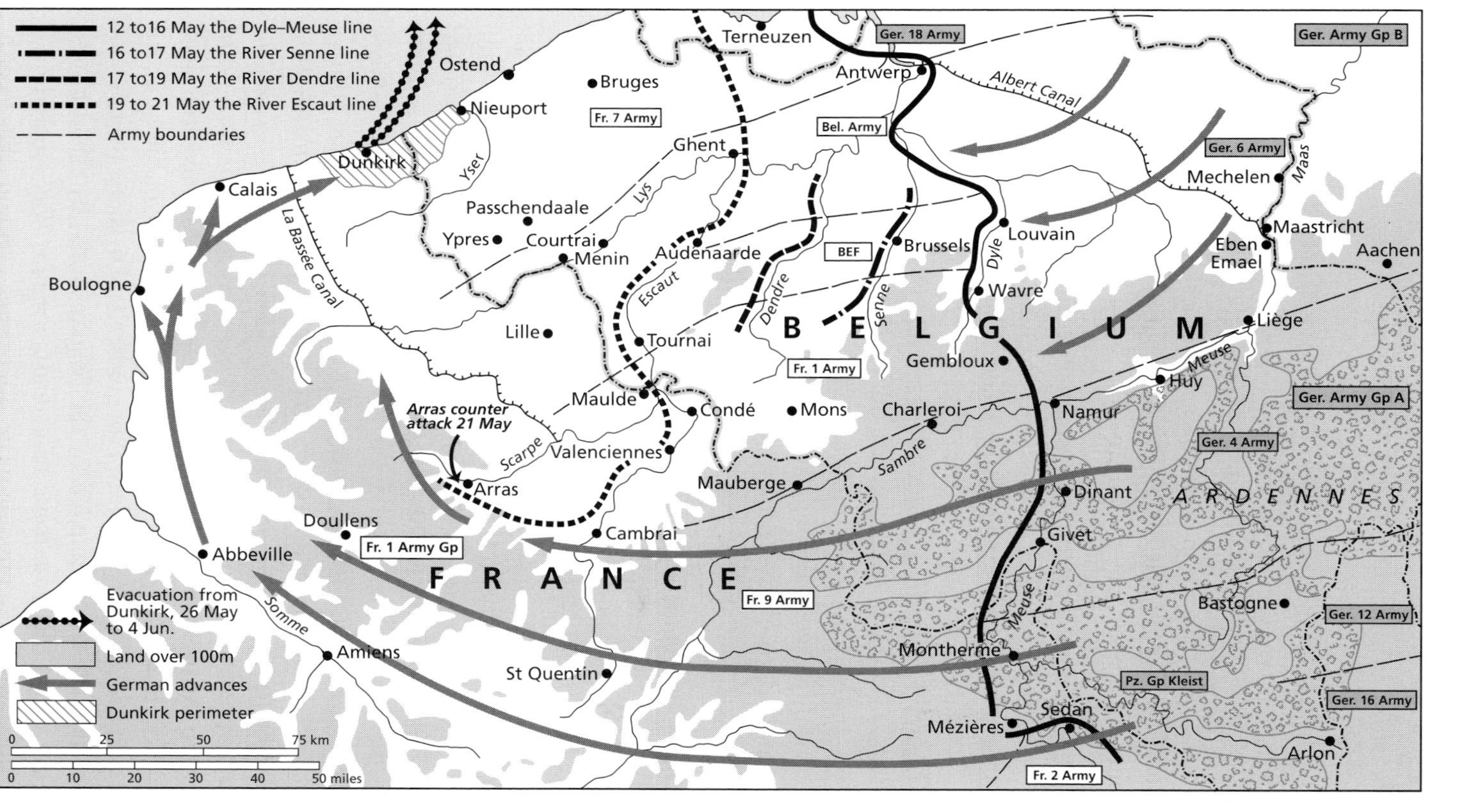

Map 3.1 The German breakthrough and the Allied retreat, 10 May–4 June 1940

to collect under various expedients from base troops and logistic units, now transformed into infantry' defended the south-western and western flanks.[30]

This meant that there were gaps in the British line, a situation, according to David French, that played into German hands:

> As soon as their reconnaissance units had made contact with the BEF's forward positions, they mounted a series of probing attacks 'which taps along the front line until a weak spot or gap is found'. Once they found it, they crossed the obstacles covering the British front, established a bridgehead, widened it, and built a bridge so that they could bring tanks and other support troops across. If the reconnaissance unit failed to find a weak spot, their follow-up forces put down a concentration of gun and mortar fire, sometimes assisted by Stukas, and crossed the obstacle behind a curtain of fire. Once they had established a bridgehead, they infiltrated between the British-defended localities, with apparent disregard for their flanks, and pushed mobile troops well forward to further disrupt the defenders by seizing focal points such as town and road junctions.[31]

In the face of these tactics and the aggressive German infiltration techniques, the British line did not hold for long. That night, 23 May, Army Group A broke into the British positions on a 20-mile front. A chaotic retreat ensued.[32]

Matters now began to deteriorate rapidly as concentric attacks were launched directly on the BEF and on its flanks. By 25 May, Army Group B had driven back the Belgian Army leaving a gap on the British left, thus increasing the possibility of encirclement. Gort was left in an impossible position. He had been ordered by Weygand to launch a counter-attack from the north on 26 May (unknown to the C-in-C BEF, the French had abandoned the idea on 24 May). The 5th and 50th Northumbrian Divisions were again to be used for the attack, but it looked destined to fail. The prospects of a more general breakout to join the French Army south of the Somme also looked highly doubtful. At 1800hrs, on 25 May, Gort cancelled the preparations for the counter-attack and ordered 5th and 50th Northumbrian Divisions to move to the British left to fill the gap left by the Belgian Army. By this decision 'Gort saved the BEF'; its route to at least one port was secured and evacuation was still possible. The following evening, the British

Illustration 3.1 British soldiers wade out to a waiting destroyer off Dunkirk, May/June 1940. The defeat in France opened the decisive phase of the crisis that was to engulf Britain in the first half of the war.

Government gave orders for the commencement of Operation 'Dynamo', the evacuation of the Army from Dunkirk.[33]

Evacuation, as desirable a prospect as it was for the increasingly exhausted BEF, was, nevertheless, no easy matter (see Illustration 3.1).

Supported by French troops, the BEF 'had to hold their positions, and then embark, against attacks by a total of about nine divisions'. The crowded bridgehead was a prime target for air attack, and, as the perimeter shrank, German guns were brought within range of the beaches and the harbour.[34] Ironside estimated that only 30,000 men could be saved. Brooke, the commander of II Corps, thought it would be 'lucky' if 25 per cent of the BEF made it back to the United Kingdom.[35] In the end, the BEF fared much better than either feared. The German High Command's remarkable and much-debated decision on 24 May to halt the advance of the *panzers* at the 'gates' of Dunkirk for over three days was, undoubtedly, a key factor in the 'miracle' that was to ensue. The Arras counter-attack had played no small part in convincing Hitler and key personnel in the German High Command that the Allies were preparing a decisive counter-offensive against the massively exposed flanks of the German advance. At the key moment, in spite of the chaos that was engulfing the higher echelons of the Allied military organisation, Hitler and his key generals lost their nerve.[36]

Even before the official evacuation commenced, 26,402 British and 1,534 Allied casualties and non-combatant personnel were repatriated. On 26 May, as the majority of German *panzers* waited passively on the road to Dunkirk, Allied forces began the process of withdrawing into the defensive perimeter around the town. When, on the following day, the German advance resumed, the troops holding the newly prepared perimeter fought with a steely determination. As the battle raged on the outskirts of the town, the Royal Navy organised arriving units and oversaw the evacuation. With the docks in Dunkirk destroyed, personnel were transferred directly off the beaches by inshore boats and the famous little ships before being offloaded onto larger vessels. From 28 May, more numerous evacuations took place from the East Mole (harbour sea defence), where personnel could be embarked directly onto destroyers and larger civilian ships.[37]

Britain had played its 'trump card', sea power, to rescue its Army. Nevertheless, the *Luftwaffe* took a heavy toll; of the eighty-four 'big ships' involved, fifty-two were sunk or sustained damage. Of the thirty-eight destroyers involved, six were sunk and twenty-six were damaged. Of forty-six personnel carriers, nine were sunk and eleven damaged. Overall, nearly one in five of the 848 vessels of all descriptions that had come under the control of Vice-Admiral Bertram Ramsay's Naval HQ in Dover were lost, and nearly half were damaged.[38]

The evacuation continued until 4 June. On that day, at 0900hrs, around 40,000 French troops, who had held on bravely to support the removal of as many troops as possible, surrendered. In total, 338,226 Allied personnel, including 198,315 British, were evacuated in 'Dynamo'. Of these, approximately 100,000 were saved from the beaches, the rest being lifted from the East Mole.[39] Nevertheless, there were still 150,000 British troops in France serving with the French Army south of the Somme (including 1st Armoured Division and 51st Highland Division). With French resolve having stiffened after Dunkirk, and with more effective tactics being employed, the Battle of France was not yet over. On 13 June, Brooke returned to the Continent to take control of what was to be a new BEF. The 52nd Lowland Division was already disembarking in France and the 1st Canadian Division, which had arrived in Britain at the end of 1939, was preparing to sail for France. There was still, it was hoped, a chance that France could fight on.[40]

On 14 June, Brooke met with Weygand and Georges. He was to be bitterly disappointed by the experience and quickly realised that there was almost no prospect of success. That evening he spoke to Dill, who had replaced Ironside as CIGS, and Churchill. Another evacuation had to be launched before it was too late. Two days later, Churchill made one last 'extraordinary' offer, an indissoluble union between the two countries; 'France and Great Britain', he promised, would 'no longer be two nations, but one Franco-British union'. Churchill hoped to legalise 'the continuation of French military action, from overseas' if necessary. The French Cabinet eventually rejected the proposal, believing it would render them a British dominion. Paul Reynaud, the Prime Minister, resigned, and the following day, 17 June, Marshal Philippe Pétain, the hero of Verdun, who had returned to government as Vice-President of the Council, broadcast to the French nation that resistance would cease. By then, nearly all of the remaining British troops, except 51st Highland Division, which had been captured on 12 June at St Valéry, had been evacuated.[41] Overall, 'the Royal Navy brought away from the area south of the Somme 191,870 Allied troops including 144,171 BEF personnel'.[42] It was a 'second deliverance'. The campaign in France and Flanders was over.[43] The BEF had suffered 68,111 casualties of whom 3,500 were killed and 40,000 were prisoners; 88 per cent of its artillery and 93 per cent of its motor vehicles were abandoned among the wreckage of Britain's Continental Army.[44]

Assessments and Recriminations

The defeat in France opened 'the decisive phase' of the 'Imperial crisis' that was to engulf Britain in the first half of the war. It was a 'catastrophic blow, whose full implications had been scarcely imaginable before it actually happened'. Britain was exposed to invasion. France's coastline became the 'springboard' for a German assault on Allied shipping in the North Atlantic. French defeat opened the door for Italian aggression in the Mediterranean and a direct attack on British control over Egypt and Suez. It was an encouragement to Japan to threaten European dominance in South-East Asia and invade British Malaya and Singapore.[45] Britain, as a consequence, would find herself embroiled, not in Germany's nightmare scenario of a two-front war, but eventually in a three-front war, as she would have to fight in North-West Europe, the Mediterranean and the Far East.

In the immediate aftermath of the disaster, two competing narratives became particularly prevalent, one in the public discourse and another in much more guarded tones in the military. The first, which was talked about in the press and in Parliament, blamed the reverse squarely on the political establishment (the 'Guilty Men'); the second, focused on military morale, and was to a significant degree shaped by the confidential Bartholomew Commission Report on the disaster in France.

Indeed, the idea that those in charge in the interwar period fundamentally failed Britain, the 'Guilty Men' narrative, emerged with astonishing speed, in May and June 1940. *Guilty Men*, a political polemic written during the Dunkirk evacuation, by three journalists under the pseudonym 'Cato', chosen because he had cleansed the sewers of Rome, described the troops as 'defenceless' on the beaches. This bestseller (over 200,000 copies were sold before the year's end) portrayed 'an Army doomed *before* they took the field'. In reviewing the events of the 1930s, *Guilty Men* indicted a generation of politicians who 'took over a great empire, supreme in arms and secure in liberty' and 'conducted it to the edge of national annihilation'.[46] Lieutenant-General Sir Henry Pownall, Chief of Staff of the BEF, wrote in his diaries that the Army's failings had mainly been due to political vacillation and refusal to face unpleasant facts throughout the previous decade.[47] Montgomery, then the commander of 3rd Division in France, similarly placed responsibility 'for much of what happened squarely on the shoulders of the political and military chiefs in the years before the war ... the campaign in France and Flanders ... was lost in Whitehall', he wrote, 'and this cannot be stated too clearly or too often'.[48] On the grandest scale, and on the biggest stage, Britain's politicians, so it was argued, failed to align ends and means and left Britain and the Empire unforgivably vulnerable.

The second key narrative to emerge from the ashes of defeat was the idea that military morale had been at the centre of events. Such criticism was focused largely on the French Army, for the BEF had not been at the centre of the German thrust.[49] Nevertheless, it was clear that the British Army had not been immune from similar problems. The 'Phoney War' had dragged on over a series of 'dreary, dull and ... demoralising months, particularly when a ferociously cold spell set in at the end of the year'.[50] In the Army in France, between the outbreak of war and March 1940, there were so many cases of gross insubordination, AWOL and even desertion that Gort approached the Army Council with a request for the reintroduction of the death penalty for desertion on active service, a penalty that had been abolished in 1930. He argued that penal service for serious military crimes was an insufficient deterrent because offenders knew that they would probably be amnestied at the end of the war. The military members of the Army Council were fully supportive of Gort's request and lobbied the new Secretary of State for War, Oliver Stanley, to approach the Cabinet with a suitable amendment to the Army and Air Force Act. However, before he could approach the Cabinet, the Germans invaded the Low Countries and the matter was shelved.[51]

The morale situation was reflected in the letters and diaries of those that fought. Corporal W. R. Littlewood of the Royal Engineers wrote of how morale was practically non-existent among his men during the campaign. 'Personally and individually, we were beginning to think that the Germans were almost superhuman. We were becoming demoralised without realising it. At every turn he [the enemy] seemed to have the answers.'[52] Many other candid accounts of the campaign noted similar concerns over morale.[53]

Additionally, some of the types of sickness reported in the BEF in May and June 1940 were typically not 'a feature of armies' in which morale could be described as 'high'.[54] A substantial number of the sick and wounded were made up of men breaking down under the stress of battle. A regimental medical officer during the Dunkirk evacuation remembered that 'I had little time to deal effectively with psychiatric casualties. In my battalion itself they constituted about 10% of the cases that passed through Regimental Aid Posts … In addition to those cases which occurred in the regiment itself, about 50 "stragglers", a large percentage of whom were, in fact, psychiatric cases, were brought back.'[55]

Desertions during the campaign, on the whole, were 'negligible', as determination to reach Dunkirk and escape acted as a strong incentive for soldiers to remain with their units. Additionally, the widespread belief that the men 'were surrounded', even before the German offensive, 'by the Fifth Column' may have discouraged troops from deserting. Historians have pointed to the development 'of a mass "fifth Column" paranoia in the ranks of the British Field Force both before and after the commencement of *Fall Gelb*'. There was a 'pervasive obsession with spies and "fifth columnists"'.[56] The small number of desertions, therefore, should not be confused with a will to fight and defeat the enemy. Flight, not fight, was the dynamic animating the behaviour of much of the BEF.[57]

The exhaustion, that characterised so many accounts of the retreat to Dunkirk, and the breakdown of communications, especially towards the end of the campaign, fed what can be described as a descent into chaos. Disorder in turn, exacerbated the difficulty of maintaining command and control as the speed of the retreat and the fear of 'fifth columnists' told on the troops.[58] Surrenders inevitably resulted, when utterly fatigued and extremely pressurised troops found themselves in trying battle scenarios. Claims that most surrenders were only grudgingly acquiesced to by British soldiers during the campaign[59] have to be reconciled with the fact that 62 per cent of British casualties in France and the Low Countries were POWs.[60] The overwhelming body of evidence points to the fact that 'few soldiers were prepared to fight "to the death"' and morale was clearly 'not high in terms of willingness to fight'.[61]

The British Army's attempt to rationalise its experience in France came to a similar conclusion. In the immediate aftermath of defeat, the War Office set up a committee under General Sir William Bartholomew to examine in depth the lessons of the campaign.[62] Bartholomew was assisted in his task by two major-generals, two brigadiers and a secretariat of three junior staff officers. Oral evidence was taken from thirty-seven officers who had served with the BEF, most of brigadier rank or higher, and written testimonials were submitted by three more officers of general rank.[63]

The report opened on a positive note stating that many of the withdrawals in France had been 'compelled' to 'conform to the movements of Allied forces on our flanks'. 'On no occasion' had the BEF been 'forced to relinquish the main position by a frontal attack' in spite of the fact that 'in many cases attacks were made on abnormal formations holding extremely large frontages':

> We kept the enemy back and succeeded in holding him off sufficiently to enable a very large proportion of the force to be evacuated. That this was done in spite of the fact that the main striking force of the German air arm was directed against the B.E.F. is proof, if proof were needed, that given a reasonable fighting chance the British Army may fight with confidence of success.[64]

In spite of subsequent criticisms of the performance of the BEF,[65] the report concluded that the Army's 'organisation' and 'tactical conceptions' had 'on the whole stood the test'.[66] The French telecommunications system had failed, as had, to a degree, the Army's own communications apparatus; each infantry division only had seventy-five radio transmitters (R/T), many of which could only transmit Morse, lacked sufficient range and were too cumbersome for mobile operations. Nevertheless, commanders had managed to maintain a semblance of command and control by going forward to subordinate HQs and issuing verbal orders through 'orders groups'.[67] Such methods were not necessarily inferior to wireless. Even later in the war, when wireless communications had improved in performance and availability, commanders still 'exhibited a clear preference to meet with their subordinates whenever possible'. Brigade, division and corps commanders typically fought their battles from small, mobile tactical HQs; conferences were the mainstay of transmitting plans and orders.[68] The Bartholomew Committee were of the opinion that command and control had been maintained throughout, in spite of the 'considerable difficulties' faced, and that GHQ had maintained 'a grip on the situation' (a conclusion that has been challenged by some historians).[69]

Above all else, Bartholomew and his committee identified morale as the one factor that was central to explanations regarding the performance of the BEF in France. On the very first page, the report noted:

> By every means in his power, and often with great ingenuity the enemy has concentrated his means of attack on the morale of his opponents. In the application of his weapons he relies almost as much on terrorisation by noise, as on material effect. The loud burst of the shell from his infantry gun was out of all proportion to the casualties it caused, while his dive bombers and the bombs themselves are fitted with noise producing gadgets. Enemy troops on our flanks, and those who succeeded in penetrating our positions appeared to change their positions and use their fire with the object of giving impression that they were more numerous than they really were . . . Every conceivable ruse has been employed, and to counter them we must be active both mentally and physically.[70]

Other reports produced around the same time came to similar conclusions. The Army Training Memorandum, 'Morale and Fighting Efficiency', described how 'mere individual determination to refuse to succumb to "frightfulness"' was not enough. Only 'a corporate sense of discipline' would 'maintain the fighting value of a unit or sub-unit under the strain of the technique of demoralisation as now practised by the German Army and Air Force'.[71] By February 1941, the War Office's 'Periodic Notes on the German Army' highlighted that German tactics focused on speed and surprise in battle, 'on the need for concentration of all means, *moral*, physical and material, at the decisive place and time'.[72] The methods of 'lightning' warfare were as much an attack on the morale of the enemy as they were on his physical resources. 'By continuous raids and the use of loudspeakers before the attack and by the noise of whistling bombs, loud explosions and the lavish employment of grenades, the German hopes to destroy the morale of his opponents, particularly of those in the forward defences.'[73] German artillery was taught to shoot first and correct later, believing that the shock resulting from getting their artillery active before their enemies did was a crucial factor in success.[74]

Air power was another essential element in these tactical techniques, and the Bartholomew Committee highlighted its dramatic impact during the campaign. However, again, it was not so much the material impact of air operations that caught the attention of the

Committee but the devastating impact of air power on morale.[75] The Committee noted that there was 'a mass of evidence' to show that bombs 'bursting only 5 yards away' had 'practically no effect' on men in slit trenches. While the report emphasised the 'magnificent work done by the R.A.F.', it pointed out that neither the actual bombing carried out in support of the BEF nor its effect had been 'seen by the man in the field':

> All day he saw swarms of enemy bombers escorted by fighters and suffered from their attack. Occasionally he saw or heard above the clouds an attack by our fighters. Unlike the German soldier, he had never seen aircraft closely co-operating with him to defeat his own particular enemy opposite to him. All this had a very definite effect on morale and gave the impression that the enemy superiority was complete and that our own air force hardly existed.[76]

In recognition of the morale elements of the problem, the Committee recommended that the RAF must 'show the flag' to the troops in the forward areas, even at the expense of other tasks.[77]

In light of their analysis, the need for 'offensive spirit' was the first of four 'major lessons' identified by the Bartholomew Report – a lesson only reinforced, although Bartholomew and his committee was not to know it, by the impact of the engagement at Arras on the German High Command. The need for a 'fiercer, aggressive spirit' to 'hit him [the Germans] and to hit him hard at every opportunity' was allied to the second 'major lesson': the need for more 'discipline',[78] a factor which, according to doctrine, was the 'means by which the morale of a force can alone be maintained'.[79] The third lesson pointed to the need to ensure 'air superiority' in future engagements (another factor which impacted mostly on the morale of the troops).[80] The fourth lesson emphasised the necessity for more and better 'anti-tank defences'; however, even this more technical point was couched in terms that showed a desire that 'all ranks must be taught to adopt aggressive tactics' against tanks. Any tanks that succeeded in penetrating British positions 'should be hunted and ambushed by day and stalked and harried by night, relentlessly and tirelessly until they have been destroyed'.[81]

The German assault had concentrated on penetrating and encircling Allied positions. To counter this, the report, in a section on tactics, pointed to the need for 'immediate counter-attack with vigour', the implication being that this had not taken place on nearly enough occasions during the campaign. 'It was proved' that 'rapid retaliation will frequently force him to withdraw or to try to penetrate somewhere else'. In addition, units were encouraged to organise defence in depth, with localities 'capable of holding out though isolated'. Units were 'on no account' to 'withdraw because they are outflanked, or even surrounded'. The section on 'tactics' concluded with the statement that 'it is absolutely essential that all troops be thoroughly imbued with the principle that it is their job to hold their positions'. It was the view of those who wrote the report, therefore, that the solution to blitzkrieg lay not primarily in any technological or conceptual revolution but in the willingness of British troops and junior officers to hold on and fight, thus threatening German lines of communication and retarding the speed of their advance.

> It must ... be constantly and persistently rubbed into all ranks that in the defence they must be as aggressive as possible, that they must seize every opportunity of killing [the] enemy, or attacking and exterminating parties infiltrating into their position. The determination to hold on and to be aggressive depends largely on a high esprit de corps, but more particularly on a very high standard of leadership on the part of officers, W.O.s [Warrant Officers] and N.C.O.s. These are points which require immediate attention, and no opportunity should be missed, in training, to instil into everybody that on their determination and on their resourcefulness may depend the success or failure of the defence in their part of the line.[82]

The effect of the Cabinet's decision to leave the expansion of the Army to the very last moment had unquestionably led to deficiencies in its preparations for war.[83] These issues, needless to say, impacted negatively on the BEF's ability to fight and its performance in France and Flanders. It was clear also, however, that there were question marks over morale; thus the 'cocktail' of defects in training, organisation, equipment and communications were not made good, as they needed to be, by a gritting and uncompromising determination to fight.[84] The citizen soldier proved entirely incapable of compensating for the failures of the 'Guilty Men'.

Preparing for Invasion

As Britain faced up to the consequences of defeat in France, it had little time to get its house in order to prepare for what many considered the next stage of the German assault in the West: the invasion of Great Britain.[85] The BEF had left virtually all its weapons in France. 'Of 2,794 guns that had originally been sent to the Continent, only 322 came back. All but 4,739 of 68,618 vehicles were lost. More than 70 per cent of the BEF's 109,000 tons of ammunition, and 96 per cent of its 449,000 tons of supplies and stores were abandoned. Just twenty-two tanks made it back to Britain.'[86] Losses 'included 180,000 rifles, 10,700 Bren guns, 509 two-pounder anti-tank guns, 509 cruiser tanks, and 180 infantry tanks'. These 'truly shocking' losses of all kinds of supplies, from tanks to telephones and binoculars, amounted to the equivalent of ten divisions' worth of equipment. 'The British Army had been saved but had effectively been disarmed.' The Army had just 340 tanks and armoured cars, 54 anti-tank guns, 420 field guns and 163 heavy guns left to defend the shores of Britain from the threat of imminent invasion.[87]

Such losses, even with the expansion of British armament production, could not be made good overnight, and certainly not in time for the expected attack. Churchill looked to America for help and Roosevelt, fearing 'that a disarmed British Army might succumb to a German assault', ordered the US War Department to dispatch 'surplus' war material to the United Kingdom. The weapons sent included 500,000 Enfield rifles; 50,000 First World War vintage Lewis, Vickers and Browning machine guns; 130 million rounds of small-arms ammunition; 820 French 75mm field guns; and 1 million rounds of artillery ammunition.[88]

As the RAF battled the *Luftwaffe* for control of the air, 'there was no more significant body of water in the world' than the English Channel. The Royal Navy's Home Fleet remained a 'vastly superior force' to anything that the *Kriegsmarine* could amass for invasion and it was clear that German weakness at sea would make a seaborne attack on the United Kingdom an extremely risky prospect.[89] Nevertheless, Brooke, who had been appointed C-in-C Home Forces, was left with the challenge of repelling an assault on the beaches of the United Kingdom (with an army largely bereft of heavy equipment).[90] He assessed his minimum requirements at twenty-two divisions, eight of them armoured, eight independent brigade groups, and ten army tank brigades. To hold the beaches, there would have to be an additional twelve static 'County' divisions on hand.[91] Huge numbers of men were called up to meet these requirements; between June and August, 270,000 joined the Army. These new recruits had to be integrated into what was left of the Field Force after Dunkirk. With only light weapons in abundant supply, the infantry expanded fastest; 120 new battalions were formed in three months. Soldiers were billeted wherever space could be found, 'in houses, schools, inns, warehouses, outhouses and bus depots'. Every existing barracks and camp 'was crammed to capacity' and where possible 'extended by temporary constructions'. Trains were packed with men in khaki. The roads of Britain became 'ever fuller with military convoys' as factories replaced the vehicles lost in France. Side roads, playgrounds, scrap yards and paddocks became vehicle parks. The countryside 'was covered' with requisitioned firing ranges; it echoed to the sound of military manoeuvres. 'Much of the coast was designated an operational area, with civilians denied access, and obstacles laid against landing craft. Road blocks and concrete pill boxes were erected on all likely ... enemy routes inland.'[92]

Brooke understood that to repel the invasion he would have to concentrate his forces at the decisive point at the decisive time. Rather than relying on static defences, he would need mobile reserves.[93] These, in the absence of modern equipment, would initially move in requisitioned buses. 'They would be almost entirely unarmoured. But they would at least have the power of concentration; and they must attack.' To fight this kind of mobile aggressive battle, the vastly expanded Army needed 'to train, and train again'.[94] But, in the summer of 1940, time for an intensive training programme was in short supply. Perhaps then it is fortunate that Germany did not invade in those fateful months. As Max Hastings has argued, a clash on the beaches and fields of England 'would probably have ended ignominiously for the defenders'. Churchill 'merely required' the 'acquiescence' of the Army and the people 'while the country was defended by a few hundred RAF pilots and – more importantly though less conspicuously – by the formidable might of the Royal Navy'.[95]

The precondition Hitler himself had laid down for invasion, that British air power be decisively beaten, was never met.[96] On 17 September, he gave the order to cancel Operation 'Sealion', the *Wehrmacht's* plan to invade the UK.[97] The country, at least for the time being, was saved.

4 THE MIDDLE EAST

As the battle of France raged in North-West Europe, Benito Mussolini, the Italian *Duce*, sensed an opportunity to further Italian interests in the Mediterranean. On 10 June 1940, with the fighting in France having reached its dénouement, Italy declared war on Britain and France. Twelve days later, Pétain signed the armistice leaving Vichy in control of the French Empire as well as what was left of the French armed forces. These events had a direct impact on the British position in North Africa and the Middle East, as the armistice neutralised the French forces in Syria, Lebanon, Tunisia, Algeria and Morocco, forces that were central to containing Italian ambitions in the region. When Britain decided to attack the French main fleet at its moorings at Mers-el-Kebir on 3 July, to prevent this vital asset falling into German hands, any lingering positive feelings harboured by the French towards its former ally dissipated.[1] The Empire was now massively exposed. A belligerent Italy threatened Egypt and the Suez Canal; Italian naval presence in the Mediterranean shut off the most direct route to India, the Far East and the Antipodes, adding many weeks and thousands of miles to every passage; any Italian success in the Middle East would deny British access to oil and expose the western approaches to the Raj.[2]

In the face of this potentially critical situation, stood General Sir Archibald Wavell, General Officer Commanding (GOC) Middle East Command. Wavell, the son of a major-general, was one of the intellectual élite of the British Army, an officer blessed with originality and 'untrammelled by convention'. He passed fourth into the Royal Military College, Sandhurst, in 1900 and headed the list of entrants to the Staff

College nearly a decade later, graduating with a coveted 'A', one of only two awarded that year. Having already served in South Africa and India in the early part of his career, Wavell spent a year in the Russian Army on completing the Staff College. He lost an eye at Ypres in June 1915 (he was awarded the MC) and ended the First World War a brigadier-general under Sir Edmund Allenby in the Middle East (a man he held to be his mentor). In the interwar years, he continued his stellar trajectory, spending much of the 1920s in the War Office and on the Staff. In 1930, he received command of 6th (Experimental) Infantry Brigade. He went on to rewrite the *Field Service Regulations* (*FSR*) Parts II and III and command in turn 2nd Division, British forces in Palestine and Trans-Jordan, Southern Command and then set up the new command in the Middle East in 1939.[3]

Since August, Wavell had been responsible for overseeing this enormous area of strategic importance to Britain, which encompassed Egypt, Palestine, Aden, the Sudan and the British East African possessions of Kenya, Uganda, Tanganyika and British Somaliland.[4] Although the forces at his disposal were not numerous (in East Africa, the British deployed 40,000 troops, most of them local, in Egypt 36,000 and in Palestine 27,000) Middle East Command was made up of almost entirely regular formations and was, as a consequence, very different from the force that had fought against the Germans in France.[5] These units were faced by an Italian Army in Somaliland, Eritrea and Ethiopia of 91,203 Italian military personnel and police and 199,973 African troops and Italian divisions in Libya numbering around 200,000. In East Africa, the Italians had 323 aircraft, in Libya and Rhodes, 425.[6] Overall, the Italians had access to well over 5,000 aircraft in the Mediterranean; the British had about 400 and a navy that after the French surrender had a deficit of eleven cruisers, ninety-four destroyers and ninety submarines compared to its Italian opponent.[7]

It was not surprising, then, that buoyed by this massive numerical superiority, Mussolini saw an opportunity to expand the Italian Empire in Africa. On 4 July, less than two weeks after the French armistice, he instructed units from the Italian garrison in Ethiopia to occupy frontier towns in the Anglo-Egyptian condominium of the Sudan. On 15 July, Italian forces launched an incursion into the British colony of Kenya, and between 5 and 19 August, they occupied the whole of British Somaliland. The five battalions stationed in country proved insufficient to combat an Italian Army of twenty-six battalions, supported by tanks, armoured cars and aircraft. These successes were quickly followed, on 13 September, by the invasion of Egypt. Marshal Rodolfo Graziani's Tenth Army advanced 60 miles beyond the Libyan/ Egyptian border, halted, and began to construct a number of bases to consolidate gains and prepare for further operations.[8]

Operation 'Compass'

By the winter of 1940, therefore, British forces in North Africa were outnumbered and all but surrounded, opposed as they were by hostile forces to the west (Italian-controlled Libya), the south (Italian-controlled East Africa) and the north (the Italian Army in Italy and the Italian Navy in the Mediterranean). Undeniably, the Italian forces had the initiative, but for the next three months, rather than aggressively building on their advantage, they consolidated their gains and pondered what to do next. This hiatus gave Wavell and General Sir Richard O'Connor, the commander of the Western Desert Force (WDF), Britain's last remaining field army in the Western Hemisphere, the time needed to stabilise its position and consider options for a counter-stroke in Africa.

The opportunities for such an offensive increased considerably as reinforcements arrived in the Middle East. As the invasion threat to the United Kingdom receded between August and December 1940, 69,500 troops, three tank regiments (including fifty-two cruisers and fifty infantry tanks), forty-eight 2-pounder anti-tank guns, twenty Bofors light anti-aircraft guns, forty-eight 25-pounder field guns, 500 Bren guns, 250 anti-tank rifles and 50,000 anti-tank mines were transferred from Britain to Egypt. In addition, 28,000 Australians, 7,300 New Zealanders, 11,400 Indians and 2,000 British troops arrived from India and other parts of the Empire.[9] Confident in his growing strength, Wavell instructed O'Connor to plan an attack in the Western Desert to be launched at the beginning of December. He considered that this operation would be limited in its ambitions but was careful not to overly constrain his army commander. 'It is possible', Wavell wrote to O'Connor, that 'an opportunity may offer for converting the enemy's defeat into an outstanding victory.'[10] Wavell 'was prepared to see how the operation went' and adapt to circumstances as they arose.[11] Such flexible instructions placed much responsibility on the commander receiving them, and, to a large degree, they were indicative both of

Wavell's style of command and the command-and-control arrangements set out in interwar *FSR* (which Wavell of course had authored himself).[12]

Although outnumbered, O'Connor had every right to be confident of the coming offensive. He was at the head of a force largely made up of regular seasoned troops. The campaign against the Italians, in 1940 to 1941, was the only campaign of the Second World War in which the interwar Regular Army fought alone, without the presence of substantial numbers of territorial, conscript or volunteer troops.[13] Many of these men had been stationed in Palestine since 1936, suppressing the Arab rebellion. Others, such as 4th Indian Division, which had been transferred to the Middle East at the outbreak of the war, had been posted on the North-West Frontier of India in the 1930s.[14] The 7th Armoured Division had been in the Middle East since the 1938 Munich crisis and Major-General Sir Percy Hobart had trained his division 'with utmost energy' for living, moving, communicating and fighting in the harsh and challenging conditions of the desert.[15] In the weeks running up to 'Compass', O'Connor subjected his troops to an additional intense period of training and preparation.[16] As professionals, many of the division yearned for the opportunity to put this training into practice[17] and O'Connor described the WDF generally as 'in very good heart' as it prepared for battle.[18]

The attack commenced on 9 December (see Map 4.1). Two assault divisions, 7th Armoured and 4th Indian, were instructed to penetrate the gaps between the Italian fortified positions near Sidi Barrani and assault the defenders from the rear. By the end of the next day, the Italian forts had surrendered, as had Sidi Barrani itself, yielding 20,000 prisoners. O'Connor was free now to exploit the situation as he saw fit. With 4th Indian Division, which was required for a separate offensive planned in East Africa, having been replaced by 6th Australian Division, the first of the Australian divisions to arrive in the Middle East, O'Connor continued the pursuit into Libya. By 5 January 1941, Bardia had fallen, yielding another 40,000 prisoners, and by 21 January, Tobruk had also succumbed with a further 27,000 prisoners taken. O'Connor determined to cut Tenth Army off completely from its base in Tripoli in western Libya. He ordered 7th Armoured Division to drive across the neck of the bulge of Cyrenaica and block the Italian retreat at Beda Fomm, 400 miles to the west of where operations had commenced on 9 December. The pincer closed on

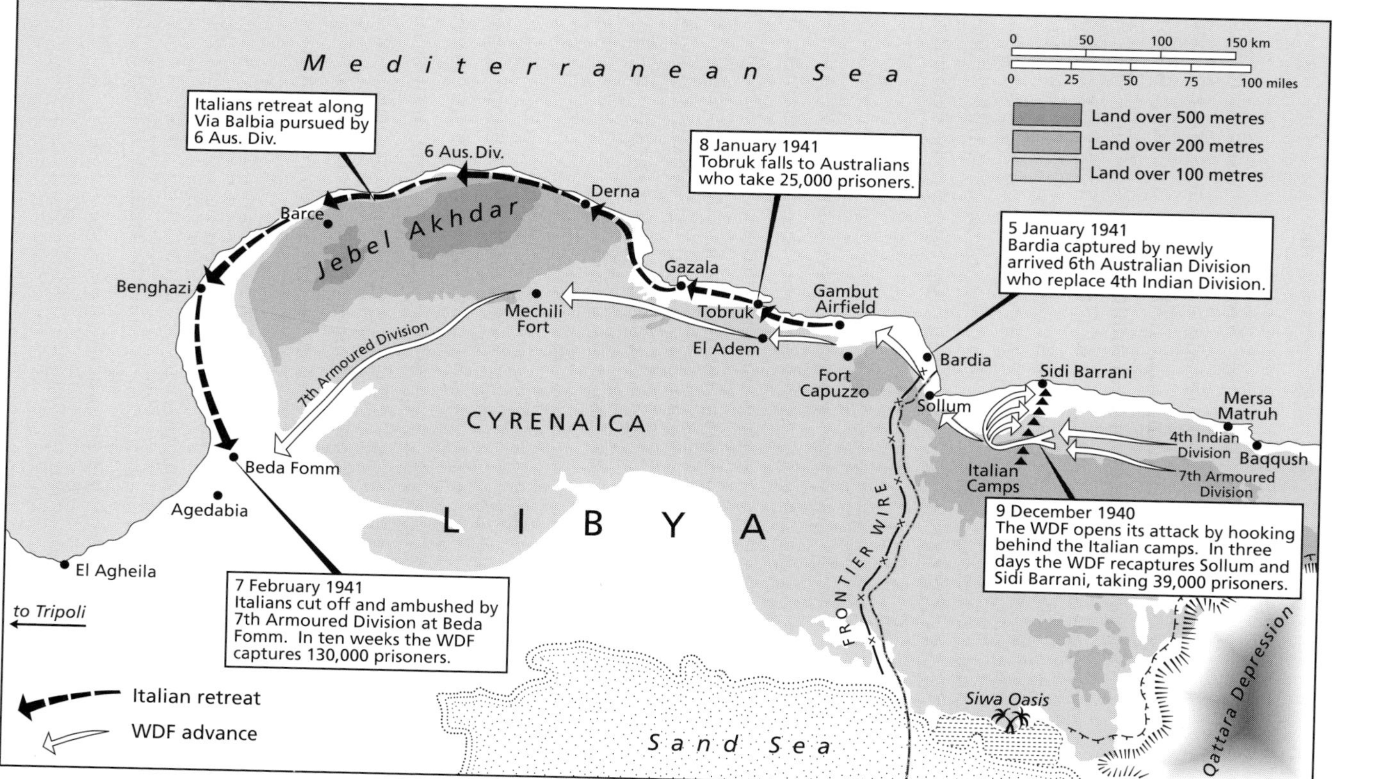

Map 4.1 Operation 'Compass', December 1940–February 1941

6 and 7 February. The 7th Armoured Division encircled the retreating Italian forces, preventing them from breaking out to the west. From the east, 6th Australian Division advanced to close the trap. The Italian Tenth Army surrendered en masse.[19]

The British and Commonwealth Armies had won their first major success of the war; the WDF, made up of 36,000 troops, had overcome a force of 200,000 Italians. Led by O'Connor, it had advanced 500 miles in the space of two months and totally destroyed an army of ten Italian divisions, for a loss of 500 killed, 1,373 wounded, and 55 missing. Around 130,000 prisoners were taken; 180 medium and more than 200 light tanks and 845 guns were captured.[20] So great were the spoils of victory that British POW cages were totally 'inadequate' for the influx of Italian soldiers and prisoners had to be evacuated in haste to 'save them from dying of thirst'.[21]

The WDF's victory over Tenth Army can be seen as the culmination of British interwar doctrinal development. A mainly regular force of seasoned troops,[22] 'perhaps the finest-trained, if not the best equipped, force that Britain possessed',[23] decisively defeated a much larger opponent by implementing the ideals of *FSR*. 'Compass' was illustrative of the extent to which interwar British doctrine had grasped the essentials of twentieth-century combat. The operation was evidence of a 'decentralised, initiative led command system in practice'. For example, in 4th Indian Division, brigade commanders were involved in operational planning from the earliest stages, becoming well versed in their superiors' intentions as a result. This greatly reduced the need to prepare and transmit detailed orders within the division during action and enabled its brigade commanders to take informed decisions with speed and confidence without recourse to higher authority.[24] A report on operations in the Western Desert in 1940 noted that:

> Recent operations have shown that ... situations develop and change so rapidly that more and more it is becoming necessary for subordinate commanders to be 'in the mind' of their superior so that they will instinctively take the right course of action in accordance with his general intention, acting upon the briefest of instructions and often upon none at all.[25]

Where co-ordination was required at corps/army level, it had been provided by O'Connor, who spent much of the battle forward with

7th Armoured Division HQ. This enabled him to observe events and wield real control over the offensive and ensure 'the energetic fulfilment of the manoeuvre [he] had conceived'.[26] While it must be recognised that the Italians were not a first-class opponent, success in the desert showed that there was nothing fundamentally wrong with British inter-war doctrine; it just needed to be implemented properly by well-trained, well-equipped and highly motivated troops.[27]

From East Africa to the Balkans

The WDF's successes in the Western Desert illustrated both the folly of Italian aggression in Africa and the latent strength of the British Empire. As vast amounts of materiel, formed units, administrative and reinforcement personnel streamed into Egypt, so too did reinforcements arrive further south. In April 1940, Wavell had visited Smuts and received a guarantee of South African support in retaking East Africa. By July, three South African brigades had arrived in Kenya to form the 1st South African Division.[28] British forces in the Sudan were also augmented; 5th Indian Division arrived from the subcontinent in September and 4th Indian Division, fresh from its success in the initial stages of 'Compass', in December.

On 19 and 20 January, the reconquest of East Africa began; 4th and 5th Indian Divisions, under the command of Lieutenant-General Sir William Platt, attacked Ethiopia from the north, through Eritrea, and the Sudan Defence Force, the equivalent of half a division of troops, crossed into Ethiopia south of the Blue Nile. These incursions were supported, on 11 February, by Lieutenant-General Sir Alan Cunningham's army of South Africans and East and West Africans, who marched out of Kenya into southern Ethiopia and Italian Somaliland.[29] As such, the campaign represented 'a massive pincer movement' (see Map 4.2).

The Italians, under the command of the Duke of Aosta, concentrated their best troops against 4th and 5th Indian Divisions (the northern pincer) and built up significant forces around what they considered the most defensible position in the region, the small town of Keren in Eritrea. This was surrounded by high peaks and approachable only along a deep and narrow gorge; the Indian divisions were faced with a formidable task. They attacked on 10 February, only to be driven off as they reached their objective.[30]

Map 4.2 East African campaign, 1941

In spite of this setback to the northern pincer, there was much to be positive about for those in London and at HQ Middle East Forces.[31] The southern pincer, with East and West African formations in the vanguard, had seized Kismayu on 14 February and had then driven on with remarkable speed to take Mogadishu eleven days later. With 'Compass' having proved a dramatic success and Mussolini continuing to overstretch his ill-prepared formations further north still, in the Mediterranean – Italian forces had invaded Greece on 28 October and were now in disarray[32] – it appeared, from a strategic perspective, that Italian military weakness offered an opportunity to seriously undermine the entire Axis war effort.

The countries bordering the Mediterranean in South-East Europe provided a convenient avenue for the Axis to circumvent the British blockade in North-West Europe and undermine what had been the Anglo-French long-war strategy. The region provided half of Germany's cereal and livestock requirements. Greece and Yugoslavia (neither of which were as yet at war with Germany) were the source of 45 per cent of the bauxite used by German industry, while Yugoslavia supplied 90 per cent of its tin, 40 per cent of its lead and 10 per cent of its copper. Romania (the Ploesti oilfields) and, to a marginal extent Hungary, provided the only supply of oil which lay within the radius of German strategic control; the rest came from Russia under the terms of the Molotov-Ribbentrop Pact.

From a British perspective, if these oilfields, and the railways which carried ores and agricultural produce out of the Balkans to Germany, were brought under British bomber attack, German ability to prosecute the war would be seriously compromised.[33] Furthermore, Turkey, which occupied a geographical position of great importance (she had land frontiers with Iraq and Syria and provided strategic depth against German aggression from the north, which might be targeted towards the Suez Canal and the Anglo-Iranian oilfields), commanded the third gateway to the Mediterranean, the Dardanelles, a route of enormous importance to Italy, who relied for much of her raw materials on access to the Black Sea.[34]

The development of a Balkan front (requiring the support of Greece, Yugoslavia and Turkey) against the Axis would, therefore, be a prize worth having.[35] In the final months of 1940, however, British intelligence began to suspect that the Germans might pre-empt a British move in South-Eastern Europe. Evidence of a German build-up in

Hungary and Romania pointed to an occupation of Bulgaria or an advance on Greece through Bulgaria. By the end of December, *Luftflotte* 4 and *Fliegerkorps* VIII, formations both previously associated with the potential invasion of Britain, were identified at bases in Romania. It was apparent that a change was taking place in German strategic planning. On 11 February, Churchill sent Anthony Eden, the Foreign Secretary, and General Sir John Dill, the Chief of the Imperial General Staff (CIGS), to the Middle East to address the situation. Churchill and Eden were convinced that 'the desert battle had been won and that they could now send troops to Greece to counter the German infiltration of the Balkans'.[36]

Much to Eden's satisfaction, he arrived in Cairo on 19 February to find that Wavell, who had been briefed by Churchill earlier in the month, had already given instructions to halt O'Connor's offensive at the frontier of Tripolitania and redirect forces to Greece. With the road to Tripoli practically defenceless, this decision was undoubtedly controversial; but it was supported by all the commanders-in-chief in the theatre at the time.[37] By 22 February, a series of conferences with the Greeks to iron-out the terms of the proposed intervention were under way. It soon became clear that a Greek venture was more complicated than heretofore imagined. The Turks and the Yugoslavs refused to commit to the British cause. The Greeks, for their part, were convinced that no less than ten divisions were necessary to make a defence of their country viable; any number short of that would only provoke a German attack and both destroy any hope of avoiding war and guarantee defeat. This, however, was simply beyond the resources of the Middle Eastern Forces (MEF). With the Greek Commander-in-Chief (C-in-C), Alexander Papagos, proving intransigent with regards to proposed dispositions for the defence of his country, serious questions began to arise over the successful outcome of a Greek expedition.[38]

When news of this filtered back to London, Churchill, the architect of the disasters at Gallipoli and Norway, began to cover his back. He urged Eden and Dill not to consider themselves 'obligated to a Greek enterprise if in your hearts you feel it will only be another Norwegian fiasco'.[39] It was too late. On 4 March, Papagos, urged on by the Greek King, accepted Britain's offer of support and a formal agreement was signed. A force consisting of an armoured brigade, two infantry divisions, an infantry brigade, some artillery and the necessary ancillary troops, services and transport would be sent to Greece; this was dramatically short of the ten divisions Athens had asked for.[40] Nevertheless, the advance guard (of what became 'W Force') began to disembark on the Greek mainland the same day and from this point on there was virtually no turning back. To renege now would have had grave consequences for the reputations of both Eden and Dill; their plan to bring Yugoslavia and Turkey into the war would have lain in tatters. Later, Eden explained that 'we had made a provisional arrangement and had started to carry it out, we could not now back out'. Whatever Eden's actual belief, which the contemporary evidence leaves uncertain, from this point on, more and more emphasis was put on 'the moral duty to stand by Greece', and less on the original aim to create a Balkan front. The fear was that, as Smuts put it in Cairo on 6 March, if Britain did not help Greece now it would be held up to public ignominy.[41]

In fact, there were even greater issues at play than strategy in the Mediterranean. By December 1940, it had become evident to Churchill and the Cabinet that the United Kingdom was facing bankruptcy. While the Empire 'could provide the British Isles with a whole range of raw materials, it could not provide all of the ships, planes, tanks and guns that Britain needed' for a world war. In the great emergency of the summer of 1940, Churchill had turned to the United States. But Roosevelt had insisted that transactions be on a 'strictly commercial basis'; British orders 'had to be paid for in gold, securities or dollars – not sterling'. By December, Britain had 'reached the end of her easily realisable assets'. Orders placed in America for December, January and February 'amounted to $1,000 million, yet the country's remaining gold reserves and dollar balance totalled just $574 million'. After just one year of fighting, the war had placed an 'intolerable burden' on Britain's finances. Its future was now 'in the hands' of the United States, for without American aid and assistance 'above and beyond the commercial basis of "cash and carry"', Britain 'would not be able to continue the war'.[42]

The solution to this problem became known as Lend-Lease: 'Britain would have to pay as much gold and dollars as she had left, but in return the United States would manufacture and supply what she needed and then lease it to her, with payment delayed until after the war.' Britain could, therefore, 'run up an astronomical debt' but avoid bankruptcy in the short term and continue the war.[43] The legislation to enable Lend-Lease passed the House of Representatives on 8 February and the Senate was due to begin debating the bill just over a week later.

None of this was lost on Wavell who met William Donovan, an 'unofficial personal representative' of President Roosevelt, in Cairo on 8 February. Donovan 'forcibly expressed the importance of keeping American public opinion on side' since the Lend-Lease Bill had yet to pass the Senate. It was this intervention, along with the pressure exerted by Churchill, that drove Wavell to halt the advance in North Africa. Strategy, as he wrote to General Marshall-Cornwall, the commander of British troops in Egypt, 'is only the hand-maid of policy, and here political considerations must come first'. British decisions over Greece, therefore, were taken in an atmosphere where the 'political repercussions in America were potentially more important than the military realities' facing a force sent to the Balkans.[44]

As formations were being transferred from the desert to Greece, the campaign in East Africa continued apace. The two Indian divisions besieging Keren had spent ten days conducting intensive mountain warfare training as they prepared for a renewed assault on 'the most strongly held natural defensive position in the whole of East Africa'. With successful psychological operations reducing the strength of the Italian garrison by nearly one-fifth, as Italian, Ethiopian and Somali troops deserted, the assault began again on 15 March. The gains were 'slow and incremental', but the defenders were gradually worn down. After twelve days of very hard fighting, and after fifty-three days of siege, at a cost of 536 killed and 3,229 wounded, the final breakthrough was achieved. The road to Eritrea was now open and the end of Italian power in East Africa was within sight.[45]

Meanwhile, General Cunningham's southern pincer continued its remarkable advance into Italian Somaliland and then on into Ethiopia. The advance from Mogadishu was led by 11th African Division reinforced by 1st South African Brigade Group and 22nd East African Brigade. They progressed on average 65 miles a day and by late March, having swung west towards central Ethiopia, they had taken the major Italian base at the ancient walled city of Harar. Thereafter, Italian fighting spirit collapsed, and, with the 12th African Division in the lead, the British and Commonwealth forces pushed on to Addis Ababa. On 5 April, the capital fell; however, the honour of entering the city first was not given to the Brigade of West African troops that had spearheaded the advance.[46] Haile Selassie, the Ethiopian Emperor, was returned to his throne; the war in Ethiopia was effectively over, although an Italian garrison at Gondar held out until November.[47] For the cost of only 500 casualties and just 150 killed, the Commonwealth Armies, ably supported by the Royal Navy and RAF, had captured 360,000 square miles of territory and destroyed an army of nearly 300,000 men (50,000 of whom were taken as POWs). Italian forces had once again been comprehensively beaten in Africa.[48]

Matters were progressing less smoothly in the Balkans. The military rationale for intervening in Greece had been subsumed by political strategy,[49] the folly of which became all the more apparent when, on 25 March, Yugoslavia, rather than aligning itself with the Allied cause, joined the Axis. Within days, a British-sponsored coup overthrew the Yugoslav Regent, but it was increasingly apparent that the British and Commonwealth forces in the Middle East had taken on more than they could cope with. By the end of March, 35,000 men of 6th Australian Division, which had been transferred from the desert, 2nd New Zealand Division, which had just finished concentrating in Egypt, and 1st Armoured Brigade, which too had only just arrived in the Middle East, had already taken up position on the Aliakmon Line, a series of defensive positions running from the mouth of the Aliakmon River on the Aegean coast north-west to the Yugoslav border.[50]

On 6 April, the long-feared German attack arrived. The *Wehrmacht*, massing 680,000 men and 1,000 serviceable aircraft, unleashed simultaneous offensives against Greece and Yugoslavia. From Bulgaria, XVIII and XXX Corps attacked into Greece and XL Corps attacked Yugoslavia,[51] where they were met with such 'feeble' resistance by the million-strong Yugoslav Army 'that the German invaders suffered only 151 fatal casualties in the course of the campaign'.[52] The rapid collapse of the Yugoslav Army fatally compromised the already questionable defensive dispositions of the Anglo-Greek forces, as it allowed the Germans to split the Aliakmon and Albanian defensive lines by attacking through the Monastir gap towards Florina (see Map 4.3). This left the western flank and rear of the Aliakmon Line exposed and 'W Force' was compelled to withdraw to defensive positions around Mount Olympus.[53]

By now, the Greek Army, having initially put up a fierce fight on the Macedonian front, was in a state of collapse. It had fought off a twenty-eight-division assault by the Italians in March, but a full-scale attack by the superiorly equipped and trained *Wehrmacht* proved too much.[54] The disintegration of the Greek Army rendered the defences

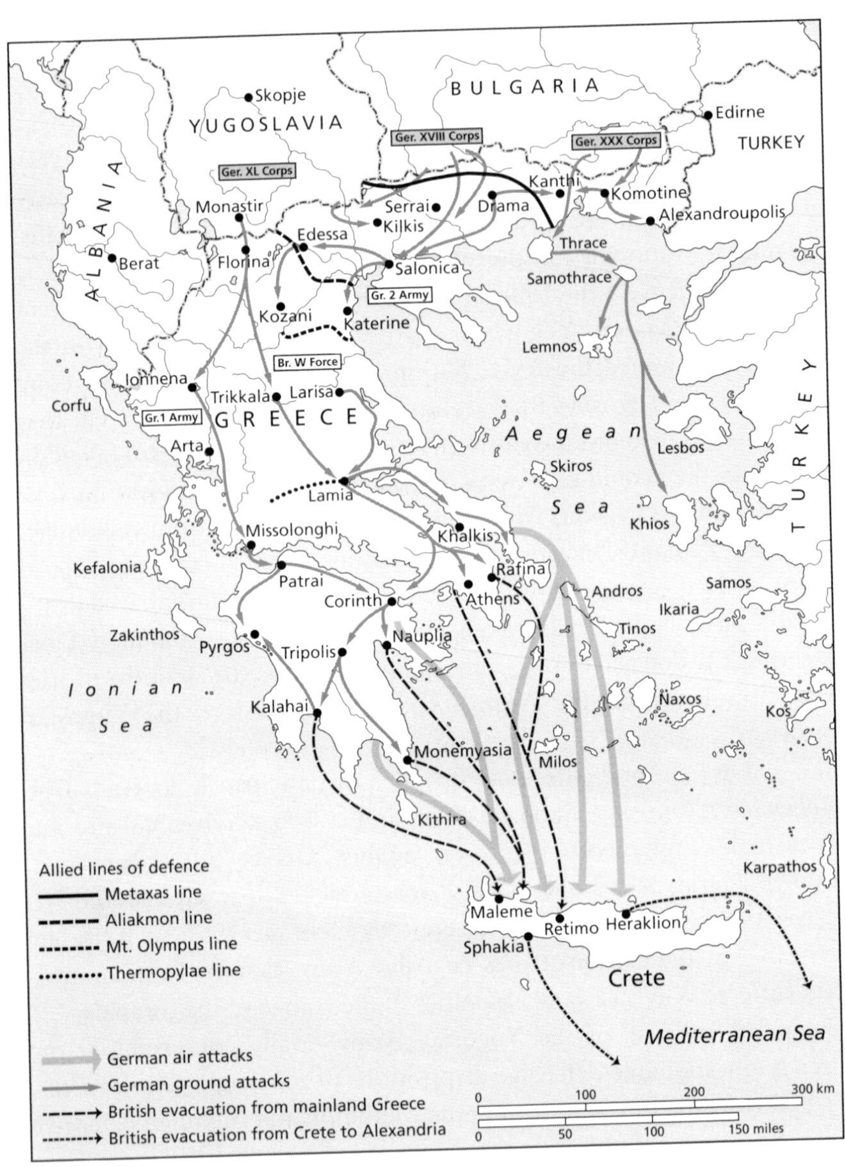

Map 4.3 The campaigns in Greece and Crete, April–May 1941

around Mount Olympus untenable and also the next position on the Thermopylae Line.[55] On 21 April, Wavell, having arrived at the HQ of the temporarily constituted ANZAC Corps, decided that Greece should be evacuated as soon as possible.[56] On the nights of 26 to 28 April, a great number of fighting troops (50,662 men, something in the order of 80 per cent of all troops eventually sent to Greece)[57] were rescued by the Royal Navy either from ports on the mainland around Athens or from those in the south of the Peloponnesus. 'W Force' suffered 12,000 casualties, 9,000 of whom were prisoners (75 per cent). All heavy equipment, including around 100 tanks and 8,000 trucks, was lost, while the RAF lost 209 aircraft and the Royal Navy 26 ships, including no fewer than five hospital ships.[58] The Germans, in their conquest of Greece and Yugoslavia, suffered 5,000 casualties.[59]

It was Norway and Dunkirk all over again and apart from the fact that the strategic calculations behind the Greek adventure had been faulty, it is hard to avoid the conclusion that many of the same operational issues that had beset the BEF in France also undermined the performance of 'W Force'. Operations were hindered by problems with co-ordination. There were too few interpreters and liaison officers and Major-General Sir Iven Mackay, the commander of 6th Australian Division, remembered that it took ages to arrive at decisions with his Greek counterparts.[60] So few units were sent to Greece that force-to-force and force-to-space ratios had been unworkable; the ANZAC Corps alone, made up of 6th Australian and 2nd New Zealand Divisions, came into contact with seven German divisions during the short campaign.[61] Mackay thought that units had been asked to defend too long frontages, with, in one case, one brigade covering 20,000 yards.[62] The RAF had initially only been able to spare eighty aircraft for Greece, which meant that British planes, when operations commenced, were outnumbered ten to one.[63]

Of the formations that fought in Greece, only 6th Australian Division had been battle-tested[64] and Commonwealth units proved all too often incapable of dealing with German infiltration tactics. 'Our troops were surprised by these tactics', recalled Mackay, and 'were NOT trained to the stage of countering them'. On too many occasions, infantry withdrew 'before it was really necessary' and 'in some cases the inf[antry] did NOT show that essential determination to stay and fight it out when the enemy did filter around their flanks'.[65] British, Australian and New Zealand morale had been undermined by the fact that the Germans had control of the air. Robert Crisp, a lieutenant in the Royal Tank Regiment, recalled:

> From dawn to dusk there was never a period of more than half an hour when there was not an enemy plane overhead ... It was

> the unrelenting pressure of noise and the threat of destruction in every hour which accentuated the psychological consequences of continuous retreat ... I had never seen so many men so unashamedly afraid as I saw on the bomb-torn roads of Greece.[66]

In spite of the undoubted fear and chaos, as Lieutenant-General Thomas Blamey, the commander of the Australian Imperial Force (AIF), concluded in his report on the operation, 'the troops successfully avoided being pinned down by greatly superior forces' even though they had been 'attacked incessantly by an overwhelmingly superior enemy air force' and had been 'deprived through no fault of their own of the opportunity of meeting the German army on reasonably equal terms'.[67] Much like the BEF at Dunkirk, one of the few positive things that could be said about 'W Force' was that most of it lived to fight another day.

The Battle for Crete

'Another day' arrived rather more quickly than the remnants of 'W Force' might have wished. Some of those rescued from Greece were transported by the Royal Navy back to Egypt to rejoin the WDF. Others were transferred to Crete, which had been occupied by the British following the Italian attack on Greece in October 1940. For the Germans, an attack on Crete was the logical extension of the Greek campaign. For the British, much like Greece, the island offered airfields that could be used to threaten Italy and Axis interests in the Balkans; it acted as a gateway for Royal Navy sorties into the Aegean, thus threatening Italian access to the Black Sea; and it provided the Royal Navy with a fuelling base between Alexandria and Malta.[68]

German intentions regarding the island became apparent to British intelligence through the Government Code and Cipher School, at Bletchley Park. Ultra, the intelligence derived from this source, had hitherto yielded little information of value to army operations against Germany. During the battle of France and the campaigns in Africa and Greece, Bletchley had struggled to break the cipher 'keys' used on the German Enigma machine, through which the different *Wehrmacht* HQs communicated. The Enigma machine was designed to make eavesdropping impossible; it provided the potential listener with no less than several million possible solutions to any intercept. However, when mistakes were made by German Enigma machine operators in encipherment procedure, it did prove possible to 'break' the German code. German Army and Navy operators made few mistakes in procedure; the less experienced *Luftwaffe* were not so proficient, providing Bletchley with regular opportunities.[69]

The *Luftwaffe's* relative lack of professionalism in encipherment procedure was to play a key role in the battle of Crete, as the German assault on the island would be spearheaded by an airborne landing. The plan, conceived by General Kurt Student, commander of XI Air Corps, involved 7th Airborne Division, supported by 5th Mountain Division, and some light tanks from 5th Panzer Division. These units would be carried in a fleet of 600 Junkers Ju-52 aircraft, some of which would also tow gliders, eighty in number, carrying light tanks as well as men. An air component of 280 bombers, 150 Stukas and 200 fighters would cover and support the operation. In all, 22,000 troops would be committed in the largest airborne operation to date in the Second World War (significant operations had already taken place in Belgium, Holland, Norway and Greece). Student's plan, envisaged using his three parachute regiments against the three towns on the north coast of the island, Maleme, Retimo and Heraklion (see Map 4.3). These towns all had airfields that once captured could be used for the landing of heavy equipment and exploitation further inland. At Maleme, which Student identified as his main effort, the intention was to commit the 1st Assault Regiment, which would crash-land in gliders directly onto the airfield. Although Student expected his forces to be outnumbered, he was sure that surprise, the high quality of his troops and German air superiority would win the day.[70]

By 29 April, detailed information on the impending attack began to reach General Sir Bernard Freyberg, the commander of 'Creforce', from London (see Illustration 4.1).[71] Freyberg, much like Gort in France, had acquired, in the years before the war, a reputation for the rarest gallantry and tremendous leadership. Although his main task during the war was as GOC the 2nd New Zealand Expeditionary Force (2NZEF), in Crete in the summer of 1941 he found himself in charge of a corps-level force preparing for the expected German invasion. Freyberg was not a New Zealander by birth. He was born in the United Kingdom and only emigrated to New Zealand as a child in 1891. There, he excelled as an athlete, if not academically. He registered professionally as a dentist in 1911 and the following year was commissioned as a second lieutenant in the territorials. In 1914, he left New Zealand in search of adventure and 'a better life overseas'. He sailed first to San Francisco and then, on the outbreak of the First World War, to Britain. He served with distinction in the Great War, earning a DSO at Gallipoli and a VC on the Somme. In April 1917, at the age of 28 he was appointed the youngest brigade commander in the British Army. On the armistice, Freyberg reverted to the rank of captain. He attended the Staff College in 1919 and after a failed attempt at Parliament, as a Liberal candidate for Cardiff South in 1922, he built his career in the Army; as an officer in the Grenadier Guards, as commander of 1st Battalion, the Manchester Regiment, and in staff positions at divisional and command levels, as well as at the War Office. In 1934, Freyberg was promoted to major-general, but three years later, having been declared medically unfit, not least due to the nine wounds he sustained during the First World War, he was retired from the British Army. For the next two years, he engaged in business activities and in 1938 he was adopted as the prospective Conservative candidate for the Spelthorne division of Middlesex. However, on the outbreak of hostilities in 1939 he was recalled to the Army and with the permission of the War Office, he offered his services to the New Zealand Government for the duration of the conflict; he was appointed commander of the 2NZEF on 23 November 1939.[72]

Freyberg was shocked at the information he received from London and immediately cabled Middle East Command and Peter Fraser, the Prime Minister in New Zealand, that there was a disconnect in strategy; the forces at his disposal were, he argued, 'totally inadequate' to meet the attack described.[73] He stressed that many of his units were disorganised and split up and that, at least in the case of 2nd New Zealand Division, the men needed to return to Egypt to replace casualties and re-equip. Such a course of action was, in the circumstances, impossible. Wavell instructed Freyberg that there was no room for manoeuvre; those troops that had been evacuated to Crete would have to remain and fight where they stood.[74]

This was not what Freyberg wanted to hear, for he knew his concerns regarding the preparedness of his troops were not exaggerated. Only a brigade of regular British infantrymen, 14th Brigade of 6th British Division, had been stationed on Crete before two brigades of New Zealanders, one brigade of Australians and other stragglers had been transported to the island after the disaster in Greece. Many of these newly arrived troops were 'in poor shape'.[75] Around 10,000 of the British Commonwealth and a further 10,000 Greek troops were without arms or discernible military organisation. In some cases, these men were found 'wandering about the island ... leading a lawless life'.[76] So great was the problem that the military police had to be reinforced and all soldiers informed that those found unattached to a unit would be court-martialled for desertion.[77]

It soon became clear, however, that London had exaggerated the scale of the impending German attack. As new projections were sent to the Middle East, Wavell became increasingly confident that with the 'magnificent troops' at Freyberg's disposal, 'Creforce' would 'be equal to [the] task'. Although there was little air support available, Freyberg did have 42,547 Allied troops (7,702 New Zealanders, 6,540 Australians, 18,047 British, and 10,258 Greeks), even if only about half of these were 'properly formed infantrymen'.[78] With every day that passed, British and Commonwealth forces were making their positions stronger; means and ends appeared increasingly to be in line.[79]

By the first week in May, Freyberg, in spite of his initial misgivings, also began to gain in confidence. He wrote to the troops stressing that the successful withdrawal in Greece had been a 'great feat of arms'. The 'fighting qualities and steadiness of the troops' had been 'beyond praise'. He warned them of what to expect. The attack would be accompanied by 'all the accustomed air activity'. But, they had learned much in the last month and this time they were ready:

> If he attacks us here in Crete, the enemy will be meeting our troops upon even terms and those of us who met his infantry in the last month ask for no better chance. We are to stand now and fight him back. Keep yourselves fit and be ready for immediate action. I am confident that the force at our disposal will be adequate to defeat any attack that may be delivered upon this island.[80]

On 5 May, he cabled the Prime Minister in London that he was 'not in the least anxious' about the impending attack. 'Have made my dispositions and feel can cope adequately with the troops now at my disposal.'[81] By 16 May, Freyberg considered himself ready. 'I have completed plans for Defence of Crete', he wrote to Wavell:

> Have just returned from final tour of defences. I feel greatly encouraged by my visits. Everywhere all ranks are fit and moral [*sic*] is now high ... We have 45 field guns in action with adequate ammunition dumped. Two infantry tanks are at each aerodrome ... I do not wish to seem overconfident but I feel that at least we will give an excellent account of ourselves ... I trust Crete will be held.[82]

Freyberg had every right to be confident, for when the German attack materialised four days later, on 20 May, not only were his defences prepared, but he also knew through Ultra 'when, where and in what strength' the parachutists and glider infantry were going to land. It was slaughter. One company of the German III Battalion, 1st Assault Regiment, lost 112 killed out of 126; 400 of the battalion's 600 men were dead before the day was out. The parachutists' 'helplessness during descent, the necessary lightness of the equipment they would use to fight if they survived, doomed them to undergo appalling losses'.[83]

In spite of these heavy casualties, remarkably, by the end of the first day, the Germans found themselves in a strong position at Maleme airfield (Student's *schwerpünkte*). During the day, what was left of the German paratroopers gradually concentrated against the key points, intensive aerial bombardment knocked out the field guns defending the airfield and that night a battalion had withdrawn from its defences 'owing to severe bombing and heavy casualties'.[84] This allowed the Germans to win a foothold on the airfield and make use of it the next day, landing forty Junkers Ju-52s bringing 650 men of the II Battalion, 100th Mountain Rifle Regiment.[85]

The position, in spite of the initial advantages enjoyed by the British and Commonwealth forces, was now according to Freyberg, 'perilous'.[86] Wavell sent him a telegram encouraging the troops to 'stick it'. 'Have great hopes the enemy cannot stay the pace much longer.'[87] Captured German prisoners reported that their morale had been 'extremely shaken' by the reception that they had received from the anti-aircraft guns and on seeing their comrades landing on telephone wires or being shot on landing. Many had reached the ground in a state of 'complete disorganization', separated as they were from their officers and NCOs.[88] Wavell emphasised the 'great difficulties' faced by the Germans and the need for 'guts and determination'.[89]

Encouraged by their commanders, the New Zealanders dutifully counter-attacked, but failed to dislodge the Germans from their

Illustration 4.1 German Junkers Ju-52 aircraft dropping paratroopers in the Galatos area, near Maleme, Crete, May 1941. The battle was an utter catastrophe for the British and Commonwealth forces; with a numerical advantage of approximately 2:1, they were defeated in circumstances where the enemy's plans and intentions had been fully known beforehand.

positions around Maleme. By 24 May, almost the whole of the mountain division had landed and 'Creforce' was clearly feeling the strain.[90] Freyberg began to continually refer to his troops as being 'tired'. In the 'fierce' fighting, he argued, German casualties had been higher than the British and Commonwealth forces. 'Man for man', he stated, 'we have beaten him.' However, there was a problem. German dominance in the air was beginning to have a dramatic impact on the troops' morale. 'I feel that you should be told scale of air attack we have been faced with has been far worse than anything I had visualized', he wrote to Wavell.

'It has been savage. Further our men are very tired ... the men I know will do their best but with lack of any [air] support whatsoever the result with tired troops must always be in balance ... Anything you can do to neutralize the air situation will help us materially.'[91]

The German breakthrough came the next day. Freyberg reported that German bombers, dive-bombers and ground straffers had attacked around 1900hrs and 'bombed our forward troops'. This was followed by an immediate ground assault. The front collapsed.[92] Wavell cabled Freyberg calling for all-out effort; the battle would go to those who could hold out the longest. 'Enemy has lost high proportion of aircraft and specially trained troops and those that survive must be tired of our troops and dismayed at their reception. They were promised cheap victory and are facing costly defeat.'[93]

It was not to be. On 26 May, six days after the initial landings, Freyberg cabled Wavell to report that defeat was now a certainty as, in his opinion, 'the limit of endurance has been reached by the troops under my command ... No matter what decision is taken by the C-in-C from a military point of view our position here is hopeless.' He explained the situation in no uncertain terms; 'a small ill-equipped and immobile force such as ours cannot stand up against the concentrated bombing that we have been faced with'.[94] The next day he cabled Wavell again exasperated at the apparent lack of action. 'It is obvious you do not realize position here.' He stressed again the centrality of the air issue. 'There is no possibility of our existing as a fighting force unless supported by adequate air.' The 'present conditions court ... disaster. Our only chance with present force which has been battered and shaken by an overwhelming Air Force is to hide by day ... Once we are engaged in battle we are easy prey for dive bombers ... We have counter-attacked and succeeded only to be bombed out in each case in course of few hours ... What we require is air support.'[95]

It does appear in hindsight that Axis air power, apart from its obvious role in transporting Student's troops to Crete, played the decisive part in the outcome of the battle. Major-General E. D. Weston wrote afterwards that air power had been a 'serious matter'. The experience of the troops, he noted, 'had engendered a ludicrous anxiety regarding the powers of aircraft and all areas were infested with self-appointed critics':

> Shouts of 'sit down' enforced by discharge of rifles greeted any movement by day if an aircraft could be detected anywhere in the sky. By night, lights could not be used as shouts of 'put that light out' followed by rifle shots greeted any attempt to use sidelights. In consequence ... movements ... were most seriously prejudiced ... little could be done to abate this nuisance, but it is considered of the first importance that in any future operations the severest disciplinary action should be taken to stamp out the ... practice.[96]

Weston's report, much like that of the Bartholomew Committee, stressed the morale rather than material impacts of air power. At Malame, after several days of straffing, 'only one N.C.O. had been killed and 3 other ranks wounded'.[97] 'The effect produced on the troops' he said, 'appear[ed] out of all proportion to the actual damage inflicted'. By comparison, he continued, 'in the last war, troops endured with fortitude dangers and casualties incomparably greater than those inflicted by air action, yet in Crete air action had produced a state of nerves in troops which seriously interfered with operations'.[98]

Such a damning assessment was not received well by other New Zealand officers. Major-General Sir Edward Puttick, who had commanded 2nd New Zealand Division in Crete, testily pointed out that in the First World War periods of great danger had been usually very short. Reliefs had been frequent and troops when out of the line lived in almost complete security. Furthermore, the enemy rarely, if ever, enjoyed complete superiority in any weapon. He stressed that inappropriate behaviours had been 'confined largely to troops not employed on normal duties to their arm ... It did *not* apply to our infantry units which carried out several counter-attacks by day.' He did accept, however, that gunners, sappers and Army Supply Corps personnel acting as infantry had lost their cohesion after six days of hard fighting. The turning point appears to have been the aerial assault on 25 May, which had been followed by a determined infantry attack. It is worth pointing out that his criticisms of Weston's report were based more on the contention that any troops would have had 'their morale impaired' in the circumstances rather than a denial of the fact that air power had produced a devastating impact on men's morale.[99]

Even taking Puttick's comments and qualifications into account, it is hard to avoid the impression that order and cohesion broke down on Crete. Addressing events in the last few days of the battle, Puttick, writing to Freyberg, advised that in future:

a) Officers and NCOs must maintain command at all times; they must take under command and re-organise all leaderless troops in their vicinity; such men must be taught immediately to place themselves under command of the nearest officer or NCO.
b) All movement of troops must be properly under command and straggling prevented.
c) All leaders must be prepared to set an example of courage and coolness to steady their men in a crisis.
d) Areas in which men are dispersed must be under continuous watch and control by officers and NCOs and any tendency on the part of the men themselves to control such areas, such as by calling out to transport to move on or to individuals to stop moving or take cover, must be rigidly suppressed. The unauthorized or accidental discharge of firearms should be severely dealt with.[100]

All of these issues were covered in training manuals, as Puttick himself pointed out, but it was clear that some of the officers and troops on Crete had failed to behave in the manner expected.[101]

To an extent, therefore, it does appear that Crete was an utter, and perhaps avoidable, catastrophe; the British Commonwealth, with a numerical advantage of approximately 2:1,[102] had been defeated in circumstances where the enemy's plans and intentions had been fully known beforehand. Although 18,000 troops were rescued from the island by the Royal Navy, 12,000 British and Commonwealth soldiers were captured on Crete and a further 2,000 were killed in the fighting.[103] In addition, the Royal Navy lost three cruisers and six destroyers and had four other capital ships severely damaged. Around 2,000 seamen were also killed.[104]

Freyberg chose afterwards to concentrate on the positives. He contended that the appalling losses suffered by the parachutists would prevent them from being 'used again for [a] similar objective'.[105] By making the Germans fight on ground suited to the defender, Crete had allowed the British and Commonwealth Armies to 'bite the head off' the German airborne apparatus. Some 220 out of 600 German transport aircraft used in the operation had been destroyed and 4,000 men had been killed, all for an objective that was not essential to German strategy.[106] Freyberg was correct, but only to a point; the impact of the Greek and Crete adventures would have a domino effect beyond the geographical confines of the Balkans; and the German airborne apparatus used in Crete only made up a tiny proportion of the growing Axis strength in the Middle East and the Mediterranean. The 'golden lining' referred to by Freyberg was not enough to compensate for the cloud now hanging over the British and Commonwealth position in the Middle East.

Strategic Overstretch

The first and perhaps most significant consequence of the Greek and Crete campaigns was overstretch in terms of theatre-wide strategy. The diversion of troops away from North Africa not only called a halt to Operation 'Compass', just as Tripoli lay potentially open to the WDF's advance,[107] but it also gave Germany and Italy the chance to reinforce their position in the desert. In February and March 1941, 13,000 men of the German 5th Light Division and 18,000 men of 15th Panzer Division, of what became known as the *Deutsches Afrika Korps* (*DAK*), arrived in Tripoli under the command of Generalleutnant Erwin Rommel.[108] The *Afrika Korps* did not waste time acclimatising to the desert and on 31 March, a week before the launch of the German Balkan campaign, Rommel's barely formed units began a counter-offensive in North Africa.

The force that remained in the desert to combat Rommel's assault was only a shadow of its former self.[109] With 6th Australian Division in Greece and 'Compass' stalled, 7th Armoured Division was withdrawn to rest, re-equip and recuperate. In its place came the under-strength and untried 2nd Armoured Division, newly arrived from Britain, and the equally fresh, partially trained and equipped 9th Australian Division.[110] In more ways than one, the make-up of the desert army in North Africa fundamentally changed. It became a mixture of regular, territorial, volunteer, and conscript soldiers.[111] These men were not of the same fighting calibre as those who had so decisively defeated the Italians at the start of the year.[112] Poorly trained and lacking in experience, 2nd Armoured Division succumbed rapidly to the battle-hardened troops of the *Afrika Korps*, many of whom had taken part in the invasions of Poland, Belgium and France.[113] By 11 April, German and Italian forces had surrounded the port of Tobruk, besieging 9th Australian Division, and captured O'Connor, the mastermind of 'Compass'.[114]

The British position in the Middle East, which had appeared so strong in January and February, was fast unravelling and Wavell spent the summer of 1941 doing all he could to 'put out fires' in all parts of his vast command. The first in a sequence of emergencies occurred in Iraq. Early in April, with the crises in Greece and in the desert of North Africa in full flow, British intelligence decrypts revealed that the Germans and Italians were jointly planning to use Vichy French Syria as a staging and basing area from which to supply an uprising by the Iraqi Army, led by the former Prime Minister Rashid Ali. On 31 March, on hearing of the plot to overthrow him, the pro-British Regent fled Baghdad; on the night of 1–2 April the Army mobilised its troops and compelled the sitting Prime Minister to resign. The following day, Ali seized power. London, conscious of Iraq's role as a source of oil and the danger of an Arab uprising, demanded action. Wavell prevaricated and encouraged a negotiated settlement, claiming that his forces were already too stretched to tackle Ali. General Sir Claude Auchinleck, the C-in-C India, was more forthcoming, and put in place a long-standing plan to send a division from the subcontinent to protect the Iraqi oilfields. On 17 April, 10th Indian Division began landing at Basra, with a second contingent of the division unloading twelve days later. With his plan fast unravelling, on 30 April Ali ordered the Iraqi Army (about 9,000 troops) to attack the RAF's airfield at Habbaniya, about 50 miles west of Baghdad. Under increasing pressure from London, with Falluja also occupied by Iraqi troops, Wavell scraped the bottom of his manpower barrel to support the position in Iraq, hastily organising 'Habforce', comprised of units from Palestine, and dispatching them on a trans-desert march towards Habbaniya.[115]

On 1 May, with the situation now critical and 'Habforce' still weeks away, the Foreign Office gave Air Vice-Marshal H. G. Smart, the Air Officer Commanding RAF Habbaniya, permission to launch a preemptive strike against the enemy massing outside his perimeter fence. He began his attack the next day and by 5 May the siege of Habbaniya was broken. On 18 May, the first elements of 'Habforce' arrived at Habbaniya and, with the Iraqi Army increasingly in disarray, it was decided to strike fast towards Baghdad. On the night of 29–30 May, with 'Habforce' and 10th Indian Division closing on the city, Ali and his co-conspirators fled. The following day, the Regent was restored and a new government took office under Jamal Madfai. A significant crisis that could have impacted on British access to oil in the Middle East, allowed the Axis to outflank Wavell's position in Egypt and emboldened the Axis to threaten India had been averted.[116]

The whole saga demonstrated, however, the extent to which Britain's oil supply could be threatened by actions out of Syria. Evidence of Vichy complicity in Iraq (Ali's coup had been supported by about thirty German and Italian aircraft flying out of Syria) made it imperative to address the problem of the French Army of the Levant in Syria and Lebanon: a garrison of 35,000 to 45,000 troops, supported by ninety tanks. On 8 June, Wavell ordered Commonwealth columns, a scratch force of 34,000 British, Australian, Indian and Free French troops, to move against Syria. 'Habforce' and 10th Indian Division, fresh from their success in Iraq, moved against Palmyra and Aleppo; the two brigades of 6th Division that had not been involved in Crete moved from northern Palestine against Damascus; and two brigades of the newly arrived 7th Australian Division attacked from Haifa towards Beirut. The short campaign which ensued involved Frenchmen fighting Frenchmen and on all fronts the fighting was 'imbued with resentment'. The British believed that they were spilling blood better saved for the Germans while the Vichy French felt that the war had been unfairly forced upon them. Of the columns closing in on Syria, 7th Australian Division, supported by naval gunfire, proved most successful. The division cracked the defensive positions south of Beirut, making the Vichy position untenable. On 11 July, General Henri Dentz, the Commander of the Army of the Levant, sued for terms, but only 5,700 of his 38,000 men rallied to the Free French cause; the rest were shipped to French North Africa.[117]

As these events unfolded in the east of his command, the problem of the *Afrika Korps* only intensified on Wavell's western flank. Throughout the spring and summer of 1941, British and Australian troops besieged in Tobruk as a consequence of Rommel's rapid advance, had repeatedly repelled Axis advances on the fortress. The doughty defence of Tobruk caused Rommel immense difficulties as his forces could not advance into Egypt with a British fortress to his rear and without the port capacity that Tobruk would provide for a drive towards the Canal. Rommel consequently pushed his men to the limit in order to take the town, but they failed repeatedly in the face of determined British, Australian and Indian resistance.[118]

For 240 days, between April and December 1941, the garrison held out.[119] Based on well-conceived defences built by the Italians,

Tobruk hardened 'into a rock-solid enclave'. Not for the last time, the troops of 9th Australian Division earned themselves a reputation for dogged and determined fighting as they were supported by the massed firepower of the British artillery.[120] Tobruk demonstrated that inexperienced and imperfectly trained troops could fight the Germans and Italians to a standstill. Instead of surrendering on being attacked or penetrated by enemy *panzers*, the defenders of Tobruk 'stayed where they were and destroyed the German infantry and artillery crews trying to follow up'. Even in the rear areas, batmen, cooks and clerks were told in no uncertain terms that they had to fight and hold their ground. Leslie Morshead, the commander of 9th Australian Division, was adamant that Tobruk would be defended in an aggressive rather than passive manner. No-man's land was to be the domain of the Australians. In reaction to newspaper articles that 'Tobruk can take it!', Morshead reacted confidently that 'we're not here to "take it", we're here to "give it"'.[121]

Morale in the garrison, which numbered by the end of April 23,000 men (of whom 15,000 were Australian, 7,500 British and 500 Indian), was 'as high as anywhere in the Middle East – truly high'. With the port at Tobruk remaining largely operational, the men were well supplied with food, cigarettes and basic welfare amenities. Sickness rates were low and there was, as one historian has put it, a 'mood of grim determination which comes to men who have been told by their commander, "There'll be no Dunkirk here . . . There is to be no surrender or retreat.'[122] By May, it was clear that the German and Italian forces could not compel the garrison to capitulate. Understanding, through Ultra, that Rommel's attack had shot its bolt, Churchill began to put sustained pressure on Wavell to go on the offensive, relieve Tobruk and secure the canal zone once and for all.[123]

Wavell, as a result, launched two offensives, codenamed 'Brevity' and 'Battleaxe', in May and June 1941. Both operations were 'ill-considered and ill-prepared' and were ultimately unsuccessful.[124] Thus, even though Wavell had presided over great victories against the Italians in North and East Africa, had quelled the Iraqi rebellion, and was on the way to securing the WDF's eastern flank by conquering Syria, his repeated defeats, and to an extent, humiliations, at the hands of the *Wehrmacht*, drained Churchill's confidence in his commander in the Middle East. On 22 June 1941, Wavell, whose taciturn character had never made him one of Churchill's favourites, was informed that he was to swap places with General Sir Claude Auchinleck, the C-in-C in India.

Operation 'Crusader'

Auchinleck, who had impressed Churchill while in charge of Southern Command in England during 1940 and with his aggressive response to the emergency in Iraq as C-in-C India,[125] took up his new role on 5 July. The son of a lieutenant-colonel in the Royal Artillery and of Ulster protestant extraction, Auchinleck passed into the Royal Military Academy, Sandhurst, in forty-fifth place in 1902.[126] The following year, he was among some thirty cadets awarded commissions in the Indian Army and in 1904 he joined the 62nd Punjabis. On the outbreak of the First World War, he accompanied his regiment to Egypt and then on to Mesopotamia, where he spent the rest of the war. Auchinleck was considered 'outstanding among the younger officers of the Indian Army who had survived the war'; he was appointed to the DSO in 1917 and thrice mentioned in dispatches. By the end of hostilities, he had experienced a brief but successful period in command of his battalion and had become a brigade major, as part of 52nd Brigade. It was after the war, however, that his career really took off. He passed the Staff College Quetta in 1919 and attended the inaugural course at the Imperial Defence College in 1927. As a full colonel, he returned to Quetta as an instructor between 1930 and 1932. In 1933, he took over command of the Peshawar Brigade and after leading successful operations on the North-West Frontier was promoted to major-general in 1936. The following year, he became Deputy Chief of the General Staff, India, playing a key role in the Chatfield committee on the modernisation of the Indian Army. On the outbreak of the Second World War, Auchinleck returned to the UK to prepare IV Corps for dispatch to France, but on account of his experience on the North-West Frontier, and his expertise in mountain warfare, was sent to Norway, taking command of the land forces in the Narvik area. Following the disaster and evacuation, he returned to England and was promoted to commander, Southern Command in July 1940. That November, once the threat of invasion had passed, he was sent east as C-in-C India.[127]

Now transferred to the Middle East, Auchinleck began immediately to prepare for a decisive blow against the Axis in Africa. The success in Syria, for the cost of only 3,300 casualties, had produced a number of very positive outcomes. It had forestalled German intentions of establishing themselves on the eastern shores of the Mediterranean; it had created a land bridge with Turkey; it had gained naval and air bases to the north of the Canal; and it had provided considerable depth to the defence of Iraq. It had also ensured the security of the British and Commonwealth Army in Egypt from the east and liberated the commander of the WDF from all preoccupations but that of beating the Axis in the deserts of North Africa.[128]

Auchinleck began to prepare his army for a new offensive, to be codenamed 'Crusader'. During the seven months from January to July 1941, vast quantities of men and stores had arrived in Egypt. The 1st South African Division and 4th and 5th Indian Divisions disembarked, hardened from their victories in East Africa. The 144,000 men landed from the UK included 50th Northumbrian Division, which had fought in France, 2nd Armoured Division, the rest of 2nd New Zealand and 7th Australian Divisions, which had been sent to the UK during the invasion crisis, and the HQ of X Corps. In addition, 60,000 men from Australia and New Zealand (including 9th Australian Division), 23,000 men from India and 12,000 men from South Africa (part of 2nd South African Division) had arrived. During the same period over a million tons of military stores, ammunition, weapons, aircraft, and vehicles were also unloaded.[129]

Even more equipment would be required, however, if Auchinleck was to successfully challenge Rommel in the desert.[130] With Lend-Lease signed into law on 11 March 1941, the British and Commonwealth forces in Egypt were supplemented by another influx of new materiel; between July and October, 300 British cruiser tanks, 300 American-made Stuart tanks, 170 'I' tanks, 34,000 lorries, 600 field guns, 80 heavy and 160 light anti-aircraft guns, 200 anti-tank guns, and 900 mortars arrived in the Middle East. British and Commonwealth factories had finally got into their stride and perhaps more crucially the vast potential of the economy of the United States was now fully on the side of the armies in the desert.[131]

With these forces at the disposal of the newly formed and newly named Eighth Army, Auchinleck found himself immediately under the kind of pressure (for rapid success) from the Prime Minister that Wavell had experienced before him.[132] The German invasion of Russia, on 22 June, had thrown Britain a life-line of sorts, as the fate of both countries now revolved around the defeat of the *Wehrmacht* (Britain and the Soviet Union signed an alliance on 12 July 1941). Stalin, more than anything else, required the opening of a 'Second Front' to distract the Germans from their onslaught in the East. 'It would be a very great reflection on us', Churchill told Auchinleck, 'if, in this vital period when the Russians were bearing the full brunt of the attack, and when conditions were so favourable, we took no action of any kind.'[133]

Auchinleck was conscious, however, of the profound difficulties he faced in the desert, not least the need to train his much-expanded citizen army; consequently, he played for more time. He informed Churchill that 'Battleaxe' had shown beyond doubt that the 'present standard' of training was 'not (repeat not) enough'.[134] This time, 'nothing' was to be 'left to chance'. He ensured that the New Zealanders, for example, undertook three brigade exercises 'under full support of artillery and ... two divisional rehearsals' prior to 'Crusader'.[135] Auchinleck also, in consultation with Air Marshal Sir Arthur Tedder, the Air Officer in Command in the Middle East, set out to solve the problem of air support for the Army which had so bedevilled the campaigns in Greece and Crete. In July, an inter-service committee was formed which conducted a series of joint practical manoeuvres aimed at improving air/land co-operation. These efforts resulted, on 30 September, in the Middle East (Army and RAF) Directive on Direct Air Support, which spelt out in detail new procedures for co-operation between the two services. It introduced an innovative joint command structure, Air Support Control (ASC), to manage air–land operations and to ensure that in future, forward troops would be able to 'make air support requests that would be considered immediately and, if granted, met promptly'.[136]

With these vital improvements made, Auchinleck handed over the planning of 'Crusader' to Alan Cunningham, fresh from his victory in East Africa and now installed as the first commander of Eighth Army. Cunningham's plan was, broadly, to meet Rommel's *panzer* forces in a climactic armoured engagement that would decide the fate of the desert war. Much like 'Compass', the plan for 'Crusader' was built around the prescriptions and understandings of interwar doctrine. It was 'deliberately flexible' as it aimed to make best use of the Army's apparent strengths, the ability of its commanders at all levels to adapt to the multitude of unforeseen circumstances presented by war.[137] Cunningham determined that there should be 'no detailed operational orders. Circumstances change with time. Enemy dispositions are liable to alter and necessitate frequent amendments to orders. Any plan made should be ... elastic'.[138] Success, thus, was to rely heavily on the skill, resolve and creativity of commanders in the field. As Brigadier G. M. O. Davy, the commander of 7th Armoured Brigade, put it in a special instruction issued before 'Crusader':

> Senior commanders will often be unable to know what is going on except in their immediate neighbourhood, and will themselves be engaged with the enemy. Orders may be few and far between and shortage of wireless sets will make control less easy. Much will depend on the cooperation and initiative of junior commanders and the enterprise of tank commanders.[139]

By November 1941, Eighth Army was ready to deploy no fewer than six full divisions and two army tank brigades in the field. The 4th Indian Division, 2nd New Zealand Division and 1st Army Tank Brigade of XIII Corps (based on the old WDF) and 7th Armoured Division and 1st South African Division of the recently established XXX Corps, were joined by 70th Division (6th Division renamed having being transferred from Syria) and 32nd Army Tank Brigade (which had been formed in North Africa in September 1941) of the Tobruk garrison,[140] and 2nd South African Division in Army Reserve (118,000 men in all). Opposing Eighth Army, the newly formed *Panzer Gruppe Afrika*, comprising 15th and 21st Panzer Divisions (21st Panzer Division was the former 5th Light Division renamed) and the newly arrived *Afrika* Division (later to be renamed 90th Light Division) of the *Afrika Korps* and the five Italian infantry divisions of XXI Corps, was supported by the two Italian divisions (the Ariete Armoured and Trieste Motorised Divisions) of the *Corpo d'Armati di Manovra XX* (an army of 65,000 Germans and 54,000 Italians, 119,000 in all).[141]

Although the two forces were in manpower terms relatively equal, Eighth Army did enjoy a considerable numerical advantage in materiel. It had at its disposal 173 light, 339 medium and 199 heavy tanks (711 in all) against 70 light and 174 medium German tanks and 146 medium Italian tanks (390 in all). The Italian mediums, however, were little better than the light Stuarts of the British Army and light *Panzer II*s of the Germans; thus, in terms of main battle (medium and heavy) tanks, Eighth Army enjoyed a 538 to 174 advantage (a ratio of 3:1).[142] The Germans had no operational armoured reserves while the British had a sizeable one, about 259 tanks (only 90 of which were light), and were expecting a further convoy (which included 1st Armoured Division from the UK) to arrive imminently with about 236 tanks (only 60 of which were light).[143] In the air, a reinforced RAF numbered some 554 serviceable aircraft. Axis air strength, just like on the ground, was limited by the fact that 'Barbarossa' had dragged on into the autumn; reinforcements that had been expected were now unavailable. In these circumstances, the Germans had 121 serviceable aircraft, while the *Regio Aeronautica* contributed another 192. The RAF, therefore, enjoyed a superiority of 554 to 313 in the air (a ratio of nearly 2:1), a 'sizeable advantage' by any measure.[144]

With Eighth Army replenished, and, to a large extent, retrained,[145] and, with the *Wehrmacht* fully committed in Russia, Auchinleck launched Operation 'Crusader' on 18 November 1941. Churchill's message to the troops on the eve of the attack captured the mood and his expectations for the battle; it stated boldly that:

> For the first time British and Empire troops will meet the Germans with an ample supply of equipment in modern weapons of all kinds. The battle itself will affect the whole course of the war. Now is the time to strike the hardest blow yet struck for final victory, home and freedom. The Desert Army may add a page to history which will rank with Blenheim and Waterloo. The eyes of all nations are upon you. All our hearts are with you.[146]

The field censorship summary for 12 to 18 November, the first summary available for one of the British and Commonwealth Armies' great battles of the Second World War, showed that the troops were as buoyant and hopeful as their Prime Minister. 'On the eve of the great Libyan offensive', it stated:

> The morale of the MEF has never been so high in the 26 months of war as at the present time ... The men's belief in success is based on faith in their commanders, the excellence and quantity of the material at their disposal, the increased amount of air support, and the certainty that, man for man, they are better than the enemy.[147]

The 'morale and offensive spirit' of the Tobruk garrison, waiting to sortie in support of the operation, was noted to be 'truly remarkable'.[148]

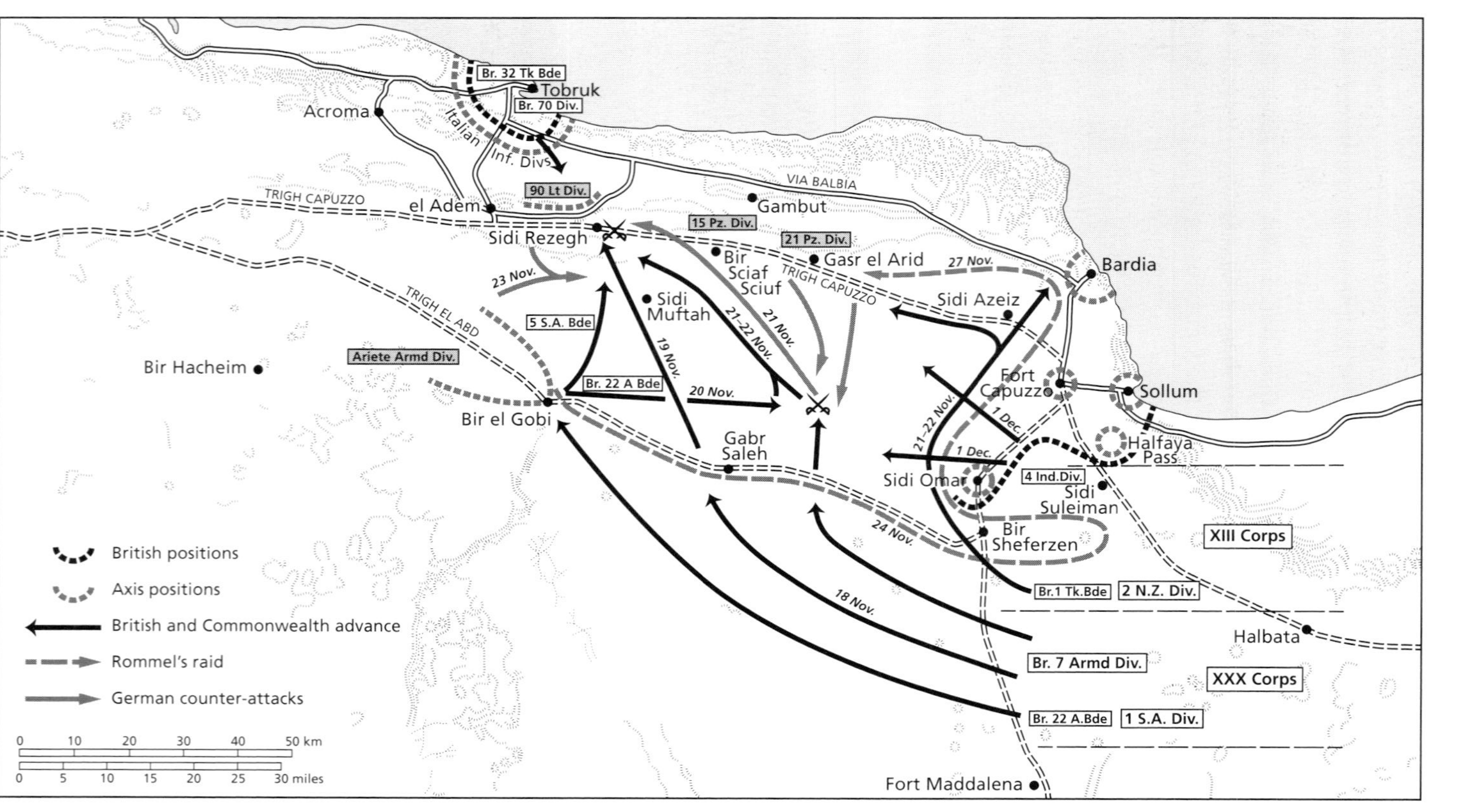

Map 4.4 Operation 'Crusader', November–December 1941

The operation, however, did not go entirely according to plan. Cunningham's broad aim for 'Crusader' revolved around the need to find and destroy the enemy armour. He intended to do this by advancing XXX Corps, under the command of Lieutenant-General Willoughby Norrie, about 40 miles into Axis-held territory, seize ground of its choosing and provoke a decisive tank engagement that would lead to the destruction of the German armour. This ploy did not work; Rommel, distracted by his own plans for an offensive to take Tobruk, treated Norrie's advance as nothing more than a reconnaissance in force. Frustrated, the next day Cunningham decided to push XXX Corps even further forward to threaten Rommel's east–west lines of communication, on the Trigh Capuzzo and Via Balbia. This bolder thrust brought 7th Armoured Division, the spearhead of the British advance, towards the airfield at Sidi Rezegh, where the decisive engagement of 'Crusader' played out (see Map 4.4).[149]

The flat ground around Sidi Rezegh was, in theory, perfect for an armoured clash. But, as Rommel began to grasp the significance of Eighth Army's advance and decided to respond, an extremely troubling dynamic emerged; the open terrain brutally exposed differences in the quality of the British and German armour. All of the British tanks in the desert were armed with the 2-pounder gun, which was both the standard anti-tank and tank gun in the British Army. This weapon was, unfortunately for British tank men, incapable of penetrating the 'face hardened' armour of the German Mark III and IV *panzers* beyond 500 yards. The German *panzers* were, therefore, able to engage the British armour and anti-tank guns at a safe distance using their superior 50mm and 75mm guns.[150] As a consequence, as one soldier put it, 'we all met Mr Death that day in Sidi Rezegh'. 'We were ... blown to pieces a bit at a time by the enemy and we could not do a thing about it.'[151] As Private Crimp of 2nd Battalion, the Rifle Brigade, 7th Armoured Division, noted:

> We may have had the greater number, but most of them were ... lanky, lightweight, gangling cruisers, pretty fast, but mounted with feeble 2-pounder guns, no earthly good against the thicker armour and much more powerful 75-mm. armament of the German Panzers. How many crews have been wasted in useless tanks, not being able to retaliate against the longer-ranged

> enemy guns before having approached several hundred yards nearer their opponents over open desert and under fire? And only then with a mere 'pea-shooter'![152]

Four VCs were awarded for the fighting at Sidi Rezegh. With the short effective range of the inferior British tank and anti-tank guns and the proneness of the British made tanks to mechanical breakdown, British armoured units resorted to charging the enemy tanks and guns in the hope of knocking them out. Commanders such as Brigadier 'Jock' Campbell, of 7th Support Group, 7th Armoured Division, had no alternative but to rely on more and more extreme ways to motivate their men to take such risks. Campbell famously led his unit into the attack in his open unprotected staff car. He believed, according to Jake Wardrop of 5th Royal Tank Regiment, 'that tanks should charge no matter the odds'. Protests from the likes of Wardrop, who admitted to 'quite frankly' not being 'so strong for this charging business', were met with the reply, 'that's what you are soldiers for – to die!'[153]

By 23 November, a pattern began to emerge in the confused fighting around Sidi Rezegh, and it was apparent that Eighth Army's losses were becoming critical. Reports suggested that so many of Cunningham's tanks had been knocked out that the enemy now possessed a numerical advantage of three to one.[154] Cunningham called for Auchinleck to fly out to the desert to assess the situation for himself. When Auchinleck arrived at Eighth Army HQ, Cunningham presented two options to his C-in-C: to withdraw and hope to save Egypt and what remained of his tank force or to continue to fight on. Auchinleck chose to fight and issued his orders to Cunningham. 'You will . . . continue to attack the enemy relentlessly using all your resources even to the last tank.'[155]

The 'Crusader' battle had now become more than a technical clash of armour; it had evolved into a climactic struggle of physical and mental endurance. Rommel, sensing that the critical moment of the battle had arrived, decided to try and break his opponents' will. On 24 November, in an effort to exploit his success at Sidi Rezegh, he used 21st Panzer Division, supported by 15th Panzer Division, to launch an armoured thrust towards the Libyan/Egyptian border (the 'dash to the wire'). He hoped that the strength and ferocity of this attack would so surprise and disorientate Eighth Army that it would be forced into a general retreat, much as had happened in April and June 1941. But

Auchinleck, who was still at Eighth Army HQ, held his nerve. The C-in-C Middle Eastern Forces wrote to his army commander and to his men:

> During three days at your Adv H.Q. I have seen and heard enough to convince me though I did not need convincing that the determination to beat the enemy of your Commanders and troops could NOT be greater and I have NO doubt whatever that he will be beaten. His position is desperate and he is trying by lashing out in all directions to distract us from our object which is to destroy him utterly. We will NOT be distracted and he WILL be destroyed. You have got your teeth into him. Hang on and bite deeper and deeper and hang on till he is finished. Give him NO rest. The general situation in NORTH AFRICA is EXCELLENT. There is only one order ATTACK and PURSUE. ALL OUT EVERYONE.[156]

There was to be no retreat. Rommel, as a consequence, found himself increasingly at the end of a long and uncertain logistics chain. His *panzers* began to run out of fuel and, back at Sidi Rezegh, 2nd New Zealand Division and 70th Division, which had sortied from Tobruk, were able to exploit the absence of the German armour and open a small corridor to the besieged fortress. Rommel's gamble had failed and he was left with little choice but to turn 21st and 15th Panzer Divisions around.[157]

The moment of greatest danger had passed, but it was clear that Cunningham was not the right man to push Eighth Army to the levels of human endurance necessary to defeat the *Wehrmacht*. On 26 November, Auchinleck removed his Commander Eighth Army and replaced him with his Deputy Chief-of-Staff, Major-General Sir Neil Ritchie. Ritchie had spent his time in the Middle East behind a desk in Cairo. Nevertheless, Auchinleck trusted him deeply and was confident that he would put into effect his ideas, for he 'showed every sign of continuing personally to direct operations'.[158] In the circumstances, this was no bad thing, as Auchinleck had shown himself more than capable of handling Rommel and the *Panzer Gruppe Afrika*.[159] By 1 December, it was clear which way the battle was going. Both sides were exhausted, but while the *Afrika Korps* was receiving few replacements and reinforcements (in November, due to shipping losses, only 40,000 of the 120,000 tons of supplies required arrived), Eighth Army was the recipient of a steady stream of men and armaments from its bases and workshops around Cairo. By 4 December, the *Afrika Korps* had only 40 tanks left; by comparison, a replenished 7th Armoured Division alone had 140. On 6 December, Rommel issued the order to retreat; Tobruk was relieved and Eighth Army spent much of December driving the Axis forces out of Cyrenaica and mopping up enemy garrisons holding out at Bardia and Halfaya.[160]

To all intents and purposes, a great victory had been achieved; Eighth Army had outfought and outlasted the *Panzer Gruppe Afrika* in a chaotic battle that had placed an enormous strain on the troops and the junior leaders in charge of them, a fact that was emphasised in the censorship summaries throughout the period of the operation.[161] The summaries following the battle, pointed to 'overwhelming evidence' that the troops were prepared to 'outfight and outstay the Germans' and that they possessed 'the desire ... to engage the enemy wherever possible and destroy him if possible, tank for tank, man for man, and hand to hand'.[162] The summary for 24 to 30 December noted:

> Briton, South African, New Zealander, Australian and Pole each readily acknowledges the Hun's stubbornness, the accuracy of his fire, and the superior quality of his equipment, but there is unanimity of feeling that they can outstay the enemy and that he will not stand up to cold steel. This mail contains no heroics; it is sober in tone and matter of fact in its description of battle field incidents; it is sprinkled throughout with a due and proper admixture of grumbling and self-deprecation; and through it all shines the real spirit of the British soldier, who may not relish the job at hand and is continually longing to be back on home soil, but who will stick it out as long as it is necessary, however hard and perilous the way.[163]

A 2nd New Zealand Division report echoed this sentiment, noting that the first lesson from the operation had been that 'there is a time in all battles when the men on both sides are exhausted. It is the man who can hold on longest and who fights with the greatest determination who will win.'[164] As one man put it:

> For 2 or 3 days round about the time General Cunningham was given sick leave [this was the official explanation for his removal] things were serious, in fact it appeared at first that

> we should lose the initiative, but no, the lads got into 'em and held on like grim death against his furious counter attacks until he finally had to retire.[165]

The result, as Ritchie and Auchinleck put it in mid-December, was that by the end of the battle, 'the German infantry had been reduced almost to the level of the Italian'.[166]

'Crusader' had been conceived and fought with the understanding that the result would depend on the determination, ingenuity and creativity of junior officers and their men.[167] That the soldiers of Eighth Army rose to the challenge was all the more important as command and control, due to the constant movement of units on the vast 'Crusader' battlefield and poor information flow, had been extremely difficult throughout. Commanders were often separated from subordinate units and even their own HQs. Armoured brigade units 'spent most of their time physically finding, rallying and concentrating units after engagements'.[168] By 24 November, six days into the battle, the damage to the HQs of XXX Corps, 7th Armoured Division, 1st South African Division and 7th Armoured Brigade had caused the corps command structure to collapse almost entirely.[169] Nevertheless, Eighth Army held on and fought the Axis forces to a standstill. This determination, along with Auchinleck's remarkable *sang-froid*, allowed Eighth Army to capitalise on its considerable reserves of materiel and outlast the *Panzergruppe* in the battle of attrition that ensued.

Spring 1942

A brief period of recuperation followed victory at 'Crusader'. Eighth Army had lost some 18,000 men and the *Panzergruppe* 38,000.[170] But the shortened lines of communications and supply following the Axis retreat allowed the German and Italian *Panzergruppe* quickly to regain its material strength. By mid-January, the Axis forces mustered 173 serviceable tanks at the front plus 300 serviceable aircraft. As Rainer Kriebel, a staff officer in the *Afrika Korps*, has argued, the rest period granted to the soldiers and the arrival of reinforcements in the beginning of January also had a 'favourable influence' on fighting spirit.[171] Eighth Army was, by comparison, still recovering from its estimated 800 tank losses and the fact that the Desert Air Force had sent 450 of its aircraft to the Far East, to support British and

Commonwealth forces in a new war against the Japanese (see Chapter 5).[172] The Japanese attack on Pearl Harbor and their invasion of Malaya were to have profound implications for Britain's war effort. Although in the short term, they would divert much needed resources away from the Middle East, the addition of the USA to the Allied cause would unleash vast industrial potential and armies for the land war against the Axis.[173]

In January 1942, the full effect of American involvement in the war was far from being realised and it was at this juncture, at the end of the month, that Rommel, unknown to the German and Italian High Commands, and, therefore, unknown to Ritchie and Auchinleck through Ultra, launched a surprise counter-offensive.[174] The parallels with what had happened after 'Compass' were striking. With the formations that had fought so hard during 'Crusader' relieved for rest and refitting, Rommel was, once again, faced with a newly arrived and underprepared division, this time 1st Armoured Division. The division had fought briefly at the end of the campaign in France in 1940. Thereafter, it had twice had its tanks removed and sent to the Middle East. The effect upon training, as the Official History recounts, 'was of course deplorable'. The 22nd Armoured Brigade, which had been sent to the Middle East in advance of the main body of the division, had fought with 7th Armoured Division during 'Crusader'. But the brigade was refitting in February 1942, leaving the rest of the division, which had only disembarked at Suez during the second half of November, to guard the gateway to Cyrenaica.[175] They proved completely incapable of dealing with the *Panzergruppe's* rapid offensive. By 4 February, Eighth Army had been driven out of the Cyrenaican bulge back as far as Gazala, 30 miles west of Tobruk, and, while casualties during the retreat were relatively modest – 1,390 men, 72 tanks and 40 field guns – the setback had a devastating impact on the men's morale.

'Crusader' had been built up as the climax of the desert war.[176] Since July 1941, many had anticipated victory and a return home by Christmas or at least early in the New Year.[177] The censorship summary for mid-February showed that there was 'no denying the fact that the tone of correspondence from British troops in the forward areas was lower than it ha[d] ever been ... and reflected the general disappointment of all ranks over our hurried withdrawal'.[178] The morale report for the same period identified a tendency among the troops to 'criticise the war effort and general conduct of operations'. The report noted that one censorship section had stated, in mid-March, that 45 per cent of the letters examined complained of being 'Browned off'.[179] Auchinleck wrote to Sir P. J. Grigg, the newly appointed Secretary of State for War, the same month, describing how one of his 'main tasks here, if not *the* main one, is to study the psychology of this very mixed array we call an Army, and I spend most of my time doing this in the hope that it will not disintegrate altogether!'[180]

In many ways, the worst aspect of the morale problem was, as Auchinleck wrote to Churchill, that personnel of the Royal Armoured Corps were 'losing confidence' in themselves and in their equipment.[181] The inferior penetration of the 2-pounder anti-tank gun left the infantry without adequate protection from tanks, the decisive arm in desert warfare. In this regard, the Army was still paying the price of the catastrophe in France. The need for a more capable anti-tank weapon had been foreseen as early as 1938, and a new 6-pounder anti-tank gun was due to enter production in 1940. But with the loss of over 500 2-pounders on the Continent, it was decided to keep producing the inferior weapon as the delays associated with retooling factories were considered, in the crisis after Dunkirk, to be too great. It was better to have an inferior weapon than no weapon at all.[182]

The infantry, therefore, demanded that it be protected by British tanks and 25-pounder batteries, in addition to the ineffective anti-tank guns; during 'Crusader,' the 25-pounder 'proved to be the best destroyer of [German] tanks'.[183] These problems were exacerbated by the fact that German *panzers* were equipped with dual-purpose guns capable of firing armour piercing and high explosive rounds. This meant that they could act both as tank killers and mobile artillery. German *panzers* could, therefore, sit out of range of Eighth Army's anti-tank gun detachments and knock them out using high explosive and machine-gun fire. British tanks, by comparison, only fired armour-piercing shot, which meant that Eighth Army had to rely on 25-pounders or medium artillery to provide such support in battle. This could be achieved, providing units co-operated closely, but this was an ideal that was not always possible in the chaotic and fast-moving conditions of desert combat.[184] Innovative tank commanders, therefore, had to resort to extreme methods to find solutions to the tactical challenges faced in the desert, such as charging German tank and anti-tank guns. This brave, or perhaps reckless, approach was arguably the best way in the circumstances to take on the *Panzergruppe*,[185] but it did prove highly dangerous and enormously expensive, leading eventually to morale difficulties as armoured units lost confidence in their ability to defeat the enemy without appalling and unsustainable casualties.[186]

By April, Auchinleck had become so concerned about the impact of these issues on Eighth Army's morale, that he began to resort to extreme measures to ensure that his troops behaved in the manner expected of them. With the unanimous agreement of his army commanders, he forwarded to the War Office, as Gort had done in 1940, a recommendation for the reintroduction of the death penalty for 'desertion in the field' and for 'misbehaving in the face of the enemy in such a manner as to show cowardice'. To back up his request, he recounted evidence that since April 1941 there had been 291 convictions for desertion and 19 convictions for cowardice in the Middle East.[187] Auchinleck's request, which eventually reached the Prime Minister and the War Cabinet, was turned down on 16 June for political and not military reasons.[188] Nevertheless, as he waited to hear back from London, Auchinleck felt the situation was so serious that he took matters into his own hands and ordered that corps and divisional commanders should establish stragglers' posts on the main axes of advances. Senior officers at these posts were instructed to:

> Take the strongest possible action against any individual of whatever rank who refuses to conform to orders. If necessary in order to stop panic, there must be no hesitation in resorting to extreme measures, such as shooting an individual who cannot otherwise be stopped.[189]

Gazala

It is difficult, therefore, to avoid the impression that Eighth Army was suffering some form of crisis in the spring of 1942 (see also Chapter 6). But, in spite of Auchinleck's concerns, the morale of his army did not disintegrate to the extent that might have been expected in the circumstances.[190] For a start, the growing strength of Allied manpower and materiel in the Middle East gave a boost to the men. Between January and May 1942, the front-line strength of Eighth Army, which had been badly damaged by the heavy fighting during 'Crusader', increased 43 per cent, from 88,000 troops to 126,000. During the same period, with Lend-Lease in full flow, 1,078 guns, 1,297 tanks,

30,566 vehicles and 320,204 tons of stores arrived from the UK and North America.[191]

These developments, combined with reports of the seizure of Vichy-controlled Madagascar on 5 May, the Red Army's successes in Russia and the growing intensity of the air war over Germany, led to a growing narrative that the war had reached a turning point. This sentiment was echoed in Churchill's speech of 10 May, marking two years since he had taken office. There was something different about this speech, 'his best ever', according to Home Intelligence. Instead of calling for more 'blood and tears and toil', it was noticed that Churchill focused more on 'good cheer' and on hope for the future.[192] 'We are moving through reverses and defeats to complete and final victory', he said. 'We are no longer unarmed; we are well armed. Now we are not alone; we have mighty Allies ... There can only be one end ... we may stride forward into the unknown with growing confidence.'[193] That reports were also beginning to appear in the press dealing with demobilisation and post-war gratuities only seemed to reinforce the impression that the end was in sight.[194] The censorship summary for 13 to 19 May noted:

> It is the considered opinion of this Section that no single event in the last six months has had such a marked influence on the morale of the men as the Prime Minister's stirring words. Coming as it did in the wake of other encouraging news ... the speech, full of fire and determination and ironic humour, has created a great feeling of confidence and satisfaction. The men feel that once again 'they are in the picture'.[195]

The following week, the censors noted that a 'widespread belief that the turn of the tide has come and that reverses, withdrawals and the like are things of the past' was now apparent. Instead 'offensive action on all fronts is expected ... and many anticipate that the war can be brought to a conclusion this year'.[196]

These were positive developments indeed. However, Eighth Army's growing confidence and materiel might mean little if the troops were not capable of making effective use of their mounting strength. The problem during 'Crusader', and the setback in the spring, had revolved, to a large extent, around the inferior quality of British tank and anti-tank guns. There was little Auchinleck could do about this in the short term, but he could compensate for technological deficiencies by training and organising Eighth Army to function as a more effective team. He decided that 'emphasis' would have to be 'laid on training the co-operation of all arms in battle' in the run-up to the next operation.[197] With that aim in mind, Major-General John Harding was appointed to the new post of Director of Military Training Middle East Command in January 1942. It was hoped that by reinvigorating the tactical training of junior officers ('the most important part of all training' according to Harding), by establishing schools, including a higher commanders' course for selected senior officers, and by allocating collective training areas, each large enough to exercise a complete division, commanders, staff and men would develop skills that would allow infantry, tank, artillery and anti-tank units to work so closely together that they would negate the qualitative advantage enjoyed by the *Afrika Korps*.[198]

In order to facilitate greater co-operation, a degree of reorganisation was required.[199] Eighth Army's armoured divisions were ordered to scrap one of their two armoured brigades and replace it with a motor brigade. This meant that a British armoured division would have less armour and more infantry, like a German *panzer* division. The artillery and anti-tank units that had previously resided in an armoured division's support group, were now reapportioned to the two 'brigade groups'. In future, therefore, an armoured division would consist of one armoured brigade group and one motor brigade group. The former would contain three tank regiments, one motor battalion, and a regiment of field and anti-tank guns, and the latter three motor battalions and a similar allotment of artillery and anti-tank guns. Following the same logic, infantry divisions were also reorganised. They maintained the same number of brigades, but whereas previously artillery, anti-tank and anti-aircraft units had been predominantly under divisional command, they were now placed under the direct control of 'infantry brigade groups'.[200]

These changes finally provided brigade commanders with direct control over a significant amount of fire-support weapons (see Chapter 1).[201] It was clear that Auchinleck recognised the organisational deficiencies of the interwar Army and was willing to do everything in his power to make the Eighth Army function in line with the basic concepts of *FSR*. Auchinleck's forces would fight the next battle of the campaign with a fully devolved system of command and control with local commanders in charge of a significantly greater proportion of the all-arms team.

A question remained, however, over whether Auchinleck had gone far enough. His reorganisation did little, for example, to address the important issue of infantry/armour co-operation. The armoured brigade group of each armoured division still possessed only one motorised infantry battalion. For effective infantry support, close co-operation with the divisional infantry brigade group was still a requirement; and collaboration between armoured and infantry brigades had proved distinctly difficult during the fluid engagements of 'Crusader' and during Spring 1942. Much, in this new arrangement, still depended on the creativity and drive of local commanders and the willingness of the men of Eighth Army to grit things out and fight to the bitter end. However, there was much evidence to suggest that morale in Eighth Army had become more, rather than less, fragile in the period following 'Crusader'.

There was some unqualified good news. The new weapons being churned out by British and American factories had begun to arrive in the Middle East; these included the Grant tank and the 6-pounder anti-tank gun. The Grant was a significant improvement on all British armour previously seen in the desert. It possessed a 75mm gun in a sponson at one side capable of firing both high explosive and armour-piercing shot.[202] This meant that from now on British crews, 'rather than charging anti-tank guns, could stand off at long range and shell suspected positions in exactly the same manner as the Germans'. The arrival of the 6-pounder anti-tank gun also made a considerable difference. It meant that Eighth Army now had an anti-tank weapon that could take on the *panzers* on an equal footing, thus, in theory, releasing the 25-pounder guns to their more traditional role of providing artillery support.[203] Moreover, the infantry, once their anti-tank regiments had received the new 6-pounders, could transfer the old 2-pounder anti-tank guns to each infantry battalion, providing them with at least a modicum of organic anti-tank capability – thus improving morale and combat effectiveness.

By May 1942, Eighth Army was clearly a hotbed of ideas, activity and reorganisation. These initiatives, however, required time to bed in, a commodity that was in increasingly short supply. Churchill had become progressively adamant that a new offensive had to be launched in June, in time to acquire landing grounds to allow the RAF to cover the passage of a proposed convoy to the island of Malta, which, at the time lay besieged in the heart of the Mediterranean.[204] The island was of immense strategic value to Britain. It formed an 'unsinkable aircraft carrier', barring the north–south route across the Sicilian channel that connected Mussolini to his African empire. Situated 1,100 miles from Gibraltar and 900 miles from Egypt, it acted as a safe haven and refuelling station between the western and eastern basins of the Mediterranean. It was an asset that Britain could ill afford to be neutralised, let alone lose.[205] Yet, by May 1942, Malta had been effectively eliminated as a naval and air base due to Axis air attack from Sicily. British surface ships and submarines had been withdrawn and air activity had been severely curtailed. As a result, Axis ships and convoys bound for North Africa could pass close east or west of the island with little danger of being attacked.[206]

In the circumstances, Auchinleck and Ritchie had little choice but to prepare to launch a new offensive to acquire the landing grounds demanded by Churchill. For this endeavour, Eighth Army had 126,000 men at its disposal, divided between XIII Corps, under Lieutenant-General William 'Strafer' Gott, which included 50th Northumbrian Division, 1st and 2nd South African Divisions and 1st and 32nd Army Tank Brigades, and XXX Corps, under Lieutenant-General Willoughby Norrie, consisting of 1st and 7th Armoured Divisions (5th Indian Division was in Army Reserve). By comparison, the renamed *Panzerarmee Afrika* had 90,000 men split between three German divisions (15th and 21st Panzer and 90th Light) and six Italian, two of which (the Trieste Motorised and Ariete Armoured) were fully mobile.[207] As regards tanks, Auchinleck had 849, including 167 of the new American Grants, whereas the Germans possessed only 332, of which 50 were obsolescent Mark II's, and the Italians had 228, some 560 in all. In the key metric of medium and heavy tanks, Eighth Army enjoyed a sizeable 2.5:1 advantage.[208] In the realm of guns, Eighth Army had a 3:2 advantage; it had 112 of the new 6-pounder anti-tank guns, although Rommel did have 48 88mm anti-tank guns.[209] Only in the air, where Axis strength had recovered significantly, did the German and Italian forces have a substantial superiority, possessing 497 serviceable aircraft in the desert while the Desert Air Force had only 190. Losses during 'Crusader', reverses in Malta and increasing transfers to India had all added up.[210]

Auchinleck had been determined to avoid launching an offensive before he had a 3:2 material superiority over the *Panzerarmee* and, indeed, it did appear that the situation was broadly in line with his intentions.[211] For 'strong psychological reasons', it was decided to give every armoured regiment a quota of the new and powerful Grants. The Grants available to Eighth Army were, therefore, spread among the armoured regiments as evenly as possible instead of concentrating them together as a powerful strike force (thus, replicating the mistake made by the French with the Char B1 in 1940). The limited number of 6-pounder anti-tank guns that had arrived in the desert prior to the proposed offensive,[212] meant that many of the anti-tank batteries that were to participate in the battle were still armed with 2-pounder guns and many of the infantry and motor battalions that were due to receive 2-pounders (once they had been replaced by 6-pounders in the anti-tank regiments) had not received their anti-tank weapons at all. Thus, while Eighth Army was on paper better equipped than ever before, many of the units designated to receive new weapons had either not received them or had not had sufficient time to train with them properly. Much as had been the case at 'Crusader' and during the spring, morale and co-operation between arms would be vital to success. Failing that, Eighth Army might need to rely on a little luck.

In the summer of 1942, however, luck was not on the side of British and Commonwealth forces in any part of the world. As the date for the new offensive neared, it became increasingly apparent, through Ultra, that Rommel, whose logistic position had also improved steadily in the first five months of the year, was preparing to pre-empt Eighth Army's offensive.[213] Ritchie, who under Auchinleck's tutelage still commanded Eighth Army, quickly repositioned his troops to address Rommel's planned offensive. In spite of his numerical superiority, Ritchie did not have the personnel to man the whole of the 50-mile Gazala Line. He, thus, organised his less mobile infantry units into 'boxes' for all-round defence, with the gaps between these covered by vast minefields. The question of what to do with his mobile armoured and motorised units was more pressing. Rommel, it appeared to Ritchie, had two options for the impending attack. He could assault Eighth Army's line frontally on the general axis of the Trigh Capuzzo – the most direct path to the port of Tobruk – or he could swing round the open desert flank, near Bir Hacheim, and attack Eighth Army from the south and from the rear (see Map 4.5). No matter what course Rommel chose, the lesson from 'Crusader', and other engagements in the desert, was clear; it was crucially important to meet Rommel's thrust with a concentrated armoured riposte. Disagreement arose over how best to achieve this end. The result, almost inevitably, was a compromise; 1st

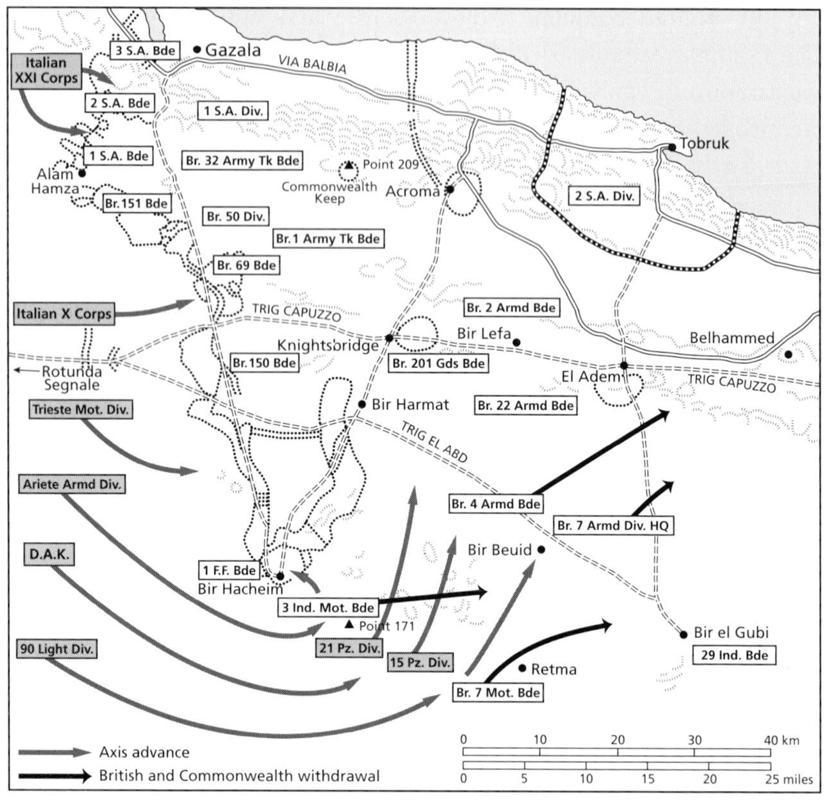

Map 4.5 Gazala, 26–27 May 1942

Armoured Division was positioned north to deal with the possibility of a direct frontal assault on the Gazala position and 7th Armoured Division was placed further south to tackle a flanking manoeuvre should it develop.[214] The armoured brigades of 1st and 7th Armoured Divisions were, therefore, placed behind the front line, spread out in a triangle of which the longest side was about 20 miles.[215]

In these circumstances, warning time was going to be all-important, as it would take about two hours to concentrate the armour at the proper place once the alarm was raised and Rommel's intentions deduced. Adequate forewarning hardly seemed a problem in the event of a frontal assault on the Gazala Line. However, if Rommel launched a flanking manoeuvre to the south, it would be vital. Norrie, consequently, was convinced that 7th Armoured Division needed additional pivots, or 'boxes', to provide bases for patrolling and for warning and to help canalise an enemy advance should it materialise to the south. These extra 'boxes', all under the command of 7th Armoured Division, were provided by the 1st Free French Brigade, 3rd Indian Motor Brigade and 29th Indian Brigade. The 1st Free French Brigade, which had arrived in the desert after its success in Syria in 1941, was placed at Bir Hacheim. The unfortunate 3rd Indian Motor Brigade, which had arrived in Suez from India in February 1941, only to get caught up in 2nd Armoured Division's chaotic retreat during Rommel's first offensive that April, was placed 5 miles south of Bir Hacheim, at Point 171. Rebuilt after the April debacle, it had done garrison work in Syria and then three months of training in Egypt, before joining Eighth Army in the desert in May 1942.[216] The 7th Motor Brigade, of 7th Armoured Division, was placed at Retma, 20 miles further to the east, and 29th Indian Brigade, of 5th Indian Division, was about the same distance east again, at Bir El Gubi.[217] Barring disaster, these dispositions should have been sufficient, in the circumstances, to allow Eighth Army's armour to concentrate and meet the *Panzerarmee* at least on equal terms.[218]

That was not the way events unfolded. Unknown to Ritchie and Auchinleck, reports sent to Washington by the US military attaché in Cairo, Colonel Bonner Fellers, were being intercepted by Italian intelligence. The Italians had achieved a 'magnificent coup'; in August 1941, a clerk working in the American embassy in Rome had been persuaded to take a photocopy of the American military attaché code. This 'proved disastrous to British fortunes' for within hours of each transmission, a translated copy of Fellers's cables 'was winging its way to Rommel's headquarters'. Fellers's reports became known as 'the Good Source' by German and Italian intelligence, and thanks to his 'unfettered access' to the High Command in the Middle East, the information he offered up was to prove crucial to unlocking the Gazala position.[219]

When the battle opened at 1400hrs on 26 May, Rommel knew the broad dispositions of Eighth Army on the Gazala Line.[220] He, therefore, began his great offensive in North Africa with a diversionary attack to the north, using the German 15th Infantry Brigade and the Italian infantry divisions of X and XXI Corps. That night, in an attempt to take advantage of this distraction, he led the three divisions of the *Afrika Korps* and the two divisions of the Italian XX Corps, using 10,000 vehicles in all, round the desert flank in what he intended to be the *schwerpunkt*. By 0200hrs the next morning, 27 May, desert patrols began to report large enemy columns heading towards Bir Hacheim.

Ritchie did not react with the kind of urgency that was required in the circumstances. He had been repeatedly warned by Auchinleck that he had to be 'most careful' not to commit his armoured striking force before he knew 'beyond reasonable doubt' where the 'main body' of Rommel's armour was heading. It was possible that Rommel's flank manoeuvre was a ruse. Moreover, Auchinleck, whom Ritchie understood to have access to secret sources of information (Ultra), had confidently predicted that Rommel would make a frontal assault on the Gazala position.[221]

Rommel's thrust, however, was not a ruse; instead, he was leading a bold advance that he hoped would first penetrate Eighth Army's position and then allow him to surround Eighth Army's armour and destroy it in a great battle at the heart of the Gazala defences. By 0700hrs, air patrols confirmed the folly of Ritchie's hesitancy. By now aware of the danger unfolding before him, Ritchie immediately ordered the commander of 1st Armoured Division, Major-General Herbert Lumsden, to send the armoured brigades of his division south. But, it was already close to too late. If the 'boxes' and pivots to the south of XXX Corps' position failed to slow the Axis advance, there would be nothing to stop Rommel penetrating Eighth Army's defences before the armour could concentrate.[222]

Even before Ritchie's message to Lumsden, the drama had begun to unfold. At 0630hrs, a startled Brigadier A. E. E. Filose, the commander of 3rd Indian Motor Brigade, informed the commander of 7th Armoured Division that he was looking at 'a whole bloody German armoured division'.[223] An hour and fifteen minutes later, the Italian Ariete Division smashed into the infantry and gunners of his brigade. The brigade had only arrived in its position at point 171 on 25 May.[224] It was short of mines, wire, 6-pounder guns and had only partially sighted its guns and dug in before the Ariete attacked.[225] It took only forty-five minutes for the brigade to be destroyed for a second time.[226] Some 500 Indians were killed and wounded and another 600 taken prisoner; the rest fled in disarray.[227]

The 7th Motor Brigade, at Retma, fared little better when at 0830hrs it found itself in the path of 90th Light Division; it retreated in haste north towards El Adem leaving 7th Armoured Division HQ defenceless; it too was overrun, at 1000hrs, leaving Major-General Frank Messervy, its commander, a prisoner and 7th Armoured Division without effective leadership at a key moment in the battle.[228]

The 15th Panzer Division found the gap between Point 171 and Retma and crashed into the tanks of 4th Armoured Brigade around 0730hrs. By 0845hrs, it and 21st Panzer Division had driven through 4th Armoured Brigade and met 22nd Armoured Brigade, of 1st Armoured Division, in position 12 miles further to the north; only seventy-five minutes after the first armoured clash Rommel was already in the heart of the Gazala defences. The plan to meet Rommel's armour with a concentrated and co-ordinated counter thrust had failed utterly.[229]

That is not to say that all was lost. By the end of 27 May, Rommel's forces were almost as scattered as those of Eighth Army, and by this stage of the battle the *Panzerarmee* was 'in a very vulnerable position'.[230] Rommel's *panzers*, much as Ritchie's armoured units had done throughout the desert war, had, in the heat of battle and with the utmost aggression, resorted to charging Eighth Army's defences 'without artillery support' and suffered heavy casualties as a consequence.[231] Over the course of the day, Rommel had lost about 200 tanks, over a third of his force. The 15th Panzer Division was already short of fuel and ammunition; 90th Light was out of touch somewhere south of El Adem; the Ariete had failed to capture Bir Hacheim and the Trieste was bogged down in minefields.[232] Rommel, in the circumstances, had little choice but to abandon his original plan of crushing XIII Corps between his tanks and the Italian infantry advancing from the west. Instead, he decided to pull his forces together and back up against Eighth Army's minefield to the west, near the 'box' of 150th Brigade, 50th Northumbrian Division, and adopt a temporary defensive position.[233]

Much now depended on Ritchie's next move. It was clear, through Ultra, that Rommel was not planning a withdrawal but a strong base from which to continue his advance. Eighth Army, however, failed to launch a concerted counter-attack on 28 May and by the end of the next day Rommel had once again concentrated his armour in a position that became known as the 'Cauldron'. By 1 June, he had crushed 150th Brigade and cleared gaps in the minefields to allow supplies to reach him directly from the west, rather than by the long precarious route around Bir Hacheim. Rommel's moves 'had a punch and urgency which his opponent lacked'.[234]

On 4 June, Ritchie finally managed to pull Eighth Army together and launch something resembling a co-ordinated counter-attack, using elements of three divisions and a tank brigade. Operation 'Aberdeen', which was intended to destroy Rommel's 'beachhead' with a forceful pincer movement from the north and east, proved to be a catastrophe. The infantry and armour fought the battle in a wholly unco-ordinated manner. In the eastern thrust, the location of the enemy's front line was incorrectly identified, so the initial artillery barrage hit empty desert. This no-man's land was then occupied by 5th Indian Division, and the armour of 7th Armoured Division passed through only to find that the German anti-tank positions were intact. 7th Armoured Division, suffering heavy casualties, sheered away and left the infantry of 5th Indian Division to look after themselves.[235] The next day, Rommel counter-attacked and for slight loss scattered the HQs of 5th Indian and 7th Armoured Divisions, knocked out sixty tanks and thrust through two Indian brigades and four regiments of field artillery, taking 4,000 prisoners. The northern pincer fared equally poorly, with 32nd Army Tank Brigade losing fifty of its seventy tanks. The battle had been so ill-co-ordinated and inadequately handled that it was almost embarrassing, 'one of the worst-conceived and worst-executed British operations of the war', according to one historian.[236] 'Aberdeen' was, in Auchinleck's view, 'probably the turning point of the whole battle'.[237]

Rommel now focused his attention on the French at Bir Hacheim, which, isolated as it was at the end of the Gazala Line, fell after determined resistance on 11 June. The *Panzerarmee's* logistic situation was now relatively secure.[238] By comparison, XXX Corps was a shadow of its former self. By this stage of the battle it was outnumbered; it had 200 tanks compared to the *Panzerarmee*'s 226 and was a hodgepodge of reconstituted units lacking in anything that could be described as cohesion. Thus, when Rommel continued his relentless offensive on 11 June and took on the British armour in a decisive clash around 'Knightsbridge' on 12 and 13 June, XXX Corps was no longer in a fit state to take on the *Panzerarmee*. By nightfall on 13 June, the tank element of Eighth Army had been reduced to some fifty machines. The infantry divisions of XIII Corps, holding the Gazala Line, and 2nd South African Division in Tobruk, were now desperately exposed.[239]

The engagements on the Gazala Line showed, in spite of the reorganisation of the armoured and infantry divisions and the devolved system of command and control employed by Eighth Army, that the British and Commonwealth forces in the desert were still unable to work effectively as a team. Empowered junior leaders had been unable to compensate for a lack of grip, control and co-ordination at army, corps and divisional level. 'Operating in a vacuum of higher direction', those engaged on the front line were required to use their initiative and judgement 'without knowing whether their decisions aided or undid the plans of their superiors'. The result was that the fighting power of Eighth Army was dissipated and dislocated, exacerbating the natural confusion of battle.[240] In the prevailing circumstances, subordinate commanders began to 'short circuit' or even 'ignore the chain of command', to 'protest and debate orders they did not like', thus further obstructing action and wasting valuable time.[241] 'A field army functions as such when the separate actions of its units can be coordinated beyond their own local battlefield, by a higher command, to produce a broader strategic effect.'[242] This did not happen at 'Knightsbridge', or at any time during the Gazala battle.

Ritchie and Auchinleck, who had flown up to Eighth Army HQ, concluded that there was little option but to retreat to the Egyptian frontier. It was decided controversially to hold on to Tobruk; all previous indications had been that Tobruk would not again be held if invested. Churchill wrote to Auchinleck on 14 June, offering his support. 'Your decision to fight it out to the end', he wrote, is 'most cordially endorsed. We shall sustain you whatever the result ... This is a business not only of armour but of will-power. God bless you all.'[243]

By now, the morale and cohesion of Eighth Army was beginning to flag. Correspondence from troops engaged in the opening phases on the Gazala Line had 'provided ample proof that the fighting spirit ha[d] stood the acid test of battle, and, indeed, ha[d] been enhanced by it'; the censors thought that Eighth Army possessed at the time a 'moral ascendancy over the Hun' born of the 'knowledge or belief that the corner has been turned in the war'.[244] In contrast, by the week beginning 17 June, the censors noted that 'the mail did show that the high morale of the troops had suffered a set back, chiefly due to utter physical exhaustion combined with the realisation of the horror of battle and the loss of comrades' and that 'optimism regarding an early finish to the campaign ha[d] been tempered by the stiff opposition encountered'.[245]

Between May and June, sickness rates, including incidences of battle exhaustion (or NYD(N) – Not Yet Diagnosed (Nervous)), rose 51 per cent from 32.9 per thousand in May, before Rommel's successful offensive, to 49.5 per thousand in June. They would rise again to 74.1 per thousand in July and 75 per thousand in August, a 125 per cent rise from the start to the end of the summer fighting, a clear suggestion that the morale of Eighth Army had deteriorated significantly (see Appendix 3 and Figure 4.1).[246]

These problems with morale were especially evident in Tobruk where the 'material and moral defences ... were in a very poor state'.[247] The root cause of this issue, according to Lieutenant-Colonel P. T. Tower, commander of 31/58 Field Battery Royal Artillery, was the decision made by Auchinleck, in his operational instruction No. 110 on 19 January,[248] and again announced at the beginning of the summer campaign on 27 May, that Tobruk would not again be held.[249] This decision was well known to all ranks of Eighth Army and a scheme for the evacuation of Tobruk had been practised several times by way of signal exercises.[250] Tower argued that:

> When the original decision was reversed, the new 'defenders' of Tobruk were caught with their 'pants down.' They had very little time to put their defences in first class shape, they had few documents, such as mine charts, to show them how their predecessors had done it, and, above all, their morale sagged considerably.

'Theirs', Tower continued, 'was almost a feeling of being sacrificed, and little was done to explain the reason for the new decision (even if there were a good one).'[251]

When the *Panzerarmee* launched its offensive at 0520hrs on 20 June, with an aerial bombardment by all available German aircraft, it was faced, therefore, not by the determined and resolute 9th Australian Division, which had been relieved, but by a garrison that was ill-prepared for the assault and that had endured the psychological blow of 'witness[ing] the decisive defeat of [the British] armour', their only potential protectors in the open spaces of the Gazala Line.[252] By 1800hrs, the Germans had entered the town and by 0600hrs on 21 June, Tobruk's commander, Major-General H. B. Klopper, had decided to surrender; 33,000 troops, nearly 20,000 of them British, 2,000 usable vehicles, 1,400 tons of fuel and 5,000 tons of food fell into German hands. The second siege of Tobruk had lasted little longer than twenty-four hours,[253] sending shockwaves throughout the British Empire. While there were

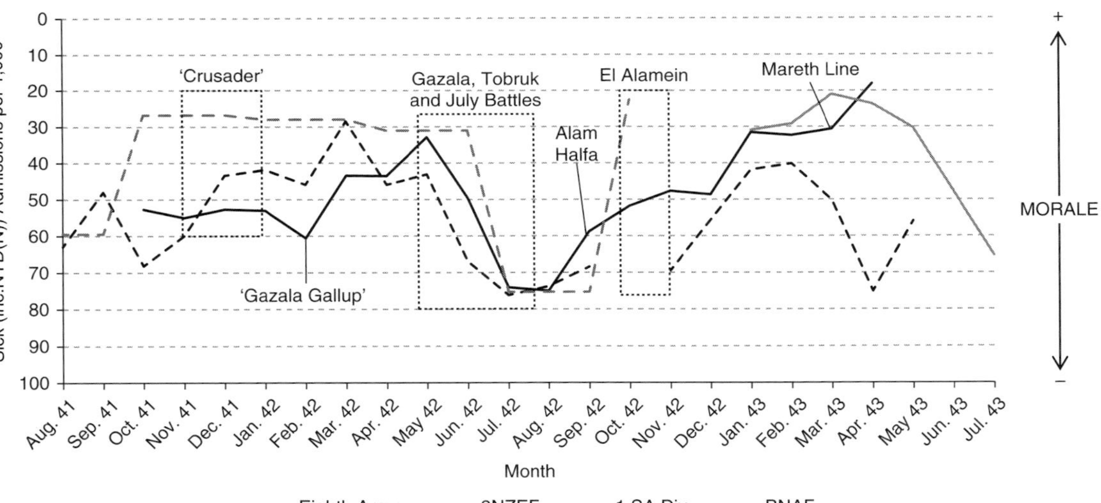

Figure 4.1 Monthly sick (including NYD(N)) admissions per thousand, Eighth Army, the British North African Force (BNAF), 2NZEF and 1st South African Division, North Africa, August 1941–July 1943

a number of reasons for the fall of Tobruk, including the fact that the town's defences had been left to decay and were no longer comparable to that of 1941, it was the issue of morale that Churchill found of most concern. He commented that 'it was a bitter moment. Defeat is one thing; disgrace is another.'[254] 'If this was typical of the morale of the Desert Army', he declaimed, 'no measure could be put upon the disasters which impended in North-East Africa.'[255]

Auchinleck was fully aware of the significance of the capitulation. He wrote to Brooke in London, accepting full responsibility for all that had occurred. He offered to vacate the post of C-in-C Middle East admitting to a 'loss of influence' with the troops 'due to lack of success, absence of luck and all other things which affect the morale of an army'.[256] His offer was not accepted, but, as Eighth Army continued to retreat east, in what the troops christened the 'Gazala Gallop',[257] Auchinleck increasingly understood that he needed to do something drastic to turn around Eighth Army's fortunes. The axe would have to fall somewhere, and Ritchie was the man. On 25 June, Auchinleck sacked his army commander and this time assumed command of Eighth Army himself, along with his position as C-in-C Middle Eastern Forces.

Auchinleck sought to take an immediate grip on the situation. One of Ritchie's last substantive decisions as commander of Eighth Army had been to abandon plans to make a stand at the Libyan/Egyptian frontier and dig in at Mersa Matruh, over 100 miles to the east of Gazala. Auchinleck, realising that Eighth Army was in no shape even to stand at Matruh, countermanded this order. Instead, he decided to conduct a fluid delaying action at Matruh and retreat further east should the need arise. The next day, 26 June, Rommel attacked once again, despite his increasingly depleted forces. By now, he had only around 10,000 men and just over 100 tanks, of which only 60 were German. He should have stood no chance against an enemy which was made up of four, admittedly weak, infantry divisions, including 2nd New Zealand Division fresh from a period of rest and retraining in Syria, and one armoured division (which had about 170 tanks, about 50 of which were Grants).[258] Nevertheless, that evening Eighth Army shattered. German reports claimed that they captured forty tanks (many more were destroyed), 6,000 prisoners and enough supplies and equipment to outfit a whole division. The 50th Northumbrian Division and

10th Indian Division, which had been transferred to North Africa from Iraq, were mauled to the extent that they were mere shells of their former selves and 2nd New Zealand Division suffered about 1,000 casualties. The *Panzerarmee* had lost only a few tanks and perhaps 300 men.[259]

The retreat from Matruh could not have been more headlong or chaotic, but, on 30 June, Eighth Army reached the next, and as it turned out last, stop on its journey east, a small railway halt some 60 miles west of Alexandria called El Alamein.[260] Unusually in the desert, the El Alamein position offered no flanks to be turned. Anchored as it was on the sea to the north and the impassable Qattara Depression to the south, it presented probably the strongest defensive line in Egypt. 'It is the only place', as one British soldier wrote, 'that we can actually call a front because from the Depression to the coast is only 40 miles and in this 40 miles we can watch Jerry very well and our lines of communications are right up to our Base Areas.'[261]

In spite of these geographical advantages, Auchinleck was increasingly faced with difficulties, not least the problem of dealing with a disorganised and demoralised army. The censorship summaries show that 'the withdrawal into Egypt ha[d] provoked expressions of very bitter disappointment from all ranks of the Eighth Army, accompanied by admissions of weariness and fatigue'.[262] A XXX Corps intelligence summary for 1 July described how 'indiscreet and defeatist talk' was rife among the troops.[263] An officer, weighing up the position at El Alamein, wrote on 2 July 1942, 'this disaster goes on and on and now it has raised a sort of impetus which takes a lot of stopping. For no good cause chaps sort of say "where do we retreat to next?" That sort of spirit is quite inevitable but very very difficult to compete with. If we do not succeed in stopping the brutes that mental aspect will be at least 50% responsible.'[264]

Much of the troops' ire appeared to be directed towards Eighth Army's recently sacked army commander, Ritchie. The censorship summary for 24 to 30 June noted that many troops 'criticised leadership in the field, and there were accusations that "someone has blundered badly"'. It stated categorically that the summary 'would not give a fair cross-section of the criticisms levelled if it did not emphasise that many letters suggested that Rommel is a better general than our own, and more than one correspondent has stated that the "8th Army have more respect for Rommel than for our own high command"'.[265] The summary for 1 to 7 July commented that 'the Eighth Army is without doubt a very angry army ... Our reverse in Libya is attributed by a number of writers from Field Rank to Trooper to the fact that "Rommel seems to be a better General".' It was commonly believed that under the right leadership, 'we would prove more than a match for the Axis forces'.[266]

As they faced the *Panzerarmee* at El Alamein, therefore, an atmosphere of bewilderment and dejection rather than focused belligerence pervaded Eighth Army. Auchinleck, aware of the situation, set out to reignite the aggressive spirit of his forces. On 30 June, he sent a message to the troops pointing out that 'the enemy is stretched to the limit and thinks we are a broken army' and 'hopes to take Egypt by bluff. Show him where he gets off.' His efforts fell on deaf ears; they made no impact on the censorship summaries or the troops' diaries and memoirs.[267] The orders and counter-orders issued at Matruh had created such a sense of mistrust that even Auchinleck, the theatre commander, was unable to penetrate it. It was unclear to many of the men whether the Eighth Army was to stand and fight at El Alamein or retreat to yet another defensive line under preparation in the Delta.[268] This, according to Gott, the commander of XIII Corps, created a 'psychological conception' that the line in the rear had to 'be better than the one occupied!'[269] With Auchinleck acting as C-in-C MEF and Commander Eighth Army, the staff at HQ Eighth Army became embroiled in GHQ staff work. In this way, strategic issues, such as the possibility of a further retreat to the Delta, became 'popular knowledge', with obvious effects on morale.[270]

With Eighth Army's morale potentially on the verge of collapse, on 1 July, Rommel launched his offensive on the El Alamein line. This time, however, he ran into a commander intellectually capable of fighting and winning a battle even with a demoralised army. In the brief period since Auchinleck had taken over command, he once again began to reorganise the way Eighth Army fought, and especially the manner in which the Royal Artillery was employed. The reforms of the summer months had led to the artillery, acknowledged by the Germans to be their opponents' most dangerous and efficient weapon,[271] being dispersed into the newly formed brigade groups. These reforms, which brought Eighth Army's organisation more in line with the understandings of *FSR* might have worked had Ritchie taken a firmer grip of operations around Gazala and had morale and motivation remained high. Now, however, Auchinleck sought to locate as much command, control and decision-making as possible in his person. Under his instruction, the artillery was concentrated once more to facilitate co-ordination and allow divisional shoots or 'stonks'.[272]

The ability of Eighth Army to unleash concentrated fire-power in the bottleneck of El Alamein had a devastating effect on the troops of the *Panzerarmee* as they tried to drive it out of the El Alamein position. The war diary of 90th Light Division reported how 'a panic' broke out in the division when the *Afrika Korps* ran headlong into the newly concentrated fire of the South African artillery on 2 July. 'Supply columns and even parts of fighting units rush[ed] back under the ever increasing enemy artillery fire.' The energetic action of the divisional commander and Chief of Staff was all that prevented a 'rout'.[273]

By this time, as the *Afrika Korps* war diary confirms, the *Panzerarmee* was even more exhausted than its British and Commonwealth enemy.[274] Alan Moorehead, one of the journalists covering the fighting, pointed out how they 'were wearied to the point where they had no more reserves either of body or of willpower, where all the goading and enticement could make no difference, where they were compelled to stop and sleep'.[275] Without doubt, the toll of a month's heavy fighting had begun to tell. By 30 June the *Afrika Korps* could muster only fifty-five battle-worthy tanks while the Italian XX Corps could manage a meagre fifteen.[276] In comparison, although an estimated 1,188 British tanks had been knocked out at Gazala, the British forces had 137 tanks at the front on 1 July. Auchinleck could also rely on another forty-two tanks in transit from base workshops to the front.[277]

The Desert Air Force had also begun to wrest control of the skies from the *Luftwaffe*. The German war diaries show that this more than any other factor seemed to drain the offensive capabilities and willpower of the Axis forces.[278] The war diaries of 90th Light Division commented that:

> The enemy throws all the Air Force at his disposal into the battle against the attacking Afrika Army. Every 20 or 30 minutes 15, 18, or sometimes even 20 bombers, with adequate fighter

> protection, launch their attacks. Although the visible success of these heavy and continuous bombing and low-flying attacks is negligible owing to the disposition of the fighting and supply units, the moral effect on the troops is much more important. Everyone prays for German fighter protection ... Sometimes German fighters appear singly, greeted by the roaring applause of the troops, but naturally they are not in a position to attack such heavy bomber formations.[279]

Rommel had pushed his army so far and so fast that the *Luftwaffe* was no longer able to provide meaningful air cover. The Axis air forces had put forth an 'enormous effort' during 'Gazala' and for the assault on Tobruk, but they could not, with the demands for the neutralisation of Malta, the Eastern Front and the defence of Germany, 'sustain this level of activity indefinitely'.[280] As the RAF fell back on its depots in Egypt, it now had 780 operational aircraft as opposed to *Fliegerführer Afrika* which had 126; a 6.2:1 advantage.[281] General Navarini, the commander of the Italian XXI Corps, considered the issue of such importance that, on 6 July, he issued an Order of the Day informing the troops that 'final victory is within your grasp. Do not let yourselves be overawed by some momentary predominance of enemy aviation.'[282]

The 'critical moment' in the battle had passed.[283] By the evening of 3 July, the *Panzerarmee* was reduced to only twenty-six German and five Italian tanks fit for action.[284] Auchinleck had taken a firm grip and, aided by the natural strength of the El Alamein position, the rapid reinforcement of Eighth Army, and the extraordinary efforts of the Desert Air Force, he had repelled Rommel's advance when all appeared to be falling apart around him. He deserved much credit for his actions, and his troops were well aware of it. The censorship summary for the second week of July recorded that it had now become 'generally known that the C-in-C had himself assumed command of the operations and this undoubtedly gave a great fillip to the troops' morale'.[285]

The July Battles

With the momentum having shifted in his favour, Auchinleck, almost instinctively and with no little aggression, chose to go on the offensive. That July, he launched no fewer than four attacks on

Rommel's attenuated *Panzerarmee*. These assaults were aided enormously by the proximity of Eighth Army's supply base in the Delta and the continued resurgence of the Desert Air Force; they were also greatly supported by the discovery of the Fellers leak (by 29 June, Fellers' reports were no longer being read by German and Italian intelligence) and a wealth of information that was increasingly available to the C-in-C through Ultra and Eighth Army's own intelligence (Y) services. Auchinleck planned his attacks, therefore, fully cognisant of the *Panzerarmee's* growing supply difficulties, order of battle and dispositions. This allowed him to target the weaker Italian formations, 'compelling Rommel to use his German units as a kind of fire brigade, rushing from point to point to prevent collapse'.[286]

Eighth Army was also able to make use of two new relatively fresh and well-trained infantry divisions and a new armoured division for the attritional warfare that was to develop in the confined spaces of the El Alamein position. Both 9th Australian and 2nd New Zealand Divisions had recently arrived after a period of rest in Syria and 8th Armoured Division began unloading from Britain in mid-July.[287] These formations, largely uncontaminated by the disasters at Gazala, Tobruk and Matruh brought new life to Eighth Army. By the second week of July, morale showed signs of recovery, with correspondence from 9th Australian Division personnel in the battle area proving 'excellent in tone'. The Australians were 'amazed at the vast amount of equipment' now available and 'were loud in their praise of the R.A.F.' The censors commented that 'the number and quality of our planes has been a revelation to all and several lamented the fact that such air support was lacking in previous campaigns'.[288] By the third week of July the censors were reporting on the 'high morale prevailing among all ranks':

> The outspoken criticisms and ranting against leaders and Government alike which were a common feature of the mail over a fortnight have now virtually ceased. It would seem that all ranks have given full expression to their feelings at our reverses and that, having got these off their minds, they are now looking forward to the next round. And such being the resilience of the Tommy's spirits that he has no doubt who is going to win; confidence in an early reversal of the present position is general, and letters from old 'Benghazi Trotters'

> and new draftees alike showed genuine anxiety to 'get down to Brass tacks and finish the . . . job'.[289]

In spite of this resurgence in morale, Auchinleck's July offensives, although they pushed the *Panzerarmee* near to its limit, failed to break the front. The first, launched on 10 July by XXX Corps, shattered one Italian division and badly damaged another. The second, the first battle of Ruweisat (14 to 15 July), was, by comparison, a failure, leading to the destruction of 4th New Zealand Infantry Brigade. The third offensive, the second battle of Ruweisat (21 to 23 July), was also a failure. Eighth Army had a massive material advantage, deploying 350 tanks, three infantry brigades, nine artillery field regiments and one medium regiment (as well as supporting fire from XXX Corps) against thirty-eight German and fifty-eight Italian tanks, four 'weak, tired and widely dispersed' German battalions and the remains of an Italian division supported by artillery units that counted their 'guns singly, or at the most, in troops or batteries of three'. Yet Eighth Army failed utterly to break the German front.[290] By the end of the attack, 1st Armoured Division had lost 131 tanks and the newly arrived 23rd Armoured Brigade, 8th Armoured Division, was destroyed. 6th New Zealand Infantry Brigade had lost nearly half its strength. By comparison, the *Afrika Korps* had lost an insignificant three tanks. Auchinleck's final offensive was made on 27 July. Once again, the operation broke down in 'doubt and muddle'. 'The two attacking infantry brigades, one Australian and one British, hit by German counterattacks while their armoured support was still in the rear, took heavy casualties, with two British battalions being overrun.'[291]

The underlying problem, again, appeared to be Eighth Army's inability to achieve effective integration of arms on the battlefield.[292] The closest of co-operation between infantry and armour, in particular, had been required for the attacks at El Alamein to succeed. Once a position was taken, usually at night, by attacking infantry, it was necessary to prepare the ground for an inevitable German counter-attack the next morning. These counter-attacks were normally led by *panzers* supported by infantry. The problem, according to Brigadier Inglis, the commander of 2nd New Zealand Division during the July battles, was that 'infantry could not protect itself against tank counter-attack for a period of 3 to 5 hours after daylight' the following day. Some reorganisation of the infantry was always necessary at first light. It then took an hour to reconnoitre the area in daylight and co-ordinate an anti-tank plan. It took a further hour for the infantry's anti-tank guns to be sighted. It then finally required a further one to three hours for everything to be dug in. Inglis argued that 'until all this is done the infantry is not in a position to meet any weighty A.F.V. [Armoured Fighting Vehicle] attack' and during the intervening period 'mobile A/Tk [Anti-Tank] weapons, that is to say, tanks must be right up prepared to support immediately'.[293]

In spite of Inglis' concerns and forewarnings, the British armour repeatedly failed to support the infantry during the July battles on the El Alamein front. The New Zealanders suffered particularly, causing much bitterness among their battalions left to face German *panzers* without support. An officer wrote:

> Our boys were supposed to have armoured support, as the Jerry always counter attack with tanks. Well our boys went through them like butter with the bayonet and gained the objective easily and started looking around for our tanks, not a tank of ours was to be seen, but they soon saw plenty of German tanks, they moved around and cut the whole lot of our boys off and shot them to pieces. As it turned out the Tommy tanks were sitting about two miles back waiting orders!!! The crews out frying sausages while our lads were being torn to pieces ... it was a disgraceful affair, it's terrible to see the best troops in the world slaughtered like sheep because of those Pommie bastards ... It was a stinking show ... The Germans regard the N.Z. as the best troops in the M.E. and they are correct, and consequently they have their best material facing us always. Our men do the job and then are let down by the armoured forces. Good as our blokes are they are not human tanks.[294]

The horrific casualties suffered by the New Zealanders during the July battles (4,000 out of a total for Eighth Army of 13,240) were roundly blamed on the incompetence of the higher command and the lack of tank support. These casualties destroyed the trust between the New Zealanders and the British and played a major role in a crisis that developed in the New Zealand division during and following the battle.[295] The censorship report for the week 29 July to 4 August reported how only about 1 per cent of New Zealand writers had a good word to say about 'Tommy'.[296]

By the end of July, Eighth Army was in an uncertain state. Although it found itself better equipped than ever before, victory had still not been achieved. Trust between the various nationalities was beginning to wane with both the British and South Africans (due to the surrender of Tobruk) seriously ridiculed for their performances during June and July.[297] Following the horrific casualties at Gazala, the armoured forces of Eighth Army had performed poorly on the El Alamein line, suggesting that they had been, perhaps unsurprisingly, profoundly affected by their experience at Gazala and had lost their self-belief.

By the end of the month the censors were reporting an increased amount of 'individual cases of depression'.[298] Many of the troops were 'beginning to lose interest in the war, to some in fact the reason for the war itself has become dimmed'.[299] The censorship report for the period 5 to 11 August stated that the soldiers' mail had shown a 'spate of grouses and an increase in the number of writers who stated they were "browned off" ... there were little or no traces of the offensive spirit, and an almost complete absence of any reference to forcing the enemy to give up the ground gained in the last two months'.[300] Such negative references were given all the more colour when compared with the usual positive picture the censors portrayed of the fighting troops' morale.[301]

Auchinleck, was by now deeply concerned by what could only be described as a morale crisis.[302] On 25 July, he wrote to Brooke noting that perhaps he had 'asked too much of [the troops]' and admitted that 'we may yet have to face a withdrawal'.[303] The previous day, the medical situation report for Eighth Army had noted a 'considerable rise' in the number of men reporting sick that was 'most disquieting'.[304] In these circumstances, Auchinleck cabled London again demanding the return of the death penalty. He provided more statistics to lend weight to the argument he had outlined in April. He reported that sixty-three absentees had been apprehended behind the front line, at Matruh, in a single day during the 'Knightsbridge' fighting in June. During the twenty-seven days of battle ending 13 July, 907 absentees had been reported to the Corps of Military Police of whom 430 were subsequently apprehended. The total number of unapprehended absentees was still 1,728 at the time of writing.[305] This figure represented around 0.9 per cent of the c.191,000 men who were engaged in operations in the desert in the summer of 1942 and about 3.6 per cent of those who were likely to have been doing the fighting on the front line. Taken at face value, this figure did not appear unduly high. However, it did suggest that the equivalent of one man from every rifle platoon (consisting of an officer and thirty-six enlisted men) went absent during the summer fighting.[306] The problem of desertion was equally problematic. Auchinleck reported that the average monthly number of soldiers sentenced for desertion in the five months from February to June 1942 had been thirty-four. There were, however, now over 120 soldiers awaiting trial by courts martial in Cairo and in one high-category unit (it is apparent that this was the Guards Brigade), twenty-three cases of desertion in the face of the enemy had been reported during the recent fighting.[307]

To bolster the impact of his absence and desertion statistics, Auchinleck also drew the Army Council's attention to the alarming ratio of 'missing' to overall casualties during the summer fighting. On 10 June, Churchill had noted in the casualty figures coming out of the desert an 'extra-ordinary disparity between killed and wounded on one hand and prisoners on the other', which to him 'revealed that something must have happened of an unpleasant character'.[308] Auchinleck confirmed these fears. Between the beginning of Rommel's offensive at the end of May and late July, Eighth Army lost 1,700 killed and 6,000 wounded, but had 57,000 categorised as missing, 'of whom the great majority must be assumed to be prisoners of war' (see Illustration 4.2).[309] These figures equated to an overall missing/surrender rate for Eighth Army of about 88 per cent of casualties; a figure that was only comparable with Italian performance during 'Crusader', when 84 per cent of casualties had been POWs.[310] The figures were not uniform throughout Eighth Army; without doubt those formations that had fought during the mobile engagements at Gazala and Tobruk suffered worst (the UK statistics were between 82 to 86 per cent; the South African and Indian 90 per cent and the New Zealand and Australian 42 and 34 per cent respectively).[311] Both Adam, the Adjutant-General, and Grigg were convinced by and 'perturbed at these figures'. They accepted that the evidence produced showed that the British soldier was 'inclined to surrender rather than to fight it out', and therefore agreed to reopen

Illustration 4.2 British prisoners captured by the Germans during the siege of Tobruk, 1942. Rates of missing/surrender were so high during the summer battles of 1942 that Auchinleck, concerned about the morale of his troops, asked the War Office to reinstate the death penalty for cowardice and desertion in the field.

the death penalty issue as demanded by Auchinleck.[312] The Army Council similarly concluded that 'the capitulation at Singapore [see Chapter 5], the fall of Tobruk and the large proportion of unwounded prisoners in the operations in Cyrenaica [the Western Desert]', were pointers to a condition existing in the Army which did 'not appear to accord with its old traditions'.[313] Something dramatic needed to happen if Eighth Army was to reverse its fortunes in the desert.

5 THE FAR EAST

The Strategic Context

The involvement of India, Australia and New Zealand in the war against Germany and Italy came at a price to the Imperial position in the Far East. Between 1939 and 1941, vast reserves of manpower were transferred away from the Indian subcontinent and the Antipodes to fight in the West. India sent its Imperial Reserve overseas on the outbreak of war, two brigades to the Middle East (these brigades plus a British one formed 4th Indian Division) and another, 12th Indian Brigade, to Malaya. The first echelon of 2nd New Zealand Division sailed west in January 1940, followed over the course of the year by 6th, 7th and 9th Australian Divisions (8th Australian Division was sent to Malaya) and 5th Indian Division. After the fall of France and the entry of Italy into the war, it became increasingly necessary to raise new formations to address the danger of an additional conflict with Japan. During 1940 and 1941, the Indian Government authorised the creation of six new divisions (the 6th, 7th, 8th, 9th, 10th and 11th). Of these, 6th, 8th and 10th Indian Divisions were sent to Iraq during the spring and summer of 1941[1] and 8th and 10th Indian Divisions, under the supervision of India Command and not Middle East Command, partook in the occupation of Persia in August 1941. This latter engagement both secured the 10 million tons of crude oil flowing from the Persian oilfields every twelve months for the British Empire and created a Persian land bridge to supply Russia.[2]

In Australia, just as in India, there was a concern that sending so many formations overseas would leave the homeland vulnerable. In July, 1st Australian Armoured Division was formed and recruiting for the 2nd Australian Imperial Force (AIF) was actually suspended between the end of June 1940 and January 1941 as efforts were made to get Australia's eighteen militia brigades (for home defence) up to strength. With its distance from the landmasses of Asia, home defence was less of a concern for New Zealand. Nevertheless, the decision to enact conscription in the summer of 1940 was partly to ensure an adequate balance between the 2nd New Zealand Expeditionary Force (2NZEF) and the territorial force. In addition to sending 2nd New Zealand Division to the Middle East, New Zealand had also agreed to provide a brigade (8th Infantry Brigade) to defend Fiji (it was joined later by a second brigade to form the 3rd New Zealand Division). To compensate for this loss of manpower, seven brigade groups, organised into three territorial force divisions, had to be raised to form a striking force for home defence in New Zealand.[3]

This rapid expansion of forces in India and the Antipodes presented a multitude of challenges. Existing units, especially in India, were 'milked' to provide a nucleus of trained manpower for new ones. With the majority of India's modern equipment sent overseas with the Imperial Reserve in 1939 and 1940, there was little left in the subcontinent with which to train. This not only prevented field formations from being prepared for active operations, but also seriously retarded the training of new formations.[4] As it built its new army, India was only allotted, let alone sent, 36 per cent of the 25-pounder guns, 27 per cent of the tanks, 23 per cent of the 2-pounder anti-tank guns and 19 per cent of the Bren guns that it required.[5] Australia and New Zealand had virtually no military equipment of any kind available for training. In fact, equipment shortages were so dire that 6th Australian Division sailed for the Middle East armed with only sixteen First World War-era 18-pounder field guns; 'not even enough to fill out a single field regiment of artillery'.[6]

These were the trade-offs made necessary by the exigencies of a world war. To a degree, however, the weakness of the British and Commonwealth Armies in the east should have mattered less than it eventually did, for Britain's strategy for the defence of the Far East had long been based not on the Army, but on the Royal Navy. In spite of the fact that the Royal Navy 'out-built all other navies' in 'nearly all classes of warship' during the interwar period,[7] its strength relative to its competitors was fundamentally weakened by 1939. In 1922, Britain had signed the Washington Naval Agreement. This accord fixed British, American and Japanese naval strength in the ratio of 5:5:3 and made the Royal Navy a one-ocean force at a time when a two-ocean navy was still arguably required to prepare adequately for a future war in Europe or Asia.[8] This strategic disconnect was not lost on the Australian or New Zealand Governments, who, throughout the 1920s and 1930s, repeatedly expressed concerns regarding Britain's ability to defend the Antipodes. To assuage these fears, the British Government promised from 1923 onwards that in an emergency the main British battle fleet would be sent to the Far East. To make this promise a reality, a massive naval base on Singapore Island was constructed to house the fleet when it arrived. The problem, apparent to some, was what would happen if trouble arose at the same time that Britain itself was already in danger, surely the most likely time for an aggressor to act. In this scenario, there was serious uncertainty regarding whether Britain would actually send a fleet to the Far East.[9]

With the fall of France, Antipodean fears regarding London's promises over Singapore became a reality. In June 1940, the Australians and New Zealanders were told that, for the 'foreseeable future', there was 'no hope' of despatching a fleet to Singapore. This had an 'apocalyptic' effect in Wellington and Canberra. The centrepiece of the strategy that as late as the last pre-war Imperial Conference, in May 1937, had been the foundation of Imperial defence in the Far East was, to all intents and purposes, shattered.[10]

With no fleet available and the Indian, Australian and New Zealand armies needed in the Middle East, the Chiefs of Staff developed a new plan to contain Japan and assuage concerns over the defence of the Antipodes. They turned to the RAF. On 8 August 1940, the Chiefs outlined their aim to bring the RAF in Malaya up to a strength of twenty-one squadrons, with 336 first-line aircraft. This, at least, would give some bite to Singapore's defences.[11] The Army's main role would be to defend the RAF's airfields on the Malayan mainland and, according to another important 'appreciation' produced by the Chiefs a week later, 'in the last resort to retain a footing from which we could eventually retrieve the position when stronger forces become available'.[12]

The adoption of an air power strategy to defend the Far East was accompanied by the creation of a new command structure. On 17 October 1940, Air Chief Marshal Sir Robert Brooke-Popham was named commander of the newly created Far East Command. The General Officers Commanding Malaya, Burma and Hong Kong were all to be subordinate to him and he was given responsibility for liaison with the Dutch and Americans, who both had imperial interests in the region. India Command was ordered to concern itself with the defence of the North-West Frontier and with providing manpower for the Middle East.[13]

As Brooke-Popham settled into his new post, the military/political dynamic in Asia began to deteriorate seriously. Since 1931, when Japan had seized the coal and iron-rich Chinese province of Manchuria, relations between Japan and China had been strained. By 1937, Japan had launched an all-out war with China, which the Western powers hoped would not escalate and affect their own areas of imperial influence. By the spring of 1941, this outcome appeared ever less likely. That April, Japan signed a neutrality pact with Russia, which, alongside the German invasion of the Soviet Union in June, secured Japan's vulnerable northern flank in Manchuria.[14] In July, Japan sought to pile more misery on an already prostrate France by occupying French Indochina. This brought Japanese aircraft within range of Singapore and spurred the Americans, who were concerned about the encirclement of the Philippines and access to trade routes, to impose economic sanctions. Despite concerns that the escalation of tensions in Asia might force Japan into war with America and Britain, London, after consulting the Dominions, followed suit. An alternative approach would have undermined American efforts at deterrence and damaged Anglo-American relations at a time when Britain was increasingly reliant on US aid.[15]

The situation was now critical for Japan; it was a question of negotiation, collapse or war with America and Britain. With the most rigid economic measures, Japan's reserves of oil could be made last for three years; in the case of war with America, Britain and the Dutch, they would last for a much shorter period. With negotiations in Washington proving fruitless, the Japanese Government decided on 1 December that they would attack.[16] By defeating the British, French, and Dutch, the hope was that Japan could gain control of the substantial natural resources of the 'Southern Resource Zone' of the East Indies. When added to the industrial capacity of Japan and the conquered territories in northern China, the oil, rubber, and rice of South-East Asia would 'give Japan the geopolitical base required to create a great and modern industrial empire'. At the same time, the defeat of the West and an extension of Japanese power into Burma, would force the Chinese Government to 'see reason and end the costly war in China on terms acceptable to Japan'.[17] On 2 December, all Japanese commanders were told that war with the United States and European Empires in Asia would begin on 8 December.[18]

Preparations

The Japanese forces gathered to attack the British Empire in the Far East were not, by any standard, overwhelmingly strong. As Twenty-Fifth Army, commanded by Lieutenant-General Yamashita Tomoyuki, prepared to assault Singapore, the lynchpin of the British position in the Far East, it could muster only three divisions (the Imperial Guards Division, 5th Division and 18th Division). The Japanese armada that approached the shores of Siam (modern-day Thailand) and Malaya, contained no more than 26,640 men, of whom 17,230 were combat troops.[19] By comparison, Lieutenant-General Arthur E. Percival, who was appointed General Officer Commanding (GOC) Malaya Command in May 1941, had 88,600 men available in December 1941, including 19,600 British, 15,200 Australians, 37,000 Indians and some 16,800 locally enlisted Asians.[20]

Percival had not set out in life to become a professional soldier, and he was certainly not in character or disposition in the Gort and Freyberg mould of senior officer. He was an intellectual soldier, more in the image of Wavell. Before 1914, he had worked as a clerk in a City of London iron-ore dealership. On enlisting for the First World War, he served with distinction on the Western Front where he was badly wounded (near Thiepval) and was awarded the MC, the DSO and the Croix de Guerre. He ended the war a battalion commander and decided to make a career of the Army. In the years immediately after the war, he served in Russia and in Ireland before attending the Staff College in 1923 to 1924. Between 1925 and 1929 he was posted to Nigeria, before returning to the Staff College as an instructor in 1931. Thereafter, his career accelerated. After commanding 2nd Battalion the Cheshire Regiment in Malta, he attended the Imperial Defence College in 1935. Now a colonel, he was sent to Malaya as a staff officer for two years before returning to the UK as Brigadier General Staff (BGS), Home Command. On the outbreak of war, he accompanied Dill, his long-time patron, to France as BGS I Corps, before periods commanding 43rd Wessex and 44th Home Counties Divisions in the UK. In 1941, he received the call to take over Malaya Command with the acting rank of lieutenant-general.[21]

Percival's forces were organised into three divisions, each with a strength of two brigades. The 11th Indian Division, which had arrived in the area at the end of 1940, and 9th Indian Division, which had landed in Malaya in March to April 1941, made up III Indian Corps, under the command of Lieutenant-General Sir Lewis Heath, who had led 5th Indian Division to victory at Keren in East Africa. The III Indian Corps was supported by 8th Australian Division, which had arrived in Singapore early in February 1941.[22] Percival also had at his disposal 12th and 28th Indian Brigades, two fortress brigades for Singapore Island (1st and 2nd Malaya Brigades), a battalion as garrison for Penang and another at Sarawak, fixed coastal defence and anti-aircraft batteries for the defence of Singapore, some airfield defence battalions and local volunteer units.[23] Although these forces comprised only thirty-one of the forty-eight infantry battalions Percival deemed necessary for the successful defence of Singapore, his numerical advantage was not inconsiderable.[24]

The position of Malaya Command was bolstered by a series of studies designed to prepare it doctrinally and conceptually for the battle to come. In 1940, well before the Japanese started to consider the problems of waging war under tropical conditions, Lieutenant-General Lionel Bond, then GOC Malaya Command, directed his General Staff to produce a small pamphlet to help units prepare for a possible war in the jungles and rubber plantations of South-East Asia. The pamphlet was based on lessons learnt during exercises conducted in Johore and Singapore between 1939 and 1940 and, although 'simplistic', got to the heart of the basics of jungle warfare. 'Tactical Notes for Malaya 1940' identified infantry as the primary arm in jungle warfare. Supporting weapons, such as artillery, mortars and Armoured Fighting Vehicles (AFV), were deemed less important than the fighting man due to the fact that they were restricted to the limited number of roads in the underdeveloped Malayan countryside. In the pamphlet, officers were directed to seize every opportunity to train in the jungle and stress was placed on the need for all-round protection in defence, with patrols and listening posts providing advance warning of attack. The pamphlet explicitly informed readers that thick country did not favour static defence, since flanks could be easily found, turned and exploited. Instead a defence in depth down the lines of communication along with offensive action whenever possible was recommended along with ambushes and ruses used to confuse and disorganise an opponent. When on the offensive, 'Tactical Notes' stipulated that success depended to a very great extent on surprise, boldness and resourceful leadership. This was because, in jungle warfare, information was extremely hard to come by, supporting fire was troublesome to arrange and command and control difficult to maintain. To influence enemy morale continual harassment by guerrilla tactics was recommended. The pamphlet emphasised the effectiveness of flank attacks by small units on enemy positions or lines of communications. Centrally organised fire plans, by comparison, were of limited effect due to the difficulty in identifying targets in the jungle.[25]

'Tactical Notes' was issued to all units arriving in Malaya Command and was also published in New Delhi and Melbourne for use in the instruction of Indian and Australian Army units preparing for dispatch to Malaya. It was 'the single most influential piece of training literature dealing with the conduct of operations in Malaya' in 1941 and 1942.[26] In 1940, another small pamphlet was prepared by GHQ India dealing with operations in tropical terrain against a modern fully equipped enemy. In conjunction with 'Tactical Notes', it was supposed to prepare the large numbers of troops in the rapidly expanding Indian Army, many of whom were destined for Malaya. 'Military Training Pamphlet (MTP) No. 9 (India): Extensive Warfare: Notes on Forest Warfare', much like 'Tactical Notes', emphasised the vital importance in jungle warfare of seizing the initiative and of mobility. Again, it noted that infantry were the primary arm and acknowledged that AFVs and artillery would have a limited role in jungle warfare since they were largely road-bound. The attack was considered broadly to be stronger than defence given the cover provided by the terrain. MTP No. 9 argued that the most effective form of attack was a turning manoeuvre combined with a holding movement on the main front. Patrolling was considered essential. An active and mobile defence was recommended as most effective, although a traditional all-round defence was also considered to have merit. On the defence, the danger posed by flanking attacks was emphasised, although patrols, large reserves and speedy counter-attacks were recommended as a solution.[27] Copies of MTP No. 9 were sent to Malaya Command during the autumn of 1940, over a year before the Japanese invasion; additionally, the key insights in 'Tactical Notes' and MTP No. 9 were repeated in the 'Army in India Training Memoranda (AITM) No. 6 War Series' of April 1941.[28]

If the forces in the Far East were relatively well prepared with regards to manpower and doctrine, they were less fortunate in terms of armour, air power and the general training of their forces.[29] Over the course of the campaign, the Japanese made use of 265 medium and light tanks. Percival, by comparison, had no armour other than carriers and some armoured cars.[30] The Japanese also enjoyed substantial air superiority. On the day that war broke out, Malaya Command had 181 serviceable aircraft; the Japanese had nearly 600, more than 200 of them first-class fighters.[31] Perhaps more importantly, given the limited utility of AFV and close air support in jungle terrain, the Japanese Army, which had been at war since 1938, was both superbly trained and experienced.[32]

While it must be accepted that by May 1941 the overall standard of preparations in Malaya Command had improved, it was clear that the quality and intensity of training 'still left much to be desired, especially regarding inter-arm co-operation and higher collective training'. The arrival of Percival that same month, 'injected a vigour' and 'a new spirit' in training. Percival had previously served in Malaya Command, 1936 to 1937, and in the Royal West African Frontier Force, a regiment with a tradition of bush warfare. Moreover, he had considerable experience of modern training methods from his pre-war time at Aldershot, his six months in France and his experience of commanding a division in the UK following Dunkirk. Under his supervision, brigade and divisional exercises took place in the autumn of 1941. In addition, Percival directed that attention should be placed on building up a solid foundation of individual, subunit and unit tactical training, and towards the end of the year new arrivals were increasingly encouraged and given the opportunity to train and live in the jungle. But the responsibility to carry out this training, just as it had been in France, was placed on the shoulders of unit and formation commanders.[33]

The problem was that 'whilst some COs eagerly grasped the challenge, most did not'.[34] One report, following the campaign, pointed out that it had been:

> Surprising to find that training in jungle fighting, jungle patrols and patrol work generally, had been neglected in so many units that had been in Malaya for many months. In certain Indian units it was admitted that no jungle work had been practiced, units limiting their training to the manning of beach posts, etc.[35]

Much as in France, up to three-quarters of a unit's time could be spent constructing fixed field defences, while some units found that key elements, such as artillery and anti-tank regiments, arrived too late in country to carry out combined armed training.[36] Such criticisms did not apply equally to all units, but few 'devoted sufficient time' to jungle training and many junior leaders 'failed' to train their formations 'to plan or conduct small battles'.[37] This was all the more inexcusable when one considers that 'Tactical Notes for Malaya 1940' stressed in capital letters that 'TROOPS NEWLY ARRIVED IN MALAYA MUST TAKE EVERY OPPORTUNITY OF TRAINING ALL RANKS IN MOVING THROUGH JUNGLE. THE DIFFERENCE IN VALUE BETWEEN TRAINED AND UNTRAINED TROOPS IS IMMENSE.'[38] (See Illustration 5.1.) Moreover, in April 1941, 9th Indian Division Training Instruction No. 1 noted that 'a very high degree of efficiency' could be 'obtained in short time provided really hard work is put in and practice is insisted upon as opposed to theory'.[39]

The insights and practices encompassed in doctrine were, thus, not disseminated evenly throughout the Army. In some cases, it is questionable whether these pamphlets were read at all. Apart from the Officer Cadet Training Unit at Changi, training centres or schools, where doctrine could be disseminated clearly, and through which new units and individual replacements could pass to receive an introduction to jungle fighting, were notably 'marked by their absence'.[40] 'This was in direct contrast to the Middle East where all newly arrived troops passed through desert warfare training centres before going into combat'.[41]

Percival understood that in these circumstances, his primary mission was little more than damage limitation. His aim was to defend the base at Singapore so that it could be used to house the fleet and receive reinforcements when they arrived; a decisive defeat of an invading Japanese Army was not essential to this plan. It was self-evident that he needed to prevent an assault on and occupation of Singapore Island itself, but, more problematically, he also needed to prevent the Japanese from getting their hands on the airfields of northern Malaya, which

Illustration 5.1 Soldiers of 2/18th Australian Infantry Battalion making their way through dense jungle during training exercises, May 1941. Those units and formations that trained to live and fight in the jungle performed significantly better than those that were not given such opportunities in Malaya and Burma, 1941 and 1942.

could be used, if captured, to bomb Singapore harbour and put it out of action. Percival, therefore, placed III Indian Corps including 28th Indian Brigade in the north of the country to defend against Japanese landings there or against an advance through Siam, and 8th Australian Division with 12th Indian Brigade in the south, around Johore. The two Malaya brigades were placed on Singapore Island.[42] These dispositions seemed entirely sensible. A direct assault on Singapore Island was deemed highly unlikely considering its substantial defences and there was only one suitable place for a landing in Johore, where the towns of Endau and Mersing on the east coast were both well defended by the Australians.[43] Any attack was likely, therefore, to come from the north where, should the Japanese advance via the long tortuous main road from Siam to Singapore, a distance of about 600 miles, it was thought that the nature of the country would lend itself to 'long delaying actions and costly ambushes so that an invading force would take months or even years to negotiate this long distance, if indeed ... [it] could ever succeed'.[44]

The Malaya Campaign

Percival's expectations of Japanese intentions proved well founded. On 8 December 1941, the Japanese 18th Division stormed ashore at Kota Bharu on the north-east tip of Malaya (see Map 5.1). In spite of the heavy surf and considerable fire, they quickly infiltrated inland and forced the Indian troops on the beaches to withdraw.[45] From that moment on, it seemed that everything that could go wrong did go wrong for the British and Commonwealth forces. In the chaos that ensued, the airbase at Badang, close to the landings, was abandoned, leaving the runway and large stocks of petrol and bombs intact. 'At least four bases were left as valuable gifts' in this manner in the first days of the campaign. The demolition of air bases behind Commonwealth positions had been deemed so 'disastrous' to morale that Percival had persuaded Air Vice-Marshal C. W. H. Pulford, Air Officer Commanding Far East, to order that 'buildings should be broken up as much as possible and petrol allowed to run to waste' rather than 'fired'. This made it nearly impossible to deny facilities properly to the enemy.[46]

Further north, in neutral Siam, the main Japanese landings took place unopposed at Singora and Patani. The pre-war plan for the defence of Malaya, a pre-emptive invasion of Siam by 11th Indian Division (codenamed 'Matador'), 'had precluded British violation of Thai sovereignty unless and until the Japanese attacked'. By the time they had done so, 'it was too late to defend Malaya by launching a pre-

Map 5.1 The Malaya campaign, 8 December 1941–15 February 1942

emptive strike across the border, and the dithering over the question of respect for Thai neutrality hampered the planners and commanders in Singapore', much as it had with the BEF and Belgium in 1940.[47]

It was apparent, in the crucial first days after the invasion, that, just like at Gazala, those in command were failing to take the initiative and demonstrate drive and determination. Matters were made worse when 3/16 Punjabi Regiment, 11th Indian Division, failed to take 'the

Ledge', a stretch of road carved precariously along the edge of a steep hill south of Singora and Patani. The road, which stretched for several winding miles, could have been destroyed, imposing many weeks of delay. Instead, 3/16 Punjabi took fifty-one hours to reach its objective (it had taken two and a half hours in the last training exercise before war broke out).[48]

As a consequence of the decision to cancel 'Matador' and the failure to hold 'the Ledge', 11th Indian Division fell back south to prepared positions at Jitra, in the north-west corner of Malaya, abandoning the airfields and the rationale that had required III Indian Corps to defend Singapore so many miles to the north in the first place.[49] Between 11 and 13 December, the Japanese rushed forward to engage III Indian Corps on the Jitra defences. In an appalling setback, 14,000 troops of 11th Indian Division, supported by more than fifty field and thirty-six anti-tank guns, occupying a defensive position that had been worked on for months, were routed by less than 1,500 Japanese infantry supported by a tank company. It was, as Major-General D. M. Murray-Lyon, the Commander of 11th Indian Division, recalled, reminiscent of March 1918, when the British Army had retreated in disarray following the German 'Michael' offensive. The War Diary of 2nd East Surreys called the defeat and subsequent retreat 'a pitiful sight'; some historians have described it as 'disgrace'. The disappointment over the decision not to launch 'Matador', news of the loss of the Royal Navy capital ships HMS Prince of Wales and Repulse (which had been sent East in a last gasp attempt to deter the Japanese), the dominance of the Japanese air force, the abandonment of airbases, and the incessant rain, had led the division to fall into, what Brian Farrell has termed, 'a funk of self-pity before being seriously engaged' in the Jitra position. Lieutenant-Colonel Tsuji Masanobu, Chief Operations Officer at Japanese Twenty-Fifth Army HQ, was so unimpressed by the British and Commonwealth forces that he concluded that 'we now understood the fighting capacity of the enemy. The only things we had to fear were the quantity of munitions he had and the thoroughness of his demolitions.'[50]

The rout at Jitra gave the Japanese the initiative and the chance to fight the campaign on their own terms. By the time 11th Indian Division pulled itself together following the engagement, it was 'a shadow of its former self', having lost half its fighting strength, more than two dozen guns and great quantities of ammunition and supplies. About 75 per cent of its casualties were POWs. The Japanese advance south played on British and Commonwealth weaknesses. It was usually led by a battle group with tanks, motorised infantry, light artillery and engineers. They were trained to fight as an aggressive combined arms team and make maximum use of manoeuvre. They were 'light and fast enough to keep up the pressure but strong and balanced enough to deal with anything short of determined resistance'.[51] This was the key dynamic, much as it had been in France in 1940; British and Commonwealth forces when penetrated or surrounded appeared unwilling, or unable, to offer 'determined resistance'.[52]

This was tacitly admitted by Malaya Command. Percival accepted that British and Indian units were inexperienced in jungle warfare.[53] But he did not think that the Army was incapable of adapting to the environment or the situation if it showed the requisite determination and energy. There appeared to be two aspects to the issue. First, as GHQ Far East communicated to its formations on 18 December, the British and Commonwealth forces had to stand and fight on positions chosen as best suited to facilitate determined resistance:

> Our experience to date has shown that linear defence is no use since the enemy has invariably outflanked us and also infiltrated in thick country. It is considered, therefore, that we must choose ground upon which to fight where a) there is a formidable obstacle with few communications leading to it b) the main communications pass through a restricted area in this obstacle which can be easily blocked c) the position is sited for all round defence and provisioned for a prolonged defence which will not be easily prejudiced by any infantry infiltration round the flanks.[54]

Second, as Percival pointed out in a note issued around the same time, there was a greater requirement for discipline; it was imperative that Japanese infiltration and outflanking attacks did not consistently lead to withdrawals. To counter Japanese methods, Percival recommended digging in on the main axis of communication with smaller forces deployed on either flank ready to attack as soon as the enemy made contact. Percival emphasised that offensive methods must be employed whenever possible to beat the Japanese at their own game.[55]

It is clear that those in charge felt capable of handling the Japanese 'driving charge' and that Percival understood the character of jungle warfare. But, as 11th Indian Division, along with the rest of III Indian Corps, retreated south to the strong defensive positions at Kuantan and Kampar, the problem became less one of understanding and tactics and increasingly one of action and morale. Much as had happened in the desert in the summer of 1942, a 'widespread concern about morale' began to grow in the Army.[56] Every time Malaya Command turned to fight there was a sense that it was already looking over its shoulder to the next possible position.[57]

At Kampar, at the end of December, the plan was to hold the position for ten days. The new commander of 11th Indian Division, Archibald Paris, called it to arms as it prepared its defences:

> The present situation has GOT TO CEASE – and the Japanese have got to become frightened of us. I decline to believe that British and Indian troops are incapable of bringing about this desirable state of affairs ... it is up to us to establish local and personal ascendancy over the enemy immediately opposed to us.[58]

Paris' units, in spite of his exhortations, did not rise to the challenge. The battle lasted only four days. Commanders became increasingly reluctant to make counter-attacks, even when there was good reason to believe that they might prove decisive; such engagements, it was feared, could easily degenerate into a brawl and officers had little faith in the determination of their men in such circumstances.[59]

In another 'fiasco', at Slim River on 7 January, thirty Japanese tanks, supported by no more than 1,000 infantry, engineers and gunners, destroyed the fighting power of two of 11th Indian Division's brigades in a morning. The Japanese for the cost of less than 150 casualties took around 3,000 prisoners, a month's worth of supplies for two brigades, fifty Bren carriers and dozens of trucks. This was a windfall that eased their supply difficulties as they advanced further and further south into Malaya.

On 4 January 1942, Wavell, who had been Commander-in-Chief (C-in-C) India since his replacement by Auchinleck in the desert, was given overall command of the newly created American British Dutch Australian (ABDA) Command, known as South-West Pacific Command to the British. Wavell's new position, a product of the first Anglo-American summit meeting of the war (the Arcadia Conference held in Washington, December 1941 and January 1942), gave him overall responsibility for an area stretching in an arc from Burma to Australia. More importantly, it superseded Far East Command and now meant that he was in charge of defending Malaya, Singapore and Burma.[60] Wavell, who regarded the Japanese as much overrated, was confident that Malaya Command could adapt to the tactical challenges posed by their advance. He believed that the Japanese progress owed more to mistakes by the defenders than to his opponent's combat power[61] and that 'effective counter to these tactics' could 'easily be devised'.[62]

On 9 January, he wrote to the Chiefs of Staff in Melbourne, outlining his plan for the as yet uncommitted 8th Australian Division and the defence of Malaya. He concluded that 11th Indian Division and the rest of III Indian Corps were too spent to continue the fighting retreat and ordered them to break contact and retreat to Johore in the south of the country.[63] Major-General H. Gordon Bennett, commander of 8th Australian Division, would be given command of the Johore defences and it was hoped that under his leadership the British, Indian and Australian forces in southern Malaya would 'delay [the] enemy till collection of reserves enables us to deliver counter-stroke which will not be before middle of Feb'. He pointed out that as the Japanese approached Johore, their maintenance problems would worsen and they would increasingly come under attack from Commonwealth fighter aircraft and bombers stationed in the south of the country. It was going to be, as he dryly remarked, a 'time problem between rate of Japanese advance and arrival of our reinforcements'.[64]

Bennett's 8th Australian Division had been freed from working on the defences up north and had been given time and opportunity to train intensively in the jungles, plantations and swamps of Johore. It had also taken the opportunity to profit from training instructions and conferences that had circulated lessons learned following the early disasters in the campaign.[65] Thus, when the battle of Johore began on 14 January, the fresh, highly motivated and well-trained Australians gave the Japanese a nasty surprise and the following day, Wavell wrote to the Chiefs of Staff in London assuring them that, provided his reinforcements arrived at the front intact, he could hold Singapore.[66]

Bennett's battle plan for the 'Johore Line' assumed, however, that the Japanese would advance along a single axis and was, according to one commentator, 'so flawed it would have been failed by any officer cadet course'.[67] On 16 January, the Imperial Guards Division, searching for weak points in the British and Commonwealth position, crossed the Muar River on the west flank of the 'Johore Line'. There it attacked 45th Indian Brigade, which had arrived as part of the first reinforcement convoy, that much to Wavell's relief had reached Singapore on 3 January. The brigade was spread out along 24 miles of riverbank and was woefully inexperienced; originally part of 17th Indian Division, it had been organised, trained and equipped in India for desert warfare before being diverted to Malaya en route to Iraq where further training had been planned. Its ranks were filled by 'young, raw and largely untrained' Indian other ranks (ORs) deficient in basic military skills. On first contact with the enemy, the brigade splintered, thus threatening the lines of communication of the Australians and other units to the north. The exhausted III Indian Corps was ordered to fill the gap. Two newly landed battalions of 53rd Brigade, of British 18th Division, were also flung into battle, despite the fact that they lacked both 'experience and training in jungle fighting'; they had originally been en route to the Middle East before being diverted east to land as part of the second reinforcement convoy to reach Singapore on 13 January.[68]

The position on the 'Johore Line' gradually became more and more untenable. Bennett, who was fiercely critical of the British and Indian troops under his command, identified a 'lack of fighting spirit' and a 'withdrawal complex' as having played a big part in undoing the position.[69] Whether these criticisms were deserved or not, after Johore, there was nowhere left to go but onto Singapore Island. The retreat 'fostered a save-yourself-first mentality'. Australian war diaries complained about constant fatigue, enemy air pressure, and the absence of friendly air support, noting 'general despondency', 'physical exhaustion', 'many crack ups and general lowering of morale'. The 22nd Indian Brigade disintegrated, finishing 9th Indian Division as a fighting formation. The force that crossed the causeway on the morning of 31 January 1942 'was more an exhausted horse being corralled than a fighting mad rat being cornered'. Bennett reflected in his diary:

> This retreat seems fantastic. Fancy 550 miles in 55 days – chased by a Jap army on stolen bikes without artillery. It was a war of patrols. All that happened was that they patrolled outside our resistance and sat on a road behind us. Thinking we were cut off, we retreated … Never felt so sad and upset. Words fail me. Why? This should not have been. The whole thing is fantastic.

> I thought I could hold Johore – but I assumed that British troops would have held their piece.[70]

For a cost of 4,500 casualties, the equivalent of a regiment, the Japanese had taken Malaya along with more than 300 guns, 50 carriers, large quantities of supplies of all kinds, some 3,600 vehicles, 800 items of rolling stock and about 35,000 prisoners.[71]

The Invasion of Burma

As the situation deteriorated in Malaya, matters hardly looked more promising elsewhere in the Far East. A few hours after the landings at Kota Bharu, the Japanese Twenty-Third Army attacked Hong Kong. The British Chiefs of Staff had long held that Hong Kong was indefensible. In October 1940, that position was reversed as the Chiefs rather ironically considered Britain's position in the Far East to have improved. More importantly, the Americans encouraged the British to fight for the colony; it was reasoned that along with their own recently reinforced forces in the Philippines, the garrison at Hong Kong might contain or delay a Japanese attack. Reinforcing Hong Kong now took on symbolic importance as Churchill strived to drag the United States into the war. The 'new orthodoxy' was that Hong Kong could not be held, but that it must be defended. In November, reinforcements arrived in the form of two battalions of half-trained Canadian troops. The plan was for the colony to hold out for ninety days, until the US fleet from Pearl Harbor arrived. In the end, the British and Commonwealth garrison, amounting to almost 12,000 troops, lasted only eighteen days against the combat-hardened troops of Twenty-Third Army (which was made up initially of 15,000 men);[72] the garrison of six infantry battalions, two Indian, two British and two Canadian, surrendered on Christmas Day 1941. In spite of the capitulation, the troops at Hong Kong fought well in comparison to Malaya Command; in the short campaign, the garrison inflicted upwards of 3,000 casualties on the Japanese for the cost of 4,000 of their own. The rest of the garrison went into captivity.[73] Nevertheless, Hong Kong was only an outpost, and, in this sense, was not central to the British strategic position in the Far East. Burma, by comparison, was (see Map 5.2).[74]

There was a six-week intermission between the invasion of Malaya and the attack of Japanese Fifteenth Army on Burma.

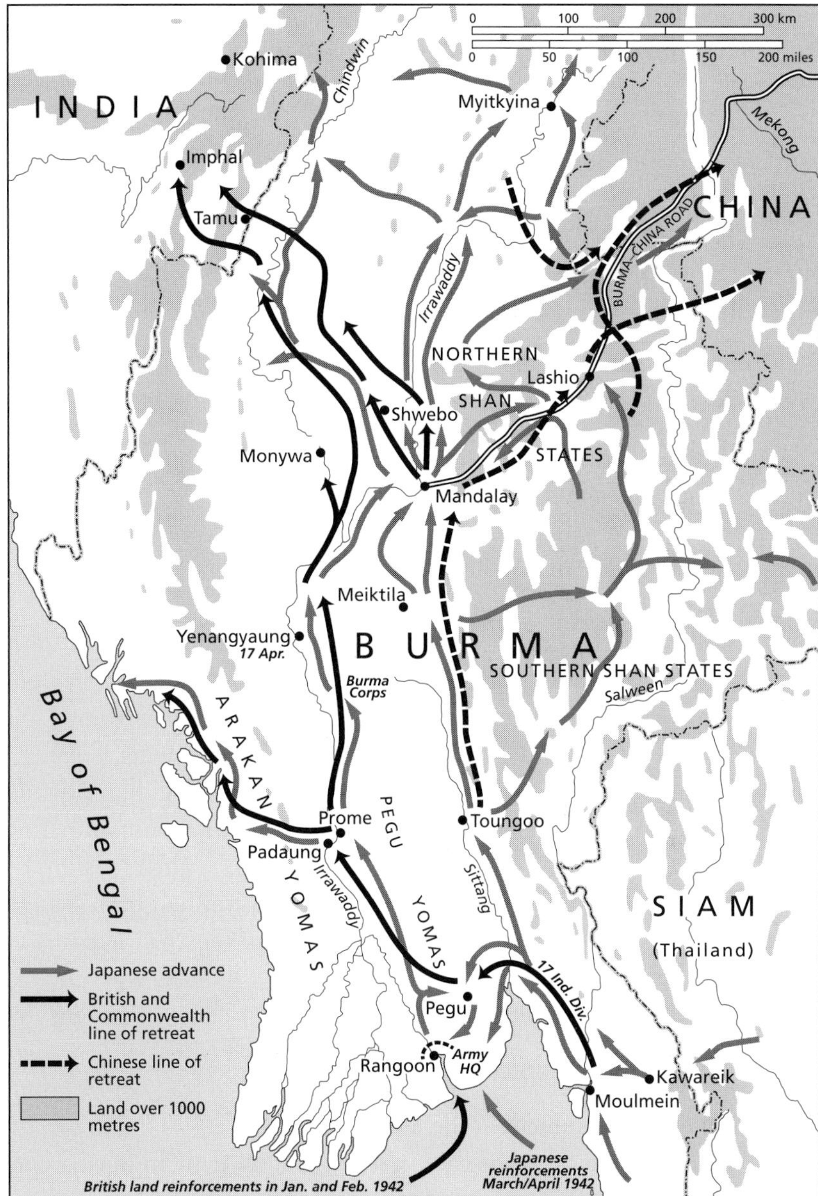

Map 5.2 The Japanese invasion of Burma, January–May 1942

The possession of Burma was of no little importance to the Japanese. It would provide airfields to protect the flank of their conquests in Malaya; it would allow the control of the Burma Road, an artery of supply to Nationalist China, which stretched north from the port of

Rangoon and then north-east from Mandalay into eastern Burma and the Yunnan province; and it would give Japan access to rich natural resources of rice, oil and wolfram.[75] For the attack, Fifteenth Army comprised two well-trained divisions, the 33rd and 55th, and accompanying support troops, 35,440 men in total, plus 701 horses, 53 troop-carrying vehicles, 570 trucks and 200 aircraft.[76]

In autumn 1941, the forces available to defend Burma were 1st Burma Division, consisting of 1st and 2nd Burma Brigades and 13th Indian Brigade. The 13th Indian Brigade had landed in Rangoon in April 1941. The two Burmese infantry brigades had been raised only that July. The division 'lacked transport, signals, guns, and collective training – everything in fact except the divisional designation'. A second Indian brigade, the 16th, which arrived on the eve of war in the Far East, was the sole reserve. In the air, the RAF had a single squadron (16 aircraft) of obsolete American-built Brewster Buffalo fighters, whereas the air defence of Burma was estimated to require at least 280 aircraft.[77]

Following the Japanese attack on Malaya on 8 December, 46th and 48th Indian Brigades and the HQ of the 17th Indian Division were also sent to Burma, bringing Burma Army, including RAF personnel, up to a strength of around 45,000 men. These reinforcements began to unload in Rangoon on 9 January 1942. Along with 16th Indian Brigade they were to form the nucleus of 17th Indian Division, commanded by Brigadier (acting Major-General) J. G. Smyth, VC.[78] This division, of which two of its original brigades, the 44th and 45th, had been sent to Malaya before moving to Burma, was a product of the 1941 expansion programme and had been in existence only a few months when it was sent overseas. Pronounced unfit to face a first-class opponent by Brigadier D. T. 'Punch' Cowan, India's Director of Military Training, it had been promised six weeks of intensive training in Iraq before going into action, it was assumed, in the Middle East.[79]

Much as had been the case in Malaya, the Army in Burma was broadly aware of the character of the challenge it was about to face. Copies of MTP No. 9: Forest Warfare were sent to the country and in early January 1942 Army HQ Burma issued an operation instruction highlighting tactics that were understood to be central to successful fighting in jungle conditions. Such tactics included the importance of offensive action, aggressive patrolling and mounting ambushes. The instruction stressed that 'every effort' had to be made 'to accustom troops fresh from INDIA in fighting in the jungle'. However, again, much as was the case in Malaya, there is little evidence that troops actually trained according to these guidelines. Moreover, all the Indian troops sent to Burma had been heavily 'milked' and were lacking both equipment and experienced officers.[80]

Matters were made more complex by regular changes in higher command and the poor dispositions employed by commanders in country. Up until the outbreak of hostilities with Japan, responsibility for the defence of Burma had lain with Far East Command. On 12 December, it was handed to Wavell in India, who placed his own Chief of Staff, Lieutenant-General Thomas Hutton as C-in-C Burma.[81] Hutton was ordered to hold the Japanese away from Rangoon in the south, the only port through which reinforcements could arrive in the area. This job he gave to Smyth while 1st Burma Division, which had 2nd Burma Brigade transferred south to support 17th Indian Division, was left in the Shan States to the east, covering another potential invasion route from Thailand.[82] Thus, the brigades of 17th Indian Division ended up being spread over 400 miles of mountainous jungle country to the south, with widely dispersed formations operating at the end of long lines of communication.[83]

It was here, on 20 January, that the Japanese Fifteenth Army, led by Lieutenant-General Shojiro Iida, poured across the jungle-covered mountainous border with Siam. The 55th Division headed for Moulmein while 33rd Division advanced along jungle tracks towards the River Salween.[84] Nothing seemed to go right for the British and Commonwealth forces. In a grim foretaste of things to come, 16th Indian Brigade was routed at Kawkareik by 55th Division. Barely a week after the commencement of hostilities, events in Burma were unfolding in a pattern no different to what had happened so recently in Malaya. In a similar vein to Percival, Hutton became concerned that the problem lay principally with the morale and determination of his troops. On 27 January, he issued an Order of the Day outlining what he expected and needed of his men:

> It is the duty of the forces present in the front line to hold their ground without yielding, to halt the enemy and to drive him back. There must be no question of further withdrawal. Troops who cannot go forward must defend the posts entrusted to them to the last. It was thus in 1914 that the original British

> Expeditionary Force and Indian Expeditionary Force stopped the German advance and saved Europe.
>
> The Japanese have so far been allowed to win their successes too cheaply and easily by the method of sending quite small bodies round the flanks to spread confusion in the rear and give the impression of a much larger force. All troops must understand that they must on no account give ground because enemy parties have penetrated to their rear; these parties will be dealt with by other of our troops disposed in depth.[85]

The order had little effect. On 31 January, Moulmein was captured by the Japanese after 7th Burma Rifles 'disintegrated' and 'large-scale desertions affected other units'. Against 'increasingly demoralised' men night attacks and 'jitter' tactics designed to scare the troops 'worked to perfection'.[86]

The 17th Indian Division fell back behind the Salween River where Smyth desperately tried to recalibrate his force. Experienced troops were attached to advance parties of units yet to engage the Japanese to try and pass on what lessons had been learnt about jungle fighting. On 6 February, Smyth issued instructions outlining again the principles of jungle warfare. These were accompanied a few days later by another Operation Instruction produced by Burma Army HQ. These efforts made little difference. On 8 February, the Japanese 55th Division crossed the river. By 14 February, with his lines of communication increasingly threatened by Japanese infiltrations, Smyth decided to fall back to a more defensible position.[87]

The Fall of Singapore

At Singapore, as the final retreat onto the island took place, further reinforcements started to arrive; 44th Indian Brigade and 7,000 Indian replacements landed on 22 January; the Australian 2/4 Machine-Gun Battalion and 1,900 Australian replacements arrived on 24 January; and the bulk of 18th Division landed on 29 January.[88] The Japanese entry into the conflict had coincided with a short breathing space in the war against Germany and Italy. Unexpected Russian victories in the East had temporarily reduced the threat of a German thrust through the Caucasus to Iraq and Persia. Eighth Army's success in Operation 'Crusader' had also eased the situation in North Africa. Reinforcements previously earmarked for the Middle East could, therefore, be transferred to the Far East.[89] As a consequence, by the end of January, an additional 33,939 men had arrived in Malaya Command, bringing its strength, once casualties had been accounted for, to 106,085 men.[90] Further reinforcements were also on the way, including the two trained and experienced divisions of I Australian Corps, which on the insistence of the Australian Government were steaming east after service in the Middle East, and 7th Armoured Brigade, formerly part of 7th Armoured Division, which had fought successfully in the desert.[91]

On 20 January, Churchill wrote to Wavell outlining what he required of the ABDA Commander:

> I want to make it absolutely clear that I expect every inch of ground to be defended, every scrap of material or defences to be blown to pieces to prevent its capture by the enemy, and no question of surrender to be entertained until after protracted fighting among the ruins of Singapore city.[92]

Wavell was confident he could honour Churchill's demand and intended with 'an active defence' to hold the island for three months. During this time, he planned to build up a force in Java and Sumatra to strike back and retake Malaya.[93]

The stakes were high indeed. If the British failed to hold Singapore, their power and prestige in Asia would be seriously undermined. To keep the Empire together, Malaya Command had to fight to hold the naval base.[94] In the event that matters were to end badly, the British Government would have to present the loss of Singapore in a positive light, much as it had done after Dunkirk, and limit the political fallout of defeat, but this would only be credible if there was fierce resistance to the Japanese.

By now, however, Malaya Command was a collection of units with little confidence left in their High Command or each other. While some were still full of fight, others were broken. What they found on Singapore Island made matters worse:

> The army believed what everyone else believed. Their job was to protect the naval base. They were buying time for 'Fortress Singapore' to perfect its supposedly formidable defences, then they would dig in behind those ramparts and defy the enemy to dig them out.[95]

Much to the men's consternation, however, the Navy decided to abandon the base and 'started to demolish its facilities literally before the eyes of the retreating troops'. Moreover, there were no ramparts. Units directed to the coastal defences to the north of the island found practically nothing waiting for them. 'The base was gone. There was no fortress. There would be no rescue.'[96] Bennett wrote later that many of his troops 'freely stated that it seemed absurd to defend the naval base after it was destroyed'.[97]

Singapore was, nevertheless, still a difficult prospect for the Japanese. There was no way to outflank the island's defences. They had to be stormed by a frontal amphibious assault across the Johore strait, a type of operation that, for success, typically required a force-to-force ratio of about 3:1 in the attacker's favour. Even at this stage, Malaya Command still outnumbered the Japanese, who, when they attacked on 8 February, had only 67,660 in their combat arms, supported by around 33,000 service troops.[98]

Churchill wrote again to Wavell on 10 February, emphasising this very fact. He pointed out that the 'defenders must greatly outnumber Japanese forces' and that the matter now, more than ever, was an issue of willpower.

> There must at this stage be no thought of saving the troops or sparing the population. The battle must be fought to the bitter end at all costs. The 18th Division has a chance to make its name in history. Commanders and senior officers should die with their troops. The honour of the British Empire and the British Army is at stake. I rely on you to show no mercy to weakness in any form. With the Russians fighting as they are and the Americans so stubborn at Luzon [in the Philippines], the whole reputation of our country and our race is involved. It is expected that every unit will be brought into close contact with the enemy and fight it out.[99]

Wavell passed Churchill's message on in an Order of the Day adding that 'the Chinese, with almost a complete lack of modern equipment, have held back the Japanese for 4 and a half years. It will be disgraceful if we yield our boasted Fortress of Singapore to inferior enemy forces.' He continued, 'I look to you and to your men to fight to the end to prove that the fighting spirit that won our Empire still exists to enable us to defend it.'[100]

Percival's own Order of the Day, issued on 11 February, echoed Wavell's:

> In some units the troops have not shown the fighting spirit which is to be expected of men of the British Empire. It will be a lasting disgrace if we are defeated by an army of clever gangsters, many times inferior in numbers to our own. The spirit of aggression and determination to stick it out must be inculcated in all ranks. There must be no further thought of withdrawal without orders. There are too many fighting men moving about in back areas. Every available man who is not doing other essential work must be used to stop the invader.[101]

Historians have criticised these commanders as 'weak' for passing on Churchill's 'tendentious emotional blackmail'.[102] However, such a reading of the situation was entirely consistent, at least in the case of Wavell, with his understanding of the nature of war. Both before the war, and during the many battles in the Middle East, he had constantly stressed the centrality of morale to combat outcomes.[103] As brutal as it sounds, men were expected to stand and fight, and most likely die, for the cause.[104] The Russians had behaved thus at the gates of Moscow; they would do so again in the cauldron at Stalingrad. Australians had won lasting fame at Tobruk and the Americans were building a reputation at Luzon. The Empire would survive or fall on the personal sacrifices of the tens of thousands of men trapped on the island of Singapore. Empires had always lived and died on such pitiless calculation.

In spite of the stirring words issued by their commanders and political leaders, the troops on Singapore Island, by this stage of the campaign, had little fight left in them. Once the Japanese had broken through the crust of defences on the coast, it was clear that the remaining Indian forces were strong only in numbers and that 8th Australian Division 'was a shadow of the formation' that had fought with determination in Johore.[105] Many Indian units on the island 'melted away by mass desertion' or were subverted by Japanese propaganda units.[106] For example, Bennett claimed that 12th Indian Brigade 'disappeared and only 70 men could be gathered by 15th February'.[107] Few showed any desire to fight.

The War Diary of the Assistant Director of Medical Services (ADMS), 8th Australian Division, counted 6,000 admissions due to illness during the seventy days of the campaign, an astonishingly high average monthly admission rate of 162.82 per thousand men, the highest figures encountered by this author in the war in the Far East (see Figure 8.1).[108] As many as 7,000 out of a final combat force of 12,000 Australians were unaccounted for in the final days before the capitulation. Wavell certainly thought that Australian units had deserted en masse, in spite of the fact that some had put up a determined resistance to the initial landings. Major H. P. Thomas, who compiled a report on the campaign drawn from more than sixty interviews, argued that 'beyond any doubt morale and discipline at this time had gone to pieces'.[109] The War Diary of 8th Australian Division Provost Company probably captures the situation more vividly than any other source:

> 12. [February] Many soldiers of all units finding their way into Singapore saying they needed a sleep and a meal, and giving panicky accounts of the front line actions ... Soldiers are becoming very sullen, and they are so numerous that it is very difficult to collect and return them to Assembly Area.
>
> 13. [February] Conditions as on the previous day ... Some AIF soldiers very reluctant to return to the line, saying 'there is no organisation there'. British and Indian Troops wandering aimlessly about ...
>
> 14. [February] More and more soldiers in Singapore, morale very low. All imaginable excuses being made to avoid returning to the line. Arms and equipment being discarded all over Singapore. Wharves crowded with soldiers viewing chances of getting off in boats.
>
> 15 [February] Soldiers everywhere ... morale shocking. A lot of men hid themselves to prevent and avoid return to the line ... general pandemonium and confusion.[110]

On 15 February 1942, seven days after the Japanese had stormed the straits, Singapore surrendered. By this point, Malaya Command had received fifty infantry battalions, more units than had been deemed necessary to defend Singapore in the first place.[111] The lynchpin of British power in the Far East had fallen, with a loss of over 80,000 prisoners.[112] The shockwaves were felt all throughout the British Empire.

Retreat to India

Much now depended on Burma. On 20 February Churchill cabled the Australian Prime Minister, John Curtin, urging that 7th and 6th Australian Divisions, of I Australian Corps, be diverted to Rangoon. Curtin refused, stating that it was his 'primary obligation' now, after the fall of Singapore, 'to save Australia not only for itself, but to preserve it as a base for the development of the war against Japan'.[113] I Australian Corps would return home and Hutton would have to defend Burma with the formations at his disposal and those already on the way.

The 48th Indian Brigade, of the 17th Indian Division, had arrived in Rangoon on 3 February and was quickly rushed to the front. The brigade, unlike its predecessors consisted of three well-trained pre-war Gurkha battalions; it was hoped that their previous experience on the North-West Frontier would help them perform well in Burma. It did. The 17th Indian Division stalled the Japanese advance for four days in the first major action of the campaign at the River Bilin.[114] By 19 February, however, it was becoming clear that Smyth's forces were tiring; with 17th Indian Division's reserves committed, there was a danger that the division would be unable to disengage effectively to the more formidable obstacle of the River Sittang, which lay only 30 miles to the rear.[115]

That night the division broke off the battle and moved down the rough track towards the Sittang, the last major river before Rangoon.[116] By now widespread confusion and exhaustion had begun to reign. A regiment of the Japanese 33rd Division, which had moved through the jungle parallel to the British retreat, reached the east bank of the Sittang while two-thirds of 17th Indian Division were still in retreat. Smyth, believing that most of his units were across the river, ordered the bridge blown at 0530hrs on 23 February.[117] Although some of the troops on the east bank got back, most did not. The following day 17th Indian Division massed only 3,484 men, just 41 per cent of its authorised strength. Over the course of the next week, as stragglers began to reach the western side of the river, its numbers slowly increased to 4,277. But the division was effectively destroyed; it had lost most of its transport, and it could only account for 1,400 rifles and 56 light machine guns.[118]

With the situation descending into chaos, overall control of Burma, which had been transferred to ABDA at the start of January, was returned once again, on 22 February, to India Command. This meant, due to Wavell's continued role as C-in-C ABDA, that General

Sir Alan Hartley, C-in-C India, was given responsibility for Burma. This proved to be a short-lived arrangement. With the collapse of Allied resistance in Malaya, Singapore and the Dutch East Indies, ABDA effectively ceased to exist and Wavell returned to India, resuming command there on 28 February.[119]

While these changes were taking place at the highest level, Hutton decided that Rangoon would have to be evacuated. With only the recently arrived 7th Armoured Brigade available, he saw little purpose in fighting on in southern Burma. He turned around a convoy carrying the partially trained 63rd Indian Brigade to Rangoon and prepared to retreat north. Hartley agreed with this decision, but when Wavell, having returned from ABDA, visited Rangoon on 1 March, he countermanded the order. He ordered Rangoon to be held and the convoy carrying 63rd Indian Brigade to be turned around for a second time. Wavell then visited 17th Indian Division and sacked Smyth, replacing him with 'Punch' Cowan.[120]

By mid-February, the Chiefs of Staff, along with Churchill and the Viceroy, Lord Linlithgow, had become so displeased with the speed of the withdrawal in Burma that they decided to replace Hutton (although he would remain as his successor's Chief of Staff). On 4 March, Wavell met with his replacement, General Sir Harold Alexander at Calcutta airport. He gave Alexander an unequivocal objective: 'The retention of Rangoon is a matter of pivotal importance to our position in the Far East and every effort must be made to hold it.' On taking over command the next day, Alexander ordered his remaining units to counter-attack, at Pegu, north-east of Rangoon. It was a costly error and he was soon left with little option, in spite of his clear orders, to evacuate the capital of Burma; as Alexander's forces withdrew into the Irrawaddy Valley, on 8 March the Japanese marched into Rangoon.[121]

Control of the port of Rangoon allowed the Japanese to pour in reinforcements, better than doubling the strength of Fifteenth Army. Two divisions, 18th and 56th, two tank regiments, an extra regiment for 33rd Division and heavy artillery arrived in March and early April. By contrast, on 19 March, 17th Indian Division had a strength of 6,700 men, while 'the only effective units in the 1st Burma Division were three Indian battalions, its Burmese units having been depleted by desertion or dismissal to their homes'. No reinforcements were available. In the air, the Japanese Fifth Air Division was now brought up to 420 aircraft, while the British, with American support, could only muster 150. By the end of March, 'the sky belonged to the Japanese'.[122] The 7th Armoured Brigade would have to function as the 'solid core' of the British and Commonwealth forces in Burma.[123]

In the circumstances, 17th Indian Division had little alternative but to withdraw northwards towards Prome, while 1st Burma Division covered the deployment of Chinese troops into Burma. The British had agreed with Chiang Kai-shek, the leader of Nationalist China, that he would move the Chinese Sixth Army into the Shan States in the east and concentrate the Chinese Fifth Army near Toungoo in the Sittang Valley to cover the main road and railway line towards Mandalay. After the fall of Rangoon, the Sixty-Sixth Chinese Army moved into Burma as well. These forces were roughly equivalent in size to the British formations already in the country and at a crucial moment occupied the attention of three of Fifteenth Army's four divisions, perhaps, along with 7th Armoured Brigade, saving Burma Army from complete destruction.[124]

On 19 March, yet another change in the command arrangements in Burma took place, this time with the creation of a new corps HQ ('Burcorps'), commanded by Lieutenant-General William Slim (see Illustration 5.2). 'Bill' Slim would go on to become one of the most celebrated commanders of the Second World War. As a young man, he had always hankered after a career in the Army. However, his family could not afford to send him to Sandhurst or Woolwich. Thus, after school, he took a post with an engineering firm and was due to start a job with Shell when the First World War broke out. In September 1914 he was commissioned into 9th Battalion, the Royal Warwickshire Regiment.[125] He first saw active service in Gallipoli in August 1915, where he was very badly wounded to the extent that it seemed likely that he would not see action again. After convalescing in England, where he arranged a regular commission in the West India regiment, he went, in October 1916, with a draft to his old battalion in Mesopotamia where he was again wounded, gained the MC and was evacuated to India. He joined the staff at Army HQ India in November 1917 and in May 1919 was granted a regular commission as a captain in the Indian Army. Slim finished his time at Army HQ and was posted to the 1st Battalion, 6th Gurkha Rifles, in March 1920.[126]

There is 'no doubt' that Slim, by this stage, 'was one of the outstanding talents' in the Army. He came top in the entrance exam for the Indian Army Staff College, at Quetta, in 1926. Two years later, he graduated as top student. In 1934, he was selected as the Indian Army's

Illustration 5.2 General William Slim inspecting his men, n.d. Along with Auchinleck, Slim would play a key role in turning the Indian Army from an at times hopelessly ineffective citizen force into a flexible, confident, highly motivated, innovative, increasingly culturally representative and highly trained fighting machine.

member of the directing staff at the Staff College, Camberley. He made such an impression at Camberley that he was selected for the 1937 cohort at the Imperial Defence College, a course designed to equip senior officers for higher command. In 1938, having returned to India, he took command of 2nd Battalion, 7th Gurkha Rifles and the following year he was appointed commandant of the Senior Officers School at Belgaum, now with the rank of brigadier.[127] On the outbreak of war, Slim became commander of the 10th Indian Infantry Brigade, 5th Indian Division, which went to Eritrea in the autumn of 1940. He led his brigade successfully, if unspectacularly, in the East African campaign until wounded and returned to India. There, he found himself involved in the planning to send an expeditionary force to Iraq to counter Rashid Ali's coup. He flew to Basra as the Chief of Staff to the C-in-C in Iraq, but on 15 May was given command of the 10th Indian Division, when the incumbent, Major-General W. A. K. Fraser, fell ill. Slim, now temporarily promoted to the rank of major-general oversaw the division's advance on Baghdad. He led the division with verve and confidence in Syria and took charge of two armoured brigades in the occupation of Persia in August 1941.[128]

Slim, now recalled from the Middle East, was to take control of all operations in Burma. He realised that there was no quick and easy fix to the Army's problems. The troops needed to be withdrawn from the fighting line to rebuild morale and undertake a protracted period of intensive training in jungle warfare. Such an opportunity, however, was sadly unavailable, and, as the Japanese continued to push forward with energy, 'Burcorps' withdrew north to the flat terrain of central Burma, around the oilfields at Yenangyaung.[129]

Here, 17th Indian Division tried forming a new defensive line on 3 April, but the Japanese launched a three-pronged attack to finish off the British/Chinese forces in Burma. On 10 April, Japanese 33rd Division attacked 'Burcorps' at Yenangyaung; 55th Division attacked up the main road against the Chinese and 56th Division advanced towards the Shan States to cut off the Burma Road (18th Division was in reserve). By 17 April, 1st Burma Division was surrounded at Yenangyaung, forcing it to blow up the oilfields; the division only escaped with the help of a desperate counter-attack by 17th Indian Division. The situation was now clearly beyond recovery and morale was unquestionably 'very low'; the 'inability to stop the general retreat, the lack of any air support, the constant fear of a Japanese roadblock appearing behind them, and the lack of reinforcements all took a toll on survivors of the two divisions'.[130] As Major-General Henry Davies, Slim's chief staff officer put it:

> The complete severance of all contact with homes and families bore very hardly on the spirits of the men. There was no post.

> Not a man in the army received a letter of any sort from the time Rangoon was evacuated until he emerged, months later, in Assam ...
>
> The conditions in which the troops were fighting and living were exceptionally tough. There were no tents nor any shelter from the elements. There were no replacements of clothing or equipment. The men slept on the ground. If it rained, they got wet – and stayed wet until their clothes dried on them. There were no amenities of any sort. Nothing to read, nothing to drink, nothing to smoke. Essentials were also lacking. For instance there was a lamentable absence of salt – all the salt-bearing areas were on the South Burma coast. Men died for the lack of this simple commodity.[131]

On 25 April, India Command decided that 'Burcorps' and the Chinese forces should withdraw from Burma altogether; the defence of India had to take priority. The main body of 'Burcorps' broke contact on 30 April and crossed the River Irrawaddy. The battered remnants of 'Burcorps' arrived at the Imphal Plain in mid-May 1942 ending a nearly 1,000-mile-long fighting retreat, the longest in the history of any British force. It was just in time. On 12 May, the first heavy rain of the monsoon fell, threatening to turn jungle tracks into impassable quagmires and rivers into raging torrents. In a similar vein to Dunkirk and Greece, the Army had been thoroughly defeated, but it survived and would, in due course, fight another day.[132]

The Cost of Failure

The retreat from Burma cost the British and Commonwealth Armies 13,463 casualties, of whom 4,033 were killed or wounded and 9,430 were posted as missing, presumed POWs (70 per cent of the total casualties).[133] In Malaya and Singapore, the British Commonwealth forces suffered 138,708 casualties, of whom more than 130,000 (94 per cent) were POWs.[134] By comparison, the Japanese took Burma at the cost of 2,431 casualties (1,999 of whom were killed) and Malaya and Singapore at the cost of 9,824 casualties, of whom 3,500 were killed. In other words, for the price of 5,500 lives Japan seized the greater part of Britain's Empire in the Far East.[135]

General Henry Pownall, Wavell's Chief of Staff at ABDA Command, wrote in his diary two days before the fall of Singapore, 'we were frankly out-generalled, outwitted and outfought. It is a great disaster, one of the worst in our history, and a great blow to the honour and prestige of the Army. From the beginning to the end of this campaign we have been outmatched by better soldiers.'[136] Brooke came to a similar conclusion; in the wake of the disaster, he wrote to Wavell arguing that 'we are not anything like as tough as we were in the last war ... Our one idea is to look after our comforts and avoid being hurt in any way.' Wavell agreed, blaming the catastrophe in no small measure on a society that produced what appeared to be lacklustre soldiers.[137]

The consequences of these failures were, indeed, immense. By the spring of 1942, the Axis controlled over a third of the population and mineral resources of the world.[138] 'The internal structure of Britain's pre-war system, as well as its ethos and assumptions, had been drastically destabilised by a geopolitical earthquake.'[139] The defeats in France and the Middle and Far East had 'set in motion a rapid, cumulative and irreversible transformation of the pre-war structure of British world power'. Canada had taken 'a long stride towards strategic integration' with the United States when, in August 1940, they agreed the joint planning for the defence of North America at Ogdensburg. Economic integration followed with the Hyde Park agreement of April 1941. The British connection with Canada was now, in a sense, 'limited by a third-party contract'. With the fall of Singapore and the massive build-up of American forces in the Pacific, Australia and New Zealand began to understand that they had now passed from the strategic sphere of the British system into that of the United States.[140] After the loss of *Prince of Wales* and *Repulse* and the rapid retreat in Malaya, John Curtin, the Australian Prime Minister, wrote an article published on the front page of the *Melbourne Herald* warning that Australia's traditional links with Britain might have to be rethought in favour of an American orientation to preserve Australian security.[141] The 'unstinting commitment' of the dominions to an imperial war 'had been based on the assumption that Britain would keep their homelands safe. After 1940–2, that assumption could no longer be made: another great power protector was needed.' Since the late nineteenth century, 'the mutual and unconditional loyalty of the "British" countries had lain at the core of British world power ... 1942 saw the end of this old imperial nexus'. The Empire was finished.[142]

6 THE GREAT IMPERIAL MORALE CRISIS

The Anatomy of Defeat

The well-worn argument that the British and Commonwealth Armies' early setbacks in the Second World War were the consequence of weaknesses in materiel and manpower (the 'guilty men' narrative) has been so conclusively undermined by a number of recent studies that it leaves the historian with a set of complex problems.[1] Britain and her allies were in a sufficiently strong position materially, economically and doctrinally to prevent the disasters that overtook the Empire between 1940 and 1942. The great German offensive in the West, no less than the Japanese 'driving charge' in the East, was 'a one-shot affair', an enormous gamble.[2] Hitler, as much as his generals, could not believe the scale and speed of their success. They had no scheme for what to do next, plans for the invasion of Britain only being confirmed in July 1940 when peace overtures were abruptly rejected.[3] What, therefore, went wrong?

The core of the problem, according to the most recent literature, was that the British Army 'did not desire, or appreciate the need for, a coherent institutional approach to command'; such an imposition 'ran counter to a command culture that prioritised pragmatic individual solutions to tactical problems over any form of centrally mandated process and procedures'.[4] This flexible approach to command was essential, it is accepted, in a far-flung empire where reliance on a single method was unrealistic; much better for commanders to work to a broad set of principles but in essence think for themselves.

In a world war, however, and with a citizen army, it was absolutely unworkable,[5] as the lack of uniform tactical and operational procedures meant methods could vary significantly from formation to formation and teamwork, in the ever-changing order of battle, could suffer. Major-General Raymond Briggs wrote after the war that 'everything was chaotic' as 'when you changed your commander you changed your doctrine'.[6] The historian David French has gone so far as to argue that the lack of a common understanding of command culture 'was the single most important obstacle impeding combined arms co-operation in the British army'.[7]

As authoritative as these sources are, the significance of the failure of the British and Commonwealth Armies to impose a uniform understanding of processes and procedures deserves reconsideration. The challenges faced by the BEF, Middle East Command and Malaya Command all required bespoke solutions, not just at army, corps or divisional levels, but also even at the tactical level. The suggestion that units had to 'do the same thing in the same circumstances' (an approach that this author has referred to elsewhere as the 'tactics narrative') rests on an assumption that standardised approaches to the problems of war were essential for citizen armies to be effective.[8] Such a perspective, however, rarely stands up to systematic analysis. In practice, warfare, at all levels, was a dynamic interactive process where commanders had to constantly balance the means available with the goals handed down to them by superior officers. War was, as it is now, infinitely complex and decisions and activities had to be made in light of constantly shifting and evolving events.[9]

In this context, Wavell, O'Connor, Cunningham, and Ritchie's fluid and flexible battle plans before 'Compass', 'Crusader' and 'Gazala' appear more easy to understand. Confusion in battle and the disruption of plans were so commonplace that they had to be expected as a given and addressed.[10] As S. L. A. Marshall put it, in war 'the unusual is met usually and the abnormal becomes the normal'.[11] If the British and Commonwealth Armies were to truly embrace a devolved system of command and control, army commanders could do little more than clearly express their intent, trust their subordinates' ability to act appropriately and monitor and adapt to the situation as it evolved. In essence, commanders at all levels of the Army had to take responsibility and act 'strategically'. As Sir Lawrence Freedman has argued:

> By and large, strategy comes into play where there is actual or potential conflict, when interests collide and forms of resolution are required. This is why a strategy is much more than a plan. A plan supposes a sequence of events that allows one to move with confidence from one state of affairs to another. Strategy is required when others might frustrate one's plans because they have different and possibly opposing interests and concerns … The inherent unpredictability of human affairs, due to chance events as well as the efforts of opponents and the missteps of friends, provides strategy with its challenge and drama.[12]

Warfare, more than most other endeavours, confounds the plans of belligerents; according to Helmuth von Moltke (the Elder), no plan survives first contact with the enemy.[13] Thus, in all circumstances, military actors have to act strategically, as the input of adversaries can be so devastating to even the best-laid plan, even when all formations in a military organisation understand a plan and are trained to act uniformly in accordance with a plan. Such a perspective does not champion the 'gifted amateur' or encourage a 'making it up as you go along' philosophy.[14] Common principles and language are and were extremely important, and indeed they existed in the body of the *Field Service Regulations* (*FSR*). Nevertheless, the best that British and Commonwealth commanders could do, as Clausewitz argued in *On War*, was to recognise the components of each military problem at each level of war and manage and balance them appropriately in each scenario faced; that is to say, behave strategically.[15] As Clausewitz wrote:

> Theory cannot equip the mind with formulas for solving problems, nor can it mark the narrow path on which the sole solution is supposed to lie by planting a hedge of principles on either side. But it can give the mind insight into the great mass of phenomena and of their relationships, then leave it free to rise into the higher realms of action.[16]

The British and Commonwealth Armies' rather irreverent attitude to common tactical and operational procedures was not, therefore, the fundamental problem identified in much of the literature, but an approach and philosophy not wholly inappropriate when the nature of war is taken into consideration. It also created, as a direct, and, in fact, intended consequence, 'a seasoned body' of 'officers who sought to use their own independent judgement in battle, and expected to apply it within their own sphere of command'.[17] This could again be seen as an appropriate approach and outcome when the character of modern warfare, and especially the fighting in France, the Middle East and the Far East is considered. War in those environments placed enormous responsibility and stress on junior and middle-ranking officers. Timothy Moreman has argued in the context of Malaya and Burma that:

> As a result of the dispersion and difficulties exercising command and control inherent in jungle fighting, due to dense foliage and limited visibility, responsibility devolved down the chain of command and rested on the shoulders of company and platoon commanders and NCOs, as well as the ordinary infantryman who often fought out of sight and supervision of his immediate superiors. A premium was placed on individual aggressiveness, mobility and personal skills and the proficiency of individuals and sub-units, rather than at battalion and brigade level. An extremely fit, highly trained and self-reliant infantryman, possessing considerable initiative, emerged as a key requirement for victory given the prevalence of close quarter combat.[18]

There does appear, therefore, to be a disconnect between the frequent contention in the literature on the British and Commonwealth Armies in the Second World War that military success depended upon the imposition of common tactical and operational procedures and the argument, equally forcefully made, that devolved command, control and responsibility was essential for successful operations in the fast-moving, fluid battles of 1940 to 1942. Standardised approaches would have made sense, perhaps, under a centralised command-and-control arrangement, where commanders sought to control, constrain and direct behaviours, but this was not the approach followed by the British and Commonwealth Armies in the first half of the war (see Chapter 1). As Patrick Rose has argued in relation to North Africa, 'the operation of a rigid and hierarchical system of command that limited the role of subordinates, rendering them unable to exercise initiative or command in their own right, was little evident at brigade, division and corps level'.[19] The goal was, thus, not that everyone did the same thing in the same circumstances, but that commanders did the right thing in each circumstance. It was the failure of the British and Commonwealth

Armies to behave thus, not the lack of a common implementation of doctrine, that was its undoing in France, North Africa, Malaya and Burma.

The question that necessarily arises out of this understanding is why did the British and Commonwealth Armies fail to take advantage of what was an essentially sophisticated and appropriate approach to the challenges of modern warfare? The evidence presented in this book suggests two key interrelated reasons for this failure. The first was the need for high-quality and effective training. The 'laissez-faire' doctrine in the British Army asked a lot of the men who were tasked with adapting to, controlling and conquering the vast array of challenges they might face in a battle environment. In order to meet these challenges, all officers and men had to be superbly trained. This, however, was rarely the case for most of 1940, 1941 and 1942, as the troops who fought in Europe, North Africa (with the possible exception of 'Compass') and the Far East were handicapped by a training regime that was inadequately prepared for war. As one historian has put it, 'not only should it not be surprising but it should also be forgivable if troops sent into the ... fray in 1941 and 1942 lacked the full range of professional tactical skills one should expect in fully trained career soldiers'.[20]

The British Army, as a whole, increased its numbers on an enormous scale following the declaration of war in September 1939.[21] By June 1941, its fully trained cadre of regular soldiers made up at most just over 10 per cent of the forces available.[22] Almost all of the Australian, Canadian, New Zealand and South African soldiers, that began to swell the numbers of the British and Commonwealth forces early in 1941, were amateurs. The Indian Army, which experienced a tenfold expansion over the course of the war,[23] had 'milked' or 'bled' regular units of their trained officers, NCOs and men to provide a nucleus around which new units could be formed. As Major-General James Elliot, Director of Military Training in India from 1942 to 1943, later explained:

> A Colonel might think himself lucky if he had two pre-war officers besides himself; and of the new entry one or two would still be wrestling with the language their men spoke; half the V.C.O.s [Viceroy's Commissioned Officers] and

> N.C.O.s [Non-Commissioned Officers] would be recently promoted; and more than half the men would be recruits with less than a year's service.[24]

It was close to impossible to turn these newly raised forces into highly trained armies overnight. The War Office in the UK faced chronic shortages in 'equipment, accommodation, ammunition, and land for training' due to the understandable fact that 'priority was given to field force units rather than to the training organization'. It was not until March 1942, 'with the opening of battle-training areas on the South Downs, that Home Forces had sufficient land for a whole brigade to exercise with live ammunition and air support'.[25] There were also problems with a paucity of skilled instructors, the dispersal of billets, 'which made collective training difficult to organize', the wholesale conversion of units from one arm of service to another, 'which meant that troops who had just mastered one set of skills had to begin to acquire another set from scratch', and the requirements of home defence which 'consumed time that might have been spent in field training'.[26]

Similar problems were faced in India and the Dominions. The training time given to Emergency Commissioned Officers (ECOs), both British and Indian, 'was drastically shortened from the normal schedule as a result of wartime expansion'. Before the war, British officers received eighteen months of training at Sandhurst and Indian officers thirty months at Dehra Dun. Both British and Indian officers would then receive a further year of training in a battalion before being posted to take up their commission. But, with the outbreak of war, ECOs received only four to six months of training at officer training schools in India. When an officer was subsequently posted to a battalion or regiment, his instruction continued, 'at least in theory'.[27]

Shortening the training time also affected the way that officers learned Urdu (a version of Hindustani), the language of the Indian Army. All commands to NCOs and men were traditionally given through this medium. Before the war, instruction for officers involved a year of training with a personal *munshi*, or language teacher. At the end of this period, the officer had to pass an exam and earn a certificate. Wartime conditions meant that instruction in the *lingua franca* of the Indian Army 'was seriously curtailed', which 'in practice meant that, at least at first, neither British nor Indian officers had sufficient knowledge of the language of command to give orders'.[28]

Matters were little different in the armies of the Antipodes; a 6th Australian Division report, written in July 1941, pointed out that 'generally' the standard of training fell 'far short of what we are looking for'. Many recruits had 'fired as few as 5–10 rounds' in training in Australia before they came overseas.[29] In South Africa, numerous units were faced with so many shortages (in transport and equipment) that they were unable to begin any serious military training at all.[30] The War Office was forced to admit that the best it could do under these circumstances was to try and ensure that formations were 'supplied with the latest tactical lessons and general information' from the theatres of war to which they might be posted. This would 'enable them to make a special study of the fighting in such areas'.[31] This solution, however, was limited by the exigencies of security and the quality of the information provided. In general, formations were rarely given much warning whether they were being sent to Egypt, India or Burma. This made a realistic training programme, specific to a particular theatre, all the harder to implement. An officer wrote, in 1942, for example, that 'although we saw regular pamphlets about the German Army', his Brigade's knowledge of fighting in the desert was 'extremely poor' as these pamphlets 'gave little idea of the actuality' of combat in North Africa. Tank troops, fresh from England, were often sent into battle without knowledge of how to find a hull-down position in the small folds of ground in the desert, or without training in how to cope with dust clouds or how to navigate properly in the prevailing conditions. There was a general perception within Middle East Command that the level of training received by units from the United Kingdom was insufficient and inappropriate for desert conditions.[32]

As a consequence, training, in many ways, became the remit of commanders in theatre. In the West, a 'laissez-faire' doctrine was often confused with a necessity also to devolve responsibility when it came to training. While senior officers seemed to fully understand the fundamental importance of training, too many 'failed to translate' that realisation into meaningful action.[33] A similar narrative is apparent in an assessment of the war against Japan in Malaya, where undoubtedly the key criticism has been in relation to training.[34] In spite of all the difficulties faced in the Far East, it is hard to avoid the conclusion that when given the freedom to manage training as they saw fit, too many commanders inexcusably failed to prepare their men adequately. This led to a 'slowness in appreciation, decision and action in a war whose tempo was extreme'.[35] There was, according to Lieutenant-Colonel Ian Stewart, the Commanding Officer (CO) of the 2nd Argyll and Sutherland Highlanders, one of the 'few battalions' to emerge from Malaya 'having added to its reputation', only 'one way to practical efficiency, namely continual practice under realistic conditions'. This applied to commanders, staffs and services as well as to units. Training was, in line with the doctrine of the time, supposed to make people 'capable of meeting unexpected problems and environments, so that they may never be either physically or emotionally surprised'.[36] The jungle environment, much like the deserts of North Africa, presented a singular challenge to armies. 'The only solution' to overcoming these trials was to hold 'frequent exercises under active service conditions' to prepare for what was to come.[37] Under the pressures of a rapid expansion, and inadequate time and facilities, this clearly did not happen. In this sense, at least, the problem was not with what appears to have been a sensible doctrine, but that units were not prepared properly to operationalise the precepts of that same doctrine.

The second key influence on success and failure in the early years of the war was the requirement for junior officers and their men to win the battle of wills at the tactical level. British officers, NCOs and other ranks were expected to be extremely practical with high levels of determination, creativity and imagination. Because 'unforeseen circumstances' always arose in war,[38] the soldier, as the 1934 Training Regulations pointed out, was required to 'be intelligent, adaptable, and capable of acting on his own initiative'.[39] Individual initiative, however, was to a large extent a function of military morale. 'Military Training Pamphlet No. 1 (India): Armoured Units in the Field, Characteristics, Roles and Handling of Armoured Divisions 1941' noted for instance that:

> Initiative is largely a state of mind, psychological. It is retained by commanders and troops who refuse to take counsel of fears or to conform to enemy action; and who seek and make opportunity to surprise and inflict loss on the enemy, and to impose their will on him.[40]

Once battle began, matters were typically in the hands of junior officers and troops, and all too often in the early years of the war, these men failed to defeat the enemy in tactical actions that eventually accumulated into operational and strategic setbacks.

The apparent inability of field commanders to control battles in this period, which has often been blamed on deficient communications and command-and-control systems, was to a great degree the consequence of the behaviour of the troops. If British and Commonwealth commanders appeared to be slower, less decisive and time-poor compared to their German and Japanese equivalents, it was because they genuinely had less time than their opponents. Whereas British offensives might be held up for seconds, minutes, hours or days by determined local resistance, providing German and Japanese commanders with time to react and save the situation, too often, between 1940 and 1942, British and Commonwealth units at the tactical level melted away in the face of Axis assaults. Great battles, decided usually by fine margins, hinged on the willingness of small groups of individuals to fight with determination and, if necessary, sell their lives dearly. It was only in these circumstances that commanders could truly seek to 'control' and influence events.

The Bartholomew Report into the causes of the defeat in France, the censorship summaries, sickness, battle exhaustion, desertion/AWOL and POW rates from North Africa and report after report on the causes of the Malayan debacle, could not have been clearer on the centrality of morale to the setbacks suffered. Percival wrote in the midst of the Malayan disaster, in 'Operational Instruction No. 30', 6 January 1942, that the Japanese Army was 'an Army of gangsters, relying for success more on weakening the morale of the troops than on any particular skill with his weapons'.[41] Whatever the hyperbole of his assessment, it was a fair summary of the impact of Japanese methods on the fighting efficiency of the British and Commonwealth troops. Bennett, in a similar vein, pointed out after the defeat that 'leadership, especially on the part of Junior leaders' had 'lacked the offensive spirit'.[42] He noted that many 'units were quite valueless as fighting troops. They were unable to stand against even the slightest pressure and they frequently withdrew in a disorganised body of their own volition. This applied mainly to the tired Indian units whose Commanders openly admitted ... could not be relied upon.' Bennett went so far as to state that 'the very low morale displayed by the Indian troops throughout this campaign was the most important influence responsible for the failure to hold Malaya'. Over and over again, he said, 'the slightest opposition was allowed to check an advance, the slightest threat bringing about a retirement. Very often the "threat" was more imaginary than real. Having started retreating the rearward move gained momentum, the "step back" soon became a long stride back, unnecessarily.'[43]

Stewart wrote in December 1942 that there had been 'no fire in any British or Indian troops of any rank' in Malaya. By contrast, the Japanese soldier was:

> Eager though fanatical. He was quite ready to be killed, our men were not. As a result he was aggressive. We were passive he was daring, mobile, quick and mentally alert for somebody was ready to go in front and be the first to buy it; we were cautious, static and ineffective.[44]

He pointed to an 'extraordinary apathy, almost the lethargy-making influence that a weasel has on a rabbit'. Officers and men had been 'less keen and much less efficient than on training' and 'reserves of emotional energy' had been 'much less than anticipated'.[45] As the Cameron Report on the experience of 17th Indian Division, probably the 'most detailed source of tactical and administrative lessons learnt from the retreat from Burma', noted, 'nothing of tactical theory will avail' if 'guts are lacking' in our fighting in the East.[46]

In a similar vein, at Gazala, unlike 'Crusader', junior officers and their men failed to demonstrate the ingenuity and determination to wear the *Panzerarmee* down. Brigade boxes surrounded by Axis forces chose to retreat or surrender rather than fight it out. The 'brave to the point of foolhardiness'[47] behaviour of the armoured regiments in 'Crusader' was not repeated at Gazala as the armour had lost confidence in their ability to fight the enemy with equal weapons on equal terms.[48] Brigadier H. E. Pyman, who had been a staff officer in 7th Armoured Division, spoke of the trust he and others had in the Army's 'spirited' armoured commanders before the Gazala fighting. Such feeling had however evaporated by July, at which time 'confidence between the leaders and the led, from the highest level downwards, was sadly lacking'.[49]

The crux of the problem was that between 1940 and 1942, the British Empire, a socio-political system that had been built largely on the ingenuity and energy of 'private enthusiasts in search of wealth, virtue or religious redemption',[50] was dependent, for the second time in a generation, on an unprecedented mass mobilisation of its citizens and subjects (see Chapter 2). When all else failed, ministers and generals hoped to be 'rescued by the "poor bloody infantry"'. From the beginning of the campaign in the Far East, for example, British resources were stretched due to the fact that they were already engaged in Europe and in the Middle East. The Commonwealth forces could no longer rely on the arrival of the Royal Navy (the basis of the Singapore strategy during the interwar years). In the air, the Japanese enjoyed almost complete superiority. The desire to hold the naval base on Singapore Island left very little room for manoeuvre at the operational level; Japanese forces had to be engaged as far north as possible in order to prevent the capture of air bases from which Japanese bombers could raid the Island. Thus, the Army was forced to fight on ground that it would not necessarily have chosen if given a free hand. There were only two ways, therefore, to fundamentally influence the strategic calculus. London could either change policy and allow Percival to abandon Singapore, thus authorising him to fight the campaign as he saw fit, carrying with it enormous political risks given the repeated assurances regarding Singapore made before the war; or, London could rely on the British and Commonwealth soldiers to fight and buy time for the promised reinforcements.[51]

As the Government 'did not want to drink political poison', the fate of Singapore was ultimately left in the hands of the bottom link of the strategic chain, the men at the sharp end.[52] From Churchill to Wavell to Percival, those in charge of strategy were convinced that ordinary English, Welsh, Scots, Irish, Australians and Indians would fight with the required determination and intensity to save the Empire. This was the key assumption, or understanding, that drove strategy during much of the first half of the war. It was recognised that in a newly raised citizen army the men would be poorly trained. It was comprehended that in some cases they were not provisioned with the theoretically ideal scale or quality of materiel. But, it was expected, in this great crisis, the 'great crisis of Empire', that in spite of these drawbacks they would rise to the challenge.[53]

When they did not, the fundamental disconnect in British and Commonwealth strategy was laid bare. Brooke wrote in his diary on 18 February, three days after the surrender of Singapore, 'cannot work out why troops are not fighting better. If the army cannot fight better than it is doing at present we shall deserve to lose our Empire!'[54] One of Churchill's close friends and confidents, Lady Violet Bonham Carter, related that 'for the first time in their long friendship she had found him depressed ... underneath it all was a dreadful fear, she felt, that our soldiers are not as good fighters as their fathers were'. 'In 1915', said Winston, 'our men fought on even when they had only one shell left and were under a fierce barrage. Now they cannot resist dive bombers. We have so many men, in Singapore, so many men – they should have done better.'[55] Why did they display what appeared to have been less determination and motivation than their predecessors in the First World War?

Morale Crisis

An individual's fighting morale is influenced by a complex range of multidimensional factors that can be grouped into two broad categories; these have been termed endogenous factors (primarily focused within the military organisation) and exogenous factors (primarily associated with issues broadly outside of the control of the military organisation).[56] Tarak Barkawi has referred to these categories as the 'organisational' and 'societal' views on combat motivation while Anthony King has captured these ideas in the concepts of 'masculine honour' and 'patriotic duty'.[57]

There can be no doubt, however, that since 1945, the 'endogenous' view, which focuses on the design and quality of military institutions, has dominated the literature on what maintains morale in modern war. In particular, primary group theory has become a catch-all explanation for combat motivation.[58] Primary group theory stresses 'that men fight not for a higher cause but for their "mates" and "buddies", bound by war in a relationship which ... can achieve great intensity'.[59]

For the British and Commonwealth Armies in the Second World War, like all armies in all conflicts, 'the effectiveness of primary group loyalty' in persuading men to fight depended 'on the human stability of each primary group and the fact that leaders and men knew each other intimately'. Heavy casualties sustained over a brief period made it difficult to sustain such relationships.[60] In assessing the effect of casualties on front-line units during the war, J. H. A. Sparrow, who was responsible for compiling the Army morale reports, made it very clear that junior officers within the British Army were 'always handicapped' by 'heavy casualties, a rapid turnover of men, and reinforcements from strange units – which prevented [them] from getting to know [their] men'.[61] For example, in relation to Malaya:

> When the handful of trained and experienced officers – the framework of the 'family' atmosphere pervading Indian regiments and often the focus of individual loyalty – were killed, without good junior leaders providing effective command and stiffening morale cohesion was fragile at best. Instead of counter-attacking or immediately trying to rejoin, many Indian units rapidly disintegrated and scattered into the jungle. Few of the young, immature and inexperienced individual soldiers were sufficiently resourceful, self-reliant or had the initiative to escape.[62]

The problem with using primary group loyalties as a tool to explain fluctuations in morale and cohesion in battle, however, is that victorious battles were often as dear in terms of casualties as defeats. For example, perhaps two-fifths of the British infantrymen who fought in the front line during Operation 'Crusader' were casualties. South African infantry casualties during 'Crusader' were about 43 per cent while New Zealand infantry casualties during the same operation were as high as perhaps 81 per cent. Overall, between December 1940 and November 1942, 2nd New Zealand Division suffered a casualty rate among its front-line infantry units perhaps as high as 300 per cent. Casualties were no less extreme for the armoured units engaged in 'Crusader' and around half of the crews that fought during the operation suffered some disruption to their primary group.[63]

Of the other endogenous factors that are known to influence combat motivation, leadership and training have also received a considerable amount of attention in the literature.[64] In September 1939, there were 53,500 officers in the British Army. By October 1941, this number had more than doubled to 136,500 officers. However, the army list had comprised only 13,800 regular officers in September 1939; the rest had been made up of territorials and reserves who all required a significant amount of further training. By October 1941, therefore, at most 10 per cent of serving officers had been regulars at the outbreak of war. 'The vast majority of regimental officers during the Second World War had ... been civilians in 1939 and the wartime officer corps was composed overwhelmingly of amateur soldiers.'[65] This massive increase in both manpower and training requirements for the officer corps put a great strain on the capacity of the Army to deliver the appropriate level of quality leadership. To exacerbate the problem, many of the best officer candidates, just like many of the best other ranks, were drawn into the RAF and Royal Navy. The War Office, as Sparrow wrote after the war, 'had to work on the material that came to its hand and of this, it is enough to say that the shortage of good officer material was perhaps the gravest of all the enemies to military morale'.[66]

In early 1942, reports reached the War Office that officers in field units were struggling to cope with the challenges of military leadership.[67] In the desert, Auchinleck wrote of the extent of 'criticism of officers in the letters of other ranks'.[68] The field censorship summary for 5 to 11 March 1942 admitted that it could not 'be denied that criticism of the ability and enterprise of officers both in the field and at the base is increasing'.[69] The censorship summary for 8 to 14 July 1942 pointed out that 'many officers fail to inspire confidence in their men'.[70] A 1st South African Division memorandum, written in August 1942, on the 'Morale of SA troops in the Middle East', highlighted that the problem of inefficient officers was a 'theme of endless discussion' among the men.[71] Similar problems were evident in the Australian Imperial Force (AIF). A report submitted by 6th Australian Division, in 1941, pointed out that there was 'a general criticism throughout th[e] division' that officers arriving in the Middle East were 'very poorly trained'.[72] The Commander-in-Chief (C-in-C) Home Forces noted when referring to the death penalty debate in August 1942, that the solution to the problems being faced in the desert lay principally 'in the training of a corps of officers, whose efficiency, example and instinctive interest in their work and the troops would compel the respect of the men'.[73]

The Ideological Deficit

It appears that the performance of the British and Commonwealth troops in the early years of the war was undermined by a training regime that inadequately prepared both leaders and men for the challenges of modern war. In combat, they were often members of highly unstable primary groups and were expected to fight under junior officers who often exhibited poor leadership skills. These deficiencies had a negative impact on the tactical proficiency of the troops, but also, importantly, on their will to fight.[74]

Undertrained, poorly led troops, who were denied the support of effective primary groups, could, however, still perform well in battle if highly motivated. Russian units, for example, in a process called 'front mobilisation', would often 'shanghai' civilians into their formations in the midst of active operations. These men were not sent to reserve regiments for training but were clothed, armed and usually sent into battle woefully underprepared. Such units rarely produced sophisticated or efficient military performance at the tactical level, and they usually suffered appalling casualties, but their willingness to fight, usually as a consequence of coercion or ideological conviction, produced incremental gains at the tactical level that eventually converted into operational-level success.[75] Undertrained German units also demonstrated extraordinary cohesion in the final years of the war. As Robert Rush has argued:

> Most German infantry regiments during 1944 did not have much time to train before being committed to combat, but even in the early years of the war many units had only very short training periods before being dispatched to the front. The twenty Regular Army regiments of the 100,000-man *Reichheer* split three times before 1939 to form new organizations, and those formed after 1939 generally had from one to six months of training from inception to entry into combat.[76]

It is not unreasonable to suggest that had untrained and poorly organised British soldiers had to fight on the cliffs of Dover in 1940 or 1941, they too might have fought with desperate and selfless intensity (much as the RAF did in the Battle of Britain). Indeed, on 26 May 1940, the Chiefs of Staff pondering the possibilities of defeat in France and an invasion of Britain, concluded that 'the real test' to come was 'whether the morale of our fighting personnel and civil population' would 'counter balance the numerical and material advantages which Germany enjoys'. They concluded unequivocally, in spite of all the challenges facing the British Army, 'we believe it will'.[77]

In the absence of a recourse to coercion, commanders in the field failed on four occasions during the war to persuade their political masters to restore the death penalty for desertion and cowardice in the face of the enemy,[78] it does appear that much rested on the relationship between the soldier, the cause for which he was fighting, the state and the home front. In a citizen army, it did matter enormously that men should, as Cromwell said, know what they fight for and love what they know.[79] However, for much of the early years of the war, the British and

Commonwealth soldier appeared to either not know the cause he was fighting for or he was too disillusioned to care. This kind of attitude was, in opinion of H. Willans, the Director-General of Welfare and Education at the War Office, 'liable in times of pressure to transform a retreat into a rout or a setback into a disaster'.[80] Glyn Prysor has noted with regards to France in 1940, for example, that:

> When examining the accounts of British servicemen, it becomes clear that over the course of the campaign a profound, if abstruse, mentality grew among the soldiers. It was a sense of disillusionment: with themselves, with their army, with their allies and with their leaders. It was a distinct, though often implicit, sense of betrayal.[81]

If there was 'a defining characteristic of the shared experience of all British servicemen who took part in the retreat in 1940', it was 'the almost overwhelming sense of isolation from everything except one's immediate comrades or, in some cases, everyone except oneself'. Many British soldiers felt that they were 'essentially alone'. It is striking that the accounts given by those who experienced the campaign in France often evoke not a nation united in a common cause, but 'a decidedly solitary experience'.[82]

'Middle East Training Pamphlet No. 10', which dealt with the lessons from Operation 'Compass', December 1940 to February 1941, described the dangers of such a mentality:

> The maintenance of discipline on active service was difficult enough when troops fought and moved in close order. In modern war … wide frontages and great dispersion prevent close control of individuals by their superiors. Instead, the individual must discipline himself and this is only possible where the individual has learnt to understand and respect the cause for which he fights and to take pride in his army, his unit and himself. Where these incentives are lacking, lamentable things happen which bring disgrace on our cause and may expose the Army to a dangerous reverse.[83]

By July 1941, after the disasters in Norway and France, with the Western Desert Force having been routed from Cyrenaica and having suffered two defeats in its attempts to recapture the territory lost, it seemed to the War Office that British morale was not resolute enough to stand up to the trials of modern warfare against a politically indoctrinated foe. The censorship summaries from the desert reported, in the spring and summer of 1941, that the army was thoroughly 'browned off', bored and lacking in any personal commitment to the war. P. J. Grigg, the future Secretary of State for War, noted that spring that the majority of soldiers were 'listless and lazy', doing 'what was absolutely required of them but nothing more ... civilians in khaki' in the worst sense of the term.[84]

In many ways, Grigg was right, but this ideological deficit was not the result of an inherent disregard for politics and the world around them; many soldiers were crying out for a cause for which they deemed it worth fighting. In the early years of the war, it was possible to discern both a yearning for political engagement and a palpable sense of frustration with, and alienation from, the state that was supposed to provide meaning to the men's sacrifices. It must not be forgotten, for example, that even as late as April 1940, over 1 million people were still unemployed in the United Kingdom.[85]

It was only after the battle of France, as a genuine threat to national survival emerged, that this desire to imbue the war with a greater meaning began to take coherent form in the public discourse. A much-quoted *Times* leader reflected in July 1940:

> If we speak of democracy, we do not mean a democracy which maintains the right to vote but forgets the right to work and the right to live. If we speak of freedom, we do not mean a rugged individualism which excludes social organisation and economic planning. If we speak of equality we do not mean a political equality nullified by social and economic privilege. If we speak of economic reconstruction, we think less of maximum production (though this too will be required) than of equitable distribution.[86]

The crisis of 1940 was much more than a military crisis; it was a 'political-military crisis'.[87] It had the effect of undoing Conservative dominance in Parliament, but also 'of radicalizing much of the population'. Before May 1940, little had been asked of the British people by the state; as a consequence, 'little was given' in return. From that moment, however, 'attitudes changed'. In the weeks following Dunkirk, 'Home Intelligence reported strong support generally for state direction and intervention, if only to guarantee equality of sacrifice.'[88] This led to

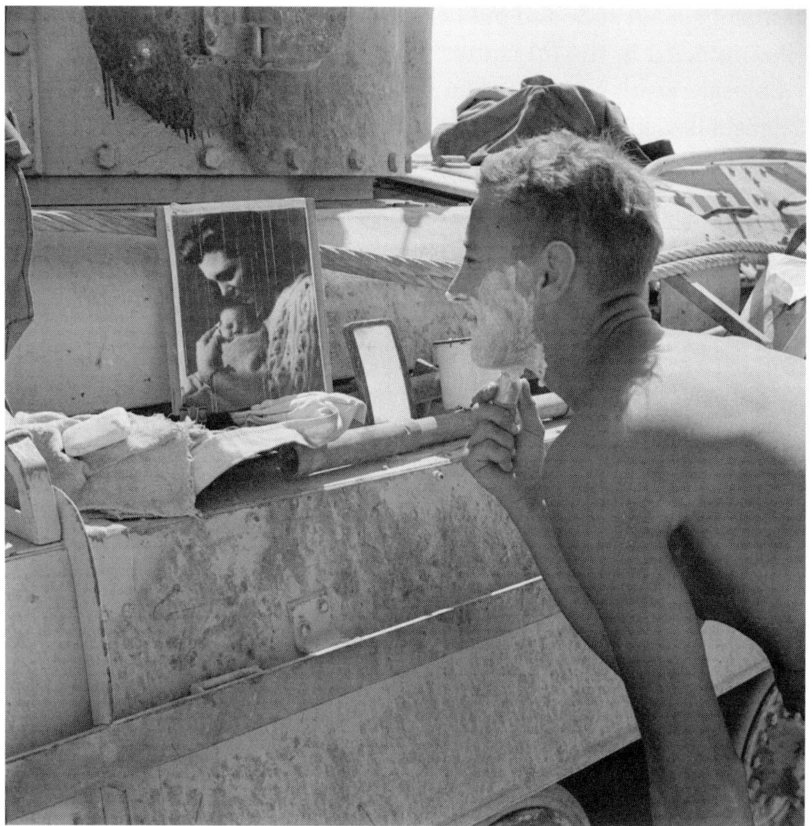

Illustration 6.1 A soldier of 50th Battalion, Royal Tank Regiment, shaving beside his Valentine tank, October 1942. The manner in which the individual, the home front and the state interacted, had a big impact on the morale of the troops, and, therefore, the performance of the British and Commonwealth Armies in the Second World War.

a redrawing of the political landscape in Britain,[89] and entreaties that individuals should put the community's interests and needs above their own became widespread.[90] Herbert Morrison, the Minister of Supply, called for workers to 'Go To It', moving to seven-day-a-week working and giving up their Whit holidays in order to:

> work our fingers to the bone for our sons and their future. We are going to do whatever lies in our power to match, and to be worthy of, the sacrifices that are being made for us. We are going to cut down our leisure, cut down our comfort, blot out of our thought every private and sectional aim.[91]

These shifts in attitude and public opinion on the home front have been well chronicled in the literature,[92] but little is known about how this ideological awaking impacted on the troops and their behaviour on the battlefield (see Illustration 6.1).[93]

The British Army

As the war progressed, military morale reports began to point both to the emergence of political feelings as a consequence of the war and to the fundamental need for the Army and the Government to fill the ideological vacuum that was so clearly undermining the morale of the troops. The report for February to May 1942, a period that included both the fall of Singapore and the initial setbacks at Gazala in the desert, noted that 'certainty of employment in what they consider satisfactory conditions is the nearest thing to a "war aim" that most soldiers can be said to have at the moment. Vague assurances from politicians or others, and exhortations to join in a "crusade", do not reassure them on this point.' Commanders' reports confirmed 'that a very large proportion of the rank and file' were 'preoccupied by the question of what, if any, social and economic changes will take place after the war'. The vast array of setbacks and problems faced in the early years of the war were blamed on 'the whole of "the existing system"' and an 'increasingly large number of soldiers' expressed 'resolve that the system must be different "after the war"'. Such reflections, according to the writers of the report, were 'too frequent to be dismissed as the stock complaints of the professional "grouser" or the amateur politician'.[94]

It is here that one begins to grasp the futility of Wavell and Percival's exhortations to the troops at Singapore. The men had no interest in fighting a 'crusade' for the Empire. As the historian Bernard Porter has argued, British people, and the working classes in particular (who made up a very large portion of the Army), felt little attachment to the Empire. While there is little doubt that there was some affection for and interest in the Dominions, not least because of family connections, a Gallup Poll carried out in November 1939 showed that 77 per cent of respondents thought that India should be granted independence soon; 26 per cent felt that this should happen during the war, 51 per cent just after the war.[95] The first 'proper' survey of attitudes to Empire was carried out by the Colonial Office in 1948. The survey of 1,921 people from all classes, showed that most 'were both ignorant of the empire, and not particularly enamoured of it'. It found, for example, that 75 per cent of respondents were unaware of the distinction between a colony and a dominion, that 49 per cent could not name a single colony, and that 3 per cent believed that the United States was still a colony of the British Empire. A mere 4 per cent reckoned that they had any kind of 'connection' with the colonies.[96] If the wartime Army mirrored the attitudes expressed in the post-war poll, and there is nothing to suggest that it did not, instead of itching to fight for the Empire, British soldiers had little interest in it. As shall become clear, what they were interested in was change at home, change in the social and economic realities that governed their everyday existence.

The Morale Report for May to July 1942, a period encompassing the fall of Tobruk and a month of prolonged fighting on the El Alamein line, addressed the multiple interlinking factors that engendered these attitudes and were producing 'some cause for concern' among military authorities. The Army at home, training for the Second Front, was particularly 'bored and "browned off"'. Those stationed and training in the UK were keen for 'activity', but this was not manifested in a desire for action, or as the report put it, 'clamour for a Second Front'. With regards to the Army overseas, in a section that was ultimately deleted from the final report, it was noted that 'the full effects' of the fighting of the past few months were 'only now beginning to make themselves felt, and that the prospect, not of defeat, but of a long war and a delay of perhaps years before the M.E.F. [Middle East Forces] will get home, is beginning to produce apathy and even despondency'.[97]

In attempting to explain this poor morale, the report referred to a lack of self-respect among the troops. This was caused by a sense of inequality, both of sacrifice and of pay. The report concluded:

> Every available source ... shows that the subject of pay and allowances baulks very large in soldiers' minds. It is by far the most frequent subject of the letters and inquiries addressed to the newspapers and the B.B.C. by soldiers and their families, and practically every Commander's report presses the soldiers' claim for an increase in pay or allowances or both. The topic is thrown into prominence by the contrast between the soldiers' rate of pay and
>
> (i) the remuneration of munition workers, building trade workers, and civil workers generally;

(ii) the pay of U.S. and Dominion troops, and
(iii) the pay of the R.A.F.[98]

Indeed, an ordinary private soldier in early 1942 earned 17s 6d a week. At the same time, workers in the metal, engineering and shipbuilding trades might bring home almost £6. 'Even taking into account the fact that soldiers did not have to pay for their own food and lodging, this still left them with less than half the disposable income that they might have had if they had remained on civvy street.'[99]

Many of the men, for the duration of the war, sent home large portions of their pay to support their loved ones.[100] It was not uncommon for men in the desert to send home items such as food and cigarettes as well[101] or to encourage wives to work in the war economy to support themselves. This upset those who felt that their sacrifice was enough for the whole family. One man in 1st Army Tank Brigade wrote to his wife, 'I do hope you like being back at work again but when I think that such a step was made necessary because the miserable pittance allowed by the Army is not sufficient to keep you and John going, I feel like getting up and hitting somebody's head off. It's b … y disgusting and the more I think about it the worse I feel. To say the least it can hardly be said to encourage any feeling of patriotism.'[102]

The Morale Report pointed out that 'many soldiers' were not able to provide their families with the 'necessaries of life at the present cost of living' and it was 'generally accepted as *axiomatic* that a private soldier's wife with children in an urban area who had no resources other than his pay and allowances simply could not manage'.[103] The censors in the desert noted that 'one has only to recall the important part played by similar fears in the decay of German front-line morale in 1918 to realise how important it is that troops serving overseas should be convinced' that their loved ones at home were okay.[104] Additionally, commanders' reports suggested, and censorship reviews confirmed, that wives 'frequently' tried to 'dissuade their husbands from accepting promotion on the grounds that any resulting increase in their pay will involve a corresponding decrease in the amount of the grant [to families]'. This meant that many men were reluctant to take commissions, the report pointing out that this dynamic was 'wide-spread' in the Army.

'The average soldier's attitude towards his military and political leaders' was also a problem; it was not influenced by newspaper campaigns or subversive tendencies but by what the Morale Report referred to as 'a lack of solidarity':

> To judge by the tone of his letters, the ordinary soldier does not fully identify himself with the Army; he looks with detachment upon it and those who control it, and thinks of those in authority, whether political or military, as his governors rather than as his leaders. The morale and fighting spirit of the Army as a whole would be enhanced if the ordinary soldier could be reassured that differentiations due to social tradition and the subordination involved in military discipline do not imply a fundamental conflict of interests. Anything, on the other hand, that strengthens his belief in the existence of a fundamental gulf or barrier between himself and his leaders has an immediate and marked adverse effect on morale.[105]

The report continued that where soldiers perceived or experienced inequality or unfairness, it usually resulted in 'an outburst of political reflections' such as 'references to capitalism, democracy, Russia, and the like', even among 'men who do not seem to be by nature politically minded'.[106] Other reports also recounted that there was a notable 'demoralising effect' when soldiers were left feeling a sense of 'unfairness', 'inequality' or 'injustice'. These feelings, since they were concerned with the whole sense of 'justice', had a 'particularly strong bearing on the attitude of the troops towards their own leaders'.[107] As the May to July Morale Report pointed out, 'there is nothing to suggest that political feeling creates a discontented atmosphere in units' but that 'there is much to suggest that discontent ... creates political feeling'.[108]

Closely connected with the foregoing, was the question of war aims. The May to July 1942 Morale Report confirmed again that 'the nearest thing' that the ordinary soldier had to a conscious 'war aim' was 'to make sure that he will have a home and a job and what he regards as a fair deal after the war'. The experience of the First World War generation had taught men 'to be sceptical of easy promises and high-sounding assurances in this matter'. But the report made it clear that men did 'crave for an assurance that those who control affairs have his interests at heart and are planning for the realisation of this aim'. One man wrote:

> The men ... are interested, above all, in the position of labour ... after the war ... If only we could get rid of the firmly planted idea that ... the soldiers are going to return to unemployment and the wretched conditions of 1920–39, then there would not be the faintest need to worry about morale. That is the one lurking, disturbing thought in the men's minds; otherwise they are all for fighting this war quietly and effectively and getting fascism down once and for all.[109]

An officer wrote describing a debate held by a unit in Iraq during the same period:

> Evident in the debate was a fear of unemployment and insecurity after the war, and a distrust of there being any radical changes. I feel that if the Government outlined plainly reforms in education and industrial control and a possible method of seeing that demobilised men in the Army were given employment, a great strengthening of morale would be given to the men out here.[110]

Another soldier wrote, 'take it from me it will be the same story too after this war as it was after the last one. All the plum jobs etc., will be plucked before we get home. If I could believe that things would be better after this war than they were pre-war, I wouldn't mind putting up with all this.'[111]

The significance of these issues was not lost on those at the highest level. 'Attlee remained convinced that "practical socialism" was not only an absolute good but also essential to win the war.' As early as July 1940, he began pressing for:

> A definite pronouncement on ... policy for the future. The Germans are fighting a revolutionary war for very definite objectives. We are fighting a conservative war and our objects are purely negative. We must put forward a positive and revolutionary aim admitting that the old order has collapsed and asking people to fight for the new order.[112]

A post-war Britain was 'too controversial a topic', however, for the new Coalition to agree on. 'Socialism was the sticking point.' The Conservatives could just about get behind a commitment that 'the abuses of the past' should 'not be allowed to reappear'. 'Unemployment, education, housing and the abolition of privilege' could 'form the main planks of such a platform'. But Churchill was fundamentally against such a move. He was 'far too busy with the war to think about subsequent reforms'. As Daniel Todman has argued:

> The prime minister was a man who was moved by grand visions – and those visions could include projects of social progress – but in practice his idea of domestic reforms tended more towards Edwardian electioneering stunts than the construction of a social democracy. Allergic as usual to planning for the future, he was reluctant to over-promise on what would happen next. Given his simultaneous dependence on Labour co-operation in government and on the gloomy and angry Conservative majority in the Commons, he had little reason to open up issues that would lead to party political dissent.[113]

Attlee, nevertheless, pushed on and on 23 August the War Cabinet agreed to set up a War Aims Committee to 'consider means of perpetuating the national unity achieved ... during the war through a social and economic structure designed to secure equality of opportunity and service among all classes of the community'.[114] In practice, however, 'the formation of a new committee meant very little. It did not actually meet until October. When it dispatched its recommendations to Number 10, they disappeared without trace. This was a topic that Churchill's "restless and probing mind" preferred for the moment to leave undisturbed.'[115]

The consequences of Churchill's unwillingness to engage with a vision for the future were profound for the fighting men. The morale reports could not have been clearer on the importance of exogenous motivational factors to combat morale. The Report for May to July 1942 stated that 'the morale of the soldier abroad, like that of the soldier at home', was 'evidently determined not so much by his immediate surroundings or the course of the battle or campaign as (a) by the efficiency and "tone" of his unit, (b) by his concern for his home and family, and (c) by his hopes and fears regarding the post-war world'.[116] Thus, the soldiers' morale was dependent, to an extent largely underplayed in the literature, by family, friends and politicians. The war, at this stage, was not viewed as a 'crusade', but as 'a bad business that would have to be endured while it lasted – rather like a particularly painful but unavoidable piece of surgery'.[117] This left

British soldiers psychologically 'unarmed' compared to the highly motivated ranks of the *Wehrmacht* and Imperial Japanese Army. They were not 'unarmed' because they had no interest in home or politics, as some have contended,[118] but because the home front and their political leaders failed to give them a coherent and compelling reason to fight. As Stewart wrote in his 'Lessons from Malaya', 'the cultivation of ideals for which we fight so as to make them real and alive to individuals' had simply not been 'practiced' by politicians and commanders. This, in his view, should have been one of the 'first duties' of military and national leaders in war.[119] The implications of the fact that this was clearly not the case for Churchill warrant considerable reflection.

The Indian Army

In India, that part of the Empire where anti-colonial nationalism had been fiercest during the 1930s,[120] the soldiers' relationship with the state, and the cause for which he was fighting, had the potential to destabilise front-line morale to an extent even greater than in the British Army. The interwar period had been one of 'significant political upheaval', characterised by the 'growing influence of political discussion and protest on national thought'. British rule in India depended on the cooperation of the Indian population, a point not lost on Gandhi, Congress or the Muslim League as they sought to use Indian support for the war as a tool to leverage independence.[121]

The antagonistic attitude to the war adopted by many Indians meant that during much of the conflict, fifty infantry battalions, the equivalent of four and a half divisions, had to be deployed on internal security duties.[122] To many, and to Congress in particular, Churchill's refusal to apply the principles of the Atlantic Charter to the subcontinent was hard to believe.[123] Throughout February and March 1942, as the Japanese Army advanced into Burma threatening India, internal intelligence reports pointed out that morale in the country was 'unsatisfactory'. The report for 20 February noted 'deepening gloom', 'signs of alarm' and an 'accelerated exodus from the danger zones'. In December 1941, about 38 per cent of the population of Calcutta fled the city; the following April, in Bombay, where there was 'a feeling bordering on panic among certain sections of the city's population', almost 25 per cent of the total industrial workforce were reported absent. Citizens were hoarding 'gold and food supplies'.[124] By July, 'the cumulative effect of the prolonged absence of their men folk, the lack of news of victories, rising prices, and food shortages' had 'engendered a feeling of defeatism amongst the families of some Indian soldiers'.[125] Some authors have associated these accounts of 'panic' with a more general 'anti-British and pro-independence sentiment'.[126]

Such problems also spread among troops serving in India and those on the front line[127] in spite of the fact that the 'army's broadly rural, Muslim recruiting base helped to insulate it [to a degree] from the mainly urban, Hindu Congress'.[128] Bennett wrote in his report on the Malayan campaign, for example, that 'for some time prior to the commencement of hostilities it was known that homesickness existed among many of the Indian troops who were straining to be returned to India'.[129] In Egypt, in March 1942, there was a sense that the British had 'lost India'. With the departure of 6th and 7th Australian Divisions to the Far East, a 'feeling that the Indian Divisions should also be allowed to return to defend India from the "Yellow Peril"' was prevalent.[130] The Internal Intelligence Summary for 31 July noted that:

> The Army shares the anxiety felt by the civil population at rising prices. This is a matter of vital concern to the Indian soldier, as it affects his family; it occupies a bigger place in his thoughts than the war situation . . . Soldiers have reported that in some villages the rise in prices is as much as 300%, and represent that if this state of affairs cannot be altered immediately, a corresponding increase must be made in their pay.[131]

Many new soldiers, especially those from outside of the 'martial classes', 'seemed less reliable' than their interwar predecessors as, according to military intelligence, 'they looked over their shoulders towards home, becoming easily alarmed by the stories of famine and revolution which they read in vernacular newspapers or in letters'. A CO commented, 'I feel sometimes that I do not command this Battalion; it is commanded by forces in the Punjab.' It seemed that the great expansion of the Indian Army had made 'its loyalty much less certain' and that it had afforded the enemy, both external and internal, 'a far better target for propaganda than the carefully selected and trained pre-war army'.[132]

Indeed, the question of the Indian Army's 'loyalty' during the Second World War has attracted much attention. While some have argued that 'nationalism had little impact on the ranks' during the interwar years,[133] others have postulated that Indian officers were typically 'well acquainted with the nationalist movement'; often recruited from the elite, they 'frequently socialized in the same circles as leading nationalist politicians'.[134] Apurba Kundu, who surveyed 108 Indian officers commissioned before or during the war, noted that a fifth of them had friends or family who were active in nationalist politics.[135] During the war, with the dramatic expansion of the Indian Army, the proportion of Indian officers and other ranks who were both politically aware and antagonistic to British presence in India increased markedly. During the 'Quit India' campaign (see Chapter 8), for example, officers were cautioned to avoid suggestions of 'scorn for the "unenlightened Indian" who wants independence' since freedom, as it was put, was 'probably sought after by the troops themselves'.[136] It was 'no use', as Auchinleck put it at the time, 'shutting one's eyes to the fact that any Indian officer worth his salt is a Nationalist'.[137]

It does seem clear that 'the attitudes of Indian officers towards the British were marked by ambivalence and conditionality' throughout the war:

> By and large, they served professionally but not with the kind of loyalty to cause and country often taken for granted in national militaries. As one later noted ... 'loyalty is not quite as general as is believed by senior British Officers. A number of people are loyal but they will only remain so as long as it suits them'. This was due to the fact that in his opinion 'every Indian (soldiers included) desires a higher political status for India. The difference is only in degrees'.[138]

The fact that many Indian officers and men were politically orientated towards Indian independence was clearly inconsistent with British war aims, which included a determination to hold on to India and preserve the Empire. Indian morale, as a consequence, was typically not bolstered by firm political or ideological commitments to the British war effort, meaning that there was little 'morale capital' to fall back on when endogenous motivational factors, such as the primary group, leadership and training, were found wanting. Thus, when organisation broke down, as in Singapore, 'politics' came 'to play a decisive role in ... behaviour'.[139]

The defection, in 1942, of a large number of Indian soldiers captured in Malaya and Singapore to the Japanese sponsored Indian

National Army (INA), an organisation whose avowed aim was the attainment of India's freedom from British rule, seems to support this contention.[140] In many ways, the creation of the INA stands as one of the two 'largest rebellions in British military history';[141] it was certainly an historical phenomenon as, with few prominent exceptions, the POWs of defeated armies 'are not normally organized into armed formations which wage war on their former comrades'.[142]

Accounts vary as to the extent to which Indian troops defected; during the debacle in Malaya, there were examples of entire companies surrendering under the command of their Indian Commissioned Officers (ICOs). Indian and Japanese sources put the total number at something like 40,000 of the 65,000 Indian prisoners taken, while British sources put the figure between 20,000 and 30,000. About thirty-five of the around fifty ICOs captured at Singapore 'volunteered', alongside a further one hundred VCOs; all told, 400 Indian officers joined the INA.[143] Not all 'volunteers' for the INA were politically motivated. For many, the choice between the INA and Japanese captivity was no choice at all. Conditions in Japanese prison camps in the Second World War were horrific and many of those who fell into captivity knew what to expect. The death rate among Allied prisoners was over 27 per cent in Japanese camps as compared to 4 per cent for those interned by the Germans and Italians. Thus, many 'volunteered' for the INA 'in order to avoid hardship'.[144]

Nevertheless, the 'very idea of forming an INA can only be understood against the backdrop of Indian nationalist politics'. Key figures, such as Mohan Singh, the C-in-C of the INA, 'were motivated by deeply-held commitments'.[145] Of the 23,266 military personnel of the INA who were captured and then interrogated by British Military Intelligence after the war (up to 28 January 1947), only 3,880 men, or 17 per çent, were deemed to be 'unconditionally loyal to the crown'.[146] Indeed, a report by the Directorate of Military Intelligence in India, on 12 November 1942, noted that 'we cannot afford to disregard the possibility that there is genuine belief that adherence to the INA is a service to the motherland'.[147] Another report written on 6 November, by the Combined Services Detailed Interrogation Centre (India), an organisation set up to interrogate detainees, defectors and POWs suspected of harbouring detailed information about the enemy, noted that:

> If one thinks 'From where do our recruits come?' it will be found that they are [of] the same material and come from the same places where the Congress made frantic efforts to win over 'the rural population of India'. These seemingly inarticulate millions have in fact been made politically conscious to an appreciable degree by Congress propaganda. The modern recruit of the Indian Army is very different to his predecessor of 1914–18. Hence this lurking danger, this already prepared foundation for [the] INA.[148]

'The early conclusion reached by British Intelligence in India was that the *sipahis* who had joined the INA were all "black" [i.e. of a nationalist bent] and were merely reflecting the dark thoughts that simmered in the hearts of all Indians.'[149] Wavell certainly thought that 'consistent "nationalist" propaganda' was 'sapping the foundation on which the morale and loyalty of the old Indian Army was based'.[150] One Indian officer serving in Singapore later reported that the Indian officers in Malaya had been discontented over the political situation in the subcontinent, particularly the resignation of the Congress ministries at the outbreak of the war. Another noted 'he'd be damned if he'd lift even his little finger to defend these Europeans', while yet another remembered that 'our anti-British feelings were intense. The war in Europe and Africa was going badly for the Allies, and most of us greeted the news of a British defeat with delight.'[151] It was estimated by another Indian officer that about 60 per cent of his fellow Indian officers were '"Nationalists" and desire an early independence for India. The remaining 40% are in a general way dissatisfied with British rule in India but hold no strong political views.'[152]

The INA, and its much smaller German equivalent, were formed from POWs and groups of deserters after military disasters.[153] Ultimately, the Indian Army in Malaya and Burma, like the British Army in France, was defeated in large measure because it was poorly trained and led and, as a consequence, lacked many of the endogenous factors key to maintaining morale. In this context, in a campaign where military leadership, organisation and training proved inadequate, the Indian Army was forced to rely on more visceral and deep-seated motivations, such as ideological conviction, to maintain morale and cohesion. It was this link in the chain that was supposed to give strategy in the Far East its coherence. When it failed, Indian Army morale was fatally weakened, to the point of collapse. The deficit in leadership and training could not be made good by political and ideological zeal.

The Union Defence Force

The dynamic interplay between the soldier, the cause for which he was fighting, the state and the home front was also central to the South African experience during the first half of the war. As early as the East African campaign, the South African Intelligence Corps (IC), who were in charge of military censorship in South Africa, wrote to the Director of Military Intelligence, Dr E. G. Malherbe, that 'total censorship of outgoing mail to the troops should be immediately introduced' in certain parts of the Union due to the 'subversive propaganda ... calculated to depress the troops and make them discontented' that was being sent to the front by those opposed to South Africa's participation in the war.[154]

Most of this 'subversive' mail came from the Afrikaner right, made up of movements such as the *Ossewa Brandwag* (OB), New Order and the Greyshirts.[155] Initially, attempts by the OB to 'sow seeds of dissention among South African troops', through acts of sabotage and by writing anonymous letters alleging infidelity by wives and sweethearts back home, were a 'dismal failure'. The dominant reaction appeared to be a determination to deal with the OB once soldiers returned home. As one man put it, 'God save and help the Brandwag when we get back again', while another Afrikaner wrote, 'believe me, when we come home, there will be a real civil war'.[156]

By 1942, however, the cumulative effect of friction on the home front was beginning to tell on front-line troops. The South African Military Censorship Summary for 16 to 28 February 1942 pointed out that 'sabotage activities' by the OB figured 'prominently in nearly all letters' to the front:

> The general tone in such letters is the feeling of insecurity and impotency. Whilst descriptions of the sabotage acts are generally culled from Press reports, there is no doubt that, because of the unknown quantity of this underground menace, i.e. where it will strike next, letter-writers also draw on their imaginations and personal suspicions. Indictments, therefore, that certain friends and acquaintances of the writers are O.B.'s [*sic*] are frequently found.[157]

Censorship for units at the Sonderwater and Kafferskraal camps at home in South Africa noted that it was 'with disturbing frequency' that dependants of men on service were 'being persecuted by O.B.'s [*sic*], even to physical maltreatment'.[158] It was not uncommon to read reports of OB ladies 'spitting at servicemen's wives when they pass them'.[159] Some RAF personnel serving in South Africa started to travel in and out of town through the 'coloured people's quarters of the town, as they were safe there at any time of the night'.[160] Many soldiers felt that the only place that they were really secure was in camp.[161]

On 24 February 1942, the IC wrote a memorandum on the state of civilian morale for Malherbe. It pointed out that 'demoralising and disheartening' statements were continually made in letters not only about OB activities, but also about the futility of promises on 'things being different after this war' and the veracity of press and radio reports 'about our ability to win this war'. The failure to capitalise on the initial success of Operation 'Crusader' after press reports 'on the inevitable destruction of General Rommel's army', the surrender of Singapore 'after its much-boasted invincibility', and the threat to the Union by Japan's 'possible occupation of Madagascar' had all rattled the civilian population. Military censorship from Durban talked of the 'growing wave of defeatism … and pessimism which seems to be spreading even amongst the reliable and pro Government section of the community who are now by their despondency and low spirits unwittingly acting as "fifth columnists"'. Women were increasingly 'telling their menfolk "to get out of the damned Army"' and criticisms of the efficiency of army administration were 'rampant'. The memorandum went on to outline how 'relatives of soldiers are advising their menfolk up North':

(a) To injure themselves – "I think it would be quite an idea to get your little toe shot off … see what can be done".
(b) To be taken prisoner – "Now take my advice, do not risk your life, but rather be taken prisoner".
(c) To exaggerate existing ailments or create ailments in order to get Union leave – "can't you work your passage back to the Union … Your kidneys will work the oracle or stomach trouble such as an ulcerated stomach".[162]

The impact of poor domestic morale on the troops' morale was of grave concern to the IC, as the memorandum outlined:

> The morale of our troops on the fighting front is bound up with the morale on the home front and in particular with the morale of relatives of troops and HOME FRONT MORALE

> IS DISTINCTLY SHAKY – PARTICULARLY THE MORALE OF OUR WOMENFOLK WRITING IN ENGLISH.[163]

The memorandum stated that it was 'doubtful' that the 'élan' of the troops could be 'maintained' under these circumstances.[164] A censorship report from the same period pointed out more explicitly that 'this increase in depressing letters from the South African home front might have serious consequences on the fighting determination of our troops in the field'.[165] The memorandum went on, remarkably, to quote a lengthy passage from *Mein Kampf* as being applicable to South Africa's current situation:

> Letters coming directly from home had long been exercising their effect. There was now no further necessity for the enemy to broadcast such letters in leaflet form. THE WHOLE FRONT WAS DRENCHED IN THIS POISON WHICH THOUGHTLESS WOMEN AT HOME SENT OUT, without suspecting for a moment that the enemy's chances of final victory were thus strengthened or that the suffering of their own men at the front were thus being prolonged and rendered more severe.[166]

Substitute for 'German women' the words 'South African women', and particularly 'English-speaking South African women', and, the memorandum concluded, the 'whole situation' would be 'fittingly summarized'. There was no doubt in the minds of the IC that 'the gravest consideration should be accorded to this memorandum'.[167]

Soldiers travelling home on leave were desperately disappointed by the situation that they found in South Africa. The censorship summary for 16 to 31 April 1942 noted that men who had come home were 'bitter' about their 'treatment by the military authorities' and the 'attitude that everyone has towards the war ... No one cares a darn about it so long as they get their pay or have a good time.' One man wrote that 1st Division were 'treated almost like criminals; everybody seems to look at us with suspicion as though we had committed some awful crime up North, whereas the only mistake we made was to come home on leave and most of us have regretted that over and over again ... we're not even allowed to wear our first division flashes now'.[168]

These attitudes and experiences, as the IC feared, filtered back to front-line troops in North Africa. At this time, according to Brigadier A. J. Orenstein, the Director of Medical Services, Union Defence Force

(UDF), the number of 'anxiety neurosis and hysteria cases' in the desert was 'abnormally high', as were the number of cases of 'undiagnosed backache, headache and stomach troubles'.[169] So severe was the problem of desertion among South African units, that, in April 1942, the UDF requested the establishment of a permanent courts martial in the South African base depot to deal with the number of cases.[170] All these issues were 'giving rise to considerable concern' regarding the morale of the troops.[171]

It is remarkable how the tone of South African mail changed between the idealistic days at the start of the East African campaign and the increasing pessimism presented in the censorship summaries in the run up to the summer of 1942. Many felt that as the war progressed 'the spirit of patriotism and desire to defend the country' had swung right round. Those at home were 'doing too well ... to worry about the future, being content to let the original crowd [of volunteers] continue to hold the baby', in spite of the fact that they were increasingly 'few in number'.[172] The 4th South African Infantry Brigade, which surrendered at Tobruk along with the rest of 2nd South African Division, was predominantly from Natal, an English-speaking area, while each of the three infantry brigades in 1st South African Division had an infantry battalion from Natal. In many ways, therefore, it is hard to avoid the conclusion that, in the summer of 1942, the performance of the UDF was, to a perhaps critical extent, undermined by problems with morale. This crisis was caused by a cocktail of deficiencies, in equipment, the quality of manpower, welfare, leadership and training.[173] But, it was also triggered by a widespread disaffection and disenchantment with the war effort on the home front; the potentially destructive link between family and the front line had been exposed in a most unfortunate and damaging fashion.

The Australian Imperial Force

Similar dynamics were at work in Australia. As the military crisis in the Far East deepened in early 1942 and Australia grappled with the threat of a potential Japanese invasion, it became increasingly evident that winning the war depended 'just as much on civilian morale as on Army morale' (see Illustration 6.2). 'Over and over again', according to an article submitted to the Australian Army Educational Journal, *SALT*, by the Director of Welfare and Vocational Training, R. B. Madgwick, 'Armies have been beaten in the field simply because civilian morale has collapsed behind them. That is what happened to the

German Army in 1918 and to the French Army in 1940, and that is what could happen to us unless the Home Front remains solid behind us.' If the 'soldier goes home to a dispirited community or receives dispirited letters from his family and friends, it is likely that his own outlook will be affected similarly'.[174]

'At bottom', the 'whole question', according to the article, was one of 'discipline':

> For some reason or other we have got hold of the idea that discipline is something which is imposed on soldiers by their officers ... Few ideas have done more harm, and few have ever been more false. The real object of discipline is not simply to train a man to observe Army regulations and obey his officers: it is to ensure that he will do the right thing at all times, instinctively, whether he is on duty or not. True discipline is self-discipline and is the brother of self-respect. It is an individual thing, and when you get down to bedrock it is nothing else but the individual soldier's ability to recognize his duty and his readiness to carry it out of *his own free will.*[175]

The military heart of the Empire had always been built on the back of individual ingenuity and dedication. The extraordinary performance of the 'digger' in the First World War had been dependent, at least according to myth, on a 'devil-may-care but disciplined individualism'.[176] The problem was that individuals were not performing as required or expected. In the summer of 1942, the Australian Prime Minister, John Curtin, set up an Advisory Committee on Civilian Morale, attached to the Prime Minister's Department, to address the apparent disengagement of Australians from the war.[177] The Committee was chaired by A. A. Conlon, a Fellow of the Senate of the University of Sydney, and included Dr C. E. W. Bean, the editor of the Official History of Australia in the First World War who was a key figure in the foundation of the ANZAC legend. Experts in literature, science, international affairs, anthropology, the law, moral and political philosophy were also included.

The committee pointed to 'deficiencies in civilian morale' and explored some of the 'underlying factors' behind them. The first was the 'de-idealisation of the war'. The rapid approach of physical danger to Australia, with the Japanese advance in Asia, had, according to the Committee, 'tended to thrust idealism into the background and displace it with a crude physical self-preservation'. Citizens had begun to concentrate on their own 'personal safety rather than on that of the nation or of the Allied cause'. This operated inevitably 'to disrupt national solidarity and negative the common cause as between Australians'. The same tendency produced a mistrust of the intentions of other Allied nations, since 'it imputes to them a similar solicitude for their own skins and a similar lack of co-operation in the common cause'. For example, the Committee highlighted the recent reports and rumours that highly placed strategists in Washington regarded Australia as of secondary importance and were, therefore, considering leaving it to its own devices in the war against Japan.[178]

The second was the 'relation of the war to popular notions of major historic trends'. It pointed to an 'accepted mental pattern' among all classes. 'With working people this pattern is vaguely based upon the Marxist view that capitalist imperialism is to be followed by capitalist collapse. In the middle classes the pattern is a vaguer one of disintegration of their familiar world'. These patterns, according to the Committee, were 'facts of popular psychology', regardless of whether the theories they embodied were sound or not. Recent 'catastrophic events' had led people to wonder whether they were 'not in the presence of the unfolding of some such historic process before which they are helpless'. As an example, the Committee referred to 'suggestions from the Press' that British and Dutch failures in Malaya and the East Indies were attributable, at least in part, 'to native resentment of the colonial Powers' exploitation'.[179]

The third issue, the 'confusing effects of rapid social and economic change', was closely interlinked with the second. For many people, this was the 'first war' where 'social issues' were 'inextricably entangled with international relations'. The interactions taking place, whether implicitly or not, between peoples and their governments, who required their consent and commitment to the war in order to prosecute it effectively, were all too evident. The 'conflict between the patriotic and the economic motive' was being played out across the commonwealth and was a 'crucial matter, not merely for the effective conduct of the war, but for the stability and progress of the community in the post-war period'. The problem clearly was that too many citizens failed to identify their wellbeing, security and prosperity with that of their fellow citizens and the state.[180]

It was 'impossible', in the words of the Committee, to run a planned war effort 'on a laissez-faire psychology'. The solution, it concluded, lay in the adoption of a positive policy of planned cultural education and propaganda, 'both as to the nature of the war and as to social and economic change'. Such an approach would undoubtedly be 'controversial'. However, the Committee refuted suggestions that there was a 'choice' between engendering good morale 'by evading controversial issues' and fostering poor morale 'by debating them':

> In fact ... evasion tends to disintegrate belief in the common cause. The real choice is between a passive, uninspired, superficial appearance of harmony and a really inspired unity of the great mass of the people ... Propaganda which seeks to improve morale without reference to actual conditions, for instance, by the direct injection of fear, or other standardised emotions, will not only be ineffective but also harmful. For, since it will not make contact with the public mind, it will produce the feeling among the people that they are out of touch with their leaders.[181]

The Australian Government's early response to the war, much like the British Government's, had focused on imposing conformity upon the populace through censorship, propaganda, coercion, sweeping legislative powers and by emphasising the dangers faced from internal and external enemies.[182] The Committee viewed these efforts as ineffective and recommended setting up a new expanded Department of Information with the funds and know-how to 'secure from the public not simply the passive acceptance of the Government's policies but active co-operation in putting them into effect'. The Government, if it was to prosecute the war effectively, would have to realise that it needed a 'strategy of morale' as much as 'military strategy'.[183]

These were important recommendations, for, much as in the case of the UDF, frictions on the home front filtered through to the soldiers on the front line. The Field Censorship Summary for troops in North Africa, 19 June 1941, pointed out that the 'chief points in the outgoing Australian mail' were 'rather outspoken comments on the need for an intensification of the war effort in Australia'. One man wrote:

> Menzies and his gang of muddlers are well below par over here and we feel that with N.S.W. [New South Wales] Labour we might get things done and in a big way; cut everybody down to the bare necessities, no incomes above what is necessary if it means sacrificing everything we have worked all our lives for and throw everything into the production of things to kill ... for as sure as I sit here we will need it.[184]

Illustration 6.2 A mail delivery to Australian troops in a forward area in Malaya, *c.* January 1942. As the military crisis in the Far East deepened and Australia grappled with the threat of a potential Japanese invasion, it became increasingly evident that the home and battlefronts were intimately interlinked; winning the war depended on civilian morale as well as on army morale.

The summary for 28 August again noted 'criticisms of Australia's war effort' and with regards to 'the recruiting results' in particular, quoted one man as writing that 'the feeling amongst the troops is hardly one of pride at that effort'.[185] There was, in what the censors described as a 'typical letter', one thing lacking in the Government's policy, which was 'of vital importance':

> This is the statement of war aims and the announcement of a tangible outline of the new order that must follow this war if civilisation is to make any progress ... Unless the leaders of the Empire realise *now* the importance of post-war planning in advance then some new form of disorder will overtake us when peace is won. The old system will not do; it can't possibly satisfy the needs of the next generation socially or industrially.[186]

Many realised that a 'new age of peace and prosperity after the war' was, however, unlikely unless Australians accepted that there were 'greater things than ease and safety and personal gain'.[187] On returning to Australia, Blamey delivered a nationwide radio address, in November 1941, castigating his homeland on its attitude to the war. 'To come from [the Middle East] ... back to Australia gives one the most extraordinary feeling of helplessness. You are like – here in this country – a lot of gazelles grazing in a dell on the edge of the jungle, while the beasts of prey are working up toward you, apparently unseen, unnoticed.'[188]

In Malaya, impressions such as this, that the Australian domestic war effort was not 'all out', unquestionably impacted negatively on AIF morale and left many feeling 'neglected'.[189] On the fall of Singapore, the censors in the Middle East noted that 'many writers' expressed the opinion that the unfolding Japanese threat to Australia was 'a good thing' as it had finally 'aroused the Australian people to a realisation that there is a war on'.[190] One man wrote:

> You know Father how often I have urged upon you to make your friends and acquaintances more conscious of the need for the full co-operation of the Australian people. Yet until Japan forced them to it they refused to take the situation seriously. Apart from petrol restrictions nobody in Australia suffered except the families of men in the A.I.F.[191]

By the summer of 1942, criticisms of the Government and home population were still widespread, 'writers not sacrificing anything to politeness in their outspoken comments'. Affairs in Australia were consistently 'the most discussed topics in all letters',[192] and although home troubles did not undermine Australian morale to the same extent as that of the UDF, they were still to a large extent a negative influence. A field officer wrote:

> there is a singular lack of guts in the leadership and spirit of the country generally. Too much cringing … and too little fighting spirit on the part of those who should have it in plenty. In fact it is felt by quite a number of us that the attitude of the country generally is a national disgrace. Never at any stage did I think that I should be ashamed of my country but I'm afraid that is how it is.

Another man, a private, wrote, in a similar vein, 'one is *not* proud to be an Australian now. No longer can one carry the slouch hat with a prideful swagger when one's country has failed to do its duty … where is our pride? Where?'[193]

The Soldier and the State

The failures of the British and Commonwealth Armies in the early years of the Second World War have, more often than not, been linked with endogenous military factors, such as inadequate training and doctrine. This chapter, and the ones that preceded it, have shown, however, that the defeats suffered by these armies were influenced, to an extent perhaps greater than historians and commentators have realised, by a lack, both on the home front and among the citizen armies, of the levels of morale and motivation necessary for victory. These issues, which were so detrimental to the performance of the British, Indian, South African and Australian Armies would also affect the New Zealanders and Canadians later in the war (see Chapters 10 and 15). Wavell wrote to Brooke on 17 February 1942:

> The trouble goes a long way back, climate, the atmosphere of the country … lack of vigour in our peace-time training, the cumbrousness of our tactics and equipment, and the very real difficulty of finding an answer to the very skilful and bold tactics of the Japanese in this jungle fighting. But the real trouble is that for the time being we have lost a good deal of our hardness and fighting spirit.[194]

This was all the more troubling for, as Stewart later wrote, 'in jungle it is the quality of the man far more than the quality and quantity of weapons that counts'.[195]

It was in this context that pre-war socio-economic conditions, and the manner in which the individual, the home front and the state interacted, had a big impact on the performance of the British and Commonwealth Armies. For Britain chose to fight the Second World War cognisant of the limits it faced. This decision was based on a set of calculations that placed a large premium on the innate commitment and fighting ability of its citizens and subjects.[196] This commitment, however, when it came down to it, was dependent, particularly where high casualties were suffered in battle, on the citizen's relationship with the state, 'the feeling of being somebody'[197] and of 'being valued by the . . . community' more generally.[198] Many men drafted into the Army, however, in the early years of the war, 'had centuries of disillusionment behind them'.[199] 'Many' more had been told by their parents of the 'unemployment from which the latter suffered after the last war'.[200] On top of that, injustices and inequalities in the manner in which sacrifices were apportioned during the war left many men deeply dissatisfied with their lot. Morale and motivation, and combat performance, suffered as a consequence.

Such arguments do not sit easily with the majority of the Western literature on the war, which downplays the role of ideology and the home front in successful combat performance.[201] The overwhelming mass of evidence produced here, however, strongly challenges these views. By making widespread use of censorship summaries of the soldiers' mail and morale reports – sources that give a heretofore unobtainable insight into the motivations of British and Commonwealth soldiers – it is possible to see that soldiers were deeply interested in politics and the state of the home front.[202] The fact that this interest was not converted into ideological commitment to the war was not a function of the liberal democratic tradition, or innate disinterest among the troops, but the failure of the state to present a coherent, just and compelling vision of what the soldiers were fighting for. This failure, in turn, had profound and negative effects on morale and combat performance. No more powerful argument can be made for the centrality of the ideological deficit in the defeats that beset the British and Commonwealth Armies between 1940 and 1942 than the censorship summary for 12 to 18 August 1942, the height of the morale crisis that beset Eighth Army in the desert. It noted that among the reasons making men 'readier to surrender' was the fact that 'many of the troops still want to know what we are fighting for'.[203]

Part III Transformation

7 VICTORY IN NORTH AFRICA

No Retreat

By the end of July 1942, Churchill had lost faith in Auchinleck, his Commander-in-Chief (C-in-C) in the Middle East, who, at the time, was also commander of Eighth Army. On 13 August, after flying to Cairo to assess the situation for himself, he replaced Auchinleck with two men; General Bernard Law Montgomery was placed in charge of Eighth Army, and General Harold Alexander was appointed the new theatre commander.[1]

Montgomery, whose whole career had been built towards this moment, would go on to become the most famous British general of the war (see Illustration 7.1). He had spent twelve years of his childhood in Tasmania before passing into Sandhurst in 1907, seventy-second out of 170. He passed out rather better, in thirty-sixth place, and was duly commissioned into the Royal Warwickshire Regiment. He spent four years in India before the outbreak of the First World War. Between 1914 and 1918, he was wounded three times (including a bullet through the lung), mentioned in dispatches six times and was awarded a DSO and the Croix de Guerre. He spent much of the conflict in staff positions, appointments that quite likely saved his life. He attended the Staff College in 1920, after which he was sent, as a brigade major in 17th Infantry Brigade, to Ireland. He returned to the Staff College as an instructor in 1926 and then spent an extended period in command of 1st Battalion the Royal Warwickshire Regiment, before being appointed the Chief Instructor at the Indian Staff College, in Quetta, in 1934.

In 1937, he was given command of 9th Infantry Brigade and then, in 1938, of 8th Infantry Division in Palestine during the Arab Revolt. On the outbreak of war, Montgomery, now a Major-General, took 3rd Division to France; after the disaster at Dunkirk, he was appointed General Officer Commanding (GOC) V Corps and was thereafter given command of XII Corps and then of South Eastern Army in the UK.[2]

Alexander, similarly, seemed destined for the challenge ahead. The son of an earl, he spent his youth in county Tyrone before joining the Army. He was not required to sit the entrance exam for Sandhurst in 1910, as he had already sat the London University Leaving Certificate for the Army, and in July 1911, he passed out of Sandhurst eighty-fifth out of 172 and was commissioned into the Irish Guards.[3] Three years later he was in France. Unlike Montgomery, he spent most of the war on the front line. He was twice wounded, awarded the MC and was appointed to the DSO during a period of almost non-stop fighting that saw him rise rapidly through the ranks. By the end of the war, he had commanded at battalion and brigade level, serving as an acting brigadier-general in charge of 4th Guards Brigade during the retreat from Arras in March 1918. After the war, he was sent to Poland, Latvia, Constantinople and Gibraltar before attending the Staff College in 1926. Thereafter, his career continued its upward trajectory. After more command experience with his regiment, he attended the Imperial Defence College (in 1930) and then held staff positions for three years (the only staff appointments of his career) before spending the best part of four years commanding brigades on the North-West Frontier. By 1937, Alexander, at the age of 45, was the youngest general in the British Army. The following year, he was given charge of 1st Division and took the formation to France on the outbreak of hostilities in 1939. Alexander, like Montgomery, was one of the few generals to emerge from the debacle in France with any credit. He commanded the final rearguard at Dunkirk and went on to command I Corps and Southern Command in the UK before being sent to Burma in February 1942 to take over from Hutton in an attempt to rescue the deteriorating situation in the Far East. Having failed in that endeavour, a close to impossible task, he was earmarked to command First Army in the invasion of North-West Africa, before being given charge of Middle East Command in August 1942.[4]

Both men, like Auchinleck, were of Ulster Protestant extraction; they knew each other well. Montgomery had taught at the Staff College

Illustration 7.1 Montgomery engaging with soldiers of Eighth Army, likely Sicily, 1943. Montgomery understood that the key material with which he had to deal was men and that to 'handle' a citizen army well he had to go to extraordinary efforts to earn the trust of his troops and ensure that morale was as high as possible.

while Alexander was a student there and had later been one of Alexander's Corps commanders in Southern Command after the fall of France. They now had to work as a close-knit team to turn around the situation in the Middle East. To this end, their task was made significantly easier by a series of changes to command arrangements in theatre. The clear delineation between Alexander and Montgomery's roles as theatre and army commanders was designed, first and foremost, to avoid a situation where close to intolerable responsibility was placed on the shoulders of one man (as had happened with Auchinleck during the summer months). To further ensure that Alexander and his subordinate army commander were not distracted by the strategic concerns of the immense Middle East theatre, a new Persia and Iraq Command was created to prepare, should the situation deteriorate in Russia, for the potential threat of a German attack from the north. It was Alexander's and Montgomery's good fortune to take command in a greatly truncated Middle East Command. Responsibilities no longer spanned across 2,000 miles of territory; instead, they were focused on the campaign in Egypt. The war in East Africa was over; the threat to Palestine and Syria had passed; the 'looming menace' of a German attack into Persia was not now their concern. Shorn of these responsibilities, Alexander and Montgomery 'were in a position to work hard and efficiently to ensure that the now vast base organisation in Egypt could respond quickly to the growing needs of Eighth Army'.[5]

Matters were improved further as enormous quantities of supplies started to arrive in theatre to make good the losses of the summer months. During August, 446 guns, 254 tanks, 3,289 vehicles and 72,192 tons of stores landed from Britain.[6] Eighth Army now had 135,000 men[7] and 693 tanks, including 524 mediums and heavies. By 28 August, the *Panzerarmee* had also been rebuilt and compared favourably with the force that had begun the summer offensives on 26 May. There were now 84,000 German and 44,000 Italian personnel (128,000 in total)[8] with 265 German and 243 Italian tanks (508 in all) in Africa. This gave Eighth Army a barely perceptible superiority in manpower, and an advantage in medium and heavy tanks of 2.2:1. Eighth Army also had an advantage in terms of numbers of guns. Furthermore, during the next battle (Alam Halfa) Eighth Army would enjoy the support of 2,900 sorties by the Desert Air Force as compared to 1,200 by the *Luftwaffe* (a ratio of 2.4:1).[9]

From a materiel viewpoint, therefore, Eighth Army was well positioned to repel the expected renewal of the Axis advance towards Alexandria, the Suez Canal and the oilfields of the Middle East. Nevertheless, a number of serious problems remained, one of which was that after the setbacks of the summer months Eighth Army was experiencing a profound and dangerous crisis of morale. Montgomery noted in his diary on arriving in the Middle East that it was 'in a bad state'. The troops 'had their tails right down and there was no confidence in the higher command. It was clear that ROMMEL was preparing further attacks and the troops were looking over their shoulders for rear lines to which to withdraw'. The whole 'atmosphere', he continued, 'was wrong'.[10] He would write later that the 'situation here when I arrived was really unbelievable; I would never have thought it could have been so bad'.[11]

Montgomery set out to address the problem head on and issued orders to try and reinvigorate his troops; the days of retreat had to end, he said. On 13 August, he gathered his new subordinates around him. 'The defence of Egypt', he stated confidently, 'lies here at Alamein and on the Ruweisat Ridge':

> What is the use of digging trenches in the Delta? It is quite useless; if we lose this position we lose Egypt; all the fighting troops now in the Delta must come out here at once, and will. *Here* we will stand and fight; there will be no further withdrawal; I have ordered that all plans and instructions dealing with further withdrawal are to be burnt, and at once. We will stand and fight *here*. If we can't stay here alive, then let us stay here dead.[12]

This order, as historians have argued quite correctly, was strategically meaningless.[13] Auchinleck had not intended to retreat to the Delta. Nevertheless, from a psychological perspective, it was exactly what Eighth Army needed to hear. Its effect was extraordinarily dramatic.

The senior officers present on 13 August passed the message down the chain of command. Freyberg, the commander of 2nd New Zealand Division, told his commanding officers on 16 August that:

> I want you to make the Army Commander's views clear to everybody. This looking over your shoulder and cranking up to get back to the position in the rear is to cease. Here we are going to stay and here we are going to fight. There is no question of going to any back position from here. We are to make this position as complete as we can.[14]

Brigade commanders then shared Eighth Army's new ethos with their subordinates. Howard Kippenberger, the commander of 5th New Zealand Brigade, sent a circular to his formation as they prepared for the expected Axis offensive at the end of August:

> We are now facing a very severe test. For the next few weeks we will be on the defensive and it is open to the enemy to make an attack which will test us to the limit. If he does not make it or if he makes it and fails, then the tide will quickly

> turn strongly against him, but these few weeks are critical. We hold an exposed and vital position of the line. Like the Australians, the South Africans, the Indians and British we are burning our boats by sending our transport many miles away and it is our duty to stand and fight where we are, to the last man, and the last round. It is probable, almost certain that we will be subjected to extremely severe attacks by dive bombers, arty, tanks and infantry and in fact it is probable that the supreme test of the New Zealand Division is close ahead of us.[15]

Whereas Auchinleck's stirring message of 30 June 1942 to the effect that Rommel 'thinks we are a broken army' and 'hopes to take Egypt by bluff ... Show him where he gets off' made little to no impact on the censorship summaries or the troops' diaries and memoirs,[16] Montgomery's directive spread like wildfire throughout Eighth Army. Both Brian Horrocks, Montgomery's new commander of XIII Corps, and Francis de Guingand, his new Chief of Staff, described the effect of the order as 'magical'.[17] Hugh Mainwaring, Auchinleck's former General Staff Officer (GSO) 1 Operations, believed it was 'the turning point of the war'.[18] The censorship summary for 19 to 25 August reported that 'a breath of fresh, invigorating air has swept through British Troops in Egypt, and the mail has altered in tone almost overnight. Renewed optimism and confidence were everywhere apparent, and the old aggressive spirit ... is in the process of being recovered.'[19] Montgomery in one move had gripped the imagination of his army.

Alam Halfa

Thus, when the Axis forces attacked on 30 August along the Alam Halfa ridge, Eighth Army's morale had improved markedly since its low point in July and at the start of August (see Figure 4.1). It was still, nevertheless, decidedly fragile. According to the censorship summaries, a nervous optimism pervaded the Army on the eve of the battle. The report for 3 to 9 September made 'many references to past mistakes and performances', and stressed that the withdrawals of the summer 'still rankle in the minds of many' of the soldiers. These 'bitter blows of the recent past', rang 'a warning note that we must be properly led and equipped before we tackle the job, that the many weary months spent in reforming and re-equipping must not be wasted'. It was important in the eyes of the troops that 'we must not make a present of large quantities of brand new equipment to the enemy – as we did last time'.[20] Indian troops stressed 'in no equivocal terms the urgent necessity of "success for the British Army on land" involving "some major reverses" of the enemy "to restore confidence in its ability"'.[21]

Montgomery was conscious of the frailties of his army, a fact he made abundantly clear in his diaries and memoirs. He planned, therefore, to fight Alam Halfa as a limited, predominantly defensive, battle. The engagements on the El Alamein line in July had shown that the Army's strength lay in its artillery and the Desert Air Force. Its weaknesses, apart from the issue of morale, were its armour and its inability to control and co-ordinate actions at corps level and above. Alam Halfa was a battle conceived and executed with these strengths and weaknesses in mind. Whereas Auchinleck, had he remained in command, had envisioned a mobile defensive battle, Montgomery 'had no intention of allowing one to develop'. Auchinleck had planned to hold the El Alamein line with boxes which would act as 'pivots' of manoeuvre for his armour. Montgomery, on the other hand, decided on the much more conventional option of bringing up more infantry and digging them in besides armour and guns around the Alam Halfa feature.[22]

Montgomery purposely set out to prevent his armour becoming embroiled in a mobile tank versus tank battle with the *Panzerarmee*, a fight he did not think he could win. His command philosophy would echo Auchinleck's behaviour in the first week of July much more than at 'Crusader' and Gazala. He realised that his troops needed time to develop confidence in both themselves and in their weapons. There was no way, therefore, that he was going to place the outcome of the battle unduly in their hands. As a consequence, he devised an essentially static defensive battle in which he would maintain control; he would draw Rommel onto his artillery and anti-tank screen, and then destroy him with the added support of the Desert Air Force.[23]

On the whole, the operation played out as Montgomery planned. As German and Italian forces drove round the southern flank of the British and Commonwealth positions, and headed north, as they had done on so many occasions, they ran into an immovable line of tanks and anti-tank weapons. Whereas the concentrated armour of the *Panzerarmee* had cut through Eighth Army with relative ease at Gazala, this time 'at no point did the enemy break in or break through' (see Map 7.1).[24] Instead, the line held

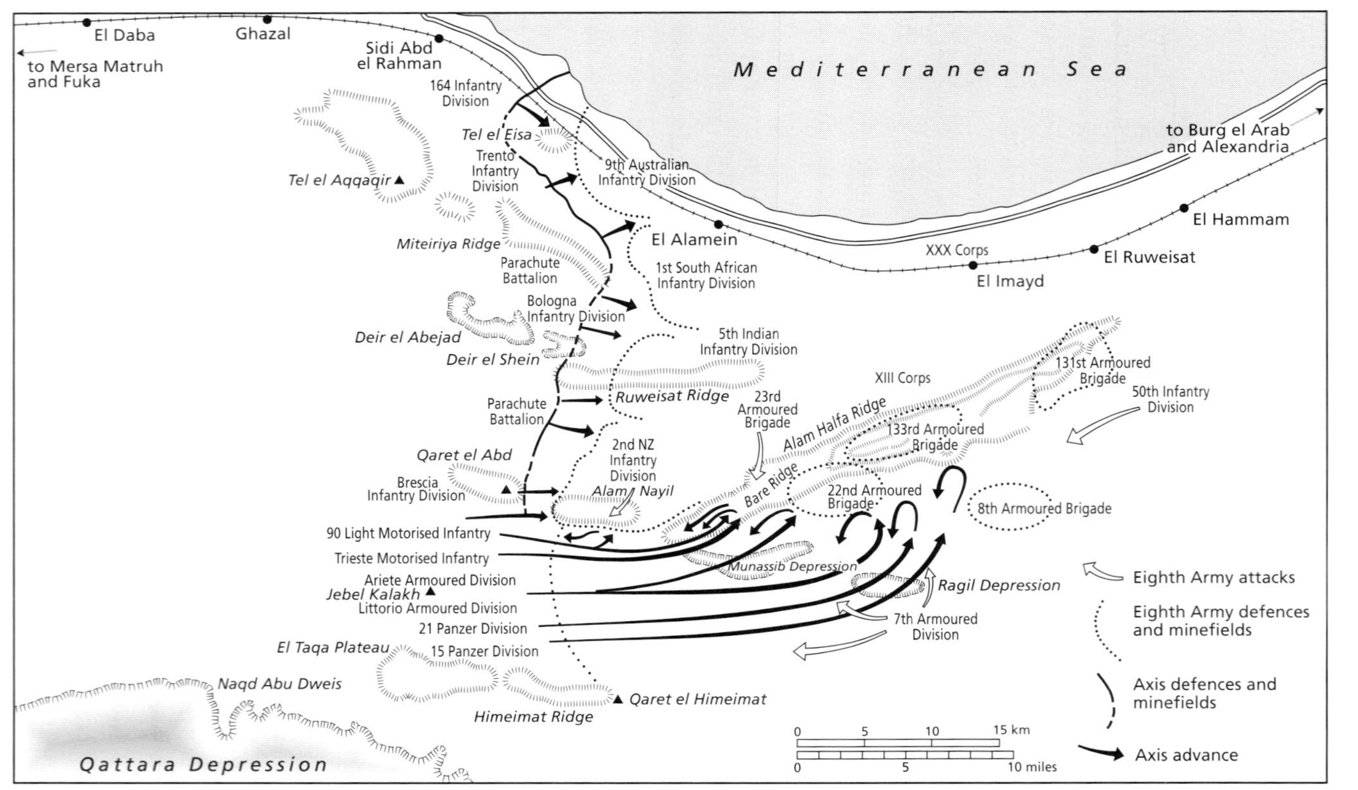

Map 7.1 The Battle of Alam Halfa, 30 August–5 September 1942

firm and the combined and co-ordinated firepower of Eighth Army had its intended effect. The *Panzerarmee's* daily report for 2 September acknowledged that the weight of fire unleashed by Eighth Army had 'caused serious losses to personnel and material' as well as affecting 'the morale of both the German and Italian troops'.[25] A report by the 19th Flak Division for *Panzerarmee Afrika* HQ noted that 15,600 bombs had been dropped by the Desert Air Force over the five days of the offensive. These had been distributed over a front averaging about 7–9 miles in length and 5–6 miles in depth. That meant approximately 250 bombs were dropped per square mile during the offensive. The effect of such action on the Axis troops was that 'in addition to the extensive material damage caused, the effect on morale was ... great. The spirit of the troops was considerably depressed owing to the totally inadequate German fighter cover. Incessant night attacks in particular served to reduce the degree of readiness for action of both officers and men', due to 'no sleep, continual waiting for the next bombs, [and the] dispersal of units etc.'[26]

The success at Alam Halfa did wonders for Eighth Army. The censorship summary for 10 to 16 September contained references to improved tactics and the fact the Army appeared to be learning from its previous mistakes. An officer wrote, 'we do not sacrifice the wretched tank crews as before, as this old fashioned idea of cavalry charges head on with tanks has been given up I'm glad to say'. Another stated, 'it does look as though the tanks are beginning to learn their lesson – and not charge straight at dug in 88mm A/Tk guns two up with their flag flying'.[27] The same summary recorded that 'the predominant feature of correspondence from all ranks of British troops in the Western Desert' was the 'general appreciation of the massive support given to our land forces by the Allied Air Forces'.[28] The summary for 17 to 23 September told a similar story. A gunner wrote, 'air co-operation was perfect and we'd only to name a target to have the R.A.F. bombing it ten minutes later; artillery combined shoots ... worked perfectly. We drove their stuff ... into groups and then left them to the R.A.F.' Another soldier stated:

> [W]e harried him a good deal on his way back but didn't get really heavily involved. Our artillery and the R.A.F. gave him absolute hell and I sat on one ridge all day about 5,000 yards from a *Panzer* Division which the R.A.F. bombed every 45 mins and which the big gunners put about 10,000 shells into in

> one day. It was the most incredible sight I have ever seen and gave our chaps considerable satisfaction. We took some of those particular Germans prisoner the following day and they said it was [by] far the worst day they had ever experienced.[29]

Improved morale and what can only be described as a simple yet profoundly pragmatic approach to the battle had played their part in the victory. Montgomery had devised a plan that catered for the actual situation on the ground – namely an under-trained citizen army that had just experienced an atrocious run of serious defeats. As a consequence, he avoided 'asking too much' of his men, unlike Auchinleck in July.[30] The success of Eighth Army had also hinged significantly on the part played by the Allied Air Forces and the Royal Navy. Allied air and naval dominance in the Mediterranean, supported by intelligence from Ultra, had produced a devastating effect on the Axis supply lines. Considerable quantities of materiel destined for North Africa were either destroyed on the way to the desert or held back for lack of shipping. Something like 2,000 trucks and 100 guns for German formations awaited transport from Italy with a further 1,000 trucks and 120 tanks held in Germany.[31] As a result of these logistic failures, the *Panzerarmee* lacked fuel, thus limiting its ability to fight Eighth Army in the manner to which it was best suited.

It was evident that a profound change had occurred in the British and Commonwealth forces in the Middle East. The three services were working together in an increasingly coherent and co-ordinated fashion. Moreover, with the concentrated support of the Royal Artillery and Desert Air Force, British and Commonwealth infantry, armour and anti-tank units had, for the first time since Operation 'Crusader', held their ground and fought the *Panzerarmee* to a standstill. 'Montgomery had perhaps not fought the battle with as much "grip" or prescience as he later claimed', but 'the real significance of Alam Halfa was its influence upon the officers and men of Eighth Army'. Montgomery had promised them that they would win the next fight with Rommel and he had been right. The morale of Eighth Army and their confidence in their new general soared; 'just as importantly, once the Panzerarmee had withdrawn, it still remained pinned to the stretch of desert near El Alamein. Having conclusively beaten off the Axis offensive, the Eighth Army could prepare to mount its own.'[32]

Colossal Cracks

In many ways, the stars began to align for Eighth Army as it commenced its preparations for the next offensive, at El Alamein. Following Alam Halfa, new shipments of weapons continued to arrive in the Middle East. The delivery mid-way through September of over 300 Sherman tanks from the United States, which Roosevelt had offered to a distraught Churchill after the loss of Tobruk, was one of the most important additions. The Sherman carried a 75mm high-velocity gun firing either armour piercing or high explosive shells. It was very reliable and unlike the Grant carried its big gun in the turret. Another arrival was the British Crusader Mark III with a 6-pounder gun. Seventy-eight of these new tanks were available by the beginning of the next battle. By the middle of October, Eighth Army also had at its disposal 849 6-pounder anti-tank guns. The introduction of these guns meant that every infantry battalion received eight 2-pounder anti-tank guns to add to its defences.[33] This would allow the infantry a better chance of dealing with German *panzers* without the complexities of co-operating closely with the armoured regiments.

Montgomery now sought to stamp his intellectual imprint on Eighth Army. Montgomery's 'own way' of fighting, dubbed the 'Colossal Cracks' approach by Stephen A. Hart,[34] marked a decisive step-change in the way the British and Commonwealth Armies fought the Second World War. Few commanders imposed their will on an army quite as ruthlessly as Montgomery[35] and he was able 'to a considerable degree, to make his own approach to battle something close to British Army doctrine' for the rest of the war.[36]

The years since 1939 had clearly demonstrated that the British operational approach as laid out in *Field Service Regulations* (*FSR*) was inadequate in the prevailing circumstances. Relying as it did on the creativity, commitment and common sense of 'empowered' officers, NCOs and other ranks (ORs), the British and Commonwealth Armies had proved largely ineffective in the context of poor training and a demotivated and alienated working- and lower-middle class (see Chapters 2 and 6). Something clearly had to change.

Montgomery decided to distance Eighth Army from *FSR* as it was judged that officers and NCOs in the expanded citizen army were incapable of applying abstract principles in practice on the battlefield.[37] Whereas, Cunningham and Ritchie had employed a system of directive command, which sought to adapt to and exploit battlefield opportunities, Montgomery recognised that his army was quite simply incapable of fighting effectively in this manner. Instead, he sought to impose a more centralised system of command and control aimed at creating opportunities through 'unity of effort'.[38] Although less dynamic and flexible, this approach, it was hoped, would limit the impact of poor training and questionable motivation on the outcome of events. By controlling operations tightly, something both Cunningham and Ritchie had manifestly been unable to do, Montgomery hoped that he could get more out of the combined resources, especially firepower, available to Eighth Army.

Montgomery's pamphlet on command and control issued to senior officers after El Alamein, in December 1942, 'captured the essence of this new approach'. It laid 'much importance on unflinching maintenance of the objective, despite the external frictions, pressures and temptations of battle'.[39] On no account were commanders to 'wait on events and then try and form a plan'. They were told to 'never react to enemy thrusts or moves', for once this happened they would 'be in trouble'.[40] At times in North Africa, battles had degenerated into chaos and 'command by committee';[41] Montgomery's contribution, therefore, was to establish 'operational coherence' engendered by clear higher direction and organisation.[42]

This approach placed an enormous burden on the Army commander to devise a coherent and effective plan of battle. But, once a plan had been devised, there were benefits. With a clear plan, it was possible to train the Army in a very specific and directed manner. Within this context also, it would be easier to motivate the Army, as units could be told exactly what they were going to be asked to do. That is not to say that subordinate initiative was unnecessary under Montgomery's new operational technique. Initiative was still recognised as an essential means of enabling the full fighting power of the Army to be developed, but the vital importance of commanders setting and maintaining an overall aim to guide actions was emphasised in a manner completely novel to Eighth Army.[43] Control rather than dynamism was to be the watchword of Montgomery's Army.

War Office Initiatives

Thus, within barely a month, a remarkable transformation had overtaken Eighth Army. The recurring problems with the human element of the Army still, nevertheless, required attention. The expansion of the pre-war professional army into a citizen army of millions had put tremendous stress on organisations and individuals responsible for managing manpower and morale.[44] Ronald Adam, the Adjutant-General of the British Army from 1941 to 1946, and the member of the Army Council responsible for morale, believed that defeats, such as the loss of Malaya and Hong Kong and the withdrawal in Burma at the beginning of 1942, had all been 'due to the low morale of our troops'.[45]

Adam is perhaps the great unsung hero of the British Army in the Second World War (see Illustration 7.2). The son of a prominent businessman and public servant, he was schooled at Eton, before passing both in and out of the Royal Military Academy Woolwich in thirty-third place (out of a cohort of thirty-nine cadets). He was commissioned into the Royal Artillery and spent time in India before serving on the Western Front and in Italy during the First World War. He finished the war a brigade major with a DSO, having three times been mentioned in dispatches. During the interwar period Adam climbed the ladder at the War Office with remarkable speed. He attended the Staff College at Camberley in 1920 and spent another five years there as an instructor or as commandant. In 1930, he passed the course at the Imperial Defence College and by 1938 was a Lieutenant-General and Deputy Chief of the Imperial General Staff (DCIGS). Shortly after the outbreak of the Second World War, he was appointed commander of III Corps in France, where he performed sufficiently well to be given charge of preparing the perimeter defences at Dunkirk. He was installed as GOC Northern Command on his return to the UK before becoming Adjutant-General the following year.[46]

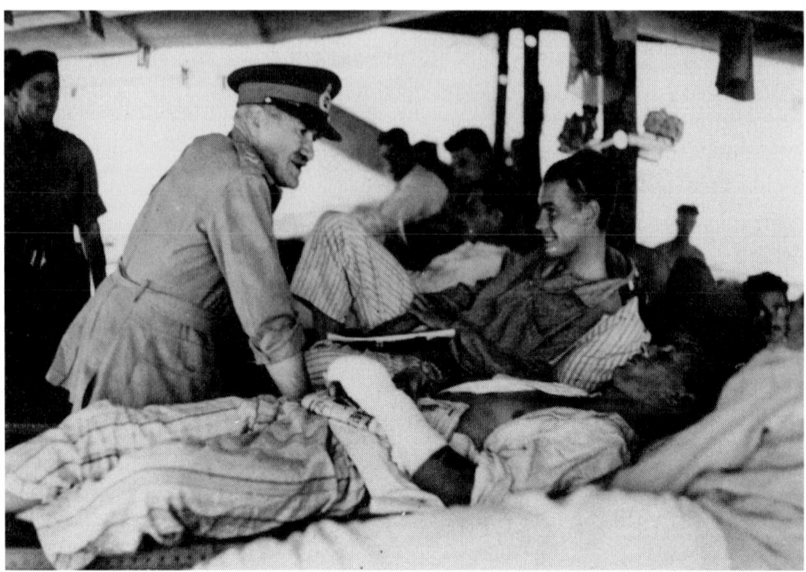

Illustration 7.2 General Adam visiting British troops in hospital during the Second World War, likely Burma, 1944. As Adjutant-General of the British Army between 1941 and the end of the war, Adam oversaw significant institutional adaptation and innovation that made the War Office more attuned to the needs of a citizen army in a world war.

Adam considered the issue of morale to be so crucial and the extent of the problem to be of such concern, that, on 27 February 1942, in the wake of the collapse at Singapore, he proposed the creation of a Morale Committee to the Executive Committee of the Army Council (ECAC).[47] He informed the ECAC that,

> The War is going to be won or lost on morale. We are too apt to leave the problem alone. Morale is a psychological problem like sex, and therefore the Britisher is almost ashamed to talk about it.[48]

It was clear to Adam that no authority either inside or outside the War Office was responsible for:

(a) surveying and analysing the state of the morale of the Army as a whole and the factors particularly affecting it at any time
(b) considering what measures should be taken from time to time for the express purpose of improving the state of morale generally

(c) judging proposed changes in army administration, regulations, etc., in the light of their probable repercussion on morale.[49]

In its meeting on 6 March 1942, the ECAC approved the setting up of the Committee,[50] its terms of reference 'to discuss, monthly, questions of morale arising from reports received from all sources, contained in the Adjutant-General's quarterly report, or brought before them by a member of the Committee, and to co-ordinate action'.[51] Adam believed that the Committee, which would report to the ECAC on a monthly basis, would 'serve a useful purpose in not only reviewing the causes adversely affecting Army Morale [both at home and with troops under British command abroad], but in planning ahead to counteract and guard against such adverse influences' in the future.[52] The Committee, thus, represented a concerted effort by Adam and the War Office to achieve cross-directorate co-ordination in dealing with morale, so that, as Adam himself said, 'quick action could be taken by those responsible in the various fields'.[53] The Morale Committee represented the final piece in a complex revolution that would bear fruit in time for the great offensive at El Alamein in October 1942. Between 1939 and 1942, the Army began to radically address the manner in which it managed that crucial factor in war, the 'human element' of the combat problem.

Training

The first, and perhaps most important, issue that was addressed, was the question of training. From early in the war, psychiatrists in the Army had argued that the root of the problem with morale was deficient training.[54] The 'value of training', as Hew Strachan has argued more recently, is 'in large part psychological: it is an enabling process, a form of empowerment, which creates self-confidence'. Training can familiarise soldiers with the confusion and noise of battle, thus helping them overcome fear; it can reproduce the continuous and exhausting nature of modern war, thus hardening troops to the trials of battle; and it can address the civilising effects of peacetime norms and accustom soldiers to the idea of killing.[55]

The German Army, which is often considered the benchmark for effective training during the Second World War, certainly saw training in this light. It focused 'less on tactical or specialist skills' in training and more on the 'psychological dimension'. 'The principal aim', declared a German High Command training directive in February 1941, 'is to educate leaders and men for ruthless aggression ... based on confidence in the superiority of the German soldier against any opponent and unwavering faith in ultimate victory.' Again, on 8 December 1941, a German High Command directive made it clear that the key attributes of training were not technical but 'the inner, psychical attitude of each individual'.[56]

The British understanding of training was not dissimilar to the German. The 1922 committee on shell-shock noted, for example, that 'the production of good morale is the most important object in military training'. Wavell, who, as an umpire, as GSO1 of a division, as a brigade commander, as a divisional commander and as General Officer Commanding-in-Chief (GOC-in-C) of a command, was responsible for fourteen consecutive training seasons between 1926 and 1939, made similar observations in a lecture in 1933 on 'training for war' at the Royal United Services Institute. The purpose of training, he said, was psychological as much as tactical, to produce 'formidable fighting men – fit, active, inquisitive and offensive – confident of making ground with their own weapons'.[57]

In March 1942, the battle-training area on the South Downs was created, providing Home Forces with sufficient land for a whole brigade to exercise with live ammunition and air support.[58] Whereas the Army only had 235,000 acres of land at its disposal, for all purposes including training, in September 1939, by January 1943 it had an additional 317,238 acres for training purposes and temporary training rights over a further 7,882,079 acres of land. By February 1944, the figures were 391,000 acres and 9,378,000 acres respectively.[59]

The most important improvements to training between 1940 and 1942, were in three key areas. First, exercises became more realistic; second, battle drills were introduced to provide junior officers with ready-made solutions to common tactical problems; and third, battle inoculation was developed to prepare troops for the sights and sounds of war.[60]

These changes began almost as soon as the BEF returned from France. Brooke, who was appointed C-in-C Home Forces in July, insisted that exercises had to become more realistic if they were to properly prepare men for battle. They were now to take place both during the summer and winter; they were to last for several days; and troops were to be hardened so that they could march 30 miles or more and still be ready to fight. Under Brooke and his successors 'exercises came to reflect some of the confusion of the battlefield'. Len Waller, a Guardsman in the Grenadier Guards, remembered them as:

> Highly disorganised affairs, and we couldn't help thinking that if real war was going to be anything like this it was God help us. Whenever we were supposed to meet up with somebody or other you could bet they wouldn't be there; the cook house got lost and there'd be no hot meal for us; we stumbled for miles across fields in the wrong direction; at nightfall we were told that 'the enemy' had captured our blankets. But the worried expressions on the faces of the senior officers confirmed our suspicions that the enemy were in our midst. Some of these exercises were more physically arduous than anything we were to experience in true combat.[61]

Training, thus, began to resemble more closely the chaotic nature of battle. The introduction of more realistic training was also accompanied by the reintroduction of a First World War innovation into the British Army, battle drills.[62] These provided the ordinary section or platoon commander with standard solutions to common tactical problems. Such drills could inculcate uniformity of practice throughout the Army; this made it easier to absorb new replacements in units, as well as facilitating the development of confidence through knowledge and understanding of how to deal with stressful and difficult tactical situations. Battle drills were to function when exhaustion made 'rational thought impossible', or when 'fear has taken over'. The logic was that they would replace the need for initiative by allowing individuals to 'react without thinking'.[63]

The Army had entered the war with a doctrine that laid down general principles but gave individual commanders a great deal of latitude to interpret them. Battle drills ran counter to this doctrinal standpoint. The concern, shared by many at the time, was that drills 'would inhibit leaders from using their knowledge, intelligence, and initiative to adapt the principles [of war] to the particular situation they faced'.[64] However, by 1941 senior officers were beginning to accept that the massive expansion of the Army from its pre-war cadre of regular soldiers required a far more prescriptive method of fighting, or, as it was put in 'Army Training Memorandum No. 44' (1944), 'tactics by numbers'.[65] After the defeat in France, commanders such as Alexander, Montgomery and Sir John Dill, Chief of the Imperial General Staff (CIGS) between May 1940 and December 1941, began to accept that the best way to solve the problem of deficient performance at the tactical level was through the development of these tactical drills. While Dill feared that tactics could become stereotyped if such measures were introduced, the priority, after Dunkirk, was really on the absolute basics, the necessity for officers and men to develop the ability to cope with danger and disorganisation and fight. The inculcation of tactical flexibility could come later.[66]

Alexander was the driving force behind the changes. From his experience in France, he was convinced that the Army's propensity to shun tactical drills had been a mistake. He acknowledged that under stress most soldiers were too beset by fear and doubt to exercise their initiative. While British troops had been paralysed, German units had penetrated between positions and forced British units to retire. In August 1940, he urged the divisional commanders of I Corps to consider tactical drills in training 'both to save time and to cater for the officer who lacks training and initiative'.[67] In October, he issued a set of 'Tactical Notes' to I Corps in which he insisted that it was:

> Better to know instinctively some orthodox line of conduct than to be paralysed by the uncertainty of what to do. Let us, therefore, study and draw up lines of conduct for the simple soldier – so that we may ensure that our soldiers when faced with problems on the battle-field will have an answer to them.[68]

Dill had 'Tactical Notes' reprinted and issued throughout the Army. The first divisional Battle School, set up to teach battle drills, was established in Britain by 47th Division in July 1941. By December, GHQ was in the process of establishing its own Battle School at Barnard Castle to provide instructors for the schools that had been ordered to form in every division in the country.[69]

Montgomery, on arriving in the desert, insisted that these training innovations be disseminated throughout Eighth Army,[70] and, indeed, it is not hard to see how these initiatives facilitated his more centralised, structured and systematic approach to battle. In his first training memorandum for El Alamein, written on 30 August 1942, he stressed that:

> Battle drill must be highly developed. By means of this battle drill we ensure a common line of approach to the sub-unit battle problem, and a common procedure within the sub-unit. The fact that every Officer, N.C.O. and man is taught this common procedure ensures full co-operation in the battle area, even when casualties necessitate changes in junior commanders and reinforcements to replace wastage.[71]

Montgomery was aided in his efforts by Alexander's close connection with the battle-drill movement,[72] and 'much practice of battle drills, both on the ground and in TEWTS, was undertaken before the battle'. Many formations exchanged methods and procedures, and 'valuable experience was passed to novice formations'.[73]

The battle-drill and battle-school movement introduced another training innovation, battle inoculation.[74] These techniques were designed to provide the soldier with experiences that would 'help him to face unmoved, the attack on his morale involved in battle'.[75] It was supposed to undermine the 'pacifist propaganda' that had, in the words of a report written in 1942, 'exaggerated the horror and danger of war, until the individual has a false inner mental picture of it as an overwhelmingly terrifying thing to which the only logical attitude is escape or extreme passivity'. This attitude of defence and retreat could 'only be resolved by letting each man learn for himself that his inner image is over-drawn' and that the 'real truth' was 'not so terrifying'. Battle inoculation was the slow application of battle effects, such as noise and gunfire, graduated in severity up to battle conditions that were as near reality as possible. By steady inoculation, applied with patience and understanding, the average man could be made tolerant of the worst noises and sights of war and the 'unreal fears from his imagination' could be dissolved.[76] Battle inoculation was of particular value to leaders and potential leaders on active service, as they needed to learn how to make decisions under the stress and noise of battle.[77]

Captain Lionel Wigram, who was commandant of 47th Division's battle school at Chelwood Gate, hoped that the combination of realistic battle inoculation and battle drill training would so raise the morale of British infantrymen that they would soon be able to win battles 'against exceedingly quick and bold opponents' such as the Germans. 'We shall find ourselves at a grave disadvantage', he said, 'if we cannot be as fit, as quick, as bold and as enterprising as they are'.[78]

Montgomery heartily agreed with this assessment and championed both initiatives in the lead up to El Alamein. Battle drill and battle inoculation were, thus, not solely or even primarily about developing technical tactical skills; they were about fostering morale, drive, initiative and determination.

Manpower

The second key aspect of the 'human problem' addressed by the War Office, was the question of the quality of manpower available to the Army. The British Government had made a conscious decision to limit the overall size of the Army in the Second World War; many skilled workers were in reserved occupations, while the Royal Navy and RAF received many of the most intelligent recruits (see Chapter 2). This left the Army with what Brigadier Rees, the Consultant Psychiatrist to the Army, called 'the psychopathic tenth'[79] of the country's manpower, the least intelligent and often the least ambitious of the recruits. Accelerated expansion post-1939 did not help matters. The Cabinet, hoping to frighten Hitler and Mussolini, rushed headlong into a rapid enlargement that the Army was ill-equipped to manage,[80] and it was clear that all too little attention had been given to the problems of morale and selection in a conscript army during the interwar years. Adam recalled that:

> I was as much to blame as anyone, for I was a chief instructor at the Staff College for more than three years and Commandant for a few months. I can recall only one lecture dealing with morale in a conscript army, and that an excellent one, given by Lt Colonel A. E. Nye, then an instructor at the college and later VCIGS.[81]

The War Office was, therefore, forced to relearn, by trial and error, the policies and practices necessary to select and motivate a citizen army.[82]

The process began on return from France in 1940. Adam was installed as GOC Northern Command and immediately set about studying the problem of manpower. With the co-operation of the Northern Command psychiatrist, Lieutenant-Colonel G. R. Hargreaves, he initiated a study to ascertain the intelligence of the men under his leadership and their suitability for the jobs to which they had been posted. In his findings, sent to the War Office in January 1941,[83]

Adam found a wide gap between the ideal of employing every man on the work most suited to him and the actual position as it pertained in the Army. The figures he produced were quite staggering. He recorded that 50 per cent of every Royal Armoured Corps (RAC) intake and 20 per cent of every infantry intake did not have the intelligence for full efficiency in the corps to which they had been posted. Furthermore, 20 per cent of every infantry intake and 50 per cent of every pioneer intake in Northern Command were 'misplaced' and capable of more efficient service in a corps other than the one to which they had been posted. Overall, he found that 4 per cent of intakes were totally useless for any training as a soldier.[84] The Army was making extremely poor use of the human assets available to it.

In general, men of low intelligence were more likely to develop neurotic features, poor morale, low personal esteem, disciplinary problems and see themselves as useless in their jobs.[85] A study carried out in Western Command, in August 1941, found that, of 300 soldiers under sentence for going AWOL, 'one half had the intellectual capacity found in the least intelligent quarter of the population, i.e. this group of men contained twice the number of dullards and defectives usually found in homologous conscript groups'.[86] Another study, carried out in 1942, found that nine out of ten men who reached a minimum level in intelligence tests were successful in training. Below that level, four out of five men either failed in training, or were reported as unsatisfactory by their field units.[87] Men of low intelligence were also more likely to break down if they were placed in the wrong post ('misfits') or put in a position of heavy stress.[88] 'Misfits', who also included intelligent men placed in jobs below their capabilities, tended to feel, and become, 'outsiders' in their unit.[89] Their loyalty to their unit was therefore always doubtful and they were liable, as a circular to all Medical Officers written later in the war on 'Morale Discipline and Mental Fitness' noted, on slight cause to become openly resentful of authority. Their 'poor individual morale' could, therefore, 'affect group morale'.[90]

The situation convinced Adam that proper selection procedures had to be introduced.[91] Since July 1940, recruits had undergone intelligence tests subsequent to joining a corps in the Army.[92] Unco-ordinated testing had also taken place in various commands under the supervision of Command Psychiatrists. However, no central authority had been concerned with the allocation, transfer or discharge of personnel in the Army. The system clearly required an immediate overhaul.[93] Not only did the state require the Army to apply its resources 'to the best possible advantage', but the 'efficiency and contentment of the Army depended to a large extent upon putting the right man in the right place'.[94] Adam brought the issue before the ECAC in June 1941. His view was that the Army was 'wasting its man-power in this war almost as badly as it did in the last'. He pointed out that men were being posted to a corps almost entirely on the demand of the moment and without any effort to determine their fitness for the corps in question. He argued that the Army in the United States, which had carried out selection testing on every man in the Great War, was continuing the policy into this period of crisis and that the German Army was employing as many as 1,000 psychologists on testing. He thought the Red Army was also conducting intelligence tests.[95]

As a result of Adam's proposal, the Directorate of Selection of Personnel was set up, in June 1941, under Brigadier Alick Buchanan Smith. The purpose of the Directorate was to provide testing, at medical examination centres, for all new recruits, as well as for units in formations due for conversion to other corps, in particular for transfer to the RAC.[96] The new Directorate was advised by a committee of civilian psychologists, including the Professors of Psychology at Cambridge, Edinburgh and London Universities, as well as Dr Charles Myers, who had experience of psychiatry in the First World War (as Chief Specialist in Nervous Shock and as Consulting Psychiatrist to the British Army in France). The Directorate's staff consisted of a nucleus of officers who were professional psychologists and approximately 150 NCOs. The officers devised suitable selection procedures and the NCOs carried out the tests.[97] Matrix tests (general intelligence tests similar to modern-day aptitude tests), seen as 'the best established and most reliable' form of evaluation at the time, were designed to assess recruits by testing their reasoning abilities and spatial awareness. The intelligence levels for various army jobs were established and it was then up to recruits to meet the standard required. Those scoring particularly low on the tests were referred to psychiatrists to ascertain the best use of their abilities.[98]

The extent of the challenge facing the new Directorate was immense. By the second half of 1941, the Army was discharging about 1,300 men every month because of diagnosable, and therefore avoidable, psycho-neurotic problems during training.[99] Testing began in some commands in August 1941, and, by November, two-thirds of intakes were being subjected to proper examination on enlistment.[100]

Table 7.1 Intelligence levels of a group of 2,000 RAC reinforcements sent to the Middle East, 1942

Selection groups	Ideal make-up of draft based on job analysis	Actual RAC drafts to Middle East
SG1, 2 and 3 plus	72.8%	72.4%
SG3 minus	17.1%	15.6%
SG4 and 5	10.1%	12%

By July 1942, the system was fully up and running, with some 23,000 men a month being tested on entering the Army.[101]

These innovations were to have profound implications for Eighth Army as it prepared its offensive at El Alamein. For years units had used drafts for the Middle East 'as a means of getting rid of their worst personnel'.[102] But, by August 1942, as a result of the efforts of Adam and others, the issue was well on the way to being solved. The Secretary of State for War, James Grigg, provided the Army Council and War Cabinet with a report by the Directorate of Selection of Personnel on a 'test audit' carried out on 2,000 drafts of the RAC who were due to leave for the Middle East that summer. Grigg's sample was made up of one-third of the total RAC drafts sent to the desert during the period. Recruits were banded into groups, based on their scores in selection tests designed to identify their suitability for active operations. Selection Group 1 (SG1) were the best material; SG2 were above average; SG3 were average; and SG4 and SG5 were below average and useless for active operations.[103]

As Table 7.1 shows, the quality of men being sent to the desert at this juncture matched the 'ideal make up of drafts based on job analysis'. In the words of the Deputy Adjutant-General, Grigg's report provided strong proof 'that the increased use of selective testing is bearing fruit', and that the quality of drafts, from this point of view, should 'certainly show progressive improvement' into the future. If the RAC figures were representative of the Army as a whole, and there was 'no reason to think that they are not', the Army had 'already achieved a satisfactory standard of drafting'.[104] By September 1942, a Joint Memorandum by the Lord Privy Seal, the First Lord of the Admiralty, the Secretary of State for War, and the Secretary of State for Air, noted that many of the manpower problems besetting the Army had been solved. It stressed that men who were 'definitely sub-normal mentally' and who were effectively 'unemployable' in civilian life were by this time fitted into jobs within their capacity and in some cases were sent to the new unarmed units of the Pioneer Corps where they were 'happy, efficient, clean, and useful members of the Army'. Overall, the report concluded that there could 'be no doubt' that morale had 'gained as a result of the introduction of psychiatry'.[105]

There is evidence to support this view from theatres of operation, not least from the desert. By August 1942, there were some thirty psychiatrists in the Middle East.[106] Brigadier J. R. Rees, the Consultant Psychiatrist to the Army, regarded these men as 'the cream of the psychiatrists available at the time when they were sent out'. Brigadier G. W. B. James, the Consultant Psychiatrist Eighth Army, for instance, had received a MC and bar in the First World War and was, in the view of Major H. B. Craigie of the Department of Army Psychiatry in the Middle East, 'an excellent man'.[107] In July, Craigie reported that 'the position' in the Middle East was 'improving' and that the 'indiscriminate posting overseas of backward or unstable men' had become 'less likely'.[108] Adam, on a tour to the Middle East the following month, expressly to ascertain the state of the fighting troops' morale, noted that 'so far as the "fighting troops" are concerned ... the reinforcements appeared to be satisfactory'.[109] Later he stated that the application of selection procedures to the 363,000 men inducted into the Army in 1942 had provided it with an intake 'predominantly of an age, medical category and type suitable for the fighting arms'.[110] Thus, it is fair to say that the approximately 60,000 reinforcements received by Eighth Army between 1 August and 23 October 1942 were generally of a higher calibre than those that arrived before them in the desert. These were the men who made up the replacements needed after the Gazala and Tobruk disasters and the July battles on the El Alamein line. These were the men who, alongside the desert veterans, would fight under Montgomery in the critical battle to come in October and November 1942.

Officers

Even more important than the selection of ORs, in the eyes of Adam and the War Office, was the quality of officers inducted into the Army.[111] The average platoon, as Colonel T. N. Grazebrook, of 78th Division, noted later in the war, typically included 'three or four heroes, three or four irreconcilables' and a remainder of men who responded 'in direct relationship to the quality of their leaders'.[112] By March 1942, the situation was arousing enough attention that Grigg stated at a press conference that the question of getting 'the right leadership' and of promoting 'the right officers', was one which was 'being taken seriously by the military'. Grigg stressed that it was his belief that the quality of officers was 'about the most important single consideration affecting the morale of the Army' and 'the most important thing to get done'.[113]

Such concerns were not new. Adam, since taking over the role of Adjutant-General, had adopted a two-sided approach to the problem of poor-quality officers. First, he concentrated on better officer selection procedures and, secondly, he focused on educating potential officers in the essentials of man-management.[114] Traditionally, officers were selected in the Army by a small Command Interview Board in a ten- or fifteen-minute interview designed to test whether the personality of the officer candidate matched traditional requirements. By the summer of 1941, it was evident that this system was not working. Selection boards were turning down approximately 30 per cent of COs' nominations[115] and as many as 20 to 50 per cent of candidates sent to Officer Corps Training Units (OCTUs) were failing the course.[116] By mid-1941, the Secretary of State for War was receiving as many as thirty parliamentary questions each week that were critical of the officer selection system.[117] It was clear that many men felt they were poorly treated by the single command interview,[118] and that the lack of transparency in the system was dissuading many potential candidates from putting their names forward for commissions. As a result, during 1941, OCTUs were frequently running below capacity because enough willing recruits could not be found.

Adam was aware that the Germans had a far more scientific method of selecting their officers. Since 1926, they had subjected their potential candidates to two days of rigorous personality and psychological testing along with more traditional selection procedures. Adam put the possibility of instituting a similar type of test for OCTU candidates to the Army Council in June 1941.[119] In the same month, at the suggestion of Rees, the Consulting Psychiatrist to the Army, the Psychiatrist Scottish Command began investigations designed to test the value of psychological methods in the assessment of officer candidates. An effort was made to reproduce and try out the German Army methods of officer selection and the results of the study proved encouraging.

As a consequence of these preliminary investigations, a conference was held in Edinburgh, in late 1941, at which the tests used were demonstrated to Adam, Buchanan Smith, the Director of Selection of Personnel, and General Sir Andrew Thorne, the GOC Scottish Command. By 20 October 1941, Adam had brought the War Office round to the opinion 'that an intelligence test supplemented by a commanding officer's report and a really well planned interview might produce a good result'.[120]

The new officer selection procedure was introduced in January 1942 in Scottish Command and the first batch of officer candidates were examined there in February.[121] The tests became widespread throughout all commands the following month and later with overseas OCTUs.[122] Overall, seventeen new War Office Selection Boards (WOSBs) were set up in 1942.[123] The selection procedure itself was lengthened from a single interview to three days of rigorous psychological and military situation tests. Cutting-edge selection techniques, such as leaderless group tests, were introduced to observe men's capacity for maintaining personal relationships in situations of strain that tempted them to disregard the interest of their fellows for the sake of their own.[124] At the end of the course, individuals underwent an interview of the old type to ascertain whether candidates' personalities fitted the more traditional view of an officer.[125]

The reaction to the new selection procedures was extremely positive. Candidates at several WOSBs, who were surveyed in the summer of 1942, expressed unanimous enthusiasm about the new process.[126] A man who attended a board in North Africa later in the war wrote:

> At the moment of writing I am at one of the new fangled ideas, a WOSB, I must say after my first day here that I am very agreeably surprised. I had expected one of the usual red-tape shows, but find that it was quite the opposite. It is one of the soundest things I have ever contacted since I came into the Army and if I do not make the grade, then it will be because I haven't got what it takes to be an officer. The whole idea of this place is simplicity and it is so run that the examining officers really do get to know with whom they are dealing. One thing I am supremely confident of win or lose I shall go away from here much improved in the ways of man and his deeds.[127]

Psychiatrists involved in the testing procedures noticed that new candidates felt they were getting a square deal from a more 'fair' procedure.[128] The upshot was that the supply of candidates to OCTUs rose by a remarkable 65 per cent over the summer of 1942.[129]

Not only did these initiatives improve the experience of those put forward for selection as officers, but there is much evidence to suggest that the quality of officers improved as a consequence of the new system too. The old system of the command interview had rejected at least one out of three of the best candidates appearing before selection boards.[130] The new system also rejected about one in three candidates. However, the better candidates did not get discarded to the same extent in the revised selection procedures.[131] An investigation, carried out at the end of the war on men selected for OCTUs by the two methods, showed that the standard of men who passed out selected under the WOSBs was higher than those selected under the old command interview system.[132] The increased number of candidates willing to put themselves before selection boards, combined with the more efficient selection techniques introduced in 1942, resulted 'in nearly two-and-a-half times as many above average candidates being sent to OCTUs than would have been sent under the old system'.[133] *Picture Post* declared that the new system was one of the 'most progressive initiatives of the war'.[134]

The morale reports back up these contentions. The report for home forces, May to July 1942, noted that the standard of junior leadership and man-management had improved; favourable references to their officers outnumbered the unfavourable references in the men's letters.[135] The report also stated that a decrease in minor cases of absence had occurred and that 'several Commanders' had suggested that this was 'due to an improvement in officers' care for their men and an increase in the attention paid to the men's domestic difficulties'.[136] Much credit for these improvements could be given to the OCTUs and lectures given at battle schools throughout the UK. By May 1942, 'training in these establishments' was 'concentrated on Leadership and not, as [be]fore, on training the cadet to be the perfect private soldier'.[137]

These improvements fed through to the desert also. The censorship summary for 5 to 11 August 1942 stated that officers who passed out of the Middle East OCTU were of a far higher quality than those who had gone before them. These officers, the summary stated, were granted their commissions on 'merit and experience after what must be one of the most exacting courses existing'.[138] The censorship summary for 3 to 9 September reported that mail from 'training units and Base Depots' offered:

> Many interesting comments on Senior and Junior Officers. The majority of these were favourable and gave the impression that officers who inspire their men by their ability and courage by far outnumber those who do not. For some time past much adverse criticism was registered and it is therefore a pleasant feature to see this change of tone.[139]

The summary for 10 to 16 September commented that 'one of the happiest features of the mail was the confidence expressed by other ranks in their officers [and] unit commanders'.[140]

The second initiative that Adam focused on, in order to improve the quality of officers, was education in the essentials of man-management. In the British Army, the welfare of the soldier had always been regarded as the responsibility of the regimental officer. Major-General H. Willans, who was appointed Director-General at the new Directorate of Welfare in December 1940,[141] realised that the weight of responsibility on newly commissioned officers was overwhelming for many of the new citizen army.[142] 'The present war' was, in his opinion 'far more complicated' than those in the past, including the Great War. The duties of the officer were more numerous, more varied and more difficult to master. Moreover, the ordinary recruit also had 'many more problems', some of which were 'beyond the reasonable scope of the Regimental Officer's knowledge and experience' such as difficulties raised by the bombing of the soldier's home, the evacuation of his relations and those connected with his business and property.[143]

Willans summarised the significance of these issues in a speech that he gave at the beginning of 1942:

> You will agree with me, or, at any rate you will not quarrel with me, for saying that leadership is the most important of all the sinews of war, and it is not too much to say that one instant of toil denied at this moment by any leader, great or small, senior or junior, may well make the difference between victory or defeat ... And I say, without fear of contradiction that no part of the leader's duty is more insistent or more unforgiving than

> that part which charges him to cater for the spiritual, moral, physical and mental well-being of the men who are under his command; to cater for them in such a way that it will bring out their best qualities, courage, resolution, and stiffen their fibre and their morale and will make them in due course better soldiers; so much better soldiers that they may be described as the 'Crusaders', as we hope they will be, of 1942, or 1943, or of the following years.[144]

Willans believed that the responsibilities of leadership in such times were 'crushing', the opportunities 'endless'. The officers and men of the Army would 'not fail us' as long as their welfare was properly considered. The problem, as he saw it, was that such a situation had been far from reality at the beginning of 1941.[145]

Throughout 1941, therefore, Willans oversaw the publication of a series of pamphlets on the subject of welfare in the Army in an attempt to educate officers in man-management. 'The Officer and Fighting Efficiency', for instance, told officers that 'in order to care for their men properly, they must first know and understand them'.[146] Another pamphlet, 'The Soldier's Welfare, Notes for Officers', released by order of the Army Council, also in 1941, clearly listed the two main aims of welfare work in the Army as:

(1) To make the men as happy and contented as possible, in the varying circumstances of war, so that they would be at all times fighting fit and fit to fight.
(2) To link officers and men together in a bond of mutual friendliness and respect, which would, not only stand the hardest tests of war, but would be strengthened by them.[147]

The pamphlet went on to list a number of principles the officer should adhere to in order to realise these two aims. Among them were the following:

> The care of his men is an officer's first concern, which he puts before his own comfort and convenience.
>
> Discontent seldom arises from hardship, provided that the men feel the hardship is reasonable, i.e. that it is a necessary part of the business of winning the war. They are ready to endure cheerfully anything which they believe to be unavoidable, but they are easily disgruntled if they feel that the hardships are

> caused by red tape or inefficiency or by lack of understanding, rather than by military necessity.
>
> Every man is entitled to be treated as a reasonable human being, unless he has shown himself unworthy of such treatment. Whenever possible, therefore, the reason for irksome orders or restrictions should be explained to him . . . Such action strengthens discipline and is not a sign of weakness.
>
> Men are more easily upset by treatment that they believe to be unfair and by supposed inequality of sacrifice than by any other cause.[148]

The pamphlet concluded that the reward for officers would be not only 'happy and efficient men, but a loyalty and devotion from them out of all proportion to the services rendered'.[149]

Lectures to regimental officers on man-management, welfare and morale were given on a large scale by consultant and specialist psychiatrists, and were a standard part of staff courses, OCTUs and battle schools throughout 1941 and 1942. These focused on topics such as measures to maintain the mental health of the soldier; how to weed out unsuitable men before battle; the handling of incipient breakdowns during a campaign; the principles of group feeling (esprit de corps); the place of discipline in mental health; the foundations of morale; the morale effects of various enemy weapons; the proper place and use of battle inoculation; factors militating against individual and group morale; methods of upholding mental health under difficulties; and the function of leadership in the field of morale.[150]

These pamphlets and lectures represented a concerted drive by Willans and Adam to educate officers in the art of leadership and man-management. They also demonstrated that, although the War Office was determined to be accountable for the welfare of its soldiers, ultimately responsibility rested on the shoulders of the regimental officer, just as it had done in the First World War. The censorship summaries in the desert provide ample evidence of the success of these initiatives. The summary for 23 to 29 September remarked that 'there is much pleasing evidence to show that officers, senior and junior, are putting their best into their work, a fact which never fails to be appreciated by the men'. The censor believed that 'a good deal of [the] friendliness and understanding between officers and men' was due to a 'keener appreciation [by officers] of the importance of man-management'.[151] A sapper wrote:

> We have new officers and we hardly know what has happened to us. We feel imbued with new courage because these new officers consider us as the old ones never did. We are not accustomed to officers having much interest taken in our welfare and it almost makes one feel as if you have just started so pleasant is the atmosphere. While the old officers always ignored us or tried to get rid of us with the least trouble, these new officers are doing all they can for us. They have to travel over more than a 100 miles of desert to bring our post to us, but they do it whereas the others would not have bothered about it. Yes, I thank God that the old crowd have gone, and I hope I never see them again. It was just the treatment meted out to us by our former officers that upset me, hard work and hardship never affected me or made me despondent.[152]

Education

War Office inspired improvements in training and manpower selection and man-management, were accompanied also by a further initiative deemed central to improving the morale of the troops: army education. On accepting Adam's recommendation for the setting up of the Morale Committee in March 1942, the ECAC noted that it regarded the setting up of the Committee 'as a sound first step', but were concerned 'that bigger issues may well be involved' which were 'probably far more fundamental and deep-set than those arising from internal administration'. Some of the possible causes, the ECAC concluded, were 'outside the control of the Army Council' and would 'require action at the highest level' if they were to be addressed; these included the 'attitude of the Press', the 'wider question of the morale of the British people as a whole' and 'the fact that there is no very clear objective for the soldier of today'.[153]

The problem was that the Conservative-dominated Government had hardly any interest in addressing such issues (see Chapter 6). Churchill 'engaged little with domestic politics' during the war and saw debate about social change and reconstruction 'as a distraction from his main task'.[154] In this respect, he differed markedly from Roosevelt's handling of the American war effort. Roosevelt believed that the efforts demanded by the state to meet the global cataclysm that was the Second World War, 'required legitimacy, accorded by citizens who were invested somehow – materially or ideologically – in the power of the national government'. In this sense, he linked intimately the questions of social change and social justice with the performance of American armies on the battlefield.[155]

In the absence of a similar ethos in the handling of the British and Commonwealth war effort, the Army Council supported the development of army education as a proxy for real government led engagement with the broader meaning of the war. It began this process in January 1940, when concerns about morale became evident during the 'phoney war'. In the circumstances, the Army Council assigned a committee chaired by Lieutenant-General Sir Robert Haining, the Vice-Chief of the Imperial General Staff, to consider among other things educational needs in the Army. The Haining Report led to the creation of the Directorate of Welfare but also to the introduction, that September, of a voluntary education scheme for those that were interested when off-duty. An education officer was appointed in each unit and the Army Education Corps (AEC), which had almost died away during the interwar years, was expanded and returned to work. The Directorate of Education, which was formed in the autumn of 1940, was intended to co-operate with its welfare counterpart and this arrangement was formalised at the end of 1940 when General Willans was appointed Director-General of Welfare and Education.[156]

The creation and expansion of the Directorate of Welfare and Education was, as Jeremy Crang has argued, a direct result of the experiences in France and Flanders.[157] In order to inculcate morale, it was emphasised to education officers that it was especially important to educate the troops about what they were fighting for. 'There should be constant opportunities', an Army Council Instruction noted, 'of showing to all the destructive nature, both as regards material and culture, of the forces set against us, and of illustrating how the British Empire stands for the essential factors of a new and better life.'[158]

Nevertheless, by the spring of 1941, it was estimated that only 20 per cent of troops in the UK were receiving educational provisions.[159] At the same time, news of defeats in the Middle East and the prospect of a continued sedentary existence for the troops at home raised fresh concerns over morale.[160] Willans was convinced that education and welfare had to go hand in hand. 'Welfare was concerned with the morale of the army' and, in his mind, 'so too was education'.[161] In June 1941, he proposed to the Army Council a new project designed, above all, 'to maintain the morale of the troops'. It would also have the added effect of forcing junior officers to get to know their men better and prepare men for the requirements of the post-war world.[162]

The proposal, encapsulated in a paper, 'Current Affairs in the Army: The Outline of a New Plan' made a number of far reaching recommendations that linked education and morale in an intimate relationship that was designed to drive towards success in battle. It stated that the soldier, who neither knew nor cared why he was under arms, was a danger to national safety. Morale was 'fundamentally a matter of discipline' and true discipline was 'a matter of understanding'.[163] In brief, the argument amounted to this:

a) The soldier who understood the cause for which he was fighting was likely to be a more reliable soldier than the one who did not.
b) Many soldiers in the British Army had no such understanding, and many others were losing touch with the sources of knowledge and information they used to possess.
c) It was the business of the Army [in the absence of a Government led initiative] to make good this deficiency of knowledge and therefore to devise what means were possible to keep the men abreast of Current Affairs.[164]

To oversee this radical new plan, a new directorate, the Army Bureau of Current Affairs (ABCA), was formed. It was headed by W. E. Williams, who was, at the time, secretary of the British Institute of Adult Education[165] and was viewed by Willans as a 'pioneer' of his profession.[166]

The new plan for current affairs instruction was to be introduced as a part of the soldiers' general training. The regimental officer would take his men aside once a week and lead a discussion on current events.[167] In order to help the already overloaded regimental officer carry out these new duties, ABCA issued two fortnightly, alternating bulletins. The first was 'War', the second 'Current Affairs'. 'War' provided military intelligence in the widest sense. It printed vivid narratives of what was happening in the various theatres of war and illustrated these records with accounts of outstanding achievements by the British Army, Royal Navy and RAF. It was designed to educate the troops about the march of events.[168] 'Current Affairs', on the other hand, aimed to provide a background of knowledge against which events could be assessed and understood.[169] It was expected that these publications would contain sufficient material to enable officers of average ability to talk usefully to their men on a particular topic for at least half an hour every week.[170]

In August 1941, Williams officially became Director of ABCA and, in the same month, 'Current Affairs in the Army: The Outline of a New Plan' was released in pamphlet form to all commanding officers.[171] ABCA, unquestionably, represented the strongest effort deemed possible by the War Office to inculcate morale amongst the troops by keeping them informed about the war and giving them a cause for which it was deemed worth fighting.

By November 1941, army education along the same lines as in the UK was up and running in the Middle East.[172] Although courses were initially only available to officers, by May 1942 they were made accessible to all British officers and ORs.[173] That same month, General Ritchie, at the time the commander of Eighth Army, announced that all units of a strength equal to or over that of a battalion were to have both a Unit Welfare and a Unit Education Officer.[174] In June 1942, a Middle East School of Education was formed to train Unit Education Officers on the same lines as the syllabus in Britain. The Unit Education Officers were given an outline of the Army Education Scheme, background information about current affairs and direction on the general principles of instruction. According to the commandant of the school, 'the personnel attending were for the most part keen and appreciative, and the results achieved proved ... that much good had been derived from the School's peregrinations'.[175]

Besides these courses, staff from the Middle East School of Education gave numerous talks during two lecture tours, the second of which was with Eighth Army on the eve of the El Alamein offensive. This tour was received 'with unparalleled enthusiasm by the seventy audiences who listened to the talks of which they themselves had chosen the subject'. Before El Alamein, the school embarked on an additional programme, with the objective of making units 'ABCA conscious'. This involved holding courses of two and a half days' duration for junior officers at any location where a sufficient number of units were stationed.[176] ABCA pamphlets, similar to those in use in Britain, were reproduced in the Middle East and circulated widely.[177] At the same time, touring teams of AEC personnel held short courses to give demonstrations of the main principles of ABCA instruction.[178] In the first year of the school's existence, its staff conducted thirty-four courses and delivered more than 150 lectures to units. During that period, more than 650 trainee instructors passed through the school, representative of all branches of the Army, and including small numbers of RAF and Royal Navy officers, as well as members of the Free French Forces.[179]

The War Office Historical Monograph for the 'History of Army Education' stated that, by August 1942, education had begun 'to take definite root in the Eighth Army'.[180] That month, the censorship summaries reported that many men referred to attending lectures on 'war aims' and 'our plans after the war'.[181] In addition, a Command Education Officer arrived in the desert in September 1942, his main focus being education of 'a field nature' due to the forthcoming battle at El Alamein.[182] Montgomery, even, 'pragmatically incorporated' army education 'into his plan to build up the efficiency and esprit de corps of the units under his command', and his efforts 'proved', by all accounts, 'a great success'.[183]

By the second half of 1942, Education Officers had become integral parts of units in the desert. Both personal diaries and mail show that the men were interested in current affairs and concerned about their future following the war.[184] Education, thus, was able to provide the soldier with a link to home and the future for which he was fighting. The establishment and strengthening of education in the desert meant that another element in the intricate web of human needs and motivation had been put in place in time for what would prove to be the decisive battle of the desert war and a turning point in the Second World War more generally.

El Alamein

By October 1942, the pieces of a complex strategic jig-saw were beginning to fall into place for Montgomery and Eighth Army; a new operational doctrine had been introduced and the broad issue of morale had begun to be addressed by multiple War Office initiatives. These qualitative improvements were accompanied by quantitative enhancements. In the weeks following Alam Halfa, Eighth Army decisively won the logistics battle. With Tripoli, Benghazi and Tobruk 1,300, 800 and 375 miles respectively from the front at El Alamein, the Axis forces were using between one-third and one-half of their total fuel deliveries just to run vehicle convoys taking supplies into Egypt. As Allied reinforcements piled into the Middle East, Rommel's logistic chain went into a catastrophic 'death spiral'. In August 1942, 35 per cent of Axis tonnage bound for Africa was sunk in the Mediterranean. In September, the figure was 30 per cent and in October more than 50 per cent. In the first three weeks of August, the Italians received 15,000 tons of supplies and the Germans 8,500. By comparison, British and Commonwealth forces were unloading 400,000 tons a month in Suez.[185]

By late October, Eighth Army had twice as many troops as the *Panzerarmee* (around 220,000 versus 108,000).[186] Its advantage in materiel was also considerable. It had twice as many tanks (around 1,029 versus 548),[187] and over four times as many medium and heavy tanks.[188] It had a 3:2 advantage in artillery (around 892 versus 552) and anti-tank guns (1,451 versus 1,063) and nearly 200 more planes (around 530 versus 350).[189] Eighth Army had, however, enjoyed quantitative advantages previously and still been defeated by the *Panzerarmee*. What had appeared to be good morale in May 1942 had disintegrated quickly into full-blown crisis during Rommel's successful advance. British and Commonwealth forces had suffered approximately 80,000 casualties over the summer months, and the 'reborn Eighth Army was full of untrained units'. It was clear, therefore, that Montgomery would have to 'stage-manage' the coming battle so that the 'troops would be able to do what was demanded of them' and that he had to be not 'too ambitious' in his demands. By doing 'foolish or stupid things' Eighth Army could 'lose heavily in the first few days of the battle' and 'negative [its] superiority'. Much like Alam Halfa, therefore, Montgomery aimed to ensure that the battle was fought '*in our own way*' and that 'formations and units were not given tasks which were likely to end in failure'.[190]

His first task, a necessity given his new operational approach, was to devise a clear and coherent plan for the coming offensive. With this aim in mind, on 6 October, a memorandum was issued outlining the Commander's intentions for the forthcoming battle. Ordinarily, Eighth Army's approach to operations had been first to eliminate the enemy's armour in a battle of manoeuvre and then to destroy the remaining unarmoured portion of the *Panzerarmee*. At El Alamein, Montgomery decided he would reverse the process 'because of the low state of the training' of the troops. The modified plan was to contain the German *panzer* units facing him in the desert, while Eighth Army carried out a methodical destruction of the unarmoured troops on the Axis side. He referred to this tactic as a 'crumbling' process.[191] In essence, as 9th Australian Division's report on the battle of El Alamein confirmed, Montgomery accepted that his armoured forces were incapable of beating the *Afrika Korps* in a straight fight.[192] He therefore concentrated his best troops, the Australian, New Zealand, South African and Scottish infantry of XXX Corps, against the infantry of the Germans and Italians. This would force the Axis armour to react and counter-attack Eighth Army's plentiful anti-tank guns and armour. Montgomery judged that it was far easier to train units for a frontal assault and then to fight behind anti-tank guns than to train them in the intricate combined arms operations that the Germans were so efficient at in the open spaces of the desert.

Montgomery set about perfecting the training of his formations for the battle of attrition to come. He removed five divisions from the line for intensive preparations; these were 1st, 10th and 8th Armoured Divisions from X Corps, and 2nd New Zealand Division and 51st Highland Division from XXX Corps. There were good reasons for choosing these formations. The armoured divisions of X Corps were required to break through the gaps in the Axis defences once the four attacking infantry divisions of XXX Corps had 'broken in' and they needed specific training for this key task. The 2nd New Zealand Division needed training after its heavy casualties during the July fighting. The newly arrived 51st Highland Division, which had been reconstituted after its destruction in France in 1940, had not been tested in battle and, therefore, required extra training as it was going to take part in the initial assault on 23 October. The remaining formations in Eighth Army were required to hold the line and train a brigade at a time, as each brigade was relieved to take on the role of reserve.[193]

The extent, intensity and attention to detail of Montgomery's training programme dwarfed any that had preceded it during the war. The 51st Highland Division, in the two months leading up to El Alamein, laid out exact replicas of the parts of the enemy's defences that they were supposed to attack. Douglas Wimberley, the division's commander, recalled that:

> I took my troops, a Brigade at a time, and practised every Battalion in the exact job I had decided it was to do in the initial attack ... The dummy trenches were made the exact distance from the mock start line as were the real entrenchments ... held by the enemy, on the frontage on which I had been told to attack. Then, I used our Divisional artillery to fire the exact barrage they would have to fire in the battle, at the same rate and with the same pauses for leap frogging. Meanwhile Div Signals carried out the same outline plan, reporting the capture of objectives: and the Sappers did their clearing of mines through dummy minefields, of what we believed were the same breadth as the ones we had actually to gap in the battle.[194]

J. B. Salmond, who wrote the history of 51st Highland Division, recalled that the whole operation had been 'rehearsed to such an extent [in total there were four divisional scale exercises[195]] that every man ... knew absolutely in detail what he was expected to do'.[196] In addition, the 'Jocks' were given the opportunity to send troops to learn from the veteran Australian and New Zealand Divisions. Wimberley remembered that 'this went on throughout most of September. Our officers in the line were attached to Australian officers, our sergeants to their sergeants. If the Australians sent out patrols they were composed of a mixture of Aussies, and Jocks under instruction.'[197]

All divisions benefited directly or indirectly from this process. Freyberg wrote to the Minister of Defence in New Zealand, in September 1942, noting that 2nd New Zealand Division had 'been hard at training' since they came out of the line on 10 September. 'The period of training was very necessary because we now have almost a complete change in infantry battalion commanders.' As a result of Montgomery's training regime, Freyberg was able to report that 'as a fighting force although reduced in numbers' the division would be 'fit to take our part in every way'.[198]

With a clear plan of action devised and a heretofore unparalleled training regimen in place, Montgomery directed his focus once again to morale. He grasped that this issue was at the heart of the problem facing Eighth Army, and the British and Commonwealth Armies more generally in the first half of the war.[199] In his first memorandum before the forthcoming battle, he began with the clear statement that 'I consider that we must get the troops, both officers and men, so tuned up to this battle that every single man will be determined to go all out 100 per cent.'[200] The battle, he warned, would 'involve hard and prolonged fighting. Our troops must not think that, because we have a good tank and very powerful artillery support, the enemy will all surrender. The enemy will NOT surrender and there will be bitter fighting. The infantry must be prepared to fight and kill, and to continue doing so over a prolonged period.'[201]

In the two days running up to the battle, 'intensive propaganda' was put in place; this was designed to let the attacking troops know their role and to get them enthusiastic for the coming operation. All ranks, noted 'Lightfoot (the codename for the offensive) Memorandum No. 1', 'must be told that this battle is probably the decisive battle of the war; if we win this battle and destroy the Panzer Army it will be the turning point of the war.'[202] Wimberley recalled how, on 21 October, he was allowed to let 51st Highland Division know 'what they were in for, and their part in the battle explained to them'.[203] The 9th Australian Division report on the operation stated that, during the two days preceding the offensive, an intensive drive was made to ensure that every man knew the object of the battle, the part his formation and unit had to play and the part that he himself had to play.[204] The soldiers, according to the memorandum, had to 'be worked up to that state', which would 'make them want to go into battle and kill Germans'.[205]

As part of these preparations, Montgomery sought to address one of the issues that had so undermined Eighth Army's performance in the summer months. In 'Lightfoot Memorandum No. 2', on 6 October, he wrote:

> It is essential to impress on all officers that determined leadership will be very vital in this battle, as in any battle. There have been far too many unwounded prisoners taken in this war. We must impress on our Officers, N.C.O.'s and men that when they are cut off or surrounded, and there appears to be no hope of survival, they must organise themselves into a defensive locality and hold out where they are. By so doing they will add enormously to the enemy's difficulties; they will greatly assist the development of our own operations; and they will save themselves from spending the rest of the war in

> a prison camp. Nothing is ever hopeless so long as troops have stout hearts, and have weapons and ammunition.[206]

Leslie Morshead, the Commander of 9th Australian Division, passed on Montgomery's concerns to his senior officers. 'There must be no wavering', he informed them. 'If you have anyone you are not sure of, then don't take the risk of taking him in. Give him some other job other than fighting.' He went on:

> I cannot stress too greatly the value and necessity for *determined* leading, and it will apply in this battle as never before. Whatever the shelling or dive bombing, or the mortaring, we must stand firm, and not give way or run away. In the war there have been far too many unwounded prisoners taken. The modern term 'in the bag' is too excusable, it is not harsh enough, and it seems to mitigate having failed to make a proper stand and even to having just merely surrendered. We must make it unfashionable. I have closely questioned escaped prisoners and I know what actually happened in some instances, I am sure that those who did not put up a fight must often ruminate over it in their prison camps especially in the winter months.
>
> You must impress on your officers, NCOs and men that when they are cut off or surrounded and there appears no hope of survival they must organise themselves into a defensive locality and hold out. They must be a good staunch Australian and not emulate the Italians. By so doing they will add enormously to the enemy's difficulties and will assist materially the development of our own operations. And they will live to have pride and satisfaction in themselves instead of spending the rest of the war and a long time afterwards in prison camps. Nothing is ever hopeless so long as troops have stout hearts, and have weapons and ammunition. In this too is the test of real leadership and manhood.[207]

To reinforce the point, Montgomery's personal message (from the Army Commander) to his troops on the eve of the battle of El Alamein had one section standing out in bold and in capitals so that it could not be missed. It read, 'LET NO MAN SURRENDER SO LONG AS HE IS UNWOUNDED AND CAN FIGHT', a remarkable point of emphasis considering Eighth Army was about to go on one of the decisive offensives of the war.[208]

The Battle

At 2140hrs on 23 October, the guns of Eighth Army opened fire at El Alamein (see Map 7.2). The exact time for each gun was calculated so that every one of the first 882 shells would land on its target at the same time. The guns fired for fifteen minutes at the known positions of the enemy's batteries. Then, after a five-minute silence, they opened up again, this time on the forward positions of the German and Italian infantry. At 2200hrs, XXX Corps, under Lieutenant-General Sir Oliver Leese, comprising 9th Australian Division, 51st Highland Division, 2nd New Zealand Division and 1st South African Division (with 4th Indian Division carrying out diversionary tasks), advanced on a 6-mile front and attacked the northern part of the Axis line. Behind them came 1st and 10th Armoured Divisions of X Corps, under Lumsden, the newly formed 'corps de chasse'.[209] X Corps' job was to follow closely on the heels of XXX Corps and clear lanes through the estimated 445,358 mines laid by Rommel in his 'devil's garden'. Having done this, X Corps would 'debouch' from the corridors, pass through the infantry and advance 2 miles beyond the objectives of XXX Corps. The armour would then hold the ring beyond the main defensive area and destroy the enemy's tanks when the expected German counter-attacks commenced, thus facilitating the 'crumbling' process envisaged by Montgomery.[210] In the south, XIII Corps, under Horrocks, comprising 7th Armoured Division, 44th Home Counties Division, which had arrived from the UK in the late summer, and 50th Northumbrian Division, were tasked with a diversionary attack with the aim of holding as many of Rommel's armoured forces away from the main attack as possible.[211]

'Lightfoot', as the plan was appropriately named considering the profusion of mines around the Axis defences, started well, with all the infantry divisions making substantial gains. However, it soon became apparent that the Axis main defensive belt had mostly survived the heavy bombardment.[212] By dawn on 24 October, none of the armour of X Corps had advanced through XXX Corps.[213] Chaos reigned as, in the few lanes that had been cleared of mines, an enormous traffic jam developed not least due to 'the complexity of deploying one

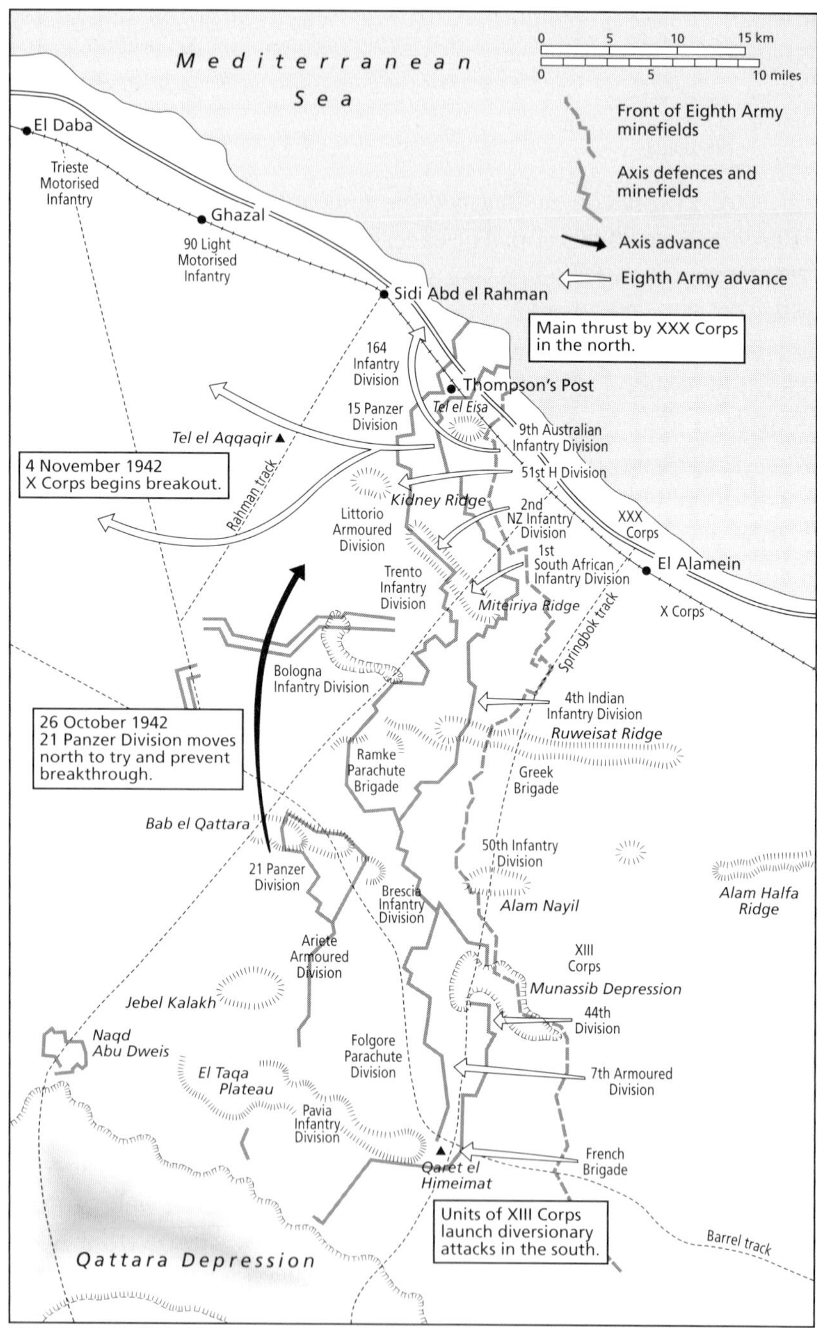

Map 7.2 The Battle of El Alamein, 23 October–5 November 1942

corps through another already heavily engaged, and on a very tight timetable'.[214] Throughout the day, Montgomery 'drove Lumsden on – to force his armoured divisions through the minefields', but his efforts were frustrated by the *Panzerarmee's* line of tanks and anti-tank guns.[215]

Although the operation had not gone quite according to plan, Eighth Army's advance did have the effect intended. On 25 October, the *Panzerarmee* launched its first set of counter-attacks. These proved to be costly; the next day, fearful of a breakout in the north, the armoured forces in the south, 21st Panzer and half of the Ariete Division, were ordered to move to the northern half of the line.[216] Montgomery's controlled and deliberate approach to the battle began to pay dividends. By 29 October, X Corps had suffered considerable losses; 213 tanks had been knocked out and recovered; many more had been damaged beyond repair. But, by comparison, the entire complement of German tanks had, by 28 October, been reduced to eighty-one. By 1 November, the German total had increased to 109, but on the same day, Eighth Army was able to field 487 medium and 100 heavy tanks.[217]

That night, Montgomery launched his knockout blow, Operation 'Supercharge'. In spite of heavy losses, he had been able in the midst of the battle to remove 2nd New Zealand Division and 1st, 7th and 10th Armoured Divisions to create a new mobile reserve under the command of X Corps. This new reserve was employed to launch a fresh attack in the north of the line and this time it was successful. By 0600hrs the next morning, 1st Armoured Division had broken through as far as the Rahman track.[218] By now, the German war diaries conceded that their troops were 'exhausted' and that, taking all things into consideration, 'it had to be admitted that after a desperate 10-day struggle against an enemy superior on land and in the air the Army was in no condition to prevent a further attempt at breaking through'.[219]

By 4 November, the battle was all but over. The balance of forces had swung decisively against Rommel. At the start of the battle the ratio of British medium and heavy tanks to the Axis had been just greater than 4:1, the ratio in terms of artillery had been 3:2 and in anti-tank guns 1.4:1. By 5 November the ratio of medium and heavy tanks was 15:1; by 9 November, Eighth Army would enjoy a superiority in artillery of 12:1 and in anti-tank guns of 30:1.[220] As he pondered the situation, Rommel estimated that he had only twelve tanks left. All his 88mm anti-tank guns had gone and the Army was 'almost totally without air cover'.[221] The man that had brought the Axis so close to victory in the desert had little choice but to retreat and save the *Panzerarmee* so that it could live and fight another day.

Rommel left behind around 7,000 killed and wounded and 30,000 prisoners at El Alamein.[222] By comparison, Eighth Army suffered 13,560 casualties, about the same number it had experienced during the July fighting. The German war diaries from the battle were gracious in their praise of the Commonwealth soldier who had 'demonstrated his tenacity and hardiness in fighting and in enduring losses ... in spite of the very heavy losses which he is known to have sustained, he attacked repeatedly'.[223] By the end of the battle, 'Eighth Army had virtually run out of formed infantry units that could still be used in the attack.'[224] Many of these units had suffered well over 50 per cent casualties among their front-line troops in the space of thirteen days.[225]

It was for this very reason that Montgomery had been right to focus so greatly on the related issues of training and morale before the battle. Following El Alamein, 'Middle East Training Memorandum No. 7', which dealt with the lessons from the operation, highlighted that 'all formations from Headquarters to sub-units trained systematically ... and to this must be attributed a large measure of the success obtained'.[226] The morale report for November 1942 to January 1943 showed a general 'appreciation of the careful and exact rehearsal of the El Alamein battle in preliminary divisional schemes'.[227] The 9th Australian Division Report on the battle stated that 'the operations proved the general soundness of our principles of training for war, some of which had been neglected during previous fighting in the desert'.[228]

Formations such as 51st Highland Division, which arrived in North Africa after the disasters of the summer of 1942, had certainly out-performed other new formations that had fought before them in the desert. This had been due, in no small part, to the fact that they had benefited from Adam's training, manpower and education revolution. Both the 2nd and 1st Armoured Divisions had been routed in their first contact with the enemy in the spring of 1941 and 1942, while 50th Northumbrian Division had suffered heavy casualties for little gain in its engagements in the summer of 1942. 51st Highland Division, by comparison, had profited from better selection procedures before it left the UK; it had spent six weeks attending battle schools at Aldershot in April and May 1942, where medical officers 'did their bit by purging units of the unfit' and officers had attended classes on welfare and man-management.[229] Wimberley, the commander of the division, believed that its quality 'owed not a little' to the innovations introduced by Adam.[230]

After El Alamein many units recognised the vital contribution of battle drill to the operation. A report by 26th Australian Infantry Brigade considered 'a sound and practised battle drill capable of carrying troops through heavy continuous fighting' as the most important lesson of the operation.[231] A number of troops in 1st South African Division were questioned following El Alamein about their experiences. The men were asked whether they considered that 'battle drill, as taught during training and as rehearsed during ... exercises ... produced as smooth a working machine as possible?' All respondents agreed that this had been 'most beneficial' throughout. The troops were also asked whether they considered their 'basic infantry tactics stood the test in the "Lightfoot" operation?' Once again, all agreed that Eighth Army's basic tactics had stood the test excellently.[232]

Eighth Army's sponsorship of battle inoculation facilitated and enhanced its performance also. A psychiatrist, assessing the success of the practice in the Middle East in November and December 1942, reported that fighting men and officers were 'strongly' of the opinion that battle inoculation had played 'a most important part of the training of battle reinforcements and should be given to all troops before their first action'. The troops, he found, 'were emphatic that their first experience of a set battle at Alamein had been well prepared for' and that they had been 'the steadier for it'.[233] A few months later, another report concluded that 'without a preliminary battle inoculation on active service, even the best troops will suffer unnecessary casualties and fail to make the best of an unexpected situation'.[234]

These training initiatives, and the other myriad innovations introduced by the War Office and Montgomery in the lead-up to El Alamein, meant that by 23 October morale among forward troops in Eighth Army had 'never reached a higher level'. 'All ranks', wrote the Australian censors during the battle period, 'are convinced that this time they will be able to clear the Axis forces out of Libya once and for all, although they realise that the task is a heavy one and casualties must inevitably be high.'[235] The Indian censors noted that morale left 'nothing to be desired',[236] while by October, the British censors were reporting that 'the offensive spirit' was 'dominant in correspondence', and it was 'obvious that all ranks expect and are ready for a flare up on a grand scale at any moment. And what is more, they are absolutely convinced that this time there can be but one result to the impending campaign, since, as one man said, "we've got the stuff and a General who knows how to use it".'[237]

The morale report, compiled by Adam's Morale Committee in London, for August to October 1942, pointed out that:

> Morale reached its peak as a result of the Army Commander's message to his troops on the eve of the offensive, and of the fact (commented on widely in the mail) that all ranks, down the whole chain of command, were taken into confidence about the plan of attack. In the words of the censor 'the fact that the G.O.C.-in-C., 8th Army, took the whole army into his confidence right down to the last man and stated exactly what he hoped to do and how he was going to do it, the belief that the plan was good, and the knowledge that the tools at their disposal were more numerous and effective than they have ever been, brought the spirit of the troops to a new high level and intensified their assurance and grim determination which was to be fully tested and proved to the hilt in the twelve historic days that followed. On the evidence of this mail no army ever went to battle with higher morale.[238]

The assessment of the censorship summaries and morale reports was supported by the sickness, Not Yet Diagnosed (Nervous) (NYD(N)) and surrender rates during the battle. The rate of NYD(N) and sickness decreased dramatically (see Figure 4.1) after the July and August battles. The monthly statistical reports on the health of Eighth Army for October and November 1942 stated that the incidences of NYD(N) were much smaller during the El Alamein offensive than they had been in previous battles, the total number of cases for the two months combined being 209. The number for the July battles alone had been 557.[239] Although the exact number of NYD(N) casualties for the El Alamein battle itself is unknown, it is generally accepted that the incidence of breakdown during the days of fighting was remarkably low, especially for an attritional infantry battle.[240]

The sick admission rate was also notably low. By November, the rate was 47.7 per thousand per month, a considerable drop from 75 per thousand in August. The report for November 1942 made it clear that the majority of the sick were non-divisional troops and not those involved in the fighting. The incidence of surrender and desertion also dramatically decreased. At El Alamein, instances of missing/surrender only made up 17 per cent of casualties. Even considering that this was an offensive rather than defensive battle, this was a substantial reduction from the height of the crisis in the summer of 1942 when figures were around 88 per cent. Two days after the end of the battle, replying to an enquiry by the Secretary of State for War on the continuing need to consider the reintroduction of the death penalty, Alexander was able to report that desertion and cowardice cases were 'decreasing and I think they will continue to do so'.[241] As Brigadier A. B. McPherson pointed out in his post-war War Office monograph on 'Discipline', in 1942 and 1943, 'as the tide turned in the Allies' favour, and repeated withdrawals and uncertainty gave way to advances and confidence in their leaders, especially in the Eighth Army, morale improved and crime as a whole decreased. This was particularly so among troops in the forward areas.'[242]

Montgomery had devised a relatively simple, conventional approach to tackle the *Panzerarmee* on the El Alamein line, one from which he would rarely stray until the latter years of the war. To make maximum use of the massive material resources provided to him by the factories of Britain and the USA, he had trained his men carefully for the specific roles he required of them and he had ensured that they went into the fight with, as he put it, 'the light of battle in their eyes'; in this sense, Eighth Army's turn around in morale had been crucial.[243] In the context of a poorly trained army with uncertain morale, this approach was wholly logical and profoundly strategic; he aligned ends and means effectively and it won him the battle. Indeed, for the first time since Operation 'Compass', a British and Commonwealth commander had obeyed the fundamental rule of warfare of only asking of the troops what they were capable of and trained to do.[244]

El Alamein did not lead, however, to the total destruction of Rommel's forces in North Africa. As many historians have pointed out, Montgomery's new slow and cautious 'Colossal Cracks' approach almost certainly precluded such an outcome.[245] But, the battle did put a first and decisive nail in the Axis coffin in Africa. The second was to be delivered a couple of days later with the Allied landings in the north-west corner of the continent.

The Tunisian Campaign

The plan to send a second army to Africa had been agreed by a new Anglo-American body set up to oversee the higher direction of the war, the Combined Chiefs of Staff. Talks aimed at military and political co-operation between the two countries had begun as early as the summer of 1940, long before the United States entered the war. Between January and March the following year, formal American–British 'Conversations', known as ABC-1, took place to set out the 'necessary machinery' for a Supreme War Council for the co-ordination of the political and military direction of a future Anglo-American alliance.[246] On the United States entering the conflict in December 1941, Churchill and his staff soon set off for the first of the great Anglo-American meetings of the Second World War, the Arcadia Conference in Washington. In the discussions that took place between 23 December 1941 and 12 January 1942, it was decided that British and American strategy would henceforth be formulated together; 'through face-to-face [weekly] meetings between the respective military heads of each service [the Combined Chiefs of Staff], who, in dialogue with the Prime Minister and President, would then hammer out the priorities, resources and purpose of Allied strategy'. To further cement Allied co-operation and co-ordination, each theatre of operation would have 'one man in command of the air, ground and maritime forces'. As General George C. Marshall, the Chief of Staff of the US Army, put it, 'we cannot manage by cooperation. Human frailties are such that there would be emphatic unwillingness to place portions of troops under another service. If we make a plan for unified command now, it will solve nine-tenths of our troubles.' Arcadia also led to other significant agreements and discussions; the defeat of Germany was prioritised over that of Japan; the need to reinforce the Far East was considered as was the longer-term possibility of occupying French North Africa, in a prospective operation codenamed 'Gymnast'.[247]

In the aftermath of Arcadia, events on the ground soon impacted on the significance of Africa to Anglo-American strategy. 'Gymnast' was dropped 'due to the worsening situation in Libya' and an increasing American determination to focus Allied efforts where they considered them most needed, on the European Continent against the *Wehrmacht*. By 27 March, Dwight D. Eisenhower, who at the time was at the War Plans Division of the US Army General Staff, had prepared an outline conception for 'Operations in Western Europe', which was wholeheartedly supported by Marshall and Henry L. Stimson, the US Secretary of State for War. There were three main parts to the American plan. The first, was a proposal to concentrate the majority of American combat troops in the United Kingdom. This would require the shipping of vast quantities of men and materiel across the Atlantic in an operation codenamed 'Bolero'; importantly, from the British perspective, it would ensure the safety of the United Kingdom from any lingering threat of invasion. The second part, codenamed 'Roundup', involved a cross-Channel attack in the spring of 1943, with as much force as could be mustered at the time. The third revolved around the American desire to make Europe an 'active sector' as soon as possible; it involved 'making an emergency landing in France' in the autumn of 1942 in the twin eventualities of a Russian collapse or an unexpected weakening of the German position. This operation, codenamed 'Sledgehammer', was somewhat less well received by the British than the first two parts although they agreed to consider the proposal; the main concern being that there were insufficient forces available in 1942 to support an attack of this kind.[248]

Calculations soon changed as disaster struck in North Africa in the summer of 1942. The defeat at Gazala, the fall of Tobruk and the failure of the July battles convinced Churchill and the British Chiefs of Staff that 'Gymnast' was a more achievable object for Anglo-American forces than an invasion of North-West Europe. On 22 July, the British Chiefs of Staff 'conclusively' put an end to 'Sledgehammer'. This 'threw all of the Allied plans against Germany into flux and called into question the feasibility of Operation Roundup as well'. The Americans considered 'Gymnast' to 'have almost no military value', it would 'not provide any succour to the Russians while at the same time making a cross-Channel assault virtually impossible until 1944'. Worse still, they suspected that British enthusiasm for 'Gymnast' 'disguised an attempt to subvert American strength for their own imperial objectives'.[249]

Marshall 'was faced with an intractable dilemma'. If Britain would not support a major cross-Channel attack in 1942/3 – the 2nd Canadian Division had been launched on a 'disastrous one day raid' on the French port of Dieppe in August – where was the growing strength of the US Army to be applied? Roosevelt's response was 'unequivocal'; the United States would have to agree to some sort of operation, and the best option on the table was 'Gymnast'. The invasion of North-West Africa, soon to be renamed 'Torch', was on. Marshall and the American

Chiefs of Staff had 'lost a vital battle' and had been 'forced to bend to British views' on strategy.[250]

The plan for Operation 'Torch', which was to be overseen by Eisenhower as the C-in-C, Allied Expeditionary Force, involved the utilisation of the American Army, which had been gathering in the United Kingdom since the spring of 1942, and the first of the ninety new divisions being mobilised in the United States. 'Torch' would make use also of part of Britain's home reserve, surplus now to strategic requirements as the danger of a German invasion had receded. The landings would involve three task forces (Western, Central and Eastern), 65,000 men in total, alighting respectively at Casablanca on the Atlantic coast of Morocco and at Oran and Algiers inside the Mediterranean (see Map 7.3). The Western Task Force, consisting of the American 2nd Armored, 3rd and 9th Divisions, would be transported direct from the United States; the Central Task Force comprising the American 1st Armored Division and part of the future 82nd Airborne Division would set out from Britain; and the Eastern Task Force, which would eventually become British First Army, composed of the British 78th Division, which had been recently formed of veteran brigades from France specifically for the assault, and the American 34th Division, would also set out from the United Kingdom.[251]

'Torch' began at 0100hrs on 8 November 1942. The landings went broadly according to plan. However, amid uncertainty over whether the French Army in North Africa, made up of 120,000 men (mostly Africans) would stay loyal to Vichy and fight, or defect to the Allied side, and with the three task forces separated by considerable distances, consolidation was not as rapid as hoped or envisaged. With the Allies struggling to exploit the element of surprise, the initiative shifted perceptibly towards the Axis. Hitler and Mussolini poured reinforcements into Tunisia. From a strategic perspective, it was considered 'imperative' for the Axis to retain a bridgehead on the continent to keep the Allies at maximum distance from the resources of the Balkans and the Italian mainland.[252]

The benefit of interior lines of communication and the comparatively short distance from Italy and Sicily enabled the Axis to win the 'race' for Tunis.[253] These reinforcements prevented First Army, under Lieutenant-General Kenneth Anderson, from seizing the ports of Tunis and Bizerta, the Axis' last supply line to Africa. As a consequence, First Army, now reinforced by 6th Armoured Division, which had been

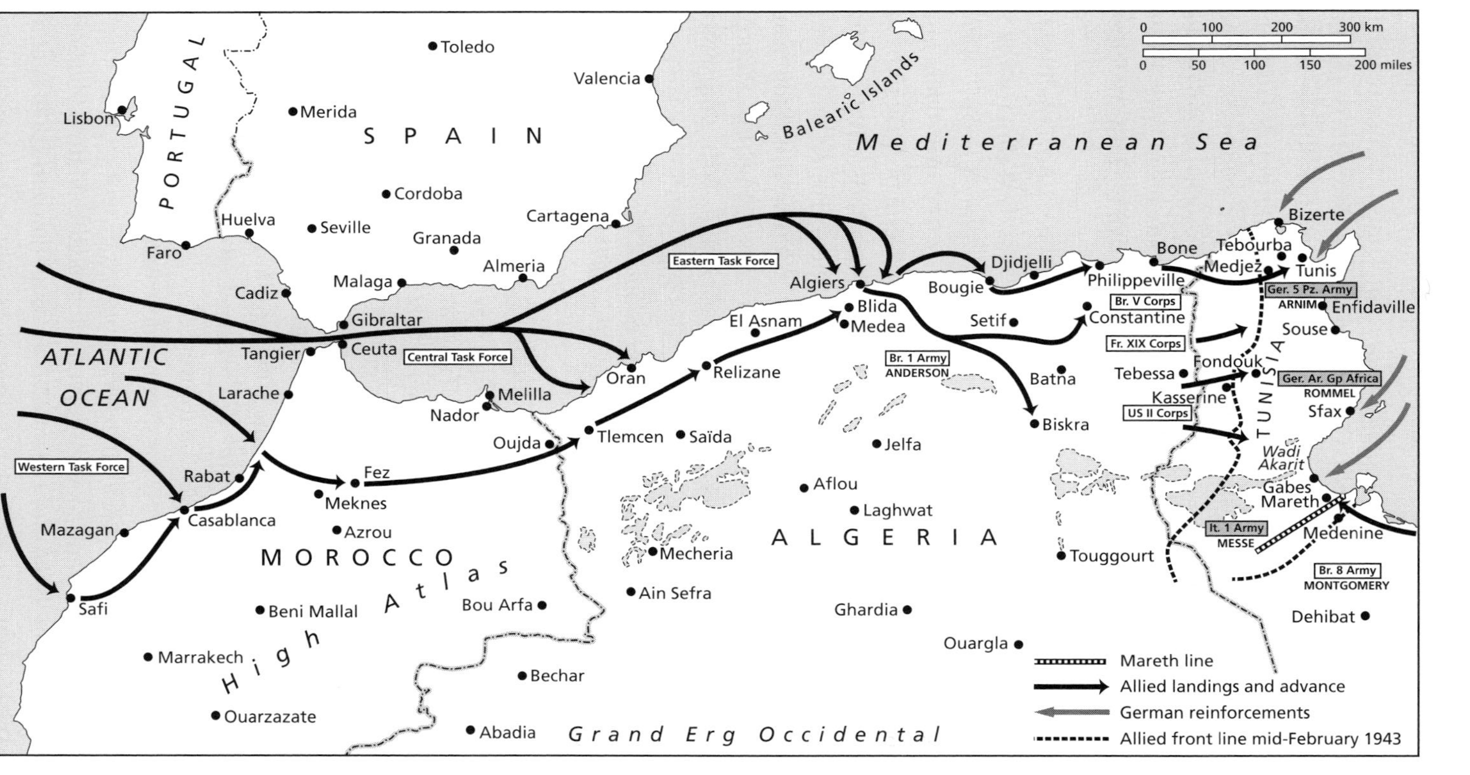

Map 7.3 The Tunisian campaign, November 1942–May 1943

formed in the UK in late 1940, spent November and December bogged down in heavy fighting in the mountains west of Tunis.[254] Poor weather and the difficult terrain brought a lull in activities in January 1943, but by mid-February the Allied forces in Tunisia were ready to strike. In the west, First Army, which was now made up of three corps – V Corps in the north, XIX French Corps in the middle, made up of soldiers who had defected to the Allied cause, and II US Corps to the south – stood poised to attack. To the east was Eighth Army, having advanced over 1,000 miles from El Alamein. Together, these forces were ready to close a massive pincer on the Axis in Tunisia.[255]

Rommel, who had fallen back from Cyrenaica and Tripolitania to link up with the newly arrived reinforcements was, by February 1943, in overall command of what was now termed Army Group Africa, comprising the Fifth Panzer Army under General Jürgen von Arnim and the Italian First Army, which included the original German *Afrika Korps*, under General Giovanni Messe.[256] Rommel, characteristically, and in spite of the difficulties faced, decided to go on the offensive, employing his now concentrated army group in a series of strikes intended to regain the initiative. On 14 February, he launched attacks against US II Corps near the Kasserine Pass, routing the Americans and destroying more tanks (235) than he himself employed at the start of the battle (228). The inexperienced Americans held on long enough, however, to rush up reinforcements and on 22 February Rommel called off the offensive.[257] On 6 March, he launched another attack, this time at Medenine, using his three *panzer* divisions against the Eighth Army as it began to edge up the Tunisian bulge towards the Mareth Line, a set of defences built by the French in the interwar years to defend Tunisia from the Italians in Libya. The attack was a failure. Montgomery, who had been given ample warning of Rommel's intentions through Ultra, was able to place 460 anti-tank guns, 300 field and medium guns and 300 tanks in the way of the 150 tanks of the *Afrika Korps*. By the end of the day, the Germans had lost a third of their attacking force as it ran headlong into Montgomery's trap. A few days later, sick and disillusioned, Rommel handed over command to Arnim and left Africa forever.[258]

The stage was now set for the final destruction of the Axis forces in Africa. Between 20 and 28 March, Montgomery, in another El Alamein style battle, broke into and then through the formidable Mareth position. But, much like in November, he failed to trap the retreating enemy. On 5 April, Eighth Army began a frontal assault on the next line of

German defences, at the significant 'natural barrier' of the Wadi Akarit. Once more, the position was taken but the defenders slipped away, caught neither by the advance of Eighth Army nor the efforts of the reinforced First Army as it tried to cut off the Axis retreat with a drive east towards Fondouk.[259] By 10 April, First and Eighth Armies had joined together and the noose tightened ever closer around the Axis forces. For the final push on Tunis, in addition to Allied forces, the British and Commonwealth Armies deployed three armoured and nine infantry divisions, with Eighth Army launching its final attack in Africa at Enfidaville on 19 April. Responsibility for the final assault on Tunis fell to First Army. On 12 May, with the Axis forces surrounded and cut off from escape by the Royal Navy, the German–Italian forces in Africa surrendered.[260]

As Leese, Commander of XXX Corps, remarked, Eighth Army had finally reaped 'the full reward of Alamein'.[261] The men, many of whom had fought in France in 1940, felt that Dunkirk had at last been avenged. The censorship summary for 2 to 8 May 1943 was replete with references to the 'pluck and fighting qualities of the British Infantry',[262] while the report for 16 to 22 May noted that 'victory in North Africa has brought about a realisation that the British Army has lived up to its best traditions once again'. Victory, 'in addition to bringing out pride of Regiment and admiration for the unequalled fighting qualities of the British Tommy, has crystallised for many writers the feeling of confidence on a wider basis'.[263]

Montgomery wrote to the CIGS that 'the high morale of my soldiers is almost unbelievable ... they believe that this Army is invincible and can do nothing wrong'. A 'feature of this morale', he said, 'is the low sick rate'; Montgomery was able to report proudly that the rate of admissions was now as low as 18 per thousand, a 76 per cent drop from the bad old days of August 1942 (see Figure 4.1).[264] We now 'have two grand armies', Alexander wrote to Brooke, 'and lots of good young commanders. It is most cheering.'[265] The fighting in Tunisia had cost the British and Commonwealth Armies dearly; First Army suffered 25,742 casualties among its Imperial troops, while Eighth Army suffered an additional 12,618.[266] Nevertheless, the months from October 1942 to May 1943 witnessed the destruction of Axis forces at El Alamein (around 50,000 killed and captured)[267] and Tunisia (around 250,000 captured).[268] By May 1943, more Axis soldiers had surrendered at what the German soldiers called 'Tunisgrad' than the Russians captured at Stalingrad.[269] A remarkable turnaround had taken place.

8 NEW GUINEA AND BURMA

The 'Battle for Australia'

The catastrophe at Singapore demonstrated the inability of Britain to defend the Empire and the necessity for the Pacific Dominions to defend themselves. While New Zealand, to an extent, was sheltered by its larger neighbour to the north-west, there was no comparable barrier between Australia and the Japanese forces that advanced southwards during the spring and summer of 1942. Two brigades of 8th Australian Division had been lost at Singapore. The remnants of the division, stationed at Rabaul in New Britain and at Ambon and Timor in the Dutch East Indies were overrun in January and February 1942.[1] Most of the rest of the Australian Imperial Force (AIF), Australia's only contingent of full-time soldiers, were in the Middle East or at sea as they steamed towards the evolving crisis in Burma. On 19 February, the Japanese air force attacked Darwin. Eight days later, the Australian Chiefs of Staff advised the Government that Japan was 'now at liberty to attempt an invasion of Australia should she so desire'.[2] 'For the first and only time since European settlement', Australia faced what appeared to be a real 'threat of invasion' (see Map 8.1).[3]

Defensive positions were established around the major cities.[4] 'There was an element of panic' in the reactions of many Australians. Some residents in Sydney 'moved inland to escape a possible Japanese landing'. The Government developed 'scorched-earth' policies in threatened areas. Some citizen groups planned guerrilla bands 'to harass the

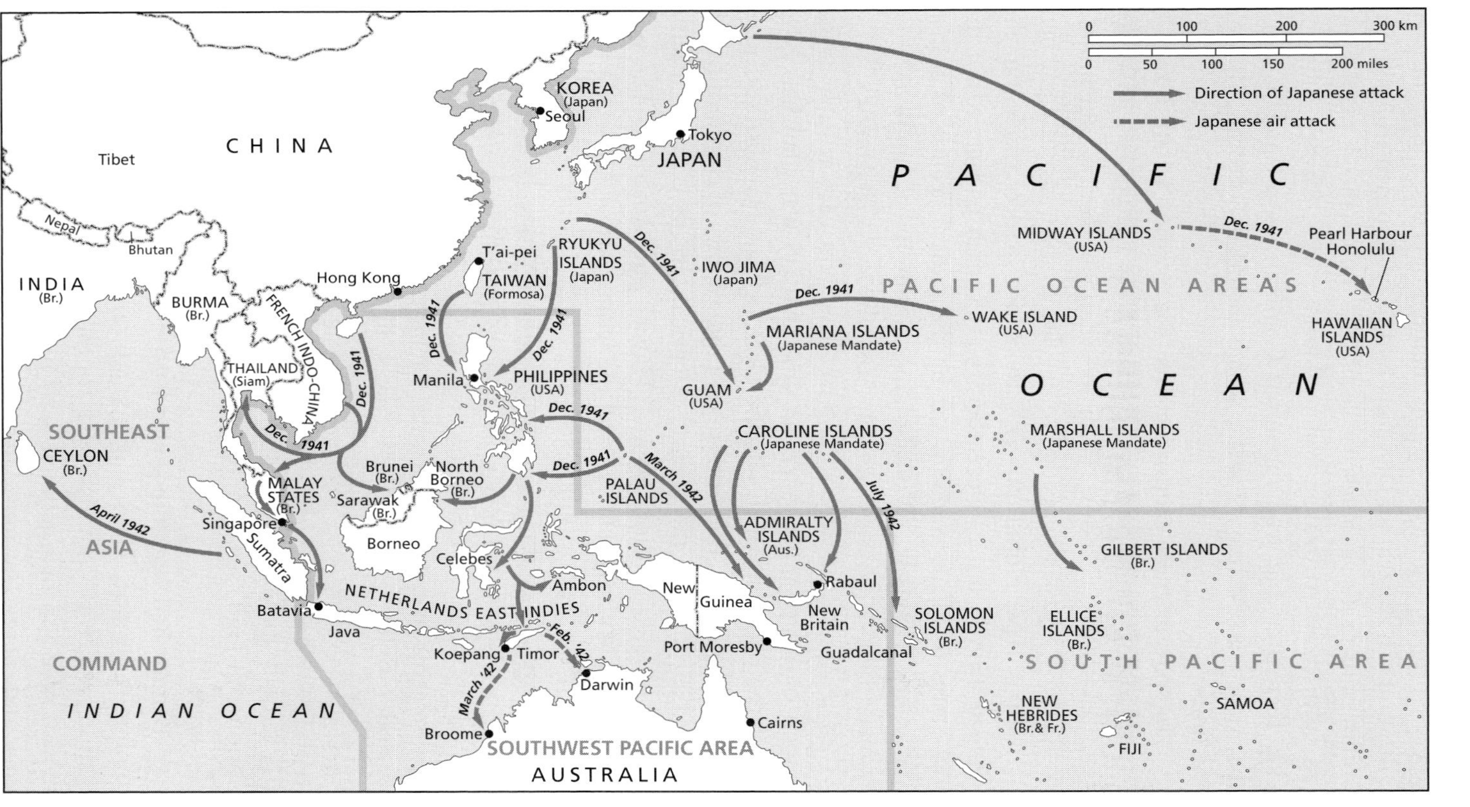

Map 8.1 Extent of the Japanese advance, 1941–2

Japanese when they landed'.[5] In this moment of crisis, Curtin insisted that 6th and 7th Australian Divisions had to be returned to Australia. Churchill reluctantly acquiesced and these experienced formations began landing on Australian soil in March 1942. Blamey followed quickly thereafter and was appointed Commander-in-Chief (C-in-C) of the Australian Military Forces, which included both the AIF and militia units.[6]

In spite of these reinforcements, the position of Australia, in what was to become known as the South-West Pacific Area (SWPA), was still extremely perilous. 'With its small population and limited industrial base', Australia needed to develop a 'close strategic partnership' with a new global power.[7] In a newspaper article, in the *Melbourne Herald* on 27 December 1941, Curtin had called on the United States to fill the vacuum left by the critical decline of British power in the Far East. 'Without any inhibitions of any kind', he declaimed, 'I make it quite clear that Australia looks to America.'[8]

The Americans were willing to answer the call; as early as the afternoon of 8 December 1941, an amended US war plan had been issued to the remnants of the Pacific Fleet at Pearl Harbor. This plan included, 'as a priority, the protection of the sea lines of communication to Australia'. In fact, the 'entire' American strategy in the Pacific 'depended on two cardinal points': Hawaii and Australia. The sea-lanes between Midway, Hawaii and the west coast of America had to be secured as a first priority. The second priority, in only a 'small degree less important', was the protection of the life-line between North America and Australia. Every other concern was to be 'ruthlessly subordinated' to what the Commander of the US Navy, Admiral Ernest J. King, referred to as those 'two vital Pacific tasks'.[9] On 17 March, the commander of the defeated US forces in the Philippines, General Douglas MacArthur, arrived in Australia; the following month, he took over command of all forces in the SWPA.[10] MacArthur set up his GHQ, initially in Melbourne, and appointed commanders to oversee operations on land, sea and air, with Blamey as Commander Allied Land Forces.[11]

Blamey had been the senior Australian Army officer since the beginning of the war. The son of a small farmer, he was interested in education and was commissioned to the Australian Cadet Forces Administrative and Instructional Staff in Melbourne in 1906. 'Full of promise and energy', he moved to the Australian military forces in 1910 and attended the Staff College at Quetta in 1912, graduating with a 'B' Pass.[12] He landed at Gallipoli in 1915 and went on to serve on the Western Front as Chief of Staff in 1st Australian Division until June 1918, when he was promoted to temporary brigadier and made Chief of Staff of the Australian Corps. In the interwar years, he held a number of senior staff positions until 1925 when he left the army to become Commissioner of Police in Victoria. Blamey served in this post until 1936, when he was forced to resign for 'issuing an untrue statement in an attempt to protect the reputation of one of his senior police officers'. Then, in September 1938, the Australian Government appointed him to organise manpower planning and recruiting as Australia rearmed in preparation for war. Soon after the outbreak of hostilities, Blamey was promoted to Lieutenant-General and was appointed General Officer Commanding (GOC) 6th Australian Division, the first formation in the newly raised 2AIF, before taking over command of the Australian Corps and the 2AIF in the Middle East in 1940.[13]

With the arrival of MacArthur and Blamey, it was clear that it was no longer, to use the much-derided phrase of Menzies, 'business as usual' in Australia.[14] By April 1942, 46,000 men of the AIF had returned from the Middle East; a further 63,000 AIF men had completed their training in Australia. They were joined by 280,000 militiamen, who were now mobilised for full-time service.[15] These forces were arranged into the main force, the First Australian Army, responsible for the defence of New South Wales and Queensland, and the Second Army, which covered the rest of Australia.[16] With the Army now consisting of some eight infantry divisions, two motorised divisions and one armoured division, it appeared on paper that Australia was increasingly ready for war.[17] The situation was improved further when 41st US National Guard Division arrived in April, bringing with it another 33,000 troops, followed in May by the arrival of 32nd US National Guard Division.[18] By August, there were 100,000 US troops on the continent.[19]

As well as the increase in troop numbers, the Government set out to address the perception 'that Australia was not solidly behind the war'.[20] Between 1939 and 1941, Australia had, in many ways, remained psychologically and physically remote from the conflict.[21] Few had to endure any hardships. Bereavement had not yet deeply touched the population as a whole. Up to the end of November 1941 the total of service losses (deaths from all causes, missing and POW) was 9,000 and the wounded less than 5,000. The number of deaths on war service from all causes (2,745) in two years had been considerably less than the average number of deaths from accidents in Australia for a single year (3,766) at that time.[22] The sluggish recruitment campaign for the AIF was matched by the poor performance of the Government's 1941 war loan appeal, with subscribers 'less than half that of the Great War'. In one opinion survey carried out at the start of 1942, 95 per cent of respondents believed that the country was not making an 'all-in war effort'.[23]

In February, Curtin announced 'a complete mobilisation of all Australia's resources, human and material' for the battles to come. 'Every human being in this country, whether he likes it or not', Curtin explained, was now 'at the service of the Government to work in the defence of Australia'.[24] All men aged between 18 and 60 were directed to register for military service[25] and rationing was initiated in June. These undertakings were 'supported by extensive official propaganda and enforced by coercive measures'.[26] Through regulation issued under the National Security Act, 'the Commonwealth came to control where people worked, what they consumed, the information they received and a myriad of other things that Australians took for granted before the war'.[27] In effect, 'the whole productive system of the nation was placed under government control and direction and many of the incentives for individuals operating in a market system were suspended'.[28] In early May, Curtin called on the nation:

> I put it to any man whom my words may reach ... that he owes it to those men [fighting in the air, on land and at sea], and to the future of the country, not to be stinting in what he will do now for Australia. Men are fighting ... today; those who are not fighting have no excuse for not working.[29]

The change in ethos was captured by the changing lexicon; 'Military Districts' were renamed 'Lines of Communication Areas' and the regional commands replaced by the First and Second Armies.[30]

These reforms put the country materially and psychologically on a sounder defensive footing. But, only the AIF units had combat experience. In July, the Australian Army rated its brigades as well as the two US divisions now in Australia on the basis of an 'A' to 'F' scale for efficiency ('A' being the highest). Of the thirty-two brigades and two

US divisions in the order of battle, only the four AIF brigades from 6th and 7th Divisions were rated 'A'. No brigade was rated 'B', four were rated 'C', six rated 'D', nine rated 'E' and eight rated 'F'. The 32nd US Division was rated 'C' and 41st US Division an 'F'.[31]

In the prevailing circumstances, it is fortuitous, perhaps, that Japan had little intention of invading Australia in 1942. Japanese strategy was focused instead on holding on to its newly won 'Greater East-Asia Co-Prosperity Sphere' (see Map 8.1). The achievement of this ambition would be no easy task for the Imperial Japanese forces. The United States, after Pearl Harbor, was 'clearly in no mood to make peace' and with American men and supplies building up in Hawaii and Australia, it would not be long before the Allies were in a position to launch attacks in the Central and Southern Pacific. Tokyo aimed, therefore, to blunt the Allies' capacity to manoeuvre by both destroying American sea power in a decisive battle with the US Navy (by function of another assault on Hawaii) and by preventing Australia from becoming a base for offensive operations.[32] To achieve the second of these goals, the Japanese High Command concluded that it had to 'isolate' Australia 'through air and naval action' and the seizure of key points in the string of islands to the north and east of the Australian continent, including New Guinea, the southern Solomons, Fiji, Samoa and New Caledonia (see Map 8.2).[33] If all went to plan, such actions might draw the US Navy into a major engagement, or, even, encourage Australia to 'withdraw from the war' altogether.[34]

The central piece in the isolation of Australia was possession of Port Moresby on the south coast of Papua, on the island of New Guinea. At the time, the western portion of the island of New Guinea was part of the Dutch East Indies. The eastern half, modern-day Papua New Guinea, was divided into two parts; the south and south-eastern portion was the territory of Papua, which the British had transferred to Australian control early in the twentieth century; to the north lay the territory of New Guinea, which after the First World War was transferred from Germany to Australia as a mandate.[35] If the Japanese did not take and hold Port Moresby, then Australian and American air forces stationed on Papua could attack Rabaul, Japan's key base in its newly conquered territories in the South Pacific. If Rabaul, with its important port and airfield, was taken, 'the door to the Philippines and the Southern Resource Zone itself was wide open'.[36] Moreover, if Port Moresby, with its good airfields and a fine harbour, was captured,

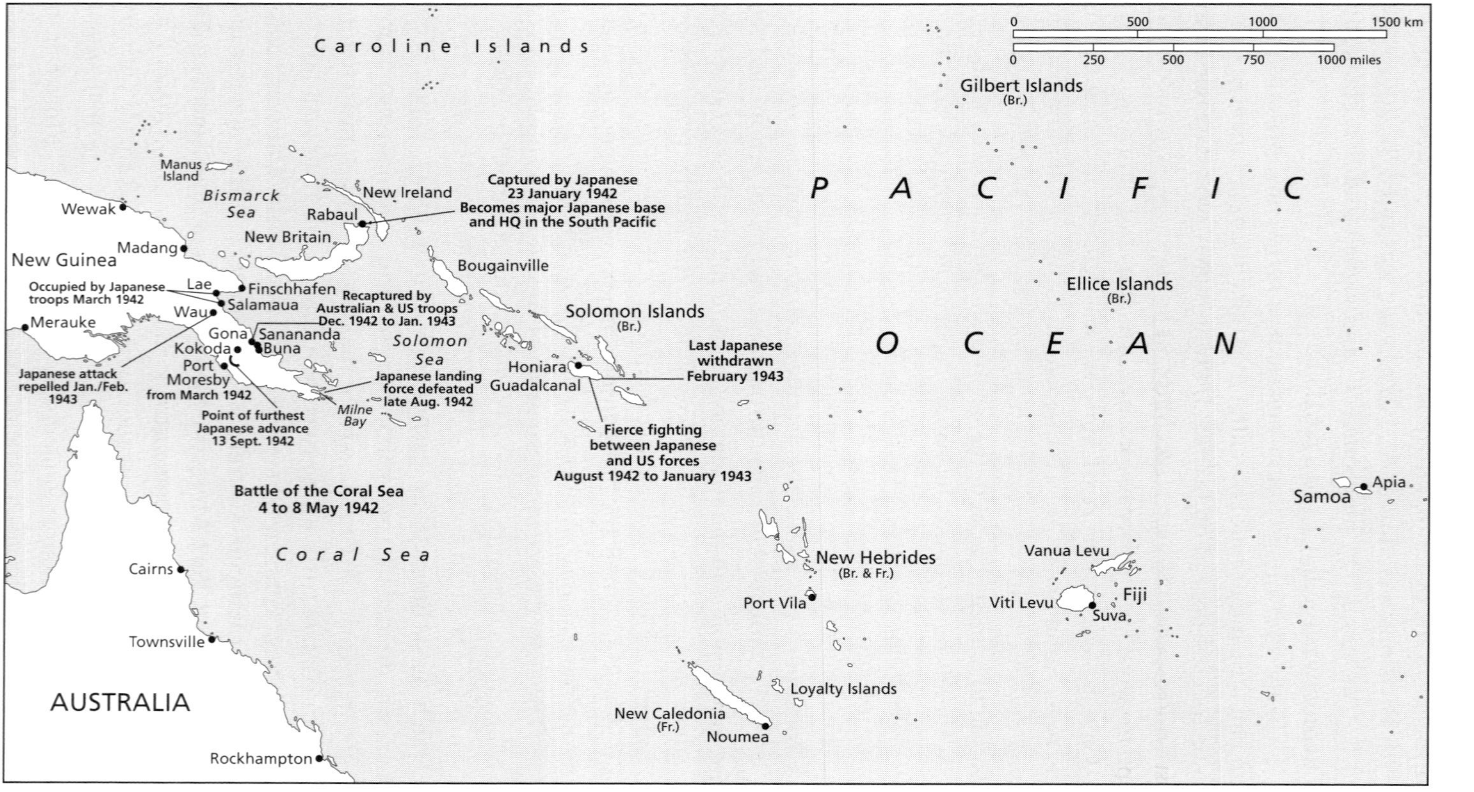

Map 8.2 Allied operations: New Guinea to Guadalcanal, January 1942–February 1943

the Japanese would be in a position to 'strike at will at the north coast' of Australia.[37]

On 8 March, the Japanese took the first step towards occupying Port Moresby by seizing Lae and Salamaua on the east coast of New Guinea. The operation did not go according to plan; two days after the landings US carrier-borne aircraft surprised Japanese ships as they unloaded, sinking four vessels and damaging seven.[38] Such losses, the worst the Japanese had experienced to that point in the Pacific, delayed the planned attack on Port Moresby, as it was now evident that an invasion force would require the protection of aircraft carriers.

Two months later, Japanese convoys once more set off from Rabaul, this time to attack Port Moresby directly. By now, however, the Allies could read portions of the Japanese Naval codes and the taskforce was intercepted in the battle of the Coral Sea, off the south-east tip of Papua. The Japanese lost one small aircraft carrier and suffered damage to another large one. In the circumstances, it was decided to delay the sea-borne assault on Port Moresby. That June, the Americans surprised and sank four Japanese carriers at the Battle of Midway in the Central Pacific. Without its carriers, plans for another attack on Hawaii and the seizure of New Caledonia, Fiji and Samoa would have to be abandoned. The capture of Port Moresby now became even more urgent and important. But, with an amphibious operation out of the question, responsibility for the isolation of Australia would have to rest with the Imperial Japanese Army.[39]

Kokoda

The initiative appeared to have shifted towards the Allies. With the forward defences of the SWPA secured by the victory at the Coral Sea in May, and with the sea-lanes between Midway and Hawaii secured by the victory at Midway, the Americans and Australians started planning for an offensive of their own. MacArthur aimed to occupy Papua and launch offensive action towards Rabaul;[40] King meanwhile decided that his first point of counter-attack would be the island of Guadalcanal in the South Pacific Area (SOPAC), which had already been seized by the Japanese. The two main campaigns in the Pacific during the second half of 1942 and most of 1943 would, therefore, focus on objectives that would do much to ensure that communications would remain open between America and Australia.[41]

Before MacArthur could act in the SWPA, however, intelligence revealed a large Japanese convoy departing Rabaul with its destination assessed as Buna, in Papua. On 18 May, the Imperial Japanese Army had activated the Seventeenth Army at Rabaul for the purpose of commanding an overland assault on Port Moresby.[42] In the Army's eyes, 'the Navy had failed badly at both the Coral Sea and Midway'. It decided, therefore, to take matters into its own hands in Papua. Consequently, the Seventeenth Army assembled an elite formation of shock troops designated the South Seas Detachment (or *Nankai Shitai*),[43] which on 21 and 29 July 1942 landed unopposed at Buna and Gona on the north coast of Papua.[44]

The South Seas Detachment, a Japanese light division built around two infantry regiments and a 'stronger than usual proportion' of engineers, labourers and medical units, was made up largely of long-service veterans who had experienced fighting in campaigns in China, Malaya and the Philippines.[45] Although the initial landings comprised 4,057 men, the formation eventually reached a size of about 16,000 and 16 artillery pieces. On landing in New Guinea, its commander, Major-General Tomitaro Horii, decided to go immediately on the offensive, launching a force of four infantry battalions, a mountain artillery battalion and two engineer companies (a total of about 3,500 fighting men and 13 guns) into the mountains.[46]

Facing the South Seas Detachment was New Guinea Force (NGF), which was effectively the HQ of I Australian Corps, under Lieutenant-General Sydney Rowell. NGF was made up of 30th Militia Brigade, which had been in country since January, the 14th Militia Brigade, which had arrived after the victory at the Coral Sea, and two brigades of 7th Australian Division, under Major-General Arthur 'Tubby' Allen, the 18th and 21st, which had arrived in Papua in early August. A small force from 39th Militia Battalion, 30th Militia Brigade, codename 'Maroubra Force', had set out from Port Moresby towards Buna on 8 July and it was this formation that first came into contact with the Japanese in Papua.[47]

To reach Port Moresby, the South Seas Detachment had to tackle some of the most formidable terrain confronting any army in the Second World War, the 60-mile-long Kokoda Trail, a narrow, muddy foot track running through the thick jungle of the Owen Stanley mountains, which, at their peak, reach an altitude of 13,000 feet.[48] The militia forces in their path conducted a fighting withdrawal towards the defensive position at Isurava (see Map 8.2). With the terrain proving 'far more formidable than the Japanese had anticipated',[49] the militia held the South Seas Detachment there until mid-August, when reinforcements from 21st Brigade, 7th Australian Division, began to arrive. The 21st Australian Brigade, under Brigadier Arnold Potts (who also took over command of 'Maroubra Force') proved unable, however, to stop the Japanese, when, having also been reinforced, they renewed their offensive along the Kokoda Trail on 26 August. Isurava was overrun and abandoned, prompting the dispatch of Blamey to Port Moresby and the sacking in due course of Potts and Allen.[50] On 1 October 1942, Rowell too was replaced, by Lieutenant-General Edmund 'Ned' Herring. With all these changes at the top, there was little doubt that responsibility for events in New Guinea now rested on Blamey's shoulders.[51]

It was clear that the Japanese with their mountain artillery, mortars and medium machine guns 'completely overmatched' the Australians in these early battles; 'Maroubra Force' had nothing heavier than Bren light machine guns to counter the Japanese thrusts.[52] Morale, due to the appalling hardships and setbacks, could hardly be described as high during this period. Forces actively engaged on the Kokoda Trail, according to one report, could become 'so depleted' due to illness 'as to approach ineffective levels – certain groups were reduced by 90% in six weeks, and the efficiency of the individual soldier deteriorated partly from exhaustion and poor nutrition but mainly from malaria'.[53] One report put the total number of sick between 6 August and 19 September at 883. As the average strength of Maroubra Force during this period was 2,000 men, this equates to a monthly sickness rate of around 294 men per thousand, although it is difficult, with the outbreak of malaria, to gauge how accurate this figure is as an indicator of morale.[54] The official histories recorded 'few neurotic casualties', for example, reflecting, according to the Official Medical Historian of the Australian Army, 'the spirit of the men and their leaders'.[55] 'Maroubra Force' just about held together and it does appear that the fact that the men were clearly fighting in defence of their homeland played a role in preventing complete disintegration.

On 25 August, another Japanese force landed at Milne Bay on the east coast of Papua, where there was a natural deep-water harbour, a large base and a number of airstrips. The Allies had decided in early June to develop Milne Bay in order to protect against a further Japanese amphibious attempt on Port Moresby and to provide a route for allied aircraft to attack Rabaul without having to cross the Owen Stanley Range.[56] The Japanese Navy did indeed intend for Milne Bay to be used as a jumping-off point for another attack on Port Moresby (and to support the Army's push across the mountains). They underestimated, however, the Allied forces available, and the 2,800 men landed were unable to progress against the nearly 9,000 Australians (including 18th Brigade, of the veteran 6th Australian Division, and 7th Militia Brigade) and Americans in the area. By the end of August, the attacking forces were in full retreat and on 4 September the Japanese Navy began evacuating what was left of the landing force. For the cost of only 162 Allied dead, approximately 1,500 Japanese perished.[57]

The fighting and conditions had been brutal; according to one man in 6th Australian Division, the Greek and Crete campaigns had been 'like a Sunday school picnic' compared to what he had experienced in the mountains and jungle of Papua.[58] At one point, at the end of December 1942, malaria at Milne Bay reached a high of 82 cases per thousand troops per week.[59] Nevertheless, the men were beginning to show that it was possible to defeat the Japanese in jungle warfare (see Illustration 8.1).

On the Kokoda Trail, the South Seas Detachment reached Ioribaiwa, about 30 miles from Port Moresby, in mid-September. With their target almost literally in sight, matters now began to deteriorate seriously for the Japanese forces. After the defeat at Isurava, Blamey had ordered the third of 7th Australian Division's three brigades, the 25th, to Port Moresby. There, they were sent forward to confront the increasingly exhausted and starving South Seas Detachment. With 'Maroubra Force' systematically destroying supply dumps before withdrawals, the South Seas Detachment was unable to sustain itself using captured stores, as had been done so often by the Japanese in Malaya and Burma. The Imperial Japanese Army's penchant for taking risks with logistics now backfired as the men's rations were cut to a handful of rice per day.[60]

To complicate matters further, the US offensive in the SOPAC was launched at Guadalcanal on 7 August. Japanese efforts to destroy the US 1st Marine Division on the island did not go well, forcing the Japanese commanders at Rabaul to divide their forces and 'ultimately choose the pursuit of the recapture of Guadalcanal over their assault on Port Moresby'. On 16 September, with Japanese forces in the South

Illustration 8.1 A patrol of the 2/31st Battalion negotiates a path through the swampy river flats bordering the Brown River on the Kokoda Trail, October 1942. During the New Guinea campaign, the Australians learnt how to fight in the jungle and, ultimately, how to beat the Japanese, lessons that would be put to good effect in the years to come.

Pacific seriously overstretched, the offensive in Papua was cancelled. The surprised and disappointed South Seas Detachment began a 'bitter and demoralising' retreat towards the north coast. By mid-November, the Kokoda campaign was over.[61]

The AIF, perhaps unsurprisingly, had borne the brunt of the fighting and as a result suffered the majority of the casualties, about 66 per cent up to 12 September and no less than 74 per cent the week after. For these reasons, and others, 'ill feeling' developed between AIF and militia units, with morale suffering as a consequence. One man wrote in November 1942:

> The Jap is certainly finding a big difference fighting the A.I.F. to having the Militia in front of him. After this campaign I do not think that they will ever heal the breach between A.I.F. and C.M.F. [the militia] after their work over here. We have read extracts of the wonderful work

> the 'chocos' are supposed to have done ... but you can take it from me that outside one or two battalions the rest are not worth the tucker they eat.[62]

As morale was inevitably degraded by the frictions between AIF and militia units, and by the debilitating conditions, much depended on the basic military competence of the well-trained AIF units.

Although it has been argued that much of the training undertaken by 7th and 6th Australian Divisions in the six months before they were deployed to Papua 'was not directly relevant', as it focused overly on the experience of 8th Australian Division in Malaya (where the terrain was markedly different) and on anti-invasion exercises in Australia, it did ensure that the men were extremely hard and fit when they arrived at the front.[63] Moreover, the AIF, not least as a consequence of their considerable battle experience, were able to learn effectively from their mistakes.

During the months following Kokoda, NGF expanded to an army-level command. The 7th Australian Division, 'the principal strike weapon' of the NGF, reinforced by additional formations from 6th Australian Division, militia units and the US 32nd Division, eliminated the Japanese forces (of *c.*12,000 men) on the beachheads to the north, at Buna, Gona and Sananda.[64] During this period of bitter and prolonged fighting, the Australians gradually wore the Japanese down. They continually modified and adapted their platoon tactics; new techniques for co-operating with artillery and air support were developed; methods of camouflage and moving at night were adapted; and logistics challenges were overcome.[65] By 21 January 1943, six months to the day after the campaign commenced, the fighting in Papua was over.[66]

Wau

With the destruction of the South Seas Detachment in Papua and with the unfolding disaster at Guadalcanal,[67] the Japanese Army began to appreciate the 'full dimensions' of Allied power in the South Pacific. More forces would be required to maintain their beachheads west in New Guinea. On 16 November 1942, the Eighth Area Army at Rabaul was activated, under Lieutenant-General Hitoshi Imamura; this included the Seventeenth Army fighting on Guadalcanal and the new Eighteenth Army, under Lieutenant-General Hatazō Adachi, in New

Guinea. The creation of Eighth Area Army 'represented a major increase in commitment from the Imperial Japanese Army to operations in the South Pacific'. The Japanese still had 1,200 men at Lae and Salamaua. In December, they seized further bases at Finschhafen and Wewak, beginning the process of rebuilding their forces on the island.[68] A detachment of one reinforced infantry regiment, the 102nd Infantry Regiment from 51st Japanese Division, arrived in Lae on 7 January 1943. The main elements of 20th and 41st Japanese Divisions landed far to the west (in order to be out of range of Allied aircraft) at Wewak on 19 January and 12 February.[69]

These reinforcements brought the strength of the Lae-Salamaua garrison up to about 4,500 men and Adachi immediately ordered his forces to go on the offensive. The objective was the Allied base and airfield at Wau, which Adachi saw as valuable, not only for the defence of the bases on the north shore of New Guinea, but as a key launching point for a renewed offensive against Port Moresby.[70] Blamey, who had effectively taken over command of NGF during the height of the crisis on the Kokoda Trail, was aware that Japanese troops had landed in the north and reacted with considerable haste. With the garrison at Wau, codenamed 'Kanga Force', made up of only several hundred men, he moved the as yet uncommitted 17th Brigade, which had fought with 6th Australian Division in the Middle East, from Milne Bay Force to Wau to bolster its defences.[71] The 2/6th Battalion arrived first and on advancing to meet the Japanese threat ran into the full force of the 102nd Infantry Regiment at Wandumi on 28 January. Here, in an action characterised by incredible tenacity, Captain Bill Sherlock's A Company held up the Japanese spearhead:[72]

> The attack began at 4 a.m. Three and a half hours later Sherlock signalled: 'Holding them nicely. Only disadvantage JAPS above us'. That afternoon, at 2.55 p.m., he reported that 'he was cut off and looked like being overrun'. By 3.40 p.m., he was down to just 40 men and running out of ammunition. Sherlock's final message came through at 6.23 p.m.: 'Don't think it will be long now. Close up to flank and front, about 50 yds in front'.[73]

Sherlock, along with many of his men, was killed in the fighting at Wandumi, but the stand of A Company, 2/6th Battalion, bought time for the defence of Wau. By 29 January, the rest of 17th Brigade had been flown in and by the start of February 'Kanga Force' numbered 3,166 all ranks. In the face of determined and sustained resistance, hungry and disease ridden, the Japanese abandoned their offensive on 9 February.[74]

Between the summer of 1942 and January 1943, the fighting in Papua had cost the Australians 5,698 casualties, 2,165 of whom lost their lives. The battle for Wau added another 349 to the casualty list. The Americans, who entered the campaign at Buna in November, lost 2,848 casualties, 930 of them dead. The casualties of the Australian and US troops at the beachheads were greater per capita than the US Marine Corps at Guadalcanal. The approximate losses for the Japanese were 12,000 dead from 16,000 committed in Papua, with a further 1,200 dying in the assault on Wau in New Guinea;[75] by comparison, Japan lost 5,500 lives from the 136,000 committed in seizing Malaya, Singapore and Burma earlier in the year.[76] The victories achieved in Papua and New Guinea, therefore, marked a considerable turning point, and represented 'Japan's first real defeat on land' in the Second World War.[77]

The lessons that emerged from the fighting were little different from those in Malaya, Singapore and Burma. As Major-General George Vasey, the new commander of 7th Australian Division, noted in January 1943, in jungle warfare 'for success in either attack or defence ... high morale, [and] a high standard of tng [training], both individual and collective' was necessary.[78] The militia units that fought in Papua were inadequately prepared compared to their AIF compatriots; these conscripts were initially provided with only ninety days of training.[79] It is not unfair to argue that their morale was not of the same level as that of the AIF either; for example, the proportion of sick to wounded in AIF units was approximately 2:1, whereas in militia units it was 4:1.[80] With inadequate training and less resolute morale, militia performance was generally not up to the standards of the AIF. Blamey considered the 14th Militia Brigade at Port Moresby a 'poor show'; the Army rated it level 'E', meaning 'a considerable' amount of training was required. The 7th Militia Brigade at Milne Bay was seen as only 'efficient in a static role' and 30th Militia Brigade was considered level 'F', the lowest possible rating, meaning unit training was 'not complete'.[81] Nevertheless, when operations were going badly at the start of the campaign, retreats never turned into routs, and, when the Australians turned to the offensive in late September, most AIF and militia units stuck to their tasks with a dogged resolve.

This level of grit and steely determination had been markedly absent in previous campaigns against the Japanese. Whereas Australian units broadly held their ground in Papua and New Guinea, in Malaya and Burma Commonwealth formations had retreated almost on first sight of the enemy. Whereas in Papua and New Guinea, vital stores had been destroyed before necessary withdrawals, in Malaya and Burma they were left behind as unintended gifts to the advancing Japanese. These behaviours made a significant difference at the tactical level, but, also, and perhaps more importantly, at the operational and strategic level. By holding on to ground with determination, Australian units were able to delay Japanese advances, thus granting time to commanders to make and execute decisions. Blamey's move of 17th Brigade from Milne Bay Force to Wau, for example, was only made possible and meaningful by the stand of Sherlock's A Company, 2/6th Battalion, which delayed the Japanese advance long enough to provide time for the rest of 17th Brigade to land and defend Wau. The criticisms levelled at commanders in Malaya and Burma, and even in France and the Middle East, must be understood in this light; they were rarely provided with sufficient time to allow them to genuinely control, or even manage, events. The challenges of command proved distinctly more achievable when officers found themselves in charge of an army that would stand and fight.

Nevertheless, in spite of the dramatic improvement in the performance of one element of the British and Commonwealth Armies, it must be recognised that success in Papua and New Guinea in 1942 and early 1943 'did not save Australia' all by itself. These campaigns 'taught the Australians how to fight in the jungle and, ultimately, how to beat the Japanese', lessons that would be put to good effect in the years to come.[82] The 'victories were only possible' because the Americans (in some cases with Australian support) had engaged the Japanese Army and Navy in extremely costly campaigns elsewhere in the Pacific. The air attacks at Lae and Salamaua in March 1942, the battles of the Coral Sea in May and at Midway in June, and the destruction of the Japanese forces on Guadalcanal (with the loss of 20,800 men of the Imperial Army), prevented Japanese commanders in Rabaul from concentrating overwhelming force against the Australian mainland and its surrounding islands. Had the Americans not played their part, the 'Battle for Australia' might have ended very differently.[83] Now that the Japanese assaults in Papua and New Guinea had been defeated, the Australian and American forces in the SWPA were in a position to finally go on the offensive.

Quit India

As Australia lurched from crisis to recovery and finally began to fully mobilise, India, in many respects, had the opposite experience. The dismal failure to defend Malaya, Singapore and Burma raised serious questions regarding the willingness and ability of the Indian people and the Indian Army to fight if attacked or invaded.[84] On 2 February 1942, Clement Attlee, the leader of the Labour Party and Deputy Prime Minister, presented a 'Memorandum on the Indian Political Situation' to the War Cabinet. In it he called for an urgent 'act of statesmanship' to draw Indian political leaders behind London and the war. 'To mark time is to lose India', he concluded. Attlee's initiative led to the establishment of a special India Committee of the War Cabinet and to the decision to make a new constitutional offer to India, promising that, as soon as the war ended, India's political future would be handed over to a constitution-making body, free to withdraw India from the Empire.[85] In the meantime, Indian participation in the Viceroy's Government would be substantially increased.

Sir Stafford Cripps brought the offer to India on 23 March, but his mission ran immediately into two intractable problems. The first, 'was the Congress insistence on a direct say in defence operations', a demand to which London, the Viceroy and Cripps were unanimously opposed. The second, which was even more fundamental, 'was the British insistence that, whatever the model of independence proposed after the war, the Muslim provinces and the princely states would be free to opt out and make their own arrangements in negotiation with Britain'. This, in the eyes of Congress was the recipe for 'Pakistan' or, worse still 'Ulsterisation' or 'balkanisation'; Congress rejected it completely.[86] The most vital zones of the Indian war effort were Muslim majority provinces. Bengal contained 'more than half of India's industrial capacity' and the Punjab was the main recruiting ground for the Indian Army. Britain quite simply needed Muslim India and its 'tacit but deepening' commitment to the war. By supporting these claims, however, Britain worsened its relationship with Congress and the rest of India. By early April, the negotiations were over and Cripps was on his way home.[87]

Months later, on 8 August, Congress passed the 'Quit India' resolution sanctioning 'a mass struggle on non-violent lines on the widest possible scale' to bring British rule in India to an immediate end.[88] The next day, more than 30,000 members of the Indian National Congress (INC) were arrested.[89] The detention of the principal leaders of Congress 'marked the start of spontaneous and popular outbursts across the subcontinent. The first phase consisted of a wave of industrial strikes in mills and steelworks, and a large number of street demonstrations led by the urban middle classes, especially students.' In the weeks that followed, unrest spread to the countryside. Telephone lines, railways, post offices, courts, and revenue offices were attacked; 208 police stations, 332 railway stations, 749 government buildings and 945 post and telegraph offices were fully or partially destroyed. The destruction of 268 items of rolling stock and the sabotage of railway lines in 411 places delayed troop movements and disrupted the construction of air bases and the delivery of essential coal supplies. Strikes resulted in the reduction of vital steel production by 10 per cent.[90] Linlinthgow informed Churchill that he was engaged 'in meeting by far the most serious rebellion since that of 1857, the gravity and extent of which we have so far concealed for reasons of military security'. The rebellion in parts of eastern India, according to one historian, 'approached that of a fully fledged insurgency'.[91]

By early September, the situation was so fraught that the censors recorded that 'many' British civilians were, as Congress wished, 'considering quitting India'. Mail from India to the front was 'gloomy' and 'full of depression'; 'politics in India have gripped, perhaps for the first time, since 1857 the year of the Indian Mutiny, the imaginations of the wives of Army men in India', wrote the censors. One woman wrote:

> India is frightfully anti-British just now ... I must say I do think it is no place for English women or indeed white people at all. We are finished out here, unwanted and most unpopular. There is talk of compulsory evacuation for white families now, but nothing official yet as far as I know, but it is being discussed.[92]

A Bengali professor in Calcutta wrote:

> Whole of India is now in great turmoil. From the big cities the movement is spreading to smaller ones. In Calcutta ... Buses

> and trams have stopped running except in one or two sections. The Medical College Hospitals are full of wounded patients. Shops on the main streets don't dare to open. All nationalist journals in Calcutta ... are going to suspend their publication from Friday next as a protest against censoring of local news ... The situation in Bihar and Bombay is bad.[93]

Conscious of the threat Quit India posed to both the war effort and the future of the Raj, the British suppressed the rising with considerable ruthlessness. Fifty-seven battalions, including twenty-four drawn from the Field Army and seven formed from manpower from Reinforcement Camps and Training Centres, were called out to act as aid to the civil power.[94] Nearly 3,000 people were killed or wounded and over 90,000 arrested.[95] By the end of September, the uprising had been crushed. Quit India never managed to seriously threaten 'the overall security of the Raj'.[96] It did, however, encourage many to boycott the British war effort; it paralysed the lines of communications in north-east India; and it delayed all training and offensive preparations, at a key moment in the war, by about six weeks.[97]

It also adversely affected the morale of the Army, as it desperately tried to regroup after the disasters of the first half of the year.[98] British servicemen, in particular, were dismayed at the turn of events and welcomed the 'severe repressive measures' taken by the Government.[99] A British officer wrote from Poona at the end of August, 'the main issue at stake is winning the war and then we can settle the Indian problem after that. It seems ridiculous that after all these years that this problem should come up as blackmail at this important stage of the war.' A Signals corporal in an Indian unit in the Middle East was more forthright:

> I see the Indians are taking advantage of our troubles. I wonder if they think they will get away with it. We can't allow it, so they must be treated in a rough way ... I am all for teaching them a few lessons. We have too much at stake to treat anyone with kid gloves.[100]

Although Indian soldiers were broadly behind the swift suppression of the rebellion, their reactions to the political implications of Quit India were more mixed. The potential for 'future political freedom' and the 'excitement caused in political circles' made 'the old soldier (and especially the V.C.O. [Viceroy Commissioned Officer])' of the martial races 'keep "looking over his shoulder" with unsettled feelings at the prospect of disappearing stability'. By contrast, 'newly enlisted classes' were 'more influenced by hostile propaganda and political cross-currents' and likely to have at least some sympathy for the Congress movement.[101] Nevertheless, it was clear from censorship that while the ramifications of Quit India were not lost on the Indian soldier, the majority were preoccupied with how the political uncertainty would affect their homes and families. One man wrote in August 1942:

> Since things are changing in India, conditions going worse, you should keep the children like [the] hen keeps the chickens under her wings . . . If the danger grows, Mian should not go to school even . . . Don't trust anybody.[102]

By October, military intelligence was sure that 'the cumulative influence of the present political ferment in India must consciously, or unconsciously, affect the army in general, and the ICO in particular, to an increasing extent'.[103]

The following month, with the uprising quashed, interest in the political situation died down. But, the effects of the Cripps Mission, Quit India and, what reports referred to as, 'the hostile attitude of the Indian civilians towards the army' all contributed to a decline in morale, just as preparations were under way to reengage the Japanese Army in Burma.[104]

The Arakan

As early as April 1942, Churchill had informed the Chiefs of Staff that he wanted plans framed for 'a counter-offensive' in Burma.[105] Neither the Prime Minister nor Wavell, the C-in-C India, wished to wait long for a second round with the Imperial Japanese Army.[106] Only the rapid reconquest of the territories lost could undo the damage done to the reputation of Britain and its empire. With this aim in mind, it was broadly agreed that an amphibious strategy rather than a ground campaign was preferable for retaking Burma. As Churchill would write later, 'going into swampy jungles to fight the Japanese' was like 'going into the water to fight a shark'.[107] However, the amphibious resources required to cross the Bay of Bengal and retake Rangoon and then move on to Singapore were not available in the Far East in the autumn and winter of 1942. These precious resources, instead, were sent to seize Madagascar from the Vichy French. Then, just as it seemed they would be transferred east, they were assigned to North Africa for Operation 'Torch', the Anglo-American invasion of Tunisia and Morocco.[108]

In the circumstances, Churchill, and the Chiefs of Staff, were willing to forgo an offensive in 1942. But, Wavell wanted to act with 'boldness and determination'. He had written to his Chief of Staff in September noting that 'we may find Japanese opposition very much lower than we expect in Burma ... The Jap has never fought defensively and may not be much good at it.'[109] Efforts had been made to document the mistakes of the preceding year. Doctrine had been adapted and veterans had been sent to formations to disseminate recommended techniques.[110] 'Both the morale of the Indian Army and the prestige of the Raj', he said, required at least some 'demonstration of offensive capacity'.[111]

On 19 November, Wavell ordered 14th Indian Division, which had been advancing cautiously down the Arakan coast since September, to launch a full-scale attack south. The primary objective was to seize a jumping off place, at the tip of the Mayu peninsula, for an assault on Akyab island, where there was one of two serviceable ports in the eastern Bay of Bengal and a strategically important airfield. Success, should it be achieved, would sharply reduce the Japanese air threat to the industrial region around Calcutta, provide a forward air base to cover amphibious operations in the next campaigning season, and erode Japanese air strength in Burma (see Illustration 8.2).[112]

Wavell's plans were certainly aggressive and proactive, but there remained a plethora of problems besetting the Indian Army. The troops still lacked a cause for which they deemed it worth fighting and Quit India had only served to complicate and exacerbate this situation. Although, in general, lessons had been learnt, there had been insufficient time to retrain since the end of the first Burma campaign (in May) and put new understanding into practice. Moreover, each unit was still 'left to its own devices' to implement changes in doctrine and training. Thus, teamwork, trust and morale were still deficient in the force that advanced south and east into the Burmese jungle in November 1942.[113] Nothing resembling the transformation of the Army in the UK and in North Africa had yet materialised in Burma.

The outcome of the Arakan campaign was perhaps unsurprisingly, therefore, little different to what had occurred in Malaya and

Illustration 8.2 Mahrattas lined up for an attack on Japanese positions in the Arakan, n.d. The almost intolerable setback in the Arakan would eventually compel India Command to fundamentally rethink its doctrine for fighting in the jungle.

Burma in the first half of the year. The 14th Indian Division, under Major-General W. T. Lloyd, comprising four brigades, advanced steadily against limited Japanese opposition, of just two battalions, until it was only 10 miles from the southern tip of the Mayu peninsula, near Donbaik. Here it ran into a complex bunker system and the newly arrived Japanese 55th Division. Wavell hurried reinforcements to the front and pressed Lloyd, whose division, by mid-March, commanded an unworkable nine brigades, to crush the Japanese by sheer weight of numbers.[114] Repeated assaults failed to dislodge the considerably outnumbered defenders whose '"fanatical" willingness to stand and fight quite literally to the last man and round, required each position to [be] carefully cleared of all surviving Japanese infantrymen' before the attack could progress. As the British and Commonwealth advance ran out of steam, the Japanese prepared to counter-attack. On 7 March, the Japanese launched their own offensive and the British Commonwealth forces in the Arakan disintegrated. By the end of May, after a humiliating retreat, with casualties of 916 dead, 2,889 wounded and 1,252 missing, Wavell's forces were back to their original start line.[115]

This was an almost intolerable setback. Once again, a British and Commonwealth Army, with superior artillery and a monopoly on tanks, had been decisively beaten by a force only half its size. On 9 April, Wavell wrote to his Army Commander, Lieutenant-General N. M. S. Irwin, asking 'has there been any surrender without fighting or desertion to the enemy by Indian troops? I am more worried about the morale aspect both of the troops and to India [*sic*] than anything else.'[116] He was right to be concerned. As Raymond Callahan has outlined:

> On at least two occasions British battalions fell apart in something like panic. Many of the Indian troops were in an equally bad state. Poorly trained and terrified of the jungle, patrols, unless accompanied by a British officer, would simply lie up and return after a suitable interval to report that they had seen nothing. On one occasion a critical position was lost because its jittery defenders had fired off all their ammunition at night noise in the jungle. One unit refused an order to advance, another threw away its rifles during a retirement, and, perhaps not surprisingly, 'defeatist and disloyal' talk was reported rife among the wounded.[117]

A liaison officer who visited the front in May reported that:

> I came away unfortunately with the definite impression, gained from personal observation and conversations with senior and junior officers, NCOs, men and escaped POW that on this front the Japanese soldier, with the notable exception of the gunners, was definitely superior to the troops forming the bulk of our forces in the area.
>
> Outstanding was the fact that our troops were either exhausted, browned off, or both, and that both Indian and British troops did not have their hearts in the campaign. The former were obviously scared of the Jap and generally demoralised by the nature of the campaign, i.e. the thick jungle and the subsequent blindness of movement, the multiple noises of the jungle at night, the terror stories of the Jap brutality, ... the undermining influence of fever, and the mounting list of failures; the latter also fear the jungle, hate the country, and see no object in fighting for it, and also have the strong feeling that

> they are taking part in a forgotten campaign in which no one in authority is taking any real interest ...
>
> Reinforcements that have arrived have consisted mostly of untrained men, many of whom according to the CO of the L.F. [10th Lancashire Fusiliers] had never even seen a Bren Gun. All complained of the lack of pre-campaign training ...
>
> To sum up the man to man situation the seasoned and highly trained Jap troops are confronted by a force which, although impressive on paper, is little better, in a large number of cases, than a rather unwilling band of raw levies.[118]

The liaison officer concluded with the observation that the majority of COs and staff officers he had met no longer had confidence in the men under their command.[119]

Morale reports showed that the experience in the Arakan had certainly exerted a 'damping effect' on British troops.[120] Many wanted to leave India and appeared to be driven by 'a strong conviction that their "contract" was to fight the Germans' and not the Japanese. 'The present citizen army is more interested in fighting for home and family than for Empire possessions', noted the compilers of the reports.[121] It was certainly clear that British troops exhibited 'little enthusiasm for defending India for the Indians'.[122] Soldiers asked themselves, as a later report outlined, '"what do I get out of India"? "Is it worth defending it if, as we are told, we are going to hand it over to Congress when the war is over".' Morale among British troops was, therefore, 'a tender plant' and the 'complete lack of real enthusiasm for service in India and for the necessity of beating the Japanese' was considered 'almost universal' and not 'a sound foundation upon which to base a prolonged campaign'.[123]

Indian troops 'on the Arakan front, and those on Lines of Communication' were 'generally speaking' also in a not very 'happy frame of mind':

> Men returning to back areas or proceeding on leave, are indulging in a good deal of gloomy, alarmist, or defeatist talk. The Japanese 'I' [Information] offensive has recently been intensified, and subversive propaganda has been instrumental in lowering morale, even to the extent of causing a few Indian ranks to desert to the enemy in the field.[124]

By the end of the campaign, it was clear that 'general confidence in the allied cause and in final victory' had been 'shaken by the withdrawal from [the] Arakan, and [by] the crop of wild rumours which followed in its trail'.[125] 'An appreciable victory over the Japanese on the Eastern Frontier' was desperately needed to restore the prestige and morale of the Indian Army.[126]

Sickness figures available for Eastern Army during the period reinforce this picture (see Figure 8.1).[127] They show that between February and May 1943, the sick rate jumped by 45 per cent, from 68 per thousand to 98 per thousand. It would rise again to 138 per thousand in July, a 75 per cent increase from February (figures are not available for 1942).[128] The medical services were so 'overwhelmed' with cases of battle exhaustion, that one report pointed out that 'no purpose would be served by counting Psychiatric heads in this campaign. The whole of 14th Ind. Div. was for practical purposes a Psychiatric casualty.'[129] As significant as these morale problems were, the army in Burma was also let down by its commanders. Clear direction had been distinctly lacking;[130] 14th Indian Division's HQ had been incapable of managing nine whole brigades; remarkably it was only on 14 April that Slim's XV Corps HQ was activated to oversee the final phases of the disastrous campaign (much as had happened at the end of the first Burma campaign).[131] Wavell unquestionably had to shoulder some of the blame too. He wrote to Brooke on 22 May:

> I knew the difficulties and dangers, since I was employing troops not fully trained or of best quality ... We have found weakness in the present Indian Army which we knew to exist owing to the great expansion, but which are more pronounced than we realised.[132]

Wavell had clearly overestimated the fighting abilities of his troops. It was time to face facts, and, as he told Brooke, 'do our best to remedy' the situation. The same day, he wrote a letter to all officers serving in India Command. 'It is most certainly not our way to lose heart when we have been worsted', he affirmed. 'We have never yet failed to avenge a defeat or to regain what we have lost. We must examine calmly and with confidence the reasons for our failure and work to remedy them before we fight the next round.'[133] The remarkable turnaround that had happened in the desert now desperately needed to be replicated in the jungle.

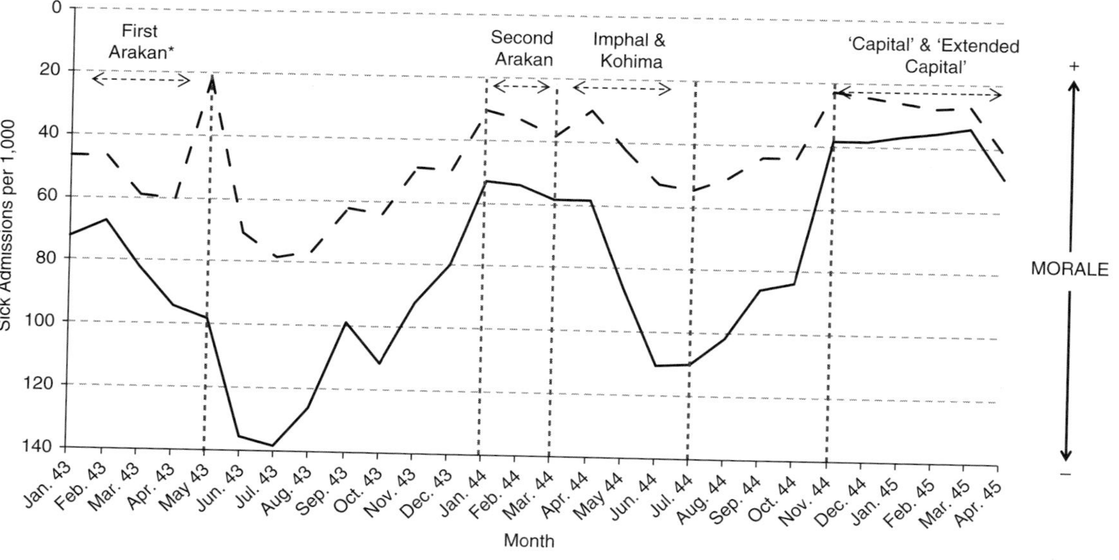

Figure 8.1 Sick rate, Eastern Army, 11 Army Group and Allied Land Forces South-East Asia, January 1943–April 1945 * The decrease in sickness less malaria in May 1943 was caused not by an improvement in health, but by a massive increase in the prevalence of Malaria in those forces engaged in the Arakan. Whereas Malaria had represented 36 per cent of sickness in Apr. 1943, it represented 78 per cent of sickness in May 1943.

Part IV The Limits of Attrition

9 THE MEDITERRANEAN

Strategy and Preparation

By the last months of 1942, with the successes at El Alamein and the 'Torch' landings behind them, Allied thoughts turned increasingly to the next step in the war in the West. The most obvious move, an invasion somewhere along the North-West coast of Europe was, even with growing American participation and the Russian victories in the East, extremely risky. In the circumstances, the British Chiefs of Staff pushed strenuously for an Anglo-American strategy that would build on accomplishments in North Africa and focus on the achievable rather than the desirable. For Britain, knocking Italy out of the war was the obvious answer to the strategic conundrum. In British eyes, in many ways, the war had always been 'Italy first', not 'Germany first'.[1]

Intelligence projections suggested that knocking Italy out of the war would put potentially crippling stresses on the German war machine. Hitler would have little choice but to cover the loss of Italy and of Italian garrisons in the Balkans. If he attempted also to hold the existing front in the USSR, he would find himself short by 54 divisions and 2,200 combat aircraft. To add to these difficulties, Hitler would face an intractable logistic and transportation challenge, 'for while a highly developed and efficient lateral railway system enabled the Germans to switch forces across Europe between the East and the West, there was no such system to the south – only two lines into Italy and one into Greece, all of them potentially vulnerable to disruption by bombing'.[2] Additionally, taking the Italian Navy out of the equation in the Mediterranean would free up a million tons of British shipping, while a reopened Suez Canal would knock thousands of miles off the journey between the United Kingdom and the armies massing in India to retake Britain's lost territories in the Far East.[3]

At the 'Symbol' Conference at Casablanca in January 1943, the British Chiefs of Staff put their position to the Americans. After heated debate, they carried the day; an attack on North-West Europe would be postponed until 1944. Instead, the Allies would focus on the Mediterranean with the first step being an invasion of the Italian island of Sicily. 'Symbol' has generally been regarded as a diplomatic triumph for Britain; it ensured, at least in the short term, that British interests would remain at the heart of Allied strategy. The price, an agreement that preparations for the long-awaited second (North-West Europe) front would, in the long term, take priority over activities in the Mediterranean, seemed well worth paying.[4]

In the wake of 'Symbol', planning for the invasion of Sicily, Operation 'Husky', began almost immediately. Eisenhower would be Commander-in-Chief (C-in-C), but the three component commanders would be British: Alexander (ground forces), Tedder (air forces) and Sir Andrew Browne Cunningham (naval forces). The initial plan, drawn up by the Joint Planning Staff in London and then amended by Major-General Charles H. Gairdner, the Chief of Staff of Force 141 (the inter-Allied, inter-service force designated for the invasion of Sicily), was driven by logistic and air power considerations; it envisaged two widely separated landings, one on the East and one on the West of the island. This approach was agreed by Eisenhower and his three commanders in March 1943, only to be unilaterally rejected by Montgomery in April. Montgomery, emboldened by his success in Africa, insisted on a more concentrated landing area, so that the full force of the invading Armies could be thrown into battle in a co-ordinated and controlled manner. Not for the last time, he got his way. With different aspects of the plan assigned to HQs at opposite ends of the Mediterranean and in London and Washington, and with key men responsible fully engaged in active operations in Tunisia, co-ordinating the plan for 'Husky' had been unquestionably challenging.[5]

After the collapse of Axis resistance in Tunisia, attention focused more clearly on Sicily. The planning for the assault was ironed out and a period of rest, regrouping, re-equipping, and where possible retraining, began.[6] There was little doubt that control of the air was a prerequisite for a successful amphibious assault, as was the capture of the fortified island of Pantellaria, which lay along the sea route from Tunisia to Sicily.[7] For these purposes, the Allied forces had use of 3,462 combat aircraft. In comparison, by the beginning of July 1943 there were about 775 *Luftwaffe* aircraft capable of intervening against 'Husky' and a further 63 bombers scheduled to arrive in theatre. The *Regia Aeronautica* had 600 aircraft in theatre. About 289 German and 145 Italian aircraft (434 in all) were based in Sicily, most of which were fighters or fighter-bombers.[8]

Between 16 May and 9 July, the Allied air forces began to systematically destroy Axis air power in the region.[9] An enormous bombing campaign over Pantelleria, between 6 and 11 June, ensured that the fortified island with its important long-range radar outpost, airfields and shipping observation stations fell without much resistance.[10] The 1st Division, which had fought in France and in the later stages of the Tunisian campaign, captured it on 11 June taking 11,399 Italian POWs; the local newspapers in North Africa noted that the only casualty suffered was a soldier bitten by a donkey – 'this turned out to be a Guardsman who gave it an army biscuit!'[11] By 10 July, the planned D-Day for Operation 'Husky', only two Axis airfields on Sicily were fully usable. The German and Italian air forces had retreated from the island, and were compelled to operate at extreme range from airfields near Naples. The Allies had, to a considerable degree 'broken Axis air power in the Mediterranean'.[12]

The foundations for success in Sicily had, therefore, largely been laid. But there was no guarantee of victory in what even the most optimistic of Allied planners considered a high-risk operation. There were grave concerns, not least among Eisenhower and his 'Committee of Three' (Alexander, Tedder and Cunningham), that anything over two German divisions in Sicily might prove difficult to defeat.[13] The Germans quite simply could not be allowed to build up reserves before the landings. With this in mind, a series of deception operations were initiated to fix enemy forces as far away from Sicily as possible. Operation 'Barclay', focused on convincing the German High Command that Allied operations in the Mediterranean would be aimed not at Italy or Sicily, but at the Balkans. A fictitious British Twelfth Army in Egypt was depicted as poised to invade Greece in the early summer. Turkey was portrayed as ready to join the Allied side and together they would link up with an advance by the Red Army through southern Russia. The Allies, so the fiction went, had decided to bypass Sicily and mainland Italy as the risk, ironically enough, of a 'laborious advance through the mountainous terrain' with 'the formidable barrier of the Alps at the far end' was deemed too great.[14]

'Barclay' was supported by another deception launched on 30 April, Operation 'Mincemeat'. It involved the deliberate planting by a British submarine of a body off the Spanish coast purporting to be that of a major in the Royal Marines killed in an air crash. Attached to the body, was a briefcase carrying 'important documents' along with personal items that lent credibility to the story. The documents indicated that the Allies planned to land in Greece and Sardinia in 1943. The Spanish passed this information on to German Intelligence who believed the story as it offered evidence supporting their own expectations of Allied strategy. 'Barclay' and 'Mincemeat' 'ensured that whatever German forces could be found to reinforce the Axis southern flank went to the Balkans'. In March 1943, there were eight German divisions in the Balkans; by July there were eighteen, with the number in Greece having increased from a single division to eight; two divisions were sent to reinforce Sardinia and Corsica. That left just two for Sicily.[15]

By July 1943, therefore, it was clear to the Allies (through Ultra) that 'Sicily was very far from being the German-dominated fortress feared initially in Allied planning'. The island was garrisoned by four field divisions of the Italian Sixth Army (around 50,000 men) together with a number of second-rate formations: five coastal divisions, two coastal brigades and mobile groups (around another 150,000 men). These forces were reinforced by the Hermann Göring Panzer Division (reconstituted after its destruction in Tunisia) and the 15th Panzer Grenadier Division; in all, the German forces amounted to around 32,000 troops, 160 tanks, 140 field guns, 36 rocket projectors (*nebelwerfers*) and a large number of anti-aircraft guns.[16] These not insignificant combined Italian and German forces were expected to fight with great intensity, as Sicily was part of the Axis homeland.

Nevertheless the scale of the forces now available to the Allies was immense and they 'certainly began Operation Husky with a marked numerical advantage'.[17] The force that the Allies intended to land on Sicily consisted of the newly formed 15th Army Group, under Alexander, which was made up of two armies, the British and Commonwealth Eighth Army, under Montgomery, which included a number of formations and units from the now disbanded First Army, and the American Seventh

Army, under General George Patton. These formations included seven infantry divisions, two airborne divisions, one armoured division, three armoured brigades and four battalions of commandos and rangers. A further three infantry divisions were held in reserve, a total of 450,000 troops.[18] The assault was to be accompanied by 400 tanks and 540 artillery pieces. The number of warships, assault craft and transports available for 'Husky' exceeded 2,500 and included 6 battleships, 15 cruisers, 3 monitors, 5 gunboats and 128 destroyers. 'This was an extremely powerful concentration of firepower, whose long range and high manoeuvrability allowed precise concentrations of devastating fire at particularly threatened points.'[19] The Eighth and Seventh Armies were also, by this stage, fielding fully trained and in many cases battle-experienced divisions.[20]

The Sicilian Campaign

On 10 July, 'Husky' was launched. Patton's Seventh US Army and Montgomery's Eighth Army landed in the south-east of Sicily, Seventh Army on the left and Eighth Army on the right (see Map 9.1). The latter, consisting of XIII Corps, under Lieutenant-General Sir Miles Dempsey, and XXX Corps, under Leese, was tasked with capturing Catania and advancing on Vizzini while Seventh Army was to push west towards Agrigento.[21] Alexander 'was keen to allow the land battle to develop before any decisions were made about specific measures by each of the two armies'. However, there is little doubt that Montgomery and Patton were quite clear that the ultimate objective was the capture of Messina in the north-east of the country and the sealing off of the Axis life-line to mainland Italy. With the towering volcano of Mount Etna standing as a considerable barrier between the landings and this objective, only two viable routes for the capture of Messina were available. One was along the plain of Catania to the east – a broad, marshy lowland 12 miles wide and 18 miles long – and another was through the mountainous terrain to the west of Etna. As such, initially at least, Eighth Army had operational priority in Sicily as it was best placed to assault Catania and advance along the easier eastern route.[22]

The amphibious landing got off to a good start. Shortly after H-Hour, the four assault divisions of Eighth Army, 50th Northumbrian and 51st Highland Divisions (veterans of North Africa), 5th Division, which had fought in France and taken part in the seizure of Vichy-

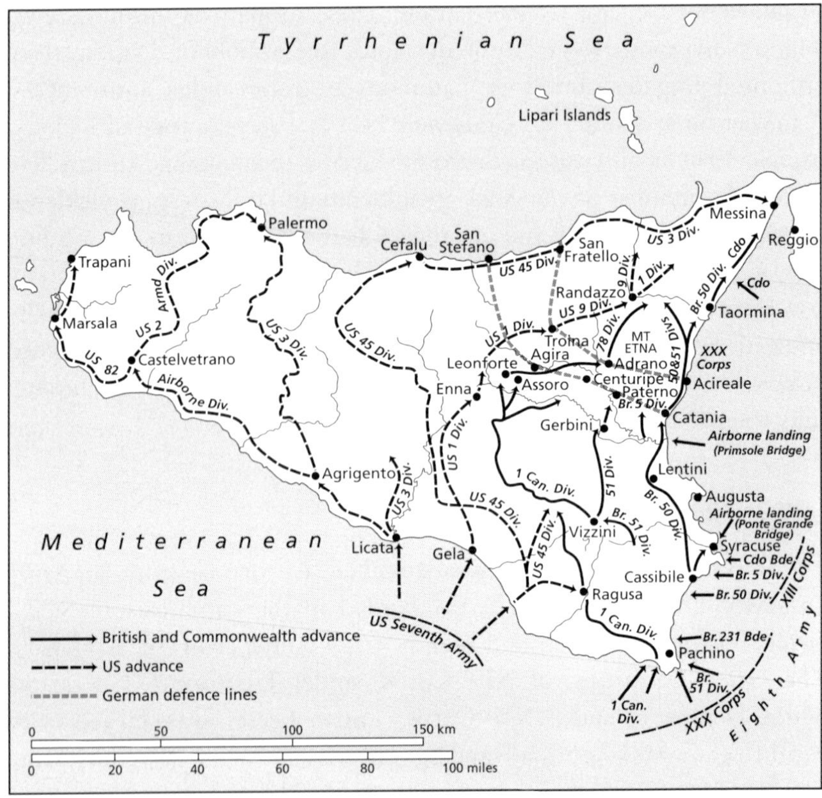

Map 9.1 The Sicilian campaign, 1943

controlled Madagascar, and the as yet untested 1st Canadian Division, landed on six beaches on the Pachino peninsula. Opposition was rapidly overcome and deep penetrations inland were made with remarkably few casualties, 1,517 in the first week of the operation, only a sixth of the 9,434 expected.[23] The Italian Coastal Divisions, made up mainly of inexperienced troops, many of them older reservists, lacked motivation, training and equipment. Many gave up after token resistance or took to the hills.[24] As one Canadian soldier put it, 'we were lucky that we only ran into the Wops first', as 'they haven't got their heart in it at all – we had no trouble'.[25]

The landings were supported by the first major allied airborne operation of the war. Airborne troops were used to 'secure defiles along the line of advance of the assaulting troops after they were ashore'. By doing this, it was hoped that the momentum of the attack would be maintained. The task was given to 1st Airborne Division.[26]

The operation did not go entirely to plan. British 1st Airlanding Brigade, which was tasked with capturing the operationally important Ponte Grande Bridge inland of the assault beaches, experienced appalling casualties. Inexperienced pilots and navigators lost their way and became dispersed, veering off their assigned flight paths. They mistakenly flew into the invasion fleet's anti-aircraft defence zone and took heavy flak. In the fear and confusion that followed, some tug pilots released their gliders early; sixty-nine went down into the sea and hundreds of men drowned. Only two gliders reached their objective; another twenty-two came down within 1 mile; a further forty-nine were dispersed even further from the target bridge. In spite of these difficulties, the airborne troops stuck to their tasks and broadly achieved their objectives.[27]

British and Commonwealth units demonstrated no little drive in the immediate period following the landings.[28] The key ports of Syracuse and Augusta on the east coast were captured by 11 July.[29] Morale was unquestionably 'very high' in all units. In the weeks leading up to the invasion, the censors reported that the men were 'exceedingly keen ... their one desire being to put up what they describe as a terrific fight on the Continent which many consider would finish Nazism once and for all'.[30] Letters written on board ship, as the troops steamed towards Sicily, showed that 'morale and fighting spirit' remained 'extremely high amongst all ranks'. For the men of 1st Canadian Division:

> The monotony of three years training was being left behind. They were full of confidence ... and it can be said that with hardly an exception they were going into battle joyfully. Their only regret seemed to be that their people would worry about them.[31]

The lessons on the importance of welfare, learnt in the preceding years, were not forgotten in the cramped conditions of the troopships. Although some officers wrote that 'they were very sorry for their men, especially after "blackout" when the ventilation was poor', it was clear that 'grousing' was much 'less than the normal in troopship mail'. Canteens were 'well stocked' while 'as far as space would allow everything possible seems to have been done to keep the men from being bored. Cinema, concerts, games, P.T., boat drill etc. are all frequently mentioned; also there seemed to be plenty of reading matter on board':

> The fact that these troops were going to become part of the Eighth Army and be under the leadership of General Montgomery gave them tremendous confidence and writer after writer, Canadians and British mentions it with pride. A C.S.M. [Company Sergeant Major] makes a typical remark:- 'Monty says that we can do it and that is good enough for all of us.'[32]

Montgomery's visits to the troops before the operation had, according to the censors, given the 'greatest satisfaction. His personal magnetism imbued all ranks with supreme confidence.' Many wrote 'that they would follow him anywhere'.[33]

By 13 July, the 'battle situation', as Montgomery put it, looked 'very good'. With the bridgehead increasingly secure, Alexander issued orders that Seventh Army was to expand westwards and adopt a mostly defensive posture while Eighth Army should drive on Catania in the east and also capture the central road network towards Enna in the centre of the island. Sicily, thus, would be cut in two, trapping enemy formations in the West and East.[34]

Montgomery assigned Dempsey's XIII Corps the task of advancing along the east coast road. After a series of bitter and costly assaults, they failed to dislodge the German defenders and break out towards Catania. As the east coast route appeared blocked, Montgomery switched focus to thrust north through the centre of the island, but an attack by XXX Corps towards Enna failed also to break through the German line.[35] Eighth Army's efforts were not producing the desired outcomes.[36] By 18 July, with Patton straining on the leash, Alexander changed tack. He instructed Montgomery to focus on Catania and ordered Patton to drive north and 'split the island in two'.[37]

The Germans, by this stage, had already decided on an orderly withdrawal from Sicily. General Hube who, with the HQ of XIV Panzer Corps, had arrived in Sicily to take over direction of operations, put in place a plan to rescue as many Axis forces as possible. He decided on a 50-mile coast-to-coast defensive line from Catania in the east to San Stefano in the north with successive withdrawal positions falling back towards Messina in the north-east. Troops would have to be brought back from central and western Sicily to defend this new line and it was necessary, as a consequence, for the Germans to hold very firmly in the east. Eighth Army's advance towards Catania, therefore, was aimed at the position upon 'which the whole enemy operation hinged' and the advance turned into a period of 'bitter fighting' where little progress was made.[38] Eighth Army suffered 3,103 casualties in the second week and as the campaign wore on sickness rates began to climb on account of admissions for 'minor complaints', particularly diarrhoea and septic skin conditions.[39] By 23 July, the Axis forces had withdrawn fully to the Catania/San Stefano line. Three German divisions, the 29th Panzer Grenadier (which had just arrived), 15th Panzer Grenadier and Hermann Göring Panzer Division, each having under command part of an Italian division (Assietta, Aosta and Napoli respectively) manned the new defences. Against this line the Allies had in aggregate some eleven divisions and formidable air power.[40]

With the repeated assaults by XIII Corps in the east making little progress, Montgomery once again decided to use XXX Corps to attack the centre of the German defensive line. Bolstered by the news of Mussolini's fall from power, the battle began on 29 July and lasted the best part of four days. The 78th Division (newly arrived), 51st Highland Division and 1st Canadian Division attacked the German defences but failed to break through in a battle described by the 78th Division historian as 'worse than Longstop' (some of the toughest fighting in Tunisia).[41] Hube ordered his divisions to fall back to the next defensive line on 2 August and by 11 August German units were evacuating the island. The campaign 'became a slow and cautious follow-up' that 'never seriously threatened the enemy's escape'.[42] On 17 August, Alexander signalled Churchill to report that 'the last German soldier was flung out of Sicily'.[43]

Opportunity Lost

In spite of the apparent success of 'Husky', controversy still surrounds the operation. In the space of thirty-eight days the Allies had pushed the Axis out of Sicily for the relatively minor loss of 11,843 casualties in Eighth Army (9,617 British and 2,226 Canadian) and 8,781 in Seventh Army (20,624 in total). By comparison, the Germans lost nearly 29,000, around 41 per cent of their forces, which had eventually amounted to about 70,000. The Italians lost 144,000, about 72 per cent of their forces engaged.[44] This was not an inconsiderable achievement, especially considering Kesselring had thought on 13 July that the island could be held for a prolonged time.

Nevertheless, more than 50,000 German troops and much of their equipment, including some 47 tanks, 94 guns and nearly 10,000 vehicles, were successfully evacuated from the island. Some 60,000 Italian troops, along with 227 vehicles, 41 artillery pieces and 12 mules also escaped.[45] A German force of around 70,000 men with little assistance from the Italians 'had been able to hold off almost half a million troops for five weeks'.[46] To a degree, therefore, an opportunity to inflict a devastating blow to the Axis in the Mediterranean had been lost.[47]

Much of the blame for this apparent failure has fallen on Montgomery whose approach in Sicily has been criticised for being unforgivably slow and cautious.[48] Historians have argued that he could have taken Catania 'in one or two days if he had been "less conservative and his forces more mobile"'. Having taken Catania, he could then probably have stormed Messina in the first week, thus cutting off the bulk of the Axis forces in Sicily.[49]

By this point in the war, however, Eighth Army had been fully indoctrinated into the Montgomery 'Colossal Cracks' operational approach. Infantry were taught to rely heavily on the hitting power of concentrated artillery (see Figure 9.1).[50] On meeting resistance, infantry knew what they had to do; they halted and called down artillery support, 'rather than trying to outflank the enemy or fight their way forward with their own weapons'. They would then advance close behind the barrage, so that they arrived on top of German positions before they could react. Eighth Army had discovered a battle winning formula, and by the time of Sicily its organisation began to reflect that. Whereas during the summer fighting of 1942, those in the artillery had made up 29 per cent of the British infantry, armour and artillery personnel engaged, by the end of the Tunisian campaign, they made up 37 per cent.[51]

The problem was that in the rugged terrain and the mountainous countryside of Sicily, a more aggressive approach was required. The geography made it challenging for artillery to dominate the battlefield, as the craggy mountains prevented forces from concentrating (thus, presenting a target). Moreover, there was little open country in which tanks could manoeuvre. The primary determinant of tactical success in Sicily was the endurance and ability of the soldier.[52]

Lieutenant-Colonel Lionel Wigram, who had played a key role in developing battle drill in the UK in 1941 and 1942, was sent to Sicily

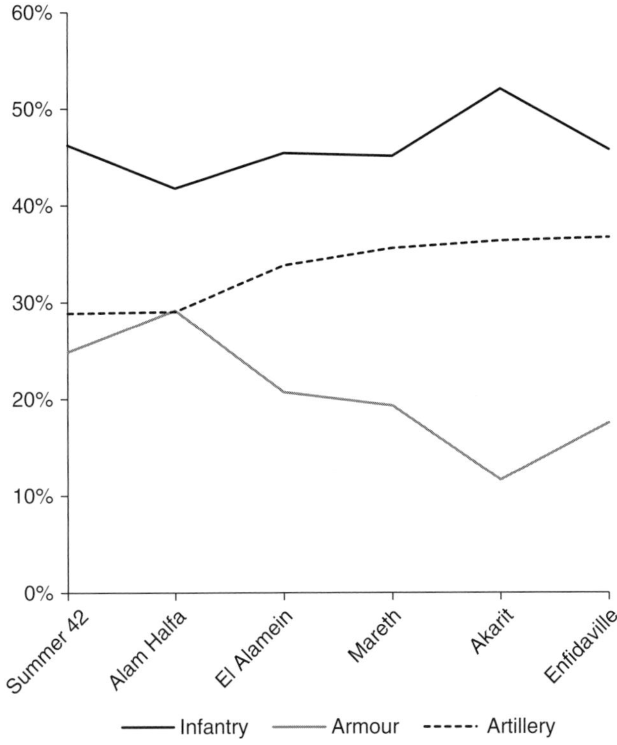

Figure 9.1 Ratio of infantry to armour and artillery personnel (British troops only), Eighth Army, North Africa, 1942–3

in 1943 to observe and study the tactical challenges presented by the Sicilian terrain. Wigram believed that the combat environment put a premium on small-unit manoeuvre to work through and around Axis defences. The Germans did not offer 'last ditch' stands in Sicily like they were to do later in the war. Aggressive manoeuvre and fire and movement could, therefore, produce very positive results.[53] Once the Germans were compelled to retreat, close pursuit by British and Canadian troops was necessary to reduce the time the enemy had to organise the next defensive line. It was in this context 'that the physical stamina and endurance required to overcome the ground and the heat needed to be combined with an aggressive initiative and resourcefulness in order to overcome the obstacles and minefields left in the enemy's wake'.[54]

Wigram 'rejected the view, heard on all sides [and still prevalent today], that the mountainous and difficult country was ideal for defence and impossible for attack'. He argued that the terrain, covered as it was with olive groves, plantations and crops and cut by numerous irrigation ditches and dividing walls, was 'positively advantageous' for the attack. He pointed to German small-unit tactics from earlier in the war and, especially Japanese performance in Malaya, where they had used small teams to infiltrate British positions at night to undermine them from the rear. 'Operating in ones and twos and armed with light automatic weapons and machine guns, ... [Japanese] troops had made good use of the prevailing cover to harass communications, isolate and pick off observation posts and generally to cause disorder and confusion.'[55]

Dynamic and aggressive infiltration and exploitation operations, however, required highly motivated and committed troops, and, the experience in North Africa suggested that this was not a luxury enjoyed by Eighth Army. Montgomery had relied heavily on materiel and massed firepower in North Africa for these very reasons. As he told an audience of senior officers in February 1943, 'I limit the scope of operations to what is possible, and I use the force necessary to ensure success.'[56]

There is much evidence, however, that the character of Eighth Army had changed markedly as a consequence of success in North Africa. Morale, in particular, had improved considerably in the lead-up to and early stages of the Sicilian campaign. In this context, it is not inconceivable that Montgomery might have profited from a more aggressive approach. The censorship summary for 1 to 15 July pointed out that 'all ranks are in great heart and full of confidence ... There are several comments expressing willingness to suffer the hardships of active service and to be away from home, as the writers are determined to destroy Nazism once and for all.' Some men apparently were 'dying to get into action again'.[57] By the start of August, morale was still described as 'very high' and it was clear that it had been managed more thoughtfully than in previous campaigns; for example, the troops were 'both surprised and delighted' that mail services were established so rapidly after the landing.[58] The sickness rates for the first three weeks of the operation were the lowest of the Sicilian and Italian campaigns (4.5, 6.4 and 8.5 per thousand per week respectively). Battle exhaustion figures tend to reinforce this picture; psychiatric casualties in the British contingents of Eighth Army amounted to around 11 per cent of battle casualties.[59] The Canadian figure was as low as 1 per cent.[60]

Nevertheless, given the seemingly endless sequence of setbacks suffered by the British and Commonwealth Armies between 1940 and 1942, it would have been surprising if Eighth Army had abandoned, or fundamentally altered, a winning formula so quickly after it had been discovered. In many ways, the kind of organisational flexibility necessary to adapt to the changing character of war required self-confidence and Eighth Army, at least in Montgomery's view, lacked such confidence at this stage of the war. Formations such as 50th Northumbrian and 51st Highland Divisions and 78th Division were highly experienced and battle hardened but there was little time, and perhaps willingness, following success in Tunisia, to retrain or fundamentally alter their tactical methods.[61]

More recent additions to Eighth Army, such as 1st Canadian and 5th Divisions, were, by comparison, less indoctrinated in Montgomery's new way of doing things (a point that could equally be applied to 78th Division which had fought as part of First Army in Tunisia). They had undergone a broad and extensive training programme that, in some ways, prepared them better for the type of warfare encountered in Sicily.[62] The Canadians had also, during their extended period of training in the United Kingdom, embraced the battle-drill movement and by December 1941, 'all infantry units in the Canadian Corps were enthusiastically conducting their own battle drill training' which focused extensively on the centrality of fire and movement.[63]

In its first few weeks after its introduction to action, the 1st Canadian Division systematically 'used brains and initiative to find the weak spots in the German defences'; they tended to try 'to outflank the Germans or to make German forward positions untenable'. German reports praised the Canadians and described them as 'very mobile at night', inclined to employ 'surprise break-ins' and 'clever infiltrations ... with small groups between our strong points'.[64] The attack of the Hastings and Prince Edward Regiment on the German-held mountain-top village of Assoro late on 20 July is an excellent example. The battalion ascended the steep eastern face of the mountain from which direction its commander, Major the Lord Tweedsmuir, rightly considered the Germans would never expect an attack. The troops carried nothing but their rifles, automatic weapons, and ammunition; the only food each man took with him was a ration of chocolate. It was a punishing climb, but it saved what otherwise might have been a very costly frontal attack. Such was the surprise achieved, that the Canadians took their objective by dawn without a single casualty.[65]

The assault was 'remarkable', a demonstration of 'intelligent, imaginative and bold manoeuvre'. It showed what the Canadians could do. But, rather than trusting in this method for the next assault, on the town of Agira, the divisional commander, Major-General Guy Simonds, changed tactics. He issued orders 'for what can perhaps best be called a set-piece advance to contact'. Five field and two medium artillery regiments as well as medium bombers and Kittyhawks, for close air support, were placed in support of the attacking infantry of the Royal Canadian Regiment (RCR), who were supposed to advance behind a creeping barrage at a rate of 100 yards in two minutes.[66]

Perhaps predictably, as the infantry reached rougher ground they slowed and the barrage 'began to draw ahead leaving an increasing gap between it and the forward troops'. Three of the RCR's companies took cover in a gully, advanced, and found themselves out of wireless range behind German positions, but in a good spot to cut off the forward elements of the enemy defence. Instead of attacking, however, they awaited further orders. When those orders eventually came through they were instructed to withdraw rather than attack. The change in philosophy was marked, and it is apparent that the division had, after just two weeks of action, come under the influence of Montgomery and his 'Colossal Cracks' approach. A fixed, rigidly timed fire-support programme was used instead of infiltration and Agira was not taken for five more days at a cost to the division of 438 casualties.[67]

Thus, Eighth Army found itself in a position where its veteran units were accustomed to a type of warfare that left them ill-prepared for the particular challenges faced in Sicily. The new additions to Eighth Army were less inhibited by past events, and perhaps more open to innovation, but suffered the uncertainties and fears of untried troops. Regardless, they soon adopted the prevailing tactical methods in Eighth Army. As a consequence, an opportunity to hit the Axis hard while it was on the back foot, and Eighth Army was riding high on victory in North Africa, was arguably missed. The British and Commonwealth forces had, at this stage of the Mediterranean campaign, the materiel and the morale resources to shatter the Axis, but there was not the will at the higher levels, or perhaps the ability, to radically alter its offensive techniques in so short a period of time. Much would depend in the future on its ability to show a greater propensity to learn and adapt in contact with the enemy.

The Invasion of Italy

Plans for the next move in the Mediterranean had been put in place even before the conclusion of the Sicilian campaign. In May 1943, Churchill and Roosevelt met at the 'Trident' conference in Washington and directed Eisenhower to mount such operations in exploitation of 'Husky' as were 'best calculated to eliminate Italy from the war and to contain the maximum number of German forces' in the Mediterranean. Eisenhower would have to do this, however, with reduced forces, as seven experienced divisions, four American and three British (50th Northumbrian, 51st Highland and 7th Armoured), and considerable shipping and air power, would at some stage be withdrawn from the Mediterranean for 'Overlord'.[68]

Two options were on the table, an invasion of Sardinia, or, a fully fledged campaign on the Italian mainland. Opinion coalesced behind the latter. It was considered more likely to impact on Italian morale; it would open up airfields that could be used to strike at strategic targets currently beyond bomber range; and it would, most likely, divert a greater number of German divisions away from the impending invasion of North-West Europe. With 'Husky' progressing well, Eisenhower decided on 18 July to progress the Italian option. Lieutenant-General Mark W. Clark, commanding the as yet non-operational US Fifth Army in Morocco, was ordered to prepare plans for a landing near Naples, codenamed 'Avalanche'. This would be accompanied by another landing near Reggio in Calabria to secure the Strait of Messina, which was assigned to Eighth Army and codenamed 'Baytown'. In August 1943, this approach was signed off by Churchill and Roosevelt at the 'Quadrant' Conference in Quebec.[69]

'Baytown' was launched on 3 September 1943. Eighth Army's XIII Corps crossed the Strait of Messina in face of only desultory resistance. Two German battalions were deployed near the invasion area, while the Italian Seventh Army had four coastal divisions in Calabria, units that experience in Sicily had shown to be of little value. The Germans began to retreat almost as soon as the operation began. That left the Italian 211th Coastal Division on the receiving end of the enormous bombardment that preceded the landings. The 1st

Map 9.2 The invasion of Italy, September–December 1943

Canadian and 5th Divisions landed mostly unopposed. The Canadians found empty beaches lacking wire, mines or any serious defences. Most Italian soldiers had little interest in fighting and many helped unload Allied landing craft. The *Luftwaffe* and *Regia Aeronautica* played almost no part in the defensive efforts and by 10 September, Eighth Army had advanced about a hundred miles to reach Catanzaro and Nicastro in the 'neck' of the 'toe' of Italy (see Map 9.2).[70]

'Avalanche' was more risky than 'Baytown'. The beaches for the landing were in some ways ideal; they were in range of Allied fighter cover (just) and there was an airfield 3 miles inland which would facilitate the immediate basing of fighter squadrons on the mainland. However, the Bay of Salerno, where the landing was to take place, was ringed by high ground which gave 'excellent observation' and afforded a defender 'ideal fire positions'. For an invader from the sea, 'it would be like landing into an overlooked amphitheatre'.[71]

Moreover, Allied intelligence estimated that the German position in Italy was strong. In the North, Army Group B, to which Rommel had been appointed, had eight divisions, including one Panzer and one SS. In the South, Tenth Army (General von Vietinghoff), made up of XIV and LXXVI Panzer Corps, had a further six divisions (including Hube's divisions from Sicily), five of them Panzer or Panzer Grenadier. It was thought that the Germans might well be capable of repulsing a landing in the area of Salerno with these forces. They had 16th Panzer Division, with over 100 tanks, near the Bay. The 15th Panzer Grenadier Division was just north of Naples and the Hermann Göring Division was stationed around the city. Additionally, all evidence pointed to the likelihood that the Germans would build up forces in the Salerno area faster than the Allies could move units from Sicily and North Africa.[72] As Ian Gooderson has argued, 'planners must sometimes through necessity accept, not the best option, but the "least worse", and this was the case with "Avalanche"'. The only other real option available was a landing north of Naples near Gaeta, which would have been well beyond the range of Allied single-engine fighters.[73]

In the first week of September, German reconnaissance aircraft spotted Allied convoy activity in the Mediterranean; it was quickly concluded that a major landing was imminent. Matters became even more complicated when, on 8 September, the day before the operation was to commence, Italy surrendered. The Italian Navy defected to the Allies, but the Army dispersed and the Germans took over their equipment and positions. German units were rushed to the coast and as the invasion armada neared the shoreline, 16th Panzer Division near Salerno and the Hermann Göring Division just to the north, were on full alert. There was to be no strategic or operational surprise on this occasion.[74]

Fifth Army put three divisions ashore on 9 September. Two of them, 46th North Midland and West Riding and 56th London, part of British X Corps, had fought in France in 1940 and with First Army in North Africa, but neither had been involved in the fighting in Sicily. X Corps landed under considerable fire. The Germans took good advantage of the terrain and employed snipers and small machine-gun teams to hold up the advance; by the end of the first day most of the British units had moved little more than 3 miles inland.[75]

The situation at this stage was potentially precarious. The Germans rushed the 15th Panzer Grenadier and Hermann Göring Divisions, of XIV Panzer Corps, from the Naples area to pressurise the Salerno beachhead from the north and prevent a breakout. The 26th Panzer Division and the 29th Panzer Grenadier Divisions were transferred from the south, leaving the rest of LXXVI Panzer Corps to delay Eighth Army's advance as best it could. A battle group of 3rd Panzer Grenadier Division was also to be sent from Rome. Shortly after the landing, therefore, there were strong elements of six divisions facing the three assault divisions of Fifth Army.[76] The German counter-attack came on 12 and 13 September. It cut through to within 2 miles of the beaches and Clark had to commit all his reserves.[77] Some battalion officers burned their secret documents and maps as a precaution against capture. Michael Howard, then a young officer in the Coldstream Guards, wrote that 'shells whined swiftly over us like lost souls. Moan, moan, moan, they wept.' The mood among the men was one of desperation; the Official History of the Scots Guards later recorded that 'there was a general feeling in the air of another Dunkirk'. By D-Day plus three, casualties in X Corps had reached 3,000 killed, wounded and missing, as much as 7 per cent of the force engaged.[78]

With the situation appearing grave, on 14 September, Clark initiated tentative contingency planning for a re-embarkation of either US VI or X Corps. The next day, Alexander arrived at the beachhead to assess the situation. He put a stop to thoughts of evacuation, well aware, much as Montgomery had been before Alam Halfa, that even the slightest rumour of retreat would be fatal to morale. Alexander was right to hold his nerve; by 16 September, the decisive phase of the Salerno battle had ended.[79] Resolute defence and a timely and devastating bombardment from the air and sea had broken the German assault.[80] The employment of naval gunfire support, which was considered 'an improvisation' at the time, had, according to after-action reports, 'brought about the decision'.[81] With reinforcements pouring in from around the Mediterranean and with Eighth Army linking up from the south, the crisis was over.[82]

While the Italian campaign had thus begun successfully, there were still many imponderables. Following the fall of Sicily, 'a slight reaction' had 'set in' among the troops. Morale was described as 'good' rather than 'very high' in the censorship summaries. The announcement en route to Salerno that Italy had surrendered did much to relax the men, but as the CO of 201st Guards Brigade put it, 'from the point of view of the soldier who had to do the landing the time chosen was an unfortunate one. It aroused in the troops a quite unjustified hope that the landing itself would be a pleasant picnic, to be followed by a speedy and easy advance on Naples.'[83] Sick levels were extremely high in Eighth Army, mostly due to an epidemic of malaria; one report referred to the disease as 'enemy number 1 at the start of the Italian campaign'.[84]

Eighth Army's advance from Reggio had been painstakingly slow too; Montgomery 'did not play Blucher to Clark's Wellington'.[85] Fifth Army had been forced to fight it out on its own at Salerno and, as Alexander commented later, the Germans could 'claim with some justification to have won if not a victory at least an important success'. For 3,470 casualties, they had inflicted 8,659 on the Allies. The Allied troops had shown resilience and determination in defence, but both British and American assessments of 'Avalanche' argued that they demonstrated a lack of drive and initiative in attack.[86] For great success to be achieved in Italy, matters would have to improve.

Advance to the 'Gustav Line'

In light of the German performance at Salerno, Hitler decided to stand and fight in southern Italy and not fall back, as had been envisaged, to preprepared positions in the north of the country. A winter line, the 'Gustav Line', was hastily improvised and a string of defences laid out from the Tyrrhenian coast in the west to the Adriatic in the east. The 'Gustav Line' followed the course of the River Garigliano, then that of its tributaries, the Gari and Rapido, as far as the town of Cassino, crossed the Maiella Mountains and then ran through the Sangro Valley to the Adriatic. South of this, the Germans planned a number of intermediate positions, two of which were the 'Viktor Line', following the Volturno River in the west and the Biferno River in the east and the 'Bernhardt Line', following the Garigliano River in the west, then crossing by Monte Camino to join the 'Gustav Line'.[87]

Eighth Army, whose job it was to advance up the east coast, was now comprised of V and XIII Corps. These were made up of 1st Airborne, which had landed at Taranto, 1st Canadian and 5th Divisions, who took part in 'Baytown', 78th Division and 4th Armoured Brigade, newly arrived from Sicily, and 8th Indian Division, from Persia and Iraq. On the western side of the country, X Corps, made up of 46th North Midland and West Riding and 56th London Divisions and 7th Armoured Division, was still, after 'Avalanche', with Fifth Army. Opposing these units was the newly formed Army Group C, under Field-Marshal Albert Kesselring. The Army Group was comprised of Fourteenth Army in the north, under General von Mackensen, and Vietinghoff's Tenth Army in the south. Tenth Army in turn was made up of LXXVI Panzer Corps on the eastern Adriatic coast and XIV Panzer Corps facing Fifth Army in the west.[88]

On 1 October, three weeks after the landing at Salerno, the first Allied troops, the King's Dragoon Guards of X Corps, entered Naples; twenty-one days later, the port was handling 5,000 tons of cargo a day.[89] By mid-October, X Corps, as part of a wider Fifth Army offensive, had crossed the River Volturno, 46th North Midland and West Riding Division crossing the river without a preliminary bombardment having caught the Germans by complete surprise. In the east, Eighth Army employed a bold amphibious landing to outflank the River Biferno position and land at Termoli; the 'Viktor Line' had been taken.

As Eighth Army closed up against the River Sangro, it was reinforced in October by 2nd New Zealand Division, fresh from a rest after its exploits in North Africa.[90] Alexander and Montgomery, in spite of the addition to their order of battle, were increasingly pessimistic about the situation in Italy. Initial operations had resulted in heavy casualties. Montgomery wrote to Brooke on 14 October complaining that X Corps could not continue to sustain such 'severe casualties', about 8,000 in his estimation, nearly all of which had been concentrated in 46th North Midland and West Riding and 56th London Divisions. 'A Division that suffers such losses', he said, 'requires time to absorb its new drafts, to build up the broken teams, and so on. From what I hear of 46 Div it requires a good period of rest and training.'[91] Morale appears to have been affected and sickness rates in X Corps were becoming extremely high, an average of 88 per thousand for the months of October and November 1943. These figures exceeded what had been experienced in the desert in the summer of 1942 and were just about as high as any in Italy between 1943 and 1945 (see Figures 4.1 and 9.2).[92]

Alexander was even more concerned with the balance of forces in Italy. He reported to Eisenhower, on 24 October, that the rate of build-up favoured the Germans and that the situation was unlikely to improve even in the New Year. In November, seven divisions were to leave Italy to prepare for the invasion of North-West Europe. Reductions in landing craft, also needed for 'Overlord', ruled out flanking moves of any size, while the German demolition of roads, bridges, railways and port facilities meant that many of those which were available in theatre were also needed to run supplies along the coast. 'It would therefore appear', wrote Alexander, 'that we are committed to a long and costly advance to Rome ... a "slogging match" with our present slight superiority in formations on the battlefront offset by the enemy opportunity for relief; for without sufficient resources in craft no out-flanking amphibious operation of a size sufficient to speed up our rate of advance is possible.'[93]

Although Alexander could not have known the force-to-force ratios exactly, he does appear to have been somewhat disingenuous on this point. His claims that the Allies had insufficient forces to achieve their goals certainly appeared valid when numbers of divisions were compared on paper. However, respective strengths within Allied and German formations 'were in fact very different and invariably meant that an equal number of divisions gave the Allies a considerable superiority of fighting troops'. By January 1944, Allied battalions contained about seven to eight times more men than the equivalent German units; the ratios cannot have been decisively different between September and December 1943. Allied superiority in tanks, guns and aircraft 'was overwhelming'. By the end of November, they had about a 5:1 advantage in tanks, a 'considerable' superiority in artillery and about a 10:1 advantage in aircraft.[94] In January 1944, on the Eastern Front, the Soviets' numerical superiority over the Germans was far less advantageous, a ratio of 1.31: 1 in men, 1.75: 1 in artillery and 3.4: 1 in aircraft; there was parity in terms of armour. The problem appeared, therefore, not to be resources, as the successes of the Red Army on the Eastern Front attest, but how these resources were to be employed in the prevailing battle conditions.[95]

By early November, Fifth and Eighth Armies faced some undoubtedly formidable terrain; the mountain and river barriers of the 'Bernhardt' and 'Gustav' lines, collectively referred to as the 'Winter Line', were incredibly tough nuts to crack. The terrain, much like in Sicily, shaped the character of the fighting and put huge demands on the human body and spirit. 'The Apennine mountain range running the length of the peninsula faced the Allies with narrow plains along the

Tyrrhenian and Adriatic coasts, cut with rivers, rock-strewn valleys and gullies.'[96]

In these circumstances, the infantryman and his skill in minor tactics was again key.[97] However, much as in Sicily, there had not been adequate time since the cessation of hostilities in North Africa and the landings in the Mediterranean to fundamentally retrain and reorientate Eighth Army's tactical approach to battle. The same problems which had undermined performance in Sicily were all too evident also in Italy. In December 1943, the Director of Military Training at 15th Army Group circulated, with Alexander's endorsement, a report on recent operations that concluded:

> Our tactical methods are thorough and methodical but slow and cumbersome. In consequence our troops fight well in defence and our set-piece attacks are usually successful, but it is not unfair to say that through lack of enterprise in exploitation we seldom reap the full benefit of them.[98]

This was an even-handed assessment of British and Commonwealth performance that fully illustrated the limits of Montgomery's 'Colossal Cracks' approach; senior commanders were massively limited in the options available to them. Highly ambitious infiltration operations through the mountains could only work with troops possessing maximum levels of initiative, motivation and training. Such troops, Montgomery and his commanders believed, were still unavailable to Eighth Army.

Montgomery's firepower-heavy mechanised approach could not compensate for this deficiency, requiring as it did a huge logistical tail which, in turn, required good roads, a rare commodity in Italy. Only the state highways could meet Eighth Army's needs. In the west, these were Highway 7, running along the Tyrrhenian coast to Rome, and Highway 6, leading to Rome through Cassino and the Liri Valley. In the east, Highway 16 skirted the Adriatic coast with Highway 17 inland of it abutting the Apennines. The principal lateral roads from East to West were Highway 87 from Termoli to Naples, Highway 86 from Vasto to Mignano, and Highway 5 from Pescara to Rome.[99]

The lack of good roads meant that the Allied advance could, in many ways, be 'predicted, and even to a large extent channelled by a resolute and skilled defender'.[100] Much depended, therefore, on two key factors. One was the ability of Alexander and his commanders to develop sufficiently high force-to-force ratios at the operational level to break through at one of the limited number of points where advance was supported by good roads. The second was the willingness of the troops, once committed to battle, to fight with greater determination, resolve and endurance than their German enemy.

With regards to the first of these challenges, a number of options were open to Alexander. The first and probably best route through the 'Winter Line' required the Allies to advance along Highway 6 into the Liri Valley and then on to Rome (see Map 9.2). Highway 6, however, was overlooked by Monte Camino, Monte la Difensa and Monte Rotondo in the 'Bernhardt Line' (the Mignano Gap) and was dominated by Monte Cassino in the 'Gustav Line'. The area around Cassino was the strongest point of the German defence. The second option, along Highway 7, which skirted the west coast, was easily blocked from the overlooking mountains and could be flooded from the Pontine Marshes. The third option, an advance along the Adriatic coast (to the east), would eventually require a lateral attack towards Rome across the Apennine range with its very limited road network. In the circumstances, Alexander decided to attack along two axes; Clark's Fifth Army would fight its way towards Rome along Highway 6 in the west while Montgomery and Eighth Army would break through to Pescara along Highway 16 in the east. The two armies would then close in a massive pincer on Rome.

The battle opened on 5 November with 56th London Division and US 3rd, 45th and 34th Divisions, of Fifth Army, attacking the 'Bernhardt Line'. In what has been described as a 'truly remarkable effort', Fifth Army gained footholds on Monte Camino, Monte La Difensa and Monte Rotondo. 'The tenacity of the attack and the intensity of the fighting was a shock to the German command.' It stretched their forces and brought them close to breaking point. But they held on. On each occasion, Allied infantry were just too exhausted and depleted by casualties to push the enemy to the point of collapse. On 15 November, Alexander called off the attack.[101]

Attention switched to the east coast where Montgomery began his assault on the Germans defending the River Sangro on 20 November. After a pause due to bad weather, Eighth Army 'shattered' the German defences, taking over 1,000 prisoners including the commander of 65th Division.[102] However, much like in the west, the Germans showed a remarkable ability to adapt and threw up a new defensive line at the next river, the River Moro. They simply refused to break.

On 2 December, Fifth Army, in an attempt to keep the pressure on, resumed the assault on the mountains west of Highway 6 on the 'Bernhardt Line'. Supported by 800 guns, 46th North Midland and West Riding and 56th London Divisions attacked Monte Camino. The Americans took on Monte La Difensa and Monte Maggiore. By 10 December, the mountains were in Allied hands. Clark now ordered an assault on the Germans holding the mountains on the other side of the highway. By 18 December, Monte Maggiore and Monte Lungo were taken. The Allied infantry, and especially the Americans, were beginning to demonstrate no little skill and determination in mountain fighting. However, while Fifth Army had pushed the Germans out of the 'Bernhardt Line' it was in no position to continue the fight to break the 'Gustav Line'.[103]

On the Adriatic flank, Eighth Army resumed its drive north on 4 December. The 2nd New Zealand Division and 8th Indian Division struck 12 miles inland at the hilltop village of Orsogna. In spite of three full-scale divisional attacks, the Germans stubbornly held out.[104] Further to the east, 1st Canadian Division assaulted the German positions at the River Moro. They had more success. By 20 December, after two weeks of heavy fighting, the Canadians had broken the enemy line and advanced on the seaside town of Ortona. The Germans had turned the town into a 'hornet's nest of mutually-supporting strongpoints'. In a week of fierce house-to-house fighting, the Canadians evicted the defenders.[105]

The success at Ortona marked the end of Eighth Army's offensive. Much like Fifth Army in the west, it had run out of steam. As the winter took hold, Eighth Army was tasked with maintaining just enough pressure to ensure that German units could not be transferred to the Fifth Army front where Alexander in due course planned another attack on the 'Winter Line'.

Winter in Italy

In three and a half months, the British and Commonwealth Armies had made steady but unspectacular progress up the boot of Italy.[106] While on many occasions Eighth Army and X Corps had come close to breaking the German line, each time they had lacked the numbers, the supplies or the will to continue the advance and achieve decisive victory. The Italian campaign had become a war of attrition and, to their credit, the German forces facing X, XIII and XXX Corps had wavered but not cracked.

Although morale at the Army level had gradually improved following 'Baytown' and 'Avalanche' (see Figure 9.2),[107] and the censorship summary for 16 November to 15 December had described it as 'probably higher than it has ever been',[108] it is evident that morale fluctuated across nationalities and within formations in the British and Commonwealth Armies during the early days of the campaign in Italy.

By the second half of December, the censors noted that hard fighting and bad weather had begun to cause 'a definite decline of the immense optimism recently observed' in some units. Though 'not so extreme as to be described as poor morale', this problem was 'particularly noticeable' in units of 5th Division and in 44th Royal Tank Regiment.[109] The 1st Canadian, 78th and 5th Divisions, supported by 8th Indian Division, had shouldered the majority of the heavy lifting in October.[110] By November and December these formations were beginning to show the strain. For example, there appears to be little doubt that the Canadians struggled in their assault at the Moro River and in the house-to-house fighting in Ortona, where, according to Terry Copp and Bill McAndrew, their 'morale was badly shaken'.[111] The sick rate in 1st Canadian Division jumped 248 per cent from 9.9 per thousand in the week ending 4 December, a period when it was resting around Campobasso, to 34.6 per thousand in the second week of fighting to cross the Moro River (the week ending 18 December).[112] The sick rate remained extremely high during what the Official History described as the 'desperately slow work'[113] around Ortona at the end of the month, the figure being 28 per thousand during the week ending 1 January 1944 (these were extremely high sickness rates in the context of the Italian and North-West Europe campaigns; see Figures 11.4 and 14.3).[114] Battle exhaustion made up 24 per cent of casualties between 28 November and 12 February, a figure comparable to those experienced in the desert in the summer of 1942, when battle exhaustion represented 28 per cent of New Zealand and about 26 per cent of South African casualties. In addition, sixty-seven cases of self-inflicted wounds (SIW) were recorded between December 1943 and February 1944. Overall, the Canadian rate for SIW in 1944 was 2.4 per thousand, a considerably higher rate than the British (0.21) and the New Zealanders (0.10).[115]

Across the board, casualty rates in Eighth Army were higher in December than in any other month during the Italian campaign.

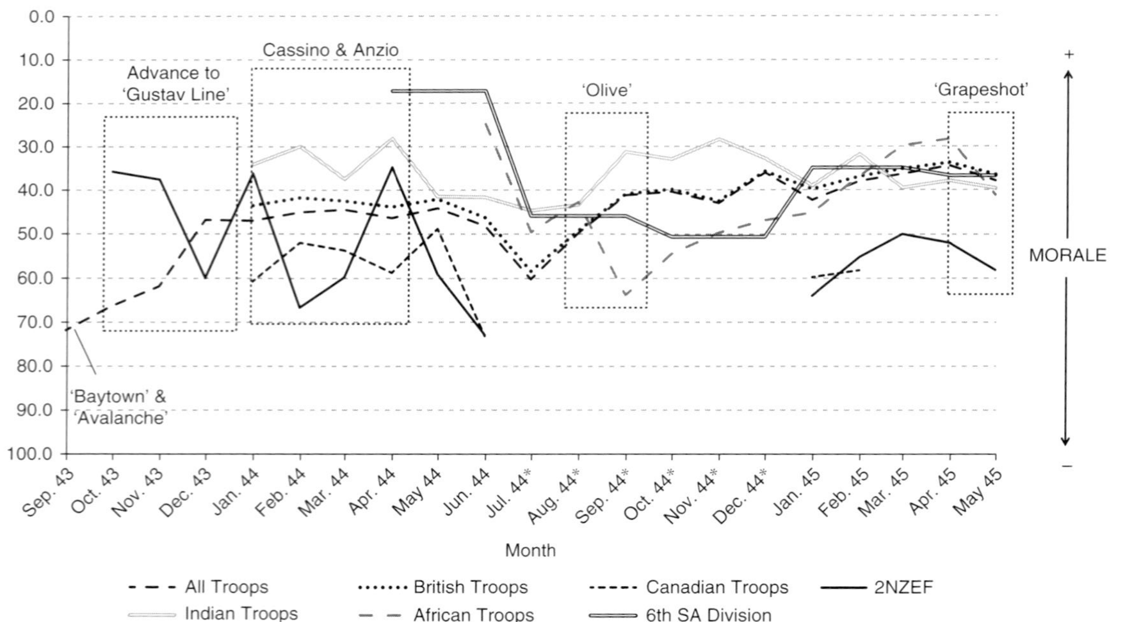

Figure 9.2 Monthly sick admissions per thousand, the Italian campaign, September 1943–May 1945 * The Canadian and New Zealand figures for July–Dec. 1944 are distorted by an outbreak of Infective Hepatitis and have, therefore, been left out (see LAC Vol. 12559).

Table 9.1 Monthly gross battle casualty rates, percentage of troops engaged (as shown on operational order of battle), Italian campaign, 1943–4

Month	British	Indian	Canadian	NZ*	SA*	Poles	Greeks	Average
Sept. 43	4.9		0.3					2.6
Oct. 43	2.7		3.2					3.0
Nov. 43	1.9	4.2	1.2	0.5				2.0
Dec. 43	2.2	8.9	6.0	7.2				6.1
Jan. 44	3.3	2.2	1.2	0.8				1.9
Feb. 44	5.8	2.8	3.6	2.4				3.7
Mar. 44	2.2	5.3	1.9	5.5				3.7
Apr. 44	1.2	1.0	0.8	1.3	0.5			1.0
May 44	3.1	4.5	3.6	1.3	2.9	8.3		4.0
June 44	2.5	1.3	2.1	1.5	3.9	4.3		2.6
July 44	1.9	9.4	1.3	2.2	3.9	5.0		4.0
Aug. 44	1.5	2.7	1.2	3.6	4.0	2.5		2.6
Sept. 44	4.6	5.2	8.0	4.2	2.3	0.3		4.1
Oct. 44	1.7	4.5	1.6	1.1	3.1	0.8	3.7	2.4
Average	2.8	4.3	2.6	2.6	2.9	3.5	3.7	3.1

* NZ=New Zealand; SA=South Africa.

The Indians, New Zealanders and Canadians suffered especially (see Table 9.1).[116] That month, 1st Canadian Division lost 176 officers and 2,163 other ranks. Most of these came from the rifle companies of the infantry battalions in the division, the cohort of fighting troops (about 3,000 men) that did the majority of the fighting. 'A large number' were 'platoon and section commanders, essential forward leaders'. Reinforcements did arrive, 150 officers and 2,258 other ranks, 'but some were ill-trained at best. Many joined their units in the midst of an action and were killed or wounded before anyone knew their names.' About half of the battle exhaustion cases came from these reinforcements. In the wake of Ortona, the divisional commander, Major-General Christopher Vokes, wrote to Lieutenant-General Charles Allfrey, the commander of V Corps that the infantry units of the division were not in 'fit condition to undertake further offensive operations'.[117] By the middle of November, 5th Division's sick rate was as high as 21 per thousand per week; it remained at that level for the best part of a month.[118] 8th Indian Division was in a similar state by the middle of December,[119] and 78th Division was in a bad way too; its sickness rate rarely dropped below 20 per thousand during October and November. Battle exhaustion cases were so prevalent in the division in November that they represented an incredible 37 per cent of casualties.[120] After the battle of the Sangro, it was taken out of the line by Montgomery on account also of its very large number of desertions and cases of AWOL. Much like 5th Division, it spent the winter months in the bleak mountains north of Isernia where it recorded 108 cases of exposure (of which five men died).[121] By December, the division was unquestionably tired and in need of a rest. It had been almost continuously in contact with the enemy since the beginning of October, suffering 1,468 casualties.[122] By 7 November, casualties among unit leaders were so high that Montgomery reckoned that no platoon in the division was commanded by an officer.[123] It had been to the fore in difficult hill fighting in Tunisia, where it had 'earned a high reputation', and in Sicily, where it had received high praise from Montgomery for its performance.[124] A strong rumour had begun to circulate in the division after Sicily that it would be sent home, like 51st Highland Division; when it became clear that this was not going to happen, it was hardly surprising that morale suffered.[125]

There was unquestionably, therefore, a need for the British and Commonwealth forces in Italy to regroup. As Adam, the Adjutant-General of the British Army, put it after a whirlwind tour of commands in Europe and the Far East in November and December 1943:

> I have discussed with corps and divisional commanders the general question of morale in Italy. The importance of morale, as stated to me by one divisional commander, was that Napoleon's dictum 'morale is to the physical as three is to one' should be in this war at least six to one, and we must do much more than we are doing.[126]

The situation was not improved when, in December, it was announced that Montgomery would depart to command 21st Army Group in the invasion of North-West Europe. Most accepted that he was the right man to lead the invasion, but he would be greatly missed in Italy; as the censors noted, his 'hold upon the imagination of the troops' had been 'unique'.[127] Rueful jokes that the CMF (Central Mediterranean Force) now stood for 'Chaps Monty Forgot' were common in the mail. 'You ask what the Eighth Army thinks about losing Montgomery', wrote one man:

> The army, as a whole, is very, very sorry to see him go. He was extremely, almost fantastically popular with the men. What really endeared him to the Army was the frequent personal contact near the front, the knowledge that he would never ask for the performance of the impossible, the flair for success, the friendly chat as between man and man, and his concern for those things that mean so much to a soldier's life – mail, rations, news and cigarettes.

For another man, it was Montgomery's efforts to always 'avoid if possible letting his men into situations that call for the old 1914–18 slogging efforts' that mattered most. 'If he is called upon to sacrifice men, then he makes sure that the returns for doing so are considerable'.[128] The men, as one Canadian wrote, 'idealize him', while another noted that he had 'never heard a man say one word against him. The men who have been with him practically love him.' He was 'a soldier's general ... by words and deeds he has won the hearts of those who fight for him'.[129]

In spite of much depression at Montgomery's departure, considerable satisfaction was expressed that Alexander was remaining in Italy. Though less well known to the average soldier, he was generally referred to 'in admiring terms' and officers laid great stress upon his reputation as a 'brilliant strategist'.[130] News of the appointment of General Oliver Leese as successor to Montgomery also 'met with marked approval'.[131] It felt to many of the men that 'we have another Monty with us ... he is very popular with all the boys already'. He had, as they put it, the 'Monty touch'.[132]

More, perhaps, would be required in Italy than the 'Monty touch'. By mid-November, even Montgomery admitted that the Allies had 'made a great many mistakes and we have made a sad mess of it'.[133] With little scope for change at the strategic level, as 'Overlord' unquestionably had priority over resources by this stage of the war, Alexander and Leese had to produce results with what they already had at the operational level. Much would depend on their creativity and imagination and their ability to motivate their soldiers to stand up to the increasing horrors of war in Italy and the hardships of the Italian winter.

With victory at El Alamein, in 'Torch' and in Sicily, the war against Germany had clearly moved into a new phase. The issue for Churchill was no longer whether the British and Commonwealth

Armies could win the war but how to shape victory to support Imperial interests. The Army's new materiel-based 'Colossal Cracks' approach to operations 'limited risk, eschewed manoeuvre, emphasized firepower and . . . sought to impose the superiority in resources' held by the British compared to its enemies. By the winter of 1943/4, it was becoming evident that this approach could not provide the answers for the new strategic challenge facing the British and Commonwealth Armies.[134]

10 REMOBILISATION?

By the turn of the year 1943/4, the British and Commonwealth troops fighting in the Mediterranean 'were tired, not only in body, but in spirit also'. A report on 'The British Soldier in Italy' noted that the number of exhaustion cases was now posing 'a real problem'. A Rehabilitation Centre was set up in January 1944 to help cope with 'the flood of psychiatric cases that were arriving at the rate of about 50 a day after the start of the new offensive':[1]

> It was generally recognised, both by Commanders and men themselves, that 3 years was the longest a soldier should be kept overseas. Repeated cases showed that after 2½ years woman's fidelity was liable to break down, moreover there was often a subtle psychological change in the man himself, to put it colloquially, he became 'browned off', and might even under stress do something foolish.[2]

At the start of August 1943, the censorship reports identified that many veteran units in Eighth Army felt that they had 'earned a rest'.[3] 'We often wonder why we are always in the forefront of the battle', wrote a man in the 1st Argyll and Sutherland Highlanders, 51st Highland Division, 'can't some other Div get going'.[4] The return to European 'civilised' conditions seemed to have an impact on the troops. One man wrote in January 1944:

> In previous letters I have given you the idea that I have settled down to army life well, and that I now take the good with the

> bad and most things for granted, well that was all well and good in the desert where men were men and women were a mirage only, but here things are different, as I am now seeing something nearer to civilization and it is having its effect on me. This taste of Italy is making me more homesick everyday. I want now to get back to real civilization which I left behind, and I think that most of my mates are suffering from the same complaint, and now instead of waiting patiently for the final whistle we find that we are fed up with this long drawn out war, in other words we have had enough, and though we try to keep cracking we find that army life has lost all its glamour if it ever had any, we are all ready for Civvy Street once more with the well founded notion that we have done our bit.[5]

Homesickness was linked directly with family problems in the UK. One man in the 1st SAS Regiment described the dynamic as 'the triumphant and victorious tragedy of the Eighth Army'. The censors were unequivocal about the importance of the matter. Letters written in 'affectionate terms' had 'a beneficial effect upon morale'. On the other hand, where friction existed there was 'almost invariably evidence of lowered morale'. The problem was clearly becoming 'a major source of anxiety to many'. For example, a man at GHQ 2nd Echelon wrote:

> You can write a decent letter if you want – why the hell don't you? Take your time and tell me something that is going on in the town and what you and the children do in the evenings. The children started to write and then packed up … and another thing please get it out of your head that I am having a bloody good time here because I'm not.[6]

A related issue was, as the censors put it, the 'alleged immorality wave' back home. One man working in a base area wrote 'Nan, perhaps I'm wrong, but I have a queer impression from your letter that you are not bothering yourself whether you write to me or not and seem to delight in flaunting about your dancing with the Americans', while yet another in a logistics unit wrote that 'if the Yanks could fight as well as they can break up homes we would be better off'.[7] Some were able to see the funny side of the issue and many Americans would be greeted with the question 'How's my wife and your kids?'[8] Most, however, were not. Approximately 40,000 British women married Americans during the war. The Canadians, whose forces were roughly one-sixth the size of the American, married about the same number.[9] The issue cut two ways; at one point it was estimated that around 45,000 military 'clients' were being 'serviced' every month by the working girls in Cairo alone.[10]

Many soldiers believed that their long period in action 'morally entitle[d] them' to leave.[11] In light of the prevailing mood, in the first half of 1943, the New Zealand Government decided to give 6,000 men in the 2nd New Zealand Expeditionary Force (2NZEF) furlough, or leave, back home. This equated to about 20 per cent of the forces in theatre and a third of 2nd New Zealand Division.[12] Later that year, a somewhat less generous scheme was introduced ('Python') to post British men home after they had completed six years' service. This did not apply to very many and the length of service was reduced to 4.5 years in 1944. Even this change was greeted with reserve.[13] Matters were made even worse when, in January 1944, it was announced that the Americans would be eligible for return to the United States after eighteen months overseas.[14]

The situation was exacerbated by the constant fear that men would be transferred to the Far East once victory in Italy had been achieved. 'In many thousand letters examined', wrote the censors:

> one man alone expressed a desire to fight against the Japanese. The almost universal attitude does not appear to be due to fear of the Japanese as an enemy, but to be based solely on the time factor, i.e. those who have fought in Africa and Europe will have 'done their bit' and should be allowed to return to their families, leaving any further operations elsewhere to those who have not seen overseas service.

As a man in the 1st Irish Guards wrote in January 1944, the threat of service in the Far East 'definitely does not give us much heart here for fighting'.[15]

It was abundantly clear that 'every soldier' had his 'breaking point' and that there was a danger of a disengagement of soldiers from the war, with morale potentially weakening to the point of jeopardising military performance.[16] Some form of 'remobilisation' was required. This in turn begged the question not just of the organisational resources available to the state for such an operation (2.6 million British soldiers served overseas during the war) but of the terms on which to conduct it and the changes it might demand.[17]

The profound challenge of remobilisation was to manifest most significantly in the British, New Zealand and South African forces in the Middle East and Mediterranean in 1943/4. For the British Army, the remobilisation process hinged on the social change encapsulated by Sir William Beveridge's report on 'Social Insurance and Allied Services'. The Beveridge Report, as it became widely known, had been published in December 1942. It presented a vision of 'cradle to grave' social security ensuring all citizens of a basic minimum standard of living. It included proposals for a commitment to full employment, a state system of medical care and family allowances.[18] Government inaction on the plan enraged and disappointed the troops, and, in many ways, they had to engage in self-remobilisation as they began to realise that they could take ownership of the war effort and make use of their franchise to shape the post-war world.

In New Zealand, the soldiers' frustration with the remobilisation process escalated into outright mutiny. Those 6,000 men lucky enough to return home on furlough were appalled by what they found. The Government had promised to avoid conflict about equality during the war; powers to conscript wealth were to equal those to conscript men. However, in reality, the war served to exacerbate inequalities between sections of society. By 1943, there were 35,000 Grade 'A' men at home, fit enough to go overseas but who held jobs in 'essential industry'. The furlough men were stunned by this apparent injustice and insisted, in the interest of fairness, that these men had to be used on the front line in the Middle East, to replace those who had already done their duty.[19]

The Government refused to bend to the furlough men's wishes, leading to a revolt that would result in only 13 per cent of the men returning to the Middle East.[20] The 'Furlough Mutiny', as it became known, would escalate to the extent that it arguably represents the most severe outbreak of indiscipline in any British and Commonwealth force in both world wars. The 'only serious' incident of 'group disobedience' in the British Army in the First World War, the Étaples mutiny, had centred on the treatment of veteran soldiers in a training camp.[21] The 'Furlough Mutiny', by comparison, involved criticism about the very conduct of the war. It can be compared, perhaps provocatively, to the French mutinies following the Chemin des Dames offensive in 1917, a series of incidents that represented 'the most significant internal challenge to the prosecution of World War I in any of the victorious powers'.[22] The 'Furlough Mutiny' constituted a dramatic act of defiance of state mobilisation and, much like the French mutinies, demonstrated 'a highly embittered disengagement from "the war" writ large'.[23]

The situation that evolved in South Africa was not dissimilar in terms of its significance. With the return of 1st South African Division to the Union in early 1943, attention turned to raising sufficient troops for two armoured divisions (ideally constituted under a South African Corps) to replace it in the field. In order to recruit these men, and ensure that they could accompany the Allied Armies as they advanced beyond the shores of Africa, Smuts announced, on 11 December 1942, that he would ask Parliament to sanction a new oath for general service anywhere in the world. Parliament passed the motion, on 27 January 1943, to allow persons who signed the General Service Oath, also known as the 'Blue Oath', to fight outside of Africa. As long as 60 per cent of serving soldiers took the oath, South Africa would be able to play a full part in the closing stages of the war in North Africa and in the campaigns beyond. Remarkably, nowhere near that figure signed up for the 'Blue Oath', and South Africa was forced to dramatically reconsider its contribution to the Allied Armies in the Second World War. In the end, the Union struggled to keep even one division up to strength in the field; South Africa, much like New Zealand, would fail dramatically to remobilise a significant proportion of its citizen soldiers for the second half of the war.[24]

Political legitimacy was central to these failures. It was the ability of the state to reimagine itself and effect considerable political, economic and social change that was key to remobilising citizen soldiers, and ensuring the survival of the state in the first place (something the Wilhelmine German and Tsarist Russian regimes failed to do in 1917/18). Thus, 'ultimately, deeply political questions of will and consensus lay at the heart of the mobilization process'. As John Horne has argued in relation to the First World War but with considerable relevance to the situation unfolding during the Second, 'the terms and language of national mobilization and "self-mobilization"' were 'a vital dimension of "total war" without which neither the combatants' tenacity nor the duration of the conflict is readily explicable'. The 'radical heart' of the war lay in the encounter between national mobilisation and the front line. This interaction, or negotiation, 'tested the legitimacy' of states and the 'sense of national community to the limit'. The way ordinary soldiers rationalised their experience on the front line, 'and either rebelled or kept fighting, had a good deal to do with the varying capacity of different powers to keep mobilizing their soldiers' will to continue'.[25] It mattered enormously, to return to Cromwell, that men should know what they fight for and love what they know.[26]

The British Army and the Beveridge Report

For citizens and soldiers of the United Kingdom, the Beveridge Plan became the catalyst for the remobilisation process. Beveridge's aim was 'not merely to abolish physical want, but to give a new sense of purpose to democracy, to promote national solidarity and to define the goals of the war'.[27] It captured the public imagination and 'it soon achieved the status of a kind of social "Magna Carta"'. The report sold over 100,000 copies in the first month and over 630,000 in total; the night before its publication, long queues of eager purchasers formed outside His Majesty's Stationery Office in London.[28] The report, in many ways, played surrogate to a government-sponsored plan for remobilisation of the war effort. Only a fortnight after its release, Gallop reported that 95 per cent of the population had heard of it, with 86 per cent favouring its implementation and only 6 per cent opposed. It seemed that the public's vaguely formulated desires for social reform had been turned into a concrete programme by Beveridge. Sections of the Conservative Party looked for ways to shelve the Plan and the right-wing press reacted with hostility. They believed that the country had already moved too far in the direction of socialism. Some argued that it was too costly, would smother individual initiative and encourage excessive dependence on the state.[29]

A summary of the plan, written by Beveridge himself, was issued as an Army Bureau of Current Affairs (ABCA) pamphlet on 19 December, but two days later the War Office withdrew it on the ground that it 'could not permit ABCA discussion groups, which were compulsory, to discuss such a controversial subject'. Many saw the ABCA affair 'as a clear sign that the Government disapproved of the report'.[30] Nevertheless, mounting pressure for a parliamentary debate on Beveridge proved irresistible and in February 1943 the issue provoked a serious anti-government revolt in the Commons. With Conservative speakers intent on making no commitment to the Plan and the Labour front bench unwilling to break up the

Coalition, Labour's rank-and-file MPs carried out the biggest parliamentary rebellion of the war, with all but two voting against the Government.[31]

It was at this point that the majority of soldiers overseas became aware of the plan. The censorship summaries from First Army in Tunisia noted that 'the Beveridge Report meets with general approval'. One man in the 2nd Lancashire Fusiliers, remarked that 'it is a step forward' while another serving at the HQ of 78th Division wrote that 'I am praying night & day now that the Beveridge plan will be unanimously accepted by the government'.[32] The outcome of the debate was much commented on in North Africa. The censors noted that 'disappointment [wa]s expressed at the failure of the Beveridge Plan to pass the "House"'. A serviceman in a Heavy Anti-Aircraft Regiment wrote, 'it amuses me to think that the man in the street put these people into the house and yet when they get there they refuse to do anything which is going to benefit the man in the street'.[33]

Over the next number of months, the censors noted keen and growing interest in the report and other matters relating to politics, along with concerns about post-war conditions and troops' families in the United Kingdom. A man in the 10th Battalion the Rifle Brigade wrote that 'nearly all the chaps seem to take a keen interest in the Beveridge Report. Whenever there is any news about the Report there is always a number round the news sheet.'[34] The censorship summary for 23 April to 1 May noted that 'anxiety exists and is much discussed with regard to the deal that the fighting man may expect from the politicians at the end of the war'.[35] At the start of May, the summaries introduced a new subject heading, 'Home Affairs', to address the growing focus on domestic issues.[36] In the second half of September a further section on 'Family Problems' was introduced, followed in October by a new section on 'Post-War Problems'.[37] The censors pointed to a growing frustration among the men regarding government prevarication regarding Beveridge and social change more generally; 'many men … express their opinions in no uncertain manner, that it [the plan] should pass into law with few amendments'. A soldier in 6th Inniskilling Fusiliers wrote, 'I have been reading a few more articles on the "Beveridge Plan" and I feel like doing a soap box act myself to let off steam. You should hear some of the things the Boys here have got to say about the way the Government is treating the plan. They don't believe in picking and choosing their words.'[38]

By May, with victory in North Africa assured, the men's minds turned even more towards home affairs. The censorship summary for the second week of the month reported that 'there are intelligent criticisms of the Government's attitude to the Beveridge Report, the Budget, Politics and the Prime Minister. Much interest is also taken in post-war politics, education and employment and considerable speculation is evident with regard to the condition that will prevail for the fighting man after the war.' The more phlegmatic of the men realised that the 'rejection of the report' did 'not mean much' because 'Parliament is now 8 years old and out of touch with public opinion. There has been undoubtedly a great swing to the left.' Indeed, the Labour rebellion had done much to associate the party with the Beveridge Plan. A man in a Light Anti-Aircraft Regiment commented in May that:

> Chaps are still arguing about the Beveridge Report ... it seems to me a good step in the right direction and it is a pity that the Govt. can't be big minded enough to do something about it now ... Churchill ... is I think an admirable man for the present task, but for the future he is too bellicose and too steeped in Toryism. He must not handle the peace ... What sort of Govt. is this when the elected person to bear a responsibility avoids his duty ... This much is certain, that the fellows in the Army are more than ever left-wing in their politics.[39]

The censors continued to note 'great interest' in Beveridge throughout the summer of 1943.[40] One of the most popular lectures given by army education speakers in Tunisia was on the Beveridge Report. The Army Education Corps (AEC) team gave around forty talks per week to audiences ranging from 5 to 500 men on topics such as 'the Soldier's Vote' and 'Full Employment'. With ever present shortages of wireless sets and home newspapers, it is likely that the men's interest in Beveridge was to a significant degree a product of the AEC's work. In total, the team addressed 538 groups, comprising over 21,000 troops in Tunisia alone, a contribution, which, according to the censors, was much appreciated.[41]

There does appear to be little doubt that army education played a key role in helping the ordinary soldier articulate his developing awareness of the goals for which he was fighting. In late 1943, a survey conducted among 5,000 soldiers in transit camps and convalescent depots revealed that in 60 per cent of all home units ABCA sessions were being carried out with complete success and adequately in another 10 per cent, while 83 per cent of those questioned indicated that they would still attend ABCA sessions if they were made voluntary. The latter percentage was recognised as rather suspect, as transit camps and convalescent depots lacked more popular distractions. But, it must be noted that these soldiers were away from their home units; the men surveyed were under no compulsion to exaggerate how well the scheme was being performed by their COs and officers. Another questionnaire circulated to a cross-section of units at around the same time revealed roughly the same picture; 59 per cent of the 8,500 respondents were in units which did ABCA regularly, 24 per cent irregularly. A coverage of 60 to 70 per cent meant that over a million men and women were participating, 'a very satisfactory state of affairs', as the Adjutant-General put it. The coverage overseas in combat zones was probably more limited; figures from North Africa at this time showed that 30 per cent of units were conducting ABCA sessions regularly while 45 per cent did so when they could. Another questionnaire circulated to a cross-section of units at around the same time revealed that 78 per cent of respondents were interested in ABCA discussions, as opposed to 17 per cent who were indifferent and 5 per cent who were just plain bored.[42]

In the absence of trust in the political sponsorship of the remobilisation process, the Beveridge Report, disseminated and discussed as part of army education, was 'the axis' about which remobilisation took place (see Illustration 10.1).[43] The themes explored in army education clearly reflected many of the issues raised in the Beveridge Report. The topic chosen for the first *British Way and Purpose* (*BWP*) booklet, a new initiative sponsored by Adam, designed to complement current affairs education with a study of the basic characteristics of British society, dealt directly with the question animating the minds of the troops: 'what we are fighting for'. The first chapter of *Citizen of Britain*, released in November 1942, covered what Britain was trying to preserve – freedom of speech, democratic institutions, religious liberty etc. – and what Britain was fighting against. The author, A. D. K. Owen, 'however, went beyond listing the traditional values of British society and touched on the question of a better life after the war: what the nation was fighting to create rather than just protect'.[44] He pointed out that while the 'condition of Britain' was 'almost heavenly' compared with what the Nazis might impose:

Illustration 10.1 An ABCA course for officers stationed in the Middle East, April 1943. The Beveridge Report, disseminated and discussed as part of army education, was 'the axis' about which remobilisation took place in the British Army.

> Few people are likely to confuse masses without work, half-derelict mining communities, the slums of Glasgow, the under-sized bodies of ill-nourished children, or the shocking scars on the loveliness of the English countryside with any heavenly thing. The fact is that, in spite of all the social progress in the years between the wars, there is still a great deal which cries out to be remedied in the condition of Britain.[45]

While the booklet was explicitly apolitical, it was unmistakably radical in its proposals. Its 'Big Idea', 'the dynamic idea of democracy', would lead to 'several startling changes – in the distribution of employment and wealth, in the provision of education and other social services, and in the creation of new opportunities for adventure and public service'. What is more, Owen was clear that 'it is up to us' to ensure that 'there is no unreasonable delay in translating the[se] ideas into carefully thought-out working propositions'. He went on to outline what the Coalition Government and organisations such as Nuffield College, Oxford, and the Fabian Society were planning to do once the war was won. In a section headed 'Our Responsibility' he stated strongly that:

> These things are good so far as they go, but the responsibility still rests with the ordinary citizen to see that the Government takes the measures necessary for carrying out a sound progressive policy. When the next General Election comes along, reconstruction problems will doubtless play an important part in the campaign and electors will have to be prepared to judge between the various programmes which are put forward.[46]

To a degree, therefore, the Beveridge Report, in conjunction with the AEC, played a key role in remobilising interest and commitment to the war effort. Here, at last, was a cause for which it was worth fighting, even if the Government did not explicitly support it.[47] As the censors in India and South-East Asia Command (SEAC) put it, 'for those who look forward to social and political changes', the Beveridge Report was:

> The yard stick by which the sincerity of the Government is estimated . . . The majority . . . interpret its having been shelved as a manoeuvre on the part of vested interests, reactionaries, the 'haves', and the like to deprive the returning soldier of that for which he has been fighting.[48]

One officer wrote from North Africa in August 1943:

> Since the battle here ended we have had many discussions with the troops about the post war world. Gosh, how difficult it was at first to get them to think. At first their only idea was to get out of the Army as soon as possible, go back to their old jobs and settle down comfortably again in the old way of life. There are improvements they want but there were very few who even considered the part they must play to get them. Now however, we have got them thinking and even discussing.[49]

Over time, soldiers came to realise that they would have to act for themselves if they were to live in the new world to which they aspired.

The 'only common factor' found in all the mail, according to the censors, was 'the idea that it is our way of living for which we are fighting and that, if the conditions when peace comes are found wanting, the fighting will have been in vain'. A report on 'Post-War Prospects: A Note on British Forces Opinions as Seen in Censorship' pointed out that there was 'a general demand that all soldiers must be given an opportunity of voting for their respective choices ... the majority ... only ask that, at the correct moment, schemes may be offered to them and explained, and they themselves given an opportunity to express their opinions'.[50] As the morale report for British troops in India, May to July 1943, noted:

> Some units record that there is doubt, and even apprehension, that post-war conditions will not justify the years of blood and sweat; the opinion has been expressed that proposals more concrete than the Beveridge Plan, involving actual legislation, are necessary to counter such catch phrases as 'troops in India will be handicapped in the race for jobs after the war'.[51]

The men, according to morale reports, were 'eager for more information' and the lack of concrete proposals suggested to many that the Beveridge plan was 'being shelved in the hope that it will be possible to "circumvent the New Deal"'.[52]

The men, quite simply, as a soldier in 5th Buffs put it, were looking for 'a fair deal' and 'won't be contented to sit back and be treated like a doorstop as our fathers were in 1918'.[53] 'I have read the Beveridge and Keynes reports with interest and hope', wrote yet another, 'and learned of the torpedoing of the former by financial interests with disgust and determination. The Army, a very different body of men from that of 1919, will not, this time, permit the sabotage of the people. If they find that the brave new world is really a financiers' paradise, tempers will be ugly and leaders will not be lacking.'[54] It was quite evident according to the censorship summaries that the men would 'not be contented with unfulfilled promises of a "better world"'.[55] The Beveridge report had 'a 100% backing in the army'.[56]

The British Army, it could be argued, therefore, engaged somewhat in self-remobilisation. The soldiers recognised, perhaps at times inarticulately or vaguely, that by carrying out their duties to the state, they also had claim to certain rights and benefits. Furthermore, in a democratic country, they could take ownership of their war effort in the firm understanding that the franchise gave them the opportunity to shape the post-war world. In that regard, they bypassed Government inaction on the plan (see Chapter 16). The troops could decide their own vision of what it was worth fighting for. As a soldier wrote in October 1944:

> The social security scheme ... is very sound and something worthy of our people at last, and it does mean the generation to come will have a better time and that alone has made this war worth fighting for because it is after all a fight against evil things and an attempt to keep common decencies and a reasonable way of life.[57]

The New Zealand Furlough Mutiny

The extent to which, as the war wore on, soldiers were prepared to challenge the legitimacy of the demands made upon them by the state and take control of the remobilisation process is well illustrated by the Furlough Mutiny in the New Zealand Army, an affair that has received little attention in the literature on the Second World War.[58] By April 1943, the 2nd New Zealand Division, like other veteran formations in Eighth Army, was tired and in need of rest.[59] The 'Main Body' of original volunteers, made up of the first three echelons, had been overseas for the best part of three years. Over this period the division had suffered around 18,500 casualties, 43 per cent of the total force that had been sent to the Middle East. Of the first three echelons, only 9,281 remained as of 30 April 1943.[60] Since mid-1942 Maori officers had been petitioning their Members of Parliament to send their battalion home. The men were homesick, exhausted and war weary.[61]

All signs pointed to the likely return of 2nd Division from the Middle East. The Australian divisions had been withdrawn to fight in the South-West Pacific Area (SWPA). The 3rd New Zealand Division was committed to support the Americans against the Japanese. The situation in North Africa looked secure after victory at El Alamein and the landing of US and British troops in Tunisia. With American troops pouring into the Pacific theatre, the demand for food and services was increasing sharply; the New Zealand War Cabinet estimated, in March 1943, that an additional 10,200 males were required in essential industry.[62] New Zealand could not maintain major expeditionary forces in two theatres, and, at the same time, keep up the flow of goods and services on which the Allied war effort in the Pacific increasingly depended.[63]

On 19 November 1942, Fraser put the case personally to Churchill. There was, he wrote, a 'general feeling in the country that our men have a strong claim to return, particularly in view of the extremely heavy casualties which our Division has suffered'. Churchill pleaded with Fraser to keep the New Zealand Division in the Middle East and referred him to the Combined Chiefs of Staff in Washington. On 3 December, the New Zealand Parliament agreed to keep the division in the Middle East.[64] As a consequence, two other major considerations entered into the New Zealand War Cabinet's calculations, the question of the willingness of the men to continue serving abroad, and, the domestic political situation.

The Minister of Defence, Frederick Jones, who was visiting the Middle East in March/April 1943, investigated the matter and reported to Wellington with what one of the official historians has referred to as 'exasperating but probably accurate obscurity'. There was, according to Jones, 'a general desire on the part of the Division to return to New Zealand'. The expectation was, however, that any period of home leave would be followed by further service in the Pacific. But, few wanted to serve in the Pacific; conditions in the Solomons and New Guinea were well known to be awful. Therefore, Jones continued, 'if given the option the majority [of soldiers] would prefer this theatre of war'. Nevertheless, he finished, if each man was individually consulted 'the great majority would wish to return'. General Freyberg reported more succinctly 'if your Division can remain in the Middle East, ... your decision will be welcomed on all sides'.[65]

On the domestic political front, the decision to retain the division in the Middle East could easily undermine Fraser's position in the Labour Party. Since the breakdown of the War Administration in September 1942, party politics had resumed 'a lusty if not much respected life'. It was expected that a general election would be held when the war situation permitted.[66] However, most of those who thought the 2nd Division should be recalled to New Zealand were members of Fraser's own party and Labour supporters more generally were understood to be behind its return.[67] There was a further danger in the possibility that Democratic Labour, founded by

J. A. Lee on his expulsion from the Labour Party in 1940, could outflank Labour on the left by directing an appeal to mothers, wives and families, to return their sweethearts home, under the guise of furthering New Zealand's true Pacific interests.[68] As a consequence, and as a condition of Parliament's approval to keep 2NZEF in the Middle East, it was decided that those who had served longest overseas would be sent back to New Zealand for three months' furlough, or leave. This, it was envisaged, would not only improve morale, both military and domestic, but, also, strengthen Labour's position in the forthcoming election.[69]

In the Middle East, Freyberg and his senior officers, while pointing out the 'great dislocation' that would be caused by the replacement of 'one third of the division', accepted the Furlough Scheme on the understanding that 5,000 men, 3,500 of whom would be veterans, would return to the division in time for the resumption of operations, probably in November or December 1943.[70] The first furlough draft, codenamed 'Ruapehu', sailed in June 1943, comprising just about all of the married men, the railway contingent (needed in New Zealand) and 20 per cent of the single men from the first three echelons. The draft, consisting of 5,855 soldiers in all, arrived back in New Zealand on 12 July.[71]

The furlough did not get off to a good start; the day the draft arrived back in Wellington was very wet and cold and no street parade or mass welcome had been organised (see Illustration 10.2). They were given a new issue of battle dress, an extra 'subsistence allowance', travelling privileges and told to get on their way.[72] The men were appalled by what they found. The apparent lack of commitment to the war effort demonstrated by ordinary New Zealanders reaffirmed their worst fears. Labour had promised to avoid conflict about equality during the war; powers to conscript wealth were to equal those to conscript men. However, in reality, the war served to exacerbate inequalities between sections of society. Big business was booming; 'businessmen and manufacturers had guaranteed markets, sure sales, a disciplined labour force with set wages and conditions, and price margins which provided uninterrupted profitability, capital growth, and resources for further investment'.[73] For those at the top it was a financial bonanza.

On the other hand, the employee classes were determined to share in the newfound prosperity. While workers' jobs were secure and

Illustration 10.2 The Ruapehu furlough draft of the 2NZEF arrives back in Wellington, July 1943. The 'Furlough Mutiny' represented arguably the most severe outbreak of indiscipline in any British Commonwealth force in both world wars.

wages did increase (26 per cent between 1939 and 1945), the war years were wracked by industrial disputes. In 1939, 53,800 working days were lost to strikes; in 1941, 28,100; in 1942, 51,200; in 1943, 14,700 (the unions exercised restraint partly due to the forthcoming election); in 1944, 52,600; and in 1945, 66,600. The six years of the war (1940 to 1945) saw a 45 per cent increase in days lost to strike action compared with the six years preceding the conflict.[74]

Such 'slackness and selfishness in the community' angered men who had suffered for three long years on the front line.[75] Where was the justice, they said, in 'wharfies' earning 3s 2d an hour for an ordinary shift, 6s an hour for night shifts and 7s 4d for weekend shifts, when in the Middle East soldiers could expect only 4s 6d a day with no overtime rates. On top of that, watersiders had the cheek to demand 'danger money' for loading and unloading ammunition ships.[76] The Prime Minister could not disprove the soldiers' claim that equality of sacrifice was far from the reality in New Zealand. In February 1944, he admitted that 'these things are unfortunately true, the question is how far can they be rectified and counteracted and the people roused once more'.[77] By 1943, there were 35,000 Grade 'A' men at home, fit enough to go overseas but who held jobs in 'essential industry'. These men, according to the soldiers, their families and friends, had, in the interest of fairness, to be used on the front line in the Middle East, to replace the furlough draft.[78]

In fact, some confusion had arisen over whether the men were expected to return to the Middle East at all. W. G. Stevens, Officer in Charge of Administration in the NZEF, had written in April that 'there should be no mention of any return to 2NZEF at a later date. As far as is known here, men would be going back [to New Zealand] for good.'[79] By May, on the other hand, it was being stated that the men would 'in general be liable to further overseas service'.[80] This was communicated to them in the final routine order (RO) instructing them on their embarkation for New Zealand; however, the RO also stated that on completion of the leave period, those who wished to return to the Middle East would 'be given fullest consideration, and their wishes will, as far as possible, be observed'. This wording was imprecise and did lead men to the misapprehension that they would be given a choice on whether or not they were to return to the Middle East.[81] The censors certainly noted that some writers 'wondered what would happen after the 3 months home leave was over'.[82]

The forthcoming election also complicated matters. The men had originally been due to return to the Middle East at the start of October. This clashed with the expected polling day at the end of September. The Government hoped that the presence of the division would not only please loved ones but 'lend credibility' to its 'handling of the war'. Thus, it extended the men's leave to ensure positive sentiments in the run-up to the vote.[83] The longer the men stayed in New Zealand, however, the less they wanted to leave. On 31 August, the Leader of the Opposition opened his election campaign with a broadcast speech that castigated the Government for overcommitting New Zealand's manpower in the war adding that 'in my opinion no man should be sent to the war twice before everybody has gone once'. This remark received coverage in the press and Holland's phrase became the rallying call of the Furlough men as a full-blooded campaign ensued.[84]

Family and friends and the soldiers themselves began bombarding newspapers with bitter letters calling for them to remain in New Zealand. One man wrote to the *Auckland Star* stating:

> I am a member of the furlough party. Would some kind person please inform a poor bewildered soldier what we are fighting for ... I wonder if the people who are earning 15–20 pounds a week ever give thought to the hollow-eyed, nerve-strained men who are dodging bombs and machine-gun bullets on their behalf, or ... the girls who bestow their favours on anyone but New Zealand furlough men ... And what of the women who betrayed their husbands while they were away defending their homes ... We had faith in the people of New Zealand once, we know better now. Their apathy is hard to understand.

The letter was signed, rather pointedly, 'Cannon Fodder'.[85] The War Cabinet could not tolerate such dissent and banned newspapers from mentioning the possibility of 'replacing soldiers on furlough by exempted men now working on farms or in other essential occupations'.[86] The furlough men began their own publicity campaign; posters sent out the message that 'while we faced death and the hard rigours of warfare, our fellow New Zealanders have taken our places in industry'. The Returned Servicemen Association and various public organisations began to take the furlough men's side. As a result of the growing controversy and increasing public pressure, and with the general election won (see Chapter 16), the Government decided that all married men aged 41 and over or with children, and all Maori, were excused from further service and would not have to return to the Middle East. Additionally, a further 2,664 men were downgraded on medical grounds, leaving only 1,637 men due to return to the Middle East.

By the turn of the New Year, with embarkation due on 12 January 1944, it was becoming increasingly clear to the authorities that they faced an organised revolt rather than a mélange of individual objections.[87] On 28 December, a meeting was held in Hamilton attended by ninety furlough men. A further meeting on 4 January, attended by over a hundred, agreed that they would refuse to return to camp for embarkation. The next day, the soldiers paraded in the local drill hall before joining the train to bring them to camp. They handed their CO a letter (see Figure 10.1)[88] and then 'very smartly right-turned and walked out of the Drill Hall'. The men then proceeded to the rail

To the Staff Officer,
Army Office,
Hamilton.

Sir,

We have paraded here today as ordered. We now respectfully request that arrangements be made to place us on leave without pay until such time as every Grade One man in New Zealand has done his duty overseas.

Our slogan is:

'Every man once, before volunteers are called upon twice'.

Please convey this message to the Ministry of Defence and Members of the War Cabinet that we now desire to change places with the Grade One men in industry and to enjoy the many privileges of the Home Front.

Thanking you,
From 'Other Ranks Only'
Furlough Draft

Figure 10.1 Furlough men's letter of protest, 5 January 1944

station where they attempted to get others to join in the 'revolt' and there were 'similar occurrences' throughout the rest of the country.[89]

In the face of this growing unrest, three members of the War Cabinet – the Minister of Defence, the Minister of National Service and the Minister of Rehabilitation – along with the Deputy Chief of the General Staff, Brigadier Gentry, met a deputation of furlough men at Linton on 7 January. Exhortations were made and concessions offered, but to no avail.[90] On the day that the men were due to sail with the 11th Reinforcement for the Middle East, 248 of them failed to report for duty and a further 700 refused to obey orders to embark. Only 680 men, 13 per cent of the original furlough party and 42 per cent of those expected to embark on the day, set sail – a far cry from the 3,500 trained veterans Freyberg was expecting to receive in the Middle East.[91]

The Government suppressed all media reports of the 'rebellion' with some success. Some months later, enemy controlled Radio Paris in France reported that there had been 'a mutiny among the troops due to embark for the European front from Hamilton'. No other use, however, was made of the incident by German propaganda. The denial of any publicity forced the men to make alternative arrangements to acquaint the public with their grievances. On 14 January, a hundred soldiers attempted to raise awareness by marching down Wellesley and Queen Streets in Auckland. On 22 January, displays were organised at the Wellington Cup race at Trentham.[92] In the face of this open 'rebellion', the Army ordered court-martial proceedings to begin on 27 January. Over the next two months, different contingents of the 'mutineers' were tried under section 12(1)(a) of the Army Act for desertion and sentenced to ninety days' detention. In light of the men's previous service, the sentences were suspended on the understanding that they would embark with the next Reinforcement. Warrant Officers and NCOs were reduced to the ranks.[93]

The Army's position, as expressed by Brigadier L. M. Inglis in a press statement on 9 February 1944, was clear. 'Every soldier, sailor or airman had not done his bit until either the war is over or he was dead or incapacitated.' The problem, in spite of his efforts, did not go away. On 22 February, furlough men went so far as to barricade District Army HQ in Christchurch when one of their leaders, Sergeant Major Locke, was detained. The situation was only defused when, through the use of an intermediary, it was agreed that two soldiers from each camp holding furlough men would have the opportunity to state their case to the War Cabinet. On 26 February the War Cabinet, together with two other ministers and the Adjutant-General, met the men and their counsels. Again, the men stressed 'the inequality of sacrifice between themselves and fit men held on appeal in industry'. While the War Cabinet agreed that equality of sacrifice was desirable, it maintained that equal outcomes were impossible in the circumstances. It was agreed that the Government would pay the cost of the men taking their case to the Court of Appeal.[94] The same message was delivered again when the Prime Minister and Minister of Manpower came to visit the detained men on 14 March. Efforts were made to reason with the men and hear their grievances. However, Fraser was adamant that 'the letter of the law should be obeyed'.[95]

As far as the 'mutineers' were concerned, they were making headway. The authorities had baulked at the idea of coercing the men to obey legal orders. The 'mutineers' were negotiating with the Prime Minister of New Zealand about the terms of their continued service, a remarkable situation in the context of the Second World War.[96] The men had additional success at the end of March when they brought their case first to the Supreme Court and then to the Court of Appeal. In the first hearing of its kind, the Court of Appeal quashed a number of the men's sentences on the grounds that the charge as framed did not amount to desertion. The judgment made clear, however, that the men had been 'guilty of insubordination and possibly mutiny'.[97] On 31 March, the authorities tried again to get the furlough men to embark for the Middle East as part of the second section of the 11th Reinforcement. Their attempts substantially failed; only 148 agreed, the great majority refusing to embark.[98] At this stage, the situation threatened to get violent. A group from Trentham Camp wrote to the Minister of Defence warning that 'there can be no foretelling what men who have faced but never feared the very cream of the German Army might contemplate if the present state of affairs is allowed to continue'. On 3 April, the Minister of Defence received a telegram from Linton Military Camp stating that they had 'read Trentham's ultimatum' and were 'in full concurrence' with it. The following day, about 200 men from Trentham broke camp and boarded the train for Wellington. They marched on Parliament carrying banners pointing out that they represented '1,000 furlough men' and demanded 'Equality of Sacrifice'. Precautions had been taken and the men did not gain entry to Parliament, but they did manage to gain an 'interview' with the Minister of Defence.[99]

That afternoon, the War Cabinet finally decided to act, and act decisively. They resolved to dismiss the 'rebels' from the Army for misconduct and insubordination under section 6(b) of the Defence Act 1909. The men would be removed without mufti allowance, discharge privileges, deferred pay, rehabilitation benefits or a war gratuity.[100] Furthermore, they would be ineligible for appointment or reappointment to the public service. The War Cabinet hoped that this action might deter the Second Furlough Draft, which was about to arrive in New Zealand, from following in the steps of the first and help maintain discipline in the armed forces more generally. Their hopes were not to be realised. The second draft, codenamed 'Wakatipu', arrived in New Zealand on 10 February with the remaining 1,904 men of the first three echelons. As early as 3 April, the Adjutant-General noted that 'they had already shown unmistakable signs of infection and so there is every prospect of a repetition of all the trouble we have gone through with Ruapehu'.[101] Events played out in a now familiar manner; 1,100 men were medically downgraded and eliminated from the service in other ways. Of the 450 men who were ordered to re-embark at the end of June 1944, 100 refused to do so (thus, only 18 per cent of the original draft returned to the Middle East).[102] These men were court-martialled on 15 June and eventually dismissed dishonourably, on 26 July 1944, just like those from the first draft.[103]

By this stage, it was becoming abundantly clear that getting the furlough men to return to the front line was close to impossible. Fraser and Freyberg discussed the matter when the Prime Minister visited Italy at the end of May. No decision had yet been made with regards to a furlough for the 4th Reinforcement, an issue that was expected to become a 'problem in [the] near future'.[104] On 7 June, Freyberg wrote to the Prime Minister that in the circumstances and 'after careful consideration' there were 'strong reasons why 2NZEF should be withdrawn to New Zealand'. While he was certain that the division 'could carry on and add fresh honours to its record', there were 'various factors affecting the efficiency of the Force' which had to be taken into consideration. Aside from the Furlough Mutiny, signs were 'not lacking that many of the old hands require[d] a prolonged rest':

> I feel therefore that . . . a replacement scheme would be required for all long service personnel. Such a change-over would not be easy but I feel it would be essential in the interests of the efficiency of the Force. That being so, and taking into consideration your manpower difficulties and probable future commitments in the war against Japan I have come to the conclusion that the time may well be opportune for the complete withdrawal of 2 NZEF.[105]

Indeed, it was time to act. In September, the Government decided, in light of Freyberg's comments, the strategic situation laid out at the Quebec conference, and the continuing manpower shortage, that New Zealand was no longer in a position to maintain two divisions overseas. It decided to concentrate efforts in Europe and disband 3rd Division in the Pacific. This made it possible to introduce a new scheme to replace furlough and progressively relieve, on a permanent basis, all men in 2nd Division who had been overseas for three years or more. Replacement drafts from New Zealand comprising Grade A men held on appeal in industry (5,000 were transferred to the Middle East in the first three months of 1945) and men left over from 3rd Division, who were still fit and of the required age and status, were sent to replace the old hands of 2nd New Zealand Division.[106] Many of the men sent from New Zealand were not happy to go; Armed Forces Appeals Boards dismissed or rejected close to 5,000 appeals against military service in the first quarter of 1945 alone.[107]

Whether intentionally or otherwise, the Government had in spirit and in practice adopted an approach consistent with the arguments of the furlough men. By the end of March 1945, some 9,800 veterans had arrived back in New Zealand after three long years of service in the Mediterranean and Middle East.[108] Between April 1943, when the idea of furlough began to gain traction, and August 1945, 19,084 men under appeal in industry were made available for service in the armed forces. Whereas only 570 men per month were released from industry between April 1943 and March 1945, 819 men per month were released between April and August 1945, a 44 per cent increase.[109] In March 1944, 41,617 men were held on appeal in reserve industries in New Zealand. By February 1945, that figure had dropped to 28,441.[110] The role of fairness and equality of sacrifice had clearly become more important in New Zealand's approach to mobilising for the final years of the war.

The Government's inability to get more than a portion of the 'Ruapehu' and 'Wakatipu' drafts back to the Middle East stands out nevertheless as 'a striking instance' of the 'limited effectiveness of the impressive array of wartime powers' that the New Zealand Government had been given in law. The Government was reluctant to use physical force to coerce the furlough men to return to the Middle East. In many ways, the legal right to coerce 'became unreal' as public opinion was clearly behind the mutineers. As the official histories have argued, 'no one could well deny that any country which accepted the principle that soldiers could retire on their own initiative after three years' service would be withdrawing itself from effective participation in the war'.[111] As one man put it, 'we knew in 1943 or 1944 no Government would ever attack us physically, not in that day and age. Well we didn't think they would. We didn't think the country would stand for it.'[112]

It is clear, that the strength of the men's case trumped the Government's legal rights. As John McLeod has put it, it was the appeal to the basic tenet of 'egalitarianism' that mattered.[113] Equality of sacrifice was much more than a catchphrase; the men believed that they had the right to expect others to do as much as them. After all, they were fighting for a free, democratic and egalitarian society. The remarkable fact that the cohort of men (volunteers of the first three echelons) who, it could be argued, were most committed to the war effort ended up rejecting the demands made of them by the state bears reflection. The New Zealand soldier, to all intents and purposes, was able to negotiate the terms of his service in the second half of the war. As a result, 2nd New Zealand Division would fight some of its hardest battles without its most experienced veterans.

The UDF and the 'Blue Oath'

The narrative that emerges from the South African experience of remobilisation resonates in many ways with that of the furlough mutineers. By the middle of 1941, 'the UDF [Union Defence Force] was scraping the barrel for fighting soldiers'. Following the fall of Tobruk in June 1942, with the loss of 10,722 South Africans as POWs, another (second) mobilisation was attempted to fill the void in the manpower of the UDF.[114] This recruiting drive, the 'Avenge Tobruk' campaign, focused more on urban areas than previous efforts, resulting in a higher percentage of recruits from social classes I and II (13 and 18 per cent for 1942 and 1943 compared to 11 and 8 per cent for 1940 and 1941).[115] Recruitment jumped 46 per cent from the April/June to the July/September quarters of 1942. However, it fell again, by 56 per cent, in the fourth quarter of the year.[116] One factor negatively affecting the response to the appeal of General Smuts for recruits was that many soldiers, especially in the Transvaal, warned friends and relatives 'against joining up' because they themselves were 'dissatisfied with service conditions'.[117]

It is clear, for example, from recruitment statistics, the Defence Personnel Records, censorship summaries and 'Gallup Polls', that many South Africans who volunteered for service in the Second World War never saw combat, spending much, if not all of their time, in training camps and on garrison duty in South Africa.[118] By 1943, Smuts had serious doubts about the continued utility of the UDF. After serious defeats in the desert, with the security risk from Afrikaner nationalists, and with recurring problems in keeping establishments at full strength, he announced the formation of Inland and Coastal Commands. South Africa would look to its own defence first. 'Nobody', Smuts said, 'knew where Japan would halt' its expansionist agenda, 'we are the gateway to India, which I look upon as the most important part of the Globe today'.[119] Available statistics suggest that from 1942/3 between two-thirds and three-quarters of the South African Army were stationed at home.[120] These men, many of whom were keen to see combat, became deeply dissatisfied with the Government and the war effort, a problem that was exacerbated by the fact that at no point during 1943 was a South African infantry, armour or artillery unit actually fighting the enemy.[121] One man in Kimberley wrote that his officers used to get the men to pick up stones around their tents and on the parade ground as they had nothing else to do. 'Just imagine us, fully trained men who should be in the front line ... picking up stones ... I am sick of this damn regiment ... and often wish I could get out of it ... I may tell you I am not the only one.'[122] The extent of the malaise was illustrated by a letter sent by a member of the Tank Corps who complained that their camp contained 4,000 men, of whom 100 were ex-North, 600 to 700 were new recruits undergoing training, and the rest, the vast majority, were doing nothing. Another trooper wrote that his service had been 'two years of wasted effort and time, humiliation beyond endurance'.[123] Such problems attracted considerable public attention[124] and in this context it is perhaps not very surprising that absence and desertion in the Union were very high.[125]

By the late summer of 1942, a 'serious general discontent' had developed among South African troops at home. In an attempt to get to the bottom of the problem, the Directorate of Military Intelligence commissioned a 'Gallup Poll' on 'Soldiers' Grievances'. The results showed that 'inactivity and stagnation' represented 25 per cent of the total unfavourable comments, while 'general living conditions' and 'training' made up 19.5 and 16.5 per cent respectively. These problems were especially evident among members of the South African Tank Corps, many of whom would go on to fight in Italy as 6th Armoured Division.[126]

Veterans were not immune to these challenges either. The decision to bring 1st South African Division home, and then disband it, proved 'disastrous to army morale'. Some units were dissolved, others were merged; in the process the esprit de corps built up over many years was lost.[127] Many ex-North men also complained of the appalling treatment they received on return to the Union (see Chapter 6). 'You are no hero in the Cape' wrote one man.[128]

When a third phase of mobilisation took place at the beginning of 1943, the response was decidedly lukewarm. With the thought that the end of the war in Africa was drawing near, General Smuts introduced the 'Blue Oath' in early 1943.[129] This produced, in the first quarter, a 30 per cent increase in white and 42 per cent increase in black recruitment. Thereafter, however, recruitment dropped considerably and did not pick up again during the remaining period of the war.[130]

Most soldiers already in service declined to take the new oath and extend their service outside of Africa.[131] Analysis of the Defence Personnel Records indicates that only 23 per cent of the men opted for the 'Blue Oath',[132] the majority of these, 76 per cent, being English-speaking South Africans. Only 17 per cent of Afrikaners as compared to 26 per cent of English-speakers opted to take the oath.[133] A South African Military Censorship Special Report on 'Reactions to [the] New Oath' tried to engage with the question of 'why the men were not coming forward in a better spirit?' The veteran 3rd Armoured Car Company of 1st South African Division was most negative about the oath (75 per cent being against it). They thought that they were being treated 'very, very unfairly' as they felt, much like the New Zealand furlough mutineers, that they had already done their bit. Interestingly, the report showed that of three infantry battalions assessed, the higher the percentage of Afrikaans-speakers in the unit the less likely it was to support the oath.[134] Smuts, who had intended to send two armoured divisions to Italy, would have to settle for one.[135]

This report, and others like it, laid the blame squarely on the home front, stating that 'civilian influence seems to have been largely responsible'; more specifically, it blamed women 'whose hostility to the new oath' seemed to be particularly 'deep-rooted'. Many men, especially older ones with families, left 'the final decision entirely to their wives'. 'I'm telling you now', wrote one woman:

> That if you *dare* volunteer for any service overseas or in Madagascar, you need never come back to me. I'll never never forgive you as long as I live. I'll leave Doreen [their child] with my mother and I'll go away and be a nurse and have a damn good time . . . Why must some people do all the sacrifices and the others stay here and get all the benefits . . . so remember I've given you for North Africa and its nearly killing me, so if you went overseas it will be my end.[136]

A central issue appeared to be the need for fairness; it was perceived that some families made all the sacrifices while others benefited from the booming war economy. This factor, along with the overwhelming desire to be reunited with family, played with the motivations of soldiers as much as it did with their wives, sweethearts and families. Indeed, according to the censors, the men were 'reluctant' to leave their families again 'for any considerable length of time'. Significantly, the 'call from their homes seemed to be stronger than comradeship' and 'loyalty' to their country.[137] There is evidence that many units had to go so far as to resort to threats of 'garrison duty' in Egypt and coercion to get men to sign the new oath.[138]

As the war wore on, the danger grew of a disengagement of soldiers and their families from the war effort. The censors commented that 'surprisingly few [soldiers] seem to have patriotic motives for their decision' to take the new oath,[139] while a survey on morale in the Army in September 1943 pointed to a 'disturbing increase of despondency in the UDF'. After nearly four years, it was clear that 'a feeling of war-weariness' had emerged and that 'the issues of the war had been lost sight of'. This was typified by comments such as, 'I honestly feel that I do not care who wins this war as long as it ends soon.' An 'ex-North' Sergeant wrote, 'the papers write how we are itching to go into action. I laugh, the fellow who wrote that does not know how our hearts ache to return to our loved ones.' A Corporal stated, 'I feel no obligation to this country or any country any more. I had my ideals when the war started but they no longer exist'. A 'very large number of writers', according to the censors, 'could find no justification for their sacrifice, and a Trooper felt "sorry to say that patriotism does not pay. I gave up everything for fighting but I find that it is only a fool who gives up everything"'.[140] Some form of 'remobilisation' was indeed required. This in turn begged the question not just of the organisational resources available to the South African state for such an effort but of the terms on which to conduct it and the changes that might be demanded.[141]

On the whole, the South African state failed to rise to this challenge. Fewer men joined up in the later years of the war (see Table 2.2), a fact that caused great bitterness in those families who had loved ones in the services.[142] The dramatic drop in recruitment post-1942 meant that many units struggled to keep up to strength.[143] As the war dragged on, satisfaction with Smuts and the United Party diminished dramatically (see Chapter 16). Civilians at home, and soldiers at the front, increasingly talked about the inevitability of a new government after the war. This made prospective recruits, and

Table 10.1 UDF, percentage of enlistees English-speaking versus Afrikaans-speaking by year, 1939–45

	1939	1940	1941	1942	1943	1944	1945
Sample size	37	569	140	150	82	74	30
English-speaking	49%	73%	46%	53%	51%	69%	87%
Afrikaans-speaking	51%	27%	54%	47%	49%	31%	13%

Afrikaners in particular, less likely to rally around Smuts and the war effort.[144] Of those who did volunteer late in the war, the South African Military Censorship Summary for 8 to 21 June 1944 pointed to two key motivations: adventure and financial hardship. It commented that for the 'majority' the Normandy invasion had 'stirred the imagination' and induced them to join the Army. Many of these recruits appeared to be young men who were 'just dying to get away'. '"I've waited long enough to get into the army, and now that I'm in I want to see some action", was the kind of statement frequently found in letters.' A 'few' enlisted for the 'less noble' reason that they could 'not get work'.[145]

It does appear that the prevailing circumstances were particularly damaging to Afrikaner enlistment (see Table 10.1). During the first four years of the war (apart from the great ideological awaking of 1940, when English-speaking South Africans had been roused in Britain's great moment of danger), Afrikaner enlistment broadly kept up with English-speaking South Africans. Between 1941 and 1943, for example, northern parts of the country were stricken by a devastating drought, which resulted in large-scale crop failures. Localised infestations of 'streak disease' and 'army-worms' also impacted negatively on agriculture during these years. Such problems primarily impacted on poor white farmers (and, of course, black labourers) in rural areas. Price inflation and the shortage of housing brought many hardships to the towns as well. Thus, many poor whites, who were in the main Afrikaners, joined up rather than face destitution.[146] Afrikaner enlistment was also likely maintained by the 'Avenge Tobruk' recruiting campaign, as 2nd South African Division had contained a large number of Afrikaans-speakers.

By 1944 and 1945, however, with the increasing 'groundswell of antagonism toward the government', widespread dissatisfaction in the Army, and an increasing awareness that those 'who had stayed at home were financially better off' than those who had joined up, it was only those few (young people) who had a yearning for adventure, and who perhaps had a commitment to the Imperial war effort, who joined up. As Table 10.1 shows, these men were almost entirely English-speakers.[147]

The remarkable power of citizens to in effect negotiate the terms of their continued military service and perhaps reform their relationship with the state is borne out by the heated debates that raged over whether black and coloured soldiers should take the new oath in January 1943. The following month, the censors carried out an evaluation of mail from black and coloured members of the Cape Corps at Kimberley in South Africa. Of the thousands of letters sent, 231 commented on the new oath and of these, 70 per cent were in favour, as compared to 21 per cent against and 9 per cent undecided. The censors pointed out that those openly opposed to the new oath came largely from the 'more intelligent and better educated men of the Corps' whose object appeared to be a 'desire to use the new oath as a lever to improve their existing ... conditions'. Most of these men had no 'fundamental objection' to service overseas. However, 'there was commonly the proviso that some measure of social and economic security must be obtained for themselves and their dependents' if they were to volunteer for further service. As far as ex-North coloured soldiers were concerned, the new oath appeared to provide 'an avenue of escape from the colour bar in this country'.[148]

It must be noted that the vast majority of men did not mention the new oath in their letters home.[149] This might reasonably be taken as an indication that for the great bulk of men the new oath was not even an issue worth commenting on. On the whole, black and coloured soldiers' letters demonstrated nothing but antipathy for the European war. 'Let the white bastards kill one another' said one, while another despaired that he had been forced to 'fight for King and Country and not for my country. I got no country of my own, the country I got the white man is boss over.' This 'objection against racial discrimination' the censors argued was not based on 'exclusion from European social life' but rather the 'economic inequality' which made their lives so difficult; 'I have no intention of taking the new oath ... until the Cape Corps are paid to the same level as the whites.' Thus, economic opportunity was a driving force behind those taking the oath and 'economic injustice' the 'most prominent reason for refusal to sign the new attestation'.[150]

It appears that those against continued participation in the war effort eventually won out. Table 2.2 shows that black recruitment decreased dramatically in 1943; the number of recruits fell a remarkable 96 per cent between the first and second quarters of the year.[151]

Procedural Justice

'In short', as a morale report for British troops in India put it, '"the Home and Post-War position peg" is that on which morale hangs'.[152] British, New Zealand and South African attempts to remobilise their societies for a fourth year of war hinged on governments' willingness to manage the war effort in a manner consistent with the aims and political aspirations of citizen soldiers. In a context where popular support for the war stemmed mostly from persuasion much more than from coercion,[153] the concept of procedural justice became ever more important.[154] As a report on 'The British Soldier in Italy, September 1943 to June 1944' put it:

> The soldier centred his thoughts and hopes on the day when he would return home. Not that he expected to find any great recompense for his services awaiting him there. Indeed in his blacker moments he seems to have felt alienated from his country, seeing it as a land 'peopled largely by overseas troops and highly paid civilian workers, living a life of ease and contributing little to the war effort'. The British soldier ... was a stickler for justice, in the full sense of the word, and the ruling principle that he required of his superiors was 'fair shares'.[155]

The unwillingness of Churchill and the Conservative-led coalition to countenance implementation of the Beveridge Report and the inability of Fraser in New Zealand and Smuts in South Africa to guarantee anything close to equality of sacrifice led to the psychological disengagement of soldiers from the war effort, with concomitant negative implications for morale and combat effectiveness.

The remarkable power of citizens to implicitly negotiate the terms of their continued military service and perhaps reform their relationship with the state had other consequences too. In South Africa, where service was voluntary, citizens could simply refuse to participate in the war. In order to provide two armoured divisions for the conflict in the Mediterranean, South Africa required 60 per cent of those serving to take the 'Blue Oath'. In the end, only 23 per cent signed up and South Africa struggled to keep even one division, 6th South African Armoured Division, up to strength in the field. By November 1943, South Africa's commitment to the war was so questionable that the British Government was forced to agree to subsidise it by paying £5.5 million towards the estimated £17.5 million annual cost of its overseas forces.[156] In New Zealand, where a voluntary system was not in play, the men, in a manner not dissimilar to the French Army in 1917, mutinied, depriving 2nd New Zealand Division of a third of its most experienced veterans at a time that it needed them most – during the extremely challenging battles at Cassino in February and March 1944 (see Chapter 11). In Britain, soldiers came to realise, through army education, that they could, in the absence of a government-sponsored vision for a post-war world, take control and back their own idea for social change (as articulated in the Beveridge Report). In time, through use of the franchise, the men would get the chance to ensure the future of the country coincided with their desires. The 'road to 1945' would pass through the battlefields of Africa, Asia and Europe.

11 CASSINO

Anzio and the First Battle of Cassino

The short break in the fighting at the height of the winter of 1943/44 allowed for a reassessment of approach in Italy. The question of how to break the stalemate on the 'Winter Line' had been discussed at the 'Sextant' Conference in Cairo and the 'Eureka' Conference in Tehran in late November and early December 1943. On 19 December, Churchill signalled the British Chiefs of Staff: 'there is no doubt', he said, 'that the stagnation of the whole campaign on the Italian front is becoming scandalous'. It was known that the success of German defensive operations south of Rome had encouraged Hitler to transfer the best part of five divisions to the Eastern Front. Something had to be done to ensure that German formations were not diverted away from the Mediterranean to the decisive campaigns being planned by the Soviets in the East and the Western Allies in North-West Europe; this, after all, was, to a large extent, the strategic logic behind the Italian campaign.[1]

To this end, something radically different had to be tried. The war in Italy had become, according to Alexander, a 'slugging match'. In such circumstances, much depended on the hard arithmetic of combat numbers and the morale of the troops. With the remobilisation of the British, New Zealand and South African war efforts having largely failed, and with casualties high and reinforcements in short supply (in January 1944, 5th, 46th and 56th Divisions received 219 reinforcements against a requirement of 4,686), Eighth Army was experiencing problems with both morale and manpower that it was ill-equipped to address (see Chapter 15).[2] In the circumstances, Alexander decided to try a different approach.

His plan revolved around making use of Allied command of the sea to outflank the 'Gustav Line' and open the door to Rome. The amphibious assault that would be required, codenamed 'Shingle', was to be undertaken by VI US Corps, comprising the fresh 1st Division (which had arrived from North Africa in December and which was now transferred from Eighth Army to VI Corps) and 3rd US Division. 'Shingle' would be accompanied by a renewed assault by Fifth Army on the 'Gustav Line' around Cassino. With Fifth Army pushing hard at Cassino, it was envisaged that VI Corps would move swiftly inland from Anzio and convince, or bluff, the Germans holding on at Cassino to withdraw. It was, as Alexander admitted later, a gamble. Nevertheless, it was one that appeared worth the risk.[3]

The first of many problems was that of landing craft. The Allies possessed plenty of conventional warships and merchantmen in the Mediterranean; however, the majority (68 out of 104) of the highly specialised landing craft needed for a successful amphibious assault were due to be transferred to Britain for 'Overlord'. Once these units had left the Mediterranean, Alexander would only have the resources for a one-division assault, a force too weak to land behind the German lines. Alexander contacted Churchill, who, in turn, wrote to Roosevelt in December requesting an extension of three weeks before the landing craft departed for Britain. 'If this opportunity is not grasped', he wrote, 'we may expect the ruin of the Mediterranean campaign of 1944.' Roosevelt agreed providing that the timetable for 'Overlord' was not affected.[4]

The beaches south of Rome around Anzio and Nettuno were chosen for the landing (see Map 11.1). Good roads led from there to the Alban Hills which, situated between Highways 6 and 7, offered an excellent location to threaten German lines of communication. The extension granted by Roosevelt did not give much time for planning; whereas the scheme for 'Husky' had taken five months to design and 'Avalanche' six weeks, the landings at Anzio had to be completed in a three-week period.[5] It was, therefore, hardly surprising that planning was rushed and informed by what one historian has described as 'a spirit of excessive optimism'.[6]

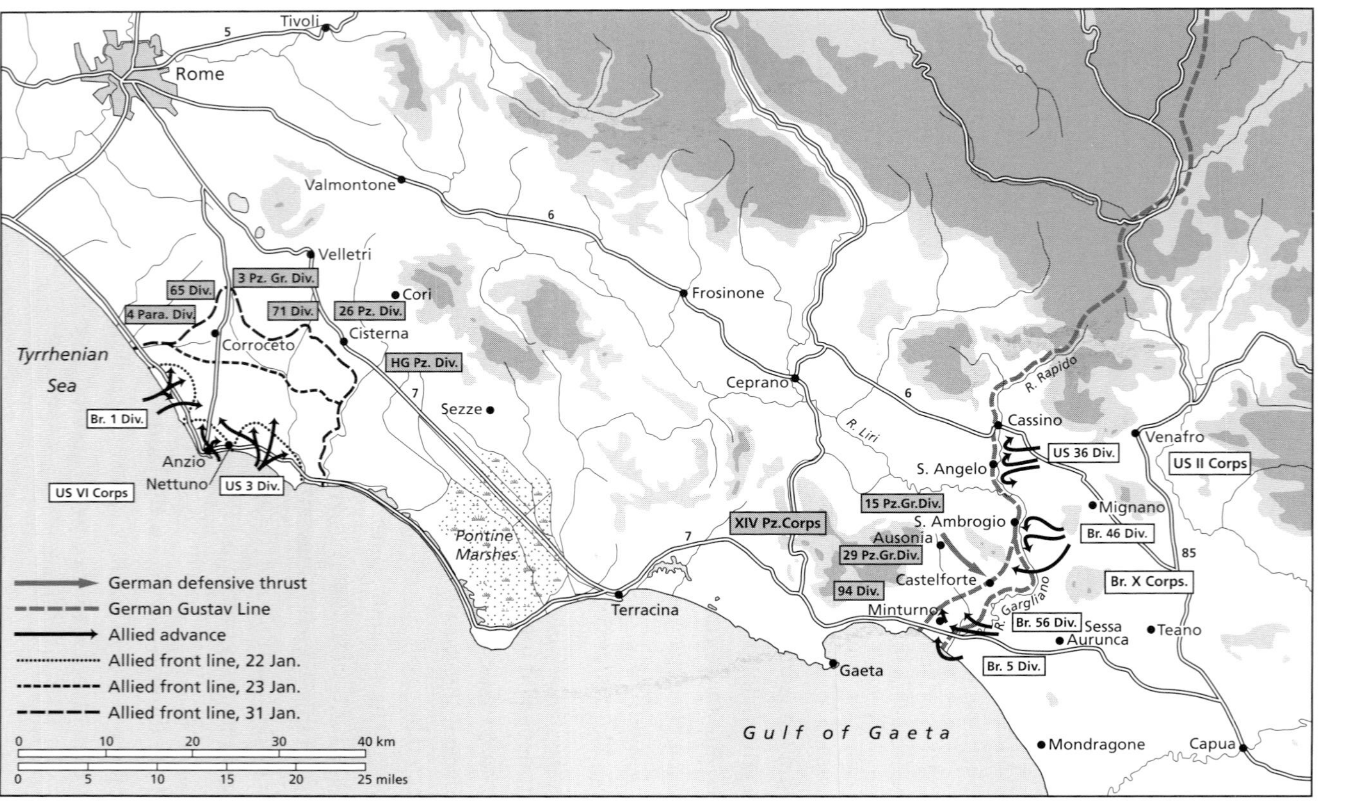

Map 11.1 Anzio and the First Battle of Cassino, January 1944

The assault on the 'Gustav Line' began on 17 January. X Corps, comprising 5th Division, which had also been transferred from Eighth Army, and 56th London Division, assaulted the defences on the River Garigliano. Two days later, 46th North Midland and West Riding Division, as part of US II Corps, crossed the Garigliano near San Ambrogio. The 2nd New Zealand Division was in 15th Army Group Reserve poised for the planned breakout into the Liri Valley. The offensive was supported by an Allied Air Force that now mustered 2,700 operational aircraft, compared to the *Luftwaffe*'s 300. The Allies had in the region of 2,000 tanks, close to ten times the German number. Kesselring had thirteen divisions in central Italy under Tenth Army, and eight in the north. Alexander had some twenty divisions in Italy, twelve of which faced the 'Gustav Line' and three were earmarked for 'Shingle'.[7]

X Corps attacked along an 8-mile front and caught the Germans by surprise. The 5th Division mounted an amphibious assault to support its crossing of the Garigliano at the coast, but, much like 56th London Division further east, it got held up by extensive minefields. By the end of the next day, a bridgehead had been established across the river and Kesselring found himself in a desperate position as he received calls to release his reserves to prevent the total collapse of the line. The 29th and 90th Panzer Grenadier Divisions were available, but they were held in case of an Allied amphibious landing behind German lines. Kesselring had little option in the circumstances; he sent his reserves to the front. This quick decision stabilised the situation and prevented the British from breaking through the 'Gustav Line'.

The 46th North Midland and West Riding Division's assault across the Garigliano River near San Ambrogio was less successful. The Germans had opened the sluices of an irrigation dam to the north, making the current too strong for assault boats. Surprise was lost and after artillery fire began to concentrate on the attacking troops, the assault was called off; the division was then redirected to support the overstretched 56th London Division fighting to hold on to its bridgehead across the river to the south. The failure of 46th North Midland and West Riding Division undermined the US 36th Division's attack across the River Rapido further to the north, as the high ground near San Ambrogio covered their crossing. The assault failed, with the Americans losing 1,681 men compared to the Germans' 243.[8]

With X and US II Corps' attacks having stalled, everything now rested on the success of Operation 'Shingle'. US VI Corps, under Lieutenant-General John Lucas, landed at Anzio before dawn on 22 January and caught the few defenders in the area (two companies of 29th Panzer Grenadier Division) completely by surprise. There were no other Germans within 25 miles of the beachhead; the attacks of X and US II Corps in the south had, to that extent, done their job. By the end of the day, Lucas had 36,000 troops ashore along with some 3,000 vehicles.[9] The Allied advance inland, however, was extremely slow and cautious. Clark had warned Lucas not to 'stick his neck out' and Lucas himself was pessimistic about the landings. Captured German documents reported that:

> Allied infantry carried out attacks at a walking pace and without taking advantage of the terrain. A vigorous defence with effective use of the MG42 stopped every advance immediately. Mutual fire support within companies and platoons while working their way forward was nowhere in evidence.[10]

The 'wildcat' that Churchill had hoped to hurl ashore at Anzio became a 'stranded whale'.[11]

The character of the Allied landing at Anzio quickly became apparent to Kesselring. Under pressure from von Vietinghoff to withdraw Tenth Army from the 'Gustav Line', Kesselring showed immense confidence and resolve and decided to stand his ground. He issued the predesignated code word, 'Richard', for the German response to an Allied assault on 'Fortress Europe'. Reinforcements poured in from every part of the expanded Reich, France, the Balkans, Germany, Crete and Greece.[12] By the end of the first day, two German divisions were beginning to form in the area around Anzio. By 28 January, the best part of four divisions had arrived around the beachhead and by 4 February five divisions were in place. To the extent that the Germans had been lured into removing their forces from other theatres, the overall Allied strategy was working. This was little consolation for the troops on the front line; Allied reinforcements (including 56th London Division, which arrived in mid-February, and which in turn was replaced by 5th Division on 11 March), while also impressive, did not match the German build-up and the German infantry 'greatly outnumbered' the Allies as they strove to throw them back into the sea. It was only the 'determination of the defence and the accuracy of the artillery fire', along with heretofore-unmatched levels of direct air support, that saved the day. In spite of savage fighting, by 29 February, German attempts to destroy the beachhead had failed.[13]

That debacle had not turned into disaster was scant consolation for Alexander. Brooke blamed the setback on a 'lack of initiative in the early stages', while Churchill wrote to Alexander complaining, 'I have a feeling that you may have hesitated to assert your authority because you were dealing so largely with Americans and therefore *urged* an advance instead of *ordering* it.' There had certainly been no clear understanding regarding the goals of the operation. Alexander saw 'Shingle' as the key move in loosening the German grip on the Cassino position. Clark, however, considered the attack on the 'Gustav Line' the main effort and that 'Shingle' would be employed to help mop up the already defeated Germans by threatening their flank and rear. This unresolved disagreement about the goal of Lucas's corps, the sort of muddle that a more clear-thinking and less 'agreeable' commander than Alexander might have avoided, lay at the heart of the failure at Anzio.[14] Ends and means could not be aligned if there was a lack of clarity over the goal of the operation.

To make matters worse, casualties were absolutely appalling: they amounted to 4.5 per cent of the British beachhead force in January, rising to an astonishing 21.6 per cent in February, twice the rate experienced in Normandy in June 1944 (see Table 14.1). As always, the infantry suffered most, with line rifle companies suffering 35 per cent and the Foot Guards suffering a staggering 49 per cent casualties in February.[15] The conditions, as the journalist Wynford Vaughan-Thomas wrote, 'bore a close resemblance to the Somme or Ypres in 1916–1917'.[16] Morale suffered accordingly; in the first two months after the landing at Anzio, 1st Division had 2,961 men admitted sick, of whom 810 were classified as suffering from battle exhaustion. The sick and battle exhaustion admission rate per month for this period was an extremely high 90 per thousand (see Figure 9.2 for context).[17] On the one hand, the key British and Commonwealth formations in the combined offensive had not had an opportunity to recover from the high levels of attrition and exhaustion during the hard fighting between September and December 1943. On the other, a 'large proportion of these cases of "exhaustion"', according to a report on 'Medical Aspects of the Campaign in Italy, 1943 to 1945'

> were undoubtedly . . . frightened men. It happened frequently on this beach-head that reinforcements, who had never heard a shot fired in anger before, landed at the port one day and were in the line a day or two after. There was no time to acclimatize them to war conditions.[18]

Similar difficulties were evident in 56th London Division after it was moved from the Garigliano to the Anzio beachhead. In this case the primary origin of the problems lay, not so much in the trauma experienced by untried battle replacements, as in the wearing down of unrested veterans. In a two-week period between 17 February and 4 March, the division had 1,139 men admitted to medical units on account of sickness. Of these, 366 cases were admitted for physical and mental exhaustion. These figures, if applied on a monthly basis, equate to a sick and exhaustion rate even higher than that of 1st Division (114 per thousand), a rate, according to medical officers, that reflected the 'physical and mental condition of a Division which, after some five months of very hard fighting, was flung without rest or reinforcements into this beach-head'.[19] Cases of desertion were so prevalent at Anzio, that sentences of five years penal servitude were imposed, in place of the standard three years, in an attempt to deter soldiers from illegally removing themselves from combat.[20]

The situation on the River Garigliano in X Corps was little better. By the end of January, 5th and 56th London Divisions had together over 4,000 casualties.[21] The majority of these were in the assault battalions, each suffering around 170 casualties, or about one-third of its strength. When these figures are translated to the level of the rifle platoon (the real front-line effective strength of a division), they amounted to an even more damaging casualty rate of between 40 and 50 per cent.[22] Sickness rates in X Corps were very high, averaging around 74 per thousand per month for the three months between December 1943 and February 1944 (see Figure 9.2 for context).[23] The monthly battle exhaustion rate in X Corps alone, for January 1944, came to 8.1 per thousand.[24] On multiple levels, it appeared that the British and Commonwealth formations in Italy were physically and psychologically struggling to cope. When the lack of clear agreed objectives was added to the mix, it is hardly surprising that little drive had been demonstrated in the first major attempt to break through the 'Gustav Line' at Cassino.

The Second Battle of Cassino

The failure at Anzio put considerable pressure on Fifth Army. With US VI Corps trapped behind enemy lines, another attempt at breaking through at Cassino was initiated. During the first half of February, American troops had advanced to within 1,500 yards of the monastery atop Monte Cassino. Signals intelligence suggested that the German defences were beginning to show signs of strain and that their situation was desperate.[25] Fifth Army's troops were, however, also exhausted. As a consequence, Alexander decided to send some of Eighth Army's most experienced divisions to support Clark and Fifth Army, initially 2nd New Zealand and the mountain-trained and experienced 4th Indian, which had arrived from North Africa, and later 78th Division (together forming the New Zealand Corps under Freyberg). The Second and Third Battles of Cassino were not to be Alexander's or Clark's but Freyberg's.[26]

Freyberg did not waste time in coming up with a new plan. For the capture of Cassino, Operation 'Avenger', he envisaged 4th Indian Division storming Monte Cassino and 2nd New Zealand Division attacking across the Rapido River into Cassino town from the south-east. The Indians, once they had taken the peak of Monte Cassino, would descend from the west to complete a pincer on the town itself.[27] This would allow the Allies to exploit Highway 6 and break into the Liri Valley. The plan was not without controversy. Major-General Sir Francis Tuker, the commander of 4th Indian Division, was adamant that it was impossible to capture Monte Cassino unless an attack was preceded by the complete destruction of the abbey which was perched atop the imposing mountain. Agreement had been reached with the Vatican that neither side would use the abbey for military purposes, an agreement which by all accounts the Germans observed.[28] Tuker was highly sceptical of such assurances and firmly believed that the enemy were taking advantage of the commanding and apparently invulnerable abbey building. He communicated his concerns firmly to Freyberg:

> To go direct for Monastery Hill now without 'softening it' properly is only to hit one's head straight against the hardest part of the whole enemy position and to risk the failure of the whole operation.[29]

Freyberg passed these concerns on to Clark, who, in turn, passed them on to the Commander-in-Chief. Alexander's position was that he would consent to the bombing of the abbey if Freyberg believed that its destruction was 'a military necessity'. Freyberg was certain that it was. As Fraser has argued:

> Nobody should underestimate the influence of the monastery on the morale of our own troops, none of whom could believe that its brooding presence was of no military significance, that it did not hide enemy observers at the least. And the beliefs of soldiers, even if mistaken, are military realities if the soldiers are to be required to attack and to die.[30]

The bombing went ahead on 15 February. The monastery was shattered into ruins, but the impact of this demonstration of Allied air power was substantially lost as 4th Indian Division had not been informed that the timing of the raid had been brought forward to take advantage of a brief period of good weather. By the time the attack commenced, it was too late; the Germans had occupied the still very substantial ruins of the monastery and turned them into a major strongpoint.[31] In spite of the weight of the bombardment, the enemy, according to intelligence summaries, showed 'no sign of diminished will to resist'.[32] The whole operation was a costly failure.[33]

The 2nd New Zealand Division fared little better in its attack on Cassino town. Two companies of Maori crossed the Rapido on bridges and causeways repaired by engineers. They fought their way as far as the town's railway station but the engineers failed to complete the last of several bridges to enable tanks to follow up. Thousands of rounds of smoke shell concealed the engineer's work from the German observers on the mountain but it was 'to no avail ... A serious lack of drive ... amongst the engineers, who admittedly came under heavy fire, had caused the bridging operation to be abandoned.' In the late afternoon the survivors in the station were attacked by a few tanks. Their anti-tank ammunition exhausted, they withdrew.[34]

The Third Battle of Cassino

Attention now turned to a third attempt at Cassino, Operation 'Dickens' (so named because someone recalled that Charles Dickens had once visited Monte Cassino). This time, the main offensive effort would

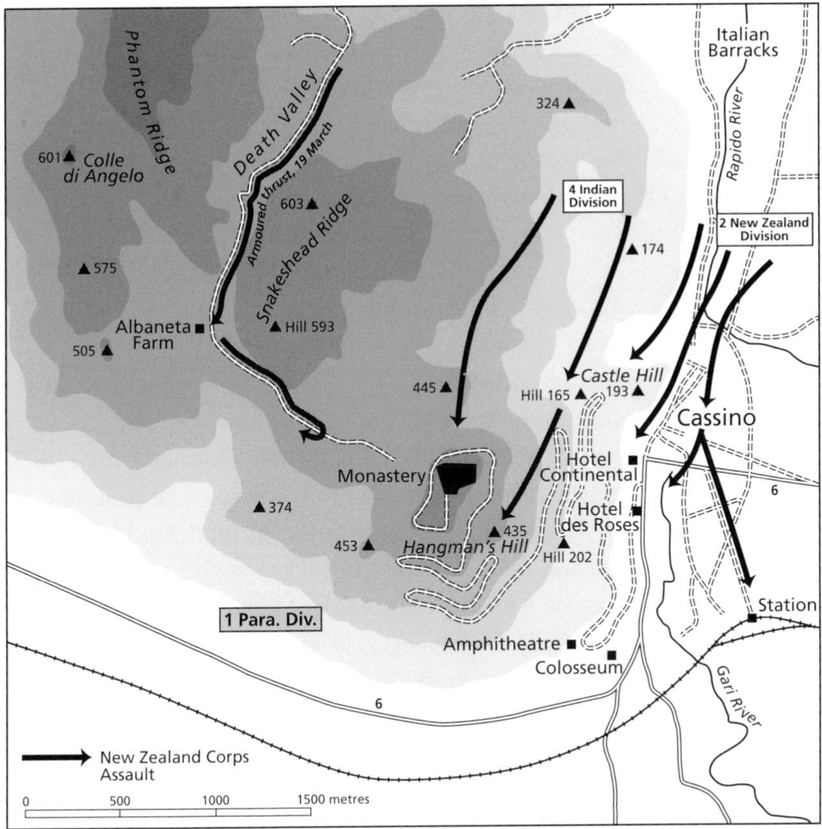

Map 11.2 The Third Battle of Cassino, March 1944

be launched through the town itself. The 2nd New Zealand Division would capture Cassino and Castle Hill (Point 193), a height above the town that Freyberg stressed was 'fundamental to success'. The 4th Indian Division would then use Point 193 as a firm base from which to attack Hangman's Hill and then move on to the monastery. With the Indian assault to be supported by a small group of tanks specially assembled to attack the monastery from the west and create 'chaos', it was hoped that the conditions would be set for the long-awaited break-out up the Liri Valley (see Map 11.2).[35]

Major-General Alexander Galloway, in temporary command of 4th Indian Division (Tuker had become ill), stressed the extent to which the success of the division was dependent on the performance of the New Zealanders. Unless 2nd New Zealander Division could protect its left flank from 'fatal enfilade' by clearing Cassino town, its job would be 'almost impossible'.[36] All told, the New Zealand Corps was putting five battalions into the initial attack (three Indian and two New Zealand), a total of 3,000 troops. They estimated that the Germans had about 1,000 troops in the 'sector of attack', so the New Zealanders, British and Indians of the two divisions would have a 3:1 advantage in men, the ratio deemed necessary by Alexander to have 'a reasonable chance of effectively penetrating organized defences in Italian terrain'.[37] The New Zealand Corps would also have an advantage of about 6:1 or 7:1 in terms of tanks.[38]

Freyberg had intended to launch his second attack on Cassino almost as soon as the first had failed. With US VI Corps still in danger at Anzio, it appeared that he had little choice. Alexander, however, laid down two conditions for the renewed assault: it had to be preceded by three good days of weather to ensure that the ground could properly accommodate tanks; and there had to be good visibility on the day of the attack, to ensure that the Allied Air Forces could play a full role. Bearing these restrictions in mind, the earliest day the attack could go in was 24 February. The weather broke on 23 February and the troops were forced to endure a three-week wait in conditions not conducive to the maintenance of morale.[39]

The battle eventually commenced on 15 March. The assault was preceded by a massive aerial blitz; 514 aircraft dropped 1,140 tons of bombs on the town.[40] Some 900 pieces of artillery added their fire in a prolonged barrage[41] that allocated 4 or 5 tons of explosive for every German defender.[42] The bombardment was heavier than the one preceding the attack at El Alamein.[43] At first, the assault met little opposition and casualties were light. Prisoners taken were stunned by the sheer weight of Allied firepower. However, in the crater-strewn rubble of what was left of Cassino (see Illustration 11.1), it proved 'impossible to keep control' of the advance and progress slowed.[44] There had been 'a disgraceful delay over bringing the 24th and 26th [New Zealand] Battalions into the fight':

> A private soldier of the 26th recalled that he had been told that the tanks would lead the way for his second wave, but when the tanks were halted by debris on the outskirts of the town, instead of pushing on alone they hung about waiting for something to happen.[45]

When 4th Indian Division moved forward, Cassino town had not been cleared, resulting in more delays and a 'loss of cohesion'.[46] Partly as a consequence of these difficulties, in addition to signal failures and 'a lack of enterprise', 5th Indian Brigade failed to reach Point 193 before midnight on the first day; it had been due to arrive at dusk, around 1800hrs. The speed and initiative necessary to exploit the suppressive impact of the heavy bombardment had been sorely lacking.[47]

There can be little doubt that German opposition had been fierce. The New Zealand Corps intelligence summaries noted that the paratroopers had 'continued to resist with their characteristic and fanatical tenacity in houses turned into strongpoints'.[48] The force-to-force ratios, were, however, massively in favour of the British and Commonwealth forces. By the time of the attack, it is estimated that there were only about 300 German paratroopers occupying positions in the town, and about half of these had become casualties in the bombardment or were buried under the rubble. This meant that although the attacking units were canalised by the ground during the assault, they broadly had a numerical advantage of 8:1 over the German defenders.[49]

Over the subsequent days, slow but sustained pressure was exerted as the New Zealand Corps looked to exploit its numerical advantage. These efforts were of little avail; casualties, which were extremely low (only 130 men and 12 tanks by the close of 17 March), did not suggest that many risks were being taken or that excessive drive was being exhibited.[50] Even where more imagination was in evidence, the British and Commonwealth forces made little progress. The armoured assault on 19 March, of over thirty tanks, along Snakehead Ridge to the west of the Cassino Massive became stuck, unable to manoeuvre on the narrow trail. With insufficient protection provided 'by lagging infantry', it was forced to withdraw.[51]

The cumulative effect of the assault, was, however, beginning to tell. Intelligence summaries commented that unless the Germans could 'produce more substantial reinforcements soon Hitler's "last man, last round" orders' were likely to be 'literally fulfilled'.[52] Reinforcements did arrive, mostly from the 15th Panzergrenadier Division. But these men, according to the intelligence summaries, showed 'less anxiety to die for the Fuehrer than the parachutists'. As a result, 'fairly numerous' prisoners were taken.[53] By 20 March, the fifth day of 'Dickens', the heavy casualties sustained in counter-attacks, especially on Point 193, began to 'temper' the German 'ardour'. Enemy POWs were beginning to take a more 'pessimistic view of the situation' as their strong points were gradually reduced one by one by the Commonwealth infantry.[54]

The decisive phase of the battle was at hand. The intelligence officers in the New Zealand Corps believed that when the attack had started, the Germans had intended to give up Cassino and withdraw to a defensive line, the 'Adolf Hitler Line', some 10 miles to the west. 'When they saw their defence was being more successful than they first expected', they decided to change plans and 'to hold their ground and try to restore the situation by local counterattack'; 1st Paratroop Division was 'hanging on in the hope that we [the New Zealanders] will give up first'. By 21 March, it was estimated that the paratroopers were 'certainly now very reduced in strength'. The intelligence summaries noted that they 'must be getting tired':

> They cannot be expected to continue indefinitely if we go on developing the strength of our ... available divisions against them in their present state. It is true that they are now receiving more arty and mortar support than before, but this can only be very small compared with our large resources both in guns and ammunition. In conclusion, therefore, I feel that assuming we continue to attack with the superior resources which are available to us, the German 1 Para Div is facing the alternative of destruction or withdrawal.[55]

That this scenario did not play out as and when expected raises a number of questions. Those reinforcements that were sent to 1st Parachute Division were typically employed in quiet sectors rather than on the front line.[56] They had, at least according to the intelligence summaries, not added substantially to the ferocity of the defence. Alexander had left Freyberg in no doubt that the operation had to succeed.[57] Did the New Zealand Corps fold at the crucial moment?

Brooke certainly thought so; he noted in his diary on 31 March that:

> In the afternoon I received an interesting letter from Wilson and Alexander. Evidently, just as I suspected, Freyberg has been fighting with a casualty conscious mind. He has been sparing the NZ infantry and hoping to accomplish results by use of heavy bombers ... without using too much infantry.

> As a result he has failed. In the evening saw Kenneth Anderson just back from Italy, who was very interesting and confirmed all my impression as to Freyberg's weakness.[58]

The scale of air support had, indeed, been immense. Over the ten days of the battle, the Allies launched 2,629 sorties dropping 2,362 tons of bombs. A further 194 sorties dropped supplies for Allied troops. By comparison, the Germans launched 214 sorties, barely 8 per cent of the Allied total.[59]

Brooke wrote after the war intimating that he had been a bit harsh on the New Zealand commander. He accepted that the need for casualty avoidance had been 'frequently impressed' on Freyberg by the New Zealand Government. But, he noted, 'it is hard in war to make omelettes without breaking eggs, and it is often in trying to do so that we break most eggs!'[60] To an extent, he was right. Both of the New Zealand Corps' Cassino battles had been fought in the manner decided 'in view of the paucity of our infantry'.[61] From that perspective, the 'basic cause' of the stalled attack was either a 'lack of troops' at the decisive point, as a number of historians have intimated,[62] or an unwillingness to push those troops that were available to the required extent.

It is difficult to reconcile the 'lack of troops' explanation with the facts as they are known. When compared to broadly similar assaults, the force-to-force ratios at Third Cassino were sufficiently in New Zealand Corps' favour to facilitate success. The 6,000 men of 1st Parachute Division were faced by the two assault divisions of the New Zealand Corps, which amounted to about 35,000 troops.[63] Freyberg estimated that the attacking infantry, about 3,000 men in the initial assault, would have a 3:1 advantage[64] and that 4th Indian Division would have a 4:1 advantage in their assault from Point 193.[65] It is conceivable, if no more than 150 Germans in Cassino town survived the bombardment preceding the attack, that these ratios could have been significantly higher, even 8:1. When taking into account force-to-force ratios on the Eastern Front, which were often much lower than this, and even acknowledging the extraordinarily difficult terrain, which had the effect of 'canalising' troops and reducing the number of viable axes of advance, it would appear that the relative numbers of troops engaged at Third Cassino could not, of themselves, explain the failure of the New Zealand Corps.[66]

This raises again the question of morale and the failure to remobilise the British and Commonwealth troops in Italy. The importance of determined leading had been drilled into Eighth Army since the arrival of Montgomery. At a conference held at Divisional HQ on 15 February, the necessity for speed to 'gatecrash the pillbox line before they [the enemy] can man it' was stressed. It was fully understood that risks might have to be taken and that there was 'going to be real difficulty in exercising command'. Much would depend on the determination and ingenuity of junior leaders and their men. Freyberg was clear, 'I will give tasks to Comds who will go out and do them.'[67] On 2 March, he stressed that the battle was 'going to be a slogging match. There is no question about it, it is an all-out go.' He tried to put the battle in context:

> I want you to consider what you would feel like if you were to be attacked by 450 heavy bombers, 480 guns of all classes and 3,000 men and 400 tanks. You would take a poor view of it so don't enlarge on your difficulties. The enemy's difficulties are much greater.[68]

By February 1944, however, after three and a half months of winter fighting, all the armies in Italy 'were suffering to a lessor or greater degree from disillusionment and lack of enthusiasm. Among the Allies, desertion was becoming a problem. Men were sometimes charged with it, although cowardice in the face of the enemy was the crime, because it was less difficult to prove in law but bore the same penalty.'[69]

Nowhere were these problems more apparent than in 2nd New Zealand Division. Morale had been excellent on embarkation for Italy from the Middle East; the censors noted that 'in many cases the spirit on show was exuberant to a degree that is remarkable'.[70] By Christmas 1943, morale had deteriorated. The censors remarked that it was 'good, but not as spontaneously good as it has been':

> The mud is inclined to get under the skin. Xmas conjured up wistful and longing thoughts of home, and many (about 5%) who were feeling somewhat tired became very dispirited and 'fed up with the whole darned thing'.[71]

By the start of January, there were 'definite signs of war weariness and homesickness in almost 25% of the letters'. This was especially evident in the mail of the Maori battalion, 'which was feeling its losses and casualties rather keenly'.[72] By mid-January, 50 per cent of letters had a 'homesick' tone, although only 4 per cent were described as 'war weary'. Of note, the censors compared the 'war weariness' being experienced to that which had overtaken the division in the static positions at El Alamein in July 1942. Ten per cent of letters showed a distinct sense of dissatisfaction at the unequal sacrifices being made in the war effort. A sergeant wrote:

> It's foolish to try and blink the fact that men over here are becoming more and more aware of the extent to which they have been 'carrying the baby' for years for lots of people at home who have every reason to hope the war will never end.[73]

By the beginning of the Second Battle of Cassino, the censors noted that there had been a 'decided drop in morale, and letters are distinctly gloomy'. The prevailing conditions had 'made the men "furlough conscious"' with 10 per cent of letters referring to the mishandling of the scheme in New Zealand and the thousands of 'essentials' that could be used to replace them on the front line.[74] The following week, an 'alleged announcement' that no further furlough schemes were being considered for overseas personnel attracted much comment 'agin [against] the Gov't'[75] and the phrase that the people in New Zealand 'don't know that there is a war on' became increasingly common.[76] In the run-up to the Third Battle of Cassino, the censors again noted 'a slight drop [in morale] over the whole of the Div'[77] and by the outbreak of the battle, on 15 March, it was noted that morale was only 'fairly good'.[78]

Undoubtedly, the furlough scheme and the news of the mutiny was having a 'psychological effect' on those remaining in the Mediterranean.[79] 'We have to face the fact', said Freyberg in December 1943, 'that once [a] man knows his turn is coming he ceases to be such a good soldier.'[80] When the issue of furlough was first raised with the command in the Middle East, Freyberg had been adamant that the matter 'should not be mentioned'.[81] 'The effect of this getting about with further operations pending would be devastating and I feel it is a mistake to discuss it in the Division until we are freed from an operational role'.[82] Montgomery, when considering a similar scheme for British troops, pointed out that 'we are playing with a very highly explosive material when dealing with the question of formations and personnel returning to UK'.[83]

The departure of the furlough men from the Middle East left many of those remaining wondering why they should not go too.[84] The censors confirmed that 'the question of home leave' continued to 'exercise the minds' and that many were 'becoming restless at delay in continuing the scheme'. This applied to men, not only of the 4th Reinforcement (who were next in line for leave), but to men who had travelled overseas in the 5th, 6th and 7th Reinforcements and who would be aware that their turn for leave could not be too far away.[85] The censorship report for the week ending 12 December 1943 noted that:

> The extension of the Ruapehu scheme personnel's leave to four months and the consequent delay in the departure of the Wakatipu scheme personnel has been very poorly regarded by remaining Echelon men and the reinforcements who are possible 'eligibles' in the near future.[86]

The return of the 3rd New Zealand Division from the Pacific in February only made matters worse, as these men had experienced, in the minds of the 2NZEF, only a fraction of the hardships that they themselves had endured.[87] Furthermore, it was difficult to hide from the troops that there was a mutiny developing in New Zealand that directly impacted on when they might return home. Notwithstanding widespread censorship, it is clear that the men became aware of the events unfolding in New Zealand in the first few months of 1944. As a result, there was a real fear that the mutiny could weaken 'authority and control and risk spreading disobedience'.[88] Letters from home, the *NZEF Times* and first-hand contact with those that had returned to the Middle East, who, the censors noted, were 'often critical of the "peacetime atmosphere and the smug complacency"' to be found in New Zealand, had a detrimental effect on the troops' morale. Such news created 'discontent and bitterness', and left many questioning the 'sincerity of the Government'. Some started to believe that the furlough scheme had only been a 'vote catcher'[89] and the oft-mentioned fact that '35,000 men in essential services' were safe at home making plenty of money became 'rather a blister' for the men in Italy, as it had been for the furlough men in New Zealand.[90]

The Furlough Mutiny moreover had the effect of depriving 2NZEF of many of its veteran troops just as the division was to face one of its greatest challenges. In September 1943, Stevens, much like

Illustration 11.1 New Zealand soldiers and tanks in the ruins of Cassino, April 1944. The Furlough Mutiny undoubtedly had a 'psychological effect' on those remaining in the Mediterranean; it also deprived 2NZEF of many of its veteran troops just as the division was about to face one of its greatest challenges.

Freyberg, had made it clear to the New Zealand War Cabinet that 'there was a maximum' number of men that could be removed from the division for furlough 'beyond which it would NOT repeat NOT be safe to go'. He had stated that the return of 3,500 'old hands' to the Middle East would be 'adequate provided the total draft reached 5,000' and arrived by mid-December.[91] By the end of November, Stevens had returned to the Middle East and reported the deteriorating situation in New Zealand to Freyberg. The General Officer Commanding (GOC) warned that the delays would 'have a serious effect upon the fighting efficiency of the Division during the ensuing year'.[92] Freyberg had expected about 60 per cent of the

Ruapehu and Wakatipu drafts to return to the Middle East. In the end, only 13 per cent of the Ruapehu and 18 per cent of the Wakatipu drafts returned and the total embarked from New Zealand in the first section of the 11th Reinforcement in mid-January 1944, about 3,400, was well below the 5,000 that had been envisaged to arrive in December. The second section of the 11th Reinforcement would not sail until the end of March.[93] The New Zealand Division, therefore, had a shortage of reinforcements for the coming campaign season and would have a 'very high' proportion of new personnel, a fact that was not lost on the troops.[94]

Freyberg had been concerned that the shortage of experienced reinforcements might require him to send partly trained men into battle, if casualties during the early months of campaigning in Italy were 'heavy', which, in the event, they were.[95] By December 1943, it was clear that not only would the division have to fight with inadequately trained personnel, but it would have 'to fight below W[ar] E[stablishmet]' until the Wakatipu draft returned from New Zealand.[96] What is more, training establishments, such as the Middle East Officer Training Corps Unit (OCTU) at Acre, were 'singled out for exceptionally bitter denunciation' due to 'poor food, the bug-ridden beds, and the inefficient instruction'.[97]

The Director of Medical Services (DMS) 2NZEF commented during the desperate fighting around Cassino in March 1944:

> I have referred on previous occasions to the factors which influence nervous breakdown in our troops, and my reason for again touching on the subject is the high incidence of such cases at the present time. The majority appear to be coming ... from recent arrivals.

Apart from the exclusion of those already disposed to psychological breakdown through better selection procedures in New Zealand, the DMS pointed out that:

> The most important factor in prevention, or in the reduction of the incidence of these breakdowns is the inculcation of sound discipline, which can only derive from proper military training. Medical officers dealing with these cases frequently remark – and more so in recent months – upon the almost complete lack of training many of these men appear to have had in New

> Zealand. Some of these 'breakdowns' assert that they have attended practically no parades, have done no rifle drill, have never seen a Lewis gun, have not even done a route march ... When such men join a line battalion it is only natural that they should develop acute feelings of inadequacy and inferiority, especially in times of stress. These feelings breed various phobias, anxieties, insomnia and depression, and the first step towards functional nervous disorder is well established before the man has any chance of adjusting himself to his completely new and strange environment. I feel that these facts should be recorded. We frequently hear it said that the RMO [Regimental Medical Officer] or the Company Officer is largely to blame. In these cases the blame would appear to lie in the scheme which makes it possible for such men to be sent overseas.[98]

In many ways 'the sense of purpose that had been universal ... in the first months in Italy had fast eroded around the Cassino battles ... Cassino proved to be a strain on the morale of all ranks.'[99] Much of this failure revolved around the Furlough Mutiny and the inability of the New Zealand Government to remobilise its people and the Army for war. As a consequence, veterans felt decidedly let down and reinforcements, pushed prematurely into battle due to the shortage of manpower caused by the mutiny, suffered from feelings of inferiority due to a lack of proper battle preparation; morale and combat effectiveness suffered accordingly. More immediate problems did not help either: the three-week delay before launching 'Dickens' 'unavoidably' affected the 'spirits of the troops' and a 'feeling of physical and mental staleness spread'. As the Official Historian remarked, 'soldiers can key themselves up to begin a great battle at zero hour on a fixed date, and once engaged they can meet the various shocks of battle with astonishing resilience and resolution. But soldiers who can renew their resolves daily to order are supermen and scarce.' The loss of the acting divisional commander, General Kippenberger, who had served in all the division's battles since Greece, on 2 March did not help matters either.[100]

A quantitative assessment of the morale of 2NZEF supports the contention that there were problems during this period. The sickness rate, 'a good barometer' of morale, rose in the lead up to 'Dickens'.[101] Between embarkation for Italy and the Cassino battles in March 1944,

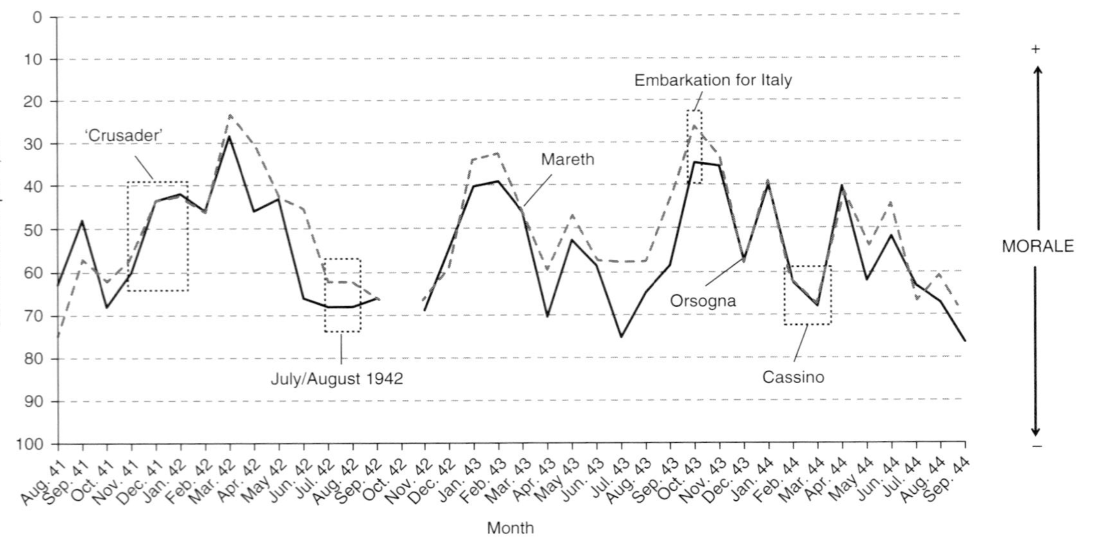

Figure 11.1 Monthly sick admissions per thousand, 2NZEF 1941–5

* The figures for autumn 1942 and from autumn 1944 have been left out as they were skewed due to the only two large epidemics (those of infectious jaundice and hepatitis) to affect 2NZEF (ANZ WAII/1/DA21.3/1/24 Report of Medical Services 2 NZ Div., Oct. 1942, p. 3).

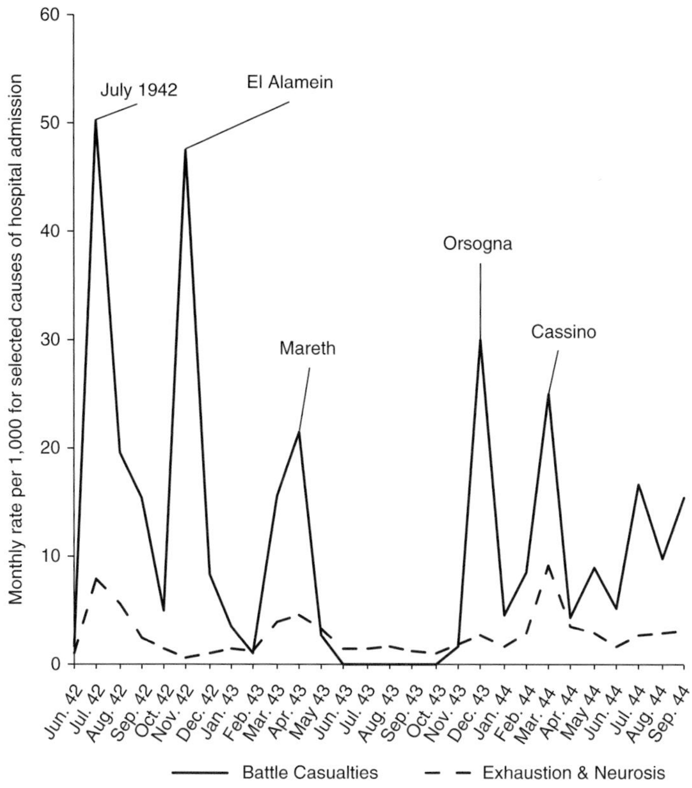

Figure 11.2 2NZEF exhaustion and neurosis casualties in relation to battle casualties, June 1942–September 1944

the sickness rate for other ranks increased by 96 per cent, that for officers by a remarkable 162 per cent (see Figure 11.1).[102]

The battle exhaustion rate was also alarming. Whereas cases of battle exhaustion and neurosis had accounted for 9 per cent of casualties in the heavy fighting around Orsogna in December 1943, they amounted to 34 per cent of casualties in February and 36 per cent in March 1944 (see Figure 11.2), worse than during the morale crisis in the desert in the summer of 1942.[103]

The desertion rate had also increased dramatically, although it compared favourably with some of the British formations in Italy (see Figure 11.3).[104] In the second half of 1942 in North Africa, desertions from New Zealand units had averaged about three per month. In Tunisia they averaged about one per month. In Italy, the average rose to eight per month.[105] Many of these men were old

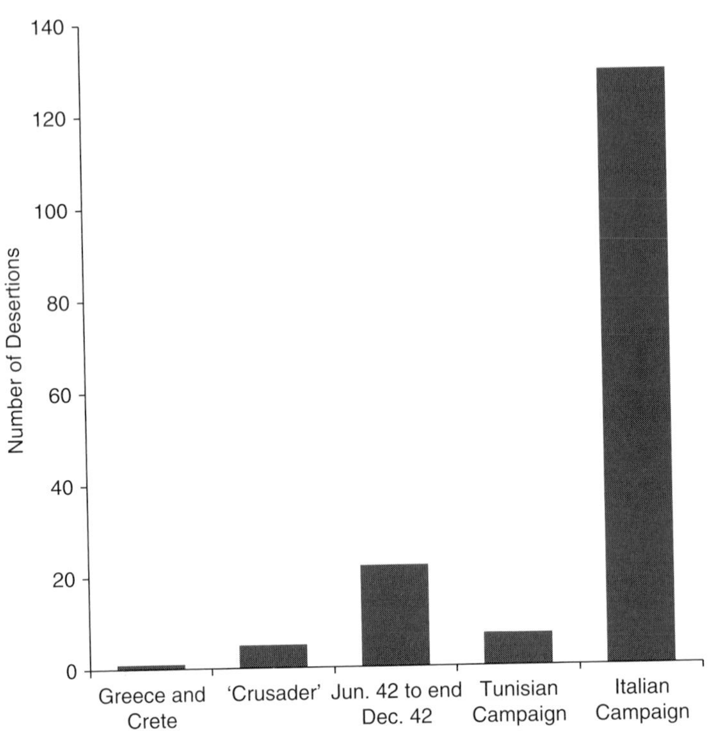

Figure 11.3 2NZEF desertion statistics, 1941–5

timers who had increasingly had their fill of the horrors and risks of battle.[106]

Freyberg, who was always 'sensitive to the spirit – "the feel" – in his division',[107] accepted that by 1944 the division was a 'tired force as compared with previous years' and could not 'easily absorb indifferent personnel'.[108] In June, a few months after the battle, he wrote to the New Zealand Prime Minister that 'after careful consideration' there were 'strong reasons why 2NZEF should be withdrawn to New Zealand'. While he was certain that the division 'could carry on and add fresh honours to its record', there were 'various factors affecting the efficiency of the Force' which had to be taken into consideration:

> The inevitable effect of fierce fighting over a long period, on even the best troops in the world, is becoming apparent. There is no doubt in my mind that the high-water-mark of our battleworthiness was reached at Sidi Rezegh and Belhamed in November 1941.

> In that campaign and in the other costly Western Desert battles which followed many of our best men became casualties, and gradually the keen fighting edge of the Force was blunted. For a period the gradual reduction in offensive spirit was offset by the increased efficiency of the Divisional machine and the ever increasing battle experience of our commanders. Time has gone on. Another long campaign in Italy has followed. I know the great stress of battle which large numbers of men have been through and we cannot disregard its effect, especially on battleweary leaders. Signs are not lacking now that many of the old hands require a prolonged rest ... I have come to the conclusion that the time may well be opportune for the complete withdrawal of 2NZEF.[109]

As far as the men were concerned, 2nd New Zealand Division 'was like a family business' where everybody was a 'shareholder'. 'If there was a characteristic that Freyberg's men had in marked degree it was sensitivity to unfair treatment and unwillingness to put up with it.'[110] As mostly volunteer participants in a war on which the fate of the Western World rested, the men felt distinctly badly treated, and, in particular, they believed that they had been let down by the home front. In a citizen army, made up of a high proportion of volunteers, this mattered very much.

The question of morale had certainly played a key role in the Cassino fighting. Second and Third Cassino had been, according to Freyberg, 'one of the hardest sectors' that he had fought in during the war. In many ways, it was 'like fighting on the western front in the last war' and the experience had taken its toll; casualties at Second Cassino came to 816, while Third Cassino eventually cost 2,106 losses.[111] It was apparent to Freyberg that it was unlikely that the 2NZEF would be withdrawn to New Zealand. In this context, he realised that:

> We have got to a stage which was reached in the last war where by encouragement and discipline people have got to be made to fight ... we have to fight now with some second-class material. The Germans are doing it and we have to harden our hearts and make as many fight as possible.[112]

Something was going to have to change if the British and Commonwealth Forces were going to last the distance in Italy.

The Fourth Battle of Cassino (Operation 'Diadem')

Third Cassino had unquestionably been a disappointment. Not only had the Allies failed to out-think or outwit their opponents, but, it would appear, they had also been outfought. The New Zealand Corps, in Freyberg's estimation, had failed.[113] He wrote to Clark, his army commander, on 3 April that he was 'sorry that we did not accomplish our mission, capture Cassino and the Monastery'.[114] A week later, he also apologised to Leese for handing over to XIII Corps such a difficult position; he wished it 'had been possible to make a bigger contribution'.[115] The American soldiers magazine *Stars and Stripes* certainly felt that the battle had been a 'failure' and that 'no objective observer could deny that the Germans had scored a defensive success'.[116] The troops thought so too, the censors noting that the battle was described as the 'hardest fighting yet experienced' and 'it is felt that the engagement must be regarded as a set-back'. Some wrote 'despondently of the casualties suffered' while others referred to Freyberg as 'the butcher'.[117]

The setback left many men dejected, perhaps unsurprisingly. The censorship summary for British troops for the first half of April noted that there 'was some evidence' that morale was 'not as universally high' as on previous occasions:

> Sarcastic remarks such as: 'if we are not quick we shall be meeting Russian patrols in Italy' have not been infrequent. It is certain that strikes in England have had a very depressing effect, as they are considered to impede the war effort and delay the invasion of Europe.[118]

There were 'definite' and continued 'expressions of war weariness from units of 5th Division' and the casualties in British 1/4 Essex Battalion, 4th Indian Division, had 'told on the morale of the unit', with some talking 'openly of desertion' and others showing 'definite signs of real disinclination to go back into action'. Letters from men in action, or just relieved, revealed 'a sense of frustration due to our apparent inability to dislodge the Germans'. The bitterness of the fighting, 'pure unadulterated hell just now', was stressed by all, while there was 'a tendency' for troops at Anzio 'to criticise those on the Cassino Front for their lack of progress'.[119]

The New Zealanders seemed to take the setback in a strangely detached manner. The censors noted that there was a 'common mood':

> not easy to define, but perhaps best described as a 'don't give a damn' attitude, which seems to have resulted to a large extent from dissatisfaction over affairs in New Zealand and a feeling that people at home are making but little sacrifice of any kind towards the war effort; and also from disappointment on the part of the troops over the lack of Allied progress in Italy. It is as though the Division has come to the conclusion that 'everything is in a mess', so it is no use their having any interest or enthusiasm over anything, except their own purely personal affairs.[120]

The summary for 16 to 30 April noted that British morale appeared to be little better than 'sound' and that the 'lack of forward movement' had 'bred a certain mental restlessness, and an anxious seeking for some indication that the end of the war is not too remote'. There was, as one man put it, 'a terrific homesickness among most of the chaps'. There were 'numerous references by forward troops to the strain of prolonged action, particularly in mail from the Anzio bridgehead', and some criticisms were made of the 'length of time units are sometimes kept in the line'.[121]

In many ways, the old Eighth Army had finally reached the limits of endurance. The men, many of whom had been away from their families for between three and five years, longed for a break. Alexander, who had a 'sixth sense about morale' decided, therefore, to almost completely replace the fighting formations of Eighth Army.[122] Four British and Commonwealth divisions arrived from the Middle East. These were 6th Armoured; 4th Division, which as well as the battle of France had partaken in the final stages of the campaign in Tunisia; 10th Indian, which had been undertaking mountain and combined operations training in Cyprus, Syria and Palestine; and the newly formed 6th South African Armoured Division. Two armoured brigades (9th and 7th Armoured) and one tank brigade (25th) also arrived from the Middle East. These were joined by the Polish Corps (Lieutenant-General Anders), the US IV Corps HQ plus two infantry divisions, and two French infantry divisions.[123] Although the number of British soldiers in Eighth Army remained broadly the same, as formations rotated in and out of theatre, by June, 22,000 Indian troops and 30,000 South Africans had been added to the order of battle.[124] The influx of French and Polish troops was even more significant; by the beginning of the next offensive, the Polish Corps stood at 45,626, while the French Expeditionary Corps, which would fight under the Americans, amounted to 71,827 men.[125]

The new British and Commonwealth and Polish formations would make up the bulk of Eighth Army in the offensive to come. With both his armies exhausted, a fact which 'made it impractical to maintain pressure on both sides of the Apennines', Alexander reasoned that Eighth Army would be better employed in the west, reinforcing Fifth Army on the march towards Rome.[126] As a result, nearly the entire Eighth Army was secretly transferred from the Adriatic side of the Italian peninsula across to join Fifth Army in the West. Leese's Army, Alexander decreed, would attack the German front in two places: in the Liri Valley below Cassino with the almost completely fresh XIII Corps (4th British, 8th Indian, 78th and 6th Armoured Divisions) commanded by Lieutenant-General Sydney Kirkman[127] and once more at Cassino with the Polish Corps. It was hoped that once XIII Corps had seized crossings over the Garigliano River, facilitated by the Polish Corps' capture of Monte Cassino, it would open the way for Lieutenant-General 'Tommy' Burns' I Canadian Corps (1st Canadian Infantry Division and 5th Canadian Armoured Division, which had arrived in Italy in December 1943, fresh after its extended period of training in the UK), to drive towards Valmontone. There, it would link up with elements of US Fifth Army, specifically US VI Corps breaking out from the Anzio beachhead, the plan on which 'Shingle' had originally been based. I Canadian Corps would also have the much-reduced South African forces available (in Army Reserve). If successful, Eighth and Fifth Armies would trap the retreating Tenth Army in a German-style battle of annihilation; the capture of Rome would quickly follow.[128]

The core of the new plan, therefore, was to attack the enemy with overwhelming force using almost completely fresh formations. The 2nd New Zealand Division and 4th Indian Divisions, after their ordeal in 'Avenger' and 'Dickens', would remain in reserve as part of X and V Corps respectively, which were tasked with holding Eighth Army's flanks. The 46th North Midland and West Riding Division and 56th London Divisions had already been withdrawn from Italy to rest and refit in the Middle East,[129] while 1st and 5th Divisions, which had suffered so much at Anzio, were allotted only subsidiary roles in the advance to come (Operation 'Diadem').[130]

At a conference on 10 May, Leese outlined the part that the forthcoming offensive would play in the 'three-pronged thrust' from Russia, from Italy, and from North-West Europe, which would ultimately wear down the German reserves and lead to the collapse of the Nazis. He warned against expecting 'a quick battle, as they were bound to have a hard fight'. The Army was better equipped than ever before and this offensive had a 'big advantage over previous shows' as there had been plenty of time to prepare and the weather conditions were such that 'the going was 100%'.[131] He wrote to the troops, 'I say to you all – Into action, with the light of battle in your eyes. Let every man do his duty throughout the fight and the Day is ours!'[132] Alexander's message to the men frankly recognised the difficulties and disappointments that had been experienced in the past, but emphasised the role the Italian campaign was playing in a much wider Allied strategy:

> Perhaps you are disappointed that we have not been able to advance faster and farther ... The results of the past months may not appear spectacular, but you have drawn into Italy and mauled many of the enemy's best divisions which he badly needed to stem the advance of the Russian Armies in the East ... The Allied armed forces are now assembling for the final battles on sea, on land, and in the air to crush the enemy once and for all. From the East and the West, from the North and the South, blows are about to fall which will result in the final destruction of the Nazis and bring freedom once again to Europe, and hasten peace for us all. To us in Italy, has been given the honour to strike the first blow.[133]

'Diadem' started at 2300hrs on 11 May with a thunderous barrage by 1,700 field and medium guns, nearly double the number employed at El Alamein.[134] A clever deception plan confused the Germans to such an extent that they were completely caught out by the timing of the operation; the commanders of Tenth Army and XIV Panzer Corps were both on leave in Germany.[135] Eighth Army alone had 1,121 guns. Opposite them, Tenth Army possessed 351. The ratio of anti-tank guns was 1,055 to 235.[136] Alexander had twenty-five divisions under his command, twelve of which were British and Commonwealth.[137] With the onset of spring, the improvement in the weather had also allowed the Allies to launch as many as 50,000 air sorties, playing havoc with the German lines of communication.[138]

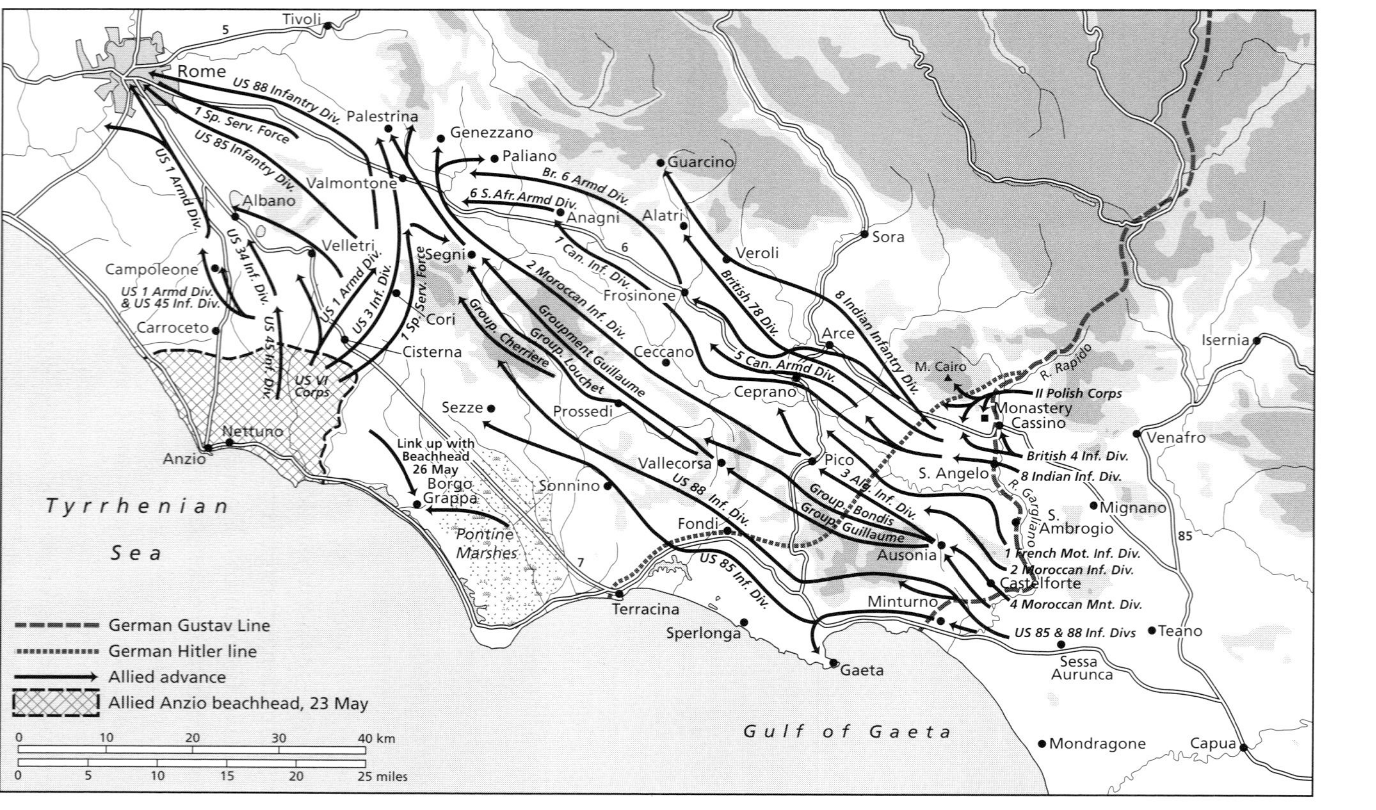

Map 11.3 Operation ‘Diadem’, 11 May–4 June 1944

Facing Eighth and Fifth Armies on the main position was von Vietinghoff's Tenth Army, which had a total of six divisions, while von Mackensen's Fourteenth Army covered Rome and Anzio with a further five. In reserve, Kesselring had another three divisions, one of them Panzer. By 20 May, some German divisions had about the same number of men as an Allied battalion; 'the Germans were, therefore, outnumbered significantly overall and even more at the chosen point of attack'.[139] Whereas Second and Third Cassino had involved effectively a two-division attack in the Cassino sector, 'Diadem' involved three Corps – XIII British, II Polish and I Canadian – a total of six infantry divisions, three independent armoured brigades, two armoured divisions with a third, 6th South African Armoured Division, available in Army Reserve if needed.[140]

During the first five days of the battle, nearly half a million shells were fired in support of XIII Corps' advance alone.[141] By 16 May, Kesselring realised that neither Cassino nor the 'Gustav Line' could be held in face of such a concentrated assault and authorised withdrawal to a fall-back position across the Liri Valley some 10 miles west of Cassino, the 'Hitler Line'. By 18 May, the 'Gustav Line' had fallen and Monte Cassino was finally conquered, by the Poles. When I Canadian Corps was loosed for exploitation, it ran headlong into the 'Hitler Line' and a full-frontal assault was prepared for 23 May. On the same day, Alexander issued orders for Truscott's US VI Corps to break out from Anzio. This was the left pincer of Alexander's encirclement battle. US VI Corps achieved complete tactical surprise and by 25 May had broken through the German defences penning them in around Anzio.[142] The battle, in spite of local setbacks, could hardly have unfolded much better. The Germans were falling back from the 'Gustav' and 'Hitler' lines and were in disarray around Anzio. The Allies had not only outthought and outmanoeuvred the Germans, and finally made effective use of their massive material resources, but it appears they were also now outfighting them.

The decision to 'rotate' Eighth Army had proved vital to a remarkable turnaround in morale that was to prove key to success. At the start of the battle, whereas the censors noted that there were 'inevitable expressions of war-weariness among troops who have had a large share of the fighting', elements recently arrived from North Africa and the Middle East were described as being in 'excellent spirits and eagerly looking forward to action'. A man in the Warwickshire

Yeomanry wrote, 'we have all taken on a new lease of life after the soul-destroying and super expensive Middle East. I am almost sane again with the positive prospect of adventures to come.' 'Similar expressions of high morale were noted in mail from British units in Indian Divisions.'[143] The newly arrived 10th Indian Division, more generally, were 'full of cheerful spirit and adventure and keen to get into action'.[144] Among the Canadians, who had been out of the line for a period of rest and training, morale was 'high'. There was 'an air of great expectancy ... which indicates a spirit of real hope and optimism regarding the coming struggle'.[145] It was among the Poles, however, that morale appeared to be highest. The censors noted 'an excellent fighting spirit, allied with fervent patriotism'; 'all ranks' 'frequently' referred to 'their presence in the line as a very welcome change from inactivity in the Middle East':

> Despite the strong anti-Russian sentiments constantly expressed, these views do not appear to have resulted in any weakening of loyalty to the Allies' present cause, nor to have lessened the writers' eagerness to aid in the defeat of Germany as the first stage in the liberation of Poland. Hatred of Nazi Germany is often very evident.[146]

'Russian victories, our heavy raids on Germany, and better weather' had all 'heartened the troops'. The 'opening of the 2nd Front' was also 'anticipated with the utmost optimism, the general feeling being:- "As soon as the big show starts everybody will go to it with 100% more life. Morale could never be higher".'[147] The Government had recently decided to increase pay and family allowances and news of this decision also had a powerful effect; comments on the subject in the men's mail were 'innumerable'.[148]

The communications from Alexander and Leese to the troops before 'Diadem' had a most heartening effect too; many troops indicated that their messages had been inspiring and left them feeling 'proud' to be British. Others appreciated the fact that they were taken into confidence regarding the plan of attack. Leese, especially, was beginning to have a Montgomery-like hold on the troops. One man at HQ Eighth Army noted that 'I think his personal influence ... is one of the greatest possible battle-winning factors.'[149]

By the start of the offensive, the censorship summaries noted that there was 'abundant evidence' that in the 'majority of units morale' was 'excellent and the fighting spirit of the troops has never been better'.[150] All ranks were clearly in 'excellent fighting form' and there was 'an invincible determination to carry on to victory'.[151] A key characteristic of this remarkable surge in the soldiers' will to engage in combat was what the censors referred to as a 'noticeable trend', the 'increasingly aggressive spirit among fighting troops'. The summary for the first half of June gave the example of an NCO who wrote:

> Damn the Jerries, they have kept me away from my dear ones too long, and I will never forget it. I will have no pity whatsoever for any of them – they have caused a lot of sorrow and tears and they ought to be taught a lesson that they will forever remember.

A private added:

> He is running now, a damn sight faster than we ever ran in France in 1940, and we're the chaps that really realise that, and have the satisfaction of seeing the sods go through hell, like we had to in France. Roads littered with transport of every kind, tanks, equipment, and the very many cold Bosche that could no longer run lying over the countryside. It may sound pretty horrible to you, but to me it is a tonic of the best type.[152]

Sickness and battle exhaustion rates confirm that morale improved during these critical battles. The weekly sickness rate for Eighth Army, which had reached 14.3 per thousand the week ending 15 April, dropped to 13.0 per thousand by the weekend ending 13 May, the start of the operation, and fell again to 10.8 per thousand by the end of the operation (a 24 per cent drop from April to June).[153] The weekly sickness rate for I Canadian Corps, which had peaked at 21.9 per thousand the week ending 25 December 1943, had dropped due to a prolonged period of rest and retraining to 12.5 per thousand by the start of 'Diadem'. It declined again to 8.8 per thousand by the fall of Rome (see Figure 11.4).[154]

Morale in the British and Commonwealth forces had improved markedly. As a consequence, there would be no let up this time in the pressure being mounted on the German defenders on the Cassino front. By comparison, at least according to the British and Commonwealth soldiers, the resolve of the German defenders had deteriorated. Whereas, the censorship summaries during Third Cassino had been

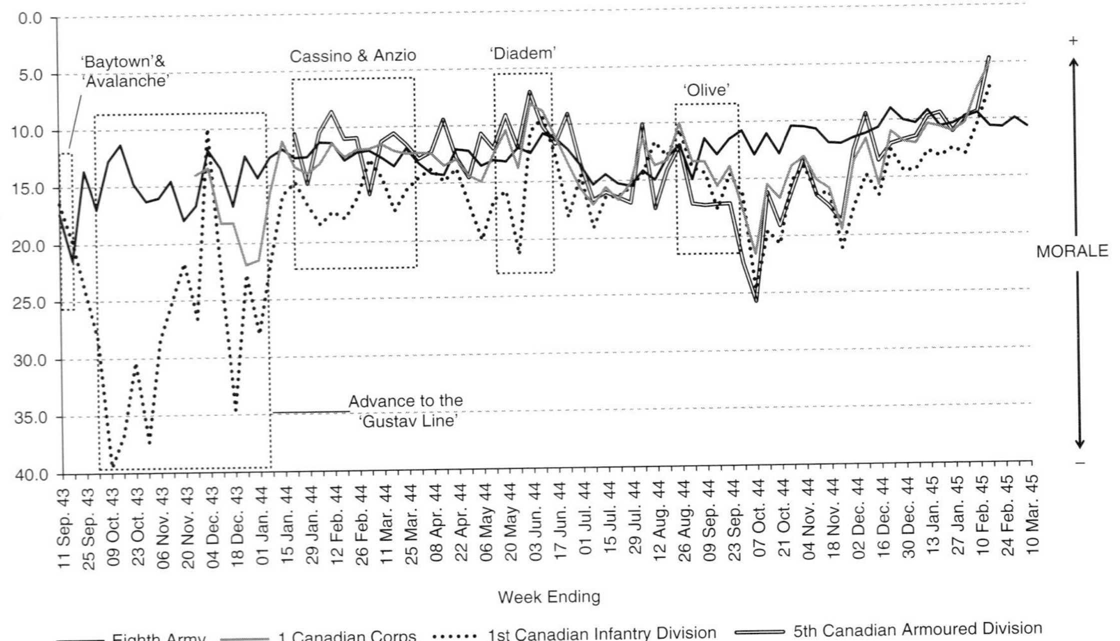

Figure 11.4 Weekly sick admissions per thousand, Eighth Army, I Canadian Corps, 1st Canadian Division and 5th Canadian Armoured Division, 1943–5

* Canadian figures for July–Dec. 1944 impacted by an outbreak of Infective Hepatitis (see LAC Vol. 12559).

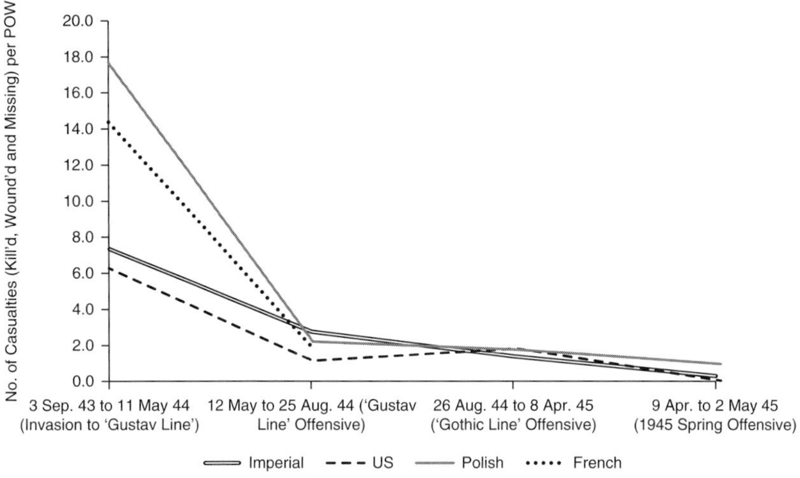

Figure 11.5 Cost of a prisoner, Italian campaign, September 1943–May 1945

full of references to the 'fanaticism' of the defenders on the 'Gustav Line',[155] an NCO writing that he had 'come to the conclusion that either he [the German] has a ton of guts or he is bloody well mad',[156] by 'Diadem', the censors were noting that there were 'indications that he is not as good as he was . . . The attitude of German prisoners is stated to be one of resignation . . . Other writers maintained that the Germans were cracking and their morale not too good, particularly the younger ones who seemed very disillusioned.'[157] The summary for the first half of June noted that 'the demoralised condition of German prisoners' was the 'subject of frequent comment'.[158] This appears to be borne out by a dramatic change in the German soldiers' performance, as measured by how many casualties the Allies suffered for each German POW captured. Whereas the 'cost' of a prisoner had been as high as 7.3 British and Commonwealth casualties per POW during the advance to the 'Gustav Line' and the first three battles of Cassino, between May and August 1944 this figure dropped to 2.7 casualties per POW, a reduction of 63 per cent (see Figure 11.5).[159]

An opportunity for decisive success in Italy was clearly, in these circumstances, on the cards. However, the effects of the setbacks in February and March now played out in another way, as the increasingly strained relations at the top of the Allied command chain intervened. Clark ignored clear orders for US VI Corps to complete the encirclement of the retreating German Army. Instead of directing the whole of US VI Corps towards Valmontone (where the trap was supposed to close), he sent only one division while the rest of the corps swung in the direction of Rome. The German Tenth Army made maximum use of the opportunity presented and escaped to live and fight another day. From the very beginning, the aim of 'Diadem' had been to destroy the German formations in Italy. If that could be done, or even partly done, the liberation of a large part of Italy, the fall of Rome and the movement of German forces from Normandy would follow.[160] Churchill wrote to Alexander on 28 May reminding him that 'the glory of this battle' would be measured 'not by the capture of Rome ... but by the number of German divisions cut off'.[161] Clark, it appeared, had let the team down badly; his decision to turn towards Rome was castigated by many, at the time and since, as glory hunting, driven by the lure of liberating the first of the occupied European capitals. The blame, however, does not rest entirely with him, as irresponsible as his actions might appear in hindsight. For a start, the speed of Eighth Army's advance, which was still determined to a great degree by the 'Colossal Cracks' approach, offered no guarantee that the two pincers would meet at Valmontone in time to cut off the Germans. Furthermore, the failure to encircle the increasingly desperate German Army was the responsibility also of Alexander, who quite simply should have kept a firm grip on his subordinate. While it can never be known what might have happened, there is nevertheless a lingering suspicion that an excellent opportunity was lost to effectively finish off the Germans in Italy.[162]

By the start of June, it was apparent to Kesselring that he could no longer prevent the Allies from taking Rome. He ordered his armies to begin a slow withdrawal to the 'Gothic Line', which covered the approaches to the Po Valley and the Alpine passes leading north from Italy to the heart of Europe. Clark's victorious army entered the Eternal City on 4 June, two days before the eyes of the world turned to the beaches of Normandy.[163] The British and Commonwealth Armies took little joy in their victory; they were focused 'far more on the ordeal being faced by the men in Normandy than on ... their own great success in Italy'. Those few who did enjoy the liberation of Rome wrote that it was impossible to describe 'the scenes of enthusiasm and welcome. We were shaken by the hand, patted, petted, kissed, and made to feel as if we'd done something.' The city itself was almost untouched by the war and many of the men had the best of times in the ensuing celebrations. Some were even received by the Pope in the Vatican, who blessed them and praised them for their success.[164]

The five-month struggle to take the German Cassino position and break the 'Gustav Line' was finally over. It had been 'an epic infantry combat, fought out in ghastly weather and nightmarish terrain',[165] a pure war of attrition. 'Diadem' had cost the Allies some 42,000 casualties, an indication of the relentless pressure that had been exerted on the German defenders. The Germans by comparison had lost 30,000 (10,000 battle casualties and 20,000 POWs).[166] Four of their infantry divisions had been 'destroyed', and three more were 'so shattered' that they had to be withdrawn for rebuilding, while a fourth was broken up to provide reinforcements. In the face of such losses, Hitler and the German High Command were forced to send four replacement divisions, and reinforcements on a scale equivalent to three more, to Italy.[167] Much heavy equipment and most of the German tank strength had also been lost (2,100 machine guns, 306 artillery pieces and 250–300 tanks and other armoured fighting vehicles).[168] Here at last 'was vindication for the Italian campaign'.[169] When it mattered most, large numbers of German divisions were diverted from the decisive points: the invasion of Normandy and the Eastern Front. All that mattered now was that the troops storming the beaches of North-West Europe made the most of that opportunity.

12 TRANSFORMATION IN THE JUNGLE

Training and Doctrine

By 1943, there was little doubt that the British and Commonwealth Armies in the West had discovered an operational approach that systematically, if not dramatically, wore the *Wehrmacht* down in battle. Montgomery's 'Colossal Cracks' method was a step away from the *Field Service Regulations* (*FSR*); rather than leaving the outcomes of battles in the hands of empowered junior officers, Montgomery determined that those at the top of the strategic chain should centralise command and control and create opportunities through 'unity of effort'.[1] Although less dynamic and flexible, this approach, it was intended, would limit the impact of poor training and questionable motivation on the outcome of events. By controlling operations tightly, Montgomery hoped that he could get more out of the materiel advantages enjoyed by his armies.

The same operational techniques could not work for the British and Commonwealth Armies in the East. The success of the Australian Army in Papua and New Guinea had demonstrated that devolved command and control was absolutely essential in the jungle. The Indian Army in the fighting in the Arakan had been considerably less successful than the Australians in New Guinea, but conditions there too had shown the necessity for a form of warfare far more in line with interwar *FSR* than with Montgomery's new operational method. The challenge in the East, therefore, was to find a way to implement and adapt more fully the understandings of *FSR* so that the Japanese could be beaten in the jungle.

Substantial army-wide reform and learning had to take place and it began in Australia. As early as March 1942, Blamey had instigated the production of new Australian Army training memoranda, 'which consolidated material issued in Mediterranean and Indian Army training memoranda, supplemented with some material on the Japanese armed forces'.[2] By the middle of 1943, this process had produced doctrine more suitable for the challenges faced by a citizen army in the jungle of New Guinea. In May, 'Military Training Pamphlet No. 23 (Australia): Part XX Jungle Warfare' was released and disseminated widely. The pamphlet, which became known as the 'Jungle Soldier's Handbook', emphasised many of the same understandings as *FSR*. The Handbook noted that 'all our experience shows':

> that in the jungle or similar enclosed country, command in battle is decentralised so that junior leaders are often confronted with a situation in which they must make decisions and act without delay on their own responsibility ... Junior leaders in particular must be trained and capable of taking the place of their superiors in the event of casualties.[3]

Continuous patrolling, in both offensive and defensive scenarios, was considered 'most important'. Advancing formations, usually in columns protected by active patrols, would seek to avoid frontal assaults and outflank the enemy, by fixing and then outmanoeuvring the defending force. Attacks would be delivered from the flank or rear once the enemy's lines of communication had been cut.[4] The tactics espoused in the 'Jungle Soldier's Handbook' drove the training of 6th and 7th Australian Divisions once they had been withdrawn from New Guinea 'for rest, refitting, and retraining', and of 9th Australian Division, on its return from the Middle East in early 1943.[5]

To disseminate this new doctrine, the Australian Army began expanding its schooling and training system. In November 1942, it established the Land HQ Training Centre (Jungle Warfare) at Canungra in southern Queensland to provide reinforcements with an extra twenty-eight days of preparation in jungle conditions.[6] Canungra had an immediate impact; by May 1943, the course was graduating 500 men a week and 60 platoon commanders every six weeks for service in New Guinea. By the end of 1943, 'there were 4500–5000 men undergoing training' at any one time.[7] To improve training for field forces, an extensive training area was also developed on the Atherton Tablelands in northern Queensland.[8]

According to the censors, the 'intensive training', 'toughening up exercises' and 'realistic "mock" battle[s]' carried out in these jungle warfare schools was 'enthusiastically appreciated by most troops'.[9] A man wrote in June 1943, 'I saw some time ago about 300 men who were thoroughly trained come out of the jungle from a fortnight's ordinary infantry jungle training – all they could do for about 3 days was lie around and recover.'[10] Training was so intense and realistic that it was not unusual for writers to report casualties due to the 'use of live ammunition'.[11] By August/September 1943, there was no doubt that training was preparing the men both physically and psychologically for the challenges to come. As one man put it, 'when we get stuck into the Japs we will be 100% fit and I feel sure we will give him a helluva hiding'.[12]

To better suit the requirements of the new doctrine, the Australians decided to reorganise their divisional structures. In future, the Army would field three types of divisions, 'armoured, standard infantry, and jungle infantry'. The 5th and 11th Militia Divisions, and 6th, 7th and 9th Divisions of the Australian Imperial Force (AIF) were selected for modification to the new jungle infantry format.[13] In recognition of the increasingly devolved command-and-control requirements for jungle warfare, local commanders would be given a far greater quota of organic fire support. Jungle divisions would field 129 per cent more medium machine guns, 492 per cent more sub-machine guns, 350 per cent more medium mortars and 25 per cent more light mortars than their standard equivalents.[14]

Thus, by the second half of 1943, 'great strides' had been taken towards developing a doctrine, training regime and divisional structure more suitable for the challenges of jungle warfare.[15] The Australian Army had unquestionably adapted and moved beyond *FSR* and begun to think for itself,[16] but the essential principles of *FSR* were maintained.

These developments did not go unnoticed in the other part of the British and Commonwealth Armies grappling with the challenges of fighting the Japanese in the jungle, the Indian Army. In November 1942, in the wake of the successful fighting on the Kokoda Trail and Milne Bay, Wavell corresponded with Blamey seeking to learn from the Australians' success. 'I should be very grateful', he wrote, 'if you could send me as much detailed information as possible.'[17] The following February, a War Information Circular issued by GHQ India, 'described enemy defensive tactics in New Guinea at Buna and ... on the Kokoda Trail'.[18] In the wake of the debacle in the Arakan, two experienced Australian officers were sent on a tour of the subcontinent, between July and October 1943, to 'pass on lessons they had learnt' from fighting the Japanese. These men played an important role as the British and Commonwealth Armies began not only to learn from their own individual experiences, but from each other. They lectured on minor tactics at GHQ and throughout India and prepared 'detailed reports for the Director of Military Training' dealing with tactical problems. In the autumn, Brigadier 'Jack' Lloyd, the former commander of 16th Australian Infantry Brigade began a six-month posting in India and Burma where he 'carried out an extensive lecture tour, visiting units, formations and training establishments ... with the aim of bolstering Anglo-Indian morale and spreading the Australian gospel of jungle warfare'. In addition to these initiatives, a party of fifty British and Indian officers arrived in Australia in October 1943 to learn directly from the Australians. They underwent the training course at Canungra and were then attached to 7th and 9th Australian Divisions in New Guinea. These men later returned to India where they were 'used as lecturers, instructors at GHQ schools and also assigned to units to pass on what they had learnt about Australian jungle fighting methods'.[19]

As important as this cross-fertilisation of techniques undoubtedly was for the Indian Army, it would be unfair to overlook the doctrinal and training revolution that took place independently in India between 1943 and 1944. Wavell began this process, at the end of May 1943, when he convened the Infantry Committee, India, chaired by Major-General Roland Richardson, the Deputy Chief of the General Staff (India), and ordered it to examine the problems facing his forces in the Far East and provide recommendations. After two weeks of deliberations, the committee came to the view that the fundamental problem was training. Drafts of British personnel, either directly from the UK or 'milked' from internal security duties in India, had been sent into action with alarmingly low standards of basic military skills, discipline and physical fitness. The quality of Indian recruits had been even worse, with most completely lacking skill-at-arms, fieldcraft and musketry training. Those who had reached the Arakan had been, in the Committee's view, little more than an undisciplined 'mob of partially trained village youth'.[20]

The findings of the Infantry Committee made for difficult reading, but they did provide the blueprint for a way forward. Wavell, however, did not get the chance to oversee the rebuilding of the Indian Army. Churchill had by now lost confidence in his Commander-in-Chief (C-in-C) and decided to remove him and once more put Claude Auchinleck in his place. The blow was softened for Wavell when in June the Prime Minister appointed him Viceroy of India.[21] The morale reports recorded that both appointments were received 'with universal approval'. 'The appointment of Lord Wavell as Viceroy designate', the report for May to July noted, 'has been welcomed, and has tended to relieve anxieties regarding the position and interest of Indian troops in the immediate post war period'. Auchinleck, in particular, was 'held in high esteem' by Indian troops. Those who had served under him in the Middle East were understood to be 'particularly pleased that he has now been appointed their Commander-in-Chief'.[22]

In a further attempt to revamp the fortunes of the Indian Army, it was also decided that responsibility for conducting the war in Burma would be transferred to a new South-East Asia Command (SEAC), under the stewardship of Lord Louis Mountbatten. The creation of SEAC and the appointment of Mountbatten as Supreme Commander gave 'great satisfaction' to the troops. There was 'widespread anticipation' that his appointment meant that the Indian Army would 'be committed to action in the near future', thus 'bringing nearer the ultimate defeat of the Japanese'.[23] India Command would now focus solely on organising, equipping and training units destined for the front, while SEAC would manage their employment on the front line once they had been adequately trained and prepared.[24]

As Mountbatten established his new command, Auchinleck set to his task with considerable zeal. The Infantry Committee had pointed to the need for a simple consistent, and recognised jungle warfare technique. There were, it noted, as a consequence of the flurry of intellectual activity after the Japanese assault, numerous doctrines in circulation, some of them fundamentally different from others; divisions and even battalions often produced their own pamphlets. It was recommended that, in future, GHQ India should oversee the production of doctrine so that trained soldiers could follow one, and one only, approach.[25]

This new operational method was set out in the fourth edition of 'Military Training Pamphlet No. 9 (India): Jungle Warfare', more commonly known as the 'Jungle Book'. Published in September 1943, and issued on a scale of one copy per officer and NCO in British units and to every officer in Indian units (80,000 copies were produced), the 'Jungle Book' effectively played the role of the 'Jungle Soldier's Handbook' in the Australian Army.[26]

The 'Jungle Book', just like its Australian equivalent, emphasised the necessity for devolved command and control. The close character of the fighting in Burma required junior leaders to make rapid decisions when they came into contact with the enemy; acting 'without delay' could be the difference between life and death, success and failure.[27] At the operational level, by comparison, the 'Jungle Book' resonated more with the attritional approaches being employed in the West. It proposed to counter Japanese combat techniques by the use of 'boxes', of fighting and administrative troops organised for all-round defence. Instead of thinking about well-defined fronts, these 'boxes', an idea that originated in the attempts to tackle Axis forces in the desert, would be used both on the defensive and on the offensive. Half of a formation's troops would be stationed along the perimeter of a box. Another quarter would be assigned to attack any Japanese penetration of the defences, and the last quarter would be earmarked to attack the Japanese outside the perimeter by use of fighting patrols.[28] The 'boxes' would, therefore, both in attack and defence, require the Japanese to assault British and Commonwealth forces in fixed and well-defended positions. This would, in turn, allow the Indian Army to make maximum use of its superiority in firepower (artillery) to wear the Japanese down in battle.

Forces held in reserve would then be used to crush Japanese formations like a hammer on an anvil, the mobile force being the hammer and the 'box' the anvil. The idea that a force which is surrounded is in a hopeless position', stated the 'Jungle Book', 'must not be permitted':

> Troops must realise that the enemy who are behind them are just as much cut off from their comrades as they themselves are. Resolute, offensive action against them will not only bring about their destruction, but will make such tactics much less likely in future.[29]

To facilitate this doctrinal revolution, Auchinleck insisted, in a way that none of Wavell, Percival or Hutton had done before, that all field units undergo intensive collective training under jungle conditions. Auchinleck wrote to Brooke in September 1943 promising that 'all divisions' would be prepared 'by the end of this year'. 'I can assure you', he said, 'that I shall not allow any formation to go into battle until it is adequately trained.'[30]

The Infantry Committee had recommended that basic training should be extended from three to at least eight months. To address this new requirement, instruction at Regimental Training Centres was immediately extended by a month. Additionally, a new two-month period of specialist jungle training, at one of two freshly created training divisions (14th and 39th Indian Divisions), was added to the recruit induction programme. Each regiment in the Indian Army was ordered to provide these training divisions with a battalion; it was from these battalions that future replacements for regiments would be provided; for example, 6th Battalion, the 2nd Punjab Regiment became the training battalion for the whole 2nd Punjab Regiment.[31] As Slim later wrote:

> There were infantry battle schools, artillery training centres, co-operation courses with the R.A.F., experiments with tanks in the jungle, classes in watermanship and river crossing and a dozen other instructional activities, all in full swing. Our training grew more ambitious until we were staging inter-divisional exercises over wide ranges of country under tough conditions. Units lived for weeks on end in the jungle and learnt its ways.[32]

In a similar vein to the training revolution in Britain, the Indian Army began also to embrace clear and defined battle drills to facilitate rapid teamwork on meeting the enemy. A copy of GHQ Home Forces new 'Instructors' Handbook on Fieldcraft and Battle Drill' had arrived in New Delhi in December 1942, where 'it was eagerly examined'. Over the following months its recommendations were adapted to a jungle context and in the summer of 1943 a modified version was issued by the Indian High Command. The 'Instructors' Handbook on Fieldcraft and Battle Drill (India)' laid down 'easily understood section, platoon and company battle drills that gave precise guidance to junior officers, NCOs and other ranks' on what to do in the noise and confusion of battle. Some 45,000 copies of 'Battle Drill for Thick Jungle' were issued around the same time and together these pamphlets described a series of section-, platoon- and company-level battle drills for advance, assault and offensive defence in the jungle.[33]

The failure of the Arakan offensive had 'finally convinced military leaders to formally establish a centrally controlled tactical training program'.[34] In terms of overall ethos, this new programme, and the doctrine that accompanied it, strongly resembled that of the Australian Army in the South-West Pacific Area (SWPA). However, in key ways, it also adopted some of the characteristics of the 'Colossal Cracks' approach. At the operational level, it intended to use 'boxes' to draw the Japanese into set-piece battles that would allow the Indian Army to make use of its superiority in firepower. At the tactical level, it would embrace 'tactics by numbers' as encapsulated in battle drill.[35] While such prescriptive methods could lead to tactics becoming stereotyped, it was thought that they best suited the requirements in India in the prevailing circumstances.

These efforts had the desired effect. The morale reports confirmed that 'the harder and more realistic and more varied the training', the 'more contented and confident' were the troops.[36] Whereas the report for February to April 1943 had noted that morale 'suffered' and a 'feeling of frustration' had set in as a consequence of inadequate training,[37] by the end of July 1943, it was clear that 'keen interest' was being shown by troops 'undergoing training in jungle warfare, combined operations, and other special forms of warfare'. The report concluded that the men mentioned 'the hardships' they were experiencing, but fully 'appreciate[d] that their training will stand them in good stead when they meet the enemy'.[38]

One last piece of the puzzle remained. Much as was the case in the Australian Army, the doctrinal revolution in India needed to be facilitated by an organisational revamp. In the past, battalions had used either mechanised transport or animal transport. This structural delineation meant that some units had been mostly tied to roads, a real problem in jungle terrain where there were few metalled carriageways. A new mixed-transport model was introduced, with all units instructed to employ a combination of mule and mechanised transport, with the emphasis on having animal transport. This innovation eased the logistic challenges of fighting in 'boxes', as isolated units could be more easily resupplied using animal transport or, as air superiority was gradually attained, from the air, than by the use of mechanical transport.[39]

The first phase of the rebuilding of the Australian and Indian Armies was complete.

Institutional Reform

By the second half of 1943, doctrine and the disconnect between understanding and action (the poor quality of training), had finally begun to be seriously addressed in the British and Commonwealth Armies in the East.[40] In this respect, the dark clouds of 1942 and early 1943 had a golden lining; 'officers at all levels' began to recognise that the only 'way forward' was through institutional adaptation and innovation. The transformation in doctrine and training was accompanied by new divisional structures;[41] but the question of reform was not left there, for much like in the West, significant efforts needed to be made to adapt the military institution better to the needs of a citizen army.

Personnel selection was one of the first issues to be addressed. In Australia 'the rapid expansions of the armed Services and war industries' after the entry of Japan into the war, made the 'correct allocation of men' ever 'more important'. In September 1942, 'a psychological section' was formed at Allied Land HQ and by March 1943 all states were covered by the services of this section with recruits 'subjected to a degree of psychological control'. By the middle of 1943, pre-selection boards for officers had also been introduced, with psychiatrists and psychologists added to the process in October.[42] Similar initiatives were introduced in India. In March 1943, a senior officer from the Directorate of Selection of Personnel and three psychiatrists arrived on the subcontinent to establish a Directorate of Selection of Personnel (India) at Meerut.[43] In the summer of 1943, the successful War Office Selection Board system for officers was also introduced. These innovations were supported by the appointment of a large number of psychiatrists to divisions, who set to work immediately on weeding out unsuitable men from fighting formations.[44]

The ideological deficit that had left such a 'gaping hole' in the morale armour of the front-line soldier was also addressed. In Australia, with the immediate threat of invasion having receded by 1943, the short-lived remobilisation of the home front had begun to peter out. It seemed in many ways that Australia had reverted to a 'business as usual' mentality. The number of days lost to strikes increased dramatically between 1942 and 1943, from 378,200 to

990,200 (a rise of 162 per cent).[45] The censors commented on this change in ethos and its effect on the troops; in June, they noted that 'industrial conditions on the mainland' were forming 'the subject of many biting comments by writers' and that they helped make 'the average soldier in a forward area somewhat dissatisfied with his own lot'. A lieutenant in 22nd Battalion, 5th Australian Division, wrote, 'is it any wonder we sometimes feel bitter and fall to thinking whether or not the struggle worth while'.[46] A corporal in the same division wrote at length:

> It's an irremovable disgrace to the British race that munition [*sic*] workers – the suppliers of arms & protection of fighting men – should be allowed to strike whenever they feel inclined ... Why not immediately send strikers into the army to a forward area and replace them with men who have lost their health through military service? Men, who having seen war and the horrors of it, having their friends killed beside them, knowing the bestial ruthlessness of the enemy, would bend every effort to supplying in full all the essential requirements to those still in service. The present situation is not in keeping with the rudiments of justice.[47]

Faced with the renewed apathy of the home front, army education would play an important role in maintaining the morale of the combat soldier. In fact, an Australian Army education scheme had been approved by the Australian War Cabinet as early as March 1941. It was modelled largely on the British Army Bureau of Current Affairs (ABCA) initiative and became fully operational in June 1941. The role of education, according to the 'War History of the Australian Army Education Service', 'involved finding solutions for a number of allied problems, all of which had to be solved if the welfare and morale of troops was to be maintained at the highest possible level'.[48] The Australian Army Education Service (AAES) was designed explicitly to meet the 'demands of total war' and combat the 'fanatical faith' of the German and Japanese Armies. 'This was done by breeding confidence in the soldier that the ideals for which he fought are worth far more than the sacrifices required to preserve them.' Education, in other words, was to toughen the soldier's 'spirit so that he resolutely faced privation and loss and ever strove toward the goal'.[49]

As the Army faced renewed pressures to maintain morale among the troops, funding for the AAES increased dramatically, nearly doubling between 1941–2 and 1942–3. By the middle of 1943, 'the total full-time staff of Army Education had increased from the initial establishment of 43 to almost 600'. In addition, there were more than 1,200 units with part-time education officers. New discussion groups were set up, the support of hobbies expanded, a range of correspondence courses was made available through technical colleges and universities, and a limited number of vocational training classes were offered, particularly in hospitals and training camps.[50] Lectures were the most important aspect of this expanded education programme. In 1942, 16,238 lectures were given, attended by 1,481,683 personnel. In 1943, 49,771 lectures were delivered, attended by 3,109,416. To cater for growing demand and its growing importance, the AAES was established as a stand-alone directorate in October 1943, with an Army Education school set up near Sydney to train forty students a month.[51]

By any standards, the AAES was a major success.[52] The censorship summaries were consistently complimentary about its contribution,[53] and post-war assessments were almost universally positive too. The Australian War Cabinet supported the scheme not for 'idealistic' reasons but for very 'pragmatic' ones; it was 'regarded as helping the Army, and therefore the nation, meet its objectives'.[54]

The need for army education was no less keen in India. The failure of the Cripps mission and the violence sparked by Quit India had demonstrated the extent to which the British Government in India had failed to fully mobilise the people, and their representatives, for total war. Doubt over the future of India, in turn, did much to undermine morale in the Indian Army. It is clear from the morale reports that 'one of the chief anxieties among the soldier class of the martial races, the backbone of the Army',[55] was the 'feeling of uncertainty as to what will happen ... when the war is over':

> The Congress, it is known, will certainly cut down the Army and thus the standard of living of the soldier-farmer class. The sepoy from the village feels that he may be left to face such a reduction with no one to fight battle on his behalf ... His future is, therefore, uncertain and ... there is a feeling in some quarters, therefore, that the sepoy is looking over his shoulder. This is particularly unfortunate as the class affected

> is not the new type of recruit from the towns, but the stolid soldier-agriculturalist who has always been the backbone of the Indian Army. Were a clear pronouncement possible on Great Britain's attitude to India after the war, and, in particular, a statement that we do not intend to leave our friends to the mercy of those who have proved our overt enemies in this war, much would be done to set these fears at rest.[56]

The situation was little better for British soldiers. Adam had flown to the Far East in April 1943, and visited Eastern Army HQ during operations in the Arakan.[57] He returned to London concerned that 'the British soldier regarded the war [in the Far East] as a secondary one'. As he put it in his report to the Executive Committee of the Army Council, the British soldier 'was fighting for a country that did not want us, that disliked us and did everything possible to rob the British soldier by high prices'.[58]

The solution Adam proposed was army education. 'Everything should be done', he said, 'to get A.B.C.A. going. The questions asked me by the average N.C.O. and man shewed that they were in complete ignorance of what was happening in this country, and what was likely to happen' after the war.[59] In May, India Command announced that active attempts would be made to address these concerns.[60] Between May and July, four out of six issues of the Indian Army version of 'Current Affairs' dealt with Far Eastern problems. It was apparent, according to morale reports, that 'every effort' was being made 'to focus' the attention of the troops on the importance of the far eastern war through the medium of ABCA.[61] To support these initiatives, a Current Affairs School was set up at Ranchi, where courses were held for commanding officers, regimental officers (British and Indian), Women's Auxiliary Corps (Indian) officers and army chaplains to familiarise them with the principles of ABCA. Similar courses were later arranged for senior *havildars* (Indian NCOs, equivalent in rank to a sergeant) and *jemadars* (Indian officers, equivalent in rank to a lieutenant).[62]

As the number of trained instructors increased, every unit of the Indian Army was ordered to create 'Josh' (meaning 'pep') groups to discuss current affairs and the rationale for the war.[63] These efforts were supported by various pamphlets and a weekly Josh newsletter. Any antipathy Indian soldiers had towards the war, or the Empire, was supposed to pale in comparison to the hatred that would be fanned for the Japanese through these publications and sessions.[64] An 'image of the Japanese soldier as a cruel, ruthless "fanatical", but beatable opponent' was deliberately cultivated, 'building on existing racist views of the Japanese following earlier fighting and accounts of the brutal treatment meted out to captured Commonwealth troops'. The men were told that their object was to kill or exterminate Japanese troops like vermin, rather than simply seizing ground or capturing prisoners.[65]

Morale reports demonstrate that army education, through 'correspondence courses and Current Affairs pamphlets' were 'popular'.[66] While it is clear that the Army Education Corps (AEC) struggled to cope with the challenge of introducing education to the expanded Indian Army, and their efforts were, to some extent, only 'a drop in the ocean',[67] by the end of 1943, the morale reports were noting that 'Josh training' had become 'increasingly effective' and was 'having a good effect – in some cases considerable – in promoting knowledge of the purpose and implications of the war against the Japanese'.[68] The Indian Army, in the absence of the mass mobilisation of the subcontinent, had to make the most of the resources and powers directly at its disposal; army education was one of the many vehicles it employed to achieve this end.

Another was the provision of more enlightened welfare provisions for the citizen soldier. Just as in the West, the authorities in Australia and India gradually realised that morale could be nurtured by ensuring that day-to-day interactions between the Army, the man and his family were carried out in the most positive manner possible. A Directorate of Welfare and Vocational Training was set up in Australia in February 1942, initially responsible for welfare and education, but also for Army chaplains, and philanthropic bodies such as the Red Cross and YMCA.[69] The censorship summaries from Australia and New Guinea were unequivocal in the way they linked welfare and morale. The summary for 1 to 15 May 1943 pointed out, for example, how inadequate welfare provisions could undermine the morale of even the most experienced and disciplined unit. 'Grave doubts', according to the report, had emerged regarding the morale of 9th Australian Division:

> A general atmosphere of discontent pervades the correspondence. Leave, rations, canteen services and camp conditions generally all attract their share of bitter and often intemperate criticism. A widespread belief that preferential treatment is

> accorded to militiamen and US troops deepens the sense of grievance … Domestic anxiety is another contributing factor to discontent on the part of many writers, and a connection between this anxiety and the activities of American servicemen is invariably traced.[70]

The report went on to recount the 'curious form of protest' manifested in the division as a result of discontent. A private in 20th Brigade wrote:

> I must tell you about the latest craze up here. Its dogbarking [*sic*] and has it taken a hold. The boys reckon they are being treated like dogs so are acting like them. And whenever you go within 10 miles of the camp you can hear the barking. It's in the jungle, it's on the road, it's on the river and in the tents. Two platoons meet each other marching along the road and start barking at one another. A driver will come down the road in his truck and as he is passing you lean out and give a blood chilling snarl. All this has got the powers that be very worried. One CO called his unit out on parade and said 'all this barking will cease forthwith'. His answer would have vied with a cat being dropped into the middle of dog show. So they placed a fine on it in the battalions. £5 if you were caught barking. No good, so now if you've caught its [*sic*] gaol I believe. But it's getting worse. Four lads were missing from a battalion the other morning and left a note on their beds 'gone through for a feed and a smoke' both of which are very scarce up here.[71]

In spite of these difficulties, it does appear that welfare provisions gradually improved over the course of 1943. By August, 'in general' the morale of the troops was described as 'high', particularly in 9th Australian Division. Troops in Papua were 'enthusiastic in their appreciation of quantities of fresh meat and vegetable recently issued', and there were only favourable comments with regards to the delivery of mail.[72] By December 1943, the censors were reporting that 'in general, the morale of the AMF [Australian Military Forces], as shown in their letters, has never been higher'. Factors 'contributing to this "uplift"' included, among others, 'a general improvement in rations (especially extra Xmas fare) and the high standard of Amenities now provided'.[73]

Similar dynamics were as important, if not more so, in India. Morale reports made clear that 'a large proportion of the expanded

[Indian] Army' had enlisted, 'not because of military tradition' or any great belief in a cause, 'but in order to provide for its families'. Naturally, therefore, there was 'great concern' among soldiers 'about village conditions'; village welfare assumed 'a steadily increasing importance' as the war wore on, especially with regards to 'high prices and [the] scarcity of essentials'.[74] From this perspective, it was perhaps fortunate that, as the morale reports put it, 'very few soldiers' were 'recruited from famine areas'.[75] District Soldiers Boards (DSBs) were set up on an all-India basis, to look after the domestic interests of fighting men. The Directorate of Welfare and Amenities (India), which was set up in August 1942, introduced women's welfare centres at training depots across India and also a scheme for trained women welfare workers (*Sevadarnis*), to parallel the contributions made by DSBs and Civil Liaison Officers.[76]

Efforts to better the relationship between British soldiers and their families were introduced as well. Morale report after morale report noted that 'the most important factor' affecting troops in India was 'their concern regarding the fidelity of their womenfolk at home ... This topic is mentioned in some form or other in the majority of letters to the U.K.':[77]

> In this connection one division which left England about two years ago, states that 66 illegitimate children are known to have been born to the wives of men in the division, and estimates that there are at least 100 cases in all, amounting to 2% of the married men in the division.[78]

In April 1943, Soldiers', Sailors' and Airmen's Families Association (SSAFA) sub-offices were established at Calcutta, Lahore and Bangalore to help men deal with family problems. A little later, in July, a Legal Aid Scheme was introduced for those who wanted to seek divorce or other forms of settlement.[79]

Few of these initiatives matched the significance of another development, the Indianisation of the Indian Army. Until the interwar years, only white British officers had been put in charge of battalions or regiments as 'Indians were not considered capable of leading battalions or regiments in the field ... without getting caught up in the men's religious or class issues.' The sacrifices made by the Indian Army in the First World War finally opened the door for Indian commissions,[80] but Indian officers were initially assigned solely to specific Indianised units, where they were only able to command other Indians, 'a form of ghettoization not lost on those involved'.[81]

In 1938, Indian Commissioned Officers (ICOs), who had passed through the Indian Military Academy at Dehra Dun, were given the power to command British officers in the Indian land forces. With the expansion of the army in the early years of the war, it was also decided to do away with the pre-war restrictions on Indianisation; Indian officers would now be sent wherever they were needed. However, blatant inequalities still remained. ICOs did not have the power of punishment over British other ranks.[82] Moreover, in an Indian Army battalion, an ICO was paid less, lower pay being justified by the fact that Indian officers 'did not have to travel home or bring over their wives and children'. Indian officers, although they generally did find their pay sufficient, 'resented the lower pay scale because it implied racial discrimination'.[83] Equal pay was finally introduced in early 1942, but it was not until June 1943 that it was announced that Indian officers were to have powers of punishment over British Army personnel.[84] 'It would be a poor response to the magnificent achievements of Indian officers and men in this war', noted an official communiqué on the subject, 'if we were to delay ... in according these powers':

> An Indian ... officer who is felt to exercise command is obviously to be trusted to exercise powers of punishment and if he is deprived of such powers just because he is an Indian, not only will it have a bad effect on his morale but may cause issues with the men.[85]

At the beginning of the war, there had been only 577 Indian officers in an army nearly 200,000 strong; by the end of the war, there were over 15,000, with 220 lieutenant-colonels and four temporary or acting brigadiers. Whereas in 1939 there had been ten British officers to every Indian officer in the Army, by 1945, there would be only four British officers to each Indian officer.[86]

By the second half of 1943, a spirit of reform had begun to take root in the armies in the Far East. This mirrored closely the process that had occurred in the British Army in the UK and in the desert in 1942, even if its end product was quite different. Where 'Monty's Army' sought to centralise and control, Blamey's, Auchinleck's, Mountbatten's, and, ultimately, Slim's armies, had to a far greater extent, due to the challenges of fighting in the jungle, to devolve and delegate command and control to the lowest levels. The morale reports pointed to the significance of these changes. Whereas 'general confidence in the allied cause and in final victory' had been 'shaken by the withdrawal from Arakan, and the crop of wild rumours which followed in its trail', by July 1943, 'this temporary set-back' had 'been largely restored'.[87] It was just as well, for by the end of the year, expansion of the Army in India had reached its peak and the authorities would have to make maximum use of what they already had at their disposal.[88]

From now on, all troops, from infantry to cooks, would be trained and prepared to fight.[89] As the 'Jungle book' put it, in the future 'THERE WILL BE NO WITHDRAWAL.'[90] 'We have good equipment; better is on its way. Real hard training will give us the tactical skill to use that equipment.' Quite simply, the reforms introduced in Australia and India encompassed nothing less than the transformation of the Australian and Indian Armies; citizen armies without ideological conviction were superseded by new armies motivated by professional pride.[91] The tide had finally begun to turn in the war in the East.

The South-West Pacific Area

As early as 2 July 1942, the US Joint Chiefs of Staff, who had been delegated the direction of strategy and operations in the Pacific by the Combined Chiefs of Staff in Washington, had issued orders that the main Japanese base in the south Pacific, Rabaul, had to be isolated. This plan had been delayed by the Japanese offensive in Papua in 1942, but, by January 1943, MacArthur was in a position to take the initiative.[92] Command and control for a proposed new offensive was no easy matter. In order to satisfy the US Army and Navy service chiefs, the US Joint Chiefs of Staff had divided the Pacific theatre into two separate commands, Pacific Ocean Area (subdivided into the North, Central and South Pacific commands) under the US Navy, and the SWPA under the control of the US Army. Strategy in the Pacific War 'would be undertaken along two lines of operations'.[93] One was a continuation of the counter-offensive begun in the SWPA and South Pacific Area (SOPAC) in late 1942 and early 1943, a drive 'up the ladder' of the Solomons and along the northern coast of New Guinea towards the Philippines. The other was a direct offensive by the US Navy, under Admiral Chester Nimitz, across the Central Pacific through the Gilbert, Marshall and Caroline Islands. The two prongs of the Pacific advance had the same general geographical objective, the Philippine Islands,[94] the repossession of which would sever communications between the East Indies and Tokyo and serve as an excellent springboard for an offensive against the Japanese home islands.[95]

Initially, MacArthur's campaign against Rabaul would take precedence 'as the US Navy and the forces in the Central Pacific needed until November 1943 to build up enough strength to launch their first operations'.[96] On 26 April, MacArthur produced his design for the reduction of Rabaul, Operation 'Cartwheel'. Forces in the SWPA and SOPAC, under MacArthur's strategic direction from January 1943, would engage in a six-phase envelopment of the Japanese base (see Map 12.1),[97] one part of which was assigned largely to the Australians in New Guinea. Although the Australian contribution to 'Cartwheel' appeared small, their proposed operation was central to the success of the whole plan. By securing airfields and ports in north-east New Guinea, Australian and US forces would be free to manoeuvre northwards along the New Guinea coast and protect the flank of American operations further to the east.[98] The development of Allied air power in New Guinea would also give the Allies control of the sea. Control of the sea would then provide the opportunity to occupy more terrain and use that terrain for airbases to dominate more of the sea. Thus, in this 'archipelagic region', control of the ground, led to command of the air; this, in turn, gave command of the sea; and command of the sea gave an attacking force a clear logistic edge as well as no little strategic mobility.[99]

Blamey's plan for the Australian phase of 'Cartwheel', Operation 'Postern' (see Map 12.2),[100] would be conducted by New Guinea Force (an Army level HQ). It focused initially on the main Japanese base in New Guinea at Lae, on the Huon Peninsula. To draw off Japanese forces from Lae, Blamey intended first to launch a diversionary attack from Wau to Salamaua, using 3rd Australian Division, a militia formation, supported by an amphibious landing by US 162nd Infantry Regiment, US 41st Division, at Nassau Bay. He would then launch, using I Australian Corps (commanded by Lieutenant-General 'Ned' Herring), a combined amphibious, airborne and land assault on Lae from two directions. To the east of Lae, an amphibious landing would be undertaken by 9th Australian Division; meanwhile, to the north-west, an airborne/air landing assault would be launched by the US 503rd Parachute Infantry Regiment and 7th

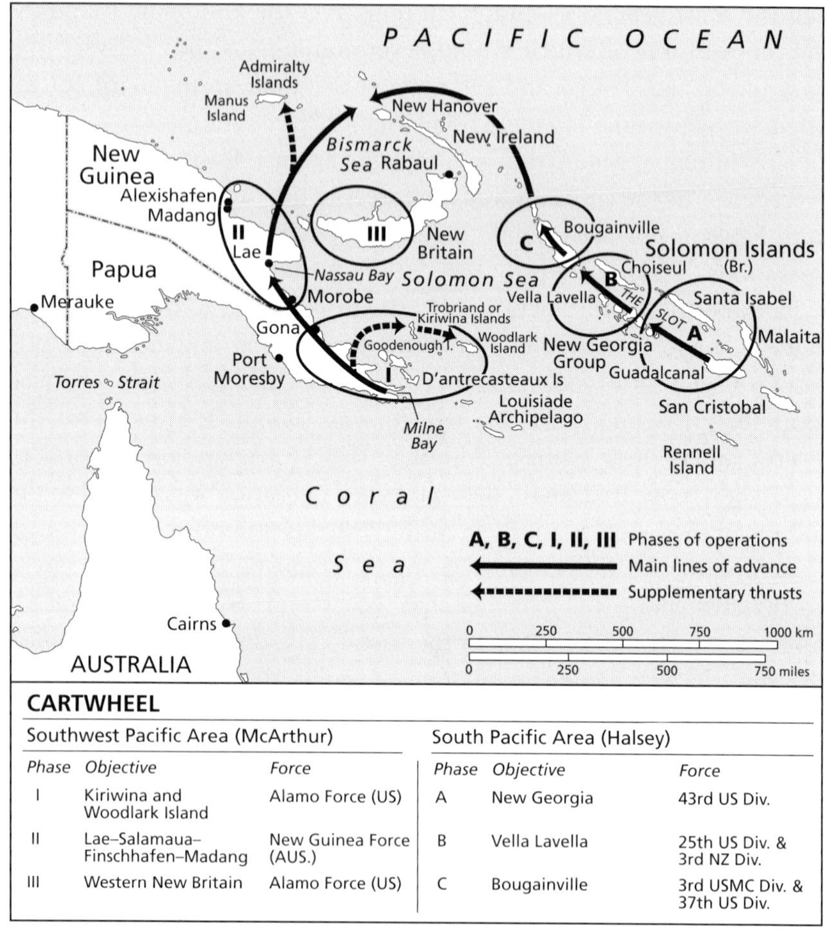

CARTWHEEL

Southwest Pacific Area (McArthur)

Phase	Objective	Force
I	Kiriwina and Woodlark Island	Alamo Force (US)
II	Lae–Salamaua–Finschhafen–Madang	New Guinea Force (AUS.)
III	Western New Britain	Alamo Force (US)

South Pacific Area (Halsey)

Phase	Objective	Force
A	New Georgia	43rd US Div.
B	Vella Lavella	25th US Div. & 3rd NZ Div.
C	Bougainville	3rd USMC Div. & 37th US Div.

Map 12.1 Operation 'Cartwheel', 1943

Australian Division. These two forces would then converge on the town.[101]

Once Lae had been taken, Phase II of Operation 'Postern' would begin. This required 7th Australian Division to advance north-west up the Markham Valley, to facilitate the construction of airfields, while 9th Australian Division conducted combined land and amphibious operations along the coast into the Huon Peninsula; their objective, to establish forward bases to support the American landings on New Britain and to open up the Vitiaz Strait (between New Guinea and New Britain).[102]

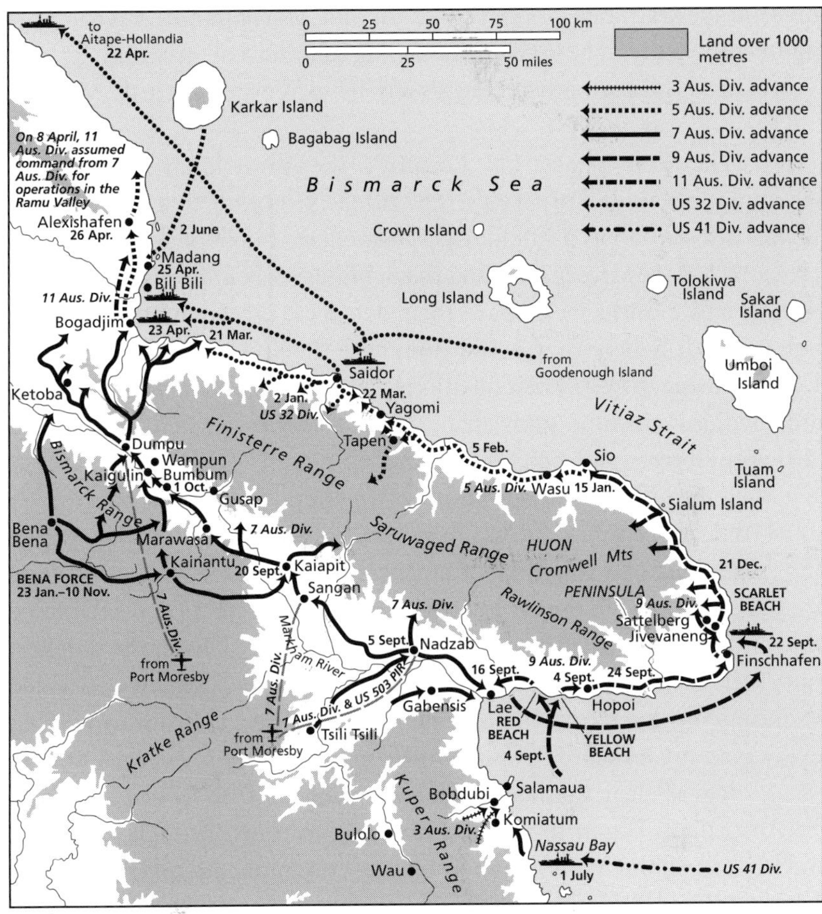

Map 12.2 Operation 'Postern', September 1943–April 1944

Operation 'Postern'

For these operations, Blamey was able to put into the field 3rd (Militia), 5th (Militia), 7th (AIF), 9th (AIF) and 11th (Militia) Australian Divisions, with 6th Australian Division (AIF) in reserve; a total of six infantry divisions. The 4th Australian Armoured Brigade (AIF), a number of independent (commando) companies plus corps, army and base troops were also available: a field force of 155,500 men. A further 106,300 were deployed in defence of the Australian mainland and as garrison troops in New Guinea, while 108,500 were in logistical and support units. All told, the Australian Army committed 370,300 men to the campaign in the SWPA in 1943. Opposing these forces in New Guinea stood 51st, 20th and 41st Japanese Divisions of Eighteenth Army. The 51st in the Salamaua and Lae area, the 41st at Wewak and the 20th advancing slowly from Wewak towards Madang and then on to Lae.[103]

The first phase of 'Postern', the diversionary attack on Salamaua, began in April 1943. The offensive got off to a steady start. It was not rapid or particularly spectacular, but it was, in spite of ferocious Japanese resistance and the debilitating conditions, successful. Having had months to prepare their defences, the Japanese dug in on high ground, 'where they could dominate the approaches to tracks or surrounding features'. Their positions were typically 'defended by heavy and medium machine guns firing from well-constructed timber and earthen pillboxes and bunkers'. These pillboxes were 'usually sited so that their fire could provide mutual support and were connected by crawl trenches or tunnels to skilfully camouflaged foxholes and weapon pits', often dug in at the base of large trees, among the roots. 'Fields of fire were cut through the undergrowth although vegetation was thinned only enough to make fire and observation possible.' Even the smallest units were instructed to prepare fortifications with 'belts of concealed positions connected to each other'. Japanese soldiers were informed that 'every man must regard his position as his grave'.[104]

It was clear that such defences 'could not be rushed'. Instead, the Australians began to isolate Japanese positions through patrolling and by cutting and harassing their lines of communication. These would then be taken by combined assaults involving air and artillery support with infantry attacking under the cover of mortar and machine-gun fire. 'Bren gunners would concentrate on suppressing the pillboxes while Owen gunners [an Australian-made submachine gun] and riflemen attacked from the flanks, closing in with grenades.' Pillboxes became death traps for their Japanese occupants, while the Australians learnt to quickly consolidate newly won positions in anticipation of Japanese counter-attacks.[105] 'This pattern of attack and counter attack was regularly repeated' and by early September, some 6,000 Japanese had been drawn towards the 'Salamaua magnet'.[106] The time was now ripe for the attack on Lae.

The assault on the main Japanese base on New Guinea began on 4 September, with the landing of 9th Australian Division 17 miles to the east of Lae. The division met little resistance as it stormed ashore in the first major Australian amphibious operation since Gallipoli in the First World

War.[107] The following day, while Japanese attention was drawn towards the coast, the US 503rd Parachute Infantry Regiment and 7th Australian Division began landing at the abandoned airfield at Nadzab to the north-west of Lae. As Lieutenant-General Yoshihara Kane, the Chief of Staff of the Japanese Eighteenth Army, put it, 'while the Lae units were keeping at bay the tiger at the front gate, the wolf had appeared at the back gate'.[108]

In marked difference to the amphibious operations in North Africa and the Mediterranean in 1943, which had been characterised too often by caution and sluggishness, 9th and 7th Australian Divisions built on the surprise and confusion generated by their landings and pushed forward relentlessly. By 8 September, the pincer closing on Lae made the Japanese position untenable and Lieutenant-General Nakano Hidemitsu, the commander of 51st Division, ordered his troops and the garrison at Lae to retreat northward. There was now an opening to encircle and wipe out the bulk of the Japanese forces in New Guinea, but both Wooten, the commander of 9th Australian Division, and Herring, the commander of I Australian Corps, failed to recognise the opportunity unfolding in front of their eyes. Instead, they stuck rigorously to the plan and focused on capturing the now undefended Lae. This 'was a major mistake and as a result approximately 8000 of the Japanese garrison escaped'.[109]

Nevertheless, by 16 September, Lae was in Australian hands. By any standards, in spite of the opportunity missed, a great success had been achieved. The first phase of Operation 'Postern' encompassed a series of important milestones. It was the 'first major coordinated sea, air and land assault in Australian history and the first in the SWPA; it involved the first tactical employment of parachute troops in the Pacific and it was the first combination of parachute troops and air-landing troops with an amphibious assault in the Pacific War'. As such, its success had clearly been heavily reliant on the contributions of the other services, especially the destruction of the 'vast majority' of the 250 aircraft of the Japanese Fourth Air Army in New Guinea by the Allied air forces. By employing a 'classic double envelopment', the Australian commanders had completely out-thought and outwitted their Japanese foes and for the cost of 689 casualties ejected the Japanese from their main base in New Guinea.[110] Perhaps even more importantly, it demonstrated that the many months of preparation and training that had taken place in 1943 had not been wasted. The Australian soldier was now, in training and morale, the superior of his enemy in the jungle.

With the capture of Lae, attention now focused on seizing the whole of the Huon Peninsula. As planned, 7th Australian Division advanced up the Markham and Ramu valleys, with the main body of Japanese troops in their path withdrawing to the 'difficult terrain of the Finisterre Range'. On the coastal route, facing 9th Australian Division, the Japanese concentrated about 5,000 troops of the 20th Division at Finschhafen.[111] Due to the absence of roads, Finschhafen functioned as a logistics hub for the movement of barges between the Japanese base in Madang and units further south. There was little doubt that it could play a similar role in the Allied drive north-west along the Huon Peninsula. Although the opportunity to throw a knock-out blow had been missed at Lae, there was still a chance to take advantage of the chaos in the Japanese ranks.

On 17 September, the day after the capture of Lae, MacArthur ordered Finschhafen to be taken. In three days, the staff of 9th Australian Division prepared and planned 'an assault landing against a hostile shore'.[112] At 0451hrs on the morning of 22 September, the 20th Brigade, commanded by Brigadier Victor Windeyer, of 9th Australian Division, stormed ashore under fire at Scarlet Beach, 6 miles to the north of Finschhafen. Confusion was rife; units became intermingled and many found that they had landed at the wrong location. The preparatory bombardment did little physical damage to the Japanese positions, while smoke and dust obscured key features along the coastline:

> The third wave was the only one to run into the right beach but due to an unexpected sandbar several landing craft dropped their ramps in 2–3 metres of water. Some troops jumped in and swam ashore; others were lucky not to drown. Several landing craft reversed and were then able to make a more successful run into the beach. Meanwhile, the Japanese defenders were engaging with machine guns to which the crews of the landing craft responded with 20-millimetre anti-aircraft guns. The fire was 'wild and undirected' but succeeded in silencing the Japanese.[113]

By 0630hrs, all of the landing beach and jungle fringe was secure and the next day the division began its drive towards Finschhafen. Progress was slow, but with 4th Brigade, of 5th (Militia) Division, advancing overland along the coast, the Japanese, fearing being cut off, once more decided to withdraw. By 2 October, Finschhafen was in Australian hands.[114]

In spite of this success, the Japanese had not given up hope of holding on to their important logistic hub at Finschhafen. Continuing Japanese patrol activity compelled Windeyer to call for reinforcements, although his request was initially denied by an increasingly hubristic and overconfident MacArthur. Windeyer maintained his stance and was able to secure, by 15 October, the reinforcements he required, in the form of 24th Australian Brigade and the HQ of 9th Australian Division.

Just two days later, the Japanese counter-attack materialised. The attack was prosecuted with the usual Japanese vigour and came all too close to success, but the Australians held their nerve and held their ground; 'assaults were smashed with automatic weapons, and artillery and mortar fire. Like water around rocks in a stream, the Japanese advance flowed around' isolated 'bastions' of Australian defenders. Japanese losses were horrific, and the margin between victory and defeat was 'narrow'; but with some Japanese units suffering 50 per cent casualties, by 24 October the counter-attack was spent. The Japanese attempt to recapture Finschhafen was called off.[115]

In many ways, in spite of the confusion, the counter-attack at Finschhafen had played into Australian hands. The men of the experienced and highly trained 9th Australian Division had already demonstrated their competence in mobile amphibious warfare. Now, under determined attack, they held their ground, inviting the Japanese to expose themselves to the Australian's superiority in firepower. The engagement became a battle of attrition, and, in this sense, Australian tactics played out in a manner not dissimilar to the 'boxes' being proposed by the Indian Army in Burma. With well-trained and highly motivated troops, commanders on the ground were able to adapt their approach to the requirements of the situation.[116]

Nevertheless, the narrowness of the victory at Finschhafen and the failure to trap the Japanese at Lae forced Blamey to rethink command arrangements in New Guinea. Herring, the commander of I Australian Corps, was clearly exhausted and his 'nerves were fraying'. It was decided, in the circumstances, to rotate corps HQs; going forward, II Australian Corps HQ, under one of Blamey's most trusted subordinates, the soon to be promoted to lieutenant-general, Frank Berryman, would direct operations at corps level. With Blamey needed in Australia, as C-in-C AMF, command of New Guinea Force would pass to the greatly experienced Leslie Morshead.[117]

With these changes in place, the advance north now began in earnest. But, Wooten, having nearly had his fingers burnt at Finschhafen, was reluctant to take further risks. The advance guard 'was always kept in gun range, seven days of supplies were to be in reach of the forward troops and dumps to the rear of the advance had to be moved forward as quickly as possible so the line of communications, and the force protecting it, would not become strung out and vulnerable'. When required, the forward troops were ordered to a halt 'to allow the supporting tail to close up'.[118] The dynamic form of warfare outlined in the new Australian jungle doctrine was beginning, in practice, to resemble a hybrid between the 'Jungle Soldier's Handbook' and the 'Colossal Cracks' approach; this was perhaps not surprising considering 9th Australian Division and the commander of New Guinea Force (NGF) had fought under Montgomery at El Alamein.[119]

With the advance progressing slowly, but purposefully, MacArthur gave permission for yet another amphibious assault to try and cut off the Japanese retreat. On 2 January, US 32nd Division landed at Saidor, far to the west of the Australian advance. However, instead of pushing rapidly inland to block and destroy the retreating Japanese, the American commanders ordered their troops to dig in. They 'completely overestimated' the capabilities of the Japanese forces in their way. As a result, some 13,000 Japanese troops managed to escape the 'road block' and retreat towards Madang.[120]

With another 'grand opportunity' to 'trap and destroy the remainder of the Japanese forces in New Guinea' lost, the caution of the Australian and American commanders began increasingly to be matched by the troops as they tired due to prolonged exposure on the front line and the debilitating jungle environment. By late December, many 'infantry battalions had less than 300 men out of an establishment of 786'.[121] Battle casualties on the Australian side during the campaign were modest, 7th and 9th Australian Divisions and 4th Militia Brigade suffered only 2,055 in the capture of the whole Peninsula;[122] but this masked a much greater cost in terms of sickness. The 7th Australian Division, engaged in slow positional warfare in the mountains of the Finisterre Range, experienced twenty times more losses due to illness than due to battle casualties. Between 18 September 1943 and 8 April 1944, it lost 13,576 men sick, mostly from tropical diseases such as malaria. These losses amounted to about 96 per cent of the average strength of the division.[123]

Not least as a consequence of these hardships and the tactics employed, it was not until 24 April 1944 that Madang was finally captured, by 5th and 11th Australian Divisions who had replaced the now exhausted 9th and 7th Divisions (on 20 January and 8 April respectively). Of approximately 12,600 Japanese troops deployed against the Australian advance along the coast, 7,000 became casualties. Of the approximately 6,000 Japanese that commenced the campaign in the Markham Valley, 1,200 became casualties; an additional 800 succumbed to illness. By the time of the fall of Madang, the Japanese Eighteenth Army had been 'virtually destroyed, losing some 35,000 men'. The Vitiaz Straits had finally been closed and the isolation of Rabaul, the main Japanese base in the South Pacific, was complete.[124]

There was an additional benefit to the outcome of 'Postern'. As the 20th Japanese Division retreated in disarray from the fighting around Finschhafen, its signallers buried their cryptography library in metal trunks at the bottom of a riverbed. A unit of 9th Australian Division fortuitously stumbled upon the trunks and discovered the division's codebooks. For the next two months, Allied intelligence was able to read all of the Imperial Japanese Army's messages in theatre. Thereafter, in spite of the Japanese changing their codes, Allied intelligence possessed enough information to continue deciphering enemy communications. This intelligence was to prove 'indispensable' to MacArthur as he planned his operations in 1944 with 'almost full access to the IJA's [Imperial Japanese Army] order of battle and operational plans for the region'.[125]

With the conclusion of Operations 'Cartwheel' and 'Postern', the main line of defence of the Japanese Greater Co-Prosperity Region had been breached. MacArthur 'could now launch forward on his campaign of maritime manoeuvre towards the Philippines' and ultimately the occupation of Japan with great confidence. Australian formations had made a steady and eventually 'decisive contribution to MacArthur's strategy'.[126]

Burma

As the Australian Army grappled with the Japanese in New Guinea, so too did the Indian Army get the chance to put their many months of preparation into practice in the jungle. By early 1944, all of the infantry and cavalry regiments on the Burmese front had been retrained in line with the Infantry Committee's recommendations. The two new training divisions were now providing reinforcements of a quality not seen before in the Far East; they were familiar with jungle warfare and had a clear understanding of the way in which doctrine and tactics could be put into practice.[127]

To improve matters further, reinforcements began to pour in from other parts of the Empire. Following the Fall of Singapore, with the loss of 80,000 POWs, the War Office had sent an East African brigade to Ceylon (modern-day Sri Lanka) to free up Indian troops for operations in Burma. Later in the year, with the situation in North Africa stabilised, the authorities began to consider using East and West African troops for the fighting in Burma as well. The 81st and 82nd West African Divisions, each consisting of 28,000 men, arrived in Burma in July and November 1943. They would be joined by 11th East African Division the following summer.[128]

From a British perspective, the presence of all these newly trained, and increasingly well-provisioned formations in Burma offered an opportunity to decisively retake the initiative in South-East Asia.[129] On 18 August 1943, the position was summarised in a paper submitted to the Combined Chiefs of Staff:

> The British Planners feel that the recapture of Singapore ... is a full and correct application of sea and air power. It will electrify the eastern world and have an immense psychological effect on the Japanese. It will ... in fact flank and undermine the whole Japanese defense structure in Southeast Asia.[130]

Such an ambitious amphibious strategy made complete sense from a British perspective but did not tally with American plans in Asia. The United States was concerned first and foremost with the possibility of unlocking the war-fighting potential of Chiang Kai-shek's nationalist China and had little interest in operations aimed at restoring the power and prestige of the British Empire.[131]

The only land route by which American supplies could be transported to China ran through Japanese-occupied northern Burma, the famous 'Burma Road'. It was here that the Americans wished to focus Allied strategy. On 6 October 1943, the Joint Planning Staff reported to the Chiefs of Staff that they considered such a strategy wholly 'unrealistic':

> We conclude, firstly that logistic considerations alone preclude the possibility of advancing very far into . . . Burma against even a scale of opposition much below that to be expected; secondly that even if we could maintain adequate forces at the end of such long and precarious L[ines] of C[ommunication], the advantages conferred on the enemy by the nature of the terrain would certainly render an advance a slow and costly affair. In consequence, we consider that any plan based primarily on an overland advance would be unrealistic. This course is therefore rejected.[132]

The Chiefs of Staff were in no position to prevent the Americans getting their way, however. With ongoing wrangling over strategy in the more important western theatres, it made little sense to expend what credits they had with the Americans over Singapore. The Indian Army was to become embroiled in a strategy that appeared to make no sense from a British perspective, except under the premise that it had to keep the Americans on side and be seen to be doing 'something'.[133]

Second Arakan

As a consequence of these strategic deliberations, the leading elements of XV Indian Corps, which included two brigades of the newly arrived 81st West African Division, and which were 'by far the best trained Commonwealth troops yet deployed in S[outh] E[ast] Asia', were sent to the Arakan in November 1943;[134] the objective once more was Akyab and its airfields. The taking of Akyab would provide a vastly increased radius for Allied aircraft in Burma. As such, Akyab was 'an essential stage' in the recapture of Rangoon, itself only a 'staging point' on the road to the ultimate goal, 'the retaking of Singapore from the Japanese'.[135]

That October, Slim had been promoted to command Fourteenth Army (previously Eastern Army) in a major reshuffle of command in the Far East. General Sir George Giffard was appointed commander of the newly created 11th Army Group, of which Fourteenth Army was the main subordinate formation, and which acted as the land forces HQ for Mountbatten's SEAC, when it became operational in mid-November 1943.[136] Slim, much like Montgomery before him in the desert, 'carefully stage managed' the cautious advance of XV Indian Corps. 'Small-scale actions' were picked which guaranteed success in an effort 'to build and improve basic skills, blood new troops and foster morale'.[137] Slim's efforts were largely successful. The morale report for November 1943 to February 1944 noted:

> The recent actions, large and small, ... have been the first 'ordeals by fire' for many untried troops. Most reports state that there is considerable enthusiasm for offensive action, though the first clash is slight[ly] disconcerting to some of the younger soldiers ... Successes in many minor actions are increasing the troops' confidence in their ability to beat the Jap.[138]

By the end of January 1944, XV Corps comprised six and a half divisions against only one Japanese division in the Arakan.[139] Nevertheless, the advance ground to a halt in the face of determined Japanese resistance around a complex bunker system at the foot of the Mayu Range near Razabil. Lieutenant-General Sir Philip Christison had taken over XV Corps from Slim when he was appointed commander of Fourteenth Army. As he began to regroup to prepare for another assault, the Japanese forces in the area, under the command of the newly created Twenty-Eighth Army (under General Sakurai Shozo), launched a surprise counter-offensive, codenamed Operation 'Ha-Go', on the night of 3/4 February.[140]

The offensive was unquestionably a risky ploy by the Japanese High Command; by the end of 1943, the Japanese position in the Pacific was becoming increasingly fragile. To the west, American naval forces were 'driving like a trident into Japanese positions'. To the north, the Americans had destroyed the Japanese garrison on the Aleutian Islands. In the centre, 'they were gathering to assault the Marshall Islands' and in the south, American and Australian forces were 'thrusting by land and sea along the coast of New Guinea'.[141] Tokyo's strategy to address this deteriorating situation aimed at establishing 'an impregnable perimeter which ran from the Kurile Islands in the north through the inner south Pacific, to "the western parts of New Guinea, the Sunda Strait and Burma"'.[142] Though overall defensive in posture, at the operational and tactical levels the focus still lay very much on the attack.

With this aim in mind, the Japanese High Command wished to launch a limited offensive in Burma.[143] With the newly built Siam to Burma railway opened in October 1943, two divisions and an independent brigade of reinforcements arrived in country. This brought the number of Japanese divisions available for offensive activities to seven, together with one Indian National Army (INA) division. All told, by March 1944, there would be over 300,000 Japanese troops in Burma. Japanese Fifteenth Army, under the command of Lieutenant-General Renya Mutaguchi, who was responsible for the defence of central and northern Burma, proposed an attack into the Bengal plains. If successful, this would cut off Anglo-American supplies to China, where another Japanese offensive, Operation 'Ichi-Go', was planned. If all went well, Mutaguchi's offensive could even knock India out of the war.[144]

The first Arakan campaign had shown that the Indian Army was far from being an effective fighting force. Indeed, in many ways, the Indo-Burmese frontier appeared 'to be the weakest sector' of the whole long Japanese perimeter. In addition, 'India was seething with discontent. Newly inspired by Subhas Bose, the Indian National Army was now a fighting force of 40,000 men, spurred to greater efforts by news of the suffering of the [Bengal] famine. If it appeared on Indian soil ... it might spark a rebellion greater than ... Quit India.'[145] The Japanese High Command authorised Mutaguchi's plan on 7 January 1944, and it was to mask this major assault and draw away British and Commonwealth reserves, that the Twenty-Eighth Army was created and Operation 'Ha-Go' launched in the Arakan.

Shozo, who by now had three divisions at his disposal, only employed one division in the attack, a decision that was 'indicative of the low opinion the Japanese had of their opponents'.[146] The Japanese columns infiltrated through the British and Commonwealth positions and overnight the rear areas of XV Indian Corps 'were transformed into the front line with administrative troops bearing much of the burden of dealing with advancing Japanese troops'. However, 'to the surprise of many' British and Commonwealth, but also Japanese officers, the troops on the lines of communication 'displayed a determination and fighting spirit unknown a year before and took a heavy toll of the Japanese attackers'.[147]

Instead of withdrawing, as had happened many times before, troops were ordered to assume all-round defence and immediately go on half-rations.[148] Lieutenant-General Pownall, serving at HQ SEAC, observed, 'we've learned now to fight where we stand and NOT to be frightened of the bogey of infiltration'. The Japanese attacked XV Corps with increasingly fanatical desperation 'seeking to secure vitally needed stockpiled supplies of food, arms and ammunition'. But, with air supply providing the necessary supplies, 'including newspapers, mail, toothbrushes and other sundries', British and Indian troops held their ground and 'fought on until the . . . Japanese units had exhausted their own food and ammunition'. Over a five-week period, 714 sorties were flown by British and US transport aircraft dropping some 2,300 tons of food, ammunition and other stores. Air power had proved vital to sustaining the isolated, self-contained and all-round defensive boxes central to the Indian Army's new operational technique.[149]

Moreover, 'a new spirit was evident' among the men.[150] Cases of battle exhaustion constituted less than 10 per cent of battle casualties.[151] The morale report for the period noted the 'high' morale among British and Commonwealth troops in the Arakan. Success, at last, proved a tonic in itself. The morale reports stated proudly:

> For the first time it is possible to say that the news from the East has received as much attention as the news from the West and much pleasure is expressed at the fact that the 'Forgotten Army' has come into its own.[152]

Allied air power in Burma also had a 'highly encouraging effect', as did the new-found 'fighting ability of Indian troops'. The 'majority of reports' indicated that Josh groups and welfare education were having 'a good effect' and that there had 'been an increase of anti-Jap feeling'. While the troops consistently showed 'more concern with personal matters, particularly the welfare of their families', than for 'the war as a whole', as a report from the Army School of Education showed, 'out of a group of I.O.Rs. [Indian Other Ranks] questioned, 80% had no complaint' about their domestic situation.[153] Matters had certainly improved for the Indian soldier and one of the main outcomes of the man-management and welfare revolution was the success of the Indian Army in battle.

By 26 February, the enemy offensive 'had been broken', leaving 5,000 Japanese dead on the battlefield.[154] XV Corps had suffered 3,506 casualties, but the performance of the British, Indian and West African men of the corps had been highly satisfactory.[155] As Slim later wrote:

> This Arakan Battle ... was the turning-point of the Burma campaign . . . [British and Commonwealth] soldiers had proved themselves, man for man, the masters of the best the Japanese

could bring against them . . . it was a victory about which there could be no argument, and its effect, not only on the troops engaged, but on the whole XIV Army, was immense.[156]

Imphal and Kohima

The failure of 'Ha-Go' did not deter Mutaguchi from launching the main part of his ambitious offensive in Burma, Operation 'U-Go'. Mutaguchi had at his disposal Fifteenth Army, consisting of about 100,000 combat troops, including three experienced infantry divisions, 15th, 31st and 33rd, plus the 1st INA Division in support (another 7,000 men).[157] The Japanese planned a two-pronged attack towards the massive British and Commonwealth logistical base area that had been built up on the Imphal Plain since 1942. By advancing on Imphal to the south and to Kohima in the north, it was hoped through 'aggressive, bold and inventive' action that Fifteenth Army would encircle the British and Commonwealth forces and trigger a chaotic and perhaps catastrophic retreat.[158]

The attack fell on IV Indian Corps, commanded by Lieutenant-General G. A. P. Scoones, which had a strength of about 155,000 men and 11,000 animals.[159] IV Corps had 17th Indian Division, under Major-General 'Punch' Cowan, deployed in the south at Tiddim; it had 20th Indian Division, under Major-General Douglas Gracey, on the Chindwin to the east, in the area of Tamu and Sittang; and it had 23rd Indian Division, under Major-General Ouvry Roberts, in reserve north and east of Imphal, with one brigade responsible for the garrison of Kohima and the defence of Ukhrul (see Map 12.3). Scoones planned, if attacked, to concentrate the corps at the base area of Imphal, with its airfields and stockpiles. There he would fight it out, supplied by air, until a major counter-offensive could be mounted once the Japanese advance had petered out.[160]

The offensive began on 7/8 March, when Japanese 33rd Division advanced through the jungle and infiltrated into and behind 17th Indian Division around Tiddim. The 17th Division began a pre-planned withdrawal along the narrow 160-mile long road to the Imphal Plain. For once, Japanese roadblocks failed to turn a withdrawal into a rout. The division, supported by two brigades of 23rd Indian Division, employed 'vicious' counter-attacks to bulldoze its way through successive Japanese positions, its 16,000 troops, 2,500 vehicles and 3,500 animals supplied all the way from the air. On 4 April, it reached the Imphal Plain.[161]

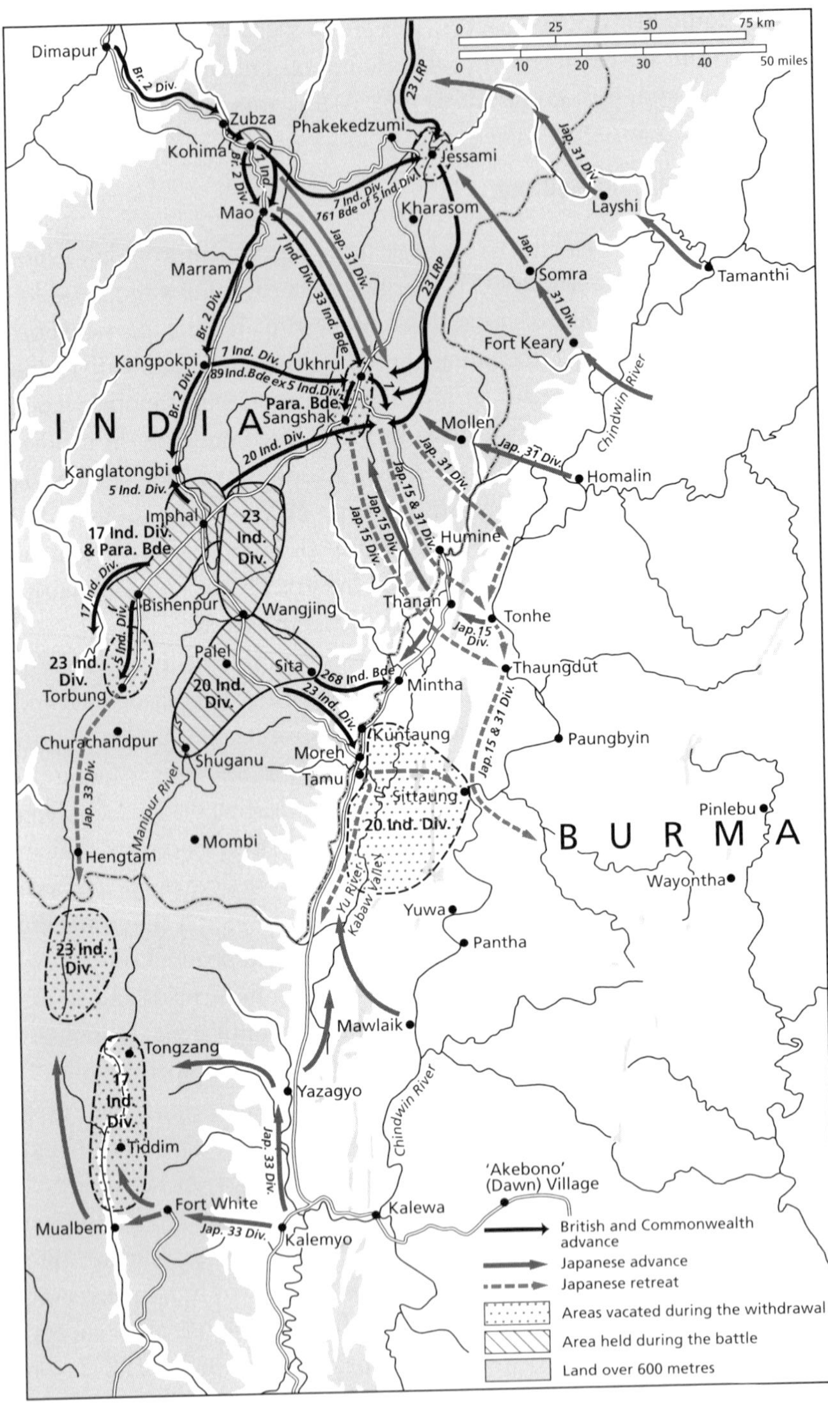

Map 12.3 The Battles of Imphal and Kohima, March–June 1944

On 12 March, a week after the attack of Japanese 33rd Division, the Japanese 15th Division entered the fray. It advanced by Ukhrul to cut the Kohima–Imphal road and then swung south to attack Imphal from the north. The 20th Indian Division, just like 17th Indian Division, withdrew in good order towards Imphal. Further to the north, the Japanese 31st Division also joined the battle and drove through the 5,000-foot-high Naga Hills towards the positions around the small hill station of Kohima, cutting the road north and south of the village.[162]

Imphal and Kohima were now cut off from the land route back to India. There was a month's supply of stocks on the Imphal Plain but the garrison of 2,500 men at Kohima was in no way similarly prepared. Slim rushed 50th Indian Parachute Brigade to Kohima and 5th Indian Division, which had returned from the Middle East, was transferred from the Arakan to reinforce Imphal, with one brigade going to Kohima. Realising that he was now fighting not one but two significant battles, Slim sent forward XXXIII Indian Corps HQ, under Lieutenant-General Sir Montague Stopford, to manage the situation at Kohima, leaving Scoones free to fight the Imphal battle unimpeded.[163]

On 4 April, the Japanese forces began their assault on Kohima. For two weeks they attacked ceaselessly, shrinking the perimeter and leaving pockets of defenders surrounded and cut off. The garrison did not surrender and slowly the tide began to turn. On 18 April, the leading troops of 2nd Division, accompanied by tanks, fought their way through to Kohima from India; after its chastening experience in France in 1940 it had arrived in India in 1942 to form an emergency reserve for the Middle and Far East theatres.[164] The Japanese forces, which had carried only twenty days' rations and ammunition with them into battle now began to 'wither on the vine'. To make matters worse, they were badly affected by cholera and malaria.[165]

The Japanese Fifteenth Army had been 'sucked into' a set of attritional battles for which it was 'badly organised' and 'ill-equipped'. Japanese units 'lacked sufficient firepower to break through the hardening British defences'. Whenever they emerged from the protective jungle, they 'were exposed to devastating attacks by massed artillery, tanks and tactical air power and suffered heavy losses'.[166] It was, in many ways, 'Stalingrad in reverse for the Japanese Fifteenth Army'.[167] In March, 1,475 sorties were flown, dropping 400 tons of bombs in support of the Imphal–Kohima forces. Between 18 April and 30 June, the RAF and United States Army Air Force 'flew in 19,000 reinforcements, 13,000 tons of cargo, 835,000 gallons of petrol and evacuated 43,000 non-combatants and 13,000 casualties to India'. The daily tonnage of supplies flown in support of IV Corps on the Imphal Plain in April was 148; by June it reached 362.[168] By comparison, the much larger besieged German Sixth Army at Stalingrad received only 90 tons a day in December 1942 and 120 tons a day in January 1943.[169]

With the British and Commonwealth troops at Imphal proving as resolute as those at Kohima, 'the Japanese offensive had by the end of March 1944 already reached its high water mark'. It was one thing, however, to hold on to ground and resist Japanese assaults; it was a totally different matter to dislodge the Japanese from the positions they still occupied around IV and XXXIII Indian Corps. The British and Commonwealth forces quickly found that their new tactical techniques, learned during the period of retraining in 1943, did not lead inevitably to the kind of battle outcomes that they had envisaged, the retreat and destruction of the Japanese Army. It became increasingly necessary to fight the Japanese out of every bunker and every defensive locality between Imphal and Kohima.[170]

The British and Commonwealth counter-offensive, when it began, therefore, was carried out in a painstakingly slow manner, requiring vast quantities of supplies and ammunition to dislodge the enemy.[171] Much like the Australians in the final stages of Operation 'Postern', the troops tired after their prolonged exposure to the debilitating jungle conditions and the hazards of the front line. Sickness rates, which had 'remained remarkably good' until the end of the siege, now soared (see Figure 8.1). By late May/June, they had nearly doubled, not least due to the arrival of the monsoon (which led to an increase in the number of mosquitos and cases of malaria), and an outbreak in dysentery.[172] To make matters worse, after months of heavy fighting malnutrition was now 'not uncommon'; many had also suffered from the reduction of the water ration at Kohima to less than a pint a day.[173] Morale suffered under these conditions and Fourteenth Army, much like Eighth Army in Italy and the Australians in New Guinea, relied on its material superiority to drive the Japanese out of their defences.[174]

The historian, Timothy Moreman, has referred to the operational technique that developed during this period, February to July 1944, as 'colossal crumps'; and, indeed, much like 'colossal cracks' in the West, the 'fast, flexible fire support' now available to Fourteenth

Army proved effective against troops in the open, but of less utility against well dug-in, determined defenders.[175] This was a problem, as, in some ways 'the Japanese army thrown against Imphal and Kohima was a kind of mass suicide squad'.[176] Slim wrote on 3 June:

> What we find is that we can kill the first 50% of a Jap formation comparatively easily, because they attack and counter-attack thus giving us our opportunity. It is the second 50%, and especially the last 25%, who cause us our losses and who hold us up. They dig in and have to be literally prized out and killed individually in the bitterest kind of fighting imaginable. That fighting is going on now, continuously.[177]

The Japanese Army – starving, sick and exhausted – finally broke around Imphal/Kohima. It retreated from Kohima on 1 June. Stopford immediately sent 2nd Division southwards to support IV Corps. On 22 June, 2nd Division, of XXXIII Indian Corps, and 5th Indian Division, of IV Indian Corps, joined together on the Imphal road, ending a siege that had lasted eighty-six days.[178] Operation 'U-Go' had failed utterly, costing Mutaguchi an estimated 50,000 dead, 'making it the worst defeat in Japan's military history'. In a stark illustration of the brutality of the fighting, only 600 Japanese were taken prisoner. The price of victory was also immense. By the end of the Second Arakan campaign, XV Indian Corps had suffered 7,951 casualties. At Imphal and Kohima, IV and XXXIII Indian Corps had lost a further 16,700 men. Overall, SEAC's total casualties between January and June 1944 came to 40,000 plus 282,000 sick.[179] In spite of the 'butcher's bill', and the privations experienced by those on the front line, by August 'the striking military successes of Fourteenth Army' were beginning to have an extremely positive effect; confidence and morale in the theatre was now 'higher than it has ever been before'.[180] Slim and Auchinleck were later knighted for the remarkable turnaround in the fortunes of the Indian Army.[181] The threat to the Raj was finally over, and 'it was now a question of how soon the enemy could be pursued across the Chindwin and the reconquest of Burma begin'.[182]

Turn Around

The year 1943 was 'seminal' in recalibrating Australian jungle warfare doctrine. As the lessons of Kokoda, Milne Bay and the

Beachheads permeated throughout the Army, 'marked improvements in the standards of training and preparation for jungle warfare' were evident across Australian formations. No less a transformation took place in the Indian Army. The British and Commonwealth Armies in the jungle would from now on be 'extremely well trained and far better armed and equipped'.[183] This turnaround resulted in dramatically improved performance on the battlefield. Japanese forces were defeated in New Guinea in the largest military operations ever conducted by Australian forces,[184] while the Indian Army, barely a year after its rout in the first Arakan campaign, inflicted at Imphal/Kohima the 'greatest land defeat of the Japanese armed forces in their history'.[185]

The British and Commonwealth Armies in the East were a hotbed of inter-theatre and inter-army learning. The more formal exchange of ideas between the Australian and Indian Armies was matched by an at times less prescribed transfer of techniques and processes from the West. As commanders and formations were moved east, to address the great emergency sparked by the Japanese victories in 1942, tactics employed in the desert were adapted and tried in the jungle. The key lessons of Adam's manpower revolution at the War Office were also applied in Australia and India. At the same time, the Australian and Indian Armies profited from a hard, and at times painful, assessment of their own performance in the early years of the war. By 1943, both institutions could fairly be described as effective learning organisations.

As a result of these changes, in both the SWPA and Burma, the form of warfare adopted by the Australian and Indian Armies reflected a hybrid between the basic principles of *FSR* and Montgomery's 'Colossal Cracks' approach. As a consequence, both Armies proved exceptionally capable of killing Japanese in battles of attrition but less accomplished in the kinds of rapid exploitation operations that were required for the annihilation of Japanese formations in the field. Nevertheless, the British and Commonwealth Armies in the jungle had made massive strides forward. High morale and a willingness to fight had, as ever, proved to be the overriding determinant of success and failure. Indeed, this is what the reform of the Australian and Indian Armies had always been about. As the 'Jungle Book' concluded, the 'guts already displayed by our troops at Sidi Barrani, Keren, Damascus, Tobruk and in the wary stubborn withdrawal from Rangoon, will prove – as ever – the "deciding factor"'.[186] A truly remarkable turnaround had taken place.

Part V Redemption

13 D-DAY

As the British and Commonwealth Armies in Italy, Burma and the South-West Pacific gradually wore the German and Imperial Japanese Armies down in battle, planning for the 'second front', the 'great crusade' in North-West Europe, gathered pace. By the second major Anglo-American conference, held in Casablanca in January 1943, it had become clear that the proposed invasion would not commence before 1944; the British timetable for the war against Germany had won out. Planning for the cross-Channel invasion, however, could not wait until 1944;[1] there had to be an individual and an organisation in charge of preparations who 'would impart a dynamic impetus' to preparing what was envisaged to be the decisive campaign of the war.[2] In April 1943, Lieutenant-General Frederick Morgan, the commander of British I Corps in the United Kingdom, was appointed to this role as Chief of Staff to the Supreme Allied Commander (Designate); the Supreme Allied Commander had not yet been appointed. Morgan rapidly put together a new organisation, which was to become known as COSSAC (derived from the first letters of his title) and began detailed planning for the invasion of North-West Europe, now codenamed 'Overlord'. By the end of July, Morgan and his staff had prepared a plan for a cross-Channel invasion in May 1944 and specifically for an assault on the beaches of Normandy on the north-west coast of France; it won approval from Churchill and the British Chiefs of Staff and was presented to the Americans at the Quebec 'Quadrant' conference in August 1943. There, Roosevelt and the US Chiefs signed it off.[3]

At last, the Allies had the beginnings of a concrete plan for the final defeat of the *Wehrmacht* on the Continent. The choice of commander for the forthcoming invasion, however, was no easy task. The two most senior officers in the British and US armies, Brooke and Marshall, harboured ambitions to return to the field, but both men were indispensable in their respective roles in London and Washington. In the circumstances, it was decided to move the experienced, and thus far successful, leadership team from the Mediterranean to London to take over the planning and execution of the invasion; Eisenhower was announced as Supreme Allied Commander on 6 December 1943, with Tedder appointed as his deputy. On 24 December, Montgomery was informed that he would take charge of the Anglo-Canadian 21st Army Group and have overall command of the Allied land forces (until Eisenhower took over). General Omar Bradley would command 12th US Army Group and Lieutenant-General Sir Miles Dempsey, who had started the war as a battalion commander in France and who had risen through the ranks to command a corps in the latter stages of the campaign in North Africa and during the fighting in the Mediterranean, would command British Second Army. Lieutenant-General Harry Crerar would take charge of First Canadian Army once sufficient Canadian formations had landed in Europe. Beneath these men, the five Anglo-Canadian Army corps (I, VIII, XII, XXX and II Canadian) would be commanded by Lieutenant-General John Crocker, Lieutenant-General Richard O'Connor, who had escaped from Italian captivity and returned to the UK, Lieutenant-General Neil Ritchie, once more given an operational command after the disaster at Gazala in 1942, Lieutenant-General Gerard Bucknall and Lieutenant-General Guy Simonds, who had commanded 1st Canadian Division in the Mediterranean.[4]

It was the good fortune of these men that they took charge of armies that, in many ways, had been 'rebuilt and reinvented' since the disasters of the early years of the war. Nevertheless, the challenge ahead of them was immense. The British and Commonwealth Armies in the United Kingdom were, as they had been throughout the war, made up of citizen soldiers; around 75 per cent of troops were conscripts, the rest being professionals and volunteers.[5] Some had experienced defeat in France and escaped from Dunkirk in June 1940. Others, such as the veteran 7th Armoured, 50th Northumbrian, 51st Highland and 1st Airborne Divisions, and 4th and 8th Armoured Brigades had fought for many years in the Middle East and Mediterranean theatres and had experienced both heady victories and devastating defeats. The rest, the majority, had experienced no combat at all and relied exclusively on training to prepare them for the challenges ahead;[6] of the twenty-five divisions stationed in the British Isles on the eve of the invasion, only five (20 per cent) had seen service overseas since the outbreak of the war.[7]

Training and Doctrine

In these circumstances, the quality of training was key; the dramatic turnaround in the basic competence of the British and Commonwealth Armies in the Middle and Far East would have to be replicated in the United Kingdom. Indeed, it was; 21st Army Group, and Home Forces before it, pursued a very similar approach to that which had been successfully initiated in these other theatres. Even before the arrival of Montgomery and his team in the UK, a centrally controlled tactical training programme for new recruits, under the Director of Military Training at the War Office, had been introduced (in 1942).[8] All new recruits in the Army were now enlisted into a General Service Corps, where 'a common syllabus of six weeks primary training' was carried out. During this period, selection tests were performed (see Chapter 7) 'to determine the type of employment for which the recruit was most suited'.[9] After the six-week primary training programme, and a week's leave, men would then move to corps training centres for the arm with which they were to serve. Infantry were given the shortest period of specialist training, ten weeks, while signals were given the longest, up to thirty weeks. The men were then transferred to one of the new 'reserve' divisions (formed in late 1942), of which there were three for most of the war. Here, they were given five weeks additional 'collective' and 'crew' training before they were sent to their field formations. Gone were the days when each regiment was left to its own devices to train its recruits.[10]

To complement this rationalisation of the training of new recruits, a plethora of 'schools' and training establishments were set up, much as had been the case in Australia and India, to prepare the Field Army for the challenges that awaited. By October 1942, there were no fewer than thirty-two schools under the Director of Military Training, including an Armoured Fighting Vehicle School at Bovington, an Advanced Handling and Fieldcraft School at Llanberis, a Mountain and Snow Warfare Training Centre at Glenfeshire and a Royal Armoured Corps (RAC) Officers Tactical School at Tidworth. By the end of 1942, the School of Infantry had been founded at Barnard Castle in Northern Command, where the training of instructors and the development of doctrine was centralised and controlled.[11]

That is where the similarities between the reform of the Australian and Indian Armies and that of the British and Canadian Armies in the United Kingdom ceased. For, whereas new doctrine, as encapsulated in the 'Jungle Soldier's Handbook' and the 'Jungle Book', had directed and animated the retraining of the armies in the East, the preparation of 21st Army Group was not guided by a similar and universally accepted evolution in doctrine. The key manual guiding the training of the British Army during this period, 'Infantry Training', had not been revised since 1937. A provisional document pending the long-awaited rewriting of 'Infantry Training', 'The Instructor's Handbook on Fieldcraft and Battle Drill' (published in October 1942), focused almost entirely on battle drill as the 'accepted' and 'orthodox way to teach tactics'.[12] The problem was that many commanding officers were sceptical about the utility of battle drill as a catch-all solution for tactical problems on the battlefield. 'The Instructor's Handbook' would, therefore, not play the role of the 'Jungle Soldier's Handbook' or the 'Jungle Book' for 21st Army Group.

Some commanders were so concerned about the utility of battle drill that they were 'reluctant' to send their junior officers and NCOs to schools because they saw the teaching in such establishments as 'not in accordance with what goes on in battle'. Many believed that Battle School trainees were 'wooden' in action, trying 'to apply a manoeuvre which they have previously seen to totally unsuited situations and ground'.[13] Moreover, when push came to shove, too many commanders had 'fundamental doubts' over the 'moral fitness of the typical infantryman' to apply 'battle drill to common tactical ends'. The adoption of such approaches required devolving, to the lowest levels of the army, decision-making, about, for example, when to go to ground and when to advance. Many held that 'once down soldiers would refuse to get up again', and that, therefore, it was far more effective to tell soldiers when to advance, to encourage them to keep their feet and rush forward by 'leaning' on a barrage.[14]

The influence of the great defeats of 1940 to 1942 was hard to shake. Crerar, the commander of First Canadian Army, wrote to his men in May 1944, that the 'temptation to "go to ground"' must be resisted and that this had to be 'thoroughly drilled into the minds of all those under command'. Those troops that allowed themselves to go to ground were 'doing exactly what the enemy wants':

> The longer they remain static, the more certain it is they lose the assistance of their own supporting fire programme, and that they will become casualties to the defensive fire of the enemy. To press on is not only tactically sound, it is, for the individual, much safer.[15]

The revised Infantry Training Manual, which was, according to some historians, the 'most important tactical manual to be issued by the British Army during the Second World War', was released in March 1944, far too late to guide the training of those formations destined for Normandy.[16]

In the absence of a universally accepted doctrinal solution to the tactical problem, such as that disseminated in the East, Montgomery had scope to take a grip of 21st Army Group and direct training as he saw fit. Indeed, it is apparent that Montgomery's thinking about his operational approach had evolved since his days in the Middle East and the Mediterranean. In light of the attritional battles of 1942 and 1943 and the fact that he was commander of an army group rather than an army, he recognised that he had to rebalance the relationship between control and initiative in his armies. Up to El Alamein, he had been adamant that the commander who was 'fighting the battle' had 'to be able to exercise full control and give quick decisions in sufficient time to influence the fast moving tactical battle'.[17] By 1944, he was stressing a very different ethos, one that began to resonate more with interwar *FSR* than with 'Colossal Cracks'. 'Within the general limits' of his 'framework' or his 'instructions or plan', he told his generals, 'subordinates do as they like'. It was 'essential' for his subordinates 'to establish confidence' and 'accept responsibility and get on with the job'. Armies, corps and divisions would 'run their own show', once they had received 'the general form from me'.[18] 'Rather than telling people how to do things', Montgomery now 'insisted on the importance of people coming up with their own answers with regard to tactical problem solving'.[19] In Normandy, he would seek a 'more rapid tempo in sequencing between phases and operations' in response to the 'tactical and operational problems' he expected to face.[20]

The shift in focus illustrated Montgomery's capacity for reflection and the continuing influence of interwar *FSR* on the thinking of senior British commanders. Before 1939, when commander of 9th Infantry Brigade, he had written that:

> We must remember that if we do not trust our subordinates we will never train them. But if they know they are trusted and that they will be judged on results, the effect will be electrical. The fussy commander, who is for ever interfering in the province of his subordinates, will never train others in the art of command.[21]

Montgomery's imposition of a centralised rather than directive command and control system on Eighth Army had not been the result of prewar doctrine, or the influence of the First World War; it evolved instead from his experience of the first years of the Second World War. In the circumstances, in the specific context faced by Eighth Army, he had acted pragmatically and found a way to win. Now, having been thoroughly frustrated by his experience in the Mediterranean, he once more sought to adapt his approach.[22]

The fact that he largely failed in this endeavour has much to do with training. Before Montgomery's arrival as Commander-in-Chief (C-in-C) in January 1944, 'the object' of collective training in the UK had 'usually' been 'determined by G.H.Q.'.[23] Sir Bernard Paget, the first commander of 21st Army Group, had no qualms about laying down 'the pattern of training for all formations'.[24] But, on taking over his new command, Montgomery explicitly forbade centrally mandated training guidelines. 'I have no training instructions', he told his generals on 13 January 1944, 'Army Comds train their armies.' 'Good troops who are well officered, well trained, mentally alert, and who are fit and active', he continued, 'will adapt themselves to any conditions. Do not cramp initiative or break the chain of command, in the issue of training instructions.' Army group Monthly Training Letters were 'to be discontinued' and 'all orders' contained in these letters 'saying that unit commanders *will* do this, or that', were to be 'cancelled'.[25]

This was radically different to Montgomery's approach to training for El Alamein when he had been more than happy to set out precisely what formations had to cover in training.[26] In hindsight, the decision to leave the direction of training in the hands of subordinates seems perplexing, especially considering the lessons of the early years of the war. The outcome was that a rather dysfunctional hybrid doctrinal formula emerged in 21st Army Group. Senior officers, left to their own devices, 'married' two approaches, battle drill and mechanised firepower. Troops were trained to employ battle drill, but only when bombardments had failed to adequately open the way for the infantry to advance. Priority was unquestionably given to the mechanised firepower-heavy approach of advancing behind a barrage, as it had been proven to work.[27]

The 'Colossal Cracks' formula would, thus, be rolled out once again in Normandy. This method, as evidenced from experience in North Africa and the Mediterranean was attritional, 'with the twin objectives of seizing ground and wearing down an enemy'. It was not elegant and it severely limited the possibilities for exploitation, but to most 'there were few better realistic options available'. Although often costly in terms of lives and resources, these tactics were 'likely to inflict serious damage' on a defender 'who was doctrinally committed to counterattacking for every lost yard of ground'. The strength of 'Colossal Cracks', therefore, 'lay in that it switched the combatants' places, so that the attacker, upon reaching the objective, could dig in and assume a defensive stance, with most of the advantages of the defence on their side if they could entrench themselves rapidly'.[28]

In spite of the doctrinal 'fluidity' that overtook 21st Army Group in the run-up to the invasion of North-West Europe, there can be little doubt that Montgomery's armies did train with great energy and focus. The exercises undertaken by 21st Army Group prior to D-Day 'represented probably the most extensive and thorough training programme the British army in the UK had ever undertaken'.[29] The censorship summaries for North-West Europe support this assessment. The reports for April and May 1944 were based on 127,797 British and 32,163 Canadian letters and each bi-weekly report had a section devoted to training. From these, it is clear that, in many respects, no military formation ever went into battle more thoroughly prepared. They note 'many references to tough training and strenuous field exercises'. By April 1944, training had 'reached a high level'; it was 'invariably enjoyed'; and the 'personal fitness' of the troops was of a high standard. The 'general picture', according to the summaries, was one of 'efficiently run units with discipline at a high level'.[30] By the start of May, the censors noted that 'strenuous and organised training schemes have contributed greatly to the confidence, and general sense of physical and mental well being of the troops'. A private in the 2nd Gordon Highlanders,[31] of 15th Scottish Division, a territorial division that had spent the war training in Britain, wrote, 'our training is simply terrific just now and we are seldom in the camp. We are certainly going through our paces these days, but it's all for the best.' A company sergeant major in the 1st King's Own Scottish Borderers, 3rd Division, which, since its evacuation from Dunkirk, had also spent its time training in Britain, remarked that 'things are going along well . . . I am feeling almost done up as we were out all night on a very hard bit of training and I reckon I must have been marched the whole length and breadth of dear old Britain.'[32]

Comments on being 'trained and ready' were 'frequent' in Canadian mail too, one man writing, 'if we don't know how to use our equipment or how to fight by now we never shall'.[33] By the end of May, British troops were writing home to the effect that they were 'like race horses waiting for the word "go"'. 'The standard of training is high', reported the censors, 'and the large number of references are usually associated with expressions of fitness and readiness for action. Writers invariably refer to training as hard and arduous, but without complaint.'[34] The Canadian censors noted that 'the many references to training' were 'linked with expressions of confidence and fitness, and emphasise the morale and preparedness of the troops'.[35]

Such evidence is backed up and given colour by the secondary literature.[36] The historian of one of the assault divisions, 3rd British Division, which had trained for over a year for its role in the invasion of the Continent, recalled that by the autumn of 1943, 'every soldier knew what to do on coming to grips with the enemy on the occupied land of Europe'.[37] Realistic training exercises (especially with regards to the initial beach assaults), battle schools and battle inoculation had taken their toll in casualties. However, as Lieutenant-Colonel Trevor Hart Dyke, of 49th West Riding Division, which had spent much of its time since Norway garrisoning Iceland and, from 1942, training in Britain, recorded, 'this policy was well rewarded when we went into battle, as we were not then unduly perturbed by the noise and danger of war'.[38] The 21st Army Group was trained and ready to go; time would tell whether the inconsistencies inherent in its doctrine and preparation for Normandy would play out detrimentally on the battlefield.

Selection and Morale

To support 21st Army Group's training programme, a major effort was made to select the right men for the coming campaign and to get the most out of the human element of the combat problem. The years of defeat had been associated with an extremely inefficient use of the human resources available to the Army. The War Office was determined to ensure that the same mistakes were not made again. Between September 1943 and D-Day, an intensive programme of personnel selection and testing was carried out on the units of 21st Army Group. About 180 personnel selection officers (PSOs) and 200 sergeant-testers were employed and by D-Day the 'great bulk of the troops in forward areas had been visited' and assessed. The procedure was then extended to reinforcements, and, in the end, nearly all arms were covered.[39] Once testing had been completed, 'ratings conferences' were held between PSOs and unit representatives to assess 'each soldier's' general character and efficiency. All information gained was entered on men's records and on their Field Conduct Sheets in the form of special Monomark codes which, when translated, gave the soldier's physique, age-group, general intelligence and knowledge, standard of education, nature of present duties and suitability for training on other duties. Every CO had this information at his disposal and, as a result, was 'better able to choose the "right man for the right job"'.[40] Those officers, NCOs and men who were considered 'unsuitable' for the forthcoming campaign were reallocated and posted to activities more appropriate to their intellect and skills.[41]

In February 1944, a psychiatric advisor was attached to 21st Army Group and provision was made for medical officers specially trained in field psychiatry to be allocated to corps and higher formation staffs.[42] One of these men, Major Robert J. Phillips, who joined VIII Corps in September 1943, recalled that he spent much of his time in the run up to D-Day lecturing and liaising with medical officers, regimental officers and padres on the problems of psychiatric casualties in battle. By March 1944, he was confident that all medical officers in the corps had 'realised the importance of watching for incipient signs of early breakdown' and 'were showing a marked interest in and keenness to learn something of psychiatry'. Between October 1943 and May 1944, 770 men in VIII Corps were psychiatrically evaluated, the majority of whom were transferred, downgraded or discharged. Just before D-Day,

Phillips distributed three pamphlets on battle exhaustion and organised a 'Study Day' for all corps medical officers. Additionally, in the final exercise before embarkation, Philips had VIII Corps practising the evacuation of 'mock psychiatric battle casualties'.[43]

The Canadian Army was equally convinced of the value of weeding out unsuitable men prior to combat on the Continent. A neuropsychiatrist was attached to each of the divisions (2nd, 3rd and 4th Armoured) that were to take part in the campaign. These specialists carried out 'psychiatric weeding' and gave 'instruction' to medical officers on the handling of breakdown cases in battle. Such screening and teaching was particularly intensive in 3rd Canadian Infantry Division, which was to assault Juno beach on 6 June. Major R. A. Gregory, the Division Neuropsychiatrist, instructed all the medical officers, and they, in turn, gave an hour-long talk to officers of their units and another one to NCOs. In all, 127 men were removed on psychiatric grounds from this division in the three months running up to the landings.[44] The other two divisions had less instruction and pre-invasion weeding.[45] Nevertheless, between 8 May and 9 June 1944, a course of five lectures on army psychiatry was given to the medical officers of 4th Canadian Armoured Division and forty-one soldiers in the division were referred to psychiatrists, of whom only thirteen were returned to their units.[46] Overall, across the Canadian Army in the UK, 5,813 men were assessed and downgraded in the six months before the invasion.[47]

Allied to the imperatives of training and manpower allocation, was the issue of morale. Indeed, morale received more attention and careful management in the period before D-Day than before any other operation of the Second World War. Over the many years of training and preparation in the UK, attempts had been made to foster a greater commitment to Britain's war effort. Army education, in particular, had sought, through discussions and citizenship instruction, to excite troops about the possibilities of broadly defined social and political reforms in Britain. However, even these educational innovations, while heightening soldiers' political awareness and increasing their understanding of the ideals of democracy, were not sufficient, in light of the Government's unwillingness to promise real reform, to produce high and enduring morale and motivation.[48]

Matters were not improved when the much-anticipated news of increases in pay for British soldiers was announced in April 1944.

The increment, in marked contrast to its reception in the Mediterranean, was widely judged as too small; the difference between military rates of pay and civilian wages was just that more apparent for those still serving on the home front. Of ten pages addressing morale in the censorship summary for Second British Army, 1 to 15 May 1944, three were dedicated to the subject. It reported that it was 'generally expected' that the increase in pay and allowances 'would be substantial all round, and the disappointment has had a marked effect on the spirit of the troops ... The increase of 3d a day is held up to ridicule by all.'[49]

The paltry improvement left many wondering about the extent to which they were valued by the state. Some wished that they were young enough to emigrate; others talked of 'revolution' and a concern for how they would be treated after the war. The company quarter master sergeant of 3rd Monmouthshire Regiment, 11th Armoured Division, remarked that 'I'm afraid I cannot think anything about him [Churchill] after those scandalous pay "concessions" ... What we want in the army is a first class trade Union now.' As regards officers, 'the general opinion' was that unless they enjoyed a private income they could 'barely manage'. A major in an unnamed British infantry brigade wrote:

> I was also surprised about the recent 'services pay increase' – and it's little short of scandalous ... Have you ever heard of the miners or railwaymen striking and being appeased by an additional 7/6 a *month* ... Either it shows up what our government thinks of 'the officer' – or as has always been the case he is expected to be a man of means. When will it be recognised that an officer *can* be a professional in his business, and make it a life study. No, seemingly it is still a hobby to be indulged in but his income must come from private sources ... the cost of living is up by 40% – taxation has been doubled – both since 1938 – and still I could get no more pay than then ... Every other person, not in the forces, is earning twice sometimes three times his pre-war wage.[50]

The War Office had neither the power nor authority to fully compensate for a government that at its heart eschewed the dramatic changes the soldiers craved. Thus, great efforts were made to manage those influences on morale that were in the Army's control. The need for 'spit and polish' could not be completely done away with, but soldiers could be treated as valued and respected citizens and be led in humane and imaginative ways. A remarkably sophisticated system to monitor and manage morale in the lead-up to, and during, the North-West Europe campaign was developed through better officer selection and training and by utilising the intelligence gained from unit censorship.[51]

The use of censorship, in particular, allowed the Army to react with great speed to the needs of the men. Those in charge of unit and base censorship, on learning of some defect or problem, would write to officers in command of units and formations.[52] These interventions would typically lead to concrete actions to address the men's concerns. The Navy, Army and Air Force Institutes (NAAFI) were able to confirm by the second half of 1943, for example, that 'every individual case' brought to their attention through the 'extremely interesting and useful' censorship reports, was addressed.[53]

Efforts were made to ensure that this important feedback loop would work on the Continent too. Whereas there had been delays in the arrival of censorship sections in previous campaigns, censorship units would now 'proceed to the theatre of war in small parties attached proportionally to formations' until a base censorship apparatus was fully up and running. This would both improve security and ensure that GHQ was provided with 'useful up to date censorship morale reports'.[54] Divisions, battalions, companies and platoons in need of cigarettes, clothing, better equipment, leadership, or rest, would be identified through censorship and action would be taken.

The 'Montgomery effect' was an important factor too; before D-Day, Montgomery took the time to address all the men in his huge command, formation by formation, to assure them that the invasion would succeed.[55] In these speeches he emphasised again and again the vital importance of morale and the need for senior and junior officers to nurture it in their men at all available opportunities.[56] The Army may have lacked one of the key ingredients of a highly cohesive organisation, a passionate commitment to a cause; nevertheless, it identified this deficit and proved adept at attempting to manage morale in other ways.

By the middle of April 1944, as 21st Army Group began to assemble in the south-east of England, it was clear that these efforts had largely paid off.[57] The censorship summaries presented a picture of 'keen, well trained troops'. Morale was described as 'high', and a 'good fighting spirit' was frequently noted in the mail.[58] Phillips recalled that the VIII Corps' move from its training area to the south of England had 'produced an uplift in morale which was very evident':

> At last our troops felt that the time would not be long before they could put all their intensive training into actual practice. The vast mixture of Corps and Divisional signs that one saw in the South added to the spirit of comradeship and served to produce a realisation that one's own Corps was not alone in the party to come.

Phillips had expected an increase in psychiatric cases due to 'embarkation fever' but was relieved to find that his fears were unfounded; he saw fewer cases per week than usual.[59] A similar situation pertained in I Corps.[60]

While morale was clearly very good, the censorship summaries show what can only be described as a 'growing tension' as D-Day approached. Expressions of anxiety 'to get on with the job' and 'to get it over' and 'get back home' were present. Inter-Allied strains rather than co-operation were evident in the mail. Unfavourable comments about American troops outnumbered favourable ones by 2:1, while 'isolated unfavourable comments' with regards to Canadian troops were also noted. Many of these tensions were driven by inequalities in pay and welfare amenities. However, it was the American and Canadian troops' relationships with British women that most upset the ordinary Tommy. A rifleman in the 2nd King's Royal Rifle Corps, 4th Armoured Brigade, commented that there had been '3 cases of men's wives leaving them for Yanks or Canadians in this [company] in the last two weeks. So do you wonder as why we can't stand them.' There was apparently 'a lot of fighting going on at dances with the Canadians'. One local dancehall was, according to a driver in the Royal Army Supply Corps, nicknamed the 'Bucket of Blood' due to the constant 'clashes between our boys and Canadians'.[61] As a private in the 2nd Gordon Highlanders, 15th Scottish Division, put it, 'you are just nothing if not a Canadian ... anyway they [the lassies] are immune to the skirl of the bagpipes as yet'.[62]

By the start of May, British morale was described as 'very high'. 'At its highest', the censors noted, 'it is expressed by real fighting men keen to get at the enemy. At its lowest by those who long for the end, and yet are ready to face the inevitable fight to achieve that end.' Throughout the mail there was again, however, 'a growing sense of tension', indicating, according to the censors, that the men had reached a 'peak of emotional readiness for action'. A corporal in the Royal Army Supply Corps wrote, 'I'm sure the lads won't stop at anything, they are like alarm clocks, wound up ready for the off. It's telling on our nerves, but what must it be like for jerry.' The prevalent attitude among troops, and most noticeably among NCOs, was a desire to get the whole thing over with so, as a sergeant in 9th Royal Tank Regiment put it, 'we can settle down to a little life'. The main worry, according to the censors, was that the high state of morale was 'often verging on over optimism'.[63]

Canadian mail told a similar story. An 'undercurrent of tension' was 'discernible in the letters' and 'a strong feeling of nostalgia ... the desire to be able to return to Canada and to resume the business of living' was 'very marked'. Nevertheless, the mail indicated that the troops were in 'mental and physical readiness for action'. Confidence in equipment and training and in victory was 'evident', and there were 'many indications of a fine esprit de corps'. Morale, it was confidently stated, was 'high', although the censors noted frankly, 'there are no heroics'.[64]

By the end of May, as the invasion creeped ever closer, the strain of what must have seemed the interminable wait was beginning to take its toll on the men. British morale was still described overall as 'very high', but the censors reported that 'the mail is subdued in tone, and there are no highlights ... The expression "browned off" is freely used throughout the whole mail and is inseparable from the desire for the long awaited Second Front to open, to get into the fight, to get home again and back to "civvy street".' 'To sum up', the censors concluded, 'this is the mail of a civilian army with absolute faith in the rightness of its cause [the necessity to defeat Germany], with no love of soldiering, but with a grim determination to see this thing through and the sooner the better'.[65]

In the days running up to D-Day at the start of June, the slightly subdued character of the British troops' mail continued, and, according to the censorship summaries, morale dropped somewhat.[66] The men did not enjoy being cooped up in camps and 'a minority showed strong resentment', especially when these camps were near large towns.[67] The censors pointed to 'frequent abuses' of twenty-four-hour leave privileges during this period; but it was not clear whether overstaying was 'deliberate or due to transport difficulties'.[68] There was clearly a strong feeling among some of the units that had fought in North

Africa and the Mediterranean that they 'should *not* be asked' to take part in the invasion. Absence without leave was particularly prevalent in these formations, notably in 50th Northumbrian Division stationed in the New Forest, with, according to one source, 'well over 1,000' cases and 'considerable unrest' reported more generally.[69] Some men in the division used 'blast grenades and Bangalore torpedoes to blow holes in the fences and liberate themselves'. Soldiers of 3rd Royal Tank Regiment, who had fought at El Alamein and who would serve with 11th Armoured Division in Normandy, were 'virtually mutinous', according to one officer, inscribing 'No Second Front' on the walls of their barracks at Aldershot.[70] It was 'clear', therefore, in the words of the censorship summaries, 'that a postponement of the operation might have had serious repercussions'.[71] Eisenhower's decision to launch the invasion on 6 June, in spite of the inclement weather and obvious risks, must be understood in this light.

As final preparations were made for D-Day, then, there were a number of issues that were acting negatively on the morale of British troops. In contrast, the morale of the Canadian troops rose noticeably in the same period. Reaction to the eventual Canadian successes in Italy 'had an inspiring effect',[72] with the censors reporting that 'fighting spirit' was 'outstanding' and morale 'very high'. The men were 'supremely confident' and 'regimental pride and fine esprit de corps is evident'. The clear message from the mail was that 'we are ready ... this is it'.[73] The Canadian troops seemed much more positively disposed towards their Commonwealth brethren than their British counterparts. They had clearly enjoyed their time in England. The censors noted that 'the Canadian appreciation of English qualities is often embarrassing'. A captain at HQ 21st Army Group wrote, 'there may be better fighters in the world than [the] English, but not many; and there are no braver fighters. No braver people. And despite the venomous implications of the British caste system there are no more democratic people in the world'. A private in the Canadian Signals wrote that 'we have come to look on this place as our home', while a signalman in 5th Canadian Infantry Brigade remarked, 'I like England quite a lot, unlike the States or Canada everybody isn't always in a rush to make money.' 'Many things have been said of the conservativeness of English people', wrote a private in the 18th Canadian Field Ambulance, 'but take it from me, there is nothing more genuine than the hospitality of England's working class.'[74]

Developments on the Canadian home front only served to reinforce this air of positivity. There was 'widespread praise for the speed of delivery of inward mail from Canada'; this had a 'marked effect on the happiness of the Troops'. The censors pointed to 'enthusiastic references to the 6th Victory Loan'. These war bonds were remarkably popular; the Army deferred a portion of the men's pay each month and many thought it good sense to buy a bond to gain a higher interest rate on their savings.[75] As D-Day approached, Canadian mail was almost exuberant. The 3rd Canadian Division as a whole, according to the divisional psychiatrist, was in fine shape. 'The general morale throughout the division is excellent. The troops are relaxed and in the highest spirits. Some of the officers and practically all of other ranks feel that our troops will go twenty-five miles in one day, that they have the firepower, the naval support and air superiority. There seems to be no talk of hazard.'[76]

Notwithstanding the domestic issues undermining British morale in the long waiting period before the invasion, by the morning of D-Day, 6 June, it appeared that all the troops, British and Canadian, were in 'fine fettle!'[77] The Canadian censors noted that their troops 'feel that their hour is about to come. They are ready, fighting fit, tough, well trained, confident t[roo]ps, proud and ... longing to show their mettle. They say that this is the moment they have lived for, trained for, left their homes for'.[78] 'First impressions', according to British censorship reports from Normandy, were that morale was 'excellent, particularly in the case of 6 Airborne Division'.[79]

The Assault

High levels of motivation and commitment were to prove essential in the hours that lay ahead. Waiting for the troops in the general area of north-west France ranged some sixty German divisions (including ten *panzer* divisions), deployed in thirteen corps and in four armies, First, Seventh, Fifteenth and Fifth Panzer (Panzer Group West). Those formations that would fight in Normandy came under Field-Marshal Erwin Rommel's Army Group B, which was in turn under the overall supervision of Field-Marshal Gerd von Rundstedt, the C-in-C West.[80]

These forces ranged themselves behind the formidable defences of the Atlantic Wall. After the Dieppe raid in 1942, the German High Command had ordered the building of a set of fortifications intended to make an attack from the air, sea or land 'hopeless'.[81] The main strength of the Atlantic Wall, which was supposed to stretch from Norway to the Spanish frontier, concentrated for obvious reasons between Dunkirk and the Somme estuary.[82] Those defences that were complete in Normandy, ranged from small concrete shelters to elaborate fortified gun positions. Most of these 'were built around a gun casement protected from air or naval assault by six feet of concrete on the seaward side and four feet on the roof'. These positions typically also included pillboxes and concrete pits, known as 'Tobruks', housing machine guns and mortar positions. The large concrete bunkers, in addition to underground installations, offered protection against bombardment. No continuous secondary line of defence existed behind the coastal strip; but, reserve companies and field and anti-tank artillery were placed inland. These units were intended to provide some depth to the defences and contain a breakthrough until help arrived in the form of mobile reserves.[83]

Since the spring of 1942, 716th Infantry Division with two *Ost*, or East, battalions of captured Russians and Poles, had been responsible for defending the area which was now marked for the Allied assault. In March 1944, 352nd Division, a 'first-class mobile infantry' outfit, arrived to strengthen the defences, assuming control of the western part of the Calvados coast. These forces were further supplemented by the arrival of 21st Panzer Division around Caen in May.[84] By 6 June, the German Army in Normandy had more formations than the Supreme Headquarters Allied Expeditionary Force (SHAEF) had originally believed safely manageable by the D-Day forces.[85]

In order to overcome this challenge, the Western Allies had forty divisions at their disposal, twenty-three of which were in Bradley's 12th US Army Group and seventeen (thirteen British, three Canadian and one Polish) in Montgomery's 21st Army Group.[86] This amounted to only two-thirds of the German divisions in theatre, but German divisions, much as was the case in Italy, were not equivalent in manpower or firepower to Allied ones; a German *panzer* division, for example, had about 160 tanks as compared to about 240 in an American or British Armoured Division, while a German division of any kind had about 50 field or medium guns, against about 90 in an Allied division. The 21st Army Group also had eight independent armoured or tank brigades, six brigades of heavy, medium and field artillery and six engineer groups. Overall, the Allies had a superiority of about 3:1 in tanks, of about 3:2 in medium and field artillery, and a rough equivalence in infantry battalions. In the air and at sea they enjoyed an overwhelming superiority.[87]

In spite of these advantages, the force-to-force ratios on land clearly left Montgomery vulnerable if the Germans could concentrate their forces in the area of the bridgehead quicker than his own.[88] The Allies had to gain operational surprise to ensure that the landing force came up against as few German formations as possible and buy time to allow the build-up of troops before the full weight of the *Wehrmacht* could be thrown against the bridgehead. To this end, a complex and multidimensional deception plan, Operation 'Bodyguard', was put in place to mislead the Germans as to the place and timing of the attack.[89] It was hoped that the Germans would be induced to deploy their troops as far away from Normandy as possible.

As part of this overall plan, Operation 'Fortitude South' was conceived to pin down German defenders in the Pas de Calais for as long as possible after the invasion. To achieve this goal, the German High Command had to be convinced that there were forces available for two attacks. One would be a diversion on the shores of Normandy and a second would be a real invasion across the Channel at the shortest point. Every effort was made to draw attention to the south-east coast of England, the obvious launching point for an attack on the German defences at the Pas de Calais. Dummy wireless traffic, troop concentrations, landing craft, vehicle parks, guns, tanks and field kitchens were set up. Men drove army trucks back and forth to leave visible tyre tracks. A dummy oil storage complex near Dover was even inspected by King George VI and Montgomery. Fighter patrols flew over tent cities in order to maintain the charade. General Patton was put in charge of the fictitious First United States Army Group (FUSAG), as the Germans fully expected the Allies 'most talented' general to command the invasion. Spies and double agents disseminated information supporting the fiction that FUSAG would launch the main invasion at the Pas de Calais.[90]

The Germans never spotted the massed FUSAG tent cities in southern England, as few German aircraft managed to penetrate Fighter Command's defences, but, by mid-1944, there was every indication that the double agents had convinced the Germans that Normandy was a diversion. This growing sense within the German High Command that the invasion would be launched at the Pas de Calais was reinforced by their misinterpretation of the intent of the massive aerial offensive launched by the Allied Air Forces to isolate Normandy from the rest of France and prevent German reinforcements reaching the front after the invasion ('The Transportation Plan'). The Germans believed that these co-ordinated aerial attacks were designed to prevent reinforcements from Normandy reaching the Pas de Calais, and not the other way around. The attacks were so successful that, by D-Day, no routes across the River Seine north of Paris remained open and only three road bridges across the river were functional between Paris and the sea.[91] Normandy, to all intents and purposes, had been cut off from the rest of the Continent.

Even with these key enablers in place, the scale of the challenge for those assaulting the beaches was immense. The plan of attack was to land on a 50-mile front along the Normandy coastline (see Map 13.1), incorporating two sectors. The Americans in the west were tasked with taking Utah and Omaha beaches and the Anglo-Canadian Second Army in the east were assigned to the taking of Gold, Juno and Sword beaches. Montgomery's operational plan for Normandy called for Second Army, on taking the beaches, to push inland and capture the high ground to the south-east between the city of Caen, about 10 miles inland, and the town of Falaise, 20 miles further to the south. It was hoped that the Anglo-Canadian force would thus threaten the road to Paris, forcing the Germans to commit in the eastern sector. This would facilitate First US Army's drive to capture Cherbourg and the Brittany ports to the west and north of the initial beachhead, a key requirement for the logistical sustenance of the invasion; then the US forces could turn east towards Paris. Second Army's push south would also involve the capture of valuable territory to the west of Caen, near Carpiquet, land suitable for airfields. Caen, it was planned, should be taken on the first day, before the Germans had the chance to react and reinforce the area. Should the Anglo-Canadian forces fail to take the city, there was a real danger that the invasion would bog down in intense and costly fighting. Should the 'eastern wall' fail, the whole bridgehead, according to Dempsey, the commander of Second Army, 'could be rolled up' from the flank.[92]

To prevent this from happening, three airborne divisions were used to protect the eastern and western extremities of the bridgehead. The 82nd and 101st US Airborne Divisions were employed in the west while 6th British Airborne Division was tasked with protecting the

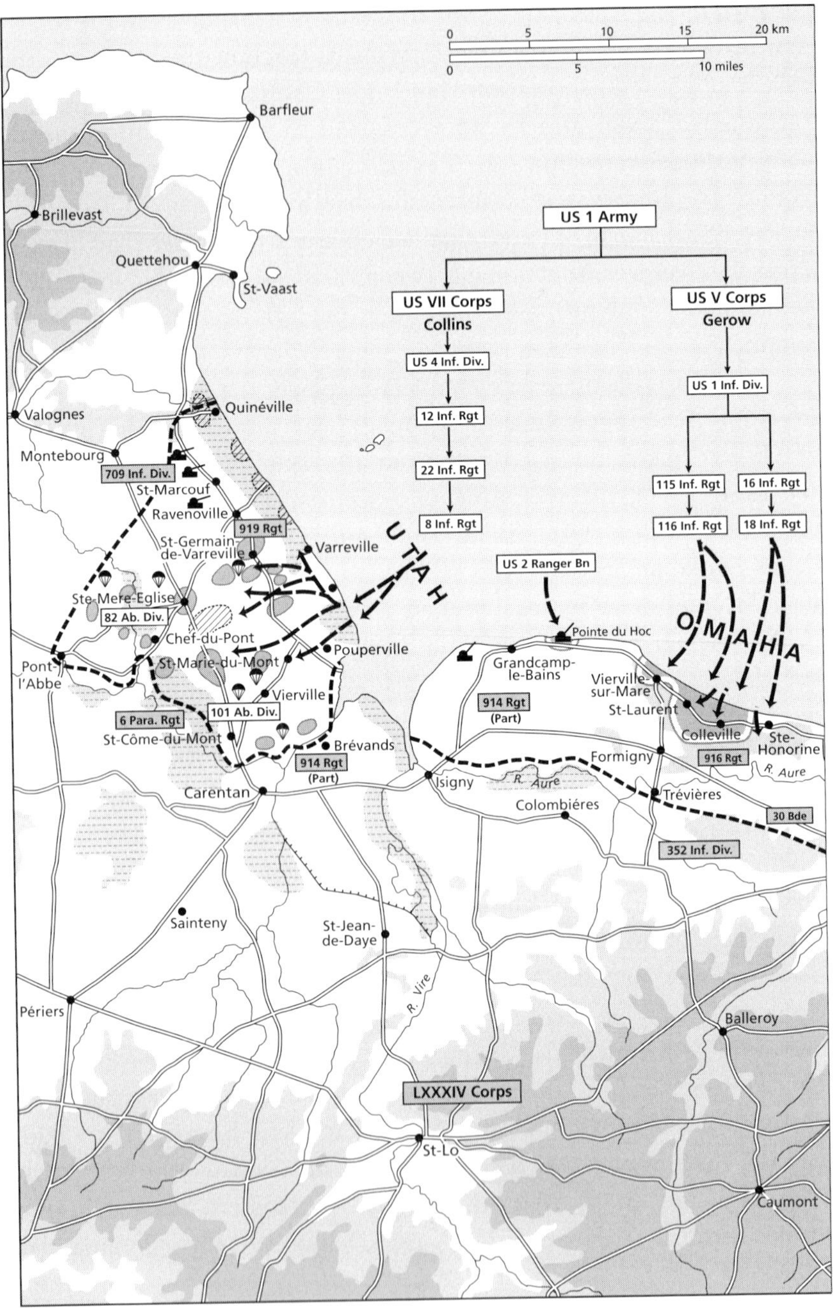

Map 13.1 D-Day, 6 June 1944

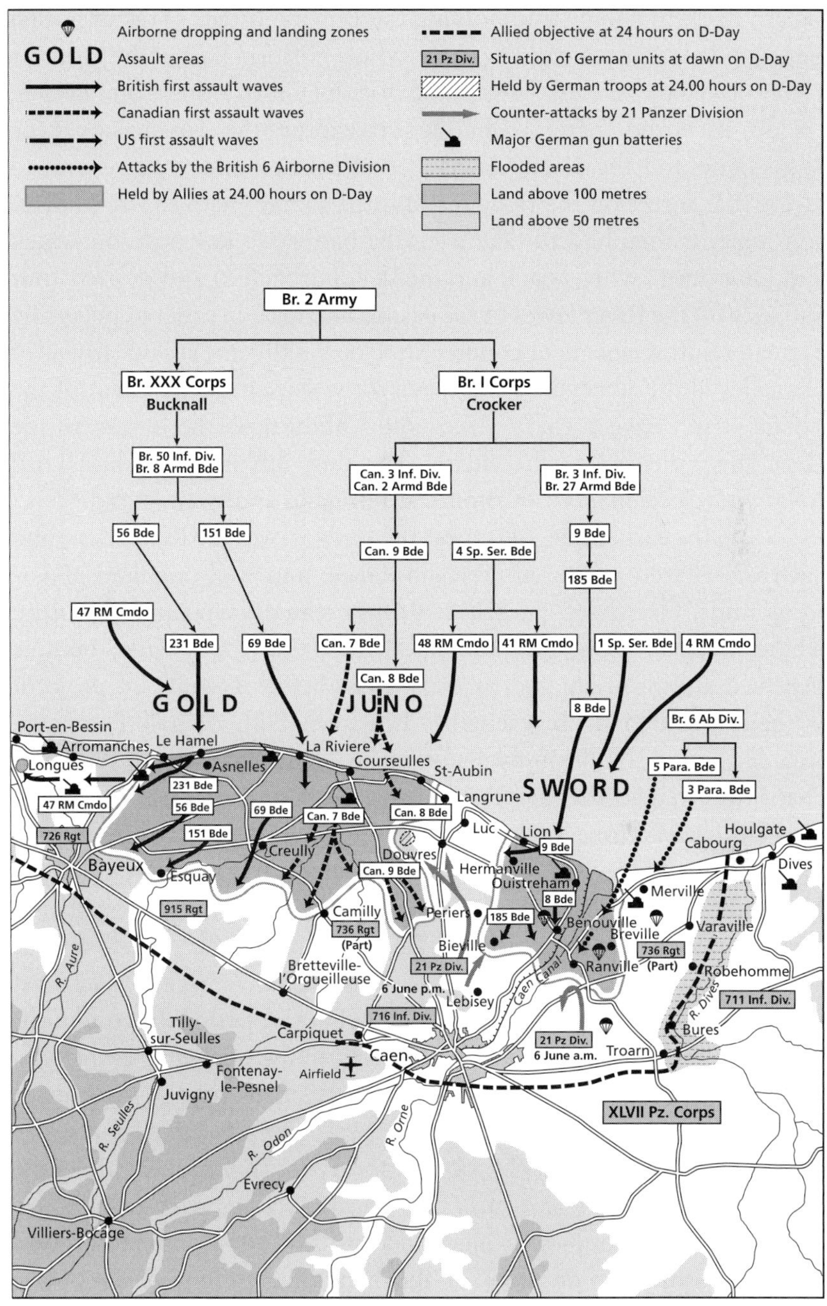

Airborne dropping and landing zones
GOLD Assault areas
British first assault waves
Canadian first assault waves
US first assault waves
Attacks by the British 6 Airborne Division
Held by Allies at 24.00 hours on D-Day
Allied objective at 24 hours on D-Day
21 Pz Div. Situation of German units at dawn on D-Day
Held by German troops at 24.00 hours on D-Day
Counter-attacks by 21 Panzer Division
Major German gun batteries
Flooded areas
Land above 100 metres
Land above 50 metres
Br. 2 Army
Br. XXX Corps
Bucknall
Br. I Corps
Crocker
Br. 50 Inf. Div.
Br. 8 Armd Bde
Can. 3 Inf. Div.
Can. 2 Armd Bde
Br. 3 Inf. Div.
Br. 27 Armd Bde
56 Bde
151 Bde
Can. 9 Bde
4 Sp. Ser. Bde
9 Bde
185 Bde
47 RM Cmdo
231 Bde
69 Bde
Can. 7 Bde
48 RM Cmdo
41 RM Cmdo
1 Sp. Ser. Bde
4 RM Cmdo
Can. 8 Bde
GOLD
JUNO
8 Bde
Br. 6 Ab Div.
5 Para. Bde
3 Para. Bde
SWORD
Port-en-Bessin
Arromanches
Le Hamel
La Riviere
Courseulles
St-Aubin
Langrune
Longues
Asnelles
47 RM Cmdo
726 Rgt
Bayeux
Esquay
Creully
Douvres
Luc
Lion
Hermanville
Ouistreham
Houlgate
Cabourg
Dives
Merville
Varaville
Breville
Benouville
Ranville
736 Rgt
(Part)
Robehomme
711 Inf. Div.
915 Rgt
Camilly
736 Rgt
(Part)
Periers
Bieville
21 Pz Div.
Bretteville-l'Orgueilleuse
6 June p.m.
Lebisey
Caen Canal
716 Inf. Div.
R. Aure
R. Dives
Bures
Tilly-sur-Seulles
Carpiquet
Caen
21 Pz Div.
6 June a.m.
Troarn
Airfield
Fontenay-le-Pesnel
Juvigny
XLVII Pz. Corps
R. Seulles
R. Odon
R. Orne
Evrecy
Villiers-Bocage

eastern flank by taking and holding the Breville Ridge. 'This imposing long wooded ridge was the key to the whole position East of the Orne' as it overlooked the 'greater part' of the British I Corps front around Caen. The 6th Airborne, therefore, had first to capture the crossings over the River Orne and the Caen Canal, between Caen and Ouistreham, to ensure that forces on the ridge maintained contact with the main invasion force. It then had to take Merville battery (a key position which could fire onto Sword beach and the sea approaches) and destroy four bridges over the River Dives to the east of the ridge, in order to delay any German reinforcements or counter attacks. Finally, the seaside towns of Salanelles and Franceville Plage were to be seized and as much of the coastal strip between these places and Cabourg on the mouth of the River Dives cleared of the enemy. For this, 6th Airborne had Lord Lovat's 1st Special Service Commando Brigade under command.[93]

In the early hours of 6 June, the bridges over the River Orne and Caen Canal were captured intact in daring and well-prepared gliderborne raids. Elsewhere, parachute drops created havoc and confusion behind German lines, in spite of the fact that many units became dispersed and disorientated (in most cases achieving only 40 per cent of their intended drop strength). Brigadier Hill, of 3rd Parachute Brigade, had warned his men not to be 'daunted if chaos reigns'.[94] Chaos did reign; the aerial bombardment intended to soften up Merville battery (one of his brigade's objectives), missed its target; only 150 out of the 600 men of 9th Parachute Battalion intended for the assault scheduled at 0430hrs could be found and brought together in time for the attack. In spite of these difficulties, the objective was eventually taken.[95] The 6th Airborne Division, in a remarkable achievement, attained all of its main objectives on D-Day, setting the conditions for the seaborne invasion that was massing in the English Channel.[96]

By the early hours of 6 June, the vast Allied armada, made up of around 130,000 troops, 12,000 aircraft, 1,200 fighting ships and 5,500 landing and naval craft, was sitting off the five assault beaches along the Normandy coast.[97] The attack opened at 0300hrs with over 1,000 British bombers dropping around 5,000 tons of bombs on and around German positions.[98] In spite of the incredible weight of firepower unleashed, the bombardment proved largely ineffective. The poor weather, which had allowed the unseen crossing of the Allied invasion fleet and the achievement of operational surprise, limited the impact of the bombing programme. Few enemy positions were hit. Typhoon

Illustration 13.1 Troops of 3rd Canadian Division disembark from a landing craft onto Nan Red beach, Juno area, near St Aubin-sur-Mer, at about 0800hrs, 6 June 1944, while under fire from German troops in the houses facing them.

squadrons assigned to attack beach targets found the winds and overcast skies a serious challenge.[99] The bombardment from the sea was only marginally more effective. Major John Fairlie, a Canadian artillery officer, who conducted an exhaustive investigation of Juno beach after the battle, concluded later that naval fire had done 'no serious damage to the defences'.[100]

It was in this context that the assault troops were to land; and, as Terry Copp has put it, 'no one who examines the events of the first hours of D-Day can fail to be impressed by the accomplishments' of these men (see Illustration 13.1).[101] The 3rd Division, of I Corps, landed on Sword beach, the furthest east of the five Allied landings; its objective was to seize Caen and, along with 6th Airborne Division, to hold the left-hand flank of Second Army. 3rd Canadian Division, also of I Corps, assaulted Juno beach, in the centre of the Anglo-Canadian sector; it was tasked with capturing the area around Carpiquet, a roughly similar distance inland. The 50th Northumbrian Division, of XXX Corps, landed on the right-hand flank (to the west) on Gold beach; it was tasked with pressing inland towards Bayeux, somewhat closer to the coast than the other two objectives, and to link up with the Americans advancing from Omaha beach to the west (on their right flank).

What the men experienced was, by any standard, an ordeal. The landing craft of 50th Northumbrian Division, with the assault brigades on board, were lowered into the water at 0415hrs. There they spent the next three hours rising and falling with the waves as they awaited touch down at H Hour +5 (H+5), namely five minutes after the landings in this sector were due to begin. At about 0600hrs the five cruisers and nine destroyers assigned to provide fire support opened up with over 100 guns. This was accompanied from H-60 by the guns on the landing ship tanks (LSTs) and by the landing crafts' own weapons. At H-12 and H-7 the four rocket ships supporting the assault discharged their fire. The roar, by all accounts, was terrifying.[102]

Though supported by the firepower of the massive Allied armada, it was perfectly clear to the individuals in the landing craft that they alone carried the terrible responsibility of assaulting the beaches. As the Queen's Own Rifles, 3rd Canadian Division, approached Juno beach, one man recalled:

> As we moved further from the mother ship and closer to the shore, it came as a shock to realise that the assault fleet just behind us had disappeared from view. Suddenly there was just us and an awful lot of ocean ... Ten boats stretched out over fifteen hundred yards is not really a whole lot of assault force. The boats began to look even tinier as the gaps widened, with more than the length of a football field between each.[103]

When the order 'down ramp' came, there was nothing for the men to do but race for the sea wall and endure the heavy machine-gun and mortar fire unleashed by the German defenders. Many of the Duplex Drive (DD) amphibious tanks, which were to plunge ashore and arrive ahead of the first wave, were not launched or became stalled in the heavy seas. Some units suffered heavily, with their platoons losing up to two-thirds of their men.[104] In the 'Queen White' and 'Queen Red' sectors of Sword beach, the first wave suffered 30 and 45 per cent casualties respectively. For the first two waves, overall the figures for 'Queen White' and 'Queen Red' were 22.5 and 28 per cent, 'the highest of any of the Anglo-

Canadian beaches'. Close to 15 per cent of all armoured vehicles landed at Sword were knocked out by enemy gunfire.[105]

Overall, casualties in the assault divisions were lighter than expected. At Sword, it was thought that casualties would amount to as high as 72 per cent in the first wave.[106] Major W. N. Lees, an Australian officer attached to the British Army in North-West Europe, who compiled a detailed 360-page report on the campaign, noted that the British and Canadians had anticipated 7,750 casualties on D-Day, approximately 3.1 times the actual casualties suffered (around 2,515). The Historical Section at the Cabinet Office estimated that 6th Airborne Division suffered 1,022 casualties up to 0600hrs on 7 June 1944, 20 per cent of its landing force on D-Day. The 3rd Division suffered 957 casualties, 9 per cent of its landing force and 3rd Canadian Division suffered 1,063 casualties, 7 per cent of its landing force. The Historical Section did not provide figures for the first day for 50th Northumbrian Division, but the casualty returns for 9 June estimated it had suffered 801 casualties by this date.[107] The invasion had by no means been a walk over.

Nevertheless, it was clear that the carefully prepared plan for the assault had to all intents and purposes worked. The Germans had been taken completely by surprise. It is apparent from German reports that they had anticipated a large-scale operation only where the point of landing was in the neighbourhood of at least one good harbour.[108] They did not expect an invasion near cliffs, unless they had a wide foreshore, or where there were strong currents, surf, reefs or shallows. The invasion was expected in fair, calm weather, with a rising tide and at a new moon. As it turned out, the Allies commenced the landing at full moon, away from large harbours, in a strong wind with low cloud ceiling and a rough sea; they landed at some points at sheer cliffs, and in water stated by German naval experts to be impassable by reason of underwater reefs and strong currents; the first wave went ashore at lowest ebb. Thus, it was possible to pass the foreshore obstacles almost without casualties, while bright moonlight had facilitated the dropping of parachutists and airborne troops on terrain that had been considered unsuitable for air landings and had not therefore been blocked or defended sufficiently.[109]

The Second Army Intelligence Summary for the end of D-Day was damning in its criticism of the German defence. The opposition had been 'less than anticipated'. It was evident that 'the place of the … invasion [had] remained a secret' and that 'a considerable measure of surprise' had been achieved. The German defence of Normandy had clearly 'failed'; 'no other conclusion' was 'possible when it is realised that within an hour of H hour the landing troops were passing through the beaches'.[110] Many of the assaulting British and Canadian troops agreed with this appraisal and were decidedly unimpressed by what they met on the beaches. Major J. N. Gordon of the Queen's Own Rifles recalled that the Germans encountered by his company were 'mere boys' and 'very frightened' and 'ran away'.[111] The British censors noted that 'comments by Air and Seaborne formations on enemy troops showed one marked difference. Airborne troops referred to the enemy with respect, whereas Seaborne troops emphasised the poor quality of the Static German Beach formations encountered during the early stages of the operation'.[112] One observer noted that in some strongly fortified positions 'the enemy fought well only submitting when he was overwhelmed by fire and assaulted with the bayonet'.[113] In others, German resistance was less determined and 'prisoners were many'.[114] The Canadian censors noted that the troops had 'a poor impression' of the POWs they had seen. A private in the Highland Light Infantry of Canada wrote that 'we have taken quite a few prisoners and they aren't the ferocious people they are described as. All of them pretty young and most of them mighty scared.'[115]

Much credit must go to the preliminary bombardment, in spite of its inaccuracy. While the material effects had been underwhelming, British, American and German reports all emphasised the extent to which it had demoralised defensive units on the beaches and the reserves further back.[116] An Allied report on 'German Views on the Normandy Landing' produced in November 1944 and based on twenty-three captured documents, emphasised that although minefields laid near the coast had been 'blown up, and proved useless' and barbed wire entanglements had been 'broken down', concrete emplacements and slit trenches, especially when covered with strong wooden lids, had allowed troops to survive the inferno. By comparison, 'the moral effect' had been immense:

> Even where it was not reinforced by simultaneous air bombing, the drum fire [naval bombardment] inspired in the defenders a feeling of utter helplessness, which in the case of inexperienced recruits caused fainting or indeed complete paralysis. The instinct of self preservation drove their duty as soldiers, to fight and destroy the enemy, completely out of their minds.[117]

The sheer scale of Allied mastery of the air undoubtedly contributed to German soldiers' feelings of helplessness. In February 1944, Allied planners had expected 1,650 first-line German aircraft on D+1, perhaps joined by 950 more. While the *Luftwaffe* did throw most of its fighters into the fray during 'Overlord', they numbered only 1,300. On D-Day itself, the *Luftwaffe* flew only 319 sorties, while the Allies flew 12,015 (a ratio of 1:38).

Moreover, many of the troops, according to captured German documents, 'were suffering from overstrain as a result of incessant labouring on field works, as they were ordered to do from the first light to dusk for weeks before the invasion'. In many front-line units, a high percentage of men were convalescent personnel, 'fit for labour service only' or 'conditionally fit', or were recruits with only four weeks training. The NCOs were mainly specialists without infantry training, for example tank repairers, German Air Force ground staff etc.[118] Poles and Alsatians, pressed into service in the army, proved particularly vulnerable and 'wholesale desertions' were reported.[119] It would appear, then, that particularly on D-Day, the performance of German troops opposing the Anglo-Canadian landings had been significantly inhibited by the psychological effects of Allied firepower and the quality of their training.

Nevertheless, in spite of the problems facing the German defenders on 6 June, by midnight, the three British and Canadian assault divisions had failed to take their D-Day objectives. In the morning, 3rd Division had cleared the beach defences. But, by the afternoon, as it pushed inland, its advance began to slow as it encountered stiffer opposition. By the end of the day, it had secured the line along the River Orne to the east, making contact with 6th Airborne Division, and a bridgehead had been established. But the furthest penetration inland had only got as far as Lebisey Wood, just to the north of Caen.[120] The assault battalions of 50th Northumbrian Division completed the first phase of the attack not long after the prescribed time; apart from 1st Hampshires, 231st Brigade, who encountered bitter fighting in Le Hamel, little trouble was experienced.[121] By the end of the day, it had linked up with the Canadians advancing inland from Juno beach but it had not connected with the Americans near Omaha. The follow-up troops of the reserve brigades, 8th Armoured, 56th and 151st Infantry, had only reached their assembly areas; this was in spite of the fact that the enemy had failed to launch a determined counter-attack. Most importantly, just like 3rd Division, it had not taken its D-Day objective, the town of Bayeux.[122] The 3rd

Canadian Division, by comparison, fared better;[123] beach clearance had 'proceeded rapidly'[124] and 'with several hours of daylight left ... there was little doubt that the 9th [Canadian] Brigade could reach Carpiquet'. But with matters unfolding less well in the British sectors, and with 3rd British Division being counter-attacked by 21st Panzer Division, Dempsey 'ordered all three assault divisions to dig in at their intermediate objectives. This decision was relayed to subordinate commanders sometime after 1900' on D-Day.[125]

Controversy

At first glance, it is hard to reconcile the failure of the assault divisions to take their objectives with the reportedly excellent morale of the British and Canadian soldiers and the poor performance of the German defenders on D-Day. As Lees put it, 'opposition on the British beaches was less than anticipated, and at the same time, the rate of advance inland was, in many cases, slower than planned'.[126] According to the Canadian Official History, the Anglo-Canadian forces had missed the opportunity to seize Caen and the original D-Day objectives because they had not followed up the initial assault with sufficient aggression.[127] German reports indicated that 'after the first infiltration in the coastal defence zone' the Allies advanced 'only hesitantly',[128] a perspective shared by Chester Wilmot, the Australian war correspondent, who thought that 3rd Division had noticeably 'dropped the momentum of the attack' as the day wore on.[129]

Montgomery had warned precisely against such behaviour. On 14 April 1944, he instructed Dempsey to advance armoured brigade groups inland from the beaches as soon as possible to secure crucial objectives, most obviously Caen:

> Armoured units and [brigades] must be concentrated quickly as soon as ever the situation allows after the initial landing on D-day; this may not be too easy, but plans to effect such concentrations must be made and every effort made to carry them out; speed and boldness are then required, and the armoured thrusts must force their way inland.
>
> I am prepared to accept almost any risk in order to carry out these tactics. I would risk even the total loss of the armoured brigade groups.[130]

He stressed the point again in an address to senior commanders on 21 May:

> Every officer and man must have only one idea and that is to peg out claims inland and to penetrate quickly and deeply into enemy territory. To relax once ashore would be fatal ... senior officers must prevent it at all costs on D-Day and on the following days. Great energy and drive will be required.[131]

The D-Day plan clearly called for both 'boldness and dash'. As Dempsey argued after the war, it was imperative to grab as much as possible in the confusion generated by the landings.[132] As one man from the Norfolks later wrote, 'you can do with a platoon on "D" Day, what you cannot do with a battalion on "D"+1 or a division on "D"+3'.[133] But, that same confusion, accompanied by friction and chance, was also the undoing of Second Army's ambitions. As events did not play out exactly as expected, platoon, company, battalion and brigade commanders all had to adapt in contact with the enemy.

This required excellent morale, but in spite of the positive appraisal offered by the censorship summaries, it is difficult to ignore the criticisms of Wilmot and others. It is not possible to conclusively assemble definitive evidence on the state of morale on 6 June; sickness, battle exhaustion and desertion/AWOL rates are not available in the archives for the first five days of the Normandy campaign; the first figures available are for the week ending 17 June. Moreover, the censorship summary for British troops, 1 to 14 June 1944, was based on 145,000 letters written before D-Day and only 8,000 written following the landings. It can be confidently concluded then that morale was 'high' before the assault, but it is less certain that it was 'excellent' both during and after D-Day. The compilers of the summary acknowledged that 'the special conditions prevailing' made it 'possible to report only on the broadest features reflected in the mail. The comparatively small proportion of overseas mail examined can only carry a first impression of the operational conditions.' The British censors picked out 6th Airborne Division for special mention, and it is notable that Richard Gale, its commander, also highlighted its high morale and the lack of military crime in the division before D-Day. 'All seemed to be imbued with the seriousness of the task in hand; all had a real and deep sense of their responsibilities; and all seemed impressed with the sacredness and justice of the cause for which they were trained and eventually going to fight.' 'Several times', according to Gale, 'the situation appeared serious [during the first day of fighting], but always it was restored by the fine leadership of the junior commanders and the determination and initiative of the troops.'[134] The 6th Airborne was the only division to secure its D-Day objectives. Similarly, Canadian morale, according to the censors, appeared to be exuberant, and, perhaps, in this context, it is not surprising that they would likely have reached their objectives had they not been halted by Dempsey on the evening of 6 June.[135]

Elsewhere, behaviour was more consistent with 'high' rather than 'excellent' morale. On Sword beach, stiff resistance at some strong points and casualties among key personnel delayed clearance of the beach. The assault engineers cleared none of the planned eight exit lanes in the first 30 minutes; it was 50 minutes before the first lane was open, with a total of seven available after 150 minutes. One strong point, 'Cod', took over three hours to clear. These delays had a 'cascading effect' as D-Day progressed;[136] combined with an 'unexpectedly high tide', they led to a great deal of congestion on the shore. This, in turn, 'delayed the start of the advance inland' (see Illustration 13.2).[137]

In the confusion that ensued, the infantry, under strict instructions to push ahead, got separated from its supporting arms. The poor weather made matters worse by inhibiting the use of close air support.[138] Tactical intelligence was poor, the price of strategic security; reconnaissance flights had been launched at a ratio of two in the Pas de Calais area to one in Normandy in an attempt to mislead the Germans regarding Allied intentions. The British, therefore, did not know that 352nd Infantry Division had raised its strength by 150 per cent on Gold beach, nor did they know that 21st Panzer Division had placed its anti-tank units and half its infantry between the River Orne and Caen, right in the path of 3rd Division's line of advance.[139]

In the context of 21st Army Group's training, the manner in which events unfolded proved problematic for the rapid advance envisaged by Montgomery. Formations had been taught primarily to move forward to designated objectives in controlled bounds and dig in at the first sign of an enemy counter-attack. On calling in artillery support, Anglo-Canadian units, even those as small as ten-man sections or thirty-man platoons, were instructed to advance to the next objective behind a curtain of bullets and high-explosive artillery shells.[140] Crerar, especially, could not have been more explicit on this matter prior to the invasion, and, indeed, it was a message continuously reiterated by

Illustration 13.2 British Commandos advance towards Ouistreham, Sword area, 6 June 1944. In spite of the notable feat of arms of D-Day, controversy still rages over whether British and Canadian forces should have pushed more aggressively inland to take their D-Day objectives.

commanders in Normandy.[141] A more dynamic approach once the beaches had been taken would have required Second Army to utilise its battle drills in preference to firepower-heavy tactics.[142] In the complex, fearful environment of D-Day, this was an unrealistic expectation.[143]

Particularly in the case of the two largely inexperienced divisions, 3rd British and 3rd Canadian, a mechanised firepower-heavy approach had been prioritised in training. Additionally, the veterans of 50th Northumbrian Division had fought under Montgomery in North Africa and Sicily and were inclined, according to some reports, to assume that they had cracked the tactical challenges of modern warfare and did not require alternative training in preparation for Normandy.[144] Thus, all three divisions, under extreme stress, relied on the practices with which they were familiar. By comparison, 6th Airborne Division was trained, according to its commander, to exercise individual initiative in battle and embrace the challenges and opportunities of mobile warfare.[145]

The hybrid doctrinal formula that had evolved in the British and Canadian Armies had conditionally embraced battle drill but clearly subordinated it to mechanised firepower. In the light of the extremely ambitious objectives set for D-Day, this conceptual balance and understanding appears to have been inappropriate, much, indeed, as it had been in Sicily and Italy. Montgomery, who wished for Second Army to fight a mobile and aggressive battle on landing in Normandy, had only himself to blame. He had stressed in his seminal 'Brief Notes for Senior Officers on the Conduct of Battle', of December 1942, that 'all commanders' had to 'understand clearly the requirements of battle; then, and only then, will they be in a position to organise the proper training of their formations and units'. 'In fact', he said, 'the approach to training is via the battle.'[146] Such an understanding, as encapsulated in the 'Jungle Soldier's Handbook' and the 'Jungle Book', had underpinned the training revolution that had taken place in the Far East. If soldiers were to truly use their initiative in combat, a key requirement for success in modern warfare, they had to be trained consistently to do so. 'The Instructor's Handbook', in the eyes of too many commanders, did not provide the solution to the tactical problems they expected to face in Normandy. Moreover, Montgomery, in spite of his increasing understanding of the limits of the 'Colossal Cracks' approach, left training to his subordinates, who were still overwhelmingly affected by the experiences of the first years of the war. In this respect, it is apparent that although Montgomery and the War Office adequately prepared their men for another 'break-in' battle (the beach assault), they did not, in light of the inevitable frictions inherent in a complex multinational and tri-service amphibious operation, prepare the men fully for the 'breakout', the exploitation phase of D-Day.

Such an observation does not take away from what the official historian described as the 'notable feat of arms' of D-Day.[147] The achievement of putting ashore 75,215 men and landing another 7,900 from the air on the first day of the invasion of North-West Europe ranks with any in the history of warfare.[148] But, the factors that prevented Anglo-Canadian units from reaching their D-Day objectives did point to problems that would affect 21st Army Group recurrently over the course of the campaign. The British and Commonwealth Armies in the West were still searching for a way not only to wear down the *Wehrmacht* in battle, but to annihilate it in great clashes of fire and manoeuvre.

14 NORMANDY

The advance inland resumed at dawn on D+1 (7 June 1944). Considerable progress was made; Bayeux was captured intact, and by the end of the day no co-ordinated counter-attack had materialised. The intelligence summaries indicated that the bulk of the German armour was concentrating in the Caen area, rather than further west; it was in the British and Canadian sector that the German counter-stroke would take place. Both 12th SS Panzer Division and the Panzer Lehr Division, which constituted two-thirds of the theatre armoured reserve under the direct control of Hitler, were moving up in force and it was estimated that by nightfall at least one of these powerful formations would be available for battle.[1] By 8 June, heavy fighting had broken out along the whole front, particularly in the Canadian sector where strong counter-attacks by German forces were repulsed, but for heavy losses.[2] Allied firepower, and naval gunfire in particular, proved decisive; the Germans would not drive the Allies back into the sea. By 9 June, the counter-attack had fizzled out and the five invasion beaches had been linked up into a continuous and coherent bridgehead.[3]

The next day, Montgomery met with his army commanders to discuss the situation. His desire for fast-moving and aggressive operations had not been tempered by the failure to take Caen on D-Day. He proposed a 'double envelopment' of Caen, with XXX Corps, spearheaded by the newly arrived 7th Armoured Division, striking to the west through Villers-Bocage and then south-east towards the Orne; 51st Highland Division and 4th Armoured Brigade, of I Corps, would attack to the east of the city. The operation would be accompanied by a drop by 1st Airborne Division, which would meet up with the two spearheads south of Caen.[4]

It was 'a bold plan', but Air Chief Marshal Sir Trafford Leigh-Mallory, the air force commander for 'Overlord', refused to support the airborne drop as it was deemed too risky. Montgomery raged as he saw his plan fall apart. He wrote to his Chief of Staff, Freddie de Guingand, 'obviously he [Leigh-Mallory] is a gutless bugger who refuses to take a chance and plays for safety on all occasions'. Montgomery searched for other options, but these diminished as events unfolded on the ground. First, the landing of 51st Highland Division was delayed, depriving him of the use of one of the formations needed for the attack. Then, 50th Northumbrian Division and 8th Armoured Brigade of XXX Corps got sucked into battle as the Panzer Lehr arrived near Caen. That left Montgomery with just 7th Armoured Division, a force arguably too small for the ambitious operation conceived.[5]

Montgomery decided to go ahead anyway. For, while Panzer Lehr was proving 'a severe obstacle' to the west of Caen, the formations further west again, in the US sector, were faring much less well. The collapse of 352nd Division, in particular, presented an opportunity to attack towards Caumont and then head towards the town of Villers-Bocage deep behind Panzer Lehr's left flank. If this thrust could be followed up by an additional push towards Caen and the Orne Valley, 7th Armoured Division might force the Germans to fall back and suffer heavy casualties in the process (see Map 14.1).[6]

Operation 'Perch' launched at 0530hrs on 13 June. Initially, 7th Armoured Division advanced with 'urgency' and at a 'rapid pace', but the attack soon lost momentum as it came into contact with the enemy around Villers-Bocage. 'Perch' quickly turned into a costly and embarrassing failure as 7th Armoured Division showed neither the tenacity nor creativity to overcome very limited but 'fierce' German resistance in the battle area. By any standard, 'Perch' was a 'badly bungled' operation that reflected poorly on the tactical skills of one of Second Army's key veteran formations. By 14 June, 7th Armoured Division, having made all too little progress, was ordered to retreat. Hopes of a quick breakout began to diminish and the battle lines in Normandy stabilised into an identifiable front. Dempsey 'was appalled by the manner in which PERCH had been prosecuted'. The 'whole handling of that battle', he said, 'was a disgrace'. It was now clear to both Montgomery and Dempsey that 'any hope of a rapid encirclement of Caen had passed'.[7]

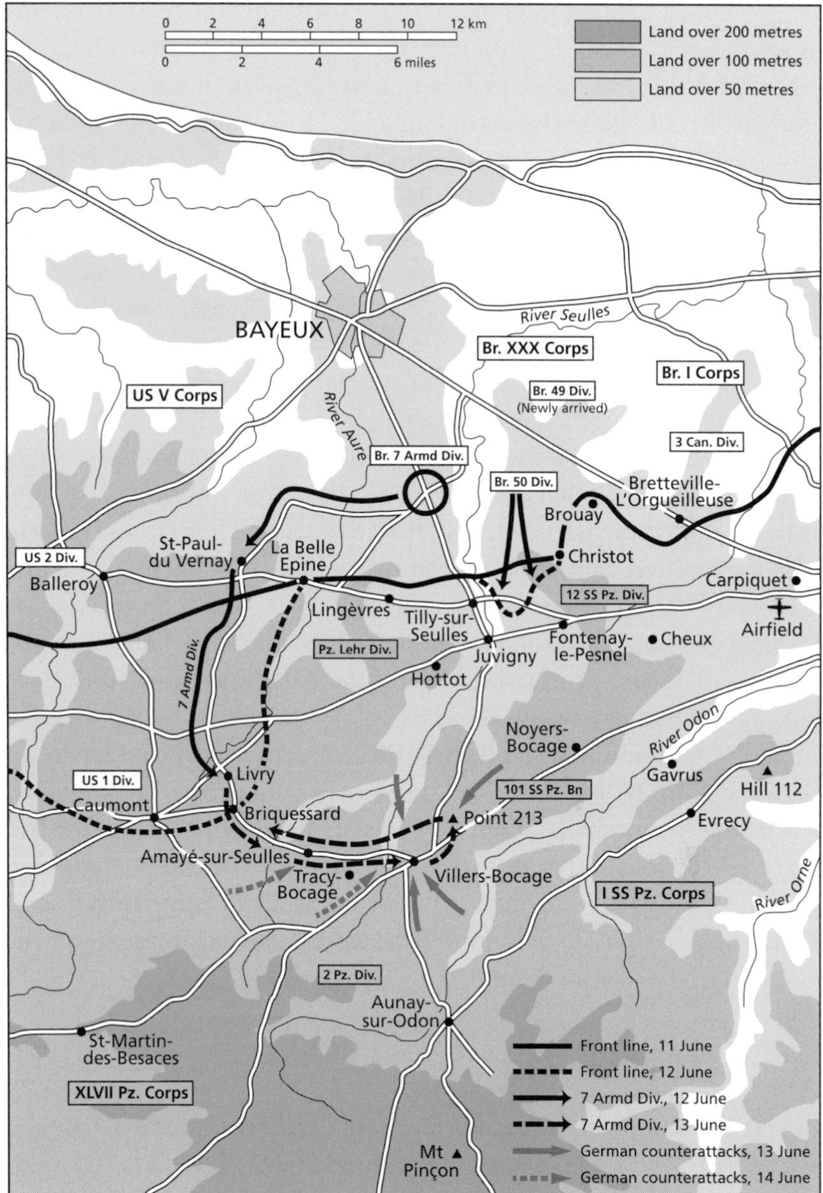

Map 14.1 Operation 'Perch', 11–14 June 1944

With the front stabilising, German reinforcements arriving, and with Second Army proving no more capable than Eighth Army in mobile warfare, it was time to return to proven methods.

On 18 June, Montgomery issued a new directive to his two army commanders. 'To-day is D plus 12', he wrote, 'and we have now been fighting since 6 June. During this time we have been working on the original directive issued by me in England.' He recognised that 'after the very great intensity' of the initial operations he had had to 'slow down the tempo'. In the circumstances, Montgomery explained, he intended to launch a very different type of operation; what he described rather ironically in his diary as a 'blitz attack' on the Second Army front.[8] With the dynamic outflanking move of 'Perch' having failed, it was time for a set-piece engagement in the El Alamein mould.

Second Army strove to build up sufficient forces to launch the offensive. The Allies knew, through air reconnaissance, that 1st SS Panzer Division, the third division in Hitler's theatre armoured reserve, had left Belgium and that II SS Panzer Corps was en route to Normandy from Poland.[9] Much depended on how quickly the Allies could offload supplies and new formations at the two artificial 'Mulberry' harbours that had been towed across the Channel and constructed at Arromanches and Saint Laurent. Fate now played a hand. On the night of 18 June, a storm swept in off the Atlantic, lasting three days and causing 'immense damage' to the landing facilities. By 22 June, the build-up of Second Army was three divisions short of the target set by planners. Montgomery feared that he would lose the initiative. The delay, he said, was exactly 'what the enemy needs'; to pause too long could court disaster; he had to strike first. He decided, therefore, to commit the newly landed VIII Corps, under Lieutenant-General Richard O'Connor, to a large offensive, codenamed 'Epsom', to the west and south-west of Caen.[10]

The Battle for Caen

'Epsom' commenced on 26 June, its goal to drive across the River Odon Valley and up on to the high ground of Hill 112 to the south of Caen (see Map 14.2). The hill offered a commanding position over the open terrain to the south of the city and was an ideal launching point for an armoured thrust to threaten the German defences in the area. The attack would be launched by some 60,000 troops and over 600 tanks supported by 696 guns, 250 medium bombers, 18 squadrons of fighter bombers and the firepower of three cruisers and one monitor from the Royal Navy.[11] The opposition facing VIII Corps initially

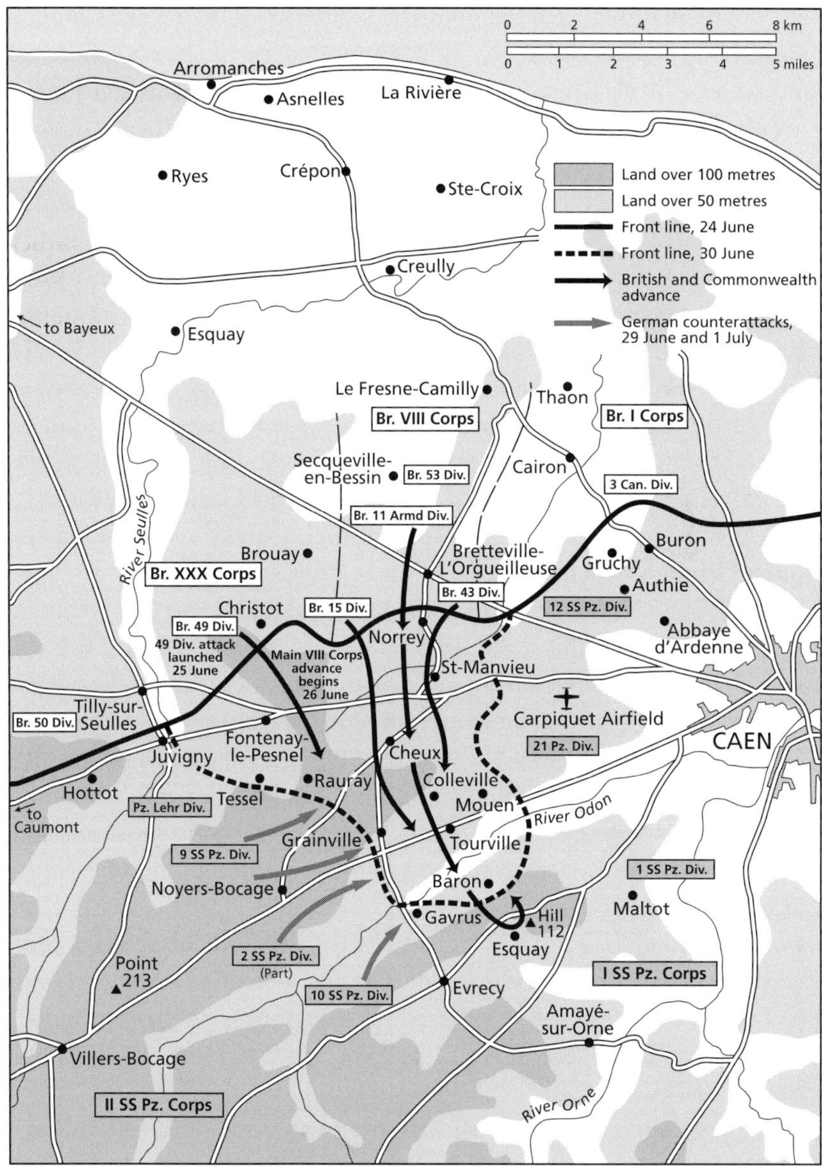

Map 14.2 Operation 'Epsom', 26 June–1 July 1944

consisted of the 12th SS Panzer and Panzer Lehr Divisions. Both formations had taken a 'battering' since the invasion, with 12th SS Panzer Division already reduced to about 75 per cent of its strength. The Germans had at their disposal just short of 200 tanks and between 60 to 80 88mm anti-tank guns.[12]

The plan required the infantry, primarily of the recently landed and untested 15th Scottish Division, supported by the heavy Churchill tanks of 31st Tank Brigade, to advance on a narrow frontage to maximise the concentration of firepower and ensure that sufficient troops were available to follow up the attack in force. In true 'Colossal Cracks' style, the advance would take place behind a rolling artillery barrage, which would move ahead at the rate of 100 yards every three minutes. Once the infantry had breached the German defences, they were to pave the way for the newly arrived 11th Armoured Division to break out to the south of Caen. The similarly untried 43rd Wessex Division would then take over the ground won by 15th Scottish Division and exploit southwards with the rest of the corps. The whole operation would be preceded by an attack to the west by 49th West Riding Division, which as part of XXX Corps had landed on 11 June. This assault would aim to capture Rauray, which lay on a spur of high ground overlooking the country through which VIII Corps was to make its attack.[13]

Things did not go quite according to plan. Due to bad weather, the promised RAF support did not materialise and the advance was far slower than expected. Determined German resistance around the village of Cheux and St. Manvieu held up 15th Scottish Division and it began to lose contact with the rolling barrage. By lunchtime, the division was still some 2 miles from its main objective of the first day, the bridges over the River Odon. Nonetheless and in spite of these delays, it appeared that the German defences were 'stretched to breaking point' and O'Connor decided to launch 11th Armoured Division into the battle earlier than planned. It failed to break through and by the end of the day, VIII Corps was still 1 mile short of the Odon. The German position had held, if only just; 12th SS Panzer Division suffered the loss of over 700 troops killed, wounded or missing, the most it had experienced in any single day of action.[14]

The next day, a successful attempt was made to cross the River Odon and on 28 June the 11th Armoured Division assaulted Hill 112, which was taken after much bitter fighting. Events now intervened. 'Epsom' had pre-empted a major German counter-offensive to be launched by the II SS Panzer Corps, which had recently arrived from Poland. Montgomery and Dempsey, fully aware that this new formation was preparing to go into action, decided to continue with 'Epsom' irrespective. Their goal was to retain the initiative and force the Germans to commit their reinforcements piecemeal and at a time and place of British choosing. With Allied artillery and naval gunfire support already in situ and ready for a battle in and around the salient created by VIII Corps' advance (the 'Scottish Corridor'), it was understood that 'Epsom' now represented an excellent opportunity to inflict serious attrition on the German Army.[15]

O'Connor ordered his men to hold on to their positions and await the expected counterblow, which was duly delivered on 29 June. Even with the prior warning, the intensity of the German offensive caught Second Army by surprise; some units fell back and others were overrun. But the German assault stalled as determined infantry supported by air attack (now that the weather had improved) and artillery fire began to inflict grievous losses on the attacking units. The battle was a 'holocaust for the Germans. Their dead lay in piles among the wheat'.[16] By the end of 1 July, the battle had burnt out. The British still held on south of the Odon, though they had given up Hill 112. The German line had not broken, but they had suffered grievous losses and sacrificed the chance of mounting a concerted counter-attack at a time and place of their choosing.[17]

The initiative still lay firmly with Second Army and in the circumstances 'Epsom' has to be viewed as a considerable success.[18] Montgomery, Dempsey and O'Connor had demonstrated the ability to adapt and balance ends and means in the continually shifting sands of major combat operations. As the situation changed, so too did their approach to the battle.[19] 'Epsom' did, however, highlight the difficulty of outflanking Caen to the south-west. An attack on the north-eastern flank looked equally unpromising, as there was too little space to manoeuvre in the small bridgehead around the River Orne and the Caen Canal. Thus, it was decided that the Germans would have to be driven out of Caen in a frontal assault if Second Army was to advance further south, take the operationally important Bourguébus Ridge to the south-east of Caen and break out into the Caen/Falaise Plain.[20] Normandy was turning into a full-on battle of attrition.

The responsibility for this new offensive was handed to I Corps, under John Crocker, which had by 5 July captured the town of Carpiquet to the west of the city (although the airfield still remained in German hands). The operation was codenamed 'Charnwood' (see Map 14.3) and involved 3rd British, 3rd Canadian and the newly arrived 59th Staffordshire Division, supported by 33rd, 27th and 2nd Canadian armoured brigades. Intelligence estimates suggested

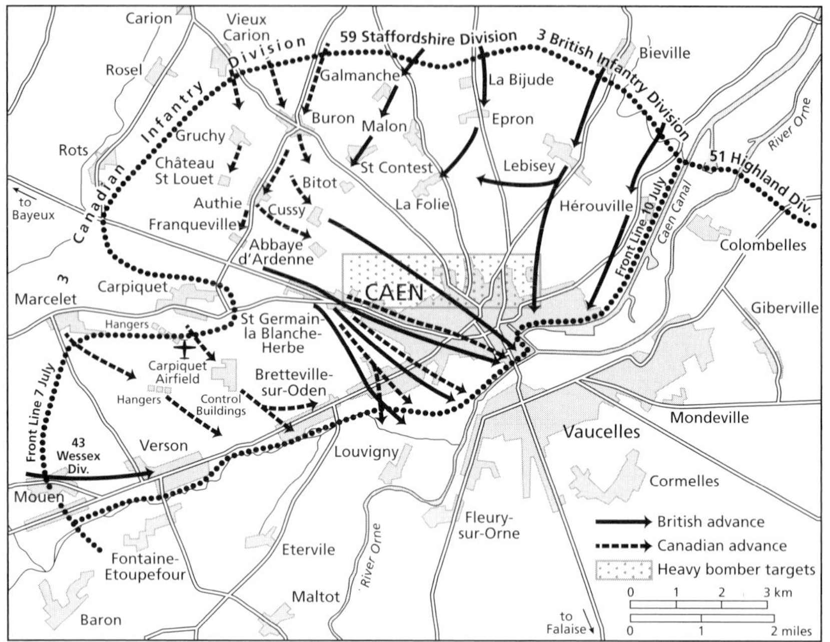

Map 14.3 Operation 'Charnwood', 8–9 July 1944

that Second Army had a marked, but not spectacular numerical advantage over the Germans; it outnumbered them 2:1 in infantry and 4:1 in tanks.[21] In the circumstances, it was hoped that massed fires would make all the difference; the attack would be supported by 656 guns of the Royal Artillery plus naval gunfire and would be preceded by the innovative use of RAF Bomber Command to saturation bomb what was known to be 'exceptionally strong' German defences. By dropping more than 2,000 tons of ordinance from 467 Lancaster and Halifax bombers, it was hoped that the RAF would 'blast a path open for the advancing ground forces'.[22]

The battle, much as was the case with 'Epsom', did not get off to the best of starts. Although the bombing 'greatly impressed' those who witnessed it, it was remarkably ineffective in its outcomes.[23] In order to avoid hitting their own troops, the target zone for the heavy bombers was set 6,000 yards from the forward Anglo-Canadian positions. With the pathfinders of 625 Squadron having been ordered not to let the bomb line 'drift back', many overcompensated. The result was that the bombers devastated the city, but left most German defences intact. In addition, in circumstances mirroring the failure of the bombing mission at Monte Cassino, the forecast of adverse weather brought forward the bombing to six hours before the start of the ground assault. Some bombs were fused to explode six hours later, to coincide with the start of the operation, but the raid alerted the Germans to the imminent attack, thus preventing rapid exploitation of the physical and morale effects of Bomber Command's contribution.[24]

When I Corps crossed the start line at 0420hrs on 8 July, therefore, the Germans were fully expecting the attack. Anglo-Canadian casualties were 'staggering'. Among infantry battalions, losses of 25 per cent 'were the rule rather than the exception'.[25] The three assault divisions lost around 3,000 men killed, wounded and missing.[26] Losses on the German side were no less severe. The infantry strength of 12th SS Panzer Division was reduced to the equivalent of just one battalion; the division was, according to its commander, at breaking point. The 16th Luftwaffe Division suffered 75 per cent casualties and 'ceased to exist as a functioning unit'.[27]

Under such pressure, the Germans were forced to retreat to the south bank of the River Orne and by 9 July the British and Canadians were in control of the northern half of the city.[28] The British press was ecstatic. But while Second Army unquestionably improved its position with 'Charnwood', the Bourguébus Ridge, the gateway to the open country to the south, still remained in German hands. The eastern industrial suburb of Colombelles was also controlled by the Germans, with its high factory chimneys providing excellent observation over the surrounding countryside.[29]

The Germans were, nevertheless, increasingly on the back foot. Second Army did not pause for long; it attacked again the next day. Operation 'Jupiter', conducted primarily by 43rd Wessex Division, focused on the south-west flank of the city and particularly the area of Hill 112. 'Jupiter' once again provoked localised casualty intensive German counter-attacks but the forces involved failed to take their key objectives, notably a launching point for a push into the more open countryside to the south. British casualties were heavy, some 2,000 in total for the two-day battle, while 31st Tank Brigade had 25 per cent of its tanks knocked out.[30]

The first five weeks of fighting in Normandy had resulted in limited gains and a serious toll on Second Army. Casualty rates were appallingly high, four times higher than those being experienced in Italy

Table 14.1 Monthly gross battle casualty rates, percentage of troops engaged (as shown on operational order of battle), British North-West Europe compared to Eighth Army, Italy (all nationalities), June–October 1944

Month	British NW Europe	Eighth Army Italy
June 44	10.7	2.6
July 44	9.8	4.0
Aug. 44	8.8	2.6
Sept. 44	9.0	4.1
Oct. 44	5.1	2.4
Average	8.7	3.1

in June 1944 (see Table 14.1).[31] By 11 July, midway through 'Jupiter', British and Canadian forces had suffered 33,417 losses. The majority of these were in the infantry: 3rd Division had suffered 3,859 casualties; 3rd Canadian Division, 4,605; 6th Airborne Division, 2,606; 15th Scottish Division, 2,378; 43rd Wessex Division 1,442; 50th Northumbrian Division, 3,723; 51st Highland Division, 1,756; 59th Staffordshire Division, 1,159; 49th West Riding Division, 2,885; and 53rd Welsh Division, which began landing on 23 June and had been fighting under VIII Corps, 580.[32] Within these formations, casualties were concentrated in the rifle companies that made up each of the nine infantry battalions in a division (*c.*3,500 men).[33] Thus, by the time they had captured the northern half of the city of Caen, of the ten Anglo-Canadian infantry divisions in contact with the enemy, three had suffered in the region of 100 per cent casualties in their fighting units, while a further four had suffered over 50 per cent.[34]

The troops' determination to fight during this extended period of heavy fighting was, nevertheless, nothing short of 'excellent'. The censorship summary for British troops in the second half of June noted that 'some of the best testimony' came from 'Field Ambulance personnel'. A private in 203 Field Ambulance, 59th Staffordshire Division, wrote, 'the British Tommy is the finest fighter ... He never quits and still wants to go back to the Front again although wounded. You have only to see them as we bring them in. They are still full of the fighting spirit.' The summary was derived from the mail of six divisions, three of which were the veteran 7th Armoured, 50th Northumbrian and 51st Highland Divisions. It is worth noting that morale in these formations was very good in spite of their initial reluctance to participate in the Normandy invasion.[35] It was pointed out, for example, that there was 'a very fine esprit de corps' in 50th Division and 'pride in the Division' was considered 'very high'. Across the British mail, there were 'many indications of fine comradeship, confidence in leadership ... and in equipment'.[36] The report noted that the morale of the troops had been 'strengthened by battle experience', and the performance of the Royal Navy and RAF had 'made a deep impression', giving the men a 'feeling of security'.[37]

Similar sentiments were expressed in the Canadian summaries. The censors reported that:

> Morale is magnificent and is still sounder because of [the] successful battle encounter with the enemy. The enemy is not despised, but though he is given credit for being tough, the Canadians are even tougher. There is true modesty in this morale, and troops are not ashamed to say they have got 'their second wind'; when wounded they have 'lots of scrap' left in them.[38]

The Canadian reports also provided a statistical analysis of the troops' reactions to certain aspects of the battle experience. For example, they presented data on the number of letters whose writers stated that they were 'optimistic' about the progress of the war or 'pessimistic', 'keen' for training or 'adverse', 'satisfied' with leave arrangements or 'dissatisfied', 'contented', or 'browned off'. They also provided data on the number of writers who stated that they were 'keen for action'. Information on 'keenness for action', or, to put it another way, willingness to fight, was arguably a better indicator of morale than the morale description contained in each summary and Figure 14.1 indicates that, on that basis, morale in the Canadian Army was higher in June 1944 than at any other time during the North-West Europe campaign.[39]

This assessment of Canadian morale is supported by reference to combined instances of sickness, battle exhaustion, desertion, AWOL and self-inflicted wounds (SIW) figures for Second Army (including Canadian troops under command) during the North-West Europe campaign. These figures, presented graphically in Figure 14.2 and aligned with levels of morale derived from the censorship summaries,

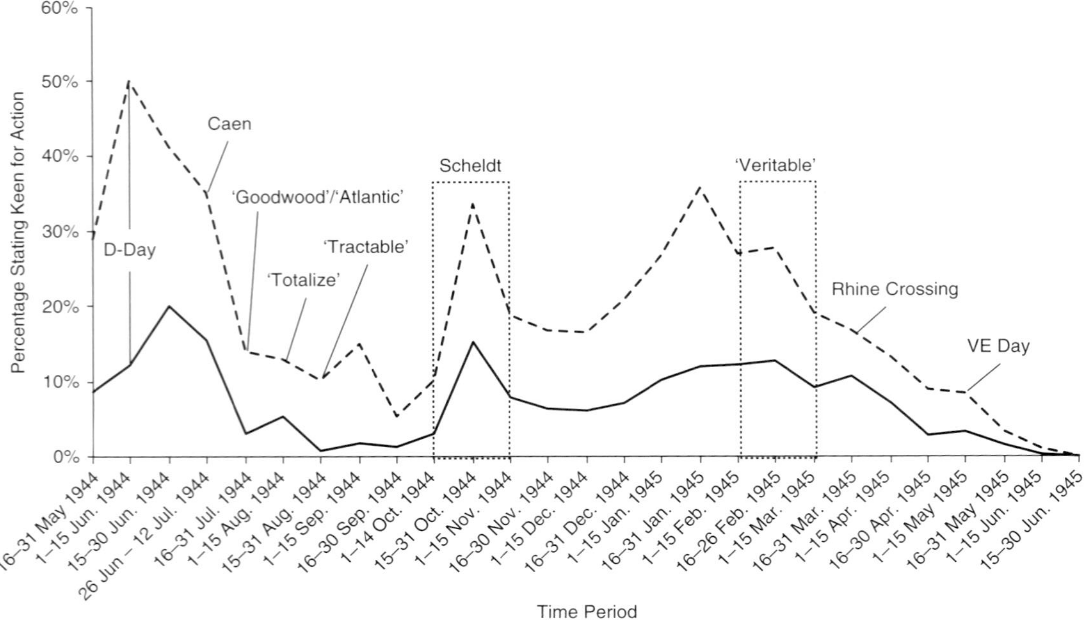

Figure 14.1 Percentage of Canadian mail that is 'keen for action' and percentage of Canadian mail that addresses the issue of morale that is 'keen for action', May 1944–June 1945

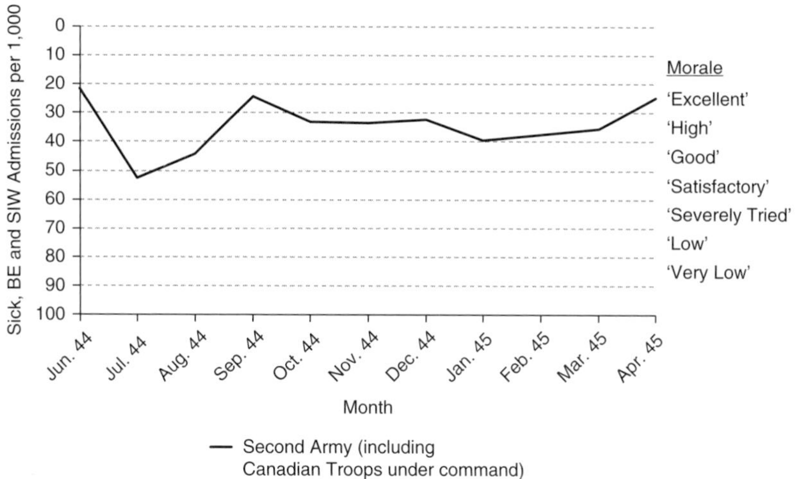

Figure 14.2 Second Army (including Canadian troops under command), monthly admissions per thousand to general hospitals and casualty clearing stations for sickness, battle exhaustion, desertion, AWOL and SIW, June 1944–April 1945

demonstrate that morale was 'excellent' in the Anglo/Canadian Second Army in June 1944.[40]

This positive picture continued during Operations 'Charnwood' and 'Jupiter', in the first two weeks of July (see Figure 14.3 for weekly rates of sickness and battle exhaustion for British Second and First Canadian Armies in North-West Europe).[41] Although morale was no longer 'excellent', it could still be described as 'good' to 'high' during this period; the British censors noted, for instance, that morale was 'thoroughly sound and the troops who have been in battle are quietly confident of their ability to meet and beat the enemy'. 'Heroics', according to the censors, were 'absent, but there is determination and ability to fight on, even when very weary'. The health of the troops had held up in spite of the 'continued bad weather and rain' and the censors commented on the fact that there had been 'no outbreak of colds or other sickness'.[42] The situation with Canadian troops was no different:

> Morale is very high and is all the sounder because it has been tested in battle ... Even when wounded or weary, no desire has been expressed to avoid resumption of battle. Pride in formation and unit is manifest.[43]

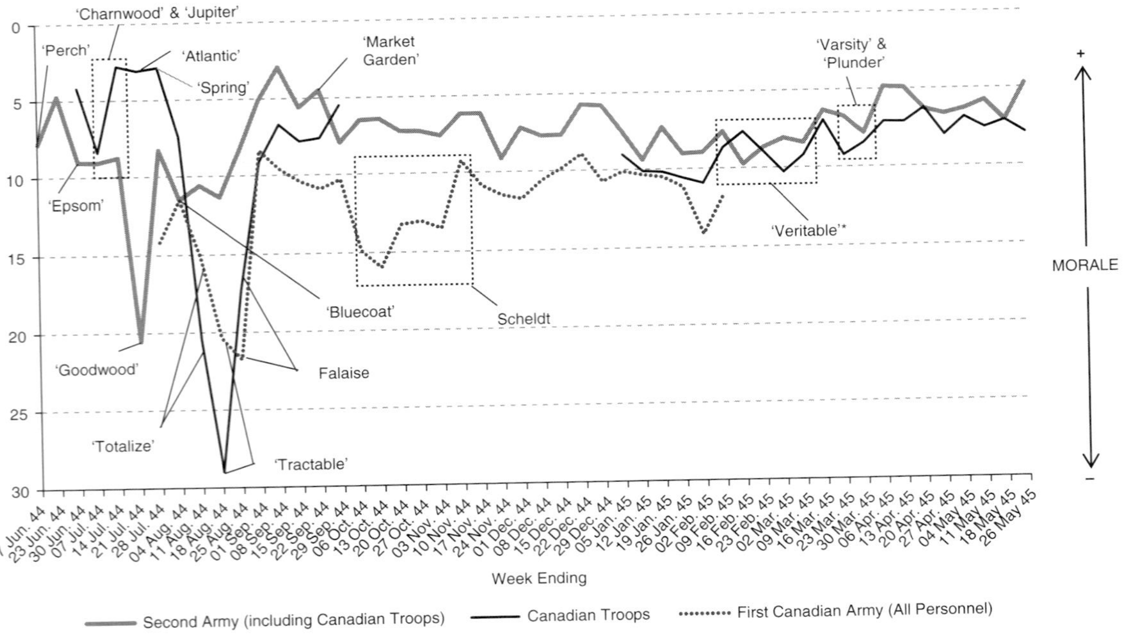

Figure 14.3 British Second Army (including Canadian troops under command), First Canadian Army (Canadian troops only) and First Canadian Army (all troops under command), weekly admissions per thousand to general hospitals and casualty clearing stations for sickness and battle exhaustion, 11 June 1944 – 5 May 1945

* 'Veritable' was a First Canadian Army operation.

It does appear, therefore, that morale was at least 'good' to 'high' during the success of 'Epsom' and during the much more limited gains of 'Charnwood' and 'Jupiter'. It follows, then, that it was a combination of other factors that played the dominant role in the outcome of events in late June and early July 1944. One of these was the interplay between Anglo-Canadian tactics and the behaviour of the enemy. The willingness of German units to stand their ground and continue fighting cost Second Army time, resources and casualties. After 'Perch' the firepower-heavy approach employed by Second Army eschewed the kind of rapid manoeuvre that might have surrounded and penetrated German positions and placed enemy units in situations of intolerable pressure, where they might have been forced to surrender.[44] Small numbers of Germans, if they could withstand the physical and morale effects of massive Allied bombardments, were able to hold up advances and force British and Commonwealth units to reset and begin another set-piece attack.[45] The 'Colossal Cracks' approach, just like in North Africa, Sicily and Italy, had severe limitations.

The level of resistance displayed by the Germans over the course of the campaign can be shown to some extent by plotting the cost in casualties of taking a German prisoner. Figure 14.4 shows the ratio of casualties in Second Army (including Canadian troops under command) to the number of German prisoners captured every week during the North-West Europe campaign.[46] These figures indicate clearly that German resistance hardened significantly in July 1944, notably during the fighting around Caen in the first two weeks of the month; for each German prisoner captured, Second Army suffered 8.18 casualties during 'Charnwood' and 3.35 casualties during 'Jupiter'.[47] The 'Charnwood' ratio was even higher than in the bitter fighting on the 'Gustav Line' in Italy between September 1943 and May 1944, a period that included the first three battles of Cassino, when British and Commonwealth troops suffered 7.3 casualties for every German prisoner captured. By comparison, Operation 'Compass', against the Italians in the winter of 1940/1 had cost the Western Desert Force 0.02 casualties per prisoner;[48] the conquest of Malaya had cost the Japanese 0.1 casualties per prisoner;[49] while the fighting in the desert between May and July 1942 had cost the Germans 0.57 casualties per prisoner.[50] The battle challenge facing Second Army around Caen was distinctly different to that which had faced the German and Japanese armies between 1940 and 1942.

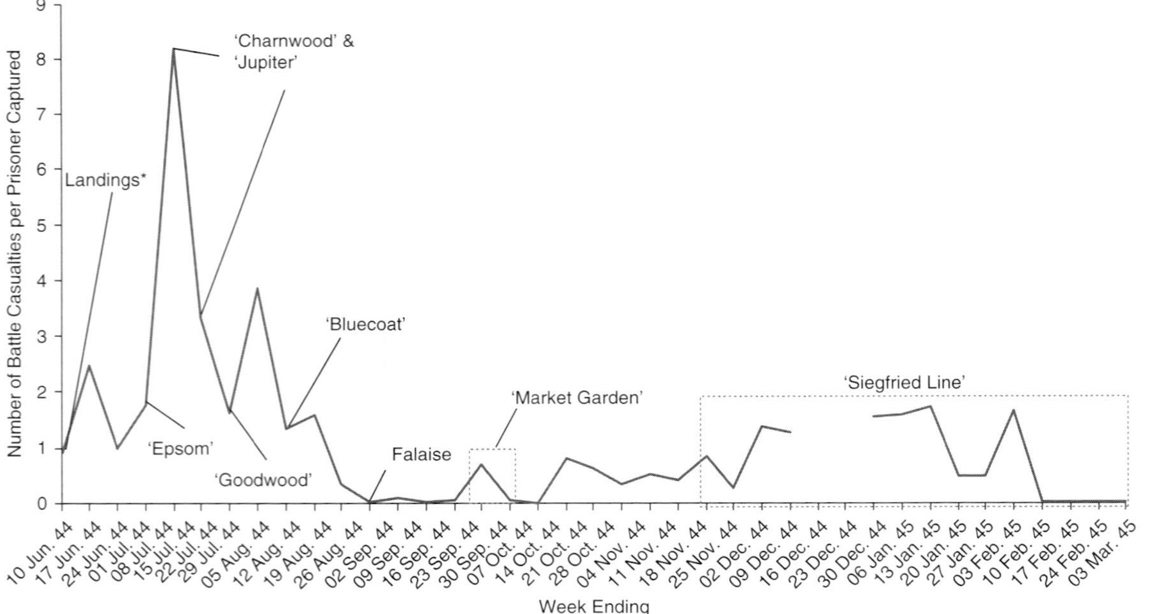

Figure 14.4 The cost of a German prisoner, British Second Army (including Canadian troops under command), North-West Europe, 1944–5

*Figure for the week ending 10 June 1944 is for the first five days of the campaign.

The censorship summaries support this contention; by early July the tone of correspondence from British and Canadian troops had shifted noticeably as the men began to develop a healthy respect for the German soldier in Normandy. 'Whether young or old', the censors noted, 'they fight well, especially the Hitler Youth troops [12th SS Panzer Division]' defending Caen. Many commented that there seemed to be 'a whole generation missing' in the German Army; 'they were a queer mixture of very old and very young'. Nevertheless, 'one thing they had in common' was 'the ability to fight and keep on fighting until their position was absolutely hopeless'. Hitler Youth 'tank boys' appeared to be extremely 'tough'. 'These boys', a guardsman in the 1st Armoured Coldstream Guards wrote, 'are 14 years of age to 20 ... The worst of them [*sic*] is they'd sooner die than be caught.' A trooper in the 23rd Hussars remarked that 'the majority of the enemy' were 'fighting to the last man'.[51] One word in particular was constantly used in the Canadian summaries to describe the German fighters, 'fanatics'. 'The real "Nazi" German', wrote a trooper in the 27th Canadian Armoured Regiment, 'fights to the very last and no fooling. They are young and tough and fanatical as hell.'[52] The result was that infantry battalions in Normandy, faced by this stiff opposition, advanced typically at a very slow rate, 'on average between 380–525 yards per hour in daylight and 305–420 yards at night'.[53] In a situation where German forces showed little propensity to surrender, small numbers of defenders were continually able to hold up advances and force British and Commonwealth units and formations to reset and begin new set-piece attacks. Fanatical German soldiers quite simply had to be killed or wounded to be removed from the battle equation; it was proving profoundly difficult to restore mobility to the battlefield.

Operation 'Goodwood'

It was in the context of stiffening German resistance and heavy casualties that planning for the next phase of operations took place. The campaign had descended into a 'dog fight' and Second Army was going to struggle to find replacements for the casualties endured in this type of combat. The apparent solution to the problem revolved around a greater use of Second Army's superiority in armour. By the start of July, the British and Canadians enjoyed a rough 4:1 advantage in tanks, so an armour-heavy operation appeared the most 'strategically appropriate use of resources'. Dempsey pressed to use the armour available for an all-out push to break out of the Normandy beachhead.[54] Initially, Montgomery embraced this plan. He wrote to Eisenhower on 12 July informing him that he expected his whole eastern flank to 'burst into flames'. Two days later he wrote to Brooke that he had 'decided that the time has come to have a real "show down" on the eastern flank . . . The possibilities are immense; with 700 tanks loosed to the S.E. of CAEN, and armoured cars operating far ahead, anything may happen.'[55]

As the day of battle neared, in the only formal written directive produced in advance of the detailed planning of an operation in the North-West Europe campaign, Montgomery changed his approach. He decided instead that 'Goodwood', the new operation to be carried out in the British sector, would continue wearing down the best of the German armoured formations and so facilitate the planned American breakout in the west, Operation 'Cobra'.[56] The 'Goodwood' plan envisaged a three-corps, seven-division, attack on a 9-mile frontage south and east of Caen. Four infantry divisions, 3rd British and 51st Highland of I Corps and 2nd and 3rd Canadian of II Canadian Corps (the Canadian portion of 'Goodwood' was codenamed 'Atlantic'), would secure the flanks and a main effort was to be launched by the three armoured divisions of VIII Corps, 11th Armoured, Guards Armoured and 7th Armoured. The armoured thrust would be massed on a front just over 1 mile wide and, all going well, would penetrate the German defences to the long-sought-after gateway to the Caen/Falaise Plain, the Bourguébus Ridge.[57] (See Map 14.4.) As Montgomery put it, 'a victory on the eastern flank will help us gain what we want on the western flank':

> The eastern flank is a bastion on which the whole future of the campaign in NW Europe depends; it must remain a firm bastion; if it became unstable the operations on the western flank would cease. Therefore, while taking advantage of every opportunity to destroy the enemy, we must be very careful to maintain our own balance and ensure a firm base.[58]

As long as these considerations were kept in mind, Montgomery ordered, armoured cars could 'push far to the south towards FALAISE, and spread alarm and despondency, and discover "the form"'.[59]

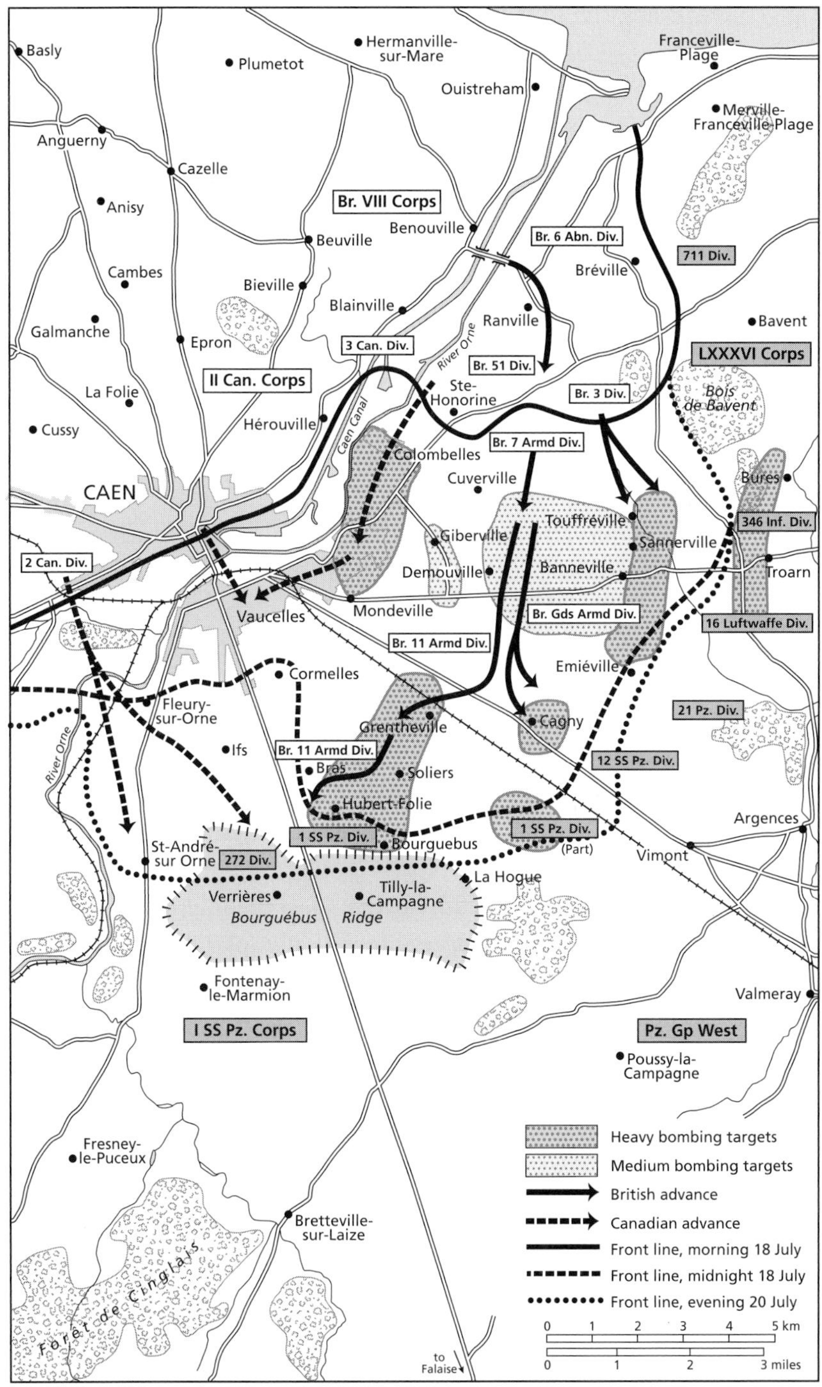

Map 14.4 Operation 'Goodwood', 18–20 July 1944

Opposing the four infantry divisions and three armoured divisions of the Anglo-Canadian forces were the remnants of three German infantry divisions (272nd, 346th and 16th Luftwaffe), and three *panzer* divisions (21st, 1st SS and 12th SS Panzer). The attritional battles around Caen had clearly had a devastating effect on the increasingly overstretched German Army. All told, Second Army enjoyed a 'truly crushing' numerical advantage. It had 1,277 tanks and 118,000 soldiers in the front line with 4,500 aircraft in support. The Germans had, by comparison, between 118 and 319 tanks and about 29,000 troops with only several hundred aircraft in support. Thus, the attackers had at least a 4:1 advantage in both personnel and armour. Moreover, at the point of main effort, the VIII Corps thrust towards the Bourguébus Ridge, the British forces enjoyed a numerical advantage of more than 22:1 in troops and more than 80:1 in tanks.[60]

These numerical and material advantages were hammered home on the morning of 18 July, when 1,000 Lancasters and Halifaxes of RAF Bomber Command deposited their payloads on the German defenders between the start line and objectives of Operation 'Goodwood'. The inferno unleashed was followed up by the firepower of 318 B25 Mitchells and B26 Marauders of the US 9th Air Force and 570 B24 Liberators and B17 Flying Fortresses of the US 8th Air Force.[61] All told, the firepower employed, not only by the Allied air forces, but also by the Royal Navy and Royal Artillery, 'struck the German positions [that morning] with the explosive power of more than eight one-kiloton tactical nuclear warheads in the span of only three hours'.[62] To take advantage of this unprecedented use of firepower, it was planned, in the first phase, to rush the armour through at the highest possible speed while the enemy was still stunned by the air and artillery bombardments. Subsequently, as distances increased, much would depend on the ability of the armour and infantry to work effectively together, as once they reached the Bourguébus Ridge they would be outside the range of effective artillery support; much of Second Army's artillery would still be on the west bank of the River Orne, due to the fact that the armour had priority crossing the few bridges over the river and the Caen Canal.[63]

When the ground assault began early in the morning of 18 July, it made rapid progress as the massed British armour overran or bypassed the shattered German forward positions. By mid-morning, 29th Armoured Brigade, the lead formation of 11th Armoured

Division, was battling at the foot of the Bourguébus Ridge, near Hubert-Folie and La Hogue, over 7 miles south of its start position.[64] However, the tanks found themselves isolated from the support of the majority of their infantry (159th Brigade), which was held up by resistance in Cuverville and Démouville near the start line.[65] At approximately 1000hrs, with the tanks of 11th Armoured Division fighting to all intents and purposes alone on the Bourguébus Ridge, O'Connor ordered 5th Guards Armoured Brigade to advance rapidly and support the left flank of this vital penetration. It ran into a line of anti-tank guns around Cagny and Emiéville, on the eastern flank of the 1-mile armoured assault frontage and failed to make further progress. The clearance of the left (eastern) flank had been the responsibility of 3rd Division, whose task had been complicated because Touffréville, one of its first objectives, had been missed by the aerial bombardment. This slowed the advance of the division, which meant that the Germans in Sannerville and Banneville, its next two objectives, had 'time to recover from the shock of the bombing and ... were able to move west to Cagny' and Emiéville.[66]

O'Connor quickly reassessed the situation facing his corps and this time ordered 22nd Armoured Brigade, of 7th Armoured Division, to advance in support of 29th Armoured Brigade, this time on the right (see Illustration 14.1). The 22nd Armoured Brigade also got held up, however, by the failure of 3rd Division to silence German resistance on the eastern flank and by the continuing battle around Cuverville and Démouville.[67] With the advance of the 11th Armoured Division stalled on the slopes of the Bourguébus Ridge, 'the critical moment in the battle' had arrived.[68] Had the increased armoured strength of Guards Armoured or 7th Armoured Division 'been brought to bear', it is possible 'that the enemy might have been forced off' the greatly desired Bourguébus feature.[69] But it was not to be; by the end of the first day, the advance had slowed to a crawl and VIII Corps was still short of the ridge. Renewed efforts to advance over the course of the following two days made little progress and the offensive ground to a halt by midday on 20 July with the ridge still in German hands.[70]

The failure to break through at 'Goodwood' led to great controversy and no little recrimination.[71] Eisenhower remarked caustically after the battle that 7,000 tons of ordinance expended for only 7 miles gained appeared little value for money.[72] Such tactical and operational

Illustration 14.1 Cromwell tanks of 7th Armoured Division assembled for Operation 'Goodwood', 18 July 1944. On being ordered forward to support 11th Armoured Division, 7th Armoured Division got held up by the failure of the infantry of VIII Corps to silence German resistance on the eastern and western flanks of the 'Goodwood' battlefield. Had the increased armoured strength of 7th Armoured Division been brought to bear, it is possible that the enemy might have been forced off the Bourguébus Ridge.

methods were, indeed, extremely expensive, but their utility depended on context. Bombing from the air was notoriously inaccurate;[73] nevertheless, the suppressive effect of massed firepower could be impressive, as evidenced by 29th Armoured Brigade's rapid advance to the Bourguébus Ridge. Problems arose, however, when tactical plans did not fully take account of the opportunities and costs of employing massed firepower, and when such plans were not pursued with sufficient willingness and energy by the troops employed.

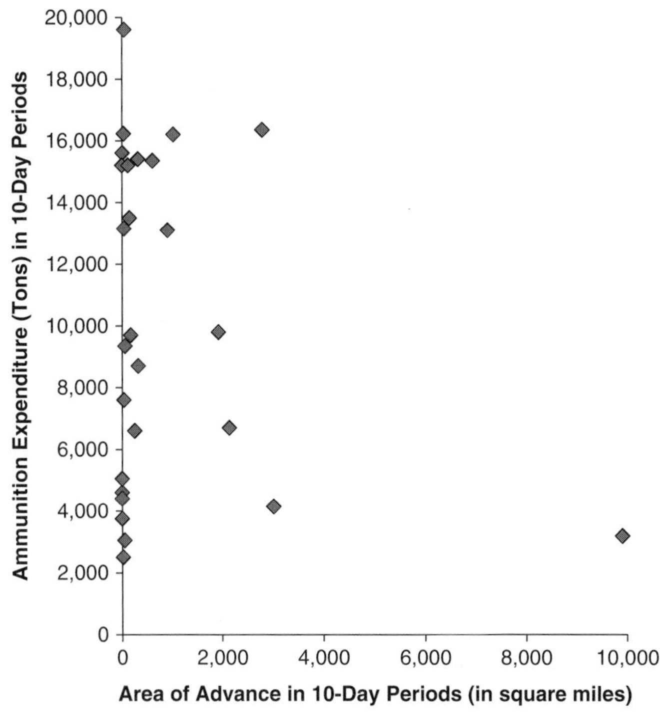

Figure 14.5 21st Army Group, area of advance in ten-day periods to ammunition expended (1 July 1944 to 28 March 1945)

Statistics for the performance of 21st Army Group in North-West Europe, compiled by the Army Operational Research Group, help to highlight this dynamic. They indicate that artillery, when assessed as an independent variable, was a poor determinant of combat success. Operational Research Memorandum No. E20, 'Some Statistics on the North West Europe Campaign', clearly demonstrated, for example, that there 'was no significant correlation between German casualties and ... Allied [Anglo-Canadian 21st Army Group and US 12th Army Group] ammunition expenditure'.[74] Furthermore, Figure 14.5 shows that there was not a strong relationship (–0.234, P=0.179) between the firepower employed by 21st Army Group, of which Second Army was a key component, and the area of ground captured from the enemy.[75] There was a similarly weak correlation (–0.160, P=0.445) between the firepower employed by 21st Army Group and the number of enemy prisoners captured.[76]

Massed firepower was only truly effective when used as part of a suitably well-thought-through concept of operations. However, there were considerable weaknesses in the 'Goodwood' plan. A number of historians have pointed out, for example, that the leading elements of the British armoured forces were required to battle against the German defenders with insufficient infantry and dwindling artillery support (as they outran the range of their guns).[77] 'Pip' Roberts, the commander of 11th Armoured Division, had requested of O'Connor prior to the battle that 159th Brigade should not be employed in mopping up Démouville and Cuverville and that the armour and infantry of 11th Armoured Division should instead be utilised together at the decisive point further forward. He had suggested that the capture of the two villages should be assigned to 51st Highland Division. However, O'Connor refused as he had received clear instructions from Montgomery that he was not to over-commit in case of a German counter-attack.[78] In hindsight, this decision appears excessively cautious, but it can hardly be argued that insufficient manpower was committed in 'Goodwood'; at the point of main effort, the VIII Corps thrust, British forces enjoyed a numerical advantage of more than 22:1.[79] The crux of the matter was that 'Goodwood', by separating the armour from its infantry and the forward elements of the advance from its artillery support, 'broke the blueprint' for the 'Colossal Cracks' approach.[80] In Dempsey's own words it had not been 'a very good operation of war tactically'.[81]

Nevertheless, there is considerable evidence to suggest that even this bad plan did not fundamentally doom 'Goodwood' to failure. It is, in fact, only in the context of a severe drop in morale that the ineffectiveness of the enormous resources applied to 'Goodwood' can be understood. By the time of the battle, as Major D. J. Watterson, the psychiatrist attached to Second Army, noted, 'the high optimism of the troops who landed in the assault and early build up phases' had 'dwindled':

> Almost certainly the initial hopes and optimism were too high and the gradual realisation that the 'walk-over' to Berlin had developed into an infantry slogging match caused an unspoken but clearly recognisable fall of morale. One sign of this was the increase in the incidence of psychiatric casualties arriving in a steady stream at Exhaustion Centres and reinforced by waves of beaten, exhausted men from each of the major battles.

> For every man breaking down there were certainly three or four ineffective men remaining with their units.[82]

This view was tacitly acknowledged by others at the time and is also to be found in assessments published after the war. Carlo D'Este has suggested that the British offensive was 'overcautious' and had it been more 'thrustful' it could have punched through the German defences (which, as Figure 14.4 shows, was not of the same intensity as during the previous battles in the Caen area) before they had recovered from the carpet-bombing.[83] After the battle, he argued, there was a 'good deal of dismay' at Army and corps level, most noticeably with 7th Armoured Division, who, it appeared, 'had been needlessly slow in closing up on 18 July', just one more example of their 'poor performance in Normandy'.[84] John Ellis has pointed out that VIII Corps, upon whose shoulders the main thrust of the offensive lay, failed to keep pace with the creeping barrage laid down by the artillery following the carpet-bombing, while many others have pointed to a more general emergence of a problem with morale in July 1944.[85]

According to the censorship summaries, this drop in morale was most noticeable in the veteran units of 7th Armoured Division, 50th Northumbrian Division and 51st Highland Division. The summary for the first half of July pointed out that:

> A jarring note comes sometimes from troops who had served in other theatres of war and who feel they had not been sufficiently rested before taking part in the invasion of Normandy ... There is a grumbling among troops who served in North Africa and Italy because they feel that insufficient leave was given before they landed in Normandy.[86]

As one man wrote, 'the lads here have figured it out their own way, just as they did with M.E.F. (Men England forgot). They reckon B.W.E.F. (British Western European Force) means "Boys without English furlough".' The censors pointed to other 'disturbing influences upon troops' such as 'the weather, the slow delivery of mail to the U.K. and the dangers to relatives of flying bombs'.[87] Montgomery was so concerned with the performance of 51st Highland Division that he informed Brooke on 15 July that, in the opinion of Dempsey, Crocker and himself, the division was not fit for front-line action; the divisional commander Charles Bullen-Smith was, as a consequence, fired and replaced by Tom Rennie, who had commanded 3rd Division on D-Day.[88]

The censorship summary for the second half of July described morale as ‘good’. However, it mostly omitted evidence from the key formations involved in ‘Goodwood’, the major battle of the period. Only one reference to 3rd Division was made, a quote from a lance corporal of the East Riding Yeomanry to the effect that ‘the lads have had some nasty knocks handed out to them since they landed, but they seem no worse for it’. The summary did not assess mail written by men from the main assault divisions over the ‘Goodwood’ period (Guards, 7th and 11th Armoured Divisions)[89] as only 326 of the 27,366 letters used in the bi-weekly summary came from these formations.[90] The picture of morale that emerged from the censorship summary, therefore, was incomplete.

The sickness, battle exhaustion, SIW and desertion/AWOL statistics for July, however, cover all formations during all phases of the month’s fighting including 3rd Division and the armoured divisions of VIII Corps. They suggest that a significant problem with morale had emerged by the second half of July. The overall rate of sickness, battle exhaustion, SIW and desertion/AWOL in Second Army rose from 21.4 per thousand in June 1944 to 52.7 per thousand in July, a 146 per cent increase (see Figure 14.2). The majority of this increase took place in the week ending 22 July, the period of Operation ‘Goodwood’; the weekly sickness and battle exhaustion rate in Second Army for this period was 20.6 per thousand per week, an increase of 133 per cent from the figure for the week ending 15 July (8.8 per thousand) and by far the highest rate reached in Second Army during the North-West Europe campaign (see Figure 14.3).

A more granular assessment of the available statistics shows that this peak in sickness, battle exhaustion and SIW can mostly be attributed to the infantry, who all too often ended up doing the majority of the fighting and dying. Morale issues were less obvious in the armoured regiments, artillery or supporting arms of Second Army. For example, between 18 and 27 July, 11th, Guards and 7th Armoured Divisions suffered 179 cases of battle exhaustion, almost all of which it must be assumed were during the fighting of 18 to 20 July.[91] The Second Army hygiene report for the week ending 22 July noted that only about fifty battle exhaustion casualties came from armoured units.[92] This is supported by evidence from the VIII Corps psychiatrist, who reported later that 'over 80% [of exhaustion cases admitted during the battle] were from the Infantry Brigades of the armoured divisions ... I took the opportunity of chatting with a number of tank crews just out of the battle; they were in excellent fettle, morale being at a very high level.'[93] Thus, it is likely that at least 129 of the 179 cases of battle exhaustion in VIII Corps during 'Goodwood' came from the three infantry brigades and three motor battalions of 11th, Guards and 7th Armoured Divisions, an establishment of 11,022 men.[94] The rate of battle exhaustion in these infantry units was, therefore, in the region of 11.7 cases per thousand men for the 9.3-day period surrounding the battle, a monthly equivalent of 36.27 per thousand (see Figure 14.2 for context). These figures (11.7 and 36.27 cases per thousand) do not include men admitted sick during battle and so the overall sick and battle exhaustion rate would have been dramatically higher; the number of men admitted sick in 7th Armoured Division in July 1944 was, for example, over three times the number admitted for battle exhaustion.[95]

However high these figures for battle exhaustion might appear, they are substantially less than those of another key infantry formation during the 'Goodwood' offensive, 3rd Division. The three infantry brigades of 3rd Division (8th, 9th and 185th), a fighting strength of 6,814 men, reported 167 sick and 464 battle-exhaustion cases between 18 and 22 July. This represents an extraordinarily high sick and exhaustion rate of 92.6 per thousand for the five days of the battle. Battle exhaustion was so high that it made up an unparalleled 40 per cent of total battle casualties during 'Goodwood'.[96] As early as 28 June, the I Corps medical diary had noted 'indications of physical and mental exhaustion' in 3rd Division.[97] According to the Divisional Monthly Medical Bulletin for July 1944, a 'disturbing feature' for the month 'was the increase of "exhaustion" cases which numbered no less than 738'. This extremely high figure was due, according to the report, to the wear and tear of modern warfare, the strain caused by the division being constantly in the line since landing on D-Day (since 6 June, it had suffered casualties on every day except 13 July) and the fact that in many cases reinforcements were not fully battle-trained, a problem well appreciated by Montgomery.[98] Indeed, during June and July, 3rd Division spent more days in 'intense combat' than any other division in 21st Army Group.[99]

It is difficult, therefore, to avoid the conclusion that morale had deteriorated substantially between June and July and that a serious problem had developed by the time of 'Goodwood'; this problem was particularly acute in 3rd Division and in the infantry battalions of VIII Corps. So significant was the problem of battle exhaustion, for example, that immediately after 'Goodwood', on 21 July, O'Connor ordered his divisional commanders to court-martial for desertion any soldiers who were discovered to have feigned 'exhaustion' as a way of escaping from the front line.[100]

This deterioration in morale helps to explain the failure of 159th Brigade and 3rd Division to quell the limited German resistance on the flanks of the VIII Corps advance, thus delaying the advance of the Guards and 7th Armoured Divisions and sealing the fate of 29th Armoured Brigade on the slopes of the Bourguébus Ridge.[101] 'The death ride of the armoured divisions'[102] was not solely the consequence of a poor tactical plan, as detrimental as this factor was to the performance of Second Army; it was also due to a morale problem that by the middle of July was having a serious impact on the effectiveness of the British infantry in Normandy. In fact, in analysing the 'Goodwood' concept, perhaps it is best to argue that the fundamental weakness in the plan was not 'tactical' in the technical sense, but that it did not make adequate allowance for an army that was, after a month and a half of heavy fighting, physically and mentally worn out from battle.

Breakout

The failure to break out at 'Goodwood' heightened tensions in the upper echelons of the Allied command chain. Montgomery had intimated to Brooke and Eisenhower, before he had reined in his ambitions on 15 July, that 'Goodwood' might 'have far reaching results'.[103] Such a suggestion had ensured the support of the strategic air arm but left Montgomery extremely vulnerable when the advance ground to a halt on the Bourguébus Ridge.[104] Eisenhower certainly felt let down. Under all this pressure, and with 'Cobra' planned in the west, it was politically important for the British and Canadians to be seen to continue the offensive. In the week following 'Goodwood', limited attacks were launched once again around Hill 112 to the south-west of Caen (Operation 'Express') and to the south of Caen (Operation 'Spring'). These operations confused the Germans as to where the next major offensive would strike and ensured that when the Americans launched 'Cobra', on 25 July, the German forces available to face them were as small as possible; the British and Canadians faced 92 infantry battalions and 645 tanks (in six *panzer* divisions), while the Americans confronted 85 infantry battalions and 190 tanks (in two *panzer* divisions).[105]

'Cobra', after initial setbacks, was a huge success, with the Americans breaking open the front in the west of the Normandy bridgehead. The 21st Army Group had played its part by pinning the heavier German formations in place around Caen. Nevertheless, the Americans took the plaudits. The collapse of the German line opened up the opportunity to free up the Brittany ports and then exploit towards Paris. General George Patton's Third US Army was activated on 1 August and soon began an all-out drive to the Seine. The German strategy in Normandy had failed. Their plan of digging in and hanging on had 'stymied' the Allies for six weeks, but it had been at considerable long-term cost, as formations 'had to be fed into the line piecemeal merely to maintain a generally static front'. Now, 'with few reserves left and all available units committed, collapsing or pinned in place, the German position in Normandy was on the point of meltdown'.[106]

The stage was set for a coup de grace. In order to exploit and support the American success, Dempsey recommended a new assault, Operation 'Bluecoat', on the boundary with the US First Army near Caumont, on the British right about 20 miles west of Caen. At this point of the line, only limited German resistance was expected.[107] For the operation to take place, the weight of Second Army would have to be moved westward away from Caen. This was no easy task as many of the formations involved would have to cross the maintenance routes of corps already in action. Nevertheless, the HQ of Second Army carried out the move secretly and efficiently, a fine example of effective staff work.[108]

'Bluecoat' launched on 30 July and consisted initially of two corps, XXX and VIII, attacking in the direction of and to the west of Mont Pinçon, the highest point in Normandy. The main thrust of the new operation was to be delivered on the left by XXX Corps, under Lieutenant-General Gerard Bucknall, initially towards Hill 361, important high ground to the west of Mont Pinçon, and then on to Pinçon itself (see Map 14.5). Bucknall had 43rd Wessex and 50th Northumbrian Divisions in the lead with 8th Armoured Brigade, which had, like 50th Northumbrian Division, transferred from the

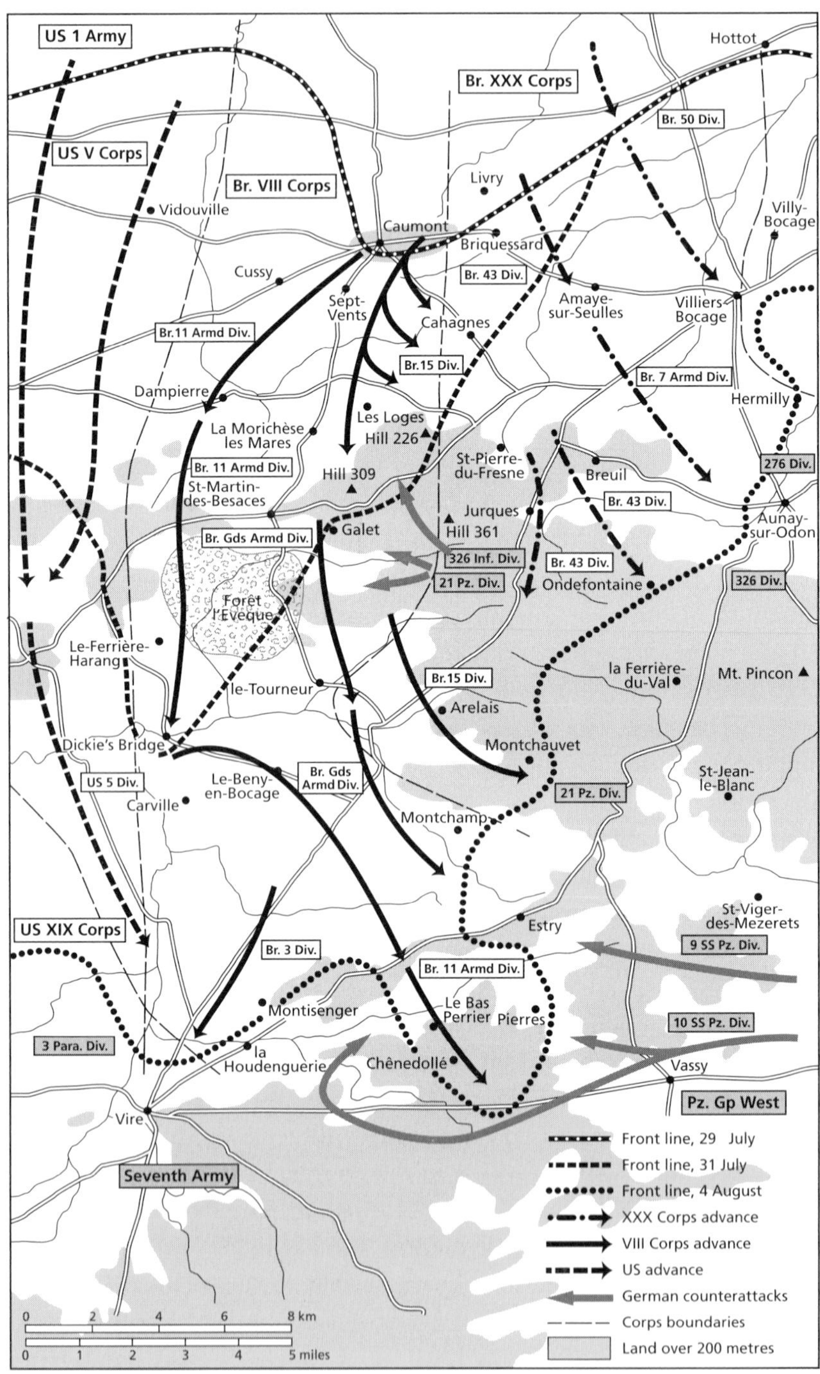

Map 14.5 Operation 'Bluecoat', 30 July–4 August 1944

Mediterranean and landed on Gold beach on D-Day, and 7th Armoured Division in support. On the right, O'Connor's VIII Corps was to strike south from Caumont towards Hill 226 and Hill 309 and then on towards Bény-Bocage Ridge and the town of Vire. O'Connor had 15th Scottish Division at his disposal, supported by 6th Guards Tank Brigade, which had recently arrived in Normandy, and 11th Armoured Division, with the Guards Armoured Division in support.[109]

All told, Second Army had a force of 115,018 men, 1,104 tanks and 536 artillery pieces in and around the battle area, west of the River Orne.[110] An air 'armada' of some 1,600 medium and heavy bombers from RAF Bomber Command and 9th US Air Force was also available.[111] The Germans deployed, by comparison, 326th Division, a proportion of 276th Division and two companies of tanks and a heavy anti-tank battalion along the 11-mile front of the British attack, a total of 18,023 men, 49 tanks and assault guns and 102 artillery pieces. Thus, Second Army had a 6:1 advantage in terms of manpower, a quite staggering 23:1 preponderance in armour, an advantage of 5:1 in artillery and an 'overwhelming superiority' in air power.[112]

The concern remained, however, that Second Army had enjoyed similar advantages in previous operations and failed to exploit them. Much to its credit, Second Army now took the 'bull by the horns' and made some important adaptations to its overall approach. For a start, the crisis in morale that had so affected operations in 'Goodwood' had to be addressed, and it was. Basic welfare provisions and amenities were overhauled and improved, and, according to the available evidence, this made all the difference. The weekly sickness and battle exhaustion rate for Second Army dropped from 20.6 per thousand for the week ending 22 July to 8.3 per thousand for the week ending 29 July (a 60 per cent decrease). A note on 'Psychiatric Casualties during the Quarter July to September 1944', explained this improvement by reference to the 'increase of morale which was perceptible at that time'. It had certainly, according to the note, not been caused by any decrease in the intensity of the fighting as 'casualties continued to increase for three weeks thereafter'.[113]

The censorship summaries support this assessment. They show that, over the course of the second half of July, a perceptible shift took place in the manner in which a number of key factors central to the wellbeing of the British and Commonwealth citizen army were managed. Whereas the censorship summary for 1 to 15 July made it clear that many of the troops were tired and in need of rest and pointed to the slow introduction of recreation and entertainment facilities, the summary for 16 to 31 July reported that:

a) The setting up of rest camps was much approved ...
b) Mobile baths were universally welcomed and their ubiquity was frequently the subject of mild astonishment.
c) Writers from at least three formations stated that the organisation of supplies was magnificent, and was considered by experienced soldiers to be a vast improvement on anything achieved before.

The censors went on to note that 'appreciation of various forms of entertainment was expressed' and that 'the arrival of beer supplies received a rapturous welcome'.[114] With regards to food, the censors pointed out that in the first half of the month the troops were 'finding tinned food more and more monotonous' and there was 'genuine demand for fresh bread in place of biscuits, of which the troops are heartily tired'. In the second half of the month, they noted that 'supplies of bread and fresh vegetables increased ... and were the subject of a large volume of comment from all formations'.[115] Regarding mail, in the first half of July the censors noted that 'the slowness in the delivery of mail from FRANCE has been a great source of worry to troops in the field and bitter complaints are registered'. By the second half of July, they reported that 'mail services in both directions were said definitely to have improved, particularly outward mail' and that 'adverse references showed a corresponding diminution'.[116] Between 1 and 15 July, the censors had pointed out that there was 'a great desire for books and reading matter' and that the seven-a-day issue of cigarettes was 'rarely considered sufficient for men in action feel the need of a smoke'. By 15 to 31 July, 'newspapers were stated to reach the troops on the evening of the day of publication' and complaints regarding cigarettes had disappeared altogether.[117] Morale in Second Army would never again reach the widespread lows of 'Goodwood'. Those in charge of providing for the welfare of the troops had improved matters just when it was needed most.

Issues regarding infantry/armour co-operation, which had been problematic in Operations 'Perch' and 'Epsom', but had really come to the fore in 'Goodwood', were also addressed. For the 'Bluecoat' operation, 'Pip' Roberts, commander of 11th Armoured Division, and Major-General Allan Adair, commander of Guards Armoured Division, were determined to avoid a repeat of 'Goodwood', where infantry and armour had fought largely separately. Instead, they decided to mix their brigades, 'such that each had two regiments of tanks and two battalions of infantry'. British armoured divisions would no longer fight with separate infantry and armoured brigades. This would encourage armour and infantry to 'support each other more readily' in combat and 'fight in a more balanced manner'. Matters were improved further by allowing soldiers to ride into battle on the backs of tanks, a procedure that had been rejected in training in the UK, as it was considered too dangerous.[118]

The tactical use of heavy bombers was also reconsidered. Following 'Goodwood', after-action reports had noted that if key areas around the Bourguébus Ridge and Cagny had been attacked one or two hours after the others, instead of at nearly the same time, 'enemy resistance would have been much less. The tactical development of the battle indicated the desirability of a bombing timetable which is progressive so that targets in depth are bombed just before the assault upon them.'[119] There would be two major bombing runs, therefore, in the 'Bluecoat' offensive.

Second Army was desperately trying to find a way to restore mobility to the battlefield and adapt the attritional approach characteristic of 'Colossal Cracks'. Nevertheless, when the battle started on 30 July, XXX Corps got off to an 'uneven' start. The 43rd Wessex Division made slow progress;[120] it had been just three days into a rest period after the 'gruelling ordeal on Hill 112 [during Operation 'Express'], and the return to action was unpopular'; the ground to be covered was also some of the densest bocage in Normandy (areas of small fields, generally between 20 and 100 yards across, surrounded by high-banked hedgerows). 'This was the *Suisse Normande*, the little Switzerland in Normandy, terrain where even depleted and surprised German defenders might sell ground dearly'.[121] The 50th Northumbrian Division made even less headway, while 7th Armoured Division, which entered the fray on 1 August, made 'only modest progress'.[122]

On 28 July, Montgomery, in language reminiscent of his instructions prior to D-Day, had issued orders to Dempsey urging him to accept heavy casualties if necessary in 'Bluecoat' and to 'step on the gas'. 'All caution' was to be 'thrown overboard, every risk to be taken, and all troops to be told to put everything into it'. Frustrated by the lack of progress of XXX Corps, Dempsey pressed Bucknall on 1 August, who, in turn told Major-General George Erskine, the commander of 7th Armoured Division, that he could lose 'every tank' he had, but that he had to take his objectives 'by midnight tonight'. Erskine failed. The next day, Dempsey informed Montgomery that he wanted Bucknall and Erskine sacked. Montgomery concurred and they were removed on 4 August. In the aftermath of the dismissals, a hundred other senior officers were also shipped out 'in an effort to pep things up in XXX Corps and 7th Armoured Division' – a truly remarkable cull.[123]

Something did, indeed, need to be done. Brigadier Gerald Verney, the commander of 6th Guards Tank Brigade (and a future commander of 7th Armoured Division), recalled later, that '1st and 5th RTR [of the division] were no longer having a go, the brigade commander (Hinde) was dead tired, and the infantry were crumbling under the pressure of heavy losses'. A 'combination of fatigue and grim operating conditions were clearly taking their toll on 7th Armoured'.[124] The censorship summaries show that the general recovery in morale in Second Army did not apply to all its formations equally. The summary for the first half of August acknowledged that there was 'some indication of weariness ... among troops who had been a long time in the line'.[125] The summary for the second half of the month was even more explicit in its characterisation of the problem. It stated that 'from letters written at the beginning of August it was apparent that individual and collective morale had been severely tried by the toughness and hardships of battle'. This was especially the case with 7th Armoured Division, whose 'letters dated between the 1 and 8 Aug 44 contained many indications that troops had been near exhaustion'.[126] The difficulties of maintaining high morale across the board under the strains of modern warfare were all too evident.

The indifferent performance of XXX Corps did not, however, fundamentally undermine Operation 'Bluecoat', for on the right-hand (western) side of the advance, VIII Corps made much better progress. At 0655hrs on the morning of 30 July, 15th Scottish Division, supported by the armour of 6th Guards Tank Brigade, with whom they had trained in Britain prior to coming to Normandy, advanced steadily towards its objectives. As the morning wore on, the infantry proved increasingly unable to keep up with the armour. The tanks of 4th Tank Coldstream Guards, on the left side of 15th Scottish Division's advance, decided to push on anyway towards the second of the objectives set for the day, 'leaving the infantry to follow up as quickly as possible'. By 1600hrs a similar dynamic had unfolded on the right-hand side of the advance. This left Verney and General MacMillan, the commander of 15th Scottish Division, 'with an awkward problem'. Although intimate co-operation between infantry and armour had been a clear lesson from Operation 'Goodwood', speed was essential in order to take advantage of the impact of the rolling barrage and the phased air support. Both men agreed that the armour should push forward without the infantry.[127] This decision was a gamble. Nevertheless, by 1530hrs, Hill 226 on the left had been occupied (the infantry following up thirty minutes later) and by 1900hrs Hill 309 on the right had been taken (the infantry completed its follow up by 0230hrs the next morning). The division's objectives for day one had been taken; an example, if one was needed, of the limitations of standardised tactical approaches and the requirement for commanders to use their own judgement in battle.[128]

It now fell to 11th Armoured Division to keep up the momentum. The division had made reasonable progress on 30 July but had got held up at the village of St Martin-des-Besaces. In the confusion of battle, a patrol of the 2nd Household Cavalry found a gap in the enemy's line, at the boundary between German Seventh Army in the British sector and Fifth Panzer Army in the American. The commander of the patrol, Lieutenant Derek ('Dickie') Powle, immediately informed 11th Armoured Division that they had penetrated several miles behind the German front, to a bridge over the River Souleuvre. This was 'not according to plan. Still notionally in a supporting role, VIII Corps should in theory have been seeking to advance on a south-easterly axis, not westward, away from XXX Corps.' But 'Pip' Roberts, the commander of 11th Armoured Division, had the 'imagination to recognise a unique opportunity and the initiative to exploit it'. Even before seeking O'Connor's approval, which arrived in due course anyway, Roberts had 'no hesitation' in changing the axis of his divisional advance. All available forces were rushed west and south to secure the bridge.[129]

By evening, as German reinforcements, comprising lead elements of 21st Panzer Division, appeared on the heights south of the bridge, the crossing was already secure. By the end of the following day, the whole of 11th Armoured Division was across the bridge and in position south of the river, holding the Bény-Bocage Ridge and the main road running in the direction of Vire. The speed and aggression of 11th Armoured Division's assault had created a genuine infiltration of the German line. Roberts wanted to push on and take Vire, but Montgomery controversially decided to shift army boundaries and leave the town to the Americans. On 2 August, the 11th Armoured Division pushed further forward to the Perrier Ridge. But by now, the fracture of the German front, along the boundary of the two German armies in Normandy, was beginning to provoke a full and fierce counter-attack.[130]

The VIII Corps salient, due to its rapid advance and the failure of XXX Corps in the east, was now dangerously exposed, especially on its left flank. The 15th Scottish Division faced ferocious and desperate counter-attacks by 326th Infantry Division and then 21st Panzer Division between Hills 226 and 309. Other reinforcements, in the form of 10th SS Panzer Division and then 9th SS Panzer Division, attacked 11th Armoured Division on the Perrier Ridge.[131] These arrivals, as well as that of the 102nd and 503rd Heavy Tank Battalions, brought the German forces in the area up to 58,913 men, 304 tanks and 185 artillery pieces. The enormous numerical advantage enjoyed by Second Army at the start of the operation had been well and truly whittled away; the British to German force ratios, not counting British casualties, were now 2:1 in manpower, 3.6:1 in tanks and 3:1 in artillery.[132]

Under increasing pressure, the British position began to resemble a series of defensive strongpoints rather than a continuous line; a desperate fight ensued. The infantry and armour of VIII Corps held on, inflicting grievous casualties on the attacking German formations. By 4 August, the counter-attack had petered out and the Germans began to fall back in a general retreat. Three days later, Second Army captured Vire and Mont Pinçon.[133] The 'dramatic and forceful' push of VIII Corps had not led to a complete breakout, such as that achieved by the Americans in the west, but it had compelled the Germans to draw troops away from the key Caen–Falaise sector. It had also prevented the Germans from massing a greater force for their effort to cut off the American breakout following 'Cobra', the Mortain counter-offensive. As the pressure from 'Bluecoat' had intensified, the Germans committed the best part of four *panzer* divisions, two Tiger tank battalions, a *Nebelwerfer* brigade and three batteries of 88mm guns to the sector. Second Army, at a crucial moment in the campaign, had adapted its tactics and welfare provisions and ensured a general, if uneven, improvement in morale and combat performance. By any standard, and especially in the context of the overall Anglo-American strategy in Normandy, the operation had been a success.[134]

Encirclement

With the success of 'Cobra' and 'Bluecoat', the German position in Normandy was ever closer to collapse. While US First Army absorbed the German counter-offensive at Mortain, US Third Army, which had broken out to the south into Brittany, hurried eastwards in an attempt to encircle the German forces remaining in Normandy. Second British Army was still to the west of Caen, while First Canadian Army, which had become operational on 23 July, was to the east of the city, facing the Germans in and around the Bourguébus Ridge. The job of closing what was becoming a massive encirclement fell to First Canadian Army, which was tasked with driving south from Caen towards Falaise and then east to the Seine in an attempt to seal off the German escape route.[135]

Command of the operation, codenamed 'Totalize', was delegated to Lieutenant-General Guy Simonds of II Canadian Corps. Simonds was determined, much like the commanders of 'Bluecoat', to ensure that the mistakes of 'Goodwood' were not repeated. Rather than allowing his armour and infantry to become separated, as had happened to VIII Corps on 18 July, this time he would ensure that all arms would fight together. The plan required the infantry of 51st Highland Division supported by 33rd Armoured Brigade, and 2nd Canadian Division supported by the 2nd Canadian Armoured Brigade, to break into the German line under the cover of darkness. They would advance in all-arms mobile columns down both sides of the Caen–Falaise road, bypassing enemy strongpoints (to be mopped up later by separate infantry battalions), thus seeking to maintain surprise and momentum. The attacking mobile columns were to advance at a pace of 200 yards every two minutes, behind a rolling barrage that was 4,050 yards wide and 6,000 yards deep. They would be pointed in the correct direction by light beams, radio beacons and tracer fired parallel to their advance.[136]

These were not the only adaptations to be employed in 'Totalize'. In order to ensure that Simonds' all-arms mobile columns worked effectively, and to prevent the infantry getting separated from its armour (as had happened at both 'Goodwood' and 'Bluecoat'), it was decided that the infantry needed a greater degree of protection when on the move. The solution came in the form of seventy-six new armoured personnel carriers or 'Kangaroos', modified Priest self-propelled guns reinforced by steel plate welded on at key places and with the gun-tubes removed. To deal with the expected depth of the German position, the innovation used in 'Bluecoat' would be broadly re-employed. Once the initial phase of the assault was completed, there would be a hiatus while another aerial bombardment would destroy the second line of German resistance. This would enable the forward troops to press on while their supporting guns moved forward to aid the next phase of the attack. Only then were the newly arrived 4th Canadian Armoured and 1st Polish Armoured Divisions to advance and break out into the German rear towards Falaise. In case further help was needed for exploitation, 3rd Canadian Division was in reserve (see Map 14.6).[137]

For the attack, Simonds assembled 85,000 troops, backed by 2,000 aircraft, 720 artillery pieces and upwards of 600 tanks. With the German forces in eastern Normandy 'denuded' of men and supplies, due to the evolving crisis in the west, initial opposition consisted of only 89th Infantry Division, a formation of 5,000 front-line troops of 'lower grade and questionable staying power' and the 12th SS Panzer Division, made up of 4,500 front-line troops. These formations were backed up by 120 artillery pieces, 54 *Nebelwerfers* and about 80 88mm guns. In all, the Germans had about 9,500 troops in the line (a British and Commonwealth advantage of 9:1), 74 tanks and tank destroyers (a British and Commonwealth advantage of 8:1) and 120 artillery pieces (a British and Commonwealth advantage of 6:1). First Canadian Army's superiority in terms of air support was overwhelming. 'There is no doubt' then that the Allies enjoyed 'considerable advantages in resources and capability' when the battle started on the night of 7/8 August; as the Canadian Official Historian put it, by this stage of the Normandy campaign, the German Army was stretched to 'breaking point and beyond'.[138]

The night-time advance proved extremely successful; for the cost of 380 casualties, 'Totalize' achieved a penetration of the German front 5 miles wide by 4 miles deep. With success potentially in their grasp, the attacking units were compelled to pause, however, as the second phase of bombing was not due until a little after midday, and, 'such a commitment could not readily be cancelled at such short

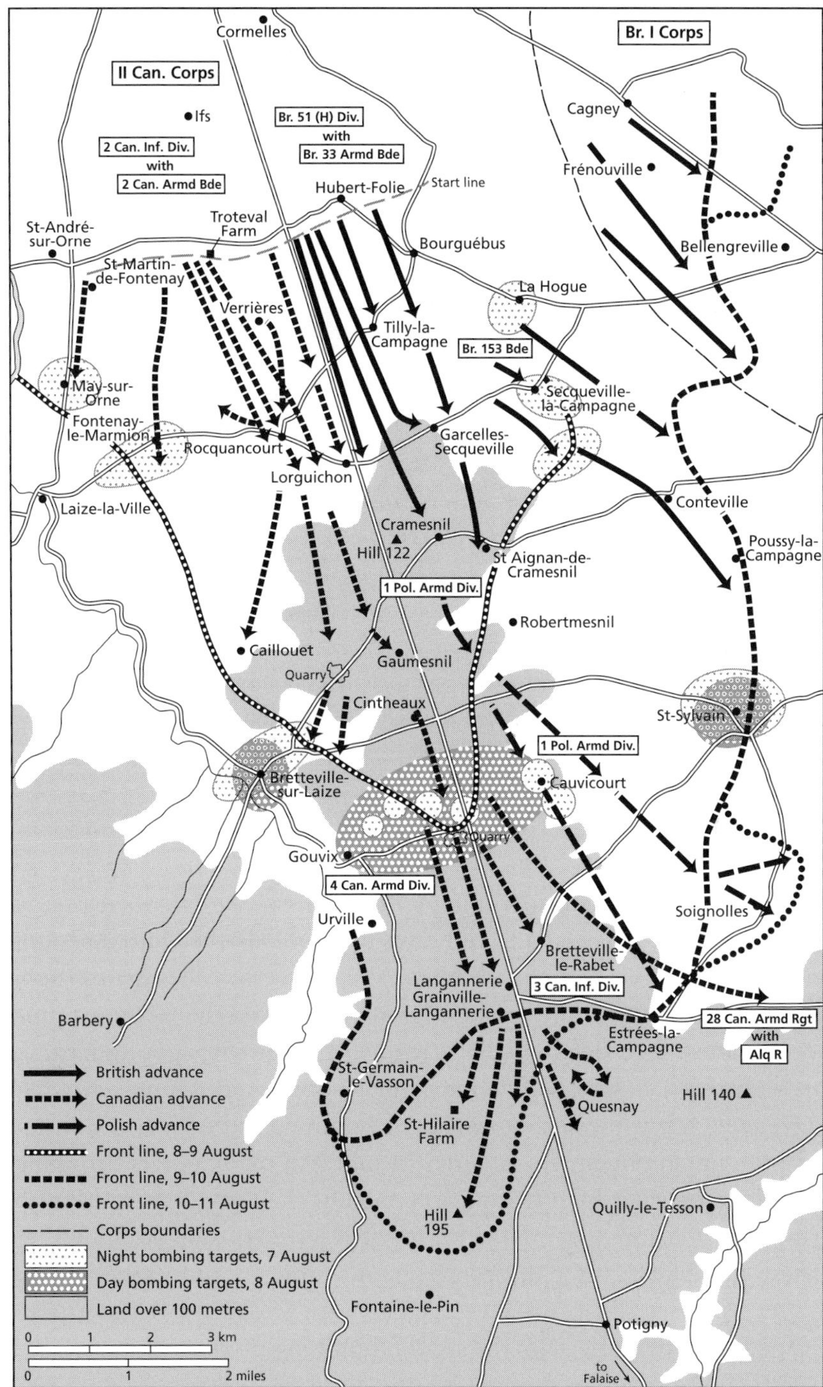

Map 14.6 Operation 'Totalize', 7–11 August 1944

e010858649

Illustration 14.2 Fires caused by the second phase of bombing for Operation 'Totalize', 8 August 1944. An error resulted in the bombers dropping munitions on their own troops, causing widespread confusion, sapping morale, and, thus, negatively affecting the advance on the road to Falaise when it resumed at 1355hrs.

notice'. This was a considerable pity, as the stoutly defended second line of resistance expected by Simonds did not exist; the initial assault had 'ruptured the German defences in the sector'. The pause now undid Simonds' carefully prepared plan; it allowed the Germans time to reorganise their defences, with 12th SS Panzer Division, in particular, launching a series of fierce if unco-ordinated counter-attacks. Moreover, when the second phase of bombing did arrive, it did not have the impact intended. An error resulted in the bombers dropping munitions on their own troops; 315 men of the Canadian and Polish armoured divisions assembling for phase II were killed or wounded.[139] 'These accidents caused widespread confusion ... and sapped troop morale.'[140] (See Illustration 14.2.) The 12th SS Panzer Division also escaped the worst effects of the second bombing by closing up with the British and Canadian forces. By the time the assault resumed at 1355hrs, the attack had lost momentum. By dusk the Poles had advanced only an extra 2.5 miles, while the Canadian 4th Armoured Division managed only a mile. That evening, Simonds tried to drive his forces on but with little success. By 10 August, the operation had 'effectively blown itself out'.[141]

The failure to break out at 'Totalize' meant that the plans of Montgomery and Bradley for a wide encirclement, trapping all German forces west of the River Seine, had to be abandoned for a smaller encirclement focusing specifically on Falaise.[142] With the Americans having made good progress, and now closing in from the south, and the Canadians, by this stage, only about 9 miles from the town, another battle was required. Patton fumed at the delay. He phoned Bradley on 13 August; 'shall we continue', he said mischievously, 'and drive the British into the sea for another Dunkirk'.[143] But Bradley, in a decision that subsequently provoked much controversy, halted Patton's forces at Argentan and waited for the Canadians to slam the door shut.[144] For the battle, codenamed 'Tractable', which was due to start the following day, Simonds again planned to use massed armour and carrier-borne infantry to break through the enemy gun screen. He positioned 4th Canadian Armoured Division on the left and 3rd Canadian Division supported by 2nd Canadian Armoured Brigade, on the right, 'only this time he chose for surprise purposes to cloak their movement with smoke rather than darkness'.[145] (See Map 14.7.)

The assault went in on 14 August. Again, it started well, but momentum was quickly lost. The Allied Air Forces once more dropped bombs on their own troops, this time causing a further 400 Canadian and Polish casualties. The River Laison, situated a little over 2 miles from the start line, proved to be a much more problematic anti-tank obstacle than planners had anticipated. First Canadian Army had clearly not been blessed with a great deal of luck; nevertheless, 'the uncomfortable fact' remains, the Canadians with four brigades of infantry and roughly 300 tanks, supported by 'massive' artillery and air resources failed to overcome two reinforced infantry regiments, 'many of whose men had not been under fire before', and some 41 tanks.[146]

Something appeared to be wrong with First Canadian Army. Montgomery, frustrated by the slow progress, 'asked the Americans', on 17 August, to step in. If they could 'lunge' 8 miles north-east from Argentan and sever the two roads remaining to the Germans, their escape could still be prevented. However, on 15 August, Bradley had dispatched 'more than half' of his combat power around Argentan, two

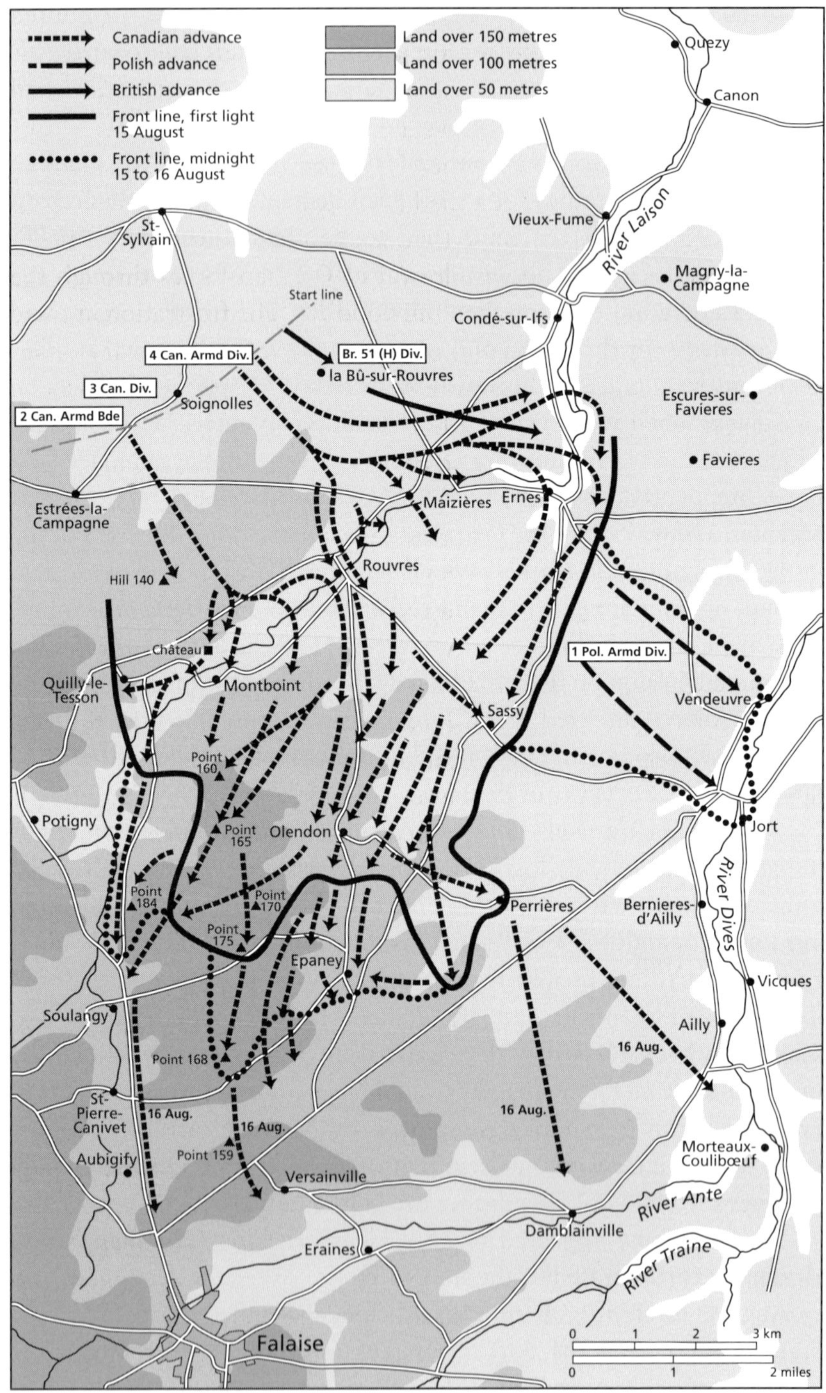

Map 14.7 Operation 'Tractable', 14–16 August 1944

divisions and fifteen artillery battalions, 65 miles to the east. 'Due to the delay in closing the gap between Argentan and Falaise', he had reasoned 'that many of the German divisions which were in the pocket' had already 'escaped'. Bradley's move both failed to trap the Germans further east and meant that there were insufficient forces around Argentan when Montgomery called for American support to make up for the lack of progress on the First Canadian Army Front.[147]

By 18 August, the withdrawal of German forces through the famous Falaise Gap had 'reached full flood'.[148] The frustration in some quarters was palpable. Estimates of the number escaping the trap 'ranged from thirty thousand to more than a hundred thousand'. In due course, it would become evident that 'those who got away included four of five corps commanders, twelve of fifteen division commanders, and many capable staff officers'.[149] The Germans ultimately managed to extricate around one-third of their forces, and, according to the Operational Research Section of 21st Army Group, about two-thirds of their transport, before the gap was finally closed on 21 August. On the same day, Simonds, who was greatly displeased with the performance of his armoured forces, relieved the commander of 4th Canadian Armoured Division.[150] Churchill was clearly disappointed by the outcome as well; on 23 August, he cabled Montgomery: 'I had, of course, rather hoped we should be in the region of hundreds of thousands [of prisoners] rather than tens of thousands.'[151] The Allied victory, 'though extraordinary, was incomplete'.[152]

The Trap

There were 'several factors' that prevented the total annihilation of the German Army in Normandy in August 1944. Among these, according to one prominent historian, were 'miscalculation, confusion … dull generalship … [and] a German reluctance to be annihilated'.[153] Others have argued that there wasn't a 'great tactical misjudgement' at Falaise.[154] It is clear, for instance, that Montgomery did everything in his power to drive 21st Army Group towards closing the gap and that Bradley's controversial halt order on 14 August was issued on the understanding that the Canadians were coming. His subsequent decision to send much of Patton's forces further east was made in light of the continued and apparently inexplicable inability of the Canadians to push south.[155]

If the failure to completely trap the German Army in Normandy was not the consequence of a command 'error', it follows that other factors must have been at play. For example, there is little doubt that 21st Army Group's continued commitment to the 'Colossal Cracks' approach did not facilitate the aggressive operations envisaged by senior officers. Simonds, who was widely recognised as an extremely able, creative and forceful commander, firmly bought into the 'Colossal Cracks' approach and although the plans for 'Totalize' and 'Tractable' were innovative, he maintained 'highly centralised' command and control arrangements throughout. As Doug Delaney has argued, Simonds tended to develop a plan on his own and then present it to his subordinates as a *fait accompli*. This did not 'foster a command climate that encouraged initiative'. 'Totalize' and 'Tractable' also highlighted weaknesses among Simonds' divisional and brigade commanders, too many of whom 'lacked tactical sense and what Simonds called the "determination and drive to get things done"'.[156]

As serious as these deficiencies were, the evidence suggests that Canadian performance in August 1944 was hindered by much more than issues related to command and control and 'tactical sense'; it was severely handicapped by the last serious drop in morale to affect the British and Commonwealth Armies in the Second World War. Figure 14.1 shows that by August 1944, morale among Canadian troops in Normandy was at a low level compared to the highs of June. Whereas in the first half of June, 50 per cent of letters mentioning morale were 'keen for action', by the first half of August it was down to 13 per cent.[157] The Canadian censorship summaries, probably the least critical of troops of all the Commonwealth forces censorship summaries during the war, described morale as 'very good' by the first half of August; morale had typically been described as 'excellent' or 'very high' in the preceding summaries. The report covering the period of 'Totalize' noted that there were 'signs of weariness and nerves' in 'a few units of 2 Cdn Div'. One man from the Royal Regiment of Canada wrote, 'there's not much to tell in this letter apart from the battlefield blues. Things are still quite hot for us over here and we are all pretty tired and worn to a nervous stage. I'm speaking of the majority of the new boys and myself.' A lieutenant in 6th Canadian Field Regiment, RCA, wrote:

> After two weeks of this sort of dangerous life one's nerves have begun to roughen ... I have all I can manage at present to keep the men in a satisfied condition ... the stickiest job is that of manning OP's [Observation Posts] ... I go up myself very often to allay their fears and stay with them.[158]

The sickness rates in First Canadian Army reinforce this picture (see Figure 14.3). Whereas the rate for Canadian troops for the week ending 29 July had been 2.9 per thousand, by the week ending 12 August ('Totalize') it had risen to 20.5 per thousand. By the week ending 19 August ('Tractable') it had risen again to a staggering 29.0 per thousand, a tenfold increase in less than a month. The rate dropped somewhat during the closure of the Falaise Gap to 17.3 per thousand.[159] The picture for 51st Highland Division and 1st Polish Armoured Division, under the command of First Canadian Army, was little different. Sickness rates in 51st Highland Division were, depending on the source used, somewhere between 16 and 19 per thousand for 'Totalize'.[160] The figures for 1st Polish Division were, at best estimate, 14 per thousand in 'Totalize', 18 per thousand in 'Tractable' and 17 per thousand during the closing of the Falaise Gap.[161] Although the censorship summaries did point to a rise in sickness due to 'stomach trouble', 'diarrhoea' and 'dysentery' caused by a 'plague of mosquitoes and other bugs',[162] it is apparent that something serious, along the lines of what happened to Second Army at 'Goodwood', was affecting morale.[163]

With regards to 3rd Canadian Division, which fought at 'Tractable', it is evident that a problem was developing from the middle of July. By then, after a 'period of seven weeks continuous over the top type of warfare' during which the division had been involved in 'every type of fighting and had been used to clear up some very tough positions', the officers and men were beginning to show signs of strain.[164] So concerned was the Assistant Director of Medical Services (ADMS) of the division, Colonel M. C. Watson, that he wrote to the General Officer Commanding (GOC) on 26 July claiming that 'the forward troops are suffering from lack of physical rest to an extent which is greatly impairing their efficiency as fighting soldiers. A number of Officers in key positions are physically and mentally tired to a degree that may result in a sudden complete breakdown under further stress.' 'In my opinion', he continued, 'the fighting elements of the Division are now capable of fighting at about 40% of the efficiency of which they were capable at the end of the first week after the original assault ... It is my opinion that certain units may crack completely under a forced operation.' Watson promised that the contents of the letter were for the GOC and the Deputy Director Medical Services (DDMS) of II Canadian Corps only. As a result of his efforts, the division was granted rest between 1 and 8 August,[165] but it is evident that this was not enough to alleviate the problems in the division; 3rd Canadian Division suffered a sickness rate of no less than 21.6 per thousand for the week ending 18 August, the period covering Operation 'Tractable'.[166]

The War Diary for 1 Canadian Exhaustion Unit for August 1944 noted similar problems in other units. There had been a 'peak' in admissions 'following the first engagement of 4 Cdn Armd Div and of the Polish Div and following the accidental bombing of our lines by Fortresses' during Operation 'Totalize'. Another 'peak', 'a very abrupt rise' during Operation 'Tractable', came 'following accidental bombing by Lancasters, in which the story we got was a mild degree of generalized panic among the units affected'. A large number of these individuals, according to the report, were recent reinforcements 'who were firmly convinced by this episode that they "couldn't take it"'. Overall, the report pointed out that there were many cases who were:

> good prospects and did well while their morale was high but who now feel that they have had enough and have no adequate motive to cause them to carry on under adverse circumstances or to exercise the necessary self-control ... We have been struck ... by the uniform pattern of inadequacy and low battle tolerance of the patients admitted of whom a large number were very recent reinforcements with short periods of service. Among these were some who had been transferred from other arms of service to Infantry just prior to arrival in France.[167]

These problems were not lost on Simonds. In the period after the hard fighting following 'Goodwood'/'Atlantic', he had tried to address the 'excuses' that were being made by some units to explain inadequate performance. He stressed the need for 'determined, courageous and skilled leadership'; a deficit in these attributes, in his view, was largely to blame for the failures south-east of Caen. He was no less forgiving of the armour after 'Totalize'. He believed that the tanks of his two armoured divisions 'had been too timid in pressing the attack ... "He quoted the heavy infantry casualties of the past month compared to armour. He demanded much greater initiative from arm[oure]d reg-[imen]ts – drive on – get amongst the enemy etc. Forget about harbouring at night – keep driving on".'[168]

A drop in morale had clearly, and seriously, impeded the performance of First Canadian Army on the drive towards Falaise. It was hardly the men's fault. The 3rd Canadian Division spent twenty-one days in 'intense combat' between June and August 1944, a figure only matched by the equally exhausted 3rd Division. The 2nd Canadian Division had only been in combat for three weeks by the launch of 'Totalize', but in that time it had suffered around 2,000 casualties. Most of these, as was typically the case in Normandy, were in the rifle companies of its nine infantry battalions. On 7 August, the division was still more than 1,000 men under-strength. It must also be noted that 4th Canadian Armoured Division and 1st Polish Armoured Division were facing combat for the first time. In the case of 4th Canadian Armoured Division, it also had to contend with a serious lack of training. In the run-up to Normandy, it 'had to content itself' with limited infantry/tank training in early April, some assault boat training in the middle of the month, and live-fire training for the infantry battalions in mid-May. The division never had a full-scale exercise, and this 'mattered later on'.[169]

The consequences of these travails were significant; those Germans that escaped through the Falaise Gap would be used as a cadre around which to rebuild the *Wehrmacht* in North-West Europe. In terms of reputations, the Americans once again took the plaudits, the rapid advance of Patton's Third Army contrasted noticeably with the slow progress of the Anglo-Canadians. An opportunity for the British and Commonwealth Armies to be centre stage in the final act in Normandy had clearly been missed.

Nevertheless, it must be recognised that the Germans paid a heavy price as they fought to prevent the complete encirclement and utter destruction of their armies around Falaise. The favourable force-to-force ratios enjoyed by First Canadian Army were proof, if proof was needed, that 'Colossal Cracks' was slowly but surely wearing the *Wehrmacht* down. In the final days of the collapse, some 10,000 were killed and 50,000 captured by the Allied Armies. Montgomery described the carnage as 'almost unbelievable', while Eisenhower said that the scene 'could be described only by Dante'. Pilots flying over Falaise recalled that the powerful stench of burning vehicles, unburied bodies and thousands of dead horses and cattle reached hundreds of feet into the air.[170]

Within a few days of the closing of the Falaise Gap, Paris was liberated by French and American troops. By any standard, a great victory had been achieved. In total, the Germans lost something like 300,000 troops in the campaign in Normandy.[171] Eisenhower reckoned that in addition to this, 1,300 tanks, 20,000 vehicles, 500 assault guns, and 1,500 field guns and heavier artillery pieces had been captured or destroyed.[172] The price had been dear. The two weeks of fighting from the beginning of 'Totalize' to the eventual sealing off of the German escape route from Normandy had cost the Canadians 5,679 casualties.[173] By the end of August, Allied casualties in North-West Europe amounted in total to 206,703, of which the Americans had suffered 124,394, the British 63,865 and the Canadians 18,444.[174] The struggle had been as intense as anything experienced in the First World War. The Battle of Normandy cost the Allies 2,354 casualties a day; the 105 days of the Third Battle of Ypres (Passchendaele), by comparison, had cost British and Canadian forces 244,000 casualties, or 2,121 a day.[175] With Russian armies closing in on Germany from the east and with the German armies in the west retreating in disarray over the Seine, the question was no longer whether the Allies would win in North-West Europe, but how quickly they would win and who would be the main beneficiary of that success.

15 THE VICTORY CAMPAIGNS

The destruction of the German armies in Normandy presented an opportunity to swiftly conclude the campaign in North-West Europe. The censors commented that it was 'the general opinion that the war in EUROPE would end in a matter of weeks'.[1] The feeling at Supreme Headquarters Allied Expeditionary Force (SHAEF) was certainly that 'the August battles' had 'brought the end of the war … in sight, almost within reach'.[2] Montgomery shared the sense of expectation;[3] on 26 August, he issued instructions that 'speed of action and movement' were 'now vital … Every officer and man must understand that by stupendous effort now we shall … hasten the end of the war.'[4] So great was the opportunity, according to Harry Crerar, the commander of First Canadian Army, that 'any tendency to be slow or "sticky"' had to be 'quickly and positively eliminated'.[5]

Montgomery ordered XXX Corps and XII Corps of Second Army[6] to drive flat out to force a crossing of the River Seine, the first major obstacle on the route north and east towards Germany. First Canadian Army was instructed to free up the ports along the north-west coast of France, to facilitate the logistical support of the advance.[7] Morale in British units was 'excellent'; as measured by sickness rates, it was the best it had ever been. By the week ending 9 September, the sickness and battle exhaustion rate in Second Army was as low as 3.0 per thousand (see Figure 14.3). The general confidence was aptly expressed by a man in 3rd Monmouthshire Regiment, 11th Armoured Division, who wrote 'we have got him on the run and now is the time to give him the same medicine as he has been giving to other people'.[8]

In addition to the obvious effects of a series of hard-won victories, morale was also bolstered by the announcement of the plan for demobilisation at the end of the war, and a special bonus for extended war service that was considered 'fair' and 'substantial' and 'a recognition of the worth of the Army'.[9]

Canadian morale had bounced back considerably since the lows of 'Tractable' and Falaise. Whereas the sickness rate had been 17.3 per thousand during the week ending 26 August, by the week ending 2 September it had dropped to 9.1 per thousand and would drop again to 6.7 per thousand the following week (see Figure 14.3).[10] The Canadian censors noted the improvement in health; 'as against 523 references to good health in the previous report, there were 1,713 references in the period covered by this report [1 to 15 September 1944]'.[11]

Much as was the case for British troops, an announcement from Ottawa regarding a gratuity to be paid to Canadian service personnel on demobilisation played a significant role in enthusing the troops. The gratuity, according to the censors, was 'enthusiastically' and 'widely' approved. 'Writers are already calculating the sums they will receive at the conclusion of hostilities.' A corporal in 30th Field Company, the Royal Canadian Engineers wrote:

> The Government is paying each soldier on his return 15 dollars a month for every month he's been overseas, and seven dollars for each six months service. Well, Betty, that would give me 1000 dollars when I get home, and on top of that we get 100 dollars for clothes. So we are going to be well looked after.[12]

A lance bombardier in 6th Canadian LAA Regiment, remarked

> This gratuity and rehabilitation scheme that the Government has passed on seems like the real McCoy to me . . . naturally I'm delighted at the prospect of such a wonderful start when I get back with you all again . . . you can see that we are going to derive some benefit from these three years of doing and dying.[13]

The realisation that the Canadian state would reward citizen soldiers for their sacrifices during the war no doubt played a key role in returning a definite bounce to First Canadian Army. The heady excitement of the dynamic drive into the north of France was important too. The 'entire' Canadian mail, according to the censors:

> was permeated with elation created by the rapid advance of the Canadian Army, and the capture of Dieppe raised morale to the highest possible pitch. The troops felt that they had avenged their comrades who fell there in 1942. Both front and rear troops displayed the same splendid spirit, and men in hospital were eager to return to their units. Weariness due to prolonged, continuous pursuit was discounted in the general desire to bring the enemy to battle. The Canadian Army, in brief, know itself to be a 'victorious army'.[14]

The 'extraordinarily cordial welcome received from the population of the liberated towns of France and Belgium brought home to troops that they were indeed an army of liberation'. This 'conviction', according to the censors, 'strengthened their determination to bring the war to the speediest possible conclusion'.[15] A trooper in a Canadian Armoured Regiment wrote, 'I never seen [*sic*] people so happy in all my life as some of these French people, it made me feel happy to be fighting when I saw those people, boy are they ever happy to be free.'[16] A private in 2nd Canadian Infantry Division recounted, 'I found tears in my eyes after passing through one town. It doesn't seem possible that people could be so overjoyed. Those are the things that make you realize that our efforts and inconveniences have been necessary for civilization which we are a part of'.[17]

By 28 August, XXX Corps, on the right-hand side of Second Army's advance, had two Forty bridges in operation across the Seine. That night, tanks of 11th Armoured Division began pouring across the river. The next day, XII Corps, on the left, followed suit, with 4th Armoured Brigade and 53rd Welsh Division in the vanguard.[18] Within three days, 11th Armoured Division had crossed the Somme at Amiens, capturing 3,000 prisoners; General Hans Eberbach, former commander of the Fifth Panzer Army and now commander of Seventh Army, was captured in his pyjamas.[19] By 3 September, Brussels had been liberated. In twelve breathless days, Montgomery's armoured regiments had travelled over 300 miles, an average of 26 miles each day (see Map 15.1). By contrast, in 1940, the German *panzers* had managed an average of 21 miles per day in their race from the River Meuse to the Channel coast.[20] As a man in the Lake Superior Rifles, 4th Canadian Armoured Division, put it, 'it's 1940 in reverse only with interest, he asked for it, by gad he got it, not defeat but disaster and annihilation'.[21]

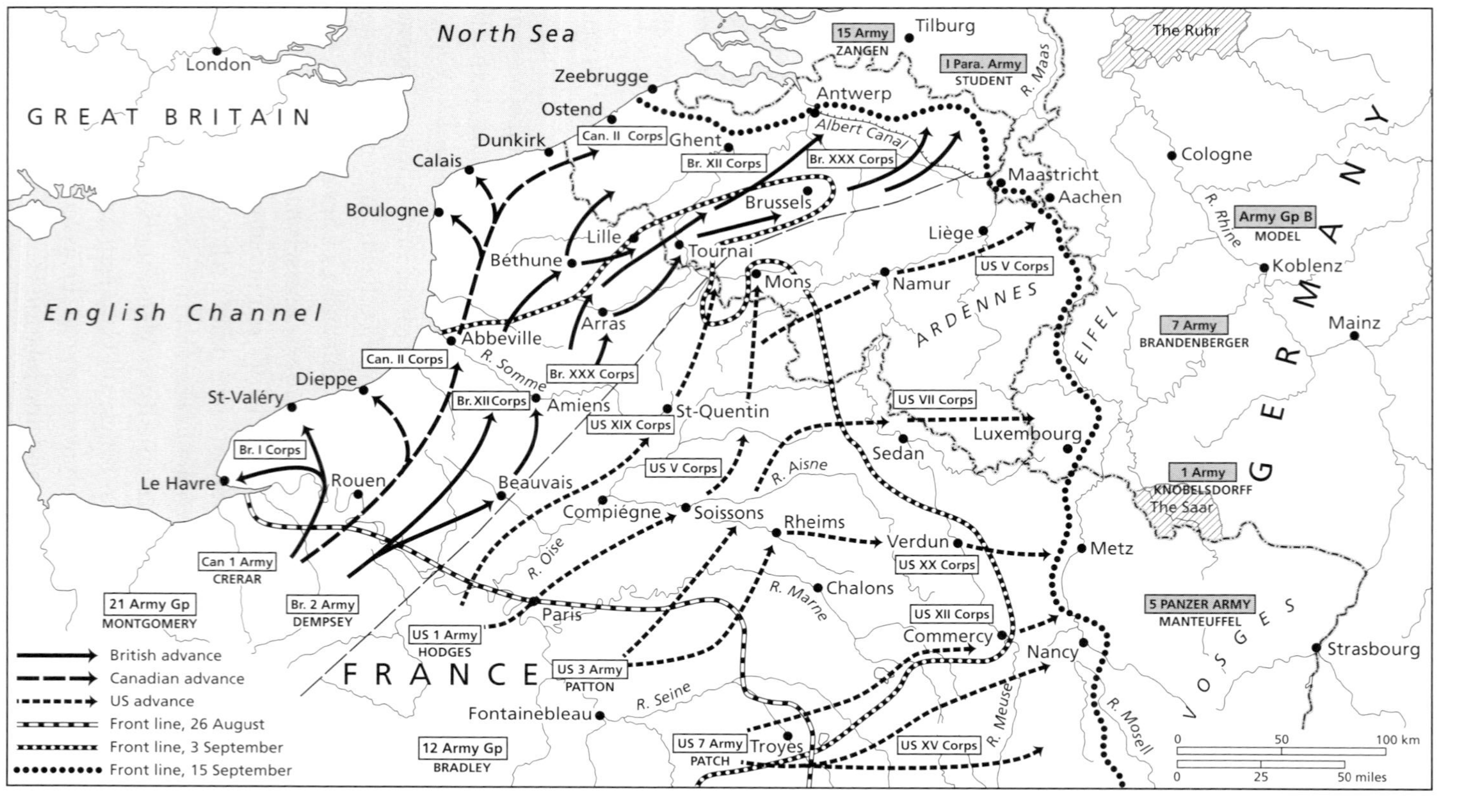

Map 15.1 The Allied advance, 26 August–15 September 1944

Operation 'Market Garden'

A by-product of this rapid and exhilarating advance was that 21st Army Group, and Second Army in particular, began increasingly to operate at the end of an extended logistics chain, still dependent as they were on supplies landed in Normandy, about 300 miles away. Antwerp, Europe's largest port, fell on 3 September, but the Germans held on determinedly to the north shore of the Scheldt estuary, making the port unusable.[22] Le Havre, the second biggest port in France, fell on 12 September. But, due to damage and sabotage, it too remained unusable for the best part of a month. The port of Boulogne fell only on 22 September and Calais was taken at the end of the month.[23]

With insufficient port capacity secured, the Allied High Command had to reconsider its plans for the defeat of Germany. Eisenhower had intended to destroy the *Wehrmacht* with twin thrusts towards the two key industrial zones in western Germany, the Ruhr and the Saar. This was the so-called 'broad front' strategy. He decided now to temporarily alter his preferred approach. The Canadian capture of Dieppe on 1 September had made it possible to land sufficient supplies to launch one major assault towards the heart of the Reich. This was also Montgomery's preferred approach (the so-called 'narrow front' strategy). Montgomery, who relinquished overall command of Allied ground forces to Eisenhower on 1 September, claimed that Allied forces could be in Berlin in three weeks. He believed that there was every chance, with Romania and Finland having dropped out of the war and with the German Army on the ropes, that one big push could bring about the collapse of Germany.[24]

As was his custom, Montgomery advocated hard for the British to lead the thrust into the heart of Germany; his determination and confidence seemed reasonable given the information available. With XXX and XII Corps taking thousands of prisoners each day, it looked like the *Wehrmacht* was in an 'identical' state to the German Army in 'August and September 1918'.[25] Over a four-week period following the closure of the Falaise Gap, British elements of 21st Army Group had suffered only 0.05 casualties for every German prisoner captured (see Figure 14.4).[26] I Corps, for example, took Le Havre at the cost of only 388 casualties. Over 11,000 prisoners were taken.[27] With the right amount of pressure applied and with the outcome of the war no longer in doubt, there appeared to be every chance that German soldiers would throw in the towel and capitulate en masse.

The *Wehrmacht* was, by any standard, on the ropes. On 5 September, of the fifty-eight infantry divisions available to the German Army Command in the West (OB West), only thirteen were considered 'completely fit for offensive operations'; another nine were 'reorganising', twelve were 'partially fit', and fourteen were 'totally unfit'. Of eleven *panzer* divisions, only three were 'completely up to scratch' while seven were 'completely unfit'. All in all, Field-Marshal Model, who commanded OB West from 16 August to 4 September, estimated that his divisions, which held a 400-mile front, had a fighting value of no more than twenty-five divisions; and even on paper these divisions were only half the strength of their Anglo-American equivalents.[28]

By comparison, the Allies had forty-eight largely up-to-strength divisions available for battle (thirty-one American, fifteen Anglo-Canadian, one French and one Polish) plus First Allied Airborne Army (the strategic reserve), which comprised five airborne divisions (three American and two British), an air transportable division (52nd Lowland Division) and the Polish Independent Parachute Brigade.[29] The discrepancies in terms of materiel were even more pronounced. On 15 September, OB West could muster only 271 serviceable tanks, with another 73 in repair and 321 in shipment (665 in all). The Allies had 5,961 medium and 1,690 light tanks (an advantage of 9:1 counting only medium tanks or 11.5:1 if all Allied tanks were included). The Allies had almost 14,000 planes; the *Luftwaffe Kommando West* was able to deploy only 573 serviceable aircraft (a ratio of 24:1).[30]

Conditions appeared excellent for a final and decisive offensive in the west. On 10 September, Eisenhower decided to back Montgomery's proposal for the defeat of Germany, signing off 'Market Garden'. This operation required XXX Corps (Guards Armoured Division and 43rd Wessex Division), of Second Army, to punch a hole in what remained of the German line and advance 64 miles towards the bridge over the Lower Rhine at Arnhem, in the eastern Netherlands. On capturing a bridgehead over the river, Montgomery hoped to push on with great speed and aggression and threaten the Ruhr or advance towards Berlin (and hopefully finish the war). It was a highly ambitious plan, as the newly appointed Field-Marshal himself recognised, one that called for risk taking and dynamic leadership.[31] XXX

Corps was to be supported by Lieutenant-General Frederick 'Boy' Browning's First British Airborne Corps, of First Allied Airborne Army, which was stationed in the UK.[32] These forces, in what was to be the largest airborne operation ever mounted, were to take a series of bridges along XXX Corps' axis of advance (see Map 15.2). The US 101st Airborne would take the area around Eindhoven; US 82nd Airborne would take the bridge over the Maas at Grave, a bridge over the Maas-Waal canal and the big bridge over the Waal at Nijmegen; and 1st Airborne, supported later by the 1st Independent Polish Parachute Brigade, would take and hold the bridge over the Lower Rhine at Arnhem. As XXX Corps moved northwards along the direction of the airborne 'carpet', VIII Corps to the east and XII Corps to the west 'were to widen the axis of advance' and protect the flanks of the narrow and extended XXX Corps thrust.[33]

When the operation commenced on 17 September, the anticipated capitulation of the German forces in the path of 'Market Garden' did not, however, materialise. When the first airborne troops were dropped, they found the German formations in their way more than willing to fight. The troops of II SS Panzer Corps, made up of 9th and 10th SS Panzer Divisions, refitting near Arnhem after their battering in Normandy, proved particularly problematic.[34] Montgomery wrote later, 'we knew it [II SS Panzer Corps] was there. But we were wrong in supposing that it could not fight effectively'.[35] The 21st Army Group intelligence summary for 12 September had noted that having been caught up in the 'great retreat', it was considered that there 'cannot be much left of them'.[36] They were wrong.

As a result, 1st Airborne Division became trapped behind enemy lines, with a small detachment of just over 700 men holding the bridge over the Lower Rhine and the rest clinging to a bridgehead on the north bank, around Oosterbeek; there they waited desperately for XXX Corps and the Poles to relieve them.[37] The dynamic offensive operation envisaged by Montgomery became a fraught defensive battle, as all the weaknesses of Second Army once more played out on the battlefield. Instead of participating in a great offensive to end the war, 1st Airborne Division found itself fighting for its very survival.

In hindsight, it is evident that the plan for 'Market Garden' was built on wishful thinking, especially with regards to the extent of German resistance to be expected. In the Canadian sector, in late August and early September (the four weeks after the closing of

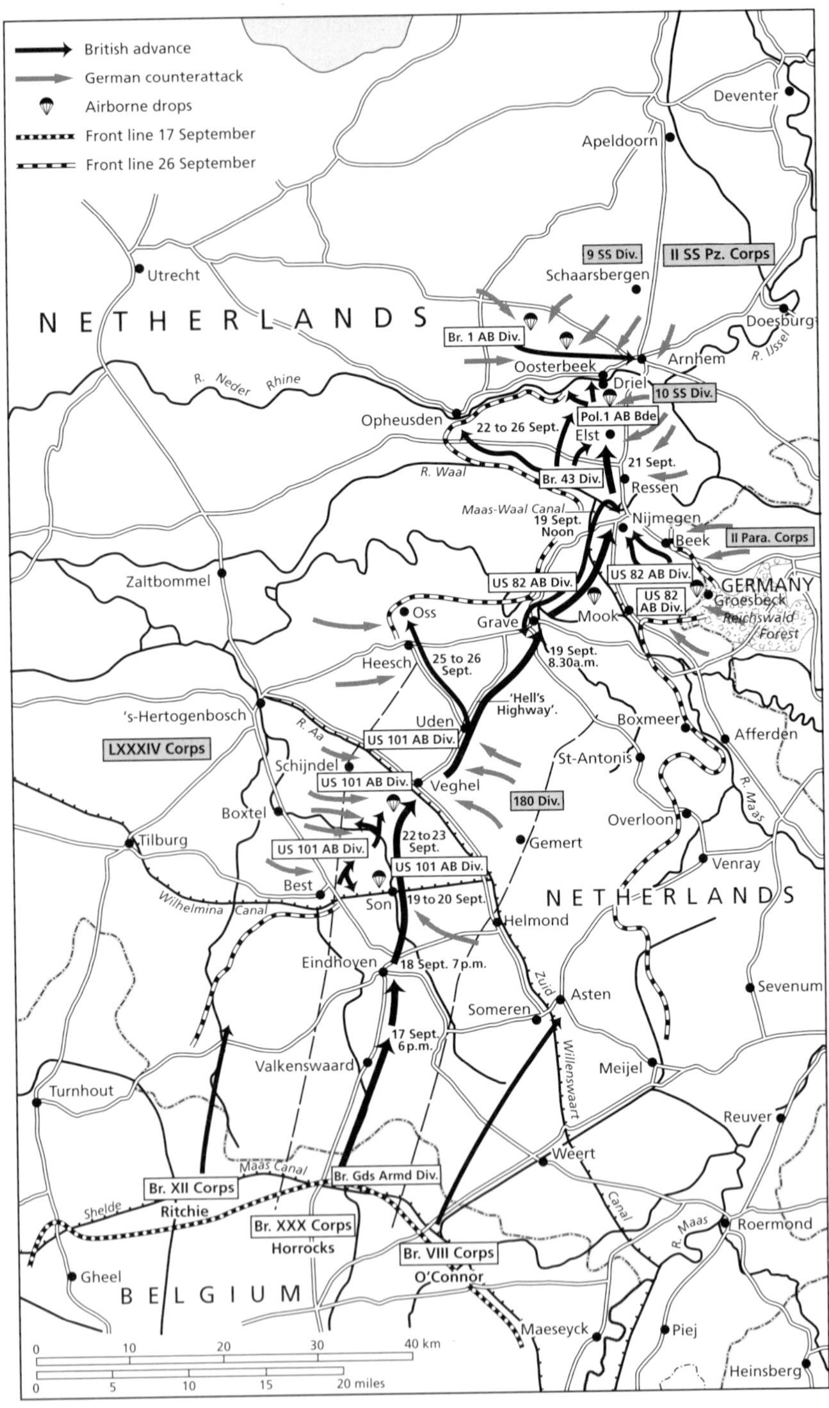

Map 15.2 Operation 'Market Garden', 17–26 September 1944

the Falaise Gap), the Canadians suffered 0.6 casualties for every German captured, twelve times the British rate.[38] In some places, a deadly cocktail of propaganda and coercion was holding the *Wehrmacht* together.[39] It was apparent 'that organized terror from above' was keeping many German soldiers 'in the line'.[40] A rifleman in 3rd Canadian Division wrote, 'we were coming up the road with about 200 [POWs] and we ran into a machine gun nest. Get this, Jerry machine gunned his own men because they surrendered. He killed a few in front of me. They were scared to death.'[41] To make matters worse, most German POWs expected 'bad treatment on capture', especially from Canadian and Polish troops.[42] A Craftsman in 2nd Canadian Division wrote in September 1944 that:

> I saw some German prisoners about a week ago and their main question was whether we were Canadians or Poles . . . of course they were more than surprised when they discovered that we were Canadians, and that a Canadian Doctor was attending to their wounds and fixing them up instead of having them shot.[43]

The censors concluded that 'enemy troops would surrender more readily, were it not for fear of their officers and for their belief that Canadian troops would shoot prisoners'.[44]

By the week ending 23 September, the period covering 'Market Garden', Second Army was suffering 0.7 casualties for every German prisoner captured, a figure much closer to what the Canadians had been experiencing, and fourteen times the average rate suffered during the preceding four weeks.[45] The ferocity of German resistance, which was driven also by the fact that the *Wehrmacht* was now fighting on the border of the *Reich*,[46] meant that US 82nd Airborne Division failed initially to capture one of its key objectives, the big road bridge over the Waal at Nijmegen. This delay held up Guards Armoured Division, the spearhead of XXX Corps' advance, when it arrived at Nijmegen on 19 September. It took until 1900hrs the following evening before troops could be pushed across the river, by which time it was deemed too late to drive on to Arnhem, a decision considered controversial then and ever since.[47]

Meanwhile, at Arnhem, bad weather had delayed the arrival of the Poles south of the Lower Rhine (until 20 September). General Stanislaw Sosabowski, the commander of the Polish Parachute Brigade, had intended to use a ferry at Driel to transfer troops and supplies to the 1st Airborne as they held on desperately at Oosterbeek. But the ferry had been destroyed; as a result, the Poles proved of little help to the surviving paratroopers north of the Rhine. The next day, 1st Airborne Division lost its hold on the bridge at Arnhem and hope of success began to diminish. In the days that followed, XXX Corps, now with 43rd Wessex Division in the lead, proved unable to advance the 10 miles to Arnhem. The fate of 1st Airborne was sealed and on 25 September it was ordered to withdraw back to friendly lines. 'Market Garden' had failed. The airborne landings cost 11,850 British, American and Polish casualties, of which 1st Airborne Division alone suffered 1,130 dead and 6,500 POWs (about 2,000 of whom were wounded). XXX Corps, in its advance along the corridor, lost 1,480 men and 70 tanks. The Germans, by comparison, lost between 6,000 and 8,000 men.[48]

It is not surprising, given the extent of the casualties and the nature of the setback, that 'Market Garden' has had its fair share of critics.[49] John Buckley, for example, has argued that the operation was 'poorly conceived, ill considered and deeply flawed', a plan 'which stood little chance of success before it had even begun'.[50] Without doubt, there were many operational and tactical shortcomings to the plan.[51] The dropping of 1st Airborne Division 8 miles from Arnhem severely hindered efforts to capture and consolidate a hold on the bridge. The decision to launch the 20,000 vehicles of XXX Corps along a very narrow axis of advance, what the Americans called 'Hell's Highway', was also questionable, especially given Second Army's recurrent inability to avoid costly 'traffic jams'. The distance was arguably too great; a single line of advance over water obstacles and through urban areas required the opposition to largely dissolve in order to succeed. Most importantly of all, the plan asked Second Army to fight in a manner to which, even at this late stage of the war, it was not suited; namely, to fight a fluid 'brawl' without the support of massed artillery.[52] The 21st Army Group, just as during D-Day, 'Perch', 'Goodwood', 'Totalize' and 'Tractable', proved mostly incapable of dynamic mobile operations.

Montgomery, nevertheless, remained an 'unrepentant advocate' of 'Market Garden'.[53] He had pushed hard for the operation believing that it would have considerable benefits for himself personally, but also more importantly for geo-strategic reasons. A successful advance by Second Army would have forced Eisenhower to support his strategy for victory in North-West Europe, a narrow thrust into the heart of Germany. 'A crossing at Arnhem' would also have led 'the advance away from the American sector, leaving First US Army to mop up the Ruhr', while Second Army could 'drive on deep into Germany'.[54] A quick end to the war thanks to the efforts of the British and Commonwealth Armies would have had important implications for Britain's standing and reputation in the post-war world.[55]

The operation at Arnhem, it can certainly be argued, was a risk worth taking from a British perspective, even if it did lead to a setback for the greater Allied cause. The theatre-wide force-to-force ratios were massively in favour of the attackers – although the plan of advancing down one easily defensible road certainly undermined this advantage.[56] Eisenhower, thus, must also shoulder a significant amount of blame for supporting a risky operation that, from a broader Allied perspective, slowed down and hindered efforts to open up the Channel ports and provide the logistic base necessary to advance into Germany on a broader front. To win big, Montgomery had been willing to bet big; with his gamble having failed, the British and Commonwealth forces in North-West Europe were about to become increasingly irrelevant as socio-political, demographic and military weaknesses limited the extent of their contribution to final victory.[57]

Operation 'Olive'

This pattern of events was to play out broadly in other theatres too as the relevance of the Imperial war effort gradually, but inexorably, decreased in comparison to that of the Americans. Churchill seethed at the reduction in British influence.[58] The opportunity to capitalise on victories in Italy, including Operation 'Diadem' and the fall of Rome, had been missed, in his view, due to the growing US dominance over strategy. In particular, he was furious that with the German Army on the run in the Mediterranean, the Americans had insisted that seven divisions be removed from the campaign to take part in Operation 'Dragoon', the Allied invasion of the South of France.[59] In July, in a fit of anger, he drafted a note to be sent to Roosevelt:

> Very grave dissatisfaction ... exists here at the way in which control of events is now being assumed, one-sidedly, by the United States Chiefs of Staff ... I consider that we are entitled to press for better and more equal treatment ... Otherwise it

> would be necessary, in particular, to devise some other machinery for conducting the war, including the separation of the command in the Mediterranean.[60]

The British Chiefs of Staff prevented the message from being sent. Brooke and his fellow Chiefs understood that there was no alternative; the Italian theatre could not be sustained on British assets alone. For strategic reasons, the Americans held the upper hand and Britain had no choice but to toe the line. The relegation of Italy to a secondary theatre mirrored the relegation of Britain to the junior partner in the Anglo-American Grand Alliance and prefigured Britain's relegation to secondary power status in the post-war settlement.[61]

It was necessary, nevertheless, to fight on. By the end of June, the pursuit of German Tenth and Fourteenth Armies after Operation 'Diadem' had come to a halt on the 200-mile-long Pisa–Rimini line, or, as it became known, the 'Gothic Line'. This belt of defences had originally been designed by the Germans 'as a bastion to hold Italy', but, due to myriad changes of strategy, it had remained unfinished as resources were sent to shore up the defences south of Rome. Now, Kesselring drove his men to make good the deficiencies. By August, a line of improvised defences ran right across the country, from the River Magra below La Spezia on the west coast inland to the Apennines, and then along the River Foglia to the 50 miles of lower ground on the Adriatic coastline near Pesaro.[62]

Operation 'Olive', which was aimed at breaking the 'Gothic Line' and driving towards the open terrain of the Po Valley, launched on 25 August (see Map 15.3). Eighth Army attacked the Tenth Army's positions in the Adriatic coastal sector on a three-corps front. To the east, II Polish Corps, made up of 3rd Carpathian and 5th Kresowa Divisions, were directed to seize the high ground to the north-west of Pesaro and isolate the town. In the middle, I Canadian Corps, made up of 1st Canadian Division and 5th Canadian Armoured Division, were to strike north towards Cattolica and then drive on to Rimini. In the west, V Corps, the main strike force – made up of the 1st Armoured Division (newly arrived after its exertions in the Tunisian campaign), 46th North Midland and West Riding and 56th London Divisions (both having returned after a much-needed period of rest in the Middle East), the 4th British and 4th Indian Divisions – was to drive inland towards Bologna and Ferrara far to the north, with the intent of breaking out

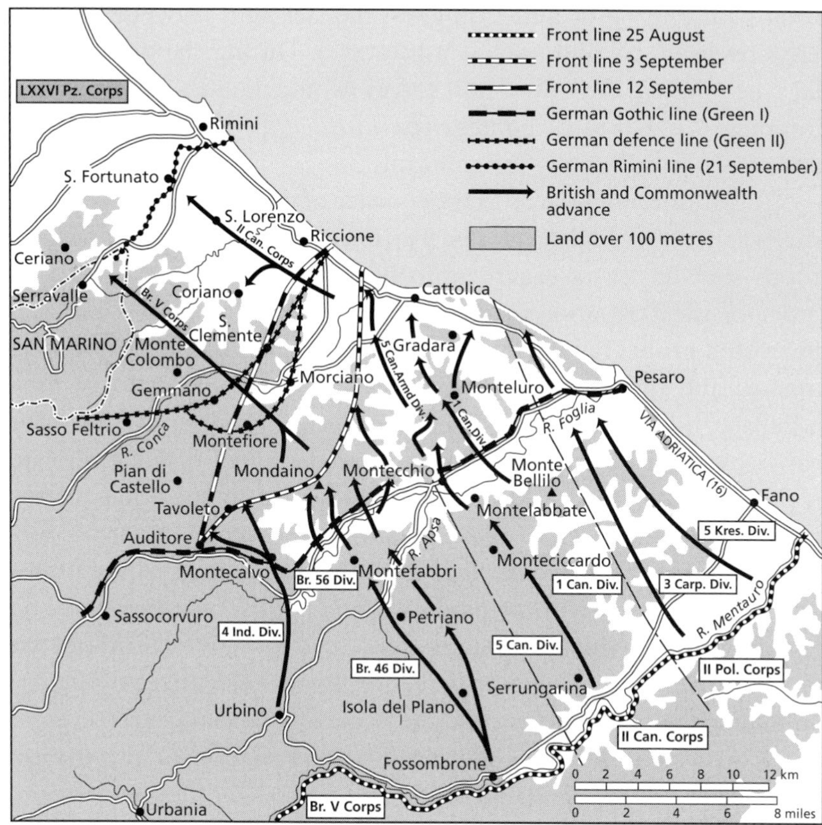

Map 15.3 Operation 'Olive', 25 August–21 September 1944

into the Po Valley and destroying the German forces in its path. The 2nd New Zealand Division was in reserve.[63]

Eighth Army and US Fifth Army enjoyed 'a tremendous superiority' over their opponents; US Fifth Army, in addition to launching supporting attacks to the west, was to be ready to exploit the hoped-for breakthrough in the east. In contrast to the three armoured divisions, seven infantry divisions and four independent armoured brigades available to Eighth Army, for example,[64] LXXVI Panzer Corps, which was to 'bear the brunt' of the assault, had initially only three divisions in the path of Leese's forces. In terms of infantry, Eighth Army had a 3.5:1 superiority. Eighth Army deployed 1,276 serviceable medium and 278 light tanks (1,554 in all); Tenth Army could muster 83 (a ratio of 19:1). Eighth Army had

1,121 guns and 1,055 anti-tank guns; the Germans had 351 and 235 respectively (a 3:1 and a 4.5:1 advantage). During the twenty-eight days of 'Olive', the Allied air forces would launch 8,507 sorties dropping 6,471 tons of bombs. The *Luftwaffe*'s efforts by comparison were almost wholly insignificant.[65]

Morale, not least as a consequence of the overall context of the war, was at a very high level. The British censors reported that fighting troops showed 'every eagerness to be "in the final party"'. Leese's Order of the Day prior to the operation 'gave the impression that this would probably be [Eighth Army's] last great battle'. There were 'innumerable references to sweepstakes on the date of the "cease fire" in Europe' in the men's mail; 'every time we hear a cheer, we think the war is over' wrote one man. The Canadians noted that morale had 'reached a new peak'. 'The lightning advance of the Allies across France' had done much to excite the men, but 'even the dramatic war news ha[d] to yield pride of place to the announcement from Ottawa regarding the gratuity to be paid to [Canadian] service personnel on demobilisation'. Much as was the case in North-West Europe, the censors noted that 'general satisfaction [wa]s evident regarding the Dominion's post-war plans', and the 'scale of financial provision envisaged' was 'considered to show a due appreciation of the troops' services and sacrifices'. As an officer put it, 'to sum up the situation, it looks as though we shall receive a chance to make a permanent notch for ourselves in civilian life. You have no idea how this has raised the morale of the boys overseas.'[66] Indeed, in spite of an outbreak of infective hepatitis, which dramatically increased sick rates in the Canadian Army between July and December 1944, the sick rate in I Canadian Corps for the week ending 26 August was only 10.06 per thousand (see Figure 11.4).[67]

The initial attack was put in, therefore, with considerable verve, especially in the Canadian sector. In fact, the Canadians, who assaulted along the more open ground of the Adriatic Plain, were in fine fettle for a number of key reasons. After 'Diadem', Burns, the I Canadian Corps commander, had instigated an intensive training programme to better prepare his men for the types of operations he expected going forward in Italy: pursuit of a retiring enemy and break-in attacks against prepared positions, such as those experienced on the 'Hitler Line'. He emphasised the ever-increasing need for 'bold action' to take advantage of a disorganised enemy and advised that in future 'firm bases', or set-piece attacks, would 'only be necessary' when resistance was 'stiff and counter attack possible'.[68]

He also expressly addressed the recurring problem of traffic control. A new system was developed that resembled that used by railways. Routes would be split into blocks. Traffic control posts and waiting areas were placed in between each of these blocks so that low-priority traffic could be shunted aside quickly if high-priority traffic needed to use the route.[69] This arrangement would give Burns a greater degree of flexibility, allowing him to take advantage of opportunities as they arose. Indeed, his plan for 'Olive' reflected this approach. Burns had devised a four-phase operation to carry I Canadian Corps through the 'Gothic Line'. In the first two phases, 1st Canadian Division would cross the Metauro River and then 'dash to the defences of the Gothic Line proper at the Foglia River'. These two stages were 'fixed'. The third phase, however, was much more flexible in its conception. Depending on what the attackers found at the Foglia, they were either to 'push [forward] with all speed and break through the GOTHIC LINE' without waiting for the arrival of the other main asset of the corps, 5th Canadian Armoured Division, or await the arrival of the armour and prepare for a set-piece attack. The fourth and final phase of the operation would involve the full pursuit and exploitation of the German Army.[70]

Remarkably, in the end, a hybrid solution emerged. In the face of initial German resistance, Burns ordered up 5th Canadian Armoured Division for a two-division set-piece attack. However, on reconnoitring the Foglia River in preparation for the assault, it became clear that the Germans were in the middle of rotating their formations on the front line and that the enemy's forward defences were not manned. Burns immediately ordered a rapid advance and within twenty-four hours both divisions had cracked the crust of the 'Gothic Line'.[71] It was clear that the speed and aggressiveness of the Canadian offensive had caught the Germans by surprise, and that the retraining and reorganisation of the Canadian Corps had paid dividends. This 'was an occasion when Canadian units were faster to the punch than the Germans, exhibiting excellent minor tactics', outfighting their opponents and 'opening the door for the Eighth Army to roll forward'.[72]

Leese, however, had erred badly in his dispositions for 'Olive'. He placed the exploitation force, 1st Armoured Division, under the command of Lieutenant-General Charles Keightley's V Corps, which was to attack, not in the open ground of the Adriatic Plain, but in the foothills of the Apennine Mountains to the west; this terrain was far less suited to armoured vehicles. Leese had let concerns about German demolitions and mining on the coast road and doubts about the ability of Burns as a corps commander cloud his judgement; he assigned his 'heaviest corps to the most mountainous sector, where tanks would have the most difficulty'. He then compounded this error by failing to act with energy to improvise and take advantage of the situation as it unfolded.[73]

With casualties mounting, the attack lost momentum. The nature of the terrain (there were thirteen rivers running across the line of advance of Eighth Army), tenacious German defence and the introduction of German reserves (eight divisions in total) began to tell. Had Leese shown more foresight or dynamism, the fleeting opportunity presented by success in the first week of 'Olive' might have been converted into a breakout. Instead, by 21 September Eighth Army had advanced only 30 miles in 'savage and intensive fighting'. The operation had cost Eighth Army 14,000 casualties, 4,511 of them Canadian, 'their highest casualties for any period of equal length either before or after the Italian campaign'. By comparison, the Germans lost 16,000 men, a 'disappointing' figure according to the Official History when the 'preponderance of material' and 'massive air support' enjoyed by Eighth Army was taken into consideration. The slow remorseless push forward in Italy resumed its steady and monotonous pattern. The rains came and in mid-December offensive operations were called to a halt, with the Allies still short of Bologna.[74]

Manpower Crisis

As the dust settled over the battlefields of 'Market Garden' and 'Olive', the consequences of the inability of the British and Commonwealth Armies to decisively overcome their German opponents became ever more apparent. In North-West Europe, Montgomery's obsession with his narrow thrust into Germany had led him to take his eyes off the perhaps even greater prize of the port of Antwerp. As a consequence, General von Zangen's Fifteenth Army, which had been trapped between the Channel coast and Second Army's rapid advance into Belgium and Holland (see Map 15.1), was able to escape across the Scheldt to the island of Walcheren and South Beveland; by 21 September, nine infantry divisions, including 82,000 men, 530 guns, 4,600 vehicles and 4,000 horses had been evacuated.[75]

Many of these men were transferred east to counter the threat of 'Market Garden' and Second Army's operations along the German frontier. Those forces that stayed behind were organised into two fortress garrisons, north and south of the Scheldt, with the object of denying the port facilities to the Allies and tying down as many troops as possible.[76] These forces had to be cleared from around the Scheldt if Antwerp was to be opened and sufficient supplies built up for a new drive into Germany. To do this, Montgomery had to reappraise his plans for the final phase of the war in the West. Proposals made before 'Market Garden' to transfer 3rd Division, 6th Airborne Division, 6th Guards Tank Brigade and a corps HQ to Burma to reinforce Fourteenth Army had to be cancelled. Montgomery wrote to Brooke on 2 October:

> We have in front of us some very hard fighting. If we emerge successfully, I suppose we shall have about won the war. But if we are seen off the war is very likely to drag on. With our present resources ... I do not see how we can fight two wars at the same time.[77]

There was, quite simply, an ever-increasing manpower crisis. Britain had already, even by 1942, fully mobilised its population for service either in the armed forces or in the wartime economy. Consequently, the manpower resources of one sector could only be expanded at the expense of the other.[78] Since D-Day, the infantry divisions of 21st Army Group had suffered an average of 7,500 casualties apiece, approximately 40 per cent of the strength of each division. Although the overall number of casualties in 21st Army Group was well within pre-'Overlord' projections, the high rate of losses in front-line infantry companies was a major cause of concern.[79] The effect of these losses was exacerbated by the situation in the Mediterranean. Eighth Army had suffered 11,842 casualties in Sicily; in Italy, British infantry divisions had suffered on average 10,750 casualties each by November 1944.[80]

Although replacements broadly kept up with these losses, they did not make good for other forms of 'wastage'.[81] In Italy, during 1944, for example, disease, as opposed to battle and accidental injuries, was responsible for more than three-quarters of admissions to hospital. In the context where medical professionals were 'conquering' epidemic diseases such as malaria, dysentery and jaundice (infectious hepatitis), it was the rise in sick admissions associated with other factors, such as morale, that caused the most serious concern.[82] On 29 August, Lieutenant-General Guy Simonds, the Commander of II Canadian Corps fighting in North-West Europe, wrote to his divisional commanders:

> I have checked the figures of our deficiencies in unit establishments with the figures for battle casualties and there is a marked discrepancy between the two. Records show that this discrepancy ... may be attributable to ... (a) Battle Exhaustion ... (b) Straggling and Absenteeism.[83]

The British Army suffered over 95,000 admissions for sickness during the North-West Europe campaign, the Canadians just short of 44,000 (139,000 in total). Of these losses, in the British Army, 13,255 were due to battle exhaustion; in the Canadian Army, 4,991 (a total of 18,246, the equivalent of a whole division).[84] The figure for sick admissions in Eighth Army in Sicily and Italy was extremely high at 250,284.[85] It is not clear how many of these were caused by battle exhaustion, but it does seem likely, given the available evidence, that the overall British battle exhaustion figure was not far off that experienced in North-West Europe.[86] The issue, as D. F. Butler wrote, 'posed a real problem for, with the great shortage of manpower, the Army could not afford to waste such material'.[87] Lieutenant-Colonel A. M. Doyle, the Neuropsychiatric Advisor at the Canadian Section Allied Forces HQ, reckoned that during the Italian campaign as a whole the Canadian Army suffered at least 5,020 neuropsychiatric casualties, of which crucially about 72 per cent were in the infantry.[88] Only about one third of such men, according to another report, ever returned to full duties in the field.[89]

The total number of court-martial convictions for desertion and AWOL in North-West Europe and Italy also lend credence to Simonds' claim. Between July 1944 and April 1945 there were 5,737 convictions in 21st Army Group.[90] Courts martial for desertion among British troops in Italy, between October 1943 and June 1945, came to a further 5,694. The total number of cases of AWOL and desertion by British troops reported to GHQ 2nd Echelon for the Central Mediterranean Force (CMF) July 1943 to June 1945 (which included Sicily, Italy, North Africa and Greece) came to a remarkable 12,929.[91]

One historian has gone so far as to argue that the desertion rate in Eighth Army in the winter of 1944 'was the worst of any Allied army in the whole war'.[92] Indeed, the rate of desertion in Italy 'so greatly exceeded' forecasts 'that for considerable periods' there were up to 800 soldiers awaiting admission to prisons for whom 'no vacancies were available'.[93]

Figures were comparable for Canadian troops. There were 463 field general courts martial in North Africa, Sicily and Italy in 1943, 2,088 in Italy in 1944, with another 936 in Italy 'in the first months of 1945', a grand total of 3,487.[94] Although details of the offences for which courts martial were issued are not available, it seems reasonable to assume that the proportion of these courts martial that were for desertion and AWOL was similar to that for Eighth Army as a whole; if that was the case, then there were about 2,400 cases of desertion and AWOL in the Canadian Army in the Mediterranean during this period (a British and Commonwealth total for the theatre of nearly 8,100).[95]

All told, therefore, the British and Commonwealth Armies in North-West Europe and Italy were deprived of the use of around 14,000 men due to convictions for desertion and AWOL (a figure that represents probably only a fraction of the total number of offences). Moreover, a sample of 584 of these men, from March 1945, showed that 81.7 per cent were infantry. The seriousness of the problem was indicated by the fact that a great majority of those assessed in the sample had 'previously been well-behaved soldiers' and most of the men had committed their offences in the 'face of the enemy or in anticipation of enemy action'.[96]

So great were concerns about desertion and AWOL that the question of reinstating the death penalty once again came to the fore in 1944, in Italy. It was first taken up by commanders in February when General Richard McCreery (then commanding X Corps) wrote to Lieutenant-General Harding, Alexander's Chief of Staff. Alexander was greatly perturbed when he read the letter and immediately took the matter in hand, writing to General Maitland Wilson at Allied Forces HQ. Wilson, in turn, forwarded the letter with his comments to Adam, the Adjutant-General, at the War Office in London.[97]

The problem, as before, seemed to revolve around the lack of an adequate deterrent to desertion. At the time, in light of the manpower crisis, sentences for desertion were often suspended after a short term and 'there existed a widespread belief that a general amnesty would be announced at the end of war in Europe' for deserters.[98] Alexander deplored the situation, and, like almost all his field commanders, maintained that it had been 'a great mistake to have done away with the death penalty'.[99] As one divisional commander put it, 'shootings in the early days would probably have been an effective prophylactic'.[100]

Adam, who received Wilson's correspondence at the end of April, produced a paper on the problem of desertion, which eventually came before the Army Council in June. The Army Council, and especially its chair, P. J. Grigg, the Secretary of State for War, was 'acutely aware of the political dimension' that had undermined previous attempts to reinstate the death penalty and decided not to intervene and to maintain the status quo. Grigg and Adam, however, were determined not to let the matter lie there; they continued to push for a firm declaration regarding the question of a post-war amnesty for deserters. They were adamant also that all service prior to a conviction for desertion should be discounted when it came to demobilisation at the end of the war.[101]

In November, Churchill bowed to this pressure; the following month he made a statement in the House of Commons:

> So far as concerns the present Government, it is not the intention to grant any general remission of sentences. Offences such as desertion which comprise the bulk of these sentences, involve at the best an added strain upon man-power of this country, and at worst forfeit the lives of other soldiers who have filled the places of these deserters.[102]

When the demobilisation regulations were released in early 1945, they included an announcement that any soldier convicted of desertion after 1 February would forfeit all prior service for purpose of release. 'Whether it was because of these two rulings … or because fighting was less bitter in February 1945', cases of desertion decreased dramatically in the final months in Italy.[103]

The desertion problem had certainly been of 'crisis proportions' and had been 'a significant factor in causing and exacerbating the infantry crisis' that afflicted the British and Canadian Armies in late 1944.[104] Another problem related to morale, however, has received somewhat less attention in the literature: the incidence of venereal disease (VD).

By October 1944, VD had become so prevalent in 21st Army Group in North-West Europe that Montgomery wrote to all commanding officers to address 'this lapse from high principle and conduct'. 'You are all fully aware of our manpower difficulties', he chided, 'which are such that we cannot afford to lose a single man unnecessarily'. The only 'really satisfactory method' of dealing with the problem, he stressed, was 'by a personal talk' from officers to their men, as, in the end, VD was really 'all part of man-management'. Montgomery attached a graph with the message clearly showing the incidence of VD in 21st Army Group having trebled since the end of the fighting in Normandy; 'the number of cases reported during the week ending 7 Oct[ober]' being 'equivalent in a year to the total strength of a division'.[105] By the end of the campaign, the British had suffered 4,390 losses to VD,[106] while the much less numerous Canadians had been deprived of no less than 7,000 men due to the disease (a British and Commonwealth total of 11,390) (see Figure 15.1).[107]

VD was an even greater problem in Italy. Between 17 October 1943 and 31 March 1945, Eighth Army was temporarily deprived of the service of 15,140 men due to VD.[108] As one report put it, 'in many areas the inhabitants were desperately poor and only too ready to follow the "oldest profession in the world"'.[109] In Bari alone there were 'some 2,000 clandestine prostitutes in addition to those in licensed houses'.[110] The situation was made worse by the lack of home leave and welfare amenities; only an average of 180 compassionate postings home were issued each month in Italy during 1944. It was not until November that year that leave to the UK was introduced from the CMF or other parts of the Mediterranean. Until this time, men had received a week of local leave every six months. This put tremendous strain on relationships, and, in turn made men more likely to seek what Montgomery referred to as 'horizontal refreshment'.[111]

Moreover, when on local leave, there were 'few' options for relaxation open to the men. Beer was in short supply; reading material, sports and games equipment were not plentiful; and there was little chance of seeing a film. Towards the end of 1943 the rate of VD had risen so alarmingly that Eisenhower 'circulated every command in the theatre, stating that the increase was "beyond all reasonable expectation" and that it was a sign of boredom and low morale' (see Figure 15.2).[112]

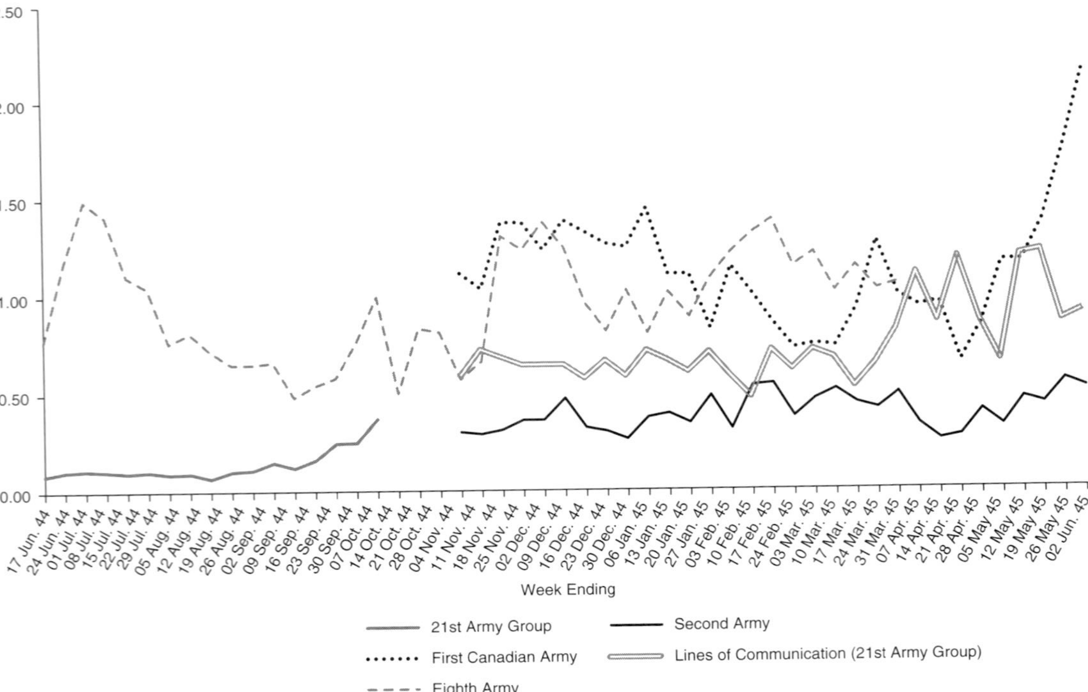

Figure 15.1 VD admissions per thousand troops, British Second Army, First Canadian Army, Line of Command troops, 21st Army Group and Eighth Army, 1944–5

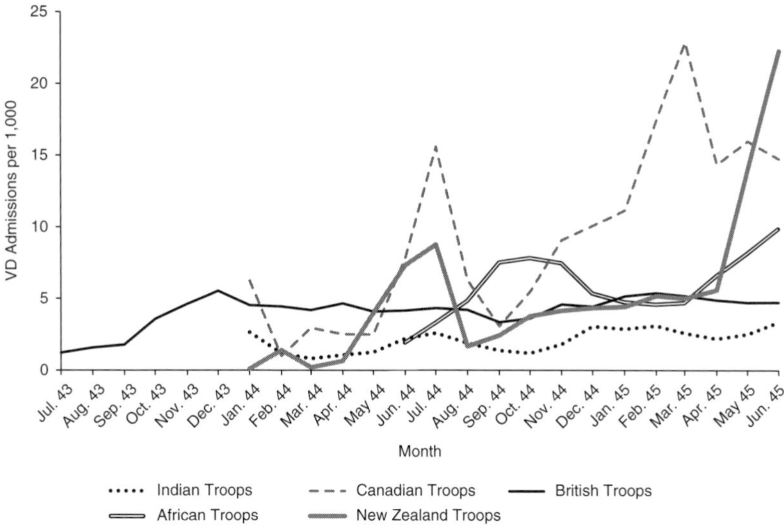

Figure 15.2 VD admissions per thousand troops, British and Commonwealth troops, Italy, 1944–5

The manpower crisis was, therefore, not solely a product of demographic limitations, or of the balance made between allocating citizens to the armed forces and the wartime economy, but also a manifestation of the continued inability of Britain and the Empire to mobilise and enthuse its citizen armies not only to join up for war but to serve with the unswerving commitment and self-discipline required. The consequences of this systemic weakness now again played out on the battlefield. With only a small percentage of replacements earmarked for the infantry, perhaps 20 per cent,[113] deficiencies had to be made up in other ways. In North-West Europe, Montgomery was forced to disband 59th Staffordshire Division (in August) and 50th Northumbrian Division, which had landed on Gold beach on D-Day, in November/December.[114] In Italy, at the end of September, Alexander ordered that 1st Armoured Division and two brigades be disbanded and every British infantry battalion be cut from four to three rifle companies.[115] A number of disparate measures were put in place to provide more troops for the infantry from other theatre resources; light anti-aircraft regiments were significantly reorganised; the anti-aircraft troops of armoured regiments, armoured reconnaissance regiments and tank battalions were disbanded; army corps and divisional defence corps and platoons were maintained at only 80 per cent strength. These measures, and others, provided an additional 30,000 infantry in North-West Europe and 29,700 in Italy.[116]

More officers were needed as well. Battalions, if they were to be kept up to war establishments, were supposed to have thirty-six on their books, but many had fought for long periods with only twenty-five, and, in one case, a battalion had been reduced to sixteen officers. To offset these deficiencies, 21st Army Group gave permission for the promotion of up to six extra NCOs (sergeants) with paid 'local rank' in excess of a battalion's war establishment.[117] In Italy, an Officer Cadet Training Unit Board was established in theatre to increase the supply of subalterns.[118]

These measures addressed the immediate problems, but, in turn, created complications of their own. The Canadian Army had adopted the same system as the British as its guide for the allocation and training of reinforcements. Accordingly, as the Canadians also had a shortage of infantry due to casualties, they had to hurriedly convert surpluses of men from other arms into infantry units.[119] Between late April 1944 and January 1945, over 12,500 other ranks were remustered into infantry.[120] Those at the front were often highly critical (much of the time unfairly so) of the skills of these replacement infantrymen.[121] The 'news' that 'undertrained' Canadian men were being sent into battle in Europe became public knowledge when Major Connie Smythe, the owner of the Toronto Maple Leafs, having been wounded commanding an anti-aircraft battery in Normandy, broke the story in September on his return to Canada.[122] The disclosure caused uproar at home and Smythe's account spread like wildfire among the troops back in Europe, only reinforcing their own negative attitudes to reinforcements.[123]

The Minister of National Defence, Colonel J. L. Ralston, informed the Canadian Cabinet that 15,000 infantrymen would have to be drawn from the trained NRMA (National Resources Mobilisation Act – home service conscript) soldiers in Canada to make good the shortfall. Ralston's position put Mackenzie King, the Canadian Prime Minister, in an extraordinarily difficult situation; he had promised French Canada at the start of the war that there would be no conscription for overseas service.[124]

To a degree, Mackenzie King had already prepared the ground for a *volte-face*. In April 1942, he had ordered a plebiscite to release him from his pledge.[125] But the results of the national poll had not been an overwhelming vote of confidence in the Government's policy. English Canadians had voted strongly in favour of releasing it from its past promises, Ontario by 82.3 per cent, Prince Edward Island by 82.4 per cent, British Columbia by 79.4 per cent, and the rest by substantial margins. However, in Quebec, only 27 per cent of the electorate voted 'Yes'.[126] Mackenzie King was free from his commitment, but the problem of alienating Quebec and destroying 'the unity of Canada' remained. His solution, announced on 10 June 1942, was to emphasise that although conscription for overseas service was now a possibility, it was not yet necessary, might never be necessary and would only be introduced as a last resort; as he put it, 'not necessarily conscription, but conscription if necessary'.[127]

By October 1944, the Government found itself backed into a corner and there was no more room for prevarication. Mackenzie King sacked Ralston from the Cabinet and replaced him with General Andrew McNaughton, who had recently returned from service overseas. Mackenzie King hoped that the new Defence Minister would use his enormous prestige and popularity with the troops to persuade NRMA soldiers to volunteer and remove the necessity for overseas conscription.[128] Instructions were sent to gather all NRMA recruits capable of serving as infantry for retraining. Commanding officers were told to impress upon the men the seriousness of the situation; they were to use all measures to find the necessary volunteers from among the ranks.[129]

These efforts met with little success. Of the 60,000 trained home service conscripts in Canada, only 694 volunteered for overseas service in the first three weeks of November.[130] In fact, during the whole North-West Europe campaign, only 21,067 NRMA men opted for General Service; by comparison, 4,117 deserted.[131] On 22 November, senior officers at Army HQ raised the stakes. They sent McNaughton a memorandum stating that the voluntary system of recruiting through Army channels could not 'meet the immediate problem' faced in North-West Europe. Mackenzie King saw this interjection as nothing short of a revolt of the generals. It did, however, convince him of the immediate need for trained men in Europe and he changed policy, deciding that he would send 16,000 NRMA soldiers overseas.[132]

The decision had immediate consequences, many of which echoed those of the New Zealand Furlough Mutiny and the saga of the 'Blue Oath' in South Africa (see Chapter 10). In British Columbia, where most of the trained NRMA men were stationed, news of the Government's change in policy reached them by radio. The result 'was several disturbances'. The most serious occurred in Terrace, where a sit-down strike by two companies of the Fusiliers du St. Laurant sparked further protests involving 'most of the men in the camp'. For several days, NRMA men 'refused to appear on parade or to obey orders from their officers'; some 'broke into storerooms and seized ammunition and weapons, including Bren light machine guns and Sten sub-machine guns'.[133]

On 25 November, a large group of men paraded through the camp at Terrace 'bearing banners with slogans such as "Down with Conscription" and "Zombies Strike Back"'. General Pearkes, the General Officer Commanding-in-Chief (GOC-in-C) Pacific Command, reported to Ottawa that the situation could 'only be considered as mutiny'.[134] It was certainly the 'most serious breach of Canadian military discipline' of the war.[135] Two days later, another large group, of about 1,600 men, marched through the town. 'In a few cases loaded weapons were openly displayed. Once or twice, soldiers allegedly pointed their rifles at officers ... and threatened violence.' Other disturbances took place in Vernon, Nanaimo, Prince George, Courtenay, Cilliwack and Port Alberni.[136]

By December, order had been restored, mostly through a process of negotiation, and by January 1945 'every immediately available trained NRMA infantryman had left Pacific Command' for the journey across Canada to the eastern seaboard and the boat to North-West Europe.[137] Many of the men, however, had little intention of sailing overseas. Much like the Furlough Mutineers, the 'Zombie' rioters were driven by a broader frustration and dissatisfaction with the overall management of the war effort. They were either opposed to 'any form of Conscription for overseas service' or 'willing to go overseas if there were a "total conscription" of wealth and industry'. 'Let Them Conscript Wealth Too' and 'Conscript Wealth and Industry as well as Manpower' were commonly recurring slogans used by the mutineers.[138] The issue of political legitimacy was once again central to the remobilisation process. One local newspaper commented:

> Among the English-speaking draftees one can hear many remarks smacking of class warfare, ideological struggle and party politics. 'We can win this war right here at home',

> meaning the war for 'economic democracy', and similar phrases were common enough during the riots staged by the Zombies.[139]

It was 'small wonder' then that 'many' of the mutineers 'took their embarkation leave as the occasion to desert';[140] 7,800 of the 16,000 men (48.8 per cent) ordered overseas went absent as their units moved from British Columbia to Halifax. While many simply overstayed their embarkation leave, by the end of March, 4,082 men still remained unaccounted for (25.5 per cent of the 16,000 men due to be sent overseas). With all the delays caused by the 'Zombie Mutiny', only 2,463 NRMA men reached the front in North-West Europe before the conclusion of hostilities.[141] In a context where popular support for the war stemmed mostly from persuasion much more than from coercion,[142] the concept of procedural justice had once again taken on considerable importance.[143]

Needless to say, these events were not conducive to maintaining high morale among the volunteers on the battlefront in North-West Europe and Italy. Many felt that they showed that 'the Dominion as a whole' was 'indifferent to the sacrifices made by those serving overseas';[144] it was clear to the censors in Italy that 'in volume and in bitterness, the dissatisfaction expressed' exceeded 'the usual limits of Army grousing'.[145] The censorship summary from North-West Europe for the second half of November 1944 noted that 'the policy of the Canadian Government on conscription was the burning topic of this mail',[146] while later summaries remarked that 'there was a widespread feeling of shame at the way in which the reinforcement question had been handled, and the Prime Minister was blamed for being too much influenced by QUEBEC politicians'.[147] A soldier in 3rd Canadian Division wrote:

> If you had seen the boys that I know die before my eyes; and then have Rats like the Zombies say 'We won't go overseas' ... The German Radio puts on a program for us all day trying to break our morale, but little do they know that our own people are breaking our morale far more quickly than the Germans.[148]

The feelings among soldiers of 2nd Canadian Division were no different. One man wrote:

> At the moment there are, as you may well imagine, a great many soldiers here who are pretty ashamed at being Canadians, I'm very definitely one of the number ... this little party has certainly brought politics home to the troops. Canada to me right now looks like a country I want to have little to do with.[149]

A soldier in 4th Canadian Armoured Division echoed these sentiments:

> Honest Joan I am very sorry to say that I feel like laying down my arms right here and head back for home. I can't see how the devil they expect the boys over here to go in there against the fire Jerry puts up to try and stop us, when those yellow-bellied so and so back home won't come over and help us. The reinforcement problem is pretty serious now ... Do those fellows want us to get down on our knees and plead with them for help or what? I am going to get off that subject because it just makes me boil every time I think of it.[150]

When news reached the troops that a large number of those drafted for overseas service went AWOL, even more 'indignation', 'resentment and disappointment' was expressed, especially in Italy. 'We have put up with excuses for the last five years but this is overstepping the mark', wrote a private. Another commented that 'all fronts are doing well except the home front', while yet another wrote:

> When I read of these 6000 alleged 'men' on the loose in Canada [the number that was still reported as AWOL on 20 January], I almost hate to admit I'm a Canadian ... They're letting us guys down in a really big way and total conscription right from the start would have saved all this mess, but now it's too late.[151]

'I'll be home within a few months – with the help of Russia and NOT Canada', wrote an officer in the first half of February 1945. A trooper commented that 'it doesn't do our morale any good when we hear that while only 400 men go home on leave from here [Italy], there are 6,000 Zombies AW[O]L in Canada';[152] many believed that a lack of reinforcements had 'kept in Italy many men who would otherwise have been able to enjoy home leave', which had been introduced in November 1944.[153] An NCO added:

> It really makes a guy wonder just what he is fighting for when 6000 and some go loose when on draft over here. I don't think

> much of fighting for yellow-bellies like that and can't understand why the Government treats them so leniently, when over here I've heard of cases where a guy was two hours AWOL and is now serving out two years. It is time they quit using kid gloves on them.[154]

It is perhaps fortunate that the 'Zombie Mutiny', unlike its New Zealand 'Furlough' equivalent, occurred during a period when the Canadian forces were mostly uncommitted in Europe. The German attack in the Ardennes on 16 December, which did not directly affect the Canadians, delayed the beginning of First Canadian Army's next big operation, 'Veritable', which was due to begin on 1 January, by about five weeks. I Canadian Corps in Italy also avoided major engagements over the winter months and was then transferred to North-West Europe, as part of Operation 'Goldflake' (see later in this chapter). The 1st Canadian Division, for example, would not return to the front line until 11 April 1945.[155]

Moreover, by 1945, the worst of the problem that the 'Zombies' were supposed to fix, the manpower crisis, was behind the Canadian Army. With First Canadian Army rested for a period over the winter months, and with the infantry conversion programme in theatre paying dividends, all Canadian infantry battalions in North-West Europe were at full strength by January.[156] The Liberals under Mackenzie King, as the Opposition claimed, had 'failed to assure equality of service and sacrifice' in Canada during the war.[157] Nevertheless, it is clear from censorship that the vast improvement in the management of the human dimension that took place across the British and Commonwealth Armies in the second half of the war played a key role in keeping the spirit of the troops at a high level. Improved welfare and education arrangements, alongside the introduction of superior opportunities for leave, including provisions for furlough to the UK and Canada, and the guarantee of post-war gratuities that were far superior to those promised to British soldiers, ensured that the morale of Canadian troops stayed resolute during the final months of the war.[158]

In a similar vein, the potential fallout from the 'Zombie Mutiny' never materialised at the political level. The Minister of National Defence for Air, C. G. Power, a long-time opponent of conscription for service overseas, resigned. He was adamant that political 'convenience' should not 'give way before National interest ... I envisage the prospect of one-third of our population uncooperative, with a deep sense of injury, and the prey to the worst elements among them, and worst of all hating all other Canadians.'[159] However, other key members of the Cabinet, who had previously opposed conscription for service overseas, supported Mackenzie King. Minister of Justice Louis St. Laurent recognised that the Prime Minister's actions were a workable compromise under the circumstances; they would keep the Government in office and prevent the pro-conscription opposition from imposing an even more severe form of military compulsion. On 27 November, Mackenzie King brought the matter to Parliament and carried the day with the support of 23 out of 57 Quebec members.[160] The character of the fighting in Normandy and the experience of the Canadian Army overseas had impacted well beyond the military operational sphere; it had sparked a mass mutiny back home, threatened national unity and nearly brought down the Government in Ottawa.

As serious, and shocking, as the manpower problem was to become for the British and Commonwealth Armies in the Second World War, the extent of the crisis and the extraordinary measures taken to address it must be understood in context. Whereas by the end of 1944, the British Army was short of 42,000 infantrymen, half of them in the Mediterranean,[161] the *Wehrmacht*, by February 1945, was reporting a deficiency of 460,000. Most German formations mustered less than half the strength of their Anglo-Canadian counterparts.[162] In Italy, most divisions comprised no more than 2,500 men.[163] By 25 September, 'of the Tenth Army's 92 infantry battalions only 10 had a strength of over 400 men, 16 were over 300, 26 were over 200 and 38 had less than 200'.[164] By comparison, British battalions were rarely smaller than 700 men.[165] The British approach, of fighting with powerful allies and gradually wearing down the German Army through attrition, was working in this respect at least. It may not have been fast or spectacular, but the 'Colossal Cracks' approach did at least appear to guarantee victory.

The Scheldt and the 'Siegfried Line'

In North-West Europe, unlike Italy, there would be no respite in the fighting over the winter months. While Second Army focused on operations along the German frontier, it was also necessary to clear the low-lying territory south and north of the Scheldt estuary and open up the port of Antwerp. Nearly one-third of the fuel the Allies were bringing into theatre was being consumed in the process of getting supplies to the front; the whole Allied advance was in danger of being held up due to a lack of resources. Something had to be done. On 13 September, Montgomery assigned the First Canadian Army the job. It was no easy task; the Scheldt was below sea level and was intersected by a profusion of canals, ditches and other waterways. Roads were usually raised on dykes, leaving large flat basins known as polders in the intervening countryside. Much of the area had been flooded by the Germans and the fighting conditions as a consequence were miserable in the extreme.[166]

Simonds, who was temporarily in command of First Canadian Army (Crerar had been struck down by a severe stomach ailment), designed a three-phase scheme for the operation. First, a pocket of German troops remaining around Breskens, on the south bank of the Scheldt, would have to be eliminated, while the isthmus leading to South Beveland, on the north shore, was sealed off. It would then be necessary to exploit the land approach along South Beveland 'as far as practicable' before the final stage, an assault on Walcheren Island both from South Beveland and from the sea (see Map 15.4). With barely sufficient means for the job due to the ongoing manpower crisis and the fact that the operations along the German border took precedence, Simonds's task was made more complicated by the continuing actions to open up Boulogne and Calais and the need to drive north-east, away from the Scheldt, 'to conform with the long left flank of Second Army, now exposed after Market Garden'.[167]

To achieve all this, Simonds had under his command I Corps, 49th West Riding Division and 1st Polish Armoured Division, and II Canadian Corps, 2nd and 3rd Canadian Divisions and 4th Canadian Armoured Division; somewhere in the region of 100,000 men. In between Simonds and his goal was the German LXVII Corps, with 711th and 719th Divisions in the area east and north-east of Antwerp, the remnants of 356th and 344th Divisions in blocking positions north of Antwerp, 64th Division defending the Breskens Pocket, and most of 70th Division holding Walcheren.[168] Intelligence estimates put the defenders on the northern shores of the estuary at 15,300, those to the south at 4,400: a total of about

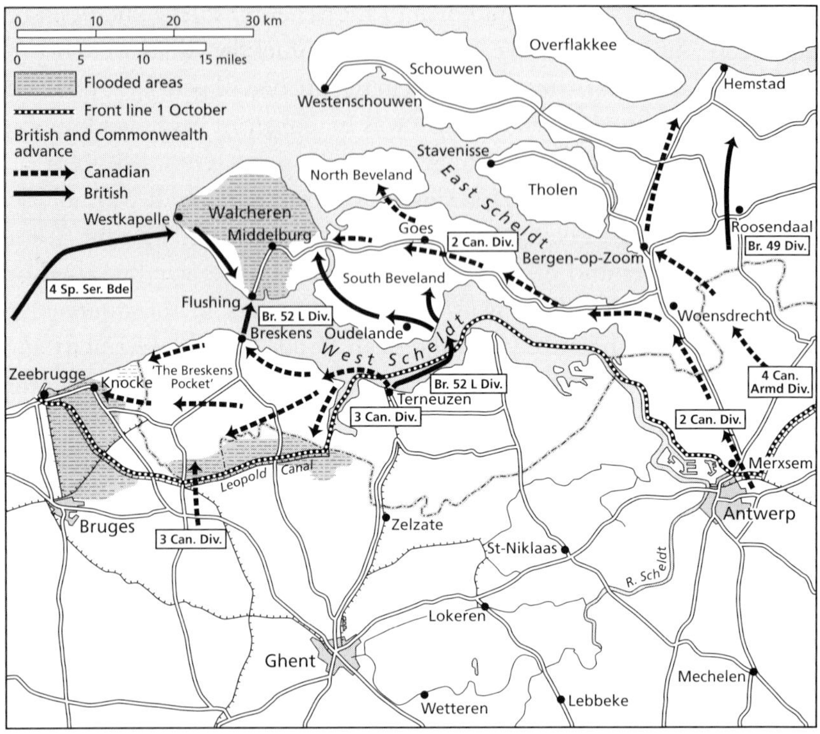

Map 15.4 The Scheldt battles, October–November 1944

20,000 men. As ever, the British and Commonwealth advantage in terms of materiel was considerable.[169]

Operation 'Switchback', the clearing of the Breskens Pocket, began on 6 October with an assault across the Leopold Canal by 7th Canadian Brigade of 3rd Canadian Division. Twenty-seven Wasp flamethrowers 'lobbed liquid fire across the ninety feet of the canal' before the Canadian Scottish Regiment and the Regina Rifles stormed across in assault boats. The fire plan for the operation was markedly different from many that went before it. Instead of utilising a timed barrage, a 'system of on-call concentrations and stonks on known or suspected enemy positions' was employed. Thus, the attacking infantry were 'no longer bound to the timings of the guns' and could call for fire support when and where it was needed. The system was 'much more responsive than the timing-rigid fire plans' characteristic of the Normandy campaign. With 'excellent' fire support and a 'determined' effort by the infantry, 7th Canadian Brigade gradually expanded its bridgehead over the Leopold Canal. When 9th Canadian Brigade launched an amphibious assault using 'Buffalo' LVTs (Landing Vehicle, Tracked) on the north-east coast of the pocket, the German position began to unravel. Breskens was captured on 21 October, although it would take until 3 November to fully clear the enemy from south of the Scheldt. The Canadians, far from facing a force of fewer than 5,000 men, had been compelled to tackle a garrison of about 15,000 troops who had been ordered to fight to the last man and the last round.[170]

On the north bank, the fighting was equally as intense. With the number of German divisions in the line roughly equivalent to those of First Canadian Army and, with each German division averaging between 6,000 and 8,000 men, Simonds' troops were faced with a considerable challenge. Without a decisive numerical advantage, the Canadians had to both outfight and out-think the enemy. In both these respects, they performed admirably. By 24 October, 2nd Canadian Division had cut the South Beveland isthmus, opening the way for the assault on South Beveland itself. The 2nd Canadian Division was aided considerably in this arduous task by an amphibious assault by 52nd Lowland Division, which had been relieved of its duties with First Allied Airborne Army and sent to reinforce First Canadian Army. This ambitious operation helped unhinge the last major German defensive line before Walcheren and by 30 October, both divisions had reached the Walcheren Causeway.[171]

The final phase of Simonds' plan was no easy task either. In order to support another set of ambitious amphibious landings to the west and south of Walcheren, at Westkapelle and Flushing, Simonds decided that a diversionary attack from the east was necessary. The problem was that the ground to the left and right of the Walcheren causeway 'was too soggy for vehicle or dismounted movement, yet lacked enough water to support an amphibious assault'. This meant that an attack would have to be restricted to the narrow neck of the causeway. 'No one' in the 2nd Canadian Division 'relished the idea of attacking across' a feature 'that was 1,100 metres long, 35 metres wide, surrounded by saturated ground, and covered by anti-tank and machine gun fire'. Nevertheless, the assault went ahead. The attacks, which went in between 31 October and 2 November, 'were gut-wrenching'. It took three separate attempts by 2nd Canadian Division to gain a foothold on the Walcheren end of the causeway. The division's valiant efforts meant that the amphibious landings could go ahead on

1 November; they were successful, and a week later, the Scheldt Estuary was completely clear of German land forces.[172]

In over a month of bitter fighting against a determined enemy, the First Canadian Army, for the cost of 12,873 casualties had captured 41,043 prisoners and destroyed the best part of three German divisions. At no stage had the Canadians enjoyed the kind of force-to-force ratios that would have been expected for such a difficult assignment. Nevertheless, they had shown both the determination and the creativity to dislodge the Germans from some of the most formidable defences to be faced by any Allied Army in the Second World War. Simonds had pushed his troops to the limit, pursuing his goal with 'a certainty and cold-bloodedness' perhaps more characteristic of an American than a British and Commonwealth general. The outcome, the opening up of the best port facility in northern Europe (supplies through port facilities increased by no less than 70 per cent) was a very great prize indeed for these efforts.[173]

That the Canadian Army could perform such a task so soon after the ordeals of Normandy was quite remarkable. In spite of the hardships and a spike in cases of battle exhaustion, morale in First Canadian Army actually improved over the course of the operation (see Figures 14.1 and 14.3).[174] Again, matters on the home front were key. Although the 'Zombie' issue back home certainly acted as a drag on morale in the run up to the battles,[175] the appointment of the 'very popular' McNaughton as Defence Minister played no small part in the uplift. The troops were 'convinced', incorrectly as it turned out, 'that he would get them a "square deal"' and that 'his appointment would be followed by the dispatch of home defence forces [the Zombies] overseas'.[176] Whereas the sickness rate for First Canadian Army was 14.9 per thousand for the week ending 7 October, it had dropped 38 per cent to 9.2 per thousand by the week ending 11 November.[177] The morale of 3rd Canadian Division was described as 'excellent' or 'extremely high' throughout and although there were 'a few' references to the troops in 2nd Canadian Division and 4th Canadian Armoured Division being 'weary', it was clear that both formations were 'determined to "see it through"'. The percentage of soldiers' letters that both addressed morale and professed to be 'keen for action' rose from 5 per cent in the second half of September to 34 per cent in the middle of the operation.[178] There is little doubt that the success on the Scheldt could not have materialised but for this considerable uplift in morale.

Barely a month and a half after its failure to close the Falaise Gap, a reinvigorated First Canadian Army showed what could be achieved when it was competently and ruthlessly led and well-motivated. A significant turnaround had taken place.[179]

As First Canadian Army battled to open up Antwerp, Second Army made slow but methodical progress as it pushed north through Holland along the German border.[180] By 8 November, 21st Army Group, as a whole, had closed up to the Meuse in the north, in a line stretching west to east from the sea to the town of Grave. One man in 11th Armoured Division remarked that the 'stiff fight' being put up by the Germans was just 'like a second CAEN'.[181] Although Second Army increasingly showed 'signs of tiredness', it was clear from censorship that morale remained high[182] and that 'there was no evidence to suggest that troops were any less willing to do all that was expected of them'.[183] By the start of December, 21st Army Group was along the Meuse to the east also (the river travels north from the Ardennes before it curves west near Grave). It now occupied an extended rectangle along the western borders of Germany, stretching from northern France, through Belgium and into Holland.[184]

The scene was set for a fresh attempt to drive towards the Rhine and on into Germany. Between 21st Army Group and its prize, however, lay the northern extension of the German 'Westwall', the 'Siegfried Line'. In this sector, woods and forests covered much of the front; near the rivers the land was flooded, making offensive operations problematic in the extreme.[185] Von Runstedt, reappointed by Hitler as Commander of German forces in the West in September 1944, had used the period of static attritional fighting after 'Market Garden' to rebalance and stabilise his forces.[186] There was little doubt that breaking the 'Siegfried Line' would take an enormous and concerted effort on behalf of the Allies.

As von Runstedt 'steadied the ship' at the front, Hitler focused on building up an armoured reserve, the Sixth Panzer Army, for a great counter-offensive in the West.[187] These divisions were to be ready for action in November, but 'were not to be tied down in defence' of the western approaches to the Reich. Hitler understood that in the long run a defensive posture could not prevent the final defeat of Germany. It was only by attack that the situation could be retrieved. His goal, therefore, was to blast a 50-mile hole between the British and American forces at the front and drive on to the Canadian's recently won prize, the port facility at Antwerp.[188]

Although the Allies were aware of the existence of Sixth Panzer Army, the ambition behind its creation remained unclear during the winter of 1944. Logic dictated that any German build-up would be used to blunt the expected Allied offensive. 'The enemy's aim', according to the 21st Army Group Intelligence Review for 3 December, 'has been to expend his infantry to stop a damaging break through; to use his "tactical reserves" to hold the infantry in line and to "blunt" the Allied assault.' No one expected Sixth Panzer Army to be used for a counter-offensive, for such an eventuality demanded, according to the intelligence review, 'five elements not readily to be found together':

> a) Vital ground, and there is nowhere obvious for him to go which would hurt us deeply. The limited drive on Antwerp, a 'dash to the wire' as of old [see Chapter 4], is just not within his potential.
> b) He needs bad weather, else our air superiority will disrupt his assembly; yet this very weather could clog his own intent.
> c) He must find us tired and unbalanced, and himself be in a position both physically and tactically to take advantage of it.
> d) He needs adequate fuel stocks not only to sustain a full-blooded operation, but also to guarantee a withdrawal in his own time when it fails, and
> e) He needs more infantry and of better quality in the present terrain and weather.[189]

It was recognised that the 'morale prize' for such an offensive 'would be great for never was there greater need of a fillip', but to lose Sixth Panzer Army in the doing of it would 'be a disaster perhaps irreparable, for the Rhine can best be defended this side [to the west] and with those five divisions [of the Panzer Army] removed might otherwise not be defended at all'. It seemed most probable that the Germans would 'wait to smash our bridgeheads' over the next river crossing.[190]

That was not how events played out. On 16 December, Hitler ordered three German Armies, with twenty divisions including, with reserves, twelve *panzer* divisions, to once more go on the offensive in the west. Some 200,000 men, supported by around 500 tanks, 1,900 artillery pieces, assault guns and mortars and 2,295 aircraft crashed into American positions in the Ardennes.[191] Initially, the attack made rapid progress as it overran the four American divisions facing it. Soon, however, the tide began to turn, due to a combination of dogged American resistance, as many units who were surrounded and cut off continued to fight on determinedly, and Allied material might; the Allies at this time were able to call on 7,079 medium tanks alone to blunt the German offensive.[192] By the end of January, the 'Battle of the Bulge', as it became known, had petered out. Montgomery, who had taken over command of First and Ninth US Armies during the height of the crisis, and 21st Army Group had played an important role in first steadying the situation on the northern flank and then in driving back the German penetration. But the battle had been overwhelmingly an American affair; 90,000 casualties had been inflicted on the Germans for the cost of 80,000 American and only 1,400 British.[193]

Attention now turned again to the challenge of breaking the Siegfried Line. During the closing stages of the German counter-offensive, 21st Army Group had in ten days of hard fighting consolidated its position on the River Roer (an eastern tributary of the Maas).[194] Having done this, Montgomery planned two convergent operations. The first, Operation 'Veritable', required 470,000 British and Canadian troops, under the command of First Canadian Army, to thrust south-east through and around the Reichswald Forest (see Map 15.5). The second, Operation 'Grenade', to be launched by the 300,000 troops of US Ninth Army (also under the command of 21st Army Group), was to head north-east across the Roer. The two armies would converge in a large pincer in the area of Wesel and ideally destroy all German forces west of the Rhine.[195]

'Veritable' launched on the morning of 8 February with a series of major air attacks and fire support involving over 1,200 guns. Refined tactics contributed greatly to ensuring that all initial objectives were seized by midnight on day one. These tactics included pepperpot bombardments that hinged on the 'number of guns firing into a given area for a sustained period of time' rather than the 'actual weight of shell', the use of armoured personnel carriers and Crocodile and Wasp flame-throwers.[196] Morale was also unquestionably high. The Canadian censors noted that the 'troops were eagerly awaiting action' while the British censors commented on 'distinctly hostile' references to the Germans in the mail.[197]

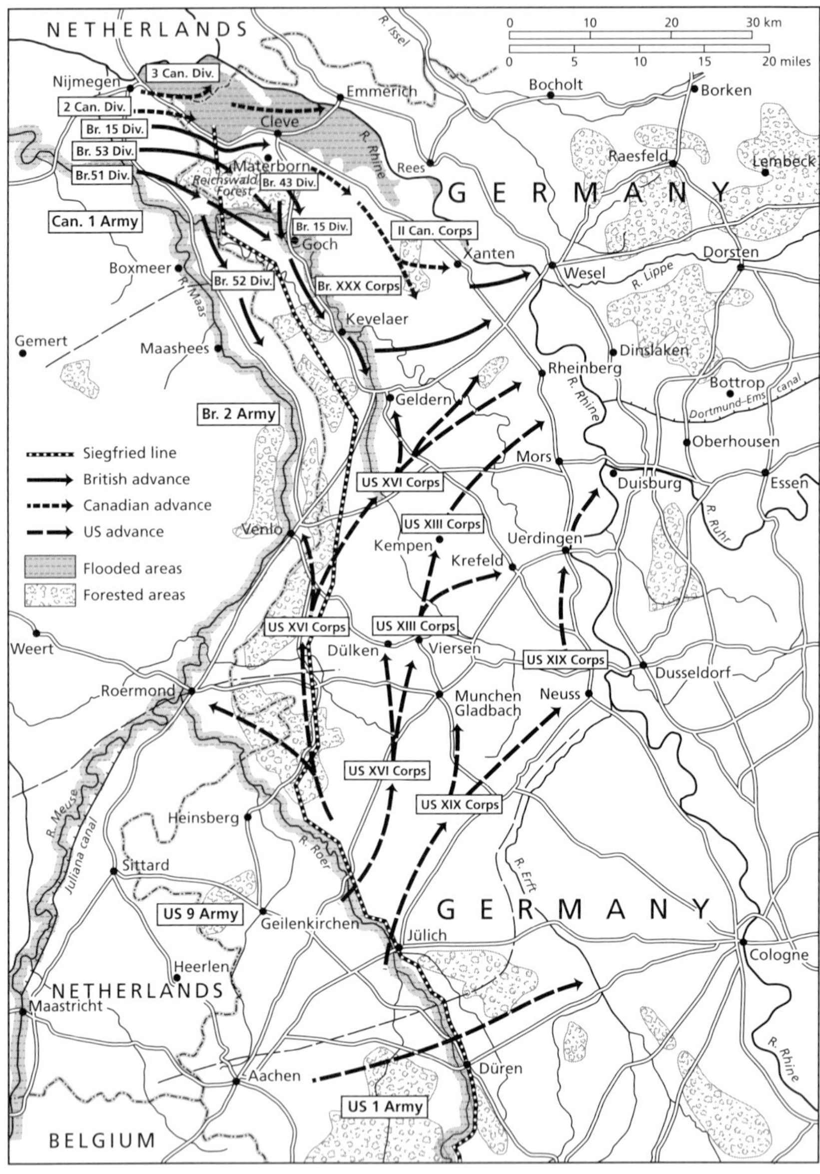

Map 15.5 Operation 'Veritable', 8 February–10 March 1945

Hundreds of prisoners were captured. A private in 7th Hampshires, 43rd Wessex Division, remarked that:

> The bombardment has been so bad that some of the Germans were still down in the cellars of the houses and we had to go

> down and get them out. They were very frightened and shook like a leaf in a wind. They must have thought we were going to shoot them, either that or our shelling had broken their nerves. It was the same in other villages we took.[198]

A gunner in the Canadian Army wrote on 9 February that 'it's so one sided it's almost pathetic'.[199]

Nevertheless, the soldiers of the German 84th Infantry Division and 2nd Parachute Regiment, no more than 13,000 men supported by a single battalion of self-propelled assault guns, refused to crack.[200] With the Rhine to the north and the Meuse to the south, First Canadian Army was forced into a funnel 10 miles wide at the start line near Groesbeek and 30 miles wide between Wesel and Venlo, the objective. The already cramped area of advance was reduced further by the German decision to flood the polder lands on the west bank of the Rhine, placing a third of the available manoeuvre space under water. Most of the towns and villages in the area had been turned into strongpoints, organised into three defensive belts. To make matters worse, the 'large and elevated' Reichswald forest 'sat squarely in the centre' of the battlefield.[201]

All this might have been overcome if the weather had held, but it did not. Horrocks' XXX Corps had been assigned the key role of advancing through the Reichswald Forest. He had identified the Materborn gap, between Cleve and the forest, as the vital ground for the battle and hoped to storm it before the Germans could push up reserves. XXX Corps would then break out into the plain beyond, which was better suited to the use of tanks. As the ground began to thaw in early February, 'it did not take a military genius to imagine that Veritable would look more like Passchendaele than it would any battle from the current war', and Horrocks reverted to a more 'conservative plan to blast his way through the enemy defences to Materborn using as much firepower as possible'.[202]

Not for the first time, such an approach did not produce the hoped-for results. By 10 February, the offensive had lost momentum as the early thaw resulted in endless mud and traffic jams (as heavy vehicles could not travel cross country). Matters were made worse by the German decision to open the floodgates of the Roer dams, thus flooding the Roer Valley and delaying the launch of Operation 'Grenade'. With 'little happening' on the US Ninth Army front, the Germans were free to direct available reinforcements towards First Canadian Army. They now 'drained their reserves' to meet the Anglo-Canadian advance; by 16 February, three infantry divisions, four parachute divisions, one *panzergrenadier* division and one *panzer* division had been committed to the Anglo/Canadian front.[203]

'Veritable', much like 'Olive', descended into a costly slogging match.[204] But, whereas in previous sustained periods of prolonged and intensive fighting, such as at 'Goodwood' and on the drive towards Falaise, where morale had broken down, it now, just as had happened during the Scheldt battles, stayed high (see Figures 14.2 and 14.3). 'The spirit of the troops was evident in the frequently-quoted slogan: "Conquerors not liberators"'.[205] The censors were generous in their praise:

> The whole tone of the mail was expressive of prolonged spells of hard fighting. Opposition had been fierce and conditions at times made any advance almost impossible. Men spoke of being weary, but in the next breath assured their correspondents of their determination not to allow anything to stop them.[206]

The first of the newly arrived conscripts from Canada, in spite of all the difficulties and heartache that had been faced, 'acquitted themselves well' and were by all accounts 'good soldiers'. Altogether, as an officer in the Royal Hamilton Light Infantry (RHLI), 2nd Canadian Division, put it on 3 March, 'we find with great satisfaction that when the chips are down, man to man, the Canadian soldier is superior to the German paratrooper (Germany's best) – we have definitely proved it'.[207] Moreover, it seemed to some that 'the old Desert Army' was 'getting into its stride again'.[208] The company quartermaster sergeant (CQMS) of the 1st Gordons, 51st Highland Division, wrote, 'I salute these young lads . . . for they have done wonders which we of the old mob are glad to admit. Not one of your lads fell out or turned his back in what has been a gruelling test to experienced and inexperienced soldiers alike.'[209]

By 22 February, in spite of the slow progress, First Canadian Army had captured more than 11,000 German troops and killed or wounded an estimated 12,000. Operation 'Grenade' finally launched on 23 February, and by 3 March contact between the two Allied Armies had been made. There was no breakthrough but by 10 March organised German resistance on the west bank of the Rhine had ceased, a not inconsiderable achievement considering the strength of the 'Siegfried Line' and the nature of the terrain. Anglo-Canadian casualties had amounted to 15,500. German losses were hard to estimate, but prisoners were coming in so fast that it was, as one man put it, 'really a problem to know how to deal with them'.[210]

'Veritable' had been 'a killing match; slow, deadly and predictable'. According to one Canadian, 'the worst we have had yet'.[211] It was the 'last great attritional battle' fought by 21st Army Group in the Second World War,[212] for although 'the German Army in the West was still capable of brave resistance by [an] individual battalion or division', its 'cohesion had largely gone'.[213] Moreover, the Anglo-Canadian Armies in the West were fast becoming as professional, capable and ruthless as was required to decisively overcome their German counterparts.

Operational and Tactical Transformations

The Scheldt battles, 'Veritable' and 'Olive' demonstrated that by the winter of 1944/1945 21st Army Group and Eighth Army were capable of cracking some of the most formidable defensive positions to be faced in the Second World War. Morale was high; the efforts made, both on the home front (in some cases) and the battlefront (more generally), had returned a certain robustness and zeal to the armies of the Empire. This renewed willingness to fight was complemented by the great quantities of material now available. High morale and considerable material advantages over the enemy were not, however, the only factors driving the improvement in the performance of the British and Commonwealth Armies in the West. These armies increasingly began to employ sophisticated and highly adaptive operational and tactical techniques; the British and Commonwealth Armies were clearly in the midst of a significant doctrinal transformation.

At the operational level, Montgomery was central to this change. As a consequence of his experience in Normandy and during 'Market Garden', he had deliberately sought to finish what he set out to do before D-Day, to re-emphasise the importance of initiative and a devolved system of command and control in battle. In two important doctrinal publications, 'Some Notes on the Conduct of War and The Infantry Division in Battle' (November 1944) and 'The Armoured Division in Battle' (December 1944), Montgomery, to a considerable extent, demanded a return to the basic tenets of interwar *Field Service Regulations* (*FSR*).[214] He determined that his armies had to move away from the 'rigid command arrangements', predefined roles and approaches that had characterised 'Colossal Cracks'; for much of the Normandy fighting, this approach had constrained commanders in battle and limited the effectiveness of his armies.[215]

Matters were no different under Alexander and Leese in Italy. Senior commanders, while recognising Eighth Army's proficiency in the break-in battle, 'bemoaned' its inability to rapidly exploit opportunities. It was generally believed that 'slow decision making in effecting the transition from break-in to break-through operations', and a 'lack of enterprise and flexibility' among higher commanders 'less accustomed to more fluid fighting' were at fault.[216]

The solution, according to Montgomery, was to ensure 'ubiquity', a term 'in contemporary usage ... to describe the "infinite variety of tasks" which infantry could undertake'. He wished to apply the concept to all units, believing that what was required was 'formations capable of ubiquitous use, equipped and trained accordingly'. This would facilitate 'flexibility when planning the battle ... It would also increase speed of action' and hopefully improve outcomes. In other words, Montgomery adopted a 'problem-solving approach—in response to his and other commanders' experience of fighting in Normandy and through the Low Countries—in which he emphasised the importance of context'. From now on, there would 'always' be 'scope for individual initiative' to suit the occasion.[217]

In Italy, a similar shift in doctrine took place, although it was not codified and disseminated at an army level as in North-West Europe. Reflective and self-critical senior officers 'actively attempted to learn from other Allied formations, notably the French Corps following ... DIADEM, and also from each other'. As a result, a command 'culture' developed which strongly resembled that of 21st Army Group. In the rapid advance following 'Diadem', 'deliberate operations' were replaced with a 'more flexible approach'. Subordinate commanders were no longer required to stop and await new orders on reaching their objectives. Instead, they were instructed to merely notify their superiors and get on with the job, thus providing them with 'considerably more opportunity to develop operations according to the tactical situation, rather than the dictates of senior HQs'.[218]

'Reliance upon the skill and temperament of the officers involved ... to judge each tactical situation on its own right' increasingly became the norm. Gradually the balance began to shift between the firepower-heavy approach of advancing behind a barrage and a method that relied on individual initiative. By the second half of 1944, it increasingly became the norm in Italy that only when small-scale actions failed would brigade or division commanders intervene to 'lay on more rigorously prepared and heavily supported attacks, forcing decision with greater numbers, firepower, or a combination of both'.[219]

The 'increasing latitude' afforded officers 'to seek and prosecute battlefield opportunities within the bounds of their available means and superior's intent' was transformative. As Patrick Rose has argued:

> It is not overstatement to suggest that by mid-1944, the British Eighth Army in Italy had coherently adopted a particular expression of mission command from brigade to army level, and its senior officers understood through experience how to apply it effectively on the battlefield.[220]

To conduct these 'new-type operations' successfully, it was recognised, even before Normandy, that revised tactical as well as operational doctrine was needed. In March 1944, the long-awaited Infantry Training Manual was released. This document was to guide the training of formations for the rest of the war and was, in many ways, the equivalent of the 'Jungle Soldier's Handbook' and the 'Jungle Book' for the British and Commonwealth Armies in the West. 'On a modern battlefield', it stated:

> The close formations of past wars cannot survive; dispersion is therefore essential. Dispersion means that small sub-units and even individuals will have to decide on the action they must take to carry out the general intention of their commander. This situation calls for initiative, intelligence, and military knowledge on the part of every private soldier.[221]

'Infantry Training' was designed to 'reconcile' battle school teaching, which, to many had become rigid with its over-emphasis on battle drill, with the requirement for creativity and flexibility, so evident from commanders' own experiences of the war.[222] As the introduction to the section on 'Fieldcraft, Battle Drill, Section and Platoon Tactics' emphasised, 'if the situation changes, each sub-unit or individual out of immediate touch with his commander must make the plan most likely to fulfil the commander's expressed intention'. Individuals quite simply had to act on their 'own initiative'.[223]

Whereas the 'Instructor's Handbook' had seen battle drill as the catch-all solution for tactical problems (see Chapter 13), 'Infantry Training' 1944, emphasised three methods of preparing the soldier for war: battle discipline, incorporating realistic training exercises and a more flexible set of battle drills; battle inoculation, to inure the soldier to the sounds of modern war; and 'measures to support morale', for soldiers had to be given a cause to fight for if they were to 'act intelligently and bravely without waiting to be told what to do in an unusual situation'.[224] The British and Commonwealth Armies' new tactical doctrine encapsulated the key lessons of the war; there could be no set solution to the infinitely complex challenges faced in modern warfare. Initiative and imagination were required in equal measure and these qualities could only be expected of soldiers who were personally invested in the meaning of the war.

To complement these doctrinal advancements, new divisional structures were also introduced. In North-West Europe, Montgomery formalised the lessons of infantry/armour co-operation that were learned in Normandy; he got rid of the distinction between tank brigades, that were designed for close infantry support, and armoured brigades, that were designed for 'fast-moving exploitation after a breakthrough'. A 'new unified role' was introduced that would require all armour to be 'capable of tactical infantry co-operation and exploitation'.[225] In Italy, a 'mixed infantry division' was developed, 'incorporating an armoured regiment in permanent support' of each division. 'The typical arrangement this encouraged was for one tank squadron to support one infantry battalion in the conduct of offensive operations.'[226]

The impact of all these developments would be hard to overstate. They marked a 'great change' away from the 'set piece-advance' characteristic of 'Colossal Cracks'. 'This had been Montgomery's own, previous approach until tactical problems became apparent in Italy and then in Normandy.' The significance of the battles in the Scheldt, and on the 'Gothic' and 'Siegfried' lines, was 'that they were the "laboratory"' for the wider adoption of the 'spirit' of these reforms, the reintroduction of fluidity to operations. The 21st Army Group and Eighth Army increasingly 'allowed a degree of latitude to individual commanders' and encouraged devolved problem solving as the best way of 'getting to the overall aim, which was the relentless imposition on the Germans of mobile war, using armoured and other units to overwhelm an increasingly less mobile enemy'.[227] Thus, what Montgomery, and others, wanted to do was to 'introduce an understanding not of how to fight but of how to think', so that commanders 'could decide how to fight'. This, in turn, required subordinate commanders to exercise their initiative and to be proactive in battle – to execute 'mission command'.[228] The British and Commonwealth Armies in Europe had completed a full circle. Whereas conditions had not been right in 1940 to facilitate a devolved system of command and control, by the spring of 1945 they certainly were.

Victory in Italy

As 'Veritable' reached its climax, the Allied Armies in the Mediterranean prepared one last push to finish off the campaign in Italy. 'Olive' had cost Eighth Army significant casualties and more men were not available to replace these losses.[229] To make matters worse, Eighth Army was deprived of a number of its best divisions for the forthcoming campaigning season; after the shock of the Ardennes, I Canadian Corps (two divisions) as well as 5th Division were transferred from the Mediterranean to strengthen Eisenhower's armies on the march into Germany. As Brooke put it in a letter to Alexander, 'we must concentrate on one main effort, and that main effort must be on the vital front'. Operation 'Goldflake', the movement by sea of 110,000 men, 28,800 vehicles and 1,200 tanks to North-West Europe (a force the same size as the original assault on Normandy), was planned in no less than twelve days; it represented a stunning administrative achievement. The German withdrawal from Greece, meanwhile, sparked a Communist uprising in its wake and the threat of civil war; a further two British divisions were sent from Italy to stabilise the situation while a settlement was negotiated.[230]

There was flux also at the top of the command chain. On 29 September, Leese, whose performance had been decidedly subpar during Operation 'Olive', was sent to the Far East. The commander of X Corps, General Richard McCreery, replaced him at Eighth Army. On the death in November of Field-Marshal John Dill, Chief of the British Joint Staff Mission in Washington, Wilson, the Supreme Commander at Allied Forces HQ in the Mediterranean, was sent to the United States in his stead. That December, Alexander was promoted to field-marshal and appointed in Wilson's place. Clark, in turn, succeeded Alexander as commander of 15th Army Group.[231]

In light of the reduced means available to the Allies in Italy and the unsettled command arrangements, the Combined Chiefs of Staff informed Alexander that his armies were to do little more than contain the Germans and prevent their withdrawal to other battlefronts. 'It was a stark acknowledgement that the Italian campaign had been relegated' to a strategic backwater.[232] Nevertheless, Alexander considered that the best way to contain the Germans in Italy was to engage them in another significant offensive as soon as the weather and supply situation permitted.[233]

Alexander's approach was undoubtedly correct, for, in spite of the advantages of the terrain (the Apennines still presented a fearsome barrier and the Adriatic flank comprised a succession of river crossings and the 20-mile-long Lake Comacchio), the German situation was at this stage, by any standard, dire.[234] Their forces in Italy, organised under Army Group C, comprised 439,000 men, whilst the Allies had 1,677,000 (a 3.8:1 advantage). Tenth and Fourteenth Armies could muster 200 tanks against some 3,000 available to 15th Army Group (a 15:1 advantage for the Allies). The 15th Army Group had a 2:1 superiority in medium guns and a 5:1 superiority in heavies.[235] With the Allied bomber force in Italy no longer required for 'strategic' operations over Germany, as the Red Army had overrun its targets, the Allies were now able to deploy 4,000 aircraft against a 'barely perceptible' *Luftwaffe*.[236]

The German logistic situation was particularly grim. Allied air interdiction along the Alpine border between Austria and Italy had reduced supply trains to an average of 2.3 per day, 'half the number needed' to keep Army Group C equipped. Those that got through were 'plagued' by partisan attacks, 'all of which transformed the German supply situation into a nightmare of logistical improvisation'. By the end of February, German ammunition and fuel stocks in Italy were sufficient for no more than fourteen days of fighting.[237] By comparison, by March 1945, Eighth Army had 1,020 guns supplied with 2 million rounds of ammunition.[238] American Fifth Army had accumulated so many artillery shells 'that they were ordered to begin firing them off to make room for new shipments'.[239]

The plan for the new offensive, codenamed 'Grapeshot', required Eighth Army to attack once again on the Adriatic front, this time along the Via Adriatica, 'which ran through a narrow gap in the German-induced floods around the village of Argenta and thence to the River Po at Ferrara' (see Map 15.6). The Argenta Gap, as it became known, was only 2 miles wide and 8 miles deep and presented a considerable challenge if it was to be breached. The main assault was entrusted to V Corps under Lieutenant-General Charles Knightley. The 56th London Division was to cross Lake Comacchio using 200 amphibious 'Fantail' LVTs ('Buffaloes' were called 'Fantails' in Italy) and attack the enemy on the flank. The New Zealand and 8th Indian Divisions were to force the passage of the Rivers Senio and Santerno. Once a bridgehead over the Santerno had been established, 78th Division would cross, wheel right, and make for the bridge over the River Reno at Bastia. If all went well at Argenta, it would then join with 56th London Division and clear the Argenta corridor. If the crossing of Lake Comacchio did not succeed, V Corps would continue its advance north-west towards Budrio, just to the north of Bologna. Eighth Army, therefore, had developed a flexible plan reminiscent of the approach to the opening phase of 'Olive'; it had two options it could pursue depending on the outcome of the first days of the battle.[240]

To prepare for the coming operation, McCreery's forces undertook an intensive period of training over the winter and spring.[241] New tactics were developed to take advantage of the new weapons available. These came in two broad categories, 'engineer assault equipment for crossing obstacles under fire, and tracked troop carriers, either armoured to enable infantry to cross open ground more safely under fire, or amphibious for river crossings'. The armoured personnel carriers, nicknamed 'Kangaroos', had first been used in Operation 'Totalize' in Normandy. Now McCreery decided to employ them in Italy. He directed his Royal Electrical and Mechanical Engineers (REME) workshops to modify 75 Sherman and 102 Priests into 'Kangaroos', thus providing armoured transportation for four infantry battalions.[242] Methods for air/land co-operation were also refined through experiments, special courses and exchange visits between the Army and RAF. Air controllers were given Sherman tanks and half-tracks to ensure that they could keep up once the battle became mobile; new 'Night Marker' flare shells 'were tried out and found satisfactory'; fresh techniques for oblique

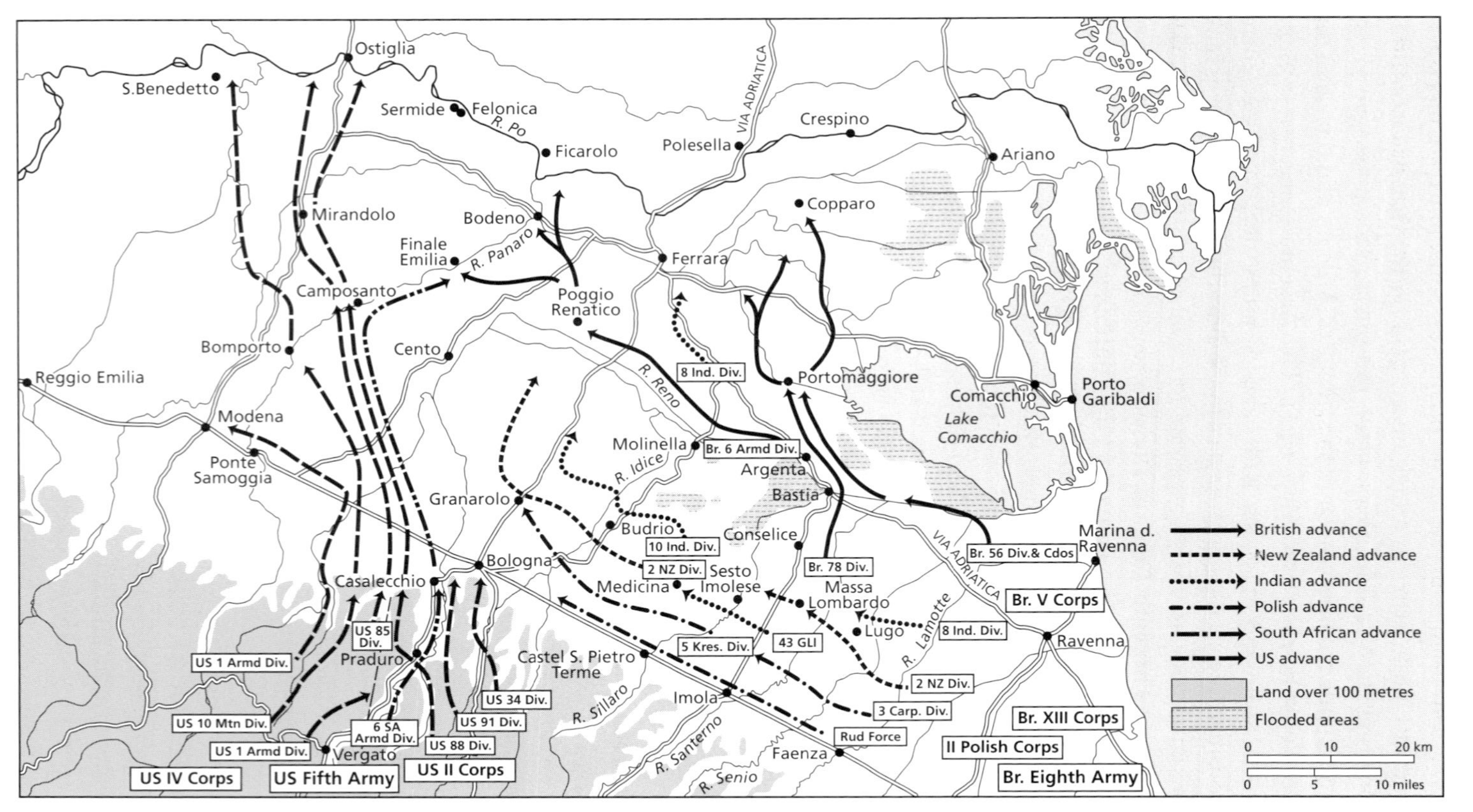

Map 15.6 Operation 'Grapeshot', April 1945

photography were developed to help the artillery; and 'Pineapple' operations were introduced 'whereby fighter-bombers accompanied tactical reconnaissance aircraft for the immediate engagement of targets discovered during the reconnaissance'.[243]

To make matters even better, by April 1945, the manpower position in Italy 'showed a marked improvement over the dark days of October 1944'. The lull in operations over the winter months had reduced battle casualties to a 'relative trickle'. Many of those wounded in the battles along the 'Gothic Line' had recovered sufficiently to return to their units. Moreover, the 'full fruits' of the conversion and retraining programme to provide more infantry, initiated during the previous summer, 'were also being garnered'. Infantry battalions were allowed to re-establish a fourth company and hold forty men over-strength 'to cover local leave'.[244]

Morale could not have been much better. According to the censors, in British and New Zealand formations, optimism was 'high', not least due to 'the fact that final victory in Europe [wa]s now regarded as being imminent'. 'Many writers' in 'fighting units' in 6th South African Armoured Division, which was part of US Fifth Army, 'were keen to "get in and finish the job"'. So 'great' was the spirit in Indian units that some men expressed 'their eagerness to serve in the Far East' once Germany had been defeated. A Rajput other rank (OR) wrote, 'I am a born soldier and like a true soldier I shall not hanker after my release from the Army till victory is achieved.'[245]

Everything appeared to be in place. The Germans, however, had demonstrated on more than one occasion their extraordinary competence at holding river lines even against the most overwhelming of odds. They too had used the winter lull to build up their forces; their defences were organised in considerable depth, and, according to Eighth Army intelligence, they were still full of fight in spite of the overall strategic situation. 'Stocks of ammunition were judged adequate for three or four weeks full scale defensive fighting on both Army fronts [British and American]; and fuel was adequate for short moves, but not for switching reserves once they had been committed'. It was clear that Eighth Army would have to perform at its best to dig them out.[246]

V Corps' plan aimed to make maximum use of the firepower available. First, strategic bombers would drop 175,000 fragmentation bombs over the German gun areas. Then some 200 bombers would strike these targets. Next, 500 fighter bombers would attack five separate times, alternating with five forty-minute artillery bombardments. After the final artillery concentration the aircraft would come in for the last time, but without attacking, to ensure that the defenders stayed deep in their dugouts while the infantry crossed no-man's land, an advance that would be supported by no less than 1,000 pieces of field artillery.[247] Once the attackers reached the Senio, German positions would be burnt out by making use of some of the new engineer assault equipment, ninety carrier- and tank-borne flamethrowers; the infantry would then follow the creeping barrage to the next river line (the River Santerno) and exploit as opportunities presented themselves.[248]

On 9 April, the offensive opened. The massive application of fire and manoeuvre shattered the German defences. By 12 April, V Corps were not only across the Senio but had bridgeheads across the next waterway, the River Santerno. The crossing of Lake Comacchio in the amphibious 'Fantails' achieved 'complete surprise' and by 17 April, 56th London Division, now supported by 78th Division, had reached and breached the bottleneck at Argenta. The 6th Armoured Division was passed through and finally Eighth Army achieved not just a break-in, but had exploited effectively to achieve the long-awaited breakout.[249] The morale of the fighting troops soared to 'probably' the highest level 'it ha[d] ever been'. The men's 'letters show[ed] a great fighting spirit, esprit de corps, and, latterly, the exhilaration of the chase. As one officer put it "it's grand to have the whip out".'[250]

On 14 April, having been delayed for two days due to bad flying weather, US Fifth Army joined the battle.[251] They punched a hole in the centre of the German line and cut the highway between Bologna and Modena. As the assault gathered pace it formed the left-hand side of a giant encirclement. By 23 April, 6th South African Armoured Division had driven as far as the River Po. There, it joined together with 6th Armoured Division of Eighth Army. With bridges downed by air attack and ferries destroyed, the German army capitulated. On 2 May, after 602 days of bitter fighting in Italy, Army Group C formally surrendered to the Allies, the first of the German battlefronts to do so.[252]

The censors reported that 'a wave of jubilation and pride' swept across Eighth Army, particularly among those troops 'who had been actively engaged in the last spectacular drive to the north'. 'Now what about the D Day Dodgers?', was the 'delighted question triumphantly asked' in the men's mail. 'It was clearly felt', according to the censors, 'to be a particularly satisfying climax to the campaign that, after their long absence from the headlines, CMF should have "stolen the limelight from BLA [British Liberation Army], and pipped them to the post!"'[253]

The Surrender of Germany

Even before the launch of the final offensive in Italy, Montgomery had pondered his next move in the war in North-West Europe. His first challenge was the great natural obstacle of the River Rhine. He took the best part of two weeks to plan and train his men for 21st Army Group's final set-piece battle of the war: Operation 'Plunder', the crossing of the Rhine, and its supporting airborne assault, Operation 'Varsity'.[254] In spite of the long, hard struggle to crack the 'Siegfried Line', 'there was a remarkable absence of war weariness' in the men's letters as they approached their next great task. Correspondence 'written on the eve of the assault stated that troops were "all keyed up" and ready for the "Big Do"'.[255]

In many ways, it was astonishing that morale was so good. The problem that had beset the British and Commonwealth Armies throughout the war, the apparent lack of connection between the soldier and the state, was still weighing heavily on the men's minds. 'Troops were worried at the thought of the post-war period, particularly with regards to employment and housing.'[256] The announcement of the Government's plans for post-war gratuities did not improve matters. The 'great majority' of writers found the proposed amounts 'insufficient', particularly when compared 'with the amounts to be paid by Canada'. A Guardsman wrote:

> I only get £87 when I come out of the Army after 5 years service – that includes everything, nest eggs money, gratuity and 2 month's leave pay. It's not good enough, is it? The Canadians get £1,000 each – It makes me wonder what we are fighting for.

A number of writers also 'expressed dissent at the difference between the gratuities to be paid to officers and to other ranks'.[257]

The men, as they had been throughout the war, were 'greatly exercised at reports of strikes in the U.K.'.[258] Whereas in 1939, 1.36 million workdays had been lost to strikes, by 1944, that figure had risen to 3.71 million.[259] A lance corporal in 43rd Wessex Division wrote:

> I've been interested to read of yet another strike ... Leith ... and especially their reasons for it which they classify under the heading 'extra pay for doing a dirty job'. I'm thinking of starting a strike here too, also under that heading, because if anyone can tell me of a dirtier, filthier job than I am doing I'd like to know what it is. Hell! I get so mad when I read of those Swine – those quislings – behaving that way. I can become grafted with filth and mud for 8 bob a day, yet they can't soil their hands for a quid a day??? And why – WHY? – in God's name are such things *allowed* to happen. Are Trade Unions bigger than laws and Government??[260]

A warrant officer in 11th Armoured Division wrote, 'could they but see these horrors, and experience the constant whistle of shells bombs or bullet perhaps then they would forget their selfishness and greed'; while a sergeant in Guards Armoured Division remarked, '98% of the fighting men out here say the same thing about strikers – they should all be treated as 5th Columnists'.[261]

Nevertheless, the British Army had by now effectively insulated itself from these problems on the home front. It had become sufficiently professional in its training, tactics, logistics, leadership and administration that it could manage regardless.[262] Through army education, it preached a vision of the post-war world as yet formally unsupported by Westminster. Improved training processes and procedures and doctrine, along with the bitter experience of battle, had taught the Army to see itself as one team, commanders and men, working together with the Air Force and Artillery. In the run-up to the crossing of the Rhine, 'there was much evidence', according to the censors, of the ever increasing 'confidence existing between ground and air forces'. 'Some writers went so far as to say that a "fortnight's really good flying weather c[ould] shorten this war by months".'[263] A lance corporal in the 2nd King's Royal Rifle Corps, 11th Armoured Division, declared that 'the Rhine shouldn't prove too difficult for us to breach. We should have enough stuff out here by now to literally eat it. We certainly give big cheers for the artillery boys who make things tons easier for us.'[264] Montgomery's presence was widely appreciated. 'Twice this week', wrote a private in the 1st Glasgow Highlanders, 52nd Lowland Division, 'I've seen Field Marshal Montgomery. Something that helps the boys a lot when we see our leaders coming among us.'[265]

By the time the attack finally began on the night of 23 March, the citizen army that had started the war so tentatively against the Germans in 1940 had fully transformed into a confident and professional martial tool. From 15 March, the entire Rhine front was enveloped in artificial fog produced by portable generators using a mixture of oil and water heated in massive boilers. The assembled array of men and machinery was truly impressive; there were 1.25 million troops (250,000 of them in the combat arms), 32,000 vehicles, including nearly 700 tanks, 30,000 tons of bridging material, 60,000 tons of ammunition and 28,000 tons of other supplies. The 21st Army Group's assault across the Rhine was launched under the covering fire of 3,500 field, medium and heavy guns and was supported on the first day by 7,700 sorties by the Allied air forces.[266] Opposite stood 100,000 troops of widely varying quality under General Alfred Schlemm's First Parachute Army, with the XLVII Panzer Corps, under General Freiherr von Lüttwitz, in support further to the rear. The defenders on the east bank of the Rhine had little in terms of air and armoured support (about 100 aircraft and 92 tanks), but 'large quantities of heavy artillery' were available, amounting to approximately 800 field and heavy anti-aircraft pieces. All told, the Germans were facing a force that was numerically about 'ten times their strength'.[267]

The 51st Highland Division, of XXX Corps, was the first to cross the Rhine (in the Rees sector) mounted in 150 'Buffalo' LVTs. Further south, 15th Scottish Division and 1st Commando Brigade, of XII Corps, also mounted in 'Buffaloes' and stormboats, crossed the Rhine north of Wesel, while the US Ninth Army (under the command of 21st Army Group) attacked to the south of the town. About 1000hrs, these forces were joined by 40,000 troops of 6th Airborne and US 17th Airborne divisions, of the US XVIII Airborne Corps (General Matthew Ridgway). Their mission was to capture bridges of strategic importance, create havoc and join up with the ground forces. By the early afternoon of 24 March, 15th Scottish Division had joined up with 6th Airborne; the US 17th Airborne Division and the Commandos had also made contact. By the end of the day, Twenty-First Army Group had gained a 'firm footing' on the east bank of the Rhine (see Map 15.7).[268]

The battles in the Rhine bridgehead were as difficult as any in the North-West Europe campaign; the defenders 'had had ample time to prepare strongpoints and plan a defence-in-depth'. But, much like

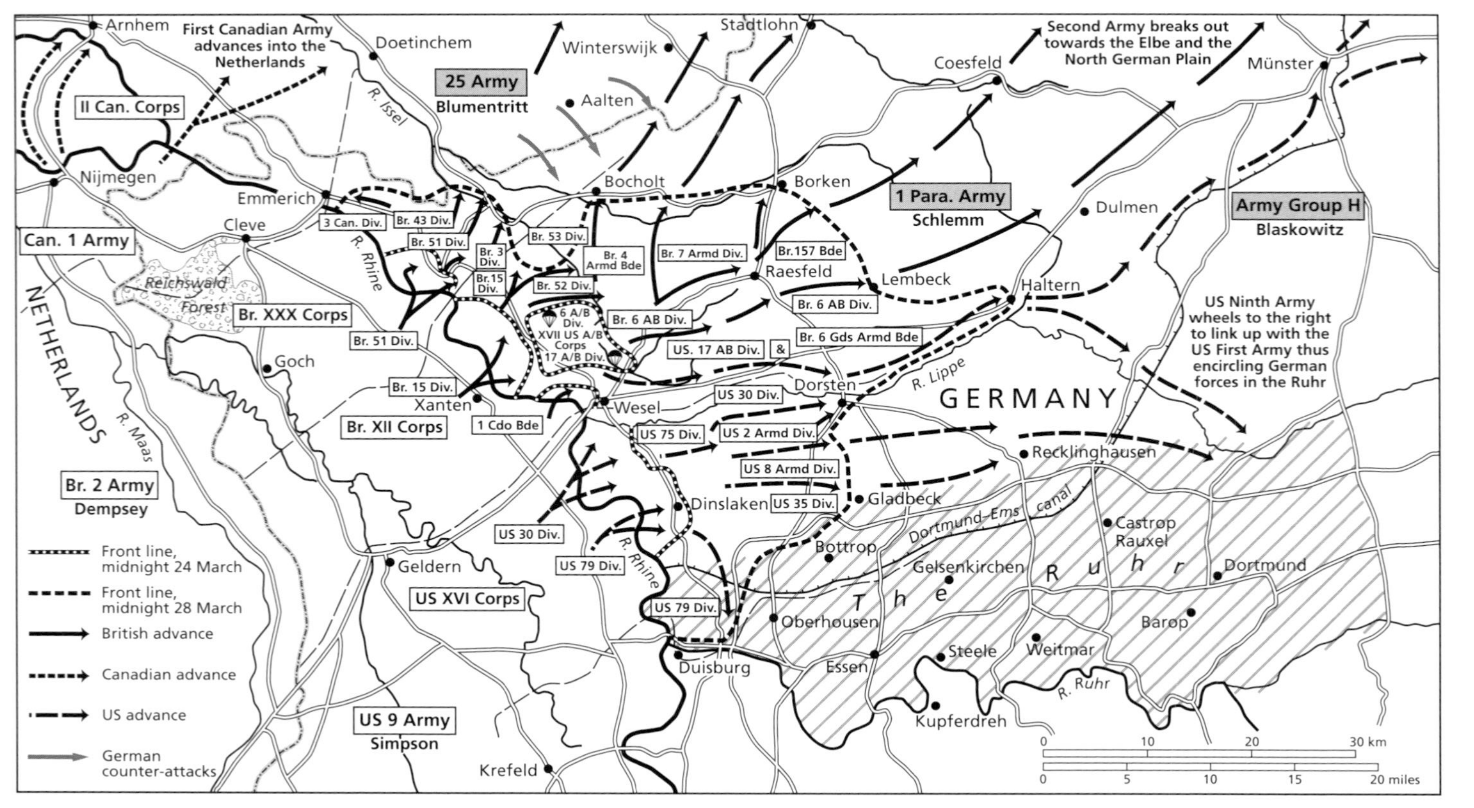

Map 15.7 The crossing of the Rhine, March 1945

'Grapeshot', the massive application of fire and manoeuvre shattered the German defences.[269] Second Army and US Ninth Army captured and expanded the bridgehead at the cost of 3,968 and 2,813 casualties respectively; during the same period, Second Army captured 11,161 prisoners, a cost of only 0.36 casualties per POW.[270] The assault, in many ways, could not have gone much better. According to the censors, 'the ... crossing was referred to as "magnificent", and examples were given by writers from all arms of the service showing how they had worked as one in this operation. Mutual support within "Monty's team" was in itself an inspiration to the troops.'[271] The Advisor in Psychiatry for 21st Army Group marvelled at the high morale of the troops and the low rate of battle exhaustion cases.[272] Even the weather, which was beautiful, seemed to indicate the final turning point of the war.[273]

Five days after the initial assault, Montgomery's armies finally broke through the German lines. An officer in HQ 46th Infantry Brigade, 15th Scottish Division, wrote:

> The crack German tps whom we had been pounding for 4 days without a break, today surrendered without firing a shot. They had had enough. They were more tired than we were. I went forward and talked with some of our chaps – their morale is superb – and they all tell me that they are ready to go to Berlin when I am.[274]

Second Army now rushed towards the River Elbe and First Canadian Army advanced into the Netherlands. To the south, US Ninth Army linked up with US First Army, surrounding and destroying the German forces in the Ruhr.[275] 'Great stress' was laid on the need to go 'flat out' and 21st Army Group delivered. By bypassing strong points and by bold thrusts it ensured that there would be no way back for the *Wehrmacht* this time.[276] Horrocks remarked that his experienced commanders were able to act with flexibility and switch their troops rapidly, 'attacking with tanks only, tanks and infantry, or infantry supported by tanks according to the situation' (see Illustration 15.1).[277]

As German opposition disintegrated, for many the horrors of the war only intensified. On 11 April, the advance guard, 11th Armoured Division, stumbled on the concentration camp at Belsen. There, the implications of the Nazi worldview became evident to British soldiers as they set eyes on 60,000 inmates suffering from disease, malnutrition and appalling

Illustration 15.1 Infantry of 5th Division, supported by Churchill tanks of 6th Guards Tank Brigade, clear a pocket of resistance south of Lübeck in Germany, 2 May 1945. The British Army's new tactical doctrine, 'Infantry Training' (March 1944), recognised that there could be no set solution to the infinitely complex challenges faced in modern warfare. Initiative and imagination were required in equal measure and these qualities could only be expected of soldiers who were personally invested in the meaning of the war.

mistreatment. Some 10,000 corpses lay about the camp and in open pits.[278] The censors captured the men's reaction to these incomparable crimes. They noted that 'the horrors of German concentration camps … hardened' the 'resolve to repay the enemy for the evils he had inflicted on the peoples of Europe'. Although many 'had formerly doubted stories of atrocities', they 'were now convinced of their truth, and of the need to eradicate the system which had perpetrated them'.[279] A corporal in 15th Scottish Infantry Division wrote, 'I shall never forget what I saw in that place as long as I live.' 'One of the most horrible things of all', according to a lance bombardier in the 249/63 Anti-Tank Regiment:

> was the thousands of dead stacked in a neat pile like anyone might stack logs of wood. All these stacked bodies were completely in the nude and what's more were stacked in between huts where people, including children were living. Seeing all these things have aroused something in us that had never been really aroused before, it was revenge, revenge to wipe out these S.S.... completely.[280]

By the second half of April, the problem of addressing the chaos into which Germany had fallen became almost as arduous as that of fighting the remnants of the *Wehrmacht*. Senior German police officers, especially if ardent Nazis, deserted their posts, undermining public order; public health officials did likewise, facilitating the spread of disease. Looting became widespread.[281] Displaced persons, ex-POWs and liberated 'slave' workers, particularly Russians, were 'roaming about the country, robbing farms and terrorising the local population'.[282] Crocker's I Corps was released from combat operations and tasked with maintaining lines of communication and reorganising civil affairs.[283]

On 16 April, Eisenhower ordered Montgomery to turn 21st Army Group north to prevent the Soviets beating the Allies to Denmark. Three days later it reached the Elbe, 200 miles from the River Rhine.[284] In some conquered cities, the scenes were truly post-apocalyptic:

> For two or three days towards the end of April 1945 Bremen was probably among the most debauched places on the face of God's earth: all sanctions broken down among those Germans who rioted in their shocking inability to accept the consequences of their own political stupidity.[285]

On 30 April, Hitler committed suicide and German troops began to surrender en masse. The spirit of fanaticism had finally died in the *Wehrmacht*. Montgomery estimated that 200,000 prisoners were taken on 2 May alone.[286]

The next day, German envoys arrived at Montgomery's HQ at Lüneburg Heath to negotiate the unconditional surrender of all German forces in Holland, North-West Germany and Denmark.[287] At 0800hrs on 5 May, almost exactly eleven months after the first units of 21st Army Group had stormed the shores of Normandy, the order to cease fire on all British and Commonwealth fronts was given.[288] The war in Europe was over. The achievement of victory was greeted by most British soldiers 'with relief and thankfulness rather than with exuberance'. The fact 'that the enemy had surrendered to 21 Army Group was referred to with great satisfaction' in the men's mail. 'It is the day that we have been fighting for and longing for and at last it has come', wrote a sergeant in 49th West Riding Division.[289] A soldier in the Calgary Highlanders, 2nd Canadian Division, noted, 'I need not say how happy I am today . . . we can go forward with a light heart once more.' 'Gosh it is a wonderful feeling', wrote a corporal in 21st Canadian Armoured Regiment, 'to know you can walk about without getting shot or shelled . . . Gee it is good to be alive.'[290] Victory, achieved at long last, was sweet indeed.

The South-West Pacific Area

As the British and Commonwealth Armies in the West learnt from their experiences, experimented, adapted and finally advanced to victory over Germany, the last year of the war proved far less rewarding and meaningful for the Australian Army.[291] In June 1943, MacArthur, the Allied Commander in the South-West Pacific Area (SWPA), had advised Curtin, the Australian Prime Minister, that 'the threat of invasion of Australia had been removed'.[292] The strategic context had turned decisively to the offensive, with the Philippines at the centre of MacArthur's considerations. The problem was that American power in the Pacific was now so great that Australian forces were no longer required to guarantee victory; it was the productive capacity of Australian industry and agriculture that was most needed to support the war effort.[293]

In the circumstances, Curtin was forced to adjudicate between the needs of industry and those of the fighting forces. At a War Cabinet meeting in October 1943, it was decided that 'by June 1944 20,000 men should be released from the armed services, 10,000 men should be released from munitions and aircraft industries and the monthly intake into the services should be fixed at 5000 men and women'. The following year, the Government insisted that a further 30,000 men from the Army be diverted to industry.[294] These cut backs, coupled with an allotment of only 4,000 male and 1,000 female recruits per month, made it impossible, as Blamey pointed out, to sustain the Army. A motor division and two armoured divisions were disbanded and the recruits sent to other formations. Only six infantry divisions and two armoured brigades would be available for the final operations of the war.[295]

Blamey railed against this diminution of the Australian contribution on the battlefront. By March 1944, it was abundantly clear that MacArthur, for personal and strategic reasons, had little intention of using Australian forces in the Philippines; Blamey argued that a new Commonwealth Army, a force of roughly 675,000 British, Australians and New Zealanders, based out of Darwin, needed to be created to retake Singapore. In April 1944, he travelled to London with Curtin to make his case. Brooke and the Chiefs of Staff were initially supportive of the idea, but, unsurprisingly, MacArthur was dead set against any dilution of his authority and influence in the SWPA. With MacArthur rallying American opposition to the proposal, Blamey's efforts came to nothing; London decided instead to focus on Burma and to send a fleet for attachment to the Central Pacific Area under Nimitz.[296]

This evolution in emphasis and strategy in the SWPA was by no means a disaster for Australia, but it was hardly devised with the continued mobilisation of the population in mind. It became increasingly difficult to convince Australians that 'shortages of consumer goods, degraded working conditions and intrusions on civil liberties were ... necessary'.[297] In 1942, 378,200 working days had been lost to strikes. By 1944, the figure was 912,800, rising again to 959,134 in the first nine months of 1945 (a 154 per cent increase).[298] From April 1943, manpower officials raided leisure facilities 'to catch absent workers and unregistered civilians'. In Queensland, the number of prosecutions rose eighteenfold, from 31 in 1943 to 567 in 1944. Authorities in New South Wales had collected £1,270 in fines for these offences up to the beginning of 1944; in the following twelve months, they collected twice that amount.[299] Fines imposed for the evasion of rationing rose in even greater proportions. Whereas the total amount of penalties imposed was £1,243 in 1943, by 1945 it was £7,909 (a 536 per cent increase).[300] 'By 1945, the Australian public's willingness to submit to the requirements of total war had worn thin.'[301]

Not to be undermined by this behaviour on the home front, and the subsidiary role set out for the Australian Army by MacArthur, the men still in action against the Japanese set themselves to face the difficult tasks ahead. In October 1944, as the Americans turned their attention to the Philippines, Australian forces relieved US formations in New Guinea, New Britain and Bougainville. Their goal, as articulated by Blamey, was: to destroy the enemy where it could be done with 'relatively light casualties'; to free the Australian mandated territories from enemy occupation, thus liberating the native population; and to create the conditions where it would be possible to 'progressively reduce' the Army's commitments and free personnel for the home front.[302]

In these endeavours, the Australian Army largely succeeded. In spite of the fact that Australian forces were starved of much-needed resources due to the prioritisation of those forces engaged in, or earmarked for, the Philippines, they killed or tied down not inconsiderable numbers of still relatively highly motivated Japanese forces. By the end of the war, for the cost of 4,030 casualties, the Australians had destroyed the 35,000-strong Japanese Eighteenth Army on New Guinea and tied down an estimated 93,000 Japanese on New Britain and a further 40,000 on Bougainville.[303]

While operations in the mandated territories continued, I Australian Corps, made up of 7th and 9th Divisions, remained without a firm objective, as it waited in the Atherton Tablelands acting as MacArthur's uncommitted theatre reserve. In the summer of 1945, MacArthur finally decided to make use of this wasting asset, when in operations of extremely questionable strategic value, he ordered that the Australians should be used to liberate Borneo. The 26th Brigade of 9th Australian Division, a force of 11,000 troops, landed at Tarakan on 1 May and for the cost of 894 casualties destroyed a garrison of 2,400 Japanese. Just over a month later, on 10 June, the other two brigades of the division, a force of 29,000 troops, attacked again, this time at Brunei Bay, and for the cost of 335 casualties killed almost 3,000 Japanese and local auxiliaries. Then, on 1 July, in 'the last Allied amphibious landing of the Second World War, and the largest ever under Australian command', 7th Australian Division, made up of 33,000 men, took Balikpapan at a cost of 863 casualties, killing a further 2,032 Japanese.[304]

I Australian Corps maintained its professionalism throughout these trying operations. By now, the quality of training and doctrine in the Australian Army, much as was the case with the British and Commonwealth Armies in Europe, had reached its 'zenith' and the quantity of material available for those operations supported by the Americans was overwhelming. On the day of the landing at Balikpapan, the 6,000 Japanese defenders facing 7th Australian Division were hit by no less than 3,000 tons of bombs, 7,361 rockets, 38,052 3- to 8-inch shells, and 14,000 rounds of automatic fire (delivered from five cruisers, eleven destroyers and planes from the Australian First Tactical Air Force and from the US Thirteenth and Fifth Air Forces). During the ten days after the landing, the division itself fired 41,800 rounds of 25-pounder ammunition.[305]

Not least due to these factors, morale among fighting units remained mostly 'good'.[306] There is no doubt, however, that it was hard for the troops to find great meaning in these operations of low strategic value. It was clear to the men that they had been sidelined in the war effort, a fact that they blamed roundly on the Australian Government and the apathy of the home front. An officer wrote:

> In my view Australia, by her actions and political policy, dating back to the complete withdrawal of all troops from the Middle East, has lost for all time any right which she once might have had for a voice in world affairs. She has demonstrated quite clearly that all she wants to do is cultivate her own cabbage patch, grumble like Hell when the world does not think as she does, and look for any necessary assistance to keep her shores safe from the nearest big neighbour – and then grumble when the job is well done and a reasonable price asked. The part we are playing up here [New Britain] seems to be part of that price, and if we have been given the job of scavengers it is mostly due to the immense complacency of the average city Australian, who in general should be publicly peed on.[307]

One man in New Guinea blamed the maltreatment of native New Guineans in the later years of the war on the apathy of those at home in Australia:

> They weren't really exploited until the Army came and used them to make up for deficiencies that would not have occurred if coal miners and unionists had pulled their weight instead of striking ... Am engaged in some slave trading this trip. The Army ... have a nice name for it and they call it recruiting

> but it's really only slaving, as the recruits are just told they are going, not asked if they want to work . . . It's a damn shame that a Government that won't conscript its own people is allowed to conscript another race to the detriment of their home life and villages. We are all against it, but just have to carry out the orders.[308]

It seemed to the troops that they were another forgotten army and that newspapers and Australians more generally were not engaged with their day-to-day exertions and the continuous dangers they faced. A private in an anti-aircraft detachment wrote that 'every paper we see is filled with pages of the Duke [referring to the visit of the Duke and Duchess of Gloucester to Australia]. It seems strange to me that those crowds of Australians can cheer themselves hoarse over the Duke and such people as film stars, yet never cheer their own men who have been fighting for them for years. It seems to me that most of them do not know there is a war on.' A private in 19th Australian Infantry Battalion wrote 'it is not much good for our morale when instead of letting you people know what we are doing, all they put over is an occasional bit about Bougainville and then fill up the news with the Duke and Duchess'.[309]

The decision by the Government to award civilians a day off to celebrate VE day in May was especially resented. '*We* can't just take days off', wrote one man, 'what the lads would have appreciated was to be put on equal terms with the civilians'. 'Generous people these Australians', wrote another:

> wave a few flags when you are leaving, then don't know you exist the next day. I can imagine all the people in Sydney shouting and shaking hands with each other, drinking beer and having a great time, a great victory for them no doubt, but I bet 75% of them don't even know what they are really celebrating. I would like some of them up here for a while.[310]

The multitude of small but significant ways in which the troops felt let down were an indication to them of the home front's apparent disregard for their sacrifices. The censorship summary for December 1944 indicated that Australian Imperial Force (AIF) troops in New Guinea and Australia were 'discontented' and exhibiting 'low morale'. Among the reasons for this low morale was the fact that the men were 'resentful' that their Christmas dinner had to be 'purchased from unit funds or individual contributions':

> I suppose you have seen or will see in the paper what the troops are going to have for Xmas dinner. Ham, turkey and all the good things that go to make a good Xmas dinner, but you don't see in the papers that the men will have these things if they pay for them out of their own pockets, which is very unfair ... if that is the way they do it I am ashamed to admit that I am Australian. The Americans will have the best but they will not pay for it out of their own pockets.[311]

'Hell I get sick of the way our Government and the Army runs things', wrote one man.[312] Many felt it was markedly unfair that due to manpower problems they had not had leave for eighteen to twenty-four months.[313] Additionally, poor mail services were clearly 'having an adverse effect on morale ... particularly with front line t[roo]ps'.[314] Payment by soldiers for conveyance in Army vehicles met with adverse criticism. This apparently had been a 'regular feature' for soldiers on leave; they were charged a halfpenny per mile.[315] Thus, when the Acting Minister for the Army, Senator Frazer, visited the men in April 1945, he received 'quite a few home truths' and 'many unflattering references' in the soldiers' mail:

> They told him that the reason for the fresh beef was his visit. Clothes fit for a bagman. For every five pairs of trousers made; another pair could be made out of the surplus ... Some of the boys took their belts off and the trousers fell right to the ankles.[316]

In circumstances where the basic welfare of the troops was not being managed effectively, the men became convinced that things would be no better after the war. While 'a generally favourable reception was given by troops to the proposed War Gratuity for service personnel', there was 'much criticism of the scale of payments'.[317] Others felt that the Government's rehabilitation plans were too vague and feared that a 'large proportion of us will end up without work and probably on the dole ... it's just talk, talk, talk'.[318] A decision in June 1945 to grant men with five years' service discharge from the Army was greeted with scepticism by the troops.[319]

The consequences of these many hardships and disillusionment was that as the war wore on, the spirit of selfish individualism on the home front seeped into the Army. It was not unusual in the final years of the war for one in every sixty men in the Army to be AWOL.[320] In some units 'dissatisfaction with officers was freely expressed' and troops felt bitter at the comforts 'enjoyed by officers as compared with ORs'. The censors reported that 'statements on these lines' were 'more frequent than heretofore' and were 'not confined to isolated cases'.[321] Complaints were also 'numerous from most areas' regarding 'black marketing' of commodities such as canteen tobacco, eggs and poultry.[322] Many concluded that 'a man is a mug to be in the Army and most of the boys can see it now'. The overriding opinion appeared to be, in spite of imminent victory in the Pacific, 'Never again.'[323]

Australia's sole goal in the last years of the war had been to find a way 'to guarantee a voice in the peace settlement'.[324] Broadly speaking, it achieved this end, but, in the absence of great victories on the battlefield, only as a second-rate power and at the price of the morale of the Army. An American rather than an Imperial peace would settle over the Pacific.

Burma

While the Australian Army was sidelined in the final year of the war, the Indian Army found itself right in the middle of the great battles that were to bring a swift end to the conflict in the Far East. As the Japanese Fifteenth Army, 'beaten, diseased, and starving', retreated from Imphal and Kohima in the late summer of 1944, Mountbatten presented the Chiefs of Staff in London with two options for continuing the war in South-East Asia. The first constituted an air and seaborne operation against Rangoon, codenamed 'Dracula'; the second, was an overland advance by Fourteenth Army, Operation 'Capital'. The Chiefs of Staff were, as they had always been, in favour of the first of these options – of manoeuvring the Japanese out of Burma, thus avoiding a costly and time-consuming advance across inhospitable terrain.[325] Churchill, ever ambitious, wished to concentrate even farther afield, on Singapore; 'here is the supreme British objective in the whole of the Indian and Far Eastern theatres', he declaimed: '*it is the only prize that will restore British prestige in this region*'.[326] Britain, however, 'in the absence of an end to the European war', simply did not have the resources to undertake the preferred amphibious strategies. To make matters worse, by the end of 1944 American interest in Burma had all but evaporated; the Ledo Road had been linked up to the old Burma Road, thus reopening the land route to Nationalist China. In these circumstances, and with fighting in Europe spilling over into 1945, resources for 'Dracula', it appeared, would not be available until after the 1945 monsoon.[327]

Bereft of other options, South-East Asia Command (SEAC) was left with the daunting challenge of another land campaign in Burma. Mountbatten and Slim did, however, have 'one immense asset' at their disposal: the reformed and retrained Fourteenth Army.[328] The victories of 1944 had been of tonic effect; 'at last the quantitative and qualitative superiority of British artillery, tanks and aircraft' had been 'exploited with deadly effect'. 'We have proved to our own satisfaction and to the discomfiture of the Jap', wrote Slim, 'that, man for man, the British, Indian and Gurkha soldier is more than a match for him.'[329] By August 1944, the morale reports for British troops in SEAC indicated that morale was at an all-time high. Having experienced victory at last, the troops now felt 'superior to the Japanese'. Allied victories in the West led the troops 'to the conclusion' that the war could not last 'many months longer' and the 'recent recognition' given by the British Press and Prime Minister to the Fourteenth Army began to dispel the long-held belief that the forces in Asia were a 'forgotten army'.[330] These sentiments were echoed in the mail of Indian and African troops. The morale report for the Army in India, August to October 1944, noted that:

> Those who have seen active operations in Burma ... have returned to India confident of their ability to defeat the enemy wherever they meet him and are eager to go into action again. Those who have yet to see action are encouraged by successes won by other units of their Corps or Regiments and are generally keen to have the opportunity to emulate them.[331]

The askari (soldiers) of the newly arrived 11th East African Division, which, along with 5th Indian Division, had pursued the retreating Japanese from Imphal and Kohima, was particularly 'high'. According to the writers of the morale reports:

> Letters from British ranks serving with the division show that they are very pleased with the way the askari is shaping in action ... The askari's own letters show a distinct contempt for the Japanese, and they describe their own activities with the panga [machete] with great gusto. They are as happy, they say, as 'fishes in the water'.[332]

These immediate improvements, for once, tended to 'overshadow outstanding grievances'. For the first time, complaints 'were not in the forefront' of soldiers' minds. Nevertheless, it was clear that those in command of the Indian Army could not rest on their laurels with regards to morale. It was still apparent that the average British OR did 'not like India or Burma and never will. Country, climate and people are alike repugnant to him.'[333] The situation was little different for the West African soldier, who, like his British counterpart, 'dislikes India' and 'desires more than anything else to get home to his family'.[334] As regards Indian soldiers, it remained evident that the sepoy's 'main interest' was not in the war, but 'in the welfare of his family and village'. 'The usefulness of his service in the army', continued another morale report, 'can in fact be said to depend on the extent to which he considers that his own personal problems are receiving attention.'[335] The men, as yet another report put it, were 'almost pathologically touchy about real or imagined slights'.[336]

In June 1944, even as Japanese troops began streaming away from Imphal and Kohima, SEAC started work on commissioning its own morale reports separate from the ones already produced by GHQ India. It was hoped that these reports would offer 'a true representation of fighting morale' and give SEAC 'more chance to instigate remediable action' where necessary.[337] Two months later, on 18 August, Adam wrote to Mountbatten, asking for a SEAC morale report to add to the information already collated in the quarterly morale reports produced by the War Office. 'As the emphasis of the war shifts from West to East', he said, 'no picture would be complete which did not include the troops under your command'.[338]

These innovations had an immediate impact. The first of Mountbatten's reports for Adam was accompanied by a long letter giving 'particulars' of the actions that had already been 'initiated to remedy the cause of most of the complaints mentioned in the Report'.[339] It was clear that, as a result of the renewed emphasis on morale, 'much greater interest' was 'being shown in the welfare of troops' and that these efforts had 'definitely' improved the situation.[340] The XV Indian Corps report for the month of October noted that 'films are up to date, concert parties are increasing in number and the supply of reading matter is good'. In general, canteen stocks had 'greatly improved'; 'with few exceptions' units appeared 'satisfied with the present range of commodities'; positive comments on the 'quality and quantity' of food 'now definitely outnumbered' negative ones, some men even indulging 'in the use of superlatives'.[341]

Two white papers, one on a special bonus for those engaged in the war in the Far East, and another outlining the plan for demobilisation also 'had an extremely good effect' on British troops. 'Much stress' was laid on the 'general fairness' of the demobilisation scheme and although it was 'widely felt' that 'Japanese Campaign Pay should be considerably back-dated', some were 'stunned by the amount of the increases which they consider generous'.[342] The compilers of the morale reports concluded that British 'morale has improved during the quarter in the sense that the soldier is now to some extent prepared to believe that officialdom does actually intend to help him'.[343]

Looking forward, serious problems remained; on the first page of the new morale report the compilers noted and 'feared' that all these efforts and actions might 'have come too late to repair the harm already done'.[344] 'There is probably a good deal of truth', wrote those in charge of distributing the morale reports, 'in the allegation made ... that the promised morale raisers have come too late to this theatre to remove the deeply rooted sense of injustice felt by British troops'.[345] Notwithstanding the appreciation shown of more recent efforts to improve the lot of the troops, it seemed that the British soldiers in SEAC were, to all intents and purposes, irreparably dissatisfied with their role in the war.

This would have been more problematic had not the size of the British contingent in Fourteenth Army diminished dramatically in the subsequent months. Whereas, by September 1944, the British had 714,135 men fighting in North-West Europe and 499,207 in the CMF (mainly in Italy), there were only 242,584 men in India and South-East Asia Commands.[346] By the summer of 1944, British infantry battalions in Fourteenth Army, just like in Europe, were short of men, some 3,500 in June, rising to 10,000 by October. Most battalions were now operating 18 per cent under establishment. Some of this 'was due' to a War Office decision in September 'to shorten the period of overseas service that qualified for repatriation from five years to three years and eight months'.[347] Although this much-longed-for change in policy had an undoubted 'encouraging effect on the BOR's morale', the 'speeding-up of repatriation' left many units 'woefully short of NCOs and other seasoned campaigners'.[348] For example, the 2nd King's Own Scottish Borderers lost 59 NCOs and 205 ORs to repatriations.[349] The two British divisions in theatre, 2nd and 36th Divisions (one composed of two brigades instead of the normal three), were now 'wasting assets'. In the 1944–5 campaign, 'they would be gradually phased out and returned to India, and British battalions in Indian divisions would be swapped out as well for Indian units'. By May 1945, British personnel would make up only 13 per cent of the whole of Fourteenth Army.[350]

It was fortunate, therefore, that the rebuilt, retrained and rejuvenated Indian formations in Fourteenth Army were in such fine fettle by the end of 1944. Although welfare amenities were never as generously provided for Indian troops as they were for British contingents, the most important matters relevant to morale were addressed in a manner unparalleled for British troops. The 'reopening of leave on a larger scale' in the summer and 'the distinct improvement in economic conditions in the villages' were of profound importance. Leave, as the morale reports noted, 'is for the IOR [Indian Other Ranks] the greatest of all morale-raisers' and there had been 'very large numbers of IORs in Fourteenth Army who had had no leave for more than 18 months – or even for more than 2 years'. The imposition of rationing and government controls on the Indian home front also 'in general improved matters for the soldier's family. On balance there is a very definite preponderance of the view that, despite certain abuses, rationing has been successful and that food conditions have improved.' This was particularly evident in southern India, but food was 'now cheaper and more plentiful in the Punjab' also.[351]

Welfare conditions for West and East African troops, that other key source of manpower for the Indian Army in late 1944/early 1945, were also sufficiently good to maintain high levels of morale.[352] Although West Africans were acutely aware that no repatriation scheme, war service increment or campaign pay had yet been put in place for them (they would be in due course), they were pleased with improvements to the mail service, local leave and entertainments more generally. The same could be said, broadly speaking, for the East African troops in theatre, who, the morale report for November 1944 to January 1945 noted, showed 'splendid fighting spirit'.[353]

In addition to this uplift in morale in the key fighting formations of Fourteenth Army, the materiel available in SEAC also improved. After a slow start at the beginning of the war, large quantities of supplies were now arriving in theatre, not least due to India's inclusion in the American Lend-Lease programme.[354] Whereas only 7,500 military vehicles had been delivered to India in 1939, by 1942, with British and American factories fully on line, 35,000 arrived, increasing again to 115,000 in 1943. In September 1943, India had 1,042 2-pounder anti-tank guns, by April the following year, the number had increased to 2,149. In early 1943, it was agreed that India would receive 125,000 tons of stores every month, a figure that was broadly adhered to thereafter. All these improvements led to a far better provisioned and equipped Army. By mid-1944, for example, Indian light divisions had three artillery regiments apiece, where they had only one before.[355]

Local production also grew; the overall output of military supplies and equipment produced in Indian ordnance factories increased by over 700 per cent between March 1940 and March 1944.[356] A vast effort was made to develop the basic infrastructure in India; improvements to road and rail made moving men and equipment far easier. By the spring of 1944, 200 airfields were in full use and with 126 Dakotas available, air transport capacity was 'more than four times that which had been available one year previously'. After the success of the air operations at Imphal and Kohima, the American Chiefs of Staff agreed to increase the number of Dakotas available to Fourteenth Army yet again, to 350 by January 1945.[357]

As well as improvements in morale and supplies, the fighting in the Arakan and at Imphal and Kohima 'had shown the soundness of the various minor tactics and fighting methods' laid down in the Indian Army's new doctrinal 'bible', the 'Jungle Book'. Brigadier William Crowther of 89th Indian Infantry Brigade commented that:

> Recent ops have shown beyond all doubt that the least expensive, and often the quickest method of capturing a Jap posn [position] is to get astride the L of C [Lines of Communication] leading to it. This invariably caused the Jap to do the attacking,

> incurring heavy cas[ualties], and in most instances also forced him to abandon arms and equipment.[358]

The new emphasis on individual skills, jungle craft, manoeuvre and surprise was complemented by, and, in fact, only 'made possible' by the 'dramatic improvements' in morale and tactical training that had occurred since the disastrous defeat in the Arakan in the first half of 1943.[359] In many respects, and in spite of the disillusionment of some British troops, Fourteenth Army was in a good state to strike a decisive blow in Burma.

Operations 'Capital' and 'Extended Capital'

Slim set about planning his final offensive fully cognisant of this dramatic change in the character of his army. He admitted:

> A year ago I would not have looked at the proposal [for a major offensive]. Even now it was not so much our advantage in the air, in armour, in greater mobility in the open, which gave me confidence to go on with my plan, but in the spirit of my troops, my trust in their experienced commanders and in the high fighting value and hardihood of them all.[360]

His plan required the XXXIII and IV Indian Corps of Fourteenth Army to cross the River Chindwin and advance across the open terrain of central Burma towards Mandalay on the Irrawaddy River. This area of 'stony desert-like sun-baked plain, dotted with patches of jungle and paddy fields' and crossed by dry river courses and roads 'was very different from where all fighting had taken place since 1942'. It offered Fourteenth Army an opportunity to 'fully exploit the superior armour, mobility and firepower' of its tank, artillery and air support.[361] At the same time, XV Indian Corps, made up of 25th Indian Division, 81st West African Division, which had fought in Second Arakan, and the more recently arrived 82nd West African Division, would launch a third Arakan campaign. They would be joined by 26th Indian Division, reinforced by 3rd Commando Brigade, who were tasked with an amphibious assault on Akyab Island to provide airfields to support the main effort in central Burma.[362]

All told, by the end of 1944, 17 divisions and 1,200 British and American aircraft were available to SEAC. This was by no means an overwhelming numerical advantage; the path to victory in Burma was still blocked by no less than three Japanese Armies (Fifteenth, Twenty-Eighth and Thirty-Third), grouping eleven divisions in all. The Japanese also had access to Bose's Indian National Army (INA) and seven battalions of Major-General Aung San's Burma National Army (BNA). The Japanese Air Force was thought to have 150 fighters available and could increase that number to 300 by redeploying aircraft from elsewhere in theatre. Slim, in spite of his growing confidence in his troops, had genuine concerns that the numbers available might prove insufficient for the job ahead;[363] his Army, as Raymond Callahan has argued, was, in marked contrast to the British and Commonwealth formations in Europe, 'smaller than the Japanese force he proposed to disrupt and destroy' in the Mandalay area (see Map 15.8).[364]

In this context, he set his forces to improve and adapt their organisations, techniques and procedures in the limited time available before the launch of his great offensive. It was evident that once Fourteenth Army 'left the jungle-covered hills and debouched into the plains of central Burma' a different style of warfare would be called for. General Sir George Giffard, who was soon to be replaced by Leese as C-in-C of Eleventh Army Group (which became Allied Land Forces South East-Asia in November), outlined the nature of the challenge facing Fourteenth Army:

> It must be borne in mind that the troops at present operating have been trained primarily for fighting in the jungle. Will they be capable of applying their tactical knowledge to the plains, where cover will be scanty? They have been taught to become jungle minded and to use the jungle as a friend, but when they reach the open they may feel a horrid nakedness.[365]

To address these issues, 'training with tanks was carried out during the autumn to ensure intimate infantry-tank co-operation, involving lectures, demonstrations and exercises covering infantry and tank attacks on enemy positions'. In an effort to facilitate effective air/land co-operation, the HQs of Fourteenth Army and 221 Group RAF were integrated. At the start of October, senior commanders including Major-General Frank Messervy, the commander of IV Indian Corps, attended Exercise 'Wasp' to 'study how an Indian standard infantry division pursuing a withdrawing Japanese force, attacking defensive

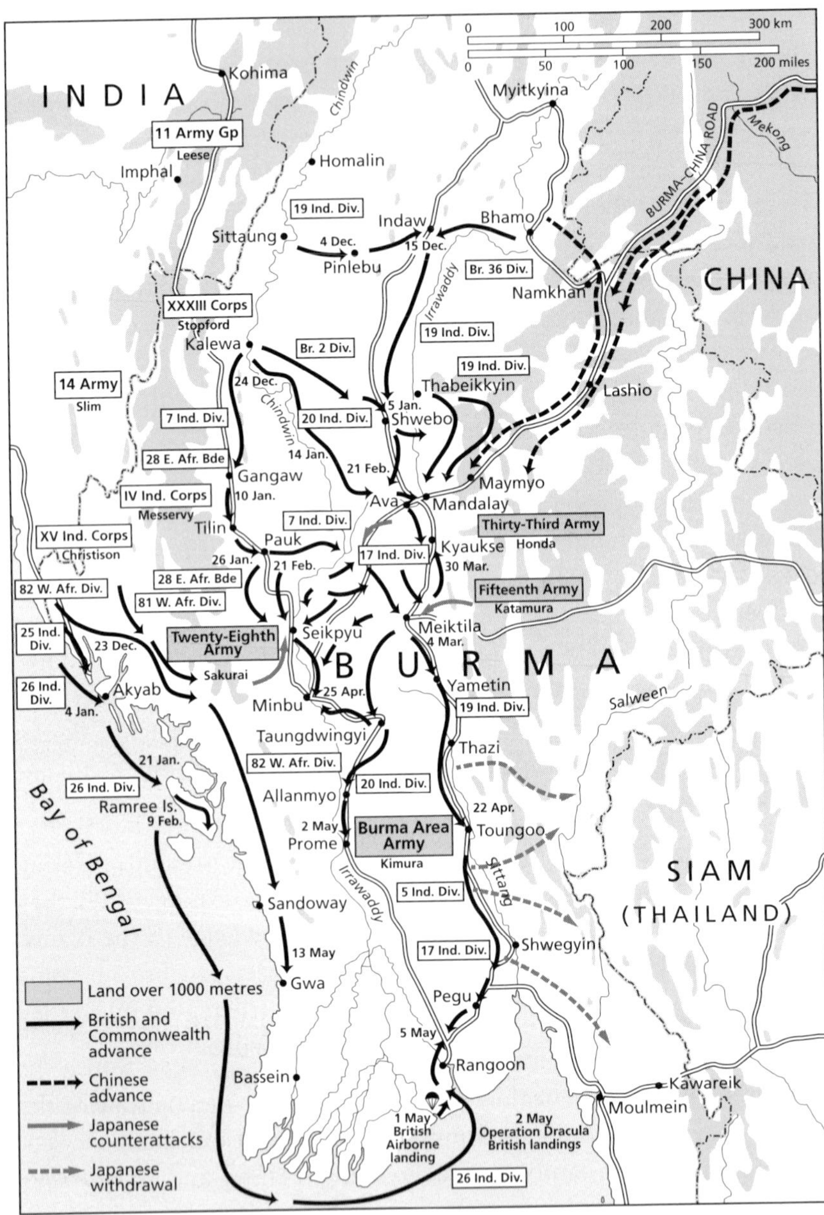

Map 15.8 Operations 'Capital' and 'Extended Capital', December 1944–May 1945

positions, protecting a road line of communications and lastly operating in open terrain should be handled'.[366]

The 5th and 17th Indian Divisions were re-motorised for the expected return of mobile warfare, while 26th Indian Division undertook specialist training in combined (amphibious) operations.[367] More generally, the infantry was able to 'fall back upon' its training in open warfare, which had formed the 'bedrock of instruction to all units' before specialised jungle training had taken place after the 'Infantry Committee' reforms. In any case, the key skills of jungle warfare – patrolling, the use of 'boxes' and infiltration – could be adapted effectively to open terrain. 'To a large degree the lesser was contained in the greater. The high standard of individual training insisted upon for the arguably far more difficult jungle fighting had of course relevance to conventional operations.'[368]

The essential soundness of British interwar doctrinal thinking now became more evident. 'The emphasis placed on the applicability of the principles of war (as laid down in FSR) to all forms of conflict' helped units to 'adjust tactical and training methods to more open terrain.' As 17th Indian Division Training Instruction No. 16, 23 January 1945, put it:

> The principles are the same always, in any type of country and on any org[anisation]. We have adapted them to fighting in enclosed country and our technique has stood the test. We must now adapt them to more open country. Battle drills, f[or]m[atio]ns and f[iel]dcraft generally must be perfected for ground where jungle will not afford concealment, but instead every use must be made of every little bump in the ground. Infiltration and hooks at all levels must still form an important part of our tactics.[369]

Major-General D. T. 'Punch' Cowan, the commander of 17th Indian Division, wrote to the officers in his division, 'I look personally to all com[man]d[er]s to see that not one minute is wasted, given even the short time we have we must, and will, leave here confident in our ability to move and fight on our new t[rans]p[or]t organisation.' He was not to be disappointed; by 31 January, after 'several training exercises in its new establishment', his division was ready to go.[370]

Operation 'Capital', Slim's new offensive, got off to a fine start.[371] By early December, in spite of the monsoon, Lieutenant-General Stopford's XXXIII Corps, comprised initially of 5th Indian and 11th East African Divisions, and then the 20th Indian and 2nd British Divisions, had secured a bridgehead on the eastern bank of the Chindwin. As the advance continued, it became increasingly clear that the Japanese were not going to fight west of the Irrawaddy but were going 'to pull back behind the river, facing Slim with the problem of an opposed river crossing' at a location where the waterway was between 800 and 2,000 yards wide with fast-flowing currents in many places.[372]

Slim quickly recast his plan and issued new orders on 18 December. XXXIII Corps, now reinforced by 19th Indian Division, would 'simulate the main advance' by closing up to the Irrawaddy and putting bridgeheads across the river near Mandalay. Meanwhile, the second of his main offensive formations, IV Corps, comprised of 28th Independent East African Brigade, 7th and 17th Indian Divisions and 255th Indian Tank Brigade, screened by a complex of deception measures, would approach the river far to the south of Mandalay. There, they would launch a surprise crossing, and then strike for the communications centre of Meiktila – the key advanced administrative base for the Japanese Fifteenth and Thirty-third armies in northern Burma and an important road and rail junction through which the Japanese lines of communication passed.[373] The loss of the town would have 'disastrous' implications for Burma Area Army, as, with Meiktila in Commonwealth hands, 'the entire Japanese position in central Burma would be unhinged'.[374]

Slim's new scheme, 'Extended Capital', was 'an operational design as audacious as the German Ardennes offensive of May 1940'. It was almost certainly 'the boldest British plan of the war'.[375] By the end of January, Slim was ready to spring his trap. With 19th Indian Division of XXXIII Corps already across the Irrawaddy to the north of Mandalay, Stopford made a second crossing, with 20th Indian Division, just south of the town on 12 February. The Japanese, believing both Commonwealth corps to be involved, began to reinforce the Mandalay area. The next day, 7th Indian Division of IV Indian Corps stormed across the 2,000-yard wide Irrawaddy far to the south, annihilating the INA division guarding the eastern shore. A week later, Messervy launched Cowan's motorised 17th Indian Division and 255th Indian Tank Brigade on a headlong drive for Meiktila. By 27 February, they were on the outskirts of the town, 'and the Japanese command had become as unhinged as had the French in 1940'.[376]

The battle of annihilation unfolding on the central Burma plain now threatened to become undone as matters outside of Slim's control impinged on the operations of Fourteenth Army. The Americans, who had always been lukewarm about British intentions in South-East Asia, threatened to divert some of Slim's transport aircraft and the Chinese divisions guarding his northern flank for a new offensive in mainland China. Regardless, Slim pushed his forces on, plunging deep into central Burma. He put his faith in Mountbatten's ability to find him aircraft somehow, believing that none of his superiors could afford to allow Fourteenth Army's advance to mire down now that victory was on the horizon.[377]

On 8 March, Mountbatten met Chiang Kai-shek to address the situation, but returned empty handed; 'the Generalissimo merely suggested that he stop his advance at Mandalay'. On the 27th, he wrote to the Combined Chiefs of Staff in Washington, with a similar result.[378] The 'increasingly serious administrative position' facing Fourteenth Army encouraged Slim to push Mountbatten for a reappraisal of the air and amphibious assault on the port of Rangoon (Operation 'Dracula'), the capture of which was now deemed vital to sustain the extended Commonwealth advance once the monsoon began.[379]

As Slim and Mountbatten grappled with the possibility that their great offensive might fall apart due to logistics, Churchill intervened. On 30 March, he wrote to the Chief of Staff of the US Army:

> As General Marshall will remember ... we greatly disliked the prospect of a large scale campaign in the jungles of Burma and I have always had other ideas myself. But the United States Chiefs of Staff attached the greatest importance to this campaign against the Japanese and especially to the opening of the Burma Road. We therefore threw ourselves into the campaign with the utmost vigour ... I feel therefore entitled to appeal to General Marshall's sense of what is fair and right between us ... to let Mountbatten have the comparatively small additional support which his air force requires to enable the decisive battle now raging in Burma to be won.[380]

The British and Commonwealth Armies were, to all intents and purposes, now reliant on American goodwill. But Slim did get to keep his transport aircraft and he secured the go ahead for 'Dracula' as well. The delays had, however, reduced his 'margins – temporal and administrative – almost to the vanishing point'. One more great push was required to destroy the Japanese Army in Burma and capture Rangoon before the monsoon set in.[381]

By 11 April, Slim was ready. XV Indian Corps had already, at the cost of 5,089 casualties, secured the airfields on Akyab Island, now vital to maintaining Fourteenth Army's renewed assault. With 300 miles to go and a one-month window before the monsoon was expected to begin, Slim figuratively threw caution to the winds. From now on, he would rely entirely on air transport to support the advance.[382] In the operation that ensued, 'tank–infantry spearheads drove over or around the disorganized but still furiously resisting Japanese; every 50 miles or so, engineers hacked out an airstrip. Then the Dakotas [aircraft] appeared, and the drive went on.'[383]

By 30 April, Cowan's 17th Indian Division, with the Sherman tanks of 255th Indian Tank Brigade in support, had reached Pegu, 50 miles from Rangoon. The IV Indian Corps, now reinforced by the motorised 5th Indian Division, had advanced 250 miles in nineteen days. Its morale was sky high; the sickness rate for the week ending 5 May was only 1.1 per thousand, while that of 17th Indian Division was even lower, at 0.5 per thousand.[384] On 2 May, the rains came early and 17th Indian Division's advance 'slowed to a crawl'. It did not matter, as Operation 'Dracula' had already been launched, and on the same day 26th Indian Division landed unopposed near Rangoon. On 3 May, Rangoon, which had already been abandoned by the Japanese, was officially 'liberated'. To all intents and purposes, for the Indian Army, the war against Japan was over.[385]

The Fourteenth Army, in what had become the largest land campaign fought by Japan outside China, and the longest campaign fought by the British and Commonwealth Armies in the war, had outmanoeuvred and outfought a much larger Japanese force than was ever encountered by the Americans in the Pacific.[386] By 1945, the Indian Army was a significantly different force from that which had begun the war. It was flexible, confident, highly motivated, innovative, increasingly culturally representative and highly trained. In more than one respect, it illustrated the extent of the transformation that had taken place in the British and Commonwealth Armies in the Second World War. In spite of ever-present tensions on the home front, Slim had turned an at times hopelessly ineffective citizen army into a competent professional one. He had truly turned 'defeat into victory'.

Part VI The Post-War World

16 SOLDIERS AND SOCIAL CHANGE

The story of the British and Commonwealth Armies in the Second World War is undoubtedly a compelling one; from the depths of defeat and despair, the armies of the Empire rose, as one historian has put it, like a 'phoenix from the ashes'.[1] The British and Commonwealth Armies demonstrated a remarkable ability to reform and adapt doctrine, training regimes and the management of manpower to the unexpected situations that unfolded between 1939 and 1945. Nevertheless, in spite of these many improvements, it was only in the last year of the conflict that the British and Commonwealth Armies began to consistently outwit, outmanoeuvre, outfight and ultimately annihilate German and Japanese forces on the battlefield. This dramatic, and at times, painful journey took longer than anyone had expected; too long perhaps.

It is hard now to believe that as the men prepared for the climactic 'Crusader' offensive in the desert in 1941, they genuinely thought that the war could be over by Christmas. The same hope persisted for those who fought in the final months of 1942, 1943 and 1944.[2] That these expectations did not materialise was to have profound implications for the place of Britain and the Empire in the post-war world. While Britain was clearly on the right side of the result in the Second World War, and the Army played its part in ensuring that this was the case, the post-war settlement was not defined, as it had largely been in 1918/19, by Britain and its empire. Instead, it was fixed by those powers that had played an even greater part in the military defeat of the Axis, the Soviet Union and the USA.[3] Britain may have started the war a first-rate power; it did not end it so. The British and Commonwealth story of the conflict, therefore, arguably requires considerable reconsideration. The meaning of the war rests not solely, or even perhaps dominantly, in martial achievement, but in how the war shaped politics, changed society and, most importantly, affected the people.

Many historians, social scientists and economists surveying the dramatic changes of the twentieth century engage with the conflict in this manner, as a catalyst for social and political change.[4] Thomas Piketty, for example, has concluded that:

> The history of the distribution of wealth has always been deeply political, and it cannot be reduced to purely economic mechanisms. In particular, the reduction of inequality that took place in most developed countries between 1910 and 1950 was above all a consequence of war and of policies adopted to cope with the shocks of war.[5]

In the *Lion and the Unicorn*, the novelist George Orwell noted that 'war is the greatest of all agents of change. It speeds up all processes, wipes out minor distinctions, brings reality to the surface. Above all it brings home to the individual that he is *not* altogether an individual.'[6]

There are a number of reasons why war can act as such a dynamic, and in some cases, radical force for change. It 'can bring into the open so much that is normally latent' and 'concentrate and magnify phenomena', thus highlighting where change is necessary.[7] Wars test citizens and states; the manner and extent to which states make demands on citizens and societies and extract resources, both material and psychological, 'provides a flare of light enabling ... [citizens] to see its features more clearly'.[8] The clarity that paradoxically can emerge from the chaos of war can, therefore, be instructive; the experience of common jeopardy can contribute to a greater knowledge of what is shared and important. Greater understanding and increased exposure to the state can transform attitudes and catalyse change.[9]

While such perspectives may be present in our understanding of the powerful effects of the war on the home front, the same cannot be said of our conception of the experience on the front line. There is still a widespread misapprehension that the Anglo-Saxon citizen armies of the Second World War were made up of apolitical and disengaged individuals, detached from the wider socio-political currents catalysed by the war. It has been argued, in relation to the Americans, that while some troops certainly engaged with the political underpinnings of the conflict, most did not; 'such ideas were extraneous to absorbing daily pursuits and consequently virtually disappeared from their thoughts'.[10] John Ellis has argued that:

> A few might be swept along by high-flown sentiments and volunteer for military service; even conscripts might balance the common good against their personal inconvenience. But once they had got to the front there was simply no place for such generalities. The world became reduced to a company or a troop and the only important thing in life was the chances of preserving one's own.[11]

As regards British and Commonwealth soldiers, it has been accepted that 'high politics', beliefs and ideals simply lacked significance for those at the front.[12] Historians have gone so far as to say that it is simply not realistic to argue that common soldiers 'develop the kind of political dedication that inspires willing sacrifice of life and limb, and that such dedication provides a firm and reliable basis for combat discipline'.[13] The apparent indifference of British and Commonwealth soldiers to a cause relates, it is argued, to Britain's liberal and democratic political culture, which, 'at its heart', is 'anti-ideological', thus tending 'to produce apathy towards politicians and causes'. The average British soldier had only three interests: 'football, beer and crumpet'.[14]

From Combat Cohesion to Social Cohesion

The evidence explored in this study indicates that these perspectives require reconsideration; the Second World War deeply affected the political persuasions of those who fought. The war made soldiers more aware of the limits of individualism and conscious of the degree to which they were dependent on their comrades and fellow citizens for prosperity, security and wellbeing. Almost every aspect of the soldiers' lives required co-operation, sharing and teamwork, the more so the closer to combat they came; extreme individualism or selfish behaviour was not only undesirable and inefficient but potentially life threatening. This experience, of front-line combat, changed and moulded opinions and profoundly influenced soldiers' broader attitudes about how society should be shaped in the post-war world.

The censorship summaries bear testimony to this transformation, especially with regards to how combat could build 'mutual trust, confidence and comradeship between all ranks'.[15] As a sergeant in 51st Highland Division wrote in March 1945:

> I have been fighting as an Infantry Platoon Commander and have formed a very strong band [*sic*] of friendship with my men. This partly due to the fact that as an infantry man I am close [*sic*] to my boys than any other officer in the other branches of the Army. We very often share a trench and even perhaps the same knife and fork or last mug of tea, all tending to make us a team instead of individuals.[16]

A gunner in the 232/67 Medium Regiment, Royal Artillery, wrote home, 'I only wish you could see for yourself the way the lads work up the line, you would think they were all brothers.'[17] 'One thing this war teaches us', wrote an officer in the 2nd Canadian Division, 'is the spirit of comradeship which in turn means that we share each others [*sic*] troubles, joys, and packages from home. That all goes to make a good Army and anyone so inclined soon loses any selfish instincts and is only too happy to share with the other.'[18] A soldier in 3rd Canadian Division wrote:

> By the way you wanted to know what my chums were like. Its [*sic*] this way. When I first joined the Boys they were nothing else but another bunch of soldiers with whom I have to contend with but after you hit several tough spots with them, go through a lot with them, they become more than mere soldiers, they are your other half upon whom your safety and integrity depends.[19]

'They share everything they have, even there [*sic*] money', wrote a soldier in the Argyle and Sutherland Highlanders of Canada, 4th Canadian Armoured Division. 'This is something which is not possible to explain. A person must see for himself.'[20]

It was quite clear, as one New Zealander put it in October 1943, that 'a stink' could 'do a lot to weld us together'.[21] 'I don't think there is a man in the Reg[imen]t who wouldn't risk his life to save another', wrote a private in the Calgary Highlanders in North-West Europe.[22] An Australian officer in New Guinea wrote:

> The boys have settled down wonderfully well and will do a good job when called on ... We had one or two visits from overhead. In the big one the boys took it well ... it was remarkable how an experience like that seemed to bring them closer together ... A dinkum action will do it to a greater degree.[23]

As a consequence of the experience of comradeship and cohesion on the front line, concepts of fairness and egalitarianism became deeply embedded in those who fought.[24] As an other rank (OR) wrote in May 1943, 'all we want is a fair deal'.[25] A report on 'The British soldier in Italy' noted that the average serviceman 'was a stickler for justice, in the full sense of the word, and the ruling principle that he required of his superiors was "fair shares".'[26] The troops railed against anything that smacked of privilege or 'the old school tie'.[27] Replacement officers arriving from New Zealand in 1943 had to revert to NCO rank upon arrival in the Middle East as it just wouldn't have been seen as fair for 'a chap with tons of desert service' to take orders from a 'rookie'.[28]

Those at the front were clearly confident that the very specific and extreme experience of 'fighting side by side' had changed opinions and would lead to 'closer co-operation' after the war.[29] 'We are all one big family', a Maori man wrote, 'with no such thing as tribal differences. Each individual works not for the good of his tribe or [Company] but for the good of the ... whole.'[30] The censorship summaries demonstrate that there was an overwhelming sense among the troops that gross inequalities and unfairness at home too had to be addressed, and it was the responsibility of the state (the Government) to do so.[31] Equality of sacrifice was much more than a catchphrase; the men believed that they had the right to expect others to do as much as them. After all, they were supposed to be fighting for free, democratic and egalitarian societies.[32]

These attitudes were reflected in the voting behaviours of the troops in the elections that took place during and immediately after the war; in Australia in 1940 and 1943, in South Africa and New Zealand in 1943 and in Canada and the United Kingdom in 1945; a referendum on state powers was held in Australia in 1944. In these national polls, those political parties that addressed issues important to the men (specifically fairness, social justice and the role of the state ('big government')) were generally more likely to receive the soldiers' support. For example, although information on voting in Britain is not published for any level/unit below that of the constituency,[33] 'there is no doubt' that the

Table 16.1 Percentages of party votes in the 1940 and 1943 Australian general elections and the 1944 referendum on state powers: the civilian and forces vote

Party	Civilian	Forces	Total
1940			
Australian Labor Party	40.1%	44.4%	40.1%
United Australia Party	30.3%	27.0%	30.3%
Country Party	13.5%	12.2%	13.5%
Rest	16.1%	16.5%	16.1%
1943			
Australian Labor Party	47.4%	52.8%	48.0%
United Australia Party	22.3%	18.7%	22.0%
Country Party	8.3%	7.7%	8.2%
Rest	21.9%	20.7%	21.8%
Referendum			
'For'	45.3%	52.8%	46.0%
'Against'	54.7%	47.2%	54.0%

Numbers have been rounded to one decimal place which may result in some columns not totalling 100 per cent.

military voted 'overwhelmingly for Labour' in 1945.[34] In Australia, the Labor Party won 44 per cent of the 15,997 valid forces votes in 1940 compared to 40 per cent of the civilian vote.[35] 'We must', Labor announced, 'substitute cooperation for competition and public service for private profit.'[36] Three years later, the party took 53 per cent of the soldiers' vote compared to 47 of civilians.[37] In 1944, in a referendum aimed at transferring considerable powers from the individual state legislatures to the Federal Government (i.e. in support of 'big government') Australian service personnel voted 53 per cent in favour, while only 45 per cent of civilians did the same.[38] (See Table 16.1.)[39]

Moreover, parties that espoused values such as fairness, social justice and a greater role for the state increased their share of the soldiers' vote the closer the soldiers were to combat. In New Zealand and Canada, where the number of votes for every candidate was recorded at every polling station in 1943 and 1945, it is possible to plot differences in voting behaviour not only between military and civilian voters, but between military voters in each theatre of operations.[40] In New Zealand, for example, Labour received 47 per cent of the civilian vote, 50 per cent of the vote of those military personnel training in New Zealand, 52 per cent of the vote of those that

Table 16.2 Percentages of party votes in the 1943 New Zealand general election: the civilian and forces vote

		Forces						
Party	Civilian	NZ	Canada	Pacific	ME	England	Total	Total
Labour	47.0%	49.9%	51.5%	54.4%	56.2%	61.6%	53.2%	47.6%
National	43.7%	37.5%	38.9%	33.5%	31.8%	30.5%	54.7%	42.8%
Dem Lab	4.0%	6.8%	4.5%	6.9%	6.8%	3.6%	6.7%	4.3%
Rest	5.3%	5.7%	5.2%	5.3%	5.2%	4.2%	5.4%	5.3%

The forces total includes 342 votes cast on the Chatham Islands and by the Mercantile Marine. NZ=New Zealand; ME=Middle East. England includes a limited number of New Zealanders stationed in Greenland, Iceland and Gibraltar.
Numbers have been rounded to one decimal place which may result in some columns not totalling 100 per cent.

had left New Zealand and were mostly training in the Air Force in Canada, 54 per cent of the vote from 3rd Division that had experienced minor operations in the Pacific and was undergoing training at Guadalcanal, 56 per cent of the vote from 2nd Division that was recovering from major operations in the desert and Tunisia and preparing for the next phase of the war in Italy, and 62 per cent of those serving in the UK, mostly Air Force personnel, who were 'almost continuously engaged' in highly hazardous bombing missions over the towns and factories of Europe (see Table 16.2).[41]

The pattern was little different in the 1945 Canadian federal election.[42] The Co-Operative Commonwealth Federation (CCF), the only popular socialist party in Canada, received 14 per cent of the civilian vote; 26 per cent of the vote of those military personnel training in Canada; 31 and 33 per cent of the vote of those that had left Canada and were mostly garrisoning isolated territories; 36 per cent of those serving in the UK, mostly Air Force personnel, who again had been engaged in hazardous bombing missions over the towns and factories of Europe; and 39 per cent of the vote of those who had been serving in the most dangerous part of the war effort for Canadians in 1944–5, with 21st Army Group as it advanced from France to the Low Countries and into Germany (see Table 16.3). 'Progressive' parties, including the Liberal Party, that appealed to the 'moderate left',[43] the CCF, and the Social Credit Party, received 58 per cent of the civilian vote, 68 per cent of the vote of those military personnel training in Canada, 73 and 75 per cent of the vote of those garrisoning isolated territories, 70 per cent of the vote of those in the UK and 71 per cent of the vote

Table 16.3 Percentages of party votes in the 1945 Canadian federal election: the civilian and forces vote

Party	Civilian	Forces						Total
		Canada	NF	Other	UK	NW Eur	Total	
Liberal	40.0%	38.7%	41.1%	40.1%	30.6%	29.0%	34.4%	39.7%
PC	27.8%	26.2%	21.6%	20.8%	26.2%	24.9%	25.5%	27.6%
CCF	14.4%	26.4%	30.6%	33.0%	36.4%	38.7%	32.0%	15.6%
SC	4.1%	3.2%	2.2%	2.0%	2.9%	3.4%	3.2%	4.0%
Rest	13.7%	5.6%	4.5%	4.0%	4.0%	4.1%	4.9%	13.1%

NF = Newfoundland; PC = Progressive Conservatives; CCF = Co-Operative Commonwealth Federation; SC = Social Credit.
Numbers have been rounded to one decimal place which may result in some columns not totalling 100 per cent.

of those serving in North-West Europe. A spirit of social cohesion had emerged from the exigencies of combat cohesion, which would have profound results for the future of Britain and the Commonwealth.

The Forces Vote and the 1945 British General Election

In Britain, the consequences of this social awakening were felt most powerfully and dramatically on 'The Road to 1945', Labour's great electoral victory at the end of the Second World War. This success laid the foundations for a political settlement that lasted a generation; accordingly, 'few topics in twentieth-century British history have attracted more attention'. Yet 'scholars remain deeply divided' about the meaning of 1945. Was it a truly radical mandate for sweeping change, or the product of a population disaffected with Conservative politics? Was it caused by the war, or the inevitable consequence of changes long in the making? Historians have argued that the sources to answer these questions are unfortunately 'patchy' and 'ambiguous' and open to a large degree of interpretation.[44]

The censorship summaries, however, show definitively that the war was a radicalising experience, at least for the British Army, a not inconsiderable portion of the male population of the United Kingdom of voting age (*c*.25 per cent). By late 1943, the military censors in the Mediterranean and India were reporting 'evidence of a swing towards the Left' in the attitudes of ordinary British soldiers.[45] 'Since joning the Army', a man in Italy wrote, 'my political views have been changed completely.

I am now as staunch Labour as you can imagine. I have had plenty of time and food for thought and I think I am quite correct in changing my views. I shall certainly be a supporter of Labour after the war.'[46]

The first morale report produced for the Army in India, in 1943, confirmed this trend. 'The main themes discussed amongst British troops', said the report:

> indicate that the soldier is intensely interested in Russia; that he hopes it is clearly understood that he is not fighting to restore the 'Status Quo' in conditions at home, especially as regards the apparent inequality of opportunity in education; and that he is critical of and antipathetic towards the existence of the old 'Vested Interests'.[47]

The quarterly report for the same period a year later, pointed clearly to 'a desire and belief' among some 'that there should be a considerable spread of socialism in the U.K. after the war',[48] while the morale report for February to April 1944 drew attention to 'the undoubted political trend towards some shade of red' among troops.[49]

Such sentiments were common in the mail of soldiers stationed in all parts of the global war. Censorship of the correspondence of Army and RAF personnel stationed in South Africa in June 1945 showed that a 'Labour vote seems to predominate'. One man wrote, 'I don't like Capitalism – think I'll vote Labour or Commonwealth [*sic*].'[50] Another censorship report produced in Durban noted after the results of the election in July 1945 that, 'throughout the war years "Left" views' had been 'very prominent' in the correspondence of British service personnel in the area.[51]

This upsurge in popular radicalism emerged as a direct consequence of the experience of shared danger and comradeship. Over time, the Beveridge Report, the Army Bureau of Current Affairs (ABCA) and left-leaning propaganda helped soldiers articulate the meaning of their experiences and directed them towards purposeful political action. As a report on 'Post-War Prospects' compiled from the censorship of British mail in India and South-East Asia Commands in 1944 put it, 'the Beveridge Report is the axis about which argument revolves. For those who look forward to social and political changes it is the yard stick by which the sincerity of the Government is estimated.'[52] Another censorship summary, from Italy in January 1944 put it similarly:

> Great interest appears to be taken in plans for an improved post-war era and the so-called return to civil life. In this respect it is of interest to note that the phrase 'a return to civil life' is often misleading; vast numbers of troops have had little or no experience of adult life under civilian conditions. Similarly, owing to the abnormal period that has elapsed since the last General Election, the larger part of the army – i.e. the great majority of those now under 30 years of age – have never voted. Perhaps as a result of this, discussion in letters of what might normally be regarded as political matters, seldom involves reference to pre-war political party labels; apart from some rather vague use of such terms as 'Tories' and 'Reds', these men usually give their ideas for post-war reconstruction without identifying their hopes in any way with an existing political party. Lectures and other sources of information regarding possible future legislation appear to be doing excellent work, however, in bringing a better appreciation of some of the problems to be faced.[53]

Over time, ABCA began to shape the soldiers' emerging political awareness. The censorship summary for North Africa, for the period 1 to 15 February 1944, pointed out that 'education on political matters is said to be much on the increase' and that 'talks and discussion upon post-war problems appear to be among the most popular'.[54] A man in the 327 Coast Battery in North Africa commented on the effect of these initiatives:

> You would be surprised to hear what the boys discuss at night. Everything that's of any importance such as demobilization, the Beveridge Report and all that's happening at home. They aren't just passing the time away either. When they do get back they know what they want and I believe they will get it too. We are greatly helped by the Army Education Corps which give lectures on current affairs twice a week and keep us right up to date with recent events. There will be another battle when this lots [*sic*] over. Its [*sic*] no use just leaving things to take care of themselves. We saw what happened last time.[55]

The troops in North Africa were so animated by these socio-political debates, that in late 1943, one of the more popular welfare clubs in

Illustration 16.1 The result of a mock 'General Election' staged by British troops in Cairo in February 1944, is displayed on a blackboard. The Forces Parliament was a manifestation of the upsurge in popular radicalism that emerged as a direct consequence of the experience of shared danger and comradeship during the war.

Cairo set up its own model parliament. The assembly 'required the men not only to talk about issues but also – through the election of a mock-government and the debating of bills and motions – to act on their beliefs along party lines'. On 2 February 1944, after discussions with the area education authorities, an election was held; of the 194 servicemen who attended, 119 (61 per cent) voted for Labour, 55 (28 per cent) for Common Wealth, 17 (9 per cent) for the Conservatives, and 3 (2 per cent) for the Liberals (see Illustration 16.1). The result was a 'fairly indicative reflection of the prevailing desire [in the Army] for change'. The elected Labour 'government' immediately called for 'socialist measures' such as the nationalisation of the banks and other financial institutions.[56]

In Italy, 'with the approach of the Second Front and the hope of an early end to hostilities' there was 'a recrudescence of interest in post-war problems' in the first half of 1944. The censors pointed towards an increasingly sophisticated understanding of politics among the men:

> The troops realise that in order to play their part in the proposed new world they must prepare themselves both educationally and politically. The following comments illustrate this:- 'I think Socialism will have the chance of a million after the war but unless the people become politically conscious and better educated I cannot see it making any real progress' (4th Indian Division Ordinance Field Park). 'We've been having a discussion on post war education this evening in our troop discussion group. Some very interesting points were raised. Thank God the chaps are getting round to serious thought in [*sic*] some of these problems' (64th Heavy A.A. Regiment). 'In the army are a number of non-thinkers who only want to get back to their firesides but there are thousands who want a better way of life and will be very vocal about it when they get home' (22 General Hospital).[57]

Whereas in late 1943 there were 'improvements' that the men wanted, but 'very few' had 'considered the part they must play to get them',[58] by 1944, the men were quite clear on what was necessary. As the report on 'Post-War Prospects', compiled from the censorship of British mail in India and South-East Asia Commands, put it, 'it can be said that there is a general feeling of apprehension about post-war conditions usually based on dissatisfaction with those existing at the present and which existed before the war, and there is a general demand that all soldiers must be given an opportunity of voting for their respective choices'.[59]

The 'loosely conceived' political awakening, or 'social democratic reform agenda', that emerged as a consequence of the war, was, it seems clear, given shape by Beveridge and ABCA, not driven by them. The wartime army education schemes had not, as some Conservative politicians claimed after the war, played a decisive role in the 'road to 1945' 'by exposing the troops to pernicious left-wing propaganda and influencing them to vote Labour'. The Labour victory in the 1945 general election was not 'the one battle honour of the Army Educational

Corps'.[60] But, army education did help the soldier 'operationalise' his emerging social and political consciousness. Williams, the Director of ABCA, writing in early 1945, certainly believed that the troops' socio-political awareness had been heightened through 'the discipline of civilized argument', while Adam, the Adjutant-General, in a speech to the British Institute for Adult Education, stated some months later that education schemes had been 'a great manifestation of democratic faith' which had done much to raise morale and civic consciousness.[61]

Much like civilians on the home front, the soldiers came to support the expansion of social services; they were convinced that the state had both an obligation and the capacity to maintain full employment; they believed that centralised planning could work; and, most importantly of all, they passionately maintained that fairness and justice should underpin all government policy.[62] As one morale report put it, 'equal opportunity is the catch phrase'.[63] A soldier in the 1st Gordons in Sicily wrote in August 1943 that 'social security must be the aim of all after the war'.[64] Another, in 62nd Bomb Disposal Section in Italy, commented in February 1944:

> What I want is a Britain on top of the world, with everyone in it having a fair chance ... good house, free education for all with the poor man's son having the same chance as the rich man's son of getting to the top. Is this too much to ask for a country that apparently can afford to spend over three millions a day to destroy life? Surely not.[65]

The report of the sixth meeting of the 'Adjutant-General in India's Committee on Morale' was unequivocal:

> Correspondence of British service personnel reveals considerable interest in post war problems. There is a determination that an improved social structure must emerge in Britain after the war and that conditions affecting employment which prevailed at the end of the last war must not be repeated ... the State must assure an improved standard of living for the people.[66]

The censorship summary for Second Army in North-West Europe, 15 to 28 February 1945, put it similarly: 'writers wanted a decent job and a decent wage, and held that their services to their country, and the sacrifices they had made, entitled them to fair treatment'.[67] 'The war', as a corporal in 3rd Division wrote the following month, 'has opened our eyes ... I can tell you this I am not going to sweat in any factory for a few bob a week ... Believe me, I can see a lot of trouble arising if we aren't given a fair deal.' The perspective was little different among officers in the division, one writing, 'we've been having a big discussion in the Mess tonight on housing. Several of our Officers want to get married and settle down after being demobbed, and the question of getting a house is a terrific problem.'[68]

The case for change was clearly a powerful motivation to vote Labour in 1945. The Labour manifesto, *Let Us Face the Future*, laid out 'a comprehensive programme including social security, housing, full employment, and healthcare. The document championed Beveridge, economic planning, and committed Labour to public ownership of specific industries and services.' The Conservative manifesto, *Mr Churchill's Declaration of Policy to the Electors*, was, by comparison, 'far less coherent' and far less enticing to the soldiers; most importantly, it failed to develop 'an adequate response to Beveridge'. Policies which predicated social reform on prosperity and that called for a speedy return to a competitive, market driven economy, did not resonate with the dominant thrust of what the men desired as expressed in morale reports and censorship summaries.[69]

While it is evident that many saw their vote as an opportunity to realise a positive vision for the future, many also wished to turn their back on the past and get rid of the Conservatives. As one assessment put it, 'had the morale reports been studied by a conservative politician (instead of the Army Council), he would have been given to think hard'.[70] The censorship summaries and morale reports pointed to a general belief that the authorities were 'out of touch with reality and indifferent to the troubles of the British soldier'.[71] When the Prime Minister toured North-West Europe in March 1945, the censors noted that his visit 'aroused little enthusiasm' and that 'the troops' reception of Mr. Churchill appeared to be apathetic'.[72]

There was, as a report on British soldiers in Italy put it, a feeling that Churchill was 'a good war leader but he would not do for peace'. There was 'small faith in the promises' of the political elite and it was generally believed that 'whenever it could' the Government kept the men 'short and did them down'.[73] The Conservatives were roundly blamed for what were perceived as miserly pay concessions in 1944. A lance corporal in 59th Staffordshire Division, wrote that 'the "increase"' was 'typical of the capitalistic attitude of the people in power'.[74] They were also castigated, to a degree unfairly, for holding the election at what the troops believed to be a wholly inappropriate moment. On the defeat of Germany, Labour had refused an invitation from Churchill to continue with the Coalition Government, arguing instead for an autumn election. The Conservatives, hoping to cash in on the euphoria of victory, went for July instead.[75] 'Some writers felt, although opportunity to vote had been arranged for serving men', that this date did not give them 'sufficient time to make a fair decision ... not enough was known about the candidates'.[76] The election, according to the men, 'had been rushed and would have been better left until a later date'. 'The lads', as a private in 7th Armoured Division wrote 'are really annoyed about it.'

The men clearly felt 'cheated'. Several writers complained that they had been 'deprived of their vote ... because the voting register was out of date'. A sapper in 43rd Wessex Division pointed out that 'that's how it's wanted to be, the future govt. are already in their seats congratulating themselves on another perfect wangle. The whole issue [*sic*] don't give two hoots for human lives except their own.' Many men described trying to register to vote, only to be told that they were ineligible for one administrative reason or another. 'I'm not bothered anyway', wrote a man in Guards Armoured Division, 'half this battery have had the same thing. It strikes me they don't want us chaps to vote anyway.' A sergeant in the Coldstream Guards mentioned that 'dozens of the lads' were in the same position while a corporal in 52nd Lowland Division pointed out that in his company 'I don't think that above twenty received their voting papers.' An officer in the same division estimated that 'at least 40% of the people who ought to have received papers just didn't'. As a driver in 53rd Welsh Division put it, 'I am one of *800,000* very angry servicemen. Through lack of interest and incompetence in certain quarters we are deprived of the right to vote!'[77]

It is clear that many men were seriously dissatisfied 'with the voting arrangements'. That only 64 per cent of the armed forces registered (a total of 2,895,466), and only 59 per cent of those who registered actually voted (1,700,653, the majority of whom were in the Army),[78] did not indicate that the men were apathetic about politics. 'Maladministration and the lack of information regarding the election were mainly responsible' for any 'indifference shown by troops in some units'. Moreover, there are very definite indications that dissatisfaction with the process was blamed squarely again on the Conservatives. 'Last night we had a political discussion in the Mess', wrote a sergeant in the Army Signals, 'of course the early election is a swindle . . . Thousands of labour men working miles away from their constituencies who will be unable to spare either the time or the fare to go and vote'. 'It almost seems as though they don't want us to know what a fast one they are pulling on the British Tommy', wrote a sergeant in 1 Corps District.[79]

It can be reasonably concluded, therefore, that the 'left's master narrative', 'the broken promises and betrayals of 1918, the dole queues and despair of the 1930s', and 'the increasing gulf between the rich and privileged and the majority of the nation' resonated powerfully with servicemen in the Army.[80] As the report on 'Post-War Prospects' from India and South-East Asia Commands put it, the soldiers felt that 'if the conditions when peace comes are found wanting, the fighting will have been in vain'. One man quoted from *The Seven Pillars of Wisdom* describing, as the censors put it, 'exactly the historical trend of which the present generation fears a repetition':

> We lived many lives in those whirling campaigns, never sparing ourselves any good or evil; yet when we achieved and the new world dawned, the old men came out again and took from us our victory and remade it in the likeness of the former world they knew. Youth could win but had not learned to keep, and was pitiably weak against age. We stammered that we had worked for a new heaven and a new earth, and they thanked us kindly and made their peace.[81]

'It would be the straw that broke the Camels [*sic*] back', wrote an NCO in 53rd Welsh Division fighting in North-West Europe, 'if things went back to what they were before the war'.[82]

Of course, not all the soldiers were die-hard reformers. The censors reported at the end of December 1943 that 'an entirely new viewpoint' had 'suddenly appeared with regard to post-war planning. Urgent suggestions as to what the Gov[ernmen]t should do, hitherto very common, have declined to a most marked extent, and many writers have begun, instead, to express uneasiness lest too much Gov[ernmen]t control will rob the future ex-servicemen of the liberty for which they are now fighting.' A man in the 156th Field Regiment wrote that he did not want to be made the 'subject of petty "Jacks in Office" under a bureaucratic system "directing" one here and "directing" one there'. Another wrote that 'few really seem to want violent changes, though a lot talk about it. Personally I have lost a lot of the enthusiasm I had for sweeping changes and am not at all sure they are a good thing. Obviously a lot was wrong with our world before the war but there was an awful lot of good too.' Yet another wrote, 'which is it going to be, the individual or the state? Everything seems to be planned for our good. A war always gives birth to wonderful ideals of this kind. Aren't we trying to do too much at once?'[83]

While it is important to avoid viewing the Army as an uncomplicated undifferentiated mass, it must be noted that 'right-leaning' sentiments such as these were, on the whole, very rarely expressed in the men's letters. The censorship summaries make it clear that most men wanted what they referred to as a 'better', 'fairer' and more 'just' Britain, and that this outcome would be best ensured by an increased level of state intervention. The experience of comradeship and shared danger at the front had laid the foundations for a popular shift to the left. With army education and citizenship education 'operationalising' these sentiments, the scene was set for the soldiers to play a considerable role in the outcome of the 1945 general election.

The Vote

The extent to which the radicalisation of the soldiers' political beliefs impacted on the outcome of the 1945 general election is still highly contested. Historians have argued, for example, that 'it must be borne in mind' that of the 25,085,978 men and women who voted in 1945, only 1,701,000, 6.8 per cent, were in the forces.[84] Moreover, as Jeremy Crang has pointed out, it is impossible to know what actually 'went through the mind' of military voters – that is to say, how can we know whether soldiers did, in fact, vote Labour.[85] In this context, it is typically understood that the service vote, while 'occasionally making a difference in marginal contests', did not make a 'decisive' contribution 'in any general sense'.[86]

The censorship summaries, however, clearly show that the men, as a consequence of their experience of the war and the influence of ABCA and Beveridge, were overwhelmingly 'left-leaning' Labour supporters. Moreover, it must be acknowledged that the views reported in the censorship summaries were derived from an analysis of letters from servicemen to their families and friends back home. Accordingly, as Herbert Morrison, who oversaw Labour's election campaign in 1945, and others have surmised, these letter-writing citizen soldiers played an important role in shaping public opinion; almost every person in the country had a father, brother, husband, boyfriend or nephew in the forces.[87]

Labour's campaign made great play of this dynamic; election posters, such as 'This is our chance to Labour for him [the soldier]' and 'Help them [the armed forces] finish their job' explicitly associated the party with the sacrifices made by the armed forces, insisting that only Labour could secure the future that these men deserved.[88] The *Daily Mirror*, which was 'especially popular with young workers and the armed forces', and whose circulation rose from 1.5 to 2.4 million copies a day during the war, also resonated with this theme. Although the paper did not explicitly endorse Labour, 'it left no doubt where its preferences lay'. It ran a 'very successful "Vote for him!" slogan'.

'Almost daily', as Geoffrey Field has argued, 'the paper appealed to wives, and indeed all civilians, to cast their vote for men in the forces, who – it was implied – had been excluded by slow and inefficient registration procedures: "Your man has fought for you. He is more entitled to have a say than anybody else".'[89]When the war against Germany ended, the paper published a 'legendary cartoon by Philip Zec: "Here you are – don't lose it again!"'. The piece, 'encompassing promises of peace and social reform', presented a wounded soldier, holding out a laurel wreath and climbing out of a war-torn landscape. The paper printed the same image on its front page on polling day, along with the call 'Vote for them!' (see Illustration 16.2).[90]

Thus, while it is accepted that the service vote only accounted for 6.8 per cent of the total votes counted in June 1945, it must also be recognised that the 3.8 million men who served in the Army during the war, and 5.8 million men who served in the armed forces more generally, had a long reach in shaping voting behaviours.[91] We can only surmise, of course, but if it is taken that, in addition to the service vote of 1.7 million ballots, each of the 3.8 million men who served in the Army influenced the electoral choice of just one voter on the home front in 1945, then 22 per cent of the 25 million votes cast would have aligned with the men's political views.[92] If, as seems reasonable given the evidence adduced here and elsewhere, about two-thirds of these votes went to Labour, then around 14 per cent of the total vote (two-thirds of 22 per cent) would have been cast by army or forces members or been

Daily Mirror THUR JULY 5 1945

FORWARD WITH THE PEOPLE

No. 12,960 ONE PENNY

Registered at G.P.O. as a Newspaper.

DON'T LOSE IT AGAIN

Vote for them

WE reproduce on this page Zec's famous VE-Day cartoon. We do so because it expresses more poignantly than words could do the issues which face the people of this country today.

As you, the electors, with whom the destiny of the nation rests, go to the poll, there will be a gap in your ranks. The men who fought and died that their homeland and yours might live will not be there. You must vote for THEM. Others, happily spared, are unable for various reasons to have their rightful say in this election. You must represent them.

Vote on behalf of the men who won the victory for you. You failed to do so in 1918. The result is known to all. The land "fit for heroes" did not come into existence. The dole did. Short-lived prosperity gave way to long, tragic years of poverty and unemployment. Make sure that history does not repeat itself. Your vote gives you the power. Use it. Let no one turn your gaze to the past. March forward to new and happier times. The call of the men who have gone comes to you. Pay heed to it. Vote for THEM.

Remember the issues. They are national not personal. Your own interest, the future of your children, the welfare of the whole country demand that today you do your duty and

VOTE

"Here you are—don't lose it again!"

(Reproduced from our VE-Day issue without apology.)

Illustration 16.2 Front page of the *Daily Mirror*, 5 July 1945. The soldiers' political beliefs were instrumental to Labour's victory in the 1945 general election; this was not solely due to the number of soldiers voting, but also because of the influence the soldiers had on the votes of their own immediate families and friends.

influenced by the troops.[93] Labour's majority over the Conservatives in 1945 was only 8 per cent; relatively small majorities in votes made big differences in overall seat numbers with Labour finishing with 393 seats as compared to 213 for the Conservatives and their allies.[94] As an NCO in Italy put it in July 1944, 'for God's sake if you have to vote before

I arrive don't give it to the government, vote for the Labour candidate even if he is only a rag and bone merchant'.[95]

The dynamic link between the home front and the battlefront, as had been the case all during the war, was capable of shaping attitudes and opinions. Although it is impossible to prove outright that the radicalisation of soldiers' attitudes was a decisive factor on 'the road to 1945', the diffusion of soldiers' views explored here does lend more weight to the contention that the soldiers' political beliefs were instrumental to Labour's victory in the 1945 general election, certainly more instrumental than the most recent literature has suggested.

Either way, Labour's victory offered exactly what many soldiers had hoped for: the removal of the Conservative party from government and an administration that would introduce a 'left-leaning' agenda. A craftsman in 79th Armoured Division wrote, 'you will have read about the Labour Party getting in. We are all glad, for now we may get houses built quicker, and a lot more.' The censors in North-West Europe noted that it was clear in terms of 'post-war prospects' that 'writers centred their hopes on the new Government'.[96] 'Many', according to the censors, 'expressed their confidence' in Labour's ability 'to tackle these [housing and employment] and other urgent problems'.[97] The following extract by a corporal in the 53rd Welsh Division in North-West Europe, according to the censors, gave a 'fair summing up of the general reaction':

> The election result was rather staggering to a staunch Conservative such as I. However, I have to admit from impartial observation, the vast majority of my Army colleagues really believe that the Service man is now assured of a square deal. Whether you and I like it or not they (the rank and file) are glad Labour is to lead us.[98]

The Forces Vote and New Zealand's Great Experiment in Social Citizenship

In New Zealand, the soldiers' political awakening was also to have effects that would last a generation.[99] In the wake of its victory in the 1935 general election, the New Zealand Labour party had successfully managed to address many of the challenges of the Great Depression. Through intervention in the economy, with reforms to pensions, healthcare and unemployment benefits, culminating in the Social Security Act of 1938, a true social citizenship was born and the gap between rich and poor narrowed.[100] By 1939, it seemed that New Zealand was firmly on the path towards building a progressive society where ordinary people were protected from the inherent uncertainty of the market and freed from anxieties and hardships caused by circumstances over which they had little control.[101]

The new 'social contract' championed by the Labour Party came under sustained pressure on the outbreak of the Second World War (see Chapter 2).[102] When the National Party withdrew from the War Administration in October 1942, 'the basis of unity in the country' appeared to be 'destroyed' and an election was called for the following year.[103] It took place in September 1943, with the Labour Party defeating the National Party by forty-five seats (plus one allied independent) to thirty-four, a majority of twelve.[104] Labour's victory ensured that it had a strong majority and a mandate to run the country and the war as it saw fit. It was able to continue its social and economic agenda, including nationalisations and social and employment reform.[105] Labour's third successive electoral success ensured that the balance in New Zealand politics lay firmly to the left. In the decades following the war, National adopted Labour's social welfare agenda and became increasingly inclined towards a policy of full employment. So great was the significance of the victory, that successive Labour triumphs in this period 'set the terms of political debate and action [in New Zealand] for the next forty years'.[106]

The election, however, was a far closer contest than Labour's majority indicated. Forty thousand, out of a total of 950,000 votes, were cast for Democratic Labour, a party to Labour's left. These votes 'cannibalised' the Labour vote and contributed to the loss of eight seats to National compared to their showing in 1938. In fact, with the civilian votes counted, the Government was heading for defeat in an additional six seats (Eden, Nelson, Oamaru, Otaki, Palmerston North and Wairarapa). It was only when the armed service votes 'were added to the [domestic] totals' that the Government survived by narrowly holding on to all six seats.[107] Had National won these constituencies, the House would have been split evenly between the two parties and there is every chance that the Government would have fallen, with profound implications for the war effort and the shape of the post-war political economy of New Zealand. Fraser later commented, 'it was not only North Africa that the Second Division had saved'.[108]

That the soldiers' vote saved Labour in 1943 is well documented in the literature.[109] The reasons behind the soldiers' vote have only more recently been explored, and it does appear that, much as was the case with the soldiers' vote in Britain, Labour's victory in 1943 was the 'culmination' of 'developments that were a direct result of the war'.[110] The attitudes of forces personnel, who, in many cases, had been affected and radicalised by the experience of combat, impacted decisively on their voting behaviours (see Table 16.2).

The Labour Party's election policy statement, which was released to troops wherever they were based all around the world, played explicitly to this dynamic – the radicalised soldier. It stressed what Labour had already done for service personnel and for their loved ones at home. It promised the 'most generous war pension system in the world'. Employment would be guaranteed for all ex-servicemen. For those who wanted to study, there would be free or subsidised education. It was full of facts and figures, but, importantly, the promise of fairness ran like a thread through the whole document; 'ex-servicemen and ex-servicewomen must come first in the national development because they have been first in the defence of our country and all that people cherish'. 'What happened after 1914–18' would 'not happen again'.[111]

The statement made great play of the Servicemen's Settlement and Land Sales Act, which had been introduced in August 1943 just before the House rose. The legislation aimed to facilitate the settlement on the land of discharged servicemen at reasonable prices, and in general to prevent speculation in land or undue increases in prices.[112] 'Pressure had been growing for some time for control of land values, which had risen spectacularly since 1939.' The failure of soldier settlement after the First World War had mainly been attributed to the high price of land. The Labour Party argued that the Government had 'to take strong action and get land at a fair price for soldiers'[113] and that this would be best achieved by giving it power to take over land suitable for subdivision and by controlling the price of all land sales.[114]

The National Party, the press, farming groups, real-estate agents, chambers of commerce and the Law Society vehemently opposed the Servicemen's Settlement and Land Sales Act. National complained that the Government was using the rehabilitation of servicemen as a cloak for pushing its socialistic schemes and that the act would operate unfairly against the holders of property in land or houses.[115] The National Party statement to the forces emphasised personal freedoms as an immutable principle. It promised to give New Zealanders:

> Freedom to live their own lives in their own way without bureaucratic dictation, to live in a system of competitive free enterprise, to own their own homes; freedom for our returning servicemen to follow the occupation of their choice without having to go cap in hand to the Government for a licence to earn a livelihood.[116]

Here lay the essential difference between the two parties. It was not that the National Party manifesto was devoid of its own narrative of fairness, but that the Labour manifesto clearly advocated fairness as it had become understood by the troops. The weakness of the National perspective, the Labour manifesto countered, was that the 'old competitive style of market values' championed by the Nationals really meant that the prosperity of ordinary citizens would be subject to the whims of 'speculators' and 'vested interests', the 'wolves of commerce'. In many other ways, the National Party policy statement echoed that of Labour. It promised to maintain wages and social services, and indeed to extend social security benefits. It pledged 'jobs for all' and to 'remove the avoidable causes of want'.[117] But, it was not the similarities in appeals that mattered to the troops; it was the underlying differences in ethos.

Having seen and experienced the war and the manner in which the state was able to mobilise its resources for destruction, the men believed that the state could also play a positive role in a prosperous and fair peace, defined by the ideals and practice of social justice.[118] The censorship summaries show that the men wrote about and were deeply concerned by issues such as social security, socialism, lack of control over profiteering, rights and class.[119] A padre wrote from North Africa in September 1943:

> I tried an experiment which proved very successful. On church parade I preached a rather controversial sermon on post war reconstruction and invited everybody in the evening to come to a kind of 'open-forum' debate in the hangar which is my recreational place. Well, when I strolled along there ten minutes before I had intended starting, the place was packed, there

> was hardly standing room ... After a few preliminary remarks from me I invited one officer to give his idea of post war things from the financial point of view – this much was pre-arranged – and after that there was no holding them, chaps popped up and said their say about all sorts of things – but the chief topics were freehold or leasehold land and state housing. They were still going strong at 10.15 when I closed it for supper and at 11.30 when I went to put out the light, there was one group still arguing. Every tent seems to have become a debating society.[120]

The basic expectation was that the men, the home front, and the state, would all 'pull together'.[121] In December 1943, as the men wrote home after the receipt of mail from New Zealand covering the period of the election campaign, it was clear to the censors that the 'large majority' appeared to 'approve of the re-election of the Labour Govt.' An officer wrote, capturing the mood of the men:

> The Labour Members may not be 'gentlemen', they are rather working men; honest and vigorous, but their policy, before and during the war, has made little NZ one of the most respected and envied countries in the world. Sir William Beveridge acknowledges the debt of his much lauded plan to the Social Security Scheme of the Labour Party ... All in all they are the only party with a definite progressive policy.[122]

In the early years of the war, Labour in New Zealand had echoed Churchill's approach to the conflict; the issues of war and social change were addressed separately, with the latter only to receive attention once the former had been won. Moreover, Labour institutionalised this split between home and front by creating dual cabinets to administer the domestic and martial aspects of the war (see Chapter 2). It was only by promising in the 1943 Labour manifesto to renew the 'social contract', so powerfully encapsulated in the 1938 Social Security Act, that the party reconnected with the citizen soldier and ultimately survived the election. The continuation of New Zealand's great adventure in social citizenship in the twentieth century hinged to no small degree on the voting preferences of the cohort of citizen soldiers who fought the Second World War.

The Forces Vote and the Formalisation of Apartheid in South Africa

The radicalising effect of the war was as profound, if not more so, in South Africa. The idea that the Second World War was a transformative event for South African soldiers is not a new one.[123] According to Neil Roos, as a consequence of the fighting and a liberal-minded Army Education Scheme, 'a "true" national identity that superseded' the long-standing conflict between Afrikaans and English-speaking white South Africans emerged in the Second World War. Captain H. B. Theunissen, of the 2nd Infantry Brigade, 1st South African Division, wrote:

> There will be no 'Jews' or 'Dutchmen' or 'English' after this war. We have seen the rough part of life and gone through everything together. We shall be 'South Africans' and I am sanguine that racial feeling and intolerance will go by the board.[124]

Such sentiments were echoed in the soldiers' letters and in the literature of the Springbok Legion, a left-leaning soldiers' rights organisation formed during the war years. The Legion noted that 'on the battlefield . . . a genuine South African nationalism was born';[125] 'ethnic identity among white volunteers was replaced by the appellation of "comrade", which described those who had volunteered to serve in the Union Defence Force (UDF) and had shared the experience of armed service'.[126] In a similar vein, the censors noted throughout the war that there was much 'evidence of complete harmony between speakers of English and of Afrikaans, respectively, within the Union Forces'. As a man in 6th South African Armoured Division wrote in December 1944, 'it is very pleasant to see that here . . . [in Italy] there is no racial hatred. If a man speaks to you in Afrikaans, you answer him in Afrikaans.'[127] This dynamic facilitated the development of a new spirit of social solidarity among white South Africans, a political movement or sentiment coined 'South Africanism' by some scholars.[128]

Evidence of a more quantitative nature confirms that the war, from a socio-political perspective, was a unifying experience for white South African soldiers. The results of the 1943 South African general election showed that a remarkable consensus had formed among service personnel, who were overwhelmingly in support of the pro-war government parties (the United Party (UP), the Labour Party and the Dominion Party).[129] No less than 92 per cent of the service vote went to the

Table 16.4 Percentages of party votes in the South African general election of 1943: the civilian and forces vote

Party	Civilian vote	Forces vote	Total
UP	46.4%	78.1%	49.3%
HNP	39.2%	3.6%	36.0%
LP	4.5%	8.2%	4.8%
DP	3.1%	5.8%	3.3%
AP	1.8%	0.5%	1.7%
CP	0.8%	0.9%	0.8%
I. Lab	0.1%	0.2%	0.1%
Ind*	4.2%	2.7%	4.0%
Government	54.0%	92.1%	57.4%

* Includes the Volkseenheid candidates.
UP = United Party; HNP = Herenigde National Party; LP = Labour Party; DP = Dominion Party; AP = Afrikaner Party; CP = Communist Party; I. Lab = Independent Labour; Ind = Independent.
Numbers have been rounded to one decimal place which may result in some columns not totalling 100 per cent.

Government, as compared to 54 per cent of civilians. The two main opposition parties, the *Herenigde* (Re-united) National Party (HNP) and the Afrikaner Party, together polled a paltry 4.1 per cent of the soldiers' vote, while they won a more impressive 41 per cent of the civilian franchise (see Table 16.4).[130] A remarkable alignment in opinion had formed among those in the services.

This extraordinary voting alignment was not, however, driven by questions of social justice and fairness as it had been in Britain and New Zealand. Instead, the election was fought, as Smuts hoped and anticipated, primarily over one issue, the great question of the day: South Africa's continued involvement in the war. The UP had warned in its manifesto, published in the forces newspaper, *Springbok*, that any votes for non-government parties would 'assist the anti-war parties and subversive elements' in the country. The Dominion Party, in the very first line of its manifesto, made a similar statement. 'Nothing can be allowed to divert the country's energies from the supreme object of winning the war. This is vital: nothing else matters.' The Labour Party played the same tune; 'in this General Election the paramount issue is the war issue'. In contrast, the opposition parties were clearly and vehemently opposed to continued participation in the war. The Afrikaner Party stated that its election aims were:

> The immediate cessation of the systematic negation of the whole spirit of South African sovereignty practiced by the present Government in its slavish obedience to overseas decisions dictated by overseas considerations and interests, as well as the immediate cessation of the exhaustion of South African resources and assets in a war which is being fought in Europe and will be decided in Europe.[131]

The HNP, while they promised to maintain the pensions and other privileges granted to European (white) soldiers and their dependants, were similarly 'opposed to our country being dragged deeper into the war'. They wanted to bring back troops within the borders of South Africa and demobilise the non-European elements on active service.[132]

The overwhelming impression from the censorship summaries is that it was this aspect of the campaign that dominated soldiers' deliberations. Having volunteered to fight, the vast majority, perhaps unsurprisingly, supported the war. They also realised 'the need for a powerful Government' if the conflict was to be prosecuted effectively. Thus, it was estimated in the summaries before the election that 95 per cent of the troops would vote for the Government.[133] 'The vital necessity' to keep the Government, and particularly Smuts, in power during the war, was the 'outstanding factor' motivating troops to vote. 'In fact', according to the censors, 'it was the only issue discussed and the consensus of opinion was that there was no option but to vote for the present Government'. After the war was over and done with, many soldiers said, 'it will be time enough to view each of the parties through party lines alone'.[134]

The Disenchanted Soldier

Beneath the dominant issue of the day, the question of South Africa's continued involvement in the war, lurked, however, a deep developing dissatisfaction with the status quo. In a similar vein to the other Commonwealth countries, the experience of war had stirred 'left-wing' tendencies among the troops. The South African Military Censorship Summary for the period 1 to 20 August 1942 pointed to a 'growing Leftist leaning among soldiers', especially among members of the Springbok Legion. Calls to win the war were 'coupled with cries for Governmental reform'. This 'reformatory spirit', continued the report, 'appears to be a direct result of the incidents which crop up continuously and which cause dissatisfaction amongst soldiers'.[135]

In an attempt to get to the bottom of the issue, the Directorate of Military Intelligence commissioned a Gallup Poll on 'Soldiers' Grievances' in September 1942. The poll pointed again to 'distinct Leftist tendencies amongst our troops,' many of whom were 'looking for a "New Order"'. These feelings, or 'the political bias of the troops', appeared, according to the poll, to emerge from 'dissatisfaction with service conditions and the general prosecution of the war effort'.[136] Later in the war, the censors reported on the radicalising effect of these feelings; 'many men in the field ... want to experiment along new lines rather than follow existing theories which have not proved infallible'.[137] It was abundantly evident that there was 'a strong socialistic trend of thought now prevalent' in the Army.[138]

Notwithstanding these widespread leftist preferences among the troops, the party that espoused the most 'left-leaning' manifesto in the 1943 election, the HNP, experienced an appalling set of results in the soldiers' vote. 'We are anti-imperialistic' read the manifesto released to *Springbok* on 17 June, but 'also anti-capitalistic ... We regard the continuance of the pre-war conditions of poverty and want ... as an infinitely greater disaster than the war itself'.[139]

Their social-economic programme had four 'cornerstones'. The first pointed out that while citizens had 'obligations towards the State', the state also had the 'obligation of creating humane and secure living conditions' for its people, including 'social security', 'proper housing', 'health services', 'employment' and 'wages'. The second 'cornerstone' considered human values above financial interests; 'the Exchequer is there for the people and not the people for the Exchequer'. The third addressed the need for the 'distribution of wealth with greater justice' and included the regulation of prices, profits and wages, and the nationalisation of key industries, such as gold mines and banks, so that workers could 'enjoy a fair share of the prosperity which they themselves helped to create'. The fourth 'cornerstone', which was undoubtedly the most controversial aspect of the HNP's vision for South Africa, clearly marked the road to formalised apartheid and the maintenance of what the manifesto referred to as a 'white man's country'. It promised to take steps to 'protect European employment and wages against deadening competition, which is now filling our urban slums with white poverty and misery'. From the HNP's perspective, social solidarity for the white races could only be achieved through the social exclusion of black and coloured South Africans; one could not exist without the other. 'Out of sacrifice and blood and tears', the manifesto continued, 'a better and happier world must arise. If not, black despair awaits us.'[140]

It is in this context that the soldiers' vote in the 1943 election gave a misleading impression of strength to the UP and weakness to the HNP. While the overall result of the election was not altered by the forces' vote (the Government parties would have been victorious even without their support), 10 of the 132 contested districts were decided by the military franchise, all 10 going to the Government rather than the HNP. In just about all the other districts, the UP performed better due to the soldiers' vote.[141] These dynamics fostered overconfidence and complacency in the UP.[142]

The problem was, as evidenced by the censorship summaries, that even by 1943 the political preferences of ordinary white South African citizen soldiers had noticeably shifted away from the liberal ideals and policies of the UP towards the reactionary socialistic policies of the HNP. During 1944 and 1945, the situation deteriorated further as cracks in the UP's relationship with the UDF began to resemble gaping holes. The Government's inability to arbitrate between competing interests in South African society, and, particularly, to ensure equality of sacrifice, increasingly undermined its popularity. It appeared to those families with loved ones in the forces that the 'stay-at-homes and the disloyal' had not only saved their own skins, but, also, benefited materially from the war.[143]

By August 1944, the censors were reporting that domestic morale had 'fallen to a very low ebb'. The war had faded into insignificance and been replaced by 'political and social matters' in the Union. The 'predominating theme in correspondence to troops was the government's (or Jannie Smuts') responsibility for the present unsatisfactory internal conditions'. 'Numerous extracts' revealed that citizens were 'distrustful and ANGRY', especially in thickly populated areas, and that they fully expected a 'sweeping victory for Dr. Malan at the next election'. The censors were concerned that these attitudes would 'undermine the confidence of our troops', but, also could lead to Malan assuming power much in the same way that General Hertzog took over shortly after the First World War.[144]

In Durban, two interlinked issues in particular were key: first, the shortage and unequal distribution of foodstuffs and, secondly, apparent 'profiteering' by segments of the Indian community.[145] By the middle of 1944, the censors were pointing to the extreme hardships being suffered by servicemen's families. 'For the monied people who are inconvenienced in obtaining only a half pound of tea or butter no tears need be shed. But for the unfortunate wives of servicemen and poor people also, who have young children to provide for, the position is desperate':

> Cases have been seen where soldiers' wives with four or five children have gone from shop to shop all over Durban in a vain endeavour to buy a quarter pound of farm butter at 4/- per lb. as they cannot purchase the controlled creamery butter at 1/10 or 1/11 per lb. The price of eggs too has been prohibitive for servicemen's families, the absence of meat – which nowadays yields no dripping – the shortage of milk, potatoes, rice together with the excessive price of fruit and vegetables generally are causing acute distress.[146]

By August, it was reported that 'under the present system there are complaints of malnutrition and in some cases starvation from the lower paid workers and soldiers' families'.[147] In September, the impact on children began to come to the fore, with some letters proving 'distressing for even censorship examiners to read'.[148]

It is not surprising, therefore, that by March 1945 'the flame of duty and sacrifice' in service families seemed 'to have been quenched'.[149] The censorship report for July outlined how 'personal readjustment during the coming decade, rather than communal or national, seems to be the first and only consideration at the moment'.[150] Having suffered so much for so long, service families wanted to see their own quality of life improve and improve quickly.

As a result, as the end of the war drew near, it became increasingly clear that a 'vast number of people' were hoping for the introduction of 'social security and reforms' in South Africa. 'In other words they are expecting many of the wartime undertakings to be implemented and it will not be so easy for Governments to pigeon hole wartime promises as it was after the last Great War.'[151] The apparent lack of progress in this regard left many disenchanted.[152] In July 1945, the Durban censors reported that only 40 per cent of letters sent from home could be described as 'cheerful or, at least, ... not depressing'. The rest were 'petulant or complaining and recorded domestic unhappiness, family quarrels, sickness' and dissatisfaction with the state of South Africa. With regards to housing and accommodation, letters were unfavourable in a ratio of 32:1; in terms of cost of living they were unfavourable in a ratio of 11:1; writers were negative about the cost and shortage of food in a ratio of 10:1.[153]

The censors fretted that it was 'impossible to prevent' such 'bitter complaints' from reaching the troops abroad and it was 'feared' that a 'state of discontent' would be created and that the men would become apprehensive, alarmed and despondent and 'not thank South Africa for permitting their families to suffer such hardships during their absence'.[154]

Indeed, censorship showed that these matters were 'uppermost in the minds' of the troops serving abroad 'who seem to be groping for some sign of security in civil life'.[155] The summaries from Italy, in 1944 and 1945, were highly critical of matters on the home front. Concern was 'evinced by the troops' at reports of food shortages in the country; 'they maintain that if this is actually the case, it can only be due to mismanagement on the part of the authorities, who are also accused by some of allowing their homeland to slump into a state of general disorder, which promises ill for post-war South Africa'.[156] 'Disgust at the alleged flourishing state of the black market' was a 'common feature of the mail', with the authorities 'indicted for "sitting back and allowing it"'.[157] The men were 'not very happy about the general position' with regards to housing either.[158] By May and July 1945, they were so dismayed that the censors referred to 'an anti-Smuts movement' that seemed to have formed in the Central Mediterranean Force (CMF) and Middle Eastern Forces (MEF).[159]

The cessation of hostilities in May 1945 did not lead to any great change in the reaction of the troops to the Government, despite plans for soldier-friendly demobilisation. The 'cornerstone' of the demobilisation scheme was the recognition of the white male veteran's right to employment.[160] Those that had given up employment prior to joining were guaranteed employment 'under conditions no less favourable' than those existing at the time of their enlistment.[161] Volunteers with no employment to which to return, were to be retained on military strength with full pay and allowances until suitable employment could be found. If the ex-soldier lost employment through no fault of his own within a year, he would be able to return to the army until another suitable position was found. No person other than an ex-soldier was supposed to be appointed to a post unless the Department of Labour could provide a certificate confirming that no suitable ex-soldier was available for the post in question.[162]

As enlightened as Government policy towards the return of the UDF to the Union appeared to be, it was 'worlds apart from the way the soldiers experienced it at first hand'; this was a substantial problem as the manner in which the Government managed demobilisation was considered an 'acid test' by the men.[163] Matters did not start well when delays in repatriation led to 'much adverse criticism of the authorities on the grounds of "muddle" and "broken promises"'[164] and eventually to a riot in Helwan camp in August 1945.[165] The South African economy was not ready to receive the ex-soldiers. Unlike the United Kingdom, the discharge of soldiers was not controlled in accordance with the conversion of industry from a war to a peacetime setting. Thus, there was no guarantee that demobilised men had employment to which to return immediately; according to the Directorate of Demobilisation, by August 1945 there were 46,475 servicemen looking for employment but only 20,944 vacancies in industry.[166]

Moreover, on getting home, the soldiers found that their standard of living was no better than it had been before they joined the Army. For some, especially those in lower income groups, it dropped considerably. The increased cost of living, which had caused so much havoc on the home front during the war, now impacted on the demobilised soldier. The post-war world was for some 'a cold hard place where everyone was out for himself'.[167] The state's inability to provide work and housing for returning servicemen challenged their sense of social justice:

> White working-class veterans saw themselves at a relative disadvantage to those who had stayed at home or worse still, had betrayed the war effort. Expensive to employ and inappropriately skilled, white ex-servicemen's lack of occupational mobility made them vulnerable to a variety of pressures.[168]

The impacts of a challenging job market were exacerbated by a shortage of housing. By 1945, it was estimated that 130,000 houses were needed nationally for whites alone. In the circumstances, the state facilitated the provision of land to white ex-servicemen who could then build homes of their own. The Government guaranteed a building society loan to help the soldiers with these costs but even with this support the costs of this buy-build scheme 'were beyond the means of poor white ex-servicemen'.[169]

The Issue of Race

It is difficult to disassociate these issues and dynamics from the direction South African politics took post-1948. While the economic position of many white servicemen and their families deteriorated during the war, that of black South Africans on the home front noticeably improved; for example, the wages of black workers rose dramatically (from a low base), faster even than those of white workers in the war economy. Faced with labour shortages, not least due to the fact that about 200,000 out of a white male working population of 790,000 were serving in the armed forces, the wartime administration authorised a greater number of black South Africans to work in skilled positions. Following the fall of Tobruk in June 1942, the demand for black labour in skilled positions increased again, as a greater proportion of new recruits were drawn from urban areas and social classes I and II.[170] Moreover, when the compulsory arbitration of industrial disputes was introduced in 1942, the Wage Boards were often the arbitrator, resolving most disputes in favour of black workers. The ratio of black to white wages rose from 22.7 per cent in 1940 to 28.9 per cent in 1946.[171] At the same time, South Africa experienced 'a mass migration' of black workers to the cities.[172] On a conservative estimate, during the war the urban black population increased by about half a million to 1,689,000.[173] The number of Africans employed in manufacturing rose by 7.7 per cent a year between 1939 and 1945. Between the beginning of the war and 1949/50, African employment in private industry more generally increased by 111 per cent in the Southern Transvaal, 190 per cent around Durban and more than 240 per cent in the Cape. The Eastern Cape, site of the country's rudimentary automobile industry, witnessed the highest increase (287 per cent). Overall, 'recording of Africans' urbanization increased from 18.9 per cent in 1936 to 27.1 per cent in 1951'.[174]

These dynamics had a direct effect on a white South African society that was accustomed to segregation and the exploitation of black workers, rather than their integration into the economy. As the war drew to a close, the censors alluded to 'grave forebodings of impending trouble', even to the possibility of 'rebellion ... unrest, revolution, bloodshed and civil war'.[175] It was generally felt that the Government's policies had 'failed lamentably' and not prevented 'rackets, ramps and profiteering'.[176] They were blamed for 'every short supply of any commodity, for the alleged "mess" and "muddle" in providing houses' and for the 'outrageous retail prices'.[177] Many felt deeply aggrieved, as they had been promised that 'THIS TIME there would be No profiteering' and much of this anger was focused on 'Jews and Coolies'.[178] Whites in Durban could not reconcile profiteering by Indian shopkeepers with their desire to 'live amongst us as equals' after the war.[179] Indeed, 'Indian encroachment' and demands for 'equal rights' were 'definitely regarded as a menace and [were] feared accordingly'.[180] By February 1945, there were growing concerns that the Indians might 'succeed in linking up with the native ... Cape Malay and Coloured elements'.[181] The high cost of black labour (relative to what it had been) was now being felt and non-European troops who had returned from 'Up North' were considered 'most disrespectful ... quarrelsome and insolent'.[182]

These issues confronted white servicemen on their return home to South Africa. Lacking artisan skills and training, they found themselves 'particularly vulnerable', not least because it was 'far cheaper to employ black men' than white veteran soldiers.[183] Additionally, as one serviceman stated in 1943, 'a large amount of surplus money was in circulation due to the Government paying unskilled and semi-skilled labourers excessive wages'.[184] This caused inflation, which in turn squeezed standards of living. In the prevailing circumstances, dissatisfaction with the Government took on a racial element,[185] a dynamic made more problematic by the fact that the war had hardened white servicemen's racial prejudices and encouraged many to seek extreme solutions to the 'colour problem'.

While there is some evidence to suggest that white and black troops served together harmoniously in the Second World War,[186] the dominant impression that emerges from censorship and intelligence reports is that the war exacerbated rather than ameliorated racial tensions between white and black South Africans. Throughout the war, 'attempts to augment white fighting units by arming black soldiers faltered' in the face of white South African racial prejudices that were 'vigorously affirmed by the

Chief of the General Staff, Sir Pierre van Ryneveld'.[187] Thus, the powerful forces of combat cohesion did not play out for white and black South African soldiers. In March 1941, for example, one man wrote from East Africa:

> It makes my blood boil to sit next to coloureds – especially Indians, and that's what we had to do on Sunday (in a cinema). They were the only seats we could get. Most of the shops here are owned by Indians and they certainly know how to profiteer.[188]

Many South Africans couldn't accept that they had 'instructions to treat *niggers* as our pals'.

> Can you imagine any European with some self-respect doing that? I'm dashed if I can, and I'm dammed if I'm going to treat one of them on equal footing. What the devil is it going to be like when we get back to the Union? Personally I'll lay the first one out that sits on a seat next to me.[189]

Censorship in the Middle East, in 1942 and 1943, regularly noted 'expressions of regret that S.A. Natives were brought to the M.E.' Writers claimed that contact with white servicemen and civilians had made black troops 'insubordinate and unmanageable and they are expected to foment trouble on their return to the Union as in their present frame of mind they are totally unsuited to S.A. conditions'.[190] In February 1943, the censors remarked that 'concern is shown over the consequences of their mixing with whites as equals, and their eventual demand for equal treatment after the war'. A trooper wrote:

> Such matters, 'post war problems', are being widely debated amongst ourselves ... The native problem is going to be one of the most urgent matters to be settled. Do you know that up here, there is practically no distinction between European and Native soldiers? They frequent the same NAAFI canteens, using the same crockery and furniture, and in many other respects, they rub shoulders with one another [*sic*] day by day. This is chiefly because they are under Imperial Command ... There is nothing we can do about it, and we fully realise that the native soldier is doing his bit in this war. But what is going to happen when we are all out of uniform, and demanding the fulfilment of all the

> solemn promises, being made by responsible people, to men who had joined up.[191]

Attitudes did not change as the war wore on. White South African troops in North Africa and Italy in 1944 and 1945 recurrently 'expressed concern' regarding the 'possible effect upon SA coloured personnel' with regards to 'social equality', fear being expressed 'that there will be unfortunate repercussions in the Union on the return home of these men'.[192] These perspectives were so prevalent in 6th South African Armoured Division, where a 'complete Europeanisation of the fighting components' was enforced, that at the start of 1944 a new 'Rational Party' was established in the South African Soldiers' Parliament (a precursor to the British Cairo Forces Parliament). The 'principal objective' of the party was 'the maintenance of white superiority in S.A.' It aimed to 'overthrow the Government' due to its 'dangerous' and 'unrealistic legislation' which focused on improving the plight of non-Europeans in the Union. As one NCO in the division wrote, the party had to be founded as the existing parties in the Parliament did 'not really' represent the opinions of 'the ordinary "men in the Div"';[193] the 'Indian question' and 'post-war Native Policy' were clearly 'sources of concern' that would require action on the cessation of hostilities.[194]

In South Africa, where the 'colour bar' did function during the war, white servicemen were particularly keen to enforce the continued subjugation of black citizens and soldiers, to ensure that they 'knew their place' and would not be 'contaminated' by the war experience. For example, white soldiers were involved in the brutal suppression of riots by black labourers and soldiers protesting against their discriminatory treatment at the hands of the South African State. One of the better-known examples is the Marabastad Riot of 28 December 1942.

On that evening, a violent stand-off developed between a few hundred black workers – who were in dispute with the Marabastad, Pretoria, municipal council over pay – and local law enforcement. As the situation deteriorated, an alarmed white civilian rushed to the Central Army Transit Depot (CATD), less than half a mile away, to ask for help. A force of four officers and eighty armed men were dispatched to the scene, but upon their arrival matters got out of hand. Corporal J. P. Coetzee, who belonged to the CATD, but was off duty and coincidentally on the scene, attached himself to the military force and began attacking a group of rioters with a stick. The rioters fought back and two officers opened fire to protect Coetzee, who himself fell to the ground. General firing then commenced.[195] The censors summarised what one staff sergeant wrote after the event, describing how South African troops had 'opened fire and shot indiscriminately':

> The poor nigs got jammed in the compound gate and were badly shot up. The natives continuously tried to break out of the gates and storm us but they were not dealing with the police but the Army, and when they rushed to stab one of our soldiers the first one dropped dead as a chap shot him through the heart. The order came 'fire' and their dead piled up three feet high.[196]

A corporal, who was at the scene, wrote that the 'soldiers got out of hand – the men just went mad and fired right into them and also charged them with fixed bayonets'. Another recalled how 'one man continued firing until his rifle was taken from him'.[197] By the time the fighting had calmed down, sixteen black workers were dead and at least another fifty-nine were wounded, of whom twenty-nine were treated in hospital. One white man, Coetzee, was killed, ironically by a bullet from an officer's service revolver. One soldier and about seven policemen received minor wounds.[198]

In reviewing the riot, the censors were struck by the 'surprisingly large number' that 'enjoyed themselves thoroughly, and were by no means averse to shooting down natives'. Many saw the riot as a welcome 'break from the monotony of camp routine' and at least one writer regretted that they had not been allowed to 'wipe the whole lot out'.[199] It was clear from the judicial commission of inquiry that took place after the event that the black workers had made use of a variety of weapons, but no firearms, and of the sixteen blacks killed, ten had received their fatal wounds in the back.[200]

Another incident took place a few days later at Sonderwater, on the night of 31 December 1942. This time, however, the rioters were men of 4th Cape Corps Battalion. Although no men were killed, physical force was again used and twenty-five 'ringleaders' were arrested. Much like the conflagration at Marabastad, but apparently not linked to it, the immediate cause of the problem was pay. A staff sergeant in the Cape Corps wrote that the officers were 'bringing ladies into camp in the evening for a dance, and fearing that if the men were paid they would drink themselves drunk and cause disturbances' they refused to give them their dues. However, as the censors reviewed the men's letters to identify the causes of the conflagration:

> It became quite clear that the course of the riot was determined largely by colour prejudice. It would appear that the minor issues were submerged in the far greater problem of colour, and the riot culminated in an out and out clash between the N.E.'s [non-Europeans] and Europeans, a clash where the righting of social injustices became the determining factor for the N.E.'s. The riot apparently served as an outlet for pent up feelings. 'Here happened a revolution with us against the Europeans. It's a long time that we suffer and always through the Europeans, not only in civilian time but all over, and we also ought to get victory over them'.[201]

The censors found that 'the Cape Coloureds' were 'more tolerant than the Europeans' and, on the whole, accepted blame for the outburst. On the other hand, 'the hatred of the Europeans for the coloureds is much more freely expressed. "Black swine", "pests", "drunken black rats", "vuil honde" [filthy dogs], are some of the phrases used.' Accounts of the riot were given 'with relish' by European soldiers and 'wishes for a recurrence of riots' were 'freely expressed'. However, the censors also pointed to the 'quite interesting' detail that 'invariably all English-speaking correspondents advocate the use of force, whereas Afrikaans-speaking writers concentrate more on the fear of revolt and fear of the coloureds being given social equality'. There were also strong criticisms of the Government, which was accused of 'appeasement' and 'being far too lenient'. One trooper wrote that 'our declared policy of dithering effeminacy prevented the coloureds from receiving a sharp enough lesson'. A very large number of writers advocated immediate action by the Smuts Government; many demanded 'subjugation by force' of the non-European community in the country. The censors continued pessimistically that:

> In discussing post-war conditions, writers invariably forecast more trouble and call these riots and strikes 'the forerunners of what is coming all over the world'. South Africa's future from this particular aspect is viewed with alarm by many and it appears to be generally accepted that 'much bloodshed will result after the war'.[202]

Following the riot at Sonderwater, 4th Cape Corps Battalion was transferred to the Dutoitspan Training Camp near Kimberley. However, here, again, on 6 February 1943, about eighty to one hundred men rioted. Many members of the unit were put in detention and sixty-seven rioters were arrested. There were no serious casualties, but seventeen men did suffer minor injuries and lacerations. Again, the censors pointed out that 'these riots have led to an increase in the expression of colour antipathy. The Europeans are the more bitter, and their comments often disclose violent hatred.'[203]

The 1948 General Election

In many ways, the decision of Smuts to turn his back on conscription and rely on a totally volunteer military effort saved South Africa from disintegration on ethnic (English-speaking versus Afrikaans-speaking) lines. However, the manner in which the war was managed dramatically deepened other divisions in South African society, divisions based on race and class. There was widespread feeling that:

> This is simply a war where the rich get richer and the poor [whites] get poorer. The poor man is forced to join up – he had no option, otherwise he starves – but the rich have sufficient money to stay at home and live on the fat of the land and make yet more money.[204]

Working-class and middle-class whites found themselves squeezed from the top by industrialists and increasingly from the bottom by black labour. In the prevailing circumstances, dissatisfaction with the Government took on a racial element,[205] while, paradoxically, there was an 'urgent desire' to be rid of 'racialism' between English- and Afrikaans-speaking segments of society.[206] Irrespective of ethnicity, all white men were understood to have the right to 'social justice' and a reasonable quality of life. Social cohesion and solidarity among whites, however, was seen, in the deeply toxic and racialised environment of the Union, to be threatened by the economic and political aspirations of black and coloured South Africans, many of whom were radicalised by the experience of the war.[207] Thus, the belief grew that, for whites to prosper in South Africa, the economic and political rights of black and coloured South Africans would have to be strictly curtailed. The conditions for institutionalised apartheid in South Africa had been substantially shaped by the experience of the war.

Given the depth of feeling and the extent to which these attitudes permeated the UDF, it does seem reasonable to suggest that they might have directly encouraged white veterans to vote for the HNP in 1948. Moreover, as the election turned out to be an extremely closely fought affair, it is conceivable that the soldiers vote proved highly influential in deciding the outcome.[208] The Nationalists won a five-seat majority with only 39.4 per cent of the votes;[209] the 'critical Nationalist gains' were generally won 'with only narrow majorities'.[210] The main electoral swing involved a twofold movement towards the HNP by Afrikaner farmers and white working-class voters. Kenneth Heard, for example, has estimated that a shift towards the Nationalists among Transvaal farmers gave the HNP fifteen extra seats, while William Beinart has argued that the Nationalist victory was probably dependent on no more than a 'protest vote of perhaps 20 per cent of English-speakers'.[211] For these reasons, historians such as Albert Grundlingh, Rodney Davenport, Christopher Saunders and Beinart have speculated that the ex-military vote may have played an important role in 1948.[212] Grundlingh has certainly intimated that Afrikaner veterans voted for the HNP. He has argued that the disenchantment of Afrikaans-speakers with Smuts and the military 'coincided with attempts' by organisations like the *Ossewa Brandwag* (OB) 'not only to temper their criticisms of Afrikaners who had enlisted but also actively to woo them back into the fold':

> Once it had become clear that the tide of war had turned against Germany, Afrikaner nationalists modified their earlier anti-war policy and this, together with a desire to bring about greater Afrikaner unity, contributed to the more conciliatory attitude towards Afrikaans-speaking soldiers. Although a range of factors account for the Afrikaner victory at the polls in 1948, it would not be inaccurate to include among these the social dynamics generated by Afrikaner participation in the war, and the impact of Afrikaner soldiers who had returned much more disgruntled with the United Party government than had been the case upon their enlistment.[213]

It must be remembered that no fewer than 23 per cent of Afrikaner volunteers during the war were farmers (approximately 10,300 of the

45,000 Afrikaners who joined up).[214] Moreover, the English-speaking cohort of the Army – around 87,000 men – was of a noticeably lower socio-economic status than the general population (see Table 2.6), and, thus, would have been especially vulnerable to the economic changes that were sweeping through South Africa at the time.[215]

There are, unfortunately, no known documentary or other sources that can definitively prove or disprove whether English-speaking and Afrikaans-speaking veterans voted for Malan in 1948. However, it certainly was the case that the Nationalists promised to honour all obligations entered into by the Smuts Government towards ex-servicemen.[216] It is also clear, from the large body of new evidence explored here, that attitudes which had developed during the war resonated with the Nationalist vision for South Africa. In this context, it does appear reasonable to conclude that this coincidence of interest and attitudes, made possible by the men's experience as part of the UDF in the Second World War, must have at least implicitly underpinned the ex-military vote in the epoch-defining election of 1948. In the unique racialised environment of South Africa, a spirit of social cohesion had emerged from the exigencies of combat cohesion, with most unfortunate and long-lasting consequences.

Soldiers, Veterans and the Partition of India

The soldiers' role in socio-political change in India was also unfortunately associated with deeply tragic outcomes. As was the case in the other British and Commonwealth Armies, many Indian soldiers, certainly in Europe, were greatly politicised by the experience of the conflict. As the war progressed, the censors increasingly pointed to radical attitudes among the men. The summary for the start of September 1944 noted that:

> Overseas service, and the consequent experience of fresh environments, has clearly affected the political outlook of some writers, who emphasise that in Italy they are 'now seeing a free country', and they are evidently somewhat unsettled by a feeling that India is not a 'free country' in the same sense.[217]

As one NCO writing in Hindi put it, 'I am not the same man now . . . my mind has undergone a metamorphosis. I feel like a free man. When the war is over and India is granted independence, then alone shall

I consider it worth while to return to my country.'[218] An Indian officer wrote in June 1945:

> Nearly every Indian officer is at present talking about the fate of India after the war. Even the ordinary Indian sepoy could not long remain unaffected by some of the conditions of political freedom and its advantages which he has had to notice in these countries (of Europe). There is going to be a great change when these sepoys go back to their villages.[219]

'When all is done and India gets Dominion Status', wrote another officer, 'then – and then alone – shall we consider that our work is over. The Indians who came out of India a few years ago will not be the same when they go back to their country after visiting several foreign lands.'[220]

Morale reports from India and South-East Asia Command broadly echoed these sentiments. The 'more intelligent' men (as they put it), such as NCOs and officers, were 'greatly interested' in 'Indian political problems and the future of their country', whereas, apparently, less interest was taken by the ordinary sepoy. The morale reports did, however, point out that all troops showed 'great interest' in the 'question of the post-war position of the soldier',[221] and, in due course, even the most apolitical of sepoys came to realise that this issue was intimately tied up with the question of independence.[222]

The men of the Indian Army were to be, as Christopher Bayley and Tim Harper have written, 'the shock troops who would finally transform the Indian village and sweep away generations of ignorance and backwardness'.[223] The censors very much saw this change coming. The report for 1 to 15 April 1945 noted that 'it appears to be a not uncommon feeling that the broadening of mental outlook produced by foreign service will prove beneficial' on the men's 'return to India'.[224] 'It becomes increasingly clear', declared the report for the second half of the same month, 'that contact with people of other countries is awakening the Indian fighting man to an awareness of the shortcomings of his native way of life, and his personal responsibility to do something about it'. An NCO in 6/13 Frontier Force Rifles wrote in Urdu:

> Mother insists on me marrying an illiterate and unmannered girl. Please tell her that I will only accept an educated one. More than four years in Egypt, Syria and Italy have made me realise

> that the true ornament of a woman is education, and parents should help to provide it.[225]

An Indian OR in 1 Sikh Battalion wrote in Gurmukhi, 'I have seen so many places and talked with men of so many different nations that I am a different man, and have learned many things which will be of great value, not only to me but also to my villagers.'[226]

It is clear that although, in many ways, the men were 'starved of political news', 'one thing' was 'certain' to them; it was 'time', as one man put it, 'to get together to obtain a substantial measure of "independence" and then to devote all our energies to building up a great country worthy of a great nation'.[227] These calls for independence and social change, however, did not reflect socio-religious differences. There was, for example, almost no mention of a separate and independent Pakistan in the many censorship reports from the Middle East and the Mediterranean and the morale reports from India and South-East Asia Commands. An NCO wrote after VE day:

> This victory has caused great rejoicing throughout the Commonwealth. India and the children of her soil have played a vital part in achieving this glorious Victory for the cause of the Democracies. We remember the days when the very existence of the Western Democracies was at stake and the loyal India has made great sacrifices in their struggle to exist. We are fully confident … [of] an appropriate reward in the shape of … Home Rule. At the same time I must assert that we Indians should sink our differences and to create unity and brotherhood should always be our topmost aim.[228]

The troops, according to the censors, were more concerned with issues such as increased 'education, particularly for women, a common language, and reforms in both social and religious spheres' than they were with perpetuating class and communal divisions. For example, the June 1945 Wavell plan for Indian self-government, which failed to gain traction due to Congress and Muslim League intransigence, 'was well received' by the troops and 'considered by many to be the basis of a settlement of old disputes and conflicting parties'.[229] The experience of combat and shared danger had blurred divisions based on communal identities. As a man in 5/5 Mahrattas wrote, 'whatever the political differences, we are held in admiration by every one who has fought side by side with us'.[230] Teamwork, not disunion, was the lesson of the front line.

Independence and Partition

These attitudes and beliefs were to play a significant role in post-war independent India, notwithstanding the fact that in the 'uncertain, transformed world after the war', the political future 'started to cleave along religious lines'.[231] Politics during the war, in many ways, prefigured this breakdown. Congress had declined to support involvement in the war, while the Muslim League and the Punjab National Unionist Party had decided to 'row in' behind Britain. Many Congress leaders, as a consequence of the decision to boycott the war, encapsulated in the ongoing 'Quit India' movement, were put in jail. The result was that the governance of Congress-led provinces in Bombay, Madras, the United Provinces, the Central Provinces, Bihar, Orissa and the North-West Frontier Province was taken over by the British and direct rule imposed. In the political vacuum that ensued, Jinnah and the Muslim League took advantage of the imprisonment of the Congress leaders, and, over time, began to propound the necessity for an independent Pakistan (not least to ensure that Muslims would not become a subjugated group under a Hindu-dominated independent India). British attempts to heal the growing rift between Hindu and Muslim political factions failed and, as the Second World War drew to an end, calls for an independent Muslim Pakistan, separate from India, grew increasingly forceful.[232]

During the war years, the 'danger' of the Muslim League had clearly been 'underestimated by the Congress leadership'.[233] Moreover, by early 1947, it was apparent too that British hopes for a quasi-federal India, still closely linked to the Commonwealth, was not going to align with the competing visions of independence held by Indians themselves. On 3 June, Mountbatten, who had replaced Wavell as Viceroy, announced to the world that the new independent India would be partitioned into two separate states (as of August that year). Recognising the necessity to partition Punjab and Bengal, a Boundary Commission, chaired by Sir Cyril Radcliffe, was established to demarcate the frontiers between a future India and Pakistan.[234] Partition into a Hindu-dominated Hindustan (India) and Muslim dominated Pakistan was now a certainty.

The consequences of the failure to build a common vision for the future of the subcontinent would prove to be immense. Fears over an independent Pakistan had 'encouraged the surreptitious collection of arms' by all sides as far back as 1940.[235] As the date for the handover of power (15 August), and the decision of the Boundary Commission neared, 'many perceived that changes in the "facts on the ground"' might yet determine the national borders of the subcontinent.[236] Communities armed themselves and 'private armies' were formed, especially in the areas most likely to be affected by partition, in the Punjab and Bengal. The 'power and strength' of these private armies was assessed in an intelligence report in February 1947; men were attending training camps where former soldiers, who were sometimes even wearing military uniform, were providing instruction. 'Many reports' on the rise of 'volunteer para-military movements' pointed to the fact that these organisations were exceptionally well drilled in military skills.[237] It was estimated that paramilitary organisations across India comprised more than 500,000 members, and it is evident that these 'private and communal armies', much like the paramilitary groups that emerged following the First World War, were led, and in many cases, manned, by ex-servicemen.[238]

The cataclysmic events of 1947 were to a great measure influenced by these groups. The boundaries of post-partition India were largely to be determined by the proportion of Muslims, Hindus and Sikhs in any territory. Muslims, Hindus and Sikhs 'caught on the wrong side' of borders, real or imaginary, found themselves, therefore, '"target" minorities' and 'large-scale' killings and population flows resulted. An estimated 17.9 million people left their homes; between March 1947 and January 1948, many thousands were slaughtered (approximations vary from 180,000 to 1 million people) as communal violence and ethnic cleansing gripped the districts on the Indo-Pakistan border.[239]

The character of this terrible bloodletting was, to a significant extent, shaped by the servicemen and ex-servicemen who had fought as part of the Indian Army during the Second World War. On the one hand, where possible, the violence was kept in check by the Army; on the other, paramilitary gangs led by demobilised veterans played an important part in the pattern, scale and intensity of population movements and ethnic cleansing.

The Indian Army's role was particularly important in the early phases of partition, in spite of the massive draw down in its numbers due to demobilisation. During this period, the Army broadly maintained its discipline, refusing to fragment along religious and communal lines, as some were concerned it would. The professionalism that had emerged after the great reforms of 1943, that had seen the Indian Army through the trials of Imphal and Kohima and the victories of 'Capital' and 'Extended Capital', now shone through again as the Army cohered round the task of internal security.

As the police and civil service crumpled under the pressure, the Indian Army managed to resist the pull towards communalism and political favouritism. Intelligence summaries from the period noted that reports from units employed on Internal Security duties continued 'to stress [the] impartiality shown by the troops in carrying out their duties'.[240] Overall, the Indian Army in Eastern Command 'was able to keep most of the violence that erupted to a manageable level during the period up to and immediately following independence',[241] while in the Punjab 'it was reported' that 'the army had performed well in its duties'.[242] The last intelligence report for the Indian Army, of 2 August 1947, noted that:

> The integrity and impartiality of the Indian troops [has] remained unchanged. The way in which the civilian population has welcomed the Army wherever it has gone has come as a pleasant surprise to the troops.[243]

Cohesion developed on the battlefields of Europe and Asia had at least, in part, tempered the destructive tensions tearing Indian society apart.

After partition, however, and coinciding with the announcement of the findings of the Boundary Commission, violence escalated to a heretofore-unimaginable level.[244] On the dissolution of the British Indian Army (in August 1947), a new organisation, the Punjab Boundary Force (PBF), was formed. It was made up of Indian and Pakistani units and put under the control of a British commander; it was now faced with the daunting challenge of internal security duties on the north-west border of India and the new Pakistan. The PBF, which initially consisted of only five brigades, was instructed 'to cover twelve districts within the Punjab: an area comprising 37,500 square miles and a population of 14.5 million, many of whom were demobilised soldiers'. It proved incapable of preventing the mass slaughter that ensued.

Nevertheless, 'although there were instances of subunits not performing their duties, there were many more examples of professionalism maintained, at times in situations of extreme stress'.[245] In an environment where the civil power had lost control of law and order, and with insufficient means available, the PBF did as best it could. Failures 'had less to do with lack of discipline in the forces during the violence, and more to do with factors that were outside of its [the PBF] control'. 'It is not an exaggeration', as Daniel Marston has concluded, 'to say that, without the intervention of the PBF, the number of people killed in the Punjab could easily have been double the number listed today.'[246]

As veterans in the Indian Army and PBF struggled to limit the negative fallout of partition, ex-servicemen were also involved in the many armed gangs and paramilitary groups that shaped the violence in other ways. These men, it has been argued, restricted more extreme behaviours, and, in places, dramatically reduced the scale of unnecessary viciousness and killing.[247] To begin with, veterans with combat experience were better able to provide their communities with 'safe havens and other infrastructure' that facilitated population movements.[248] As Ian Morrison, a reporter for *The Times* wrote from the Punjab:

> The Sikhs move in blocks of 40,000 to 60,000 and cover about 20 miles a day. It is an unforgettable sight to see one of these columns on the move. The organization is mainly entrusted to ex-servicemen and soldiers on leave who have been caught by the disturbances. Men on horseback, armed with spears and swords, provide guards in front, behind, and on the flanks. There is a regular system of bugle calls. At night a halt is called near some village where water is available, watch fires are lit, and pickets are posted.[249]

Moreover, in those districts where individuals and groups had 'enhanced organizational skill gained in combat', population exchanges were typically more peaceful, whether or not those who had attained those skills were in the majority or were a minority. As Saumitra Jha and Steven Wilkinson have argued, in cases where majority ethnic groups possessed a large proportion of veterans, 'the threat of violent ethnic cleansing' was deemed to have been more 'credible, and the actual cleansing more organized and less wasteful of life and property when it did occur'. In cases where the minority had a high proportion of veterans, it made them 'better able to leave in anticipation of violence. Thus, while minority ethnic cleansing was higher in districts with more experienced combat veterans, the population transfer was relatively more peaceful.'[250]

It does appear then that the experience of the Second World War provided Indian soldiers with 'skills at private organization of defense, offense, and mobility that' were 'particularly valuable' during the period of crisis and ethnic cleansing that accompanied partition. These enhanced organisational skills played a significant role in shaping the process of socio-political change that occurred in South Asia between 1945 and 1948. The result was a 'remarkable', but appalling, 'religious homogenization of the districts of South Asia ... While target minorities constituted an average of 13.8% of a district's population in 1931, this proportion declined by 34.8%, with minorities constituting only 9.0% over all, by 1951.'[251] The Indian subcontinent had undergone unprecedented and, for many thousands, tragic upheaval and change.

Soldiers, Veterans and Social Change

As many historians, social scientists and economists have argued, 'broad cross-country patterns' suggest that there is a strong relationship between war and socio-political change. There is, however, 'much less evidence' to evaluate the mechanisms by which this process occurs, 'whether through a change in norms of fairness, a rise in common interest or by the development of organizational skills gained in combat'.[252] The research presented here has shown that all these processes played a role in the great socio-political transformations that took place in the Commonwealth in the years during and immediately after the Second World War.

The Second World War clearly had, as so much of the literature has shown, a considerable effect on how civilians viewed their relationship with the state. But, it also profoundly affected those serving in the armed forces. Active engagement in the war effort fostered communitarian and egalitarian attitudes that were to impact greatly on voting preferences. If these ideas were not always expressed initially in explicitly political terms, it did not mean that soldiers were not intensely political. Over time, citizenship education programmes, such as ABCA, and a growing public discourse on the topic of social security, helped soldiers articulate their evolving political beliefs and shape strategies to transform these beliefs into meaningful political action.

In the case of the United Kingdom, politicised troops exhibited a strong drift to the left in their mail to friends and family. These new-found perspectives influenced citizen soldiers, and their close personal networks, to vote for Labour in 1945. Even if, as things stand, we currently lack a methodological or evidential base to prove conclusively that this was the case, an examination of the soldiers' mail does indicate clearly that this substantial cohort of the British population voted Labour not only as 'a positive endorsement of socialism', but also to reject the Conservative Party;[253] while the soldiers admired Churchill's skills as a wartime leader, they scorned him and his party when it came to 'winning the peace'.

A much richer evidential base is available for elections in other Commonwealth countries. The soldiers' voting behaviours in New Zealand and Canada, for example, show the intimate relationship between combat experience and communitarian and egalitarian attitudes at play. Taking the Labour and Democratic Labour vote in 1943 together, the 'left-leaning' vote was 51 per cent among civilians in New Zealand and 65 per cent among the mostly Air Force personnel serving in the UK, the most dangerous part of the war effort for New Zealanders in September 1943. In Canada, 'Progressive' parties, including the Liberal Party, the CCF, and the Social Credit Party, received 58 per cent of the civilian vote and 71 per cent of the vote of those Canadians who had been recently fighting on the front line in North-West Europe. For the soldiers that fought and the communities they represented, the meaning of the war clearly went far beyond victories and defeats on the battlefield. In the case of New Zealand, Labour's great experiment in social citizenship in the twentieth century could arguably have foundered had it lost the 1943 general election.[254] Although the Liberal Government was to survive the 1945 Canadian election, Mackenzie King was not so lucky; he lost his Prince Albert seat in Saskatchewan due to a protest vote among service personnel angry at what they perceived as the unjust way conscription and the provision of reinforcements for the battlefront had been managed by his government.[255]

These more benign outcomes of the politicisation of the soldier were not to be matched in other parts of the Commonwealth. In South Africa, the shared experience of danger on the front line healed old wounds between English- and Afrikaans-speaking South Africans. At the same time, the manner in which the home front was managed during the conflict exacerbated racial tensions between white and black and coloured South Africans. Thus, the conditions for institutionalised apartheid were substantially shaped by the experience of the war; for there to be security and 'social justice' for white South Africans, it became 'necessary' to exclude black and coloured South Africans from the social contract. In this context, it does appear reasonable to conclude that this coincidence of interest and attitudes, made possible by the men's experience as part of the UDF in the Second World War, led them to vote National in the epoch-defining election of 1948. The social cohesion that had emerged from combat cohesion, in this instance, had uniquely unfortunate outcomes.

Social change in this period was driven also by other dynamics. In addition to alterations in the 'norms of fairness' or a 'rise in common interest' as a consequence of the war experience, many men in the British and Commonwealth Armies learned from their Imperial colleagues and from their immersion in the cultures where they served. Indian soldiers, in particular, as the censors put it, had 'considerable knowledge' of the political currents that were affecting British soldiers during the war. An Indian officer wrote from Italy in July 1944:

> We read and hear so much about the Beveridge plan for social security in post-war Great Britain. Gigantic schemes are being worked out to discharge the nation's debt of gratitude to the soldier, when he goes back home. But we do not hear much about a corresponding plan for us when we go back to India. What we know is this – that a few odd jobs will be reserved for us. But they can't reserve jobs for an army of two million men.[256]

A year later, 'the great election uproar in Great Britain', as an Indian warrant officer put it, was also 'keenly watched' because 'of its likely results on the solution of the Indian problem'.[257]

The censorship summaries show that Indians serving abroad kept in touch with politics in India through their mail and soldiers newspapers.[258] While it is clear that some in the Indian Army were extremely uneasy at the prospect of a Congress-governed independent India, 'since it is thought that the rights of the returned soldier would be prejudiced if authority were to pass into the hands of the

Nationalists',[259] the majority expressed a firm desire for 'the dignity of national independence'.[260] When they returned to India at the conclusion of hostilities they played a role in shaping the reality of this new India. The professionalism and cohesion bought at such cost during the war years now largely insulated Indian troops, tasked with internal security duties, from the worst of the communal divisions driving violence and ethnic cleansing. Had the Indian Army fractured along communal lines, as happened with the police, it is highly likely that the death toll accompanying partition would have been even greater than the awful total that emerged. Moreover, the organisational skills of demobilised veterans, gained as a consequence of military and combat experience, played an important part in the pattern, scale and intensity of population movements and ethnic cleansing. Qualitative contemporary sources and quantitative analysis highlight the role demobilised veterans played in armed gangs and private armies during this period. These groups were highly organised, almost military, in character; where veterans were present in a district, more extreme behaviours were curtailed, and, in places, the scale of unnecessary violence and killing was dramatically reduced.

The men who made up the British and Commonwealth Armies cared deeply about conditions in the societies for which they fought. The soldiers struggled, and shed blood, not just for each other, but also for a better world. Parties on the left that harnessed this ideal and emphasised the role of the state in arbitrating between sectional interests in society, were better placed to benefit from these dynamics than those that emphasised personal freedoms and the market economy. A spirit of social cohesion had emerged from the exigencies of combat cohesion with profound and, in many cases, long-lasting results.

CONCLUSION

> If it is a case of the whole nation fighting and suffering together, that ought to suit us, because we are the most united of all the nations, because we entered the war upon the national will and with our eyes open, and because we have been nurtured in freedom and individual responsibility . . . Our people are united and resolved, as they have never been before. Death and ruin have become small things compared with the shame of defeat or failure in duty.
>
> Winston Churchill, 'The Few' Speech, 20 August 1940.[1]

The power of Churchill's speech still fires the imagination. In this moment of great danger, as Britain faced invasion, the Prime Minister and those around him remained confident that citizens would rise up and sacrifice everything for their country. The strategic calculus governing the Army's deployment, later in the war, in the Middle East, Europe and the Far East, remained little different; the Empire would rely enormously on the 'poor bloody infantry', the ordinary citizen soldier, and his willingness, when called upon, to fight and if necessary die for the cause.[2]

While Churchill, the Government and the press emphasised that Britain was engaged in a 'people's war' between 1939 and 1945, from the evidence adduced in this book it is clear that there was a distinct disconnect between the rhetoric of nations united in a collective cause and the reality as it unfolded on the ground. In the United Kingdom, given the cultural memory of the First World War and the highly fractured nature of Britain's class-based society – where structured inequality was produced and reproduced in economic, social, cultural and political relations[3] – this, perhaps, should not be all that much of a surprise. The same could be said for the ethnically fragmented dominions of Australia, Canada and South Africa and the quasi-dominion of India, where large proportions of the population, in some cases the majority, were extremely anti-British.

A Deficit of Political Legitimacy

The war began for Britain with the country far from being politically united. It was only with Churchill's accession to power in May 1940 and the formation of a coalition government, which included Labour, that some form of political accord was achieved. In India, the commencement of international hostilities sparked a major political crisis. The Indian National Congress (INC) insisted that support for the war could only be given if the London Government renounced imperialism and promised independence. When the Viceroy, Lord Linlithgow, offered no more than a post-war review of the 1935 constitution, the Congress ministries followed the Congress High Command's instructions and resigned as a body.[4]

The question of unity was as profound, if not quite as extreme, in the Dominions. In many ways Canada entered the war a divided country. Many French Canadians were decidedly against what they saw as Britain's war. Amid fears that a total war effort would wreck national unity, Mackenzie King, the Canadian Prime Minister, refrained from forming a government of national unity; a policy of 'limited liability' characterised Canada's war effort.[5] Local perspectives were no less present in the Antipodes. In Australia and New Zealand, attempts to form unity governments repeatedly failed, to the extent that in October 1942, Fraser, the New Zealand Prime Minister, was forced to admit in Parliament that 'the basis of unity in the country' had 'been destroyed – irretrievably destroyed'.[6] In South Africa, the outbreak of war tore down the veneer of stability created by the interwar Fusion Government. Anti-war sentiment among some Afrikaners extended even so far as vocal support for the Nazis and for a German victory.[7]

The struggle for unity, so evident among political elites, was matched also, in many ways, by citizens' attitudes to mobilisation. The weight of available evidence points to a far less fervent and less deferential population than that which mythically went 'willingly' to war in 1914.[8] Conscription was introduced in the United Kingdom, except Northern Ireland, from the outset of the war; New Zealand introduced compulsory service not long after.[9] It was considered in both cases that volunteering alone would not provide the requisite manpower for the services, a perspective that proved well founded.[10] In the UK, at a minimum, 10 per cent of those called up made an effort to avoid military service. With special deferment schemes in place for those in the higher echelons of society, the fighting was left predominantly to those in the lower-middle and working classes.[11] The situation was even more striking in New Zealand where, in total, 47 per cent of all those conscripted appealed against their call-up to Armed Forces Appeal Boards.[12]

In Canada and Australia, a hybrid solution to the challenges of mobilisation emerged, not least due to ethnic tensions and widespread opposition to conscription. Both countries introduced compulsory service, but only on a limited basis. Conscripts were confined, in theory at least, to home service; it was solely volunteers that could be sent overseas.[13] In Canada, this solution led to a highly unrepresentative armed forces; only 12 per cent of the Canadian Army Overseas were French Canadian,[14] in a country where, in 1939, it was estimated that 30 per cent of the population was French-speaking.[15] In Australia, a pervasive reticence to commit fully to the war meant that only 38 per cent of the Army was made up of direct volunteers. Up to the end of August 1941, voluntary enlistments from a population of 7 million amounted to only 188,587 (~2.7 per cent). In the first two years of the First World War, 307,966 had volunteered from a population of 5 million (~6.2 per cent).[16]

In the highly charged political climates of the subcontinent and South Africa, conscription was quite simply out of the question. The Indian and Union Armies would have to be expanded by volunteerism alone. On a superficial level, the Raj was extremely successful in this endeavour; the Indian Army of 2.25 million was to become the largest volunteer army in history, no small achievement.[17] However, it was raised from a population of 390 million, and, thus, represented only a small proportion of potential Indian manpower, only about 3 per cent of the entire adult male population of the region in this period.[18] The character of mobilisation in South Africa was no less driven by socio-political tensions, to the extent that there was even a 'risk of civil war'.[19] Afrikaner and Black South Africans proved far less likely to serve than their English South African compatriots.

In the main, it was the poor, the destitute and the needy that resorted to joining up.[20] These patterns mattered, as it was these less advantaged cohorts of British and Commonwealth societies (social classes III, IV and V) that were most impacted by the economic, social and psychological consequences of the Depression.[21] In the end, those citizens most connected to the British world and least able to avoid conscription (by deferment or due to their economic position) were most likely to serve in the British and Commonwealth Armies.

Thus, right across the Commonwealth, levels of enthusiasm for war reflected levels of public morale, the socio-political context and perceptions of state legitimacy. In many ways, the act of enlisting, or of being conscripted, reflected 'a dialogue' between the soldier and the state 'about citizenship' and rights more generally. Enlistment and conscription added layers of duty and obligation to the social contract; they were very much 'political' moments.[22] Mobilisation was not solely a question of demographics, but also a question of negotiation and consent.[23]

The manner in which soldiers, their families and their communities were treated by the state during the war mattered, therefore, greatly. If citizen soldiers were to risk all, and potentially sacrifice life and limb, the state had to offer something in return. The censorship summaries explored in this book show, however, that political leaders across the Commonwealth failed to live up to their side of the bargain. The necessity to defeat Germany, Churchill's overwhelming and uncompromising focus between 1940 and 1945, for example, blinded him to this key dynamic; he fundamentally undervalued and misunderstood the central aspiration of his citizen soldiers, the need for immediate and profound social change. It must be remembered that the men at the top of Britain's military machine were not 'politicians or technocrats of the left'. At the very top were Churchill and 'a tiny leavening from the left. In the bureaucratic machine an old elite, drawn from the state, industry and the military-industrial complex dominated'.[24] Churchill fundamentally saw debate about social change and reconstruction 'as a distraction from his main task'.[25] Matters were made more complicated after 'the turning of the tide' in the Second World War. With the success at El Alamein and the German defeat at Stalingrad, victory seemed inevitable; Churchill's position was, thus, 'significantly strengthened, leaving no doubts that the conflict was winnable without sweeping social and political changes'.[26]

The result of this political failure was that during the critical years of the war (most importantly), and even in the last months of fighting, many British and Commonwealth soldiers felt substantially bereft of a cause for which they deemed it worth fighting. The Morale Report for February to May 1942, a period that included both the fall of Singapore and the initial setbacks at Gazala in the desert, noted that 'certainty of employment in what they consider satisfactory conditions' was 'the nearest thing to a "war aim" that most soldiers can be said to have at the moment. Vague assurances from politicians or others, and exhortations to join in a "crusade", do not reassure them on this point.' Commanders' reports confirmed 'that a very large proportion of the rank and file' were 'preoccupied by the question of what, if any, social and economic changes will take place after the war'. Such reflections, according to the writers of the report, were 'too frequent to be dismissed as the stock complaints of the professional "grouser" or the amateur politician'.[27]

This argument might seem incomprehensible given modern-day attitudes to Nazi Germany and Imperial Japan, but the evidence is overwhelming. The morale report for British soldiers in South-East Asia, covering the period of Fourteenth Army's great 'Capital' offensive in 1945, pointed to comparable dynamics; 'the most fundamental stimulus to action', according to the writers, was only the 'desire to finish the war as soon as possible in order to get home':

> Of any widespread appreciation of a higher purpose in the war there is at present little sign, and there would appear to be an urgent need for the Government at home, by word and deed, to present the troops with a cause worth fighting for.

There was still, the report pointed out, a 'great deal of latent idealism among British troops in this theatre, waiting to be directed to a positive cause', but the 'lack of faith in the Government and in politicians generally continue[d] to be the prevalent mood among the troops'.[28]

Matters were little different in the other Commonwealth countries. The inability of Fraser in New Zealand to guarantee anything close to equality of sacrifice during the war led to the Furlough mutinies, arguably the most severe outbreak of indiscipline in any British and Commonwealth force in both world wars, an incident, perhaps comparable to the French mutinies of 1917. Problems on the home front in South Africa were so great that Smuts was unable to replace the 2nd South African Division after its loss at Tobruk. In order to provide two divisions for the campaign in the Mediterranean, South Africa required

60 per cent of those in the Union Defence Force (UDF) to sign up for further service outside of Africa. In the end, only 23 per cent volunteered and South Africa struggled to keep even one division up to strength in the field. The Union, as a consequence, to all intents and purposes forfeited a large portion of its contribution to the Commonwealth war effort in the second half of the war. The situation was analogous in Australia; in 1944 and 1945, as the country was reduced to a supporting role in the South-West Pacific Area (SWPA), enthusiasm on the home front diminished and the morale of the Army slumped. While the Americans did the fighting, the Australian Army was left with mopping-up operations in the Pacific. On the subcontinent, the obvious contradictions between a 'people's war' for the preservation of democracy and imperialism were too great to sustain morale. It led to one of the two 'largest rebellions in British military history',[29] as disenchanted soldiers defected en masse to the Japanese-sponsored Indian National Army.[30] Later in the war, the failure of the Cripps mission and the violence of 'Quit India', led to the psychological disengagement of many soldiers from the war effort.

Put simply, democracies that showed too little commitment to the fair distribution of wealth and opportunity could not expect passionate commitment from their citizens in their defence. Domestic legitimacy 'is an important but oft-ignored component of state strength'.[31] Deep-rooted factors, such as the structured inequality that characterised the class system in Britain, limited the ability and willingness of the Commonwealth states to adapt and change. This fundamentally alienated the predominately working- and lower-middle-class soldiers that made up the British and Commonwealth Armies. The failure of the state to manage narratives regarding fairness and social justice and to promise post-war reforms had immediate and long-lasting effects on the battlefield, and, as a consequence, on Britain and its Empire.

Military Performance

It is in this context that the British and Commonwealth Armies in the Second World War are best understood. In spite of the fact that it was less ready for war in 1939 than it had been in 1914, Britain, and its army, was not completely unprepared for another world war. The British Army, that part of the British and Commonwealth Armies that bore the overwhelming burden of the fighting during the first year of the conflict, was, in the main, led by a cadre of generals that were committed professionals, and, by the standards of the time, well educated. Britain planned to fight, and did fight, 'the next war, not the last'.[32] The War Office had made considerable efforts to understand the lessons of the First World War and by 1939 had successfully predicted the character of the forthcoming conflagration, with its requirement for all-arms co-operation and integration. It had also developed a doctrine that encouraged its commanders to take responsibility in battle and trust their subordinates in a manner more commonly associated with the German Army of the Second World War.[33]

Notwithstanding these many positive factors, the Cabinet's decision to leave an expansion of the Army until it was almost too late did inevitably lead to short-term deficiencies, especially in the quality of training, that essential bridge between theory and practice.[34] These military deficiencies were exacerbated by the lingering impacts of the two socio-economic catastrophes of the first years of the twentieth century, the First World War and the Great Depression, vicissitudes that had 'important economic and psychological consequences' for those that would make up the majority of the British and Commonwealth Armies.[35]

In 1939, defeat and disaster were by no means preordained; nevertheless, the British and Commonwealth Armies found themselves repeatedly overwhelmed on the battlefield. There were two key interrelated reasons for this failure. The first was the Armies' inability to make good the training deficit; the second was the incapacity of junior officers and men to win the battle of wills at the tactical level.

In terms of training, British doctrine asked a lot of the men who were tasked with adapting to, controlling and overcoming the vast array of challenges they might face in a battle environment. In order to meet these challenges, all officers and men had to be superbly prepared. This, however, was rarely the case for most of 1940, 1941 and 1942; the troops who fought in Europe, North Africa and the Far East were handicapped by a training regime that struggled to cope with the delayed and then rapid expansion of the Army. As a consequence, training, in many ways, became the remit of commanders in theatre, but too few of these senior officers rose to the task. A doctrine that focused on 'mission command' became confused with a necessity also to devolve the planning and conduct of training.[36] This led to a 'slowness in appreciation, decision and action in a war whose tempo was extreme'.[37]

The requirement for junior officers and their men to win the battle of wills at the tactical level was understood to be largely a function of military morale.[38] Once battle began, matters were typically in the hands of junior officers and troops and, all too often in the early years of the war, these men failed to defeat the enemy in tactical actions that accumulated into operational and strategic setbacks. The Bartholomew Report on the causes of the disaster in France in 1940 identified morale as the one factor above all else that was central to the performance of the BEF. The solution to the German operational approach (what became known as *blitzkrieg*) lay not primarily in any technological or conceptual revolution but in the willingness of British and Commonwealth troops and junior officers to hold on and fight, thus threatening German lines of communication and retarding the speed of their advance.[39]

The lessons from North Africa and the Far East were little different. As Eighth Army fell back in disarray from the Gazala Line in the summer of 1942, the medical situation reports documented a 'considerable rise' in the number of men reporting sick that was 'most disquieting'.[40] Those missing or having surrendered represented 88 per cent of all casualties; Auchinleck, the Commander-in-Chief, cabled London demanding the return of the death penalty for cowardice and desertion in the field.

Commanders in the Far East despaired at the performance of their men. At Kampar, in December 1941, Archibald Paris, the commander of 11th Indian Division, called his formation to arms as it prepared to defend against the coming Japanese attack:

> The present situation has GOT TO CEASE – and the Japanese have got to become frightened of us. I decline to believe that British and Indian troops are incapable of bringing about this desirable state of affairs ... it is up to us to establish local and personal ascendancy over the enemy immediately opposed to us.[41]

Percival's Order of the Day, issued on 11 February 1942, before the climactic conclusion of the battle for Singapore, echoed these sentiments:

> In some units the troops have not shown the fighting spirit which is to be expected of men of the British Empire. It will be a lasting disgrace if we are defeated by an army of clever gangsters, many times inferior in numbers to our own. The spirit of

> aggression and determination to stick it out must be inculcated in all ranks. There must be no further thought of withdrawal without orders.[42]

In the West, Montgomery was the key architect in finding a solution to these related problems. On taking over command in North Africa in August 1942, he addressed the core challenges facing his army head on. He instigated a training programme that in extent, intensity and attention to detail dwarfed any that had preceded it during the war. He also addressed the issue of morale; on 13 August 1942, he gathered his new subordinates around him. 'The defence of Egypt', he stated confidently, 'lies here at Alamein':

> What is the use of digging trenches in the Delta? It is quite useless; if we lose this position we lose Egypt; all the fighting troops now in the Delta must come out here at once, and will. *Here* we will stand and fight; there will be no further withdrawal; I have ordered that all plans and instructions dealing with further withdrawal are to be burnt, and at once. We will stand and fight *here*. If we can't stay here alive, then let us stay here dead.[43]

From a psychological perspective, Montgomery's message of defiance was exactly what the troops needed to hear; his directive spread like wildfire throughout the formations in the desert.[44] In one move, he had gripped the imagination of his army; in many ways, for the British and Commonwealth Armies, it was the turning point in the war.

The stars now aligned for Montgomery. His efforts to turn around the morale of his army were supported by a series of reforms introduced by Ronald Adam, the Adjutant-General. Adam aimed to make the Army an institution 'more careful of human values, more responsive to the needs and aspirations of the ordinary soldier, and more democratic in spirit'.[45] With this aim in mind, he initiated significant changes in personnel selection, man-management, welfare and education that began to bear fruit in the late summer of 1942. Montgomery's accession to command also coincided with the influx of vast amounts of weapons and material from the United Kingdom and the United States.

Most importantly of all, Montgomery developed a fighting method that catered for the facts as they were on the ground; he commanded an averagely trained army with uncertain morale.

Whereas those who had commanded before him had employed a system of directive command, which sought to adapt to and exploit battlefield opportunities, Montgomery recognised that his army was quite simply incapable of fighting effectively in this sophisticated manner. Instead, he sought to impose a more centralised system of command and control aimed at creating opportunities through 'unity of effort' (the 'Colossal Cracks' approach). In this way, he would make maximum use of the considerable advantages he now enjoyed in terms of materiel and fire-power in the desert.[46]

Firepower alone, however, 'could not win battles'. Against troops who were well dug-in, 'even massive concentrations of artillery killed or wounded remarkably few enemy soldiers'. The main effect of artillery and aerial bombardment was not to kill the enemy, but to degrade their morale and suppress their fire so that the troops could cross the fire-swept zone.[47] Success under Montgomery's 'Colossal Cracks' approach depended to a large extent, therefore, on the speed with which attacking infantry could follow up bombardments.[48] If too big a gap was left between the end of a bombardment and the arrival of the attacking troops, defenders were typically able to recover from the shock of massed firepower and fight effectively.[49] The ability of commanders and staff to ensure that offensives were perfectly planned was also of paramount importance. If available resources were not allocated at exactly the right place and the right time, or if unexpected events slowed the advance, allowing defenders to react and respond, operations more often than not failed shortly after H-Hour.

The level of German resistance was additionally of critical importance. The 'Colossal Cracks' approach eschewed the kind of rapid manoeuvre that could surround and penetrate German positions and place enemy units in situations of intolerable pressure where they might be forced to surrender.[50] Small numbers of Germans, if they could withstand the physical and morale effects of massive Allied bombardments, were able to hold up advances and compel British and Commonwealth units to reset and begin another set-piece attack. In this context, Montgomery's firepower-heavy approach had severe limitations. If any of these interlinking factors proved problematic, little success would be achieved. The inability of any of the British and Commonwealth Armies to progress from a break-in to a breakthrough battle during the heavy fighting of late 1942, 1943 and 1944 was largely a consequence of this reality.

In the East, training and morale were also central to the evolution in the performance of the British and Commonwealth Armies. Vast, centrally controlled, tactical training programmes were set up in Australia and India in 1942 and 1943, where new recruits and veterans alike, were taught to live and move in the jungle. The fundamental disconnect between the soldier and the state, a particularly challenging problem for the Indian Army, could not be fully overcome, but the Army learnt increasingly to better manage its human resources and treat its men with respect. The most significant of these initiatives was the Indianisation of the Army in India. By early 1942, equal pay had been introduced for Indian officers. In June 1943, it was announced that Indian officers were to have powers of punishment over British army personnel.[51]

By the second half of 1943, a spirit of reform had begun to take root in the Indian and Australian Armies. This mirrored the process that had occurred in the British Army in the UK and in the desert, even if its end product was quite different. Where 'Monty's Army' sought to centralise and control, Blamey's, Auchinleck's and, ultimately, Slim's armies, had to a far greater extent, due to the challenges of fighting in the jungle, to devolve and delegate command to the lowest levels. The close character of the fighting in the jungle required junior leaders to make rapid decisions when they came into contact with the enemy; acting 'without delay' could be the difference between life and death, success and failure.[52]

However, in both the SWPA and in Burma, it took time to fully overcome the deficiencies that had negatively affected battle performance during the early campaigns. As a consequence, the form of warfare adopted by the Australian and Indian Armies reflected a hybrid between the basic principles of pre-war doctrine and Montgomery's 'Colossal Cracks' approach. Both armies proved exceptionally capable of killing Japanese in battles of attrition at Imphal, Kohima and in New Guinea, but less accomplished in the kind of mobile warfare that was required for the annihilation of Japanese formations in the field.

As the war in both the East and West descended into costly battles of attrition in 1943 and 1944, commanders began to recognise the limits to the approaches that had emerged to address the crises of

1940 to 1942. In the West, three major initiatives were championed. The first was an incremental improvement in doctrine at the tactical and operational levels. This, in many ways, returned the Army to the basic understandings of interwar Field Service Regulations.[53] After the slog of Italy, the limited successes in Normandy and the setback of 'Market Garden', Montgomery recognised that 'Colossal Cracks' could not deliver the outcomes he desired in the timeframes required. As a consequence, he encouraged and formalised a return to a more devolved system of command and control. 'Rather than telling people how to do things', Montgomery now insisted on the 'importance of people coming up with their own answers with regard to tactical problem solving'.[54] A similar understanding developed in the Mediterranean where by mid-1944, Eighth Army had adopted, from brigade to army level, 'a particular expression of mission command'.[55]

The second initiative was an improvement in the type and intensity of training made available for troops. By 1945, improved training processes and procedures, along with the bitter experience of battle, had taught the Army to work effectively as a team with all arms closely co-operating. In the great battles that preceded the Axis collapse, Montgomery in North-West Europe and Richard McCreery, the commander of Eighth Army, in Italy, undertook intensive periods of training. Tactics were refined and new weapons integrated into existing formations. British and Commonwealth commanders finally and consistently obeyed that fundamental rule of war, of only asking of their troops what they were capable of and trained to do.

To accompany this improvement in doctrine and training, a renewed effort was made to monitor and manage morale. Attempts to remobilise Commonwealth societies in the second half of the war largely failed, hinging as they did on governments' willingness to manage the war effort in a manner consistent with the aims and political aspirations of citizen soldiers. Adam's efforts to reform the Army, which were largely repeated throughout the Commonwealth, were to play a fundamentally important role in this context. Adam understood that when the stress of combat pushed men to, and beyond, their limits, they did not, in the prevailing circumstances, have strong ideological motivations as a bulwark to crisis. It was in those situations in particular that the soldier's welfare needed to be managed carefully; he needed rest, a letter from his family, a clean pair of clothes, some beer, a cigarette and a shower. When the Army failed in these endeavours, a setback could turn into a rout and a rout could easily turn into a disaster. As the war progressed, formations in the field became increasingly effective at using censorship to gauge when and if units were experiencing vital shortages in welfare amenities, or if they needed to be rotated and rested. This reflective and remarkably sophisticated system of monitoring and managing the human factor in war was to make all the difference.

With the refined application of the lessons of the first half of the war, the path towards the victory campaigns of 1945 was opened up. In the West, once the formidable natural barriers of the 'Gothic' and 'Siegfried' lines had been breached, Eighth Army and 21st Army Group broke through German defences and destroyed enemy formations in massive battles of annihilation. In the East, a now highly trained and motivated Fourteenth Army was able to reap the rewards of the doctrinal revolution of 1942 and 1943. In Operations 'Capital' and 'Extended Capital', it outmanoeuvred and outfought a much larger Japanese force than was ever encountered by the Americans in the Pacific.[56] Citizen armies without an ideological underpinning had been superseded by new armies motivated by professional pride and martial conviction. The transformation of the British and Commonwealth Armies in the Second World War was complete.

Consequences

As impressive as this transformation in the performance of the British and Commonwealth Armies was, especially in light of the socio-political context, it came too late to achieve the ambitious ends set out for it by wartime leaders. In order to maintain its international prestige and influence after the war, Britain needed not only to be seen to play a significant part in the defeat of the Axis but also to maintain sizeable and powerful armed forces in the post-war world.[57] The British and Commonwealth Armies were to be a key part in this equation. In Britain, 66 per cent of the manpower allocated to the armed forces was in the Army, and it accounted for 38 per cent of defence expenditure (compared with 26 per cent for the RAF and 36 per cent for the Royal Navy).[58] Theoretically, with access to American Lend-Lease, limitless material resources were available. However, the time would come when Britain would have to pay her debts. It was decidedly in the Imperial interest that the war end quickly with the British and Commonwealth

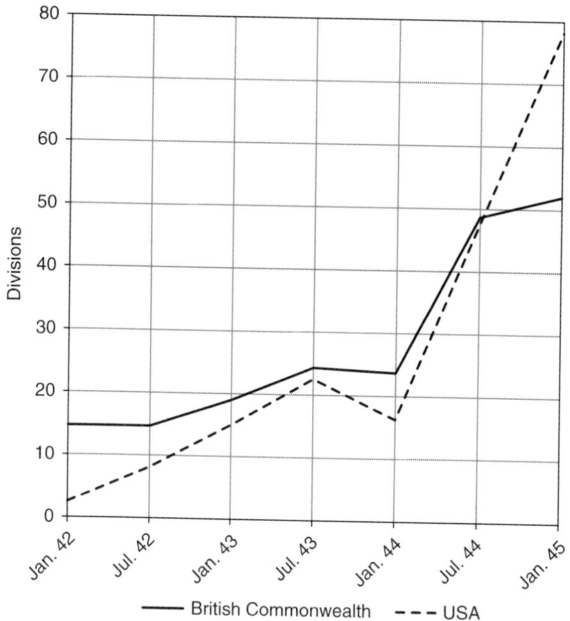

Figure 17.1 Number of British Commonwealth and American Army divisions in fighting contact with the enemy (Western and Eastern theatres), 1942–5

Armies fully functional having played a major role in the defeat of the Axis.

However, in the end, 'Britain did not even achieve her initial reason for going to war: the restoration of a free, independent Poland.'[59] As the war dragged on, the British and Commonwealth Armies played an increasingly smaller role proportionally in fighting the Axis (see Figure 17.1).[60] On 1 September 1944, with the Normandy campaign finished, Montgomery reverted to commanding an army group of roughly fifteen divisions. 'His erstwhile [American] subordinate, Bradley, on the other hand, rose to command close to 50 in what clearly signalled a changing of the guard.'[61] By the end of March 1945, of the 4 million uniformed men under the command of Eisenhower in North-West Europe, over 2.5 million were American, with only 866,575 British and about 180,000 Canadian.[62] The 21st Army Group advanced across Europe 'into an imperial retreat'.[63] The Americans were now the essential part of the transatlantic alliance. 'Heaven knows', Chamberlain had written in January 1940, 'I don't want the Americans to fight for us – we should have to pay too dearly for that if they had a right to be in on the peace terms.'[64]

How right he was. Smuts had feared during the First World War that if the conflict continued into 1919 or 1920, Britain would be reduced to virtual dependence on America. 'If peace comes now', he wrote in October 1918, 'it will be a British peace ... given to the world by the same Empire that settled the Napoleonic wars a century ago.' But, Smuts warned, in 1919 or 1920 the peace which would then be imposed 'on an utterly exhausted Europe will be an American peace' because 'in another year of war the United States will have taken our place as the first military, diplomatic and financial power of the world'.[65] What Smuts feared for 1920 came to pass between 1942 and 1945. Additionally, the delay of 'Overlord' until June 1944 made it almost certain that the Soviets would play a decisive role in the future of Eastern Europe.[66] As one man in 2nd Parachute Brigade wrote in January 1944, 'if we are not careful the final result will be that we went to war to prevent Germany controlling Europe, so that when we had won we could give the control to Russia'.[67]

As a direct consequence of the inability of the British and Commonwealth Armies to rapidly defeat Axis forces on the battlefield, 'the post-war empire was a pale shadow of its former self. The cohesion of its constituent parts had been badly damaged. Much of its wealth had been lost or redistributed.'[68] 'Unable to win a short war, unable to sustain a long one, here was the dilemma of an Empire whose resources and home-base ... failed' to provide an 'adequate' solution to the problem faced.[69] Nowhere was this more apparent than in the Far East. The loss of Singapore was not only a serious military defeat, but it was also a blow to British prestige.[70] General Henry Pownall wrote in his diary that the capitulation was 'a great disaster, one of the worst in our history'.[71] Some historians have gone so far to describe it as the biggest single defeat the British Empire ever suffered.[72]

It signalled 'the definite end of India's special place in the British system'. In its desperate scramble for a constitutional settlement amid the political fallout of the surrender, Churchill's Cabinet was forced to play almost all its trump cards. The failure of Cripps and the unrest of the 'Quit India' campaign left the Raj a political bankrupt. It could repress disorder and gaol the Congress leadership, but it had nothing left to trade with India's political leaders or its people. In what John Darwin has called the 'great imperial crisis', Britain 'sold off' what remained of its Indian empire to meet the pressing demands of the war in the East.[73] Barely two years after the war, and five years after Churchill had uttered his famous words, that he had 'not become the King's first minister in order to preside over the liquidation of the British Empire', Britain's Imperial presence in India had ended.[74] The loss of the subcontinent 'removed three-quarters of King George VI's subjects overnight', reducing Britain to a second-rate power and proved 'that the practice of European Imperialism was no longer sustainable'.[75]

The history of Britain and the Commonwealth cannot, therefore, be understood outside of the context of the performance of the British and Commonwealth Armies in the Second World War. Churchill certainly viewed battlefield success as politically essential.[76] The Empire failed not only because of economic decline, or a greater desire for self-determination among its constituent peoples, but also because it failed to fully mobilise its subjects and citizens for a second great world war. Africans, Asians and even the citizens of Britain and the Dominions demonstrated, at times, an unwillingness to commit themselves fully to a cause or a polity that they believed did not adequately represent their ideals or best interests. When the human element failed, the Empire failed.

The domestic implications of fractures on the front line were no less dramatic than the geopolitical. 'Wars cause death and destruction, but important political and social reforms often follow in their wake.'[77] Compared with the outcome of the First World War, when there was only a 'modest improvement in working-class living standards and security',[78] the Second World War led to profound changes in the relationship between the ordinary citizen and the state.[79] In its most obvious form, Britain developed a fully functioning welfare state.[80]

Much of this change has been explained through the lens of the civilian experience of the war, a trade-off for the exertions, suffering, hardship and death experienced on the home front. This has made the conflict 'feel like more of a "people's" than a "soldiers'" war'.[81] But the troops' political beliefs, many of which emerged as a consequence of their experience on the front line, were instrumental to the socio-political changes that materialised post-war. Labour's victory in the British general election of 1945 was dependent in no small measure on the votes of soldiers and their immediate social groups (friends and families); it was only with Labour's electoral triumph that 'full social citizenship for British workers' was introduced in the United Kingdom.[82] As a consequence of the election, the Conservatives too began to embrace radical social reform, albeit reluctantly.[83]

The soldiers' contribution to the outcome of the Australian federal election of 1943 was arguably no less important. In New Zealand, the continuation of the great experiment in social citizenship that had been set in motion by Labour's victory in the 1935 general election, and consolidated in the 1938 Social Security Act, hinged also on the voting preferences of citizen soldiers. With the civilian votes counted in the 1943 general election, it appeared that the Government was heading for defeat. It was only when the armed service votes 'were added to the [domestic] totals' that the Government survived by narrowly holding on to six seats.[84] Had National won these constituencies, the House would have been split evenly between the two parties and there is every chance that the Government would have fallen, with profound implications for the war effort and the shape of the post-war political economy of New Zealand. Fraser later commented, 'it was not only North Africa that the Second Division had saved'.[85]

The war nearly destroyed the unity of Canada and South Africa; in the latter case, the conditions for institutionalised apartheid were substantially shaped by the soldiers' experience on the front line. Leo Marquard, the Chief Education Officer in the UDF, understood that the United Party's 'only hope of retaining the soldiers' vote after the war' lay in making room in the party 'for a strong left wing'.[86] Marquard, perhaps due to the fact that his Information Officers were responsible for army censorship, understood better than most that the UDF had become decisively 'left-leaning'. The inability of Smuts to manage frictions on the home front during the war played to this dynamic; the families of many working-class and middle-class white soldiers found themselves squeezed from the top by industrialists and from the bottom by black labour. In the prevailing circumstances, dissatisfaction with the Government took on a racial element,[87] while, paradoxically, due to shared experiences on the front line, there was an 'urgent desire' to be rid of 'racialism' between English- and Afrikaans-speaking white segments of society.[88] Thus, the belief grew that, for whites to prosper, black and coloured South Africans would have to be excluded from sharing equally in South African society. The conditions for institutionalised apartheid in South Africa had been substantially shaped by the soldiers' experiences at the front and it does appear that the nationalists rather than the United Party tapped into this dynamic in 1948. The Nationalists won an outright majority with only 39.4 per cent of the votes[89] and the 'critical Nationalist gains' were generally won 'with only narrow majorities'.[90] For these reasons, it seems plausible that the ex-military vote was the deciding factor in delivering the Nationalist victory in 1948.[91]

On the Asian subcontinent, the very character of partition and the birth of an independent India and Pakistan in 1947 were influenced by veterans of the war. While some in the Indian Army were extremely uneasy at the prospect of a Congress-governed independent India,[92] the majority expressed a firm desire for 'the dignity of national independence'.[93] When Indian soldiers returned home at the conclusion of hostilities, they played a role in shaping the reality of this new India. The cohesion and professionalism bought at such cost on the front line largely insulated Indian troops tasked with internal security duties from the worst of the communal divisions driving violence and ethnic cleansing. Had the Indian Army fractured along communal lines, as happened with the police, it is highly likely that the death toll accompanying partition would have been even greater than the awful total that emerged. Moreover, the development of organisational skills among demobilised veterans, gained as a consequence of military and combat experience, played an important part in the pattern, scale and intensity of population movements and ethnic cleansing. Where military veterans were present in a district, more extreme behaviours were curtailed, and, in places, the scale of unnecessary violence and killing was dramatically reduced. The role of Indian soldiers during partition was arguably as significant as their contribution during the war itself.[94]

Fighting the People's War

The story that emerges from the study of the British and Commonwealth Armies in the Second World War, therefore, is far more radical and challenging than that which is found in much of the public discourse. While there can be little doubt that the majority of soldiers did their duty in the war, not least the 217,809 who lost their lives (see Table 17.1),[95] others mutinied, some ran away, surrendered too readily or broke down under pressure. It is important that such observations should not be construed as criticism of the natural courage of the average British and Commonwealth soldier.[96] Given the extraordinary and terrifying sacrifices that were demanded and expected of ordinary young men, it is hardly surprising, in the prevailing socio-economic circumstances, that the largely working- and lower-middle-class individuals that made up the vast majority of the Army would

Table 17.1 Casualties, the British and Commonwealth Armies, 1939–45

	Australian	British	Canadian	Indian	NZ	UDF & NEAS	Total
Killed	18,713	146,346	17,492	24,000	6,793	4,465	217,809
Wounded	22,116	239,575	51,660	64,000	15,324	8,137	400,812
POW	20,746	152,076	6,623	60,000	7,863	12,313	259,621
Total	61,575	537,997	75,775	148,000	29,980	24,915	878,242

have, at times, failed to live up to the martial ideal. Unequal, class-conscious societies breed disengaged and under-motivated citizen soldiers. The blame for the 'great imperial crisis' of 1940 to 1942, or the rather 'sluggish' operations of 1943 and 1944, does not lie dominantly with the institution of the Army or the ordinary citizen soldier, but to a very large extent with the political classes and the British and Commonwealth states more generally. It was the British Imperial system, of which its armed forces were just one part, that was to blame for the loss of Britain's place in the world.

The British and Commonwealth Armies, in fact, demonstrated a remarkable ability to reform and adapt their doctrine, training regimes and management of manpower in the extraordinarily challenging situation that unfolded between 1939 and 1945. Had the complex array of state systems that made up the British Empire demonstrated a similar willingness and ability to reflect and reform, issues with morale and combat performance might not have developed to the same extent.

In the end, a sufficiently large number of key individuals in the British and Commonwealth Armies, such as Montgomery, Adam, Auchinleck and Slim, came to understand the character of the challenge faced in the Second World War. Strategy was iterative and multi-levelled, a decision-making continuum where decisions on means and ends at each level affected decisions on means and ends at all other levels; strategy could be driven from below to the same extent as it was defined at the top. This insight escaped some national leaders, including Churchill, with profound consequences. In his obsession with defeating Germany, the British Prime Minister lost sight of the goals and ambitions of the ordinary man, the smallest cog in the 'machinery of strategy', but a vital one all the same. For the citizen soldier, the war was not an end in itself; it was a step on the road towards a greater aspiration, political and social reform. To endure, power had to be built on a bedrock of justice and social cohesion.

A critical understanding of the place of the Second World War in British and Commonwealth history is perhaps now more than ever important. The dominant narrative, which characterises the British and Commonwealth soldier as stolid, but apolitical and uninterested in the broader meaning of the war, encourages the perception that the outcomes of these great events were in the hands of a small group of elite and powerful persons. The soldier, in this version of history, lacks agency; he appears as a pawn in the games of great men. The reality was really quite different; bitter contestation characterised much of the interaction between the state and the individual and from that interaction, the post-war settlement was forged. The censorship summaries and morale reports indicate that the war made soldiers more aware of the limits of individualism and the degree to which they were dependent on their fellow citizens for prosperity, security and wellbeing. As General Alan Brooke, who would become the Chief of the Imperial General Staff, wrote in October 1940, through all the 'destruction, uselessness and havoc I can see some progress':

> Progress that could never be achieved without the upheaval of war. Long standing institutions and social distinctions are shattered by war and make room for more modern methods of life. Those that would never release what they hold in peace, are forced to do so in war, to the benefit of the multitude. Ultimately I suppose that human beings from much suffering will become wiser and will appreciate that greater happiness can be found in this world by preferring their neighbours to themselves![97]

Brooke understood that almost every aspect of the soldiers' lives required co-operation, sharing and teamwork; extreme individualism or selfish behaviour was not only undesirable and inefficient in times of war but potentially life threatening.

The war had demonstrated the extent to which combat effectiveness was dependent on the cohesion of British and Commonwealth societies. It was also apparent that the experience of the front line had spawned a dynamic desire for reform, that the troops yearned for the camaraderie and equality of the battlefront to be present on their return home to 'civvy street'. This great political awaking as a consequence of the war was to have profound implications for the future of the Empire and the socio-political history of all the British and Commonwealth countries.

Appendix 1
THE CENSORSHIP SUMMARIES

In studying the war in the West, against Germany and Italy, this book has made use of 901 censorship summaries (see Table A1). These remarkable sources were based on an assessment of approximately 11 million letters sent by British and Commonwealth soldiers during the war.[1] The twenty-four censorship summaries examined for the war in the East, against Japan, were produced from an assessment of over 6 million letters. Thus, it is likely that in total, the censorship summaries used in this study are based on an assessment of no fewer than 17 million letters. From those summaries that list both the number of letters sent and the number of letters examined, it is possible to deduce that the censors examined about 7 to 8 per cent of all letters mailed in any period.[2]

As exciting as these new sources are for the historian, they must still 'be used with caution'.[3] As Bernard Porter has argued in relation to the study of imperialism, 'people who look for things sometimes find them when they are not there; especially ... if they are looking through distorting lenses. Even when you can avoid that, there is still the temptation to exaggerate the significance of what you have found.'[4] C. P. Stacey, the Canadian Official Historian, admitted:

> The truth of any statement made in a soldier's letter cannot be accepted without investigation; the writer may well be ignorant, malicious or actually mendacious; he may write to vent his spite against an individual; he may exaggerate or misrepresent experiences in order to make himself appear to his correspondent as a hero or a martyr; and sometimes letters are written

Table A1 Number of censorship summaries used in this study

Army	HomeFront	Campaign						Total
		E. Africa	Middle East[i]	Sicily	CMF[ii]	NW Europe	SWPA	
British	9		100	6	48	38		**201**
Australian	[iii]		68				24	**92**
NZ			101		148[vi]			**249**
Indian	[iv]		20		60			**80**
Canadian				2	32	35		**69**
SA	89[v]	45	85		15			**234**
Total	**98**	**45**	**374**	**8**	**303**	**73**	**24**	**925**

[i] Includes the North African and Tunisian campaigns as well as forces stationed in Palestine, Syria, Transjordan, Lebanon, the Sudan, Eritrea, Iraq and Persia.

[ii] Central Mediterranean Force includes the Italian campaign and forces stationed in North Africa, Palestine, Syria, Transjordan and Cyprus.

[iii] The Australian censorship summaries for the SWPA include assessments of mail from units stationed in Australia.

[iv] The Indian censorship summaries include assessments of civilian and military mail sent from India.

[v] Many of the censorship summaries for units stationed in South Africa contain detailed sections on mail sent by units 'Up North' and in Italy.

[vi] Forty-four of these summaries were bi-weekly censorship reports which were produced as part of the CMF censorship reporting apparatus (Nov. 1943–Sept. 1945). These reports summarised and replicate the information from the weekly reports produced by the 2NZEF.

> under the influence of passing circumstances – very bad weather, lack of mail from home, etc., etc. – which lead the author to paint an unduly black picture.[5]

A possible concern, therefore, is that the censorship summaries might paint a distorted and overly negative picture, that the censors might focus on those passages that were 'most critical or most dramatic' at the expense of run-of-the-mill positive sentiments.[6] It cannot be ignored that the War Office explicitly used censorship as a tool to assess the extent of problems such as absence and desertion, shortages, pay, conditions affecting families and relations between officers and other ranks.[7]

On the other hand, there is much evidence to suggest that the censorship process was inclined to report an overly upbeat picture. Paul Fussell, for example, has argued that certainly in the context of the First World War, letters tended to focus excessively on the positive rather than the negative for the reason that they were 'composed largely to sustain the morale of the folks at home, to hint as little as possible at the real, worrisome circumstances of the writer. No one wrote: "Dear Mother, I am scared to death".'[8] Where letters were unit-censored, it was also evident during the Second World War that men 'usually refrain[ed] from criticism of their officers and administration'.[9] Censorship regulations typically forbade 'criticism or statements calculated to bring [the Army] into disrepute', or that outlined the 'moral' state of 'our forces or those of our allies'. 'Any remark which might tend, if published, to encourage the enemy', or 'to cause despondency in our own forces or people' was strictly to be censored.[10]

In spite of these inherent complexities, the available evidence strongly suggests that, on the whole, censorship was carried out in as reflective and balanced a manner as possible. E. Sachs, the Assistant Adjutant-General noted in April 1942, as he wrote seeking information on the financial conditions of the men in the Army, 'we assume that – in order to give a complete picture – favourable as well as adverse comments will be included'.[11] The instructions given to MI12 censors explicitly outlined that they were looking for 'favourable' and 'unfavourable', 'optimistic' and pessimistic' and 'praise' and 'abusive' comments.[12] The general rule was that 'the outstanding subjects' and 'any marked changes since the last report' were the key topics to be reported, with the most talked-about issues typically at the start of the report.[13] Overall, the censors noted, the policy had 'always been to conduct censorship not as a form of "Gestapo" but rather on the lines of a soldier's forum'.[14] In this respect, it does appear that they were successful in their endeavours.

Appendix 2
THE MORALE REPORTS

In researching this study, every effort was made to find the British and Commonwealth censorship summaries that survived the war. It proved impossible, however, to find summaries for every campaign of the Second World War. This problem was particularly acute for the disastrous operations of the early years of the conflict, as many contemporary records were destroyed in France and Singapore to prevent them falling into enemy hands.[1] It proved equally difficult to find censorship summaries for those British, Indian and African formations that fought in Burma between 1943 and 1945.[2] Nevertheless, in the overall context of the war against Japan, a number of morale reports (sixteen in total) were available for the period November 1942 to October 1945.[3]

The morale reports, an innovation instigated by the Adjutant-General of the British Army, General Sir Ronald Adam, were designed specifically to provide the authorities with a picture of the morale of the troops. These reports were produced typically on a quarterly basis and were compiled 'mainly from two sources': from reports submitted by commanders in the UK and overseas and from the censorship reports submitted by MI12 on the mail of the troops.[4]

In total, forty-four morale reports were used in this study (see Table A2).[5] The commanders' reports, of which something like a hundred were included in the morale reports produced in London,[6] often challenged the picture emanating from the censorship summaries. In assessing the value of these sources, therefore, it has been 'borne in mind' that the commanders' reports could 'be coloured by the peculiar experience or views' of the writer. This was also true of the

Table A2 Number of morale reports used in this study

Morale reports	Number
War Office (Home and Overseas)	25
India Command	8
South-East Asia Command	1
11th Army Group	1
Allied Land Forces South-East Asia	5
Far Eastern Inter-Services Committee	1
Allied Forces HQ (Italy)	3
Total	**44**

censors' reports, 'but in a lesser degree', since the 'volume of letters' acted 'as a check on the subjective impressions of the compiler'. Once a draft morale report was produced, 'a final check' was provided by the Morale Committee itself, with 'nothing' being published in the final Report which had 'not received approval of the Committee as a whole'.[7]

Appendix 3
QUANTITATIVE INDICATORS OF MORALE

As well as the censorship summaries and morale reports, other more quantitative measures were used in this study to assess morale in the British and Commonwealth Armies, most importantly rates of sickness, battle exhaustion, desertion, AWOL, self-inflicted wounds (SIW) and POW. Certainly, in the campaigns of the Second World War, contemporaneous historical sources suggest that morale in an army affected and was affected by these factors. In fact, the relationship between these dynamics was so close that a knowledge of such metrics can provide a useful indicator of the levels of morale at different stages of any campaign. Furthermore, when these quantitative 'measures' are considered together with the qualitative indicators of morale from the censorship summaries and morale reports, the overall assessment of morale can be particularly robust.

Table A3 presents a correlation matrix, outlining the relationship between these factors in British Second Army in North-West Europe in the Second World War and morale as described in censorship summaries. The censorship summaries for the campaign, compiled from 1,494,479 letters, were used by this author to build a 'morale scale'.[1] The censorship reports used a fairly consistent language and usually described the level of morale in a summary at the start. In order to turn a qualitative assessment of morale into a scale, all typical descriptions of morale were first graded from the 'best' to the 'worst' morale. The different descriptions were then put in categories of meaning that were as far as possible of equal intervals apart. Then each description of morale was given a score.

Table A3 Correlation matrix for rates of sickness, battle exhaustion, desertion/AWOL, SIW, a 'composite measure' (total/1,000) and morale as described in the censorship summaries for British Second Army in the North-West Europe campaign of the Second World War

	Sick/1,000	BE/1,000	Des/1,000	SIW/1,000	Total/ 1,000	Morale scale
Sick/1,000	1.000	0.190	0.395	0.207	0.919	−0.875
BE/1,000	0.190	1.000	−0.758	0.912	0.556	−0.502
Des/1,000	0.395	−0.758	1.000	−0.802	0.038	−0.076
SIW/1,000	0.207	0.912	−0.802	1.000	0.517	−0.452
Total/1,000	0.919	0.556	0.038	0.517	1.000	−0.949
Morale scale	−0.875	−0.502	−0.076	−0.452	−0.949	1.000

Source: Figures derived from Jonathan Fennell, 'Reevaluating Combat Cohesion: The British Second Army in the Northwest Europe Campaign of the Second World War', in Anthony King (ed.), *Frontline: Combat and Cohesion in the Twenty-First Century* (Oxford University Press, 2015).

Where morale was described as 'excellent', it was awarded a score of 3. 'High' morale was given a score of 2 and 'good' morale was scored 1. 'Satisfactory' morale was given a score of 0 (neither positive or negative). Morale described as 'severely tried' was scored −1, while 'low' and 'very low' morale were scored −2 and −3 respectively.[2]

The morale scale was then correlated with rates of sickness, battle exhaustion, desertion, AWOL, SIW and POW, and a composite measure that combined all these factors. The results of the correlation analysis showed that the composite measure (the combined rate of sickness, battle exhaustion, desertion, AWOL and SIW) had an extremely strong negative correlation with morale (−0.949, $P<0.001$); that is to say, when morale was low the 'composite measure' was high, and when moral was high the 'composite measure' was low. This is a remarkably strong relationship and shows that these factors when taken together can be used as a quantitative method to assess levels of morale, at the very least for Second Army in North-West Europe. Of the other factors used by medical officers to gauge morale, sickness and battle exhaustion combined (−0.937, $P<0.001$) and sickness on its own (−0.875, $P<0.001$) had almost as strong a negative correlation with morale as the 'compound measure', while battle exhaustion (−0.502,

$P<0.115$) and SIW (-0.452, $P<0.163$) were also useful, if not entirely reliable, indicators.[3]

The results of this correlation matrix have underpinned the use in this study of figures of sickness, battle exhaustion, desertion, AWOL and SIW to assess and graph levels of morale during the campaigns of the Second World War. This integrated and comprehensive approach, it is argued, allows a much more robust and dynamic assessment of morale than that attempted in many other studies.[4] Any one source or approach is of its nature limited. The censorship reports, for example, occasionally omitted mail from key formations during critical phases of campaigns and the morale reports covered such extended periods that major fluctuations in levels of morale could be overlooked or inadequately dealt with. The tabulated figures, in contrast, typically included sick and battle exhaustion for all units during all phases of a campaign. Additionally, by assessing these factors as a composite measure (i.e. where possible including desertion, AWOL and SIW as well), reporting irregularities can be rendered irrelevant. Such irregularities could arise from the fact that formations often classified similar battle behaviours in very different manners (for example, some classified breakdowns in battle as exhaustion while others classified them as military crimes, such as desertion); note the strong relationship between rates of battle exhaustion, desertion and SIW above. The overall picture that emerges from this approach to assessing morale allows this study to engage with one of the critical dynamics in war in a novel manner that hopefully provides new and convincing insights into the history of the British and Commonwealth Armies in the Second World War.

Appendix 4
DEFINING MORALE

In the context of the significance accorded to morale in this study, it is important to fully understand and define this military dynamic. The multi-authored censorship summaries and morale reports refer to morale in a number of different ways, as an affective state (psychological orientations that are an expression of or dependent on emotions or feelings), as an aspect of group dynamics and as motivation. As has been argued by this author and others, there are major problems with approaches that include affective states or group dynamics as necessary elements in the definition of morale. These problems arise particularly when the relationship between levels of morale and military performance is considered.[1]

Almost all treatments of the subject point to a strong connection between high levels of morale and military effectiveness. However, there is much evidence to suggest that troops can experience positive affective states while also behaving in manners that are contrary to the objectives set them by the military establishment. For instance, a combatant might feel 'happy', 'satisfied' or 'optimistic' due to the fact that he has run away and is now safe from harm, or, equally, he might fight with great determination whilst being personally quite miserable. Similarly, strong group bonds can undermine positive military performance. A soldier might stop to aid a wounded comrade in spite of orders to press the attack. Group desertions and mutiny can evidence small group cohesion, yet they are clearly actions contrary to the needs of the military institution.[2]

As a result, military professionals tend to link morale closely with motivation and explicitly distance it from associations with positive affective states and group dynamics. For example, Montgomery, in a paper he wrote on the subject in April 1946, defined morale as 'endurance and courage in supporting fatigue and danger ... the quality which makes men go forward in an attack and hold their ground in defence'. He stated categorically that high morale 'is not contentment or satisfaction' or 'happiness'. Happiness, according to Montgomery, 'may be a contributory factor in the maintenance of morale over a long period, but it is no more than that. A man can be unhappy but can still, regularly and without complaining, advance and defend.' He saw group dynamics in very much the same light.[3] Morale can thus be defined as the willingness of an individual or group to engage in an action required by an authority or institution; this willingness may be engendered by a positive desire for action and/or by the discipline to accept orders to take such action. The degree of morale of an individual or group relates to the extent of their willingness or discipline to act, or their determination to see an action through.[4]

NOTES

Introduction

1. NA WO 32/9735 W. E. Williams, Current Affairs in the Army: The Outline of a New Plan, 21 July 1941.
2. S. P. MacKenzie, *Politics and Military Morale: Current-Affairs and Citizenship Education in the British Army, 1914–1950* (Oxford University Press, 1992), p. 75. See also, S. L. A. Marshall, *Men against Fire: The Problem of Battle Command in Future War* (New York, 1966), pp. 161–2.
3. Michael Howard, 'The Use and Abuse of Military History', *The Royal United Services Institution Journal*, 107(625) (1962), p. 7; John Buckley, *Monty's Men: The British Army and the Liberation of Europe* (London: Yale University Press, 2013), p. 16.
4. Douglas E. Delaney, *The Imperial Army Project: Britain and the Land Forces of the Dominions and India, 1902–1945* (Oxford University Press, 2018); Ashley Jackson, *The British Empire and the Second World War* (London: Hambledon Continuum, 2006), pp. 2, 23. Although, at their core, the British and Commonwealth Armies were made up of formations from Britain, India and the Dominions, many Colonial units and formations supplemented its ranks. These included men from East and West Africa, the Caribbean/Bermuda, the Falklands, St Helena, Gibraltar, Malta, Cyprus, Palestine/Transjordan, Aden, Mauritius, the Seychelles, Ceylon, Malaya/Borneo, Sarawak, Hong Kong, Fiji, Tonga, New Hebrides, Gilbert/Ellice/Ocean, the Solomons, Basutoland, Bechuanaland and Swaziland (see Ashley Jackson, 'The Evolution and Use of British Imperial Military Formations', in Alan Jeffreys and Patrick Rose (eds.), *The Indian Army, 1937–47: Experience and Development* (Farnham: Ashgate, 2012), p. 24).
5. Jeremy Black, *War in the New Century* (London: Continuum, 2001), p. 114.
6. Albert Grundlingh, 'The King's Afrikaners? Enlistment and Ethnic Identity in the Union of South Africa's Defence Force During the Second World War, 1939–45', *The Journal of African History*, 40(3) (Nov. 1999), p. 351.
7. E. J. Hobsbawm, *On History* (London, 1998), p. 118. Quoted in Grundlingh, 'The King's Afrikaners?', p. 351.
8. George Orwell, 'The Lion and the Unicorn', in *The Collected Essays, Journalism and Letters* (Harmondsworth: Penguin, 1970), II, p. 117.

9. Indivar Kamtekar, 'A Different War Dance: State and Class in India 1939–1945', *Past and Present*, 176(1) (2002), p. 189.
10. Ibid., p. 215. See Neil Roos, *Ordinary Springboks: White Servicemen and Social Justice in South Africa, 1939–1961* (Aldershot: Ashgate, 2005); Corelli Barnett, *The Audit of War: The Illusion and Reality of Britain as a Great Nation* (London: Pan, 1996), p. xi.
11. Elizabeth Kier, 'War and Reform', in Elizabeth Kier and Ronald R. Krebs (eds.), *In War's Wake: International Conflict and the Fate of Liberal Democracy* (Cambridge University Press, 2010), p. 140. See also, Arthur Marwick, *War and Social Change in the Twentieth Century: A Comparative Study of Britain, France, Germany, Russia and the United States* (London: Macmillan Press, 1974), p. 222.
12. Kate Darian-Smith, 'War and Australian Society', in Joan Beaumont (ed.), *Australia's War, 1939–45* (Crows Nest: Allen & Unwin, 1996), p. 55.
13. SANDF, DOC, AI Gp I Box 42/I/37 DFMS No. 96, May 1945.
14. Quoted in Srinath Raghavan, *India's War: The Making of Modern South Asia 1939–1945* (London: Penguin: 2017), p. 346.
15. Darian-Smith, 'War and Australian Society', in Beaumont (ed.), *Australia's War*, pp. 76–7; John Pomeroy, 'A. P. Elkin: Public Morale and Propaganda', in Geoffrey Gray, Doug Munro and Christine Winter (eds.), *Scholars at War: Australian Social Scientists, 1939–1945* (Canberra: ANU Press, 2012), p. 40.
16. NA CAB 101/224 D. F. Butler, The British Soldier in Italy, Sept. 1943–June 1944, p. 21.
17. MacKenzie, *Politics and Military Morale*, pp. 181–2.
18. NA WO 32/15772 Report of the Morale Committee on the summary of Divisional and District Reports at Home and Censorship Reports, Feb.–May 1942, p. 1.
19. SANDF, DOC, AI Gp 1 Box 81/I/71/B South African Military Censorship, Special Report No. 8, Reactions to New Oath, 1–20 Feb. 1943, p. 2.
20. For studies that place 1940–2 as a turning point in British history see: commentary by John Barnes on Eric Hobsbawm, 'Britain: A Comparative View', in Brian Brivati and Harriet Jones (eds.), *What Difference Did the War Make?* (London: Leicester University Press, 1993); C. L. Mowat, *Britain Between the Wars* (London: Methuen, 1955). For studies that emphasise the continuities between interwar and post-war Britain, see e.g. Malcolm Smith, 'The Changing Nature of the British State, 1929–59: The Historiography of Consensus', in Brian Brivati and Harriet Jones (eds.), *What Difference Did the War Make?* (London: Leicester University Press, 1993). Others have argued that the war 'accelerated' change: David Morgan and Mary Evans, 'The Road to Nineteen Eighty-Four: Orwell and the Post-War Reconstruction of Citizenship', in Brian Brivati and Harriet Jones (eds.), *What Difference Did the War Make?* (London: Leicester University Press, 1993), p. 60. Some historians have cast doubts over the radicalizing effects of the war on British society. See e.g. Angus Calder, *The People's War: Britain 1939–1945* (London: Jonathan Cape, 1969), pp. 17–18; Henry Pelling, *Britain and the Second World War* (London: Collins, 1970), pp. 325–6.
21. Smith, 'The Changing Nature of the British State, 1929–59', in Brivati and Jones (eds.), *What Difference Did the War Make?*, p. 38. According to Smith, the 'state' can be understood as the ideology of the institutions of government, the network of laws and assumptions which construct the individual as citizen in relation to other citizens, with duties as well as rights.
22. Ross McKibbin, *Parties and People: England 1914–1951* (Oxford University Press, 2010), p. vii. See also Kier, 'War and Reform', in Kier and Krebs (eds.), *In War's Wake*, p. 157.

23. Relatively few scholars have investigated how citizens at the battlefront have affected social and political change. For some notable exceptions see, Grundlingh, 'The King's Afrikaners?'; Gajendra Singh, *The Testimonies of Indian Soldiers and the Two World Wars: Between Self and Sepoy* (London: Bloomsbury, 2014); Richard Vinen, *National Service: Conscription in Britain 1945–1963* (London: Allen Lane, 2014); Suzanne Mettler, *Soldiers to Citizens: The G.I. Bill and the Making of the Greatest Generation* (Oxford University Press, 2005); Geoffrey G. Field, '"Civilians in Uniform": Class and Politics in the British Armed Forces, 1939–1945', *International Labor and Working-Class History*, 80 (Fall 2011); James T. Sparrow, *Warfare State: World War II Americans and the Age of Big Government* (Oxford University Press, 2011). For some of the few scholarly works that specifically assess the impact of the soldiers' attitudes and voting behaviours on political and social change, see: Jeremy A. Crang, 'Politics on Parade: Army Education and the 1945 General Election', *History*, 81(262) (1996); F. D. Tothill, 'The Soldiers' Vote and Its Effect on the Outcome of the South African General Election of 1943', *South African Historical Journal*, 21 (1989); F. D. Tothill, 'The 1943 General Election' (Master's thesis, University of South Africa, 1987); J. R. S. Daniels, 'The General Election of 1943' (Master's thesis, Victoria University, 1961); J. L. Granatstein, 'The Armed Forces' Vote in Canadian General Elections, 1940–1968', *The Journal of Canadian Studies*, 4(1) (Feb. 1969); Jonathan Fennell, 'Soldiers and Social Change: The Forces Vote in the Second World War and New Zealand's Great Experiment in Social Citizenship', *English Historical Review*, 132(554) (2017); Guy Grossman, Devorah Manekin and Dan Miodownik, 'The Political Legacies of Combat: Attitudes toward War and Peace Among Israeli Ex-Combatants', *International Organisation*, 69(4) (Sept. 2015). Jonathan W. White, *Emancipation: The Union Army and the Reelection of Abraham Lincoln* (Baton Rouge: Louisiana State University Press, 2014).
24. David Edgerton, *Britain's War Machine: Weapons, Resources and Experts in the Second World War* (London: Allen Lane, 2011), p. 1.
25. Kate Darian-Smith, 'War and Australian Society', in Joan Beaumont (ed.), *Australia's War, 1939–45* (Crows Nest: Allen & Unwin, 1996), p. 55; Geoffrey G. Field, *Blood, Sweat and Toil: Remaking the British Working Class, 1939–1945* (Oxford University Press, 2011), p. 1.
26. See e.g. Kier and Krebs (eds.), *In War's Wake;* Calder, *The People's War*; Harold L. Smith (ed.), *War and Social Change: British Society in the Second World War* (Manchester University Press, 1986); Ross McKibbin, *Classes and Cultures: England 1918–1951* (Oxford University Press, 2000); Kamtekar, 'A Different War Dance'; Tony Judt, *Reappraisals: Reflections on the Forgotten Twentieth Century* (London: Penguin, 2008), pp. 8–12; Thomas Piketty, *Capital in the Twenty-First Century*, trans. Arthur Goldhammer (London: Belknap Press, 2014), p. 20.
27. Calder, *The People's War*; Adrian Gregory, *The Last Great War: British Society and the First World War* (Cambridge University Press, 2008), p. 4.
28. For those studies which address some of the thematic issues relevant to the British and Commonwealth Armies during the war, see F. W. Perry, *The Commonwealth Armies: Manpower and Organisation in Two World Wars* (Manchester University Press, 1988); Glen St. J. Barclay, *The Empire Is Marching: A Study of the Military Effort of the British Empire, 1800–1945* (London: Weidenfeld and Nicolson, 1976); Andrew Stewart, *Empire Lost: Britain, The Dominions and the Second World War* (London: Continuum, 2008); Jackson, *The British Empire and the Second World War*; Ian E. Johnston-White, *The British Commonwealth and Victory in the Second*

World War (London: Palgrave Macmillan, 2016); Delaney, *The Imperial Army Project*.

29. The foundational texts in this group, apart from the official histories, include important works by David French, *Raising Churchill's Army: The British Army and the War against Germany 1919–1945* (Oxford University Press, 2000); Jeffrey Grey, *The Australian Army* (Oxford University Press, 2001); Ian van der Waag, *A Military History of Modern South Africa* (Johannesburg: Jonathan Ball, 2015); John McLeod, *Myth and Reality: The New Zealand Soldier in World War II* (Auckland: Reed Methuen, 1986); Daniel Marston, *Phoenix from the Ashes: The Indian Army in the Burma Campaign* (Westport: Praeger, 2003); Timothy Moreman, *The Jungle, the Japanese and the British Commonwealth Armies at War, 1941–45: Fighting Methods, Doctrine and Training for Jungle Warfare* (London: Frank Cass, 2005); Terry Copp, *Cinderella Army: The Canadians in Northwest Europe 1944–1945* (London: University of Toronto Press, 2006); Terry Copp, *Fields of Fire: The Canadians in Normandy* (London, University of Toronto Press, 2003). David Killingray, *Fighting for Britain: African Soldiers in the Second World War* (Woodbridge: James Currey, 2010) is also a key source when dealing with the contribution of African soldiers during the war.
30. A number of key campaign narratives are central to our understanding of the British and Commonwealth Armies in the Second World War. These works make contributions not only to our understanding of individual campaigns but also to our comprehension of how the British and Commonwealth Armies worked more generally. See Niall Barr, *Pendulum of War: The Three Battles of El Alamein* (London: Pimlico, 2005 [2004]); Brian Farrell, *The Defence and Fall of Singapore 1940–1942* (Stroud: Tempus, 2005); Louis Allen, *Burma: The Longest War, 1941–45* (London: Phoenix Press, 2000 [1984]); Buckley, *Monty's Men*; Peter J. Dean, *MacArthur's Coalition: US and Australian Operations in the Southwest Pacific Area, 1942–1945* (University Press of Kansas, 2018).
31. Stephen A. Hart, *Colossal Cracks: Montgomery's 21st Army Group in Northwest* Europe, *1944–45* (Mechanicsburg: Stackpole, 2007 [2000]); Peter Stanley and Mark Johnson, *Alamein: The Australian Story* (Oxford University Press, 2002); John A. English, *The Canadian Army and the Normandy Campaign: A Study of Failure in High Command* (London: Praeger, 1991).
32. John Darwin, *The Empire Project: The Rise and Fall of the British World-System, 1830–1970* (Cambridge University Press, 2009), p. xii.
33. Ibid., p. 12.
34. Delaney, *The Imperial Army Project*, Chs. 1 and 2.
35. French, *Raising Churchill's Army*.
36. LAC Vol. 18,826 File No. 133.065 (D689) List of Commonwealth Forces in Fighting Contact with the Enemy, 1940–5. The number of divisions is for the first day of the month indicated. Graph includes formations which were earmarked, or held, in immediate reserve for any particular theatre, that is why Malta is included. It does not include troops in the UK or formations in garrisons throughout the world, except in the case of Malta. Belgian, Czech, Dutch, Greek and Polish formations fighting under the command of Imperial Forces are not included. A number of assumptions were made in assessing the number of divisions: (a) three brigades (infantry, armoured, commando or special service, parachute, army tank) are equivalent to one division; (b) Army Group Royal Artillery (AGRA) is equivalent to one brigade; three AGRA are equivalent to one division.
37. Jackson, *The British Empire and the Second World War*, p. 1.

38. Field, '"Civilians in Uniform"', p. 121.
39. For those few studies that address the role of service personnel in fomenting socio-political change in the Commonwealth, see, ibid.; Grundlingh, 'The King's Afrikaners?'; Singh, *The Testimonies of Indian Soldiers and the Two World Wars*; Vinen, *National Service: Conscription in Britain 1945–1963*; Crang, 'Politics on Parade'; Tothill, 'The Soldiers' Vote'; Tothill, 'The 1943 General Election'; Daniels, 'The General Election of 1943'; Granatstein, 'The Armed Forces' Vote in Canadian General Elections, 1940–1968'; Alan Allport, *Browned Off and Bloody-Minded: The British Soldier Goes to War 1939–1945* (London: Yale University Press, 2015); Fennell, 'Soldiers and Social Change'. Some key studies that address these issues for other countries include, Mettler, *Soldiers to Citizens*; Sparrow, *Warfare State*; Grossman, Manekin and Miodownik, 'The Political Legacies of Combat'.
40. For more on this understanding of strategy, see Jonathan Fennell, 'Re-evaluating Combat Cohesion', in Anthony King (ed.), *Frontline: Combat and Cohesion in the Twenty-First Century* (Oxford University Press, 2015), pp. 153–6.
41. Elizabeth Kier and Ronald R. Krebs, 'Introduction: War and Democracy in Comparative Perspective', in Elizabeth Kier and Ronald R. Krebs (eds.), *In War's Wake: International Conflict and the Fate of Liberal Democracy* (Cambridge University Press, 2010), p. 5.
42. Leonard V. Smith, *Between Mutiny and Obedience: The Case of the French Fifth Division during World War I* (Princeton University Press, 1994), p. 13.
43. See e.g. Eliot A. Cohen, 'Churchill and Coalition Strategy in World War II', in Paul Kennedy (ed.), *Grand Strategies in War and Peace* (New Haven: Yale University Press, 1991); David Reynolds, *In Command of History: Churchill Fighting and Writing the Second World War* (London: Allen Lane, 2004).
44. Hew Strachan, *Carl von Clausewitz's On War: A Biography* (London: Atlantic Books, 2007), p. 82.
45. Jonathan Fennell, *Combat and Morale in the North African Campaign: The Eighth Army and the Path to El Alamein* (Cambridge University Press, 2011), p. 2.
46. Marshall, *Men against Fire*, pp. 157–8.
47. Allport, *Browned Off and Bloody-Minded*, p. xvii.
48. For some other studies that have used this methodology, see, Fennell, *Combat and Morale* in the North African Campaign; David French, '"Tommy Is No Soldier": The Morale of the Second British Army in Normandy, June–Aug. 1944', *Journal of Strategic Studies*, 19(4) (2006), pp. 154–78; Buckley, *Monty's Men*; Alexander Watson, *Enduring the Great War: Combat, Morale and Collapse in the German and British Armies, 1914–1918* (Cambridge University Press, 2008); and Jonathan Boff, *Winning and Losing on the Western Front: The British Third Army and the Defeat of Germany in 1918* (Cambridge University Press, 2012).
49. These sources have been used in some national accounts, or thematic assessments, of the British and Commonwealth experience during the war, but, to date, no study has sought to interrogate the totality of these remarkable sources and integrate them into the historiography of the Second World War. For those studies that have used censorship summaries, see: J. L. Scoullar, *Battle for Egypt: The Summer of 1942. Official History of New Zealand in the Second World War 1939–1945* (Wellington: Historical Publications Branch, 1955); McLeod, *Myth and Reality*; Fennell, *Combat and Morale in the North African Campaign*; Singh, *The Testimonies of Indian Soldiers and the Two World Wars*; Copp, *Cinderella Army*; William Pratt, 'Medicine and Obedience: Canadian Army Morale, Discipline, and Surveillance in the Second World War, 1939–1945' (DPhil thesis, University of Calgary, 2015); Robert Engen, *Canadians Under Fire: Infantry Effectiveness in the Second World*

War (London: McGill-Queen's University Press, 2009). Watson, *Enduring the Great War* and Boff, *Winning and Losing on the Western Front 1918* have also used similar sources in the context of the First World War.

50. DHH File No. 146.11.2009 (D2) War Office Notes for Censorship Lectures, 1941.
51. While the majority of censorship was carried out by officers in each unit of the Army, every week soldiers were also permitted to send up to three letters in a 'green envelope', which was delivered to base and censored centrally, rather than regimentally. This allowed soldiers some freedom to write without their CO reading their correspondence. The base censors would then examine 'a proportion of the Green Envelopes' and 're-censor a proportion of the unit censored mail to check the efficiency of the unit censorship and to check the officers' letters'. It was the base censors that compiled the censorship summaries. The principle of base rather than regimental censorship was extended to airmail letters in Oct. 1943. See ANZ WAII/1/DA21.1/9/G4/11 Pt 1, Notes on Green Envelope, HQ NZ Div. 7 Nov. 1940; DHH File No. 146.11.2009 (D2) War Office Notes for Censorship Lectures, 1941; DHH File No. 760.001 (D1) Notes by Mr E. Pye on Censorship of Service Mail in Two World Wars; NA WO 165/143 Lecture on Unit Censorship, n.d.; NA WO 165/143 Censorship in Relation to the War Office, n.d.; NA WO 277/16 J. H. A. Sparrow, Morale, 1949, pp. 28–36; NA WO 165/143 Lecture on Clerical Work in the Deputy Chief Censor's Office of a Field Force, Dec. 1948; NA DEFE 1/381 Duties and Responsibilities of M.I.12, 9 Mar. 1944; DHH CMHQ Report 51 Censorship of Mail, CAO. Field Censors' Notes as Material for History, 31 Oct. 1941. Field censorship for South African forces was carried out by the IC of Military Intelligence (see SANDF, DOC, AI Gp 1 Box 46 I/40/(F) IC to the Director-General of Operations, 4 Sept. 1940); NA DEFE 1/381 Note on M.I.12 Organisation, 6 July 1944.
52. NA WO 165/143 Lecture on Unit Censorship, n.d.; NA WO 165/143 Censorship in Relation to the War Office, n.d.; NA WO 277/16 J. H. A. Sparrow, Morale, 1949, pp. 28–36; NA WO 165/143 Lecture on Clerical Work in the Deputy Chief Censor's Office of a Field Force, Dec. 1948; NA DEFE 1/381 Duties and Responsibilities of M.I.12, 9 Mar. 1944; DHH CMHQ Report 51 Censorship of Mail, CAO. Field Censors' Notes as Material for History, 31 Oct. 1941; SANDF AI Gp 1 Box 46 I/40/(F) IC to the Director-General of Operations, 4 Sept. 1940. One censorship section, of two officers and five other ranks, was required for every 20,000 troops in the field, while a 'special mails section' was required for every 60,000 men in a force. As each division, of about 18,000 men, was usually accompanied by about another 36,000 men (on the lines of communication, at GHQ, and as army and corps troops), the presence of a division in the field typically required the Army to send three censorship sections (i.e. six officers and 15 other ranks) and a 'special mails section' to the theatre of war (see NA WO 165/42 Despatch of Censor Sections to BEF, 1 June 1943.)
53. ANZ WAII/1/DA508/1 Vols. 3 and 4 Memorandum, Distribution of Censorship Summary, 21 Oct. 1942; AWM 54 175/3/4 1 Memorandum, Monthly Censorship Report, 5 May 1945; NA WO 165/42 Army Mail Censorship Reports, Subject Headings in Use in Great Britain, 1942.
54. SANDF, DOC, AI Gp 1 Box 81/I/71/B General Report of Military Censorship, East Africa Forces, 1–31 July 1941, pp. 3–4.
55. NA WO 204/6756 Brig. V. J. E. Westropp, Director of Postal Services, to X Corps, Eighth Army, 8 Jan. 1944.
56. NA WO 204/6756 CMF and BNAF, ACR, 8 Jan. 1943.

57. NA WO32/15772 Note on Compilation of the Reports of the War Office Committee on Morale in the Army, 2 Jan. 1943.
58. SANDF, DOC, AI Gp 1 Box 46 South African Military Censorship Regulations, June 1942.
59. Sanjoy Bhattacharya, *Propaganda and Information in Eastern India 1939–45: A Necessary Weapon of War* (Richmond: Curzon Press, 2001), pp. 178–9.
60. DHH CMHQ Report 51 Censorship of Mail, CAO. Field Censors' Notes as Material for History, 31 Oct. 1941.
61. Ibid.
62. NA WO 165/143 Lecture on Unit Censorship, n.d.; SANDF AI Gp 1 Box 43/I/38/D MCS No. 13, EAFHQ, 21 Mar.–20 Apr. 1941, p. 1.
63. AWM 54 883/2/97 MEFCWS, No. I (12–18 Nov. 1941), p. 1.
64. NAA MP742/1 52/1/20 Allied Land Forces SWPA, Memorandum on FCRs, 2 Apr. 1943.
65. Field, *Blood, Sweat and Toil*, p. 306; Sparrow, *Warfare State*, pp. 30–1. One might include the 'mail briefs' used by President Franklin D. Roosevelt as a 'feedback mechanism' to assess public morale in the United States in this list.
66. Brian Bond, *British Military Policy between the Two World Wars* (Oxford: Clarendon Press, 1980), p. 9.
67. McKibbin, *Parties and People*, p. vii.
68. LHCMA Adam 3/13 Narrative covering aspects of work as AG, WWII, Ch. 1: Manpower.
69. For some notable exceptions see e.g. Mark Johnston, 'The Civilians Who Joined Up, 1939–45, *Journal of the Australian War Memorial*, 29 (Nov. 1996).
70. Ibid.
71. John Horne, 'Introduction: Mobilizing for "Total War", 1914–1918', in John Horne (ed.), *State, Society and Mobilization in Europe during the First World War* (Cambridge University Press, 1997), p. 2.
72. Ibid., p. 17.
73. Darwin, *The Empire Project*, pp. 9–14.
74. Ibid., pp. 9–14. For other studies that identify this period as critical moment in the end of the British Empire see e.g.: David French, *The British Way in Warfare, 1688–2000* (London: Unwin Hyman, 1990); and Patrick French, *Liberty or Death: India's Journey to Independence and Division* (London: Penguin, 2011).
75. Horne, 'Introduction': Mobilizing for "Total War", in 1914–1918', in Horne (ed.), *State, Society and Mobilization in Europe during the First World War*, pp. 2–3.
76. McLeod, *Myth and Reality*, p. 138. It could be argued that the mutiny stands out even in the context of the history of the British Empire.
77. Adrian Threlfall, 'The Development of Australian Army Jungle Warfare Doctrine and Training, 1941–1945' (Doctoral thesis, Victoria University, 2008), p. 247.
78. Brendan Nelson, 'Foreword', in Peter J. Dean (ed.), *Australia 1943: The Liberation of New Guinea* (Port Melbourne: Cambridge University Press, 2014), p. viii.
79. Christopher Bayly and Tim Harper, *Forgotten Armies: Britain's Asian Empire & the War with Japan* (London: Penguin, 2005 [2004]), p. 362.
80. John Buckley, 'Introduction', in John Buckley (ed.), *The Normandy Campaign 1944: Sixty Years On* (London: Routledge, 2006), p. 1. 'Of the seven armoured divisions that participated ... only 24 tanks and 1,300 troops escaped across the Seine to flee back to Germany.'
81. Carlo D'Este, *Decision in Normandy: The Unwritten Story of Montgomery and the Allied Campaign* (London: Penguin, 2001 [1983]), p. 14.

82. Buckley, *Monty's Men*, p. 114. Allied losses in Normandy were 2,000 men per division per month, with the infantry in the rifle companies incurring 70% of all casualties, even though they made up only about 15% of the army as a whole.
83. Ibid., pp. 137–8.
84. Martin Middlebrook, *Arnhem 1944: The Airborne Battle* (London: Penguin, 1995), pp. 441–2.
85. Moreman, *The Jungle, the Japanese and the British Commonwealth Armies at War*, p. 5; Tarak Barkawi, 'Culture and Combat in the Colonies: The Indian Army in the Second World War', *Journal of Contemporary History*, 41(2) (2006), p. 329; Allen, *Burma*, p. xviii.
86. Allport, *Browned Off and Bloody-Minded*, pp. 218–19. For an overview of the historiography on the Chindits, see Raymond Callahan, *Triumph at Imphal–Kohima: How the Indian Army Finally Stopped the Japanese Juggernaut* (Lawrence: University Press of Kansas, 2017), pp. 145–9.
87. Jackson, 'The Evolution and Use of British Imperial Military Formations', in Jeffreys and Rose (eds.), *The Indian Army, 1937–47*, p. 24; Killingray, *Fighting for Britain*, p. 8; David Killingray and Richard Rathbone, 'Introduction', in David Killingray and Richard Rathbone (eds.), *Africa and the Second World War* (London: Macmillan, 1986), p. 14. See also Timothy H. Parsons, *The African Rank-and-File: Social Implications of Colonial Military Service in the King's African Rifles, 1902–1964* (Oxford: James Currey, 1999); H. Moyse-Bartlett, *The King's African Rifles: A Study in the Military History of East and Central Africa, 1890–1945* (Aldershot: Gale & Polden, 1956); Malcolm Page, *KAR: A History of the King's African Rifles and East African Forces* (London: Leo Cooper, 1998).
88. Keith Jeffrey, 'The British Army and Ireland since 1922', in T. Bartlett and K. Jeffrey (eds), *A Military History of Ireland* (Cambridge University Press, 1996), p. 438 (quoted in Allport, *Browned Off and Bloody-Minded*, p. 66).
89. Lucy Noakes, *Women in the British Army: War and the Gentle Sex, 1907–1948* (London: Routledge, 2006), pp. 125–31. See also, Eileen Bigland, *Britain's Other Army: Story of the ATS* (London: Nicholson & Watson, 1946).
90. Allport, *Browned Off and Bloody-Minded*, p. xvii; Noakes, *Women in the British Army*, pp. 119, 128. By 1942, more women were working on anti-aircraft sites than men; in Jan. 1945, no fewer than 4,000 women were serving in the decisive and climactic campaign in North-West Europe.
91. This was partly a consequence of scale; all projects have to draw a line under what can be studied. But, in this case, it was determined also by the sources available. Although scholarship on the contribution of Colonial soldiers, Southern Irish and women to the war effort has advanced since the turn of the century, it still lags considerably behind that of the British, Indian and Dominion Armies. Additionally, there was very little reference to Colonial, Southern Irish and female soldiers in the key primary sources employed in this study – the censorship summaries, morale reports and quantitative indicators of battle morale.
92. Delaney, *The Imperial Army Project*.
93. Peter Howlett (ed.), *Fighting with Figures: A Statistical Digest of the Second World War* (London: The Central Statistics Office, 1995), pp. 5, 39 and 41; Steven I. Wilkinson, *Army and Nation: The Military and Indian Democracy since Independence* (London: Harvard University Press, 2015), p. 65; Perry, *The Commonwealth Armies*, p. 117; C. P. Stacey, *Arms, Men and Governments: The War Policies of Canada, 1939–1945* (Ottawa: The Queen's Printer for Canada, 1970), p. 590; Dominion Bureau of Statistics, *The Canada Year Book, 1946* (Ottawa: Edmond Cloutier, 1946), p. 127;

Grundlingh, 'The King's Afrikaners?', p. 354. Roos, *Ordinary Springboks*, p. 1; Union Office of Census and Statistics, *Official Year Book of the Union of South Africa, No. 23 – 1946* (Pretoria: The Government Printer, 1948), Ch. XXIX: The Union of South Africa and the War, p. 20; Bureau of Census and Statistics, Pretoria, *Union Statistics for Fifty Years: 1910–1960* (Pretoria: The Government Printers, 1960), p. A13; Johnston, 'The Civilians Who Joined Up, 1939–45'; McLeod, *Myth and Reality*, p. 18.

Chapter 1 Interwar

1. Ross McKibbin, *Parties and People: England 1914–1951* (Oxford University Press, 2010), p. vii.
2. The literature on the British and Commonwealth Armies in the Second World War is split broadly between the 'declinists', who argue that these armies were 'unprepared for war, materially, tactically and – perhaps above all – psychologically' and the 'revisionists', who argue that Britain and its Empire entered the war in a strong position. Some of the key 'declinists' include: David Fraser, *And We Shall Shock Them: The British Army in the Second World War* (London: Cassell & Co., 1999), pp. 3–24; Alan Allport, *Browned Off and Bloody-Minded: The British Soldier Goes to War 1939–1945* (London: Yale University Press, 2015), p. 28; John A. English, *The Canadian Army and the Normandy Campaign: A Study of Failure in High Command* (London: Praeger, 1991), p. xiv; David Bercuson, *Maple Leaf against the Axis: Canada's Second World War* (Calgary: Red Deer Press, 1995), p. 6; H. J. Martin and Neil Orpen, *South Africa at War: Military and Industrial Organization and Operations in Connection with the Conduct of the War, 1939–1945* (Purnell: Cape Town, 1979), p. 27; Ian McGibbon, *New Zealand and the Second World War: The People, the Battles and the Legacy* (Auckland: Hodder Moa Beckett, 2004), p. 36; Stephen P. Cohen, *The Indian Army: Its Contribution to the Development of a Nation* (Berkeley: University of California Press, 1971), pp. 138–9; Jeffrey Grey, *A Military History of Australia* (Cambridge University Press, 1999), p. 139. The key 'revisionist' texts include: David Edgerton, *Warfare State: Britain 1920–1970* (Cambridge University Press, 2006), pp. 1–59; G. C. Peden, *Arms, Economics and British Strategy: From Dreadnoughts to Hydrogen Bombs* (Cambridge University Press, 2007), pp. 35, 126–7; John Ferris, 'Treasury Control: The Ten Year Rule and British Service Policies, 1919–1924', *Historical Journal*, 30 (1987), p. 865.
3. G. C. Peden, 'The Burden of Imperial Defence and the Continental Commitment Reconsidered', *The Historical Journal*, 27(2) (June 1984), pp. 416–18.
4. Iain Edward Johnston, 'The Role of the Dominions in British Victory, 1939–1945' (DPhil thesis, University of Cambridge, 2014), pp. 204–6.
5. David Edgerton, *Britain's War Machine: Weapons, Resources and Experts in the Second World War* (London: Allen Lane, 2011), p. 11.
6. John Darwin, *The Empire Project: The Rise and Fall of the British World-System, 1830–1970* (Cambridge University Press, 2009), p. 476.
7. Ibid., pp. 482–3.
8. Adam Tooze, *The Wages of Destruction: The Making and Breaking of the Nazi Economy* (London: Penguin Books, 2007), p. xxiii.
9. Edgerton, *Britain's War Machine*, p. 12.
10. See e.g. Glen St. J. Barclay, *The Empire Is Marching: A Study of the Military Effort of the British Empire, 1800–1945* (London: Weidenfeld and Nicolson, 1976), Ch. 7.
11. Peden, *Arms, Economics and British Strategy*, pp. 126–7.

12. Joseph Maiolo, 'Between the Two World Wars: Introduction', in Thomas Mahnken, Joseph Maiolo and David Stevenson (eds.), *Arms Races in International Politics: From the Nineteenth to the Twenty-First Century* (Oxford University Press, 2016), p. 64.
13. Ibid., p. 64.
14. Archives Nationale, 313AP, Vol. 230, Painlevé papers, French War Ministry memorandum, n.d. [1929]. My thanks to Professor Joe Maiolo for sharing this file with me. Figures are in 1928 francs.
15. Quoted in Peter Jackson, 'British Power and French Security, 1919–1939', in Keith Neilson and Greg Kennedy (eds.), *The British Way in Warfare: Power and the International System, 1856–1956* (Farnham: Ashgate, 2010), p. 131.
16. Peden, *Arms, Economics and British Strategy*, pp. 151–2. It was only in 1937/8 that spending on the Air Force overtook that on the Army.
17. George Peden, 'Financing Churchill's Army', in Keith Neilson and Greg Kennedy (eds.), *The British Way in Warfare: Power and the International System, 1856–1956* (Farnham: Ashgate, 2010), pp. 279–80; Robin Higham, *Armed Forces in Peacetime: Britain, 1918–1940, A Case Study* (London: G. T. Foulis & Co., 1962), p. 326.
18. Peden, 'Financing Churchill's Army', in Neilson and Kennedy (eds.), *The British Way in Warfare*, p. 280; David French, *Raising Churchill's Army: The British Army and the War against Germany 1919–1945* (Oxford University Press, 2000), pp. 82–3.
19. Peden, 'Financing Churchill's Army', in Neilson and Kennedy (eds.), *The British Way in Warfare*, p. 280.
20. Jackson, 'British Power and French Security, 1919–1939', in Neilson and Kennedy (eds.), *The British Way in Warfare*, p. 120; Peden, 'Financing Churchill's Army', in Neilson and Kennedy (eds.), *The British Way in Warfare*, pp. 281–2.
21. Peden, 'Financing Churchill's Army', in Neilson and Kennedy (eds.), *The British Way in Warfare*, pp. 282–3.
22. Peden, *Arms, Economics and British Strategy*, pp. 151–2.
23. Peden, 'Financing Churchill's Army', in Neilson and Kennedy (eds.), *The British Way in Warfare*, pp. 284–7; Peden, *Arms, Economics and British Strategy*, pp. 151–2; Brian Bond, *British Military Policy between the Two World Wars* (Oxford: Clarendon Press, 1980), p. 305. The Army's defence expenditure had been £39.66 million in 1934/5.
24. Paul Hasluck, *Australia in the War of 1939–1945, Series Four: Civil, Vol. I: The Government and the People, 1939–1941* (Canberra: AWM, 1965), p. 33; Wray Vamplew (ed.), *Australians: Historical Statistics* (Broadway, NSW: Fairfax, Syme and Weldon Associates, 1987), p. 412; C. P. Stacey, *Six Years of War: The Canadian Army in Canada, Britain and the Pacific, Official History of the Canadian Army in the Second World War, Vol. I* (Ottawa: Queen's Printer, 1955), pp. 4–13; C. P. Stacey, *Arms, Men and Governments: The War Policies of Canada, 1939–1945* (Ottawa: The Queen's Printer for Canada, 1970), pp. 3–17; Daniel Byers, *Zombie Army: The Canadian Army and Conscription in the Second World War* (Vancouver: University of British Columbia Press, 2016), p. 45; LAC Vol. 18,826 File No. 133.065 (D683) Canada's Defence: Information of Canada's Defence Achievements and Organisation, 1947, p. 14; SANDF DOC CGS (War) Box 169 File Number 10/2/9 Annual Report of the Department of Defence, 1934, p. 7; *Official Year Book of the Union of South Africa, No. 23 – 1946*, Ch. XXIX: The Union of South Africa and the War, p. 27; Philippa Mein Smith, *A Concise History of New Zealand* (Melbourne: Cambridge University Press, 2005), p. 159;

G. C. Peden, 'The Burden of Imperial Defence and the Continental Commitment Reconsidered', *The Historical Journal*, 27(2) (June 1984), p. 418; Bond, *British Military Policy between the Two World Wars*, pp. 98–126.

25. G. C. Peden, 'The Burden of Imperial Defence and the Continental Commitment Reconsidered', *The Historical Journal*, 27(2) (June 1984), pp. 416–8. In absolute terms, spending came to about £265.2 million in Britain, £34.5 million in India, £7.2 million in Canada, £6 million in Australia, £1.7 million in South Africa and £1.6 million in New Zealand.
26. Raymond Callahan, *Burma, 1942–1945* (London: Davis Poynter, 1978), pp. 19–20; Peden, 'The Burden of Imperial Defence', p. 418; Bond, *British Military Policy between the Two World Wars*, pp. 112, 121–3; Srinath Raghavan, *India's War: The Making of Modern South Asia 1939–1945* (London: Penguin: 2017), p. 37. Moreover, 93% of the Indian defence budget was spent on land forces (see Bond, *British Military Policy between the Two World Wars*, p. 117).
27. French, *Raising Churchill's Army*, p. 156; French, *The British Way in Warfare*, p. 194; Darwin, *The Empire Project*, pp. 487–8; Jackson, 'British Power and French Security, 1919–1939', in Neilson and Kennedy (eds.), *The British Way in Warfare*, pp. 107–8; Peden, 'The Burden of Imperial Defence', p. 406.
28. Fraser, *And We Shall Shock Them*, p. 29.
29. Edgerton, *Britain's War Machine*, p. 64.
30. Fraser, *And We Shall Shock Them*, p. 29.
31. Edgerton, *Britain's War Machine*, p. 57.
32. Peden, *Arms, Economics and British Strategy*, p. 144.
33. Martin S. Alexander, 'The Fall of France, 1940', *Journal of Strategic Studies*, 13(1) (1990), p. 33.
34. Wesley K. Wark, *The Ultimate Enemy: British Intelligence and Nazi Germany, 1933–1939* (London: I. B. Tauris, 1985), pp. 83, 122, 248. It would double again between 1938 and Sept. 1939.
35. NA WO 277/12 Manpower Problems, pp. 2–11.
36. Peter Dennis, *The Territorial Army, 1907–1940* (Woodbridge: Boydell Press, 1987), p. 262. See also Ian F. W. Beckett, *Britain's Part-Time Soldiers: The Amateur Military Tradition 1559–1945* (Manchester University Press, 1991).
37. W. K. Hancock and M. M. Gowing, *British War Economy* (London: HMSO, 1949), p. 136; Peter Howlett (ed.), *Fighting with Figures: A Statistical Digest of the Second World War* (London: The Central Statistics Office, 1995), p. 39; NA WO 277/12 Manpower Problems, pp. 2–11, 80; LHCMA Adam 3/1 Notes for Secretary of State Estimates Speech, AG Department, 1941; Dennis, *The Territorial Army*, p. 262. The total 'book strength' of the Army, which included those not yet called up was *c.*900,000 men.
38. Hancock and Gowing, *British War Economy*, p. 136; Sri Nandan Prasad, *Official History of the Indian Armed Forces in the Second World War, 1939–45: Expansion of the Armed Forces and Defence Organisation, 1939–45* (Calcutta: Orient Longmans, 1956), p. 54; Perry, *The Commonwealth Armies*, pp. 161, 192; English, *The Canadian Army and the Normandy Campaign*, p. 14. For more details, see Chapter 2 of this volume.
39. Matthew Cooper, *The German Army 1933–1945: Its Political and Military Failure* (Lanham: Scarborough House, 1978), p. 131.
40. Mark Harrison (ed.), *The Economics of World War II: Six Great Powers in International Comparison* (Cambridge University Press, 2000), p. 14.
41. See e.g. Elizabeth Kier, *Imagining War: French and British Military Doctrine Between the Wars* (Princeton University Press, 1997).

42. David French, 'Colonel Blimp and the British Army: British Divisional Commanders in the War against Germany, 1939–1945', *The English Historical Review*, 111(444) (Nov. 1996), pp. 1184–5. A total of 160 major-generals commanded field-force divisions in the war against Germany and Italy. This figure excludes Dominion officers who commanded Dominion formations and those British officers who commanded anti-aircraft divisions, Indian Army and Colonial divisions, and the ten country divisions raised and disbanded in 1941, which were intended to fulfil a semi-static home defence role. Those who were in temporary command of a division in the absence of the permanent commanders are also not included.
43. Ibid., pp. 1185–6. The First World War figure included 95 MCs, 66 DSOs and 4 VCs. Those officers too young to have served in the First World War, or who had served but not been decorated, gained decorations for leadership or gallantry during the Second World War before they were promoted to command divisions.
44. Ibid., p. 1200.
45. Allport, *Browned Off and Bloody-Minded*, p. 29.
46. French, 'Colonel Blimp and the British Army', pp. 1187–8.
47. Quoted ibid., p. 1190.
48. *The Times*, 23 Sept. 1937, quoted in French, 'Colonel Blimp and the British Army', p. 1185.
49. See e.g. Patrick Rose, 'British Army Command Culture 1939–1945: A Comparative Study of British Eighth and Fourteenth Armies' (PhD thesis, King's College London, 2008); Patrick Rose, 'Allies at War: British and US Army Command Culture in the Italian Campaign, 1943–1944', *Journal of Strategic Studies*, 36(1) (February, 2013); Terry Copp, *Fields of Fire: The Canadians in Normandy* (London, University of Toronto Press, 2003); John Buckley, *Monty's Men: The British Army and the Liberation of Europe* (London: Yale University Press, 2013); French, *Raising Churchill's Army*; Kier, *Imagining War*. Doctrine provides 'a guide to the principles by which all parts of an army work in combination' (War Office, *Field Service Regulations, Vol. II: Operations – General* (*FSR II*) (London: HMSO, 1935), p. 1). Ministry of Defence, *Joint Doctrine Publication 0–01: British Defence Doctrine Fourth Edition* (Shrivenham: The Development, Concepts and Doctrine Centre, 2011), p. iii; Ministry of Defence, *Army Doctrine Publication: Operations* (Shrivenham: The Development, Concepts and Doctrine Centre, 2010), p. iii both define doctrine as the 'broad philosophy and principles underpinning the employment of the Armed Forces'.
50. French, *Raising Churchill's Army*, pp. 168–9.
51. Ibid., p. 13; Tim Moreman, 'Jungle, Japanese and the Australian Army: Learning the Lessons of New Guinea', Paper to the Remembering the War in New Guinea Symposium, 19–20 Oct. 2000 (http://ajrp.awm.gov.au/AJRP/remember.nsf/pages/NT0000130A, accessed 15 Mar. 2016); Jeffrey Grey, *The Australian Army* (Oxford University Press, 2001), p. 151.
52. Allport, *Browned Off and Bloody-Minded*, p. 27.
53. See French, *Raising Churchill's Army*, Ch. 1.
54. Ibid. p. 168.
55. French, 'Colonel Blimp and the British Army', p. 1189.
56. French, *Raising Churchill's Army*, pp. 26–34.
57. Ibid., p. 34.
58. David Hall, *Strategy for Victory: The Development of British Tactical Air Power, 1919–1943* (Westport: Praeger Publishers, 2007), Ch. 1, p. 1 of 12.
59. Ibid., Ch. 1, p. 9 of 12.

60. Ibid., Ch. 2, pp. 2–4 of 13.
61. Ibid., Ch. 1, pp. 9–10 of 12.
62. Ibid., Ch. 2, pp. 5–6 of 13.
63. Rose, 'British Army Command Culture 1939–1945'; Patrick Rose, 'Allies at War'; Copp, *Fields of Fire*; Buckley, *Monty's Men*.
64. French, *Raising Churchill's Army*, Chs. 1 and 5. For other critical appraisals of the doctrine of the British Army see Brian Farrell, *The Defence and Fall of Singapore 1940–1942* (Stroud: Tempus, 2005), p. 137; French, *Raising Churchill's Army*, p. 12; Buckley, *Monty's Men*, p. 9; Basil Liddell Hart, *The Other Side of the Hill* (London: Cassell, 1951); John Ellis, *Brute Force: Allied Strategy and Tactics in the Second World War* (London: André Deutsch, 1990); Chester Wilmot, *The Struggle for Europe* (Bungay: Richard Clay and Company, 1954 [1952]).
65. War Office, *Field Service Regulations, Vol. III: Operations – Higher Formations* (London: HMSO 1936), p. 9; Rose, 'Allies at War', pp. 47–8.
66. Quoted in Rose, 'British Army Command Culture 1939–1945', p. 31.
67. War Office, *FSR II*, pp. 27–8.
68. Rose, 'British Army Command Culture 1939–1945', pp. 24–9. *FSR III* proposed that light aircraft be the primary means by which commanders should 'go and see their battle', although use of armoured vehicles, conferring the joint benefits of protection and mobile communications, was also suggested. It also followed the Kirke Committee recommendations that commanders 'must go and see their battle' whilst a designated deputy acted in their stead.
69. Rose, 'Allies at War', pp. 47–8.
70. Rose, 'British Army Command Culture 1939–1945', p. 296. The situation was very much the same in the Indian Army (see Alan Jeffreys, *Approach to Battle: Training the Indian Army During the Second World War* (Solihull: Helion, 2016), pp. 41–4, 50–1).
71. French, *Raising Churchill's Army*, p. 36.
72. Ibid., pp. 168–74. In a similar vein, the Australian Army only undertook one amphibious training exercise in the interwar years, a form of warfare that would prove central to the Allied advance across the Pacific theatre (see Rhys Crawley and Peter J. Dean, 'Amphibious Warfare: Training and Logistics, 1942–45', in Peter Dean (ed.), *Australia 1944–45: Victory in the Pacific* (Cambridge University Press, 2016). p. 260.
73. Wark, *The Ultimate Enemy*, p. 95.
74. French, *Raising Churchill's Army*, p. 174.
75. Ibid., p. 169.
76. Ibid., p. 172.
77. Ibid., pp. 168–74.
78. Ibid., pp. 36–7.
79. Ibid., pp. 38–40.
80. Hall, *Strategy for Victory*, Ch. 2, pp. 5 of 13.
81. French, *Raising Churchill's Army*, p. 43.
82. See the *FSR* and French, *Raising Churchill's Army*.
83. Laurence Van Ypersele, 'Mourning and Memory, 1919–45', in John Horne (ed.), *A Companion to World War I* (Oxford: Wiley-Blackwell, 2012), pp. 576–85; Mein Smith, *A Concise History of New Zealand*, pp. 124, 135.
84. Van Ypersele, 'Mourning and Memory', in Horne (ed.), *A Companion to World War I*, pp. 581–2.

85. Martin Ceadel, 'The First British Referendum: The Peace Ballot, 1934–1935', *English Historical Review*, 95(377) (1980), p. 838; Daniel Todman, *Britain's War: Into Battle, 1937–1941* (London: Allen Lane, 2016), p. 76.
86. Van Ypersele, 'Mourning and Memory', in Horne (ed.), *A Companion to World War I*, pp. 581–2.
87. Quoted in J. M. Bumsted, *The Peoples of Canada: A Post-Confederation History* (Oxford University Press, 2004), p. 211.
88. Bernard Harris, 'Unemployment and the Dole in Interwar Britain', in Paul Johnson (ed.), *20th Century Britain: Economic, Social and Cultural Change* (London: Longman, 1994), pp. 203–5.
89. H. M. D. Parker, *Manpower: A Study of War-Time Policy and Administration* (London: HMSO, 1957), p. 22.
90. Figure derived from Harris, 'Unemployment and the Dole in Interwar Britain', in Johnson (ed.), *20th Century Britain*, pp. 203–5; Margaret Gowing, 'The Organisation of Manpower in Britain during the Second World War', *Journal of Contemporary History*, 7(1/2) (Jan.–Apr. 1972), p. 147.
91. Parker, *Manpower*, p. 25.
92. Dudley Baines, 'Recovery from Depression', in Paul Johnson (ed.), *20th Century Britain: Economic, Social and Cultural Change* (London: Longman, 1994), p. 189.
93. Allport, *Browned Off and Bloody-Minded*, p. 79.
94. Baines, 'Recovery from Depression', in Johnson (ed.), *20th Century Britain*, p. 189.
95. Parker, *Manpower*, pp. 20–16.
96. John Stevenson, *British Society, 1914–45* (London: Penguin, 1984), pp. 117–19; Baines, 'Recover from Depression', in Johnson (ed.), *20th Century Britain*, p. 190. See also e.g. D. H. Aldcroft and H. W. Richardson, *The British Economy, 1870–1939* (London, Macmillan, 1969); S. Glynn and J. Oxborrow, *Interwar Britain: A Social and Economic History* (London: Allen & Unwin, 1976).
97. Baines, 'Recovery from Depression', in Johnson (ed.), *20th Century Britain*, p. 198.
98. Parker, *Manpower*, pp. 36–7.
99. Ibid., pp. 20–16.
100. Kevin Jefferys, *The Churchill Coalition and Wartime Politics, 1940–1945* (Manchester University Press, 1991), p. 10.
101. Ross McKibbin, *Classes and Cultures: England 1918–1951* (Oxford University Press, 2000), p. v.
102. McKibbin, *Parties and People*, p. vi.
103. Jefferys, *The Churchill Coalition and Wartime Politics*, p. 10.
104. Jose Harris, 'Political Ideas and the Debate on State Welfare, 1940–45', in H. L. Smith (ed.), *War and Social Change: British Society in the Second World War* (Manchester University Press, 1986), p. 236.
105. David Morgan and Mary Evans, 'The Road to Nineteen Eighty-Four: Orwell and the Post-War Reconstruction of Citizenship', in Brian Brivati and Harriet Jones (eds.), *What Difference Did the War Make?* (London: Leicester University Press, 1993), p. 50.
106. David Reynolds, *The Long Shadow: The Great War and the Twentieth Century* (London: Simon & Schuster, 2013), pp. 128, 160.
107. Arthur Marwick, *The Deluge: British Society and the First World War* (London: The Bodley Head, 1965), pp. 310–12; Elizabeth Kier, 'War and Reform', in Elizabeth Kier and Ronald R. Krebs (eds.), *In War's Wake: International Conflict and the Fate of Liberal Democracy* (Cambridge University Press, 2010), pp. 157.
108. Neil Roos, *Ordinary Springboks: White Servicemen and Social Justice in South Africa, 1939–1961* (Aldershot: Ashgate, 2005), pp. 13–21.

109. Ibid., pp. 19–20.
110. Ibid., p. 13.
111. J. W. Hofmeyr and Gerald J. Pillay (eds.), *A History of Christianity in South Africa, Vol. I* (Pretoria: Haum Tertiary, 1994), p. 196.
112. Roos, *Ordinary Springboks*, pp. 13–21.
113. Ibid., p. 21.
114. Darwin, *The Empire Project*, p. 496.
115. Ibid.
116. John Lambert, 'An Identity Threatened: White English-Speaking South Africans, Britishness and Dominion South Africanism, 1934–1939', *Kleio*, 37(1) (2010), p. 64.
117. Hofmeyr and Pillay (eds.), *A History of Christianity in South Africa*, pp. 195–9.
118. Roos, *Ordinary Springboks*, p. 13.
119. Ibid., p. 42.
120. Bumsted, *The Peoples of Canada*, p. 209.
121. R. Douglas Francis, Richard Jones, Donald B. Smith, *Destinies: Canadian History Since Confederation* (Toronto: Nelson Education, 2008), pp. 270–1.
122. Ibid., pp. 289–91.
123. M. C. Urquhart (ed.), *Historical Statistics of Canada* (Cambridge University Press, 1965), p. 61.
124. Francis, Jones, Smith, *Destinies*, pp. 289–91.
125. Generally, recipients of relief had to be in arrears in rent, having received notice of discontinuation of electricity and water service, and be under threat of eviction.
126. Francis, Jones, Smith, *Destinies*, pp. 289–91.
127. Ibid.
128. H. L. Wesseling, *The European Colonial Empires, 1815–1919* (Harlow: Pearson, 2004), p. 234.
129. J. L. Granatstein, *Conscription in the Second World War* (Toronto: McGraw-Hill Ryerson, 1969), pp. 3–9.
130. Ibid., p. 9.
131. Robert Bothwell, *The Penguin History of Canada* (Penguin: Toronto, 2006), p. 338.
132. Granatstein, *Conscription in the Second World War*, pp. 3–9.
133. Lawrence Leduc, Jon H. Pammett, Judith I. McKenzie and André Turcotte, *Dynasties and Interludes: Past and Present in Canadian Electoral Politics* (Toronto: Dundurn Press, 2010), pp. 108–10.
134. Bothwell, *The Penguin History of Canada*, p. 313.
135. Leduc et al., *Dynasties and Interludes*, p. 127.
136. Francis, Jones, Smith, *Destinies*, pp. 289–91.
137. Leduc et al., *Dynasties and Interludes*, p. 135.
138. Ibid., pp. 114–20. The Progressives, always uneasy at the prospect of acting like a conventional political party, forming a government or an opposition, creating formal organisations, compromising their positions and diversifying their programs, gradually lost momentum and dissolved.
139. Ibid., pp. 133–6.
140. Kate Darian-Smith, 'War and Australian Society', in Joan Beaumont (ed.), *Australia's War, 1939–45* (Crows Nest: Allen & Unwin, 1996), p. 63.
141. Stuart Macintyre, *The Oxford History of Australia, Vol. IV: 1901–1942: The Succeeding Age* (Oxford University Press, 1986), p. 275.
142. Stuart Macintyre, *A Concise History of Australia* (Cambridge University Press, 2009), pp. 178–9.

143. Ibid., pp. 180–6.
144. Wray Vamplew (ed.), *Australians: Historical Statistics* (Broadway, NSW: Fairfax, Syme and Weldon Associates, 1987), p. 152.
145. David Lee, 'Politics and Government', in Joan Beaumont (ed.), *Australia's War, 1939–45* (Crows Nest: Allen & Unwin, 1996), pp. 82–5. Except for the short interlude of the Scullin Government between 1929 and 1931, the ALP was in the political wilderness.
146. Macintyre, *A Concise History of Australia*, p. 169.
147. Ibid., p. 180.
148. Lee, 'Politics and Government', in Beaumont (ed.), *Australia's War*, pp. 84–5.
149. Mein Smith, *A Concise History of New Zealand*, p. 146.
150. Ibid, pp. 142–51; Margaret McClure, *A Civilised Community: A History of Social Security in New Zealand, 1898–1998* (Auckland University Press, 1998), p. 49.
151. Mein Smith, *A Concise History of New Zealand*, pp. 151–3.
152. Tom Brooking, 'Economic Transformation', in Geoffrey W. Rice (ed.), *The Oxford History of New Zealand* (Melbourne: Oxford University Press, 1992), p. 251.
153. Mein Smith, *A Concise History of New Zealand*, pp. 152.
154. Ibid., p. 146.
155. Ibid., p. 155.
156. Ibid., p. 154–6.
157. Ibid., pp. 154–6; McClure, *A Civilised Community*, pp. 48–93; Michael Bassett and Michael King, *Tomorrow Comes the Song: The Life of Peter Fraser* (Auckland: Penguin, 2000), p. 160.
158. Brooking, 'Economic Transformation', in Rice (ed.), *The Oxford History of New Zealand*, p. 251.
159. McClure, *A Civilised Community*, pp. 48–93.
160. James T. Sparrow, *Warfare State: World War II Americans and the Age of Big Government* (Oxford University Press, 2011), pp. 43–6. Roosevelt's four freedoms were freedom of speech, freedom of worship, freedom from want, and freedom from fear.
161. Quoted in McClure, *A Civilised Community*, p. 60.
162. Ibid., p. 83; Margaret Galt, 'Wealth and Income in New Zealand, *c.*1870 to *c.*1939' (PhD thesis, Victoria University of Wellington, 1985); Mein Smith, *A Concise History of New Zealand*, p. 124.
163. Sumit Sarkar, *Modern India 1885–1947* (London: Macmillan, 1983), pp. 257–61; Sumit Sarkar, *Modern Times: India 1880s–1950s* (Ranikhet: Permanent Black, 2014), pp. 121–30; Dietmar Rothermund, *India in the Great Depression, 1929–1939* (New Delhi: Manohar Publications, 1992), p. 203.
164. Graham Dunlop, *Military Economics, Culture and Logistics in the Burma Campaign, 1942–1945* (London: Pickering & Chatto, 2009), pp. 31–4.
165. Sarkar, *Modern India*, pp. 257–61; Sarkar, *Modern Times*, pp. 121–30; Rothermund, *India in the Great Depression, 1929–1939*, p. 203.
166. Bond, *British Military Policy between the Two World Wars*, p. 98.
167. Tarak Barkawi, 'Culture and Combat in the Colonies: The Indian Army in the Second World War', *Journal of Contemporary History*, 41(2) (2006), pp. 329–30; Darwin, *The Empire Project*, p. 497.
168. Kier, *Imagining War*, p. 96.
169. Tooze, *Wages of Destruction*, p. 212. In a similar vein, Ian van der Waag has pointed out that while there were many deficiencies in South Africa's preparation for war, the country's 'defences reached a peak in 1939 and were in a better state of

preparation than at any other time in its peacetime history': Ian van der Waag, *A Military History of Modern South Africa* (Johannesburg: Jonathan Ball, 2015), p. 170.

170. Edgerton, *Britain's War Machine*, p. 3.
171. NAA SP109/16 NN Propaganda: Lord Mayor's Committee on Morale, 1943. India's population at the time was, according to the pamphlet, 388,800,000.
172. Edgerton, *Britain's War Machine*, pp. 45–6.
173. Williamson Murray, 'The Collapse of Empire: British Strategy, 1919–1945', in Williamson Murray, MacGregor Knox and Alvin Bernstein (eds.), *The Making of Strategy: Rulers, States and War* (Cambridge University Press, 1994), p. 395.
174. Edgerton, *Britain's War Machine*, p. 2.
175. Rose, 'British Army Command Culture 1939–1945'.
176. Peden, 'Financing Churchill's Army', p. 288; Kier, *Imagining War*, p. 96.
177. Macintyre, *A Concise History of Australia*, pp. 168–9.
178. Parker, *Manpower*, pp. 36–7.
179. Alexander, 'The Fall of France, 1940', p. 34.

Chapter 2 Mobilisation

1. Sonya O. Rose, *Which People's War? National Identity and Citizenship in Britain 1939–1945* (Oxford University Press, 2003), pp. 1–2; Jeffrey A. Keshen, *Saints, Sinners and Soldiers: Canada's Second World War* (Vancouver: University of British Columbia Press, 2004), p. 3; Andrew Stewart, *A Very British Experience: Coalition, Defence and Strategy in the Second World War* (Eastbourne: Sussex Academic Press, 2012), p. 1.
2. Eric Hobsbawm, 'Britain: A Comparative View', in Brian Brivati and Harriet Jones (eds.), *What Difference Did the War Make?* (London: Leicester University Press, 1993), p. 25.
3. Stuart Macintyre, *A Concise History of Australia* (Cambridge University Press, 2009), pp. 198–9. See also, Philippa Mein Smith, *A Concise History of New Zealand* (Melbourne: Cambridge University Press, 2005), p. 124.
4. Geoffrey G. Field, *Blood, Sweat and Toil: Remaking the British Working Class, 1939–1945* (Oxford University Press, 2011), pp. 4–5.
5. Ross McKibbin, *Parties and People: England 1914–1951* (Oxford University Press, 2010), p. 106.
6. Kevin Jefferys, *The Churchill Coalition and Wartime Politics, 1940–1945* (Manchester University Press, 1991), pp. 16–17.
7. Ibid., pp. 9–36.
8. McKibbin, *Parties and People*, p. 106.
9. Jefferys, *The Churchill Coalition and Wartime Politics*, pp. 38.
10. Daniel Marston, *The Indian Army and the End of the Raj* (Cambridge University Press, 2014), Ch. 2.
11. John Darwin, *The Empire Project: The Rise and Fall of the British World-System, 1830–1970* (Cambridge University Press, 2009), p. 497.
12. Ibid., p. 506.
13. Tarak Barkawi, 'Culture and Combat in the Colonies: The Indian Army in the Second World War', *Journal of Contemporary History*, 41(2) (2006), pp. 329–30.
14. Darwin, *The Empire Project*, p. 497.
15. John A. English, *The Canadian Army and the Normandy Campaign: A Study of Failure in High Command* (London: Praeger, 1991), pp. 63–4.

16. J. L. Granatstein, *Conscription in the Second World War* (Toronto: McGraw-Hill Ryerson, 1969), p. 19.
17. Darwin, *The Empire Project*, pp. 494.
18. Granatstein, *Conscription in the Second World War*, p. 75.
19. Tim Cook, *Warlords: Borden, Mackenzie King, and Canada's World Wars* (London: Penguin, 2012), p. 207.
20. Granatstein, *Conscription in the Second World War*, p. 13.
21. Cook, *Warlords*, pp. 220–4. See also, Keshen, *Saints, Sinners and Soldiers*, p. 14.
22. Ibid., pp. 225–6.
23. J. L. Granatstein, *Canada's War: The Politics of the Mackenzie King Government, 1939–1945* (Toronto: Oxford University Press, 1975), pp. 74–6.
24. Ibid., pp. 76–80; Cook, *Warlords*, pp. 231–3.
25. Cook, *Warlords*, pp. 231–3.
26. Granatstein, *Conscription in the Second World War*, p. 27.
27. Ibid.
28. David Lee, 'Politics and Government', in Joan Beaumont (ed.), *Australia's War, 1939–45* (Crows Nest: Allen & Unwin, 1996), p. 87. They entered formal coalition five months into the war.
29. Quoted in Darwin, *The Empire Project*, p. 495.
30. Kate Darien-Smith, 'World War 2 and Post-War Reconstruction, 1939–49', in Alison Bashford and Stuart Macintyre (eds.), *The Cambridge History of Australia, Vol. III: The Commonwealth of Australia* (Cambridge University Press, 2013), p. 88.
31. Quoted in J. M. Main (ed.), *Conscription: The Australian Debate, 1901–1970* (Melbourne: Cassell Australia, 1970), p. 109.
32. Paul Hasluck, *Australia in the War of 1939–1945, Series Four: Civil, Vol. I: The Government and the People, 1939–1941* (Canberra: AWM, 1965), p. 254.
33. Lee, 'Politics and Government', in Beaumont (ed.), *Australia's War*, pp. 88–9; Hasluck, *The Government and the People*, pp. 248–53.
34. Hasluck, *The Government and the People*, p. 250.
35. Ibid., pp. 244–5.
36. Ibid., p. 256.
37. Lee, 'Politics and Government', in Beaumont (ed.), *Australia's War*, pp. 90–2. The forces vote, which came to 15,997 valid ballots, was marginally more directed to Labor than the governing coalition (see Chapter 16 of this volume and Hasluck, *The Government and the People*, pp. 262–3).
38. Lee, 'Politics and Government', in Beaumont (ed.), *Australia's War*, pp. 90–2.
39. Macintyre, *A Concise History of Australia*, p. 190.
40. Economically, however, 'war-related industrialisation and sharp increases in government revenues and expenditures transformed the South African economy' (see Ian van der Waag, *A Military History of Modern South Africa* (Johannesburg: Jonathan Ball, 2015), pp. 191–5).
41. Darwin, *The Empire Project*, p. 496.
42. Neil Roos, *Ordinary Springboks: White Servicemen and Social Justice in South Africa, 1939–1961* (Aldershot: Ashgate, 2005), p. 25.
43. Albert Grundlingh, 'The King's Afrikaners? Enlistment and Ethnic Identity in the Union of South Africa's Defence Force During the Second World War, 1939–45', *The Journal of African History*, 40(3) (Nov. 1999), p. 353.
44. Roos, *Ordinary Springboks*, pp. 25–6; F. D. Tothill, 'The 1943 General Election' (Master's thesis, University of South Africa, 1987), p. 3.

45. Christopher Vasey, *Nazi Intelligence Operations in Non-Occupied Territories: Espionage Efforts in the United States, Britain, South America and Southern Africa* (Jefferson: McFarland & Co., 2016), pp. 278–89; Neil Roos, 'The Second World War, the Army Education Scheme and the "Discipline" of the White Poor in South Africa', *History of Education: Journal of the History of Education Society*, 32(6) (2003), p. 651.
46. F. D. Tothill, 'The Soldiers' Vote and Its Effect on the Outcome of the South African General Election of 1943', *South African Historical Journal*, 21 (1989), pp. 73–4.
47. Tothill, 'The 1943 General Election', p. 3; Tothill, 'The Soldiers' Vote'.
48. Darwin, *The Empire Project*, p. 496; Ian McGibbon, 'New Zealand's Strategical Approach', in John Crawford (ed.), *Kia Kaha: New Zealand in the Second World War* (Oxford University Press, 2000), pp. 9–10; Michael Bassett and Michael King, *Tomorrow Comes the Song: The Life of Peter Fraser* (Auckland: Penguin, 2000), pp. 170–1.
49. John E. Martin, *The House: New Zealand's House of Representatives, 1854–2004* (Palmerston North: Dunmore Press, 2004), p. 212.
50. Margaret McClure, *A Civilised Community: A History of Social Security in New Zealand, 1898–1998* (Auckland University Press, 1998), p. 95; See also, J. R. S. Daniels, 'The General Election of 1943' (Master's thesis, Victoria University, 1961), p. 240.
51. McClure, *A Civilised Community*, p. 96.
52. Ibid., pp. 97–8.
53. Robert Chapman, 'From Labour to National', in Geoffrey W. Rice (ed.), *The Oxford History of New Zealand* (Oxford University Press, 1992), pp. 367–8; Bassett and King, *Tomorrow Comes the Song*, pp. 171, 200–1.
54. Miles Fairburn and S. J. Haslett, 'Stability and Egalitarians: New Zealand, 1911–1951', in Mark Fairburn and Erik Olssen (eds.), *Class, Gender and the Vote: Historical Perspectives from New Zealand* (University of Otago Press, 2005), p. 25.
55. Daniels, 'The General Election of 1943', p. 11; Bassett and King, *Tomorrow Comes the Song*, p. 230.
56. Guy H. Scholefield, *New Zealand Parliamentary Record, 1840–1949* (Wellington: R. E. Owen, 1950), p. 52; Bassett and King, *Tomorrow Comes the Song*, p. 197.
57. Bassett and King, *Tomorrow Comes the Song*, p. 230.
58. Daniels, 'The General Election of 1943', pp. 7–10; Bassett and King, *Tomorrow Comes the Song*, p. 198.
59. F. L. W. Wood, *Political and External Affairs* (Wellington: Historical Publications Branch, 1958), pp. 229–30 and 241–2.
60. Ibid., pp. 230–3; Scholefield, *New Zealand Parliamentary Record, 1840–1949*, p. 50; Martin, *The House*, p. 214; Bassett and King, *Tomorrow Comes the Song*, p. 230.
61. Wood, *Political and External Affairs*, p. 235; Bassett and King, *Tomorrow Comes the Song*, p. 231.
62. Wood, *Political and External Affairs*, pp. 236–9; Bassett and King, *Tomorrow Comes the Song*, p. 232.
63. Wood, *Political and External Affairs*, pp. 236–9; Bassett and King, *Tomorrow Comes the Song*, p. 232.
64. Catriona Pennell, *A Kingdom United: Popular Responses to the Outbreak of the First World War in Britain and Ireland* (Oxford University Press, 2012), p. 228; Adrian Gregory, *The Last Great War: British Society and the First World War*

(Cambridge University Press, 2008), p. 278; Alan Allport, *Browned Off and Bloody-Minded: The British Soldier Goes to War 1939–1945* (London: Yale University Press, 2015), p. 63.

65. David Edgerton, *Britain's War Machine: Weapons, Resources and Experts in the Second World War* (London: Allen Lane, 2011), p. 197.
66. H. M. D. Parker, *Manpower: A Study of War-Time Policy and Administration* (London: HMSO, 1957), pp. 150–1. It took until the end of 1941 for all these men to be called up. Thus, this first cohort of registrations and enlistments carried Britain through the first two years of the war.
67. LHCMA Adam 3/1 Notes for Secretary of State Estimates Speech, AG Department, 1941; LHCMA Adam 3/2 Use of Manpower in the Army 1941, Appendix A; NA WO 277/12, Manpower Problems, pp. 1–11 and 80; Jeremy A. Crang, 'The British Army as a Social Institution', in Hew Strachan (ed.), *The British Army, Manpower and Society into the Twenty-First Century* (London, 2000), p. 16; Allport, *Browned Off and Bloody-Minded*, p. xviii. The figure for the 'mobilised and embodied' strength of the Army varies in the historiography. W. Franklin Mellor (ed.), *Casualties and Medical Statistics* (London: HMSO, 1972), pp. 831–2 and LHCMA Adam Box 2, White Paper on Strengths and Casualties, 1939–45 put the figure at 402,000. LHCMA Adam 3/1 puts the figure at 410,000, while NA WO 277/12 p. 80 puts it at 485,000.
68. NA WO 277/12, Manpower Problems, p. 80.
69. Ian Beckett, 'The Nation in Arms, 1914–18', in Ian F. W. Beckett and Keith Simpson (eds.), *A Nation in Arms: A Social Study of the British Army in the First World War* (London: Tom Donovan, 1990), p. 8. Between 4 Aug. 1914 and 31 Oct. 1917, 2,675,149 men volunteered for the British Army, fully 54% of all those recruited (see J. M. Winter, 'Britain's "Lost Generation" of the First World War', *Population Studies: A Journal of Demography*, 31(3) (1977), p. 451).
70. Statistics derived from figures available in Peter Howlett (ed.), *Fighting with Figures: A Statistical Digest of the Second World War* (London: The Central Statistics Office, 1995), pp. 5, 39 and 41.
71. Winter, 'Britain's "Lost Generation" of the First World War', p. 450.
72. George Peden, 'Financing Churchill's Army', in Keith Neilson and Greg Kennedy (eds.), *The British Way in Warfare: Power and the International System, 1856–1956* (Farnham: Ashgate, 2010), p. 289.
73. David French, *Raising Churchill's Army: The British Army and the War against Germany 1919–1945* (Oxford University Press, 2000), p. 27.
74. Margaret Gowing, 'The Organisation of Manpower in Britain during the Second World War', *Journal of Contemporary History*, 7(1/2) (Jan.–Apr. 1972), p. 158.
75. See ibid.; Parker, *Manpower*.
76. Figures derived from Parker, *Manpower*, pp. 157 and 488–90. The total number of male registrations came to 8,356,686.
77. Ibid., pp. 158 and 497; *Report of the Ministry of Labour and National Service, 1939–1946* (London: His Majesty's Stationary Office, 1947), pp. 16–17. Deferments could be granted on the grounds of the importance of the work of the firm, the importance of the contribution that the individual man was making to it and the possibility of replacing him by another worker not liable to be called up. Occupations deemed important to the life of the community included the legal profession, accountancy, banking and insurance, the press, the theatrical profession and officials of employers' organisations and trade unions.
78. Parker, *Manpower*, p. 29

79. Ibid., p. 161. For example, 660,400 applications for deferment made between Jan. 1942 and Apr. 1945 were rejected, suggesting that they were made on spurious grounds. This constitutes 8% of all male registrations made during the war (see ibid., p. 497).
80. Indivar Kamtekar, 'A Different War Dance: State and Class in India 1939–1945', *Past and Present*, 176(1) (2002), pp. 190.
81. Sri Nandan Prasad, *Official History of the Indian Armed Forces in the Second World War, 1939–45: Expansion of the Armed Forces and Defence Organisation, 1939–45* (Calcutta: Orient Longmans, 1956), p. 54. On 1 Oct. 1939, the total strength of the Indian Army was 352,213. This included regular troops of the Indian army, 205,038; British troops, 63,469; and miscellaneous troops including Indian States Forces etc. 83,706.
82. Daniel Marston, *Phoenix from the Ashes: The Indian Army in the Burma Campaign* (Westport: Praeger, 2003), p. 42. The term 'martial classes' (or 'martial races') goes back to the nineteenth century, when the British designated certain groups, such as Sikhs and Gurkhas, as 'martial' on the basis of their presumed fighting abilities and traditions as well as their proven loyalty to British interests (see Steven I. Wilkinson, *Army and Nation: The Military and Indian Democracy since Independence* (London: Harvard University Press, 2015), p. 41). The Official History puts the number of recruits in the Indian Army by May 1940 at 53,000 (see S. W. Kirby, *The War against Japan, Vol. I: The Loss of Singapore* (Uckfield: The Naval & Military Press, 2004 [1957]), p. 38).
83. Prasad, *Expansion of the Armed Forces and Defence Organisation, 1939–45*, pp. 78, 84–6 and Appendix 2; Wilkinson, *Army and Nation*, p. 65.
84. Wilkinson, *Army and Nation*, p. 65; F. W. Perry, *The Commonwealth Armies: Manpower and Organisation in Two World Wars* (Manchester University Press, 1988), p. 117.
85. Robert Aldrich and Christopher Hilliard, 'The French and British Empires', in John Horne (ed.), *A Companion to World War I* (Oxford: Blackwell, 2010), p. 525.
86. Prasad, *Expansion of the Armed Forces and Defence Organisation, 1939–45*, p. 78; Wilkinson, *Army and Nation*, p. 72; Kamtekar, 'A Different War Dance', pp. 190–3.
87. Saumitra Jha and Steven Wilkinson, 'Does Combat Experience Foster Organisational Skill? Evidence from Ethnic Cleansing during the Partition of South Asia', *American Political Science Review*, 106(4) (Nov. 2012), p. 884; Tarak Barkawi, *Soldiers of Empire: Indian and British Armies in World War II* (Cambridge University Press, 2017), p. 147.
88. Kamtekar, 'A Different War Dance', pp. 190–4.
89. Raymond Callahan, *Burma, 1942–1945* (London: Davis Poynter, 1978), p. 61.
90. Kamtekar, 'A Different War Dance', pp. 190–4; Prasad, *Expansion of the Armed Forces and Defence Organisation, 1939–45*, pp. 84–5.
91. Kamtekar, 'A Different War Dance', p. 200.
92. Ibid., pp. 205–6.
93. Ibid., pp. 190–4; Wilkinson, *Army and Nation*, p. 65.
94. Barkawi, 'Culture and Combat in the Colonies', p. 330; Kamtekar, 'A Different War Dance', pp. 210–11 and 218; Marston, *Phoenix from the Ashes*, p. 2.
95. Kamtekar, 'A Different War Dance', pp. 190–3.
96. BL IOR L/WS/1/939 Report on the Morale of the Army in India, Feb.–Apr. 1943, p. 8.

97. Kamtekar, 'A Different War Dance', pp. 190–4.
98. Srinath Raghaven, *India's War: The Making of Modern South Asia, 1939–1945* (London: Penguin, 2017), pp. 78–9.
99. Prasad, *Expansion of the Armed Forces and Defence Organisation, 1939–45*, p. 78, 84–6 and Appendix 2.
100. Ibid., p. 89. See also, Andrew N. Buchanan, 'The War Crisis and the Decolonization of India, December 1941–September 1942: A Political and Military Dilemma', *Global War Studies*, 8(2) (2011), pp. 22–3.
101. Wilkinson, *Army and Nation*, pp. 64, 73–5. Only about 30,000 men from the non-martial races ended up as infantry and most of these were assigned to duties on the line of command or on internal security.
102. Raghaven, *India's War*, p. 76–7.
103. H. L. Wesseling, *The European Colonial Empires, 1815–1919* (Harlow: Pearson, 2004), p. 234.
104. Granatstein, *Conscription in the Second World War*, pp. 3–9.
105. Ibid., p. 16.
106. English, *The Canadian Army and the Normandy Campaign*, p. 69.
107. Ibid., p. 14.
108. Ibid., p. 69.
109. Granatstein, *Conscription in the Second World War*, p. 27.
110. DHH CMHQ Report 51 Censorship of Mail, CAO. Field Censors' Notes as Material for History, 31 Oct. 1941.
111. Granatstein, *Conscription in the Second World War*, p. 27.
112. Ibid., p. viii.
113. C. P. Stacey, *Arms, Men and Governments: The War Policies of Canada, 1939–1945* (Ottawa: The Queen's Printer for Canada, 1970), p. 590; Dominion Bureau of Statistics, *The Canada Year Book, 1946* (Ottawa: Edmond Cloutier, 1946), p. 127. By comparison, 640,000 Canadians served in the First World War (see Wesseling, *The European Colonial Empires*, p. 235). A further 12,000 troops from Newfoundland served during the war also.
114. Daniel Byers, *Zombie Army: The Canadian Army and Conscription in the Second World War* (Vancouver: University of British Columbia Press, 2016), pp. 187–8.
115. Stacey, *Arms, Men and Governments*, p. 590; Vol. 18,826 File No. 133.065 (D697) GS, NRMA, & CWAC Appointments and Enlistments and Enrolments in World War II by Place of Birth by Province. 7.7% of those born in Ontario also enlisted in provinces other than their province of birth.
116. Stacey, *Arms, Men and Governments*, p. 590.
117. Robert Engen, *Strangers in Arms: Combat Motivation in the Canadian Army, 1943–1945* (London: McGill-Queen's University Press, 2016), p. 21. The National Defence HQ calculated, in Mar. 1944, that French Canadians made up 19.1% of the total strength of the Army (including conscripts). See Byers, *Zombie Army*, p. 7.
118. Cook, *Warlords*, p. 207.
119. Michael D. Stevenson, *Canada's Greatest Wartime Muddle: National Selective Service and the Mobilization of Human Resources during World War II* (Kingston: McGill-Queen's University Press), p. 38; Byers, *Zombie Army*, p. 138.
120. Byers, *Zombie Army*, pp. 180–1. In the six months leading up to Mar. 1944, call-up notices for almost 185,000 men had to be issued to find 34,000 recruits for the Army (see ibid., p. 185).
121. Stacey, *Arms, Men and Governments*, p. 406.
122. Byers, *Zombie Army*, pp. 182–3, 191.

123. Stacey, *Arms, Men and Governments*, p. 588. 170,730 were in farming, 2,257 in fishing, 4,611 in lumbering, 4,968 in mining, 32,195 in essential industries, 14,729 students, 10,843 conscientious objectors, 4,751 in the merchant marine, 6,295 on compassionate grounds and 16,089 for other reasons.
124. Stacey, *Arms, Men and Governments*, p. 589; Byers, *Zombie Army*, p. 192.
125. Daniel Byers, 'Mobilising Canada: The National Resources Mobilization Act, the Department of National Defence, and Compulsory Military Service in Canada, 1940–1945', *Journal of the Canadian Historical Association*, 7(1) (1996), p. 175. These men, according to Byers, enrolled for four months' training between Mar. 1941 and July 1945. This figure does not include some men called up from Oct. 1940–Mar. 1941 for shorter training under NRMA, although most completed the full training after 1941.
126. Andrew Stewart, *Empire Lost: Britain, The Dominions and the Second World War* (London: Continuum, 2008), p. 23.
127. Grundlingh, 'The King's Afrikaners?', p. 354.
128. H. J. Martin and Neil Orpen, *South Africa at War: Military and Industrial Organization and Operations in Connection with the Conduct of the War, 1939–1945* (Purnell: Cape Town, 1979), p. 27; van der Waag, *A Military History of Modern South Africa*, p. 185.
129. Grundlingh, 'The King's Afrikaners?', p. 354. Roos, *Ordinary Springboks*, p. 1 put the number as 'roughly 200,000'.
130. Van der Waag, *A Military History of Modern South Africa*, p. 133.
131. Union Office of Census and Statistics, *Official Year Book of the Union of South Africa No. 23 – 1946* (Pretoria: The Government Printer, 1948), Ch. XXIX: The Union of South Africa and the War p. 20; Bureau of Census and Statistics, Pretoria, *Union Statistics for Fifty Years: 1910–1960* (Pretoria: The Government Printers, 1960), p. A13. An additional 877 volunteered for the South African Naval Force.
132. Van der Waag, *A Military History of Modern South Africa*, p. 133.
133. SANDF, DOC, War Records Box 55 Memorandum, Attestations NMC, 31 Aug. 1944; SANDF, DOC, War Records Box 55 Memorandum, Attestations CC and IMC, 16 Sept. 1944; SANDF War Records Box 55 Memorandum, Attestations UDF, 28 Aug. 1944; SANDF, DOC, DAG-P Box 54 Weekly Recruiting Graph, 1944–5. The figures for the UDF include male officers and ORs in the Army and Air Force and members of the WADC and South African Military Nursing Service. The UDF figures do not include those who served in the Navy, permanent forces or non-Europeans.
134. J. S. M. Simpson, *South Africa Fights* (London: Hodder & Stoughton Ltd, 1941), pp. 88–104.
135. Darwin, *The Empire Project*, p. 11.
136. Grundlingh, 'The King's Afrikaners?', p. 354.
137. South African Defence Personnel Archive, Pretoria, Service Records. The archive contains 573 boxes of service records for the white troops who served during the war, organised alphabetically. Two records were chosen at random from each box and 1,112 usable records were accessed in this manner; at 95% confidence a random sample of 1,112 has a sample error of ± 2.9%.
138. J. W. Hofmeyr and Gerald J. Pillay (eds.), *A History of Christianity in South Africa, Vol. I* (Pretoria: Haum Tertiary, 1994), p. 195.
139. The 1946 census showed that 59% of the white population of South Africa spoke Afrikaans at home and the 1960 census showed that 56% of the white population attended Afrikaans churches. See Census Special Report No. 189, Home Languages, 1946; Edward Higgins, 'The Sociology of Religion in South Africa',

Archives de Sociologie des Religions, 32 (1971), p. 147. The same report, p. 153, shows that white membership of Christian churches changed between 1 and 3% between 1921 and 1960.

140. Hofmeyr and Pillay (eds.), *A History of Christianity in South Africa*; Peter Hinchliff, *The Church in South Africa* (London: SPCK, 1968); Peter Hinchliff, *The Anglican Church in South Africa: An Account of the History and Development of the Church of the Province of South Africa* (London: Darton, Longman & Todd, 1963).
141. Census Special Report No. 189, Home Languages, 1946.
142. SANDF, DOC, War Records Box 55 Total Figures of Religious Denominations, 26 Oct. 1941; SANDF, DOC, DAG-P Box 54 Quarterly Religious Denominational Returns, 30 Aug. 1940.
143. SANDF, DOC, War Records Box 55 Statement Showing Religious Denominations in, and Chaplains appointed to, Brigades, n.d. but likely 1941; SANDF, DOC, War Records Box 55 Religious Denominations Potchefstroom Camp, n.d. but likely 1941.
144. Roos, *Ordinary Springboks*, p. 25; van der Waag, *A Military History of Modern South Africa*, pp. 178–9.
145. Louis Grundlingh, 'The Recruitment of South African Blacks for Participation in the Second World War', in David Killingray and Richard Rathbone (eds.), *Africa and the Second World War* (London: Macmillan Press Ltd, 1986), pp. 181–90.
146. Ibid., pp. 191–4.
147. SANDF, DOC, AI Gp 1 Box 81/I/71/B South African Military Censorship, Special Report No. 7, The Riot at Kimberley, 9–25 Feb. 1943.
148. Defence Personnel Archive. These men became known as 'red tabs' as they wore orange/scarlet shoulder tabs on their uniform (Simpson, *South Africa Fights*, pp. 88–104; Andre Wessel, 'The First Two Years of War: The Development of the Union Defence Forces, Sept. 1939 to Sept. 1941', *Military History Journal*, 11(5) (June 2000)).
149. Roos, *Ordinary Springboks*, pp. 34–5.
150. SANDF, DOC, War Records Box 55 Memorandum, Attestations NMC, 31 Aug. 1944; SANDF, DOC, War Records Box 55 Memorandum, Attestations CC and IMC, 16 Sept. 1944; SANDF, DOC, War Records Box 55 Memorandum, Attestations UDF, 28 Aug. 1944; SANDF, DOC, DAG-P Box 54 Weekly Recruiting Graph, 1944–5. The figures for the UDF include male officers and ORs in the Army and Air Force and members of the WADC and South African Military Nursing Service. The UDF figures do not include those who served in the Navy, permanent forces or non-Europeans.
151. David Horner, 'Australia in 1942: A Pivotal Year', in Peter J. Dean (ed.), *Australia 1942: In the Shadow of War* (Cambridge University Press, 2013), pp. 14–15.
152. Albert Palazzo, 'The Overlooked Mission: Australia and Home Defence', in Peter J. Dean (ed.), *Australia 1942: In the Shadow of War* (Cambridge University Press, 2013), p. 55.
153. Main, *Conscription*, pp. 64–5; Wesseling, *The European Colonial Empires*, p. 234.
154. Palazzo, 'The Overlooked Mission', in Dean (ed.), *Australia 1942*, p. 63.
155. Hasluck, *Australia in the War of 1939–1945*, p. 399 and Appendix 8.
156. Kate Darian-Smith, 'War and Australian Society', in Joan Beaumont (ed.), *Australia's War, 1939–45* (Crows Nest: Allen & Unwin, 1996), p. 54.
157. Hasluck, *Australia in the War of 1939–1945*, pp. 399–400 and Appendix 8. Wesseling, *The European Colonial Empires*, p. 234, notes that 7.5% of the Australian population volunteered in the First World War.

158. Jeffrey Grey, *The Australian Army* (Oxford University Press, 2001), p. 115. In 1939 the age limit was 20 to 35 for recruits, but higher for officers and some NCOs.
159. Darian-Smith, 'War and Australian Society', in Beaumont (ed.), *Australia's War*, p. 59.
160. Mark Johnston, 'The Civilians Who Joined Up, 1939–45', *Journal of the Australian War Memorial*, 29 (Nov. 1996).
161. Ibid.; AWM 54 903/1/3 Pt 1 Australian Military Forces: Some Comparative Figures of Army Strengths and Casualties, 1914–18 War with 1939–45 War puts the figures at 727,703. Grey, *The Australian Army*, p. 107 puts the figure at 735,781
162. Johnston, 'The Civilians Who Joined Up, 1939–45'. This figure includes direct enlistments up until 18 Aug. 1945.
163. Taken from the last census completed before the war: *Census of the Commonwealth of Australia*, 30 June 1943, Pt IX – Age. L. E. Ball, in his history of recruiting in the AMF, has estimated that between 300,000 and 500,000 young men between the ages of 18 and 35 (married and single) did not serve during the war (NAA P617 527/1/126 L. E. Ball, Recruiting for AMF, 1939–45, p. 106).
164. Taken from the last census completed before the war: *Census of the Commonwealth of Australia*, 30 June 1943, Pt IX – Age; Grey, *The Australian Army*, pp. 118, 155. The recruiting age for the CMF was between 18 and 60 (NAA P617 527/1/126 L. E. Ball, Recruiting for AMF, 1939–45, p. 4).
165. John McLeod, *Myth and Reality: The New Zealand Soldier in World War II* (Auckland: Reed Methuen, 1986), p. 18.
166. New Zealand Defence HQ Library, Report of the National Service Department, 1946, p. 17. Perry, *The Commonwealth Armies*, pp. 180–1 and McLeod, *Myth and Reality*, p. 18, put the figure at 59,644. The First New Zealand Expeditionary Force had fought in the First World War.
167. Mein Smith, *A Concise History of New Zealand*, p. 133.
168. Ian McGibbon, *New Zealand and the Second World War: The People, the Battles and the Legacy* (Auckland: Hodder Moa Beckett, 2004), p.49. Service in the Air Force, Navy and among the Maori remained voluntary for the duration of the war.
169. Wood, *Political and External Affairs*, p. 147.
170. New Zealand Defence HQ Library, Report of the National Service Department, 1946, pp. 18–9. McLeod, *Myth and Reality*, p. 18; Census and Statistics Department, *New Zealand, Population Census, 1945* (Wellington: Gisborne Herald, 1945–52). The appeal procedure required an employer to lodge a request that a man should not be withdrawn from industry.
171. Ibid., p. 17.
172. Ibid., pp. 15–6.
173. Mein Smith, *A Concise History of New Zealand*, p. 124.
174. Figures derived from: Census and Statistics Department, New Zealand, Population Census, 1945; John Crawford, 'Introduction', in Crawford (ed.), *Kia Kaha*, p. 3; New Zealand Defence HQ Library, Report of the National Service Department, 1946, p. 19.
175. Darian-Smith, 'War and Australian Society', in Beaumont (ed.), *Australia's War*, p. 54.
176. Figures derived from: Census and Statistics Department, *New Zealand, Population Census, 1945*; John Crawford, 'Introduction', in Crawford (ed.), *Kia Kaha*, p. 3; New Zealand Defence HQ Library, Report of the National Service Department, 1946, p. 19.

177. Mein Smith, *A Concise History of New Zealand*, p. 124; War Office, *Statistics of the Military Effort of the British Empire During the Great War, 1914–1920* (Eastbourne: CPI Antony Rowe, 1922), p. 363.
178. New Zealand Defence HQ Library, Report of the National Service Department, 1946, pp. 21.
179. J. E. Cookson, 'Appeal Boards and Conscientious Objectors', in John Crawford (ed.), *Kia Kaha: New Zealand in the Second World War* (Oxford University Press, 2000), p. 173. Cookson has estimated that, public interest appeals aside (usually but not invariably put in by employers), nearly a fifth of those called up sought conscientious objection status or postponement on hardship grounds.
180. New Zealand Defence HQ Library, Report of the National Service Department, 1946, pp. 21–33.
181. Nancy M. Taylor, *The Home Front, Vol. I* (Wellington: Historical Publications Branch, 1986), p. 72.
182. Hasluck, *Australia in the War of 1939–1945*, p. 7.
183. John Pomeroy, 'A. P. Elkin: Public Morale and Propaganda', in Geoffrey Gray, Doug Munro and Christine Winter (eds.), *Scholars at War: Australian Social Scientists, 1939–1945* (Canberra: ANU Press, 2012), p. 41.
184. See also, Gregory, *The Last Great War*, p. 81 and 317; David Littlewood, '"Should He Serve?": The Military Service Boards' Operations in the Wellington Provincial District, 1916–1918' (Master's thesis, Massey University, 2010), pp. 55–74.
185. Jonathan Fennell, 'Soldiers and Social Change: The Forces Vote in the Second World War and New Zealand's Great Experiment in Social Citizenship', *English Historical Review*, 132(154) (2017). Byers, *Zombie Army*, pp. 138–40, categorises a part of the Canadian Army in the Second World War, 158,056 NRMA conscripts, by occupational grouping based on the type of work they had performed, which is an indicative rather than conclusive measure of their social-class status. As for Table 2.3, see W. B. Elley and J. C. Irving, 'A Socio-Economic Index for New Zealand Based on Levels of Education and Income from the 1966 Census', *New Zealand Journal of Educational Studies*, 7 (1972), p. 159; Defence Library, New Zealand Defence Force, Nominal Rolls 1–15, Second New Zealand Expeditionary Force, 1940–5. Elley and Irving did not name their different levels (or classes), but the terms 'higher professional', 'lower professional', 'clerical & highly skilled', 'skilled', 'semi-skilled' and 'unskilled' seem appropriate given the occupations included in each level (or class). As the 1945 census did not include social-class categories, it was not possible to compare the 2NZEF social-class composition directly with a contemporary social-class breakdown of the New Zealand population. The 1966 census data on occupations grouped into classes by Elley and Irving is the earliest acceptable social-class categorisation; thus it was used as a proxy for the 1945 New Zealand national social-class profile. There is, therefore, a twenty-one-year gap between the Army sample and the analysis of the general population. Nevertheless, the social-class composition of societies tends to change at a sufficiently gradual rate to make comparisons meaningful (see Elley and Irving, 'A Socio-Economic Index for New Zealand', p. 159).
186. While Neil Roos has provided some information on the generic industries South African soldiers hoped to work in after the war, no systematic social-class survey of the UDF during the war has been carried out (see Roos, *Ordinary Springboks*, pp. 104–5).
187. David Rose, 'Official Social Classifications in the UK', *Social Research Update*, 9 (July 1995), p. 2. Social classes or groups are based on a number of criteria, including the kind of work done, the nature of the operation performed, the degree

of skill involved, the physical energy required, the environmental conditions and, perhaps most importantly, the social and economic status associated with the occupation. See, The Registrar General's Decennial Supplement: England and Wales, 1951. *Occupational Mortality, Pt II, Vol. I: Commentary* (London: HMSO), pp. 12–13.

188. Erik Olssen and Maureen Hickey, *Class and Occupation: The New Zealand Reality* (Dunedin: University of Otago Press, 2005), p. 13.

189. The list used the Ministry of Labour and National Service occupational classifications (ED 526) instead of the census classifications. Nevertheless, the descriptions of each classification within ED 526 was sufficiently clear to allow a comparison of the classifications used in the census. As for Table 2.4, see NA WO 365/87 British Army Other Ranks: Analysis by Main Occupational Classification, 20 Oct. 1944; NA WO 365/87 Key to Main Occupational Classification Codes in Column 1 of AG Stats Return, Dated 20 Oct. 1944; The Registrar General's Decennial Supplement: England and Wales, 1951. *Occupational Mortality, Pt II, Vol. I: Commentary*, pp. 12–13.

190. DHH File No. 113.3R4003(D1) Research and Information Section, AG Branch, Special Report No. 180: Rehabilitation 1945: A Survey of Opinions in the Canadian Army, n.d.; English, *The Canadian Army and the Normandy Campaign*, p. 73. Similar surveys considered to be equally representative and statistically valid were conducted during the first twelve days of Aug., Sept. and Oct. 1945 on a total of 3,629 officers and men awaiting discharge in depots. A high degree of internal consistency was noted among the Aug., Sept. and Oct. samples and these reports were similarly considered to be consistent with the findings recorded in Special Report No. 180. See, DHH File No. 113.3R4003(D1) AG Coord 2 AG Branch, Rehabilitation: A Survey of Opinions among Army Personnel Awaiting Discharge, August 1945; DHH File No. 113.3R4003(D1) AG Coord 2 AG Branch, Rehabilitation: A Survey of Opinions among Army Personnel Awaiting Discharge, September 1945; DHH File No. 113.3R4003(D1) AG Coord 2 Adjutant-General Branch, Rehabilitation: A Survey of Opinions among Army Personnel Awaiting Discharge, October 1945.

191. John Porter, *The Vertical Mosaic: An Analysis of Social Class and Power in Canada* (University of Toronto Press, 1965), pp. 160–1; Bernard R. Blishen, 'The Construction and Use of an Occupational Class Scale', *The Canadian Journal of Economic and Political Science*, 24(4) (Nov. 1958), pp. 519–31. Blishen's scale provided a class 'score' for each occupation in the census by combining average income and average years of schooling in each occupation. He also made use of the author's 'awareness of the relative prestige' of each occupation. Blishen ranked occupations into seven classes:

I e.g. judges, dentists, engineers, architects
II e.g. stock brokers, managers, chemists, professors
III e.g. laboratory technicians, draughtmen, artists, teachers
IV e.g. book-keepers, office clerks, foremen
V e.g. farmers, plumbers, postmen, fitters
VI e.g. millers, blacksmiths, bakers, truck drivers
VII e.g. labourers, cooks, janitors, hunters and trappers.

As for Table 2.5, where the list in Special Report No. 180 did not record the sample percentage for a particular occupation (because members of that occupation made up less than 0.045% of the total sample), that occupation could not be included in the status categorisation. As the total of such excluded occupations amounted to only 4.6% of the whole sample, it was deemed that the exclusion of these occupations would not adversely affect the accuracy of the army/country comparison. While there was considerable consistency between the occupational descriptions used in the Army survey and Blishen's scale, there were some areas where best judgement had to be used. For example, in categorising restaurant managers (not listed by Blishen), retail managers (who were categorised by Blishen as status 2) were used instead. One difficulty that did recur arose from the multiple use in the survey of the same occupation description under different headings. For example, in the survey list, 'machine shop' occupations were included in the skilled category, in the semi-skilled category and also in the unskilled category. However, in Blishen, 'machinists, metal' have only one listing and they were given a status 5. It was decided, where no other information was available, to rely throughout on the Blishen status in situations like this and to effectively give no status recognition to the survey distinctions between skilled, semi-skilled and unskilled listings of the same general occupation. The rationale for this decision was that, whereas the survey of army personnel did not have any direct focus on occupational status in their study, Blishen, in his scientific and detailed analysis of occupational status, had this as his primary focus and most likely took all these factors into account in his categorisations.

192. Consideration was given to using the occupation classifications used in Owen Crankshaw's *Race, Class and the Changing Division of Labour under Apartheid* (London: Routledge, 1997). However, while Crankshaw's use of Manpower Surveys in constructing his index has many strengths, it has a basic weakness for the purposes required here, in that the surveys do not, in particular, include the agricultural sector – 108 recruits in the sample from the Defence Personnel Archives listed their occupation as Farmer. I would like to thank Prof. Jeremy Seekings, the University of Cape Town, for corresponding with me on this matter.
193. The UK census identifies farmers as social class II. However, many farmers in South Africa in this period would have been far from affluent, thus, in this study they have been assigned to social class III.
194. South African Defence Personnel Archive, Pretoria, Service Records; Union Office of Census and Statistics, *Union of South Africa Population Census, 7 May 1946, Vol. V: Occupations and Industries* (Pretoria: The Government Printer, 1955); The Registrar General, *Census 1951: Classification of Occupations* (London: HMSO, 1956). Table 2.6 is derived using a sample of service records from the South African Defence Personnel Archive, Pretoria; *The Union of South Africa Population Census, 7 May 1946*; and The Registrar General, *Census 1951: Classification of Occupations* (London: HMSO, 1956). Only records where it was possible to identify the ethnicity and social class of the recruit were used. The Army figures for English-speakers, therefore, are based on a sample of 667 records; the Army figures for Afrikaans-speakers are based on a sample of 336 records; the total Army figures are based on a sample of 1,003 records giving a sampling error of 3.15% at 95% confidence.
195. NA WO 163/50 Use of Manpower in the Army, Pt Two, Appendix A, Notes on the Growth of the Army, 21 Nov. 1941.
196. Engen, *Strangers in Arms*, p. 21. This depiction of the Canadian Army is supported by Byers's occupational classification of NRMA men during the war (see Byers, *Zombie Army*, p. 140).

197. Parker, *Manpower*, pp. 488–90; NA WO 277/12, Manpower Problems, p. 80; Howlett, *Fighting with Figures*, p. 41; Byers, *Zombie Army*, p. 140.
198. Allport, *Browned Off and Bloody-Minded*, p. 71.
199. Ibid., p. 75.
200. The proportion of unskilled workers in the Army appears to have fallen almost exactly in between the 1931 and 1951 census figures for the general population; thus, it is likely that the Army was representative in this class.
201. One of these records was 'farm boy' rather than 'farmer'. The next best represented occupation was 'labourer' with twenty-one.
202. Grundlingh, 'The Recruitment of South African Blacks for Participation in the Second World War', in Killingray and Rathbone (eds.), *Africa and the Second World War*, p. 194; John Lambert, '"The Finest Hour?" English-Speaking South Africans and World War II', *South African Historical Journal*, 60(1) (2008), p. 72. See also the Farming Report sections in AI Gp Box 42/I/37/B Durban Forces Censorship Summaries, June 1944–July 1945.
203. Roos, *Ordinary Springboks*, p. 32–3.
204. SANDF, DOC, AI Gp 1 Box 81/I/71/B South African MCS No. 4, 1–15 Apr. 1942.
205. Kamtekar, 'A Different War Dance'.
206. NAA MP729/6, 58/401/485 Census of Army Personnel, 1942–3. The population statistics were taken from those aged 20 to 45 in the 1933 census.
207. Johnston, 'The Civilians Who Joined Up'.
208. Ibid.; Jonathan Kelley and M. D. R. Evans, 'Trends in Educational Attainment in Australia', *Worldwide Attitudes*, 08-26 (1996).
209. Bernard Harris, 'Unemployment and the Dole in Interwar Britain', in Paul Johnson (ed.), *20th Century Britain: Economic, Social and Cultural Change* (London: Longman, 1994), pp. 204–6. See also, Tom Brooking, 'Economic Transformation', in Geoffrey W. Rice (ed.), *The Oxford History of New Zealand* (Melbourne: Oxford University Press, 1992), p. 251–2.
210. There were 146,794 clerks in the Oct. 1944 sample of 2,518,827 ORs (5.8% of the total).
211. Brooking, 'Economic Transformation', in Rice (ed.), *The Oxford History of New Zealand*, p. 251–2; James Belich, *Paradise Reforged: A History of New Zealanders from the 1880s to the Year 2000* (London: Allen Lane, 2001), p. 292; J. M. Bumsted, *The Peoples of Canada: A Post-Confederation History* (Oxford University Press, 2004), p. 219.
212. Johnston, 'The Civilians Who Joined Up'. See also François Oosthuizen, 'Soldiers and Politics: The Political Ramifications of the White Union Defence Forces Soldiers' Demobilisation Experience after the Second World War', *South African Journal of Military Studies*, 24(1) (1994), p. 24; F. D. Tothill, 'The Soldiers' Vote', p. 91. Later in the war, a wish to be part of the AIF tradition appears to have played an important role in encouraging CMF soldiers, who by this time were required to fight in the SWPA anyway, to volunteer and transfer to the legendary AIF. Some also volunteered in order that they might have a better chance of getting into the service they preferred (Parker, *Manpower*, p. 159).
213. Such a perspective does not reflect the consensus in the literature that concepts of duty and ideology had 'little immediate currency' among those 'who volunteered to serve' (see e.g. Roos, *Ordinary Springboks*, pp. 37–8).
214. Johnston, 'The Civilians Who Joined Up'.

215. Hasluck, *The Government and the People*, Appendix 8.
216. Roos, *Ordinary Springboks*, pp. 37–8; Lambert, '"The Finest Hour?"', pp. 71–3.
217. SANDF, DOC, AI Gp 1 Box 43/I/38/D MFF Censorship Summary No. 1, 24 Oct.–4 Nov. 1940, p. 2; SANDF, DOC, AI Gp 1 Box 43/I/38/D EAFHQ MCS No. 18, 22 May–5 June 1941, p. 7.
218. SANDF, DOC, AI Gp 1 Box 81/I/71/B South African MCS No. 5, 16 to 30 Apr. 1942, p. 2.
219. SANDF, DOC, AI Gp 1 Box 43/I/38/D EAFHQ MCS No. 20, 19 June–3 July 1941, pp. 6–7.
220. SANDF, DOC, AI Gp 1 Box 43/I/38/D EAFHQ MCS No. 18, 22 May–5 June 1941, p. 7.
221. SANDF, DOC, AI Gp 1 Box 43/I/38/D MCS No. 13, EAFHQ 21 Mar.–20 Apr., p. 6.
222. SANDF, DOC, AI Gp 1 Box 43/I/38/D EAFHQ MCS No. 19, 6–18 June 1941, pp. 6–7; SANDF, DOC, AI Gp 1 Box 43/I/38/D EAFHQ MCS No. 17, 7–21 May 1941, p. 3.
223. SANDF, DOC, AI Gp 1 Box 43/I/38/D EAFHQ MCS No. 15, 21 Apr.–6 May 1941, p. 5.
224. SANDF, DOC, AI Gp 1 Box 43/I/38/D EAFHQ MCS No. 18, 22 May–5 June 1941, p. 2.
225. Roos, *Ordinary Springboks*, pp. 11, 43.
226. Ibid., p. 43.
227. Howlett, *Fighting with Figures*, p. 5; John Ellis, *The Sharp End: The Fighting Man in World War II* (London: Pimlico, 1990), p. 156; McLeod, *Myth and Reality*, p. 18; Census and Statistics Department, *New Zealand, Population Census, 1945*; Hasluck, *Australia in the War of 1939–1945*, pp. 399–400; Roos, *Ordinary Springboks*, p. 26; Cook, *Warlords*, p. 207; Stacey, *Arms, Men and Governments*, p. 590; Dominion Bureau of Statistics, *The Canada Year Book, 1946*, p. 127; Prasad, *Expansion of the Armed Forces and Defence Organisation, 1939–45*, p. 78; Wilkinson, *Army and Nation*, p. 72.
228. Gowing, 'The Organisation of Manpower', p. 148.
229. John Horne, 'Introduction: Mobilizing for "Total War", 1914–1918', in John Horne (ed.), *State, Society and Mobilization in Europe during the First World War* (Cambridge University Press, 1997), p. 12.
230. Field, *Blood, Sweat and Toil*, p. 5.
231. Harris, 'Unemployment and the Dole in Interwar Britain', in Johnson (ed.), *20th Century Britain*, pp. 205–6.
232. Darwin, *The Empire Project*, p. 11. The large 'English' minority among South African whites also tended to have a loyalty to Britain.
233. Statistics in Table 2.7 are derived from figures available in: WO 277/12, Manpower Problems, p. 80; Howlett, *Fighting with Figures*, pp. 5 and 41; *Canadian Yearbook, 1946*, p. 102; Stacey, *Arms, Men and Government*, p. 590; Jha and Wilkinson, 'Does Combat Experience Foster Organisational Skill?', p. 884. By July 1945, the strength of the Indian Air Force and Royal Indian Navy was 75,725 and 37,863 respectively (see Prasad, *Expansion of the Armed Forces and Defence Organisation*, p. 409); *Census of the Commonwealth of Australia*, 30 June 1943, Pt IX – Age; Johnston, 'The Civilians Who Joined Up'; Census and Statistics Department, *New Zealand, Population Census, 1945*.
234. Darwin, *The Empire Project*, p. 43.

Chapter 3 Defeat in the West

1. David Fraser, *And We Shall Shock Them: The British Army in the Second World War* (London: Cassell & Co., 1999), p. 24.
2. Cyril Falls, revised by Brian Bond, 'Vereker, John Standish Surtees Prendergast, sixth Viscount Gort', *Oxford Dictionary of National Biography* (Oxford University Press, 2004), online edn, Jan. 2011, www.oxforddnb.com/view/10.1093/ref:odnb/9780198614128.001.0001/odnb-9780198614128-e-36642, accessed 3 Jan. 2018; Edward Smalley, *The British Expeditionary Force, 1939–40* (Basingstoke: Palgrave Macmillan, 2015), p. 17.
3. Fraser, *And We Shall Shock Them*, pp. 24–6.
4. Ibid., p. 28; Smalley, *The British Expeditionary Force*, p. 19; Brian Bond, 'Introduction: Preparing the Field Force, Feb. 1939–May 1940', in Brian Bond and Michael Taylor (eds.), *The Battle for France and Flanders Sixty Years On* (Barnsley: Pen & Sword, 2001), Location 217 of 5795; L. F. Ellis, *The War in France and Flanders* (Uckfield: The Naval & Military Press, 2004 [1953]), p. 19. The rest of the total of nearly 400,000 men was made up of line of communication troops, reinforcements etc. To strengthen the territorials, the regular divisions were asked to give them some of their experienced battalions, and, with the exception of 50th Northumbrian Division, all the territorial brigades were given a stiffening of one regular battalion.
5. David Reynolds, '1940: Fulcrum of the Twentieth Century', *International Affairs*, 66(2) (Apr. 1990), p. 328; John Ellis, *Brute Force: Allied Strategy and Tactics in the Second World War* (London: André Deutsch, 1990), p. 5; Matthew Cooper, *The German Army 1933–1945: Its Political and Military Failure* (Lanham: Scarborough House, 1978), p. 214; Adam Tooze, *The Wages of Destruction: The Making and Breaking of the Nazi Economy* (London: Penguin Books, 2007), p. 369.
6. Ellis, *Brute Force*, pp. 5–6.
7. David Ian Hall, *Strategy for Victory: The Development of British Tactical Air Power, 1939–1943* (Westport: Praeger, 2008), Ch. 3, p. 9 of 12.
8. Hew Strachan, *European Armies and the Conduct of War* (Oxford: Routledge, 2004 [1983]), p. 167; Hall, *Strategy for Victory*, fnn. p. 17 of 50. 1,665 fighters, 1,120 bomber, 501 reconnaissance, 342 dive-bomber, 42 ground-attack and 154 seaplane aircraft.
9. Hall, *Strategy for Victory*, Ch. 3, pp. 7–9 of 12, fnn. p. 17 of 50; Julian Jackson, *Fall of France: The Nazi Invasion of 1940* (Oxford University Press, 2004), p. 41 of 368.
10. Wesley K. Wark, *The Ultimate Enemy: British Intelligence and Nazi Germany, 1933–1939* (London: I. B. Tauris, 1985), pp. 96–9.
11. David French, *Raising Churchill's Army: The British Army and the War against Germany 1919–1945* (Oxford University Press, 2000), pp. 159–60. Although David French has questioned whether officers paid them any attention.
12. Wark, *The Ultimate Enemy*, p. 97.
13. Fraser, *And We Shall Shock Them*, pp. 26–30.
14. Ibid., p. 30.
15. French, *Raising Churchill's Army*, p. 179; Smalley, *The British Expeditionary Force*, pp. 78–83.
16. Fraser, *And We Shall Shock Them*, pp. 31–2; John Kiszely, *Anatomy of a Campaign: The British Fiasco in Norway, 1940* (Cambridge University Press, 2017), pp. 5–6, 277; François Kersaudy, *Norway 1940* (London: Collins, 1990), pp. 15–20.

17. Ibid., p. 32; Antony Beevor, *The Second World War* (London: Weidenfeld & Nicolson, 2012), p. 43. Churchill had also undertaken this role in the early years of the First World War.
18. Fraser, *And We Shall Shock Them*, pp. 33–7. As it transpired, the army never had more than four brigades ashore, two of them territorial, during the whole of the Norwegian campaign.
19. Ibid., p. 40.
20. SANDF, DOC, UWH Box 345 Medical Histories: The Campaign in Norway, Apr.–June 1940, p. 4. See also, Kiszely, Anatomy of a Campaign, pp. 276–85; Jack Adams, *The Doomed Expedition: The Norwegian Campaign of 1940* (London: Leo Cooper, 1989), pp. 169–77.
21. Ibid.; John Connell, *Auchinleck: A Biography of Field-Marshal Sir Claude Auchinleck* (London: Cassell, 1959), p. 86.
22. Fraser, *And We Shall Shock Them*, pp. 47–52.
23. Ibid., pp. 55–6. See also Karl-Heinz Frieser, *The Blitzkrieg Legend: The 1940 Campaign in the West* (Annapolis: Naval Institute Press, 2005).
24. Fraser, *And We Shall Shock Them*, pp. 55–6.
25. Ibid, p. 57. See also Frieser, *The Blitzkrieg Legend.*
26. Fraser, *And We Shall Shock Them*, pp. 55–60.
27. Ibid., p. 59–62.
28. David Edgerton, *Britain's War Machine: Weapons, Resources and Experts in the Second World War* (London: Allen Lane, 2011), pp. 62–3; Fraser, *And We Shall Shock Them*, p. 61–2. British tanks, much like their French counterparts, were more than a match for German equivalents. The 2-pounder gun was, for example, arguably superior to the German 37.2mm gun on the Panzer III and 38t tanks. The Panzer IV did have a 75mm artillery piece which facilitated the support of infantry. The British forces on the Continent were, therefore, on paper, 'exceptionally well-supplied with modern light and medium tanks'.
29. Ellis, *The War in France and Flanders*, p. 89; Edgerton, *Britain's War Machine*, pp. 62–3; Fraser, *And We Shall Shock Them*, pp. 28, 74.
30. Fraser, *And We Shall Shock Them*, pp. 63–4; French, *Raising Churchill's Army*, p. 175. As French has argued, 'throughout the campaign, the shortage of troops meant that the BEF was compelled to hold far longer stretches of front than was practicable'.
31. French, *Raising Churchill's Army*, pp. 175–6.
32. Fraser, *And We Shall Shock Them*, pp. 63–4; French, *Raising Churchill's Army*, p. 175.
33. Fraser, *And We Shall Shock Them*, pp. 65–7.
34. Ibid., p. 71.
35. Smalley, *The British Expeditionary Force*, p. 33.
36. Frieser, *The Blitzkrieg Legend*, pp. 291–314.
37. Ibid. See also Hugh Sebag-Montefiori, *Dunkirk: Fight to the Last Man* (London: Penguin, 2015).
38. Glynn Prysor, *Citizen Sailors: The Royal Navy in the Second World War* (London: Penguin, 2012), p. 81.
39. Ibid., pp. 33–4.
40. Fraser, *And We Shall Shock Them*, pp. 71–7; Smalley, *The British Expeditionary Force*, pp. 34–5; C. P. Stacey, *Six Years of War: The Army in Canada, Britain and the Pacific* (Ottawa: Edmond Cloutier, 1955), p. 189; Martin S. Alexander, 'After Dunkirk: The French Army's Performance against "Case Red", 25 May–25 June 1940', *War in History*, 14(2) (2007), p. 253.

41. Fraser, *And We Shall Shock Them*, pp. 71–7; Smalley, *The British Expeditionary Force*, pp. 30–5; Alex Danchev and Daniel Todman (eds.), *War Diaries 1939–1945: Field Marshal Lord Alanbrooke* (London: Phoenix, 2002 [2001]), pp. 80–2. The Highlanders had been deployed to the Maginot Line on 30 Apr. to gain experience of combat under French command. When the German assault penetrated the French line in the centre they were separated from the main body of the BEF. The armistice was signed on 22 June 1940.
42. Smalley, *The British Expeditionary Force*, p. 33.
43. Fraser, *And We Shall Shock Them*, pp. 71–7.
44. French, *Raising Churchill's Army*, p. 156.
45. John Darwin, *The Empire Project: The Rise and Fall of the British World-System, 1830–1970* (Cambridge University Press, 2009), p. 499.
46. 'Cato', *Guilty Men* (London: Gollanz, 1940), pp. 16, 19. The authors were Michael Foot, Frank Owen and Peter Howard. Reynolds, '1940', p. 326; Geoffrey G. Field, *Blood, Sweat and Toil: Remaking the British Working Class, 1939–1945* (Oxford University Press, 2011), p. 308.
47. Brian Bond, 'The British View', in Brian Bond and Michael Taylor (eds.), *The Battle for France and Flanders: Sixty Years On* (Barnsley: Pen & Sword Books, 2001).
48. B. L. Montgomery, *The Memoirs of Field-Marshal Montgomery of Alamein* (Barnsley: Pen & Sword, 2005 [1958]), p. 49. See also, Danchev and Todman (eds.), *Alanbrooke War Diaries*, p. 131.
49. Edgerton, *Britain's War Machine*, p. 57.
50. Bond, 'Introduction: Preparing the Field Force, Feb. 1939–May 1940', in Bond and Taylor (eds.), *The Battle for France and Flanders Sixty Years On*, Location 182 of 5795.
51. David French, 'Discipline and the Death Penalty in the British Army in the War against Germany during the Second World War', *Journal of Contemporary History*, 33(4) (Oct. 1998), pp. 538–9. Between Sept. 1939 and June 1940, 243 individuals were court-martialled for unauthorised absences and 49 for desertion (see Smalley, *The British Expeditionary Force, 1939–40*, p. 158).
52. Quoted in Glyn Prysor, 'The "Fifth Column" and the British Experience of Retreat, 1940', *War in History*, 12(4) (2005), p. 428.
53. Prysor gives examples of these, such as Anon., *Infantry Officer: A Personal Record* (London: B. T. Batsford Ltd, 1943) and 'Gun Buster', *Return via Dunkirk* (London: Hodder & Stoughton, 1940).
54. Prysor, 'The "Fifth Column" and the British Experience of Retreat, 1940', p. 432.
55. AWM 54 624/2/6 Report on Functions of AG's Branch during Invasion of Western Europe, 1944, p. 166.
56. Prysor, 'The "Fifth Column" and the British Experience of Retreat, 1940', p. 426; Brian Bond, 'The British Field Force in France and Belgium, 1939–40', in P. Addison and A. Calder (eds.), *Time to Kill: The Soldier's Experience of War in the West, 1939–1945* (London: Pimlico, 1997), p. 43.
57. Prysor, 'The "Fifth Column" and the British Experience of Retreat, 1940', pp. 444–5. Many units 'disbanded and dissipated' in the confused fighting and very few retreated and evacuated in 'formal battle order'.
58. Ibid., p. 434.
59. Mark Connelly and Walter Miller, 'The BEF and the Issue of Surrender on the Western Front in 1940', *War in History*, 11(4) (2004); Prysor, 'The "Fifth Column" and the British Experience of Retreat, 1940', p. 445.
60. See John Ellis, *The World War II Databook: The Essential Facts and Figures for all the Combatants* (London: Aurum Press, 1993), p. 251, Table 53: 'Army Battle Casualties in Major Campaigns, 1939–45 – France 1940'. The number killed and

missing is given as 11,010; wounded, 14,070; and captured, 41,340, although it should be noted that this figure almost certainly includes wounded that were left behind in the course of the battle; Prysor, 'The "Fifth Column" and the British Experience of Retreat, 1940', p. 444. There was no great capitulation at the end of the fighting, where men could reasonably be described as having been 'led' into captivity; all the British soldiers on the beaches at Dunkirk were evacuated.

61. Prysor, 'The "Fifth Column" and the British Experience of Retreat, 1940', pp. 444–5.
62. NA WO 106/1775 Bartholomew Committee Final Report, 1940.
63. Hall, *Strategy for Victory*, Ch. 4, p. 2 of 11.
64. NA WO 106/1775 Bartholomew Committee Final Report, 1940.
65. French, *Raising Churchill's Army*, pp. 177–8.
66. NA WO 106/1775 Bartholomew Committee Final Report, 1940.
67. French, *Raising Churchill's Army*, pp. 180–1. These orders groups were followed, only if time allowed, by brief written confirmation or map tracings showing objectives and boundaries between units.
68. Patrick Rose, 'British Army Command Culture 1939–1945: A Comparative Study of British Eighth and Fourteenth Armies' (PhD thesis, King's College London, 2008), pp. 186–7; Alan Jeffreys, *Approach to Battle: Training the Indian Army During the Second World War* (Solihull: Helion, 2016), pp. 115–17.
69. NA WO 106/1775 Bartholomew Committee Final Report, 1940. See e.g. Smalley, *The British Expeditionary Force*, pp. 84–140.
70. NA WO 106/1775 Bartholomew Committee Final Report, 1940.
71. NA WO 277/7 Brig. A. B. McPherson, *Army: Discipline* (The War Office, 1950), pp. 6–7.
72. SANDF, DOC, Div. Docs., Gp 1, Box 49 Periodic Notes on the German Army No. 35, Feb. 1941, p. 7 (emphasis added.)
73. Ibid., p. 9.
74. Ibid., p. 14.
75. For other accounts of the campaign that share this perspective see: Ellis, *Brute Force*, pp. 12–13; Connelly and Miller, 'The BEF and the Issue of Surrender on the Western Front in 1940' and Prysor, 'The "Fifth Column" and the British Experience of Retreat, 1940'. A very similar story emerged from the Norwegian campaign, see, Adams, *The Doomed Expedition*, pp. 172–3.
76. NA WO 106/1775 Bartholomew Committee Final Report, 1940.
77. Ibid.
78. Ibid.; Frieser, *The Blitzkrieg Legend*, pp. 286–90.
79. War Office, *Training Regulations* (1934), p. 4.
80. See also, Jonathan Fennell, 'Air Power and Morale in the North African Campaign of the Second World War', *Air Power Review*, 15(2) (2012).
81. NA WO 106/1775 Bartholomew Committee Final Report, 1940.
82. Ibid. For a similar perspective on the French Army, see Alexander, 'After Dunkirk', p. 238.
83. George Peden, 'Financing Churchill's Army', in Keith Neilson and Greg Kennedy (eds.), *The British Way in Warfare: Power and the International System, 1856–1956* (Farnham: Ashgate, 2010), p. 288; Elizabeth Kier, *Imagining War: French and British Military Doctrine Between the Wars* (Princeton University Press, 1997), p. 96.
84. Ross McKibbin, *Parties and People: England 1914–1951* (Oxford University Press, 2010), p. vii.
85. Danchev and Todman (eds.), *Alanbrooke War Diaries*, pp. 90, 106–8.

86. Alan Allport, *Browned Off and Bloody-Minded: The British Soldier Goes to War 1939–1945* (London: Yale University Press, 2015), p. 56.
87. Niall Barr, *Yanks and Limeys: Alliance Warfare in the Second World War* (London: Jonathan Cape, 2015), p. 88; Allport, *Browned Off and Bloody-Minded*, p. 56.
88. Barr, *Yanks and Limeys*, pp. 90–1.
89. Prysor, *Citizen Sailors*, pp. 94–8; Christina Goulter, Andrew Gordon and Gary Sheffield, 'The Royal Navy Did Not Win the "Battle of Britain"', *The RUSI Journal*, 151(5) (2006), pp. 66–7.
90. Prysor, *Citizen Sailors*, p. 94.
91. Fraser, *And We Shall Shock Them*, p. 85. Nine 'County' divisions were eventually formed.
92. Ibid., p. 84.
93. Danchev and Todman (eds.), *Alanbrooke War Diaries*, p. 94.
94. Fraser, *And We Shall Shock Them*, pp. 85–7.
95. Max Hastings, *All Hell Let Loose: The World at War, 1939–1945* (London: Harper Press, 2011), pp. 79–80. See also Danchev and Todman (eds.), *Alanbrooke War Diaries*, p. 108.
96. Fraser, *And We Shall Shock Them*, p. 96.
97. Hastings, *All Hell Let Loose*, p. 92.

Chapter 4 The Middle East

1. John Keegan, *The Second World War* (London: Pimlico, 1989), p. 265; Barrie Pitt, *The Crucible of War: Wavell's Command* (London: Cassell & Co., 2001 [1980]), p. 55.
2. David Fraser, *And We Shall Shock Them: The British Army in the Second World War* (London: Cassell & Co., 1999), p. 114.
3. Hew Strachan, *Military Lives* (Oxford University Press, 2002), p. 485; Bernard Fergusson and Judith M. Brown, 'Wavell, Archibald Percival, first Earl Wavell (1883–1950)', rev. Robert O'Neill, Judith M. Brown, *Oxford Dictionary of National Biography* (Oxford University Press, 2004), online edn, Jan. 2011, www.oxforddnb.com/view/article/36790, accessed 24 Apr. 2017; Harold E. Raugh, *Wavell in the Middle East, 1939–1941: A Study in Generalship* (Oklahoma University Press, 2013 [1993]), pp. 7–38.
4. Fraser, *And We Shall Shock Them*, p. 114. The Command was also tasked with operations, should they occur, in an area between the Mediterranean, the Caucasus and the Indian Ocean
5. John Bierman and Colin Smith, *Alamein: War without Hate* (London: Penguin, 2003), p. 29. Fraser, *And We Shall Shock Them*, pp. 114–15. There were a few territorials and conscripts involved to fill up the establishment. The BEF in France in May 1940 had five territorial infantry divisions.
6. Fraser, *And We Shall Shock Them*, pp. 114–15; Andrew Stewart, *The First Victory: The Second World War and the East Africa Campaign* (London: Yale University Press, 2016), p. 51; Keegan, *The Second World War*, p. 266; Douglas Porch, *Hitler's Mediterranean Gamble: The North African and the Mediterranean Campaigns in World War II* (London: Weidenfeld & Nicolson, 2004), p. 42. These armies were also supported by 460 tanks and 2,000 guns.
7. John Ellis, *Brute Force: Allied Strategy and Tactics in the Second World War* (London: André Deutsch, 1990), p. 229.
8. Keegan, *The Second World War*, p. 272.

9. I. S. O. Playfair, *The Mediterranean and Middle East, Vol. I: The Early Successes against Italy* (Uckfield: The Naval & Military Press, 2004 [1954]), pp. 190, 244–7; Fraser, *And We Shall Shock Them*, p. 120; David Edgerton, *Britain's War Machine: Weapons, Resources and Experts in the Second World War* (London: Allen Lane, 2011), p. 65. The reinforcements from Britain included 5,000 Australians and 700 New Zealanders plus an additional 7,500 RAF personnel.
10. Quoted in Fraser, *And We Shall Shock Them*, p. 120.
11. Fraser, *And We Shall Shock Them*, p. 120.
12. Patrick Rose, 'British Army Command Culture 1939–1945: A Comparative Study of British Eighth and Fourteenth Armies' (PhD thesis, King's College London, 2008)', p. 97. Wavell authored *FSR II* (1935) and *FSR III* (1936).
13. Correlli Barnett, *The Desert Generals* (London: Cassell, 1983), p. 27; Pitt, *Wavell's Command*, p. 9; Bierman and Smith, *Alamein*, p. 29. Fraser, *And We Shall Shock Them*, pp. 114–15. There were a few territorials and conscripts involved to fill up the establishment.
14. Pitt, *Wavell's Command*, p. 9.
15. Bierman and Smith, *Alamein*, p. 29; Fraser, *And We Shall Shock Them*, p. 115; NA WO 201/352 Report on Lessons of the Operations in the Western Desert, Dec. 1940.
16. NA WO 201/3526 O'Connor to 4th Indian and 7th Armoured Divisions, 29 Nov. 1940. In early Dec., he ordered an exercise with troops 'firing live shell and machine gun ammunition' that resembled the requirements of the coming operation.
17. Ibid.; Pitt, *Wavell's Command*, p. 86.
18. Barnett, *The Desert Generals*, p. 35; Pitt, *Wavell's Command*, p. 86.
19. Fraser, *And We Shall Shock Them*, pp. 121–4.
20. Pitt, *Wavell's Command*, p. 190.
21. NA WO 177/41 DDMS, Descriptive Account of the Work of the Medical Services in Egypt, Quarter ending Dec. 1940, p. 8.
22. Pitt, *Wavell's Command*, p. 9.
23. Niall Barr, *Pendulum of War: The Three Battles of El Alamein* (London: Pimlico, 2005 [2004]), p. 46.
24. Rose, 'British Army Command Culture', p. 104.
25. War Office Report on Operations in the Western Desert, 1940. Quoted in Land Warfare Development Centre, *Army Doctrine Publication AC71940, Land Operations* (Bristol: MOD Crown Copyright, 2017), Section 6-17.
26. Quoted in Rose, 'British Army Command Culture', p. 98.
27. NA WO 201/352 Report on Lessons of the Operations in the Western Desert, Dec. 1940. Andrew Stewart has made similar points in his assessment of British Commonwealth success later on in East Africa (see Andrew Stewart, *A Very British Experience: Coalition, Defence and Strategy in the Second World War* (Eastbourne: Sussex Academic Press, 2012), pp. 63–4).
28. Keegan, *The Second World War*, pp. 267–8; Ian van der Waag, *A Military History of Modern South Africa* (Johannesburg: Jonathan Ball, 2015), p. 196.
29. Keegan, *The Second World War*, pp. 267–8; Ian van der Waag, *A Military History of Modern South Africa* (Johannesburg: Jonathan Ball, 2015), p. 196; LAC Vol. 18,826 File No. 133.065 (D689) List of Commonwealth Forces in Fighting Contact with the Enemy, 1940–5; Andrew Stewart, *The First Victory: The Second World War and the East African Campaign* (London: Yale University Press, 2016), p. 38.

30. Stewart, *A Very British Experience*, p. 50; Keegan, *The Second World War*, pp. 267–8.
31. Porch, *Hitler's Mediterranean Gamble*, p. 139.
32. Matthew Cooper, *The German Army 1933–1945: Its Political and Military Failure* (Lanham: Scarborough House, 1978), p. 251.
33. Keegan, *The Second World War*, p. 117; AWM 54 534/2/36 Medical History, The Campaign in Greece, 6–28 Apr. 1941, p. 1.
34. Playfair, *The Mediterranean and Middle East, Vol. I*, pp. 25 and 49.
35. Keegan, *The Second World War*, p. 117; AWM 54 534/2/36 Medical History, The Campaign in Greece, 6–28 Apr. 1941, p. 1.
36. Ian Wards, 'The Balkan Dilemma', in John Crawford (ed.), *Kia Kaha: New Zealand in the Second World War* (Oxford University Press, 2000), pp. 20–4; Niall Barr, *Yanks and Limeys: Alliance Warfare in the Second World War* (London: Jonathan Cape, 2015), p. 124; The Rt Hon. The Earl of Avon, *The Eden Memoirs: The Reckoning* (London: Cassell, 1965), pp. 184–96.
37. Ronald Lewin, *The Chief: Field Marshal Lord Wavell, Commander-in-Chief and Viceroy, 1939–1947* (London: Hutchinson, 1980), pp. 90–6, 113; Barr, *Yanks and Limeys*, p. 126; John Connell, *Wavell: Scholar and Soldier, to June 1941* (London: Collins, 1964), pp. 369–72; Porch, *Hitler's Mediterranean Gamble*, p. 140; John Terraine, *The Right of the Line: The Royal Air Force in the European War, 1939–1945* (Ware: Wordsworth Editions, 1985), p. 330.
38. Wards, 'The Balkan Dilemma', in Crawford (ed.), *Kia Kaha*, pp. 20–6.
39. Terraine, *The Right of the Line*, pp. 329–30.
40. Porch, *Hitler's Mediterranean Gamble*, pp. 148.
41. Wards, 'The Balkan Dilemma', in Crawford (ed.), *Kia Kaha*, pp. 30–1; Barr, *Yanks and Limeys*, pp. 125–6. The Lend-Lease Bill was also making its way through Congress at this time. Niall Barr has argued that 'the British decisions over Greece were . . . taken in an atmosphere where the political repercussions in American were potentially more important than the military realities facing any British force sent to the Balkans'.
42. Barr, *Yanks and Limeys*, pp. 114–16.
43. Ibid., pp. 116–17.
44. Ibid., pp. 89, 123–7. The Lend-Lease Bill passed the Senate and was signed into law on 11 Mar. 1941.
45. Stewart, *The First Victory*, pp. 165–90; Stewart, *A Very British Experience*, pp. 47–64; Playfair, *The Mediterranean and Middle East, Vol. I*, p. 439.
46. Smuts controversially requested that the South Africans enter the city first in order to 'strengthen domestic support for the war' effort back home. See Stewart, *The First Victory*, p. 206.
47. Ibid., pp. 135–43; Stewart, *A Very British Experience*, pp. 47–64; Keegan, *The Second World War*, pp. 268–9.
48. Stewart, *The First Victory*, pp. xii, 236, 243.
49. Wards, 'The Balkan Dilemma', in Crawford (ed.), *Kia Kaha*, p. 31.
50. Keegan, *The Second World War*, p. 120; AWM 54 534/2/36 Medical History, The Campaign in Greece, 6–28 Apr. 1941, p. 1. The 17th and 19th Australian Brigades had not yet reached the line at this stage. The 7th Australian Division and the Polish Brigade were not sent as they were needed to counter renewed Axis activity in the desert. 'W force' would eventually total 58,000 men, of whom 35,000 were fighting personnel.

51. Cooper, *The German Army 1933–1945*, p. 251; I. S. O. Playfair, *The Mediterranean and Middle East, Vol. II: The Germans Come to the Help of their Allies* (Uckfield: Naval & Military Press, 2004 [1956]), p. 85.
52. Keegan, *The Second World War*, pp. 124–6.
53. AWM 54 534/2/37 Report on Operations of ANZAC Corps Greece, 1941, p. 2; AWM 54 534/2/37 Wavell to CIGS, 26 Apr. 1941, p. 1; AWM 54 534/2/37 Blamey to Minister for Army Melbourne, 12 Apr. 1941.
54. Porch, *Hitler's Mediterranean Gamble*, p. 146. On paper, the Greek Army disposed of fourteen divisions in Albania and three and a half on the Bulgarian border. See John Sadler, *Operation Mercury: The Battle for Crete 1941* (Barnsley: Pen & Sword, 2007), p. 28.
55. AWM 54 534/2/37 Report on Operations of ANZAC Corps in Greece, 1941, p. 6; AWM 54 534/2/37 Wavell to CIGS, 26 Apr. 1941, p. 2.
56. AWM 54 534/2/37 Report on Operations of ANZAC Corps in Greece, 1941, p. 10.
57. AWM 54 534/2/36 Medical History, The Campaign in Greece, 6–28 Apr. 1941, p. 16. This number included several thousands of Cypriots, Palestinians, Greeks and Yugoslavs.
58. Ibid., p. 1; Playfair, *The Mediterranean and Middle East, Vol. II*, p. 104; Sadler, *Operation Mercury*, p. 28.
59. Keegan, *The Second World War*, p. 129.
60. AWM 54 534/2/34 Report on Operations of 6 Australian Division in Greece, by Maj. Gen. I. G. Mackay, n.d. but 1941, pp. 2–7.
61. AWM 54 534/2/37 Report on Operations of ANZAC Corps in Greece, 1941, p. 2.
62. AWM 54 534/2/34 Report on Operations of 6 Australian Division in Greece, by Maj. Gen. I. G. Mackay, n.d. but 1941, p. 3.
63. Porch, *Hitler's Mediterranean Gamble*, p. 153.
64. Ibid., pp. 146–7.
65. AWM 54 534/2/34 Report on Operations of 6 Australian Division in Greece, by Maj. Gen. I. G. Mackay, n.d. but 1941, pp. 4–5.
66. Quoted in Porch, *Hitler's Mediterranean Gamble*, pp. 154.
67. AWM 54 534/2/37 Report on Operations of ANZAC Corps in Greece, 1941, p. 11.
68. Playfair, *The Mediterranean and Middle East, Vol. II*, pp. 121 and 128.
69. Keegan, *The Second World War*, p. 158–9. 'Breaks' into the *Luftwaffe* key had considerably assisted the air defence of the UK during the winter blitz of 1940–1 as well. See also, John Keegan, *Intelligence in War: Knowledge of the Enemy from Napoleon to Al-Qaeda* (London: Pimlico, 2004), pp. 167–92.
70. Keegan, *The Second World War*, p. 130–1.
71. ANZ WAII/8/14 TROPPERS LONDON to MIDEAST, 29 Apr. 1941.
72. Hew Strachan, *Military Lives* (Oxford University Press, 2002), pp. 151–3; Ian Wards, 'Freyberg, Bernard Cyril, first Baron Freyberg (1889–1963)', *Oxford Dictionary of National Biography* (Oxford University Press, 2004), online edn, Jan. 2011, www.oxforddnb.com/view/article/33276, accessed 24 Apr. 2017; Glyn Harper and Joel Hayward, *Born to Lead? Portraits of New Zealand Commanders* (Auckland: Exisle, 2003), pp. 97–8.
73. ANZ WAII/8/14 CREFORCE to MIDEAST, n.d.; ANZ WAII/8/14 Gen. Freyberg to Prime Minister, 1 May 1941.
74. ANZ WAII/8/14 Gen. Freyberg to Prime Minister, 1 May 1941.
75. ANZ WAII/8/D Dispatch by Maj. Gen. E. D. Weston Covering Operations in Crete, 22 Apr.–31 May 1941, p. 2; Playfair, *The Mediterranean and Middle East, Vol. II*, p. 125.
76. ANZ WAII/8/14 CREFORCE to MIDEAST, 5 May 1941.

77. ANZ WAII/8/D HQ Z Force, Memorandum on Discipline, 8 May 1941.
78. T. Duncan and M. Stout, *New Zealand Medical Services in Middle East and Italy* (Wellington: Historical Publications Branch, 1956), pp. 157–8; Little local assistance was available as 5th Cretan Division had been mobilised for war against the Italians and captured on the mainland. The only Cretan soldiers left on the island were recruits and reservists. See Antony Beevor, *Crete: The Battle and the Resistance* (London: John Murray, 2005 [1991]), pp. 346–8.
79. ANZ WAII/8/14 MIDEAST to CREFORCE, 2 May 1941; ANZ WAII/8/14 CREFORCE to MIDEAST, 3 May 1941.
80. ANZ WAII/8/D Special Order of the Day by Maj. Gen. B. Freyberg, Commander British Troops in Crete, 1 May 1941.
81. ANZ WAII/8/14 Gen. Freyberg to PRIME MINISTER ENGLAND, 5 May 1941.
82. ANZ WAII/8/14 CREFORCE to MIDEAST, 16 May 1941.
83. Keegan, *The Second World War*, pp. 132–5.
84. ANZ WAII/8/14 CREFORCE to MIDEAST, 22 May 1941.
85. Keegan, *The Second World War*, p. 137.
86. ANZ WAII/8/14 CREFORCE to MIDEAST, 22 May 1941.
87. ANZ WAII/8/14 MIDEAST to CREFORCE, 22 May 1941.
88. ANZ WAII/8/D Report on Operation Heraklion Sector, 1–28 May 1941, Appendix C, Data Collected by Interrogation of Prisoners, and Gen. Observation, pp. 1–2.
89. ANZ WAII/8/14 MIDEAST to CREFORCE, 23 May 1941.
90. Keegan, *The Second World War*, pp. 137–8.
91. ANZ WAII/8/14 CREFORCE to MIDEAST, 24 May 1941.
92. ANZ WAII/8/14 CREFORCE to MIDEAST, 25 May 1941; ANZ WAII/8/D Dispatch by Maj. Gen. E. D. Weston Covering Operations in Crete, 22 Apr.–31 May 1941, p. 8.
93. ANZ WAII/8/14 MIDEAST to CREFORCE, 25 May 1941.
94. ANZ WAII/8/14 CREFORCE to MIDEAST, 26 May 1941.
95. ANZ WAII/8/14 CREFORCE to MIDEAST, 27 May 1941.
96. ANZ WAII/8/D Dispatch by Maj. Gen. E. D. Weston Covering Operations in Crete, 22 Apr.–31 May 1941, p. 2.
97. Ibid., p. 5; NA WO 106/1775 Bartholomew Committee Final Report, 1940.
98. ANZ WAII/8/D Dispatch by Maj. Gen. E. D. Weston Covering Operations in Crete, 22 Apr.–31 May 1941, p. 15.
99. ANZ WAII/8/D Puttick to Freyberg, 27 June 1941. See also a report by Brig. B. H. Chappel, Commander 14th Infantry Brigade (ANZ WAII/8/D Report on Operation Heraklion Sector, 1–28 May 1941).
100. ANZ WAII/8/D Puttick to Freyberg, 27 June 1941. See also ANZ WAII/8/D Address to NCOs at Helouan Camp by Maj. Gen. B. C. Freyberg, n.d.
101. ANZ WAII/8/D Address to NCOs at Helouan Camp by Maj. Gen. B. C. Freyberg, n.d.
102. R. Wilkinson, 'Both Sides of the Hill: Intelligence in the Crete and Arnhem Campaigns', *The RUSI Journal*, 149(3) (2004), p. 79; Hanson Baldwin, *Battles Lost and Won: Great Campaigns of World War 2* (London: Hodder and Stoughton, 1966), p. 70.
103. Keegan, *The Second World War*, p. 139. Most of those rescued were British Commonwealth rather than Greek. The figures for New Zealand were 671 killed, 1,455 wounded and 1,692 POW. This was on top of the losses in Greece: 291 killed, 599 wounded and 1,614 POW. See Michael Bassett and Michael King, *Tomorrow Comes the Song: The Life of Peter Fraser* (Auckland: Penguin, 2000), p. 215.

104. Porch, *Hitler's Mediterranean Gamble*, p. 173.
105. ANZ WAII/8/14 CREFORCE to MIDEAST, 24 May 1941.
106. ANZ WAII/8/D Unknown Author, Response to a report sent by the Military Attaché, US Embassy, Cairo, 26 Aug. 1941; Keegan, *The Second World War*, p. 139.
107. There is, of course, an argument that O'Connor's advance had culminated by this stage. His forces were tired and his equipment in need of repair. There were also six Italian divisions still intact in Tripolitania in Feb. 1941 (Lewin, *The Chief*, pp. 90–1; Ellis, *Brute Force*, p. 235).
108. Porch, *Hitler's Mediterranean Gamble*, p. 209.
109. Barr, *Pendulum of War*, pp. 9–10.
110. Porch, *Hitler's Mediterranean Gamble*, p. 142.
111. Pitt, *Auchinleck's Command*, p. 5; Richard Holmes, *Acts of War: The Behaviour of Men in Battle* (London: Cassell, 2004), p. 81.
112. Timothy Harrison Place, *Military Training in the British Army* (London: Frank Cass, 2000), p. 3.
113. Barr, *Pendulum of War*, pp, 9–10; Fraser, *And We Shall Shock Them*, p. 151. Against 120 tanks of 5th Light Division, and the Italian division's light tanks and M13s, 2nd Armoured Division could muster twenty-five light tanks and twenty-two cruisers.
114. Barnett, *The Desert Generals*, p. 149.
115. Ashley Jackson, *The British Empire and the Second World War* (London: Hambledon Continuum, 2006), pp. 145–54; Keegan, *The Second World War*, p. 271; Playfair, *The Mediterranean and Middle East, Vol. II*, p. 179; John Connell, *Auchinleck: A Biography of Field-Marshal Sir Claude Auchinleck* (London: Cassell, 1959), pp. 180–233.
116. Jackson, *The British Empire and the Second World War*, pp. 145–54; Keegan, *The Second World War*, p. 271; Playfair, *The Mediterranean and Middle East, Vol. II*, p. 179; Connell, *Auchinleck*, pp. 180–233.
117. Keegan, *The Second World War*, pp. 271–2; Jackson, *The British Empire and the Second World War*, p. 155; Porch, *Hitler's Mediterranean Gamble*, pp. 579–82. Allied troops would meet them again in the Torch landing of Nov. 1942. The campaign cost 3,300 Commonwealth, 1,300 Free French and 6,000 Vichy casualties.
118. Barr, *Pendulum of War*, pp, 9–10.
119. William F. Buckingham, *Tobruk: The Great Siege 1941–2* (Stroud: Tempus, 2008), p. 7.
120. Pitt, *Wavell's Command*, pp. 267–8.
121. Barrie Pitt, *The Crucible of War: Auchinleck's Command* (London: Cassell & Co., 2001 [1980]), pp. 9–15.
122. Ibid.
123. Porch, *Hitler's Mediterranean Gamble*, p. 231.
124. Barr, *Pendulum of War*, p. 11.
125. Ibid.
126. Connell, *Auchinleck*, pp. 3–12. The total number of cadets was 360 that year.
127. Brian Bond, 'Auchinleck, Sir Claude John Eyre (1884–1981)', *Oxford Dictionary of National Biography* (Oxford University Press, 2004), online edn, Jan. 2011, https://doi.org/10.1093/ref:odnb/30774, accessed 25 Apr. 2017; Connell, *Auchinleck*, pp. 3–79.
128. Playfair, *The Mediterranean and Middle East, Vol. II*, p. 222; Keegan, *The Second World War*, p. 272.

129. Playfair, *The Mediterranean and Middle East, Vol. II*, p. 223. Some 6,000 Royal Navy and 13,000 RAF personnel were included in these contingents.
130. I. S. O. Playfair, *The Mediterranean and Middle East, Vol. III: British Fortunes Reach their Lowest Ebb* (Uckfield: Naval & Military Press, 2004 [1960]), p. 4. 'These consignments, as large as they were, were not large enough to replace all the losses and wastage that had occurred and allow any considerable reserves to be built up.'
131. Ibid., p. 4; Barr, *Yanks and Limeys*, p. 149. In Sept. 1940, the first contract for 2,085 American-built tanks was signed with a US manufacturing company (ibid., p. 101).
132. Connell, *Auchinleck*, pp. 250–1. The Eighth Army became operational on 26 Sept. 1941.
133. Quoted in Daniel Todman, *Britain's War: Into Battle, 1937–1941* (London: Allen Lane, 2016), Ch. 24.
134. LHCMA Alanbrooke MSS 6/2/11, Auchinleck to Churchill, 15 July 1941; ANZ WAII/2 Accession W3281, Box 1, 101b Pt 1, The New Zealand Division in Cyrenaica and Lessons of the Campaign, Pt 1 Narrative and Lessons, p. 2.
135. ANZ WAII/8/18 Freyberg to Fraser, 9 Oct. 1941.
136. David Ian Hall, *Strategy for Victory: The Development of British Tactical Air Power, 1939–1943* (Westport: Praeger, 2008), Ch. 7, pp. 2–6 of 12.
137. Rose, 'British Army Command Culture', p. 109.
138. Quoted ibid., pp. 109–10.
139. NA WO 201/514 Battle Memorandum, Nov. 1941. Quoted ibid., p. 109.
140. The 9th Australian Division had been relieved by these forces.
141. Playfair, *The Mediterranean and Middle East, Vol. III*, pp. 4, 19–20, 37, 97; Fraser, *And We Shall Shock Them*, p. 165.
142. Ellis, *Brute Force*, pp. 243–4.
143. Fraser, *And We Shall Shock Them*, p. 166; Playfair, *The Mediterranean and Middle East, Vol, III*, p. 31. The Eighth Army's advantage in tanks was somewhat blunted by the presence of thirty-five German 88mm anti-tank guns and ninety-six 50mm anti-tank guns in the battle area. Most of the tanks in operational reserve were in workshops undergoing repairs or modifications.
144. Hall, *Strategy for Victory*, Ch. 7, p. 1 of 12; Robert S. Ehlers Jr, *The Mediterranean Air War: Airpower and Allied Victory in World War II* (Lawrence: University Press of Kansas, 2016), p. 150.
145. ANZ WAII/8/18 Draft Cipher Message, Freyberg to Fraser, 19 Sept. 1941; ANZ WAII/8/18 Freyberg to Fraser, 9 Oct. 1941.
146. ANZ WAII/8/18 Special Order of the Day by Lt. Gen. Sir A. Cunningham, 17 Nov. 1941.
147. AWM 54 883/2/97 MEFCWS, No. I (12–18 Nov. 1941), p. 1.
148. AWM 54 883/2/97 MEFCWS, No. II (19–25 Nov. 1941), p. 1. This assessment was based on 3,500 letters written over a period of three weeks which had accumulated in Tobruk Fortress in the period running up to the offensive.
149. Quoted in Fraser, *And We Shall Shock Them*, p. 166.
150. Barr, *Pendulum of War*, p. 59. The Mark III, for example, could engage British tanks and anti-tank units up to 1,000 yards away with its 50mm gun. In addition, all the British tanks remained notoriously prone to mechanical breakdown. The American Stuart, a new introduction to Eighth Army, was mechanically reliable and its 37 mm gun used capped ammunition which gave it greater penetration against the German armour. However, its fuel capacity was modest, which only

allowed it a small radius of action. This was a disadvantage in the wide expanses of the desert, a problem which equally affected the laborious and heavy 'I' tanks.

151. Latimer, *Alamein*, p. 36.
152. IWM 96/50/1 Crimp, The Overseas Tour of a Conscript Rifleman, p. 73.
153. George Forty, *Tanks Across the Desert: The War Diary of Jake Wardrop* (Stroud: Sutton Publishing, 2003), pp. 33–4.
154. See e.g. ANZ WAII/8/18 Godwin Austen, GOC XIII Corps, to Freyberg, 23 Nov. 1941; Playfair, *The Mediterranean and Middle East, Vol. III*, p. 52.
155. Playfair, *The Mediterranean and Middle East, Vol. III*, pp. 52–6.
156. ANZ WAII/8/18 Auchinleck to Cunningham, n.d. but probably 25 Nov. 1941.
157. Playfair, *The Mediterranean and Middle East, Vol. III*, pp. 52–3; Fraser, *And We Shall Shock Them*, pp. 170–2.
158. Fraser, *And We Shall Shock Them*, pp. 176–7.
159. Rose, 'British Army Command Culture', p. 200.
160. Fraser, *And We Shall Shock Them*, pp. 172–7; Playfair, *The Mediterranean and Middle East, Vol. III*, p. 70; Ehlers, *The Mediterranean Air War*, pp. 163–8
161. AWM 54 883/2/97 MEFCWS, No. IV (3–9 Dec. 1941), p. 1.
162. AWM 54 883/2/97 MEFCWS, No. VI (17–23 Dec. 1941), p. 1. For more on why Eighth Army's morale was high during the 'Crusader' operation, see Jonathan Fennell, *Combat and Morale in the North African Campaign: The Eighth Army and the Path to El Alamein* (Cambridge University Press, 2011).
163. AWM 54 883/2/97 MEFCWS, No. VII (24–30 Dec. 1941), p. 1.
164. ANZ WAII/2 Accession W3281, Box 1, 101b Pt 1, The New Zealand Division in Cyrenaica and Lessons of the Campaign, Pt 1 Narrative and Lessons, p. 26; See also ANZ WAII/8/18 Report on Operations of New Zealand Division in Libyan Campaign, n.d. but 1941, pp. 2–3; ANZ WAII/8/18 Ritchie to Freyberg, 7 Dec. 1941.
165. AWM 54 883/2/97 MEFCWS, No. VII (24–30 Dec. 1941), p. 1.
166. ANZ WAII/8/18 Copy of a letter by Ritchie and a Cable by Auchinleck sent to authorities in New Zealand, 12 Dec. 1941.
167. ANZ WAII/8/18 13 Corps Instructions for Battle, 12 Nov. 1941, p. 3.
168. Rose, 'British Army Command Culture', p. 112–17; ANZ WAII/8/18 Lessons, 3 Dec. 1941.
169. NA WO 201/364 30 Corps Report, Western Desert 'Crusader' Operation, 15 Dec. 1941, p. 14. Quoted in Rose, 'British Army Command Culture', p. 109.
170. Keegan, *The Second World War*, p. 276.
171. SANDF, DOC, UWH Box 203 Foreign Documents, Rainer Kriebel, *History of the Campaign in North Africa*, p. 116.
172. Hall, *Strategy for Victory*, Ch. 7, p. 9 of 12; Playfair, *The Mediterranean and Middle East, Vol. III*, p. 140. The British still retained about 280 serviceable aircraft in theatre.
173. The Americans declared war on Japan on 8 Dec. and responded to the German declaration of war on the USA with a declaration of their own on 11 Dec.
174. Raymond Callahan, *Churchill and His Generals* (Lawrence: University Press of Kansas, 2007), p. 96.
175. Playfair, *The Mediterranean and Middle East, Vol. III*, pp. 73, 136.
176. Robin Neillands, *Eighth Army: From the Western Desert to the Alps, 1939-1945* (London: John Murray, 2004), p. 118.
177. AWM 54 883/2/97 British Troops in Egypt, No. 92 FCR Week Ending 31 July 1941, p. 1.
178. AWM 54 883/2/97 MEFCWS, No. XIV (11–17 Feb. 1942), p. 1.
179. NA WO 163/51 Morale Report, Dec. 1941–Apr. 1942.

180. Connell, *Auchinleck*, pp. 459–60.
181. Neillands, *Eighth Army*, p. 118.
182. Barr, *Pendulum of War*, p. 53.
183. NA WO 201/527 HQ Eighth Army MEF, Role of Armoured Formations (n.d. but clearly written after 'Crusader').
184. NA WO 202/33 Notes on Desert Warfare compiled by Capt. E. E. Tomkins, IC, and Capt. C. J. Fitzgerald, Recce Corps for the French, 26 Dec. 1941. It must also be noted that 25-pounder guns were not as mobile as tanks.
185. Barr, *Pendulum of War*, pp. 59–60.
186. Shelford Bidwell and Dominick Graham, *Firepower: British Army Weapons and Theories of War 1904–1945* (London: Allen & Unwin, 1982), pp. 221–47.
187. NA WO 32/15773 Auchinleck to the Under Secretary of State, the War Office, 7 Apr. 1942.
188. NA WO 32/15773 ECAC, The Death Penalty for Offenses Committed on Active Service, 21 July 1942; NA WO 32/15773 Death Penalty for Offences Committed on Active Service. Memorandum by the Secretary of State for War (P. J. Grigg) 12 June 1942.
189. NA WO 201/538 Corbett to 8, 9 and 10 Armies, 24 May 1942. Quoted in David French, 'Discipline and the Death Penalty in the British Army in the War against Germany during the Second World War', *Journal of Contemporary History*, 33(4) (Oct. 1998), p. 539.
190. AWM 54 883/2/97 MEFCWS, No. XXVI (6–12 May 1942), p. 1; AWM 54 883/2/97 MEFCWS, No. XXVII (13–19 May 1942), p. 1; AWM 54 883/2/97 MEFCWS, No. XXVIII (20–26 May 1942), p. 1.
191. Playfair, *The Mediterranean and Middle East, Vol. III*, pp. 371–2.
192. Richard Toye, *The Roar of the Lion: The Untold Story of Churchill's World War II Speeches* (Oxford University Press, 2013), pp. 139–40.
193. Winston S. Churchill (ed.), *Never Give In! The Best of Winston Churchill's Speeches* (London: Pimlico, 2003), p. 331.
194. AWM 54 883/2/97 MEFCWS, No. XXIX (27 May–2 June 1942), p. 3.
195. AWM 54 883/2/97 MEFCWS, No. XXVII (13–19 May 1942), p. 2.
196. AWM 54 883/2/97 MEFCWS, No. XXVIII (20–26 May), p. 2.
197. Callahan, *Churchill and His Generals*, pp. 110–12; NA WO 201/527 Harding to 1st Armoured and 4th Indian Divisions, 4 Jan. 1942.
198. NA WO 201/2591 Notes on the Training Conference Held at GHQ ME, 10 May 1942; David French, *Raising Churchill's Army: The British Army and the War against Germany 1919–1945* (Oxford University Press, 2000), p. 233; Alan Jeffreys, *Approach to Battle: Training the Indian Army During the Second World War* (Solihull: Helion, 2016), p. 106.
199. NA WO 201/357 Operation 'Battleaxe', Lessons of the Campaign, June–Nov. 1941. Lessons from Recent Operations, 7th Armoured Division.
200. Playfair, *The Mediterranean and Middle East, Vol. III*, pp. 213–14; George Forty, *British Army Handbook, 1939–1945* (Stroud: Sutton Publishing, 1998), pp. 148–50.
201. Bidwell and Graham, *Firepower*, p. 225.
202. Playfair, *The Mediterranean and Middle East, Vol. III*, pp. 214–15.
203. Barr, *Pendulum of War*, pp. 53–61.
204. Callahan, *Churchill and His Generals*, pp. 110–12.
205. Porch, *Hitler's Mediterranean Gamble*, pp. 14–15.
206. Playfair, *The Mediterranean and Middle East, Vol. III*, p. 194.

207. Ibid., p. 372; Martin Kitchen, *Rommel's Desert War: Waging World War II in North Africa, 1941–1943* (Cambridge University Press, 2009), p. 492; Fraser, *And We Shall Shock Them*, p. 213.
208. Ellis, *Brute Force*, p. 263. The 1st and 32nd Army Tank Brigades had 276 Valentine and Matilda tanks and 1st and 7th Armoured Divisions had 573 Crusaders, Honeys and Grants.
209. Stephen Bungay, *Alamein* (London: Aurum Press, 2002), p. 23; Barr, *Pendulum of War*, p. 13; Callahan, *Churchill and His Generals*, pp. 112–13; Fraser, *And We Shall Shock Them*, p. 212.
210. Playfair, *The Mediterranean and Middle East, Vol. III*, pp. 220–1; Ehlers, *The Mediterranean Air War*, pp. 179–88, 204–5. The Axis also enjoyed a superiority in serviceable aircraft for the whole Mediterranean theatre of about 1,000 compared to 739. Tedder estimated that, by Mar. 1942, 530 aircraft had been diverted to the Far East.
211. Callahan, *Churchill and His Generals*, p. 109.
212. Playfair, *The Mediterranean and Middle East, Vol. III*, p. 215.
213. Callahan, *Churchill and His Generals*, pp. 110–11. With Malta virtually unusable due to Axis bombing, few inroads were made into Axis shipping in the Mediterranean during this period.
214. Playfair, *The Mediterranean and Middle East, Vol. III*, p. 218.
215. Fraser, *And We Shall Shock Them*, pp. 214–15.
216. Ibid., pp. 214–15; Callahan, *Churchill and His Generals*, p. 113.
217. Fraser, *And We Shall Shock Them*, pp. 214–15.
218. Callahan, *Churchill and His Generals*, p. 113; Fraser, *And We Shall Shock Them*, p. 225. For a criticism of these dispositions see e.g. Carver, *Dilemmas of the Desert War*, p. 141.
219. Barr, *Yanks and Limeys*, pp. 177–8.
220. Ibid., p. 178.
221. John Parker, *The Desert Rats: From El Alamein to Basra* (London: Headline, 2005), p. 174.
222. Fraser, *And We Shall Shock Them*, pp. 217–18; Kitchen, *Rommel's Desert War*, pp. 220–3.
223. Playfair, *The Mediterranean and Middle East, Vol. III*, p. 223. The Italians were supported by a few tanks of 21st Panzer Division.
224. SANDF, DOC, UWH 322 The German Assault on the Gazala Position and the Fall of Tobruk, 26 May–21 June 1942.
225. G. L. Verney, *The Desert Rats* (London: Greenhill Books, 1990), p. 105; Fraser, *And We Shall Shock Them*, p. 218.
226. SANDF, DOC, UWH 322 The German Assault on the Gazala Position and the Fall of Tobruk, 26 May–21 June 1942.
227. Kitchen, *Rommel's Desert War*, p. 225 and Callahan, *Churchill and His Generals*, p. 113 say that it took ninety minutes for the brigade to be destroyed. Pitt, *Auchinleck's Command*, p. 196, argued that it took only thirty minutes.
228. Messervy pretended to be the general's batman and only returned to 7th Armoured Division, having escaped captivity on 29 May.
229. Fraser, *And We Shall Shock Them*, p. 218; Kitchen, *Rommel's Desert War*, pp. 222–6; Verney, *The Desert Rats*, p. 104.
230. Callahan, *Churchill and His Generals*, p. 113.
231. B. H. Liddell Hart (ed.), *The Rommel Papers* (New York: Harcourt, Brace and Company, 1953), p. 206.
232. Playfair, *The Mediterranean and Middle East, Vol. III*, p. 225.

233. Callahan, *Churchill and His Generals*, p. 114.
234. Fraser, *And We Shall Shock Them*, p. 220.
235. Callahan, *Churchill and His Generals*, pp. 114–15. Ritchie used elements of 5th Indian Division, 7th Armoured Division, 50th Northumbrian Division and 32nd Army Tank Brigade.
236. Callahan, *Churchill and His Generals*, pp. 115; Kitchen, *Rommel's Desert War*, p. 236.
237. Liddell Hart (ed.), *The Rommel Papers*, p. 216.
238. Kitchen, *Rommel's Desert War*, pp. 321–6.
239. Callahan, *Churchill and His Generals*, pp. 116–17.
240. Rose, 'British Army Command Culture', p. 145.
241. Ibid., p. 133.
242. Brian Farrell, *The Defence and Fall of Singapore 1940–1942* (Stroud: Tempus, 2005), p. 293.
243. NA WO 236/1 The Egyptian Gazette, Sunday Oct. 29 1950. The Hinge of Fate – XV The Battle for Tobruk; Andrew Stewart, '"The Klopper Affair": Anglo-South African Relations and the Surrender of the Tobruk Garrison', *Twentieth Century British History*, 17(4) (2006), p. 541.
244. AWM 54 883/2/97 MEFCWS, No. XXXI (10–16 June 1942), p. 1. Of interest, the censors thought that morale was higher than in Dec. 1941, during Operation 'Crusader'.
245. ANZ WAII/1/DA/508/1 Vol. 1 MEFCWS, No. XXXII (17–23 June 1942), p. 1.
246. NA WO 177/324 Monthly Report on Health Eighth Army, Mar., July, Aug. 1942. The summer fighting began in May and ended in July. As for Figure 4.1, NA WO 177/324 Medical Diaries DDMS 8th Army Oct. 1941–Dec. 1942; NA WO 177/325 Medical Diaries DDMS 8th Army Jan.–Dec. 1943; SANDF, DOC, UWH Box 345 Medical Histories; SANDF, DOC, UWH Box 346 1 and 2 Div Weekly and Quarterly Medical Reports; SANDF, DOC, War Diaries Box 728 DMS UDF MEF; SANDF, DOC, War Diaries Box 730A War Diary ADMS 1 SA Division, 1941–2; SANDF, DOC, War Diaries Box 730B War Diary ADMS 1 SA Division, 1942; Duncan and Stout, *New Zealand Medical Services in Middle East and Italy*, p. 692; W. Franklin Mellor (ed.), *Casualties and Medical Statistics* (London: HMSO, 1972), pp. 237–67; NA WO 177/163 AFHQ DDMS, 1942–5. Note, the New Zealand figures for Autumn 1942 are affected by one of two large epidemics (those of infectious hepatitis) to have impacted on the 2NZEF during the war and have, therefore, been left out. The figures for 1 SA Div. were only available on a quarterly basis between July 1941 and Sept. 1942. The SA figure for Oct. 1942 relates to 12–25 Oct. only. However, the sickness rate for 21 Sept.–11 Oct. was 19.1. Thus, the Oct. figure of 22.6 appears broadly accurate. While absolute sickness (including NYD(N) figures for the AIF and Indian Army are available, I was unable to work out rates as I have not, as yet, found monthly strengths for these formations.
247. SANDF, DOC, UWH Draft Narratives, Box 364, Tobruk, Accounts from British Sources. A Provisional narrative of the Fall of Tobruk, 1942 by Agar-Hamilton: General notes and criticisms by Lt. Col. P. T. Tower, then commander of 31/58 Fd Bty RA.
248. Connell, *Auchinleck*, p. 430.
249. NA WO 216/85 Some Notes on Operations, 26 May–8 July, GHQ MEF for CGS, 12 July 1942, p. 13; SANDF, DOC, UWH Draft Narratives, Box 364, Tobruk, Accounts from British Sources. Some Personal Opinions on the fall of Tobruk 1942, Brig. L. F. Thompson, Comd. 88 Area Tobruk June 1942.

250. SANDF, DOC, UWH Draft Narratives, Box 364, Tobruk, Accounts from British Sources. A Provisional Narrative of the Fall of Tobruk, 1942 by Agar-Hamilton: General notes and criticisms by Lt. Col. P. T. Tower, then commander 31/58 Fd Bty RA; SANDF, DOC, UWH Draft Narratives, Box 364, Tobruk, Accounts from British Sources. Some Personal Opinions on the fall of Tobruk 1942, Brig. L. F. Thompson, Comd. 88 Area Tobruk June 1942.
251. SANDF, DOC, UWH Draft Narratives, Box 364, Tobruk, Accounts from British Sources. A Provisional narrative of the Fall of Tobruk, 1942 by Agar-Hamilton: General notes and criticisms by Lt. Col. P. T. Tower, then commander 31/58 Fd Bty RA.
252. SANDF, DOC, UWH, Draft Narratives, Box 364: Tobruk, Accounts from British Sources. Some personal opinions on the fall of Tobruk 1942, Brig. L. F. Thompson, Comd. 88 Area Tobruk June 1942.
253. Playfair, *The Mediterranean and Middle East, Vol. III*, p. 274; Fraser, *And We Shall Shock Them*, pp. 222–3; Callahan, *Churchill and His Generals*, p. 119.
254. Winston Churchill, *The Second World War: With an Epilogue on the Years 1945 to 1957* (London: Pimlico, 2002), p. 565.
255. Ibid.
256. Barnett, *The Desert Generals*, pp. 180–1.
257. Bungay, *Alamein*, p. 23.
258. Fraser, *And We Shall Shock Them*, p. 223; Callahan, *Churchill and His Generals*, p. 123. This included 5th and 10th Indian Division, 50th Northumbrian Division and 2nd New Zealand Division and 1st Armoured Division.
259. Callahan, *Churchill and His Generals*, p. 124.
260. Bungay, *Alamein*, p. 23.
261. BL L/P&J/12/654 MEMCWS No. CXXVI, 26 Aug.–1 Sept. 1942, p. 5.
262. ANZ WAII/1/DA/508/1 Vol. 1 MEMCWS, No. XXXIV (1–7 July 1942), p. 1.
263. NA WO 169/4035 XXX Corps Intelligence Summary, 1 July 1942, War Diary XXX Corps G Branch.
264. ANZ WAII/1/DA/508/1 Vol. 1 MEMCWS, No. XXXIV (1–7 July 1942), p. 1.
265. AWM 54 883/2/97 MEFCWS, No. XXXIII (24–30 June 1942).
266. ANZ WAII/1/DA/508/1 Vol. 1, MEFCWS, No. XXXIV (1–7 July 1942), pp. 3–5.
267. Connell, Auchinleck, p. 628.
268. See, Fennell, *Combat and Morale*, pp. 200–7; NA WO 216/85 Some Notes on Operations, 26 May–8 July, GHQ MEF for CGS, 12 July 1942, p. 14; AWM 54 526/6/19 The Crisis at El Alamein, 30 June–4 July 1942, p. 12.
269. NA WO 216/85 Some Notes on Operations, 26 May–8 July, GHQ MEF for CGS, 12 July 1942, p. 14.
270. Hugh S. K. Mainwaring, *Three Score Years and Ten with Never a Dull Moment* (Printed Privately, 1976), pp. 64–7.
271. Bidwell and Graham, *Firepower*, p. 225.
272. Fennell, *Combat and Morale*, p. 79.
273. SANDF, DOC, UWH, Narratives, Box 376, Crisis in the Desert, May–July 1942, Pt III, El Alamein, p. 78.
274. SANDF, DOC, UWH, Draft Narratives, Box 316, War Diary of the German Africa Corps, 2 and 3 July 1942.
275. Alan Moorehead, *African Trilogy: The Desert War 1940–1943* (London: Cassell, 1998 [1944]), pp. 389–90.
276. NA CAB 146/13 Enemy Documents Section, Appreciation No. 9, pp. 477–86.
277. Barr, *Pendulum of War*, pp. 39–40. This was due to more efficient battlefield recovery techniques.

278. SANDF, DOC, Div. Docs., Box 54, Index to Advanced Air HQ Western Desert Intelligence Summary no. 167, Effects of our Bombing; SANDF, DOC, UWH, Narratives, Box 376, Crisis in the Desert, May–July 1942, El Alamein, p. 5.
279. AWM 54 526/6/19 The Crisis at El Alamein, 30 June–4 July 1942, p. 58.
280. Barr, *Pendulum of War*, pp. 35–6.
281. Ehlers, *The Mediterranean Air War*, p. 218.
282. SANDF, DOC, Div. Docs. Box 54, Index to Advanced Air HQ Western Desert Intelligence Summary no. 167, Effects of our Bombing.
283. Callahan, *Churchill and His Generals*, 127.
284. Ellis, *Brute Force*, p. 275.
285. ANZ WAII/1/DA508/1 Vol. 1, MEMCWS, No. XXXV (8–14 July 1942), p. 1.
286. Callahan, *Churchill and His Generals*, p. 128; Barr, *Yanks and Limeys*, p. 181.
287. Callahan, *Churchill and His Generals*, p. 129. 2nd New Zealand Division had taken part in the debacle at Matruh.
288. ANZ WAII/1/DA 508/1 Vol. 1, MEFCWS, No. XXXV (8–14 July 1942), pp. 1 and 22.
289. ANZ WAII/1/DA 508/1 Vol. 1, MEFCWS, No. XXXVI (15–21 July 1942), pp. 1–2.
290. Ellis, *Brute Force*, p. 276.
291. Callahan, *Churchill and His Generals*, p. 129.
292. Playfair, *The Mediterranean and Middle East, Vol. III*, p. 352; Callahan, *Churchill and His Generals*, p. 129.
293. ANZ WAII DA441/23/5 Brig. L. M. Inglis, Private Diary while GOC 2 NZEF, 25 July 1942.
294. ANZ WAII/1/DA 508/1 Vol. 1, MEFCWS, No. XXXVIII (29 July–4 Aug. 1942), pp. 17–8.
295. See Fennell, *Combat and Morale*, p. 80; Duncan and Stout, *New Zealand Medical Services in Middle East and Italy*, p. 348. The total wastage for the division between 27 June and 31 July was 6,005, made up of: 2,400 killed or POW, 1864 wounded and 1,662 sick.
296. ANZ WAII/1/DA 508/1 Vol. 1, MEFCWS, No. XXXVIII (29 July–4 Aug. 1942), p. 16.
297. Fennell, *Combat and Morale*, pp. 81, 88. On the home front, stories of 'fifth column' work on the part of the South Africans were prevalent (see Stewart, '"The Klopper Affair"', p. 536.
298. ANZ WAII/1/DA 508/1 Vol. 1, MEFCWS, No. XXXVII (22–28 July 1942), p. 1.
299. ANZ WAII/1/DA/508/1 Vol. 1 MEMCWS, No. XXXVIII (29 July–4 Aug. 1942), p. 2.
300. ANZ WAII/1/DA/508/1 Vol. 1 MEMCWS, No. XXXIX (5–11 Aug. 1942), p. 1.
301. IWM BLM 57 Wimberley to Montgomery, 9 June 1953.
302. See Fennell, *Combat and Morale*.
303. LHCMA Alanbrooke Papers, Auchinleck to Brooke, 25 July 1942.
304. NA WO 177/324 Medical Situation Report, 24 July 1942.
305. NA WO 32/15773 C-in-C Middle East to the War Office, 24 July 1942.
306. Jonathan Fennell, 'Courage and Cowardice in the North African Campaign: The Eighth Army and Defeat in the Summer of 1942', *War in History*, 20(1) (2013), pp. 102–3.
307. NA WO 32/15773 C-in-C Middle East to the War Office, 24 July 1942; NA WO 32/15773 C-in-C Middle East to the War Office, 9 Aug. 1942.
308. Churchill, *Hinge of Fate*, p. 366. Quoted in Callahan, *Churchill and His Generals*, pp. 116.

309. NA WO 32/15773 The Army Council, Death Penalty in Relation to Offences Committed on Active Duty, 31 July 1942, p. 1.
310. LHCMA Adam Papers, Box 2, Notes on ACS Paper Comparison of Casualties, Libya, AG Stats, 6 Aug. 1942; NA WO 163/51 The Army Council, Death Penalty in Relation to Offences Committed on Active Service, 11 Aug. 1942; NA WO 32/15773 ECAC, The Death Penalty for Offences Committed on Active Service, 21 July 1942. These surrender and casualty figures tally with other reports sent to the War Office in July and Aug. 1942. For Italian and German rates of surrender in the desert war see Fennell, *Combat and Morale*, p. 45.
311. Fennell, *Combat and Morale*, p. 44.
312. NA WO 163/89 ECAC, The Death Penalty for Offences Committed on Active Service, 21 July 1942.
313. NA WO 32/15773 The Army Council, Death Penalty in Relation to Offences Committed on Active Duty, 31 July 1942, p. 3.

Chapter 5 The Far East

1. Daniel Marston, *Phoenix from the Ashes: The Indian Army in the Burma Campaign* (Westport: Praeger,, 2003), p. 43; S. W. Kirby, *The War against Japan, Vol. I: The Loss of Singapore* (Uckfield: The Naval & Military Press, 2004 [1957]), pp. 37–9; Raymond Callahan, *Burma, 1942–1945* (London: Davis Poynter, 1978), p. 23. The 5th Indian Division departed for the Sudan in Sept. 1940.
2. Ashley Jackson, *The British Empire and the Second World War* (London: Hambledon Continuum, 2006), pp. 157–62. On 29 June 1941, command of the land forces in Iraq had been transferred back to India Command. The oilfields of the Middle East had traditionally fallen under India's strategic remit and it had only been the exigencies of the rising in Iraq and the subsequent Syrian campaign that had forced Middle East Command to get involved (see I. S. O. Playfair, *The Mediterranean and Middle East, Vol. II: The Germans Come to the Help of their Allies* (Uckfield: Naval & Military Press, 2004 [1956], p. 250). In Jan. 1942, the creation of a new independent Iraq Command once more relieved India of its responsibilities in the Middle East. The occupation of Persia allowed the Allies, and the Americans in particular, to send vast quantities of equipment to the Red Army; by Nov. 1942, the USA had delivered 27,000 aircraft and 28,000 tanks. In total, over 41 million tons of Lend-Lease supplies, 23% of the aid sent to the Soviet Union, would arrive by this route.
3. Doug Delaney, *The Imperial Army Project: Britain and the Land Forces of the Dominions and India, 1902–1945* (Oxford University Press, 2018), Ch. 6.
4. Kirby, *The War against Japan, Vol. I*, pp. 39, 48; Jackson, *The British Empire and the Second World War*, pp. 159–62.
5. Kirby, *The War against Japan, Vol. I*, pp. 47–8.
6. Delaney, *The Imperial Army Project*, Ch. 6.
7. David Edgerton, *Warfare State: Britain 1920–1970* (Cambridge University Press, 2006), p. 32.
8. G. C. Peden, *Arms, Economics and British Strategy: From Dreadnoughts to Hydrogen Bombs* (Cambridge University Press, 2007), pp. 99 and 128.
9. Raymond Callahan, *Churchill and His Generals* (Lawrence: University Press of Kansas, 2007), p. 88; Brian Farrell, *The Defence and Fall of Singapore 1940–1942* (Stroud: Tempus, 2005), p. 19.

10. Farrell, *The Defence and Fall of Singapore*, p. 62; Callahan, *Burma*, p. 16; Michael Bassett and Michael King, *Tomorrow Comes the Song: The Life of Peter Fraser* (Auckland: Penguin, 2000), p. 203.
11. Callahan, *Burma*, pp. 21–2.
12. Quoted in Farrell, *The Defence and Fall of Singapore*, p. 63.
13. Callahan, *Burma*, p. 22.
14. Kirby, *The War against Japan, Vol. I*, pp. 59–61; Eric Bergerud, *Touched with Fire: The Land War in the South Pacific* (London: Viking, 1996), pp. 2–3.
15. Kirby, *The War against Japan, Vol. I*, pp. 44, 69–70; Daniel Todman, *Britain's War: Into Battle, 1937–1941* (London: Allen Lane, 2016), Ch. 24.
16. Kirby, *The War against Japan, Vol. I*, pp. 44, 71, 88; Todman, *Britain's War*, Ch. 24.
17. Bergerud, *Touched with Fire*, pp. 3–4.
18. Kirby, *The War against Japan, Vol. I*, pp. 44, 71, 88; Todman, *Britain's War*, Ch. 24.
19. Kirby, *The War against Japan, Vol. I*, pp. 522–7. The 56th Division was in reserve, then reassigned to Fifteenth Army in Burma. This does not include an additional 10,000 men who were air and air service troops.
20. Kirby, *The War against Japan, Vol. I*, p. 163; Farrell, *The Defence and Fall of Singapore*, p. 101; Timothy Moreman, *The Jungle, the Japanese and the British Commonwealth Armies at War, 1941–45: Fighting Methods, Doctrine and Training for Jungle Warfare* (London: Frank Cass, 2005), pp. 23–4; NA WO 106/2580 Singapore, Summary of Approximate Effective Strength at 31 Jan. 1942. This figure is reached by adding the 33,939 reinforcements that had arrived by 31 Jan. to the original total and then subtracting 16,716 casualties.
21. Roger T. Stearn, 'Percival, Arthur Ernest (1887–1966)', *Oxford Dictionary of National Biography* (Oxford University Press, 2004), online edn, May 2013, www.oxforddnb.com/view/article/61472, accessed 18 July 2017.
22. Farrell, *The Defence and Fall of Singapore*, p. 415–16; Kirby, *The War against Japan, Vol. I*, pp. 39, 57.
23. Farrell, *The Defence and Fall of Singapore*, p. 101. Bennett claimed that the Malay troops that he came in contact with fought 'quite as well as the Indian troops' (AWM 54 553/5/16 PART 2 Maj. Gen. Gordon Bennett, Report on Malayan Campaign, 7 Dec. 1941–15 Feb. 1942, p. 42).
24. NA WO 106/2580 Malaya Garrison, Programme of Major Reinforcements, 1939–1941, Table 1; Kirby, *The War against Japan, Vol. I*, p. 163; Farrell, *The Defence and Fall of Singapore*, p. 101; Moreman, *The Jungle, the Japanese and the British Commonwealth Armies at War*, pp. 23–4. Thirty-one infantry battalions were the equivalent of about three and a half infantry divisions. Forty-eight infantry battalions were the equivalent of five full-strength divisions. Moreman estimates that Malaya Command was seventeen infantry battalions short of Percival's requirements by Dec., while Farrell puts the figure at sixteen.
25. Moreman, *The Jungle, the Japanese and the British Commonwealth Armies at War*, pp. 18–25.
26. Ibid., pp. 18–23.
27. Ibid., p. 19.
28. Ibid., p. 20.
29. See also Alan Jeffreys, *Approach to Battle: Training the Indian Army During the Second World War* (Solihull: Helion, 2016), pp. 55–80.
30. Kirby, *The War against Japan, Vol. I*, p. 503; NA WO 106/2580 Malaya Garrison, Programme of Major Reinforcements, 1939–41, Table 1. He did, however, have

266 field guns at his disposal (Jeffrey Grey, *A Military History of Australia* (Cambridge University Press, 1999), p. 167).

31. Farrell, *The Defence and Fall of Singapore*, pp. 101, 144, 153–4, 415. Seventy-nine of them were Buffalo fighters.
32. Jeffreys, *Approach to Battle*, p. 142.
33. Moreman, *The Jungle, the Japanese and the British Commonwealth Armies at War*, pp. 23–4; Jeffreys, *Approach to Battle*, pp. 137–8.
34. Moreman, *The Jungle, the Japanese and the British Commonwealth Armies at War*, p. 21.
35. AWM 54 553/5/16 PART 2 Maj. Gen. Gordon Bennett, Report on Malayan Campaign, 7 Dec. 1941–15 Feb. 1942, p. 29.
36. Moreman, *The Jungle, the Japanese and the British Commonwealth Armies at War*, p. 22. It is also fair to say that an underestimation of the capabilities of the Imperial Japanese Army doused enthusiasm for training.
37. AWM 54 553/5/16 PART 2 Maj. Gen. Gordon Bennett, Report on Malayan Campaign, 7 Dec. 1941–15 Feb. 1942, p. 29.
38. Quoted in Jeffreys, *Approach to Battle*, p. 134.
39. Quoted in Moreman, *The Jungle, the Japanese and the British Commonwealth Armies at War*, p. 21.
40. Moreman, *The Jungle, the Japanese and the British Commonwealth Armies at War*, p. 20. A small jungle warfare training team was formed in mid-Jan., consisting of two experienced officers and two NCOs, to assist newly arrived units and formations (ibid., p. 32).
41. Jeffreys, *Approach to Battle*, pp. 138–9.
42. David Fraser, *And We Shall Shock Them: The British Army in the Second World War* (London: Cassell & Co., 1999), pp. 185–6.
43. Farrell, *The Defence and Fall of Singapore*, p. 102.
44. AWM 54 553/5/16 PART 2 Maj. Gen. Gordon Bennett, Report on Malayan Campaign, 7 Dec. 1941–15 Feb. 1942.
45. Moreman, *The Jungle, the Japanese and the British Commonwealth Armies at War*, p. 25.
46. Farrell, *The Defence and Fall of Singapore*, pp. 143–6.
47. Grey, *A Military History of Australia*, p. 164; Farrell, *The Defence and Fall of Singapore*, pp. 155–61.
48. Farrell, *The Defence and Fall of Singapore*, pp. 153–4. The battle group, made up of at least 800 infantrymen, advanced less than 2 miles on the first night; it was held up when its lead scout was killed by a sniper and the column was engaged by about fifty Thai police. The next day it managed another 3 miles against 'little opposition' (a police patrol, according to Farrell). Once reinforced the next day, the unit advanced to 'the Ledge' to find that the Japanese were there already
49. Farrell, *The Defence and Fall of Singapore*, pp. 155–61; Moreman, *The Jungle, the Japanese and the British Commonwealth Armies at War*, pp. 29–30.
50. Farrell, *The Defence and Fall of Singapore*, pp. 155–61.
51. Ibid., pp. 155–63.
52. AWM 54 553/2/3 Top Secret Messages from Australian Force Malaya, to AHQ Melbourne, Jan.–Feb. 1942; Farrell, *The Defence and Fall of Singapore*, p. 183.
53. Moreman, *The Jungle, the Japanese and the British Commonwealth Armies at War*, pp. 29–30.
54. Farrell, *The Defence and Fall of Singapore*, p. 191.
55. Moreman, *The Jungle, the Japanese and the British Commonwealth Armies at War*, p. 30.

56. AWM 54 553/2/3 Top Secret Messages from Australian Force Malaya, to AHQ Melbourne, Jan.–Feb. 1942; Farrell, *The Defence and Fall of Singapore*, p. 183.
57. Farrell, *The Defence and Fall of Singapore*, p. 166.
58. Ibid., p. 188. Murray-Lyon was relieved of his command on 24 Dec. 1941.
59. Ibid., p. 190.
60. Marston, *Phoenix from the Ashes*, p. 73; Callahan, *Burma*, pp. 33–4; F. A. E. Crew, *The Army Medical Services: Campaigns, Vol. V: Burma* (London: HMSO, 1966), p. 5.
61. NA CAB 106/38, Wavell Despatch; PT, Vol. 4, Wavell to COS, 14–15 Jan. 1942. Quoted in Farrell, *The Defence and Fall of Singapore*, p. 206.
62. Quoted in Farrell, *The Defence and Fall of Singapore*, p. 205; Callahan, *Burma*, pp. 33–4.
63. Farrell, *The Defence and Fall of Singapore*, pp. 201–2.
64. AWM 54 553/2/3 Wavell to Chiefs of Staff Melbourne, 9 Jan. 1942.
65. Moreman, *The Jungle, the Japanese and the British Commonwealth Armies at War*, pp. 22–33.
66. NA CAB 106/38, Wavell Despatch; PT, Vol. 4, Wavell to COS, 14–15 Jan. 1942. Quoted in Farrell, *The Defence and Fall of Singapore*, p. 206.
67. Farrell, *The Defence and Fall of Singapore*, p. 235; Moreman, *The Jungle, the Japanese and the British Commonwealth Armies at War*, p. 33; Kirby, *The War against Japan, Vol. I*, p. 249.
68. Moreman, *The Jungle, the Japanese and the British Commonwealth Armies at War*, pp. 33–4; Kirby, *The War against Japan, Vol. I*, p. 253.
69. AWM 54 553/2/3 Top Secret Messages from Australian Force Malaya, to AHQ Melbourne, Jan.–Feb. 1942; Farrell, *The Defence and Fall of Singapore*, p. 246. See also AWM 54 553/2/3 Bennett to Sturdee, 19 Jan. 1942 and AWM 54 553/2/3 Austforce Johore to Army Melbourne, 22 Jan. 1942.
70. Farrell, *The Defence and Fall of Singapore*, pp. 301–12.
71. Ibid., p. 311 and 418; Moreman, *The Jungle, the Japanese and the British Commonwealth Armies at War*, p. 1; AWM 54 553/3/4 Campaign in Malaya, Operation Reports of 8th Division, 1941–1942; Gajendra Singh, *The Testimonies of Indian Soldiers and the Two World Wars: Between Self and Sepoy* (London: Bloomsbury, 2014), p. 157.
72. Philip Snow, *The Fall of Hong Kong: Britain, China and the Japanese Occupation* (London: Yale University Press, 2003), pp. 40–73. This force grew to 20,000 during the fighting on Hong Kong Island.
73. Fraser, *And We Shall Shock Them*, pp. 181–3; Kirby, *The War against Japan, Vol. I*, p. 473. The Canadians were particularly unlucky having only arrived in October.
74. Snow, *The Fall of Hong Kong*, p. 40.
75. Marston, *Phoenix from the Ashes*, p. 57; S. W. Kirby, *The War against Japan, Vol. II: India's Most Dangerous Hour* (Uckfield: The Naval & Military Press, 2004 [1958]), p. 442; Crew, *The Army Medical Services: Campaigns, Vol. V: Burma*, pp. 5–6.
76. Moreman, *The Jungle, the Japanese and the British Commonwealth Armies at War*, p. 37; Kirby, *The War against Japan, Vol. II*, pp. 25, 442.
77. Callahan, *Burma*, p. 29; Moreman, *The Jungle, the Japanese and the British Commonwealth Armies at War*, p. 36; Jeffreys, *Approach to Battle*, p. 150.
78. Marston, *Phoenix from the Ashes*, pp. 51, 58; Moreman, *The Jungle, the Japanese and the British Commonwealth Armies at War*, p. 37; Crew, *The Army Medical Services: Campaigns, Vol. V: Burma*, p. 11.
79. Callahan, *Burma*, p. 32.

80. Moreman, *The Jungle, the Japanese and the British Commonwealth Armies at War*, pp. 36–8; Jeffreys, *Approach to Battle*, p. 149.
81. Marston, *Phoenix from the Ashes*, p. 58. Callahan, *Burma*, p. 33; Moreman, *The Jungle, the Japanese and the British Commonwealth Armies at War*, pp. 36–7.
82. Callahan, *Burma*, p. 40.
83. Moreman, *The Jungle, the Japanese and the British Commonwealth Armies at War*, p. 37.
84. Ibid.; Kirby, *The War against Japan, Vol. II*, pp. 25, 442.
85. Quoted in Moreman, *The Jungle, the Japanese and the British Commonwealth Armies at War*, p. 38.
86. Moreman, *The Jungle, the Japanese and the British Commonwealth Armies at War*, pp. 38–9.
87. Ibid., pp. 39.
88. Farrell, *The Defence and Fall of Singapore*, p. 310. The 18th Division, made up largely of territorials from eastern England, had been rounding the Cape and was bound for the Middle East when Japan attacked (Callahan, *Churchill and His Generals*, p. 101).
89. Kirby, *The War against Japan, Vol. I*, pp. 252–3.
90. NA WO 106/2580 Singapore, Summary of Approximate Effective Strengths at 31 Jan. 1942.
91. Farrell, *The Defence and Fall of Singapore*, p. 171; I. S. O. Playfair, *The Mediterranean and Middle East, Vol. III: British Fortunes Reach their Lowest Ebb* (Uckfield: Naval & Military Press, 2004 [1960]), p. 125. These forces did not play a role in the drama that unfolded, as the fortress fell before they arrived. The 7th Armoured Brigade, comprising 7th Hussars, 2nd RTR and 414th Battery, RHA, were eventually sent to Burma.
92. Farrell, *The Defence and Fall of Singapore*, p. 291.
93. Quoted ibid., p. 324.
94. Ibid., p. 173.
95. Ibid., p. 311.
96. Ibid., p. 311.
97. AWM 54 553/5/16 PART 2 Maj. Gen. Gordon Bennett, Report on Malayan Campaign, 7 Dec. 1941–15 Feb. 1942, p. 10.
98. Kirby, *The War against Japan, Vol. I*, pp. 522–7.
99. Farrell, *The Defence and Fall of Singapore*, p. 355.
100. Ibid.
101. Ibid., p. 356.
102. Ibid., p. 355. Callahan has also argued that it was 'unrealistic to expect a heroic last stand' (Callahan, *Churchill and His Generals*, p. 102).
103. See e.g. Field-Marshal Earl Wavell, *The Good Soldier* (London: MacMillan and Co., 1948).
104. Farrell, *The Defence and Fall of Singapore*, p. 327.
105. Quoted ibid., pp. 335–6.
106. Ibid., p. 359.
107. AWM 54 553/5/16 PART 2 Maj. Gen. Gordon Bennett, Report on Malayan Campaign, 7 Dec. 1941–15 Feb. 1942, p. 39.
108. AWM 52 11/1/20 War Diary, ADMS 8 Division, 1940–5.
109. Farrell, *The Defence and Fall of Singapore*, p. 359.
110. Quoted ibid., pp. 360–1.
111. NA WO 106/2580 Malaya Garrison, Programme of Major Reinforcements, 1939–41, Table 1; Farrell, *The Defence and Fall of Singapore*, pp. 101, 178, 415.

At its peak, Malaya Command had on paper 130,246 all ranks, a force outnumbering the Japanese Twenty-Fifth Army which totalled on paper about 125,408 men but never in reality exceeding two-thirds of this number. According to Farrell, 'in the end Twenty-Fifth Army committed barely enough infantry to accomplish its ambitious mission; only nine and two-thirds of its fourteen regiments actually fought in Malaya and Singapore'.

112. Moreman, *The Jungle, the Japanese and the British Commonwealth Armies at War*, p. 1.
113. Kirby, *The War against Japan, Vol. II*, p. 57; Callahan, *Burma*, pp. 36–7.
114. Moreman, *The Jungle, the Japanese and the British Commonwealth Armies at War*, p. 40.
115. Kirby, *The War against Japan, Vol. II*, p. 62.
116. Moreman, *The Jungle, the Japanese and the British Commonwealth Armies at War*, p. 40.
117. Callahan, *Burma*, p. 35.
118. Marston, *Phoenix from the Ashes*, p. 66.
119. Callahan, *Burma*, pp. 34–5.
120. Ibid.; Kirby, *The War against Japan, Vol. II*, p. 86.
121. Callahan, *Burma*, pp. 35–6; Graham Dunlop, *Military Economics, Culture and Logistics in the Burma Campaign, 1942–1945* (London: Pickering & Chatto, 2009), p. 1.
122. Callahan, *Burma*, pp. 36–7; Dunlop, *Military Economics, Culture and Logistics in the Burma Campaign*, p. 26; Louis Allen, *Burma: The Longest War, 1941–45* (London: Phoenix Press, 2000 [1984]), p. 59.
123. Nigel Nicolson, *Alex: The Life of Field Marshal Earl Alexander of Tunis* (London: Weidenfeld and Nicolson, 1973), p. 139.
124. Callahan, *Burma*, pp. 39; Nicolson, *Alex*, p. 139.
125. Raymond Callahan, 'Slim, William Joseph, first Viscount Slim (1891–1970)', *Oxford Dictionary of National Biography* (Oxford University Press, 2004), online edn, Jan. 2011, www.oxforddnb.com/view/10.1093/ref:odnb/9780198614128.001.0001/odnb-9780198614128-e-36120, accessed 26 Apr. 2017.
126. Ibid.; Hew Strachan, *Military Lives* (Oxford University Press, 2002), pp. 433–5.
127. Robert Lyman, *Slim, Master of War: Burma and the Birth of Modern Warfare* (London: Robinson, 2005), pp. 3–6; Strachan, *Military Lives*, pp. 433–5.
128. Ronald Lewin, *Slim: The Standardbearer* (Ware: Wordsworth, 1999 [1976]), pp. 63–78.
129. Moreman, *The Jungle, the Japanese and the British Commonwealth Armies at War*, pp. 42–3.
130. Marston, *Phoenix from the Ashes*, pp. 3, 72–3; Moreman, *The Jungle, the Japanese and the British Commonwealth Armies at War*, p. 44.
131. Nicolson, *Alex*, p. 139.
132. Marston, *Phoenix from the Ashes*, pp. 3, 72–3; Moreman, *The Jungle, the Japanese and the British Commonwealth Armies at War*, p. 44.
133. Moreman, *The Jungle, the Japanese and the British Commonwealth Armies at War*, p. 52.
134. Kirby, *The War against Japan, Vol. I*, p. 473.
135. Allen, *Burma*, pp. 637–8.
136. Quoted in Moreman, *The Jungle, the Japanese and the British Commonwealth Armies at War*, pp. 35–6.
137. Quoted in David French, *Raising Churchill's Army: The British Army and the War against Germany 1919–1945* (Oxford University Press, 2000), pp. 1–2.

138. Alfred E. Eckes, Jr, *The United States and the Global Struggle for Minerals* (Austin: University of Texas, 1979), p. 84. Quoted in David Reynolds, '1940: Fulcrum of the Twentieth Century', *International Affairs*, 66(2) (Apr. 1990), p. 344.
139. John Darwin, *The Empire Project: The Rise and Fall of the British World-System, 1830–1970* (Cambridge University Press, 2009), p. 513.
140. Ibid., pp. 501–2.
141. Callahan, *Churchill and His Generals*, pp. 100–1
142. Darwin, *The Empire Project*, pp. 501–2.

Chapter 6 The Great Imperial Morale Crisis

1. David Edgerton, *Britain's War Machine: Weapons, Resources and Experts in the Second World War* (London: Allen Lane, 2011), p. 219; David French, *Raising Churchill's Army: The British Army and the War against Germany 1919–1945* (Oxford University Press, 2000), p. 273; Stephen Biddle, *Military Power: Explaining Victory and Defeat in Modern Battle* (Princeton University Press, 2004); David Reynolds, '1940: Fulcrum of the Twentieth Century', *International Affairs*, 66(2) (Apr. 1990), p. 325.
2. Reynolds, '1940: Fulcrum of the Twentieth Century', p. 325. Quote is from Williamson Murray, *The Change in the European Balance of Power, 1938–1939: The Path to Ruin* (Princeton University Press, 1984), p. 361.
3. Reynolds, '1940: Fulcrum of the Twentieth Century', *International Affairs*, p. 345.
4. Patrick Rose, 'Allies at War: British and US Army Command Culture in the Italian Campaign, 1943–1944', *Journal of Strategic Studies*, 36(1) (February, 2013), p. 50. See also, French, *Raising Churchill's Army*, p. 202.
5. John Buckley, *Monty's Men: The British Army and the Liberation of Europe* (London: Yale University Press, 2013), pp. 31–2.
6. Quoted in French, *Raising Churchill's Army*, p. 173.
7. French, *Raising Churchill's Army*, p. 173.
8. John Gooch, 'Series Editors Preface', in Timothy Harrison Place, *Military Training in the British Army* (London: Frank Cass, 2000), p. vii; Jonathan Fennell, 'Re-evaluating Combat Cohesion', in Anthony King (ed.), *Frontline: Combat and Cohesion in the Twenty-First Century* (Oxford University Press, 2015), p. 136.
9. See e.g. Brian Farrell, *The Defence and Fall of Singapore 1940–1942* (Stroud: Tempus, 2005), p. 157; Terry Copp, *Fields of Fire: The Canadians in Normandy* (University of Toronto Press, 2003); Buckley, *Monty's Men*.
10. Ibid.
11. S. L. A. Marshall, *Men against Fire: The Problem of Battle Command in Future War* (New York, 1966), p. 184.
12. Lawrence Freedman, *Strategy: A History* (Oxford University Press, 2013), p. xi.
13. Daniel J. Hughes (ed.), *Moltke on the Art of War: Selected Writings* (Novato: Presidio Press, 1993), p. viii.
14. A concern rightly highlighted in the foreword to the Ministry of Defence, *Army Doctrine Publication: Operations*, p. iii and in John Kiszely, *Anatomy of a Campaign: The British Fiasco in Norway, 1940* (Cambridge University Press, 2017), pp. 282–3.
15. Carl von Clausewitz, *On War* (Everyman Library: London, 1993 [1832]).
16. Ibid., p. 698.
17. Rose, 'Allies at War', p. 50.

18. Timothy Moreman, *The Jungle, the Japanese and the British Commonwealth Armies at War, 1941–45: Fighting Methods, Doctrine and Training for Jungle Warfare* (London: Frank Cass, 2005), pp. 14–15. See also, AWM 54 553/5/15 Lessons from Malaya, Copy of a secret document issued to War Department, Washington, by Lieut. Col. T. J. Wells, Assistant Military Attaché, London, 1943, p. 2.
19. Patrick Rose, 'British Army Command Culture 1939–1945: A Comparative Study of British Eighth and Fourteenth Armies' (PhD thesis, King's College London, 2008), p. 96.
20. Harrison Place, *Military Training in the British Army, 1940–1944*, p. 3. See also Edward Smalley, *The British Expeditionary Force, 1939–40* (Basingstoke: Palgrave Macmillan, 2015), pp. 37–83.
21. NA WO 277/12 Piggott, Manpower Problems, p. 80.
22. NA WO 163/50 Use of Manpower in the Army, Pt Two, Appendix A, Notes on the Growth of the Army, 21 Nov. 1941.
23. Farrell, *The Defence and Fall of Singapore*, p. 115; Indivar Kamtekar, 'A Different War Dance: State and Class in India 1939–1945', *Past and Present*, 176(1) (2002), pp. 190–3.
24. Quoted in Moreman, *The Jungle, the Japanese and the British Commonwealth Armies at War*, p. 20.
25. French, *Raising Churchill's Army*, p. 199.
26. Ibid., pp. 199–200.
27. Daniel Marston, *Phoenix from the Ashes: The Indian Army in the Burma Campaign* (Westport: Praeger, 2003), p. 43.
28. Ibid.
29. AWM 54 839/1/2 Notes for Liaison Officers (Australia), Submitted by 6 Australian Division, July 1941.
30. Neil Roos, *Ordinary Springboks: White Servicemen and Social Justice in South Africa, 1939–1961* (Aldershot: Ashgate, 2005), pp. 45–6.
31. NA WO 260/16 DSD to C-in-C Home Forces, 9 Mar. 1942. Quoted in French, *Raising Churchill's Army*, p. 234.
32. Niall Barr, *Pendulum of War: The Three Battles of El Alamein* (London: Pimlico, 2005 [2004]), pp. 157–9.
33. French, *Raising Churchill's Army*, p. 179; Smalley, *The British Expeditionary Force*, pp. 37–83.
34. Moreman, *The Jungle, the Japanese and the British Commonwealth Armies at War*, passim; Farrell, *The Defence and Fall of Singapore*, pp. 110–23; S. W. Kirby, *Singapore: The Chain of Disaster* (London: Cassell, 1971), p. 150; AWM 54 553/5/15 Lessons from Malaya, Copy of a secret document issued to War Department, Washington, by Lieut. Col. T. J. Wells, Assistant Military Attaché, London, 1943, p. 1.
35. AWM 54 553/5/15 Lessons from Malaya, Copy of a secret document issued to War Department, Washington, by Lieut. Col. T. J. Wells, Assistant Military Attaché, London, 1943, p. 2.
36. Ibid., p. 3; Farrell, *The Defence and Fall of Singapore*, p. 111.
37. Moreman, *The Jungle, the Japanese and the British Commonwealth Armies at War*, p. 14.
38. NA CAB 21/914 Committee on the work of Psychologists and Psychiatrists in the Services, 1940–2, Summary of Lectures on Psychological Aspects of War, p. 4.

39. War Office, *Training Regulations 1934*, p. 4. See also, NA CAB 21/914 Directorate of Army Psychiatry, Technical Memorandum No. 2, Suppose You Were a Nazi Agent – or Fifth Column Work for Amateurs, June 1942.
40. BL IOR L/MIL/17/5/2244 'Military Training Pamphlet No. 1 (India): Armoured Units in the Field, Characteristics, Roles and Handling of Armoured Divisions 1941', p. 11. Issued by the General Staff, India, 1942.
41. Quoted in Moreman, *The Jungle, the Japanese and the British Commonwealth Armies at War*, p. 31.
42. AWM 54 553/5/16 PART 2 Maj. Gen. Gordon Bennett, Report on Malayan Campaign, 7 Dec. 1941–15 Feb. 1942, p. 26.
43. Ibid., pp. 10, 27, 32, 45.
44. AWM 54 553/5/15 Lessons from Malaya, Copy of a secret document issued to War Department, Washington, by Lieut. Col. T. J. Wells, Assistant Military Attaché, London, 1943, p. 3.
45. Ibid.
46. Quoted in Moreman, *The Jungle, the Japanese and the British Commonwealth Armies at War*, pp. 54–5.
47. AWM 54 883/2/97 MEFCWS No. VI. (17–23 Dec. 1941), p. 5.
48. Shelford Bidwell and Dominick Graham, *Firepower: British Army Weapons and Theories of War 1904–1945* (London: Allen & Unwin, 1982), pp. 221–47.
49. Barr, *Pendulum of War*, pp. 85–88.
50. John Darwin, *The Empire Project: The Rise and Fall of the British World-System, 1830–1970* (Cambridge University Press, 2009), p. 3. See also Niall Ferguson, *Empire: How Britain Made the Modern World* (London: Penguin, 2003).
51. Farrell, *The Defence and Fall of Singapore*, pp. 144, 153–4.
52. Ibid., p. 312–13.
53. French, *Raising Churchill's Army*, p. 179. See also, Kiszely, *Anatomy of a Campaign*, pp. 282–3.
54. Raymond Callahan, *Churchill and His Generals* (Lawrence: University Press of Kansas, 2007), p. 102; Alex Danchev and Daniel Todman (eds.), *War Diaries 1939–1945: Field Marshal Lord Alanbrooke* (London: Phoenix, 2002 [2001]), p. 231.
55. Nigel Nicolson (ed.), *The Diaries and Letters of Harold Nicolson, Vol. II: The War Years, 1939–1945* (New York: Atheneum, 1967), p. 211, entry for 12 Feb. Quoted in Callahan, *Churchill and His Generals*, p. 263.
56. Jonathan Fennell, 'In Search of the "X" Factor: Morale and the Study of Strategy', *Journal of Strategic Studies*, 37(6–7) (2014), pp. 9–12.
57. Tarak Barkawi, 'Culture and Combat in the Colonies: The Indian Army in the Second World War', *Journal of Contemporary History*, 41(2) (2006), p. 329; Anthony King, *The Combat Soldier: Infantry Tactics and Cohesion in the Twentieth and Twenty-First Centuries* (Oxford University Press, 2013), p. 204.
58. Hew Strachan, 'The Soldier's Experience in Two World Wars', in P. Addison and A. Calder (eds.), *Time to Kill: The Soldier's Experience of War in the West, 1939–1945* (London: Pimlico, 1997), p. 371.
59. Hew Strachan, 'The Morale of the German Army 1917–18', in Hugh Cecil and Peter H. Liddle (eds.), *Facing Armageddon: The First World War Experienced* (London: Leo Cooper, 1996), p. 388.
60. French, *Raising Churchill's Army*, p. 147.
61. NA WO 277/16 Sparrow, Army Morale, p. 13.

62. Moreman, *The Jungle, the Japanese and the British Commonwealth Armies at War*, pp. 28–9.
63. Jonathan Fennell, *Combat and Morale in the North African Campaign: The Eighth Army and the Path to El Alamein* (Cambridge University Press, 2011), pp. 246–57.
64. Hew Strachan, 'Training, Morale and Modern War', *The Journal of Contemporary History*, 41(2) (2006), pp. 215–16; Marshall, *Men against Fire*, p. 37.
65. French, *Raising Churchill's Army*, p. 73.
66. NA 20 277/16, J. H. A. Sparrow, Army Morale, p. 21.
67. NA WO 163/51 Retention and Review of Suitability of Officers, Jan. 1942.
68. NA WO 163/51 Morale Report, Dec. 1941–Apr. 1942.
69. AWM 54 883/2/97 MEFCWS, No. XVII (5–11 Mar. 1942), p. 4.
70. ANZ WAII/1/DA 508/1 Vol. 1 MEFCWS, No. XXXV (8–14 July 1942), p. 5.
71. SANDF, DOC, Div. Docs., GP 1, Box 1, Memorandum on Morale of SA Troops in ME, 8 Aug. 1942, p. 6.
72. AWM 54 839/1/2 Liaison Officer Reports on Officer Reinforcements, Reinforcements Generally and Standard of Training of Other Ranks Arriving in the Middle East, July 1941. Notes for LO (Australia) – submitted by 6 Aust. Div.
73. NA WO 32/15773 The Army Council, Minutes of the Fourteenth Meeting, 11 Aug. 1942. Army Morale: The Death Penalty in Relation to Offences Committed on Active Service, p. 4.
74. See e.g. Fennell, *Combat and Morale in the North African Campaign*, Ch. 7.
75. Roger R. Reese, *Why Stalin's Soldiers Fought: The Red Army's Military Effectiveness in World War II* (University Press of Kansas, 2011), pp. 138–9.
76. Robert S. Rush, 'A Different Perspective: Cohesion, Morale and Operational Effectiveness in the German Army, Fall 1944', *Armed Forces and Society*, 25(3) (Spring 1999), p. 496; King, *The Combat Soldier*, p. 203.
77. Quoted in Farrell, *The Defence and Fall of Singapore*, p. 58.
78. David French, 'Discipline and the Death Penalty in the British Army in the War against Germany during the Second World War', *Journal of Contemporary History*, 33(4) (Oct. 1998), pp. 538–40. Gort made an effort in France in 1940, Auchinleck twice asked for it to be reintroduced in North Africa in 1942 and Alexander once again in Italy in 1944.
79. S. P. MacKenzie, *Politics and Military Morale: Current-Affairs and Citizenship Education in the British Army, 1914–1950* (Oxford University Press, 1992), p. 75.
80. NA WO 32/9735 ABCA, Current Affairs in the Army: The Outline of a New Plan, 21 July 1941, p. 2.
81. Glyn Prysor, 'The "Fifth Column" and the British Experience of Retreat, 1940', *War in History*, 12(4) (2005), pp. 445–6.
82. Ibid., pp. 447.
83. NA WO 201/2586 Middle East Training Pamphlet No. 10. Lessons of Cyrenaica Campaign: Training Pamphlet, Dec. 1940–Feb. 1941, p. 60.
84. MacKenzie, Politics and Military Morale, p. 86. See also, Omer Bartov, *The Eastern Front, 1941–45: German Troops and the Barbarisation of Warfare* (Basingstoke: Palgrave, 2001); Adam Tooze, *The Wages of Destruction: The Making and Breaking of the Nazi Economy* (London: Penguin Books, 2007), p. xxv. To a degree, this is not a novel argument. The mass surrenders of Italian soldiers in the Second World War have been explained universally by reference to the ordinary Italian's indifference to the aims of the war and alienation from the Fascist state that ruled, broadly, without his loyalty or consent. In a similar vein, the extraordinary cohesion demonstrated by German forces on the Eastern Front

between 1941 and 1945 has been explained by reference to the *Wehrmacht's* political indoctrination and faith in and connection with the National Socialist State.

85. Kevin Jefferys, *The Churchill Coalition and Wartime Politics, 1940–1945* (Manchester University Press, 1991), p. 19.
86. *The Times*, 1 July 1940.
87. Ross McKibbin, *Parties and People: England 1914–1951* (Oxford University Press, 2010), p. vii.
88. Ibid, pp. 132–8.
89. Ibid., p. vii.
90. Sonya O. Rose, *Which People's War? National Identity and Citizenship in Britain 1939–1945* (Oxford University Press, 2003), p. 15.
91. Quoted in Daniel Todman, *Britain's War: Into Battle, 1937–1941* (London: Allen Lane, 2016), Ch. 15.
92. See e.g. Ian McLaine, *Ministry of Morale: Home Front Morale and the Ministry of Information in World War II* (London: Allen & Unwin, 1979; Robert MacKay, *Half the Battle: Civilian Morale in Britain During the Second World War* (Manchester University Press, 2002).
93. Those studies that have looked at this question include Jeremy A. Crang, *The British Army and the People's War, 1939–1945* (Manchester University Press, 2000); MacKenzie, *Politics and Military Morale*; and Field, *Blood, Sweat and Toil.*
94. NA WO 32/15772 The Army Council, Morale in the Army: Report of the War Office Morale Committee, Feb.–May 1942, pp. 2–3.
95. Bernard Porter, *The Absent-Minded Imperialists: Empire, Society, and Culture in Britain* (Oxford University Press, 2004), p. xiv.
96. Ibid., pp. 225, 267.
97. NA WO 32/15772 Morale Committee, Draft Morale Report, May–July 1942, p. 4.
98. NA WO 32/15772 War Office Committee on Morale in the Army. Second Quarterly Report, May–July 1942.
99. Alan Allport, *Browned Off and Bloody-Minded: The British Soldier Goes to War 1939–1945* (London: Yale University Press, 2015), p. 292.
100. NA WO 204/10381 First Army Mail: ACR No. 28, 16–31 Aug. 1943, p. 14.
101. AWM 54 883/2/97 MEFCWS, No. XXIV (23–29 Apr. 1942), p. 3.
102. AWM 54 883/2/97 British Troops in Egypt No. 102 FCR Week Ending 7 Oct. 1941, p. 2. See also, SANDF, DOC, Div. Docs., GP 1, Box 1, Army Routine Orders by Lieut. Gen. N. M. Ritchie, GOC-in-C, Eighth Army, 23 May 1942; NA WO 193/453 Morale Report, Aug.–Oct. 1942. The increase in family allowances paid to soldiers' families in Mar. 1942, and the increase in soldiers' basic pay that accompanied it in the autumn, all played a role in placating such worries.
103. NA WO 32/15772 War Office Committee on Morale in the Army. Second Quarterly Report, May–July 1942.
104. AWM 54 883/2/97 MEFCWS, No. XIX (19–25 Mar. 1942), p. 3.
105. NA WO 32/15772 War Office Committee on Morale in the Army. Second Quarterly Report, May–July 1942.
106. Ibid.
107. NA WO 222/124 The Moral Effect of Weapons, Investigation into the Reactions of a Group of 300 Wounded Men in North Africa, 1943.
108. NA WO 32/15772 War Office Committee on Morale in the Army: Second Quarterly Report, May–July 1942.
109. Ibid.

110. Ibid.
111. Ibid.
112. Quoted in Daniel Todman, *Britain's War: Into Battle, 1937–1941* (London: Allen Lane, 2016), pp. 397–8.
113. Ibid., pp. 413–14. See also Richard Toye, *The Roar of the Lion: The Untold Story of Churchill's World War II Speeches* (Oxford University Press, 2013), pp. 97–205.
114. Quoted in Todman, *Britain's War*, p. 414.
115. Ibid., p. 414.
116. NA WO 32/15772 War Office Committee on Morale in the Army: Second Quarterly Report, May–July 1942.
117. MacKenzie, *Politics and Military Morale*, pp. 181–2.
118. Buckley, *Monty's Men*, p. 45; French, *Raising Churchill's Army*, pp. 133–4; Terry Copp and Bill McAndrew, *Battle Exhaustion: Soldiers and Psychiatrists in the Canadian Army, 1939–1945* (London: McGill-Queen's University Press, 1990), p. 82.
119. AWM 54 553/5/15 Lessons from Malaya, Copy of a secret document issued to War Department, Washington, by Lieut. Col. T. J. Wells, Assistant Military Attaché, London, 1943, p. 4.
120. Darwin, *The Empire Project*, p. 483.
121. Daniel Marston, *The Indian Army and the End of the Raj* (Cambridge University Press, 2014), Ch. 1.
122. Max Hastings quote, BBC, 'Singapore 1942: End of Empire', episode 2. See also Srinath Raghaven, *India's War: The Making of Modern South Asia, 1939–1945* (London: Penguin, 2017), p. 67.
123. Raghaven, *India's War*, pp. 216–18.
124. BL IOR L/WS/1/1433 War Staff Papers: India Internal Intelligence Summary No. 16, 20 Feb. 1942, p. 1; BL IOR L/WS/1/1433 War Staff Papers: India Internal Intelligence Summary No. 20, 20 Mar. 1942, p. 3; Raghaven, *India's War*, pp. 265–6.
125. BL IOR L/WS/1/1433 War Staff Papers: India Internal Intelligence Summary No. 38, 24 July 1942, p. 3.
126. Andrew N. Buchanan, 'The War Crisis and the Decolonization of India, December 1941–September 1942: A Political and Military Dilemma', *Global War Studies*, 8(2) (2011), p. 22. See also Christopher Bayly and Tim Harper, *Forgotten Armies: Britain's Asian Empire & the War with Japan* (London: Penguin, 2005 [2004]), pp. 190–7.
127. Rajit K. Mazumder, 'From Loyalty to Dissent: Punjabis from the Great War to World War II', in Kaushik Roy (ed.), *The Indian Army in the Two World Wars* (Leiden: Brill, 2012), pp. 482–4.
128. Barkawi, 'Culture and Combat in the Colonies', p. 328.
129. AWM 54 553/5/16 PART 2 Maj. Gen. Gordon Bennett, Report on Malayan Campaign, 7 Dec. 1941–15 Feb. 1942, p. 46.
130. BL IOR L/WS/1/1433 War Staff Papers: India Internal Intelligence Summary No. 20, 20 Mar. 1942, p. 3.
131. BL IOR L/WS/1/1433 War Staff Papers: India Internal Intelligence Summary No. 39, 31 July 1942, p. 3.
132. Kamtekar, 'A Different War Dance', p. 192.
133. David Omissi, *The Sepoy and the Raj: The Indian Army, 1860–1940* (London: Macmillan, 1994), p. 151.
134. Barkawi, 'Culture and Combat in the Colonies', p. 336.
135. Quoted ibid., p. 331.

136. BL IOR L/WS/1/1337 Brig. Gen. Cawthorn, Director of Military Intelligence, 31 Aug. 1942. Quoted in Robert Johnson, 'The Army in India and Responses to Low-Intensity Conflict, 1936–1946', *Journal of the Society for Army Historical Research*, 89(358) (2011), p. 176.
137. Barkawi, 'Culture and Combat in the Colonies', p. 344.
138. Ibid., p. 336.
139. Ibid., pp. 336–45.
140. Ibid, pp. 330, 339; Chandar S. Sundaram, 'A Paper Tiger: The Indian National Army in Battle, 1944–1945', *War & Society*, 13(1) (May 1995), pp. 35–6.
141. Gajendra Singh, *The Testimonies of Indian Soldiers and the Two World Wars: Between Self and Sepoy* (London: Bloomsbury, 2014), p. 157. The other being the Indian mutiny of 1857.
142. Barkawi, 'Culture and Combat in the Colonies', p. 331.
143. Ibid., pp. 338–41; Raghaven, *India's War*, p. 283. Some 250 of these officers were from the medical corps. Singh, *The Testimonies of Indian Soldiers and the Two World Wars*, p. 157, estimates that 50,000 of the 85,000 prisoners taken on Singapore Island were Indian.
144. Barkawi, 'Culture and Combat in the Colonies', pp. 341–4.
145. Ibid., p. 345.
146. Singh, *The Testimonies of Indian Soldiers and the Two World Wars*, p. 159. All save 176 of that number were *sipahis* or VCOs in the Indian Army before being captured. The remaining 176 were commissioned officers of the rank of second lieutenant or higher.
147. Quoted ibid., p. 161.
148. Ibid., p. 162.
149. Ibid.
150. General HQ, India to General Staff Branch, New Delhi, Subversive Activities Directed Against the Military, 18 Mar. 1942. Quoted in Singh, *The Testimonies of Indian Soldiers and the Two World Wars*, p. 163.
151. Quoted in Barkawi, 'Culture and Combat in the Colonies', p. 337.
152. Raghaven, *India's War*, p. 284.
153. Barkawi, 'Culture and Combat in the Colonies', p. 338. The Indian Legion was made up of 2,000 Indian volunteers (see Raghaven, *India's War*, p. 280).
154. SANDF, DOC, AI Gp Box 46 I/40(F) IC to DDMI, Military Counter Propaganda on the Home Front, n.d. but 1941; E. G. Malherbe, *Never a Dull Moment* (Aylesbury: Timmins, 1981), pp. 238–9; Saul Dubow, 'Scientism, Social Research and the Limits of "South Africanism": The Case of Ernst Gideon Malherbe', *South African Historical Journal*, 44(1) (2001), p. 128.
155. Neil Roos, 'The Second World War, the Army Education Scheme and the "Discipline" of the White Poor in South Africa', *History of Education: Journal of the History of Education Society*, 32(6) (2003), p. 651.
156. SANDF, DOC, AI Gp 1 Box 43/I/38/D MCS No. 10, EAFHQ 6–20 Mar. 1941, pp. 1–2; AI Gp 1 Box 43/I/38/D MCS No. 13, EAFHQ 21 Mar.–20 Apr., p. 2. The last quote came from a man in the air force.
157. SANDF, DOC, AI Gp 1 Box 81/I/71/B South African MCS No. 3, 16–28 Feb. 1942, p. 2.
158. SANDF, DOC, AI Gp 1 Box 81/I/71/B South African MCS No. 4, 1–15 Apr. 1942.
159. SANDF, DOC, AI Gp Box 42/I/37 DFMS No. 88, Sept. 1944.
160. SANDF, DOC, AI Gp 1 Box 81/I/71/B South African MCS No. 5, 16–30 Apr. 1942, p. 9.

161. SANDF, DOC, AI Gp 1 Box 81/I/71/B Memorandum on Morale of Union Defence Forces, p. 5, n.d. but probably 1943.
162. SANDF, DOC, AI Gp 1 Box 46 I/40/(H) IC to Director of Military Intelligence, Memorandum on Low Level of Morale on the Home Front, 24 Feb. 1942. Other reports, such as AI Gp 1 Box 81/71/B South African MCS No. 3, 16–28 Feb. 1942, point to a similar dynamic.
163. Ibid.
164. Ibid.
165. SANDF, DOC, AI Gp 1 Box 81/I/71/B South African MCS No. 3, 16–28 Feb. 1942, p. 1.
166. SANDF, DOC, AI Gp 1 Box 46 I/40/(H) IC to Director of Military Intelligence, Memorandum on Low Level of Morale on the Home Front, 24 Feb. 1942.
167. Ibid.
168. SANDF, DOC, AI Gp 1 Box 81/I/71/B South African MCS No. 5, 16–30 Apr. 1942, p. 11.
169. SANDF, DOC, UWH Box 345 Brig. A. J. Orenstein, DMS UDF, Memorandum on Anxiety Neurosis and Hysteria, 13 Apr. 1942.
170. SANDF, DOC, Div. Docs. Box 119 UDF Admin HQ MEF to GOC 1st and 2nd SA Divs., President: Permanent Court Martial, 29 Apr. 1942.
171. SANDF, DOC, UWH Box 345 Brig. A. J. Orenstein, DMS UDF, Memorandum on Anxiety Neurosis and Hysteria, 13 Apr. 1942.
172. SANDF, DOC, AI Gp 1 Box 23/CE10/2 MCS No. 46 (Final Special Report Relating to Libyan Campaign), 24 July 1942.
173. See Fennell, *Combat and Morale in the North African Campaign*; J. A. I. Agar-Hamilton and L. C. F. Turner, *Crisis in the Desert, May–July 1942* (London: Oxford University Press, 1952).
174. NAA MP508/1, 89/716/326 The Home Front and the Soldier, Article submitted to SALT, July 1942, p. 1. See also John Pomeroy, 'A. P. Elkin: Public Morale and Propaganda', in Geoffrey Gray, Doug Munro and Christine Winter (eds.), *Scholars at War: Australian Social Scientists, 1939–1945* (Canberra: ANU Press, 2012), pp. 35–40.
175. Ibid., p. 4.
176. Ibid., p. 2.
177. NAA SP109/16 John Curtin to A. A. Conlon, 26 May 1942.
178. NAA SP109/16 Report of the Committee on Civilian Morale Made Under Direction of the Prime Minister, n.d. but clearly 1942, pp. 1–3.
179. Ibid., p. 4.
180. Ibid.
181. Ibid., p. 5. See also Pomeroy, 'A. P. Elkin: Public Morale and Propaganda', in Gray, Munro and Winter, *Scholars at War*, p. 46.
182. Kate Darian-Smith, 'War and Australian Society', in Joan Beaumont (ed.), *Australia's War, 1939–45* (Crows Nest: Allen & Unwin, 1996), p. 55.
183. NAA SP109/16 Prime Minister's Committee on National Morale, Interim Report to the Prime Minister, n.d. but clearly 1942, pp. 1–2.
184. SANDF, DOC, AI Gp 1 Box 43 I/38/G FCR No. 87, British Troops in Egypt, 19 June 1941, p. 2.
185. AWM 54 883/2/97 FCR No. 96, British Troops in Egypt, 28 Aug. 1941, p. 3.
186. AWM 54 883/2/97 FCR No. 94, British Troops in Egypt, 14 Aug. 1941, p. 2.
187. AWM 54 883/2/97 MEFCWS No. XII, 28 Jan.–3 Feb. 1942, p. 7.

188. Quoted in David Horner, 'Australia in 1942: A Pivotal Year', in Peter J. Dean (ed.), *Australia 1942: In the Shadow of War* (Cambridge University Press, 2013), p. 11.
189. NAA MP729/7, 55/421/49 Publicity, AIF in Malaya, 27 Sept. 1941.
190. AWM 54 883/2/97 MEFCWS, No. XV, 18–25 Feb. 1942, p. 7; AWM 54 883/2/97 MEFCWS, No. X, 14–20 Jan. 1942, p. 10.
191. AWM 54 883/2/97 MEFCWS, No. XVI, 26 Feb.–4 Mar. 1942, p. 9.
192. AWM 54 883/2/97 MEFCWS, No. XXX, 3–9 June 1942, p. 16; AWM 54 883/2/97 MEFCWS, No. XXIX, 27 May–2 June 1942, p. 17.
193. AWM 54 883/2/97 MEFCWS, No. XXIX, 27 May–2 June 1942, p. 17.
194. Quoted in Moreman, *The Jungle, the Japanese and the British Commonwealth Armies at War*, p. 36.
195. Quoted ibid., pp. 14–5.
196. Quoted in Farrell, *The Defence and Fall of Singapore*, p. 58.
197. CAB 21/914 Directorate of Army Psychiatry, Technical Memorandum No. 2, Suppose You Were a Nazi Agent – or Fifth Column Work for Amateurs, June 1942.
198. CAB 21/914 Committee on the work of Psychologists and Psychiatrists in the Services, 1940–2, Summary of Lectures on Psychological Aspects of War, p. 1.
199. MacKenzie, *Politics and Military Morale*, pp. 181–2.
200. NA WO 32/15772 Report of the Morale Committee on the summary of Divisional and District Reports at Home and Censorship Reports, Feb.–May 1942, p. 1.
201. See e.g. P. Addison and A. Calder (eds.), *Time to Kill: The Soldier's Experience of War in the West, 1939–1945* (London: Pimlico, 1997), p. 371; Ellis, *The Sharp End*, p. 315; Marshall, *Men against Fire*; Samuel A. Stouffer et al., *The American Soldier: Combat and its Aftermath, Vol. II* (Princeton University Press, 1949); Edward A. Shils and Morris Janowitz, 'Cohesion and Disintegration in the Wehrmacht in World War II', *Public Opinion Quarterly*, 12 (Summer 1948); Stephen G. Fritz, *Frontsoldaten: The German Soldier in World War II* (Lexington: University Press of Kentucky, 1995); Richard Holmes, *Acts of War: The Behaviour of Men in Battle* (London: Cassell, 2004); Anthony King, *The Combat Soldier: Infantry Tactics and Cohesion in the Twentieth and Twenty-First Centuries* (Oxford University Press, 2013); Anthony King (ed.), *Frontline: Combat and Cohesion in the Twenty-First Century* (Oxford University Press, 2015); Roger R. Reese, *Why Stalin's Soldiers Fought: The Red Army's Military Effectiveness in World War II* (Lawrence: University Press of Kansas, 2011); Catherine Merridale, *Ivan's War: The Red Army 1939–45* (London: Faber and Faber, 2005).
202. Dissatisfaction with the home front was to manifest itself most powerfully for the 2NZEF during the Furlough Mutiny of 1943–4 (see Chapter 10 of this volume). Nevertheless, negative rumblings were evident in New Zealand unit censorship as early as 1941, the censorship summary for 14 Aug., for example, pointing out that many troops were 'frankly critical of their own Government and people' (see AWM 54 883/2/97 FCR No. 94, British Troops in Egypt, 14 Aug. 1941, p. 2).
203. NA WO 193/453 Draft Morale Report, May–July 1942; ANZ WAII/1/DA508 Vol. 3, MEMCWS, No. XL (12–18 Aug. 1942), pp. 2–3.

Chapter 7 Victory in North Africa

1. Niall Barr, *Pendulum of War: The Three Battles of El Alamein* (London: Pimlico, 2005 [2004]), pp. 202–5. Lieut. Gen. William 'Strafer' Gott had been Churchill's first choice to take over Eighth Army, but he was killed when his plane was shot down on 7 Aug.

2. Nigel Hamilton, 'Montgomery, Bernard Law [Monty], First Viscount Montgomery of Alamein (1887–1976)', *Oxford Dictionary of National Biography* (Oxford University Press, 2004), online edn, May 2011, www.oxforddnb.com/view/article/31460, accessed 18 July 2017; Hew Strachan, *Military Lives* (Oxford University Press, 2002), pp. 309–12; B. L. Montgomery, *The Memoirs of Field-Marshal Montgomery of Alamein* (Barnsley: Pen & Sword, 2005 [1958]), pp. 23–48.
3. Nigel Nicolson, *Alex: The Life of Field Marshal Earl Alexander of Tunis* (London: Weidenfeld and Nicolson, 1973), pp. 21–2.
4. David Hunt, 'Alexander, Harold Rupert Leofric George, first Earl Alexander of Tunis (1891–1969)', *Oxford Dictionary of National Biography* (Oxford University Press, 2004), online edn, Sept. 2014, www.oxforddnb.com/view/article/30371, accessed 19 July 2017; Strachan, *Military Lives*), pp. 1–4.
5. Barr, *Pendulum of War*, pp. 202–5.
6. Ibid., p. 216. I. S. O. Playfair, *The Mediterranean and Middle East, Vol. III: British Fortunes Reach their Lowest Ebb* (Uckfield: Naval & Military Press, 2004 [1960]), p. 371, put the number of tanks at 386.
7. NA WO 201/2834 HQ Middle East Casualty Statistics. 8th Army, Summary of Battle Casualties (excluding sick) for Major Operations in Egypt, Libya and Tunisia during the period 2nd July 1942–14th May 1943 (based on figures reported by GHQ O2E MEF).
8. NA CAB 146/14 Enemy Documents Section, Appreciation No. 9, pp. 58–62.
9. John Ellis, *Brute Force: Allied Strategy and Tactics in the Second World War* (London: André Deutsch, 1990), pp. 263–7; Martin Kitchen, *Rommel's Desert War: Waging World War II in North Africa, 1941–1943* (Cambridge University Press, 2009), p. 295.
10. IWM BLM 27/1 Situation in Aug. 1942.
11. IWM BLM 50 Montgomery to Maj. Gen. F. E. W. Simpson, 12 Oct. 1942.
12. NA CAB 106/703 Address to Officers of HQ Eighth Army by Gen. Montgomery on Taking Over Command of the Army, 13 Aug. 1942.
13. Barnett, *The Desert Generals*, p. 304.
14. ANZ WAII/8/24 Conference HQ NZ Div., Sunday 16 Aug. 1942, Note of GOC's Address to COs.
15. ANZ WAII/1/DA508/1 Vol. 3 MEMCWS No. XLII (26 Aug.–2 Sept. 1942), p. 18.
16. J. L. Scoullar, *Battle for Egypt: The Summer of 1942. Official History of New Zealand in the Second World War 1939–1945* (Wellington: Historical Publications Branch, 1955), p. 148.
17. Brian Horrocks, *A Full Life* (London: Leo Cooper, 1974 [1960]), p. 114; IWM BLM 56 Francis de Guingand to the Editor of the *Sunday Times*, 15 Dec. 1958.
18. Hugh S. K. Mainwaring, *Three Score Years and Ten with Never a Dull Moment* (Printed Privately, 1976), p. 67.
19. ANZ WAII/1/DA/508/1 Vol. 3 MEMCWS, No. XLI (19–25 Aug. 1942), p. 1
20. ANZ WAII/1/DA 508/1 Vol. 3, MEMCWS, No. XLIII (3–9 Sept. 1942), p. 1.
21. BL L/P&J/12/654 MEMCWS No. CXXVI, 2–8 Sept. 1942, p. 6.
22. Raymond Callahan, *Churchill and His Generals* (Lawrence: University Press of Kansas, 2007), p. 141.
23. Jonathan Fennell, *Combat and Morale in the North African Campaign: The Eighth Army and the Path to El Alamein* (Cambridge University Press, 2011), pp. 82–3.
24. David Fraser, *And We Shall Shock Them: The British Army in the Second World War* (London: Cassell & Co., 1999), p. 237.
25. AWM 54 492/4/77 Panzerarmee Afrika Daily Report, 2 Sept. 1942.

26. SANDF, DOC, UWH, Draft Narratives, Box 316 War Diary of Panzer Army Africa 28 July–23 Oct. 1942, pp. 79–83. Reply to query about bombs dropped made on 6 Sept. 1942 by 19th Flak Division, 8 Sept. 1942.
27. ANZ WAII/1/DA 508/1 Vol. 3, MEMCWS, No. XLIV (10–16 Sept. 1942), p. 2.
28. Ibid., p. 1.
29. ANZ WAII/1/DA 508/1 Vol. 3, MEMCWS, No. XLV (17–23 Sept. 1942), p. 1.
30. LHCMA Alanbrooke Papers, Auchinleck to Brooke, 25 July 1942.
31. Barr, *Pendulum of War*, p. 219.
32. Ibid., pp. 231, 249–52.
33. I. S. O. Playfair and C. J. C. Molony, *The Mediterranean and Middle East, Vol. IV: The Destruction of the Axis Forces in Africa* (Uckfield: Naval & Military Press London, 2004 [1966]), pp. 8–10. These were the guns freed up by the equipping of the anti-tank regiments with 6-pounders.
34. Stephen A. Hart, *Colossal Cracks: Montgomery's 21st Army Group in Northwest Europe, 1944–45* (Mechanicsburg: Stackpole, 2007 [2000]).
35. John Buckley, *Monty's Men: The British Army and the Liberation of Europe* (London: Yale University Press, 2013), pp. 31–2.
36. Callahan, *Churchill and His Generals*, p. 145; Charles Forrester, 'Field Marshal Montgomery's Role in the Creation of the British 21st Army Group's Combined Armed Doctrine for the Final Assault on Germany', *The Journal of Military History*, 78 (Oct. 2014), p. 1301.
37. Tim Moreman, 'Jungle, Japanese and the Australian Army: Learning the Lessons of New Guinea', Symposium Paper, available at http://ajrp.awm.gov.au/ajrp/remember.nsf/pages/NT000015DE, accessed 6 June 2018, p. 6 of 13.
38. Patrick Rose, 'British Army Command Culture 1939–1945: A Comparative Study of British Eighth and Fourteenth Armies' (PhD thesis, King's College London, 2008), pp. 138–9.
39. Ibid., p. 136.
40. Ibid., p. 203.
41. Callahan, *Churchill and His Generals*, p. 112.
42. Rose, 'British Army Command Culture', p. 197.
43. Ibid., pp. 197–206; Stephen Brooks (ed.), *Montgomery and the Eighth Army* (London: The Bodley Head, 1991), p. 52; IWM BLM 11/3 9th Infantry Brigade Individual Training, 1937/1938, Memorandum No. 2.
44. Conscription was introduced in Apr. 1939.
45. NA WO 193/453 ECAC, Morale in the Army, Note by AG for consideration by the ECAC at their forty-eighth meeting to be held on 27 Feb. 1942, 25 Feb. 1942; NA WO 32/15772 Extract from the Minutes of the Forty-Ninth Meeting of the ECAC, 6 Mar. 1942.
46. Jeremy A. Crang, *The British Army and the People's War, 1939–1945* (Manchester University Press, 2000), p. 8; Roger Broad, *The Radical General: Sir Ronald Adam and Britain's New Model Army, 1941–46* (Stroud: Spellmount, 2013), pp. 15–88.
47. NA WO 193/453 ECAC, Morale in the Army, Note by AG for consideration by the ECAC at their forty-eighth meeting to be held on 27 Feb. 1942, 25 Feb. 1942; NA WO 32/15772 Extract from the Minutes of the Forty-Ninth Meeting of the ECAC, 6 Mar. 1942.
48. NA WO 259/62 Note by AG for consideration by the ECAC at their forty-eighth meeting to be held on 27 Feb. 1942.
49. NA WO 277/16 J. H. A. Sparrow, Army Morale, p. 5.
50. NA WO 32/15772 Extract from the Minutes of the Forty-Ninth Meeting of the ECAC, 6 Mar. 1942.

51. Ibid., p. 24; WO 193/453 Note by the AG for consideration by the ECAC at their forty-ninth meeting on 6 Mar. 1942.
52. NA WO 193/453 ECAC, Minutes of the Forty-Eighth Meeting held on 27 Feb. 1942; NA WO 32/15772 Extract from the Minutes of the Forty-Ninth Meeting of the ECAC, 6 Mar. 1942; NA WO 32/15772 Adam to Wilson, C-in-C Persia and Iraq, 2 Jan. 1943. From the start of 1942, Adam had been receiving monthly morale reports from divisional and district commands in the UK and Middle East Command, with the setting up of the Morale Committee, in March, the monthly reports were changed to quarterly reports.
53. LHCMA Adam 3/13 Narrative covering aspects of work as AG, WWII, Ch. 5: Morale and Discipline.
54. Robert H. Ahrenfeldt, *Psychiatry in the British Army in the Second World War* (London: Routledge & Kegan Paul, 1958), pp. 204–5.
55. Hew Strachan, 'Training, Morale and Modern War', *The Journal of Contemporary History*, 41(2) (2006), pp. 216–17.
56. Quoted ibid., p. 222.
57. Field-Marshal Earl Wavell, *The Good Soldier* (London: MacMillan and Co., 1948), p. 96; Strachan, 'Training, Morale and Modern War', p. 223. See also, James Kitchen, *The British Imperial Army in the Middle East: Morale and Military Identity in the Sinai and Palestine Campaigns, 1916–18* (London: Bloomsbury, 2014); Jonathan Boff, *Winning and Losing on the Western Front: The British Third Army and the Defeat of Germany in 1918* (Cambridge University Press, 2012); Alexander Watson, *Enduring the Great War: Combat, Morale and Collapse in the German and British Armies, 1914–1918* (Cambridge University Press, 2008).
58. David French, *Raising Churchill's Army: The British Army and the War against Germany 1919–1945* (Oxford University Press, 2000), p. 199.
59. NA WO 277/36, J. W. Gibb, Training in the Army, p. 197.
60. French, *Raising Churchill's Army*, p. 203.
61. Quoted in French, *Raising Churchill's Army*, p. 203.
62. Timothy Harrison Place, *Military Training in the British Army* (London: Frank Cass, 2000), p. 49. Battle drills (in their modern form) had been introduced to the British Army in June 1918 by Ivor Maxse, Inspector General of Training. His innovations came too late to have any significant effect on the performance of the British Expeditionary Force in the First World War.
63. Strachan, 'Training, Morale and Modern War', p. 217.
64. French, *Raising Churchill's Army*, p. 203.
65. Quoted ibid., p. 204.
66. Strachan, 'Training, Morale and Modern War', pp. 222–4; Alex Danchev, 'Dill, Sir John Greer (1881–1944)', *Oxford Dictionary of National Biography* (Oxford University Press, 2004), online edn, Jan. 2011, www.oxforddnb.com/view/article/32826, accessed 31 July 2017.
67. Harrison Place, *Military Training in the British Army*, p. 49.
68. French, *Raising Churchill's Army*, p. 204.
69. Ibid., pp. 204–6.
70. Harrison Place, *Military Training in the British Army*, Ch. 4; French, *Raising Churchill's Army*, p. 250. Patrick Rose has pointed out that by early 1942 many of Eighth Army's formations utilised battle drills, but to varying degrees of sophistication (see Rose, 'British Army Command Culture', p. 127).
71. IWM 99/1/2 Briggs, Eighth Army Training Memorandum No. 1 by B. L. Montgomery, 30 Aug. 1942; 'Montgomery's Address to the Middle East

Staff College, Haifa, 21 Sept. 1942', in Brooks (ed.), *Montgomery and the Eighth Army*, p. 54; Rose, 'British Army Command Culture', p. 139.

72. Harrison Place, *Military Training in the British Army*, p. 49.
73. Rose, 'British Army Command Culture', p. 139.
74. NA CAB 21/914 The Work of Army Psychiatrists in Relation to Morale, Jan. 1944, p. 2; French, *Raising Churchill's Army*, pp. 205–6.
75. NA WO 199/799 Note on Object of Battle Inoculation, n.d. but 1942.
76. Ibid.
77. NA WO 199/799 Training Noise Effects. To Under Sec of State, The War Office, 12 Aug. 1942 from Lieut. Gen. C-in-C, Eastern Command. Copy to GHQ Home Forces.
78. Quoted in French, *Raising Churchill's Army*, p. 206; Stephen Bull, *Second World War Infantry Tactics: The European Theatre* (Barnsley: Pen & Sword, 2012), p. 68.
79. LHCMA Adam 3/13 Narrative Covering Aspects of Work as AG, WWII, Ch. 2: Selection of Men and Leaders; Ahrenfeldt, *Psychiatry in the British Army in the Second World War*, p. 32.
80. LHCMA Adam 3/13 Narrative Covering Aspects of Work as AG, WWII, Ch. 1: Manpower, p. 3. In fact, the expansion had been carried out largely without the input of the War Office.
81. LHCMA Adam 3/13 Narrative Covering Aspects of Work as AG, WWII, Introduction.
82. Ibid.
83. Ahrenfeldt, *Psychiatry in the British Army in the Second World War*, pp. 37–8.
84. NA WO 163/50 The Army Council, Selection Tests for the Army (Report by the ECAC for Consideration by the Army Council on Tuesday, 17 June 1941), Paper No. A.C./P(41)40, 13 June 1941.
85. Ahrenfeldt, *Psychiatry in the British Army in the Second World War*, pp. 77–81.
86. Ibid., p. 78.
87. NA WO 32/11972 Notes on the Use Now Being Made of Psychologists in the Army, 1942.
88. Ahrenfeldt, *Psychiatry in the British Army in the Second World War*, p. 78.
89. NA WO 222/218 Circular to all Medical Officers, n.d., Morale, Discipline and Mental Fitness.
90. NA CAB 21/914 The Work of Army Psychiatrists in Relation to Morale, The War Office Director of Army Psychiatry, Jan. 1944.
91. LHCMA Adam 3/13 Narrative Covering Aspects of Work as AG, WWII, Ch. 1: Manpower, p. 9. Adam became AG about the same time as the Beveridge Committee was set up to look into manpower allocation in the Army.
92. NA WO 32/11972 Memorandum on Army Psychiatry, 1942.
93. Ahrenfeldt, *Psychiatry in the British Army in the Second World War*, p. 77; The extent of this problem is also highlighted in French, *Raising Churchill's Army*, pp. 243–4.
94. NA WO 163/50 The Army Council, Selection Tests for the Army (Report by the ECAC for Consideration by the Army Council on Tuesday, 17 June 1941), Paper No. A.C./P(41)40, 13 June 1941.
95. Ibid.
96. NA WO 163/50 Army Council, WO Progress Report June 1941 Selective Testing of Personnel.
97. NA WO 32/11972 Notes on the Use Now Being Made of Psychologists in the Army, 1942; WO 163/50 The Army Council, Selection Tests for the Army (Report

by the ECAC for Consideration by the Army Council on Tuesday 17 June 1941), Paper No. A.C./P(41)40, 13 June 1941.

98. Ahrenfeldt, *Psychiatry in the British Army in the Second World War*, p. 39.
99. NA WO 32/4726/MAC19 Detection of Psycho-neurosis by Medical Boards, Jan. 1942.
100. NA WO 163/50 Army Council, WO Progress Reports for Aug. and Oct. 1941; Use of Manpower in the Army, Pt 2 Appendix 'G', Selective Testing.
101. NA WO 163/51 Army Council, WO Progress Report July 1942; Crang, *The British Army and the People's War*, p. 15.
102. NA WO 32/11972 Extract from Conclusions of the 103rd (42) Meeting of the War Cabinet, Tuesday 4 Aug. 1942; G. W. B. James, 'Psychiatric Lessons from Active Service', *The Lancet*, 246(6382) (December, 1945), p. 801.
103. NA WO 165/101 War Diary of Directorate of Selection of Personnel, 25 Aug. 1941.
104. NA WO 32/11972 Correspondence between the ACS and the DAG, Letter from DAG to ACS, 7 Aug. 1942.
105. NA CAB 21/914 Extract from a Joint Memorandum by the Lord Privy Seal, the First Lord of the Admiralty, the Secretary of State for War, and the Secretary of State for Air, 17 Sept. 1942.
106. Ibid.
107. NA CAB 21/914 Expert Committee on the Work of Psychologists and Psychiatrists in the Services, Note by Maj. H. B. Craigie of the Dept of Army Psychiatry in the Middle East to Sir Stafford Cripps (Lord Privy Seal) on Psychiatric Cases in the Middle East, 21 July 1942.
108. Ibid.
109. LHCMA Adam 3/6/1 Report by the AG on his Tour to the Middle East, India and West Africa, Aug. 1942.
110. LHCMA Adam 3/3 Notes on the S. of S. Estimates Speech, Feb. 1943, AG's Department. As Adam suggested, these men would have started reaching the Middle East around Aug. 1942.
111. NA WO 163/51 Retention and Review of Suitability of Officers, Jan. 1942.
112. NA WO 231/14 Notes by Col. T. N. Grazebrook, lately Comd. in N. Africa, Sicily and Italy, 3 Jan. 1944.
113. NA WO 259/64 War Office, Press Conference, Wednesday 18 Mar. 1942.
114. NA WO 277/16 J. H. A. Sparrow, Army Morale, p. 22.
115. NA WO 216/61 Training of Officers, Report of a meeting called by the Secretary of State for War, 29 Jan. 1941.
116. NA WO 163/89 AG, The Officer Situation, 28 Sept. 1942; Ahrenfeldt, *Psychiatry in the British Army in the Second World War*, p. 54.
117. French, *Raising Churchill's Army*, p. 74.
118. NA WO 32/11972 Memorandum on Army Psychiatry, 1942.
119. NA WO 163/50 Army Council, War Office Progress Report, June 1941; Ahrenfeldt, *Psychiatry in the British Army in the Second World War*, p. 53.
120. NA WO 163/123 Army No. 72. Allocation of Man-Power in the Army: Statement of the WO views on the 22nd Report of the Select Committee on National Expenditure (Session 1940–1). Memorandum by the WO 20 Oct. 1941; Crang, *The British Army and the People's War*, pp. 30–1.
121. Ahrenfeldt, *Psychiatry in the British Army in the Second World War*, p. 57.
122. Ibid., p. 58.
123. LHCMA Adam 3/3 Notes for the S. of S. Estimates Speech, Feb. 1943. AG's Department.

124. Ahrenfeldt, *Psychiatry in the British Army in the Second World War*, pp. 60–1.
125. NA WO 32/11972 Memorandum on Army Psychiatry, 1942.
126. Ahrenfeldt, *Psychiatry in the British Army in the Second World War*, p. 66.
127. NA WO 204/10381 CMF and BNAF, ACR No. 32, 16–31 Oct. 1943, p. 15.
128. NA WO 32/11972 Memorandum on Army Psychiatry, 1942.
129. Crang, *The British Army and the People's War*, p. 34.
130. Ahrenfeldt, *Psychiatry in the British Army in the Second World War*, p. 66.
131. LHCMA Adam 3/3 Notes for the S. of S. Estimates Speech, Feb. 1943. AG's Department.
132. Parliamentary Debate, 5th Serv., Lords, 155: 1064–6; 26 May 1948.
133. Crang, *The British Army and the People's War*, p. 34.
134. Ibid., p. 33. For an overview of the very similar story of officer selection in the British Army in the First World War, see Gary Sheffield, *Leadership in the Trenches: Officer-Man Relations, Morale and Discipline in the British Army in the Era of the First World War* (London: Macmillan, 2000), pp. 29–40.
135. NA WO 193/453 Morale Committee Papers, Draft Morale Report, May–July 1942.
136. Ibid.
137. NA WO 199/1656 Extracts from Minutes of the Commander-in-Chief's Conference Held at GHQ, 14 May 1942.
138. ANZ WAII/1/DA508/1 Vol. 1 MEMCWS, No. XXXIX (5–11 Aug. 1942), p. 7. David C. Quilter, *No Dishonourable Name: The 2nd and 3rd Battalions, Coldstream Guards, 1939–46* (London: Clowes and Sons, 1947), p. 113 noted that an OCTU had been set up in Cairo at the end of 1940.
139. ANZ WAII/1/DA508/1 Vol. 3 MEMCWS, No. XLIII (3–9 Sept. 1942), p. 7.
140. ANZ WAII/1/DA508/1 Vol. 3 MEMCWS, No. XLIV (10–16 Sept. 1942), p. 2.
141. LHCMA Adam 3/13 Narrative Covering Aspects of Work as AG, WWII, Ch. 6: Welfare, pp. 1–3.
142. For this reason, he helped to introduce a centralised welfare system in the British Army to help regimental officers bear the load.
143. LHCMA Adam 3/13 Narrative Covering Aspects of Work as AG, WWII, Ch. 6: Welfare, pp. 4–5.
144. NA WO 277/4 Brig. M. C. Morgan, *Army Welfare* (The War Office, 1953), p. 28.
145. Ibid., p. 15.
146. Ibid.; NA WO 163/123 Army Pamphlet 'Welfare and Education', produced by the Director-General of Army Welfare and Education, Maj. Gen. H. Willans, in Mar. 1941, used the same language, p. 3.
147. NA WO 163/123 The Soldier's Welfare, Notes for Officers, 1941.
148. Ibid.
149. Ibid.
150. NA CAB 21/914 The Work of Army Psychiatrists in Relation to Morale, The War Office Director of Army Psychiatry, Jan. 1944; NA CAB 21/914 The Work of Army Psychiatrists in Relation to Morale, Appendix 'C', Battle Inoculation, Jan. 1944.
151. ANZ WAII/1/DA508/1 Vol. 3 MEMCWS, No. XLIII (23–29 Sept. 1942), p. 2.
152. ANZ WAII/1/DA508/1 Vol. 1 MEMCWS, No. XXXIX (5–11 Aug. 1942), pp. 18–19.
153. NA WO 32/15772 Extract from the Minutes of the Forty-Ninth Meeting of the ECAC, 6 Mar. 1942.
154. Richard Toye, *The Roar of the Lion: The Untold Story of Churchill's World War II Speeches* (Oxford University Press, 2013), pp. 97–205.

155. James T. Sparrow, *Warfare State: World War II Americans and the Age of Big Government* (Oxford University Press, 2011), pp. 3–9.
156. Ibid., p. 116; Mackenzie, *Politics and Military Morale*, p. 74.
157. See Crang, *The British Army and the People's War*, pp. 92–94.
158. NA WO 32/9429 Army Council Instruction 1415/1940.
159. LHCMA Adam 3/13 Various Administrative Aspects of the Second World War, Ch. 6, p. 3.
160. Crang, *The British Army and the People's War*, p. 116.
161. NA WO 163/123 Pamphlet: Army Welfare and Education by Maj. Gen. H Willans, Director-General of Army Welfare and Education. Reprint of an address given on 7 Mar. 1941 to the Royal Society of the Arts, p. 14.
162. NA WO 32/9735 Extract from the Minutes of the Eighth Meeting of the Army Council held on Tuesday 17 June 1941.
163. NA WO 32/9735 ABCA, Current Affairs in the Army: The Outline of a New Plan, 21 July 1941, p. 1.
164. Ibid., p. 4.
165. LHCMA Adam 3/13 Narrative Covering Aspects of Work as AG, WWII, Ch. VI, Welfare, p. 4.
166. NA WO 32/9735 ABCA, Current Affairs in the Army: The Outline of a New Plan, 21 July 1941, p. 6.
167. Ibid., p. 2.
168. NA WO 163/123 Army no. 71, Army Welfare and Education, Memorandum by the War Office, 12 Sept. 1941.
169. Ibid.
170. NA WO 32/9735 ABCA, Current Affairs in the Army: The Outline of a New Plan, 21 July 1941, p. 4.
171. MacKenzie, *Politics and Military Morale*, p. 94.
172. NA WO 32/10462, Appendix 'A' to EC.C/P(43)98, Brief Notes on the Development of Army Education from 1939–43. In Nov. 1940, it had been decided that the education initiative would be extended overseas and, as a result, a war establishment for the AEC was approved for the Middle East.
173. SANDF, DOC, Div. Docs., GP 1, Box 1: Army Routine Orders by Lieut. Gen. N. M. Ritchie, GOC-in-C, Eighth Army, 6 May 1942; Div. Docs., GP 1, Box 49, British Council Lecture Scheme, UDF Admin, HQ, MEF, 4 Apr. 1942.
174. SANDF, DOC, Div. Docs., GP 1, Box 1: Army Routine Orders by Lieut. Gen. N. M. Ritchie, GOC-in-C, Eighth Army, 6 May 1942. In small units and detachments, it was accepted that 'Welfare, Education and A.B.C.A.' could be organised by one officer.
175. T. H. Hawkins and L. J. F. Brimble, *Adult Education: The Record of the British Army* (London: Macmillan, 1947), p. 244.
176. Ibid., pp. 244–5.
177. 'British Way and Purpose' booklets were also produced locally.
178. Hawkins and Brimble, *Adult Education*, pp. 240–1. An interesting feature of ABCA in the Middle East, according to Hawkins and Brimble, was that it was well received by field force units but with little enthusiasm by the base units.
179. Ibid.
180. NA WO 277/35 War Office, Historical Monographs: 'History of Army Education'.
181. ANZ WAII/1/DA508 Vol. 1, MEMCWS, No. XL (12–18 Aug. 1942), p. 3.
182. Ibid.
183. MacKenzie, *Politics and Military Morale*, pp. 157–8.

184. NA WO 193/453 Draft Morale Report, May–July 1942; AWM 54 883/2/97 British Troops in Egypt No. 92 FCR Week Ending 31 July 1941, p. 4.
185. Robert S. Ehlers Jr, *The Mediterranean Air War: Airpower and Allied Victory in World War II* (Lawrence: University Press of Kansas, 2016), pp. 215–41.
186. NAA A5954/69: 529/9 AIF Participation in 8th Army Offensive, Oct./Nov. 1942; T. Duncan and M. Stout, *New Zealand Medical Services in Middle East and Italy* (Wellington: Historical Publications Branch, 1956), p. 376.
187. Barr, *Pendulum of War*, p. 276.
188. Ellis, *Brute Force*, p. 263.
189. Barr, *Pendulum of War*, p. 276.
190. IWM BLM 27 Diary Notes, 12 Aug.–23 Oct. 1942. pp. 7–8; AWM 3DRL 2632 2/2 Lightfoot, Memorandum No. 2 by Army Commander, 6 Oct. 1942.
191. IWM BLM 27 Diary Notes, 12 Aug.–23 Oct. 1942, pp. 7–8.
192. AWM 54 527/6/1 Pt 1, 9th Australian Division Report on Operations. El Alamein, 23 Oct.–5 Nov. 1942, p. 12.
193. Ibid.
194. IWM 430 PP/MCR/182 Wimberley, Scottish Soldier, pp. 36–7.
195. Barr, *Pendulum of War*, p. 264.
196. J. B. Salmond, *The History of the 51st Highland Division 1939–1945* (Durham: Pentland Press, 1994 [1953]), p. 22.
197. IWM 430 PP/MCR/182 Wimberley, Scottish Soldier, p. 35.
198. ANZ WAII/8/26 Freyberg to NZ Minister of Defence, 14 Oct. 1942.
199. Callahan, *Churchill and His Generals*, p. 140.
200. IWM BLM 28/4 Lightfoot, Memorandum No. 1 by Army Commander, 28 Sept. 1942.
201. Quoted in Keegan, *The Second World War*, p. 279.
202. IWM BLM 28/4 Lightfoot, Memorandum No. 1 by Army Commander, 28 Sept. 1942.
203. IWM 430 PP/MCR/182 Wimberley, Scottish Soldier, p. 40.
204. AWM 527/6/1 Pt 1, 9th Australian Division Report on Operation. El Alamein, 23 Oct.–5 Nov. 1942, p. 4.
205. IWM BLM 28/4 Lightfoot, Memorandum No. 1 by Army Commander, 28 Sept. 1942.
206. AWM 3DRL 2632 2/2 Lightfoot, Memorandum No. 2 by Army Commander, 6 Oct. 1942.
207. AWM 3 DRL 2632 Morshead Papers, El Alamein, 10 Oct. 1942.
208. IWM, BLM 53 Eighth Army, Personal Message from the Army Commander, 23 Oct. 1942.
209. Fraser, *And We Shall Shock Them*, p. 241; Barr, *Pendulum of War*, p. 308; Playfair and Molony, *The Mediterranean and Middle East, Vol. IV*, pp. 36, 42.
210. Fraser, *And We Shall Shock Them*, p. 240; Barr, *Pendulum of War*, p. 276.
211. Fraser, *And We Shall Shock Them*, p. 241.
212. NA WO 201/2596 Lessons from Operations: Training. Preliminary Draft Lessons from Operations Oct. and Nov. 1942. (Referring to the battle of El Alamein), p. 24.
213. Fraser, *And We Shall Shock Them*, pp. 241–2.
214. Callahan, *Churchill and His Generals*, p. 144.
215. Fraser, *And We Shall Shock Them*, pp. 241–2.
216. Ibid.
217. Ellis, *Brute Force*, p. 281.
218. Fraser, *And We Shall Shock Them*, pp. 244–5.

219. ANZ WAII/11/20 German–Italian Forces in Africa 23 Oct. 1942–23 Feb. 1943. From German War Narrative, 2 Nov. 1942.
220. Ellis, *Brute Force*, pp. 262–5; Barr, *Pendulum of War*, p. 276.
221. Ellis, *Brute Force*, p. 283.
222. Barr, *Pendulum of War*, p. 404. The figure for prisoners includes the pursuit up to 11 Nov. 1942.
223. SANDF, DOC, UWH, Draft Narratives, Box 316, 15th Panzer Division Report on the Battle of Alamein and the Retreat to Marsa El Brega, 23 Oct.–20 Nov. 1942.
224. Barr, *Pendulum of War*, p. 397.
225. See Fennell, Combat and Morale, Ch. 8.
226. IWM 99/1/2 Briggs, METM No. 7, Lessons from Operations, Oct. and Nov. 1942; NA WO 201/2596 Preliminary Draft Lessons from Operations Oct. and Nov. 1942.
227. NA WO 193/453 Morale Report, Nov. 1942–Jan. 1943.
228. AWM 54 527/6/1 Pt 1, Appendix 'A' to 9 Australian Division Report on Operations, El Alamein, 23 Oct.–5 Nov. 1942, Extracts from Draft Report by 30 Corps, 21 Nov. 1942, p. 1.
229. IWM BLM 62 Notes on the Maintenance of the Eighth Army and the Supporting Royal Air Force by Land, Sea and Air from El Alamein to Tunisia. Compiled by Q Staff, GHQ Cairo, 1942, p. 2; Salmond, *The History of the 51st Highland Division*, p. 25.
230. IWM 430 PP/MCR/182 Wimberley, 'Scottish Soldier', p. 26.
231. AWM 54 527/6/9 26 Australian Infantry Brigade, Report on Operation 'Lightfoot', 23 Oct.–5 Nov. 1942.
232. SANDF, DOC, CGS Papers (CGS) Gp 2 Box 654, Summary of Replies to a Questionnaire Submitted to Battalions in the 1st SA Div. Based on their Experiences in the 'Lightfoot' Operation in the Western Desert, Oct.–Nov. 1942, 22 Mar. 1943.
233. NA CAB 21/914 The Work of Army Psychiatrists in Relation to Morale, Appendix 'C', Battle Inoculation, Jan. 1944.
234. NA WO 231/10 Lessons from Tunisian Campaign, 1942–3.
235. AWM 54 423/11/43, MEMCFS, No. XLIX (21 Oct.–3 Nov. 1942), p. 27.
236. BL IOR L/PJ/12/654 Middle East Military Censorship Fortnightly Summary, No. CXXXIII (21 Oct.–4 Nov. 1942), p. 7.
237. ANZ WAII/1/DA 508/1 Vol. 3, MEMCWS, No. XLVII (30 Sept.–6 Oct. 1942), p. 1.
238. NA WO 193/453 Morale Report, Aug.–Oct. 1942.
239. NA WO 177/324 Monthly Statistical Report on Health of Eighth Army, Oct. and Nov. 1942.
240. Ben Shephard, *A War of Nerves: Soldiers and Psychiatrists 1914–1994* (London: Pimlico, 2002), p. 217; Mark Harrison, *Medicine and Victory: British Military Medicine in the Second World War* (Oxford University Press, 2004), p. 123.
241. NA WO 32/15773 Alexander to Sir James Grigg (Secretary of State for War) 6 Nov. 1942.
242. NA WO 277/7 Brig. A. B. McPherson, *Army: Discipline* (The War Office, 1950), p. 46.
243. IWM BLM 52 Eighth Army, Some Brief Notes for Senior Officers on the Conduct of Battle, Dec. 1942.

244. See e.g. AWM 54 527/6/1 Pt 1, Appendix 'A' to 9 Australian Division Report on Operations, El Alamein, 23 Oct.–5 Nov. 1942, Extracts from Draft Report by 30 Corps, 21 Nov. 1942, p. 1.
245. See e.g. Ellis, *Brute Force*, pp. 278–84; Keegan, *The Second World War*, p. 279.
246. Niall Barr, *Yanks and Limeys: Alliance Warfare in the Second World War* (London: Jonathan Cape, 2015), pp. 119–20. The idea of the Joint Chiefs of Staff was 'clearly based upon the Great War experience of both the British and Americans in working with the French'.
247. Ibid., pp. 156–61; NA WO 277/20 Planning, 1939–45, p. 204.
248. Barr, *Yanks and Limeys*, pp. 168–71.
249. Ibid., pp. 178–85.
250. Ibid., pp. 185–6; Douglas E. Delaney, *Corps Commanders: Five British and Canadian Generals at War, 1939–45* (Vancouver: University of British Columbia Press, 2011), p. 76.
251. Keegan, *The Second World War*, p. 280; Playfair, *The Mediterranean and Middle East, Vol. IV*, p. 126; Ken Ford, *Battleaxe Division: From Africa to Italy with the 78th Division, 1942–45* (Stroud: Sutton Publishing, 1999), p. 1.
252. Fraser, *And We Shall Shock Them*, pp. 246–7; Ian Gooderson, *A Hard Way to Make a War: The Allied Campaign in Italy in the Second World War* (London: Conway, 2008), pp. 19–20; Playfair, *The Mediterranean and Middle East, Vol. IV*, p. 116.
253. Gooderson, *A Hard Way to Make a War*, pp. 19–20.
254. Callahan, *Churchill and His Generals*, p. 149; Fraser, *And We Shall Shock Them*, p. 248.
255. Fraser, *And We Shall Shock Them*, pp. 250–1.
256. Gooderson, *A Hard Way to Make a War*, pp. 19–20.
257. Ellis, *Brute Force*, p. 298.
258. Callahan, *Churchill and His Generals*, p. 151; Playfair, *The Mediterranean and Middle East, Vol. IV*, pp. 323–6.
259. Reinforcements arriving for First Army would include 1st, 4th, 46th and 56th Infantry Divisions.
260. Fraser, *And We Shall Shock Them*, pp. 256–7; Callahan, *Churchill and His Generals*, p. 154; Playfair, *The Mediterranean and Middle East, Vol. IV*, pp. 338–53. These included 6th Armoured, 1st, 4th, 46th and 78th Divisions in First Army and 1st and 7th Armoured and 2nd New Zealand, 4th Indian, 50th Northumbrian, 51st Highland and 56th Infantry Divisions in Eighth Army.
261. AWM Morshead Papers, 3DRL 2632 2/16 Telegram from Leese to Morshead, 14 May 1943.
262. NA WO 204/10381 BNAF: ACR No. 18, 2–8 May 1943, p. 1.
263. NA WO 204/10381 BNAF: ACR No. 20, 16–22 May 1943, pp. 1–2.
264. IWM BLM 49 Montgomery to Alan Brooke, 15 Apr. 1943.
265. Quoted in David French, 'Colonel Blimp and the British Army: British Divisional Commanders in the War against Germany, 1939–1945', *The English Historical Review*, 111(444) (Nov. 1996), p. 1192.
266. Playfair, *The Mediterranean and Middle East, Vol. IV*, p. 460.
267. Stephen Bungay, *Alamein* (London: Aurum Press, 2002), pp. 196–7.
268. Rick Atkinson, *An Army at Dawn: The War in North Africa, 1942–1943* (London: Little, Brown, 2003), p. 537.
269. John Bierman and Colin Smith, *Alamein: War without Hate* (London: Penguin, 2003), p. 407.

Chapter 8 New Guinea and Burma

1. Jeffrey Grey, *A Military History of Australia* (Cambridge University Press, 1999), pp. 160–8. 2/2 Independent Company, 'Sparrow Force', continued to fight on in Timor for months after its capture in Feb. 1942.
2. Quoted in David Horner, 'Australia in 1942: A Pivotal Year', in Peter J. Dean (ed.), *Australia 1942: In the Shadow of War* (Cambridge University Press, 2013), pp. 15–16.
3. Peter J. Dean, 'Introduction', in Peter J. Dean (ed.), *Australia 1942: In the Shadow of War* (Cambridge University Press, 2013), p. 2.
4. Horner, 'Australia in 1942', in Dean (ed.), Australia 1942, p. 20; Karl James, 'On Australia's Doorstep: Kokoda and Milne Bay', in Peter J. Dean (ed.), *Australia 1942: In the Shadow of War* (Cambridge University Press, 2013), p. 200.
5. Horner, 'Australia in 1942', in Dean (ed.), *Australia 1942*, p. 16.
6. Jeffrey Grey, *The Australian Army* (Oxford University Press, 2001), p. 136.
7. Peter J. Dean, 'Military History and 1943: A Perspective 70 Years On', in Peter J. Dean (ed.), *Australia 1943: The Liberation of New Guinea* (Port Melbourne: Cambridge University Press, 2014), p. 1.
8. Albert Palazzo, 'The Overlooked Mission: Australia and Home Defence', in Peter J. Dean (ed.), *Australia 1942: In the Shadow of War* (Cambridge University Press, 2013), p. 59.
9. Peter J. Dean, *MacArthur's Coalition: US and Australian Operations in the Southwest Pacific Area, 1942–1945* (University Press of Kansas, 2018), Ch. 5; Grey, *A Military History of Australia*, p. 170.
10. Horner, 'Australia in 1942', in Dean (ed.), *Australia 1942*, p. 25; Kate Darian-Smith, 'The Home Front and the American Presence in 1942', in Peter J. Dean (ed.), *Australia 1942: In the Shadow of War* (Cambridge University Press, 2013), p. 76; David Horner, 'MacArthur and Curtin: Deciding Australian War Strategy in 1943', in Peter J. Dean (ed.), *Australia 1943: The Liberation of New Guinea* (Cambridge University Press, 2014), p. 26.
11. Dean, *MacArthur's Coalition*, Ch. 3.
12. He came twenty-second out of twenty-five in his first year and forty-seventh out of fifty-two in his second year at Quetta (see David Horner, *Blamey: The Commander-in-Chief* (St Leonards: Allen & Unwin, 1998), pp. 22, 585).
13. Carl Bridge, 'Blamey, Sir Thomas Albert (1884–1951)', *Oxford Dictionary of National Biography* (Oxford University Press, 2004), online edn, 2011, https://doi.org/10.1093/ref:odnb/31918, accessed 2 May 2017; Dean, *MacArthur's Coalition*, Ch. 3.
14. Grey, *The Australian Army*, p. 141.
15. Grey, *A Military History of Australia*, pp. 173–4.
16. Grey, *The Australian Army*, p. 138.
17. Dean, *MacArthur's Coalition*, Ch. 3.
18. Grey, *A Military History of Australia*, pp. 141, 173–4.
19. Darian-Smith, 'The Home Front and the American Presence in 1942', in Dean (ed.), Australia 1942, p. 77.
20. Grey, *The Australian Army*, p. 141.
21. Ibid., p. 115; John Pomeroy, 'A. P. Elkin: Public Morale and Propaganda', in Geoffrey Gray, Doug Munro and Christine Winter (eds.), *Scholars at War: Australian Social Scientists, 1939–1945* (Canberra: ANU Press, 2012), pp. 35–8.
22. Paul Hasluck, *Australia in the War of 1939–1945, Series Four: Civil, Vol. I: The Government and the People, 1939–1941* (Canberra: AWM, 1965), p. 413.

23. Pomeroy, 'A. P. Elkin: Public Morale and Propaganda', in Gray, Munro and Winter, *Scholars at War*, pp. 37–47.
24. Quoted in Michael Molkentin, 'Total War on the Australian Home Front, 1943–45', in Peter J. Dean (ed.), *Australia 1944–45: Victory in the Pacific* (Cambridge University Press, 2016), p. 98.
25. Grey, *The Australian Army*, p. 138.
26. Darian-Smith, 'The Home Front and the American Presence in 1942', in Dean (ed.), *Australia 1942*, pp. 73–4.
27. Molkentin, 'Total War on the Australian Home Front', in Dean (ed.), Australia 1944–45, p. 99.
28. David Lee, 'Politics and Government', in Joan Beaumont (ed.), *Australia's War, 1939–45* (Crows Nest: Allen & Unwin, 1996), pp. 82–106 (quoted in Molkentin, 'Total War on the Australian Home Front, 1943–45', in Dean (ed.), *Australia 1944–45*, p. 99).
29. Ross McMullin, 'Dangers and Problems Unprecedented and Unpredictable: The Curtin Government's Response to the Threat', in Peter J. Dean (ed.), *Australia 1942: In the Shadow of War* (Cambridge University Press, 2013), p. 96.
30. Grey, *The Australian Army*, p. 138.
31. Dean, *MacArthur's Coalition*, Ch. 3.
32. Eric Bergerud, *Touched with Fire: The Land War in the South Pacific* (London: Viking, 1996), pp. 8, 15; Horner, 'Australia in 1942', in Dean (ed.), *Australia 1942*, p. 20; Dean, *MacArthur's Coalition*, Ch. 5.
33. Grey, *A Military History of Australia*, p. 172.
34. Horner, 'Australia in 1942', in Dean (ed.), *Australia 1942*, pp. 19–20.
35. Dean, 'Military History and 1943', in Dean (ed.), *Australia 1943*, p. 3; Bergerud, *Touched with Fire*, pp. xvi–xvii.
36. Bergerud, *Touched with Fire*, p. 16. Rabaul was also significant as its possession helped protect the main Imperial Japanese Navy Pacific naval base at Truk (see Dean, *MacArthur's Coalition*, Ch. 5).
37. Dean, 'Introduction', in Dean (ed.), *Australia 1942*, p. 1; Horner, 'Australia in 1942', in Dean (ed.), *Australia 1942*, p. 20.
38. Horner, 'Australia in 1942', in Dean (ed.), *Australia 1942*, p. 19.
39. Ibid., p. 22; Bergerud, *Touched with Fire*, p. 9.
40. Rabaul was defended by extensive positions including 367 anti-aircraft weapons; 43 coastal guns; 6,543 machine guns, mortars, howitzers and grenade launchers; and 100,000 men (see Dean, *MacArthur's Coalition*, Ch. 5).
41. Ibid.
42. Dean, *MacArthur's Coalition*, Ch. 5.
43. Bergerud, *Touched with Fire*, p. 17.
44. Peter Williams, *The Kokoda Campaign 1942: Myth and Reality* (Melbourne: Cambridge University Press, 2012), p. 36, 46. Japanese divisions usually had three infantry regiments.
45. Ibid., pp. 36, 46, 79–80.
46. Ibid., pp. 152–5.
47. Dean, *MacArthur's Coalition*, Chapter 5.
48. James, 'On Australia's Doorstep', in Dean (ed.), *Australia 1942*, p. 202; Allan S. Walker, *Australia in the War of 1939–1945: Series Five, Medical, Vol. III: The Island Campaigns* (Canberra: AWM, 1957), p. 15.
49. Bergerud, *Touched with Fire*, p. 22.
50. James, 'On Australia's Doorstep', in Dean (ed.), *Australia 1942*, pp. 204–7.

51. Dean, *MacArthur's Coalition*, Ch. 5.
52. Ibid.
53. AWM 54 267/3/9 A Study of the Effects of Malaria Prevention in the Conservation of Manpower in the AMF, Oct. 1943–Mar. 1945, p. 1.
54. Williams, *The Kokoda Campaign 1942*, p. 168.
55. Allan S. Walker, *Clinical Problems of War* (Canberra: AWM, 1952), p. 689.
56. Dean, *MacArthur's Coalition*, Ch. 5.
57. James, 'On Australia's Doorstep', in Dean (ed.), *Australia 1942*, pp. 209–11.
58. AWM 61 S5/1/223 3rd and 4th Field Censorship Sections, Report to 0900 Hours, 30 Nov. 1942, p. 3.
59. NAA MP 742/1 211/7/139 Report on the Visit of ADMS to New Guinea, 12 June–23 June 1943.
60. James, 'On Australia's Doorstep', in Dean (ed.), *Australia 1942*, pp. 208–13; Dean, *MacArthur's Coalition*, Ch. 5.
61. James, 'On Australia's Doorstep', in Dean (ed.), *Australia 1942*, pp. 208–13; Peter J. Dean, 'Anzacs and Yanks: US and Australian Operations at the Beachhead Battles', in Peter J. Dean (ed.), *Australia 1942: In the Shadow of War* (Cambridge University Press, 2013), p. 224.
62. AWM 61 S5/1/223 3rd and 4th Field Censorship Sections, Report to 0900 Hours, 30 Nov. 1942, p. 4.
63. Adrian Threlfall, 'The Development of Australian Army Jungle Warfare Doctrine and Training, 1941–1945' (Doctoral thesis, Victoria University, 2008), pp. 130, 153.
64. Dean, 'Anzacs and Yanks', in Dean (ed.), *Australia 1942*, pp. 235–7; Dean, *MacArthur's Coalition*, Ch. 6.
65. Threlfall, 'The Development of Australian Army Jungle Warfare Doctrine and Training', pp. 204–6; Dean, *MacArthur's Coalition*, Ch. 7.
66. Dean, *MacArthur's Coalition*, Ch. 7.
67. Bergerud, *Touched with Fire*, p. 31. The Japanese would lose 25,000 men killed, 600 aircraft and twenty-four warships in the campaign.
68. Hiroyuki Shindo, 'The Japanese Army's Search for a New South Pacific Strategy', in Peter J. Dean (ed.), *Australia 1943: The Liberation of New Guinea* (Port Melbourne: Cambridge University Press, 2014), p. 70; Bergerud, *Touched with Fire*, p. 35; Dean, *MacArthur's Coalition*, Ch. 6.
69. Shindo, 'The Japanese Army's Search for a New South Pacific Strategy', in Dean (ed.), *Australia 1943*, pp. 70–1.
70. Peter J. Dean, 'MacArthur's War: Strategy, Command and Plans for the 1943 Offensives', in Peter J. Dean (ed.), *Australia 1943: The Liberation of New Guinea* (Port Melbourne: Cambridge University Press, 2014), p. 47; Dean, *MacArthur's Coalition*, Ch. 8.
71. The organisation of the Australian Army became very complicated in 1942/3. While 17th Brigade started out life in 6th Division, and would go back there later in the war, in 1942/3 it moved between formations. In this period, brigades (both AIF and militia) were used as the core combat formations of the Army in the SWPA and they were swapped between Division and Force HQs depending on the conditions on the ground. This only settled down in 1945 when the AIF had to be maintained in its traditional formations as the militia was restricted to fighting in Australian mandated territory only. My thanks to Peter Dean for corresponding with me on this matter.

72. Karl James, 'The "Salamaua Magnet"', in Peter J. Dean (ed.), *Australia 1943: The Liberation of New Guinea* (Port Melbourne: Cambridge University Press, 2014), pp. 189–90.
73. Quoted ibid., pp. 191.
74. Ibid., pp. 191–2.
75. Grey, *The Australian Army*, p. 143; James, 'The "Salamaua Magnet"', in Dean (ed.), *Australia 1943*, p. 192; Dean, *MacArthur's Coalition*, Ch. 7.
76. Louis Allen, *Burma: The Longest War, 1941–45* (London: Phoenix Press, 2000 [1984]), pp. 637–8; S. W. Kirby, *The War against Japan, Vol. I: The Loss of Singapore* (Uckfield: The Naval & Military Press, 2004 [1957]), pp. 522–7; S. W. Kirby, *The War against Japan, Vol. II: India's Most Dangerous Hour* (Uckfield: The Naval & Military Press, 2004 [1958]), pp. 25, 442; Timothy Moreman, *The Jungle, the Japanese and the British Commonwealth Armies at War, 1941–45: Fighting Methods, Doctrine and Training for Jungle Warfare* (London: Frank Cass, 2005), p. 37.
77. Moreman, *The Jungle, the Japanese and the British Commonwealth Armies at War*, p. 77.
78. Dean, 'Anzacs and Yanks', in Dean (ed.), *Australia 1942*, p. 236.
79. Dean, *MacArthur's Coalition*, Ch. 6.
80. James, 'On Australia's Doorstep', in Dean (ed.), *Australia 1942*, pp. 201–2; AWM 54 481/1/25 Report of the ADMS Visit to Maroubra Force, 1942, p. 2 and Appendix A; AWM 54 481/1/25 Medical Situation Maroubra Force as at 19 Sept. 1942, Pt II.
81. Dean, *MacArthur's Coalition*, Ch. 6.
82. James, 'On Australia's Doorstep', in Dean (ed.), *Australia 1942*, p. 213.
83. Horner, 'Australia in 1942', in Dean (ed.), *Australia 1942*, p. 24; Richard B. Frank, 'South Pacific Turning Point: Guadalcanal', in Karl James (ed.), *Kokoda: Beyond the Legend* (Cambridge University Press, 2017), p. 87.
84. Andrew N. Buchanan, 'The War Crisis and the Decolonization of India, December 1941–September 1942: A Political and Military Dilemma', *Global War Studies*, 8(2) (2011), p. 6.
85. Ibid., p. 14.
86. John Darwin, *The Empire Project: The Rise and Fall of the British World-System, 1830–1970* (Cambridge University Press, 2009), pp. 507–8.
87. Ibid., pp. 506–8. See also Nicholas Owen, 'War and Britain's Political Crisis in India', in Brian Brivati and Harriet Jones (eds.), *What Difference Did the War Make?* (London: Leicester University Press, 1993), pp. 106–29; Buchanan, 'The War Crisis and the Decolonization of India', p. 20. Cripps left India on 12 Apr. 1942; Darwin, *The Empire Project*, pp. 508–11.
88. Owen, 'War and Britain's Political Crisis in India', in Brivati and Jones (eds.), *What Difference Did the War Make?*, p. 109; Darwin, *The Empire Project*, pp. 507–8, 516.
89. Daniel Marston, *The Indian Army and the End of the Raj* (Cambridge University Press, 2014), Ch. 2 fn. 286.
90. Robert Johnson, 'The Army in India and Responses to Low-Intensity Conflict, 1936–1946', *Journal of the Society for Army Historical Research*, 89(358) (2011), p. 174; Owen, 'War and Britain's Political Crisis in India', p. 116; Darwin, *The Empire Project*, pp. 507–8; Srinath Raghaven, *India's War: The Making of Modern South Asia, 1939–1945* (London: Penguin, 2017), p. 272.
91. Quoted in Johnson, 'The Army in India and Responses to Low-Intensity Conflict', p. 175; Raghaven, *India's War*, p. 272.

92. BL L/P&J/12/654 MEMCWS No. CXXVI, 2–8 Sept. 1942, pp. 2–5.
93. BL L P&J/12/654 MEMCWS No. CXXV, 19–25 Aug. 1942, p. 3.
94. Raymond Callahan, *Burma, 1942–1945* (London: Davis Poynter, 1978), p. 48; Moreman, *The Jungle, the Japanese and the British Commonwealth Armies at War*, p. 64; Marston, *The Indian Army and the End of the Raj*, Ch. 2.
95. Owen, 'War and Britain's Political Crisis in India', in Brivati and Jones (eds.), *What Difference Did the War Make?*, p. 116; Darwin, *The Empire Project*, pp. 507–8, 516.
96. Judith M. Brown, *Modern India: The Origins of an Asian Democracy* (Oxford University Press, 1994), pp. 324–5.
97. Moreman, *The Jungle, the Japanese and the British Commonwealth Armies at War*, p. 64.
98. NA WO 222/1571 Psychiatry – Arakan Campaign, n.d., p. 3.
99. BL L P&J/12/654 MEMCWS No. CXXV, 19–25 Aug. 1942, pp. 2–7; BL L P&J/12/654 MEMCWS No. CXXVI, 26 Aug.–1 Sept. 1942, pp. 1, 4–5, 8.
100. BL L P&J/12/654 MEMCWS No. CXXV, 19–25 Aug. 1942, pp. 5–8.
101. BL L/WS/1/939 The AG in India's Committee on Morale of the Army in India, 1st Quarterly Report, Nov. 1942–Jan. 1943, p. 5.
102. BL L/P&J/12/654 MEMCWS No. CXXVI, 26 Aug.–1 Sept. 1942, p. 10.
103. Quoted in Raghaven, *India's War*, p. 275.
104. WO 222/1571 Psychiatry – Arakan Campaign, n.d., p. 3.
105. Quoted in Callahan, *Burma*, p. 43.
106. Around the same time, as Slim withdrew Burcorps through the blazing oilfields at Yenangyaung, Wavell sent a similar note to his Chief of Staff.
107. Callahan, *Burma*, p. 13.
108. Ibid., 43–61; Daniel Marston, *Phoenix from the Ashes: The Indian Army in the Burma Campaign* (Westport: Praeger, 2003), p. 86.
109. Callahan, *Burma*, pp. 48–9.
110. Marston, *Phoenix from the Ashes*, p. 79; Moreman, *The Jungle, the Japanese and the British Commonwealth Armies at War*, pp. 50–8.
111. Callahan, *Burma*, pp. 43–61; Marston, *Phoenix from the Ashes*, p. 86.
112. Callahan, *Burma*, pp. 43–61; Marston, *Phoenix from the Ashes*, p. 86; Raghaven, *India's War*, p. 308.
113. Marston, *Phoenix from the Ashes*, p. 79; Moreman, *The Jungle, the Japanese and the British Commonwealth Armies at War*, pp. 50–8.
114. Marston, *Phoenix from the Ashes*, pp. 88–90; Callahan, *Burma*, pp. 62–3; Patrick Rose, 'British Army Command Culture 1939–1945: A Comparative Study of British Eighth and Fourteenth Armies' (PhD thesis, King's College London, 2008), p. 139.
115. Moreman, *The Jungle, the Japanese and the British Commonwealth Armies at War*, pp. 67–76.; Marston, *Phoenix from the Ashes*, pp. 88–90; Callahan, *Burma*, pp. 62–3; Rose, 'British Army Command Culture', p. 139.
116. Callahan, *Burma*, p. 63; Moreman, *The Jungle, the Japanese and the British Commonwealth Armies at War*, p. 77.
117. Callahan, *Burma*, pp. 63.
118. Quoted in Moreman, *The Jungle, the Japanese and the British Commonwealth Armies at War*, p. 75.
119. Ibid.
120. BL L/WS/1/939 General Staff Branch (MI Directorate), Report on the Morale of the Army in India, Feb.–Apr. 1943, p. 1.

121. BL L/WS/1/939 The AG in India's Committee on Morale of the Army in India, 1st Quarterly Report, Nov. 1942–Jan. 1943, pp. 1–2, 5.
122. BL L/WS/1/939 General Staff Branch (MI Directorate), Report on the Morale of the Army in India, Feb.–Apr. 1943, p. 2.
123. BL L/WS/1/939 Morale Report Aug.–Oct. 1943, Pt 1, British Troops, p. 9.
124. BL L/WS/1/939 General Staff Branch (MI Directorate), Report on the Morale of the Army in India, Feb.–Apr. 1943, p. 5.
125. BL L/WS/1/939 General Staff Branch (MI Directorate), Report on the Morale of the Army in India, May–July 1943, p. 4.
126. BL L/WS/1/939 General Staff Branch (MI Directorate), Report on the Morale of the Army in India, Feb.–Apr. 1943, p. 6.
127. F. A. E. Crew, *The Army Medical Services, Campaigns, Vol. V: Burma* (London: HMSO, 1966), p. 608 Table 50.
128. Ibid.
129. WO 222/1571 Psychiatry – Arakan Campaign, n.d., p. 3. The division was not used in action again and was converted later into a training formation.
130. Rose, 'British Army Command Culture', Ch. 4.
131. Callahan, *Burma*, p. 63.
132. Quoted in Moreman, *The Jungle, the Japanese and the British Commonwealth Armies at War*, p. 78.
133. Quoted ibid., pp. 78–80.

Chapter 9 The Mediterranean

1. Ian Gooderson, *A Hard Way to Make a War: The Allied Campaign in Italy in the Second World War* (London: Conway, 2008), pp. 27–8.
2. Ibid., p. 30.
3. Ibid., p. 33; Niall Barr, *Pendulum of War: The Three Battles of El Alamein* (London: Pimlico, 2005 [2004]), Map 2.
4. Gooderson, *A Hard Way to Make a War*, pp. 30–33; Carlo D'Este, *Bitter Victory: The Battle for Sicily 1943* (London: Aurum, 1988), p. 51.
5. D'Este, *Bitter Victory*, pp. 72–9; Gooderson, *A Hard Way to Make a War*, pp. 39–79; David Fraser, *And We Shall Shock Them: The British Army in the Second World War* (London: Cassell & Co., 1999), p. 262.
6. D'Este, *Bitter Victory*, pp. 154–5.
7. SADF UWH Box 346 Medical History of the Campaign in Sicily, July–Aug. 1943, p. 1.
8. Gooderson, *A Hard Way to Make a War*, pp. 75–8; Robert S. Ehlers Jr, *The Mediterranean Air War: Airpower and Allied Victory in World War II* (Lawrence: University Press of Kansas, 2016), pp. 294–300.
9. They launched 42,227 sorties, destroying 323 German and 105 Italian aircraft for the loss of 250 of their own.
10. Gooderson, *A Hard Way to Make a War*, pp. 75–8. The attack involved the release of 5,324 tons of bombs over 8 square miles of island.
11. NA WO 204/10381 BNAF: ACR No. 24, 20–30 June 1943, p. 9; D'Este, *Bitter Victory*, p. 216.
12. Gooderson, *A Hard Way to Make a War*, pp. 75–8.
13. Ibid., p. 49; D'Este, *Bitter Victory*, pp. 84–5.
14. Gooderson, *A Hard Way to Make a War*, p. 66; D'Este, *Bitter Victory*, pp. 188–9.
15. Gooderson, *A Hard Way to Make a War*, p. 66–7; D'Este, *Bitter Victory*, pp. 181–8.

16. Ibid., pp. 66–8, 72–3; Fraser, *And We Shall Shock Them*, p. 261; John Ellis, *Brute Force: Allied Strategy and Tactics in the Second World War* (London: André Deutsch, 1990), pp. 307–9.
17. Ellis, *Brute Force*, p. 307.
18. D'Este, *Bitter Victory*, p. 579; J. B. Higham and E. A. Knighton, *Movements* (London: The War Office, 1955), p. 351.
19. Ellis, *Brute Force*, pp. 307–9.
20. Fraser, *And We Shall Shock Them*, p. 261; Gooderson, *A Hard Way to Make a War*, p. 61.
21. Fraser, *And We Shall Shock Them*, p. 262; Gooderson, *A Hard Way to Make a War*, p. 61. These corps comprised of four infantry divisions, 5th, 50th, 51st and 1st Canadian, one independent infantry and two armoured brigades, and one Canadian army tank brigade. The 46th and 78th Divisions were in reserve. The 1st Airborne Division was to provide one airlanding brigade (glider-borne) for operations immediately north of the beachhead.
22. D'Este, *Bitter Victory*, pp. 145–50.
23. SANDF, DOC, UWH Box 346 Medical History of the Campaign in Sicily, July–Aug. 1943, pp. 12–14.
24. Gooderson, *A Hard Way to Make a War*, pp. 71–2.
25. LAC T 17,924 Extract from Middle East Field Censorship Summary No. 69, 28 July–10 Aug. 1943.
26. R. N. Gale, *With the 6th Airborne Division in Normandy* ((London: Sampson Low, Marston & Co., 1948), pp. 21–2.
27. Gooderson, *A Hard Way to Make a War*, pp. 80–1; Gale, *With the 6th Airborne Division in Normandy*, pp. 21–2.
28. Gooderson, *A Hard Way to Make a War*, p. 105.
29. D'Este, *Bitter Victory*, p. 310.
30. NA WO 204/10381 BNAF: ACR No. 24, 20–30 June 1943, p. 3.
31. LAC T 17,924 Field Censors (Home): HM Transports, Report on Mail Received from the Sicilian Invasion Force, 1–9 July 1943.
32. Ibid.
33. NA WO 204/10381 BNAF: ACR No. 25, 1–15 July 1943, p. 5.
34. Fraser, *And We Shall Shock Them*, p. 263.
35. Gooderson, *A Hard Way to Make a War*, pp. 93–5; D'Este, *Bitter Victory*, pp. 356–96.
36. Ellis, *Brute Force*, pp. 314;
37. Fraser, *And We Shall Shock Them*, p. 264.
38. Ibid., pp. 264–5; SANDF, DOC, UWH Box 346 Medical History of the Campaign in Sicily, July–Aug. 1943, p. 1.
39. SANDF, DOC, UWH Box 346 Medical History of the Campaign in Sicily, July–Aug. 1943, pp. 12–14.
40. Fraser, *And We Shall Shock Them*, pp. 266–7.
41. Cyril Ray, *Algiers to Austria: A History of 78 Division in the Second World War* (London: Eyre & Spottiswoode, 1952), p. 69.
42. Fraser, *And We Shall Shock Them*, pp. 267–8.
43. Gooderson, *A Hard Way to Make a War*, p. 100.
44. D'Este, *Bitter Victory*, pp. 552, 597; SANDF, DOC, UWH Box 346 Medical History of the Campaign in Sicily, July–Aug. 1943, pp. 1–2; LAC Vol. 18,576 File No. 133/065 (D8) Allied Casualties in Sicilian Campaign, puts the total for Eighth Army at 11,843 and Seventh Army at 6,896. Anglo-Canadian casualties can be broken down into 2,062 killed, 7,137 wounded and 2,644 missing in action. The American

statistics were 2,237 killed, 5,946 wounded and 598 missing. German casualties were 4,325 killed, 17,944 wounded and 4,325 POWs, while the Italian figures were 2,000 killed, 5,000 wounded and approximately 137,000 missing or captured.

45. Gooderson, *A Hard Way to Make a War*, pp. 93, 100; D'Este, *Bitter Victory*, pp. 513–15.
46. Alan Allport, *Browned Off and Bloody-Minded: The British Soldier Goes to War 1939–1945* (London: Yale University Press, 2015), p. 154.
47. Fraser, *And We Shall Shock Them*, p. 265.
48. See e.g. Ellis, *Brute Force*, p. 313.
49. Ibid., p. 313.
50. As for Figure 9.1, NA WO 201/2834 HQ Middle East Casualty Statistics. Eighth Army, Summary of Battle Casualties (excluding sick) for Major Operations in Egypt, Libya and Tunisia during the period July 1942–May 1943 (based on figures reported by GHQ O2E MEF). Figures for infantry include those designated 'infantry' and 'foot guards'. Figures for artillery include only 'Field and Anti-Tank Units'. They do not include 'Anti-Aircraft and Coastal' units.
51. David French, *Raising Churchill's Army: The British Army and the War against Germany 1919–1945* (Oxford University Press, 2000), pp. 265–7.
52. Gooderson, *A Hard Way to Make a War*, pp. 104, 128, 131.
53. Ibid., pp. 104, 131.
54. Gooderson, *A Hard Way to Make a War*, p. 104, 131.
55. Ibid., p. 127.
56. Stephen Brooks (ed.), *Montgomery and the Eighth Army* (London: The Bodley Head, 1991), p. 145.
57. NA WO 204/10381 BNAF, ACR No. 25, 1–15 July 1943, p. 3.
58. NA WO 204/10381 BNAF, ACR No. 27, 1–15 Aug. 1943, pp. 2–3.
59. Robert H. Ahrenfeldt, *Psychiatry in the British Army in the Second World War* (London: Routledge & Kegan Paul, 1958), pp. 185–6.
60. NA WO 177/325 Consolidated Statistics for Eighth Army, 10–31 July 1943; NA WO 177/325 Eighth Army, Statistics for Month of Aug. 1943; David J. Bercuson, *Maple Leaf against the Axis: Canada's Second World War* (Calgary: Red Deer Press, 2004), p. 163.
61. Alan Jeffreys, *Approach to Battle: Training the Indian Army During the Second World War* (Solihull: Helion, 2016), p. 118.
62. Gooderson, *A Hard Way to Make a War*, pp. 103–4.
63. John A. English, *The Canadian Army and the Normandy Campaign: A Study of Failure in High Command* (London: Praeger, 1991), pp. 107–19.
64. Bercuson, *Maple Leaf against the Axis*, p. 160. See also William J. McAndrew, 'Fire or Movement? Canadian Tactical Doctrine, Sicily – 1943', *Military Affairs*, 51(3) (July 1987), pp. 141–5.
65. Gooderson, *A Hard Way to Make a War*, p. 108; McAndrew, 'Fire or Movement?', pp. 141–2.
66. McAndrew, 'Fire or Movement?', pp. 142–3.
67. Ibid., pp. 142–4; Bercuson, *Maple Leaf against the Axis*, pp. 149–50.
68. Gooderson, *A Hard Way to Make a War*, pp. 37–8.
69. Ibid., pp. 145–7.
70. Ibid., pp. 186–7.
71. Ibid., p. 191.
72. Fraser, *And We Shall Shock Them*, pp. 270–2; Gooderson, *A Hard Way to Make a War*, pp. 176, 192.
73. Gooderson, *A Hard Way to Make a War*, p. 189.

74. Ibid., pp. 183–4, 197.
75. Ibid., pp. 199–206.
76. Ibid., pp. 212–13.
77. Fraser, *And We Shall Shock Them*, p. 272.
78. Rick Atkinson, *The Day of Battle: The War in Sicily and Italy, 1943–1944* (London: Little, Brown, 2007), p. 221; Hugh Pond, *Salerno* (London: William Kimber, 1961), pp. 155–60.
79. Gooderson, *A Hard Way to Make a War*, p. 215. Gooderson argues that he would most likely have removed VI Corps and used it to reinforce X Corps.
80. Fraser, *And We Shall Shock Them*, p. 272.
81. LAC Vol. 10708 File No. 56-16-3/Int, German Army Special Tactical Study No. 30, German Views on the Normandy Landing, 28 Nov. 1944.
82. Gooderson, *A Hard Way to Make a War*, p. 215.
83. NA WO 204/10381 BNAF, ACR No. 29, 1–15 Sept. 1943, p. 2.
84. NA CAB 101/224 D. F. Butler, The British Soldier in Italy, Sept. 1943–June 1944, p. 8.
85. Fraser, *And We Shall Shock Them*, p. 269.
86. Gooderson, *A Hard Way to Make a War*, pp. 210–11, 219.
87. Fraser, *And We Shall Shock Them*, p. 274.
88. Ibid., pp. 274–5.
89. Gooderson, *A Hard Way to Make a War*, p. 226.
90. Ibid., pp. 229–33; Fraser, *And We Shall Shock Them*, p. 277; C. J. C. Molony, *The Mediterranean and Middle East, Vol. V: The Campaign in Sicily 1943 and the Campaign in Italy, 3rd September 1943 to 31st March 1944* (Uckfield: Naval & Military Press, 2004 [1973]), p. 475.
91. Brooks, *Montgomery and the Eighth Army*, p. 305.
92. AWM 54 624/5/6 Medical Aspects of the Campaign in Italy, 1943–45; WO 177/345 DDMS 10 Corps; WO 177/346 DDMS 10 Corps.
93. Quoted in Gooderson, *A Hard Way to Make a War*, p. 227.
94. Ellis, *Brute Force*, pp. 323–8. By the end of Nov. 1943, the Germans had 229 tanks and 173 assault guns compared to almost 2,000 medium tanks deployed by the Allies.
95. C. J. Dick, 'The Operational Employment of Soviet Armour in the Great Patriotic War', in J. P. Harris and F. H. Toase (eds.), *Armoured Warfare* (London: B. T. Batsford Ltd, 1990), p. 107.
96. Gooderson, *A Hard Way to Make a War*, pp. 102, 225, 234.
97. Fraser, *And We Shall Shock Them*, pp. 275–6.
98. NA WO 231/8 Directorate of Military Training, Lessons from the Italian Campaign, 18 Dec. 1943. Quoted in French, *Raising Churchill's Army*, p. 273.
99. Gooderson, *A Hard Way to Make a War*, p. 225.
100. Ibid.
101. Ibid., pp. 234–6.
102. WO 177/326 Quarterly Report of DDMS Eighth Army, Dec. 1943–Feb. 1944; Gooderson, *A Hard Way to Make a War*, p. 237.
103. Gooderson, *A Hard Way to Make a War*, pp. 241–6.
104. Fraser, *And We Shall Shock Them*, p. 277.
105. Gooderson, *A Hard Way to Make a War*, pp. 246–7.
106. Fraser, *And We Shall Shock Them*, p. 277.
107. NA WO 177/325 Medical Diaries DDMS 8th Army Jan.–Dec. 1943; SANDF, DOC, UWH Box 345 Monthly Bulletin of Health Statistics, The War Office, May 1945; W. Franklin Mellor (ed.), *Casualties and Medical Statistics* (London:

HMSO, 1972), pp. 237–71; NA WO 177/163 AFHQ DDMS, 1942–5; ANZ Freyberg Papers; WAII/1/DA3/1/1 to DA3/1/16 DDMS 2NZEF, Jan. 1941–Jan. 1946; T. Duncan and M. Stout, *New Zealand Medical Services in Middle East and Italy* (Wellington: Historical Publications Branch, 1956), pp. 230–1, 579, 638-40, 692; SANDF, DOC, UWH Box 344 Medical, Campaign in Italy, 6 Division, 1944–5.

108. NA WO 204/10381 CMF and BNAF, ACR No. 34, 16 Nov.–15 Dec. 1943, p. A2.
109. NA WO 204/10381 CMF and BNAF, ACR No. 35, 16–31 Dec. 1943, pp. A3–4.
110. Molony, *The Mediterranean and Middle East, Vol. V*, pp. 429–73.
111. Terry Copp and Bill McAndrew, *Battle Exhaustion: Soldiers and Psychiatrists in the Canadian Army, 1939–1945* (London: McGill-Queen's University Press, 1990), p. 58.
112. NA WO 177/326 Quarterly Report of DDMS Eighth Army, Dec. 1943–Feb. 1944; LAC Vol. 12,559 Medical History of the War, 1 Canadian Corps; LAC Vol. 12,559 File No. 11/AAI 1 Div/1 1 Can. Inf. Div., Quarterly Reports, 1943–5; LAC Vol. 15,651 War Diary, Medical Branch HQ 1 Canadian Corps; LAC Vol. 12,559 File No. 11/AAI 1Corps/1 General Medical Correspondence, 1st Canadian Corps.
113. Molony, *The Mediterranean and Middle East, Vol. V*, p. 508.
114. NA WO 177/326 Quarterly Report of DDMS Eighth Army, Dec. 1943–Feb. 1944; LAC Vol. 12,559 Medical History of the War, 1 Canadian Corps; LAC Vol. 12,559 File No. 11/AAI 1 Div/1 1 Can. Inf. Div., Quarterly Reports, 1943–5; LAC Vol. 15,651 War Diary, Medical Branch HQ 1 Canadian Corps; LAC Vol. 12,559 File No. 11/AAI 1Corps/1 General Medical Correspondence, 1st Canadian Corps.
115. Copp and McAndrew, *Battle Exhaustion*, pp. 65, 206; Jonathan Fennell, *Combat and Morale in the North African Campaign: The Eighth Army and the Path to El Alamein* (Cambridge University Press, 2011), pp. 32–3.
116. Figures for the fighting from Nov. 1944–May 1945 were not available, but it is highly likely that they did not reach the levels of Dec. 1943. As for Table 9.1, see LHCMA Adam Papers Box 2 Casualties General, Monthly Gross Battle Casualty Rates, Percentages of Troops Engaged (as Shown on Operational Order of Battle, n.d. but 1945. It is noticeable that the New Zealand casualty rate is lower than that indicated in Figure 11.2. This is likely caused by the fact that the rates in Figure 11.2 are for the whole NZEF, while the figures presented here are for units engaged on the front line only. Figures are adjusted for a thirty-day month.
117. Copp and McAndrew, *Battle Exhaustion*, pp. 55–63.
118. NA WO 177/326 Quarterly Report of DDMS Eighth Army, Dec. 1943–Feb. 1944; AWM 54 624/5/6 Medical Aspects of the Campaign in Italy, 1943–5, p. 59; F. A. E. Crew, *The Army Medical Services, Campaigns, Vol. III: Sicily, Italy and Greece (1944–45)* (Uckfield: Naval & Military Press, 2014 [1957]), p. 512.
119. NA WO 177/326 Quarterly Report of DDMS Eighth Army, Dec. 1943–Feb. 1944; Crew, *The Army Medical Services, Vol. III: Sicily, Italy and Greece*, p. 512. Its weekly sickness rates for the weeks ending 18 and 25 Dec. and 1 and 8 Jan. 1944 were 17.5, 17.1, 20.1 and 19.3 respectively.
120. Crew, *The Army Medical Services, Vol. III: Sicily, Italy and Greece*, pp. 512–16.
121. NA CAB 101/224 D. F. Butler, The British Soldier in Italy, Sept. 1943–June 1944, pp. 9–12.
122. AWM 54 624/5/6 Medical Aspects of the Campaign in Italy, 1943–5, p. 21.
123. Brook, *Montgomery and the Eighth Army*, p. 318.

124. Gooderson, *A Hard Way to Make a War*, p. 97.
125. NA WO 204/10381 CMF and BNAF, ACR No. 34, 16 Nov.–15 Dec. 1943, p. A3.
126. LHCMA Adam 3/6/3 Report by the AG to the Forces on his Tour Overseas, Nov.–Dec. 1943.
127. NA WO 204/10381 CMF and BNAF, ACR No. 35, 16–31 Dec. 1943, p. B4.
128. NA WO 204/10381 CMF and BNAF, ACR No. 37, 16–31 Jan. 1944, p. A7.
129. NA WO 204/10381 CMF and BNAF, ACR No. 35, 16–31 Dec. 1943, p. B4.
130. Ibid., pp. A3–7; NA WO 204/10381 CMF and BNAF, ACR No. 36, 1–15 Jan. 1944, p. A3; NA WO 204/10381 CMF and BNAF, ACR No. 36, 1–15 Jan. 1944, p. A7.
131. NA WO 204/10381 CMF and BNAF, ACR No. 36, 1–15 Jan. 1944, p. A7.
132. NA WO 204/10381 CMF and BNAF, ACR No. 37, 16–31 Jan. 1944, p. A7.
133. Brook, *Montgomery and the Eighth Army*, p. 330.
134. Raymond Callahan, *Churchill and His Generals* (Lawrence: University Press of Kansas, 2007), p. 146; John Buckley, *Monty's Men: The British Army and the Liberation of Europe* (London: Yale University Press, 2013), p. 29.

Chapter 10 Remobilisation?

1. NA CAB 101/224 D. F. Butler, The British Soldier in Italy, Sept. 1943–June 1944, pp. 10–12. Over one-third of cases of battle exhaustion were able to return to their units within five days. A further 10% were also able to return after longer treatment.
2. Ibid., pp. 19–20.
3. NA WO 204/10381 BNAF, ACR No. 27, 1–15 Aug. 1943, p. 3.
4. NA WO 204/10381 BNAF, ACR No. 28, 16–31 Aug. 1943, p. 2.
5. NA WO 204/10381 CMF and BNAF, ACR No. 37, 16–31 Jan. 1944, p. A5.
6. NA WO 204/10381 BNAF, ACR No. 30, 16–30 Sept. 1943, pp. 6, 17.
7. Ibid., pp. 1, 17.
8. NA WO 204/10381 BNAF, ACR No. 31, 1–15 Oct. 1943, p. 4. It must be noted also that 'an increasing number of men' questioned the advantage of going home as those returning would 'probably be drafted later to a Second Front', which many thought would be a bloodbath (see NA WO 204/10381 CMF and BNAF, ACR No. 34, 16 Nov.–15 Dec. 1943, p. A4).
9. David Reynolds, *Rich Relations: The American Occupation of Britain, 1942–1945* (London: Phoenix Press, 2000 [1966]), p. 422. See also DHH CMHQ Report 119 Relations with People in UK and Problems with Morale, 1939–45, p. 20. 44,886 Canadian service personnel were married in Britain between 1940 and 1946, the vast majority to British women
10. Alan Allport, *Browned Off and Bloody-Minded: The British Soldier Goes to War 1939–1945* (London: Yale University Press, 2015), p. 147.
11. NA WO 204/10381 CMF and BNAF, ACR No. 43, 16–30 Apr. 1944, p. A3.
12. John McLeod, *Myth and Reality: The New Zealand Soldier in World War II* (Auckland: Reed Methuen, 1986), p. 138; ANZ WAII/1/DA1/9/40/16 W. G. Stevens to B. Freyberg, Future Leave Drafts, 31 May 1943; ANZ WAII/1/DA1/9/40/16 Telegram, Prime Minister to Freyberg, 23 May 1943; ANZ WAII/8/39 Freyberg, Memorandum for the Minister of Defence, Reinforcements for 2nd NZEF, n.d. but probably mid-1943.
13. NA CAB 101/224 D. F. Butler, The British Soldier in Italy, Sept. 1943–June 1944, p. 20.
14. NA WO 204/10381 CMF and BNAF, ACR No. 37, 16–31 Jan. 1944, p. A5.

15. NA WO 204/10381 CMF and BNAF, ACR No. 36, 1–15 Jan. 1944, p. A5.
16. LAC Vol. 12,631 File No. 11/Psychiatry/1/2 Col. F. H. van Nostrand, RCAMC, Neuropsychiatry in the Canadian Army (Overseas), Paper to the Inter Allied Conference on War Medicine at the Royal Society of Medicine, 9 July 1945.
17. John Horne, 'Introduction: Mobilizing for "Total War", in 1914–1918', in John Horne (ed.), *State, Society and Mobilization in Europe during the First World War* (Cambridge University Press, 1997), p. 14; Allport, *Browned Off and Bloody-Minded*, p. 131.
18. Jose Harris, *William Beveridge: A Biography* (Oxford: Clarendon Press, 1997), p. 416.
19. New Zealand Defence HQ Library, Report of the National Service Department, 1946, p. 6.
20. F. L. W. Wood, *Political and External Affairs* (Wellington: Historical Publications Branch, 1958), p. 269, puts the number at 663 who embarked for the Middle East on 12 Jan. 1944, while the CGS, Lieut. Gen. Puttick reported the number as 662 (ANZ WAII/8/70 Defender to Main 2 NZ Div., 13 Jan. 1944).
21. Alexander Watson, *Enduring the Great War: Combat, Morale and Collapse in the German and British Armies, 1914–1918* (Cambridge University Press, 2008), p. 154.
22. Leonard V. Smith, 'The French High Command and the Mutinies of Spring 1917', in Hugh Cecil and Peter H. Liddle, *Facing Armageddon: The First World War Experienced* (London: Leo Cooper, 1996), p. 87.
23. Leonard V. Smith, 'Remobilizing the Citizen-Soldier through the French Army Mutinies of 1917', in John Horne (ed.), *State, Society and Mobilization in Europe during the First World War* (Cambridge University Press, 1997), p. 144; Smith, 'The French High Command and the Mutinies of Spring 1917', in Cecil and Liddle, *Facing Armageddon*. While some have argued that the French mutinies involved a limited protest against years of tried-and-failed offensive tactics, others have contended that the main cause of the disturbances was a feeling of betrayal, of having been forgotten by those at home, those people that soldiers were supposed to be fighting for.
24. H. J. Martin and Neil Orpen, *South Africa at War: Military and Industrial Organization and Operations in Connection with the Conduct of the War, 1939–1945* (Purnell: Cape Town, 1979), pp. 122–33.
25. Ibid., pp. 4–5, 7, 12, 17.
26. S. P. MacKenzie, *Politics and Military Morale: Current-Affairs and Citizenship Education in the British Army, 1914–1950* (Oxford University Press, 1992), p. 75. See also, S. L. A. Marshall, *Men against Fire: The Problem of Battle Command in Future War* (New York, 1966), pp. 161–2.
27. Harris, *William Beveridge*, p. 416.
28. Geoffrey G. Field, *Blood, Sweat and Toil: Remaking the British Working Class, 1939–1945* (Oxford University Press), p 336.
29. Ibid., pp. 336–7.
30. Angus Calder, *The People's War: Britain 1939–1945* (London: Jonathan Cape, 1969), p. 531.
31. Field, *Blood, Sweat and Toil*, pp. 337–8.
32. NA WO 204/10381 First Army Mail, ACR No. 8, 19–25 Feb. 1943, pp. 6–7.
33. NA WO 204/10381 First Army Mail, ACR No. 9, 26 Feb.–4 Mar. 1943, pp. 6–7.
34. NA WO 204/10381 BNAF, ACR No. 14, 2–8 Apr. 1943, p. 6.
35. NA WO 204/10381 BNAF, ACR No. 17, 23 Apr.–1 May 1943, p. 8.
36. NA WO 204/10381 First Army Mail, ACR No. 18, 2–8 May 1943, pp. 6–7.

37. NA WO 204/10381 First Army Mail, ACR No. 31, 1–15 Oct. 1943.
38. NA WO 204/10381 First Army Mail, ACR No. 18, 2–8 May 1943, pp. 6–7. See also, H. Marshall, *Over to Tunis* (London: Eyre & Spottiswoode, 1943), p. 58.
39. NA WO 204/10381 First Army Mail, ACR No. 19, 9–15 May, pp. 6–7.
40. NA WO 204/10381 First Army Mail, ACR No. 22, 30 May–5 June 1943, p. 6. Comments continued until Report No. 28, 16–31 Aug. 1943.
41. NA WO 277/35 W. E. Williams, The History of Army Education, 1939–45, p. 136; NA WO 204/10381 First Army Mail, ACR No. 27, 1–15 Aug. 1943, p. 8.
42. MacKenzie, *Politics and Military Morale*, pp. 184–5.
43. BL, IOR, L/WS/1/939 Report on the Morale of British, Indian and African Troops in India Command and SEA Command, Feb.–Apr. 1944, Appendix A, Post-War Prospects: A Note on British Forces Opinions as Seen in Censorship.
44. MacKenzie, *Politics and Military Morale*, pp. 118–21.
45. BL, The Directorate of Army Education, The British War and Purpose: Consolidated Edition of B.W.P. Booklets 1–18 (1944), p. 17.
46. Ibid., pp. 17–8.
47. The Government eventually published a White Paper accepting the gist of the report, but Churchill and the Conservatives remained reluctant to guarantee that it would be enacted (see Field, *Blood, Sweat and Toil*, p. 340).
48. BL IOR L/WS/1/939 Report on the Morale of British, Indian and African Troops in India Command and SEA Command, Feb.–Apr. 1944, Appendix A, Post-War Prospects: A Note on British Forces Opinions as Seen in Censorship.
49. NA WO 204/10381 British North Africa Force, ACR No. 28, 16–31 Aug. 1943, p. 8.
50. BL IOR L/WS/1/939 Report on the Morale of British, Indian and African Troops in India Command and SEA Command, Feb.–Apr. 1944, Appendix A, Post-War Prospects: A Note on British Forces Opinions as Seen in Censorship.
51. BL IOR L/WS/1/939 General Staff Branch (MI Directorate), Report on the Morale of the Army in India, May–July 1943, p. 3.
52. BL IOR L/WS/1/939 General Staff Branch, Report on the Morale of the Army in the India Command, Aug.–Oct. 1943, p. 3.
53. NA WO 204/10381 BNAF, ACR No. 23, 6–19 June, p. 8.
54. NA WO 204/10381 BNAF, ACR No. 24, 20–30 June, p. 8.
55. NA WO 204/10381 BNAF, ACR No. 27, 1–15 Aug. 1943, p. 13.
56. NA WO 204/10381 First Army Mail, ACR No. 23, 6–19 June 1943, p. 8.
57. NA WO 204/10381 BNAF, ACR No. 27, 1–15 Aug. 1943, p. 13.
58. For some works that do engage with the mutiny see: McLeod, *Myth and Reality*; Wood, *Political and External Affairs*; Shane Capon, 'The Hamilton Furlough Mutiny' (Master's thesis, University of Waikato, 1986); Ian McGibbon, *New Zealand and the Second World War* (Auckland: Hodder Moa Beckett, 2004), pp. 161–3.
59. ANZ WAII/8/39 Freyberg to Fraser, 17 May 1943.
60. Turnbull Library MS Papers 2183–31 Frederick Jones Papers, First Middle East Furlough Draft, p. 1; ANZ WAII/1/DA1/9/40/16 W. G. Stevens, Notes on Relief of First Contingent, 22 Apr. 1943; Wood, *Political and External Affairs*, pp. 243–8.
61. McLeod, *Myth and Reality*, p. 141.
62. Ibid., p. 139.
63. Wood, *Political and External Affairs*, pp. 243–8.

64. Ibid., pp. 248–50. This decision was reinforced by the vehement opposition of the Combined Chiefs, at their meeting on 4 Dec., to the idea of returning 2nd New Zealand Division home.
65. Ibid., pp. 258–9.
66. Ibid., p. 259.
67. McLeod, *Myth and Reality*, p. 138.
68. Wood, *Political and External Affairs*, p. 259.
69. ANZ WAII/8/71 W. G. Stevens to B. Freyberg, 24 June 1944; ANZ WAII/8/71 2 NZ Div. to NEWZMIL London, 28 June 1944.
70. ANZ WAII/1/DA1/9/40/16 W. G. Stevens to B. Freyberg, Future Leave Drafts, 31 May 1943; ANZ WAII/1/DA1/9/40/16 Telegram, Prime Minister to Freyberg, 23 May 1943; ANZ WAII/8/39 Freyberg, Memorandum for the Minister of Defence, Reinforcements for 2nd NZEF, n.d. but probably mid-1943.
71. Turnbull Library MS Papers 2183–32 Frederick Jones Papers, Middle East Furlough Draft: Report on Circumstances Surrounding Refusal of Large Number to Return to Service Overseas, p. 1. Wood, *Political and External Affairs*, p. 266 states that 6,012 men returned in July 1943 and 115 men in October. Of these, 863 men were from the Railway Operating Group. Some married men were held back if they were deemed to be in key positions. The single men were selected by ballot.
72. Turnbull Library MS Papers 2183–31 Frederick Jones Papers, First Middle East Furlough Draft, pp. 1–2.
73. Robert Chapman, 'From Labour to National', in Geoffrey W. Rice (ed.), *The Oxford History of New Zealand* (Oxford University Press, 1992), pp. 367–8.
74. G. T. Bloomfield, *New Zealand: A Handbook of Historical Statistics* (Boston: G. K. Hall & Co., 1984), pp. 148–50.
75. Wood, *Political and External Affairs*, p. 262.
76. McLeod, *Myth and Reality*, p. 143.
77. Wood, *Political and External Affairs*, p. 262.
78. New Zealand Defence HQ Library, Report of the National Service Department, 1946, p. 6.
79. ANZ WAII/1/DA1/9/40/16 W. G. Stevens, Notes on Relief of First Contingent, 22 Apr. 1943; Wood, *Political and External Affairs*, pp. 243–8.
80. McLeod, *Myth and Reality*, p. 140.
81. ANZ WAII/1/DA1/9/40/16 Telegram from Fernleaf Cairo to Defender Wellington, 2 Nov. 1943.
82. ANZ WAII/1/DA508/1 Vol. III MEMCFS No. LXV, 2–15 June 1943.
83. ANZ WAII/1/DA1/9/40/16 Telegram from Fernleaf Cairo to Defender Wellington, 2 Nov. 1943.
84. Wood, *Political and External Affairs*, p. 267.
85. Quoted in McLeod, *Myth and Reality*, p. 144.
86. Wood, *Political and External Affairs*, p. 267.
87. Turnbull Library MS Papers 2183–31 Frederick Jones Papers, First Middle East Furlough Draft, p. 4.
88. Quoted in McLeod, *Myth and Reality*, pp. 145–6.
89. Turnbull Library MS Papers 2183–31 Frederick Jones Papers, 'First Middle East Furlough Draft', p. 4 and Appendix 2; McLeod, *Myth and Reality*, p. 146. In fact, an identical letter was handed to the CO in the Auckland area.
90. McLeod, *Myth and Reality*, p. 146.
91. Wood, *Political and External Affairs*, p. 269, puts the number at 663 who embarked on 12 Jan. 1944, while the CGS, Lieut. Gen. Puttick reported the number as 662 (ANZ WAII/8/70 Defender to Main 2 NZ Div., 13 Jan. 1944).

92. McLeod, *Myth and Reality*, p. 148.
93. Turnbull Library MS Papers 11256–4 Ralph Haig Nicholson, Court-Martial papers, 1944.
94. Turnbull Library MS Papers 2183–31 Frederick Jones Papers, First Middle East Furlough Draft, pp. 6–10; McLeod, *Myth and Reality*, p. 146; Wood, *Political and External Affairs*, p. 269.
95. Turnbull Library MS Papers 11256–4 Ralph Haig Nicholson, Letter Re Meeting with PM and Minister of Manpower, 14 Mar. 1944.
96. Ibid.
97. Turnbull Library MS Papers 2183–31 Frederick Jones Papers, First Middle East Furlough Draft, p. 15.
98. McLeod, *Myth and Reality*, p. 151 and Wood, *Political and External Affairs*, p. 269 put this number at 125. According to Jones, a further forty-six members of the first furlough draft proceeded overseas with the 12th Reinforcement on 29 June 1944 (this included ten men previously dismissed from the Army).
99. Turnbull Library MS Papers 2183–31 Frederick Jones Papers, First Middle East Furlough Draft, p. 17; McLeod, *Myth and Reality*, p. 152.
100. On appeal, it was later agreed that mufti allowances and deferred pay would be granted.
101. McLeod, *Myth and Reality*, p. 154.
102. Wood, *Political and External Affairs*, p. 269.
103. McLeod, *Myth and Reality*, p. 154. After the war, in Sept. 1945, the 'rebels' were forgiven, their discharge was revoked and they were given status comparable to the rest of the men of 2NZEF.
104. ANZ WAII/8/52 Gen. Freyberg to the Prime Minister, 18 May 1944; Michael Bassett and Michael King, *Tomorrow Comes the Song: The Life of Peter Fraser* (Auckland: Penguin, 2000), p. 269.
105. ANZ WAII/8/53 Gen. Freyberg to the Prime Minister, 7 June 1944.
106. ANZ WAII/8/72 External to Fernleaf, 21 Sept. 1944; New Zealand Defence HQ Library, Report of the National Service Department, 1946, p. 6.
107. New Zealand Defence HQ Library, Report of the National Service Department, 1946, p. 22.
108. Ibid., p. 6.
109. Ibid., p. 127. An average of 679 men were released in the period Apr. 1944–Mar. 1945.
110. Ibid., p. 22.
111. Wood, *Political and External Affairs*, p. 265.
112. McLeod, *Myth and Reality*, pp. 150–5.
113. Ibid., p. 155.
114. Neil Roos, *Ordinary Springboks: White Servicemen and Social Justice in South Africa, 1939–1961* (Aldershot: Ashgate, 2005), pp. 34–5.
115. Defence Personnel Files; Roos, *Ordinary Springboks*, p. 35.
116. SANDF, DOC, War Records Box 55 Memorandum, Attestations NMC, 31 Aug. 1944; SANDF, DOC, War Records Box 55 Memorandum, Attestations CC and IMC, 16 Sept. 1944; SANDF, DOC, War Records Box 55 Memorandum, Attestations UDF, 28 Aug. 1944; SANDF, DOC, DAG Personnel (DAG-P) Box 54 Weekly Recruiting Graph, 1944–5. The figures for the UDF include male officers and ORs in the Army and Air Force and members of the WADC and South African Military Nursing Service. The UDF figures do not include those who served in the Navy, permanent forces or non-Europeans.

117. SANDF, DOC, AI Gp 1 Box 81/I/71/B South African MCS No. 10, 16–31 July 1942, p. 6. Another issue, as a report compiled in late 1942 concluded, was that early volunteers who had already been demobilised had struggled to find work (see Roos, *Ordinary Springboks*, p. 36).
118. John Lambert, '"The Finest Hour?" English-Speaking South Africans and World War II', *South African Historical Journal*, 60(1) (2008), p. 67.
119. Ian van der Waag, *A Military History of Modern South Africa* (Johannesburg: Jonathan Ball, 2015), p. 204.
120. This assessment is supported by a number of reports carried out in 1942 and 1943. The DCS reported on 31 Dec. 1942, that the three services totalled 318,148 in number. This was broken down into 188,062 full time personnel in the Union, including over 75,000 non-whites, and 55,883 part-time personnel. Some 74,203, or 23% of all personnel, were serving outside of the country, including over 25,000 non-whites (coloureds and blacks were not differentiated). However, this figure included 17,030 whites, 1,080 coloureds and 2,132 blacks killed, missing, wounded and POW, leaving an effective strength overseas of only 53,961 full-time personnel. In Aug. 1943, the DAG (Organisation), Col. R. D. Pilkington Jordan, wrote to the DCS that coloured personnel inside the Union were reported to number 23,974; those outside the Union, 12,014. The Native Military Corps' effective strength was put at 10,996 outside and 45,945 inside the Union. Another memorandum prepared by Pilkington Jordan, this time for the AG, Maj. Gen. Len Beyers, showed that of the 148,249 white men in the UDF in June 1942, 98,546 were stationed in the Union and 49,703, or 34%, in the Middle East and East Africa. See F. D. Tothill, 'The 1943 General Election' (Master's thesis, University of South Africa, 1987), pp. 285–6; SADF AG Group 3/154 Box 19 Memorandum for the AG, Electoral Scheme: UDF, 30 June 1942.
121. SANDF, DOC, AI Gp 1 Box 81/I/71/B Memorandum on Morale of Union Defence Forces, p. 1, n.d. but probably 1943; AI Gp 1 Box 81/I/71/B South African MCS No. 10, 16–31 July 1942, p. 6; Roos, *Ordinary Springboks*, p. 36.
122. SANDF, DOC, AI Gp 1 Box 81/I/71/B Memorandum on Morale of Union Defence Forces, p. 1, n.d. but probably 1943.
123. SANDF, DOC, AI Gp 1 Box 81/I/71/B South African MCS No. 12, 21–31 Aug. 1942, p. 4.
124. Roos, *Ordinary Springboks*, p. 36.
125. SANDF, DOC, AI Gp 1 Box 81/I/71/B Summary of Extracts by IC, p. 1, n.d. but likely 1943.
126. SANDF, DOC, AI Gp 1 Box 81/I/71/B South African MCS No. 13, 1–29 Sept. 1942, pp. 1–11. The poll was based on 10,164 censored letters. The other factors causing discontent were: 'leave', 15%; 'red tape and organisation', 13.5%; and 'other causes', 10.5%.
127. Lambert, '"The Finest Hour?"', p. 79.
128. SANDF, DOC, AI Gp 1 Box 81/I/71/B South African MCS No. 4, 1–15 Apr. 1942, p. 16.
129. Andre Wessel, 'The First Two Years of War: The Development of the Union Defence Forces, Sept. 1939 to Sept. 1941', *Military History Journal*, 11(5) (June 2000).
130. SANDF, DOC, War Records Box 55 Memorandum, Attestations NMC, 31 Aug. 1944; SANDF, DOC, War Records Box 55 Memorandum, Attestations CC and IMC, 16 Sept. 1944; SANDF, DOC, War Records Box 55 Memorandum, Attestations UDF, 28 Aug. 1944; SANDF, DOC, DAG-P Box 54 Weekly Recruiting Graph, 1944–5. The figures for the UDF include male officers and

ORs in the Army and Air Force and members of the WADC and South African Military Nursing Service. The UDF figures do not include those who served in the Navy, permanent forces or non-Europeans.

131. Roos, *Ordinary Springboks*, p. 95.

132. Of the 1,112 records, 931 had details of the men's medals or sufficient information about their service history to make it clear whether they served in Italy. Of these men, only 217 served in Italy. While it is accepted that some men who took the 'Blue Oath' might not have made it to Italy, it can be estimated broadly that the rest (77%) chose not to take the oath and serve outside of Africa. These figures appear to be supported by evidence presented in the official histories. At Kaferskraal, for example, where the Armoured Fighting Vehicle Training Centre was established, only 500 out of 3,000 men had taken the 'Blue Oath' by the middle of Feb. 1943 (see Martin and Orpen, *South Africa at War*, p. 226).

133. Of the 931 records with details of the men's medals or information about their service history, 920 were identifiable as English- or Afrikaans-speaking as a consequence of their religious affiliation; 52 of the 309 Afrikaner records indicated service in Italy; 161 of the 611 English-speaker records indicated service in Italy.

134. SANDF, DOC, AI Gp 1 Box 81/I/71/B South African Military Censorship, Special Report No. 8, Reactions to New Oath, 1–20 Feb. 1943, p. 1. The Prince Alfred Guards with 16% Afrikaans-speakers were 77% for, 8% undecided and 15% against. The Witwatersrand Rifles with 19% Afrikaans-speakers were 74% for, 11% undecided and 15% against. The Pretoria Regiment with 28% Afrikaans-speakers were 44% for, 11% undecided and 45% against. See SANDF, DOC, War Records Box 55 Statement Showing Religious Denominations in, and Chaplains appointed to, Brigades, n.d. but likely 1941.

135. Lambert, '"The Finest Hour?"', p. 79.

136. SANDF, DOC, AI Gp 1 Box 81/I/71/B South African MCS No. 3, 16–28 Feb. 1942, p. 12.

137. SANDF, DOC, AI Gp 1 Box 81/I/71/B South African Military Censorship, Special Report No. 6, Reactions to New Oath, 12 Dec. 1942–10 Feb. 1943; SANDF, DOC, AI Gp 1 Box 81/I/71/B South African Military Censorship, Special Report No. 8, Reactions to New Oath, 1–20 Feb. 1943, pp. 2–3.

138. SANDF, DOC, AI Gp 1 Box 81/I/71/B South African Military Censorship, Special Report No. 10, Alleged Coercion in Administering New Oath, 1 May–1 June 1943, p. 1; SANDF, DOC, AI Gp 1 Box 81/I/71/B South African MCS No. 20, Selective Censorship, 2nd Regiment Botha, 7 May–11 June 1943, p. 3; SANDF, DOC, AI Gp 1 Box 81/I/71/B South African MCS No. 23, Selective Censorship, ILH Piet Retief, 13–21 July 1943, p. 1.

139. SANDF, DOC, AI Gp 1 Box 81/I/71/B South African Military Censorship, Special Report No. 6, Reactions to New Oath, 12 Dec. 1942–10 Feb. 1943.

140. SANDF, DOC, AI Gp 1 Box 81/I/71/B South African MCS No. 27, A General Survey on Morale in the Army, 22 Feb.–21 July 1943, pp. 1–3.

141. Horne, 'Introduction', in Horne (ed.), *State, Society and Mobilization in Europe during the First World War*, p. 14.

142. SANDF, DOC, AI Gp Box 42/I/37/B Durban MCS No. 85, June 1944.

143. SANDF, DOC, AI Gp 1 Box 81/I/71/B South African Military Censorship, Special Report No. 2, Memorandum on Intended Move North of Armoured Car Regiments, 25 Nov.–9 Dec. 1942.

144. SANDF, DOC, AI Gp Box 42/I/37/B Durban MCS No. 85 and 86, June and July 1944. There was also an understandable fear that a national government

under Malan would renege on the UP's demobilisation plans, thus making joining substantially more risky.

145. SANDF, DOC, AI Gp 1 Box 40 I/35, SA MCS No. 58, 8–21 June 1944.
146. Louis Grundlingh, 'The Recruitment of South African Blacks for Participation in the Second World War', in David Killingray and Richard Rathbone (eds.), *Africa and the Second World War* (London: Macmillan Press Ltd, 1986), p. 194; Lambert, '"The Finest Hour?"', p. 72. See also the Farming Report sections in AI Gp Box 42/I/37/B Durban Forces Censorship Summaries, June 1944–July 1945.
147. Grundlingh, 'The King's Afrikaners?', p. 364. The figures in Table 10.1 are from the South African Defence Personnel Archive, Pretoria, Service Records.
148. SANDF, DOC, AI Gp 1 Box 81/I/71/B South African Military Censorship, Special Report No. 7, The Riot at Kimberley, 9–25 Feb. 1943.
149. SANDF, DOC, AI Gp 1 Box 81/I/71/B South African Military Censorship, Special Report No. 8, Reactions to New Oath, 1–20 Feb. 1943, p. 1.
150. SANDF, DOC, AI Gp 1 Box 81/I/71/B South African Military Censorship, Special Report No. 7, The Riot at Kimberley, 9–25 Feb. 1943.
151. SANDF, DOC, War Records Box 55 Enlistment and Religious Statistics; DAG-P Box 54 Weekly Recruiting Graph, 1944.
152. BL IOR L/WS/1/939 Morale Report Aug.–Oct. 1943, Pt 1, British Troops, p. 2.
153. Horne, 'Introduction', in Horne (ed.), *State, Society and Mobilization in Europe during the First World War*, pp. 2–3.
154. Elizabeth Kier, 'War and Reform: Gaining Labor's Compliance on the Homefront', in Elizabeth Kier and Ronald R. Krebs, *In War's Wake: International Conflict and the Fate of Liberal Democracy* (Cambridge University Press, 2010), pp. 142–50.
155. NA CAB 101/224 D. F. Butler, The British Soldier in Italy, Sept. 1943–June 1944, p. 42.
156. George Peden, 'Financing Churchill's Army', in Keith Neilson and Greg Kennedy (eds.), *The British Way in Warfare: Power and the International System, 1856–1956* (Farnham: Ashgate, 2010), pp. 296–7.

Chapter 11 Cassino

1. Ian Gooderson, *A Hard Way to Make a War: The Allied Campaign in Italy in the Second World War* (London: Conway, 2008), p. 239; C. J. C. Molony, *The Mediterranean and Middle East, Vol. V: The Campaign in Sicily 1943 and the Campaign in Italy, 3rd September 1943 to 31st March 1944* (Uckfield: Naval & Military Press, 2004 [1973]), p. 588.
2. Molony, *The Mediterranean and Middle East, Vol. V*, pp. 421–3, 602.
3. Ibid.
4. Gooderson, *A Hard Way to Make a War*, p. 251.
5. Ibid., pp. 252–3.
6. Raymond Callahan, *Churchill and His Generals* (Lawrence: University Press of Kansas, 2007), p. 172.
7. Gooderson, *A Hard Way to Make a War*, p. 260; David Fraser, *And We Shall Shock Them: The British Army in the Second World War* (London: Cassell & Co., 1999), p. 278; John Ellis, *Brute Force: Allied Strategy and Tactics in the Second World War* (London: André Deutsch, 1990), pp. 325–6.
8. Gooderson, *A Hard Way to Make a War*, p. 264; Fraser, *And We Shall Shock Them*, p. 279.
9. Gooderson, *A Hard Way to Make a War*, p. 268.

10. LAC Vol. 10708 File No. 56-16-3/Int, German Army Special Tactical Study No. 29, German View of Allied Combat Efficiency, 17 Nov. 1944.
11. Fraser, *And We Shall Shock Them*, pp. 283–4.
12. Gooderson, *A Hard Way to Make a War*, pp. 269–70.
13. Fraser, *And We Shall Shock Them*, pp. 283–4; F. A. E. Crew, *The Army Medical Services, Campaigns, Vol. III: Sicily, Italy and Greece (1944–1945)* (Uckfield: Naval & Military Press, 2014 [1957]), p. 235; Molony, *The Mediterranean and Middle East, Vol. V*, pp. 744–50.
14. Callahan, *Churchill and His Generals*, pp. 172–3.
15. LHCMA Adam Papers Box 2 Casualties General, Monthly Gross Battle Casualty Rates, Percentages of Troops Engaged (as Shown on Operational Order of Battle, n.d. but 1945; LHCMA Adam Papers Box 2 Casualties General, Battle Casualties (All Ranks), Italy, Estimated Percentage of Casualties to Approximate Total Numbers Engaged Under British Army Command, Mar. 1944; Crew, *The Army Medical Services, Campaigns, Vol. III: Sicily, Italy and Greece*, pp. 231–7. The figures for Mar., Apr. and May were 7.1, 3.3 and 4.5% respectively.
16. Brian Bond, *Britain's Two World Wars against Germany: Myth, Memory and the Distortion of Hindsight* (Cambridge University Press, 2014), p. 80.
17. AWM 54 624/5/6 Medical Aspects of the Campaign in Italy, 1943–5, p, 52. These figures are for the period 22 Jan.–18 Mar. 1944.
18. Ibid., p, 55. Most of these men, after a good rest, encouragement and good food, realising perhaps that things were not so bad as they had imagined, went back to the line and became good soldiers.
19. Ibid., p, 56.
20. CAB 106/453 Cabinet Office Military Narratives of the War, Operations of British, Dominion and Indian Forces in Italy Monograph No. 5, p. 5.
21. Gooderson, *A Hard Way to Make a War*, p. 263.
22. Fraser, *And We Shall Shock Them*, p. 280.
23. NA WO 177/346 DDMS X Corps, War Diary, 1944–5.
24. LAC Vol. 12,631 File No. 11/Psychiatry/1/2 Lieut. Col. A. M. Doyle, RCAMC, Neuropsychiatrist, I Canadian Corps, to DDMS I Canadian Corps, 19 Mar. 1944.
25. ANZ WAII/8/50 Notes on Taking Over Conference at HQ II US Corps, 12 Feb. 1944 and Conference of Brigadiers, Heads of Services at Divisional HQ, 3 Feb. 1944.
26. Callahan, *Churchill and His Generals*, pp. 173–4; Gooderson, *A Hard Way to Make a War*, p. 272.
27. ANZ WAII/8/50 Extract from 2 NZ Div. Operation Instruction No. 20, 13 Feb. 1944.
28. Shelford Bidwell and Dominick Graham, *The Tug of War: The Battle for Italy, 1943–45* (London: Hodder & Stoughton, 1986), p. 181: Fraser, *And We Shall Shock Them*, pp. 285–6.
29. ANZ WAII/8/50 Tuker appears to have sent two messages to Freyberg on the matter on 12 Feb. 1944.
30. Fraser, *And We Shall Shock Them*, pp. 285–6. See also; Gooderson, *A Hard Way to Make a War*, p. 274.
31. Gooderson, *A Hard Way to Make a War*, pp. 274–5; Chris Mann, 'Failures in Command and Control: The Experience of 4th Indian Division at the Second Battle of Cassino, February 1944', in Andrew Hargreaves, Patrick Rose and Matthew Ford (eds.), *Allied Fighting Effectiveness in North Africa and Italy, 1942–1945* (Leiden: Brill, 2014), pp. 198–203.

32. ANZ WAII/8/50 Extract from NZ Corps Intelligence Summary No. 26, 16 Feb. 1944.
33. Bidwell and Graham, *The Tug of War*, p. 202. The Indians had nearly 40 officers and 600 men killed, wounded and missing.
34. Ibid.
35. Molony, *The Mediterranean and Middle East, Vol. V*, p. 807; John Ellis, *Cassino: The Hollow Victory* (London: Sphere Books, 1985), p. 226; Rick Atkinson, *The Day of Battle: The War in Sicily and Italy, 1943–1944* (London: Little, Brown, 2007), p. 468.
36. Molony, *The Mediterranean and Middle East, Vol. V*, p. 807.
37. ANZ WAII/8/50 Notes of Divisional Commanders Conference, HQ NZ Corps, 24 Feb. 1944; Bidwell and Graham, *The Tug of War*, p. 179; C. J. C. Molony, and W. Jackson, *The Mediterranean and Middle East, Vol. VI, Pt I: Victory in the Mediterranean* (Uckfield: Naval & Military Press, 2004), p. 1.
38. ANZ WAII/8/EE Notes of Conference held at NZ Corps HQ, 2 Mar. 1944.
39. Molony, *The Mediterranean and Middle East, Vol. V*, p. 779.
40. ANZ WAII/8/51 The Air Report in the Battle for Cassino, 14–24 Mar. 1944. On the first day, in total, 869 sorties were flown, dropping 1,358 tons of bombs, against enemy air activity of three reconnaissance flights by ME109s.
41. Gooderson, *A Hard Way to Make a War*, p. 276.
42. Bidwell and Graham, *The Tug of War*, p. 214.
43. ANZ WAII/8/51 The Air Report in the Battle for Cassino, 14–24 Mar. 1944.
44. ANZ WAII/8/52 Freyberg to Defence Minister, 4 Apr. 1944.
45. Bidwell and Graham, *The Tug of War*, p. 218.
46. ANZ WAII/8/52 Freyberg to Defence Minister, 4 Apr. 1944.
47. Bidwell and Graham, *The Tug of War*, pp. 218–19; ANZ WAII/8/50 Notes of Divisional Commanders Conference, HQ NZ Corps, 24 Feb. 1944; ANZ WAII/8/EE Notes of Conference Held at NZ Corps HQ, 2 Mar. 1944.
48. ANZ WAII/8/51 Extract, NZ Corps Intelligence Summary No. 56, 18 Mar. 1944.
49. William J. McAndrew, 'Fire or Movement? Canadian Tactical Doctrine, Sicily – 1943', *Military Affairs*, 51(3) (July 1987), p. 141; Gooderson, *A Hard Way to Make a War*, p. 277; Molony, *The Mediterranean and Middle East, Vol. V*, p. 802.
50. Molony, *The Mediterranean and Middle East, Vol. V*, p. 792.
51. Ellis, *Cassino*, p. 252; Atkinson, *The Day of Battle*, p. 468.
52. ANZ WAII/8/51 Extract, NZ Corps Intelligence Summary No. 56, 18 Mar. 1944.
53. ANZ WAII/8/51 Extract, NZ Corps Intelligence Summary No. 57, 19 Mar. 1944.
54. ANZ WAII/8/51 Extract, NZ Corps Intelligence Summary No. 58, 20 Mar. 1944; ANZ WAII/8/51 Enemy Situation Cassino Area, 21 Mar. 1944.
55. ANZ WAII/8/51 Enemy Situation Cassino Area, 21 Mar. 1944; Fraser, *And We Shall Shock Them*, p. 289.
56. Molony, *The Mediterranean and Middle East, Vol. V*, pp. 777–808.
57. ANZ WAII/8/50 Alexander to Freyberg, 23 Feb. 1944.
58. Alex Danchev and Daniel Todman (eds.), *War Diaries 1939–1945: Field Marshal Lord Alanbrooke* (London: Phoenix, 2002 [2001]), p. 536 (entry for 31 Mar. 1944).
59. ANZ WAII/8/51 The Air Report in the Battle for Cassino, 14–24 Mar. 1944.
60. Danchev and Todman (eds.), *Alanbrooke War Diaries*, p. 536 (entry for 31 Mar. 1944).
61. ANZ WAII/8/50 Notes on Conference held at Divisional HQ, 15 Feb. 1944.

62. See e.g. Bidwell and Graham, *The Tug of War*, p. 219; Ellis, *Cassino*, Chs. 10 and 11.
63. Molony, *The Mediterranean and Middle East, Vol. V*, p. 780; NA WO 177/326 Quarterly Report of DDMS Eighth Army, Dec. 1943–Feb. 1944; ANZ WAII/8/52 Historical Operational, 1944.
64. ANZ WAII/8/50 Notes of Divisional Commanders Conference, HQ NZ Corps, 24 Feb. 1944; Bidwell and Graham, *The Tug of War*, p. 179.
65. ANZ WAII/8/EE Notes of Conference held at NZ Corps HQ, 2 Mar. 1944.
66. Gooderson, *A Hard Way to Make a War*, p. 277. The New Zealand Official History didn't recognise this numerical advantage, but it counted battalions rather than men, and German battalions were often severely below strength by this stage of the war (see N. C. Phillips, *Italy, Vol. I: The Sangro to Cassino* (Wellington: Historical Publications Branch, 1957), p. 339). By comparison, the Soviet Korsun-Shevchenkovskiy offensive of 24 Jan.–17 Feb. 1944 had a 1.5:1 force-to-force ratio; the Belorussian offensive, 23 June–29 Aug. 1944, a 2:1 ratio; the Lvov-Sandomir offensive, 13 July–29 Aug. 1944, a 1.2:1 ratio; the Yassy-Kishinev offensive, 20–29 Aug. 1944, a 1.4:1 ratio: the East Prussian offensive, 13 Jan.–3 Feb. 1945, a 2.1:1 ratio; the Visla-Oder offensive, 12 Jan.–3 Feb. 1945, a 3.9/4.2:1 ratio and the battle for Berlin, 16 Apr.–8 May 1945, a 2.5:1 ratio (see C. J. Dick, 'The Operational Employment of Soviet Armour in the Great Patriotic War', in J. P. Harris and F. H. Toase (eds.), *Armoured Warfare* (London: B. T. Batsford Ltd, 1990), p. 108. The higher figure for the Visla-Oder offensive is the German estimate).
67. ANZ WAII/8/50 Notes on Conference held at Divisional HQ, 15 Feb. 1944 and Notes of Conference at Divisional HQ, 13 Feb. 1944.
68. ANZ WAII/8/EE Notes of Conference held at NZ Corps HQ, 2 Mar. 1944.
69. Bidwell and Graham, *The Tug of War*, p. 184.
70. ANZ WAII/1/DA508/1 Vol. III MEMCFS No. LXXV, 20 Oct.–2 Nov. 1943.
71. ANZ WAII/1/DA508/3 2 NZ FCSWR, 1 Jan. 1944.
72. ANZ WAII/1/DA508/3 2 NZ FCSWR, 8 Jan. 1944.
73. ANZ WAII/1/DA508/3 2 NZ FCSWR, 15 Jan. 1944.
74. ANZ WAII/1/DA508/3 2 NZ FCSWR, 19 Feb. 1944.
75. ANZ WAII/1/DA508/3 2 NZ FCSWR, 26 Feb. 1944.
76. ANZ WAII/1/DA508/3 2 NZ FCSWR, 18 Mar. 1944.
77. ANZ WAII/1/DA508/3 2 NZ FCSWR, 11 Mar. 1944.
78. ANZ WAII/1/DA508/3 2 NZ FCSWR, 18 Mar. 1944.
79. ANZ WAII/8/70 Telegram, 2 NZ Div. to 2 NZEF, 28 Dec. 1943; ANZ WAII/1/DA508/1 Vols. 3 & 4 MEMCFS No. LXXXI, 12–25 Jan. 1944.
80. ANZ WAII/8/70 2 NZ Div. to 2 NZEF, 28 Dec. 1943.
81. ANZ WAII/8/39 Telegram, Freyberg to Fraser, 15 Feb. 1943.
82. ANZ WAII/8/39 Telegram, Freyberg to Stevens, 10 Feb. 1943.
83. Stephen Brooks (ed.), *Montgomery and the Eighth Army* (London: The Bodley Head, 1991), p. 298.
84. Bidwell and Graham, *The Tug of War*, p. 185.
85. ANZ WAII/1/DA508/1 Vol. III MEMCFS No. LXXXI, 12–25 Jan. 1944; ANZ WAII/1/DA508/3 2 NZ FCSWR, 12 Dec. 1943.
86. ANZ WAII/1/DA508/3 2 NZ FCSWR, 12 Dec. 1943; NA WO 204/10381 CMF and BNAF, ACR No. 34, 16 Nov.–15 Dec. 1943, p. C2.
87. Bidwell and Graham, *The Tug of War*, p. 185.
88. ANZ WAII/8/70 Defender to Main NZ Corps, 7 Feb. 1944.
89. ANZ WAII/1/DA508/1 Vol. III MEMCFS No. LXXVII, 17–30 Nov. 1943.

90. ANZ WAII/1/DA508/3 2 NZ FCSWR, 26 Feb. 1944.
91. ANZ WAII/8/70 Defender to Fernleaf, 6 Sept. 1943.
92. ANZ WAII/8/70 Main NZ Div. to Fernleaf Cairo, 23 Nov. 1943.
93. ANZ WAII/8/70 Defender to Main 2 NZ Div., 13 Jan. 1944. The second section of the 11th Reinforcement sailed at the end of Mar., the beginning of Apr. 1944.
94. ANZ WAII/8/70 HQ 2 NZ Div. to Premier Wellington, 14 Dec. 1943; ANZ WAII/8/70 Brig. Stevens to Commander, 18 Dec. 1943; ANZ WAII/1/DA508/1 Vol. III MEMCFS No. LXXV, 20 Oct.–2 Nov. 1943; ANZ WAII/1/DA508/3 2 NZ FCSWR, 5 Dec. 1943.
95. ANZ WAII/8/70 2 NZ Div. to 2 NZEF, 28 Dec. 1943.
96. ANZ WAII/8/70 Telegram, 2 NZ Div. to 2 NZEF, 28 Dec. 1943; Christopher Pugsley, 'The Second New Zealand Division of 1945: A Comparison with its 1918 Predecessor', in John Crawford (ed.), *Kia Kaha: New Zealand in the Second World War* (Oxford University Press, 2000), p. 97.
97. ANZ WAII/1/DA508/1 Vols. 3 & 4 MEMCFS No. LXXXI, 12–25 Jan. 1944; ANZ WAII/1/DA508/1 Vols. 3 & 4 MEMCFS No. LXXV, 20 Oct.–2 Nov. 1943, p. 27.
98. ANZ WAII/1/DA3/1/28 – DA/3/1/43 War Diary, DMS, 2NZEF, Monthly Report, Mar. 1944.
99. Bidwell and Graham, *The Tug of War*, p. 185.
100. Molony, *The Mediterranean and Middle East, Vol. V*, p. 784.
101. Ibid., p. 211.
102. T. Duncan and M. Stout, *New Zealand Medical Services in Middle East and Italy* (Wellington: Historical Publications Branch, 1956), p. 692; W. Franklin Mellor (ed.), *Casualties and Medical Statistics* (London: HMSO, 1972), pp. 253–67.
103. ANZ WAII/8/BBB Morale; WAII/1/DA3/1/1 to DA3/1/16 DDMS 2NZEF, Jan. 1941–Jan. 1946.
104. ANZ WAII/8/BBB Cases of Desertion, 14 Feb. 1945.
105. Ibid.
106. ANZ WAII/8/BBB Desertion Cases, 10 Dec. 1944; WAII/8/GGG Freyberg to Jones, the Minister of Defence, 25 Jan. 1944 and Memo: GOC, 20 Jan. 1944.
107. Bidwell and Graham, *The Tug of War*, p. 185.
108. ANZ WAII/8/71 2 NZ Div. to Defender Wellington, 3 July 1944.
109. ANZ WAII/8/53 Gen. Freyberg to the Prime Minister, 7 June 1944.
110. Bidwell and Graham, *The Tug of War*, pp. 185–6.
111. ANZ WAII/8/52 Freyberg to Leese, 10 Apr. 1944; Jonathan Fennell, *Combat and Morale in the North African Campaign: The Eighth Army and the Path to El Alamein* (Cambridge University Press, 2011), p. 252; Phillips, *Italy, Vol. I*, p. 341; Molony, *The Mediterranean and Middle East, Vol. V*, p. 722.
112. ANZ WAII/8/52 Notes on Conference Held at Divisional HQ, 20 May 1944.
113. He said no less in a cable to the Defence Minister on 31 Mar. 1944: ANZ WAII/8/52 Freyberg to Defence Minister, 31 Mar. 1944.
114. ANZ WAII/8/52 Freyberg to Clark, 3 Apr. 1944.
115. ANZ WAII/8/52 Freyberg to Leese, 10 Apr. 1944.
116. ANZ WAII/8/51 Extract from *The Stars and Stripes*, No. 113, 27 Mar. 1944.
117. NA WO 204/10381 CMF and BNAF, ACR No. 42, 1–15 Apr. 1944, p. C1.
118. Ibid., pp. A2–3.
119. Ibid.
120. Ibid., p. C1.
121. NA WO 204/10381 CMF and BNAF, ACR No. 43, 16–30 Apr. 1944, p. A2.
122. Bidwell and Graham, *The Tug of War*, pp. 185, 245, 256, 330, 341–2.

123. Molony and Jackson, *The Mediterranean and Middle East, Vol. VI, Pt I*, p. 13; Alan Jeffreys, *Approach to Battle: Training the Indian Army During the Second World War* (Solihull: Helion, 2016), p. 122.
124. LAC Vol. 18,824 Summary of Approximate Effective Strengths of the British, Indian, Colonial and Dominion Military Forces in the CMF, 1943–5.
125. Molony and Jackson, *The Mediterranean and Middle East, Vol. VI, Pt I*, p. 97.
126. Ibid., p. 1.
127. The 78th Division, with 6th Armoured Division, were tasked with exploiting XIII Corp's crossing of the Garigliano.
128. Callahan, *Churchill and His Generals*, pp. 175–8; Fraser, *And We Shall Shock Them*, pp. 287–8; Molony and Jackson, *The Mediterranean and Middle East, Vol. VI, Pt I*, pp. 12, 15, 18.
129. Molony and Jackson, *The Mediterranean and Middle East, Vol. VI, Pt I*, pp. 12–13, 18, 61.
130. Bidwell and Graham, *The Tug of War*, pp. 185, 245, 256, 330, 341–2.
131. ANZ WAII/8/52 Conference at HQ X Corps, 10 May 1944.
132. ANZ WAII/8/52 Personal Message from the Army Commander, May 1944.
133. ANZ WAII/8/52 Personal Message from the C-in-C, Allied Armies in Italy, May 1944.
134. Callahan, *Churchill and His Generals*, p. 182.
135. Bidwell and Graham, *The Tug of War*, p. 246.
136. Ellis, *Brute Force*, p. 326.
137. Fraser, *And We Shall Shock Them*, p. 287.
138. Gooderson, *A Hard Way to Make a War*, p. 277.
139. Fraser, *And We Shall Shock Them*, p. 288; Ellis, *Brute Force*, p. 324.
140. Bidwell and Graham, *The Tug of War*, p. 246.
141. Callahan, *Churchill and His Generals*, p. 182. By this stage of the war, it was possible to put an entire division's guns at the support of a single infantry company in ten minutes.
142. Fraser, *And We Shall Shock Them*, pp. 290–1.
143. NA WO 204/10381 CMF and BNAF, ACR No. 44, 1–15 May 1944, pp. A2–3.
144. NA WO 204/10381 CMF and BNAF, ACR No. 42, 1–15 Apr. 1944, p. A3.
145. NA WO 204/10381 CMF and BNAF, ACR No. 44, 1–15 May 1944, p. B2. See also, LAC Vol. 12559 File No. 11/AAI 1Corps/1 Brig. E. A. McCusker, DDMS I Canadian Corps, Monthly Hygiene Report, I Canadian Corps, May 1944.
146. NA WO 204/10381 CMF and BNAF, ACR No. 42, 1–15 Apr. 1944, p. F1.
147. Ibid., p. A3.
148. NA WO 204/10381 CMF and BNAF, ACR No. 44, 1–15 May 1944, p. A6. It does seem clear that up until this point 'most married infantry' found it 'almost impossible to put anything aside against an emergency' and that 'many of their families' were 'suffering real hardship'. Until 1942 a private's wife with two children drew 38s a week in allowances and compulsory allotment. This was raised to 43s and then, in 1944, to 60s (see NA CAB 101/224 D. F. Butler, The British Soldier in Italy, Sept. 1943–June 1944, pp. 21–2).
149. NA WO 204/10381 CMF and BNAF, ACR No. 45, 16–31 May 1944, pp. A2–5, B2. See also, NA WO 204/10381 CMF and BNAF, ACR No. 46, 1–15 June 1944, p. A3.
150. NA WO 204/10381 CMF and BNAF, ACR No. 44, 1–15 May 1944, pp. A2–3.
151. NA WO 204/10381 CMF and BNAF, ACR No. 45, 16–31 May 1944, p. A2.
152. NA WO 204/10381 CMF and BNAF, ACR No. 46, 1–15 June 1944, pp. A1–2.

153. NA WO 177/325 Medical Diaries DDMS 8th Army Jan.–Dec. 1943; WO 177/326 Medical Diaries DDMS 8th Army, Jan.–Dec. 1944; WO 204/7647; SANDF, DOC, UWH Box 346/U/Med 60/12 The Campaign in Sicily, July–Aug. 1943.
154. NA WO 177/325 Medical Diaries DDMS 8th Army Jan.–Dec. 1943; WO 177/326 Medical Diaries DDMS 8th Army, Jan.–Dec. 1944; WO 204/7647; SANDF, DOC, UWH Box 346/U/Med 60/12 The Campaign in Sicily, July–Aug. 1943; LAC Vol. 15651 War Diary, Medical Branch HQ 1 Canadian Corps; LAC Vol. 12559 Medical History of the War, 1 Canadian Corps; LAC Vol. 15651 Folder 4 War Diary DDMS, 1 Corps, Sept. 1943–Feb. 1944; LAC Vol. 12559 File No. 11/AAI 1Corps/1 General Medical Correspondence, 1st Canadian Corps.
155. NA WO 204/10381 CMF and BNAF, ACR No. 42, 1–15 Apr. 1944, p. C2; NA WO 204/10381 CMF and BNAF, ACR No. 39, 16–29 Feb. 1944, p. A3.
156. NA WO 204/10381 CMF and BNAF, ACR No. 42, 1–15 Apr. 1944, p. C2.
157. NA WO 204/10381 CMF and BNAF, ACR No. 45, 16–31 May 1944, p. A3.
158. NA WO 204/10381 CMF and BNAF, ACR No. 46, 1–15 June 1944, p. A4.
159. LAC RG24 Vol. 18,824 File No. 133.065(D597) Casualty Stats Italian Campaign, Sept. 1943–May 1945.
160. Bidwell and Graham, *The Tug of War*, p. 246.
161. Callahan, *Churchill and His Generals*, pp. 178–9.
162. Fraser, *And We Shall Shock Them*, p. 291; Ellis, *Brute Force*, pp. 337–8.
163. Fraser, *And We Shall Shock Them*, p. 291.
164. NA WO 204/10381 CMF and BNAF, ACR No. 46, 1–15 June 1944, pp. A1–2.
165. Callahan, *Churchill and His Generals*, p. 173.
166. Gooderson, *A Hard Way to Make a War*, pp. 279–80. Ellis, *Brute Force*, p. 343 puts this figure at 38,024.
167. Gooderson, *A Hard Way to Make a War*, p. 280.
168. Bidwell and Graham, *The Tug of War*, p. 342.
169. Gooderson, *A Hard Way to Make a War*, p. 280.

Chapter 12 Transformation in the Jungle

1. Patrick Rose, 'British Army Command Culture 1939–1945: A Comparative Study of British Eighth and Fourteenth Armies' (PhD thesis, King's College London, 2008), pp. 138–9.
2. Jeffrey Grey, *The Australian Army* (Oxford University Press, 2001), pp. 151–2; Alan Jeffreys, *Approach to Battle: Training the Indian Army During the Second World War* (Solihull: Helion, 2016), p. 145. These memoranda were issued monthly from May 1942 onwards.
3. Quoted in Daniel Marston, 'Learning and Adapting for Jungle Warfare, 1942–45: The Australian and British Indian Armies', in Peter J. Dean (ed.), *Australia 1944–45: Victory in the Pacific* (Cambridge University Press, 2016), p. 130; Adrian Threlfall, 'The Development of Australian Army Jungle Warfare Doctrine and Training, 1941–1945' (Doctoral thesis, Victoria University, 2008), pp. 229 and 283.
4. Marston, 'Learning and Adapting for Jungle Warfare', in Dean (ed.), *Australia 1944–45*, pp. 130–1.
5. Grey, *The Australian Army*, p. 149; Threlfall, 'The Development of Australian Army Jungle Warfare Doctrine and Training', p. 275; Timothy Moreman, 'Jungle, Japanese and the Australian Army: Learning the Lessons of New Guinea' (Symposium Paper available at http://ajrp.awm.gov.au/ajrp/remember.nsf/pages/

NT000015DE), p. 5 of 13. An advance copy of the pamphlet was distributed to 6th and 7th Australian Divisions in Mar. 1943.

6. Grey, *The Australian Army*, p. 153; Threlfall, 'The Development of Australian Army Jungle Warfare Doctrine and Training', p. 228.
7. Grey, *The Australian Army*, p. 153.
8. Moreman, 'Jungle, Japanese and the Australian Army: Learning the Lessons of New Guinea', p. 4 of 13.
9. AWM 54 175/3/3 Advanced Land HQ, FCR No. 15, 17–31 July 1943, p. 2; AWM 54 175/3/3 Advanced Land HQ, FCR No. 16, 1–15 Aug. 1943, p. 2.
10. AWM 54 175/3/3 Advanced Land HQ, FCR No. 12, 1–15 June 1943, p. 5.
11. AWM 54 175/3/3 Advanced Land HQ, FCR No. 16, 1–15 Aug. 1943, p. 2.
12. AWM 54 175/3/3 Advanced Land HQ, FCR No. 17, 16 Aug.–15 Sept. 1943, p. 2.
13. Grey, *The Australian Army*, p. 149; Threlfall, 'The Development of Australian Army Jungle Warfare Doctrine and Training', p. 275.
14. Figures derived from Grey, *The Australian Army*, p. 154.
15. Threlfall, 'The Development of Australian Army Jungle Warfare Doctrine and Training', p. 306.
16. Grey, *The Australian Army*, pp. 151–2.
17. Moreman, 'Jungle, Japanese and the Australian Army: Learning the Lessons of New Guinea', pp. 7 of 13. For a study on inter-theatre learning in the British Army in the First World War, see Aimée Fox-Godden, 'Beyond the Western Front: The Practice of Inter-Theatre Learning in the British Army during the First World War', *War in History*, 23(2) (2016).
18. Timothy Moreman, *The Jungle, the Japanese and the British Commonwealth Armies at War, 1941–45: Fighting Methods, Doctrine and Training for Jungle Warfare* (London: Frank Cass, 2005), p. 100.
19. Moreman, 'Jungle, Japanese and the Australian Army: Learning the Lessons of New Guinea', pp. 8–9 of 13; Moreman, *The Jungle, the Japanese and the British Commonwealth Armies at War*, pp. 144–5.
20. Quoted in Moreman, *The Jungle, the Japanese and the British Commonwealth Armies at War*, pp. 80–1.
21. Daniel Marston, *Phoenix from the Ashes: The Indian Army in the Burma Campaign* (Westport: Praeger, 2003), p. 96; Moreman, *The Jungle, the Japanese and the British Commonwealth Armies at War*, p. 84; Raymond Callahan, *Burma, 1942–1945* (London: Davis Poynter, 1978), pp. 71–2.
22. BL IOR L/WS/1/939 General Staff Branch (MI Directorate), Report on the Morale of the Army in India, May–July 1943, pp. 1 and 4.
23. BL IOR L/WS/1/939 General Staff Branch, Report on the Morale of the Army in the India Command, Aug.–Oct. 1943, p. 1.
24. Marston, *Phoenix from the Ashes*, p. 96; Moreman, *The Jungle, the Japanese and the British Commonwealth Armies at War*, p. 84.
25. Marston, *Phoenix from the Ashes*, p. 96.
26. Ibid., p. 108; Threlfall, 'The Development of Australian Army Jungle Warfare Doctrine and Training', pp. 229 and 283; Marston, 'Learning and Adapting for Jungle Warfare, 1942–45', in Dean (ed.), *Australia 1944–45*, pp. 121–2; Jeffreys, *Approach to Battle*, p. 162.
27. Quoted in Marston, *Phoenix from the Ashes*, pp. 105–7.
28. Marston, *Phoenix from the Ashes*, p. 108.
29. Quoted in Moreman, *The Jungle, the Japanese and the British Commonwealth Armies at War*, pp. 57, 99, 104.
30. Ibid., p. 87.

31. Marston, *Phoenix from the Ashes*, pp. 96–7; Moreman, *The Jungle, the Japanese and the British Commonwealth Armies at War*, p. 92. The 39th Indian Division was the old 1st Burma Division renamed (see Graham Dunlop, *Military Economics, Culture and Logistics in the Burma Campaign, 1942–1945* (London: Pickering & Chatto, 2009), p. 76).
32. Field Marshal Viscount Slim, *Defeat into Victory* (London: Pan Books, 1999 [1956]), p. 146. Quoted in Moreman, *The Jungle, the Japanese and the British Commonwealth Armies at War*, p. 110.
33. Moreman, *The Jungle, the Japanese and the British Commonwealth Armies at War*, p. 102; Jeffreys, *Approach to Battle*, pp. 186–7.
34. Marston, *Phoenix from the Ashes*, pp. 80–1.
35. Quoted in David French, *Raising Churchill's Army: The British Army and the War against Germany 1919–1945* (Oxford University Press, 2000), p. 204.
36. BL IOR L/WS/1/939 The AG in India's Committee on Morale of the Army in India, 1st Quarterly Report, Nov. 1942–Jan. 1943, p. 2.
37. BL IOR L/WS/1/939 General Staff Branch (MI Directorate), Report on the Morale of the Army in India, Feb.–Apr. 1943, p. 1.
38. BL IOR L/WS/1/939 General Staff Branch (MI Directorate), Report on the Morale of the Army in India, May–July 1943, pp. 1–2.
39. Marston, *Phoenix from the Ashes*, pp. 86, 93, 98–9, 108.
40. Moreman, *The Jungle, the Japanese and the British Commonwealth Armies at War*, p. 53; Marston, *Phoenix from the Ashes*, pp. 80–1.
41. Marston, *Phoenix from the Ashes*, pp. 3, 86.
42. Allan S. Walker, *Clinical Problems of War* (Canberra: AWM, 1952), pp. 696–7.
43. WO 222/1571 Army Psychiatry, Psychiatric Services Overseas and in Forward Areas, India and South-East Asia, p. 75; Moreman, *The Jungle, the Japanese and the British Commonwealth Armies at War*, p. 85.
44. Moreman, *The Jungle, the Japanese and the British Commonwealth Armies at War*, p. 91.
45. Wray Vamplew (ed.), *Australians: Historical Statistics* (Broadway, NSW: Fairfax, Syme and Weldon Associates, 1987), p. 165.
46. AWM 54 175/3/3 Advanced Land HQ, FCR No. 12, 1–15 June 1943, pp. 3, 13.
47. AWM 54 175/3/3 Advanced Land HQ, FCR No. 11, 16–31 May 1943, pp. 15–16.
48. AWM 54, 492/4/34 War History of the AAES 1939–45, pp. 1–6.
49. Ibid., p. 7.
50. Darryl Dymock, *A Sweet Use of Adversity: The Australian Army Education Service in World War II and its Impact on Australian Adult Education* (Armidale: University of New England Press, 1995), pp. 37–8.
51. Ibid., pp. 38–40.
52. Ibid., p. 114. 'Between June 1942 and January 1946 an estimated ten million soldiers in aggregate attended AAES lectures, two million heard music recitals, seven million watched documentary films, and more that 66,000 enrolled in correspondence courses … Over one and a half million discussion pamphlets were distributed, up to 180,000 copies of Salt [the service magazine] were published each issue, and the AAES library collection reached 620,000 volumes.'
53. AWM 54 175/3/3 Advanced Land HQ, FCR No. 21, 16 Dec. 1943–15 Jan. 1944, p. 3. The censorship summary for 16 Dec. 1943–15 Jan. 1944 commented, for example, that 'the usual favourable comments were noted regarding the work done by all philanthropic organisation – Army Education Service, the Lending Library, the various concert parties touring remote areas, etc.'
54. Dymock, *A Sweet Use of Adversity*, pp. 132–3.

55. BL IOR L/WS/1/939 Morale Report Aug.–Oct. 1943, Pt II, Indian Troops, pp. 12–13. Even at the end of the war, the old martial races made up the majority of front-line troops (see Marston, *Phoenix from the Ashes*, pp. 218–21).
56. BL IOR L/WS/1/939 Morale Report Aug.–Oct. 1943, Pt II, Indian Troops, pp. 12–13.
57. LHCMA Adam 3/6/2 Note by AG for consideration by the ECAC, 4 June 1943.
58. LHCMA Adam 3/6/2 Report by the AG on his Overseas Tour, Apr.–May 1943, p. 3.
59. Ibid.
60. Gajendra Singh, *The Testimonies of Indian Soldiers and the Two World Wars: Between Self and Sepoy* (London: Bloomsbury, 2014), pp. 163–4.
61. BL IOR L/WS/1/939 General Staff Brance (MI Directorate), Report on the Morale of the Army in India, May–July 1943, Appendix I; Jeffreys, *Approach to Battle*, pp. 192–6.
62. T. H. Hawkins and L. J. F. Brimble, *Adult Education: The Record of the British Army* (London: Macmillan, 1947), p. 264.
63. Singh, *The Testimonies of Indian Soldiers and the Two World Wars*, pp. 163–4.
64. Srinath Raghaven, *India's War: The Making of Modern South Asia, 1939–1945* (London: Penguin, 2017), p. 398; GHQ (India), New Delhi, to All Commanding Officers of Indian Army Units, May 1944, Instructions on Josh Work and Josh Group Organisation within Units (quoted in Singh, *The Testimonies of Indian Soldiers and the Two World Wars*, pp. 163–4).
65. Moreman, *The Jungle, the Japanese and the British Commonwealth Armies at War*, p. 103.
66. BL IOR L/WS/1/939 Morale Report, Aug.–Oct. 1943, pp. 6, 12.
67. BL IOR L/WS/1/939 General Staff Branch, Report on the Morale of the Army in India Command and SEA Command for the months ending 15 Oct., p. 5; BL L/WS/1/939 Morale Report, Aug.–Oct. 1943, p. 2.
68. BL IOR L/WS/1/939 General Staff Branch, Report on the Morale of the Army in India Command and SEA Command for the month ending 15 Jan., p. 8.
69. Dymock, *A Sweet Use of Adversity*, p. 28.
70. AWM 54 175/3/3 Advanced Land HQ, FCR No. 10, 1–15 May 1943, pp. 3–4.
71. Ibid., p. 7.
72. AWM 54 175/3/3 Advanced Land HQ, FCR No. 16, 1–15 Aug. 1943, pp. 1–3.
73. AWM 54 175/3/3 Advanced Land HQ, FCR No. 21, 16 Dec. 1943–15 Jan. 1944, p. 1.
74. BL L/WS/1/939 General Staff Branch (MI Directorate), Report on the Morale of the Army in India, Feb.–Apr. 1943, pp. 8–9; BL L/WS/1/939 General Staff Branch, Report on the Morale of the Army in the India Command, Aug.–Oct. 1943, p. 7.
75. BL L/WS/1/939 General Staff Branch (MI Directorate), Report on the Morale of the Army in India, May–July 1943, Appendix I.
76. BL L/WS/1/939 General Staff Branch (MI Directorate), Report on the Morale of the Army in India, Feb.–Apr. 1943, Appendix I; NA WO 277/4 Morgan, Army Welfare, p. 119. The Directorate of Welfare and Amenities was initially called the Directorate of Welfare and Education.
77. BL L/WS/1/939 General Staff Branch, Report on the Morale of the Army in the India Command, May–July 1943, p. 2.
78. BL L/WS/1/939 General Staff Brance (MI Directorate), Report on the Morale of the Army in India, Feb.–Apr. 1943, p. 2.

79. Ibid., Appendix I; BL L/WS/1/939 GHQ India, Memorandum on Morale of British Troops Serving in India, 30 Dec. 1943; NA WO 277/4 Morgan, Army Welfare, p. 120.
80. Marston, *Phoenix from the Ashes*, pp. 15–16.
81. Quoted in Tarak Barkawi, 'Culture and Combat in the Colonies: The Indian Army in the Second World War', *Journal of Contemporary History*, 41(2) (2006), p. 331.
82. Marston, *Phoenix from the Ashes*, pp. 3, 22–3.
83. Barkawi, 'Culture and Combat in the Colonies', p. 332.
84. Marston, *Phoenix from the Ashes*, pp. 222–4.
85. BL IOR L/MIL/7/19158 Secretary of State, Military Department, India, 5 June 1943. Quoted in Marston, *Phoenix from the Ashes*, p. 224.
86. Tarak Barkawi, *Soldiers of Empire: Indian and British Armies in World War II* (Cambridge University Press, 2017), p. 103.
87. BL IOR L/WS/1/939 General Staff Branch (MI Directorate), Report on the Morale of the Army in India, May–July 1943, p. 4.
88. Sri Nandan Prasad, *Official History of the Indian Armed Forces in the Second World War, 1939–45: Expansion of the Armed Forces and Defence Organisation, 1939–45* (Calcutta: Orient Longmans, 1956), pp. 67 and 91–3.
89. Marston, *Phoenix from the Ashes*, p. 108.
90. Moreman, *The Jungle, the Japanese and the British Commonwealth Armies at War*, p. 105.
91. For a compelling take on what motivated citizen and professional armies in the twentieth century, see Anthony King, *The Combat Soldier: Infantry Tactics and Cohesion in the Twentieth and Twenty-First Centuries* (Oxford University Press, 2013). See also the extensive work of Tarak Barkawi including e.g. 'Culture and Combat in the Colonies'.
92. David Horner, 'MacArthur and Curtin: Deciding Australian War Strategy in 1943', in Peter J. Dean (ed.), *Australia 1943: The Liberation of New Guinea* (Port Melbourne: Cambridge University Press, 2014), pp. 26–31. Rabaul possessed a first-rate harbour and excellent airfields.
93. Peter J. Dean, 'MacArthur's War: Strategy, Command and Plans for the 1943 Offensives', in Peter J. Dean (ed.), *Australia 1943: The Liberation of New Guinea* (Port Melbourne: Cambridge University Press, 2014), pp. 49–51.
94. Evan Mawdsley, *World War II: A New History* (Cambridge University Press, 2009), p. 238.
95. Eric Bergerud, *Touched with Fire: The Land War in the South Pacific* (London: Viking, 1996), p. 19.
96. Peter J. Dean, 'MacArthur's War: Strategy, Command and Plans for the 1943 Offensives', in Peter J. Dean (ed.), *Australia 1943: The Liberation of New Guinea* (Port Melbourne: Cambridge University Press, 2014), pp. 49–51.
97. For the source of Map 12.1, see ibid., p. 55.
98. The American operations, most notably at Vella Lavella, were supported by the understrength 3rd New Zealand Division. See Oliver A. Gillespie, *The Pacific* (Wellington: Historical Publications Branch, 1952), pp. 125–94.
99. Dean, 'MacArthur's War', in Dean (ed.), Australia 1943, pp. 49–55.
100. For the source of Map 12.2, see Jeffrey Grey, *A Military History of Australia* (Cambridge University Press, 1999), p. 185
101. Dean, 'MacArthur's War', in Dean (ed.), *Australia 1943*, p. 61.
102. Ibid., pp. 48, 62; Hiroyuki Shindo, 'The Japanese Army's Search for a New South Pacific Strategy', in Peter J. Dean (ed.), *Australia 1943: The Liberation of New Guinea* (Port Melbourne: Cambridge University Press, 2014), p. 69. The Vitiaz

Strait was a critical line of communication into the Bismarck Sea, the possession of which was vital not only for the reduction of Rabaul but also for the Allied advance to the Philippines.

103. Peter J. Dean, *MacArthur's Coalition: US and Australian Operations in the Southwest Pacific Area, 1942–1945* (University Press of Kansas, 2018), Ch. 11. In Jan. and Feb. 1943, much of 20th and 41st Japanese Divisions had been landed at Wewak, far to the west of Lae, in order to be out of range of Allied aircraft. This had been a sensible decision, for in March, 2,000 men, 300,000 ft^3 of supplies and 12,000 drums of aviation gasoline were lost in the Battle of the Bismarck Sea on their way to reinforce Japanese 51st Division in Lae. It had been intended that 20th Japanese Division would advance overland to Madang and then on to Lae, but the rugged terrain meant that little progress had been made by the time the Australian offensive began (see Shindo, 'The Japanese Army's Search for a New South Pacific Strategy', in Dean (ed.), *Australia 1943*, pp. 70–2).
104. Karl James, 'The "Salamaua Magnet"', in Peter J. Dean (ed.), *Australia 1943: The Liberation of New Guinea* (Port Melbourne: Cambridge University Press, 2014), pp. 187–202.
105. Ibid.
106. Ibid., pp. 203–5.
107. Peter J. Dean, 'From the Air, Sea and Land: The Capture of Lae', in Peter J. Dean (ed.), *Australia 1943: The Liberation of New Guinea* (Port Melbourne: Cambridge University Press, 2014), pp. 210–21. A smaller amphibious operation had taken place in Oct. 1942 when 'Drake Force' had landed at Goodenough Island (see Dean, *MacArthur's Coalition*, Ch. 9).
108. Dean, 'From the Air, Sea and Land', in Dean (ed.), *Australia 1943*, pp. 210–21.
109. Ibid., pp. 220–9.
110. Ibid., pp. 229–30; Dean, *MacArthur's Coalition*, Ch. 11.
111. Lachlan Grant, 'Operations in the Markham and Ramu Valleys', in Peter J. Dean (ed.), *Australia 1943: The Liberation of New Guinea* (Port Melbourne: Cambridge University Press, 2014), pp. 233–42; Garth Pratten, 'Applying the Principles of War: Securing the Huon Peninsula', in Peter J. Dean (ed.), *Australia 1943: The Liberation of New Guinea* (Port Melbourne: Cambridge University Press, 2014), p. 261.
112. Pratten, 'Applying the Principles of War', in Dean (ed.), *Australia 1943*, pp. 257–8.
113. Ibid., pp. 262–3.
114. Ibid., pp. 264–5. In the interest of consistency and narrative coherence, operations have typically been described from the perspective of divisions in this study. Divisions were arguably the key operational formation in the British and Commonwealth Armies. Nevertheless, it must be recognized that the Australian Army played 'loose and fast' with the brigades in its divisions in order to adapt to conditions on the ground. Brigades (both AIF and militia) were used as the core combat units of the Army in the SWPA and they were swapped between Division and Force HQ depending on the need. (The author is grateful to Peter Dean for corresponding with him on this matter.)
115. Ibid., pp. 266–9.
116. Ibid., p. 279.
117. Dean, *MacArthur's Coalition*, Ch. 12.
118. Pratten, 'Applying the Principles of War', in Dean (ed.), *Australia 1943*, p. 279.
119. Ibid., pp. 271–9.
120. Dean, *MacArthur's Coalition*, pp. 322–3.

121. Ibid.; Pratten, 'Applying the Principles of War', in Dean (ed.), *Australia 1943*, p. 279.
122. Peter J. Dean, 'Military History and 1943: A Perspective 70 Years On', in Peter J. Dean (ed.), *Australia 1943: The Liberation of New Guinea* (Port Melbourne: Cambridge University Press, 2014), p. 13; Grant, 'Operations in the Markham and Ramu Valleys', in Dean (ed.), *Australia 1943*, pp. 251–2.
123. Grant, 'Operations in the Markham and Ramu Valleys', in Dean (ed.), *Australia 1943*, p. 251.
124. Ibid., pp. 251–2; Pratten, 'Applying the Principles of War: Securing the Huon Peninsula', in Dean (ed.), *Australia 1943*, pp. 279–81; Dean, *MacArthur's Coalition*, Ch. 12. On 8 Apr., the 11th Division assumed command from 7th Division for operations in the Ramu Valley.
125. Dean, *MacArthur's Coalition*, Ch. 12.
126. Ibid., pp. 251–2; Pratten, 'Applying the Principles of War: Securing the Huon Peninsula', in Dean (ed.), *Australia 1943*, pp. 279–81; Dean, *MacArthur's Coalition*, Ch. 12. On 8 Apr., the 11th Division assumed command from 7th Division for operations in the Ramu Valley.
127. Marston, *Phoenix from the Ashes*, p. 125.
128. David Killingray, *Fighting for Britain: African Soldiers in the Second World War* (Woodbridge: James Currey, 2010), pp. 150–1; Timothy H. Parsons, *The African Rank-and-File: Social Implications of Colonial Military Service in the King's African Rifles, 1902–1964* (Oxford: James Currey, 1999), pp. 28–35.
129. Moreman, *The Jungle, the Japanese and the British Commonwealth Armies at War*, p. 109.
130. Quoted in Callahan, *Burma*, p. 89.
131. Max Hastings, *Nemesis: The Battle for Japan, 1944–45* (London: Harper Perennial, 2008 [2007]), p. 67.
132. Quoted in Callahan, *Burma*, p. 108.
133. Ibid., p. 113.
134. Moreman, *The Jungle, the Japanese and the British Commonwealth Armies at War*, pp. 85–6, 109–11.
135. Louis Allen, *Burma: The Longest War, 1941–45* (London: Phoenix Press, 2000 [1984]), pp. 170–4.
136. Moreman, *The Jungle, the Japanese and the British Commonwealth Armies at War*, pp. 85–6, 109–11.
137. Ibid., p. 110.
138. BL IOR L/WS/1/939 Morale Report, Nov. 1943–Feb. 1944, p. 1.
139. John Ellis, *Brute Force: Allied Strategy and Tactics in the Second World War* (London: André Deutsch, 1990), p. 521.
140. Moreman, *The Jungle, the Japanese and the British Commonwealth Armies at War*, p. 117.
141. Christopher Bayly and Tim Harper, *Forgotten Armies: Britain's Asian Empire & the War with Japan* (London: Penguin, 2005 [2004]), p. 360.
142. Ibid.
143. Raymond Callahan, *Triumph at Imphal–Kohima: How the Indian Army Finally Stopped the Japanese Juggernaut* (Lawrence: University Press of Kansas, 2017), p. 69.
144. Mawdsley, *World War II*, p. 236; Bayly and Harper, *Forgotten Armies*, p. 371; David Fraser, *And We Shall Shock Them: The British Army in the Second World War* (London: Cassell & Co., 1999), p. 306; Callahan, *Burma*, p. 131; Allen, *Burma*, p. 662.

145. Bayly and Harper, *Forgotten Armies*, p. 361; Fraser, *And We Shall Shock Them*, p. 306.
146. Callahan, *Triumph at Imphal–Kohima*, p. 72; Fraser, *And We Shall Shock Them*, p. 306; Allen, *Burma*, pp. 166–7
147. Moreman, *The Jungle, the Japanese and the British Commonwealth Armies at War*, pp. 118–19.
148. Ibid.
149. Ibid., pp. 118–20; Fraser, *And We Shall Shock Them*, p. 308.
150. Moreman, *The Jungle, the Japanese and the British Commonwealth Armies at War*, pp. 119–20.
151. NA WO 222/1571 Psychiatry – Arakan Campaign, p. 6.
152. BL IOR L/WS/1/939 General Staff Branch, Report on the Morale of British, Indian and African Troops in India Command and SEA Command, Feb.–Apr. 1944, pp. 1–2, 7.
153. Ibid., pp. 3–10.
154. Bayly and Harper, *Forgotten Armies*, p. 379.
155. NA WO 222/1571 Psychiatry – Arakan Campaign, p. 6; Moreman, *The Jungle, the Japanese and the British Commonwealth Armies at War*, p. 122. The XV Indian Corps was made up of 81st West African Division and 24,000 British and 45,000 Indian soldiers.
156. Slim, *Defeat into Victory*, pp. 246–7. Quoted in Moreman, *The Jungle, the Japanese and the British Commonwealth Armies at War*, p. 122.
157. Moreman, *The Jungle, the Japanese and the British Commonwealth Armies at War*, p. 124.
158. Bayly and Harper, *Forgotten Armies*, p. 380; Moreman, *The Jungle, the Japanese and the British Commonwealth Armies at War*, p. 125.
159. Moreman, *The Jungle, the Japanese and the British Commonwealth Armies at War*, p. 131.
160. Fraser, *And We Shall Shock Them*, pp. 308–9.
161. Moreman, *The Jungle, the Japanese and the British Commonwealth Armies at War*, pp. 127–8; Fraser, *And We Shall Shock Them*, p. 311.
162. Fraser, *And We Shall Shock Them*, p. 309; Moreman, *The Jungle, the Japanese and the British Commonwealth Armies at War*, p. 125.
163. Fraser, *And We Shall Shock Them*, pp. 311–13; Moreman, *The Jungle, the Japanese and the British Commonwealth Armies at War*, p. 129.
164. Fraser, *And We Shall Shock Them*, pp. 313; F. A. E. Crew, *The Army Medical Services, Campaigns, Vol. V: Burma* (London: HMSO, 1966), p. 273. The 2nd Division had been trained in combined operations and in jungle warfare.
165. Moreman, *The Jungle, the Japanese and the British Commonwealth Armies at War*, p. 126; Bayly and Harper, *Forgotten Armies*, p. 381.
166. Moreman, *The Jungle, the Japanese and the British Commonwealth Armies at War*, pp. 126.
167. Callahan, *Burma*, p. 137. Quoted in Moreman, *The Jungle, the Japanese and the British Commonwealth Armies at War*, pp. 131.
168. Moreman, *The Jungle, the Japanese and the British Commonwealth Armies at War*, pp. 131.
169. Callahan, *Burma*, p. 137. The German Sixth Army at Stalingrad was initially 300,000 strong.
170. Moreman, *The Jungle, the Japanese and the British Commonwealth Armies at War*, pp. 130, 137–9.
171. Ibid., pp. 137–9.

172. Crew, *The Army Medical Services, Campaigns, Vol. V: Burma*, pp. 287–9, 320–2.
173. Ibid., pp. 269, 289.
174. Moreman, *The Jungle, the Japanese and the British Commonwealth Armies at War*, pp. 154–5.
175. Ibid.
176. Bayly and Harper, *Forgotten Armies*, p. 388.
177. Slim quoted in Moreman, *The Jungle, the Japanese and the British Commonwealth Armies at War*, p. 140.
178. Fraser, *And We Shall Shock Them*, p. 315; Moreman, *The Jungle, the Japanese and the British Commonwealth Armies at War*, pp. 140.
179. S. W. Kirby, *The War against Japan, Vol. III: The Decisive Battles* (London: HMSO, 1962), pp. 372, 526–7; Moreman, *The Jungle, the Japanese and the British Commonwealth Armies at War*, p. 144; Bayly and Harper, *Forgotten Armies*, p. 390; Callahan, *Burma*, p. 137.
180. NA WO 203/4538 Report on the Morale of British, Indian and Colonial Troops of Allied Land Forces South-East Asia, Aug.–Oct. 1944, p. 1; NA WO 203/4536 Morale Report for British Troops of SEAC, June–Aug. 1944, p. 1; NA WO 203/4536 Report on the Morale of British Army Personnel under the Command of 11 Army Group for the Month Ending Aug. 1944, p. 1.
181.. Bayly and Harper, *Forgotten Armies*, p. 390.
182. Fraser, *And We Shall Shock Them*, p. 315.
183. Threlfall, 'The Development of Australian Army Jungle Warfare Doctrine and Training', pp. 247, 305.
184. Brendan Nelson, 'Forward', in Peter J. Dean (ed.), *Australia 1943: The Liberation of New Guinea* (Port Melbourne: Cambridge University Press, 2014), p. viii.
185. Bayly and Harper, *Forgotten Armies*, p. 362.
186. Quoted in Moreman, *The Jungle, the Japanese and the British Commonwealth Armies at War*, p. 57. The 'Jungle Book' had been distributed in Aug./Sept. 1942, too late to influence the tactics of the units sent to the Arakan.

Chapter 13 D-Day

1. Carlo D'Este, *Decision in Normandy: The Unwritten Story of Montgomery and the Allied Campaign* (London: Penguin, 2001 [1983]), pp. 25–33; Max Hastings, *Overlord: D-Day and the Battle for Normandy 1944* (London: Michael Joseph, 1984), p. 21.
2. W. G. F. Jackson, *'Overlord': Normandy 1944* (London: Werner Degener, 1978), pp. 84–5. Quoted in D'Este, *Decision in Normandy*, p. 33.
3. D'Este, *Decision in Normandy*, pp. 33–8.
4. Ibid., pp. 41–54; Andrew Stewart, *Caen Controversy: The Battle for Sword Beach 1944* (Solihull: Helion & Company, 2014), p. 23.
5. John Buckley, *Monty's Men: The British Army and the Liberation of Europe* (London: Yale University Press, 2013), pp. 5, 42.
6. Alan Allport, *Browned Off and Bloody-Minded: The British Soldier Goes to War 1939–1945* (London: Yale University Press, 2015), p. 181; L. F. Ellis, *Victory in the West, Vol. I: The Battle of Normandy* (Uckfield: The Naval & Military Press, 2004 [1962]), p. 132. XXX Corps HQ and Corps troops were also transferred from the Mediterranean to North-West Europe.
7. Buckley, *Monty's Men*, p. 19.
8. NA WO 277/36, J. W. Gibb, Training in the Army, pp. 3, 14.
9. Ibid., p. 115.

10. Ibid., pp. 33–4.
11. Ibid., pp. 5, 31, 105.
12. Stephen Bull, *Second World War Infantry Tactics: The European Theatre* (Barnsley: Pen & Sword, 2012), p. 77.
13. David French, 'Invading Europe: The British Army and its Preparations for the Normandy Campaign, 1942–44', *Diplomacy and Statecraft*, 14(2) (2003), pp. 281–2.
14. Timothy Harrison Place, *Military Training in the British Army* (London: Frank Cass, 2000), p. 78–9.
15. LAC, Crerar Vol. III, File No. 958C/009/D75 Extracts from Address by Commander First Canadian Army given on 14 May 1944. Appendix to Tactical Directive by Commander First Canadian Army, 22 July 1944.
16. Bull, *Second World War Infantry Tactics*, p. 77.
17. Montgomery's Address to the Middle East Staff College, Haifa, 21 Sept. 1942 (quoted in Stephen Brooks (ed.), *Montgomery and the Eighth Army* (London: The Bodley Head, 1991), pp. 51–9).
18. Montgomery's notes for 'Talk to Generals, 13 Jan. 1944' (quoted ibid., p. 25).
19. Charles Forrester, 'Field Marshal Montgomery's Role in the Creation of the British 21st Army Group's Combined Armed Doctrine for the Final Assault on Germany', *The Journal of Military History*, 78 (Oct. 2014), p. 1316.
20. Charles Forrester, *Montgomery's Functional Doctrine: Combined Arms Doctrine in British 21st Army Group in Northwest Europe, 1944–45* (Solihull: Helion & Company, 2015), p. 58.
21. IWM BLM 11/3 9th Infantry Brigade, Individual Training, 1937/38, Memorandum No. 2.
22. Patrick Rose, 'British Army Command Culture 1939–1945: A Comparative Study of British Eighth and Fourteenth Armies' (PhD thesis, King's College London, 2008), pp. 136–45; Forrester, 'Field Marshal Montgomery's Role', pp. 1295–9.
23. NA WO 277/36, J. W. Gibb, Training in the Army, p. 191.
24. French, 'Invading Europe', p. 280.
25. Montgomery's notes for 'Talk to Generals, 13 Jan. 1944' (quoted in Stephen Brooks (ed.), *Montgomery and the Battle of Normandy* (Stroud: The History Press, 2008), p. 32). See also, French, 'Invading Europe', pp. 279–91.
26. IWM Montgomery Papers BLM 28/3 'Lightfoot', General Plan of Eighth Army, 14 Sept. 1942.
27. David French, *Raising Churchill's Army: The British Army and the War against Germany 1919–1945* (Oxford University Press, 2000), p. 207.
28. Robert Engen, *Canadians Under Fire: Infantry Effectiveness in the Second World War* (London: McGill-Queen's University Press, 2009), p. 106.
29. NA WO 277/36, J. W. Gibb, Training in the Army, p. 191.
30. French, 'Invading Europe', p. 281.
31. The 2nd Gordon Highlanders had originally been a regular battalion. It was lost at Singapore and then reconstituted as part of the territorial 15th Scottish Division.
32. LAC T 17,924 21 AGCR, 1–15 May 1944, p. 6; Patrick Delaforce, *Monty's Iron Sides: From the Normandy Beaches to Bremen with the 3rd (British) Division* (Stroud: Sutton Publishing Ltd, 1995), pp. 5–6.
33. LAC T 17,924 CMCR, 1–15 May 1944, p. 5.
34. LAC T 17,924 21 AGCR, 16–31 May 1944, p. 4.
35. LAC T 17,924 CMCR, 16–31 May 1944, p. 5.
36. For a good example, see Stewart, *Caen Controversy*, pp. 24–8.

37. Norman Scarfe, *Assault Division: A History of the 3rd Division from the Invasion of Normandy to the Surrender of Germany* (London: Collins, 1947), p. 34.
38. Quoted in Buckley, *Monty's Men*, p. 44; Patrick Delaforce, *The Polar Bears, Monty's Left Flank: From Normandy to the Relief of Holland with the 49th Division* (Stroud: Alan Sutton, 1995), p. 1.
39. NA WO 277/19 B. Ungerson, Personal Selection, p. 88.
40. AWM 54 624/2/6 Report on Functions of AG's Branch during Invasion of Western Europe, 1944, pp. 162–82.
41. See General Routine Order No. 30 dated 14 Apr. 1944 contained in AWM 54 624/2/6 Report on Functions of AG's Branch during Invasion of Western Europe, 1944, p. 138.
42. AWM 54 624/2/6 Report on Functions of AG's Branch during Invasion of Western Europe, 1944, p. 160; Terry Copp and Bill McAndrew, *Battle Exhaustion: Soldiers and Psychiatrists in the Canadian Army, 1939–1945* (London: McGill-Queen's University Press, 1990), p. 109.
43. AWM 54 624/2/6 Report on Functions of AG's Branch during Invasion of Western Europe, 1944, pp. 162–82. Thus, plans for dealing with the efficient allocation of manpower and psychiatric casualties 'were well formulated' by the invasion of Normandy and Phillips was able to report that he had 'made personal contact with practically every medical officer' in a corps with over 65,000 troops.
44. Copp and McAndrew, *Battle Exhaustion*, pp. 111–12; LAC RG 24 Vol. 15661 Maj. R. A. Gregory, Neuropsychiatrist 3 Can. Inf. Div., to Col. F. H. van Nostrand, Chief Neuropsychiatrist CMHQ, 8 Apr. 1944.
45. LAC Vol. 12631 File No. 11/Psychiatry/1/3 Lieut. Col. J. C. Richardson RCAMC, Neuropsychiatry with the Canadian Army in Western Europe, June 1944–May 1945; Copp and McAndrew, *Battle Exhaustion*, p. 111.
46. LAC Vol. 12631 File No. 11/Psychiatry/2/2 Maj. B. H. McNeel, Officer Commanding 1 Canadian Exhaustion Unit to ADMS 4 Canadian Armoured Division, 28 June 1944. It is apparent that at least one of the armoured regiments received a lecture on 'personality, morale and the recognition of break down' also.
47. LAC Vol. 12,631 File No. 11/Psychiatry/1/2 Lieut. Col. J. C. Richardson, Commentary on Morbidity and Military Loss from Neuropsychiatric Disorders Based on a Survey of Medical Boards, 1 Jan.–30 June 1944.
48. See Chapters 6 and 10.
49. LAC T 17,924 21 AGCR, 1–15 May 1944, p. 8; NA WO 277/16 J. H. A. Sparrow, Army Morale, p. 14.
50. LAC T 17,924 21 AGCR, 1–15 May 1944, pp. 9–11.
51. NA WO 165/143 Lecture on Clerical Work in the Deputy Chief Censor's Office of a Field Force, Dec. 1948.
52. Ibid.
53. NA WO 165/42 NAAFI Army Mail Censorship Reports, 29 July 1943.
54. NA WO 165/42 Despatch of Censor Sections to BEF, 1 June 1943. Censorship was, in fact, imposed on 21st Army Group on 1 Apr. 1944. Efforts to ensure that censorship was up and running quickly on the Continent were so that this important feedback loop was not interrupted (see NA WO 165/42 Imposition of Unit Censorship on Formations to be Engaged in Operation Overlord and Subsequent Operations, 30 June 1945).
55. David Fraser, *And We Shall Shock Them: The British Army in the Second World War* (London: Cassell & Co., 1999), p. 326.
56. Buckley, *Monty's Men*, p. 25.

57. AWM 54 624/2/6 Report on Functions of AG's Branch during Invasion of Western Europe, 1944, p. 54. The US Army was concentrated in south-west England.
58. LAC T 17,924 21 AGCR, 4–30 Apr. 1944, p. 1.
59. AWM 54 624/2/6 Report on Functions of AG's Branch during Invasion of Western Europe, 1944, p. 166.
60. NA WO 177/335 Minutes of Medical Conference at Painshill Park, Cobham, 27 Apr. 1944.
61. LAC T 17,924 21 AGCR, 4–30 Apr. 1944, pp. 1–3, 6–7.
62. LAC T 17,924 21 AGCR, 1–15 May 1944, p. 9.
63. Ibid., p. 3.
64. LAC T 17,924 CMCR, 1–15 May 1944, pp. 1–2.
65. LAC T 17,924 21 AGCR, 16–31 May 1944, pp. 1–2.
66. It was described as 'high'. It had been described as 'very high' in the previous summary.
67. LAC T 17,924 21 AGCR, 1–14 June 1944, p. 1.
68. LAC T 17,924 21 AGCR, 16–31 May 1944, p. 5. Disciplinary action, nevertheless, was severe, usually resulting in the withdrawal of leave privileges from units, and a stoppage of pay for the offender. 'In most cases', the offenders considered 'the offence worth the punishment'.
69. NA CAB 106/1060 Hargest Papers, 21 June 1944, Notes; LAC T 17,924 21 AGCR, 16–31 May 1944, p. 5; Allport, *Browned Off and Bloody-Minded*, p. 181.
70. Allport, *Browned Off and Bloody-Minded*, p. 181.
71. LAC T 17,924 21 AGCR, 1–14 June 1944, p. 1. Eisenhower had already postponed the operation once, on 4 June.
72. LAC T 17,924 CMCR, 1–15 June 1944, p. 5.
73. LAC T 17,924 CMCR, 16–31 May 1944, p. 2.
74. LAC T 17,924 CMCR, 1–15 May 1944, pp. 6–10.
75. Ibid.
76. LAC RG 24 Vol. 15661 Maj. R. A. Gregory, Neuropsychiatrist, 3 Can. Div., Psychiatric Report, 17 May 1944.
77. AWM 54 624/2/6 Report on Functions of AG's Branch during Invasion of Western Europe, 1944, p. 166; NA CAB 106/1060 Hargest Papers, 21 June 1944, Notes.
78. LAC T 17,924 CMCR, 1–15 June 1944, pp. 1–2.
79. LAC T 17,924 21 AGCR, 1–14 June 1944, p. 2.
80. Fraser, *And We Shall Shock Them*, pp. 321–3. Until 1 Aug. 1944 Bradley commanded First US Army, the assaulting American Army.
81. Terry Copp, *Fields of Fire: The Canadians in Normandy* (London, University of Toronto Press, 2003), pp. 36–7.
82. Antony Beevor, *D-Day: The Battle for Normandy* (London: Viking, 2009), pp. 32–4.
83. Copp, *Fields of Fire*, pp. 36–7.
84. Copp, *Fields of Fire*, pp. 36–7.
85. Buckley, *Monty's Men*, p. 53.
86. Fraser, *And We Shall Shock Them*, pp. 321–3. Until 1 Aug. 1944 Bradley commanded First US Army, the assaulting American Army.
87. Ibid, p. 321–3.
88. Morgan's initial plan had involved three divisions assaulting the beaches in Normandy.
89. Mary Kathryn Barbier, 'Deception and Planning of D-Day', in John Buckley (ed.), *The Normandy Campaign 1944: Sixty Years On* (London: Routledge, 2006), p. 170.

90. Ibid., pp. 171–7. Two of the more famous agents involved in the deception were Dusko Popov, codenamed 'Tricycle', and Juan Garcia, codenamed 'Garbo'.
91. Ibid., pp. 171–8. In the days after D-Day, it would take less time for armoured divisions to move from the Eastern Front to France than it did for them to proceed from Eastern France to Normandy. In the first week of the invasion the Germans failed to run a single supply train into Normandy across the Seine and Loire.
92. Buckley, *Monty's Men*, p. 51; D'Este, *Decision in Normandy*, p. 74; AWM 54 624/2/6 Report on Functions of AG's Branch during Invasion of Western Europe, 1944, p. 50.
93. R. N. Gale, *With the 6th Airborne Division in Normandy* (London: Sampson Low, Marston & Co., 1948), pp. 35–6, 45; Napier Crookenden, *Dropzone Normandy: The Story of the American and British Airborne Assault on D Day 1944* (London: Ian Allan Ltd, 1976); Flint Whitlock, *If Chaos Reigns: The Near-Disaster and Ultimate Triumph of the Allied Airborne Forces on D-Day, June 6, 1944* (Newbury: Casemate, 2011). The bridges to be destroyed over the Dives were at Varaville, Robehomme, Bures and Troarn.
94. Copp, *Fields of Fire*, p. 42.
95. Buckley, *Monty's Men*, pp. 55–6.
96. Gale, *With the 6th Airborne Division in Normandy*, p. 87.
97. Ibid., pp. 47–50.
98. Buckley, *Monty's Men*, p. 57.
99. Copp, *Fields of Fire*, p. 43. Following the invasion, operational research investigators found no evidence that fighter-bomber air attack played any role in the destruction of German positions. Bomb craters and especially the shallow elongated marks left by rocket projectiles could easily be identified, and none were found at strongpoints and resistance nests in the Anglo-Canadian sector.
100. Ibid.
101. Ibid., p. 51. This is a view also held by Buckley, *Monty's Men*, p. 58.
102. NA CAB 106/1060 Hargest Papers, Notes, Neptune, 6 June 1944.
103. Copp, *Fields of Fire*, p. 45.
104. Ibid., pp. 45–6; NA CAB 106/1060 Hargest Papers, Notes, Neptune, 6 June 1944; Buckley, *Monty's Men*, p. 59.
105. Stewart, *Caen Controversy*, pp. 96–7.
106. Ibid., p. 96.
107. SANDF, DOC, UWH Box 310 The Assault Landings in Normandy, Correspondence between the UWH Section and the Historical Section, the Cabinet Office, 1958; NA WO 365/54 North-West Europe, Battle Casualties and Captures (All Ranks), No. 54, Situation at 2359hrs 9 June. The Official Historians have estimated that up to Midnight 6/7 June, 75,215 landed by sea (suffering 3,000 casualties) and 7,900 landed by air suffering 1,300 casualties). So, 83,115 landed all told, suffering 4,300 casualties. Andrew Stewart estimates that the total losses across the ten Anglo-Canadian beaches on D-Day were 1,848 (Stewart, *Caen Controversy*, p. 143).
108. In this regard, the Allied ploy of bringing their harbours with them (the 'Mulberries') was a substantial advantage, not only in adding to deception, but also in subsequently providing supplies close to the point of attack.
109. LAC Vol. 10708 File No. 56-16-3/Int, German Army Special Tactical Study No. 30, German Views on the Normandy Landing, 28 Nov. 1944; Stewart, *Caen Controversy*, pp. 50–3.

110. AWM 54 624/2/6 Report on Functions of AG's Branch during Invasion of Western Europe, 1944, pp. 3–4. See also, LHCMA De Guingand Papers, The Administrative History of the Operations of 21st Army Group on the Continent of Europe, 6 June 1944–8 May 1945, p. 8.
111. Quoted in Copp, *Fields of Fire*, p. 46.
112. LAC T 17,924 21 AGCR, 1–14 June 1944, p. 2. See also WO 165/42 Review of Submissions Arising from the Examination of Captured Enemy Mail from the Western Front Since D-Day, 24 June 1945.
113. NA CAB 106/1060 Hargest Papers, Notes, Neptune, 6 June 1944.
114. NA CAB 106/1060 Hargest Papers, Casualties and Prisoners, D-Day and Afterwards.
115. LAC T 17,924 CMCR, 15–30 June 1944, pp. 2, 6.
116. Buckley, *Monty's Men*, p. 58. The Air Force claimed that it had helped to 'demoralize' the enemy, while the Navy claimed that a good deal of neutralization had been achieved. See also LAC Vol. 10708 File No. 56-16-3/Int, German Army Special Tactical Study No. 30, German Views on the Normandy Landing, 28 Nov. 1944.
117. LAC RG24 Vol. 10708 File No. 56-16-3/Int, German Army Special Tactical Study No. 30, German Views on the Normandy Landing, 28 Nov. 1944.
118. Ibid.
119. LAC RG24 Vol. 10708 File No. 56-16-3/Int, German Army Special Tactical Study No. 29, German View of Allied Combat Efficiency, 17 Nov. 1944.
120. AWM 54 624/2/6 Report on Functions of AG's Branch during Invasion of Western Europe, 1944, p. 190; LHCMA De Guingand Papers, The Administrative History of the Operations of 21st Army Group on the Continent of Europe, 6 June 1944–8 May 1945, p. 8.
121. AWM 54 624/2/6 Report on Functions of AG's Branch during Invasion of Western Europe, pp. 3–4.
122. NA CAB 106/1060 Hargest Papers, Notes, Neptune, 6 June 1944; Buckley, *Monty's Men*, p. 59.
123. Copp, *Fields of Fire*, p. 55.
124. AWM 54 624/2/6 Report on Functions of AG's Branch during Invasion of Western Europe, pp. 3–4.
125. Copp, *Fields of Fire*, pp. 55–6.
126. AWM 54 624/2/6 Report on Functions of AG's Branch during Invasion of Western Europe, p. 335.
127. C. P. Stacey, *The Victory Campaign: The Operations in North-West Europe, 1944–1945, Official History of the Canadian Army in the Second World War, Vol. III* (Ottawa: Queen's Printer, 1966), p. 118.
128. LAC Vol. 10708 File No. 56-16-3/Int, German Army Special Tactical Study No. 30, German Views on the Normandy Landing, 28 Nov. 1944.
129. Chester Wilmot, *The Struggle for Europe* (London: Collins, 1952), pp. 304–6.
130. Buckley, *Monty's Men*, p. 52.
131. Ibid.
132. Ibid.
133. Stewart, *Caen Controversy*, p. 153.
134. LAC T 17,924 21 AGCR, 1–14 June 1944, pp. 1–2; Gale, *With the 6th Airborne Division in Normandy*, pp. 59, 70, 85.
135. LAC T 17,924 CMCR, 1–15 June 1944, pp. 1–2.
136. Stewart, *Caen Controversy*, pp. 86–97.
137. Ellis, *Victory in the West, Vol. I*, p. 212.

138. See e.g. Copp, *Fields of Fire*, pp. 51–8; Buckley, *Monty's Men*, pp. 52–9.
139. John Ferris, 'Intelligence and OVERLORD: A Snapshot from 6 June 1944', in John Buckley (ed.), *The Normandy Campaign 1944: Sixty Years On* (Abingdon: Routledge, 2006), pp. 195–6.
140. Copp, *Fields of Fire*, p. 57; Buckley, *Monty's Men*, pp. 53, 134.
141. Buckley, *Monty's Men*, p. 134.
142. Copp, *Fields of Fire*, p. 57; Buckley, *Monty's Men*, p. 53.
143. Buckley, *Monty's Men*, p. 134.
144. French, *Raising Churchill's Army*, p. 272. A similar narrative would become prevalent in the 1st Airborne Division before Operation 'Market Garden' (see William F. Buckingham, *Arnhem 1944: A Reappraisal* (Stroud: Tempus, 2002), p. 27).
145. Gale, *With the 6th Airborne Division in Normandy*, pp. 26, 56–7.
146. IWM BLM 52 Eighth Army, Some Brief Notes for Senior Officers on the Conduct of Battle, Dec. 1942.
147. Ellis, *Victory in the West, Vol. I*, p. 213.
148. LAC Vol. 18,826 File No. 133.065 (D696) Strength Returns and Casualty Figures, Assault Landing in Normandy up to 0600, 7th June; Ellis, *Victory in the West, Vol. I*, p. 223.

Chapter 14 Normandy

1. AWM 54 624/2/6 Report on Functions of AG's Branch, pp. 4–5; LHCMA De Guingand Papers, The Administrative History of 21st Army Group, p. 8; L. F. Ellis, *Victory in the West, Vol. I: The Battle of Normandy* (Uckfield: The Naval & Military Press, 2004 [1962]), p. 119.
2. Marc Milner, *Stopping the Panzers: The Untold Story of D-Day* (Lawrence: University Press of Kansas, 2014), p. 313. In the first six days ashore, the Canadians suffered 2,831 casualties.
3. David Fraser, *And We Shall Shock Them: The British Army in the Second World War* (London: Cassell & Co., 1999), p. 329.
4. John Buckley, *Monty's Men: The British Army and the Liberation of Europe* (London: Yale University Press, 2013), pp. 64–5.
5. Ibid., pp. 65–6.
6. Ibid.
7. Ibid., p. 68–9.
8. Quoted in Stephen Brooks (ed.), *Montgomery and the Battle of Normandy* (Stroud: The History Press, 2008), pp. 149–57.
9. Buckley, *Monty's Men*, p. 73; Ellis, *Victory in the West, Vol. I*, pp. 119, 261.
10. Buckley, *Monty's Men*, pp. 72–4.
11. AWM 54 624/2/6 Report on Functions of AG's Branch during Invasion of Western Europe, 1944, pp. 10–12; Buckley, *Monty's Men*, pp. 74–5. The attack, according to John Ellis, *Brute Force: Allied Strategy and Tactics in the Second World War* (London: André Deutsch, 1990), p. 358, enjoyed a 3:1 advantage in tanks.
12. Ellis, *Victory in the West, Vol. I*, p. 277; G. S. Jackson, *Operations of Eighth Corps: Account of Operations from Normandy to the River Rhine* (Buxton: MLRS, 2006), pp. 23–4; Buckley, *Monty's Men*, pp. 74–5; Ellis, *Brute Force*, pp. 358–61.
13. AWM 54 624/2/6 Report on Functions of AG's Branch during Invasion of Western Europe, 1944, pp. 10–12; Buckley, *Monty's Men*, pp. 74–5; Ellis, *Victory in the West, Vol. I*, pp. 275–9.

14. Buckley, *Monty's Men*, pp. 78–81.
15. Ibid., pp. 82–5.
16. Ned Thorburn, *The 4th KSLI in Normandy: June to August 1944* (Shrewsbury: Castle Museum, 1990), p. 50. Quoted in Buckley, *Monty's Men*, p. 85.
17. Buckley, *Monty's Men*, pp. 84–5.
18. AWM 54 624/2/6 Report on Functions of AG's Branch during Invasion of Western Europe, 1944, pp. 10–12; Buckley, *Monty's Men*, pp. 74–5.
19. Buckley, *Monty's Men*, p. 87.
20. Carlo D'Este, *Decision in Normandy: The Unwritten Story of Montgomery and the Allied Campaign* (London: Penguin, 2001 [1983]), p. 298.
21. Ibid., p. 325.
22. Buckley, *Monty's Men*, p. 88; LAC T 17,924 21 AGCR, 1–15 July 1944, p. 8; D'Este, *Decision in Normandy*, p. 309.
23. LAC T 17,924 21 AGCR, 1–15 July 1944, p. 8.
24. John Keegan, *Six Armies in Normandy: From D-Day to the Liberation of Paris* (London: Pimlico, 1988), pp. 187–8; Buckley, *Monty's Men*, pp. 88–90.
25. D'Este, *Decision in Normandy*, pp. 316–7; AWM 54 624/2/6 Report on Functions of AG's Branch during Invasion of Western Europe, 1944, p. 195.
26. Terry Copp, *Fields of Fire: The Canadians in Normandy* (London, University of Toronto Press, 2003), pp. 101–2.
27. Buckley, *Monty's Men*, p. 90–1. Stacey, *The Victory Campaign*, pp. 163–4.
28. Buckley, *Monty's Men*, p. 90–1. Stacey, *The Victory Campaign*, pp. 163–4.
29. D'Este, *Decision in Normandy*, p. 298.
30. Buckley, *Monty's Men*, pp. 92–3.
31. With reference to the table, see LHCMA Adam Papers Box 2 Casualties General, Monthly Gross Battle Casualty Rates, Percentages of Troops Engaged (as Shown on Operational Order of Battle), n.d. but 1945.
32. NA WO 365/54 North-West Europe, Battle Casualties and Captures (All Ranks) Actually Reported to GHQ 2nd Echelon 21st Army Group, No. 61, to 0600hrs 11 July; Patrick Delaforce, *The Polar Bears, Monty's Left Flank: From Normandy to the Relief of Holland with the 49th Division* (Stroud: Alan Sutton Publishing, 1995), p. 33; C. N. Barclay, *The History of the 53rd (Welsh) Division in the Second World War* (London: William Clowes and Sons, 1956), p. 60.
33. NA CAB 106/1060 Hargest Papers, 21 June 1944, Notes. To give an example, by 20 June, Hargest estimated that of the 2,735 casualties suffered by 50th Northumbrian Division, about 95% came from its infantry units.
34. The casualty percentage figure is computed on the basis of the established strength of formations. Normally a formation would be kept at the establishment figure, in spite of casualties, by use of replacements and reserves.
35. LAC T 17,924 21 AGCR, 15–30 June 1944, p. 1. This is a perspective also held by David French, 'Invading Europe: The British Army and its Preparations for the Normandy Campaign, 1942–44', *Diplomacy and Statecraft*, 14(2) (2003).
36. LAC T 17,924 21 AGCR, 15–30 June 1944, p. 1. The other three divisions were 11th Armoured Division, 3rd Division and 49th Division.
37. Ibid., p. 1.
38. LAC T 17,924 CMCR, 15–30 June 1944, p. 2.
39. The source for Figure 14.1 is LAC T 17,924 CMCRs, May 1944–June 1945.
40. The censorship summary for the second half of June noted that sickness levels were extremely low. 'It's amazing', said one man, 'when one thinks of the sick parades during our training.' See LAC T 17,924 21 AGCR, 15–30 June 1944, p. 2. Incidences of excellent morale coincided with figures of between 20 and 30 sick,

battle exhaustion, desertion, AWOL and SIW per 1,000. Incidences of high morale coincided with figures between 30 and 40 per 1,000 etc. These findings were verified statistically by use of principal co-ordinate analysis and a T-Test (see Jonathan Fennell, 'Reevaluating Combat Cohesion: The British Second Army in The Northwest Europe Campaign of the Second World War', in Anthony King (ed.), *Frontline: Combat and Cohesion in the Twenty-First Century* (Oxford University Press, 2015), pp. 144–7.

41. Figure 14.3 sources: WO 177/321 DDMS 2nd Army, War Diaries, 1943–4; WO 177/322 DDMS 2nd Army, War Diaries, 1945; LAC Vol. 12630 File No. 11/Psychiatry/1/2 Lieut. Col. J. C. Richardson, Memorandum about Current Neuropsychiatric Problems in the Canadian Army in the European Theatre of Operations, 27 Oct. 1944; WO 285/18 2nd Army, Health Reports, Dec. 1944–June 1945. WO 222/1652 DDMS Quarterly Reports, First Canadian Army, 1944–5. Second Army figures include Canadian troops under command. Figures were not available for First Canadian Army for the weeks ending 7 Oct.–30 Dec. 1944.
42. LAC T 17,924 21 AGCR, 1–15 July 1944, p. 3.
43. LAC T 17,924 CMCR, 1–15 July 1944, p. 1.
44. David French, *Raising Churchill's Army: The British Army and the War against Germany 1919–1945* (Oxford University Press, 2000), p. 266; Buckley, *Monty's Men*, p. 133.
45. LHCMA Dempsey Second Army Intelligence Reports, No. 2, 15 Aug. 1944. Quoted in Buckley, *Monty's Men*, p. 133.
46. For Figure 14.4, see: WO 219/1531 Casualty Reports, British, Canadian and US Forces Daily Summaries, including enemy prisoners taken, June–Oct. 1944; WO 219/1532 Casualty Reports, British, Canadian and US Forces Daily Summaries, including enemy prisoners taken, Oct. 1944–Mar. 1945; WO 177/316 Medical Diaries, DDMS 21st Army Group, 1944; LHCMA Papers of Gen. Sir Harold English Pyman 5/21, A Short Account of the Operations of the Second British Army; WO 365/54 Casualties NW Europe; WO 177/321 DDMS 2nd Army, War Diaries, 1943–4; WO 177/322 DDMS 2nd Army, 1945; Brooks (ed.), *Montgomery and the Battle of Normandy*, p. 131. The figures for the week ending 10 June 1944 to the week ending 8 July 1944 include prisoners captured by both British and Canadian troops. Thereafter, the figures are based on prisoners captured by British troops only.
47. WO 219/1531; WO 219/1532; WO 177/316; WO 177/321 DDMS 2nd Army, War Diaries, 1943–4; WO 177/322.
48. I. S. O. Playfair, *The Mediterranean and Middle East, Vol. I: The Early Successes against Italy* (Uckfield: The Naval & Military Press, 2004 [1954]), p. 362.
49. Brian Farrell, *The Defence and Fall of Singapore 1940–1942* (Stroud: Tempus, 2005), pp. 311 and 418; Timothy Moreman, *The Jungle, the Japanese and the British Commonwealth Armies at War, 1941–45: Fighting Methods, Doctrine and Training for Jungle Warfare* (London: Frank Cass, 2005), p. 1; AWM 54 553/3/4 Campaign in Malaya, Operation Reports of 8th Division, 1941–2; Gajendra Singh, *The Testimonies of Indian Soldiers and the Two World Wars: Between Self and Sepoy* (London: Bloomsbury, 2014), p. 157.
50. Jonathan Fennell, *Combat and Morale in the North African Campaign: The Eighth Army and the Path to El Alamein* (Cambridge University Press, 2011), p. 41.
51. LAC T 17,924 21 AGCR, 1–15 July 1944, pp. 1, 7.
52. LAC T 17,924 CMCR, 1–15 July 1944, p. 6.
53. French, *Raising Churchill's Army*, p. 266; Buckley, *Monty's Men*, p. 133.
54. Buckley, *Monty's Men*, p. 93.

55. Brooks (ed.), *Montgomery and the Battle of Normandy*, pp. 201–8.
56. Buckley, *Monty's Men*, pp. 93–5. The directive was issued on 15 July 1942.
57. Stephen Biddle, *Military Power: Explaining Victory and Defeat in Modern Battle* (Princeton University Press, 2004), p. 109.
58. Brooks (ed.), *Montgomery and the Battle of Normandy*, pp. 213–14.
59. Ibid.
60. Biddle, *Military Power*, pp. 109–16.
61. Buckley, *Monty's Men*, p. 101.
62. Biddle, *Military Power*, p. 111.
63. Jackson, *Operations of Eighth Corps*, p. 110; Buckley, *Monty's Men*, p. 99.
64. Jackson, *Operations of Eighth Corps*, pp. 92–100; Copp, *Fields of Fire*, p. 137.
65. Biddle, Military Power, pp. 127, 294–6.
66. Jackson, *Operations of Eighth Corps*, pp. 92–100.
67. Ibid.; D'Este, *Decision in Normandy*, pp. 373–4; Biddle, *Military Power*, p. 111. Cuverville had been taken at 1030hrs by 3rd Monmouthshire Regiment, 159th Brigade, but their assault on Demouville had been delayed until 1200hrs because 51st Highland Division had been slow to relieve them at Cuverville. Demouville was not taken until 1530 hours and 159th Brigade did not start to arrive near the Bourguébus Ridge until the early evening of 18 July.
68. D'Este, *Decision in Normandy*, p. 378.
69. Jackson, *Operations of Eighth Corps*, pp. 92–100.
70. Biddle, *Military Power*, p. 111.
71. Buckley, *Monty's Men*, p. 96.
72. D'Este, *Decision in Normandy*, p. 391.
73. Buckley, *Monty's Men*, pp. 117–19. In a similar vein, studies carried out during the Normandy campaign would show that only 3% of artillery shells typically fell into trenches and enemy positions during a bombardment.
74. NA CAB 106/1084 Army Operational Research Group Memorandum No. E20, Some Statistics of the North West European Campaign, June 1944–May 1945, p. 27.
75. Figure 14.5 figures derived from statistics presented ibid. The extent to which the ten-day periods coincide with bombardments and advances could possibly distort these relationships, but probably not sufficiently to take from the overall thrust of the argument outlined here.
76. WO 219/1531 Casualty Reports, British, Canadian and US Forces Daily Summaries, including enemy prisoners taken, June–Oct. 1944; WO 219/1532 Casualty Reports, British, Canadian and US Forces Daily Summaries, including enemy prisoners taken, Oct. 1944–Mar. 1945; WO 177/316 Medical Diaries, DDMS 21st Army Group, 1944; LHCMA Papers of Gen. Sir Harold English Pyman 5/21, A Short Account of the Operations of the Second British Army; NA CAB 106/1084 Some Statistics of the North West European Campaign, June 1944–May 1945.
77. Buckley, *Monty's Men*, p. 99.
78. D'Este, *Decision in Normandy*, pp. 373–4.
79. Biddle, *Military Power*, p. 116.
80. Buckley, *Monty's Men*, p. 101.
81. D'Este, *Decision in Normandy*, p. 370.
82. WO 177/321 Report by Psychiatrist Attached to 2nd Army for Month of July 1944.
83. Biddle, *Military Power*, p. 130; D'Este, *Decision in Normandy*, p. 388.
84. D'Este, *Decision in Normandy*, p. 380.

85. Ellis, *Victory in the West, Vol. I*, p. 340; *Decision in Normandy*, pp. 291–6; Chester Wilmot, *The Struggle for Europe* (London: Collins, 1952); Russell A. Hart, *Clash of Arms: How the Allies Won in Normandy* (Norman: University of Oklahoma Press, 2004 [2001]), p. 308. More recent studies have questioned the emergence of a morale crisis in Second Army in July 1944 (see David French, '"Tommy Is No Soldier": The Morale of the Second British Army in Normandy, June–Aug. 1944', *Journal of Strategic Studies*, 19(4) 1996); and Buckley, *Monty's Men*).
86. LAC T 17,924 21 AGCR, 1–15 July 1944, pp. 1–3.
87. Ibid.
88. Buckley, *Monty's Men*, p. 143.
89. The summary did, however, include a very small number of letters from Guards Armoured Division on 18 July 1944.
90. LAC T 17,924 21 AGCR, 16–31 July 1944, p. 2.
91. AWM 54 624/2/6 Report on Functions of AG's Branch during Invasion of Western Europe, 1944, p. 326.
92. WO 177/321 DDMS Second Army, Hygiene Report, Week Ending 22 July 1944.
93. AWM 54 624/2/6 Report on Functions of AG's Branch during Invasion of Western Europe, 1944, p. 175. Indeed, he pointed out that this was the case in all three armoured divisions.
94. AWM 54 624/2/6 Report on Functions of AG's Branch during Invasion of Western Europe, 1944, pp. 319–26; George Forty, *British Army Handbook, 1939–1945* (Stroud: Sutton Publishing, 1998), p. 162.
95. WO 177/335 DDMS 1 Corps, Monthly Hygiene Report, Aug. 1944; F. A. E. Crew, *The Army Medical Services, Campaigns, Vol. IV: North-West Europe* (London: HMSO, 1962), pp. 236, 421, 485; WO 171/182 War Diaries, Deputy Judge Advocate General, 21st Army Group, Apr.–Dec. 1944. AWM 54 624/2/6 Report on Functions of AG's Branch during Invasion of Western Europe, 1944, p. 326. Whereas the infantry units of VIII Corps, made up of 11,022 men, had suffered a battle exhaustion rate of 11.7 for the 9.3 days surrounding the battle. By comparison, the other 33,308 men in the corps suffered a rate of only 1.5 per 1,000.
96. AWM 54 624/2/6 Report on Functions of AG's Branch during Invasion of Western Europe, 1944, p. 197 and 323.
97. NA WO 177/335 DDMS I Corps War Diary, 28 June 1944.
98. AWM 54 624/2/6 Report on Functions of AG's Branch during Invasion of Western Europe, 1944, pp. 196–201. See Montgomery to Brooke, 14 July 1942 (quoted in Brooks (ed.), *Montgomery and the Battle of Normandy*, p. 208).
99. Terry Copp, 'To the Last Canadian?: Casualties in the 21st Army Group', *Canadian Military History*, 18(1), p. 6.
100. French, '"Tommy Is No Soldier"', p. 165.
101. The slow progress of 159th Infantry Brigade through Cuverville and Demouville was also affected by problems in 51st Highland Division, whose sickness rate went up by 59% between June and July. See WO 177/321 Maj. D. J. Watson, Monthly Report for June 1944 by Psychiatrist Attached to 2nd Army, 7 July 1944; WO 177/335 War Diary ADMS 51 (H) Division, Monthly Hygiene Report, Aug./Sept. 1944; WO 177/335 War Diary DDMS 1 Corps, Monthly Hygiene Report, Aug. 1944 and Quarterly Report Ending 30 Sept. 1944; Crew, *The Army Medical Services, Campaigns, Vol. IV: North-West Europe*, pp. 260 and 565; WO 177/405 ADMS 51 HD, War Diary June–Aug. 1944.

102. Alexander McKee, *Caen: Anvil of Victory* (London: Pan, 1966). Quoted in D'Este, *Decision in Normandy*, p. 385.
103. Montgomery to Brooke, 14 July 1944 (quoted in Brooks (ed.), *Montgomery and the Battle of Normandy*, p. 211).
104. Buckley, *Monty's Men*, p. 96.
105. B. L. Montgomery, *The Memoirs of Field-Marshal Montgomery of Alamein* (Barnsley: Pen & Sword, 2005 [1958]), p. 259.
106. Buckley, *Monty's Men*, p. 151.
107. Ian Daglish, 'Operation BLUECOAT – A Victory Ignored?', in John Buckley (ed.), *The Normandy Campaign 1944: Sixty Years On* (London: Routledge, 2006), p. 92.
108. Jackson, *Operations of Eighth Corps*, p. 123.
109. Buckley, *Monty's Men*, p. 153; Ellis, *Victory in the West, Vol. I*, p. 132.
110. Kevin Oliveau, 'Bluecoat', in Barry R. Posen (ed.), *Breakthroughs: Armored Offensives in Western Europe 1944* (MIT/DACS Conventional Forces Working Group, 1994), p. 4, http://docplayer.net/21335961-Breakthroughs-armored-offensives-in-western-europe-1944.html; Ellis, *Victory in the West, Vol. I*, p. 387.
111. Jackson, *Operations of Eighth Corps*, p. 126.
112. Oliveau, 'Bluecoat', in Posen (ed.), *Breakthroughs*, p. 5; Ellis, *Victory in the West, Vol. I*, p. 387.
113. SANDF, DOC, UWH Box 345 Medical History, North-West Europe, Note on Psychiatric Casualties During the Quarter July–Sept. 1944.
114. LAC T 17,924 21 AGCR, 1–15 July 1944, p. 1; LAC T 17,924 21 AGCR, 15–31 July 1944, pp. 1, 5–6. See also, Patrick Delaforce, *The Black Bull: From Normandy to the Baltic with the 11th Armoured Division* (Stroud: Alan Sutton, 1993), pp. 69–71.
115. LAC T 17,924 21 AGCR, 1–15 July 1944, p. 4; LAC T 17,924 21 AGCR, 15–31 July 1944, p. 4.
116. LAC T 17,924 21 AGCR, 1–15 July 1944, p. 11; LAC T 17,924 21 AGCR, 15–31 July 1944, pp. 1, 4. In the first half of July, incoming mail had a time lag of four to five days and outgoing mail took an average of six to nine days to reach the Base Censor, with a further lag of three to four days to reach an address in the UK. In the second half of July, incoming mail took about two to three days to reach the troops while the improvement in some outgoing mail meant that some correspondence reaching loved ones within one day of sending.
117. LAC T 17,924 21 AGCR, 1–15 July 1944, p. 1, 5; LAC T 17,924 21 AGCR, 15–31 July 1944, p. 5.
118. Buckley, *Monty's Men*, pp. 131–2.
119. NA WO 291/1331 Bombing in Operation Goodwood, No. 2 Operational Research Section Report No. 6.
120. Buckley, *Monty's Men*, pp. 156–7.
121. Daglish, 'Operation BLUECOAT', in Buckley (ed.), *The Normandy Campaign 1944*, pp. 92–3.
122. Buckley, *Monty's Men*, p. 157.
123. Ibid., pp. 154–60; Ellis, *Victory in the West, Vol. I*, p. 402.
124. Buckley, *Monty's Men*, p. 157.
125. LAC T 17,924 21 AGCR, 1–14 Aug. 1944, p. 3.
126. LAC T 17,924 21 AGCR, 15–31 Aug. 1944, pp. 3–4. A lieutenant in 5th RHA wrote 'during the last month we have had a pretty difficult time. It has been hard going ... Most of our fellows have had enough of war, and although I have only been in it a short time I am beginning to feel the same.' A captain in 1/6 Queens

confided that 'there is no doubt, though, that one's nerves are not what they were, and a lot of us begin to feel we've had all we want.'

127. Jackson, *Operations of Eighth Corps*, pp. 127–9.
128. Daglish, 'Operation BLUECOAT', in Buckley (ed.), *The Normandy Campaign 1944*, pp. 91–5.
129. Ibid., pp. 96–8.
130. Ibid., pp. 96–100.
131. Ibid.
132. Oliveau, 'Bluecoat', in Posen (ed.), *Breakthroughs*, p. 17.
133. Daglish, 'Operation BLUECOAT', in Buckley (ed.), *The Normandy Campaign 1944*, pp. 96–100.
134. Buckley, *Monty's Men*, pp. 167–9.
135. Ibid., pp. 169.
136. David J. Bercuson, *Maple Leaf against the Axis: Canada's Second World War* (Calgary: Red Deer Press, 2004), p. 228; John A. English, *The Canadian Army and the Normandy Campaign: A Study of Failure in High Command* (London: Praeger, 1991), pp. 265–6; Douglas E. Delaney, *Corps Commanders: Five British and Canadian Generals at War, 1939–45* (Vancouver: University of British Columbia Press, 2011), pp. 229–30.
137. Bercuson, *Maple Leaf against the Axis*, p. 228; English, *The Canadian Army and the Normandy Campaign*, pp. 265–6; Delaney, *Corps Commanders*, pp. 229–30.
138. Stephen A. Hart, *The Road to Falaise* (Stroud: Sutton Publishing, 2004), pp. 23–34; Stephen A. Hart, '"The Black Day Unrealised": Operation TOTALIZE and the Problems of Translating Tactical Success into a Decisive Breakout', in John Buckley (ed.), *The Normandy Campaign 1944: Sixty Years On* (London: Routledge, 2006), p. 107; English, *The Canadian Army and the Normandy Campaign*, pp. 269–89; Buckley, *Monty's Men*, p. 171; Stacey, *The Victory Campaign*, p. 222. The 88mms mostly belonged to three Luftwaffe Flak regiments, and, according to Hart, were not deployed to counter the ground offensive. Brian A. Reid, in *No Holding Back: Operation Totalize, Normandy, August 1944* (Mechanicsburg: Stackpole, 2004), pp. 388–91, estimates that 89th Division had a strength of 8,000 troops and that 12 SS Panzer Division had between 11,000 and 11,500 troops. These figures, however, appear to be the total establishment of these divisions rather than front-line troops. The figure for 89th Division was calculated thus: the division had two infantry regiments with three battalions each; given that a German battalion normally numbered 600 to 800 men (and 89th Division was still 'fresh'), this would add up to about 3,600–4,800 men. The total number of 'front line' troops, i.e. in addition to infantry, was calculated to be a bit higher than this, so about 5,000 men. The author is grateful to Dr Peter Lieb for corresponding with him on this matter.
139. Buckley, *Monty's Men*, pp. 172–6.
140. Hart, '"The Black Day Unrealised"', in Buckley (ed.), *The Normandy Campaign 1944*, p. 109.
141. Buckley, *Monty's Men*, pp. 173–6.
142. Ibid., p. 177.
143. Rick Atkinson, *The Guns at Last Light: The War in Western Europe, 1944–1945* (London: Little, Brown, 2013), p. 161; Delaney, *Corps Commanders*, Map 13.
144. D'Este, *Decision in Normandy*, pp. 437–60; Atkinson, *The Guns at Last Light*, pp. 158–70.
145. English, *The Canadian Army and the Normandy Campaign*, pp. 292–3.

146. Ibid., pp. 296–8. On the whole, only one in twenty German tanks in Normandy was a Tiger (Alan Allport, *Browned Off and Bloody-Minded: The British Soldier Goes to War 1939–1945* (London: Yale University Press, 2015), p. 232).
147. Atkinson, *The Guns at Last Light*, pp. 161–6.
148. English, *The Canadian Army and the Normandy Campaign*, pp. 299–300; Bercuson, *Maple Leaf against the Axis*, p. 233; Stacey, *The Victory Campaign*, p. 270.
149. Atkinson, *The Guns at Last Light*, p. 169.
150. English, *The Canadian Army and the Normandy Campaign*, pp. 299–300; Bercuson, *Maple Leaf against the Axis*, p. 233; Stacey, *The Victory Campaign*, p. 270.
151. D'Este, *Decision in Normandy*, p. 437.
152. Atkinson, *The Guns at Last Light*, p. 169.
153. Ibid., p. 160.
154. D'Este, *Decision in Normandy*, p. 459.
155. Ibid., pp. 437–60; Atkinson, *The Guns at Last Light*, pp. 158–70.
156. Delaney, *Corps Commanders*, pp. 189, 217, 233–7. See also, Reid, *No Holding Back*.
157. LAC T 17,924 CMCRs, May 1944–June 1945.
158. LAC T 17,924 CMCR, 1–15 Aug. 1944, p. 3.
159. WO 222/1652 DDMS Quarterly Reports, First Canadian Army, 1944–5.
160. The rate for its supporting armoured unit, 33rd Armoured Brigade, was even higher, 24 per 1,000 for the week ending 12 Aug. LAC RG24 Vol. 18,712 File No. 133.065(D327B) Medical Statistics, First Canadian Army, 1945C; NA WO 177/321 Maj. D. J. Watson, Monthly Report for June 1944 by Psychiatrist Attached to 2nd Army, 7 July 1944; NA WO 177/335 War Diary ADMS 51 (H) Division, Monthly Hygiene Report, Aug./Sept. 1944; NA WO 177/335 War Diary DDMS 1 Corps, Monthly Hygiene Report, Aug. 1944 and Quarterly Report Ending 30 Sept. 1944; F. A. E. Crew, *The Army Medical Services, Campaigns, Vol. IV: North-West Europe* (London: HMSO, 1962), pp. 260 and 565; NA WO 177/405 ADMS 51 HD, War Diary June–Aug. 1944.
161. LAC RG24 Vol. 18,712 File No. 133.065(D327B) Medical Statistics, First Canadian Army, 1945C.
162. LAC T 17,924 CMCR, 1–15 Aug. 1944, p. 4; LAC T 17,924 CMCR, 16–31 Aug. 1944, p. 3.
163. LAC RG24 Vol. 15652 Rear HQ 2 Canadian Corps, Memorandum on Diarrhoea, 3 Aug. 1944.
164. LAC RG24 Vol. 15661 ADMS 3 Can. Div., Quarterly Report, 1 July–1 Oct. 1944, p. 6.
165. LAC RG24 Vol. 15661 Col. M. C. Watson, ADMS 3 Can. Div., to GOC 3 Can. Div., 26 July 1944.
166. LAC RG24 Vol. 15661 War Diary ADMS 3 Can. Inf. Div.
167. LAC RG24 Vol. 15951 War Diary No. 1 Canadian Exhaustion Unit RCAMC, Aug. 1944.
168. Delaney, *Corps Commanders*, pp. 227–33.
169. Copp, 'To the Last Canadian?', p. 6; Copp, *Fields of Fire*, p. 196; Delaney, *Corps Commanders*, p. 216.
170. Carlo D'Este, 'Falaise: The Trap Not Sprung', in Robert Cowley (ed.), *No End Save Victory* (London: Cassell & Co., 2002), pp. 466–7; Buckley, *Monty's Men*, p. 183.
171. Buckley, *Monty's Men*, p. 183.

172. Stacey, *The Victory Campaign*, p. 269. Montgomery's casualty estimates can be found in Montgomery, *Memoirs*, p. 263.
173. English, *The Canadian Army and the Normandy Campaign*, pp. 299–300; Bercuson, *Maple Leaf against the Axis*, p. 233; Stacey, *The Victory Campaign*, p. 270.
174. Stacey, *The Victory Campaign*, p. 270.
175. Terry Copp, 'If This War Isn't Over, and Pretty Damn Soon', in P. Addison and A. Calder (eds.), *Time to Kill: The Soldier's Experience of War in the West, 1939–1945* (London: Pimlico, 1997), pp. 148–9.

Chapter 15 The Victory Campaigns

1. LAC T 17,924 21 AGCR, 1–15 Sept. 1944, p. 1. A large proportion of the letters covered in this report were written in the period just after the closing of the Falaise pocket. See also, LAC T 17,924 CAO, Censorship Report, 1–15 Sept. 1944, pp. 10–11.
2. Quoted in Terry Copp, *Cinderella Army: The Canadians in Northwest Europe 1944–1945* (London: University of Toronto Press, 2006), p. 17.
3. B. L. Montgomery, *The Memoirs of Field-Marshal Montgomery of Alamein* (Barnsley: Pen & Sword, 2005 [1958]), p. 266.
4. Quoted in John Buckley, *Monty's Men: The British Army and the Liberation of Europe* (London: Yale University Press, 2013), p. 184.
5. Quoted in Copp, *Cinderella Army*, p. 25.
6. XXX Corps, after Bucknall's sacking during 'Bluecoat', was now under the command of Lieut. Gen. Brian Horrocks. XII Corps, under the command of the rehabilitated Lieut. Gen. Neil Richie, had played a largely supporting role in Normandy (Ritchie had been the victim of Rommel at Gazala in the summer of 1942).
7. Buckley, *Monty's Men*, pp. 184–8; Copp, *Cinderella Army*, p. 21.
8. LAC T 17,924 21 AGCR, 1–15 Sept. 1944, p. 3.
9. LAC Vol. 10706 File No. 46-3-6/Int Vol. 1, 21 AGCR, 16–30 Sept. 1944, pp. 3–4; NA WO 277/16 Morale, p. 14.
10. NA WO 222/1652 DDMS Quarterly Reports, First Canadian Army, 1944–5.
11. LAC T 17,924 CMCR, 1–15 Sept. 1944, pp. 1–2.
12. LAC T 17,924 CMCR, 16–31 Aug. 1944, pp. 8–9.
13. Ibid., p. 9.
14. LAC T 17,924 CMCR, 1–15 Sept. 1944, pp. 1–2.
15. Ibid., p. 1.
16. LAC T 17,924 CMCR, 16–31 Aug. 1944, p. 11.
17. LAC T 17,924 CMCR, 1–15 Sept. 1944, p. 9.
18. Buckley, *Monty's Men*, pp. 184–8. 11th Armoured Division had been transferred to XXX Corps.
19. Ibid., pp. 195–7; Ronald Gill and John Groves, *Club Route in Europe: The Story of 30 Corps in the European Campaign* (Hanover: Werner Degener, 1946), p. 54.
20. French, *Raising Churchill's Army*, p. 263.
21. LAC T 17,924 CMCR, 1–15 Sept. 1944, p. 11.
22. Copp, *Cinderella Army*, p. 38; John Buckley and Peter Preston-Hough, 'Introduction', in John Buckley and Peter Preston-Hough (eds.), *Operation Market Garden: The Campaign for the Low Countries, Autumn 1944: Seventy Years On* (Solihull: Helion, 2016), p. xv; James M. Gavin, *On to Berlin: Battles of an Airborne Commander 1943–1946* (London: Leo Cooper, 1979), p. 137. For an

analysis of the controversy surrounding the failure to clear the northern bank of the Scheldt estuary, see Buckley, *Monty's Men*, pp. 200–6.

23. Copp, *Cinderella Army*, p. 83.
24. Buckley, *Monty's Men*, pp. 202–4. Montgomery now commanded 21st Army Group and Bradley commanded 12th Army Group. The impact of this effective 'demotion' was somewhat smoothed by promoting Montgomery to the rank of field-marshal.
25. Robert S. Rush, 'A Different Perspective: Cohesion, Morale and Operational Effectiveness in the German Army, Fall 1944', *Armed Forces and Society*, 25(3) (Spring 1999), p. 501.
26. NA WO 219/1531; NA WO 219/1532; NA WO 177/316; NA WO 177/321 DDMS 2nd Army, War Diaries, 1943–4; WO 177/322; Buckley, *Monty's Men*, pp. 194–7.
27. Buckley, *Monty's Men*, pp. 192–4. Le Havre fell on 12 Sept. These casualties were British as I Corps was fighting under First Canadian Army at the time.
28. John Ellis, *Brute Force: Allied Strategy and Tactics in the Second World War* (London: André Deutsch, 1990), p. 394; Jack Didden, 'A Week Too Late?', in John Buckley and Peter Preston-Hough (eds.), *Operation Market Garden: The Campaign for the Low Countries, Autumn 1944: Seventy Years On* (Solihull: Helion, 2016), p. 77.
29. LAC Vol. 18,502 File No. 133(D2) Number of US and British Commonwealth Divisions in Theatres of Operations, Europe and Far East, Oct. 1944; Roger Cirillo, 'Market Garden and the Strategy of the Northwest Europe Campaign', in John Buckley and Peter Preston-Hough (eds.), *Operation Market Garden: The Campaign for the Low Countries, Autumn 1944: Seventy Years On* (Solihull: Helion, 2016), p. 41; James M. Gavin, *On to Berlin: Battles of an Airborne Commander 1943–1946* (London: Leo Cooper, 1979), p. 134; Lloyd Clarke, *Arnhem: Operation Market Garden, Sept. 1944* (Thrupp: Sutton, 2002), p. 15.
30. Ellis, *Brute Force*, pp. 395–6.
31. Buckley, *Monty's Men*, 208–14; Montgomery, *Memoirs*, p. 288; Sebastian Ritchie, 'Learning to Lose?: Airborne Lessons the Failure of Operation Market Garden', in John Buckley and Peter Preston-Hough (eds.), *Operation Market Garden: The Campaign for the Low Countries, Autumn 1944: Seventy Years On* (Solihull: Helion, 2016), p. 19; Gavin, *On to Berlin*, p. 134.
32. The First Allied Airborne Army was Eisenhower's strategic reserve, representing about one-sixth of his total fighting strength (see Geoffrey Powell, *The Devil's Birthday: The Bridges to Arnhem 1944* (Barnsley: Pen & Sword, 2012 [1984]), p. 11). The 82nd and 101st Airborne were transferred to Browning's Corps for the 'Market Garden' operation.
33. Buckley, *Monty's Men*, 208–14; Montgomery, *Memoirs*, p. 288; Clarke, *Arnhem*, pp. 14–22. Both the American Divisions had recently seen action in Normandy, but the 1st British Airborne Division had not fought since 1943 and the Polish Parachute Brigade was as yet untested.
34. Buckley, *Monty's Men*, 214.
35. Montgomery, *Memoirs*, p. 297.
36. Ritchie, 'Learning to Lose?', in Buckley and Preston-Hough (eds.), *Operation Market Garden*, p. 19.
37. Powell, *The Devil's Birthday*, p. 70; William F. Buckingham, *Arnhem 1944: A Reappraisal* (Stroud: Tempus, 2002), p. 119.

38. WO 219/1531; WO 219/1532; WO 177/316; WO 177/321 DDMS 2nd Army, War Diaries, 1943–4; WO 177/322.
39. See Rush, 'A Different Perspective', p. 480.
40. Ibid., p. 500.
41. LAC T 17,924 CMCR, 1–15 Sept. 1944, p. 12.
42. LAC Vol. 10706 File No. 46-3-6/Int Vol. 1, 21st AGCR, 1–15 Oct. 1944, p. 15.
43. LAC T 17,924 CMCR, 1–15 Sept. 1944, p. 12.
44. LAC T 17,924 CMCR, 16–31 Aug. 1944, p. 8. For more on this dynamic see Niall Fergusson, 'Prisoner Taking and Prisoner Killing in the Age of Total War: Towards a Political Economy of Military Defeat', *War in History*, 11(2) (2004), pp. 185–92.
45. NA WO 219/1531; NA WO 219/1532; NA WO 177/316; NA WO 177/321 DDMS 2nd Army, War Diaries, 1943–4; NA WO 177/322.
46. Robert J. Kershaw, *'It Never Snows in September': The German View of Market Garden and the Battle of Arnhem, September 1944* (Addlestone: Ian Allan Ltd, 1994), p. 53.
47. Ibid., pp. 221–7; Buckingham, *Arnhem 1944*, pp. 135–42; Powell, *The Devil's Birthday*, pp. 159–64; Gavin, *On to Berlin*, pp. 179–81.
48. Buckley, *Monty's Men*, 221–30; Ellis, *Brute Force*, p. 405; Montgomery, *Memoirs*, p. 295; David Fraser, *And We Shall Shock Them: The British Army in the Second World War* (London: Cassell & Co., 1999), p. 346; Kershaw, *'It Never Snows in September'*, p. 311. Only 125 officers, 400 glider pilots and 1,700 NCOs and men from 1st Airborne Division made it back to Second Army.
49. See, e.g., Kershaw, *'It Never Snows in September'*; Buckingham, *Arnhem 1944*; Powell, *The Devil's Birthday*; Gavin, *On to Berlin*.
50. Buckley, *Monty's Men*, 208.
51. Martin Middlebrook, *Arnhem 1944: The Airborne Battle* (London: Penguin, 1995), pp. 442–4.
52. Ibid., 214–18; David Bennett, *A Magnificent Disaster: The Failure of Market Garden, The Arnhem Operation September 1944* (Newbury: Casemate, 2008), p. 26; Buckingham, *Arnhem 1944*, p. 123.
53. Montgomery, *Memoirs*, p. 298.
54. Buckley, *Monty's Men*, 212.
55. Middlebrook, *Arnhem 1944*, pp. 441–2.
56. For example, combat ratios on 20 Sept. were 3:1 in favour of the Germans in the Arnhem area and 2:1 in favour of the Germans in the Nijmegen–Groesbeek area (see Kershaw, *'It Never Snows in September'*, p. 305. 'Market Garden' involved around 35,000 airborne troops (Ritchie, 'Learning to Lose?', in Buckley and Preston-Hough (eds.), *Operation Market Garden*, p. 28).
57. Max Hastings, *Armageddon: The Battle for Germany, 1944–45* (London: Pan Books, 2005 [2004]), pp. 392–3. By the beginning of 1945, only fifteen of the seventy-three divisions in North-West Europe were Anglo-Canadian. Twelve were British and three were Canadian.
58. Buckley, *Monty's Men*, pp. 251–2; Fraser, *And We Shall Shock Them*, p. 382; Hastings, *Armageddon*, pp. 392–3.
59. These were the four French divisions, the only mountain troops of 'high quality' in Italy and three American divisions from Fifth Army (see Fraser, *And We Shall Shock Them*, p. 351). The operation took place in Aug. 1944.
60. Quoted in Raymond Callahan, *Churchill and His Generals* (Lawrence: University Press of Kansas, 2007), p. 180.

61. Buckley, *Monty's Men*, pp. 251–2; Fraser, *And We Shall Shock Them*, p. 382; Hastings, *Armageddon*, pp. 392–3.
62. Ian Gooderson, *A Hard Way to Make a War: The Allied Campaign in Italy in the Second World War* (London: Conway, 2008), pp. 281, 287–8.
63. Ellis, *Brute Force*, p. 326; C. J. C. Molony and W. Jackson, *The Mediterranean and Middle East, Vol. VI, Pt II: Victory in the Mediterranean* (Uckfield: Naval & Military Press, 2004), pp. 128, 225–30.
64. The 2nd New Zealand Division was classed as an armoured division as it contained 4th New Zealand Armoured Brigade.
65. Ellis, *Brute Force*, p. 326; Molony and Jackson, *The Mediterranean and Middle East, Vol. VI, Pt II*, pp. 128, 225–30.
66. NA WO 204/10381 CMF ACR No. 51, 16–31 Aug. 1944, pp. A1, B1–2.
67. LAC RG24 Vol. 15651 War Diary, Medical Branch HQ 1 Canadian Corps; LAC RG24 Vol. 15651 Folder 4 War Diary DDMS, 1 Corps, Sept. 1943–Feb. 1944; LAC RG24 Vol. 12559 File No. 11/AAI 1Corps/1 General Medical Correspondence, 1st Canadian Corps; LAC RG24 Vol. 12559 Medical History I Canadian Corps, July–Sept. 1944, p. 25; LAC RG24 Vol. 12559 Medical History I Canadian Corps, Oct.–Dec. 1944, p. 16; Molony and Jackson, *The Mediterranean and Middle East, Vol. VI, Pt II*, pp. 231–2. Between Oct. and Dec. 1944, infectious hepatitis accounted for 25.2% of all sickness in I Canadian Corps.
68. Douglas E. Delaney, *Corps Commanders: Five British and Canadian Generals at War, 1939–45* (Vancouver: University of British Columbia Press, 2011), pp. 102–4.
69. Ibid.
70. Ibid., pp. 110–11.
71. Ibid., pp. 115–16.
72. Shelford Bidwell and Dominick Graham, *The Tug of War: The Battle for Italy, 1943–45* (London: Hodder & Stoughton, 1986), p. 353; Gooderson, *A Hard Way to Make A War*, p. 290–1.
73. Delaney, *Corps Commanders*, pp. 110–11; Bidwell and Graham, *The Tug of War*, pp. 357–8; Molony and Jackson, *The Mediterranean and Middle East, Vol. VI, Pt II*, p. 128.
74. Gooderson, *A Hard Way to Make A War*, p. 290–1; Bidwell and Graham, *The Tug of War*, pp. 353–9; Fraser, *And We Shall Shock Them*, pp. 352–6; Douglas Porch, *Hitler's Mediterranean Gamble: The North African and the Mediterranean Campaigns in World War II* (London: Weidenfeld & Nicolson, 2004), pp. 622–3; Molony and Jackson, *The Mediterranean and Middle East, Vol. VI, Pt II*, pp. 263, 300–4.
75. Fraser, *And We Shall Shock Them*, p. 377. Kershaw, *'It Never Snows in September'*, pp. 23–4, puts the figures at 65,000 men, 225 guns, 750 trucks and wagons, and 1,000 horses.
76. DHH CMHQ Report No. 188, Canadian Operations: The Clearing of the Scheldt Estuary, 1 Oct.–8 Nov. 1944, pp. 11–17.
77. Quoted in Buckley, *Monty's Men*, p. 251.
78. Stephen A. Hart, *Colossal Cracks: Montgomery's 21st Army Group in Northwest Europe, 1944–45* (Mechanicsburg: Stackpole, 2007 [2000]), p. 44.
79. Buckley, *Monty's Men*, p. 133; Hart, *Colossal Cracks*, pp. 46–7. The British had estimated that 48% of casualties would be infantrymen, but, in fact, due to the character of the fighting in Normandy and Italy, up to 75% of casualties were

among infantry units (see J. L. Granatstein, *Conscription in the Second World War* (Toronto: McGraw-Hill Ryerson, 1969), pp. 55–6).

80. Christine Ann Bielecki, 'British Infantry Morale during the Italian Campaign, 1943–1945' (PhD thesis, University College London, 2006), p 130.
81. Ibid., pp. 135–42, 166; NA WO 177/322 Second Army, Quarterly Medical Report for period 1 Apr. 1945–25 June 1945. Although replacements after Sicily did not keep up with casualties (6,645 replacements were immediately provided, only 56% of the requirement), all told, battle casualties in Eighth Army were matched by replacements (casualties in Eighth Army had reached 85,994 by Dec. 1944, an average of 5,375 a month. In 1944, 63,543 British reinforcements arrived in Italy (an average of 5,295 a month).
82. NA CAB 101/224 D. F. Butler, The British Soldier in Italy, Sept. 1943–June 1944, p. 8.
83. LAC Crerar Vol. IV, File No. 958C.009 (D110) Lieut. Gen. C. G. Simonds, GOC 2nd Canadian Corps, to Maj. Gen. C. Foulkes, GOC 2nd Can. Inf. Div., Maj. Gen. D. C. Spry, GOC 3rd Can. Inf. Div., and Maj. Gen. H. W. Foster, GOC 4th Can Armd Div, 29 Aug. 1944.
84. WO 177/321 DDMS 2nd Army, War Diaries, 1943–4; WO 177/322 DDMS 2nd Army, War Diaries, 1945; LAC Vol. 12630 File No. 11/Psychiatry/1/2 Lieut. Col. J. C. Richardson, Memorandum about Current Neuropsychiatric Problems in the Canadian Army in the European Theatre of Operations, 27 Oct. 1944; WO 285/18 2nd Army, Health Reports, Dec. 1944–June 1945; LAC RG24 Vol. 12631 File No. 11/Psychiatry/1/3 Lieut. Col. J. C. Richardson RCAMC, Neuropsychiatry with the Canadian Army in Western Europe, June 1944–May 1945; LAC RG24 Vol. 12631 File No. 11/Psychiatry/5 Reports, Divisional Neuropsychiatric Report, 27 June 1944; NA CAB 106/1084 Some Statistics of the North-West European Campaign June 1944–May 1945; LAC Stuart MG30/E520; Copp, *Cinderella Army*, Appendix C. A detailed examination of the weekly figures for Second Army puts the total figure of battle exhaustion at 13,295 while Lieut. Col. J. C. Richardson, the senior Canadian psychiatrist in North-West Europe, thought that battle exhaustion cases were probably in the neighbourhood of 6,000 in the Canadian Army in North-West Europe (see LAC RG24 Vol. 12631 File No. 11/Psychiatry/1/3 Lieut. Col. J. C. Richardson RCAMC, Neuropsychiatry with the Canadian Army in Western Europe, June 1944–May 1945).
85. NA WO 177/325 Medical Diaries DDMS 8th Army Jan.–Dec. 1943; NA WO 177/326 Medical Diaries DDMS 8th Army, Jan.–Dec. 1944; WO 204/7647; SANDF, DOC, UWH Box 346/U/Med 60/12 The Campaign in Sicily, July–Aug. 1943.
86. F. A. E. Crew, *The Army Medical Services, Campaigns, Vol. III: Sicily, Italy and Greece (1944–45)* (Uckfield: Naval & Military Press, 2014 [1957]), pp. 516–21.
87. NA CAB 101/224 D. F. Butler, The British Soldier in Italy, Sept. 1943–June 1944, p. 10.
88. LAC RG24 Vol. 12,631 File No. 11/Psychiatry/1/2 Lieut. Col. A. M. Doyle, RCAMC, Neuropsychiatric Advisor Canadian Section, AFHQ, 'Psychiatry with the Canadian Army in Action in the C.M.F.', n.d., p. 6. This total, he estimated, represented about 20% of those personnel lost due to battle casualties. Of those cases classified as neuropsychiatric casualties, 9.1% were in the artillery and 6.8% engineers. About 7.4% were in the armoured corps.
89. NA WO 177/322 Second Army, Quarterly Medical Report for period 1 Apr. 1945–25 June 1945, pp. 24–5.
90. LHCMA De Guingand, Administrative History of 21 AG.

91. NA CAB 106/453 Cabinet Office Military Narratives of the War, Operations of British, Dominion and Indian Forces in Italy, pp. 10–13.
92. Alan Allport, *Browned Off and Bloody-Minded: The British Soldier Goes to War 1939–1945* (London: Yale University Press, 2015), p. 159.
93. NA CAB 106/453 Cabinet Office Military Narratives of the War, Operations of British, Dominion and Indian Forces in Italy, pp. 10–13.
94. Copp and McAndrew, *Battle Exhaustion*, p. 106; LAC RG 24 Vol. 18,571 File No. 133.055(D1) Summary: Trials by Courts Martial, 1939–49.
95. ANZ WAII/8/BBB Summary of Cases Tried by FGCM, Eighth Army, Jan. 1944–Jan. 1945.
96. LAC RG24 Vol. 12,631 File No. 11/Psychiatry/1/2 Report of Survey of Canadian Soldiers under Sentence in the CMF 1945. 84% were incarcerated due to AWOL or desertion. A report on British soldiers in Italy noted a similar dynamic, pointing out that absence and desertion occurred 'almost always among front line troops' and 'by far the greatest number of desertions took place either when the troops were moving up for action or on the eve of a major assault' (see NA CAB 101/224 D. F. Butler, The British Soldier in Italy, Sept. 1943–June 1944, pp. 33–6).
97. NA CAB 101/224 D. F. Butler, The British Soldier in Italy, Sept. 1943–June 1944, pp. 35–40.
98. NA CAB 101/224 D. F. Butler, The British Soldier in Italy, Sept. 1943–June 1944, pp. 35–40.
99. Quoted in David French, 'Discipline and the Death Penalty in the British Army in the War against Germany during the Second World War', *Journal of Contemporary History*, 33(4) (Oct. 1998), p. 540.
100. John Peaty, 'The Desertion Crisis in Italy, 1944', *The RUSI Journal*, 147(3) (2002), pp. 78–80.
101. Ibid.
102. Ibid.
103. NA CAB 101/224 D. F. Butler, The British Soldier in Italy, Sept. 1943–June 1944, pp. 39–40; NA CAB 106/453 Cabinet Office Military Narratives of the War, Operations of British, Dominion and Indian Forces in Italy, p. 10.
104. Peaty, 'The Desertion Crisis in Italy, 1944', p. 82.
105. AWM 54 624/2/6 Report on Functions of AG's Branch during Invasion of Western Europe, 1944, p. 187, B. L. Montgomery, C-in-C 21 Army Group, Memorandum on Venereal Disease, Oct. 1944.
106. WO 177/321 DDMS 2nd Army, War Diaries, 1943–4; WO 177/322 DDMS 2nd Army, War Diaries, 1945; WO 285/18 2nd Army, Health Reports, Dec. 1944–June 1945. Figure covers the period 11 June 1944–26 May 1945.
107. WO 222/1652 DDMS Quarterly Reports Canadian First Army, 1944–5, June–Sept. 1944 and Jan.–June 1945; LAC Vol. 18,712 File No. 133.065(D327B) Health of the Troops, First Canadian Army, Oct.–Dec. 1944. Figure covers the period 16 July 1944–26 May 1945. For Figure 15.1 see F. A. E. Crew, *The Army Medical Services, Campaigns, Vol. IV: North-West Europe* (London: HMSO, 1962), pp. 592–3; AWM 54 624/2/6 Report on Functions of AG's Branch during Invasion of Western Europe, 1944, p. 188. It is interesting to note that the incidence of VD among Allied contingents of 21st Army Group was even higher. For example, the incidence among Allied contingents for the week ending 24 Feb. 1945 was 3.07 per thousand, approximately 'five times higher' than the combined Anglo-Canadian rate (see NA WO 285/18 Medical SITREP, 21 Army Group, Week Ending 24 Feb. 1945).

108. NA WO 177/325 Medical Diaries DDMS 8th Army Jan.–Dec. 1943; NA WO 177/326 Medical Diaries DDMS 8th Army, Jan.–Dec. 1944; NA WO 204/7647; SANDF, DOC, UWH Box 346/U/Med 60/12 The Campaign in Sicily, July–Aug. 1943. This does not include figures for the weeks ending 20 and 27 Nov. 1943 and for the final weeks of the campaign when the incidence of VD increased massively.
109. NA CAB 101/224 D. F. Butler, The British Soldier in Italy, Sept. 1943–June 1944, p. 9.
110. AWM 54 624/5/6 Medical Aspects of the Campaign in Italy, 1943–5, p. 5.
111. NA CAB 106/453 Cabinet Office Military Narratives of the War, Operations of British, Dominion and Indian Forces in Italy, pp. 29–37. The new home leave scheme, or LIAP (leave in addition to PYTHON) resulted in about 3,000 men receiving leave to the UK every month. By comparison, from Nov., men in North-West Europe could expect nine days home leave every six months.
112. Ibid., p. 50; NA CAB 101/224 D. F. Butler, The British Soldier in Italy, Sept. 1943–June 1944, p. 9. For Figure 15.2 see W. Franklin Mellor (ed.), *Casualties and Medical Statistics* (London: HMSO, 1972), pp. 247–71; NA WO 177/163 AFHQ DDMS, 1942–5; NA WO 177/325 Medical Diaries DDMS 8th Army Jan.–Dec. 1943; SANDF, DOC, UWH Box 345 Monthly Bulletin of Health Statistics, The War Office, May 1945.
113. Bielecki, 'British Infantry Morale during the Italian Campaign, 1943–1945', pp. 135–42, 166; NA WO 177/322 Second Army, Quarterly Medical Report for period 1 Apr. 1945–25 Jun. 1945.
114. Buckley, *Monty's Men*, pp. 251–2; Fraser, *And We Shall Shock Them*, p. 382. Judging by the censorship summaries, morale in 50th Division appeared poor and their disbandment appears to have been a good choice. See e.g. LAC RG24 Vol. 10706 File No. 46-3-6/Int Vol. 2, 21st AGCR, 1–15 Dec. 1944, pp. 5–6.
115. Bidwell and Graham, *The Tug of War*, p. 365; Porch, *Hitler's Mediterranean Gamble*, p. 628; Peaty, 'The Desertion Crisis in Italy, 1944', pp. 81–2.
116. AWM 54 624/2/6 Report on Functions of 'AG's' Branch during Invasion of Western Europe, 1944, pp. 122–4; Bielecki, 'British Infantry Morale during the Italian Campaign, 1943–1945', pp. 152; John Robert Peaty, 'British Army Manpower Crisis 1944' (DPhil thesis, University of London, 2000), pp. 169–70. In North-West Europe, a considerable saving in manpower was also achieved through the utilisation of local personnel, such as resistance groups, to guard important bridges and POW cages. Civilian labour and volunteers from British Civil Defence and the National Fire Service were employed on docks and in cook-houses. In the Middle East, a further 19,000 redundant anti-aircraft artillerymen were also retrained, half of whom were drafted to the infantry. In Aug., in the UK, 11,200 RAF and Royal Navy personnel were transferred to the Army. Some 6,000 were also transferred from the RAF Deferred List (containing men waiting to join the RAF as aircrew).
117. AWM 54 624/2/6 Report on Functions of AG's Branch during Invasion of Western Europe, 1944, pp. 123–4. If the officer strength of the unit reached thirty or above, however, all local appointments were to be withdrawn until such time as the officer strength fell below thirty again.
118. Bielecki, 'British Infantry Morale during the Italian Campaign, 1943–1945', p. 150.
119. Granatstein, *Conscription in the Second World War*, pp. 55–6. As the Canadians had far fewer formations in Europe, they did not consider disbanding formations as a solution to the manpower problem (see Copp, *Cinderella Army*, p. 6).

120. Daniel Byers, *Zombie Army: The Canadian Army and Conscription in the Second World War* (Vancouver: University of British Columbia Press, 2016), p. 212.
121. Andrew Brown, 'New Men in the Line: An Assessment of Reinforcements to the 48th Highlanders in Italy, Jan.–Oct. 1944', *Canadian Military History*, 21(3) (2012), pp. 35–47.
122. Granatstein, *Conscription in the Second World War*, pp. 55–6; Byers, *Zombie Army*, p. 217.
123. LAC Microfilm T17925 Censorship Report, CAO, 1–15 Oct. 1944, pp. 1–5; LAC Microfilm T17925 Censorship Report, CAO, 15–31 Oct. 1944, pp. 1–5; LAC Microfilm T17925 Censorship Report, CAO, 16–30 Nov. 1944, pp. 1–5.
124. Granatstein, *Conscription in the Second World War*, p. 43.
125. Ibid. The question was framed in a careful manner so as to leave out the hated word 'conscription'.
126. Ibid. Unsurprisingly, those in the forces were, overall, more likely to vote 'Yes' than their civilian compatriots; 72% of those serving overseas and 84% of those serving in Canada supported the 'Yes' campaign, as compared to a national approval vote of 64%.
127. Ibid., pp. 47–8, 57–64.
128. Ibid., pp. 57–64.
129. Byers, *Zombie Army*, pp. 223–4.
130. Granatstein, *Conscription in the Second World War*, pp. 57–64; Byers, *Zombie Army*, p. 227.
131. LAC RG24 Vol. 18824 File Number 133.065(D592) Canadian Army Statistics, 1939–45: NRMA Discharges, Deaths and Desertions by Month and Year Struck off Strength.
132. Granatstein, *Conscription in the Second World War*, pp. 57–64.
133. Byers, *Zombie Army*, p. 233.
134. C. P. Stacey, *Arms, Men and Governments: The War Policies of Canada, 1939–1945* (Ottawa: The Queen's Printer for Canada, 1970), p. 475.
135. Peter A. Russell, 'BC's 1944 "Zombie" Protests against Overseas Conscription', *BC Studies*, 122 (Summer 1999), p. 65.
136. Byers, *Zombie Army*, p. 233–5; Stacey, *Arms, Men and Governments*, p. 475.
137. Ibid., p. 234–8.
138. Russell, 'BC's 1944 "Zombie" Protests against Overseas Conscription', pp. 68–9.
139. Quoted ibid., p. 67.
140. Ibid., p. 70.
141. Byers, *Zombie Army*, pp. 234–8. Sixty-nine NRMA men were killed, 232 wounded and 13 taken POW in North-West Europe. In the end, all 16,000 NRMA men were eventually transferred overseas.
142. John Horne, 'Introduction: Mobilizing for "Total War", in 1914–1918', in John Horne (ed.), *State, Society and Mobilization in Europe during the First World War* (Cambridge University Press, 1997), pp. 2–3.
143. Elizabeth Kier, 'War and Reform', in Elizabeth Kier and Ronald R. Krebs (eds.), *In War's Wake: International Conflict and the Fate of Liberal Democracy* (Cambridge University Press, 2010), pp. 142–50.
144. NA WO 204/10382 CMF ACR No. 53, 16–30 Sept. 1944, p. B1.
145. NA WO 204/10382 CMF ACR No. 55, 16–31 Oct. 1944, p. B2.
146. LAC Microfilm T17925 Censorship Report, CAO, 16–30 Nov. 1944, p. 1.
147. LAC Microfilm T17925 Censorship Report, CAO, 1–15 Dec. 1944, p. 1.
148. LAC Microfilm T17925 Censorship Report, CAO, 16–30 Nov. 1944, p. 6.
149. Ibid.

150. Ibid., p. 7.
151. NA WO 204/10382 CMF ACR No. 61, 16–31 Jan. 1945, p. B2; Stacey, *Arms, Men and Governments*, p. 479.
152. NA WO 204/10382 CMF ACR No. 62, 1–14 Feb. 1945, p. B2.
153. NA WO 204/10382 CMF ACR No. 63, 15–28 Feb. 1945, p. B2; Stacey, *Arms, Men and Governments*, p. 481.
154. NA WO 204/10382 CMF ACR No. 62, 1–14 Feb. 1945, p. B2.
155. Stacey, *Arms, Men and Governments*, pp. 479–80.
156. Copp, *Cinderella Army*, pp. 10, 298.
157. Stacey, *Arms, Men and Governments*, p. 475.
158. See the censorship summaries for Nov. 1944–Mar. 1945.
159. Granatstein, *Conscription in the Second World War*, pp. 57–64.
160. Ibid., pp. 64–6. In many ways, Mackenzie King's job was made easier by the Conservative reaction. Arthur Meighen, the man who had led the party during the conscription plebiscite, raged that Mackenzie King's actions were 'dishonest and foul trickery of the meanest kind'. By attacking the Government policy, however, as Granatstein has argued, the Conservatives made it clear that the voluntary system was still in effect. They showed Quebec that there was, in fact, a clear difference between total conscription and the limited step taken by Mackenzie King.
161. Porch, *Hitler's Mediterranean Gamble*, p. 628; Molony and Jackson, *The Mediterranean and Middle East, Vol. VI, Pt I*, p. 448
162. Hastings, *Armageddon*, p. 393.
163. Gooderson, *A Hard Way to Make A War*, p. 283.
164. Bidwell and Graham, *The Tug of War*, p. 365.
165. Bielecki, 'British Infantry Morale during the Italian Campaign, 1943–1945', pp. 135–40; Ellis, *Brute Force*, p. 325.
166. Delaney, *Corps Commanders*, p. 244; NA WO 177/336 War Diary HQ (Medical) 1 British Corps, Jan. 1945, Appendix IV: Quarterly Report by Brig. Q. V. B. Wallace, DDMS 1 Corps, Quarter Ending 31 Dec. 1944; LAC Microfilm T17925 Censorship Report, CAO, 16–30 Nov. 1944, p. 13.
167. Delaney, *Corps Commanders*, pp. 242–4.
168. Ibid., p. 244. Source: LAC Vol. 12631 File No. 11/Psychiatry/1/3 Lieut. Col. J. C. Richardson RCAMC, Neuropsychiatry with the Canadian Army in Western Europe, June 1944–May 1945; LAC Vol. 12631 File No. 11/Psychiatry/5 Reports, Divisional Neuropsychiatric Report, 27 June 1944; NA CAB 106/1084 Some Statistics of the North West European campaign June 1944–May 1945.
169. DHH CMHQ Report No. 188, Canadian Operations: The Clearing of the Scheldt Estuary, 1 Oct.–8 Nov. 1944, p. 12; Copp, *Cinderella Army*, p. 125.
170. Ibid., pp. 245–6; DHH CMHQ Report No. 188, Canadian Operations: The Clearing of the Scheldt Estuary, 1 Oct.–8 Nov. 1944, p. 52. 'Buffaloes were equipped with "grousers" attached to their tracks. These propelled them in water and enabled them to churn through mud flats and climb slopes up to thirty degrees' (Copp, *Cinderella Army*, p. 104).
171. Delaney, *Corps Commanders*, pp. 248–50.
172. Ibid.
173. Ibid., pp. 244–51; Patrick Rose, 'Allies at War: British and US Army Command Culture in the Italian Campaign, 1943–1944', *Journal of Strategic Studies*, 36(1) (February, 2013), pp. 54–6; Copp, *Cinderella Army*, p. 125.
174. NA WO 222/1654 DDMS 2 Canadian Corps, Quarterly Report, Oct.–Dec. 1944; LAC T 17,924 CMCRs, 1–15 Oct., 15–31 Oct. and 1–15 Nov. 1944.

175. LAC T 17,924 CMCRs, 16–30 Sept. 1944, p. 7.
176. LAC T 17,924 CMCRs, 1–15 Nov. 1944, p. 1.
177. LAC Vol. 18,712 Medical Statistics, First Canadian Army, 1944–5.
178. LAC T 17,924 CMCRs, 15–30 Sept. 1944; LAC T 17,924 CMCRs, 1–15 Oct. 1944, p. 1; LAC T 17,924 CMCRs, 15–31 Oct. 1944, p. 1; LAC T 17,924 CMCRs, 1–15 Nov. 1944, pp. 1–3.
179. Delaney, *Corps Commanders*, pp. 244–51; Rose, 'Allies at War', pp. 54–6; NA WO 222/1654 DDMS 2 Canadian Corps, Quarterly Report, Oct.–Dec. 1944; LAC T 17,924 CMCRs, 1–15 Oct., 15–31 Oct. and 1–15 Nov. 1944.
180. Fraser, *And We Shall Shock Them*, pp. 379–81; Buckley, *Monty's Men*, pp. 232–50.
181. LAC RG24 Vol. 10706 File No. 46-3-6/Int Vol. 1, 21st AGCR, 16–30 Oct. 1944, p. 7.
182. LAC RG24 Vol. 10706 File No. 46-3-6/Int Vol. 1, 21st AGCR, 1–15 Nov. 1944, p. 1; Jonathan Fennell, 'Reevaluating Combat Cohesion: The British Second Army in The Northwest Europe Campaign of the Second World War', in Anthony King (ed.), *Frontline: Combat and Cohesion in the Twenty-First Century* (Oxford University Press, 2015), p. 146.
183. LAC RG24 Vol. 10706 File No. 46-3-6/Int Vol. 2, 21st AGCR, 1–15 Dec. 1944, p. 1.
184. Fraser, *And We Shall Shock Them*, pp. 379–81; Buckley, *Monty's Men*, pp. 232–50.
185. Fraser, *And We Shall Shock Them*, p. 382. The scheduled launch date was 12 Jan. 1945.
186. Copp, *Cinderella Army*, p. 37.
187. Buckley, *Monty's Men*, pp. 259–60.
188. L. F. Ellis, *Victory in the West, Vol. II: The Defeat of Germany* (London: HMSO, 1968), pp. 175–9.
189. AWM 54 624/2/6 Report on Functions of AG's Branch during Invasion of Western Europe, 1944, pp. 22–3.
190. Ibid.
191. Fraser, *And We Shall Shock Them*, p. 382; Buckley, *Monty's Men*, p. 260; Ellis, *Brute Force*, pp. 422–3.
192. Fraser, *And We Shall Shock Them*, p. 383; Ellis, *Brute Force*, p. 421.
193. Buckley, *Monty's Men*, p. 261; Niall Barr, *Yanks and Limeys: Alliance Warfare in the Second World War* (London: Jonathan Cape, 2015), pp. 424–35.
194. Ibid., p. 265; Fraser, *And We Shall Shock Them*, pp. 386–7. This was Operation 'Blackcock'.
195. Buckley, *Monty's Men*, pp. 268–9.
196. Ibid., pp. 271–3. See e.g. NA WO 291/1331 M. M. Swan (ed.), Operational Research in North-West Europe, the Work of No.2 Operational Research Section and 21 Army Group, June 1944–July 1945, Memorandum No. 7, The Morale Effects of Artillery.
197. LAC T 17,924 CAO, Censorship Report, 1–15 Feb. 1945, pp. 1–5; LAC Vol. 10706 File No. 46-3-6/Int Vol. 2, 21st AGCR, 1–14 Feb. 1945, p. 1.
198. LAC RG24 Vol. 10706 File No. 46-3-6/Int Vol. 2, 21st AGCR, 1–14 Feb. 1945, p. 4.
199. LAC T 17,924 CAO, Censorship Report, 1–15 Feb. 1945, p. 5.
200. Copp, *Cinderella Army*, p. 203.
201. Delaney, *Corps Commanders*, pp. 42–3.
202. Ibid., pp. 42–7.

203. Buckley, *Monty's Men*, pp. 274–5; Delaney, *Corps Commanders*, pp. 41–55; Hastings, *Armageddon*, p. 401.
204. Ibid.
205. LAC T 17,924 CAO, Censorship Report, 16–28 Feb. 1945, p. 1. The censors reported that 'only 56 complaints of ill health were noted ... out of over 9,000 letters examined. Troops were apparently coming through exceptionally trying operating conditions in good physical shape.'
206. LAC T 17,924 CAO, Censorship Report, 1–15 Mar. 1945, p. 1.
207. Ibid., pp. 1–5.
208. LAC RG24 Vol. 10706 File No. 46-3-6/Int Vol. 2, 21st AGCR, 1–14 Feb. 1945, p. 5.
209. LAC RG24 Vol. 10706 File No. 46-3-6/Int Vol. 3, 21st AGCR, 15–28 Feb. 1945, p. 5.
210. Fraser, *And We Shall Shock Them*, p. 390; Copp, *Cinderella Army*, p. 222; LAC RG24 Vol. 10706 File No. 46-3-6/Int Vol. 3, 21st AGCR, 1–15 Mar. 1945, p. 3.
211. LAC T 17,924 CAO, Censorship Report, 13–31 Mar. 1945, p. 4.
212. Copp, *Cinderella Army*, p. 224.
213. Fraser, *And We Shall Shock Them*, pp. 390–1.
214. Charles Forrester, 'Field Marshal Montgomery's Role in the Creation of the British 21st Army Group's Combined Armed Doctrine for the Final Assault on Germany', *The Journal of Military History*, 78 (Oct. 2014), pp. 1299–303.
215. Ibid., pp. 1308–13.
216. Patrick Rose, 'British Army Command Culture 1939–1945: A Comparative Study of British Eighth and Fourteenth Armies' (PhD thesis, King's College London, 2008), p. 231. See also Porch, *Hitler's Mediterranean Gamble*, pp. 627–8.
217. Forrester, 'Field Marshal Montgomery's Role', pp. 1308–9, 1318.
218. Rose, 'British Army Command Culture 1939–1945', pp. 230–2.
219. Ibid., p. 237.
220. Ibid., pp. 68–9.
221. JSCSC Library, 2773A Infantry Training, Pt VIII, Fieldcraft, Battle Drill, Section and Platoon Tactics, 1944, p. 1.
222. Timothy Harrison Place, *Military Training in the British Army* (London: Frank Cass, 2000), p. 60.
223. JSCSC Library, 2773A Infantry Training, Pt VIII, Fieldcraft, Battle Drill, Section and Platoon Tactics, 1944, p. 2.
224. Stephen Bull, *Second World War Infantry Tactics: The European Theatre* (Barnsley: Pen & Sword, 2012), p. 79.
225. Forrester, 'Field Marshal Montgomery's Role', pp. 1310–12.
226. Rose, 'British Army Command Culture 1939–1945', pp. 235–6.
227. Forrester, 'Field Marshal Montgomery's Role', p. 1310–16.
228. Ibid., p. 1319–20.
229. Bidwell and Graham, *The Tug of War*, p. 365.
230. Gooderson, *A Hard Way to Make A War*, p. 292; Molony and Jackson, *The Mediterranean and Middle East, Vol. VI, Pt III*, pp. 18, 145, 161–3, 355–6; J. A. H. Carter and D. N. Kann, *Maintenance in the Field, Vol. II: 1943–1945* (London: The War Office, 1961), pp. 225–6 and 360–1; J. B. Higham and E. A. Knighton, *Movements* (London: The War Office, 1955), p. 359; Fraser, *And We Shall Shock Them*, p. 360; G. W. L. Nicholson, *The Canadians in Italy, 1943–1945: Official History of the Canadian Army in the Second World War, Vol. II* (Ottawa: Queen's Printer, 1956), pp. 660–6. The divisions sent to Greece were the 4th and 46th Divisions.

231. Gooderson, *A Hard Way to Make A War*, p. 292; Porch, *Hitler's Mediterranean Gamble*, p. 623. Fifteenth Army Group, which had been in charge of operations in Italy, was renamed HQ Allied Central Mediterranean Force in early 1944 when it took over administrative as well as operational responsibilities for the campaign; it was shortly thereafter renamed Allied Armies in Italy (AAI). In Dec. 1944, AAI was returned to its original designation, Fifteenth Army Group, when AFHQ, having moved from Algiers to Caserta, took back control of administrative functions for the campaign (see Higham and Knighton, *Movements*, pp. 321–2).
232. Gooderson, *A Hard Way to Make A War*, p. 292; Porch, *Hitler's Mediterranean Gamble*, p. 614.
233. Bidwell and Graham, *The Tug of War*, p. 386.
234. Ibid., p. 387; Fraser, *And We Shall Shock Them*, p. 358.
235. Ellis, *Brute Force*, p. 326. Porch puts the Allied advantage in armour at 3:1 but does not provide exact figures (Porch, *Hitler's Mediterranean Gamble*, p. 644).
236. Ibid., p. 330; Bidwell and Graham, *The Tug of War*, p. 401.
237. Porch, *Hitler's Mediterranean Gamble*, pp. 641–2.
238. Bidwell and Graham, *The Tug of War*, p. 392.
239. Porch, *Hitler's Mediterranean Gamble*, p. 640.
240. Molony and Jackson, *The Mediterranean and Middle East, Vol. VI, Part 1*, pp. 198–204, 227; Bidwell and Graham, *The Tug of War*, p. 391. Eighth Army's part in the offensive was codenamed 'Buckland'.
241. Molony and Jackson, *The Mediterranean and Middle East, Vol. VI, Part 1*, p. 198.
242. Ibid., pp. 209, 401.
243. Ibid., p. 213.
244. Ibid., p. 207.
245. NA WO 204/10382 CMF ACR No. 66, 1–15 Apr. 1945, pp. A1, B1, C1 and D1.
246. Molony and Jackson, *The Mediterranean and Middle East, Vol. VI, Part 1*, p. 217.
247. Fraser, *And We Shall Shock Them*, pp. 360.
248. Molony and Jackson, *The Mediterranean and Middle East, Vol. VI, Part 1*, p. 219. They also made use of flamethrowers carried on the backs of the men.
249. Fraser, *And We Shall Shock Them*, pp. 360.
250. NA WO 204/10382 CMF ACR No. 67, 16–30 Apr. 1945, p. A1.
251. Eighth Army's assault had originally been intended to distract the Germans from the main Allied thrust, which was to be delivered by the Americans in the centre.
252. Gooderson, *A Hard Way to Make A War*, p. 295; Bidwell and Graham, *The Tug of War*, pp. 393–5; Porch, *Hitler's Mediterranean Gamble*, p. 653.
253. NA WO 204/10382 CMF ACR No. 68, 1–15 May 1945, p. A1.
254. Buckley, *Monty's Men*, p. 283.
255. LAC RG 24 Vol. 10706 File No. 46-3-6/Int Vol. 3, 21st AGCR, 16–31 Mar. 1945, p. 1.
256. Ibid., p. 2.
257. LAC RG 24 Vol. 10706 File No. 46-3-6/Int Vol. 3, 21st AGCR, 1–15 Mar. 1945, pp. 2, 9. Alan Allport has estimated that an unmarried private released in June 1945 who had served for five years, including three years overseas, could expect a gratuity of £109 on demobilisation – worth perhaps £10,000 in today's money (Alan Allport, *Demobbed: Coming Home after the Second World War* (London: Yale University Press, 2009), p. 147).
258. LAC RG 24 Vol. 10706 File No. 46-3-6/Int Vol. 3, 21st AGCR, 16–31 Mar. 1945, p. 1.
259. Geoffrey G. Field, *Blood, Sweat and Toil: Remaking the British Working Class, 1939–1945* (Oxford University Press), p. 103.

260. LAC RG 24 Vol. 10706 File No. 46-3-6/Int Vol. 3, 21st AGCR, 16–31 Mar. 1945, p. 6.
261. Ibid.
262. Forrester, 'Field Marshal Montgomery's Role', p. 1296.
263. LAC RG 24 Vol. 10706 File No. 46-3-6/Int Vol. 3, 21st AGCR, 1–15 Mar. 1945, pp. 1, 6.
264. LAC RG 24 Vol. 10706 File No. 46-3-6/Int Vol. 3, 21st AGCR, 16–31 Mar. 1945, p. 3.
265. LAC RG 24 Vol. 10706 File No. 46-3-6/Int Vol. 3, 21st AGCR, 1–15 Mar. 1945, p. 5. See also, LAC RG 24 Vol. 10706 File No. 46-3-6/Int Vol. 3, 21st AGCR, 1–15 Apr. 1945, p. 5.
266. Ellis, *Victory in the West, Vol. II*, pp. 288–92.
267. Derek S. Zumbro, *Battle of the Ruhr: The German Army's Final Defeat in the West* (Lawrence: University Press of Kansas, 2006), pp. 123–7, 145; Ellis, *Brute Force*, pp. 426–7.
268. Ellis, *Victory in the West, Vol. II*, pp. 288–92.
269. Copp, *Cinderella Army*, p. 254.
270. Ellis, *Victory in the West, Vol. II*, p. 294. The US Ninth Army captured 5,098 POWs at a price of 0.55 casualties per POW.
271. LAC RG 24 Vol. 10706 File No. 46-3-6/Int Vol. 3, 21st AGCR, 1–15 Apr. 1945, p. 1.
272. LAC Vol. 12,631 File No. 11/Psychiatry/1/2 Quarterly Report, Advisor in Psychiatry 21 Army Group, Jan.–Mar. 1945; WO 177/322 Second Army, Quarterly Medical Report, for Quarter Ending 31 Mar. 1945.
273. NA WO 177/322 Second Army, Quarterly Medical Report, for Quarter Ending 31 Mar. 1945.
274. LAC RG 24 Vol. 10706 File No. 46-3-6/Int Vol. 3, 21st AGCR, 1–15 Apr. 1945, p. 5.
275. Buckley, *Monty's Men*, pp. 285–8.
276. Ellis, *Victory in the West, Vol. II*, pp. 297–308; Jeffery Williams, *The Long Left Flank: The Hard Fought Way to the Reich, 1944–1945* (London: Leo Cooper, 1988), pp. 264–7.
277. Quoted in Patrick Delaforce, *Invasion of the Third Reich: War and Peace Operation Eclipse* (Stroud: Amberley, 2011), p. 199.
278. Buckley, *Monty's Men*, pp. 285–8.
279. LAC RG24 Vol. 10547 File No. 153/Censor Reps/1/3 21 AGCR, 16–30 Apr. 1945, p. 1.
280. Ibid., p. 6.
281. Buckley, *Monty's Men*, pp. 290–1.
282. LAC RG24 Vol. 10547 File No. 153/Censor Reps/1/3 21 AGCR, 16–30 Apr. 1945, p. 8.
283. Buckley, *Monty's Men*, p. 290.
284. Ibid., pp. 291–2; Fraser, *And We Shall Shock Them*, p. 395.
285. Quoted in Buckley, *Monty's Men*, p. 293.
286. Buckley, *Monty's Men*, p. 294; Fraser, *And We Shall Shock Them*, p. 393.
287. Barr, *Yanks and Limeys*, p. 455.
288. LHCMA De Guingand Papers, The Administrative History of the Operations of 21st Army Group on the Continent of Europe, 6 June 1944–8 May 1945, p. 1.
289. LAC RG24 Vol. 10547 File No. 153/Censor Reps/1/3 21 AGCR, 1–15 May 1945, pp. 1–4.
290. LAC T 17,924 CAO, Censorship Report, 1–15 May 1945, pp. 3–5.

291. Max Hastings, *Nemesis: The Battle for Japan, 1944–45* (London: Harper Perennial, 2008), p. 363.
292. David Horner, 'Advancing National Interests: Deciding Australia's War Strategy, 1944–45', in Peter J. Dean (ed.), *Australia 1944–45: Victory in the Pacific* (Cambridge University Press, 2016), pp. 12–13.
293. Dean and Holzimmer, 'The Southwest Pacific Area: Military Strategy and Operations, 1944–45', in Dean (ed.), *Australia 1944–45*, pp. 35–6;
294. Horner, 'Advancing National Interests', in Dean (ed.), *Australia 1944–45*, 2016), pp. 12–13; Peter J. Dean, *MacArthur's Coalition: US and Australian Operations in the Southwest Pacific Area, 1942–1945* (University Press of Kansas, 2018), Ch. 13.
295. Dean, *MacArthur's Coalition*, Ch. 13.
296. Peter J. Dean and Kevin Holzimmer, 'The Southwest Pacific Area: Military Strategy and Operations, 1944–45', in Peter J. Dean (ed.), *Australia 1944–45: Victory in the Pacific* (Cambridge University Press, 2016), pp. 35–6; Dean, *MacArthur's Coalition*, Ch. 13.
297. Michael Molkentin, 'Total War on the Australian Home Front, 1943–45', in Peter J. Dean (ed.), *Australia 1944–45: Victory in the Pacific* (Cambridge University Press, 2016), pp. 99–100.
298. Wray Vamplew (ed.), *Australians: Historical Statistics* (Broadway, NSW: Fairfax, Syme and Weldon Associates, 1987), p. 165; Paul Hasluck, *Australia in the War of 1939–1945, Series Four: Civil, Vol. I: The Government and the People, 1939–1941* (Canberra: AWM, 1965), pp. 603–8. The total figure for 1945 was 2,119,600.
299. Molkentin, 'Total War on the Australian Home Front, 1943–45', in Dean (ed.), *Australia 1944–45*, p. 103.
300. S. J. Butlin and C. B. Schedvin, *War Economy, 1942–1945* (Canberra: AWM, 1977), p. 309.
301. Molkentin, 'Total War on the Australian Home Front, 1943–45', in Dean (ed.), Australia 1944–45, pp. 102–3 and 113–14.
302. Horner, 'Advancing National Interests', in Dean (ed.), *Australia 1944–45*, pp. 21–5; Dean and Holzimmer, 'The Southwest Pacific Area', in Dean (ed.), *Australia 1944–45*, pp. 34; Lachlan Grant, '"Given a Second Rate Job": Campaigns in Aitape-Wewak and New Britain, 1944–45', in Peter J. Dean (ed.), *Australia 1944–45: Victory in the Pacific* (Cambridge University Press, 2016), pp. 214–26; Karl James, 'More than Mopping Up: Bougainville', in Peter J. Dean (ed.), *Australia 1944–45: Victory in the Pacific* (Cambridge University Press, 2016), pp. 233–48; David Horner, *Blamey: The Commander-in-Chief* (St Leonards: Allen & Unwin, 1998), pp. 473–4; Dean, *MacArthur's Coalition*, Ch. 13.
303. Horner, 'Advancing National Interests', in Dean (ed.), *Australia 1944–45*, pp. 21–5; Dean and Holzimmer, 'The Southwest Pacific Area', in Dean (ed.), *Australia 1944–45*, pp. 34; Grant, '"Given a Second Rate Job"', in Dean (ed.), *Australia 1944–45*, pp. 214–26; James, 'More than Mopping Up: Bougainville', in Dean (ed.), *Australia 1944–45*, pp. 233–48; Horner, *Blamey*, pp. 473–4; Dean, *MacArthur's Coalition*, Ch. 13.
304. See a number of chapters from Peter J. Dean (ed.), *Australia 1944–45: Victory in the Pacific* (Cambridge University Press, 2016), namely: Dean and Holzimmer, 'The Southwest Pacific Area', pp. 39–45; Tony Hastings and Peter Stanley, '"To Capture Tarakan": Was Operation Oboe I Unnecessary?', pp. 278–93; Garth Pratten, '"Unique in the History of the AIF": Operations in British Borneo',

p. 314; Garth Pratten, '"Calling the Tune": Australian and Allied Operations at Balikpapan', pp. 320–37. See also Dean, *MacArthur's Coalition*, Ch. 13.

305. Dean, *MacArthur's Coalition*, pp. 360–1.
306. AWM 54 175/3/4 1 AFCC, FCRs, Jan.–June 1945.
307. AWM 54 175/3/4 1 AFCC, FCR, Jan. 1945, p. 3.
308. AWM 54 175/3/4 1 AFCC, FCR, Feb. 1945, p. 3.
309. AWM 54 175/3/4 1 AFCC, FCR, Mar. 1945, pp. 2–3.
310. AWM 54 175/3/4 1 AFCC, FCR, May 1945, p. 5.
311. AWM 54 175/3/4 1 AFCC, FCR, Dec. 1944, p. 3.
312. AWM 54 175/3/5 Censorship Extracts from Detachment 1 AFCC, 5 Australian Base Sub Area, Week Ending 23 Mar. 1945, pp. 1–2.
313. AWM 54 175/3/4 1 AFCC, FCR, Jan. 1945, pp. 3–4; AWM 54 175/3/5 HQ First Australian Army (AIF), Censorship Extracts – Leave, Week Ending 15 Jan. 1945.
314. AWM 54 175/3/5 Censorship Extracts from Detachment 1 AFCC, 5 Australian Base Sub Area, Week Ending 23 Mar. 1945, pp. 1–2.
315. Ibid., p. 4.
316. AWM 54 175/3/4 1 AFCC, FCR, Apr. 1945, p. 3.
317. AWM 54 175/3/4 1 AFCC, FCR, Mar. 1945, p. 5.
318. AWM 54 175/3/4 1 AFCC, FCR, May 1945, p. 4.
319. AWM 54 175/3/4 1 AFCC, FCR, June 1945, p. 4.
320. NAA MP 742/1 85/1/706 Illegal absentees in Army, 1943–5; NAA P617 527/1/126 L. E. Ball, Recruiting for AMF, 1939–45, p. 85.
321. AWM 54 175/3/4 1 AFCC, FCR, Feb. 1945, p. 1.
322. AWM 54 175/3/4 1 AFCC, FCR, Dec. 1944, p. 4; AWM 54 175/3/5 HQ First Australian Army, Censorship Extracts, Week Ending 24 Mar. 1945.
323. AWM 54 175/3/4 1 AFCC, FCR, Apr. 1945, p. 3.
324. Horner, 'Advancing National Interests', in Dean (ed.), *Australia 1944–45*, p. 14.
325. Callahan, *Churchill and His Generals*, p. 225; Fraser, *And We Shall Shock Them*, p. 363.
326. Raymond Callahan, *Burma, 1942–1945* (London: Davis Poynter, 1978), p. 143.
327. Callahan, *Churchill and His Generals*, p. 225; Fraser, *And We Shall Shock Them*, p. 363.
328. Callahan, *Churchill and His Generals*, p. 226.
329. Timothy Moreman, *The Jungle, the Japanese and the British Commonwealth Armies at War, 1941–45: Fighting Methods, Doctrine and Training for Jungle Warfare* (London: Frank Cass, 2005), p. 143.
330. NA WO 203/4536 Morale Report for British Troops of SEAC, June–Aug. 1944, p. 1.
331. BL IOR L WS 2 71 Army in India Morale Report, Aug.–Oct. 1944, p. 9.
332. NA WO 203/4538 Morale Report, ALFSEA, Aug.–Oct. 1944, p. 22.
333. NA WO 203/4536 Morale Report for British Troops of SEAC, June–Aug. 1944, p. 1.
334. NA WO 203/4538 Morale Report, ALFSEA, Aug.–Oct. 1944, p. 20.
335. BL IOR L WS 2 71 Army in India Morale Report, Aug.–Oct. 1944, p. 9.
336. NA WO 203/4538 Report on the Morale of British, Indian, and Colonial Troops of Allied Land Forces South-East Asia, Aug.–Oct. 1944, p. 1.
337. NA WO 203/4536 Memorandum, Morale in SEAC, 19 July 1944; NA WO 203/4536 CICA Minute, DSR Morale Policy, 7 June 1944.
338. NA WO 203/4536 Adam to Mountbatten, 18 Aug. 1944.
339. NA WO 203/4538 Clarke to ACOS, 24 Dec. 1944.
340. BL IOR L WS 2 71 Army in India Morale Report, Aug.–Oct. 1944, pp. 1–4.

341. NA WO 203/4538 Report on the Morale of British, Indian, and Colonial Troops of Allied Land Forces South-East Asia, Aug.–Oct. 1944, pp. 3–5. See also, NA WO 277/4 Army Welfare, pp. 149–58.
342. NA WO 203/4538 Report on the Morale of British, Indian, and Colonial Troops of Allied Land Forces South-East Asia, Aug.–Oct. 1944, pp. 9–10; NA WO 277/16 Morale, p. 14.
343. BL IOR L WS 2 71 Army in India Morale Report, Aug.–Oct. 1944, pp. 1–4.
344. NA WO 203/4538 Report on the Morale of British, Indian, and Colonial Troops of Allied Land Forces South-East Asia, Aug.–Oct. 1944, p. 1.
345. NA WO 203/4538 Clarke to ACOS, 24 Dec. 1944.
346. John Peaty, 'British Army Manpower Crisis 1944' (Doctoral thesis, King's College London, 2000), p. 334.
347. Callahan, *Churchill and His Generals*, p. 227; Callahan, *Burma*, p. 147. This decision added 5,700 more men to SEAC's deficiency in manpower.
348. NA WO 203/4538 Report on the Morale of British, Indian, and Colonial Troops of Allied Land Forces South-East Asia, Aug.–Oct. 1944, p. 11.
349. Moreman, *The Jungle, the Japanese and the British Commonwealth Armies at War*, p 163.
350. Callahan, *Churchill and His Generals*, p. 227.
351. NA WO 203/4538 Report on the Morale of British, Indian, and Colonial Troops of Allied Land Forces South-East Asia, Aug.–Oct. 1944, pp. 12–17.
352. By this period, three West and East African Divisions and two Independent Infantry Brigades were serving in SEAC.
353. NA WO 203/4538 Morale Report, ALFSEA, Aug.–Oct. 1944, pp. 20–3.
354. Srinath Raghaven, *India's War: The Making of Modern South Asia, 1939–1945* (London: Penguin, 2017), p. 71.
355. Ibid, p. 72; Graham Dunlop, *Military Economics, Culture and Logistics in the Burma Campaign, 1942–1945* (London: Pickering & Chatto, 2009), p. 60.
356. Dunlop, *Military Economics, Culture and Logistics in the Burma Campaign*, p. 63.
357. Ibid, pp. 71, 128, 158, 164; S. W. Kirby, *The War against Japan, Vol. IV: The Reconquest of Burma* (London: HMSO, 1965), pp. 105–6.
358. Quoted in Moreman, *The Jungle, the Japanese and the British Commonwealth Armies at War*, pp. 152–3.
359. Ibid.
360. Ibid., p. 161.
361. Ibid.
362. Callahan, *Burma*, p. 147; Moreman, *The Jungle, the Japanese and the British Commonwealth Armies at War*, p. 177; Kirby, *The War against Japan, Vol. IV*, p. 39.
363. Dunlop, *Military Economics, Culture and Logistics in the Burma Campaign*, pp. 157–63; Louis Allen, *Burma: The Longest War, 1941–45* (London: Phoenix Press, 2000 [1984]), pp. 389–93. On paper, Japanese divisions were about 10,000 men strong; but they were often reduced to half that number. Allen has estimated that the Japanese only had sixty-four planes to defend Burma. The BNA was a force of Burmese soldiers committed to winning independence from Britain.
364. Callahan, *Churchill and His Generals*, p. 228; Callahan, *Burma*, p. 154.
365. Moreman, *The Jungle, the Japanese and the British Commonwealth Armies at War*, pp. 167–70.
366. Ibid.
367. Callahan, *Burma*, p. 155; Moreman, *The Jungle, the Japanese and the British Commonwealth Armies at War*, p. 177.

368. Moreman, *The Jungle, the Japanese and the British Commonwealth Armies at War*, p. 170.
369. Ibid., pp. 170–89.
370. Ibid., p. 189.
371. Ibid., p. 176.
372. Callahan, Burma, p. 154; Fraser, *And We Shall Shock Them*, pp. 367–8; Moreman, *The Jungle, the Japanese and the British Commonwealth Armies at War*, pp. 174–84.
373. Callahan, *Churchill and His Generals*, pp. 227–8; Moreman, *The Jungle, the Japanese and the British Commonwealth Armies at War*, p. 184.
374. Callahan, *Churchill and His Generals*, pp. 227–8.
375. Ibid., p. 228; Callahan, *Burma*, p. 154.
376. Callahan, *Burma*, pp. 157–8.
377. Ibid., p. 157.
378. Ibid., pp. 158–9.
379. Moreman, *The Jungle, the Japanese and the British Commonwealth Armies at War*, p. 198.
380. Callahan, *Burma*, pp. 158–9.
381. Ibid., p. 159.
382. Moreman, *The Jungle, the Japanese and the British Commonwealth Armies at War*, p. 181; Callahan, *Burma*, p. 159.
383. Callahan, *Churchill and His Generals*, p. 229.
384. F. A. E. Crew, *The Army Medical Services, Campaigns, Vol. V: Burma* (London: HMSO, 1966), p. 564.
385. Callahan, *Burma*, p. 160; Callahan, *Churchill and His Generals*, p. 229; Moreman, *The Jungle, the Japanese and the British Commonwealth Armies at War*, p. 202; Fraser, *And We Shall Shock Them*, p. 375.
386. Moreman, *The Jungle, the Japanese and the British Commonwealth Armies at War*, p. 5; Tarak Barkawi, 'Culture and Combat in the Colonies: The Indian Army in the Second World War', *Journal of Contemporary History*, 41(2) (2006), p. 329; Allen, *Burma*, p. xviii.

Chapter 16 Soldiers and Social Change

1. Daniel Marston, *Phoenix from the Ashes: The Indian Army in the Burma Campaign* (Westport: Praeger, 2003).
2. See e.g. AWM 54 883/2/97 British Troops in Egypt, No. 93 Field Censorship Report, 7 Aug. 1941, p. 2; AWM 54 883/2/97 British Troops in Egypt. No. 101 Field Censorship Report, 29 Sep. 1941, p. 1; SANDF, DOC, AI Gp 1 Box 43 File No. CE44/2/C MEMCWS No. XLIX, 21 Oct. to 3 Nov. 1942, p. 23; NA WO 204/10381 CMF ACR No. 32, 16–31 Oct. 1943, p. 2; NA WO 204/10381 CMF ACR No. 51, 16–31 Aug. 1944, pp. A1, B1–2; LAC T 17,924 21 AGCR, 1–15 Sept. 1944, p. 1; LAC T 17,924 CAO, Censorship Report, 1–15 Sept. 1944, pp. 10–11.
3. Alan Allport, *Browned Off and Bloody-Minded: The British Soldier Goes to War 1939–1945* (London: Yale University Press, 2015), p. 267.
4. Tony Judt, *Reappraisals: Reflections on the Forgotten Twentieth Century* (London: Penguin, 2008), pp. 8–12; Thomas Piketty, *Capital in the Twenty-First Century*, trans. Arthur Goldhammer (London: Belknap Press, 2014), p. 20.
5. Piketty, *Capital in the Twenty-First Century*, p. 20.

6. George Orwell, 'The Lion and the Unicorn', in *The Collected Essays, Journalism and Letters, Vol. II* (Harmondsworth, Penguin, 1970), p. 117.
7. E. J. Hobsbawm, *On History* (London, 1998), p. 118. Quoted in Albert Grundlingh, 'The King's Afrikaners? Enlistment and Ethnic Identity in the Union of South Africa's Defence Force During the Second World War, 1939–45', *The Journal of African History*, 40(3) (Nov. 1999), p. 351.
8. Indivar Kamtekar, 'A Different War Dance: State and Class in India 1939–1945', *Past and Present*, 176(1) (2002), p. 189.
9. These provocative insights have emerged primarily from the study of home fronts during conflict. See e.g. Elizabeth Kier and Ronald R. Krebs (eds.), *In War's Wake: International Conflict and the Fate of Liberal Democracy* (Cambridge University Press, 2010); Angus Calder, *The People's War: Britain 1939–1945* (London: Jonathan Cape, 1969); Harold L. Smith (ed.), *War and Social Change: British Society in the Second World War* (Manchester University Press, 1986); Ross McKibbin, *Classes and Cultures: England 1918–1951* (Oxford University Press, 2000); Kamtekar, 'A Different War Dance'.
10. Gerald F. Linderman, *The World Within War: America's Combat Experience in World War II* (New York: The Free Press, 1997), p. 24.
11. John Ellis, *The Sharp End: The Fighting Man in World War II* (London: Pimlico, 1990), pp. 315–16.
12. Tarak Barkawi, 'Culture and Combat in the Colonies: The Indian Army in the Second World War', *Journal of Contemporary History*, 41(2) (2006), p. 345.
13. Ibid., p. 353.
14. John Buckley, *Monty's Men: The British Army and the Liberation of Europe* (London: Yale University Press, 2013), p. 45; David French, *Raising Churchill's Army: The British Army and the War against Germany 1919–1945* (Oxford University Press, 2000), pp. 133–4; Terry Copp and Bill McAndrew, *Battle Exhaustion: Soldiers and Psychiatrists in the Canadian Army, 1939–1945* (London: McGill-Queen's University Press, 1990), p. 82.
15. ANZ WAII/1/DA508/1 Vols. 3 and 4 MEMCFS No. L, 4–17 Nov. 1942, p. 17; ANZ WAII/1/DA508/1 Vols. 3 and 4 MEMCFS No. LXXXI, 12–25 Jan. 1944. See also e.g. S. L. A. Marshall, *Men against Fire: The Problem of Battle Command in Future War* (New York, 1966); Samuel A. Stouffer et al., *The American Soldier: Combat and its Aftermath, Vol. II* (Princeton University Press, 1949); Richard Holmes, *Acts of War: The Behaviour of Men in Battle* (London: Cassell, 1985).
16. LAC RG24 Vol. 10706 File No. 46-3-6/Int Vol. 3, 21st AGCR, 16–31 Mar. 1945, p. 4.
17. LAC RG24 Vol. 10706 File No. 46-3-6/Int Vol. 3, 21st AGCR, 1–15 Apr. 1945, p. 6.
18. LAC T 17,924 CAO, Censorship Report, 16–30 Apr. 1945, p. 4.
19. LAC T 17,924 CAO, Censorship Report, 1–15 Mar. 1945, p. 11.
20. LAC T 17,924 CAO, Censorship Report, 1–15 Nov. 1944, p. 4.
21. ANZ WAII/1/DA508/1 Vols. 3 and 4 MEMCFS No. LXXV, 20 Oct.–2 Nov. 1943, p. 26.
22. LAC T 17,924 CAO, Censorship Report, 1–15 Feb. 1945, p. 3.
23. AWM 54 175/3/3 Advanced Land HQ, FCR No. 12, 1–15 June 1943, p. 3.
24. ANZ WAII/1/DA508/1 Vols. 3 and 4 MEMCFS No. LXIII, 5–18 May 1943, p. 24; ANZ WAII/1/DA508/1 Vols. 3 and 4 MEMCFS No. LXVI, 8–21 Sept. 1943, p. 26; ANZ WAII/1/DA508/3 2 NZ FCSWR No. 34, 16–22 July 1944, Pt II, p. 3.
25. ANZ WAII/1/DA508/1 Vol. 4 MEMCFS No. LXIII, 5–18 May 1943, p. 24.

26. NA CAB 101/224 D. F. Butler, The British Soldier in Italy, Sept. 1943–June 1944, p. 42.
27. ANZ WAII/1/DA508/1 Vols. 3 and 4 MEMCFS No. L, 4–17 Nov. 1942, p. 18.
28. ANZ WAII/1/DA508/1 Vols. 3 and 4 MEMCFS No. LXXI, 25 Aug.–7 Sept. 1943, p. 27.
29. ANZ WAII/1/DA508/1 Vols. 3 and 4 MEMCFS No. LXV, 2–15 June 1943, p. 21. This was especially noted in relation to Maori and Pakeha.
30. ANZ WAII/1/DA508/1 Vols. 3 and 4 MEMCFS No. LVI, 27 Jan.–9 Feb. 1943, p. 23.
31. Ibid.; ANZ WAII/1/DA508/1 Vols. 3 and 4 MEMCFS No. L 4–17 Nov. 1942, p. 18; ANZ WAII/1/DA508/1 Vols. 3 and 4 MEMCFS No. LXVII, 30 June–13 July 1943, p. 24; ANZ WAII/1/DA508/1 Vols. 3 and 4 MEMCFS No. LXXVI, 3–16 Nov. 1943, p. 23; ANZ WAII/1/DA508/1 Vols. 3 and 4 MEMCFS No. LXXVII 17–30 Nov. 1943, p. 22; ANZ WAII/1/DA508/1 Vols. 3 and 4 MEMCFS No. LXXXI, 12–25 Jan. 1944.
32. Turnbull Library MS Papers 2183–31 Frederick Jones Papers, First Middle East Furlough Draft; F. L. W. Wood, *Political and External Affairs* (Wellington: Historical Publications Branch, 1958), p. 269; John McLeod, *Myth and Reality: The New Zealand Soldier in World War II* (Auckland: Reed Methuen, 1986), p. 151; ANZ WAII/8/70 Defender to Main 2 NZ Div., 13 Jan. 1944.
33. Correspondence with the Elections Centre, Plymouth University, 23 Oct. 2013.
34. Geoffrey G. Field, '"Civilians in Uniform": Class and Politics in the British Armed Forces, 1939–1945', *International Labor and Working-Class History*, 80 (Fall 2011), p. 141.
35. AEComm, *Commonwealth Electoral Office 1940a, State Statistical Returns Showing the Voting within Each Subdivision in Relation to the Senate Election 1940, and the General Elections for the House of Representatives, 1940* (Canberra: Commonwealth Government Printer, 1940); *Commonwealth Electoral Office 1940b, Statistical Returns in Relation to the Senate Elections 1940; the General Elections for the House of Representatives 1940; together with Summaries of Elections and Referendums 1903–1940* (Canberra: Commonwealth Government Printer, 1940); *Commonwealth Electoral Office 1940c, The Northern Territory, Election of One Member for the House of Representatives, Comparative Statement – Elections 1922–1940, Election, 21st Sept. 1940 – Detailed Return* (Canberra: Commonwealth Government Printer, 1940); http://psephos.adam-carr.net/countries/a/australia/1943/1943repsnsw.txt; http://en.wikipedia.org/wiki/Candidates_of_the_Australian_federal_election,_1940.
36. Paul Hasluck, *Australia in the War of 1939–1945, Series Four: Civil, Vol. I: The Government and the People, 1939–1941* (Canberra: AWM, 1965), pp. 262–3.
37. AEComm, *Commonwealth Electoral Office 1943a, State Statistical Returns Showing the Voting within Each Subdivision in Relation to the Senate Election 1943, and the General Elections for the House of Representatives, 1943* (Canberra: Commonwealth Government Printer, 1943); *Commonwealth Electoral Office 1943b, Statistical Returns in relation to the Senate Elections 1943; The General Elections for the House of Representatives 1943; together with Summaries of Elections and Referendums 1903–1943* (Canberra: Commonwealth Government Printer, 1943); *Commonwealth Electoral Office 1943c, The Northern Territory, Election of One Member for the House of Representatives, Comparative Statement – Elections 1922–1943, Election, 21st Aug. 1943 – Detailed Return* (Canberra: Commonwealth Government Printer, 1943); http://psephos.adam-carr

.net/countries/a/australia/1943/1943repsnsw.txt; http://en.wikipedia.org/wiki/Candidates_of_the_Australian_federal_election,_1943, accessed 28 June 2018.

38. NAA A406 E1944/403 Pt K Referendum 1944, Voting by Forces, Results; Michael Molkentin, 'Total War on the Australian Home Front, 1943–45', in Peter J. Dean (ed.), *Australia 1944–45: Victory in the Pacific* (Cambridge University Press, 2016), pp. 111–12.
39. See references in fnn. 35, 37 and 38.
40. Miles Fairburn and Stephen Haslett, 'The Rise of the Left and Working-Class Voting Behavior in New Zealand: New Methods', *Journal of Interdisciplinary History*, XXXV(4) (Spring, 2005), p. 533.
41. As for Table 16.2, see Appendices to the Journals of the House of Representatives, 1944 Session I, H-33a; ANZ WAII/1/DA565/1 Maj. W. A. Bryan, Report on the Conduct of the 1943 General Election in the Middle East. With reference 342 Chatham Islands and Mercantile Marine votes, Labour received 192 (56.14%), National 115 (33.63%), Democratic Labour 14 (4.09%) and Others 21 (6.14%). See also Appendices to the Journals of the House of Representatives, 1944 Session I, H-33c, p. 2. For a more detailed assessment of why New Zealand soldiers, sailors and airmen voted so overwhelmingly for Labour in 1943, see Jonathan Fennell, 'Soldiers and Social Change: The Forces Vote in the Second World War and New Zealand's Great Experiment in Social Citizenship', *English Historical Review*, 132(154) (2017).
42. Elections Canada Library Service, *Twentieth General Election, 1945: Report of the Chief Electoral Officer* (Ottawa: Edmond Cloutier, 1946); www.parl.gc.ca/About/Parliament/FederalRidingsHistory/hfer.asp?Language=E&Search=G.
43. Lawrence Leduc, Jon H. Pammett, Judith I. McKenzie and André Turcotte, *Dynasties and Interludes: Past and Present in Canadian Electoral Politics* (Toronto: Dundurn Press, 2010), p. 146.
44. Geoffrey G. Field, *Blood, Sweat and Toil: Remaking the British Working Class, 1939–1945* (Oxford University Press), p. 8; Allport, *Browned Off and Bloody-Minded*, pp. 296–7.
45. NA WO 204/10381 CMF and BNAF, ACR No. 31, 1–15 Oct. 1943, p. 19; Christopher Bayly and Tim Harper, *Forgotten Armies: Britain's Asian Empire & the War with Japan* (London: Penguin, 2005 [2004]), p. 364; Peter Howlett (ed.), *Fighting with Figures: A Statistical Digest of the Second World War* (London: The Central Statistics Office, 1995), p. 5; Allport, *Browned Off and Bloody-Minded*, p. xviii. The voting age in the 1940s was 21.
46. NA WO 204/10381 CMF and BNAF, ACR No. 31, 1–15 Oct. 1943, p. 19.
47. BL IOR L/WS/1/939 The AG in India's Committee on Morale of the Army in India, 1st Quarterly Report, Nov. 1942–Jan. 1943, p. 4.
48. BL IOR L/WS/1/939 General Staff Branch, Report on the Morale of the Army in India Command and SEAC for the months ending 15 Jan. 1944, p. 6.
49. BL IOR L WS 1 939 Post-War Prospects: A Note on British Forces Opinions as Seen in Censorship, Appendix B to the Report on the Morale of British, Indian and African Troops in India Command and South-East Asia Command for the Three Months Ending Apr. 1944.
50. SANDF, DOC, AI Gp 1 Box 42/I/37 DFMS No. 97, June 1945.
51. SANDF, DOC, AI Gp 1 Box 42/I/37 DFMS No. 98, July 1945.
52. BL IOR L WS 1 939 Post-War Prospects.
53. NA WO 204/10381 CMF and BNAF, ACR No. 37, 16–31 Jan. 1944, p. A12.
54. NA WO 204/10381 ACR No. 38, for Period 1–15 Feb. 1944, Pt F – British Troops in North Africa.

55. NA WO 204/10381 CMF and BNAF, ACR No. 33, 1–15 Nov. 1943, pp. 14–15.
56. S. P. MacKenzie, *Politics and Military Morale: Current-Affairs and Citizenship Education in the British Army, 1914–1950* (Oxford University Press, 1992), pp. 165–6.
57. NA WO 204/10381 CMF and BNAF, ACR No. 43, 16–30 Apr. 1944, p. A8.
58. NA WO 204/10381 First Army Mail: ACR No. 28, 16–31 Aug. 1943, p. 8.
59. BL IOR L WS 1 939 Post-War Prospects.
60. For more on this issue, see Jeremy A. Crang, 'Politics on Parade: Army Education and the 1945 General Election', *History: The Journal of the Historical Association*, 81(262) (Apr. 1996), p. 215.
61. MacKenzie, *Politics and Military Morale*, p. 178.
62. Field, *Blood, Sweat and Toil*, p. 341.
63. BL IOR L WS 1 939 Post-War Prospects.
64. NA WO 204/10381 BNAF, ACR No. 28, 16–31 Aug. 1943, p. 5.
65. NA WO 204/10381 CMF and BNAF, ACR No. 39, 16–29 Feb. 1944, p. A13.
66. BL IOR L/WS/1/939 AG in India's Committee on Morale, Report of Sixth Meeting, n.d. but Apr./May 1944, p. 2.
67. LAC RG24 Vol. 10706 File No. 46-3-6/Int Vol. 3, 21st AGCR, 15–28 Feb. 1945, p. 11.
68. LAC RG24 Vol. 10706 File No. 46-3-6/Int Vol. 3 21st AGCR, 1–15 Apr. 1945, p. 9.
69. Field, *Blood, Sweat and Toil*, pp. 360–1.
70. NA CAB 101/224 D. F. Butler, The British Soldier in Italy, Sept. 1943–June 1944, p. 32.
71. NA WO 203/4536 Morale Report for British Troops of SEAC, June–Aug. 1944, p. 2.
72. LAC RG24 Vol. 10706 File No. 46-3-6/Int Vol. 3, 21st AGCR, 1–15 Mar. 1945, pp. 1 and 8.
73. NA CAB 101/224 D. F. Butler, The British Soldier in Italy, Sept. 1943–June 1944, p. 31.
74. LAC T 17,924 21 AGCR, 1–15 May 1944, pp. 8–9. Broadly speaking, these increases seem to have received a more positive response in the Mediterranean than in North-West Europe.
75. Paul Addison, *The Road to 1945: British Politics and the Second World War* (London: Pimlico, 1994), pp. 256–8.
76. LAC RG24 Vol. 10547 File No. 153/Censor Reps/1/3 21 AGCR, 1–15 June 1945, pp. 1–8; LAC RG24 Vol. 10547 File No. 153/Censor Reps/1/3 21 AGCR, 16–30 June 1945, p. 7.
77. LAC RG24 Vol. 10547 File No. 153/Censor Reps/1/3 21 AGCR, 1–15 June 1945, pp. 1–8; LAC RG24 Vol. 10547 File No. 153/Censor Reps/1/3 21 AGCR, 16–30 June 1945, p. 8; LAC RG24 Vol. 10547 File No. 153/Censor Reps/1/3 21 AGCR, 1–15 July 1945, p. 9.
78. Crang, 'Politics on Parade', p. 222; R. B. McCallum and Alison Readman, *The British General Election of 1945* (Oxford University Press, 1947), p. 43. The statistics for the Forces vote do not, unfortunately, break down voters by service.
79. LAC RG24 Vol. 10547 File No. 153/Censor Reps/1/3 21 AGCR, 1–15 June 1945, pp. 1–8; LAC RG 24 Vol. 10547 File No. 153/Censor Reps/1/3 21 AGCR, 16–30 June 1945, p. 8; LAC RG 24 Vol. 10547 File No. 153/Censor Reps/1/3 21 AGCR, 1–15 July 1945, p. 9.
80. Field, *Blood, Sweat and Toil*, p. 309.

81. BL IOR L WS 1 939 Post-War Prospects.
82. LAC RG24 Vol. 10706 File No. 46-3-6/Int Vol. 3, 21st AGCR, 15–28 Feb. 1945, p. 11.
83. NA WO 204/10381 CMF and BNAF, ACR No. 35, 16–31 Dec. 1943, pp. A14–15.
84. MacKenzie, *Politics and Military Morale*, p. 178.
85. Crang, 'Politics on Parade', p. 226.
86. MacKenzie, *Politics and Military Morale*, p. 178.
87. See Laura Beers, 'Labour's Britain, Fight for it Now!', *The Historical Journal*, 52(3) (2009), p. 688.
88. Ibid.
89. Field, *Blood, Sweat and Toil*, pp. 304, 364–5.
90. Ibid., p. 365.
91. Allport, *Browned Off and Bloody-Minded*, p. xviii.
92. The calculation is 1.7 million service votes plus 3.8 million civilian votes (influenced by those serving in the army) divided by the total number of votes cast (25 million). This equals 22 per cent.
93. Penelope Summerfield, 'Education and Politics in the British Armed Forces in the Second World War', *International Review of Social History*, 26(2) (1981), pp. 133–4; Henry Pelling, 'The 1945 Election Reconsidered', *The Historical Journal*, 23(2) (1980), pp. 410–11. It is generally accepted that about 70% of the working-class vote went to Labour (see Field, *Blood, Sweat and Toil*, pp. 370–1). Mark Franklin and Matthew Ladner have argued that new voters, many of whom were in the Armed Forces, made up 20% of the electorate in 1945 and that 67% of them voted for Labour (see Mark Franklin and Matthew Ladner, 'The Undoing of Winston Churchill: Mobilization and Conversion in the 1945 Realignment of British Voters', *British Journal of Political Science*, 25(4) (1995), p. 445). Where Labour gained support from the middle classes, it was typically, according to Steven Fielding, from the lower-middle classes (see Steven Fielding, 'What Did "the People" Want?: The Meaning of the 1945 General Election', *The Historical Journal*, 35(3) (1992), pp. 636–7).
94. Crang, 'Politics on Parade', p. 215. Labour won 393 seats, with 47.8% of the total vote; the Conservatives and their allies 213 seats, with 39.8% of the vote; and the Liberals 12 seats, with 9% of the vote.
95. NA WO 204/10381 CMF and BNAF, ACR No. 49, 16–31 July 1944, p. A3.
96. LAC RG24 Vol. 10547 File No. 153/Censor Reps/1/3 21 AGCR, 1–15 Aug. 1945, p. 1.
97. DHH File No. 581.023 (D1) 21 AGCR, 15–31 Aug. 1945, p. 1.
98. Ibid., p. 7.
99. Fennell. 'Soldiers and Social Change'.
100. Margaret McClure, *A Civilised Community: A History of Social Security in New Zealand, 1898–1998* (Auckland University Press, 1998), pp. 48–93.
101. Ibid., p. 83; Margaret Galt, 'Wealth and Income in New Zealand, *c.*1870 to *c.*1939' (PhD thesis, Victoria, 1985); Philippa Mein Smith, *A Concise History of New Zealand* (Melbourne: Cambridge University Press, 2005), p. 124.
102. John E. Martin, *The House: New Zealand's House of Representatives, 1854–2004* (Palmerston North: Dunmore Press, 2004), p. 212.
103. F. L. W. Wood, *Political and External Affairs* (Wellington: Historical Publications Branch, 1958), pp. 236–9; Michael Bassett and Michael King, *Tomorrow Comes the Song: The Life of Peter Fraser* (Auckland: Penguin, 2000), p. 232.

104. Martin, *The House*, pp. 213–14; Bassett and King, *Tomorrow Comes the Song*, pp. 205, 223–4. An election had been due to take place in New Zealand in 1941, but, with the war situation deteriorating after setbacks in the Mediterranean, Labour introduced a Prolongation of Parliament Bill that autumn. National agreed to delay a vote on the understanding that there would be as little contentious legislation as possible put before the House. With the collapse of the War Administration in Oct. 1942, however, the agreement to postpone the election lapsed and the poll took place during Sept. 1943.
105. Robert Chapman, 'From Labour to National', in Geoffrey W. Rice (ed.), *The Oxford History of New Zealand* (Oxford University Press, 1992), pp. 368–9. The Bank of New Zealand and Internal Airways were nationalised (in 1945) and the coalmines were nationalised gradually; a Minimum Wage Act was introduced, also in 1945.
106. Ibid., p. 351.
107. Bassett and King, *Tomorrow Comes the Song*, pp. 255–6. The Electoral Amendment Act 1940, granted the right to vote to members of New Zealand's armed forces serving in any part of the world. See ANZ WAII/1/DA565/1 *NZEF Times*, 2 Aug. 1943.
108. Bassett and King, *Tomorrow Comes the Song*, p. 256; Appendices to the Journals of the House of Representatives, 1944 Session I, H-33a; ANZ WAII/1/DA565/1 Maj. W. A. Bryan, Report on the Conduct of the 1943 General Election in the Middle East. Nelson was won by an Independent who voted with Labour. Palmerston North was lost by an Independent who voted with National. It is also conceivable that a truly non-party war administration, as advocated by Holland, might have been installed.
109. See e.g. J. R. S. Daniels, 'The General Election of 1943' (Master's thesis, Victoria University, 1961), p. 333; Bassett and King, *Tomorrow Comes the Song*, p. 256; Michael Bassett, *The State in New Zealand, 1840–1984: Socialism without Doctrines?* (Auckland University Press, 1998), pp. 234–5; Neill Atkinson, *Adventures in Democracy: A History of the Vote in New Zealand* (Dunedin: University of Otago Press, 2003), p. 154.
110. See Fennell, 'Soldiers and Social Change'.
111. ANZ WAII/1/DA565/1 *NZEF Times*, 15 Sept. 1943.
112. Wood, *The New Zealand People at War*, p. 264; Bassett and King, *Tomorrow Comes the Song*, p. 250.
113. Daniels, 'The General Election of 1943', pp. 262–3.
114. Wood, *The New Zealand People at War*, p. 264.
115. Ibid. The bill established prices on 15 Dec. 1942 as a base price for land in spite of the fact that since then prices had risen by nearly 70% (see Bassett and King, *Tomorrow Comes the Song*, p. 250).
116. ANZ WAII/1/DA565/1 *NZEF Times*, 15 Sept. 1943; Martin, *The House*, p. 214
117. ANZ WAII/1/DA565/1 *NZEF Times*, 15 Sept. 1943.
118. See e.g. ANZ WAII/1/DA508/1 Vols. 3 and 4 MEMCFS No. L 4–17 Nov. 1942, p. 18; ANZ WAII/1/DA508/1 Vols. 3 and 4 MEMCFS No. LXVII, 30 June–13 July 1943, p. 24; ANZ WAII/1/DA508/1 Vols. 3 and 4 MEMCFS No. LXXVI, 3–16 Nov. 1943, p. 23; ANZ WAII/1/DA508/1 Vols. 3 and 4 MEMCFS No. LXXVII 17–30 Nov. 1943, p. 22; ANZ WAII/1/DA508/1 Vols. 3 and 4 MEMCFS No. LXXXI, 12–25 Jan. 1944.
119. ANZ WAII/1/DA508/1 Vols. 3 and 4 MEMCFS No. L 4–17 Nov. 1942, p. 18; ANZ WAII/1/DA508/1 Vols. 3 and 4 MEMCFS No. LXVII, 30 June–13 July 1943, p. 24; ANZ WAII/1/DA508/1 Vols. 3 and 4 MEMCFS No. LXXVI, 3–16 Nov. 1943, p. 23; ANZ WAII/1/DA508/1 Vols. 3 and 4 MEMCFS No. LXXVII

17–30 Nov. 1943, p. 22; ANZ WAII/1/DA508/1 Vols. 3 and 4 MEMCFS No. LXXXI, 12–25 Jan. 1944.

120. ANZ WAII/1/DA508/1 Vols. 3 and 4 MEMCFS No. LXXII, 8–21 Sept. 1943, p. 26.

121. ANZ WAII/1/DA508/1 Vol. 4 MEMCFS No. LVIII, 24 Feb.–9 Mar. 1943, p. 21.

122. NA WO 204/10381 CMF and BNAF, ACR No. 35, 16–31 Dec. 1943, p. C3; ANZ WAII/1/DA508/3 2 NZ FCSWR No. 4, 13–18 Dec. 1943, Pt II, p. 2. The success of Democratic Labour, which stood to the left of the Labour Party, can be explained in a similar light. It championed a comparable set of social and economic policies to Labour, but with the added carrot of a ticket home to New Zealand. Its manifesto stated: 'We believe the Middle East forces should be returned to New Zealand for a rest and that those troops with the longest period of active service should not be called upon to reinforce our division in the Pacific until men with no active service have had their turn.' See Wood, *The New Zealand People at War*, p. 265; ANZ WAII/1/DA565/1 *NZEF Times*, 15 Sept. 1943.

123. Neil Roos, *Ordinary Springboks: White Servicemen and Social Justice in South Africa, 1939–1961* (Aldershot: Ashgate, 2005); J. Crwys-Williams, *A Country at War: The Mood of a Nation, 1939–1945* (Rivonia: Ashanti, 1992), p. 34; François Oosthuizen, 'Demobilization and the Post-War Employment of the White Union Defence Force Soldiers', *Scientia Militaria*, 23(4) (1993); François Oosthuizen, 'Soldiers and Politics: The Political Ramification of the White Union Defence Forces Soldiers' Demobilisation Experience after the Second World War', *South African Journal of Military Studies*, 24(1) (1994).

124. Roos, *Ordinary Springboks*, p. 63.

125. Ibid., pp. 90–3.

126. Ibid., p. 63.

127. NA WO 204/10382 CMF ACR No. 59, 16–31 Dec. 1944, p. D2.

128. Saul Dubow, 'Scientism, Social Research and the Limits of "South Africanism": The Case of Ernst Gideon Malherbe', *South African Historical Journal*, 44 (May 2001), p. 100; John Lambert, 'An Identity Threatened: White English-Speaking South Africans, Britishness and Dominion South Africanism, 1934–1939', *Kleio*, 37(1) (2010), pp. 50–70; John Lambert, '"The Finest Hour?" English-Speaking South Africans and World War II', *South African Historical Journal*, 60(1) (2008), pp. 76–7.

129. Tothill, 'The Soldiers' Vote', p. 88.

130. For Table 16.4, see UNISA UP Archives, Kleyntons Poster Collection, Poster Number 416; SANDF, DOC, AG 3/154 Box 78 General Election, 1943.

131. SANDF, DOC, War Diaries Box 314 *Springbok*, 'Election Supplement', 17 June 1943.

132. Ibid.

133. SANDF, DOC, AI Gp 1 Box 81/I/71/B South African Military Censorship, Special Report No. 12, Reactions to General Election in the Cape Fortress Area, 1–14 June 1943, p. 1.

134. SANDF, DOC, AI Gp 1 Box 81/I/71/B South African MCS No. 21, Post Election Repercussions, 20 June–10 July 1943.

135. SANDF, DOC, AI Gp 1 Box 81/I/71/B South African MCS No. 11, 1–20 Aug. 1942, pp. 3–4.

136. SANDF, DOC, AI Gp 1 Box 81/I/71/B South African MCS No. 13, 1–29 Sept. 1942, p. 3. The poll was based on 10,164 censored letters.

137. SANDF, DOC, AI Gp 1 Box 42/I/37 DFMS No. 88, Sept. 1944.

138. SANDF, DOC, AI Gp 1 Box 42/I/37 DFMS No. 93, Feb. 1945.

139. SANDF, DOC, War Diaries Box 314 *Springbok*, Election Supplement, 17 June 1943.
140. Ibid.
141. These were Heidelberg, Johannesburg West, Kimberley District, Malmesbury, Paarl, Prieska, Uitenhage, Ventersdorp, Bryheid and Worcester.
142. Tothill, 'The Soldiers' Vote', p. 84.
143. SANDF, DOC, AI Gp 1 Box 42/I/37 Durban MCS No. 86, July 1944; Christopher Vasey, *Nazi Intelligence Operations in Non-Occupied Territories: Espionage Efforts in the United States, Britain, South America and Southern Africa* (Jefferson: McFarland & Co., 2016), p. 276.
144. SANDF, DOC, AI Gp 1 Box 42/I/37 DFMS No. 87, Aug. 1944.
145. SANDF, DOC, AI Gp 1 Box 42/I/37/B Durban MCS No. 85 and 86, June and July 1944.
146. SANDF, DOC, AI Gp 1 Box 42/I/37/B Durban MCS No. 85, June 1944.
147. SANDF, DOC, AI Gp 1 Box 42/I/37 DFMS No. 87, Aug. 1944.
148. SANDF, DOC, AI Gp 1 Box 42/I/37 DFMS No. 88, Sept. 1944.
149. SANDF, DOC, AI Gp 1 Box 42/I/37 DFMS No. 94, Mar. 1945.
150. SANDF, DOC, AI Gp 1 Box 42/I/37 DFMS No. 98, July 1945.
151. SANDF, DOC, AI Gp Box 42/I/37 DFMS No. 93, Feb. 1945.
152. See e.g. Roos, *Ordinary Springboks*, p. 11.
153. SANDF, DOC, AI Gp 1 Box 42/I/37, Forces Mail Censorship Durban Summary No. 98, July 1945.
154. SANDF, DOC, AI Gp 1 Box 42/I/37/B Durban MCS No. 85, June 1944; SANDF, DOC, AI Gp 1 Box 42/I/37 DFMS No. 87, Aug. 1944; SANDF, DOC, AI Gp 1 Box 42/I/37 DFMS No. 96 and 96, May and July 1945.
155. SANDF, DOC, AI Gp 1 Box 42/I/37 DFMS No. 88, Sept. 1944.
156. NA WO 204/10382 CMF ACR No. 57, 16–30 Nov. 1944, p. D2.
157. NA WO 204/10382 CMF ACR No. 58, 1–15 Dec. 1944, p. D2. See also, NA WO 204/10382 CMF ACR No. 63, 15–28 Feb. 1945, p. D2.
158. NA WO 204/10382 CMF ACR No. 67, 16–30 Apr. 1945, p. C2.
159. SANDF, DOC, AI Gp 1 Box 42/I/37 DFMS No. 96 and 98, May and July 1945.
160. Roos, *Ordinary Springboks*, p. 111.
161. Parliament adopted two laws to ensure that volunteers were reinstated in their pre-war jobs. These were the Public Servants Act (No. 27 of 1944) and the Act on Civil Servants (No. 40 of 1944). Both laws were meant to prevent discrimination against the ex-volunteer who had to give up his employment in order to join the war effort. The Public Servants Act decreed that the ex-volunteer had to be reinstated to his pre-war job if he had enlisted with the knowledge of his or her employer. The Act on Civil Servants decreed that an ex-volunteer, resuming his job in the civil service, would not lose any service benefits as a result of his military service.
162. Oosthuizen, 'Demobilization and the Post-War Employment of the White Union Defence Forces Soldier', pp. 33–4. Should the ex-soldier lose his second job through his own fault, he was taken back on reduced rates for a maximum of 120 days. Those refusing employment which was considered to be suitable were retained on a reduced scale of allowances for a maximum of only four months.
163. Oosthuizen, 'Soldiers and Politics', pp. 32–6; K. J. Gibbs, 'Demobilisation after World War II: The Process and Politics of Reinstating Union Defence Force Volunteers into Civilian Life, 1943–1948', University of South Africa Paper (1990), p. 31.
164. NA WO 204/10382 CMF ACR No. 70, 1–15 June 1945, p. C1.
165. Roos, *Ordinary Springboks*, p. 97.

166. Oosthuizen, 'Demobilization and the Post-War Employment of the White Union Defence Forces Soldier', pp. 32–6; Gibbs, 'Demobilisation after World War II', p. 31.
167. Oosthuizen, 'Soldiers and Politics', p. 21.
168. Roos, *Ordinary Springboks*, pp. 114–16.
169. Ibid., pp. 116–7.
170. Defence Personnel Files; Roos, *Ordinary Springboks*, p. 35; Nicoli Nattrass, 'Economic Growth and Transformation in the 1940s', in Saul Dubow and Alan Jeeves (eds.), *South Africa's 1940s: Worlds of Possibilities* (Cape Town: Double Storey, 2005) p. 24.
171. Nattrass, 'Economic Growth and Transformation in the 1940s', in Dubow and Jeeves (eds.), *South Africa's 1940s*, p. 27; Jeremy Seeking and Nicoli Nattrass, *Class, Race, and Inequality in South Africa* (London: Yale University Press, 2005), pp. 88–9; Roos, *Ordinary Springboks*, p. 35.
172. Annette Seegers, *The Military in the Making of Modern South Africa* (London: I. B. Tauris, 1996), p. 73.
173. Roos, *Ordinary Springboks*, p. 107.
174. Nattrass, 'Economic Growth and Transformation in the 1940s', in Dubow and Jeeves (eds.), *South Africa's 1940s*, p. 24; Seegers, *The Military in the Making of Modern South Africa*, p. 73.
175. SANDF, DOC, AI Gp 1 Box 42/I/37 Durban MCS No. 86, July 1944; AI Gp Box 42/I/37 DFMS No. 89, Oct. 1944
176. SANDF, DOC, AI Gp 1 Box 42/I/37 DFMS No. 88, Sept. 1944.
177. SANDF, DOC, AI Gp 1 Box 42/I/37 DFMS No. 96, May 1945.
178. SANDF, DOC, AI Gp 1 Box 42/I/37 DFMS No. 88, Sept. 1944.
179. SANDF, DOC, AI Gp 1 Box 42/I/37 Durban MCS No. 86, July 1944.
180. SANDF, DOC, AI Gp 1 Box 42/I/37 DFMS No. 95, Apr. 1945.
181. SANDF, DOC, AI Gp 1 Box 42/I/37 DFMS No. 93, Feb. 1945.
182. SANDF, DOC, AI Gp 1 Box 42/I/37 DFMS No. 95, Apr. 1945.
183. Roos, *Ordinary Springboks*, p. 106.
184. SANDF, DOC, AI Gp 1 Box 81/I/71/B South African MCS No. 27, A General Survey on Morale in the Army, 22 Feb.–21 July 1943, p. 7.
185. Saul Dubow, 'Scientism, Social Research and the Limits of "South Africanism": The Case of Ernst Gideon Malherbe', *South African Historical Journal*, 44 (May 2001), p. 112.
186. Louis Grundlingh, 'Soldiers and Politics: A Study of the Political Consciousness of Black South African Soldiers During and After the Second World War', *Historia*, 36(2) (1991), p. 60; Saul Dubow, 'Introduction: South Africa's 1940s', in Saul Dubow and Alan Jeeves (eds.), *South Africa's 1940s: Worlds of Possibilities* (Cape Town: Double Storey, 2005), p. 9.
187. Roos, *Ordinary Springboks*, p. 34.
188. SANDF, DOC, AI Gp 1 Box 43/I/38/D MCS No. 10, EAFHQ, 6–20 Mar. 1941, p. 3.
189. SANDF, DOC, AI Gp 1 Box 40 I/35, IC to Administrative HQ, UDF, MEF, 23 May 1942.
190. SANDF, DOC, AI Gp 1 Box 43 I/38(I) MEMCFS No. LIV, 30 Dec. 1942–12 Jan. 1943, p. 20.
191. SANDF, DOC, AI Gp 1 Box 43 I/38(I) MEMCFS No. LVII, 10–23 Feb. 1943, p. 20.
192. NA WO 204/10382 CMF ACR No. 60, 1–15 Jan. 1945, p. D2; NA WO 204/10382 CMF ACR No. 71, 16–30 June 1945, p. C2.

193. SANDF, DOC, AI Gp 1 Box 43 MEMCFS No. LXXX (29 Dec. 1943–11 Jan. 1944), p. 19; Roos, *Ordinary Springboks*, p. 56; MacKenzie, *Politics and Military Morale*, pp. 165–6; Ian van der Waag, *A Military History of Modern South Africa* (Johannesburg: Jonathan Ball, 2015), p. 205.
194. NA WO 204/10382 CMF ACR No. 63, 15–28 Feb. 1945, p. D2.
195. J. E. H. Grobler, 'The Marabastad Riot, 1942', *Contree*, 32 (1992), p. 27.
196. SANDF, DOC, AI Gp 1 Box 81/I/71/B South African Military Censorship, Special Report No. 3, The CATD and the Marabastad Compound Riot', 28 Dec. 1942.
197. Ibid.
198. Grobler, 'The Marabastad Riot, 1942', p. 28.
199. SANDF, DOC, AI Gp 1 Box 81/I/71/B South African Military Censorship, Special Report No. 3, The CATD and the Marabastad Compound Riot, 28 Dec. 1942.
200. Grobler, 'The Marabastad Riot, 1942', p. 28.
201. SANDF, DOC, AI Gp 1 Box 81/I/71/B South African Military Censorship, Special Report No. 4, Disturbance at Sonderwater, 31 Dec. 1942.
202. Ibid.
203. SANDF, DOC, AI Gp 1 Box 81/I/71/B South African Military Censorship, Special Report No. 7, The Riot at Kimberley, 9–25 Feb. 1943. Other riots involving gunshots, deaths, multiple casualties and widespread damage occurred among the 2nd Battalion Cape Corps at Sonderwater on 12–13 June 1943 (see SANDF, DOC, AI Gp 1 Box 81/I/71/B South African Military Censorship, Special Report No. 11, Sonderwater Cape Coloured Riot, 13 June 1943).
204. SANDF, DOC, AI Gp 1 Box 81/I/71/B South African MCS No. 27, A General Survey on Morale in the Army, 22 Feb.–21 July 1943, p. 6.
205. Dubow, 'Scientism, Social Research and the Limits of "South Africanism"', p. 112.
206. SANDF, DOC, AI Gp Box 42/I/37 DFMS No. 93, Feb. 1945.
207. For more on this dynamic see Dubow, 'Scientism, Social Research and the Limits of "South Africanism"', pp. 99–101.
208. Roos, *Ordinary Springboks*, p. 121.
209. Rodney Davenport and Christopher Saunders, *South Africa: A Modern History* (London: Macmillan, 2000), p. 372.
210. Kenneth A. Heard, *General Elections in South Africa, 1943–1970* (London: Oxford University Press, 1974), p. 46.
211. Davenport and Saunders, *South Africa*, p. 372; William Beinart, *Twentieth Century South Africa* (Oxford University Press, 2001), p. 138.
212. Davenport and Saunders, *South Africa*, p. 370; Beinart, *Twentieth Century South Africa*, p. 138. Other historians have differed from this view. Roos argues that white veterans did not shift their allegiance to the National Party in 1948 due to the fact that they were still too closely associated with fascism and Nazism (Roos, *Ordinary Springboks*, p. 11). Oosthuizen argues that while many might not have supported UP policies most still voted UP, 'if only as a vague symbol of an ideal once considered worth fighting for' (François Oosthuizen, 'Soldiers and Politics: The Political Ramification of the White Union Defence Forces Soldiers' Demobilisation Experience after the Second World War', *South African Journal of Military Studies*, 24(1) (1994), p. 27).
213. Grundlingh, 'The King's Afrikaners?', pp. 364–5.
214. South African Defence Personnel Archive, Pretoria, Service Records. The next best represented occupation was 'Labourer' with 6 per cent.
215. Davenport and Saunders, *South Africa*, p. 372.
216. Ibid., p. 371.
217. NA WO 204/10381 CMF and BNAF, ACR No. 52, 1–15 Sept. 1944, p. D2.

218. Ibid.
219. NA WO 204/10382 CMF and BNAF, ACR No. 70, 1–15 June 1945, p. D2.
220. Ibid.
221. BL IOR L/WS/1/939 AG in India's Committee on Morale, Report of Sixth Meeting, n.d. but Apr./May 1944, p. 6; BL IOR L/WS/1/939 Report on the Morale of British, Indian and African Troops in India Command the South-East Asia Command, Feb.–Apr. 1944, p. 7.
222. Daniel Marston, *The Indian Army and the End of the Raj* (Cambridge University Press, 2014); Rajit K. Mazumder, 'From Loyalty to Dissent: Punjabis from the Great War to World War II', in Kaushik Roy (ed.), *The Indian Army in the Two World Wars* (Leiden: Brill, 2012), p. 481.
223. Bayly and Harper, *Forgotten Armies*, p. 368.
224. NA WO 204/10382 CMF and BNAF, ACR No. 66, 1–15 Apr. 1945, p. D3.
225. NA WO 204/10382 CMF and BNAF, ACR No. 67, 16–30 Apr. 1945, p. D2.
226. Ibid.
227. NA WO 204/10382 CMF and BNAF, ACR No. 53, 16–30 Sept. 1944, p. D2.
228. NA WO 204/10382 CMF and BNAF, ACR No. 69, 16–31 May 1945, p. D2.
229. NA WO 204/10382 CMF and BNAF, ACR No. 71, 16–30 June 1945, pp. D1–D2.
230. NA WO 204/10381 CMF and BNAF, ACR No. 45, 16–31 May 1944, p. D2.
231. Yasmin Khan, *The Raj at War: A People's History of India's Second World War* (London: The Bodley Head, 2015), p. 308.
232. Marston, *The Indian Army and the End of the Raj*, location 6,307 of 12,996.
233. Khan, *The Raj at War*, p. 308.
234. Marston, *The Indian Army and the End of the Raj*, location 9,309 of 12,996.
235. Mazumder, 'From Loyalty to Dissent', pp. 482–3.
236. Saumitra Jha and Steven Wilkinson, 'Does Combat Experience Foster Organizational Skill? Evidence from Ethnic Cleansing during the Partition of South Asia', *American Political Science Review*, 106(4) (2012), p. 886.
237. Marston, *The Indian Army and the End of the Raj*, location 9,119 of 12,996.
238. Ibid., location 9,119–32 of 12,996; Robert Gerwarth, 'The Central European Counter-Revolution: Paramilitary Violence in Germany, Austria and Hungary after the Great War', *Past and Present*, 200(1) (2008), p. 186. See also, Robert Gerwarth and John Horne (eds.), *War in Peace: Paramilitary Violence in Europe after the Great War* (Oxford University Press, 2012).
239. Jha and Wilkinson, 'Does Combat Experience Foster Organizational Skill?', p. 886.
240. Quoted in Marston, *The Indian Army and the End of the Raj*, location 9,258 of 12,996.
241. Ibid., location 9,070 of 12,996.
242. Ibid., location 9,216 of 12,996.
243. Ibid., location 9,432 of 12,996.
244. Ibid., location 9,466 of 12,996.
245. Ibid., location 9,811–25 of 12,996.
246. Ibid., location 9,837–60 of 12,996; See Steven I. Wilkinson, *Army and Nation: The Military and Indian Democracy since Independence* (London: Harvard University Press, 2015), pp. 84–5 for some examples of failures by the PBF to protect the population.
247. Jha and Wilkinson, 'Does Combat Experience Foster Organizational Skill?', p. 884. By conducting a quantitative survey of the relationships between communal violence, population flows and the proportion of ex-servicemen in Indian districts, Jha and Wilkinson have highlighted this aspect of the military experience that

shapes socio-political change, viz., 'the role of combat experience in enhancing organizational skills' and 'collective action'.

248. Ibid., p. 884.
249. Quoted in Raghaven, *India's War*, pp. 459–60.
250. Jha and Wilkinson, 'Does Combat Experience Foster Organizational Skill?', p. 884.
251. Ibid., pp. 885–6.
252. Ibid., p. 883; Elizabeth Kier and Ronald R. Krebs, 'Introduction: War and Democracy in Comparative Perspective', in Elizabeth Kier and Ronald R. Krebs (eds.), *In War's Wake: International Conflict and the Fate of Liberal Democracy* (Cambridge University Press, 2010), pp. 1–2.
253. Field, *Blood Sweat and Toil*, pp. 368–72.
254. Bassett and King, *Tomorrow Comes the Song*, p. 256.
255. Allan Levine, *King: William Lyon Mackenzie King, A Life Guided by the Hand of Destiny* (London: Biteback, 2012), p. 368.
256. NA WO 204/10381 CMF and BNAF, ACR No. 49, 16–31 July 1944, p. D2.
257. NA WO 204/10382 CMF and BNAF, ACR No. 70, 1–15 June 1945, p. D2.
258. NA WO 204/10382 CMF and BNAF, ACR No. 53, 16–30 Sept. 1944, p. D3; NA WO 204/10382 CMF and BNAF, ACR No. 71, 16–30 June 1945, p. D1.
259. NA WO 204/10381 CMF and BNAF, ACR No. 51, 16–31 Aug. 1944, p. D2.
260. NA WO 204/10382 CMF and BNAF, ACR No. 70, 1–15 June 1945, p. D2.

Conclusion

1. www.winstonchurchill.org/learn/speeches/speeches-of-winston-churchill/113-the-few, accessed 7 Aug. 2014.
2. Brian Farrell, *The Defence and Fall of Singapore 1940–1942* (Stroud: Tempus, 2005), pp. 153–4.
3. Geoffrey G. Field, *Blood, Sweat and Toil: Remaking the British Working Class, 1939–1945* (Oxford University Press, 2011), pp. 4–5.
4. John Darwin, *The Empire Project: The Rise and Fall of the British World-System, 1830–1970* (Cambridge University Press, 2009), p. 497.
5. Tim Cook, *Warlords: Borden, Mackenzie King, and Canada's World Wars* (London: Penguin, 2012), p. 220.
6. F. L. W. Wood, *Political and External Affairs* (Wellington: Historical Publications Branch, 1958), pp. 236–9; Michael Bassett and Michael King, *Tomorrow Comes the Song: The Life of Peter Fraser* (Auckland: Penguin, 2000), p. 232.
7. Neil Roos, 'The Second World War, the Army Education Scheme and the "Discipline" of the White Poor in South Africa', *History of Education: Journal of the History of Education Society*, 32(6) (2003), p. 651.
8. Catriona Pennell, *A Kingdom United: Popular Responses to the Outbreak of the First World War in Britain and Ireland* (Oxford University Press, 2012), p. 228; Adrian Gregory, *The Last Great War: British Society and the First World War* (Cambridge University Press, 2008), p. 278; Alan Allport, *Browned Off and Bloody-Minded: The British Soldier Goes to War 1939–1945* (London: Yale University Press, 2015), p. 63.
9. David Edgerton, *Britain's War Machine: Weapons, Resources and Experts in the Second World War* (London: Allen Lane, 2011), p. 197.
10. H. M. D. Parker, *Manpower: A Study of War-Time Policy and Administration* (London: HMSO, 1957), pp. 150–1.

11. Ibid., pp. 157–8, 299, 488–97; *Report of the Ministry of Labour and National Service, 1939–1946* (London: His Majesty's Stationery Office, 1947), pp. 16–17.
12. New Zealand Defence HQ Library, Report of the National Service Department, 1946, pp. 21–33; J. E. Cookson, 'Appeal Boards and Conscientious Objectors', in John Crawford (ed.), *Kia Kaha: New Zealand in the Second World War* (Oxford University Press, 2000), p. 173.
13. Albert Palazzo, 'The Overlooked Mission: Australia and Home Defence', in Peter J. Dean (ed.), *Australia 1942: In the Shadow of War* (Cambridge University Press, 2013), p. 63. Some Canadian conscripts were sent overseas in 1945 (see Chapter 15 of this volume).
14. Robert Engen, *Strangers in Arms: Combat Motivation in the Canadian Army, 1943–1945* (London: McGill-Queen's University Press, 2016), p. 21. The National Defence HQ calculated, in Mar. 1944, that French Canadians made up 19.1% of the total strength of the Army (including conscripts). See Daniel Byers, *Zombie Army: The Canadian Army and Conscription in the Second World War* (Vancouver: University of British Columbia Press, 2016), p. 7.
15. Cook, *Warlords*, p. 207.
16. Paul Hasluck, *Australia in the War of 1939–1945, Series Four: Civil, Volume I: The Government and the People, 1939–1941* (Canberra: AWM, 1965), pp. 399–400 and Appendix 8.
17. Indivar Kamtekar, 'A Different War Dance: State and Class in India 1939–1945', *Past and Present*, 176(1) (2002), p. 190.
18. Saumitra Jha and Steven Wilkinson, 'Does Combat Experience Foster Organisational Skill? Evidence from Ethnic Cleansing during the Partition of South Asia', *American Political Science Review*, 106(4) (Nov. 2012), p. 884.
19. Andrew Stewart, *Empire Lost: Britain, The Dominions and the Second World War* (London: Continuum, 2008), p. 23.
20. Kamtekar, 'A Different War Dance', pp. 190–3.
21. See also, Gregory, *The Last Great War*, pp. 81 and 317; David Littlewood, '"Should He Serve"?: The Military Service Boards' Operations in the Wellington Provincial District, 1916–1918' (Master's thesis, Massey University, 2010), pp. 55–74.
22. Roos, *Ordinary Springboks*, p. 43.
23. John Horne, 'Introduction: Mobilizing for "Total War", in 1914–1918', in John Horne (ed.), *State, Society and Mobilization in Europe during the First World War* (Cambridge University Press, 1997), pp. 2–14. Horne was addressing these issues in the context of the First World War. His arguments, however, have relevance also for the Second World War.
24. Edgerton, *Britain's War Machine*, p. 228.
25. Richard Toye, *The Roar of the Lion: The Untold Story of Churchill's World War II Speeches* (Oxford University Press, 2013), pp. 97–205.
26. Field, *Blood, Sweat and Toil*, p. 334.
27. NA WO 32/15772 The Army Council, Morale in the Army: Report of the War Office Morale Committee, Feb.–May 1942, pp. 2–3.
28. NA WO 203/4538 Report on the Morale of British, Indian, and Colonial Troops of Allied Land Forces, South-East Asia, Nov. 1944–Jan. 1945, p. 1.
29. Gajendra Singh, *The Testimonies of Indian Soldiers and the Two World Wars: Between Self and Sepoy* (London: Bloomsbury, 2014), p. 157. The other being the Indian mutiny of 1857.
30. Tarak Barkawi, 'Culture and Combat in the Colonies: The Indian Army in the Second World War', *Journal of Contemporary History*, 41(2) (2006), p. 331.

31. Elizabeth Kier and Ronald R. Krebs, 'Introduction: War and Democracy in Comparative Perspective', in Elizabeth Kier and Ronald R. Krebs (eds.), *In War's Wake: International Conflict and the Fate of Liberal Democracy* (Cambridge University Press, 2010), p. 5.
32. Edgerton, *Britain's War Machine*, pp. 2–3.
33. Patrick Rose, 'British Army Command Culture 1939–1945: A Comparative Study of British Eighth and Fourteenth Armies' (PhD thesis, King's College London, 2008).
34. George Peden, 'Financing Churchill's Army', in Keith Neilson and Greg Kennedy (eds.), *The British Way in Warfare: Power and the International System, 1856–1956* (Farnham: Ashgate, 2010), p. 288; Elizabeth Kier, *Imagining War: French and British Military Doctrine Between the Wars* (Princeton University Press, 1997), p. 96.
35. Parker, *Manpower*, pp. 36–7.
36. David French, *Raising Churchill's Army: The British Army and the War against Germany 1919–1945* (Oxford University Press, 2000), p. 179; Edward Smalley, *The British Expeditionary Force, 1939–40* (Basingstoke: Palgrave Macmillan, 2015), pp. 37–83.
37. AWM 54 553/5/15 Lessons from Malaya, copy of a secret document issued to War Department, Washington, by Lieut. Col. T. J. Wells, Assistant Military Attaché, London, 1943, p. 2.
38. BL IOR L/MIL/17/5/2244 'Military Training Pamphlet No. 1 (India): Armoured Units in the Field, Characteristics, Roles and Handling of Armoured Divisions 1941', p. 11. Issued by the General Staff, India, 1942.
39. NA WO 106/1775 Bartholomew Committee Final Report, 1940.
40. NA WO 177/324 Medical Situation Report, 24 July 1942.
41. Farrell, *The Defence and Fall of Singapore*, p. 188.
42. Ibid., p. 356.
43. NA CAB 106/703 Address to Officers of HQ Eighth Army by Gen. Montgomery on Taking Over Command of the Army, 13 Aug. 1942.
44. ANZ WAII/1/DA/508/1 Vol. 3 MEMCWS, No. XLI (19–25 Aug. 1942), p. 1
45. Jeremy A. Crang, *The British Army and the People's War, 1939–1945* (Manchester University Press, 2000), p. 139.
46. Rose, 'British Army Command Culture 1939–1945', pp. 138–9.
47. French, *Raising Churchill's Army*, pp. 266–7.
48. Ian Gooderson, *A Hard Way to Make a War: The Allied Campaign in Italy in the Second World War* (London: Conway, 2008), p. 126.
49. Ibid., p. 124.
50. French, *Raising Churchill's Army*, p. 266; John Buckley, *Monty's Men: The British Army and the Liberation of Europe* (London: Yale University Press, 2013), p. 133.
51. Daniel Marston, *Phoenix from the Ashes: The Indian Army in the Burma Campaign* (Westport: Praeger, 2003), pp. 222–4.
52. Ibid., pp. 105–7.
53. Charles Forrester, *Montgomery's Functional Doctrine: Combined Arms Doctrine in British 21st Army Group in Northwest Europe, 1944–45* (Solihull: Helion & Company, 2015); Charles Forrester, 'Field Marshal Montgomery's Role in the Creation of the British 21st Army Group's Combined Armed Doctrine for the Final Assault on Germany', *The Journal of Military History*, 78 (Oct. 2014), pp. 1295–320; Buckley, *Monty's Men*, pp. 255–7.
54. Forrester, 'Field Marshal Montgomery's Role', p. 1316.
55. Patrick Rose, 'Allies at War: British and US Army Command Culture in the Italian Campaign, 1943–1944', *Journal of Strategic Studies*, 36(1) (February, 2013), p. 69.

56. Timothy Moreman, *The Jungle, the Japanese and the British Commonwealth Armies at War, 1941–45: Fighting Methods, Doctrine and Training for Jungle Warfare* (London: Frank Cass, 2005), p. 5; Barkawi, 'Culture and Combat in the Colonies', p. 329; Louis Allen, *Burma: The Longest War, 1941–45* (London: Phoenix Press, 2000 [1984]), p. xviii.
57. Buckley, *Monty's Men*, p. 28.
58. Peden, 'Financing Churchill's Army', in Neilson and Kennedy (eds.), *The British Way in Warfare*, p. 298; Allport, *Browned Off and Bloody-Minded*, p. xviii.
59. Brian Bond, *Britain's Two World Wars against Germany: Myth, Memory and the Distortion of Hindsight* (Cambridge University Press, 2014), p. 7.
60. LAC Vol. 18,826 File No. 133.065 (D689) List of Commonwealth Forces in Fighting Contact with the Enemy, 1940–5; W. K. Hancock and M. M. Gowing, *British War Economy* (London: HMSO, 1949), p. 367.
61. John A. English, *The Canadian Army and the Normandy Campaign: A Study of Failure in High Command* (London: Praeger, 1991), p. 300.
62. Max Hastings, *Armageddon: The Battle for Germany, 1944–45* (London: Pan Books, 2005 [2004]), p. 437; NA CAB 106/1084 Some Statistics of the North West European Campaign 1944 June–1945 May.
63. English, *The Canadian Army and the Normandy Campaign*, p. 300.
64. David Reynolds, '1940: Fulcrum of the Twentieth Century', *International Affairs*, 66(2) (Apr. 1990), p. 332.
65. Ibid., p. 335; Ashley Jackson, *The British Empire and the Second World War* (London: Hambledon Continuum, 2006), p. 4. For a different view on the strategic impact of the performance of the British and Commonwealth Armies, see Buckley, *Monty's Men*, p. 5.
66. Reynolds, '1940: Fulcrum of the Twentieth Century', p. 341.
67. NA WO 204/10381 CMF and BNAF, ACR No. 36, 1–15 Jan. 1944, p. A10.
68. Darwin, *The Empire Project*, p. 476.
69. John Charmley, *Churchill: The End of Glory* (London, Sceptre 1993), p. 367.
70. Gooderson, *A Hard Way to Make a War*, p. 26.
71. Brian Bond (ed.), *Chief of Staff: The Diaries of Lieutenant-General Sir Henry Pownall* (London: Leo Cooper, 1974), p. 85.
72. Alan Warren, *Singapore 1942: Britain's Greatest Defeat* (London: Hambledon, 2002), p. xi.
73. Darwin, *The Empire Project*, pp. 508–11.
74. Sumit Sarkar, *Modern India 1885–1947* (London: Macmillan, 1983), p. 3; quoted in Robert Johnson, 'The Army in India and Responses to Low-Intensity Conflict, 1936–1946', *Journal of the Society for Army Historical Research*, 89(358) (2011), p. 175.
75. Patrick French, *Liberty or Death: India's Journey to Independence and Division* (London: Penguin, 2011), Introduction.
76. Raymond Callahan, *Churchill and His Generals* (Lawrence: University Press of Kansas, 2007), p. 187.
77. Elizabeth Kier, 'War and Reform: Gaining Labor's Compliance on the Homefront', in Elizabeth Kier and Ronald R. Krebs (eds.), *In War's Wake: International Conflict and the Fate of Liberal Democracy* (Cambridge University Press, 2010), p. 139.
78. Gregory, *The Last Great War*, p. 1.
79. John Barnes' commentary on Eric Hobsbawm, 'Britain: A Comparative View', in Brian Brivati and Harriet Jones (eds.), *What Difference Did the War Make?* (London: Leicester University Press, 1993); C. L. Mowat, *Britain Between the Wars* (London: Methuen, 1955).

80. Malcolm Smith, 'The Changing Nature of the British State, 1929–59: The Historiography of Consensus', in Brian Brivati and Harriet Jones (eds.), *What Difference Did the War Make?* (London: Leicester University Press, 1993), p. 38.
81. Daniel Todman, 'Defining Deaths', in Nicholas Martin, Tim Haughton and Pierre Purseigle, *Aftermath: Legacies and Memories of War in Europe, 1918–1945–1989* (Farnham: Ashgate, 2014), p. 60.
82. Kier, 'War and Reform', in Kier and Krebs (eds.), *In War's Wake*, p. 157.
83. Sonya O. Rose, *Which People's War? National Identity and Citizenship in Britain 1939–1945* (Oxford University Press, 2003), p. 22; Kevin Jefferys, 'British Politics and Social Policy during the Second World War', *Historical Journal*, 30 (Mar. 1987), pp 123–44.
84. Bassett and King, *Tomorrow Comes the Song*, pp. 255–6.
85. Ibid., p. 256; Appendices to the Journals of the House of Representatives, 1944 Session I, H-33a; ANZ WAII/1/DA565/1 Maj. W. A. Bryan, Report on the Conduct of the 1943 General Election in the Middle East. It is also conceivable that a truly non-party war administration, as advocated by Holland, might have been installed.
86. Neil Roos, *Ordinary Springboks: White Servicemen and Social Justice in South Africa, 1939–1961* (Aldershot: Ashgate, 2005), p. 55; Michael Cardo, '"Fighting a Worse Imperialism": White South African Loyalism and the Army Education Services during the Second World War', *South African Historical Journal*, 46(1) (2002), p. 23.
87. Saul Dubow, 'Scientism, Social Research and the Limits of "South Africanism": The Case of Ernst Gideon Malherbe', *South African Historical Journal*, 44 (May 2001), p. 112.
88. SANDF, DOC, AI Gp Box 42/I/37 DFMS No. 93, Feb. 1945.
89. Rodney Davenport and Christopher Saunders, *South Africa: A Modern History* (London: Macmillan, 2000), p. 372.
90. Kenneth A. Heard, *General Elections in South Africa, 1943–1970* (London: Oxford University Press, 1974), p. 46.
91. Davenport and Saunders, *South Africa*, p. 370; William Beinart, *Twentieth Century South Africa* (Oxford University Press, 2001), p. 138.
92. NA WO 204/10381 CMF and BNAF, ACR No. 51, 16–31 Aug. 1944, p. D2.
93. NA WO 204/10382 CMF and BNAF, ACR No. 70, 1–15 June 1945, p. D2.
94. Daniel Marston, *The Indian Army and the End of the Raj* (Cambridge University Press, 2014); Saumitra Jha and Steven Wilkinson, 'Does Combat Experience Foster Organizational Skill? Evidence from Ethnic Cleansing during the Partition of South Asia', *American Political Science Review*, 106(4) (2012).
95. Sources for Table 17.1: Allport, *Browned Off and Bloody-Minded*, p. xix; Peter Howlett (ed.), *Fighting with Figures: A Statistical Digest of the Second World War* (London: The Central Statistics Office, 1995), p. 43; Ian van der Waag, *A Military History of Modern South Africa* (Johannesburg: Jonathan Ball, 2015), p. 212; Wray Vamplew (ed.), *Australians: Historical Statistics* (Broadway, NSW: Fairfax, Syme and Weldon Associates, 1987), p. 415; AJHR H-19B Statement of Strengths and Losses in the Armed Services and Mercantile Marine, Parliamentary Paper, 1948; W. R. Feasby (ed.), *Official History of the Canadian Medical Services, 1939–1945, Vol. II: Clinical Subjects* (Ottawa: Edmund Clouthier, 1953), p. 426; Daniel Marston, *The Indian Army and the End of the Raj* (Cambridge University Press, 2014), Location 2,004 of 12,996.
96. Jonathan Fennell, 'Courage and Cowardice in the North African Campaign: The Eighth Army and Defeat in the Summer of 1942', *War in History*, 20(1) (2013).

97. Alex Danchev and Daniel Todman (eds.), *War Diaries 1939–1945: Field Marshal Lord Alanbrooke* (London: Phoenix, 2002 [2001]), p. 117.

Appendix 1 The Censorship Summaries

1. Of the 901 censorship summaries examined for the war against Germany, 234 list the number of letters examined in their compilation (2,849,131 letters in total). If the average number of letters examined in these 234 summaries (12,176) is applied to the total number of censorship summaries for the war in the West (901), then it is reasonable to conclude that approximately 11 million letters were assessed in the production of these key sources.
2. ANZ WAII/1/DA 302/15/1–31 History 1 and 2 NZ Field Censor Sections, pp. 35–54; WO 204/10381 ACRs: No. 1–29, Nov. 1942–Sept. 1943.
3. DHH CMHQ Report 51 Censorship of Mail, CAO. Field Censors' Notes as Material for History, 31 Oct. 1941.
4. Bernard Porter, *The Absent-Minded Imperialists: Empire, Society, and Culture in Britain* (Oxford University Press, 2004), p. 13.
5. DHH CMHQ Report 51 Censorship of Mail, CAO. Field Censors' Notes as Material for History, 31 Oct. 1941.
6. Ibid; LHCMA Adam Papers, 3/13 Narrative of Work as AG, Chapter VI, Morale and Discipline.
7. NA DEFE 1/381 Memorandum, Topics in Soldiers' Mail, 31 Mar. 1942.
8. Quoted in Glyn Prysor, 'The "Fifth Column" and the British Experience of Retreat, 1940', *War in History*, 12(4) (2005), p. 421.
9. NA WO32/15772 Note on Compilation of the Reports of the War Office Committee on Morale in the Army, 2 Jan. 1943.
10. DHH File No. 146.11.2009 (D2) War Office Notes for Censorship Lectures, 1941; NA WO 199/3082 Unit Censorship Instructions, n.d. but clearly intended for 'Overlord'.
11. NA DEFE 1/381 E. Sachs, AAG, 3 Apr. 1942.
12. NA WO 165/42 Examination of Letters from Soldiers, M.I.12, 8 Nov. 1943.
13. NA WO 165/143 Army Mail Censorship Reports, Subject Headings in Use in Great Britain, 1942.
14. SANDF, DOC, AI Gp 1 Box 43/I/38/E General Report of Military Censorship, East African Forces, 1–14 Sept. 1941, Appendix A.

Appendix 2 The Morale Reports

1. NA WO 106/1775 War Office, Directorate of Military Training, Notes of a Committee set up to consider the lessons to be learnt from the operations in Flanders, Wednesday 12 June 1940; NAA MP729/8, 36/431/38 Despatch by the Supreme Commander of the ABDA Area to the Combined Chiefs of Staff on the Operations in the Southwest Pacific, 15 Jan. 1942–25 Feb. 1942, p. 1; Brian Farrell, *The Defence and Fall of Singapore 1940–1942* (Stroud: Tempus, 2005), p. 6; WO 167/228 War Diary, 3rd Division Provost Company, 1 Sept. 1939–30 June 1940.
2. It is possible that these censorship summaries survive, most likely in India, hidden away in an unexplored archive; it is hoped that at some stage in the future they will come to light and add further layers to our understanding of these important campaigns.
3. Kausik Roy has used an additional morale report, for the period Nov. 1944–Jan. 1945, taking the number of available reports up to seventeen (see Kausik Roy, 'Discipline and Morale of the African, British and Indian Army units in Burma and India during World War II: July 1943 to Aug. 1945', *Modern Asian Studies*, 4(6) (2010)).

4. WO 277/16 Morale, p. 28; NA WO 193/453 Morale Committee Papers, 25 Feb. 1942–25 Oct. 1945, Assessment of Morale by Statistical Methods (Report by I.S.2). These morale reports were also based on intelligence reports from the Ministry of Intelligence, censorship reports on letters of complaint and enquiry received by the BBC and the *News of the World*, letters to the War Office and Courts Martial statistics.
5. Kausik Roy has used an additional morale report for India Command, for the period Nov. 1944–Jan. 1945 (see Roy, 'Discipline and Morale of the African, British and Indian Army units in Burma and India during World War II').
6. NA WO 32/15772 Note on Compilation of the Reports of the War Office Committee on Morale in the Army, 2 Jan. 1943. They were forwarded to the AG with accompanying comments in some cases from corps and army commanders.
7. Ibid.

Appendix 3 Quantitative Indicators of Morale

1. Each summary was based on the censorship of an average of over 40,000 letters, and, thus, gave a reliable appraisal of changes in morale in Second Army. A typical modern national opinion survey uses a sample of 1,100 to give an error margin of ±3%; if a similar methodology were used on a sample of 40,000, the error would be tiny (±0.5%).
2. The scale, therefore, approximates to what is known as an 'equal appearing interval scale'.
3. A strong correlation between two variables would produce an r-value in excess of +0.9 or –0.9. T. Lucy, *Quantitative Techniques* (Continuum: London, 1996), p. 113.
4. Other sources that have used these kinds of indicators as a tool to assess morale include Jonathan Fennell, *Combat and Morale in the North African Campaign* (Cambridge University Press, 2011); David French, '"Tommy Is No Soldier": The Morale of the Second British Army in Normandy, June – Aug. 1944', *Journal of Strategic Studies*, 19(4) 1996); John Buckley, *British Armour in the Normandy Campaign 1944* (London: Frank Cass, 2004); John Buckley, *Monty's Men: The British Army and the Liberation of Europe* (London: Yale University Press, 2013); Terry Copp and Bill McAndrew, *Battle Exhaustion: Soldiers and Psychiatrists in the Canadian Army*, 1939–1945 (London: McGill – Queen's University Press, 1990); William Deist, 'The Military Collapse of the German Empire: The Reality behind the Stab-in-the-Back Myth', *War in History*, 3(2) (1996), pp. 186–207.

Appendix 4 Defining Morale

1. Jonathan Fennell, 'In Search of the 'X' Factor: Morale and the Study of Strategy', *Journal of Strategic Studies*, 37(6–7) (2014), pp. 803–4.
2. John A. Lynn, *The Bayonets of the Republic: Motivation and Tactics in the Army of Revolutionary France* (Oxford: Westview Press, 1996), pp. 34–5.
3. Ibid, pp. 51–3.
4. Jonathan Fennell, 'Reevaluating Combat Cohesion: The British Second Army in The Northwest Europe Campaign of the Second World War', in Anthony King (ed.), *Frontline: Combat and Cohesion in the Twenty-First Century* (Oxford University Press, 2015), pp. 138–9.

SELECT BIBLIOGRAPHY

Primary Sources

Australia

Australian Electoral Commission

Australian War Memorial
Series and subjects interrogated include:

AWM 52 2nd Australian Imperial Force and Citizen Military Forces Unit War Diaries, 1939–45 War
AWM 52 1 HQ Units; AWM 52 11 Medical.

AWM 54 Written Records, 1939–45 War
AWM 54 52 Army Education; AWM 54 171 Casualties; AWM 54 175 Censorship; AWM 54 229 Courts of Inquiry and Investigations; AWM 54 267 Disease and Disabilities; AWM 54 277 Disposal of Sick and Wounded; AWM 54 306 Egypt and Palestine; AWM 54 307 Electoral; AWM 54 415 India, Mesopotamia; AWM 54 423 Intelligence; AWM 54 447 Law, Military; AWM 54 451 Lectures; AWM 54 481 Medical; AWM 54 492 Military History Section (War Records); AWM 54 506 Natives; AWM 54 515 Officers; AWM 54 534 Campaign in Greece (April 1941); AWM 54 553 Campaign in Malaya and Singapore (December 1941–February 1942); AWM 54 577 Owen Stanleys (July 1942–November 1942); AWM 54 624 Europe; AWM 54 804 Psychological Warfare; AWM 54 838 Rehabilitation; AWM 54 882 Science; AWM 54 883 Security; AWM 54 903 Statistics.

AWM 60 Northern Command

AWM 61 Eastern Command

AWM 63 2nd AIF HQ (Middle East)

AWM 68 Official History, 1939–45 War: Records of Paul Hasluck

3DRL 2632 Papers of Lieutenant-General Sir Leslie Morshead
3DRL 2632 Series 2: Official Correspondence 1916–47; 3DRL 2632 Series 6: Operational Papers, Middle East 1939–45; 3DRL 2632 Series 8: Administrative papers, 1943–5; 3DRL 2632 Series 10: Reports 1944–52.

3DRL 6643 Papers of Field-Marshal Sir Thomas Albert Blamey
3DRL 6643 Series 1: Middle East correspondence and administrative papers, 1940–4.

National Archives of Australia

Canberra, Melbourne and Sydney archives.
A406: Chief Electoral Office, Correspondence files, 1939–45; A2670: War Cabinet Secretariat, War Cabinet agenda with minutes, 1939–46; A2910: Australian High Commission, United Kingdom, Correspondence files, 1913–60; A8681: Department of Defence, Public Relations Bulletins from the Department of Air, 1940–9; A9695: Department of Defence, Folders of historical documents World War II, 1940–2; MP508/1: Department of the Army, General correspondence files, 1939–42; MP729/ 6: Department of the Army, Secret correspondence files, 1936–45; MP729/7: Department of the Army, Secret correspondence files, 1939–45; MP729/8: Department of the Army, Secret correspondence files, 1937–50; MP742/1: Department of the Army, General and civil staff correspondence files and Army personnel files, 1943–51; P617: District Headquarters, 6th Military District, Australian Military Forces, 1939–46; SP109/16: Department of Information, General Correspondence Files, 1941–5; SP112/1: Department of Information, General Correspondence Files, 1939–46; SP300/4 Chester Wilmot series (includes scripts, reports and personal files), 1936–55; SP459/1: HQ Eastern Command, Correspondence files, 1912–64; SP1048/7: HQ Eastern Command, General correspondence, 'S' (Secret) series, 1939–46.

Canada

Directorate of History and Heritage, Department of National Defence

Kardex Collection, 1939–71; Canadian Military HQ Reports, 1940–8.

Elections Canada Library Service

Library and Archives Canada

Record Group 3: Post Office Operations

Record Group 24: Department of National Defence
Volumes: 5267; 6917; 8035; 9408; 10110; 10111; 10508; 10511; 10547; 10651; 10704; 10705; 10706; 10708; 10738; 10870; 11702; 11706; 11994; 12320; 12322; 12559; 12630; 12631; 12699; 12705; 15651; 15652; 15661; 15664; 15951; 18499; 18502; 18570; 18571; 18576; 18712; 18715; 18824; 18826; 18829; 19466; 19466.

Record Group 25: Department of External Affairs

Record Group 36

Papers of General Henry Duncan Graham Crerar (MG 30/ E157)

Papers of Lieutenant-General Kenneth Stuart (MG30/ E520)

Microform Collection

New Zealand

Archives New Zealand

Series interrogated include:
WAII/1 War Diaries and Records of Supplementary Material 1939–45; WAII/2 Unclassified Material, 1939–45; WAII/4 Medical Records, 1940–5; WAII/8 Lieutenant-General B. C. Freyberg, Personal Files, 1939–45; WAII/11 War History Branch, Unregistered Papers, 1941–59.

Defence Library, HQ New Zealand Defence Forces

Turnbull Library Manuscript Collection

South Africa

Defence Personnel Archive, Pretoria

South African National Defence Force, Documentation Centre

Series interrogated include:

Adjutant-General Files; Army Intelligence Files; Chief of the General Staff (War) Files; Deputy Adjutant-General Personnel Files; Division Documents Files; Secretary for Defence Files; Union Defence Forces Files; Union War Histories Files; World War II: War Diaries Vol. 1 Files; World War II: War Diaries Vol. 2 Files

UNISA Library, United Party Archives

Collections interrogated include:
UP Private Collections; UP Central Head Office Collections; UP Transvaal Province Collections

United Kingdom

Bodleian Library

British Library

Oriental and African Studies Papers interrogated:
L/MIL/17 Military Department Library; L/PJ/12 Public and Judicial Department (Separate) Files, 1913–47; L/WS War Staff Files, 1921–50; L/WS/2 Other War Staff Files, 1940–51

Imperial War Museum

Liddell Hart Centre for Military Archives

Hobson Library, Joint Services Command and Staff College

National Archives

Series interrogated include:

CAB Cabinet Office
CAB 21 Registered Files (1916–65); CAB 66 Memoranda; CAB 98 Miscellaneous Committees: Minutes and Papers; CAB 101 Official Histories – e.g. Of Operations; CAB 106 Historical Section: Archivist and Librarian Files; CAB 121 Special Secret Information Centre: Files CAB 124 Offices of the Minister of Reconstruction, Lord President of the Council and Minister for Science Records.

DEFE Ministry of Defence

DEFE 1 Postal and Telegraph Censorship Department, predecessors and successor Papers.

LAB Labour and Employment

LAB 25 Private Office Papers: War Emergency Measures; LAB 29 Circulars and Codes of Instructions; LAB 45 National Service Registration: Specimen Documents.

WO War Office

WO 32 Registered Files (General Series); WO 33 Reports, Memoranda and Papers (O and A Series); WO 71 Judge Advocate General's Office: Courts Martial Proceedings; WO 73 Office of the Commander-in-Chief and War Office: Distribution of the Army Monthly Returns; WO 93 Judge Advocate General's Office: Miscellaneous Correspondence and Papers; WO 106 Directorate of Military Operations and Military Intelligence; WO 162 Adjutant-Generals Papers; WO 163 War Office Council; WO 165 Directorates (Various): War Diaries, Second World War; WO 167 British Expeditionary Force, France: War Diaries, Second World War; WO 169 British Forces, Middle East: War Diaries, Second World War; WO 171 Allied Expeditionary Force, North West Europe (British Element): War Diaries, Second World War; WO 172 British and Allied Land Forces, South-East Asia: War Diaries, Second World War; WO 175 Unit War Diaries British North Africa Forces; WO 177 Army Medical Services: War Diaries, Second World War; WO 193 Directorate of Military Operations and Plans, later Directorate of Military Operations: Files Concerning Military Planning, Intelligence and Statistics (Collation Files); WO 199 Home Forces: Military HQ Papers, Second World War; WO 201 Middle East Forces HQ Papers; WO 202 British Military Missions in Liaison with Allied Forces; Military HQ Papers, Second World War; WO 203 Military HQ Far East; WO 204 Allied Forces Mediterranean Theatre, Military HQ Papers, Second World War; WO 205 21 Army Group: Military HQ Papers, Second World War; WO 208 Directorate of Military Operations and Intelligence, and Directorate of Military Intelligence; Ministry of Defence, Defence Intelligence Staff: Files; WO 214 Earl Alexander of Tunis, Supreme Allied Commander Mediterranean Theatre: Papers; WO 216 Office of the Chief of the Imperial General Staff: Papers; WO 217 Private War Diaries of Various Army Personnel, Second World War; WO 219 SHAEF: Military HQ Papers, Second World War; WO 222 Medical Historians' Papers: First and Second World Wars; WO 227 Office of the Engineer-in-Chief: Papers; WO 231 Directorate of Military Training WO: 232 Directorate of Tactical Investigation: Papers; WO 236 General Sir George Erskine: Papers; WO 241 Directorate of Army Psychiatry; WO 258 Department of the Permanent Under Secretary of State: Private Office

Papers; WO 259 Department of the Secretary of State for War: Private Office Papers; WO 277 Historical Monographs WO 279 Confidential Print; WO 285 General Miles Christopher Dempsey: Papers; WO 291 Military Operational Research Unit; WO 365 Department of the Adjutant-General, Statistics Branch; WO 366 Department of the Permanent Under Secretary of State.

Published Primary Sources

AJHR H-11A (1946) H. L. Bockett, Report of the National Service Department on Activities Under the National Service Emergency Regulations 1940 and the Industrial Man-Power Emergency Regulations 1944.

AJHR H-19B (1948) Statement of Strengths and Losses in the New Zealand Armed Services and Mercantile Marine.

AJHR_1944_I_H-33 The General Election 1943.

AJHR_1944_I_H-33a The General Election 1943.

AJHR_1944_I_H-33b The Local-Option and National-Licencing Polls, 1943.

AJHR_1944_I_H-33c The General Election 1943.

Bureau of Census and Statistics, Pretoria, *Union Statistics for Fifty Years: 1910–1960* (Pretoria: The Government Printers, 1960).

Census and Statistics Department, *New Zealand, Population Census, 1945* (Wellington: Gisborne Herald, 1945–52).

Central Statistical Office, *Statistical Digest of the War* (London: HMSO, 1951).

Commonwealth Bureau of Census and Statistics, *Official Year Book of the Commonwealth of Australia No. 31* (Canberra: Commonwealth Government Printer, 1938).

Commonwealth Bureau of Census and Statistics, *Official Year Book of the Commonwealth of Australia, No. 37* (Canberra: Commonwealth Government Printer, 1946–7).

Directorate of Army Education, *The British Way and Purpose: Consolidated Edition of B.W.P. Booklets 1–18* (1944).

Dominion Bureau of Statistics, *The Canada Year Book, 1946* (Ottawa: Edmond Cloutier, 1946).

Higham, J. B. and Knighton, E. A., *Movements* (London: The War Office, 1955).

Land Warfare Development Centre, *Army Doctrine Publication AC71940, Land Operations* (Bristol: MOD Crown Copyright, 2017).

Office of Census and Statistics, *Third Census of the Population of the Union of South Africa, 3 May 1921* (Pretoria: Government Printing and Stationery Office, 1924).

Reed, Stanley, *The Indian Year Book, 1945–46* (Bombay: Bennett, Coleman, 1946).

The Canada Gazette, Statement of the Result of the Plebiscite, 23 June 1942.

Union Office of Census and Statistics, *Official Year Book of the Union of South Africa, No. 23 – 1946* (Pretoria: The Government Printer, 1948).

Union Office of Census and Statistics, *Union of South Africa Population Census, 7 May 1946, Vol. V: Occupations and Industries* (Pretoria: The Government Printer, 1955).

War Office, *Statistics of the Military Effort of the British Empire During the Great War, 1914–1920* (Eastbourne: CPI Antony Rowe, 1922).

War Office, *Field Service Regulations, Vol. II: Operations – General* (London: HMSO, 1935).

War Office, *Field Service Regulations, Vol. III: Operations – Higher Formations* (London: HMSO 1936).

War Office, *Manual of Military Law* (London: HMSO, 1939 [1929]).

Secondary Sources

Adams, Jack, *The Doomed Expedition: The Norwegian Campaign of 1940* (London: Leo Cooper, 1989).

Addison, Paul, *The Road to 1945: British Politics and the Second World War* ((London: Pimlico, 1994).

Addison, Paul and Calder, Angus (eds.), *Time to Kill: The Soldier's Experience of War in the West 1939–1945* (London: Pimlico, 1997).

Afflerbach, Holger and Strachan, Hew (eds.), *How Fighting Ends: A History of Surrender* (Oxford University Press, 2012).

Agar-Hamilton, J. A. I. and Turner, L. C. F., *Crisis in the Desert, May–July 1942* (London: Oxford University Press, 1952).

Agar-Hamilton, J. A. I. and Turner, L. C. F., *The Sidi Rezegh Battles 1941* (London: Oxford University Press, 1957).

Ahrenfeldt, Robert H., *Psychiatry in the British Army in the Second World War* (London: Routledge & Kegan Paul, 1958).

Alcalde, Ángel and Núñez Seixas, Xosé M., *War Veterans and the World after 1945: Cold War Politics, Decolonization, Memory* (London: Routledge, 2018).

Aldcroft, D. H. and Richardson, H. W., *The British Economy, 1870–1939* (London, Macmillan, 1969).

Alexander, Martin S., 'After Dunkirk: The French Army's Performance against "Case Red", 25 May to 25 June 1940', *War in History*, 14(2) (2007).

Alexander, Martin S., 'The Fall of France, 1940', *Journal of Strategic Studies*, 13 (1) (1990).

Allen, Louis, *Burma: The Longest War, 1941–45* (London: Phoenix Press, 2000 [1984]).

Allport, Alan, *Browned Off and Bloody-Minded: The British Soldier Goes to War 1939–1945* (London: Yale University Press, 2015).

Allport, Alan, *Demobbed: Coming Home after the Second World War* (London: Yale University Press, 2009).

Anderson, David M. and Killingray, David (eds.), *Policing the Empire: Government, Authority and Control, 1830–1940* (Manchester University Press, 1991).

Anon., *Infantry Officer: A Personal Record* (London: B. T. Batsford Ltd, 1943).

Aplin, Graeme, Foster, S. G., McKernan, Michael, *Australians: A Historical Dictionary* (Broadway: Fairfax, Syme and Weldon Associates, 1987).

Atkinson, Neill, *Adventures in Democracy: A History of the Vote in New Zealand* (Dunedin: University of Otago Press, 2003).

Atkinson, Rick, *An Army at Dawn: The War in North Africa, 1942–1943* (London: Little, Brown & Co., 2003).

Atkinson, Rick, *The Day of Battle: The War in Sicily and Italy, 1943–1944* (London: Little, Brown & Co., 2007).

Atkinson, Rick, *The Guns at Last Light: The War in Western Europe, 1944–1945* (London: Little, Brown & Co., 2013).

Avon, The Rt Hon. the Earl of, *The Eden Memoirs: The Reckoning* (London: Cassell, 1965).

Baldwin, Hanson, *Battles Lost and Won: Great Campaigns of World War 2* (London: Hodder and Stoughton, 1966).

Barbera, Henry, *The Military Factor in Social Change, Vol. I: From Provincial to Political Society* (London: Transaction, 1998).

Barclay, C. N., *The History of the 53rd (Welsh) Division in the Second World War* (London: William Clowes and Sons, 1956).

Barclay, Glen St. J., *The Empire Is Marching: A Study of the Military Effort of the British Empire, 1800–1945* (London: Weidenfeld and Nicolson, 1976).

Barkawi, Tarak, 'Culture and Combat in the Colonies: The Indian Army in the Second World War', *Journal of Contemporary History*, 41(2) (2006).

Barkawi, Tarak, *Soldiers of Empire: Indian and British Armies in World War II* (Cambridge University Press, 2017).

Barnett, Correlli, *The Audit of War: The Illusion and Reality of Britain as a Great Nation* (London: Pan, 1996 [1986]).

Barnett, Correlli, *The Desert Generals* (London: Cassell, 1983).

Barr, Niall, *Pendulum of War: The Three Battles of El Alamein* (London: Pimlico, 2005 [2004]).

Barr, Niall, *Yanks and Limeys: Alliance Warfare in the Second World War* (London: Jonathan Cape, 2015).

Bartlett, T. and Jeffrey, K. (eds.), *A Military History of Ireland* (Cambridge University Press, 1996).

Bartov, Omer, *The Eastern Front, 1941–45: German Troops and the Barbarisation of Warfare* (Basingstoke: Palgrave, 2001).

Bartov, Omer, *Hitler's Army: Soldiers, Nazis, and War in the Third Reich* (Oxford University Press, 1992).

Bashford, Alison and Macintyre, Stuart (eds.), *The Cambridge History of Australia, Vol. II: The Commonwealth of Australia* (Cambridge University Press, 2013).

Bassett, Michael, *The State in New Zealand, 1840–1984: Socialism without Doctrines?* (Auckland University Press, 1998).

Bassett, Michael and King, Michael, *Tomorrow Comes the Song: The Life of Peter Fraser* (Auckland: Penguin, 2000).

Bayly, Christopher and Harper, Tim, *Forgotten Armies: Britain's Asian Empire & the War with Japan* (London: Penguin, 2005 [2004]).

Baynes, John, *Morale : A Study of Men and Courage. The Second Scottish Rifles at the Battle of Neuve Chapelle 1915* (London: Cassel, 1967).

Beaumont, Joan, 'Australian Citizenship and the Two World Wars', *Australian Journal of Politics and History*, 53(2) (2007).

Beaumont, Joan (ed.), *Australia's War, 1939–45* (Crows Nest: Allen & Unwin, 1996).

Beckett, Ian F. W., *Britain's Part-Time Soldiers: The Amateur Military Tradition 1559–1945* (Manchester University Press, 1991).

Beckett, Ian F. W. and Simpson, Keith (eds.), *A Nation in Arms: A Social Study of the British Army in the First World War* (London: Tom Donovan, 1990).

Beers, Laura, 'Labour's Britain, Fight for it Now!', *The Historical Journal*, 52(3) (2009).

Beevor, Antony, *Crete: The Battle and the Resistance* (London: John Murray, 2005 [1991]).

Beevor, Antony, *D-Day: The Battle for Normandy* (London: Viking, 2009).

Beevor, Antony, *The Second World War* (London: Weidenfeld & Nicolson, 2012).

Beinart, William, *Twentieth Century South Africa* (Oxford University Press, 2001).

Belich, James, *Paradise Reforged: A History of New Zealanders from the 1880s to the Year 2000* (London: Allen Lane, 2001).

Bennett, David, *A Magnificent Disaster: The Failure of Market Garden, The Arnhem Operation September 1944* (Newbury: Casemate, 2008).

Bercuson, David J., *Maple Leaf against the Axis: Canada's Second World War* (Calgary: Red Deer Press, 2004).

Bergerud, Eric, *Touched with Fire: The Land War in the South Pacific* (London: Viking, 1996).

Bhattacharya, Sanjoy, *Propaganda and Information in Eastern India 1939–45: A Necessary Weapon of War* (Richmond: Curzon Press, 2001).

Biddle, Stephen, *Military Power: Explaining Victory and Defeat in Modern Battle* (Princeton University Press, 2004).

Bidwell, Shelford and Graham, Dominick, *Firepower: British Army Weapons and Theories of War 1904–1945* (London: Allen & Unwin, 1982).

Bidwell, Shelford and Graham, Dominick, *The Tug of War: The Battle for Italy, 1943–45* (London: Hodder & Stoughton, 1986).

Bielecki, Christine Ann, 'British Infantry Morale during the Italian Campaign, 1943–1945' (PhD thesis, University College London, 2006).

Bierman, John and Smith, Colin, *Alamein: War without Hate* (London: Penguin, 2003).

Bigland, Eileen, *Britain's Other Army: Story of the ATS* (London: Nicholson & Watson, 1946).

Black, Jeremy, *War in the New Century* (London: Continuum, 2001).

Blishen, Bernard R., 'The Construction and Use of an Occupational Class Scale', *The Canadian Journal of Economic and Political Science*, 24(4) (November, 1958).

Bloomfield, G. T., *New Zealand: A Handbook of Historical Statistics* (Boston: G. K. Hall & Co., 1984).

Boff, Jonathan, *Winning and Losing on the Western Front: The British Third Army and the Defeat of Germany in 1918* (Cambridge University Press, 2012).

Bond, Brian, 'Auchinleck, Sir Claude John Eyre (1884–1981)', *Oxford Dictionary of National Biography* (Oxford University Press, 2004), online edn, January 2011, https://doi.org/10.1093/ref:odnb/30774, accessed 25 April 2017.

Bond, Brian, *Britain's Two World Wars against Germany: Myth, Memory and the Distortion of Hindsight* (Cambridge University Press, 2014).

Bond, Brian, *British Military Policy between the Two World Wars* (Oxford: Clarendon Press, 1980).

Bond, Brian, *France and Belgium, 1939–1940* (London: Davis-Poynter, 1975).

Bond, Brian (ed.), *Chief of Staff: The Diaries of Lieutenant-General Sir Henry Pownall* (London: Leo Cooper, 1974).

Bond, Brian and Taylor, Michael (eds.), *The Battle for France and Flanders Sixty Years On* (Barnsley: Pen & Sword, 2001).

Bothwell, Robert, *The Penguin History of Canada* (Toronto: Penguin, 2006).

Bradley, Omar N. and Blair, Clay, *A General's Life* (New York: Simon and Schuster, 1983).

Bramble, Tom and Kuhn, Rick, *Labor's Conflict: Big Business, Workers and the Politics of Class* (Cambridge University Press, 2011).

Bridge, Carl, 'Australia's and Canada's Wars, 1914–1918 and 1939–1945: Some Reflections', *The Round Table: The Commonwealth Journal of International Affairs*, 90(361) (2001).

Bridge, Carl, 'Blamey, Sir Thomas Albert (1884–1951)', *Oxford Dictionary of National Biography* (Oxford University Press, 2004), online edn, January 2011, https://doi.org/10.1093/ref:odnb/31918, accessed 2 May 2017.

Brivati, Brian and Jones, Harriet (eds.), *What Difference Did the War Make?* (London: Leicester University Press, 1993).

Broad, Roger, *The Radical General: Sir Ronald Adam and Britain's New Model Army, 1941–45* (Stroud: Spellmount, 2013).

Brooks, Stephen (ed.), *Montgomery and the Battle of Normandy* (Stroud: The History Press, 2008).

Brooks, Stephen (ed.), *Montgomery and the Eighth Army* (London: The Bodley Head, 1991).

Brown, Andrew, 'New Men in the Line: An Assessment of Reinforcements to the 48th Highlanders in Italy, Jan.–Oct. 1944', *Canadian Military History*, 21(3) (2012),

Brown, Judith M., *Modern India: The Origins of an Asian Democracy* (Oxford University Press, 1994).

Buchanan, Andrew N., 'The War Crisis and the Decolonization of India, December 1941–September 1942: A Political and Military Dilemma', *Global War Studies*, 8(2) (December, 2011).

Buckingham, William F., *Arnhem 1944: A Reappraisal* (Stroud: Tempus, 2002).

Buckingham, William F., *Tobruk: The Great Siege 1941–2* (Stroud: Tempus, 2008).

Buckley, John, *British Armour in the Normandy Campaign 1944* (London: Frank Cass, 2004).

Buckley, John, *Monty's Men: The British Army and the Liberation of Europe* (London: Yale University Press, 2013).

Buckley, John (ed.), *The Normandy Campaign 1944: Sixty Years On* (London: Routledge, 2006).

Buckley, John and Preston-Hough, Peter (eds.), *Operation Market Garden: The Campaign for the Low Countries, Autumn 1944: Seventy Years On* (Solihull: Helion, 2016).

Buckley, John and Sheffield, Gary, 'The British Army in the Era of Haig and Montgomery', *The RUSI Journal*, 159(4) (2014).

Bull, Stephen, *Second World War Infantry Tactics: The European Theatre* (Barnsley: Pen & Sword, 2012).

Bumsted, J. M., *The Peoples of Canada: A Post-Confederation History* (Oxford University Press, 2004).

Bungay, Stephen, *Alamein* (London: Aurum Press, 2002).

Burnswoods, Jan and Fletcher, Jim, *Sydney and the Bush: A Pictorial History of Education in New South Wales* (Crown Copyright, 1980).

Butlin, S. J., *War Economy, 1939–1942* (Canberra: AWM, 1955).

Butlin, S. J. and Schedvin, C. B., *War Economy, 1942–1945* (Canberra: AWM, 1977).

Byers, Daniel, 'Mobilising Canada: The National Resources Mobilization Act, the Department of National Defence, and Compulsory Military Service in Canada, 1940–1945', *Journal of the Canadian Historical Association*, 7(1) (1996).

Byers, Daniel, *Zombie Army: The Canadian Army and Conscription in the Second World War* (Vancouver: University of British Columbia Press, 2016).

Byrnes, Giselle (ed.), *The New Oxford History of New Zealand* (Oxford University Press, 2009).

Calder, Angus, *The People's War: Britain 1939–1945* (London: Jonathan Cape, 1969).

Callahan, Raymond, *Burma, 1942–1945* (London: Davis Poynter, 1978).

Callahan, Raymond, *Churchill and His Generals* (Lawrence: University Press of Kansas, 2007).

Callahan, Raymond, 'Slim, William Joseph, first Viscount Slim (1891–1970)', *Oxford Dictionary of National Biography* (Oxford University Press, 2004) online edn, January 2011, www.oxforddnb.com/view/10.1093/ref:odnb/9780198614128.001.0001/odnb-9780198614128-e-36120, accessed 26 April 2017.

Callahan, Raymond, *Triumph at Imphal–Kohima: How the Indian Army Finally Stopped the Japanese Juggernaut* (Lawrence: University Press of Kansas, 2017).

Capon, Shane, 'The "Hamilton Furlough Mutiny": An Analysis of the Implementation and Consequences of the 1943 Furlough Scheme' (Master's thesis, University of Waikato, 1986).

Cardo, Michael, 'Fighting a Worse Imperialism': White South African Loyalism and the Army Education Services (AES) during the Second World War, *South African Historical Journal*, 46(1) (2002).

Carter, J. A. H. and Kann, D. N., *The Second World War 1939–1945 Army Maintenance in the Field, Vol. II: 1943–1945* (London: The War Office, 1961).

'Cato' (Foot, Michael, Owen, Frank and Howard, Peter), *Guilty Men* (London: Gollanz, 1940).

Ceadel, Martin, 'The First British Referendum: The Peace Ballot, 1934–1935', *English Historical Review*, 95(377) (1980).

Cecil, Hugh and Liddle, Peter H. (eds.), *Facing Armageddon: The First World War Experienced* (London: Leo Cooper, 1996).

Charmley, John, *Churchill: The End of Glory* (London: Sceptre 1993).

Churchill, Winston S., *The Hinge of Fate: The Second World War, Vol. IV* (London: Cassell, 1951)

Churchill, Winston, *The Second World War: With an Epilogue on the Years 1945 to 1957* (London: Pimlico, 2002).
Churchill, Winston S. (ed.), *Never Give In! The Best of Winston Churchill's Speeches* (London: Pimlico, 2003).
Clarke, Peter, *Hope and Glory: Britain 1900–2000* (London: Penguin, 2004 [1996]).
Clausewitz, Carl von, *On War* (London: Everyman's Library, 1993).
Coates, John, *Bravery Above Blunder: The 9th Australian Division at Finschhafen, Satelberg, and Sio* (Oxford University Press, 1999).
Coetzee, Emile, 'El Wak or Bust', address to *South African Military History Society*, 14 October 2010.
Cohen, Stephen P., *The Indian Army: Its Contribution to the Development of a Nation* (Berkeley: University of California Press, 1971).
Connell, John, *Auchinleck: A Biography of Field-Marshal Sir Claude Auchinleck* (London: Cassell, 1959).
Connell, John, *Wavell: Scholar and Soldier, to June 1941* (London: Collins, 1964).
Connelly, Mark, *We Can Take It! Britain and the Memory of the Second World War* (Harlow: Pearson, 2004).
Connelly, Mark and Miller, Walter, 'The BEF and the Issue of Surrender on the Western Front in 1940', *War in History*, 11(4) (2004).
Connelly, Mark and Miller, Walter, 'British Courts Martial in North Africa, 1940–3', *Twentieth Century British History*, 15(3) (2004).
Converse, Alan, *Armies of Empire: The 9th Australian and 50th British Divisions in Battle 1939–1945* (Cambridge University Press, 2011).
Cook, Tim, *Warlords: Borden, Mackenzie King, and Canada's World Wars* (London: Penguin, 2012).
Cooper, Matthew, *The German Army 1933–1945: Its Political and Military Failure* (Lanham: Scarborough House, 1978).
Copp, Terry, *Cinderella Army: The Canadians in Northwest Europe 1944–1945* (London: University of Toronto Press, 2006).
Copp, Terry, *Fields of Fire: The Canadians in Normandy* (London: University of Toronto Press, 2003).
Copp, Terry, *Guy Simonds and the Art of Command* (Kingston: Canadian Defence Academy Press, 2007).
Copp, Terry, 'Some Reflections on the Italian Campaign', Keynote, Military History Colloquium, The Laurier Centre for Military Strategic and Disarmament Studies (2010).
Copp, Terry, 'To the Last Canadian? Casualties in 21st Army Group', *Canadian Military History*, 18(1) (Winter, 2009).
Copp, Terry and McAndrew, Bill, *Battle Exhaustion: Soldiers and Psychiatrists in the Canadian Army, 1939–1945* (London: McGill-Queen's University Press, 1990).

Corum, James S., *The Roots of Blitzkrieg: Hans Von Seeckt and German Military Reform* (Lawrence: University Press of Kansas, 1992).

Cowley, Robert (ed.), *No End Save Victory* (London: Cassell & Co., 2002).

Cox, Seb and Gray, Peter (eds.), *Air Power History: Turning Points from Kitty Hawk to Kosovo* (London: Routledge, 2002).

Crang, Jeremy A., *The British Army and the People's War, 1939–1945* (Manchester University Press, 2000).

Crang, Jeremy A., 'Politics on Parade: Army Education and the 1945 General Election', *History*, 81(262) (1996).

Crankshaw, Owen, *Race, Class and the Changing Division of Labour under Apartheid* (London: Routledge, 1997).

Crawford, John (ed.), *Kia Kaha: New Zealand in the Second World War* (Oxford University Press, 2000).

Crew, F. A. E., *The Army Medical Services, Campaigns, Vol. I: 1939–1942 France and Belgium, Libya, Greece, Crete etc* (London: HMSO, 1956).

Crew, F. A. E., *The Army Medical Services, Campaigns, Vol. II: 1942–1943 Malaya, Libya etc* (Uckfield: The Naval & Military Press, 2014 [1954]).

Crew, F. A. E., *The Army Medical Services, Campaigns, Vol. III: 1944–45 Sicily, Italy and Greece* (Uckfield: Naval & Military Press, 2014 [1957]).

Crew, F. A. E., *The Army Medical Services, Campaigns, Vol. IV, North-West Europe* (London: HMSO, 1962).

Crew, F. A. E., *The Army Medical Services: Campaigns. Vol. V: Burma* (London: HMSO, 1966).

Crookenden, Napier, *Dropzone Normandy: The Story of the American and British Airborne Assault on D Day 1944* (London: Ian Allan Ltd, 1976).

Crwys-Williams, J., *A Country at War: The Mood of a Nation, 1939–1945* (Rivonia: Ashanti, 1992).

Danchev, Alex and Todman, Daniel (eds.), *War Diaries 1939–1945: Field Marshal Lord Alanbrooke* (London: Phoenix, 2002 [2001]).

Daniels, J. R. S., 'The General Election of 1943' (Master's thesis, Victoria University, 1961).

Darwin, John, *The Empire Project: The Rise and Fall of the British World-System, 1830–1970* (Cambridge University Press, 2009).

Davenport, Rodney and Saunders, Christopher, *South Africa: A Modern History* (Basingstoke: Macmillan Press, 2000).

Davenport, T. R. H., *South Africa: A Modern History* (Johannesburg: Macmillan, 1977).

David, Saul, *Mutiny at Salerno 1943: An Injustice Exposed* (London: Conway, 2005 [1995]).

Davies, Robert H., *Capital, State and White Labour in South Africa, 1900–1960: An Historical Materialist Analysis of Class Formation and Class Relations* (Atlantic Highlands: Humanities Press, 1979).

Dean, Peter J., *MacArthur's Coalition: US and Australian Military Operations in the Southwest Pacific Area, 1942–1945* (University Press of Kansas, 2018).

Dean, Peter J. (ed.), *Australia 1942: In the Shadow of War* (Cambridge University Press, 2013).

Dean, Peter J. (ed.), *Australia 1943: The Liberation of New Guinea* (Port Melbourne: Cambridge University Press, 2014).

Dean, Peter J. (ed.), *Australia 1944–45: Victory in the Pacific* (Cambridge University Press, 2016).

Deist, William, 'The Military Collapse of the German Empire: The Reality behind the Stab-in-the-Back Myth', *War in History*, 3(2) (April, 1996).

Delaforce, Patrick, *The Black Bull: From Normandy to the Baltic with the 11th Armoured Division* (Stroud: Alan Sutton, 1993).

Delaforce, Patrick, *Invasion of the Third Reich: War and Peace, Operation Eclipse* (Stroud: Amberley, 2011).

Delaforce, Patrick, *Monty's Iron Sides: From the Normandy Beaches to Bremen with the 3rd (British) Division* (Stroud: Sutton Publishing Ltd, 2002 [1995]).

Delaforce, Patrick, *The Polar Bears, Monty's Left Flank: From Normandy to the Relief of Holland with the 49th Division* (Stroud: Alan Sutton, 1995).

Delaney, Douglas E., *Corps Commanders: Five British and Canadian Generals at War, 1939–45* (Vancouver: University of British Columbia Press, 2011).

Delaney, Douglas E., *The Imperial Army Project: Britain and the Land Forces of the Dominions and India, 1902–1945* (Oxford University Press, 2018).

Dennis, Peter, *The Territorial Army, 1907–1940* (Woodbridge: Boydell Press, 1987).

D'Este, Carlo, *Bitter Victory: The Battle for Sicily 1943* (London: Aurum Press, 2008).

D'Este, Carlo, *Decision in Normandy: The Unwritten Story of Montgomery and the Allied Campaign* (London: Penguin, 2001 [1983]).

Dexter, David, *The New Guinea Offensives* (Canberra: AWM, 1961).

Dominion Bureau of Statistics, *The Canada Year Book, 1946* (Ottawa: Edmond Cloutier, 1946).

Dower, John W., *War Without Mercy: Race and Power in the Pacific War* (London: Faber, 1986).

Dubow, Saul, 'Scientism, Social Research and the Limits of "South Africanism": The Case of Ernst Gideon Malherbe', *South African Historical Journal*, 44(1) (May, 2001).

Dubow, Saul and Jeeves, Alan (eds.), *South Africa's 1940s: Worlds of Possibilities* (Cape Town: Double Storey, 2005).

Dunlop, Graham, *Military Economics, Culture and Logistics in the Burma Campaign, 1942–1945* (London: Pickering & Chatto, 2009).

Dymock, Darryl, *A Sweet Use of Adversity: The Australian Army Education Service in World War II and its Impact on Australian Adult Education* (Armidale: University of New England Press, 1995).

Echevarria II, Antulio J., *Clausewitz and Contemporary War* (Oxford University Press, 2007).

Eckes, Alfred E. Jr, *The United States and the Global Struggle for Minerals* (Austin: University of Texas, 1979).

Edgerton, David, *Britain's War Machine: Weapons, Resources and Experts in the Second World War* (London: Allen Lane, 2011).

Edgerton, David, *Warfare State: Britain 1920–1970* (Cambridge University Press, 2006).

Ehlers, Robert S. Jr, *The Mediterranean Air War: Airpower and Allied Victory in World War II* (Lawrence: University Press of Kansas, 2015).

Elley, W. B. and Irving, J. C., 'A Socio-Economic Index for New Zealand Based on Levels of Education and Income from the 1966 Census', *New Zealand Journal of Educational Studies*, 7 (1972).

Ellis, John, *Brute Force: Allied Strategy and Tactics in the Second World War* (London: André Deutsch, 1990).

Ellis, John, *Cassino: The Hollow Victory, The Battle for Rome January–June 1944* (London: Sphere Books, 1985 [1984]).

Ellis, John, *The Sharp End: The Fighting Man in World War II* (London: Pimlico, 1990).

Ellis, John, *The World War II Databook: The Essential Facts and Figures for all the Combatants* (London: Aurum Press, 1993).

Ellis, L. F, *Victory in the West, Vol. I: The Battle of Normandy* (Uckfield: The Naval & Military Press, 2004 [1962]).

Ellis, L. F, *Victory in the West, Vol. II: The Defeat of Germany* (London: HMSO, 1968).

Ellis, L. F., *The War in France and Flanders* (Uckfield: The Naval & Military Press, 2004 [1953]).

Engen, Robert, *Canadians Under Fire: Infantry Effectiveness in the Second World War* (London: McGill-Queen's University Press, 2009).

Engen, Robert, *Strangers in Arms: Combat Motivation in the Canadian Army, 1943–1945* (London: McGill-Queen's University Press, 2016).

Englander, David and Mason, Tony, 'The British Soldier in World War II', Warwick Working Papers in Social History, 1984.

English, John A., *The Canadian Army and the Normandy Campaign: A Study of Failure in High Command* (London: Praeger, 1991).

Essame, H., *The 43rd Wessex Division at War, 1944–1945* (London: William Clowes and Sons Ltd, 1952).

Fairburn, Miles and Haslett, Stephen, 'The Rise of the Left and Working-Class Voting Behavior in New Zealand: New Methods', *Journal of Interdisciplinary History*, XXXV(4) (Spring, 2005).

Fairburn, Miles and Olssen, Erik (eds.), *Class, Gender and the Vote: Historical Perspectives from New Zealand* (University of Otago Press, 2005).

Falls, Cyril, revised by Bond, Brian, 'Vereker, John Standish Surtees Prendergast, sixth Viscount Gort', *Oxford Dictionary of National Biography* (Oxford University Press, 2004), online edn, January 2011, www.oxforddnb.com/view/10.1093/ref:odnb/9780198614128.001.0001/odnb-9780198614128-e-36642, accessed 3 January 2018.

Farrell, Brian P., *The Defence and Fall of Singapore 1940–1942* (Stroud: Tempus, 2005).

Feasby, W. R. (ed.), *Official History of the Canadian Medical Services, 1939–1945, Vol. I: Organization and Campaigns* (Ottawa: Edmund Clouthier, 1956).

Feasby, W. R. (ed.), *Official History of the Canadian Medical Services, 1939–1945, Vol. II: Clinical Subjects* (Ottawa: Edmund Clouthier, 1953).

Fennell, Jonathan, 'Air Power and Morale in the North African Campaign of the Second World War', *Air Power Review*, 15(2) (2012).

Fennell, Jonathan, *Combat and Morale in the North African Campaign: The Eighth Army and the Path to El Alamein* (Cambridge University Press, 2011).

Fennell, Jonathan, 'Courage and Cowardice in the North African Campaign: The Eighth Army and Defeat in the Summer of 1942', *War in History*, 20(1) (2013).

Fennell, Jonathan, 'In Search of the "X" Factor: Morale and the Study of Strategy', *Journal of Strategic Studies*, 37(6–7) (May, 2014).

Fennell, Jonathan, 'Soldiers and Social Change: The Forces Vote in the Second World War and New Zealand's Great Experiment in Social Citizenship', *English Historical Review*, 132(554) (2017).

Ferguson, Niall, *Empire: How Britain Made the Modern World* (London: Penguin, 2004 [2003]).

Ferguson, Niall, 'Prisoner Taking and Prisoner Killing in the Age of Total War: Towards a Political Economy of Military Defeat', *War in History*, 11(2) (2004).

Fergusson, Bernard and Brown, Judith M., 'Wavell, Archibald Percival, first Earl Wavell (1883–1950)', rev. Robert O'Neill, Judith M. Brown, *Oxford Dictionary of National Biography* (Oxford University Press, 2004), online edn, January 2011, www.oxforddnb.com/view/article/36790, accessed 24 April 2017.

Ferris, John, 'Treasury Control: The Ten Year Rule and British Service Policies, 1919–1924', *Historical Journal*, 30 (1987).

Field, Geoffrey G., *Blood, Sweat and Toil: Remaking the British Working Class, 1939–1945* (Oxford University Press, 2011).

Field, Geoffrey G., '"Civilians in Uniform": Class and Politics in the British Armed Forces, 1939–1945', *International Labor and Working-Class History*, 80 (Fall, 2011).

Fielding, Steven, 'What Did "the People" Want?: The Meaning of the 1945 General Election', *The Historical Journal*, 35(3) (1992).

Ford, Ken, *Battleaxe Division: From Africa to Italy with the 78th Division, 1942–45* (Stroud: Sutton Publishing, 1999).

Forrester, Charles, 'Field Marshal Montgomery's Role in the Creation of the British 21st Army Group's Combined Armed Doctrine for the Final Assault on Germany, *The Journal of Military History*, 78 (October, 2014).

Forrester, Charles, *Montgomery's Functional Doctrine: Combined Arms Doctrine in British 21st Army Group in Northwest Europe, 1944–45* (Solihull: Helion & Company, 2015).

Forty, George, *British Army Handbook, 1939–1945* (Stroud: Sutton Publishing, 1998).

Forty, George, *Tanks Across the Desert: The War Diary of Jake Wardrop* (Stroud: Sutton Publishing, 2003).

Forty, George, *Villers Bocage* (Stroud: Sutton Publishing, 2004).

Fox-Godden, Aimée, 'Beyond the Western Front: The Practice of Inter-Theatre Learning in the British Army during the First World War', *War in History*, 23 (2) (2016).

France, John, *Perilous Glory: The Rise of Western Military Power* (London: Yale University Press, 2011).

Francis, R. Douglas, Jones, Richard, Smith, Donald B., *Destinies: Canadian History Since Confederation* (Toronto: Nelson Education, 2008).

Franklin, Mark and Ladner, Matthew, 'The Undoing of Winston Churchill: Mobilization and Conversion in the 1945 Realignment of British Voters', *British Journal of Political Science*, 25(4) (1995).

Fraser, David, *And We Shall Shock Them: The British Army in the Second World War* (London: Cassell & Co., 1999 [1983]).

Freedman, Lawrence, *Strategy: A History* (Oxford University Press, 2013).

French, David, *The British Way in Warfare, 1688–2000* (London: Unwin Hyman, 1990).

French, David, 'Colonel Blimp and the British Army: British Divisional Commanders in the War against Germany, 1939–1945', *The English Historical Review*, 111(444) (November, 1996).

French, David, 'Discipline and the Death Penalty in the British Army in the War against Germany during the Second World War', *Journal of Contemporary History*, 33(4) (October, 1998).

French, David, 'Invading Europe: The British Army and its Preparations for the Normandy Campaign, 1942–44', *Diplomacy and Statecraft*, 14(2) (2003).

French, David, *Military Identities: The Regimental System, the British Army, and the British People c.1870–2000* (Oxford University Press, 2005).

French, David, *Raising Churchill's Army: The British Army and the War against Germany 1919–1945* (Oxford University Press, 2000).

French, David, '"Tommy Is No Soldier": The Morale of the Second British Army in Normandy, June–August 1944', *Journal of Strategic Studies*, 19(4) (2006).

French, David and Holden Reid, Brian (eds.), *The British General Staff: Reform and Innovation, c. 1890–1939* (London: Frank Cass, 2002).

French, Patrick, *Liberty or Death: India's Journey to Independence and Division* (London: Penguin, 2011).

Frieser, Karl-Heinz, *The Blitzkrieg Legend: The 1940 Campaign in the West* (Annapolis: Naval Institute Press, 2005).

Fritz, Stephen G., *Frontsoldaten: The German Soldier in World War II* (Lexington: University Press of Kentucky, 1995).

Fuller, J. G., *Troop Morale and Popular Culture in the British and Dominion Armies, 1914–1918* (Oxford University Press, 1991).

Fussell, Paul, *Wartime: Understanding and Behavior in the Second World War* (Oxford University Press, 1989).

Gal, Reuven and Mangelsdorff, A. David (eds.), *Handbook of Military Psychology* (Chichester: Wiley, 1991).

Gale, R. N., *With the 6th Airborne Division in Normandy* (London: Sampson Low, Marston & Co., 1948).

Galt, Margaret, 'Wealth and Income in New Zealand, *c.*1870 to *c.*1939' (PhD thesis, Victoria University of Wellington, 1985).

Gamlen, Alan, 'The Impacts of Extra-Territorial Voting: Swings, Interregnums and Feedback Effects in New Zealand Elections from 1914 to 2011', *Political Geography*, 44 (2015).

Gatt, Azar, *A History of Military Thought: From the Enlightenment to the Cold War* (Oxford University Press, 2001).

Gavin, James M., *On to Berlin: Battles of an Airborne Commander 1943–1946* (London: Leo Cooper, 1979).

German, Daniel, 'Press Censorship and the Terrace Mutiny: A Case Study in Second World War Information Management', *Journal of Canadian Studies*, 31(4) (Winter 1996–7).

Gerwarth, Robert, 'The Central European Counter-Revolution: Paramilitary Violence in Germany, Austria and Hungary after the Great War', *Past and Present*, 200(1) (2008).

Gerwarth, Robert and Horne, John (eds.), *War in Peace: Paramilitary Violence in Europe after the Great War* (Oxford University Press, 2012).

Geyer, Michael and Tooze, Adam, *The Cambridge History of the Second World War, Vol. III: Total War, Economy, Society and Culture* (Cambridge University Press, 2015).

Gibbs, K. J., 'Demobilisation after World War II: The Process and Politics of Reinstating Union Defence Force Volunteers into Civilian Life, 1943–1948', unpublished University of South Africa Paper (1990).

Gill, Ronald and Groves, John, *Club Route in Europe: The Story of 30 Corps in the European Campaign* (Hanover: Werner Degener, 1946).

Gillespie, Oliver A., *The Pacific* (Wellington: Historical Publications Branch, 1952).

Glynn, S. and Oxborrow, J., *Interwar Britain: A Social and Economic History* (London: Allen & Unwin, 1976).

Gooderson, Ian, *A Hard Way to Make a War: The Allied Campaign in Italy in the Second World War* (London: Conway, 2008).

Goulter, Christina, Gordon, Andrew and Sheffield, Gary, 'The Royal Navy Did Not Win the "Battle of Britain"', *The RUSI Journal*, 151(5) (2006).

Gowing, Margaret, 'The Organisation of Manpower in Britain during the Second World War', *Journal of Contemporary History*, 7(1/2) (January–April, 1972).

Granatstein, J. L., 'The Armed Forces' Vote in Canadian General Elections, 1940–1968', *The Journal of Canadian Studies*, 4(1) (February, 1969).

Granatstein, J. L., *Canada's War: The Politics of the Mackenzie King Government, 1939–1945* (Toronto: Oxford University Press, 1975).

Granatstein, J. L., *Conscription in the Second World War* (Toronto: McGraw-Hill Ryerson, 1969).

Grant, Lachlan, 'The Second AIF and the End of Empires: Soldiers' Attitudes toward a "Free Asia"', *Australian Journal of History and Politics*, 57(4) (2011).

Gray, Colin S., *Modern Strategy* (Oxford University Press, 1999).

Gray, Colin S., *The Strategy Bridge: Theory for Practice* (Oxford University Press, 2010).

Gray, Geoffrey, Munro, Doug and Winter, Christine, *Scholars at War: Australian Social Scientists, 1939–1945* (Canberra: ANU Press, 2012).

Gregory, Adrian, *The Last Great War: British Society and the First World War* (Cambridge University Press, 2008).

Grey, Jeffrey, *The Australian Army* (Oxford University Press, 2001).

Grey, Jeffrey, *A Military History of Australia* (Cambridge University Press, 1999).

Grobler, J. E. H., 'The Marabastad Riot, 1942', *Contree*, 32 (1992).

Grossman, Guy, Manekin, Devorah and Miodownik, Dan, 'The Political Legacies of Combat: Attitudes toward War and Peace Among Israeli Ex-Combatants', *International Organisation*, 69(4) (September, 2015).

Groth, Alexander J., 'Totalitarians and Democrats: Aspects of Political-Military Relations 1939–1945', *Comparative Strategy*, 8(1) (1989).

Grundlingh, Albert, 'The King's Afrikaners? Enlistment and Ethnic Identity in the Union of South Africa's Defence Force During the Second World War, 1939–45', *The Journal of African History*, 40(3) (November, 1999).

Grundlingh, Louis, 'Soldiers and Politics: A Study of the Political Consciousness of Black South African Soldiers During and After the Second World War', *Historia*, 36(2) (1991).

Guardino, Peter, 'Gender, Soldiering, and Citizenship in the Mexican–American War of 1846–1848', *The American Historical Review*, 119(1) (February 2014).

Hall, David Ian, 'The Long Gestation and Difficult Birth of the 2nd Tactical Air Force (RAF)', *Air Power Review*, 5(3) (2002).

Hall, David Ian, *Strategy for Victory: The Development of British Tactical Air Power, 1919–1943* (Westport: Praeger Publishers, 2007).

Hamilton, Nigel, *The Full Monty: Montgomery of Alamein 1887–1942* (London: Penguin, 2002).

Hamilton, Nigel, 'Montgomery, Bernard Law [Monty], first Viscount Montgomery of Alamein (1887–1976)', *Oxford Dictionary of National Biography* (Oxford University Press, 2004) online edn, January 2011, www.oxforddnb.com/view/article/31460, accessed 18 July 2017.

Hancock, W. K. and Gowing, M. M., *British War Economy* (London: HMSO, 1949).

Handel, Michael I., *Masters of War: Classical Strategic Thought* (London: Frank Cass, 2001).

Handel, Michael I. (ed.), *Clausewitz and Modern Strategy* (London: Frank Cass, 1986).

Hargreaves, Andrew, Rose, Patrick and Ford, Matthew (eds.), *Allied Fighting Effectiveness in North Africa and Italy, 1942–1945* (Leiden: Brill, 2014).

Harper, Glyn and Hayward, Joel, *Born to Lead? Portraits of New Zealand Commanders* (Auckland: Exisle, 2003).

Harris, Jose, 'War and Social History: Britain and the Home Front during the Second World War', *Contemporary European History*, 1(1) (1992).

Harris, Jose, *William Beveridge: A Biography* (Oxford: Clarendon Press, 1997).

Harris, J. P., *Men, Ideas and Tanks: British Military Thought and Armoured Forces, 1903–1939* (Manchester University Press, 1995).

Harris, J. P. and Toase, F. H. (eds.), *Armoured Warfare* (London: B. T. Batsford Ltd, 1990).

Harrison, Mark, *Medicine and Victory: British Military Medicine in the Second World War* (Oxford University Press, 2004).

Harrison, Mark (ed.), *The Economics of World War II: Six Great Powers in International Comparison* (Cambridge University Press, 1998).

Harrison Place, Timothy, *Military Training in the British Army, 1940–1944* (London: Frank Cass, 2000).

Hart, B. H. Liddell, *The Other Side of the Hill* (London: Cassell, 1951).

Hart, B. H. Liddell (ed.), *The Rommel Papers* (New York: Harcourt, Brace and Company,1953).

Hart, Russell A., *Clash of Arms: How the Allies Won in Normandy* (Norman: University of Oklahoma Press, 2004 [2001]).

Hart, Stephen A., *Colossal Cracks: Montgomery's 21st Army Group in Northwest Europe, 1944–45* (Mechanicsburg: Stackpole, 2007 [2000]).

Hart, Stephen A., *The Road to Falaise* (Stroud: Sutton Publishing, 2004).
Hasluck, Paul, *The Government and the People, 1939–1941* (Canberra: AWM, 1952).
Hasluck, Paul, *The Government and the People, 1942–1945* (Canberra: AWM, 1970).
Hastings, Max, *All Hell Let Loose: The World at War, 1939–1945* (London: Harper Press, 2011).
Hastings, Max, *Armageddon: The Battle for Germany, 1944–45* (London: Pan Books, 2005 [2004]).
Hastings, Max, *The Korean War* (London: Michael Joseph, 1987).
Hastings, Max, *Nemesis: The Battle for Japan, 1944–45* (London: Harper Perennial, 2008 [2007]).
Hastings, Max, *Overlord: D-Day and the Battle for Normandy 1944* (London: Michael Joseph, 1984).
Hawkins, T. H and Brimble, L. J., *Adult Education: The Record of the British Army* (London: Macmillan, 1947).
Heard, Kenneth A., *General Elections in South Africa, 1943–1970* (London: Oxford University Press, 1974).
Heuser, Beatrice, *The Evolution of Strategy: Thinking War from Antiquity to the Present* (Cambridge University Press, 2010).
Higgins, Edward, 'The Sociology of Religion in South Africa', *Archives de Sociologie des Religions*, 32 (1971).
Higham, Robin, *Armed Forces in Peacetime: Britain, 1918–1940, A Case Study* (London: G. T. Foulis & Co., 1962).
Hinchliff, Peter, *The Anglican Church in South Africa: An Account of the History and Development of the Church of the Province of South Africa* (London: Darton, Longman & Todd, 1963).
Hinchliff, Peter, *The Church in South Africa* (London: SPCK, 1968).
Hofmeyr, J. W. and Pillay, Gerald J. (eds.), *A History of Christianity in South Africa, Vol. I* (Pretoria: Haum Tertiary, 1994).
Holborn, Andrew, *The 56th Infantry Brigade and D-Day: An Independent Infantry Brigade and the Campaign in North West Europe, 1944–1945* (London: Continuum, 2010).
Holland, James, *Italy's Sorrow: A Year of War, 1944–1945* (London: Harper Press, 2009).
Holmes, Richard, *Acts of War: The Behaviour of Men in Battle* (London: Cassell, 2004).
Horne, Alistair, *To Lose a Battle: France 1940* (London: Penguin, 1979 [1969]).
Horne, John (ed.), *A Companion to World War I* (Oxford: Wiley-Blackwell, 2012).
Horne, John (ed.), *State, Society and Mobilization in Europe during the First World War* (Cambridge University Press, 1997).

Horner, D. M., *High Command: Australia and Allied Strategy, 1939–1945* (Canberra: George Allen and Unwin, 1982).

Horrocks, Brian, *A Full Life* (London: Leo Cooper, 1974 [1960]).

Howard, Michael, *The Continental Commitment* (London: Ashfield Press, 1989 [1972]).

Howard, Michael, 'The Use and Abuse of Military History', *The Royal United Services Institution Journal*, 107(625) (1962).

Howard, Michael, 'When Are Wars Decisive?', *Survival*, 41(1) (1999).

Howard, Michael and Sparrow, John, *The Coldstream Guards, 1920–1946* (London: Oxford University Press, 1951).

Howlett, Peter (ed.), *Fighting with Figures: A Statistical Digest of the Second World War* (London: The Central Statistics Office, 1995).

Hughes, Daniel J. (ed.), *Moltke on the Art of War: Selected Writings* (Novato: Presidio Press, 1993).

Jackson, Ashley, *The British Empire and the Second World War* (London: Hambledon Continuum, 2006).

Jackson, Ashley, Khan, Yasmin and Singh, Gajendra (eds.), *An Imperial World at War: Aspects of the British Empire's Experience, 1939–1945* (London: Routledge, 2017).

Jackson, G. S., *Operations of Eighth Corps: Account of Operations from Normandy to the River Rhine* (Buxton: MLRS, 2006).

Jackson, Julian, *Fall of France: The Nazi Invasion of 1940* (Oxford University Press, 2004).

Jackson, W. G. F., *'Overlord': Normandy 1944* (London: Werner Degener, 1978).

James, G. W. B., 'Psychiatric Lessons from Active Service', *The Lancet*, 246(6382) (December, 1945).

James, Karl (ed.), *Kokoda: Beyond the Legend* (Cambridge University Press, 2017).

Jeffreys, Alan, *Approach to Battle: Training the Indian Army During the Second World War* (Solihull: Helion, 2016).

Jeffreys, Alan and Rose, Patrick (eds.), *The Indian Army, 1939–47: Experience and Development* (Farnham: Ashgate, 2012).

Jefferys, Kevin, 'British Politics and Social Policy during the Second World War', *Historical Journal*, 30(1) (March, 1987).

Jefferys, Kevin, *The Churchill Coalition and Wartime Politics, 1940–1945* (Manchester University Press, 1991).

Jenkins, Roy, *Churchill: A Biography* (London: Pan Books, 2002).

Jha, Saumitra and Wilkinson, Steven, 'Does Combat Experience Foster Organisational Skill? Evidence from Ethnic Cleansing during the Partition of South Asia', *American Political Science Review*, 106(4) (November, 2012).

Johnson, Paul (ed.), *20th Century Britain: Economic, Social and Cultural Change* (London: Longman, 1994).

Johnson, Robert, 'The Army in India and Responses to Low-Intensity Conflict, 1936–1946', *Journal of the Society for Army Historical Research*, 89(358) (2011).

Johnston, Iain Edward, 'The Role of the Dominions in British Victory, 1939–1945' (DPhil thesis, University of Cambridge, 2014).

Johnston, Mark, *At the Front Line: Experiences of Australian Soldiers in World War II* (Cambridge University Press, 1996).

Johnston, Mark, 'The Civilians Who Joined Up, 1939–45, *Journal of the Australian War Memorial*, 29 (November, 1996).

Johnston, Mark and Stanley, Peter, *Alamein: The Australian Story* (Oxford University Press, 2002).

Johnston-White, Ian E., *The British Commonwealth and Victory in the Second World War* (London: Palgrave Macmillan, 2016).

Jones, Edgar and Wessely, Simon, *Shell Shock to PTSD: Military Psychiatry from 1900 to the Gulf War* (Hove: Psychology Press, 2005).

Judt, Tony, *Reappraisals: Reflections on the Forgotten Twentieth Century* (London: Penguin, 2008).

Kamtekar, Indivar, 'A Different War Dance: State and Class in India 1939–1945', *Past and Present*, 176(1) (2002).

Kamtekar, Indivar, 'The Shiver of 1942', *Studies in History*, 18(81) (2002).

Kaufman, Burton I., *The Korean War: Challenges in Crises, Credibility, and Command* (London: McGraw-Hill, 1986).

Keating, Gavin, *A Tale of Three Battalions: Combat Morale and Battle Fatigue in the 7th Australian Infantry Brigade, Bougainville* (Canberra: Land Warfare Studies Centre Study Paper, 2007).

Keegan, John, *Intelligence in War: Knowledge of the Enemy from Napoleon to Al-Qaeda* (London: Pimlico, 2004).

Keegan, John, *The Second World War* (London: Pimlico, 1989).

Keegan, John (ed.), *The Times Atlas of the Second World War* (London: Times Books Ltd, 1989).

Kelley, Jonathan and Evans, M. D. R., 'Trends in Educational Attainment in Australia', *Worldwide Attitudes*, 08-26 (1996).

Kennedy, Paul (ed.), *Grand Strategies in War and Peace* (New Haven: Yale University Press, 1991).

Kersaudy, François, *Norway 1940* (London: Collins, 1990).

Kershaw, Robert J., *'It Never Snows in September': The German View of Market Garden and the Battle of Arnhem, September 1944* (Addlestone: Ian Allan Ltd, 1994).

Keshen, Jeffrey A., *Saints, Sinners and Soldiers: Canada's Second World War* (Vancouver: University of British Columbia Press, 2004).

Khan, Yasmin, *The Raj at War: A People's History of India's Second World War* (London: The Bodley Head, 2015).

Kier, Elizabeth, *Imagining War: French and British Military Doctrine Between the Wars* (Princeton University Press, 1997).

Kier, Elizabeth and Krebs, Ronald R. (eds.), *In War's Wake: International Conflict and the Fate of Liberal Democracy* (Cambridge University Press, 2010).

Killingray, David, *Fighting for Britain: African Soldiers in the Second World War* (Woodbridge: James Currey, 2010).

Killingray, David and Rathbone, Richard (eds.), *Africa and the Second World War* (London: Macmillan Press Ltd, 1986).

King, Anthony, *The Combat Soldier: Infantry Tactics and Cohesion in the Twentieth and Twenty-First Centuries* (Oxford University Press, 2013).

King, Anthony, *The Transformation of Europe's Armed Forces: From the Rhine to Afghanistan* (Cambridge University Press, 2011).

King, Anthony (ed.), *Frontline: Combat and Cohesion in the Twenty-First Century* (Oxford University Press, 2015).

Kinross, Stuart, *Clausewitz and America: Strategic Thought and Practice from Vietnam to Iraq* (Abingdon: Routledge, 2008).

Kirby, S. W., *Singapore: The Chain of Disaster* (London: Cassell, 1971).

Kirby, S. W., *The War against Japan, Vol. I: The Loss of Singapore* (Uckfield: The Naval & Military Press, 2004 [1957]).

Kirby, S. W., *The War against Japan, Vol. II: India's Most Dangerous Hour* (Uckfield: The Naval & Military Press, 2004 [1958]).

Kirby, S. W., *The War against Japan, Vol. III: The Decisive Battles* (London: HMSO, 1962).

Kirby, S. W., *The War against Japan, Vol. IV: The Reconquest of Burma* (London: HMSO, 1965).

Kisch, Richard, *The Days of the Good Soldiers: Communists in the Armed Forces WW2* (London: Journeyman Press Ltd, 1985).

Kiszely, John, *Anatomy of a Campaign: The British Fiasco in Norway, 1940* (Cambridge University Press, 2017).

Kitchen, James, *The British Imperial Army in the Middle East: Morale and Military Identity in the Sinai and Palestine Campaigns, 1916–18* (London: Bloomsbury, 2014).

Kitchen, Martin, *Rommel's Desert War: Waging World War II in North Africa, 1941–1943* (Cambridge University Press, 2009).

Krüger, Christine G. and Levsen, Sonja (eds.), *War Volunteering in Modern Times: From the French Revolution to the Second World War* (New York: Palgrave Macmillan, 2011).

Kumar, Kapil (ed.), *Congress and Classes: Nationalism, Workers and Peasants* (New Delhi: Manohar Publications, 1988).

Lamb, Richard, *War in Italy, 1943–1945: A Brutal Story* (London: John Murray, 1993).

Lambert, John, '"The Finest Hour?" English-Speaking South Africans and World War II', *South African Historical Journal*, 60(1) (2008).

Lambert, John, 'An Identity Threatened: White English-Speaking South Africans, Britishness and Dominion South Africanism, 1934–1939', *Kleio*, 37(1) (2010).

Latimer, Jon, *Alamein* (London, 2002).

Latimer, Jon, *Burma: The Forgotten War* (London: John Murray, 2004).

Leduc, Lawrence, Pammett, Jon H., McKenzie, Judith I. and Turcotte, André, *Dynasties and Interludes: Past and Present in Canadian Electoral Politics* (Toronto: Dundurn Press, 2010).

Levine, Allan, *King: William Lyon Mackenzie King, A Life Guided by the Hand of Destiny* (London: Biteback, 2012).

Lewin, Ronald, *The Chief: Field Marshal Lord Wavell, Commander-in-Chief and Viceroy, 1939–1947* (London: Hutchinson, 1980).

Lewin, Ronald, *Slim: The Standardbearer* (Ware: Wordsworth, 1999).

Linderman, Gerald F., *The World Within War: America's Combat Experience in World War II* (New York: The Free Press, 1997).

Littlewood, David, '"Should He Serve"?: The Military Service Boards' Operations in the Wellington Provincial District, 1916–1918' (Master's thesis, Massey University, 2010).

Littlewood, David, 'Willing and Eager to Go in Their Turn'? Appeals for Exemption from Military Service in New Zealand and Great Britain, 1916–1918', *War in History*, 21(3) (2014).

Lucy, T., *Quantitative Techniques* (London: Continuum, 1996).

Lyman, Robert, *Slim, Master of War: Burma and the Birth of Modern Warfare* (London: Robinson, 2005).

Lynn, John A., *The Bayonets of the Republic: Motivation and Tactics in the Army of Revolutionary France* (Oxford: Westview Press, 1996).

McAdam, Doug, Tarrow, Sidney and Tilly, Charles, *Dynamics of Contention* (Cambridge University Press, 2001).

McAndrew, William J., 'Fire or Movement? Canadian Tactical Doctrine, Sicily – 1943', *Military Affairs*, 51(3) (July, 1987).

McCallum, R. B. and Readman, Alison, *The British General Election of 1945* (Oxford University Press, 1947).

McCarthy, Dudley, *South-West Pacific Area – First Year: Kokoda to Wau* (Canberra: AWM, 1959).

McClure, Margaret, *A Civilised Community: A History of Social Security in New Zealand, 1898–1998* (Auckland University Press, 1998).

MacDonald, J. F., *The War History of Southern Rhodesia, Vol. I* (Government of Southern Rhodesia, 1947).

MacDonald, J. F., *The War History of Southern Rhodesia, Vol. II* (Government of Southern Rhodesia, 1950).

McGibbon, Ian, *New Zealand and the Second World War* (Auckland: Hodder Moa Beckett, 2004).

McInnes, Colin J., 'Men, Machines and the Emergence of Modern Warfare, 1914–1945', *Strategic and Combat Studies Institute*, Occasional Paper No. 2 (1992).

Macintyre, Stuart, *A Concise History of Australia* (Cambridge University Press, 2009 [1999]).

Macintyre, Stuart, *The Oxford History of Australia, Vol. IV: 1901–1942: The Succeeding Age* (Oxford University Press, 1986).

MacKay, Robert, *Half the Battle: Civilian Morale in Britain During the Second World War* (Manchester University Press, 2002).

McKee, Alexander, *Caen: Anvil of Victory* (London: Pan, 1966).

MacKenzie, J. J. G. and Reid, Brian Holden, *The British Army and the Operational Level of War* (London: Tri-Service Press, 1989).

MacKenzie, S. P., *Politics and Military Morale: Current-Affairs and Citizenship Education in the British Army, 1914–1950* (Oxford: Clarendon Press, 1992).

MacKenzie, S. P., 'The Treatment of Prisoners of War in World War II', *Journal of Modern History*, 66(3) (1994).

McKibbin, Ross, *Classes and Cultures: England 1918–1951* (Oxford University Press, 1998).

McKibbin, Ross, *Parties and People: England 1914–1951* (Oxford University Press, 2010).

McLaine, Ian, *Ministry of Morale: Home Front Morale and the Ministry of Information in World War II* (London: Allen & Unwin, 1979).

McLeod, John, *Myth and Reality: The New Zealand Soldier in World War II* (Auckland: Reed Methuen, 1986).

Mahnken, Thomas, Maiolo, Joseph and Stevenson, David (eds.), *Arms Races in International Politics: From the Nineteenth to the Twenty-First Century* (Oxford University Press, 2016).

Main, J. M. (ed.), *Conscription: The Australian Debate, 1901–1970* (Melbourne: Cassell Australia, 1970).

Mainwaring, Hugh S. K., *Three Score Years and Ten with Never a Dull Moment* (Printed Privately, 1976).

Majdalany, Fred, *Cassino, Portrait of a Battle* (Boston: Houghton Mifflin, 1957).

Malherbe, E. G., *Never a Dull Moment* (Aylesbury: Timmins, 1981).

Man, John, *The Penguin Atlas of D-Day and the Normandy Campaign* (London: Viking, 1994).

Marshall, H., *Over to Tunis* (London: Eyre & Spottiswoode, 1943).

Marshall, P. J., *The Cambridge Illustrated History of the British Empire* (Cambridge University Press, 1996).

Marshall, S. L. A., *Men against Fire: The Problem of Battle Command in Future War* (Alexandria: Byrrd Enterprises, 1947).

Marston, Daniel, *The Indian Army and the End of the Raj* (Cambridge University Press, 2014).

Marston, Daniel, *Phoenix from the Ashes: The Indian Army in the Burma Campaign* (Westport: Praeger, 2003).

Martin, H. J. and Orpen, Neil, *South Africa at War: Military and Industrial Organization and Operations in Connection with the Conduct of the War, 1939–1945* (Cape Town: Purnell, 1979).

Martin, John E., *The House: New Zealand's House of Representatives, 1854–2004* (Palmerston North: Dunmore Press, 2004).

Martin, Nicholas, Haughton, Tim and Purseigle, Pierre, *Aftermath: Legacies and Memories of War in Europe, 1918–1945–1989* (Farnham: Ashgate, 2014).

Marwick, Arthur, *The Deluge: British Society and the First World War* (London: The Bodley Head, 1965).

Marwick, Arthur, *War and Social Change in the Twentieth Century: A Comparative Study of Britain, France, Germany, Russia and the United States* (London: Macmillan Press, 1974).

Mawdsley, Evan, *World War II: A New History* (Cambridge University Press, 2009).

Mein Smith, Philippa, *A Concise History of New Zealand* (Cambridge University Press, 2005).

Mellor, W. Franklin (ed.), *Casualties and Medical Statistics* (London: HMSO, 1972).

Meredith, J. L. J., *From Normandy to Hanover, June 1944 to May 1945: The Story of the Seventh Battalion the Somerset Light Infantry* (Uckfield: Naval & Military Press, 2006).

Merridale, Catherine, 'Death and Memory in Modern Russia', *History Workshop Journal*, 42 (Autumn, 1996).

Merridale, Catherine, *Ivan's War: The Red Army 1939–45* (London: Faber and Faber, 2005).

Mettler, Suzanne, *Soldiers to Citizens: The G.I. Bill and the Making of the Greatest Generation* (Oxford University Press, 2005).

Middlebrook, Martin, *Arnhem 1944: The Airborne Battle* (London: Penguin, 1995).

Millett, Allan R. and Murray, Williamson, *Military Effectiveness, Vol. III: The Second World War* (London: Allen & Unwin, 1988).

Milner, Marc, *Stopping the Panzers: The Untold Story of D-Day* (Lawrence: University Press of Kansas, 2014).

Molony, C. J. C., *The Mediterranean and Middle East, Vol. V: The Campaign in Sicily 1943 and the Campaign in Italy, 3rd September 1943 to 31st March 1944* (Uckfield: Naval & Military Press, 2004 [1973]).

Molony, C. J. C. and Jackson, W., *The Mediterranean and Middle East, Vol. VI Parts I, II and III: Victory in the Mediterranean* (Uckfield: Naval & Military Press, 2004).

Monama, Frankie, 'Wartime Propaganda in the Union of South Africa, 1939–1945' (Doctoral thesis, Stellenbosch, 2014).

Montgomery, B. L., *The Memoirs of Field-Marshal Montgomery of Alamein* (Barnsley: Pen &Sword, 2005 [1958]).

Montgomery of Alamein, Field-Marshal the Viscount, *Normandy to the Baltic* (London: Hutchinson and Co., 1946).

Moorehead, Alan, *African Trilogy: The Desert War 1940–1943* (London: Cassell, 1998 [1944]).

Moran, Lord, *The Anatomy of Courage* (London: Constable, 1945).

Moreman, Tim, 'Jungle, Japanese and the Australian Army: Learning the Lessons of New Guinea', Paper to the Remembering the War in New Guinea Symposium, 19 to 20 October 2000, http://ajrp.awm.gov.au/AJRP/remember.nsf/pages/NT0000130A, accessed 15 March 2016.

Moreman, Timothy, *The Jungle, the Japanese and the British Commonwealth Armies at War, 1941–45: Fighting Methods, Doctrine and Training for Jungle Warfare* (London: Frank Cass, 2005).

Mowat, C. L., *Britain Between the Wars* (London: Methuen, 1955).

Moyse-Bartlett, H., *The King's African Rifles: A Study in the Military History of East and Central Africa, 1890–1945* (Aldershot: Gale & Polden, 1956).

Mulgan, Richard, *Politics in New Zealand* (Auckland University Press, 2004).

Murray, Williamson, *The Change in the European Balance of Power, 1938–1939: The Path to Ruin* (Princeton University Press, 1984).

Murray, Williamson, Knox, MacGregor and Bernstein, Alvin (eds.), *The Making of Strategy: Rulers, States and War* (Cambridge University Press, 1994).

Murray, Williamson and Millett, Allan R., *A War to be Won: Fighting the Second World War* (London: Belknap Press, 2000).

Neiberg, Michael, *Warfare and Society in Europe: 1898 to the Present* (London: Routledge, 2004).

Neillands, Robin, *The Battle for the Rhine, 1944: Arnhem and the Ardennes: The Campaign in Europe* (London: Weidenfeld & Nicolson, 2005).

Neillands, Robin, *Eighth Army: From the Western Desert to the Alps, 1939-1945* (London: John Murray, 2004).

Neilson, Keith, 'The Defence Requirements Sub-Committee, British Strategic Foreign Policy, Neville Chamberlain and the Path to Appeasement', *English Historical Review*, CXVIII(477) (2003).

Neilson, Keith and Kennedy, Greg (eds.), *The British Way in Warfare: Power and the International System, 1856–1956* (Farnham: Ashgate, 2010).

Nicholson, G. W. L., *The Canadians in Italy, 1943–1945: Official History of the Canadian Army in the Second World War, Vol. II* (Ottawa: Queen's Printer, 1956).

Nicolson, Nigel (ed.), *The Diaries and Letters of Harold Nicolson, Vol. II: The War Years, 1939–1945* (New York: Atheneum, 1967).

Noakes, Lucy, *Women in the British Army: War and the Gentle Sex, 1907–1948* (London: Routledge, 2006).

Noles, Kevin, 'Renegades in Malaya: Indian Volunteers of the Japanese F. Kikan', *British Journal for Military History*, 3(2) (2017).

North, John (ed.), *The Alexander Memoirs, 1940–1945* (London: Cassell, 1962).

O'Brien, Phillips Payson, *How the War Was Won: Air-Sea Power and Allied Victory in World War II* (Cambridge University Press, 2015).

Olsen, John Andreas and van Creveld, Martin, *The Evolution of Operational Art* (University of Oxford Press, 2011).

Olssen, Erik and Hickey, Maureen, *Class and Occupation: The New Zealand Reality* (Dunedin: University of Otago Press, 2005).

O'Meara, Dan, *Volkskapitalisme: Class, Capital and Ideology in the Development of Afrikaner Nationalism, 1934–1948* (Cambridge University Press, 1983).

Omissi, David, *The Sepoy and the Raj: The Indian Army, 1860–1940* (London: Macmillan, 1994).

Oosthuizen, François, 'Demobilization and the Post-War Employment of the White Union Defence Force Soldiers', *Scientia Militaria, South African Journal of Military Studies*, 23(4) (1993).

Oosthuizen, François, 'Soldiers and Politics: The Political Ramifications of the White Union Defence Forces Soldiers' Demobilisation Experience After the Second World War', *Scientia Militaria, South African Journal of Military Studies*, 24(1) (1994).

Orwell, George, 'The Lion and the Unicorn', in *The Collected Essays, Journalism and Letters, Vol. II* (Harmondsworth: Penguin, 1970).

Overy, Richard, *Why the Allies Won* (London: Pimlico, 2006 [1995]).

Page, Malcolm, *KAR: A History of the King's African Rifles and East African Forces* (London: Leo Cooper, 1998).

Parker, H. M. D., *Manpower: A Study of War-time Policy and Administration* (London: HMSO, 1957).

Parker, John, *Desert Rats: From El Alamein to Basra, The Inside Story of a Military Legend* (London: Headline, 2006).

Parsons, Timothy H., *The African Rank-and-File: Social Implications of Colonial Military Service in the King's African Rifles, 1902–1964* (Oxford: James Currey, 1999).

Peaty, John, 'British Army Manpower Crisis 1944' (Doctoral thesis, King's College London, 2000).

Peaty, John, 'The Desertion Crisis in Italy, 1944', *The RUSI Journal*, 147(3) (2002).

Peden, G. C., *Arms, Economics and British Strategy: From Dreadnoughts to Hydrogen Bombs* (Cambridge University Press, 2007).

Peden, G. C., 'The Burden of Imperial Defence and the Continental Commitment Reconsidered', *The Historical Journal*, 27(2) (June 1984).

Pelling, Henry, *Britain and the Second World War* (London: Collins, 1970).

Pelling, Henry, 'The 1945 Election Reconsidered', *The Historical Journal*, 23(2) (1980).

Pennell, Catriona, *A Kingdom United: Popular Responses to the Outbreak of the First World War in Britain and Ireland* (Oxford University Press, 2012).

Percival, A. E., *The War in Malaya* (London: Eyre & Spottiswoode, 1949).

Perry, F. W., *The Commonwealth Armies: Manpower and Organisation in Two World Wars* (Manchester University Press, 1988).

Phillips, N. C., *Italy, Vol. I: The Sangro to Cassino* (Wellington: Historical Publications Branch, 1957).

Piketty, Thomas, *Capital in the Twenty-first Century*, trans. Arthur Goldhammer. (London: Belknap Press, 2014).

Pitt, Barrie, *The Crucible of War: Wavell's Command: The Definitive History of the Desert War, Vol. I* (London: Cassell & Co., 2001 [1980]).

Pitt, Barrie, *The Crucible of War: Auchinleck's Command: The Definitive History of the Desert War, Vol. II* (London: Cassell & Co., 2001 [1980]).

Playfair, I. S. O., *The Mediterranean and Middle East, Vol. I: The Early Successes against Italy* (Uckfield: The Naval & Military Press, 2004 [1954]).

Playfair, I. S. O., *The Mediterranean and Middle East, Vol. II: The Germans Come to the Help of their Allies* (Uckfield: Naval & Military Press, 2004 [1956]).

Playfair, I. S. O., *The Mediterranean and Middle East, Vol. III: British Fortunes Reach their Lowest Ebb* (Uckfield: Naval & Military Press, 2004 [1960]).

Playfair, I. S. O. and Molony, C. J. C., *The Mediterranean and Middle East, Vol. IV, The Destruction of the Axis Forces in Africa* (Uckfield: Naval & Military Press, 2004 [1966]).

Pond, Hugh, *Salerno* (London, William Kimber, 1961).

Porch, Douglas, *Hitler's Mediterranean Gamble: The North African and the Mediterranean Campaigns in World War II* (London: Weidenfeld & Nicolson, 2004).

Porter, Bernard, *The Absent-Minded Imperialists: Empire, Society, and Culture in Britain* (Oxford University Press, 2004).

Porter, John, *The Vertical Mosaic: An Analysis of Social Class and Power in Canada* (University of Toronto Press, 1965).

Posen, Barry R. (ed.), *Breakthroughs: Armored Offensives in Western Europe 1944* (MIT/DACS Conventional Forces Working Group, 1994).

Powell, Geoffrey, *The Devil's Birthday: The Bridges to Arnhem 1944* (Barnsley: Pen & Sword, 2012 [1984]).

Prasad, Sri Nandan, *Official History of the Indian Armed Forces in the Second World War, 1939–45: Expansion of the Armed Forces and Defence Organisation, 1939–45* (Calcutta: Orient Longmans, 1956).

Pratt, William, 'Medicine and Obedience: Canadian Army Morale, Discipline, and Surveillance in the Second World War, 1939–1945' (DPhil thesis, University of Calgary, 2015).

Pratton, Garth M., 'The "Old Man": Australian Battalion Commanders in the Second World War', PhD thesis, Deakin University, 2005.

Price, Alfred, 'Air Power at El Alamein', *Air Power Review*, 5(3) (2002).

Prysor, Glyn, *Citizen Sailors: The Royal Navy in the Second World War* (London: Penguin, 2012 [2011]).

Prysor, Glyn, 'The "Fifth Column" and the British Experience of Retreat, 1940', *War in History*, 12(4) (2005).

Quilter, David C., *No Dishonourable Name: The 2nd and 3rd Battalions, Coldstream Guards, 1939–46* (London: Clowes and Sons, 1947).

Raina, B. L. (ed.), *Preventative Medicine (Nutrition, Malaria Control and Prevention of Diseases)* (Delhi: Combined Inter-Services Historical Section, India and Pakistan, 1961).

Raghavan, Srinath, *India's War: The Making of Modern South Asia 1939–1945* (London: Penguin: 2017 [2016]).

Raugh, Harold E. Jr, *Wavell in the Middle East 1939–1941: A Study in Generalship* (London: Brassey's, 1993).

Ray, Cyril, *Algiers to Austria: A History of 78 Division in the Second World War* (London: Eyre & Spottiswoode, 1952).

Reese, Roger R., 'Surrender and Capture in the Winter War and Great Patriotic War: Which was the Anomaly?', *Global War Studies*, 8(1) (2011).

Reese, Roger R., *Why Stalin's Soldiers Fought: The Red Army's Military Effectiveness in World War II* (Lawrence: University Press of Kansas, 2011).

Reid, Brian A., *No Holding Back: Operation Totalize, Normandy, August 1944* (Mechanicsburg: Stackpole, 2004).

Reiter, Dan and Stam III, Allan C., 'Democracy and Battlefield Military Effectiveness', *The Journal of Conflict Resolution*, 42(3) (1998).

Reynolds, David, '1940: Fulcrum of the Twentieth Century', *International Affairs*, 66(2) (April, 1990).

Reynolds, David, *In Command of History: Churchill Fighting and Writing the Second World War* (London: Allen Lane, 2004).

Reynolds, David, *The Long Shadow: The Great War and the Twentieth Century* (London: Simon & Schuster, 2013).

Reynolds, David, *Rich Relations: The American Occupation of Britain, 1942–1945* (London: Phoenix Press, 2000 [1996]).

Rhoden, Clare, 'Another Perspective on Australian Discipline in the Great War: The Egalitarian Bargain', *War in History*, 19(4) (2012).

Rice, Geoffrey W. (ed.), *The Oxford History of New Zealand* (Melbourne: Oxford University Press, 1992).

Rikihana, T. H., 'Education in the New Zealand Army, 1917 to 1964' (MA thesis, University of Auckland, 1965).

Roos, Neil, *Ordinary Springboks: White Servicemen and Social Justice in South Africa, 1939–1961* (Aldershot: Ashgate, 2005).

Roos, Neil, 'The Second World War, the Army Education Scheme and the "discipline" of the white poor in South Africa', *History of Education: Journal of the History of Education Society*, 32(6) (2003).

Rose, David, 'Official Social Classifications in the UK', *Social Research Update*, 9 (July, 1995).

Rose, Patrick, 'Allies at War: British and US Army Command Culture in the Italian Campaign, 1943–1944', *Journal of Strategic Studies*, 36(1) (February, 2013).

Rose, Patrick, 'British Army Command Culture 1939–1945: A Comparative Study of British Eighth and Fourteenth Armies' (PhD thesis, King's College London, 2008).

Rose, Sonya O., *Which People's War? National Identity and Citizenship in Wartime Britain, 1939–1945* (Oxford University Press, 2003).

Rothermund, Dietmar, *India in the Great Depression, 1929–1939* (New Delhi: Manohar Publications, 1992).

Roy, Kaushik, 'Discipline and the Morale of the African, British and Indian Army Units in Burma and India during World War II: July 1943 to August 1945', *Modern Asian Studies*, 44(6) (2010).

Roy, Kaushik (ed.), *The Indian Army in the Two World Wars* (Leiden: Brill, 2012).

Rush, Robert S., 'A Different Perspective: Cohesion, Morale and Operational Effectiveness in the German Army, Fall 1944', *Armed Forces and Society*, 25 (3) (Spring, 1999).

Rush, Robert S., *Hell in Hürtgen Forest* (Lawrence: University Press of Kansas, 2001).

Russell, Peter A., 'BC's 1944 "Zombie" Protests against Overseas Conscription', *BC Studies*, 122 (Summer 1999).

Sadler, John, *Operation Mercury: The Battle for Crete 1941* (Barnsley: Pen & Sword, 2007).

Salmond, J. B., *The History of the 51st Highland Division 1939–1945* (Durham: Pentland Press, 1994).

Sandel, Michael, *Public Philosophy: Essays on Morality in Politics* (London: Harvard University Press, 2006).

Sarkar, Sumit, *Modern India 1885–1947* (London: Macmillan, 1983).

Sarkar, Sumit, *Modern Times: India 1880s–1950s* (Ranikhet: Permanent Black, 2014).

Sarkesian, Sam C. (ed.), *Combat Effectiveness: Cohesion, Stress, and the Volunteer Military* (London: Sage, 1980).

Scarfe, Norman, *Assault Division: A History of the 3rd Division from the Invasion of Normandy to the Surrender of Germany* (London: Collins, 1947).

Schaller, Michael, *Douglas MacArthur: The Far Eastern General* (Oxford University Press, 1989).

Scholefield, Guy H. (ed.), *New Zealand Parliamentary Record, 1840–1949* (Wellington: R. E. Owen Government Printer, 1950).

Scoullar, J. L., *Battle for Egypt: The Summer of 1942. Official History of New Zealand in the Second World War 1939–1945* (Wellington: Historical Publications Branch, 1955).

Sebag-Montefiori, Hugh, *Dunkirk: Fight to the Last Man* (London: Penguin, 2015).

Seegers, Annette, *The Military in the Making of Modern South Africa* (London: I. B. Tauris, 1996).

Seekings, Jeremy, 'Social Stratification and Inequality in South Africa at the End of Apartheid', Centre for Social Science Research Working Paper No. 31 (2003).

Seekings, Jeremy and Nattrass, Nicoli, *Class, Race, and Inequality in South Africa* (London: Yale University Press, 2005).

Sheffield, Gary, *Leadership in the Trenches: Officer-Man Relations, Morale and Discipline in the British Army in the Era of the First World War* (London: Macmillan, 2000).

Shephard, Ben, *A War of Nerves: Soldiers and Psychiatrists 1914–1994* (London: Pimlico, 2002).

Shils, Edward A. and Janowitz, Morris, 'Cohesion and Disintegration in the Wehrmacht in World War II', *Public Opinion Quarterly*, 12 (Summer, 1948).

Simpkins, Major B. G., *Rand Light Infantry* (Cape Town: Howard Timmins, 1965).

Simpson, J. S. M., *South Africa Fights* (London: Hodder & Stoughton Ltd, 1941).

Singh, Gajendra, *The Testimonies of Indian Soldiers and the Two World Wars: Between Self and Sepoy* (London: Bloomsbury, 2014).

Slim, Field Marshal Viscount, *Defeat into Victory* (London: Pan Books, 1999 [1956]).

Smalley, Edward, *The British Expeditionary Force, 1939–40* (Basingstoke: Palgrave Macmillan, 2015).

Smalley, Edward, 'Qualified, but Unprepared: Training for War at the Staff College in the 1930s', *British Journal for Military History*, 2(1) (2015).

Smith, Harold L. (ed.), *War and Social Change: British Society in the Second World War* (Manchester University Press, 1986).

Smith, Leonard V., *Between Mutiny and Obedience: The Case of the French Fifth Division during World War I* (Princeton University Press, 1994).

Snow, Philip, *The Fall of Hong Kong: Britain, China and the Japanese Occupation* (London: Yale University Press, 2003).

Spanier, John W., *The Truman-MacArthur Controversy and the Korean War* (New York: The Norton Library, 1965).

Sparrow, James T., *Warfare State: World War II Americans and the Age of Big Government* (Oxford University Press, 2011).

Stacey, C. P., *Arms, Men and Governments: The War Policies of Canada, 1939–1945* (Ottawa: The Queen's Printer for Canada, 1970).

Stacey, C. P., *The Canadian Army, 1939–1945: An Official Historical Summary* (Ottawa: Edmond Cloutier, 1948).

Stacey, C. P., *Six Years of War: The Canadian Army in Canada, Britain and the Pacific, Official History of the Canadian Army in the Second World War, Vol. I* (Ottawa: Queen's Printer, 1955).

Stacey, C. P., *The Victory Campaign: The Operations in North-West Europe, 1944–1945, Official History of the Canadian Army in the Second World War, Vol. III* (Ottawa: Queen's Printer, 1966).

Stearn, Roger T., 'Percival, Arthur Ernest (1887–1966)', *Oxford Dictionary of National Biography* (Oxford University Press, 2004), online edn, May 2013, www.oxforddnb.com/view/article/61472, accessed 18 July 2017.

Stevens, W. G., *Problems of 2 NZEF* (Wellington: Historical Publications Branch, 1958).

Stevenson, John, *British Society, 1914–45* (London: Penguin, 1984).

Stevenson, Michael D., *Canada's Greatest Wartime Muddle: National Selective Service and the Mobilization of Human Resources during World War II* (Kingston: McGill-Queen's University Press).

Stewart, Andrew, *Caen Controversy: The Battle for Sword Beach 1944* (Solihull: Helion & Company, 2014).

Stewart, Andrew, *Empire Lost: Britain, The Dominions and the Second World War* (London: Continuum, 2008).

Stewart, Andrew, *The First Victory: The Second World War and the East African Campaign* (London: Yale University Press, 2016).

Stewart, Andrew, '"The Klopper Affair": Anglo-South African Relations and the Surrender of the Tobruk Garrison', *Twentieth Century British History*, 17(4) (2006).

Stewart, Andrew, *A Very British Experience: Coalition, Defence and Strategy in the Second World War* (Brighton: Sussex Academic Press, 2012).

Stouffer, Samuel A. et al., *The American Soldier: Combat and its Aftermath, Vol. II* (Princeton University Press, 1949).

Stout, Thomas Duncan MacGregor, *New Zealand Medical Services in Middle East and Italy* (Wellington: Historical Publications Branch, 1956).

Strachan, Hew, *Carl von Clausewitz's On War: A Biography* (London: Atlantic Books, 2007).

Strachan, Hew, *European Armies and the Conduct of War* (Oxford: Routledge, 2004 [1983]).

Strachan, Hew, *Military Lives: Intimate Biographies of the Famous by the Famous* (Oxford University Press, 2002).

Strachan, Hew, *The Politics of the British Army* (Oxford University Press, 1997).

Strachan, Hew, 'Training, Morale and Modern War', *The Journal of Contemporary History*, 41(2) (2006).

Strachan, Hew (ed.), *Big Wars and Small Wars: The British Army and the Lessons of War in the 20th Century* (Abingdon: Routledge, 2006).

Strachan, Hew (ed.), *The British Army, Manpower and Society into the Twenty-First Century* (London: Frank Cass, 2000).

Sullivan, John J., 'The Botched Air Support of Operation Cobra', *Parameters*, 18 (March, 1988).

Summerfield, Penelope, 'Education and Politics in the British Armed Forces in the Second World War', *International Review of Social History*, 26(2) (1981).

Sundaram, Chandar S., 'A Paper Tiger: The Indian National Army in Battle, 1944–1945', *War & Society*, 13(1) (May, 1995).

Swanston, Alexander and Swanston, Malcolm, *The Historical Atlas of World War II* (Edison, NJ: Chartwell Books, 2007).

Taylor, A. J. P., *English History, 1914–1945* (Oxford: Clarendon Press, 1965).

Taylor, Joe G., 'Air Supply in the Burma Campaigns', United States Air Force Historical Division Study No. 75 (1957).

Taylor Nancy M., *The Home Front, Vol. I* (Wellington: Historical Publications Branch, 1986).

Terraine, John, *The Right of the Line: The Royal Air Force in the European War, 1939–1945* (Ware: Wordsworth Editions, 1997 [1985]).

Thompson, Leonard, *A History of South Africa* (New Haven: Yale University Press, 2001 [2000]).

Thorburn, Ned, *The 4th KSLI in Normandy: June to August 1944* (Shrewsbury: Castle Museum, 1990).

Thorne, Christopher, *Allies of a Kind: The United States, Britain, and the War Against Japan, 1941–1945* (Oxford University Press, 1978).

Threlfall, Adrian, 'The Development of Australian Army Jungle Warfare Doctrine and Training, 1941–1945' (Doctoral thesis, Victoria University, 2008).

Todman, Daniel, *Britain's War: Into Battle, 1937–1941* (London: Allen Lane, 2016).

Tooley, Robert, 'Appearance or Reality? Variations in Infantry Courts Martial: 1st Canadian Division1940–1945', *Canadian Defence Quarterly*, 22(2/3) (October and December 1992).

Tooze, Adam, *The Wages of Destruction: The Making and Breaking of the Nazi Economy* (London: Penguin Books, 2007 [2006]).

Tothill, F. D., 'The 1943 General Election' (Master's thesis, University of South Africa, 1987).

Tothill, F. D., 'The Soldiers' Vote and Its Effect on the Outcome of the South African General Election of 1943', *South African Historical Journal*, 21 (1989).

Toye, Richard, *The Roar of the Lion: The Untold Story of Churchill's World War II Speeches* (Oxford University Press, 2013).

Urquhart, M. C. (ed.), *Historical Statistics of Canada* (Cambridge University Press, 1965).

Vamplew, Wray (ed.), *Australians: Historical Statistics* (Broadway, NSW Australia: Fairfax, Syme & Weldon Associates, 1987).

Van der Waag, Ian, *A Military History of Modern South Africa* (Johannesburg: Jonathan Ball, 2015).

Van der Waag, Ian, 'Smuts's Generals: Towards a First Portrait of the South African High Command, 1912–1948', *War in History*, 18(33) (2011).

Vasey, Christopher, *Nazi Intelligence Operations in Non-Occupied Territories: Espionage Efforts in the United States, Britain, South America and Southern Africa* (Jefferson: McFarland & Co., 2016).

Verney, G. L., *The Desert Rats* (London: Greenhill Books, 1990).

Vinen, Richard, *National Service: Conscription in Britain 1945–1963* (London: Allen Lane, 2014).

Walker, Allan S., *Australia in the War of 1939–1945: Series Five, Medical, Vol. III: The Island Campaigns* (Canberra: AWM, 1957).

Walker, Allan S., *Clinical Problems of War* (Canberra: AWM, 1952).

Walker, Allan S., *The Island Campaigns* (Canberra: AWM, 1957).

Walter, James and MacLeod, Margaret, *The Citizens' Bargain: A Documentary History of Australian Views Since 1890* (Sydney: UNSW Press, 2002).

Wards, Ian, 'Freyberg, Bernard Cyril, first Baron Freyberg (1889–1963)', *Oxford Dictionary of National Biography* (Oxford University Press, 2004), online edn, January 2011, www.oxforddnb.com/view/article/33276, accessed 24 April 2017.

Wark, Wesley K., *The Ultimate Enemy: British Intelligence and Nazi Germany, 1933–1939* (London: I. B. Tauris, 1985).

Warren, Alan, *Singapore 1942: Britain's Greatest Defeat* (London: Hambledon, 2002).

Watson, Alexander, *Enduring the Great War: Combat, Morale and Collapse in the German and British Armies, 1914–1918* (Cambridge University Press, 2008).

Wavell, Field-Marshal Earl, *The Good Soldier* (London: MacMillan and Co., 1948).

Weigel, George, 'Moral Clarity in a Time of War', The Second Annual William E. Simon Lecture, Ethics and Public Policy Centre, 24 October 2002.

Weinberg, Gerhard L., *A World At Arms: A Global History of World War II* (Cambridge University Press, 1994).

Wessel, Andre, 'The First Two Years of War: The Development of the Union Defence Forces, September 1939 to September 1941', *Military History Journal*, 11(5) (June, 2000).

Wesseling, H. L., *The European Colonial Empires, 1815–1919* (Harlow: Pearson, 2004).

Whetham, David (ed.), *Ethics, Law and Military Operations* (London: Palgrave Macmillan, 2011).

White, Jonathan W., *Emancipation: The Union Army and the Reelection of Abraham Lincoln* (Baton Rouge: Louisiana State University Press, 2014).

Whiting, Charles, *Siegfried: The Nazi's Last Stand* (London: Leo Cooper, 1983).

Whitlock, Flint, *If Chaos Reigns: The Near-Disaster and Ultimate Triumph of the Allied Airborne Forces on D-Day, June 6, 1944* (Newbury: Casemate, 2011).

Wigmore, Lionel, *The Japanese Thrust* (Canberra: AWM, 1957).

Wilkinson, R., 'Both Sides of the Hill: Intelligence in the Crete and Arnhem Campaigns', *The RUSI Journal*, 149(3) (2004).

Wilkinson, Steven I., *Army and Nation: The Military and Indian Democracy since Independence* (London: Harvard University Press, 2015).

Williams, Jeffery, *The Long Left Flank: The Hard Fought Way to the Reich, 1944–1945* (London: Leo Cooper, 1988).

Williams, Peter, *The Kokoda Campaign 1942: Myth and Reality* (Melbourne: Cambridge University Press, 2012).

Wilmot, Chester, *The Struggle for Europe* (Bungay: Richard Clay and Company, 1954 [1952]).

Wilson, Theodore A. (ed.), *D-Day 1944* (Lawrence: University Press of Kansas, 1971).

Winegard, Timothy C., *Indigenous Peoples of the British Dominions and the First World War* (Cambridge University Press, 2012).

Winter, J. M., 'Britain's "Lost Generation" of the First World War', *Population Studies: A Journal of Demography*, 31(3) (1977).

Wood, F. L. W., *Political and External Affairs* (Wellington: Historical Publications Branch, 1958).

Zaloga, Steven J., *Sicily 1943: The Debut of Allied Joint Operations* (Oxford: Osprey Publishing Ltd, 2013).

Zumbro, Derek S., *Battle of the Ruhr: The German Army's Final Defeat in the West* (Lawrence: University Press of Kansas, 2006).

INDEX